THE
WORLD
BANK
SINCE
BRETTON
WOODS

EDWARD S. MASON
ROBERT E. ASHER

THE
WORLD
BANK
SINCE ~~WITHDRAWN~~
BRETTON
WOODS

THE ORIGINS, POLICIES, OPERATIONS, AND IMPACT OF

The International Bank for Reconstruction and Development

AND THE OTHER MEMBERS OF THE WORLD BANK GROUP:

The International Finance Corporation
The International Development Association
The International Centre for Settlement of Investment Disputes

THE BROOKINGS INSTITUTION
Washington, D.C.

Library of Congress Cataloging in Publication Data:
Mason, Edward Sagendorph, 1899–
 The World Bank since Bretton Woods.
 Bibliography: p.
 1. International Bank for Reconstruction and Development.
I. Asher, Robert E., 1910–   joint author.   II. Title.
HG3881.M355   332.1'53   73-1089
ISBN 0-8157-5492-2

THE BROOKINGS INSTITUTION is an independent organization devoted to nonpartisan research, education, and publication in economics, government, foreign policy, and the social sciences generally. Its principal purposes are to aid in the development of sound public policies and to promote public understanding of issues of national importance.

The Institution was founded on December 8, 1927, to merge the activities of the Institute for Government Research, founded in 1916, the Institute of Economics, founded in 1922, and the Robert Brookings Graduate School of Economics and Government, founded in 1924.

The Board of Trustees is responsible for the general administration of the Institution, while the immediate direction of the policies, program, and staff is vested in the President, assisted by an advisory committee of the officers and staff. The by-laws of the Institution state, "It is the function of the Trustees to make possible the conduct of scientific research, and publication, under the most favorable conditions, and to safeguard the independence of the research staff in the pursuit of their studies and in the publication of the results of such studies. It is not a part of their function to determine, control, or influence the conduct of particular investigations or the conclusions reached."

The President bears final responsibility for the decision to publish a manuscript as a Brookings book or staff paper. In reaching his judgment on the competence, accuracy, and objectivity of each study, the President is advised by the director of the appropriate research program and weighs the views of a panel of expert outside readers who report to him in confidence on the quality of the work. Publication of a work signifies that it is deemed to be a competent treatment worthy of public consideration; such publication does not imply endorsement of conclusions or recommendations contained in the study.

The Institution maintains its position of neutrality on issues of public policy in order to safeguard the intellectual freedom of the staff. Hence interpretations or conclusions in Brookings publications should be understood to be solely those of the author or authors and should not be attributed to the Institution, to its trustees, officers, or other staff members, or to the organizations that support its research.

Foreword

ON JUNE 25, 1971, the International Bank for Reconstruction and Development—better known as the World Bank—completed its first quarter century as a multilateral source of financial and technical assistance. It had by then acquired two affiliates, the International Finance Corporation (IFC) and the International Development Association (IDA). The conglomerate, which termed itself the World Bank Group, also had as an autonomous member an International Centre for Settlement of Investment Disputes.

The stockholders of the Bank are its member governments. They numbered 116 as of mid-1971. The loans and credits of the Bank and IDA amounted to nearly $20 billion and the net commitments of the IFC to more than $500 million. Yet no serious analytical review of the Bank Group's policies and operations had been published. Fully aware of this fact, the management of the Bank, well in advance of the Bank's twenty-fifth anniversary, had instructed a staff committee to organize a project for writing a history of the World Bank Group.

The staff committee concluded that the study should be scholarly and—preferably—should be written outside the Bank. In the course of its inquiries, the Bank discovered that the Brookings Institution had a positive interest in the undertaking, if the study could be carried out in an independent, objective fashion. President Robert S. McNamara and his colleagues readily agreed that, for the purposes of the project, the authors would be given access to the records and staff of the Bank. Decision on publication of the manuscript would be made by Brookings in accordance with its normal procedures.

The authors have indeed enjoyed full freedom to study any records they wished to consult, to use such data as they considered relevant, and to reach judgments and conclusions to which knowledgeable people at the Bank might take strong exception. Each of the co-authors was well qualified for the undertaking.

vii

Edward S. Mason, Lamont Professor of Economics at Harvard University until his retirement in 1969 and a past President of the American Economic Association, has served as a consultant to the World Bank on a number of occasions. Relevant, previously published writings of Professor Mason include *Economic Planning in Underdeveloped Areas* (1958), *Foreign Aid and Foreign Policy* (1964), and *Economic Development in India and Pakistan* (1966).

Robert E. Asher, a senior fellow at the Brookings Institution from 1954 until his retirement in 1972 and a former Vice President of the Society for International Development, has been on numerous U.S. government and international agency assignments in the less developed world. His books include *Grants, Loans, and Local Currencies: Their Role in Foreign Aid* (1961), *Development Assistance in the Seventies: Alternatives for the United States* (1970), and co-authorship of *The United Nations and Promotion of the General Welfare* (1957).

Professor Mason and Mr. Asher were assisted by an experienced part-time research associate, Eleanor B. Steinberg, to whom they and the Institution are most grateful. Mrs. Steinberg is the co-author of *Government Controls on Transport: An African Case* (1965).

Chapter 18, dealing with the Bank as mediator in certain international disputes, was contributed by Harold N. Graves, Jr., Director of Information at the World Bank from 1950 to 1967 and since then Associate Director of the Development Services Department. Persuaded by Messrs. Mason and Asher to prepare a background memorandum on the Bank's involvement in the Anglo-Iranian oil dispute, the financing of the High Dam in Egypt, and the division of the waters of the Indus River between India and Pakistan, he produced an account wholly suitable for incorporation as a chapter of this study.

The organization and coverage of the present study, which attempts to combine historical narrative with an analysis of functions and an appraisal of performance, is explained in the introduction. That the authors of this study are United States citizens will not escape the notice of readers and reviewers. If the authors were citizens of any other country, it is probable that some other sources of information would have been consulted and possible that a different interpretation would have been given to various episodes in the Bank's history. Readers are accordingly put on notice concerning this more or less inescapable source of possible bias.

Financing for the study has been provided by the Rockefeller Brothers Fund, the Ford Foundation, the Charles E. Merrill Trust, and the World Bank. In addition to its cash contribution, the Bank provided substantial and much appreciated services in kind, including the time of the many officials consulted, the preparation of statistical tables and certain background memoranda, the provision of office space, part-time secretarial assistance, and the use of library and duplicating facilities. Without this generous help and financial support from the several sources I have mentioned, this study could not have been undertaken.

The Brookings Institution is as grateful as the authors to the persons mentioned in the acknowledgments following this foreword for their role in bringing to fruition this unique and comprehensive study. The project was conducted as part of the Institution's program of Foreign Policy Studies, which is under the direction of Henry Owen.

As is true of all Brookings studies, the views expressed in this volume are those of the authors and should not be ascribed to those who were consulted during its preparation, to the organizations that provided financial assistance to the project, or to the trustees, officers, or other staff members of the Brookings Institution.

KERMIT GORDON
President

May 1973
Washington, D.C.

Authors' Acknowledgments

As an international agency, the World Bank for better or worse has been spared the public inquisitions to which national agencies in some of its member countries are regularly subjected by congresses and parliaments. Through its Board of Governors and Executive Directors, the management of the Bank is, of course, responsible to its member governments, but the responsibility tends to be more indirect and insulated from the spotlight of publicity. National agencies in the United States and a number of other countries are accustomed to living in a goldfish bowl; opening their files to outside researchers and exposing their policy-making processes to critical scrutiny represent, at most, minor breaks with tradition.

It was a bold step, however, for President McNamara and his associates to invite two outsiders to take an inside look at the World Bank and to give them unimpeded access to its records. He and Vice Presidents Knapp, Aldewereld, Rickett, and Shoaib must have heard rumblings from time to time about critical or one-sided questions that were being asked and "unfair" conclusions that were alleged to have been reached. Yet they never wavered in their support of the effort. For this we remain profoundly grateful.

We are grateful also for the opportunity to consult the series of interviews recorded in the summer of 1961 for the Oral History project of Columbia University. By arrangement between the World Bank and the Brookings Institution, Dr. Robert W. Oliver of the California Institute of Technology became responsible for interviewing twenty-five or thirty of the people intimately and prominently connected with the Bank at Bretton Woods or between then and mid-1961. To the best of our knowledge, these histories have not previously been consulted. The footnote "Oral History" in our text means the transcript of the interview recorded by Professor Oliver in 1961. Where permission to quote or cite was required, it has been obtained.

Richard H. Demuth, Director of the Development Services Department of the Bank while this book was being written, served as the principal liaison officer between the authors and the Bank. He was a wise counselor, a meticulous reader of draft chapters, and a never-ending source of valuable information. Several others were persevering enough to read the entire manuscript in draft and to earn our thanks because of the many constructive suggestions they made. The group includes Aron Broches, Sir Alec Cairncross, Lincoln Gordon, Ravi Gulhati, P. D. Henderson, Michael L. Hoffman, John M. Leddy, Escott Reid, Jo W. Saxe, Davidson Sommers, J. H. Williams, and E. Peter Wright.

Many other friends were consulted during the course of our study. We would like to spell out the contribution that each one made and calibrate our thanks through appropriate adjectives, individually assigned. We shall, however, refrain from doing so. The list of persons to whom we are indebted includes, but is not limited to: John H. Adler, Gerald Alter, Dragoslav Avramović, Carol V. Baber, Warren C. Baum, Bernard R. Bell, Munir P. Benjenk, William L. Bennett, Eugene R. Black, Thomas A. Blinkhorn, Shirley Boskey, I. P. M. Cargill, Bernard Chadenet, Victor C. Chang, Hollis B. Chenery, William Clark, R. A. Clarke, S. R. Cope, Jack C. Corbett, William Diamond, A. Edward Elmendorf, Lota Fairall, Donald D. Fowler, Patterson H. French, Robert L. Garner, William S. Gaud, William M. Gilmartin, Arthur E. Goldschmidt, David L. Gordon, Harold N. Graves, Jr., Ann O. Hamilton, Mahbub ul Haq, Edward V. K. Jaycox, Andrew M. Kamarck, John A. King, Betty E. Kinsey, K. S. Krishnaswamy, Martin L. Loftus, Luis Machado, Agnes L. Maher, John J. McCloy, Robert A. McPheeters, Jr., M. M. Mendels, Lester Nurick, I. G. Patel, Donald J. Pryor, Moeen A. Qureshi, Vincent J. Riley, Leonard B. Rist, A. D. Spottswood, M. R. Shroff, Alexander Stevenson, Andrew V. Urquhart, Gregory B. Votaw, Albert Waterston, Mervyn L. Weiner, Christopher R. Willoughby, and George D. Woods.

We are indebted, of course, to the persons mentioned in our footnotes but not included in the foregoing list. The manuscript was edited by Virginia C. Haaga, assisted by Laurel H. Rabin. Finally, we owe a vote of thanks to Helen B. Eisenhart, who prepared the index, and to the hardy band of heroines who typed and retyped—and then retyped again—chapter after chapter of our lengthy manuscript.

EDWARD S. MASON
ROBERT E. ASHER

Contents

Text Tables

Appendix Tables

Appendix Charts

Glossary

ACC Administrative Committee on Coordination (UN Secretary-General and heads of UN agencies).

ADELA Atlantic Community Development Group for Latin America.

AID Agency for International Development (of the U.S. government). Also referred to as U.S. AID.

Aid Coordination Groups Collective term for consortia, consultative groups, and other aid-coordinating arrangements formed under Bank or other auspices to facilitate the coordination of external assistance to a less developed country.

AIOC Anglo-Iranian Oil Company.

AfDB African Development Bank.

Articles of Agreement Unless otherwise identified, means the Articles of Agreement, or charter, of the World Bank.

AsDB Asian Development Bank.

Bank In conformity with the Bank's own practice, we use the word Bank with a capital B to mean the International Bank for Reconstruction and Development (IBRD), also referred to as the World Bank.

Bank Group The IBRD itself and its affiliates, the IFC (since 1956) and the IDA (since 1960). Also referred to as the World Bank Group.

BIS Bank for International Settlements (established in 1930 to handle World War I reparations payments).

Board, or Board of Directors Unless otherwise identified, this term means the Executive Directors of the Bank or IDA, or the Board of Directors of IFC.

Board of Governors The council consisting of one governor and one alternate appointed by each member country of the Bank. Governors of the Bank whose countries are also members of IDA and IFC serve ex officio as Governors of IDA and IFC.

Bretton Woods Site in New Hampshire (USA) of the United Nations Monetary and Financial Conference (July 1944) at which the World Bank and the International Monetary Fund were born.

CCCE (France's) Caisse Centrale de Coopération Economique.

CIAP Inter-American Committee on the Alliance for Progress.

Congo, People's Republic of the Known as the Congo (Brazzaville) until December 1969.

Consortia and Consultative Groups (CGs) See Aid Coordination Groups.

DAC Development Assistance Committee of the OECD. Its members in 1971 were Australia, Austria, Belgium, Canada, Denmark, France, Germany, Italy, Japan, the Netherlands, Norway, Portugal, Sweden, Switzerland, the United Kingdom, the United States, and the Commission of the European Economic Community.

DAG Development Assistance Group (of OEEC), predecessor of DAC.

DAS Development Advisory Service of the Bank (1962–66).

DFCs Development finance companies. Known also as development banks, DFCs are financial intermediaries, such as the Industrial Credit and Investment Corporation of India and the Pakistan Industrial Credit and Investment Corporation, organized as sources of long-term and intermediate financing for private enterprises in less developed countries.

EC Used to designate certain economic papers and reports issued by the Bank Group.

ECA (U.S.) Economic Cooperation Administration. Succeeded by MSA, FOA, ICA, and AID.

ECE (UN) Economic Commission for Europe, a regional economic commission of the United Nations.

ECLA (UN) Economic Commission for Latin America.

ECOSOC Economic and Social Council of the United Nations.

EDF European Development Fund.

EDI Economic Development Institute (staff college of the World Bank).

EEC European Economic Community (the European Common Market).

EGAT Electricity Generating Authority of Thailand.

Egypt, Arab Republic of United Arab Republic until September 1971.

EIB European Investment Bank.

EPTA (UN) Expanded Program of Technical Assistance.

EPU European Payments Union (1950–59).

Eximbank Export-Import Bank of the United States.

FAC (France's) Fonds d'Aide et de Coopération.

FAO Food and Agriculture Organization of the United Nations.

Fiscal year The World Bank's fiscal year runs from July 1 to June 30.

FPC Financial Policy Committee. The Bank's FPC was established as a committee of the Executive Directors in 1946 and since November 1955 includes all Executive Directors. IDA's and IFC's FPCs were established in 1962 and 1964, respectively, and also include all Executive Directors.

Fund International Monetary Fund (IMF).

GATT General Agreement on Tariffs and Trade. Also the multilateral agency that administers the agreement.

GNP Gross national product.

IBRD International Bank for Reconstruction and Development, the official name of the World Bank.

ICICI Industrial Credit and Investment Corporation of India.

ICSID International Centre for Settlement of Investment Disputes, an autonomous member of the World Bank Group.

IDA International Development Association, an affiliate of the IBRD. Also referred to as the Association.

IDB Inter-American Development Bank.

IFC International Finance Corporation, an affiliate of the IBRD.

ILO International Labour Organisation.

IMF International Monetary Fund, also referred to as the Fund.

KESC Karachi Electric Supply Corporation.

Khmer Republic Cambodia until November 1970.

Less developed countries (LDCs) The poor countries of the noncommunist world, particularly those in Africa, Asia, Latin America, and the Caribbean region. Also known as "developing countries" and (in the early post–World War II years) as "underdeveloped countries." Statistics on LDCs issued by the Bank, the OECD, and the UN do not necessarily cover the same countries. In some Bank literature, developing countries means the Part II members of IDA.

Libyan Arab Republic Known as Libya until September 1969.

M Minutes. M67-5 would mean the minutes of the fifth regular meeting of the Executive Directors of the Bank in 1967. SM67-5 would mean the fifth special meeting of the Bank's Board in 1967. IDA/M67-5 would mean the corresponding meeting of IDA Executive Directors. IFC/M67-5 would mean the corresponding meeting of IFC Executive Directors.

NAC [U.S.] National Advisory Council on International Monetary and Financial Problems.

NEDB National Economic Development Board of Thailand.

ODA Official Development Assistance, or aid flows to less developed countries and multilateral institutions, as defined by the DAC.

OECD Organisation for Economic Co-operation and Development, successor to OEEC.

OEEC Organisation for European Economic Co-operation.

Part I countries Member countries of IDA whose subscriptions are payable in full in gold or convertible currencies—in other words, the countries that are more advanced economically.

Part II countries Members of IDA that are required to pay only 10 percent of their subscriptions in gold or convertible currencies—in other words, middle- and low-income (or less developed) countries.

PICA Private Investment Company for Asia.

PICIC Pakistan Industrial Credit and Investment Corporation.

R-1 through **R-1025** Secretary's Reports, 1946–56. Thereafter they are numbered by years, R57-1, etc. Similarly, IFC Reports from June 1956 on are numbered IFC/R56-1, etc., and IDA Reports from October 1959 on are numbered IDA/R59-1, etc.

RID Royal Irrigation Department [of Thailand].

SDRs Special Drawing Rights issued by the IMF.

SEC (U.S.) Securities and Exchange Commission.

SLC Staff Loan Committee, now called Loan Committee, of the Bank/IDA.

Sec M Secretary's Memoranda. Between 1946 and 1956, they were numbered 1 through 999 and 1–1 through 1–522. Since then, they have been numbered by years, SecM57-1, SecM58-1, etc. Those pertaining to IFC begin in 1956 with IFC/SecM56-1, and those pertaining to IDA begin in 1960 with IDA/SecM60-1.

SM See "M."

Sri Lanka Known as Ceylon until August 1972.

SUNFED Special United Nations Fund for Economic Development proposed in the United Nations in 1953 but not brought into being.

T.O.D. Technical Operations Department (of the Bank/IDA).

TSKB The development bank of Turkey.

U.K. United Kingdom.

UN United Nations.

UNCTAD United Nations Conference on Trade and Development. (UNCTAD I refers to 1964 conference held in Geneva, UNCTAD II to the 1968 conference held in New Delhi.)

UNDP United Nations Development Program.

UNEDA United Nations Economic Development Administration, proposed in the United Nations in 1949 but not brought into being.

Unesco United Nations Educational, Scientific and Cultural Organization.

UNIDO United Nations Industrial Development Organization.

UNRRA United Nations Relief and Rehabilitation Administration.

U.S. United States of America.

USSR Union of Soviet Socialist Republics.

WHO World Health Organization.

World Bank Group See Bank Group.

Yemen, People's Democratic Republic of Known as the People's Republic of Southern Yemen until November 1970.

Zaire Democratic Republic of the Congo until October 1971.

THE
WORLD
BANK
SINCE
BRETTON
WOODS

CHAPTER ONE

Introduction

LOOKING BACK, WITH the benefit of twenty-five years of hindsight, on the events leading to the formation of the International Bank for Reconstruction and Development and the International Monetary Fund, one is struck by both the magnificence of the achievement and the lack of prescience of the founding fathers.

When the representatives of forty-four of the "United Nations and the nations associated with them in the war" met at Bretton Woods, New Hampshire, in July 1944 to put the capstone on some three years of preliminary work and negotiation, the Soviet forces to the east of Germany had not yet reached the Polish border, and to the west the Allies were engaged in a sanguinary struggle whose outcome was by no means certain. The allied forces in the Pacific were still involved in the slow process of subjugating islands and advancing gingerly along the northern coast of New Guinea. A full year of desperate battle lay ahead. Yet the delegates to Bretton Woods were talking about, and indeed were already erecting a framework for, future international economic cooperation. This conference was not assembled merely to pass resolutions and then disband, as were so many in the interwar period. It met to establish two institutions that have helped to shape the postwar world.

Yet at the same time even the wisest of the Bretton Woods delegates had only a dim perception of what this postwar world would be like. In the Fund they established an institution that could begin to function effectively only when the principal trading nations of the world had reached something close to equilibrium in their balance of payments, and this was far to seek. And the delegates at Bretton Woods intended that the Bank would turn its attention first to the repair of war damage and then to making development loans. In his opening remarks at the first meeting of the Bretton Woods Commission on the Bank, Lord Keynes said:

It is likely, in my judgment, that the field of reconstruction from the consequences of war will mainly occupy the proposed Bank in its early days. But as soon as possible, and with increasing emphasis as time goes on, there is a second primary duty laid upon it, namely to develop the resources and productive capacity of the world, with special reference to the less developed countries.

The funds to be channeled through the Bank were to come primarily from private sources, with the Bank either guaranteeing private lending or selling its own securities on capital markets. Government-to-government loans could be tolerated in wartime, but with the coming of peace, private international lending would be revived. Furthermore, the Bank loans would be for sound productive projects and not for balance-of-payments support, as so many loans to governments had been in the 1920s. In fact, as things worked out, the war-devastated countries needed funds not merely for the reconstruction of capital facilities but, what was more important, for the restocking of inventories; for imports of foodstuffs, raw material, and fuel; and for other purposes that fall outside the purview of project financing. And they needed financing for these imports far beyond the ability of private lenders to provide. Even before the Bank began operating, the United Kingdom borrowed $5 billion from the United States and Canada in the form of government-to-government loans. The International Bank's first four loans went to Western European countries to finance imports that in no sense could be considered project-oriented, and it soon became clear that reconstruction would not become a primary concern of the Bank. The United States, through the Marshall Plan, took over this task for Western Europe, and the Bank was left slowly to discover reputable development projects and to establish its borrowing capacity in the New York capital market. The performance of the Bank in these early years was not as disappointing to its sponsors as was that of the Fund, but then no one had expected as much of the Bank. As is noted in Chapter 2, the Bank was in some respects an afterthought.

There were three fundamentally important tasks, as those engaged in economic planning for the postwar world saw it. First, food, clothing, and other necessities would have to be provided for "relief and rehabilitation." This called for government gifts; and since the United States was almost the only country able either to provide the finance or to supply the goods, it had to be mainly a U.S. endeavor. Because it was understood that this problem required special measures, it was not on the agenda for discussion at Bretton Woods. The relief effort became the task of a new agency—the United Nations Relief and Rehabilitation Administration (UNRRA). Second, there was the need for reconstruction and, over the horizon, for development. This was to be the task of the Bank, mainly through the mobilization of private capital. Once reconstruction was well under way, the world would be able to tackle the third and by far the most difficult task—the freeing of international payments and international trade from the restrictions of exchange controls, multiple exchange rates, competitive depreciation, import quotas, trade discrimination, excessive tariffs, and the like. This task was to be undertaken by the International Monetary Fund and later by an international trade organization. It was recognized that the period when relief and reconstruction were under way would need to be considered a "transitional" phase, during which countries could not be expected to live up to the full trade and payments obligations envisaged by the Fund. Although no terminal date was set for the transition period, it was provided in the Articles of Agreement of the Fund that five years after its inauguration, that is, in March 1952, countries still following unacceptable trade and payments practices would have to consult the Fund annually on their reasons for retaining restrictions on payments and transfers for international transactions.

If now we may substitute our hindsight for the postwar planners' foresight, it is quite easy to see where they went wrong. The framers of the Articles of Agreement for the Fund and those for the Bank had foreseen one world, but soon after the war it became evident that there were to be two. Although the Soviet Union sent delegates to Bretton Woods, who joined with the others in accepting the agreed Articles, it soon became clear that the Soviet Union would not become a signatory. Second, the Bretton Woods delegates vastly underestimated the costs of reconstruction in Europe and other devastated areas and did not envisage the kind of import programs that were needed to rehabilitate war-damaged economies. Third, and related to this underestimate, the framers of the Articles of Agreement had little conception of the time that would be required to reestablish international trade and effective payments relationships. In 1952, five years after the Fund opened its doors, only six countries in the world were able to comply with what Article VIII of the Fund Agreement specified as satisfactory trade and payments practices, and not until 1958 did major European countries accept the obligation to maintain convertible currencies. Fourth, neither the Bretton Woods delegates nor anyone else foresaw how rapidly the colonial world would disintegrate and what this disintegration would do to the organization of the Fund and the Bank and their relations with their membership. In 1947 the Bank had 45 members, of which 14 were European countries and 18 Central and South American. In 1958 the number was 67, the increase being due mainly to a rise in Asian membership from 3 to 13. In 1967 there were 106 members, and the change was due largely to the increase in African membership from 2 in 1947 to 7 in 1958, and 34 in 1967. In 1971 the Bank had a total of 116 members. Finally, insofar as the Bretton Woods delegates considered the question specifically, they saw no reason to distinguish those policies relating to trade, payments, and capital flows that were considered to be favorable to the growth and prosperity of the developed countries of the world from those favorable to less developed countries. In fact the distinction between developed and less developed and between north and south—the special problems of the "third world"—had scarcely swum into the ken of postwar planners.

It is remarkable, considering the disparity between the vision of Bretton Woods and what in fact happened, that the Bank and the Fund have continued to flourish in roles that are different from those contemplated by their founders. How these changes in the international scene influenced the development of the Bank is a theme of this book.

The authors have attempted to trace the history of the Bank, and later the Bank Group, from small beginnings to its emergence as a leading source of development lending. They have also attempted two other tasks: to analyze the principal functions of the Bank Group as borrower, lender, provider of technical assistance, stimulator of private investment, and guider of development policy; and to offer an appraisal of the Bank Group as a set of development institutions. It has not been easy to combine the historical narrative with an analysis of functions and an appraisal of performance. An attempt to do so is apt to err in one of two directions. Either the chronology is emphasized, with an account of year-to-year changes in a broad spectrum of activities that need to be analyzed independently to be understood; or the analysis so overwhelms the chronology that the reader loses all comprehension of the organic growth of a social entity. The authors cannot claim to have succeeded better than others in surmounting this difficulty, but they have made an effort to do so.

Part 1 deals with two topics: (a) the origins of the Bank, described in Chapters 2 and 3; and (b) the organizational and institutional evolution of the Bank Group (related in Chapter 4) from its beginning up to June 30, 1971, which marks the end of the twenty-five-year period covered by this study. This part is mainly descriptive and narrative. It attempts to set out the main features of the institution that was brought into being in 1946 and to trace its evolution to date as an organization.

Part 2 analyzes the principal functions of the Bank Group. The International Bank for Reconstruction and Development (IBRD) became a "group" with the creation of the International Finance Corporation (IFC) in 1956 and the International Development Association (IDA) in 1960. The special characteristics and problems of the IFC and IDA are discussed in Chapters

11 and 12. Otherwise the analysis of functions in Part 2 embraces the activities of the Bank Group, though the differing roles of the Bank, IDA, and IFC are distinguished where appropriate.

The Bank was established as an institution that had to borrow in order to lend. Only 20 percent of its initial $10 billion capitalization was to be paid in, and only 2 percent of that $10 billion was payable in gold or dollars, the remaining 18 percent being payable in the currencies of the members. Since in 1946 the United States was the only member country with a convertible currency, the Bank's usable resources when it opened its doors were the U.S. 20 percent subscription and the 2 percent subscription from each of the other member countries. Chapter 5, "Financing the Bank," deals with the expansion of the Bank's usable capital as the currencies of various member countries became convertible, as additional members joined, and as earnings were accumulated in usable reserves. But the chapter deals mainly with what was after all the principal source of loanable funds—the Bank's borrowing. For the first ten years the borrowing took place mainly in the United States and mainly in the form of long-term securities. But over time other markets have come to vie with the New York market, and the Bank has cultivated other kinds of securities, has raised money by selling off parts of its loans to private investors, and has tapped central banks and other governmental and international institutions as sources of capital.

Chapter 6 discusses the early years of Bank lending and the formulation of lending policy by the management and executive directors. Chapters 7, 8, and 9 should be read together as an account of the lending policies of the Bank Group in the period since the early 1950s. Chapter 7 deals with the expansion of Bank Group lending, its geographical and sectoral distribution, the relative share of Bank Group lending in the total flow of development assistance, the terms of lending, the reverse flow of principal and interest payments, the rapidly increasing burden of debt owed by the less developed world to the Bank Group and other lenders, and the involvement of the Bank in problems of debt renegotiation. Chapter 8 discusses the development of techniques of project lending and project appraisal. Chapter 9 considers two related types of Bank Group lending that have caused considerable controversy within the Bank and outside: the financing of the local expenditures involved in projects, and program lending.

Although the Articles of Agreement of the Bank say nothing about technical assistance, the Bank soon discovered that, in applying for loans, its less developed member countries were not likely to present well prepared project proposals without Bank assistance. Technical assistance in project identification and preparation, as well as in other investment-related activities, has steadily increased. The Bank Group has helped in establishing and advising development finance companies in Asia, Africa, Latin America, and the Middle East and has frequently found managerial personnel for these institutions. In addition to advising on projects, the Bank has advised governments on sectoral and national economic policies. In 1955 it established the Economic Development Institute (EDI), which by June 30, 1971, had enrolled more than thirteen hundred government officials in its training program. The Bank Group in recent years has financed the establishment of a group of long-term technical and managerial personnel for temporary assignment to borrowing governments. These and other aspects of the Bank Group's technical assistance activities are discussed in Chapter 10.

Bank Group lending, of course, and indeed the entire flow of external assistance to less developed countries, represents a minor part of total development expenditures. What these countries do with their own resources is the most important factor in development. By virtue of its lending activity the Bank Group is in a position to exert a certain amount of influence on the development practices and policies of borrowing countries. This leverage can be applied directly at the project level; and the conditions the IBRD attaches to its project loans are expressed in loan covenants, supplementary letters, and written and oral statements of intent by government officials concerned with the project. These conditions affect procurement policies, construction practices, the choice of management, and administrative organization; and they frequently extend beyond these to pricing policy, the financing of project expansion, and other matters. Because Bank Group lending increasingly has financed the capital expansion of a group of projects in key sectors of the economy, the Bank may be able to influence developmental policies relating to those sectors, such as policies affecting road and rail competition or the introduction of new agricultural practices. And if the Bank is a large and important provider of capital to a borrowing member country, the threat (or promise) to vary the level of lending may influence the formulation of policy at the national level. Obviously delicate questions of sovereignty and external intervention may arise. These aspects of the relation of "leverage" to "performance" are discussed in Chapter 13.

The final chapter in Part 2 examines the way in which the Bank has conceived the development process of its member borrowers at various stages in its history and how it has responded to their needs.

The origins of the Bank go back to the period immediately after World War II, when a host of international institutions were taking shape. Most of these were attached to the United Nations, but the European Recovery Program gave birth to the Organisation for European Economic Co-operation and the European Payments Union. Later the OEEC became the Organisation for Economic Co-operation and Development (OECD), of which the most important subsidiary from the Bank's point of view is the Development Assistance Committee (DAC). As the Third World emerged in the form of newly independent nations, bilateral assistance programs developed in most of the richer countries; regional development banks were established as multilateral institutions to serve Latin America, Asia, and Africa; and European institutions, such as the European Development Fund and the European Investment Bank, were set up and assigned development responsibilities. The World Bank has relations with all of these institutions and programs and has moved increasingly into a central role in assisting and coordinating cooperative efforts. Also the Bank's role as intermediary between the developed and less developed world has on occasion, usually through the actions of its president, caused the Bank to play an active part in mediating international disputes. The authors have sought to bring together these relationships and activities in the four chapters in Part 3, "The Bank in the Realm of International Diplomacy."

The relations between the Bank and various bilateral assistance programs are discussed in Chapter 15. During the 1950s this relationship mainly involved a not altogether friendly rivalry with the U.S. Export-Import Bank. It was some time before other suppliers of development assistance came into the field and before it became clear to the Bank that there was more than enough work for everyone and that borrowing countries were loath to depend on any single source of finance. A large step forward in cooperation with other assistance-providers was taken in 1958 with the organization of what subsequently became the India Consortium, shortly to be followed by a similar arrangement for Pakistan. The burgeoning flow of development assistance in the 1960s from many bilateral programs and newly formed regional banks created problems of aid coordination, to which one response was Bank-sponsored consultative groups. Between 1962 and 1971 some fifteen such groups were formed under Bank chairmanship. The Development Assistance Committee of the OECD was also interested in coordinating aid flows and, in general, worked closely with the Bank Group. Between the Bank and small bilateral programs a rather different relationship has developed than has been possible with larger aid donors. Canada, the Netherlands, and the Scandinavian countries, though not uncritical of the Bank, have frequently looked to it for advice and guidance. But the programs of some of the larger countries, shaped with political and commercial interests in view, have not been so amenable to influence. Over time, however, a growing volume of joint and parallel financing between the Bank and bilateral lenders has developed.

Because the Bank and the Fund were usually considered together during the war and in postwar deliberations, they were frequently called "the Bretton Woods twins." Certainly it was the intention of the founding fathers that these institutions would cooperate closely. Their location in adjoining buildings in Washington was intended to facilitate this objective. The relationship has indeed become closer over time, but at intervals it has been subject to institutional rivalries exacerbated by personality differences of a decidedly untwin-like character. Chapter 16 attempts to chart these ups and downs and also to discuss the not very well understood relationship between stabilization policy, which is the primary concern of the Fund, and development policy, which is, or should be, the primary concern of the Bank.

The Bank is a "specialized agency" of the United Nations, but like the Fund it is a rather "special" specialized agency. Chapter 17 discusses the Bank Group's relation to the UN family and to other international organizations. The UN agencies with which the Bank has particularly close connections are the United Nations Development Program (UNDP), the Food and Agriculture Organization (FAO), the United Nations Educational, Scientific, and Cultural Organization (Unesco), the United Nations Conference on Trade and Development (UNCTAD), and, beginning in 1971, the World Health Organization (WHO). The other international organizations with which the Bank has intimate dealings are the previously mentioned OECD, with its offshoot the DAC, and the regional development banks.

Part 3, concerning the Bank and its "foreign relations," concludes with Chapter 18, which discusses the attempts of the Bank to mediate and settle some of the economic disputes that have arisen between various member countries. The most important of these have involved the Iranian nationalization of oil properties, the financing of the High Dam on the Nile River, and the division of the waters of the Indus between India and Pakistan. These interventions have been made largely by the president of the Bank in his personal capacity, but—at least in the case of the Indus—they have involved a serious commitment of Bank financial and staff resources.

Finally, in Part 4 we attempt an assessment of the Bank Group as a set of development institutions. We do this principally by reviewing in Chapter 19 its role in five countries in which it has long been involved and by looking in Chapter 20 at those sectors in which it has concentrated its lending. The latter chapter also includes a few comments on its overall impact. In the closing chapter, attention is called to certain problems facing the Bank Group as it begins its second quarter century, and some opinions are offered on the roles it can play.

PART ONE

The Bank as an
International Organization

CHAPTER TWO

How the Bank
Came into Being

THE DELEGATES WHO ASSEMBLED at Bretton Woods in July 1944 encountered great difficulty in finding a name for their creation. The representatives of the United Kingdom thought it should be called "the International Corporation for Reconstruction and Development" or be given "some
other title omitting the word 'Bank.'" El Salvador proposed "the International Guarantee and Investment Association." France preferred the title
"International Financial Institution for Reconstruction and Development."
And as Lord Keynes remarked somewhat facetiously, "the Bank should be
called the Fund and the Fund the Bank."[1]

Whatever it was to be called, it obviously lacked some of the elementary

1. U.S. Department of State, *Proceedings and Documents of United Nations Monetary and Financial Conference* (Bretton Woods, New Hampshire; July 1–22, 1944),
Vol. 1, p. 366. (Cited hereinafter as *Proceedings and Documents.*)

In preparing this chapter the authors have also benefited from a manuscript by
Henry J. Bitterman, "The Negotiating History of the Bank" (1967; processed). As a
U.S. Treasury Department official, Bitterman was associated with the so-called technical
committee that prepared the "Preliminary Draft Outline of a Proposal for a United
Nations Bank for Reconstruction and Development," which was circulated to other
countries in 1943. He was also a member of the U.S. delegation at Bretton Woods and
later was on the staff of the National Advisory Council on International Monetary and
Financial Problems, established by the Bretton Woods Agreements Act to advise the U.S.
representatives on the boards of the International Monetary Fund and the Bank. A con-
densed version of the Bitterman study was published in *The International Lawyer,*
Vol. 5 (January 1971).

The internal U.S. government memoranda and the exchanges between the United
States and the United Kingdom referred to in this chapter are filed in the Fund archives
and records office. There is nothing in the files of the Bank that pertains to the period
before it opened its doors.

11

properties ordinarily associated with banks. It did not receive deposits; it made loans only to governments, or to public and private entities on the basis of a government guarantee of repayment; four-fifths of the subscribed capital was not paid in but was to be used as a guarantee fund against losses; its principal function was intended to be the guarantee of private investment; it was not to lend or guarantee loans to any borrower capable of borrowing on reasonable terms from other sources. But regardless of what title would most appropriately have described its functions, it has become known in fact as the World Bank.

Not only its name but its coming into being were in doubt until almost the last minute. In his letter to forty-four governments inviting them to send representatives to a conference at Bretton Woods, the U.S. secretary of state described this as being "for the purpose of formulating definite proposals for an International Monetary Fund, and possibly [sic] a Bank for Reconstruction and Development." Almost all the preliminary work on the proposed Bank had been done within the U.S. government, and until the meeting in Atlantic City of the committee that was to shape the agenda for Bretton Woods, the participation of other countries had been perfunctory.

The secretary of the U.S. Treasury, Henry Morgenthau, sent a letter in April 1943 to thirty-seven united and associated nations and enclosed a preliminary draft of a proposal for a stabilization fund, together with the Keynes plan for a clearing union. When representatives from the United Kingdom and the United States met in Washington from September 15 through October 9, 1943, to discuss issues arising out of Article VII of the Lend-Lease agreement, some attention was given to commodity arrangements, commercial policy, and international investment. But the real *pièce de résistance* was an amalgamation of the Keynes and White plans into what became, in the spring of 1944, a joint statement of the experts on the International Monetary Fund.

The first unveiling to foreign eyes of U.S. thoughts on an international bank came in November 1943, when Secretary Morgenthau sent to associated governments a memorandum whose tentative character was indicated by the title, "Preliminary Draft Outline of a Proposal for a United Nations Bank for Reconstruction and Development." Sir Roy Harrod describes the British reaction as follows: "Stripped, as it had long since been, of all the exciting features, this document was an uninspiring one. The Bank had been dressed, with an eye to Congress, to look as orthodox as possible."[2]

The British did not comment on this document until April 1944, and they did so in an equally uninspiring fashion. The main purpose of their comment

2. Roy F. Harrod, *The Life of John Maynard Keynes* (Harcourt, Brace and Company, 1951), p. 573.

was to emphasize the importance of reconstruction as well as development. The U.S. technicians had no difficulty in agreeing. They said, "The proposed Bank is intended to facilitate the provision of capital for reconstruction in the immediate post-war period as well as for development purposes." [3]

This is where the matter stood when the delegations of a number of countries assembled in Atlantic City to prepare the agenda for Bretton Woods. So little comment from other sources had the U.S. proposal received that the U.S. delegates were doubtful about the wisdom of including a discussion of the Bank on the agenda. What helped to change their minds was the fact that the U.K. delegation, along with representatives from other countries who were headquartered in London and who traveled together to Atlantic City on the *Queen Mary,* turned their attention to the question of a bank. As Harrod described it, "It was decided to have meetings on the subject of the International Bank, which had hitherto been somewhat neglected. Keynes' enthusiasm was fired. A draft was prepared."[4] A comparison of this draft with the U.S. documentation led Harry D. White of the U.S. Treasury to conclude in a memorandum to Morgenthau, "They seem to be in accord with the general approach that we have proposed, though there are some substantial differences which will have to be ironed out at Bretton Woods. It seems we are not as far behind on the Bank proposal as we had thought. . . ."[5] Two days were set aside to consider Bank matters, and by the time the delegates were ready to proceed to Bretton Woods, British and U.S. proposals and other variants had been woven into a document ready for further examination.

Although the contribution of the British delegation and their *Queen Mary* colleagues was sizable, the Bank was essentially a U.S. proposal. In describing the British preparations for a discussion of Article VII of the Lend-Lease agreement, Harrod remarked, "In regard to international investment, it was agreed that the British ought not to take an initiative, on the ground that they would not be in a position in the period immediately following the war to contribute substantial sums towards it. It was for the Americans to take the initiative in this part of the field."[6] At Bretton Woods Lord Keynes served as chairman of Commission II, which concerned itself with the Bank. He said in his opening remarks, "I believe we have before us a proposal the origins of which we owe primarily to the initiative and ability of the United States Treasury, conceived on sound and fruitful lines."[7]

3. In a memorandum of May 25, 1944.
4. Harrod, *Life of John Maynard Keynes,* pp. 575–76.
5. Memorandum, International Monetary Fund Records Office (June 25, 1944; processed).
6. Harrod, *Life of John Maynard Keynes,* p. 533.
7. *Proceedings and Documents,* Vol. 1, p. 88.

Preparatory Work on the Bank

Before considering how the Articles of Agreement of the International Bank took shape, let us examine the origins of the U.S. proposal. As in the case of the U.S. proposals for what later became the International Monetary Fund, Harry White was the central figure. White had begun thinking about a postwar stabilization fund and international bank in 1941 and in December of that year produced a memorandum entitled "Suggested Program for Inter-Allied Monetary and Bank Action."[8] At that time he was a special adviser to the secretary of the treasury. He had formerly been director of the Treasury's Division of Monetary Research. In both capacities he had a great deal of influence on Secretary Henry Morgenthau. He was also a dominant figure among the technical experts in Washington who during the war were working on postwar economic policies. In describing his character and influence we can do no better than quote from *The International Monetary Fund*.

His intellect was powerful; his ideas imaginative, but not flexible. He was no theorist, but essentially a pragmatist. In argument he wielded not the rapier but the bludgeon. He tended to exploit to the full a position of strength—such as that which he occupied during the International Monetary Fund negotiations by reason of Secretary Morgenthau's reliance on him and because the financial help of the United States would clearly be essential in the postwar world. But he could be considerate, even genial, and on occasions showed extreme patience with those less conversant than himself with the subject under discussion. Above all, he expected no one to work harder than he did himself, and these qualities enabled him to inspire and dominate for a decade a team of U.S. advisors of high caliber and intellectual achievement.[9]

Of course White was not the only one concerned with postwar planning whose attention was turned toward the possibilities of an international bank. Luther H. Gulick, president of the Institute of Public Administration, and Professor Alvin H. Hansen of Harvard University, who had been sent to London on a mission by the U.S. Department of State, proposed in January 1942 the establishment of an International Development Corporation.[10] Experts from the Departments of State and the Treasury, the Board of Governors of the Federal Reserve System, and the Federal Loan Agency had worked out a proposal for an Inter-American Development Bank, which was accepted in February 1940 by the Inter-American Financial and Economic Advisory

8. J. Keith Horsefield, *Chronicle*, Vol. 1 of Horsefield (ed.), *The International Monetary Fund, 1945–1965: Twenty Years of International Monetary Cooperation* (International Monetary Fund, 1969), p. 12.

9. *Ibid.*, pp. 55–56.

10. *Ibid.*, pp. 13–14.

Committee. Although White had been one of these experts, the leadership had been taken by the Department of State. But while many hands had been, and were to be, involved in the International Bank proposal, it was essentially White's version that was issued in April 1942 as a "Proposal for a United Nations Stabilization Fund and a Bank for Reconstruction and Development of the United and Associated Nations" and that shaped the subsequent discussion.[11]

In the introduction White says,

No matter how long the war lasts nor how it is won, we shall be faced with three inescapable problems: to prevent the disruption of foreign exchanges and the collapse of monetary and credit systems; to assure the restoration of foreign trade; and to supply the huge volume of capital that will be needed virtually throughout the world for reconstruction, for relief, and for economic recovery.

Clearly the task can be successfully handled only through international action. ... It is high time that detailed and workable plans be prepared.

For anyone reflecting in 1942 on the feasibility of an International Bank there were two possible precedents, the Bank for International Settlements established in 1930, and the Inter-American Bank, mentioned above, which had been proposed in 1940, but which had never come into existence. The Bank for International Settlements, however, was a different kind of animal. It had been created primarily to handle reparations transfers from Germany under the Young Plan and, when these lapsed, became mainly an agent for European central banks in handling gold flows. The Inter-American Bank, on the other hand, even though it had not come into existence, had important similarities with the institution envisaged in the White proposal and in some respects foreshadowed the Articles of Agreement of the IBRD.[12]

Shares in the Inter-American Bank were to be held by governments; each country was to have a member on the board of directors; and voting was to be in proportion to stock holding. The United States was to be the principal financier, and it was anticipated that borrowing would be mainly in the U.S. market. Although the proposed bank would lend for particular projects, it was not as limited as was the later World Bank to project lending. Indeed the Inter-American Bank was intended to have some of the functions later incorporated in the Monetary Fund. The Inter-American Bank could "assist in stabilizing the currencies, ... function as a clearing house for ... international payments, make loans, buy and sell the securities of any of the member

11. This is a document of 138 pages prepared at the request of Secretary Morgenthau. Part 1 presents a framework for the Stabilization Fund and the Bank. Part 2 spells out the rationale for the proposed Fund. Part 3 presents the rationale for the proposed Bank. International Monetary Fund Records Office (April 1942; processed).

12. Bitterman, "Negotiating History of the Bank," pp. 4–11.

governments or their political subdivisions or private entities, guarantee credits in gold and foreign currencies, discount bills and other credit instruments, accept deposits, and perform normal banking functions."[13]

In other words, the proposed Inter-American Bank combined the functions of an intergovernmental bank, an international stabilization fund, and an ordinary commercial bank. This proliferation of functions was one of the reasons for the failure of the project. In particular, U.S. commercial banks feared the emergence of a powerful competitor. "They argued that the Bank should be a bankers' bank which could make loans to the other banks or to governments only with appropriate guarantees."[14] Other objections were offered in House and Senate hearings, and with the coming of World War II the proposal was allowed to die in committee.

White's exposure to the technical discussions concerning the Inter-American Bank obviously influenced his April 1942 proposal for a Bank for Reconstruction and Development of the United and Associated Nations, though he attempted to guard against the objections of the commercial bankers by providing that short-term capital would be offered only where such capital was not available from private sources at reasonable rates. The statement of objectives, however, makes it clear that he contemplated a far-reaching instrument. Among these objectives were:

> To help strengthen the monetary and credit structures of the member countries by redistributing the world gold supply.
> To help stabilize the prices of essential raw materials and other important commodities, [and]
> To provide for the financing and distribution of foodstuffs and other essential commodities needed for the relief of populations devastated by war conditions.

The proposal indeed embraced functions later shared by the World Bank, the Fund, and the United Nations Relief and Rehabilitation Administration (UNRRA). Nevertheless certain elements of the proposed framework clearly foreshadowed provisions in the Articles of Agreement of the IBRD. For example,

> The servicing of the loan is fully guaranteed by the national government.
> The loan is to be made only after a careful study by a competent committee on the merits of the project and the loan.
> Whenever possible the Bank should guarantee loans made by private investors, instead of making loans directly. [This provision, however, was greatly qualified.][15]

13. *Ibid.,* p. 8. The text of the agreement on the Inter-American Bank and explanations by the Department of State were published in the *Federal Reserve Bulletin* (June 1940), pp. 517–25. The extent to which the Bank contemplated functions later assigned to the Monetary Fund is discussed in Horsefield, *Chronicle,* pp. 10–14.
14. Bitterman, "Negotiating History of the Bank," p. 10.
15. *Ibid.*

The capital of the proposed Bank for Reconstruction and Development was to be $10 billion, with voting power determined by the number of shares held by each government but with no government holding more than 25 percent of the total voting strength. Membership in the Bank was made conditional on membership in the Fund.

Secretary Morgenthau circulated White's proposal to other interested agencies of the U.S. government, reported the results to the White House, and in May 1942 was authorized by President Roosevelt to pursue these discussions in a cabinet committee, served by a technical committee of which White was chairman. It was this technical committee that drew up the U.S. proposal circulated in November 1943 to other governments and that provided most of the U.S. technical personnel for the Bretton Woods conference. Although the U.S. Treasury Department played a large part in shaping the proposals distributed to other governments, it was not alone. The Department of State presented in September 1943 a proposal for an International Development Agency very similar to the proposal made in November.[16] Emilio G. Collado, chief of the State Department's Division of Financial and Monetary Affairs, and his assistant chief, John Parke Young, were largely responsible for the latter version. Experts from many agencies in addition to the Treasury worked on the November draft, including State, Commerce, the Securities and Exchange Commission, the Export-Import Bank, the Board of Governors of the Federal Reserve System, and the Foreign Economic Administration. Nevertheless, Lord Keynes (quoted above) was substantially correct in referring to this as principally a Treasury document.

This was the draft that Harrod described as an "uninspiring one." And indeed, it proposed a much more limited institution than did White's earlier version. A number of the functions suggested in the earlier version were now transferred to the proposals for a UN stabilization fund and to UNRRA. At the hands of numerous collaborators and critics the Bank proposal was being shaped into something rather close to what it later became at Bretton Woods.

Although the preliminary draft outline of November 1943 did not, as did the Fund proposal, receive the benediction of a joint statement of the experts before Bretton Woods, it *was* subjected to scrutiny by, and discussion with, technical representatives of other countries. The U.S. Treasury, in January 1944, distributed to the allied and associated powers a set of questions and answers concerning the Bank, which went through several editions before the meeting in Atlantic City.[17] In subsequent months representatives of a

16. *Ibid.*, p. 16.
17. The edition of "Questions and Answers" cited here is dated June 10, 1944, and covers approximately one hundred pages. International Monetary Fund, Records Office (1944; processed).

number of countries visited the Treasury to obtain information and make suggestions. In general the Bank proposal received substantial approval.

The intention of the framers of the preliminary draft was quite clearly to establish an institution that would facilitate the international flow of private portfolio investment. The preamble said, "The Bank is intended to cooperate with private financial agencies in making available long-term capital for reconstruction and development and to supplement such investment where private agencies are unable to meet fully the legitimate needs for capital for productive investment."

A memorandum from Secretary Morgenthau distributed with the preliminary draft outline said, "With the return of an assured peace, private financial agencies may be expected to supply most of the needed short-term foreign capital." Long-term lending, on the other hand, would develop more slowly; and consequently an international agency was needed to facilitate this type of lending. "The primary aim of such an agency should be to encourage private capital to go abroad for productive investment by sharing the risks of private investors in large ventures."

The principal instrument for accomplishing this purpose would be the Bank's guarantee of private investments. "The most important of the Bank's operations will be to guarantee loans in order that investors may have a reasonable assurance of safety in placing their funds abroad. In this way it is expected that the international flow of capital in adequate volume will be encouraged."[18] Direct lending by the Bank was intended to be a definitely secondary function.

Article II of the preliminary draft outline proposed an authorized capital of $10 billion, 20 percent of which was initially to be paid in gold and currency. The remainder was to serve as a guarantee fund. The question was asked, "Will capital of $10 billion be adequate for the Bank, particularly if only a small part of the capital subscription is to be paid in?" And the answer was, "Because the Bank's principal function is to encourage international investment by private investors, the surety aspect of the Bank's capital will be of particular importance. . . . It is probable that a subscribed capital of $10 billion will make it possible for the Bank to act as a guarantor for two to three times this amount of loans without impairing the high quality of its guarantee."[19]

Article III of the draft proposal dealt with the proposed international monetary unit, *unitas*, which was to have the value of ten U.S. dollars. This

18. "Questions and Answers," reply to Question 7.
19. *Ibid.*, Question 2 and reply.

conception, along with the *bancor* of Keynes's Clearing Union, was dropped in the joint statement of the experts on the International Monetary Fund.

Article IV dealt with the powers and operation of the Bank. A number of the provisions of this article were carried over intact to Article IV of the Articles of Agreement of the IBRD: Payment of interest and principal must be fully guaranteed by the borrowing government; the borrower must be unable to secure funds from other sources on reasonable terms; a careful study must be made by a competent committee of the merits of "the project or program"; the Bank must be properly compensated for the use of its guarantee; no condition shall be imposed concerning the country in which the loan shall be spent (that is, there can be no tied loans); except in special circumstances, the loan shall be limited to the foreign exchange requirements of the project; the Bank shall not be influenced by the political character of the country requesting the loan (a provision included with the Soviet Union in mind).

Article V concerned the question of management and need not be considered here. The management provisions of the Articles of Agreement were essentially taken over from the relevant Articles of the Fund and were adapted to the Bank's purposes. It should be noted, however, that the draft outline made membership in the Bank conditional on membership in the Fund. As one of the architects of the draft outline later remarked, "Basically we wanted to force countries to agree to standards in the monetary field as a condition to get the benefits of the Bank."[20]

Atlantic City

This, then, was the state of affairs when the representatives of a number of countries met in Atlantic City to prepare the agenda for Bretton Woods. The work of the agenda committee continued until June 30, 1944, when the delegates who were assembled in Atlantic City repaired to Bretton Woods.[21]

As was mentioned above, the U.S. delegation had gone to Atlantic City uncertain whether the proposal for an international bank would be far enough advanced, as a result of the discussions held there, to be put on the agenda for Bretton Woods. This issue was substantially clarified by the document

20. Oral History Project of Columbia University, interviews recorded in the summer of 1961 on the International Bank for Reconstruction and Development (cited hereinafter as "Oral History"). Quotation is from interview of Ansel F. Luxford, p. 7.

21. The countries represented in Atlantic City were Australia, Belgium, Brazil, Canada, Chile, China, Cuba, Czechoslovakia, France, Greece, India, Mexico, the Netherlands, Norway, the USSR, the United Kingdom, and the United States. See Bitterman, "Negotiating History of the Bank," pp. 37–38.

presented by the United Kingdom, which had been worked out by the delegations assembled on the transatlantic liner, *Queen Mary,* and which became known as the "boat draft." The draft indicated, in general, substantial agreement with the U.S. proposal, though it suggested a number of substantive changes. It proposed a reorganization of the subjects covered in a form very similar to that of the final Articles of Agreement, and it rephrased a number of the provisions.

Perhaps the most important substantive change suggested by the "boat draft" dealt with the Bank's capital structure. In the U.S. version, 20 percent of each country's capital subscription was to be paid in "initially," with the assumption that this share might be increased over time. The U.K. draft insisted on a *limit* of 20 percent to be paid in, not more than one-fifth of which would be payable in gold. The 80 percent reserve funds would be callable only to meet losses.[22]

A number of further suggestions were offered by the United Kingdom and by other delegations at Atlantic City for later discussion at Bretton Woods. White summarized these suggestions and gave the initial reaction of the U.S. technicians in a memorandum to Secretary Morgenthau, dated June 27, 1944.[23]

1. "A number of countries wish to have the Bank make loans in gold for currency reserves."
The U.S. technical advisers are opposed.
2. "Several occupied countries wish to have the Bank make loans for procurement of essential materials and inventories depleted during the war or destroyed by enemy action."
The U.S. technicians recognize that there is some merit in this suggestion but think such loans should be "extremely limited in amount."
3. "Several of the Latin-American representatives wish to have the Bank authorized to make loans for agricultural development."
This is considered desirable, but the loans should be solely for the "development of agricultural production."
4. "Several Latin-American countries favor having the Bank make local currency loans."
This should be done only in exceptional circumstances.
5. "Some of the occupied countries favor a reduction of capital subscriptions for countries that have suffered substantial damage from enemy action or occupation."
The U.S. technical advisers oppose this suggestion. The gold contribution will be relatively small, and if a country lacks resources for foreign investment, its subscriptions to the Bank will not be utilized.

22. *Ibid.,* p. 39.
23. International Monetary Fund, Records Office.

6. "The United Kingdom favors the calling in of only a small proportion of the capital subscription, i.e., 20 percent."

The U.S. technicians do not object.

7. "A number of countries favor authorizing the Bank to invest a part of its capital in equity securities."

The U.S. technical advisers do not wish to see the Bank involved in project management.

8. "A number of countries feel that the proceeds of any loan guaranteed or made by the Bank should be free exchange available to the borrower for expenditure in any market."

The U.S. technical advisers think this is not feasible since no loan can be made without the approval of a country whose currency is loaned.

9. "The United Kingdom representatives favor a single flat-rate guarantee fee and want the guarantee fees retained as reserves to meet losses on guaranteed loans."

The U.S. advisers feel there should be more flexibility.

These and other suggestions were considered in Atlantic City, and the U.S. proposal and the "boat draft" were amalgamated into a statement to be placed before the delegates at Bretton Woods.[24] The agenda committee of Commission II (which was concerned with the Bank) proposed that it be taken as "the initial basis for discussion and amendment. It is not to be regarded as the proposal of any Delegation, nor is any Delegation committed to it."[25]

Bretton Woods

The draft presented to the delegates at Bretton Woods was, in its general outline, very similar to the Articles of Agreement that emerged from the conference. The titles of the articles and the order of their arrangement were, with minor changes, left untouched. The substance of each article, however, was presented in different versions—the U.S. version, the U.K. version, new material, and material taken from the draft of the Monetary Fund proposal. Delegates were asked to submit new suggestions and proposals.

The first week's discussion at Bretton Woods was devoted entirely to the Fund. Indeed fears began to be expressed that the conference would never get around to the Bank. The delegates from many of the less developed countries, however, were much more interested in the Bank than in the Fund, and so were a number of the European countries whose economies had been damaged by the war. The Russians, in particular, set great store by the reconstruction objectives of the Bank. As a result of pressures from these

24. This statement may be found in *Proceedings and Documents,* Vol. 1, pp. 192–215.

25. *Ibid.,* p. 191.

sources, a group was designated to work on the Bank. The four committees and a number of subcommittees, organized under Commission II, were useful in collecting additional proposals. But the actual redrafting of what became the Articles of Agreement was undertaken by a smaller group. On the U.S. side the senior representatives were Dean Acheson, then assistant secretary of state, and Edward E. Brown, then chairman of the First National Bank of Chicago. At the working level Emilio G. Collado of the Department of State, and Professor James W. Angell of the Foreign Economic Administration, on leave from Columbia University, were the principal participants. But Lord Keynes took a great interest and attended many of the working meetings. Pierre Mendes-France, head of the French delegation, J. W. Beyen, head of the Netherlands delegation, and Kyriakos Varvaressos, head of the Greek delegation, were actively interested, as were a number of the chiefs of Latin American delegations.[26]

It will serve no useful purpose to go through the various formulations of what later became, or did not become, the paragraphs and sections of the Articles of Agreement. Nor do we attempt to summarize the voluminous speeches and discussions at Bretton Woods on the subject of the Bank. It is important, however, to call attention to the principal features of the institution that was put together at Bretton Woods and to the reasons why these, rather than some other characteristics, were included in the articles.

The Bretton Woods creation was to serve the purposes of both reconstruction and development. But which purpose would have priority? The European countries quite naturally stressed reconstruction. The Russians, in particular, asserted that the primary purpose of the Bank should be to assist in the reconstruction and the restoration of economies destroyed by the hostilities.[27] The less developed countries, on the other hand, feared that if too heavy an emphasis were put on reconstruction, the Bank would never get around to development. Mexico proposed a version stating that economic

26. Letter from Collado to Edward S. Mason, June 26, 1969. In *The Life of John Maynard Keynes,* Harrod reports (pp. 579–80): "The Charter of the Bank was drawn up, not by the formal committees, but by Professor J. W. Angell and Mr. E. G. Collado, working on successive days into the small hours; they referred difficult points to Mr. Dean Acheson and sometimes to Mr. E. E. Brown, prior to assimilation by the British. The principal basis for their work was the 'boat draft,' which consisted mainly of a set of principles." It is not quite true that the principal basis of their work was the "boat draft," since, as we have seen, deliberations in Atlantic City had produced a document containing British and American suggestions, new material, and sections drawn from the IMF proposal. But it *is* true that Collado and Angell had a large hand in preparing the final draft.

27. *Proceedings and Documents,* Vol. 1, pp. 366–67. Cited by Bitterman in "The Negotiating History of the Bank," p. 55.

development was the first purpose but, second, the Bank was "to assist, during the first postwar years, in the reconstruction of member countries and in the transition from a war-time to a peace-time economy."[28]

The Articles of Agreement left the question of priority of purposes entirely to the discretion of the Bank. "The resources and the facilities of the Bank shall be used exclusively for the benefit of members with equitable consideration to projects for development and projects for reconstruction alike."[29] However, paragraph (b) of the same section directs the Bank to "pay special regard to lightening the financial burden" for countries that have suffered "great devastation from enemy occupation or hostilities." And there can be little doubt that the countries that were to hold a majority of the stock were concerned primarily with the reconstruction objective.

The provisions on the size and structure of the Bank's capitalization followed fairly closely earlier U.S. proposals as modified by British suggestions in Atlantic City. The total capital was to be $10 billion, of which 20 percent was callable and 80 percent was to serve as a guarantee fund.[30] The 20 percent, however, was divided into 2 percent payable in gold or dollars and 18 percent callable in the currency of the members.[31] Since the United States was the only member with a convertible currency, this meant that until other currencies became convertible the Bank would have loanable funds amounting only to the U.S. 20 percent, plus the 2 percent contribution from other members. When later on the Bank wanted to make use of the callable 18 percent of the subscriptions of other members, it experienced considerable difficulty in doing so. The reasons for this are discussed in Chapter 5.

Article III, section 3, provided that, "the total amount outstanding of guarantees, participations in loans and direct loans made by the Bank shall not be increased at any time, if by such increase the total would exceed one hundred percent of the unimpaired subscribed capital, reserves and surplus of the Bank." This question of maximum lending capacity had been left open at Atlantic City. But earlier U.S. pronouncements had suggested that the Bank might commit up to two or three times its total capital subscriptions.[32] Some of the participants at Bretton Woods favored a limit of three to five times the Bank's capitalization. These expectations were obviously based on the premise that the guarantee by those member countries other than the

28. Bitterman, "Negotiating History of the Bank," p. 55, and *Proceedings and Documents,* Vol. 1, p. 485.

29. International Bank for Reconstruction and Development (cited hereinafter as IBRD), Articles of Agreement, Article III, section 1(a).

30. *Ibid.,* Article II, section 5.

31. *Ibid.,* Article II, section 7(i).

32. "Questions and Answers," Question 2.

United States would mean something in the New York capital market, which was the only place where the Bank would, at least initially, think of borrowing. But as Beyen, the head of the Netherlands delegation, observed,

What the enthusiasts overlooked completely was that far from feeling at their ease with a guarantee, or unpaid capital liability, of forty-five nations for one-third of the obligations of the Bank, the private investors were not even likely to be satisfied with one hundred per cent guarantee from nations whose capacity to pay they were—either because of unfortunate experiences of the past or because of the general instability created by the war—to judge with a very critical eye. There were not many bankers among the Bretton Woods delegates. There was one highly able and wise American commercial banker in the United States delegation, but it had not been deemed necessary to invite representatives of the American investment houses—although it was from their clients that, at any rate for years to come, practically all the money for the financing of the Bank's operations was expected.[33]

Whatever limits were set on Bank commitments in the Articles of Agreement, in fact, the Bank's capacity to lend in the first few years of its existence was determined essentially by the size of the U.S. 20 percent commitment, the 2 percent from other countries, and what could be borrowed in the New York market. And in that market the only guarantee that was considered to be worth anything was the U.S. guarantee.

The specifications of conditions under which the Bank could guarantee or make loans[34] rather closely followed earlier U.S. proposals. The borrowing government or its representative must fully guarantee payment of principal and interest; the Bank must be satisfied that money is not available from other sources on reasonable terms; a competent committee must study the merits of the proposal; charges must be reasonable and the schedule of repayments appropriate to the project; the borrower must be creditworthy; and the Bank must be suitably compensated.

One of the specifications, however, calls for particular comment since it has been the subject of interpretation and debate during the Bank's history. "Loans made or guaranteed by the Bank shall, except in special circumstances, be for the purpose of specific projects of reconstruction or development."[35] The U.S. draft presented at Atlantic City had mentioned "programs and projects." While the British version emphasized "specific projects of reconstruction and development," it went on to say that in special circumstances and in agreement with the IMF the Bank could make or guarantee a loan "which provides the borrowing country with gold or foreign exchange for the purpose of establishing its exchanges and allowing a breathing space

---

33. J. W. Beyen, *Money in a Maelstrom* (Macmillan, 1949), p. 179.
34. Article III, section 4.
35. Article III, section 4(vii).

for the recovery of its economy and the balancing of its international payments."

When the Articles of Agreement of the Fund and the Bank came before the U.S. Congress for ratification, the Congress tried to make it clear that any loans "for programs of economic reconstruction and the reconstruction of monetary systems, including long-term stabilization loans," should be made by the Bank and not the Fund.[36] When the U.S. director of the Fund asked for an interpretation of the Articles of Agreement of the IMF on this issue, the board of directors agreed that the Fund could be drawn against only to give "temporary assistance in financing balance of payments deficits on current account for monetary stabilization operations."[37]

The question came before the executive directors of the Bank, pursuant to resolution no. 6 of the board of governors meeting in Savannah, March 18, 1946, which asked for an interpretation of the Articles of Agreement with respect to the authority of the Bank to make or guarantee loans for programs of economic reconstruction and the reconstruction of monetary systems, including stabilization loans. The executive directors accepted the recommendation of their committee on interpretation that in special circumstances such loans were indeed within the authority of the Bank.[38] On the basis of this interpretation the Bank made its early program loans to France, the Netherlands, Denmark, and Luxembourg.

During the time when Bank lending policy was being developed, the terms "special circumstances" and "specific projects of reconstruction and development" frequently demanded interpretation. In the U.S. discussions of the Bank proposal before Bretton Woods the argument in favor of lending for specific projects was based on the need to avoid such ill-considered loans as the balance-of-payments loans of the 1920s, when the use of the proceeds was unspecified. Essentially, a project loan was to be a productive loan. Indeed as late as the time covered by the *Fifth Annual Report* (1949–50) this was the interpretation given to "project."[39] But this view has changed over time. The evolution of project, sector, and program lending will be discussed in Chapters 8 and 9.

36. *Bretton Woods Agreements Act.* Public Law 171, 79 Cong. 1 sess. (July 31, 1945), Sections 12 and 13.

37. Horsefield (ed.), *International Monetary Fund,* Vol. 2: *Analysis,* p. 385.

38. IBRD, *First Annual Report by the Executive Directors* (Sept. 27, 1946), Appendix E.

39. IBRD, *Fifth Annual Report, 1949–1950,* p. 7:

The objective of this provision is simply to assure that Bank loans will be used for productive purposes. In effect, the only requirement which it imposes is that, before a loan is granted, there shall be a clear agreement both as to the types of goods and services for which the proceeds of the loan are to be expended and of the uses to which those goods and services are to be put.

The Bank is directed by its charter to "impose no conditions that the proceeds of a loan shall be spent in the territories of any particular member or members."[40] Loans are to be "untied," and since 1951 the Bank has adhered where possible to the practice of international competitive bidding. Since money raised in one country through the sale of Bank securities is expendable in any other, there may be adverse effects on the balance of payments of the country whose currency is used. This is recognized in Article IV, section 1(b):

The Bank may borrow funds . . . only with the approval of the member in whose markets the funds are raised and the member in whose currency the loan is denominated. . . .

Article IV, section 1(a), provides that the Bank may "make or facilitate loans . . . in any of the following ways:

(i) By making or participating in direct loans out of its own funds. . . .
(ii) By making or participating in direct loans out of funds raised in the market of a member, or otherwise borrowed by the Bank.
(iii) By guaranteeing in whole or in part loans made by private investors through the usual investment channels.

It was the all but universal expectation of the founders of the Bank that its primary function would be to guarantee private investments. In "Questions and Answers," issued by the U.S. Treasury Department in the spring of 1944, Question 7 read, "How significant will the guarantee of loans be in the operations of the Bank?" The reply was, "The most important of the Bank's operations will be to guarantee loans in order that investors may have a reasonable assurance of safety in placing their funds abroad."

Edward E. Brown, one of the architects of the Bank, in his testimony at the Senate Hearings on the Bretton Woods Agreements Act, said "The Bank will operate primarily by guaranteeing loans. . . ."[41] This was not to be, however, for reasons discussed in Chapters 3 and 5. By far the most important contribution of the Bank to capital flows has been its direct lending.

A number of delegates from less developed countries at Bretton Woods pressed for permission for the Bank to lend for the costs of projects paid in local currency as well as the foreign exchange costs. The U.S. technical advisers had been against this prior to Bretton Woods on the grounds (1) that the Bank should not compete with local suppliers of capital and (2) that this

---

40. IBRD, Articles of Agreement, Article III, section 5(a).
41. *Bretton Woods Agreements Act,* Hearings before the Senate Committee on Banking and Currency, 79 Cong. 1 sess. (1945), p. 93.

might unnecessarily burden the balance of payments of the borrowing country.[42] The Articles of Agreement reflect the views of these advisers though "the Bank may, in exceptional circumstances where local currency required for the purposes of the loan cannot be raised by the borrower on reasonable terms, provide the borrower as part of the loan with an appropriate amount of that currency." (Article IV, section 3[b].) There are many other reasons than this for financing local currency expenditures, and the Bank's policy with respect to this type of financing has changed over time.

In general the Bank was given complete discretion in setting terms on loans and guarantees, but Article IV, section 4, provides that during the first ten years of its existence the Bank shall charge a commission of not less than 1 percent and not more than 1.5 percent on the outstanding portion of loans made out of borrowed funds, and Article IV, section 5, includes the same limitation with respect to guarantees. The proceeds of these commissions were to be set aside as a special reserve to meet liabilities in case of default.

Article IV, section 10, says (with the Soviet Union principally in mind) "The Bank and its officers shall not interfere in the political affairs of any member; nor shall they be influenced in their decisions by the political character of the member or members concerned. Only economic considerations shall be relevant to their decisions, and these considerations shall be weighed impartially in order to achieve the purposes stated in Article I."

Member countries of the Bank embrace a wide spectrum of political forms. In its dealings with individual countries the management has certainly tried to avoid taking into account their positions in this political spectrum, but it has been subjected at times to considerable pressure. The pressure has come not only from those who object to a socialist tinge in the borrower but also from those who want to use the influence of the Bank to support their attacks on "colonialism" and "imperialism." Moreover "economics" and "politics" have a certain affinity for each other in the area of public policy. The prospects for development in a particular country are very much affected by its political stability and the efficiency with which the affairs of government are conducted. The Bank certainly must take these considerations into account in its lending policy. During a considerable period of its history the Bank refused to lend to manufacturing enterprises in the public sector on the ground that they were unlikely to be managed efficiently. Some might feel that this economic reasoning was politically motivated. Finally, attempts to use the leverage of Bank lending to induce or reward good economic performance can

42. "Questions and Answers," Question 11.

have political implications. Thus it can be seen that the wording in Article IV, section 10, that "only economic considerations shall be relevant" presents certain difficulties of interpretation.

These then were the main substantive characteristics of the institution conceived at Bretton Woods. Its initial, if not primary, function was the financing of reconstruction and only afterward of development; its capital subscriptions were relatively small, but its guarantee fund was intended to be large. Its dependence for funds therefore was mainly on private investors, which underlined the importance of establishing its position on capital markets; and the consent of the concerned government was required to raise funds in particular markets. The Bank was intended to operate mainly by guaranteeing private investors against loss, but it could also lend directly and participate in private loans. It was to lend primarily for specific projects and ordinarily only for the financing of foreign exchange costs; its loans were not to be tied to procurement in any particular countries, and the proceeds of the loans were to be used with due attention to considerations of economy and efficiency. Finally, its loans were to be made solely on the basis of economic considerations.

On the whole it was a conservative institution—considerably more conservative than its framers had intended, since it was not the size of the guarantee fund that mattered but what private investors thought of the nature of the guarantee. It was also, at least in its initial stages, far from being a bona fide international institution, since the United States supplied most of its loanable funds and was by far the predominant market for Bank securities. Its location in the territory of its largest stockholder further undermined its international status. The Bank has engaged in a long struggle to escape its reputation as an "Anglo Saxon institution," and whether or not it has succeeded in doing so remains questionable. Certainly the institution, as it emerged from Bretton Woods, was an Anglo Saxon creation, with the United States very much the senior partner.

Organizational Questions

Views on the organization and management of the Fund had fairly well crystallized in Atlantic City, and the Articles of Agreement of the Bank on this question almost duplicate the corresponding Articles of the Fund. Thus questions were raised by Bretton Woods participants as to whether a structure suited to the governance of the Fund was necessarily capable of satisfying the needs of the Bank.[43] Article V of the Bank's constitution ("Organization and Management") is nearly an exact copy of the Fund's Articles XII and XIII.

The boards of governors of both the Fund and the Bank consist of one governor and one alternate appointed by each member country. Typically the two boards meet in joint session once a year. All the powers necessary to the daily operation of the Bank are delegated to the executive directors, but only the board of governors of the Bank can admit new members, increase or decrease the capital stock of the Bank, suspend a member, determine the remuneration of directors, and perform certain other reserved functions.[44]

The Articles of Agreement of the Bank provided initially for twelve executive directors of whom

(i) five shall be appointed, one by each of the five members having the largest number of shares;

(ii) seven shall be elected . . . by all the Governors other than those appointed by the five members. . . .[45]

By the terms agreed to at Bretton Woods, the member countries having the largest number of shares were, in order, the United States, the United Kingdom, the Soviet Union, China, and France. But since the Soviet Union failed to ratify the Articles of Agreement, India moved into fifth place.[46]

43. Letter from Collado to Mason, cited in note 26 to this chapter. "We spent very little time on organization in the Bank Committee. As a consequence, no serious attempt was made to structure the organization in a different fashion, possibly more appropriate to its purpose." Daniel Crena de Iongh, a member of the Netherlands delegation at Bretton Woods, later alternate director of the Fund and the Bank, treasurer, and subsequently an executive director of the Bank, reflecting in 1961 on problems of organization, expressed the opinion that, while in the light of history it was clear that the Fund needed a board of directors in continuous session, it might have been to the advantage of the Bank to have a board of directors composed of high officials of member governments who met in Washington every two months or so. D. Crena de Iongh, "Oral History," p. 6.

44. Article V, section 2.

45. Article V, section 4(b).

46. Several explanations have been offered to account for the failure of the Soviet Union to ratify the Articles of Agreement of the Bank and the Fund. No veto power was given to any member, and the Fund quota relegated the Soviet Union to third place in number of votes in both the Fund and the Bank, after the United States and the United Kingdom. Fund membership required making available a substantial amount of information hitherto undivulged, and borrowing from the Bank involved exacting investigations. Furthermore, a general purpose of the Bank and Fund to promote private trade within freer markets was of little interest to the Soviet Union. At a meeting of the General Assembly of the United Nations in 1947 the Soviet representative charged that the Bretton Woods institutions were merely "branches of Wall Street" and that the Bank was "subordinated to political purposes which make it the instrument of one great power." Klaus Knorr, "The Bretton Woods Institutions in Transition," *International Organization,* Vol. 2 (February 1948), pp. 35–36.

Executive directors and their alternates were to be appointed or elected for two-year terms. "The Executive Directors shall function in continuous session at the principal office of the Bank and shall meet as often as the business of the Bank may require."[47] The interpretation of this provision brought about considerable controversy at the first meeting of the board of governors in Savannah, in March 1946, as is reported in Chapter 3.

Article V, section 3, provided that "(a) each member shall have two hundred fifty votes plus one additional vote for each share of stock held," and "(b) except as otherwise specifically provided, all matters before the Bank shall be decided by a majority of the votes cast."

Subscriptions to the capital of the Bank, which determined voting power, were in effect set by Fund quotas. But while all countries wanted a large quota in the Fund, which determined drawing rights, the less developed countries in particular pressed for lower subscriptions to the Bank's capital, recognizing that their power to borrow would be independent of their capital contribution. After several days of haggling at Bretton Woods, the impasse was broken mainly by the willingness of the United States to accept an obligation to subscribe $3,175 million to the Bank, although its Fund quota was $2,750 million. China and Canada also accepted somewhat larger Bank subscriptions than their Fund quotas, which made it possible to reduce the subscriptions of the less developed countries to some $200 million less than their Fund quotas.[48] One of the results of the adjustments was that in the early years of Bank operations, U.S. voting power was very large. At the time of the second annual report (August 10, 1947) the United States cast 37.20 percent of the vote.[49] Since then the addition of other members and the consequent increase in capital subscriptions have reduced the United States's share of the total vote to slightly less than 25 percent.

The president of the Bank was to be the chief officer "responsible for the organization, appointment and dismissal of the officers and staff, subject to the general control of the Executive Directors."[50] The president and staff owe an exclusive duty to the Bank. The U.K. delegation, led by Lord Keynes, strongly supported the view that executive directors should, like members of the staff, consider themselves to be international civil servants with an allegiance only to the Bank. This was completely unacceptable to the United States, which was putting up most of the money and wanted its representative on the board of directors to be subject to close governmental control. As Richard Gardner put it, "The political and economic circumstances of the

47. Article V, section 4(e).
48. Bitterman, "Negotiating History of the Bank," p. 62.
49. IBRD, *Second Annual Report, 1946–1947*, p. 36.
50. Article V, section 5(b).

transition period made it virtually inevitable that the American viewpoint should finally prevail."[51] It did not finally prevail, however, until the board of governors met in Savannah.[52]

In recruiting its staff the president of the Bank is not limited by geographical quotas as are most of the other United Nations agencies, and this, without question, has a great deal to do with the favorable reputation of both the Bank and the Fund as efficient institutions. In the discussion at Bretton Woods of the Articles of Agreement of the Fund, the Indian delegation had pressed for the principle that in the recruitment of staff, "due regard shall be paid to the fair representation of the nationals of member countries."[53] This version was rejected in favor of the present language of the Fund Articles, which has been copied in those of the Bank. "In appointing the officers and staff the President shall, subject to the paramount importance of securing the highest standards of efficiency and of technical competence, pay due regard to the importance of recruiting personnel on as wide a geographical basis as possible."[54]

The future location of both the Fund and the Bank was another matter on which the United Kingdom and the United States disagreed. According to Bitterman, "The British delegation prior to the meeting [at Bretton Woods] had definite instructions not to agree to the location of the office [of the Bank] in the U.S. without express instructions from the Chancellor of the Exchequer. It was the British view that the location of the Bank and the Fund offices was primarily a political matter, to be decided by governments which would take into account the location of the headquarters of the United Nations and other international agencies to be formed in the postwar period, rather than a technical economic matter which could be negotiated by the Bretton Woods conference."[55] The congressional representatives in the U.S. delegation, on the other hand, advised the delegation that since the United States was putting up most of the money, Congress would not consent to a location outside the United States. The U.S. view prevailed, and the Articles of the Fund and of the Bank have identical provisions. In the case of the Bank it is provided that "the principal office of the Bank shall be located in the territory of the member holding the greatest number of shares."[56] The location within that territory later became an issue at Savannah.

51. Richard N. Gardner, *Sterling-Dollar Diplomacy: The Origins and the Prospects of Our International Economic Order* (McGraw-Hill, 1969), p. 267.

52. See Chapter 3, below.

53. *Proceedings and Documents*, Vol. 1, p. 222; and Bitterman, "Negotiating History of the Bank," p. 100.

54. Article V, section 5(d).

55. Bitterman, "Negotiating History of the Bank," p. 104.

56. Article V, section 9.

Article VI of the Bank's charter concerning "Withdrawal and Suspension of Membership: Suspension of Operations" follows very closely the wording of Article XV of the Fund charter, except for the specification of conditions under which the Bank is directed to settle its accounts with a government that withdraws from membership. Section 3 provides that any country ceasing to be a member of the Fund shall, after three months, cease to be a member of the Bank "unless the Bank by three-fourths of the total voting power has agreed to allow it to remain a member."

Article VII on Status, Immunities and Privileges; Article VIII on Amendments; and Article IX on Interpretation, are practically the same as the corresponding Articles of the Fund charter and need not concern us here. Article XI, which specifies how the Bank is to come into being, will be discussed below.

Although the provisions concerning organization and management of the Bank follow closely those in the Fund's Articles of Agreement, certain differences should be noted. Article V, section 6, provides for an advisory council "selected by the Board of Governors including representatives of banking, commercial, industrial, labor and agricultural interests. . . ." It was through this medium that other specialized agencies of the UN system, which would be consulted in appointing members of the council, hoped to exercise some degree of influence on Bank policy. Although a distinguished group was appointed initially, the council quickly fell into disuse and has never been revived, despite the clear provision in the charter that "the Council shall meet annually and on such other occasions as the Bank may request."

Article V, section 9, also authorizes the Bank to "establish agencies or branch offices in the territories of any member of the Bank," and section 10 authorizes the establishment of regional offices, which "shall be advised by a regional council representative of the entire area and selected in such manner as the Bank may decide." The way was clearly open for the Bank to shape a decentralized agency, with lending operations concentrated in the various regions of concern to the Bank. In fact this path has not been followed. The Bank has developed as a highly centralized institution, with all fundamental decisions being made in Washington.

In contrast to the Fund, the Bank's charter gave it no authority to collect information from members. The Fund is, in an important sense, a regulatory agency, and its Articles of Agreement specify in considerable detail what kinds of data its members are required to supply. Although the Bank can and, of course, does require that information be supplied in connection with specific loans, it is given no authority to elicit information from nonborrowing members. As Bitterman points out, "This problem arose when the Bank began systematically to collect data on the indebtedness of member countries and the provision of information by the creditor countries had to be arranged on a purely voluntary basis."[57]

Article XI, section 1, of the Bank charter, entitled "Final Provisions," provides for the entry into force of the agreement, its signature by member governments, and the inauguration of the Bank. The agreement was to "enter into force when it has been signed on behalf of governments whose minimum subscriptions comprise not less than sixty-five percent of the total subscriptions . . . ," and instruments of acceptance had been deposited on their behalf with the U.S. government. Each signatory was to make a small down payment on its shares to help meet initial expenses of the Bank. As soon as the agreement had entered into force, each member was to appoint a governor, and the member with the largest number of shares was authorized to call the first meeting of the board of governors. The five largest shareholders were authorized to appoint provisional executive directors, and provision was made for the election of the other seven at the first meeting of governors. Finally, "The Bank shall notify members when it is ready to commence operations."[58]

Ratification

The agreements negotiated at Bretton Woods did not, of course, bind governments, and there remained the task of ratification by potential members having the requisite number of votes. As was to be expected, most of the governments represented at Bretton Woods waited for the United States to act, and in January 1945 President Roosevelt sent to Congress the Articles of Agreement of the Bank and the Fund, with a request for their approval. In the debate in Congress which produced the Bretton Woods Agreements Act, signed by President Truman on July 31, 1945, the opposition focused on the Fund. The Bank escaped practically unscathed; indeed there was very little discussion of the Bank. Allan Sproul, president of the New York Federal Reserve Bank, after a few words on the Bank observed, "The rest of what I have to say is centered on the fund because the bank seems to have become almost noncontroversial."[59]

John H. Williams, Professor of Economics at Harvard, who produced what Richard Gardner called "the only constructive alternative to the Bretton Woods agreements,"[60] expressed the view that "there has been a general en-

57. Bitterman, "Negotiating History of the Bank," p. 109, note 1.
58. Article XI, section 3(d).
59. *Bretton Woods Agreements Act,* Senate Hearings (cited in note 41, above), p. 304.
60. Gardner, *Sterling-Dollar Diplomacy,* p. 132.

dorsement of the bank but a widespread difference of views about the fund."[61] He had urged earlier "adoption of the bank, with modifications designed to permit it to perform some of the purposes of the Monetary Fund during the transition period from war to peace, and postponement for the present of a decision on the fund."[62]

Edward E. Brown, who had been a member of the U.S. delegation at Bretton Woods, was one of the few witnesses at the Senate Hearings who gave extensive consideration to the Bank. He described it as a "conservative institution" and, elaborating on this view, remarked, "Now, take the United States contribution of $3 billion and take Canada's and Cuba's, and the United Kingdom, the Scandinavian countries, Holland and Belgium, it is inconceivable to me that you would get a situation where even if the whole $10 billion were guaranteed that the guaranty of the Bank would not be good."[63]

Although members of the New York banking community were soon to demonstrate a different view, they withheld their fire from the Bank for the time being and concentrated it on the Fund. The late Ansel Luxford subsequently described this as a tactical maneuver. They did not want to appear negative to both.[64] Some evidence that this may have been so is provided by the difficulties later encountered by the Bank in establishing its position in the New York money market.

In the Bretton Woods Agreements Act, Congress made it clear, if it had not been clear already, that the executive directors of the Bank and the Fund were not to be international civil servants, but would be, at least so far as the United States was concerned, answerable to their own governments. The act established a National Advisory Council on International Monetary and Financial Problems (chaired by the secretary of the treasury, and with State, Commerce, the Federal Reserve System, and the Export-Import Bank represented) "in order to coordinate the policies and operations of the representatives of the United States on the Fund and the Bank. . . ."[65]

Although the U.S. administration succeeded in getting congressional approval of the Bretton Woods agreements, in so doing, it gave hostages to fortune, which later affected U.S. attitudes toward both the Bank and the Fund. These institutions were depicted as fully capable of handling the problems of

61. *Bretton Woods Agreements Act,* Senate Hearings, p. 319.

62. *Ibid.* These views had been expressed in an address before the Academy of Political Science, "World Organization—Economic, Political and Social," April 4, 1945.

63. *Bretton Woods Agreements Act,* Senate Hearings, p. 94.

64. Ansel F. Luxford, "Oral History," p. 24. Luxford, a Treasury official, was a member of the U.S. delegation at Bretton Woods and later assistant and associate general counsel of the Bank.

65. *Bretton Woods Agreements Act* (Section 4), Senate Hearings, p. 2.

reconstruction and transition from war to peace. No other help would be needed. As Harry White explained in an article in *Foreign Affairs,*

A loan to Britain to enable her to establish exchange stability and freedom from exchange control will not of itself help significantly with Britain's problem, or with the world's problem of establishing a sound postwar pattern of international payments. . . . On the other hand, the Fund and the Bank, by providing the favorable conditions necessary for expanding world trade and investment, would be of real help in establishing a sound postwar pattern of international payments and would contribute substantially to prosperity in this country and abroad.[66]

The Bretton Woods Agreements Act was hardly signed when the war with Japan ended and Lend-Lease was canceled. It became clear that, even if the Bank and Fund had then been in existence, Britain's balance-of-payments problems involved in the transition from war to peace—to say nothing of those of other countries—could not be handled by these institutions. Despite the assurances of the U.S. administration during the debate on the Bretton Woods Agreements Act that no further assistance would be needed, the United States and the United Kingdom found themselves in rather bitter and protracted loan negotiations. It was made clear by British leaders that the success of these negotiations was a prerequisite to British acceptance of the Bretton Woods institutions. The loan negotiations were not brought to an end until December 6, 1945, only a few weeks before the last possible date (December 31, 1945) for entry into force of the Bank and Fund Articles of Agreement. The circumstances under which the loan terms and the Bretton Woods agreements were accepted by Parliament and the loan was approved by the U.S. Congress made it clear that both the Bank and the Fund would come into being in a very different atmosphere than had characterized Bretton Woods, or even the congressional debate on the Bretton Woods Agreements Act.[67] Yet they did come into being. By December 31, 1945, governments with the requisite number of votes had indicated approval of the articles, and the United States called the first meeting of governors of the Bank and the Fund to be held in Savannah, Georgia, in March 1946.

66. Harry D. White, "The Monetary Fund: Some Criticisms Examined," *Foreign Affairs,* Vol. 23 (January 1945), p. 207.
67. Gardner, who has described admirably the development of public opinion and the course of government action in the United Kingdom and the United States on the Bretton Woods institutions and other aspects of postwar economic policy, speaks of the earlier attitude as follows:

When it voted on the Bretton Woods agreements Congress was not mainly concerned with technical economic considerations. The climax of the debate coincided with the end of the Second World War. The United Nations Charter had just been signed at San Francisco; a new era seemed to be dawning. Issues of monetary and financial policy were easily confused with other issues—regionalism and universalism, war and peace, isolationism and internationalism. . . . The Fund and Bank moved through the Congress on soaring hopes for a better world.

Sterling-Dollar Diplomacy, pp. 140–42.

CHAPTER THREE

The Bank Opens for Business

THE INTERNATIONAL BANK for Reconstruction and Development, freshly moved from the Washington Hotel to "temporary offices" on one floor of a building at 1818 H Street in the northwest section of Washington, D.C., opened its doors for business on June 25, 1946. The contrast between the fledgling organization that was testing its wings and striving to get off the ground during the last half of the 1940s and the World Bank of today—self-confident, esteemed, active, and influential—could hardly be greater.

The Bank, said a Swiss newspaper in March 1947, "was born under an un-lucky star." Its activity to date could be summed up in a single word: "zero."[1] This harsh assessment of an institution widely hailed at the close of the Bretton Woods conference three years earlier was not confined to the notoriously tough-minded Swiss. Under the most charitable of judgments, the early years of the World Bank would have to be characterized as inauspicious.

The Issues at Savannah

The Articles of Agreement negotiated at Bretton Woods, like all such charters, left a number of questions unanswered. Insofar as organization and management were concerned, however, their thrust was clear enough. The Bank would operate by weighted voting; it would be located for some time to come in the United States; its executive directors were to be directors, not advisers; and the president, selected by the executive directors, was to pay more attention to competence than to nationality when recruiting his staff. There was scant reason to expect that the inaugural meeting of the board of governors, to be held in Savannah, Georgia, in March 1946, would be as divisive as it became.

1. *Die Weltwoche,* Zurich, Switzerland, March 21, 1947.

Beneath the workaday agenda adopted for the Savannah meeting, however, lay a deeper issue:

Were the Fund and Bank purely financial institutions whose direction could be entrusted to a group of international civil servants? Or did their operations have such economic and political implications as to require close control by the member governments? The Articles of Agreement signed at Bretton Woods made no clear choice for either alternative. It remained for Savannah to decide between them.[2]

The first major item on the agenda was the choice of a site for the Bank and the International Monetary Fund (IMF). Should it be New York or Washington? Lord Keynes, governor for the United Kingdom, favored New York. He wanted the new institutions kept clear of "the politics of Congress and the nationalistic whispering gallery of the Embassies and Legations."[3] Others—France and India in particular—joined Keynes in the view that

the Bank as an international institution should not be too closely associated with the capital of any nation, and the staff and officials should be in an atmosphere conducive to allegiance to the Bank. New York, in addition to being a financial and economic world center, would afford a good opportunity for cooperation with the Social and Economic Councils of the United Nations Organization.[4]

The U.S. delegation, headed by Secretary of the Treasury Fred M. Vinson, favored Washington, and there was never any real doubt about the outcome of the controversy. In the memorandum (quoted above) that Keynes wrote immediately after the Savannah conference, he said,

Mr. Vinson told me that the American delegation had decided that both institutions [the Fund and the Bank] should be placed in Washington and that this was a final decision the merits of which they were not prepared to discuss. The U.S. Administration, he said, was entitled to decide for themselves what location within the U.S. was to be preferred. . . . Unfortunately Mr. Vinson, before warning us or seeking our views, had thought fit to take his proposition direct to the President [Harry S. Truman] and to obtain his authority to make this an absolute

2. Richard N. Gardner, *Sterling-Dollar Diplomacy: The Origins and the Prospects of Our International Economic Order* (McGraw-Hill, 1969), p. 257. Chapter 13, "Savannah: Two Conceptions of Financial Collaboration," contains a perceptive interpretation of what went on there and has been drawn on heavily in preparing this section.

3. This quote is from a memorandum of March 27, 1946, cited by Gardner (p. 258), who gives as his source Roy F. Harrod, *The Life of John Maynard Keynes* (Harcourt, Brace, 1951), p. 630.

4. *Inaugural Meeting of the Board of Governors of the International Bank for Reconstruction and Development, Savannah, Georgia, March 8–18, 1946, Selected Documents* (May 1946), "Report of the Committee on Site," pp. 61–62. The committee should have referred to the "Economic and Social Council" of the United Nations rather than to the "Social and Economic Councils."

instruction to the American Delegation from which they were not to be free to depart in any circumstances.[5]

Vinson may have been unnecessarily blunt in disclosing the U.S. view, but the view itself could be strongly defended, particularly with respect to the International Monetary Fund (IMF). "It must be remembered," he said in an article on the Savannah conference published in mid-1946,

that these are not ordinary institutions with ordinary stockholders. They are coöperative enterprises of governments and their chief business is with governments. Their location in Washington would have the great merit of making it easy for all the members to carry on their business with them, since all members have adequate representation in that city. But more than merely this convenience is at stake. *The Fund and Bank are not business institutions in the ordinary sense. While they must be operated so as to conserve their assets and allow the most fruitful use of their facilities, they are not profit-making institutions. The business of the Fund and Bank involves matters of high economic policy. They should not become just two more financial institutions.*[6]

The decision in favor of Washington guaranteed that they would not become "just two more financial institutions." In the eyes of the U.S. delegation, it symbolized a transfer of the control of international finance from Wall Street to Washington.

The next question that divided the British and the U.S. delegations concerned the time and attention the executive directors and their alternates should devote to the business of the Bretton Woods institutions. Lord Keynes reintroduced the argument, previously made at Bretton Woods, that directors should be persons who played an important role in the policy decisions of their own governments—for example, Treasury or central bank officials who would be available for meetings but not expected to devote full time to serving as executive directors. Directors who lived near the headquarters of the Bank and Fund would lose the necessary contacts with their own governments and might be men of lesser stature. The United States considered it essential that the executive directors devote full time to the business of the Bank and Fund. The result was a compromise. The bylaws provided that

it shall be the duty of an Executive Director and his Alternate to devote all the time and attention to the business of the Bank that its interests require, and between them to be continuously available at the seat of the Bank.[7]

The salary question caused more difficulty. The U.S. delegation, eager to make the job of executive director a full-time assignment at a salary compa-

5. Gardner, *Sterling-Dollar Diplomacy*, p. 258.
6. Fred M. Vinson, "After the Savannah Conference," *Foreign Affairs*, Vol. 24 (July 1946), p. 626. (Emphasis added.)
7. Bylaws of the International Bank for Reconstruction and Development, Section 14(d).

rable to that paid by a successful private bank, proposed $25,000 net of taxes. The Canadians and the Dutch, like the British, favored low salaries in order to discourage the formation of a Washington-based club and to encourage the designation of executive directors who would be in daily touch with monetary and financial issues in their home countries. The salaries chosen were $17,000 a year for an executive director and $11,500 for an alternate, both net of income taxes. For part-time directors and alternates, compensation would be in proportion to time served. The salary of the president of the World Bank was set at $30,000 a year.

The vice president of the United States and members of the cabinet at that time received $15,000 a year, and members of the British Parliament received less than $4,000; $17,000 a year, net of taxes, was a high salary for a public official by any standard. For Lord Keynes,

whose disappointment had been accumulating with the other reversals, it proved to be the last straw. He characterized the figures as "scandalous." They would lead, he argued, to "justified public criticism" of "such high emoluments for so large a body of officials." In the end it was the one decision made at Savannah on which he refused to place his Government's approval. . . .

Back in England Keynes's words attracted wide attention. The setback on the issue of salaries was represented as a serious contradiction of British expectations: "It had been hoped," *The Manchester Guardian* complained, "that the 'Bretton Woods' scheme would be managed by truly independent experts, judging economic needs on their merits and giving impartial advice to all. It would be difficult enough to make such a spirit grow in the political setting of Washington, but the arrangements now made seem to have made this even less likely."[8]

The first meeting of the executive directors, it was agreed, would take place on or about May 1, 1946. The principal business would be the naming of a president. The U.S. executive director, who represented the country having the largest quota, would act as temporary chairman of the executive directors until the president assumed office.

It was expected that the first president would be an American, but *which*

---

8. Gardner, *Sterling-Dollar Diplomacy,* p. 260. In addition to its vigorous criticism of the substance of the decisions reached at Savannah, *The Manchester Guardian* (March 23, 1946) denounced at least as vigorously the tactics used by the U.S. delegation:

The American Treasury, which in these matters seems at present to take the lead over the State Department, massed its voting powers and ran the conference in a rigidly domineering manner. Every proposal put forward by the American delegation was pressed through with steam-roller tactics, and the delegation seems to have made no secret of its belief that the United States, which pays the piper, has a right to call the tune. In fact, the worst fears of those who had always warned us that this was what the United States meant by international economic co-operation were borne out at Savannah.

(Quoted in Gardner, *Sterling-Dollar Diplomacy,* p. 267.)

American was not known at Savannah. Although the IMF seemed the more important of the two institutions created at Bretton Woods, the U.S. delegation, more than willing to have Harry D. White passed over as managing director of that institution, let it be known that it would accept a European in the top spot at the IMF.[9] It would, however, nominate an American as president of the Bank. Some of those closest to Fred Vinson believed that he himself was by no means averse to being nominated. However, the death of Chief Justice Harlan Stone in April 1946 created a vacancy on the U.S. Supreme Court in a lifetime post, for which President Truman on June 6 nominated Vinson.

Meanwhile, the Vinson view that the Bank and the Fund should be subject to rather close control by national governments had prevailed at Savannah over the British view of the Bank and Fund as more autonomous, technocratic institutions, divorced from the vicissitudes of national politics.

Arrival and Departure of the First President

It took time to find a president who would be acceptable to Washington, to Wall Street, and to the rest of the world. According to a widely circulated Associated Press dispatch, datelined New York, April 13, 1946,

the election of Lewis W. Douglas, 51-year-old President of the Mutual Life Insurance Company of New York, and a director of the General Motors Corporation, as the first president of the $9,100,000,000 world bank appeared to be a foregone conclusion today.

The formality of his election is scheduled for May 6 or 7 at the initial meeting of the 12 executive directors of the bank, but administration officials in Washington made clear that he was their top nominee from the field of American big business. President Truman endorsed him publicly last Thursday.[10]

That Douglas would be elected was not a foregone conclusion, however. As early as March 24, the press had reported flatly that Douglas would be

9. The reason White was not proposed as managing director of the Fund, according to J. Keith Horsefield, was that the United States believed "the Bank would have to be headed by a U.S. citizen in order to win the confidence of the banking community, and that it would be impracticable to appoint U.S. citizens to head both the Bank and the Fund." J. Keith Horsefield, *Chronicle*, Vol. 1 of Horsefield (ed.), *The International Monetary Fund, 1945–1965: Twenty Years of International Monetary Cooperation* (International Monetary Fund, 1969), p. 135.

10. *Washington Post*, April 14, 1946. The words "world bank" appear without initial capitals in the newspaper account. For a press account of Truman's endorsement, see *New York Herald Tribune*, April 12, 1946: "The President replied with an unequivocal yes to a press conference question whether Mr. Douglas had his personal support."

President Truman's choice, but within a few days thereafter it was reported that ex-Secretary of the Treasury Henry Morgenthau had protested the proposed nomination to Truman and Vinson because of what Morgenthau called Douglas's connections "with big business and Wall Street, his tie-ins with international financiers, and his general point of view."[11] Moreover, it is said that Douglas himself was not informed officially that he was wanted for the job until after the President had publicly endorsed him.

In any event, on April 20 Douglas reportedly served "final notice" to Truman and Vinson that he would not accept the presidency of the Bank because he could not "conscientiously" leave the position he had so recently resumed after various important wartime assignments. Morgenthau's opposition is said to have had a bearing on the decision,[12] but he was by no means the only influential American opposed to the nomination.

The first meeting of the executive directors ended without the naming of a Bank president. On May 7, 1946, Camille Gutt, the distinguished Belgian who had been elected as executive director for Belgium, Norway, Luxembourg, and Iceland, resigned to become the first managing director of the Fund. Emilio G. Collado, the American who was serving as temporary chairman of the executive directors, was in effect top man at the Bank. Formerly director of the Office of Financial and Development Policy at the U.S. Department of State, he had been at Atlantic City, Bretton Woods, and Savannah and knew a great deal about what the Bank was supposed to do. His link with the policymaking level of the U.S. government was the newly established high-level committee headed by the secretary of the treasury—the National Advisory Council on International Monetary and Financial Problems. The council was required by statute to instruct him and presumably would back him in the positions he would take.

The Search for a President Ends

While the executive directors were tackling other urgent problems, such as deciding when to call in a first installment on government subscriptions, the quest for a president continued. Several well known persons are reported to have turned down the job. On June 4, 1946, Eugene Meyer, a seventy-year-

11. *Washington Post,* March 30, 1946.
12. *Washington Post,* April 21, 1946. In a conversation with one of the authors twenty-five years later, Douglas said he had been sorely tempted to accept the post but had turned it down for two reasons: (1) his company was in genuine need of his services, and (2) the terms of reference of the Bank job were unsatisfactory and would not have given him the authority he needed. In early 1947 he left the Mutual Life Insurance Company to become President Truman's ambassador to the Court of St. James.

old American with a long record of distinguished public service dating back to World War I, was nominated and elected. He took office two weeks later, and on June 25 the Bank was declared open for business.

Except for his age, Meyer appeared to be an ideal candidate, who would have the confidence of government and financial leaders at home and abroad. He was a close friend of Secretary of State Byrnes and Secretary of the Treasury Vinson. He was well known to President Truman, and he was highly respected on Wall Street, having been the head of a successful investment banking house (Eugene Meyer and Company) before World War I.[13] Unfortunately his brief tenure at the World Bank was not a particularly happy period in his long and otherwise fruitful career.

Meyer was confronted by a strong board of directors, led by the young, well informed, energetic, and ambitious U.S. executive director. Much of Meyer's time and energy was spent in battling with the board for leadership of the institution. His own previous experience in domestic financial agencies did not help him particularly in understanding balance-of-payments crises, foreign exchange versus local currency requirements, and some of the other unprecedented problems that would have to be dealt with by the Bank. It is only fair to add, however, that the emerging problems of the postwar era were equally unfamiliar to almost everyone else; the architects of the Bank were clearer on how to avoid the pitfalls of the 1920s and 1930s than on how to meet new hazards.

Meyer's first appointment—of Harold Smith, a U.S. national and former director of the budget, as vice president—was made without prior consultation with the executive directors, most of whom had expected to be consulted on a matter of such potential importance. The appointment brought to the Bank a man in the prime of life, with a good reputation in the United States in the field of public administration, but with little or no knowledge of international finance or international affairs. The relationship between the president and vice president was never warm and grew cooler as time went on.

For the post of general counsel, Meyer sought the services of John J.

13. Meyer had been brought to Washington by Bernard Baruch in 1917 to head the division of nonferrous metals of the War Industries Board. He later became a special assistant to the secretary of war and a director of the War Finance Corporation. His public service during the interwar years included membership on the Federal Reserve Board and service as the first chairman of the Reconstruction Finance Corporation. During World War II he had been a member of the National Defense Mediation Board. Since 1940 he had also been editor and publisher of an influential daily newspaper, the *Washington Post*. The *Post* was having its troubles, and Meyer was reluctant to take on the new job, but was persuaded to do so through the combined efforts of President Truman and Secretary of State Byrnes.

McCloy, but was unsuccessful in his effort. He then recruited Chester A. McLain, a very able member of the New York law firm with which McCloy had been associated before World War II. Meyer leaned heavily on McLain for advice. Meyer also brought in a number of other competent North Americans and Europeans—among them, Simon Aldewereld (Netherlands), Aron Broches (Netherlands), Richard H. Demuth (U.S.A.), Daniel Crena de Iongh (Netherlands), Walter Hill (U.K.), Ansel F. Luxford (U.S.A.), Morton M. Mendels (Canada), Leonard B. Rist (France), Martin M. Rosen (U.S.A.), and Davidson Sommers (U.S.A.). Some of these men were still with the Bank as it entered its second quarter century.

The task of recruiting personnel of high quality, while paying "due regard" to geography, was time consuming and of course could not be satisfactorily delegated until a director of personnel was installed. This took place in August 1946, when William F. Howell, who had been serving as director of personnel at the United Nations Relief and Rehabilitation Administration (UNRRA) and was a friend of Harold Smith, became acting director of personnel. (After a year, he was made director of personnel, then assistant director of administration, and from 1954 until his death in 1964, director of administration.) Howell was responsible for bringing in an UNRRA colleague, Donald D. Fowler, who as of mid-1971 was deputy secretary of the Bank.

The recruitment process during the Bank's first year was necessarily on a catch-as-catch-can basis. Personnel were recommended to Meyer or Howell by their friends, by the executive directors, and by others already in the employ of the Bank. Some were borrowed from the U.S. government. Persons of other nationalities who had been in the western hemisphere on wartime and early postwar assignments, including participation in the Bretton Woods and Savannah conferences, were picked up as those assignments ended. The seemingly disproportionate number of Dutch nationals in high places during the Bank's early days (and throughout its first quarter century) is attributable to the longstanding reputation of the Dutch for competence in the field of international banking, the surplus of Dutch nationals unwilling or unable to resume their prewar careers in Indonesia, and the presence of a number of qualified Dutch nationals in the western hemisphere at the time the Bank was searching for staff.

Another of Meyer's major preoccupations was sounding out the private capital market on raising money for the Bank. The prevailing assumption at Bretton Woods, it will be recalled, was that the Bank would operate by guaranteeing securities issued by others rather than by issuing bonds of its own. But early in 1946—before the Savannah conference—a subcommittee of the U.S. National Advisory Council on International Monetary and Financial

Problems had begun conversations with banking and insurance groups in New York and had come away with the impression that large investors would prefer holding securities of the Bank itself rather than securities of foreign governments, backed by a guarantee from the Bank. U.S. private investors in the mid-1940s were still smarting from the experience with defaulted foreign loans in the 1930s. They were openly distrustful of foreign governments; and the guarantee of a foreign government issue by the Bank—an institution whose own credit was not yet established—could not be expected to enhance greatly their eagerness to lend money abroad. From the Bank's point of view, guaranteeing bonds of varying quality and rates of interest also began to appear less desirable than using the Bank's credit directly. Before the end of 1946, therefore, the Bank decided to give priority to issuing its own securities.[14]

During Meyer's regime, the board of directors met twice a week, and many committees of the board were established to wrestle with particular policy issues. It was decided, for example, that at any given time the Bank would charge every borrower the same rate of interest on loans of comparable duration, irrespective of differences in creditworthiness among eligible borrowers. The question of supervision of disbursements under Bank loans was discussed, and the general form of the contract with potential borrowers began to take shape.

Meyer was cordially received when he went to New York to solicit financial support for the Bank, but the cordiality was purely personal and did not presage the slightest interest on the part of the financial community in buying Bank securities. In addition to attitudinal obstacles (the Bank was thought by some to be an ill conceived, "do-good" creation of the New Deal era), there were the serious legal limitations on U.S. investors, which are described in Chapter 5.

In truth, the financial community in the summer of 1946 had no basis for knowing whether the Bank would in fact operate on a businesslike basis under nonpolitical management. The tug-of-war between the president and the executive directors, about which more will be said below, was not just a battle over whether a railroad should be run by a man or by a committee. More fundamentally it concerned the weight that would have to be given in day-to-day operations to the political interests of the committee members' bosses—the governments that instructed the executive directors.

Furthermore, the investment community was believed to be concerned about the relationship of the Bank to the new global political organization,

14. See also Chapter 5, below.

the United Nations. At Savannah the board of governors had received a letter from the president of the Economic and Social Council (ECOSOC) inviting the Bank and Fund to enter into negotiations to establish relations with the United Nations, as was contemplated in the UN Charter. The letter had been referred to the executive directors. The negotiations, which dragged on for more than a year, are summarized later in this chapter. The important point here is that one of the reasons for foot-dragging on the part of the Bank's negotiators was a fear that designating the Bank as a "specialized agency" of the United Nations, coordinating its activities in some way with that organization, or having its activities coordinated, would hurt its credit rating or alienate the Wall Street fraternity, whose confidence and good will the Bank was consciously cultivating.

The same fear raised questions when the initial personnel policies of the Bank were being discussed—whether or not to follow the pattern being established by the United Nations with respect to salaries, annual leave, and retirement benefits. A prior issue with respect to retirement benefits was whether to adopt a retirement plan rather than a provident fund system. Some of the people high in the councils of the Bank thought its staff should be comprised not of a hard core of permanent international civil servants, but of a rotating group of employees who would serve the Bank for periods of three to five years. Under a provident fund system they could pay into the fund a fraction of their salaries while with the Bank, but withdraw their contributions and the Bank's, plus interest, when leaving. The sum withdrawn could then be used to buy back into the retirement systems of their former employers upon return to service with them.

The idea that won out, however, was that the Bank should try to build a staff of career employees, who would have no competing loyalties and who could gradually acquire expertise in the problems of international finance and development. This meant a decision in favor of a retirement plan. But should it be the UN plan, which would require a higher ratio of contribution to payroll (21 percent) than was customary in U.S. private industry?

The Bank knew that people buying its bonds would be comparing its policies with their own and reaching judgments about the business acumen of the new institution. It accordingly opted for a retirement plan that initially cost 18 percent of its payroll instead of 21 percent, and the Fund did the same. Also, the Bank decided to give employees twenty working days of annual leave each year, as compared with thirty granted by the United Nations. (The Fund chose twenty-four as the appropriate number.) Salary scales in the Bank and Fund were reasonably generous by government standards but not so generous as to raise eyebrows on Wall Street.

Meyer's Frustration and Resignation

The principal frustration of the Bank's first president was his feeling of having responsibility without authority, of having to battle the U.S.-led executive directors for stewardship of the institution. "Matters of policy determination," the first annual report of the executive directors explained blithely,

are the responsibility of the Executive Directors, while operational, administrative, and organizational questions are the responsibility of the President, subject to the general direction and control of the Executive Directors. The President is the presiding officer of the Executive Directors and is entitled to a deciding vote in the case of an equal division.[15]

The Bank's committees on membership, financial policy, interpretation, information, and liaison, it went on to say, "are composed solely of Executive Directors, but the President has designated members of the staff to meet with each of them."[16]

The recipients of this first report, the board of governors, met in September 1946, at which time the staff of the Bank numbered seventy-two persons. Operating expenses were accruing at the rate of $1.2 million a year. The president professed to be

somewhat surprised in recent weeks to find that there are those who think it curious that the Bank has not already negotiated a number of loans. The fact is that, at the date of the annual report, letters requesting loans had been received from only two countries, and in neither case has the Bank yet received such properly documented applications as would make it possible for us to act. Since then, a letter has been received from a third country which indicates that its representatives are prepared to begin discussions, and informal advices indicate that the same may be true of several other countries.[17]

The U.S. executive director had been eager for the Bank to float its first bond issue and was inclined initially to be skeptical of Meyer's explanation that an enormous amount of educational work had to be done before any bonds could be sold. He was even more eager for the Bank to get into the lending business. The first approach to the Bank from what were later called "less developed countries" had come in September 1946 from Chile, which requested $40 million for a list of projects that it wanted to have considered

15. IBRD, *First Annual Report by the Executive Directors* (Sept. 27, 1946), p. 5.
16. *Ibid.*, p. 6.
17. Eugene Meyer, address of Sept. 30, 1946, at the third session of the First Annual Meeting of the Board of Governors of the Bank. The countries in question were France, Denmark, and Chile. U.S. Secretary of the Treasury John W. Snyder had said in his opening address, "As we all know, the International Bank must now assume the primary responsibility for underwriting reconstruction loans to countries otherwise unable to borrow on reasonable terms."

as a package. Collado, the U.S. executive director, vigorously endorsed the application and insisted that the loan ought to be approved by the end of 1946. He was convinced that Chile "was good for $40 million." President Meyer, supported by some of his principal advisers, maintained that the Bank did not know enough about the Chilean economy or about the proposed projects. In more abstract policy terms, the management thought the issue was whether the Bank should "simply hand out money" or whether it should behave as a prudent investment banker.

In the end, it was late March 1948 before the Bank made loans to Chile for two small projects—the Bank's first project lending. The management could be proud that it had resisted pressure from the U.S. government and had behaved with such exemplary prudence. But the view that the Bank may have been excessively cautious could also be sustained.[18] Perhaps it is not entirely unfortunate that the Bank's first U.S. executive director was aggressively action-oriented and sought to counterbalance rather than reinforce existing pressures for moving slowly.

The United States was not alone in having a strong personality as its executive director. Sir James Grigg (United Kingdom), J. W. Beyen (Netherlands), Pierre Mendes-France (France), Robert B. Bryce (Canada), Luis Machado (Cuba), and other early directors were not men who would readily accept a subordinate role; nor was Eugene Meyer.

On December 4, 1946, to the astonishment of his closest associates and before any private capital had been raised or loan applications acted upon, Eugene Meyer submitted his resignation as president, effective December 18. His explanation was that he had accepted the presidency initially on the understanding that he would remain only until the Bank had been organized. The basic organization had been completed, the institution was "passing from the preliminary work of preparation to the stage of operating activities," and the time had come to select a permanent head.[19]

Weariness, unwillingness to engage in bureaucratic infighting, and dissatisfaction with his anomalous position as president appear to be more plausible explanations. The Wisconsin State Banking Commission, rejecting the example set by New York State, had just voted unanimously to refuse to permit state banks, savings banks, and trust companies in Wisconsin to invest in securities issued by the World Bank. Meyer, moreover, tended to view his tug-of-war with the much younger U.S. executive director as a contest with someone who was out to get his job rather than as an almost predictable

18. For more on the first Chilean loan, see Chapter 6, below.
19. IBRD, Press release (Dec. 4, 1946).

result of ambiguities in the Articles of Agreement and specific provisions in the Bretton Woods Agreements Act adopted by the U.S. Congress. New understandings would be necessary if his successor were to have power commensurate with the responsibilities of the office.

Interregnum and Installation of a New Team

Meyer's abrupt resignation put Harold Smith, vice president of the Bank, into line for the presidency. But it quickly became apparent that the board of directors had no desire to name him president, nor, so far as we can ascertain, was there any suggestion from the U.S. government that it should do so. On December 18, the effective date of Meyer's resignation, Smith submitted his own resignation, to take effect as soon as a successor to Meyer was appointed. Smith became acting president and died suddenly within a few weeks—on January 23, 1947.

Several eminent North Americans—Graham F. Towers, Governor of the Bank of Canada, Allan Sproul, President of the Federal Reserve Bank of New York, and John J. McCloy—were reported to have turned down the opportunity to succeed Eugene Meyer. The World Bank, according to Walter Lippmann, the syndicated columnist, was "in an embarrassing position." His explanation was:

The president of the bank is selected by these executive directors. He becomes their chairman but he has no vote except in case of a tie. He may be removed "when the executive directors so decide."

The American executive director, Mr. Collado, who owes his appointment to the Administration, is a powerful figure in the bank. . . . The United States has 37 out of 100 votes, the United Kingdom 15, France 5.5. . . . It is Mr. Collado, not the president, who casts the American vote. Moreover, he casts it under the guidance of the Secretaries of State, Treasury, Commerce, and the Chairman of the Federal Reserve System [who constitute the National Advisory Council on International Monetary and Financial Problems]. . . .

In reality then, it is Mr. Collado, the American executive director, and not the president of the bank, who connects the work of the bank with the American government and the American people. . . .

Unless the president of the bank can count upon the support of the American government and is assured that his advice will be taken very seriously by the Administration and by Congress, he cannot hope to do what is expected of him. If his real authority is only that which he has legally, he is only an administrative officer and a figurehead. Yet the world will hold him responsible for the success of the bank. That is, I believe, the reason why it has become so difficult to find a man, qualified for the high post, who will accept it.

Since it may be too difficult to change the legal structure of the bank, the only remedy would seem to be an assurance, which convinced him, that President Truman, and the leaders of both parties in Congress, will throw the full weight of American support behind him, and that he will in fact exercise the American power in the bank. In this way it ought to be possible to find a qualified man who will accept.[20]

McCloy, Garner, and Black at the Helm

Before the situation got completely out of hand, the U.S. government was able to persuade John J. McCloy that he would have adequate power plus the full backing of its executive branch in exercising it. McCloy also consulted Eugene R. Black, vice president of the Chase National Bank of New York, who advised him to accept the proffered post. McCloy therefore reconsidered his previous refusal of the presidency, was elected by the board of directors on February 23, 1947, and assumed office on March 17. As part of the arrangement, he brought in his own team. The executive directors, on the day that they elected McCloy, approved his appointment of Robert L. Garner, vice president of the General Foods Corporation, to the vacant post of vice president of the World Bank. President Truman then accepted the resignation of Emilio Collado as U.S. executive director and named Eugene R. Black to succeed him.

When McCloy, Black, and Garner took over, the Bank was at its lowest ebb, its reputation considerably tarnished, its accomplishments nil, and its problems mounting because of the worsening economic situation of Western Europe. For the preceding several months the Bank had been drifting, "leaderless and in a state of dispirited confusion."[21] (In the age-old tradition of bureaucracies, its staff nevertheless grew larger during the interregnum.) The Bank's general counsel, Chester McLain, was probably as responsible as any other one person for preventing the organization from falling apart before McCloy came in. "He was a somewhat older man," said Garner. "People wept on his shoulders, and he kept them cheered up."[22]

Before the new team entered on duty, it had come from New York to Washington

for a discussion of the terms and general conditions under which the new management was to take over. There had been a difference of opinion from the beginning

20. "The Vacancy at the World Bank," *New York Herald Tribune,* Jan. 18, 1947.
21. Richard H. Demuth, "A Look Backward," in *The First Fifteen Years,* published by the IBRD Personnel Division (June 1961), p. 6.
22. Oral History Project of Columbia University, interviews recorded in the summer of 1961 on the International Bank for Reconstruction and Development (cited hereinafter as "Oral History"). From interview of Robert L. Garner, p. 5.

in the Bank as to the role of management and the role of the directors. At Bretton Woods most of the important countries had felt that the directors should not attempt to actually operate the institution. The United States representatives had rather argued in favor of a very active role for the directors. This question was not resolved during Mr. Meyer's tenure and I believe that it was one of the causes of his resignation. . . .

It was understood at the time in conversations carried on with McCloy that . . . the management would actually manage the institution and the directors would play the usual role of general supervision without interference in the conduct of the business. When we got down here, there was still some hesitation on the part of some of the directors to make that position perfectly clear. So we listened to the discussions, and then McCloy finally said that the only condition under which he felt it was possible to handle the situation would be a clear declaration as to the power of the management to manage, that if the directors were not fully in agreement with that, we would go on back to New York that afternoon.

Then the directors went into executive session and after lunch they said they were fully agreeable. So the deal was made.[23]

The forced acceptance of McCloy's conditions for assuming the presidency made him appear at the Bank as a man on horseback who would dictate to it and ride roughshod over the executive directors—an entree that to some extent clouded the whole of his administration. He established the tradition that the initiative in running the institution was to be left to the management. He obtained the cooperation of the board of directors, but it was a grudging cooperation.[24]

Fortunately, McCloy had a magnetic personality and was quick to win the respect and confidence of colleagues whose positions in the hierarchy were not downgraded by his arrival. He became well liked by the Europeans as well as by his fellow Americans. He was a lawyer, not a banker, but was respectful of, and respected by, the New York banking fraternity, having modestly described himself as "a bankers' amanuensis."[25]

Black, also a man of enormous charm, had been engaged in banking and in the marketing of securities for most of his life and had contacts that were to be invaluable in marketing the bonds of the Bank. Although McCloy's law firm had been a legal counsel to the Chase National Bank, of which Black was vice president, McCloy had not known either Black or Garner until shortly before they came to the Bank. Garner had had long experience in

23. *Ibid.*, pp. 3–4.

24. Richard H. Demuth, "Oral History," pp. 8–11.

25. From 1929 to 1940, he had been a member of the New York law firm of Cravath, de Gersdorff, Swaine and Wood (the firm from which Chester McLain had come). From 1941 to 1945, he had been assistant secretary of war. From 1945 to 1947, he had been a member of the firm of Milbank, Tweed, Hope, Hadley and McCloy.

banking before joining the General Foods Corporation, and Black and Garner did know each other. The faith of the new trio in private investment as a panacea for the economic ills of the world was almost boundless.

Garner had a more abrasive personality than did either Black or McCloy. His impatience with the board of directors was so evident that Morton M. Mendels, secretary of the Bank, felt it necessary to remind him from time to time "that the same Articles of Agreement which did not create his position did create the Board's."[26] Garner's tough, driving attitude was useful in convincing the staff that a full day's work was expected in return for a day's pay. He is reported also to have had the capacity for making employees think they were a little better than they really were, and in time they came to be better than they had been. His previous experience in banking was invaluable during the Bank's first decade.

Garner became primarily responsible for the administration of the Bank. The executive directors met less frequently; and with initiative in the hands of management, decisions were made far more rapidly than before. In addition to the offices of the president, the secretary, and the treasurer, and the Personnel Office, the Bank already had a Legal Department, Loan Department, and Research Department. Departments of Marketing and Administration were quickly added. An office in New York City was opened, primarily for bond marketing purposes, and in the fall of 1947 a Paris office was opened.

The new vice president came to the Bank from the post of financial vice president of the General Foods Corporation, where management was dedicated to a system of carefully defined organizational units, each unit having job descriptions that spelled out in detail the functions to be performed by the incumbent. Salary scales were integrated with job descriptions, so that employees were paid on the basis of the assumed value to the company of the job as described, not on a less circumscribed opinion of the value of the jobholder to his employers.

Garner believed in equal pay for equal work and wanted, through the job classification system, to create a staff at the Bank that knew what it was doing. Many employees, however, felt that he was trying to transform the Bank into an American-type corporation. Consequently there was resistance to his administrative philosophy as well as to his highly conservative economic views.

The new president was quick to recognize Europe's growing need for massive aid. The economists on the staff of the Bank convinced McCloy, Garner,

26. Morton M. Mendels, "Oral History," p. 40.

McLain, and some other top officials that the need was for balance-of-payments assistance rather than for project loans. In other words, the Bank's loans should permit European nations to import from the United States fuel, repair and maintenance supplies, and other items needed to restore their prewar levels of production.

The Articles of Agreement authorized project loans "except in special circumstances," and the thrust of the economists' argument was that circumstances in Europe were indeed sufficiently "special." In response to fears expressed by Latin American participants in the Bretton Woods conference that the Bank would allocate too large a share of its resources to reconstruction and not enough to development, the Articles of Agreement also stipulated that the "resources and the facilities of the Bank shall be used . . . with equitable consideration to projects for development and projects for reconstruction alike."[27] (This is an example of the kind of compromise language that often enables international meetings to surmount difficulties without actually resolving them.)

Business Begins

In practice, "equitable consideration" meant reconstruction first, then development.[28] The requirements of European reconstruction were urgent, visible, and basic to the reestablishment of a functioning world economy. Within two months after McCloy became president, the Bank made its first loan. It was for $250 million to a French public corporation, the "Crédit National," and was guaranteed by the French government. The original application had been for $500 million, but the Bank decided to limit its commitment to the immediate future, saying that it would be willing to consider a further application from France later in the year. In June 1947, however, the U.S. secretary of state in a speech at Harvard University introduced what became known as the Marshall Plan or, more formally, the European Recovery Program, thereby enabling France to look elsewhere than to the World Bank for help in meeting its reconstruction requirements.

The Netherlands had applied to the Bank for an even larger sum than had France—$535 million—to help cover its reconstruction requirements for 1947–49. The Bank, limiting its commitment to the 1947 portion of the program, approved a loan of $195 million in August 1947. These were followed promptly by loans of $40 million to Denmark and $12 million to Luxembourg.

The principal policy issues raised by these first four loans, which were

27. Article III, section 1(a).
28. See Chapter 2, above.

made not for specific productive projects but for the "general purpose" of financing a variety of essential dollar imports, are discussed in Chapter 9. The point to be made here is that under McCloy the Bank functioned courageously as one of the lifelines to a sinking Europe until Marshall Plan assistance was mobilized. McCloy testified in favor of the Marshall Plan when it was under consideration by the U.S. Congress, in full knowledge that passage of the measure would put the Bank out of business in one of the two principal fields in which it was set up to operate. In his judgment the Marshall Plan was essential, and a narrow jurisdictional stand on his part would be folly.[29]

The Bank then withdrew from the reconstruction field, although Czechoslovakia and Poland, prevented by the Kremlin from participating in the European Recovery Program, still had loan applications totaling nearly $1 billion before the Bank.[30] In addition to the unapproved loan applications from Czechoslovakia and Poland, the Bank as of August 1947 had loan applications on file from Chile, Iran, and Mexico. The first loan to a less developed country was made in March 1948—$16 million to Chile, of which $13.5 million was for hydroelectric equipment and $2.5 million for the production of agricultural machinery. Loans to Mexico and Brazil were made in early 1949.

Needless to say, the Bank could lend only as much capital as it had mobilized. Although the authorized capital of the Bank was $10 billion, of which more than $8 billion had been subscribed by mid-1947, the portion represented by paid-in capital amounted to $1.6 billion. Of the latter amount, only $727 million was in gold or U.S. dollars, the balance being in the currencies of other member governments. For all practical purposes, the resources of the Bank were limited initially to the $727 million; its clients needed supplies that could be obtained only in the U.S. market, with payment in gold or U.S. dollars.

Before the Bank's own bonds could be marketed, many barriers, both psychological and legal, had to be overcome. McCloy, Black, and Garner threw themselves energetically into the job of overcoming them. Convincing American investors that Bank securities were worth purchasing was in McCloy's view the major task of his administration. The travail that this entailed is described in Chapter 5, "Financing the Bank." As is reported there, the Bank in July 1947 made the first public offering of its own bonds: $100 million in ten-year, 2.25 percent bonds, and $150 million in twenty-five-year, 3 percent bonds. The $250 million offering was made through 1,700 secu-

29. Demuth, "Oral History," p. 15.
30. See Chapter 6, below.

rities dealers, the largest consortium of its kind ever organized in the United States. The Bank's bonds first appeared on the ticker of the New York Stock Exchange shortly after the exchange opened at 10 A.M. on July 15, 1947, and by noon both issues were oversubscribed. The fact that the bonds were promptly gobbled up by investors and began selling at a premium over the public offering price was a source of relief and considerable gratification to the management.

On the other hand, making such bonds eligible and attractive to the most conservative U.S. investors, though vital to the longer-run operations of the Bank, reinforced the pressures toward caution inherent in any organization dominated by persons connected with or close to treasuries, central banks, and the private financial community. Procedural safeguards that delayed the granting of loans, or limited the purposes for which they could be granted, or required ancillary modification of the borrower's policies as the price for their approval could all be justified as essential in order to gain and hold the confidence of private investors. The Bank's alleged dependence on Wall Street inevitably made it the target of considerable criticism. In presenting the Second Annual Report to the board of governors when it met in London in September 1947, McCloy reported that he had "had very close and continuous contact with the American investment community." He added that "the Bank must attach importance to the views of the American investor and must conduct its activities in such fashion that its bonds will be considered a sound business risk by the United States financial community."[31]

The development of a broader market outside the United States was hampered primarily by a lack of capital for foreign lending among pre-World War II capital exporters, but also by obstacles analogous to those encountered within the United States. During McCloy's term, however, the Bank did make its first borrowing in a currency other than U.S. dollars—the modest sum of $4 million in 2.5 percent Swiss franc serial bonds.[32]

Basic Agreement with the United Nations and Early Relations with Other International Agencies

During McCloy's presidency, the Bank, in addition to tightening its internal organizational structure, marketing its first bonds, and making its initial loans, completed an agreement formalizing its relationship with the United

31. IBRD, Second Annual Meeting of the Board of Governors, *Proceedings* (Sept. 11–17, 1947), p. 7.
32. Switzerland was not, and is not, a member of the World Bank.

Nations. The last of these achievements, seemingly the simplest, began at Savannah and was not completed until November 1947. The negotiations were not particularly cordial, and the signing of the agreement produced nothing on either side that remotely resembled the rejoicing after the Bank's first bond issue was successfully marketed.

The General Assembly and the Economic and Social Council of the United Nations had gathered for their respective first sessions in January 1946. A letter from the president of ECOSOC requesting the establishment of liaison with the Bank had been received during the Savannah conference and, understandably enough, had been referred to the executive directors, who were expected to meet in May. The drafters of the United Nations Charter and the Bank's Articles of Agreement had foreseen the need for a cooperative relationship.

The Bank's Articles of Agreement require it to cooperate—a requirement not easy to establish by fiat—and to "give consideration to the views and recommendations" of competent international organizations.[33] The UN Charter is more elaborate and specific.

Article 57 provides that the "various specialized agencies, established by intergovernmental agreement and having wide international responsibilities ... shall be brought into relationship with the United Nations in accordance with the provisions of Article 63" and that "such agencies thus brought into relationship with the United Nations are ... specialized agencies." Article 63 authorizes the Economic and Social Council to enter into agreements, subject to approval by the General Assembly, "defining the terms on which the agency shall be brought into relationship. . . ."

Article 58 of the UN Charter says that the United Nations "shall make recommendations for the coordination of the policies and activities of the specialized agencies," and Article 63 gives primary responsibility for coordination to ECOSOC. Article 64 authorizes ECOSOC to obtain regular reports from the specialized agencies, including reports on the steps taken to give effect to its recommendations. Article 70 provides for reciprocal representation at each other's deliberations, and Article 17 (3) empowers the General Assembly to "examine the administrative budgets of ... specialized agencies with a view to making recommendations to the agencies concerned."

33. Article V, section 8:
(a) The Bank, within the terms of this Agreement, shall cooperate with any general international organization and with public international organizations having specialized responsibilities in related fields. . . .
(b) In making decisions on applications for loans or guarantees relating to matters directly within the competence of any international organization of the types specified in the preceding paragraph and participated in primarily by members of the Bank, the Bank shall give consideration to the views and recommendations of such organization.

The Agreement with the United Nations

By the time the executive directors of the Bank were formally organized and in a position to discuss relations with the United Nations, a second letter had arrived asking whether the Bank would send representatives to New York to discuss liaison between the Bank and ECOSOC with a negotiating committee appointed by ECOSOC. The executive directors replied in effect that such action would be premature. David Owen, the UN assistant secretary general who had signed the letter to the Bank, answered that he recognized the difficulties of the moment in negotiating a formal agreement, but hoped that informal discussions would be continued. UN agreements had been completed with the International Labour Organisation (ILO), the United Nations Educational, Scientific and Cultural Organization (Unesco), and the Food and Agriculture Organization (FAO). Thus began the minuet.

In late June 1946 the UN secretary-general asked whether discussions with the negotiating committee of ECOSOC could begin in September. Bank and Fund representatives met and agreed that neither institution could sign an agreement similar to that put forward by the United Nations. The Bank was very fearful that becoming a specialized agency of the United Nations would subject it to undesirable political control or influence and hurt its credit rating in Wall Street, despite the government guarantee behind its bonds. Moreover, even though there were differences of view between the executive directors and the management as to which should run the Bank, both could readily agree that encroachments from outside should be resisted.

A committee of IBRD directors concluded that no useful purpose would be served by even informal exploratory discussions "at this early stage" and that the UN agreements with the ILO, Unesco, and the FAO all had the disadvantage of "trying to give a definite and rigid form to matters which are still fluid. . . ." The absence of a formal agreement did not prevent participation by the Bank in the work of ECOSOC's Administrative Committee on Coordination or attendance by Bank representatives as observers at the never-ending series of meetings of the Economic and Social Council and its subsidiary commissions and committees. Furthermore, the Bank and Fund really were in a different category than the ILO, Unesco, and FAO insofar as sources of funds and relations with clientele were concerned.

It gradually became clear that the UN secretariat and ECOSOC's committee on negotiation were prepared to take account of the special characteristics of the Bank and the Fund. Despite the feeling of at least one high official at the Bank that a formal agreement with the United Nations or any of the specialized agencies should be avoided at all costs, Richard H. Demuth drafted a document which, though more a declaration of independence from than cooperation with the United Nations, was suggested as an alternative basis for negotiation. A vigorous day-long session at UN headquarters ensued, during the course of which McCloy agreed to some watering down of the Bank's draft. As Demuth put it, "We took out a few of our declarations of independence but not very many."[34] Though it was accepted by ECOSOC's negotiating committee, the proposed agreement was roundly attacked when brought before ECOSOC itself and the General Assembly.

At the August 1947 session of the Economic and Social Council, Alexander P. Morozov of the Soviet Union attacked the draft agreement as a flagrant violation of at least four articles of the UN Charter. More disturbing to noncommunist delegates was the attack by Finn Moe of Norway (homeland of the then UN secretary-general, Trygve Lie). He said that it was impossible for Norway to accept the Bank and Fund agreements because of their special-privilege clauses, which would undermine the authority of the United Nations. The lack of coordination between the activities of the United Nations and those of other international agencies and the absence of authority to coordinate and assign priorities might arouse irritations that could endanger international cooperation. Willard L. Thorp, speaking for the United States, argued that nothing would undermine the United Nations more than a failure to make agreements with the Bank and Fund. The Council finally voted 13 to 3 for approval (Byelo-Russia, Norway, and the Soviet Union being opposed). Two ECOSOC members, Czechoslovakia and New Zealand, abstained.[35]

The agreement with the United Nations was approved by the board of governors of the Bank in September 1947. The governor of the Bank for Yugoslavia made it clear that, though willing to concur "in order to bring to an end the undesirable state of affairs caused by the absence of any agreement," he was not satisfied with its contents.[36]

When the proposed agreement reached its next stop (the UN General Assembly), the Soviet Union again fought against approval, buttressing its

34. Demuth, "Oral History," p. 20. The Fund, represented by its managing director, Camille Gutt, participated in these negotiations. The UN committee was headed by Jan Papanek of Czechoslovakia.

35. Czechoslovakia was then a member of the Bank, but New Zealand was not. At Bretton Woods, New Zealand's delegation appeared fully prepared to support the outcome, but shortly thereafter the political situation in that country changed sharply. The new government felt that it would be unwise to join the Bank, and New Zealand did not become a member until 1961.

36. IBRD, Second Annual Meeting of the Board of Governors, *Proceedings* (Sept. 11–17, 1947), p. 16.

"legal" case with arguments against specific loans that had been made or were contemplated. For example, it contended that the loan to the Netherlands would promote war in Indonesia. The draft agreement was nevertheless approved, and on November 15, 1947, the Bank and Fund became specialized agencies of the United Nations.[37] But they became rather "special" specialized agencies.

After a single unexceptionable sentence stating the purpose of the agreement, the text emphasized that "by reason of the nature of its international responsibilities and the terms of its Articles of Agreement, the Bank is, and is required to function as, an independent international organization."[38]

The agreement goes on to stress the limitations to which the Bank (and the UN) are subject in order to safeguard confidential information, and it permits the withholding not only of information which would in the Bank's judgment constitute a violation of confidence, but also of information "which would otherwise interfere with the orderly conduct of its operations."

The right of reciprocal representation is limited, representatives of the United Nations being permitted only to attend meetings of the boards of governors of the Bank and Fund. The Bretton Woods institutions agree only to give "due consideration" to the inclusion on their agendas of items proposed by the United Nations. In addition, the UN recognizes that the action to be taken by the Bank on any loan "is a matter to be determined by the independent exercise of the Bank's own judgment" and that it would be "sound policy to refrain from making recommendations to the Bank with respect to particular loans or conditions of financing by the Bank." The Bank in turn recognizes that the UN and its organs "may appropriately make recommendations with respect to the technical aspects of reconstruction or development plans, programs or projects."

With respect to budgetary and financial arrangements, the agreement provides that, in interpreting Article 17 (3) of the UN Charter, the UN "will take into consideration that the Bank does not rely for its annual budget upon contributions from its members, and that the appropriate authorities of the Bank enjoy full autonomy in deciding the form and content of such budget."

Though the agreements with the Bank and Fund were unsatisfactory in the eyes of the UN secretariat, it cannot be said that the United Nations was notably more successful later in coordinating the activities of agencies with

37. Resolution 124 (II) of the General Assembly was approved without a formal vote, by what is now known in UN circles as "consensus." After approval of the agreements with the IBRD and IMF, the late Mr. Vyshinsky, representative of the USSR, wanted it noted in the record that his government had "abstained from voting."

38. This quotation and those immediately following are from the "Text of the Agreement Between the United Nations and the Bank," in IBRD, Second Annual Meeting of the Board of Governors, *Proceedings* (Sept. 11–17, 1947), pp. 25–27.

which it negotiated "satisfactory" agreements. All the agreements promptly found their way into collections of international treaties and have been gathering dust there ever since, while the living organisms, regardless of legislative history, soon became about equally zealous and successful in maintaining their autonomy.

The protracted negotiations between the Bank and the United Nations did nothing to enhance the respect of their senior officials for each other, and the Bank for some years went to considerable pains to keep the United Nations at an unnecessarily long arm's length. McCloy could not be classified as an admirer of the United Nations, and Garner was considered anti-UN. As is pointed out below, mutual suspicions were gradually allayed during the 1950s, and reasonably harmonious relations developed in the 1960s.[39]

Relations with Other International Agencies

While laying the legal foundation for relations with the Economic and Social Council and its network of regional and functional commissions and committees, the Bank participated in the Geneva and Havana conferences to draft the charter for an international trade organization (which never came into being, although part of it survived as the General Agreement on Tariffs and Trade [GATT]). It sent representatives to FAO meetings and to annual meetings of the Bank for International Settlements. The World Bank also appointed a representative to maintain liaison in Paris with the Organisation for European Economic Co-operation (predecessor of today's Organisation for Economic Co-operation and Development) and developed a relationship with the Organization of American States. (The fluctuations in the Bank's relationship with the Fund are analyzed in Chapter 16, below.)

Indeed, so extensive did the exchange of representation among agencies become that at more than one of the early postwar international gatherings the signs around the table bearing the names of governments seemed to be outnumbered by the separate set of signs bearing the mysterious initials of newly created, as well as of long established but relatively unknown, intergovernmental organizations. The Bank's third annual report contains a plaintive paragraph about the number of international meetings held at different places throughout the world, the "severe strain" this imposed on the staff of the Bank (which totaled 435 persons as of the end of August 1948), and the resultant inability of the Bank, "without interfering with the conduct of its own work," to participate in meetings at distant points.[40]

However, since each agency was engaged not only in planting its flag

39. See Chapter 17, below.
40. IBRD, *Third Annual Report, 1947–1948,* p. 31.

squarely over its own territory, but also in extending its jurisdiction to un-protected contiguous territory, the practice of keeping a close watch on the other fellow's troops could easily be justified.

Resignation of the Second President

By March 1949, John J. McCloy had been president of the Bank for two-fifths of his five-year term. The unfortunate effects of the interregnum follow-ing Eugene Meyer's resignation had been for the most part overcome, and the Bank had begun to function as part of the cluster of international agencies created during World War II or shortly thereafter. However, in the spring of 1949, hints that McCloy might soon be resigning from the Bank to become the U.S. high commissioner in Germany began to appear in the public press. His staff by then had grown in size, but the staff structure, after his initial reorganization, had remained unchanged. William A. B. Iliff, a British Trea-sury official, had replaced Charles C. Pineo as director of the Loan Depart-ment, and Norman M. Tucker had succeeded E. F. Dunstan as director of the Marketing Department. The Research Department had been renamed the Economic Department, and the task of studying economic and financial con-ditions in member countries had been transferred from the Loan Department to the Economic Department.

On May 18, 1949, an IBRD press release announced that the "Execu-tive Directors of the International Bank for Reconstruction and Develop-ment today accepted the resignation of John J. McCloy as President of the International Bank and Chairman of the Executive Directors, and elected Eugene R. Black, President . . . and Chairman. . . ." The financial commu-nity was undismayed by this further changing of the guard; Eugene Black's election was, if anything, reassuring and helpful in solidifying confidence in the Bank.

Why did McCloy leave? He was not a banker; he had previously held high office in the executive branch of the U.S. government; the post of U.S. high commissioner in Germany in 1949 could be viewed as a more prominent and, for him, exciting job than the presidency of the World Bank; and the President of the United States wanted him to go to Germany. When he left, he asked to borrow his old associate, Chester McLain—a World Bank loan that was never repaid! He also took with him Chauncey Parker, director of administration.

A second press release, also issued on May 18, carried McCloy's state-ments that "the reconstruction phase of the Bank's activity is largely over," and "the development phase . . . is under way." While the latter statement was not untrue, it conveyed an impression of greater activity by the Bank in the field of development than most outsiders had been able to detect.

Summary

The charter negotiated at Bretton Woods paved the way for a tug-of-war between the president and the executive directors concerning the management and leadership of the Bank. The Savannah conference, which was convened to select a permanent site for the Bretton Woods institutions and to determine the functions and salaries of their top officials, found the United Kingdom and the United States bitterly at odds on the principal issues. The subsequent designation of the first Bank president was delayed and was handled with considerably less than consummate skill.

The candidate selected—seventy-year-old Eugene Meyer—resigned six months after being named. The day Meyer's resignation became effective, the vice president, forty-eight-year-old Harold Smith, who had been with the organization only five months, announced his resignation. He died suddenly a few weeks later. For several crucial months, the new multi-billion-dollar agency was rudderless.

The second president, John J. McCloy, made a strengthening of the president's role vis-à-vis that of the executive directors a condition of acceptance of the job. He brought with him Robert L. Garner as vice president. The first U.S. executive director, Emilio G. Collado, who had been functioning as temporary chairman during the interregnum, resigned and was succeeded by Eugene R. Black. Under new guidance, the Bank was rescued from its state of suspended animation. It sold its first bonds and made its first loans. McCloy's relations with executive directors other than Black, however, were worsening. After two years as president, McCloy resigned to become U.S. high commissioner for Germany—an assignment he regarded as more challenging and more prestigious than further service as president of the World Bank.

Not until Eugene R. Black became president in 1949 did the Bank achieve the kind of internal harmony that is essential to external effectiveness. But by then it was clear that the medium-term job of financing postwar reconstruction was beyond the capabilities of the organization, and it was not yet clear what the International Bank for Reconstruction and Development would be able to do in fulfillment of its other principal function—the long-term task of financing development.

CHAPTER FOUR

Organizational and Institutional Evolution

WHEN IN THE SPRING of 1949 the rumor began circulating that John J. McCloy might soon submit his resignation as president of the World Bank, a credible corollary rumor was that the post would then be offered to the U.S. executive director, Eugene R. Black. "I was in Europe," said Black some years later,

and I sent word back that under no conditions did I want my name to be put up. ... I made various suggestions of other people. I did everything on earth to prevent my taking the job. I didn't want it. I wanted to make a career in [the] Chase Bank. . . .

The pressure was put on me and the pressure was put on the Chase Bank to release me, and I finally took it. . . . Then after I got it . . . I became very interested in what I was doing, and I found there was more inner satisfaction in doing this than there was in making money. That's why I stuck it out. . . . It's been among the most interesting years of my life, the happiest years of my life. . . .[1]

Black served as president for thirteen of the first twenty-five years of the Bank's life and left his imprint on all aspects of Bank activity. While he was at the helm, the institution grew steadily in size, scope, and understanding of the development process, and he himself evolved from master marketer of bonds to statesman in the fields of development and development diplomacy.

More than most international institutions, the Bank, which is not dependent on funds from member governments for its administrative budget, can

1. Oral History Project of Columbia University, interviews recorded in the summer of 1961 on the International Bank for Reconstruction and Development (cited hereinafter as "Oral History"). Quotation is from interview of Eugene R. Black, pp. 51–52. (While serving as U.S. executive director, Black had not severed his ties with the Chase Bank.)

reflect the objectives, ambitions, personality, and prejudices of its president. The Articles of Agreement seem to give great authority to the board of governors. But the board, consisting of one governor from each member country, is too large a body to do more than ratify proposals put to it and serve as a general indicator of trends of thought. It meets only once a year, and the annual Bank-Fund gathering serves chiefly as a fraternal get-together for the international financial community.

The real "board," the executive directors, initially twelve in number but grown to twenty-one by mid-1971, is small enough to be a consultative and deliberative body. It meets frequently and plays a role in authorizing and legitimizing the activities of the staff. But ever since Eugene Meyer's departure, it has concerned itself primarily with the problems that the president chooses to put before it. Until quite recently, these have been problems on which the staff work had already been done, and the board could only say "yes" or "no" to the recommendations made by the president.

On January 1, 1963, Eugene Black was succeeded by George D. Woods, who served as president until April 1, 1968. Since then, Robert S. McNamara has been president. Under Presidents Black, Woods, and McNamara, the Bank has flourished by comparison with most other postwar international institutions, has launched the affiliates that account for the name "World Bank Group," and has taken other steps toward transforming itself from financier of the foreign exchange costs of bankable projects to development-financing institution, a term not used during the Bank's early years. This chapter continues the account that was begun in Chapter 3 of the evolution of the Bank as an institution rather than as a borrower or lender. After describing briefly the growth in membership, it focuses successively on the growth, internationalization, and organization of the staff, on the executive directors, who under the Articles of Agreement are responsible for selecting the president of the Bank, and finally on the presidents and their presidencies.

Membership and Voting

By mid-1947, 45 countries had become members of the Bank. (Of those that had been represented at Bretton Woods, the most important nonmember was the Soviet Union.) Poland and Czechoslovakia, as is noted in Chapters 5 and 6, had joined but ceased to be members in 1950 and 1955, respectively. A substantial net gain in membership was nevertheless registered during the first decade, at the end of which there was a total of 60 members— 10 of the 15 new ones being Asian countries. During the second decade, membership rose spectacularly to a total of 106, and 32 of the 46 new members were African countries. As of mid-1971, the membership was 116. The title "World Bank" has become more and more appropriate despite the continued absence of communist countries other than Yugoslavia from the membership roster.[2] Table 4-1 shows changes in World Bank membership and voting power, 1947–71.

The membership explosion of the 1960s had

the most powerful impact, both on the Bank as an institution and on the context in which it has to operate. . . . Like any population explosion, this has sharply affected the average age of its members, the balance of their needs and the urgency of their ambitions. It has put the Bank more than ever in the business of trying to show countries what they should borrow for and then helping them to borrow. It has raised in acute form the adequacy of earlier estimates of capital requirements. It has raised in equally acute form the question of what part of these needs the Bank and IDA [the International Development Association] can or should try to meet and how the Bank can cooperate effectively with other sources of development finance. . . .

It is generally true that the most recent members have been among the poorest, the least able to finance any significant part of their own development and, in many cases, the least well endowed with administrative and executive capacity.[3]

Despite the influx of Asian and African members, the weighted voting arrangements of the Bank have preserved a sizable formal balance of power for the minority of developed, industrialized nations that provide the institution's financial resources. In 1947 the European and North American countries cast 74 percent of total votes; in 1971 they still held 61 percent of the voting power. The addition of members from Asia, Africa, and the Middle East in the years from 1947 to 1971, by contrast, increased the voting strength of those regions from 15 percent to 28 percent. The voting strength of Central and South America has remained virtually unchanged: 8.39 percent in 1947 and 8.3 percent in 1971. The addition of thirty-eight African countries to the membership rolls since 1947 has brought Africa's voting strength up to that of Latin America.[4]

2. The big spurt in membership occurred between 1961 and 1964. Cuba and the Dominican Republic withdrew in 1960, but the latter rejoined in 1961. Indonesia joined in 1954, withdrew in 1965, and was readmitted in 1967.

3. J. H. Williams, "International Bank for Reconstruction and Development," unpublished paper delivered to the Fourth Maxwell Institute on the United Nations, Bretton Woods (Aug. 27–Sept. 1, 1967), pp. 7–8 and 10–11.

4. Adapted from *ibid.*, p. 11, and updated. Japan in mid-1971 was entitled to 3.92 percent of the total votes. Europe, North America, and Japan together accounted for 64.5 percent of the voting power and Asia, Africa, and the Middle East, without Japan, for 24.2 percent of the total in 1971.

Table 4-1. *Changes in World Bank Membership and Voting Power, 1947–71*
Voting power in percent

Region	August 10, 1947		June 30, 1952		June 30, 1957		June 30, 1962		June 30, 1967		June 30, 1971	
	Number of members	Voting power of region	Number of members	Voting power of region	Number of members	Voting power of region	Number of members	Voting power of region	Number of members	Voting power of region	Number of members	Voting power of region
Africa	2	1.64	2	1.57	2	1.42	8	2.94	34	7.85	40	8.58
Asia[a]	3	11.66	7	13.69	13	17.49	16	15.57	17	15.13	18	16.15
Australasia	1	2.41	1	2.31	1	2.09	2	3.35	2	2.94	3	2.94
Central and South America	18	8.39	18	8.09	20	9.66	19	8.35	22	8.38	22	8.30
Europe[b]	14	35.72	16	35.51	16	33.99	20	35.36	20	34.35	20	33.79
Middle East[c]	5	2.21	5	2.34	6	2.38	8	2.45	9	3.15	11	3.38
North America	2	37.97	2	36.49	2	32.97	2	31.98	2	28.20	2	26.86
Total	45	100.00	51	100.00	60	100.00	75	100.00	106	100.00	116	100.00

Source: IBRD, Economic Program Department, April 1972
a. Includes Israel.
b. Includes Cyprus and Turkey.
c. Includes Iran, Iraq, Jordan, Kuwait, Lebanon, Libya, Saudi Arabia, Syrian Arab Republic, United Arab Republic, Yemen Arab Republic, and Peoples Democratic Republic of Yemen.

Growth and Internationalization of Staff

The staff of the World Bank increased modestly during the 1950s, with the total number rising from 430 in 1951 to 646 in 1960, and the professional staff increasing from 159 to 283. During the 1960s the staff increased more than twice as fast as it had in the 1950s, and the total staff by mid-1971 exceeded 2,500. Nevertheless, the number of employees per million dollars of loans and credits was higher during the 1950s than it has been since then. In other words, by the simplistic measure of money loaned, the staff is more productive now than it used to be.[5]

The large increase in personnel that has paralleled the sharply increased tempo of operations under President McNamara means that, as of mid-1971, the number of professionals on the staff was 75 percent greater than in 1968. Large numbers of new personnel are difficult for a functioning organization to digest. And when the arrival of "new boys" coincides with the subtle changes in personal relationships that always accompany the settling-in of a new president, morale in some quarters is bound to suffer, at least for a while.

An American diplomat with long experience in the U.S. government recently observed, not entirely facetiously, that when the staff of a public agency exceeds 1,000, the employees deal only with each other and stop communicating with the rest of the world. In the history of the World Bank, the 1,000-employee point was reached toward the middle of the 1960s. While the IBRD continues to "communicate" with the outside world and is in many respects a more effective broker between developed and developing countries than ever before, it is also true that the Bank Group is by now a sizable bureaucracy, showing familiar signs of the hardening of the arteries that is characteristic of bureaucracies. These include extra layers of personnel that have to be penetrated (frequently by strangers dealing with strangers), extensive concern with procedural and presentational details, difficulty in getting information promptly to those who ought to have it, and on the other hand, burying the internal messenger service under an avalanche of papers for distribution to a growing list of recipients whose status and psyche require them to receive the papers but not necessarily to read or act upon them.

In the early years of the Bank it was decided that English would be the working language—a decision that saved money and enormously expedited

---

5. See Table 4-2, which shows the size of the World Bank/IDA staff, administrative expenses, and the relationship of staff size to loans and credits for selected years.

Table 4-2. Size of World Bank/IDA Staff, Administrative Expenses, Number and Amount of Loans and Credits, in Selected Years, 1951–71

Dollar amounts in millions

Fiscal year	Staff on duty at end of fiscal year			Administrative expenses	Loans and credits		Number of staff per million dollars in loans and credits
	Total	Professional	Nonprofessional		Number	Amount	
1951	430	159	271	$ 4.8	21	$ 297.1	1.45
1954	453	222	231	6.0	26	323.7	1.40
1957	543	237	306	7.6	20	387.9	1.40
1960	646	283	363	10.1	31	658.7	0.98
1963	884	406	478	18.0	45	708.8	1.25
1966	1,336	615	721	33.2	49	1,123.4	1.19
1969	1,836	917	919	45.5	122	1,784.2	1.03
1971	2,610	1,348	1,262	66.3	131	2,480.4	1.05

Source: IBRD, Program and Budgeting Department, July 1972.

67

the conduct of business by comparison with the United Nations and most other international agencies.[6]

Understandably, the Bank's two largest stockholders, the United States and the United Kingdom, initially provided the bulk of the professional talent required by the institution. (See Table 4-3.) They were in a very real sense its founders, they were making the most substantial contribution to its resources, and they could supply the administrators, economists, lawyers, and so on needed to fill available positions.[7] Their combined proportion of total professional personnel—more than 70 percent in 1951 and above 50 percent until 1966—has exceeded generously their combined proportion of total capital subscriptions. Furthermore, the concentration in key positions of U.S. and British nationals, especially the former, has been still more pronounced. In accordance with an understanding dating back to the Savannah conference, all five Bank presidents have been U.S. citizens. Of the nine men who have served as vice presidents, four have been U.S. and three U.K. nationals. More than half of the principal officers still are from those two countries. The Pres-

Table 4-3. *Nationality Distribution of World Bank/IDA Professional Staff, by Major Groupings, 1951–71*

Nationality groupings	Totals at end of fiscal year							
	1951	*1954*	*1957*	*1960*	*1963*	*1966*	*1969*	*1971*
United States	96	116	111	128	160	214	274	370
United Kingdom	17	24	29	41	60	101	157	198
Other developed countries[a]	30	59	71	83	137	206	304	446
Less developed countries[b]	16	23	26	31	49	94	182	334
Total	159	222	237	283	406	615	917	1,348
U.S. and U.K. nationals as percentage of total staff	*71*	*63*	*59*	*60*	*54*	*51*	*47*	*42*

Source: IBRD, Personnel Division of the Administration Department.

a. The Part I countries of the International Development Association.

b. The Part II countries of the International Development Association. (Because Part II countries include Greece, Israel, Spain, Turkey, and Yugoslavia, as well as the very poor countries, the category may overstate somewhat the number of professionals from less developed countries as that term is used elsewhere.)

6. Though English remains the working language of the staff, at the annual meetings of the board of governors there are now facilities for simultaneous interpretation from English into French and Spanish, and vice versa. Executive directors' meetings are normally conducted entirely in English, but arrangements have been made for interpretation from, and into, French or Spanish on request.

7. For reasons reported in Chapter 3, the Netherlands was also an early major source of high level professional talent.

ident's Council, his principal advisory body for day-to-day control over the affairs of the Bank and the International Development Association (IDA) during the presidency of George Woods (though it was somewhat reduced in importance and potency thereafter) has continued to be a predominantly U.S.-British-Dutch group. U.S. nationals alone have accounted for 40 percent or more of the council's membership and have played a greater role in establishing the policies and administrative style of the agency than their numbers would indicate.

A familiar plea, both at board meetings when the administrative budget is up for consideration and at annual meetings, is for a broader internationalization of the Bank staff, and particularly for greater representation of the less developed countries. While the management of the Bank is strongly opposed to quotas for different nationalities (and other devices that might reduce the competence and quality of its staff), it has always been aware of the importance of broad geographic representation and has tried to be responsive to the pressures of member governments for a more representative staff. The shortage of available talent in the less developed countries and the desperate need of member governments to make use of the talent at home are, of course, major handicaps. So is Washington's declining reputation as a desirable city in which to live.

It has been harder to internationalize the professional than the nonprofessional staff. The number of nationalities represented on the professional staff rose from twenty in 1951, to forty in 1963, and eighty-three in 1971. Of the eighty-three countries in 1971, twenty-four were represented by a single employee, fifty provided 5 or fewer nationals, and sixty-one countries, 10 or fewer. Only seven nations had more than 30 nationals on the professional staff: the United States (370), the United Kingdom (198), France (88), Germany (77), India (59), the Netherlands (54), and Canada (50).[8] The nonprofessional staff in mid-1971 included nationals of seventy-nine countries.

More important than the statistical data is whether staff members "think" internationally, regard themselves as custodians of the agency's international interest rather than the national interests of particular member governments, and avoid overt and covert lobbying on behalf of their governments. On these points the management and staff, insofar as we have been able to ascertain, deserve high marks.[9]

8. For country totals in various years, see Appendix Table H-7.
9. The term "management," often spelled with a capital "M," entered the Bank's lexicon shortly after McCloy, Black, and Garner appeared on the scene. For many years it meant the president and vice president (or vice presidents). Since the mid-1960s it has sometimes been more loosely used to include top level staff. (The executive directors are referred to as "the board" or the "board of directors.")

When the Bank's first loan—the 1947 reconstruction loan to France—was under consideration, the top-ranking French national on the staff, Leonard Rist, director of the Research Department, disqualified himself from staff work on the loan because he felt that as a French citizen he should not participate in the relevant economic studies. But, said Vice President Garner,

we came to the conclusion that was an unsound position. The Articles of Agreement say in regard to the personnel of the Bank that the staff should have its first allegiance to the Bank without regard to national or other interests. So we thought we had a sound basis to operate on. I think it's one of the most important factors in the success of the Bank that we broke down the feeling of nationality within the work of the Bank.[10]

The most loyal, dedicated, nonpartisan staff would, of course, be of limited value in the business of raising and lending capital for productive projects if it were not also technically competent. In the effort to acquire a professionally qualified, widely representative staff the Bank has spent funds generously. As was reported in Chapter 2, in the very early days recruitment was on a catch-as-catch-can basis, supplemented by the hope that when the organizational framework was erected, qualified applicants would seek Bank jobs. The need for a positive recruiting program became apparent in about 1953 and seemed to call first for a more vigorous effort to add European nationals to the staff. Recruiting trips were made periodically to Western Europe, usually by Donald D. Fowler of the Personnel Department, accompanied by the head of one or another of the operating departments. Gradually semiofficial committees were established in some European countries to work with the Bank in seeking out and evaluating personnel. They proved extremely useful.

A small training program was initiated in 1949. Of the 7 trainees who participated in the first course, 5 became members of the permanent staff. The program was continued, but after a few years the emphasis shifted from training recruits for the Bank itself to training a limited number from less developed countries—usually 8 to 10 people between the ages of twenty-five and thirty-two—who came from ministries of finance, central banks, planning boards, and the like, and returned home after six to twelve months at headquarters to become links between the Bank and their governments. Some 140 people completed the course, and many of them are by now in senior positions in their home governments. Others have returned to the Bank or Fund as directors or governors, or alternate directors or governors, or members of the senior staff.

---

10. See Robert L. Garner, "Oral History," p. 21. Nevertheless, with a few exceptions, the practice has been maintained that staff members do not work directly on matters concerning their own countries.

The training program was discontinued in 1964. Its functions by then could be better discharged in other ways. The fellows of the Economic Development Institute (the "staff college" of the Bank, described in Chapter 9) provided strong links between the Bank and member governments; and a Young Professionals Program, which seemed to be a better recruiting and in-service training device, was instituted. As of June 30, 1971, 118 staff members who had originally entered the Bank under the young professionals program had been assigned to regular posts in the Bank Group. An additional 60 young professionals were in training, and 30 more expected to join the program within a few months. Although this would raise the cumulative total of young professionals serving the Bank Group under this program to 230 from fifty-seven countries, twenty-six of the fifty-seven countries had provided only 1 young professional and six countries 2 professionals. Four countries—France, India, the United Kingdom, and the United States—provided 80 of the 230.

Over the years, the Bank has acquired a staff unique among the international agencies in terms of its professional competence.[11] Its reports are generally of high caliber, and its staff members are respected for up-to-date knowledge in their fields of specialization, even where they are considered insufficiently aware of, or sensitive to, the special problems of particular geographic areas. Knowledge on the part of the staff members that they are employed by a respected agency that is empowered to make or withhold ardently desired loans, coupled with the belief that they themselves are more cosmopolitan and experienced than are the representatives of low-income countries with whom they deal, is not conducive to humility.[12]

To the less developed world, the Bank often seems arrogant, remote, and demanding. Some of its own staff as well as outsiders believe that more train-

11. Some qualification of the term "unique" may be in order with respect to economists. The International Monetary Fund's reputation as a home for outstanding members of that profession is surely not below the Bank's and is probably above it.

12. See James Morris, *The Road to Huddersfield: A Journey to Five Continents* (Pantheon Books, 1963), pp. 62–63. Morris, an accomplished writer, says, "Few observers would deny that an unhappy air of superiority often issues from the place. I have sensed it all too strongly myself, from staff members who have been kind enough to read this manuscript and left me feeling as though I have just failed the entrance examination to a course of creative writing. ... I once attended the signing ceremony of a loan to some small member nation of the Bank ... for some not very grandiose project. ... Lofty indeed was the condescension with which the Bank, whose purpose is the making of loans, agreed to make this one, and fawning to a degree was the deference with which the money was accepted, the borrower's representative assuring the management that he was positively grateful for the difficulties the Bank had placed in their way, which had made them feel not only richer, but happier and more civilized too, and had convinced them, he seemed to suggest, that such obstructive and delaying tactics ought properly to be applied to the governing of all human affairs."

ing in the diplomacy of development would be helpful. Whether it would be feasible to provide such training is open to question, however.

The job classification system introduced by Vice President Garner shortly after his arrival at the Bank was never completed. From the early 1950s until 1969, salaries were fixed without any clear or consistent relationship to formal titles. All salaries of regular employees are net of income taxes—federal, state, and local. Salary scales and fringe benefits that make Bank employment attractive to qualified personnel from rich countries make it doubly attractive to personnel from poor countries—and even easier for the latter to get out of touch with the thinking and aspirations of people in the lands from which they have come and to which they will presumably eventually return.

The salary levels for the president and executive directors of the Bank, it will be recalled from Chapter 3, caused great difficulty at Savannah and in the end proved to be the one decision that was not approved by Lord Keynes. He considered them scandalously high. Once adopted, however, they gave the Bank an opportunity to be relatively generous at other levels, too. And because the Bank did not need to plead annually with national legislatures to finance its administrative budget, adjustments could be made to permit the institution to keep abreast of changes in the cost of living and to continue to hire highly qualified personnel when the competition for them was keenest.

Organizational Evolution

At the beginning the Bank was conceived of primarily as a guarantee institution. After discarding this conception, it thought of itself as a series of loan windows at which projects for reconstruction and development would be presented for approval or disapproval. For the early reconstruction loans, this image was not too far-fetched. For development lending, it proved naive. Initially there was little appreciation of the amount of field work that would be needed to facilitate the presentation of "sound" projects, to make judgments as to their priority, and to understand the economic, social, and political settings in which projects would be left to flourish or wither. The volume of annual lending to any one country was not expected to be large enough to justify a resident mission in the borrowing country. Individual representatives were soon assigned to a few countries, but no arrangements were made for a regular "foreign service," and no regional offices of the kind authorized by the Articles of Agreement were set up.

Once an agency is launched as a centralized institution, it tends to remain so. Key staff members develop a vested interest in the functions they perform and resist sharing them with field personnel. It becomes much more difficult to decide which functions can be decentralized. The dispatch of an almost infinite number of visiting missions to conduct surveys, prepare economic reports, inspect projects, and evaluate progress seems more normal than establishing a finite number of resident missions. And if in the process an embryonic "foreign service" is developed but service within it is not made essential to advancement on the career ladder, time so spent can easily become a handicap. Out of sight and without authority, the field personnel are also often out of mind when higher-level, more responsible jobs become available at headquarters.

The hope that well conceived, well prepared project applications would come cascading into headquarters was dashed almost as soon as the Bank opened for business. It quickly became clear that applicants needed technical assistance in preparing project proposals, but technical assistance had not been specifically mentioned in the Articles of Agreement, and the Bank was ambivalent concerning the proper source of this form of help. Its first annual report publicized the Bank's own willingness to supply technical assistance in the preparation of loan applications.[13] The second annual report emphasized that the Bank could not supply technical assistance from its own staff "on any large scale" but that it could help members select and procure private technicians.[14]

At first, the World Bank did not want to be identified with the broader technical assistance efforts being launched by the United Nations family. In reply to an inquiry from the UN secretary-general, the Bank in mid-1947 reported that it had received no requests for technical assistance as such and neither had, nor expected to have, the staff to provide advice and assistance on a broad scale. It was particularly worried about the recommendations that might emerge from a technical mission to prepare a comprehensive reconstruction or development program. Such recommendations, it felt, would normally be regarded as having the official sponsorship of the international agency or agencies that sent the mission. Because most of the projects recommended by field missions would probably require financial aid, the Bank would be the agency most likely to be embarrassed by the situation[15] (that is, embarrassed if it had to turn down applications for activities endorsed by the missions).

13. International Bank for Reconstruction and Development, *First Annual Report by the Executive Directors* (Sept. 27, 1946), p. 5.

14. IBRD, *Second Annual Report, 1946–1947*, p. 14.

15. United Nations Economic and Social Council, "Expert Assistance to Member Governments—Addendum to Interim Note by the Secretary-General," Doc. E/471/Add. 2 (July 29, 1947), pp. 25–27.

Despite the Bank's fear of embarrassment by other agencies in the UN family, the value of technical assistance as such was becoming increasingly clear. The 1947–1948 annual report said unequivocally that "successful development depends in most cases just as much upon the provision of technical assistance from abroad as upon the availability of foreign capital."[16] The IBRD announced its willingness to undertake broad investigations of conditions in underdeveloped member countries and thus laid the groundwork for the series of survey missions that got it fairly deeply into the technical assistance business.[17]

In addition to technical assistance in the form of survey missions, the Bank provided experts for advice on specific development problems, assigned staff members for as long as a year to help IBRD-financed development banks get into operation, and in other ways established itself as a provider of technical assistance on a scale that justified a special niche for this function shortly before the first major reorganization of the headquarters staff was undertaken. In late 1951 the "Staff Office" under Richard Demuth was renamed the "Technical Assistance and Liaison Staff." Its responsibilities included the Bank's technical assistance activities and liaison with the United Nations and the specialized agencies.

The Reorganization of 1952

The reorganization in 1952 is generally regarded not as the first but as the only fundamental organizational change during the twenty-five-year period covered by this study. It involved a major reshuffling of the Loan Department and the Economic Department. Prior to 1952, all staff members responsible for relations with member countries and for negotiating loans, and most of the technical and financial staff responsible for evaluating projects, were in the Loan Department. The Loan Department also included some economists, usually those specializing in particular countries. Most economists, whether engaged in assessing the creditworthiness of member countries, studying commodity problems, or doing general economic research, were in the Economic Department. A loan decision required both a favorable judgment by the Loan Department on the engineering, technical, and financial aspects of the project and a green light from the Economic Department on the creditworthiness of the borrowing country[18] Relations between loan officers and economists were not harmonious, and there was much jockeying for position and prestige.

16. IBRD, *Third Annual Report, 1947–1948*, p. 18.
17. For more on the work of such missions, see Chapter 10, below.
18. Williams, "International Bank for Reconstruction and Development," p. 13.

Furthermore, as operations in less developed countries began to expand, the loan director's load became excessive. An interdepartmental committee, chaired by William Iliff (later Sir William Iliff), was set up to see what organizational changes should be made. It decided that area departments were an absolute necessity; and in 1952 the personnel of the Loan and the Economic Departments were redistributed among three area departments, which were set up on a regional basis (and later increased to more than three), a Technical Operations Department (which later became the Projects Department and still later a series of projects departments), and an Economic Staff.[19]

The loan officers and economists who specialized in particular countries or areas went into the area departments. Engineers, financial analysts, and economists who were engaged in project evaluation and supervision were assigned to the Technical Operations Department. The area departments and the Technical Operations Department, along with the Marketing Department, were called "operational departments." The Economic Department, never a favorite of McCloy, Garner, or Black, was in contrast re-labeled "the Economic Staff" and was reduced in scope.[20]

The new Technical Operations Department, whose more elevated status facilitated the recruiting of additional engineers and other specialists, was organized on a functional basis, with sub-units for power, transportation, industry, agriculture, and so on. In other words, a proposal for an electric power project, whether from India or Brazil, would be reviewed by the power group and an agricultural proposal by the agriculture group.

Fear that the reorganization would result in different economic standards being applied in different area departments was to be allayed by the establishment of a committee, subsequently known as the Staff Economic Committee, which would be presided over by the director of the Economic Staff and would include the economic advisers of each of the area staffs and the prin-

19. See Appendix H for organizational charts of the Bank at various times in its history. After the reorganization of 1952, operational responsibility for technical assistance was assigned to the area departments, but the technical assistance and liaison staff retained a responsibility for recruiting personnel and advising the area departments on technical assistance policies.

20. "The economist did not speak up in those early days about longer-range problems and broad policy questions of the Bank. . . . The gap was filled by the lawyer. It's extraordinary how in the early days the legal department produced broad concepts and ideas and suggestions, and gradually management began to expect the lawyers to have these ideas rather than the economists. It wasn't that we were excluded from contributing. We failed to contribute ideas." (Harold Larsen, in de Wilde, Larsen, and Alter, "Oral History," pp. 6–7.) The key role of Chester McLain, the Bank's first general counsel, was mentioned in Chapter 3. His successor from 1949 to 1959, Davidson Sommers, was equally capable of producing concepts, ideas, and suggestions, and Sommers's advice too, on almost every aspect of the Bank's work, was sought and valued.

cipal economists in the Technical Operations Department. It would review country economic reports and perform certain other functions.

The intent and effect of the reorganization were twofold. In the first place, responsibility for judgments about the merits of individual projects was deliberately divorced from responsibility for judgments about the desirability of lending, or not lending, to particular countries or borrowers. Secondly, responsibility for economic work on countries was brought together with all other elements involved in arriving at lending attitudes towards the countries concerned. Of these two effects, the first has been by far the more crucial. Divorcing project responsibility from country and borrower responsibility limited the possibility that a defective or inadequately prepared project would be pushed through the Bank organization merely because the Bank's relations with a particular country were felt to be overriding considerations. Conversely, a project could not be pushed through merely because it was fascinating. The Bank thus protected itself simultaneously against the technocrat and the diplomat. This protection has a hidden cost in accentuating problems of coordination at the working level and securing consistency.[21]

The advantage of a built-in balance of power is a more probing, detailed review of proposed lending. The disadvantage is a loss of valuable time, diffusion of responsibility, unfriendly rivalry, and deadlocks that can be resolved only at the highest level of management. The relationship between area departments and the Technical Operations Department—"area–T.O.D." relations—after 1952 became the Bank's most difficult and pervasive organizational problem. The issues that caused strained relationships usually boiled down to matters of tactics and business judgment concerning conditions to be attached to proposed loans.

All Bank loans are conditioned on the acceptance of certain obligations by the borrowers. Where construction is involved, they invariably oblige the borrower to undertake certain supplementary activities during construction, for example, mobilizing the necessary local currency, submitting periodic progress reports, and so on. Frequently these agreements also contain covenants relating to rate policies, financial policies, actions with respect to management and organization, and other practices considered relevant to the success of the enterprise to be financed. The drafting of such covenants, as well as of "side letters" (letters indicating the expectations of the Bank on matters less formal and precise than those usually included in covenants) is the responsibility of the Legal Department. This department receives advice from the technical and the area departments, and often the advice is conflicting. In general, the technical departments are more inclined to think of enforceability within the confines of each individual project and consequently to want tightly defined documents obligating the borrower to take all the

21. Williams, "International Bank for Reconstruction and Development," pp. 13–14.

actions believed necessary to the success of a project. The area departments, as befits the "diplomatic" representatives of the Bank, tend to be more concerned with maintaining good relations with member countries over time, in the belief that the enforceability of agreements depends as much on the spirit of the relationship—the context of ongoing and prospective operations taken as a whole—as on the letter of individual project documents. We shall return to a more extensive consideration of the loan covenants and side letters in Chapter 13 on leverage and performance. Here we note only that the Legal Department is an active participant in the preparation and negotiation of loans.

Machinery for resolving interdepartmental conflict is also necessary. Therefore, early in the history of the Bank the "loan working party" was established as an instrument of coordination and until recently played an important role in shaping lending policy.[22] All documents destined for the Staff Loan Committee and the executive directors were first reviewed by the appropriate working party. These included the loan and guarantee agreements, project appraisal reports, and country economic reports. The working party made recommendations concerning the suitability of the proposed project, the amount and terms of the loan, and the conditions to be met before the loan became effective. Issues that were not resolved by working parties were referred to the Staff Loan Committee—a council made up of the principal department heads of the Bank for the purpose of focusing all the necessary expertise within the Bank on pending problems and issues.

The Staff Loan Committee was originally chaired by Vice President Garner, the only vice president of the Bank from the time of his arrival in 1947 until his transfer in 1956 to the presidency of the Bank's new affiliate, the International Finance Corporation. When Garner left, three vice presidencies were established, and J. Burke Knapp, Davidson Sommers, and William Iliff, who were already on the staff of the Bank, were promoted to the posts. Knapp became chairman of the Staff Loan Committee, which toward the end of George Woods's administration became simply "the Loan Committee."

22. According to IBRD, Operational memorandum 3 of February 26, 1953, "A loan working party for each country in which the Bank contemplates a loan operation will be established by the Director of the Area Department concerned" and will consist of the officer in charge of the loan operation as chairman; the officer responsible for the country economic appraisal; representatives designated by the Director of Technical Operations; a representative designated by the General Counsel; a representative designated by the Treasurer; and a representative from such other departments as may be concerned.

"Recommendations of the loan working party will be submitted to the Director of the Area Department concerned for presentation to the Staff Loan Committee."

In the course of time, the working party became an increasingly cumbersome operation. It was abolished by President Woods, and there has subsequently been no formal mechanism for working-level coordination. Experienced people in various departments concerned with the same operation often constitute themselves an informal group, but only because some of the staff abhor a vacuum. In recent years, even the full Loan Committee has met only rarely. Instead the relevant papers are circulated to the members of the committee with the expectation that their comments, if any, will be made by telephone or in writing. Issues that require face-to-face discussion usually are considered in ad hoc groups (generally chosen by the chairman of the Loan Committee), who holds what are called "special loan meetings."

The Technical Operations Department, as it was named in the reorganization of 1952, has for most of its life been under the direction of Simon Aldewereld. It has built up a uniquely competent staff of project appraisers in the fields in which the Bank has done the bulk of its lending. This comparative advantage that the Bank has over other sources of development finance has reinforced its dedication to the project approach and has accounted for some of the resistance to a substantial broadening of its field of lending. The resisters' attitude is: "Why mess around with program loans and hard-to-appraise types of projects if you are really best at financing electric power and transportation projects, and there are still plenty of power and transport projects to finance?"[23] The fact that the Bank's special competence was primarily technical also made it vulnerable to the charge of being overly concerned with the engineering aspects of projects (and their financial rates of return) and insufficiently concerned with the social and cultural aspects of growth and development.

All in all, the reorganization of 1952 proved good enough for the Bank to live with and prosper under. Nevertheless, as the scale and complexity of the Bank's business continued to grow, certain limitations of its organizational arrangements became increasingly apparent. Many within the institution came to feel that the structure needed changing in important respects. Among the desired changes was a modification of the built-in checks and balances which would permit the country focus to be strengthened and more decisions

23. The same thought was expressed more elegantly by one of the most respected executive directors in 1968 while stating his misgivings about a proposed industrial imports credit to India. Not only would it be balance-of-payments support rather than a project loan, he argued, but "the real value of the Bank and IDA is that we have that wonderful staff; that we have these economists and engineers who check the projects, who guide the investment effort, the development effort, who have the procurement control, who have end-use control. Here we completely neglect all these great values."

to be made below the level of the presidency. Critics also wanted greater representation from less developed countries at the various decision-making levels. We return to these issues in Chapter 21.

The Economic Development Institute (EDI), which was organized by the Bank in 1955 as part of the headquarters organization, is discussed in Chapter 10 since it offers what is basically a form of technical assistance to less developed countries. Also requiring only passing mention here is the establishment a few years later—and the early demise—of an embryo foreign service for high-level advisers who were stationed by the Bank in less developed countries. These advisers were recruited and paid on the basis of their individual professional qualifications rather than on the basis of the salaries attached to classified positions at headquarters.[24]

Creation of the Bank's Affiliates

The two principal "affiliates" of the World Bank—the International Finance Corporation created in 1956 and the International Development Association established in 1960—have already been referred to here. As is explained in the chapters devoted to them, they were carefully tailored responses to development "requirements" that were recognized by the Bank but were beyond the scope of its own charter and structure. Both could have been created by relatively simple amendments to the Bank's Articles of Agreement, but this procedure might have opened the floodgates to more controversial amendments and, in the case of IDA, might have made Bank bonds less attractive to investors in Western Europe and North America. Alternatively, Bretton Woods–type conferences might have been convened.

Instead of calling diplomatic conferences to consider the creation of the new institutions and the constituent instruments which were to govern them, it was the Executive Directors of the Bank who undertook the task of formulating charters for the new institutions and presenting them to member governments for signature. Traditional international lawyers might have raised their eyebrows at this procedure and, in fact, some of them did. The negotiating body for these agreements consisted of 18 Executive Directors who among them represented the entire membership. There was no express provision in the Charter of the Bank empowering the Directors to engage in this activity and there was no opportunity for individual governments (with the exception of those—five in number—who appoint their own Directors) to participate directly in the task of formulating these agreements. Moreover, the Executive Directors vote in accordance with the weighted-voting formula. . . . In practice plain voting strength has not been the determining factor. . . . The Executive Directors developed the technique of seek-

24. See Chapter 10, below.

ing a consensus, observing a balance between the interests of the richer and the poorer countries.[25]

The IFC's basic purpose is to facilitate economic development by investing—without requiring a governmental guarantee of the investment—in productive private enterprises in its less developed member countries, in association with private investors who can provide competent management. It has its own officers and staff, some of whom hold the same positions in the Bank.

While Robert L. Garner was president of IFC (1956–61), the president of the World Bank, Eugene R. Black, served ex officio as chairman of IFC's board of governors; since Garner's retirement, the president of the Bank has served also as president of IFC. In the early 1960s, responsibility for the appraisal and supervision of all industrial projects, including industrial development banks, whether they were financed by the Bank or IFC, was vested in the IFC. In late 1968, however, the department in IFC that was responsible for development banks was transferred back to the World Bank, which had been providing most of the Bank Group's financing for such institutions. Subsequently the Bank also resumed responsibility for handling, through an Industrial Projects Department, proposals for Bank/IDA financing of manufacturing, mining, and other industrial undertakings.[26]

The membership of IFC, which, like that of IDA is open only to countries that are already members of the Bank, has grown from 31 countries as of the date of IFC's establishment (July 24, 1956) to 59 on June 30, 1960; 78 as of the same date in 1965; and 96 in 1971. The IFC staff remained under 100 until 1963, but reached 161 in 1968 and 168 as of mid-1971.

In contrast to IFC, which is more nearly a separate international institution (though its president, treasurer, controller, and secretary hold those same positions in the World Bank), IDA is, in effect, a soft loan fund administered by the Bank. Nevertheless, the establishment of IDA had a far more profound influence on the evolution of the Bank Group than did the establishment of IFC—and not only because IDA has had a larger membership than IFC and greater resources to invest.

When IDA was created in 1960, the staff of the Bank tended to assume that it could run IDA simply by dipping periodically into its IDA pocket and producing some IDA money for use on a project that was already in the works. The director of administration, after consultation with the department heads concerned, estimated that "eight additional staff members would be

25. Aron Broches, General Counsel of IBRD, "Development of International Law by the International Bank for Reconstruction and Development," *Proceedings of the American Society of International Law* (1965), p. 34.

26. See Chapter 11, below.

required for the area departments (four operations officers and four economists) and that another 11 staff members would be required for the Technical Operations Department."[27] This forecast proved ridiculously low. By enabling the Bank staff to do business with member countries that were no longer creditworthy (or were not yet so) under Bank standards, and by increasing the volume of funds available to the Bank Group, the establishment of IDA led

to a marked increase in the number of individual operations, and to a rapid increase in total staff. In particular, the creation of IDA brought about a substantial increase in staff working on agricultural projects and, with a policy decision in 1961 to broaden the range of eligible sectors both for the Bank and for IDA, on education as well. The creation of IDA was also responsible, at least in part, for a decision, taken in 1964, to build up the Economics Department and to strengthen the economic work of the Bank Group more generally.[28]

Furthermore, it modified the relationship between the president and the executive directors.

The membership of IDA, unlike that of the Bank or of IFC, is formally divided into two categories. Part I countries are the high-income member countries, which through governmental appropriations provide virtually all of the usable resources of the association. Part II countries are the middle- and low-income members. Total membership rose from 15 in September 1960 to 93 in mid-1964 and 107 in mid-1971 (of which 18 were Part I countries).

When IDA's Articles of Ageement were being drafted, it was decided to follow the voting system of the Bank. This meant votes in proportion to subscriptions to the capital stock, except for a weighting in favor of the smaller, economically weaker countries. The weighting was achieved by giving all members a certain minimum number of votes, regardless of the amounts of their subscriptions. The subscriptions of Part I members were payable in full in gold or convertible currencies, whereas only 10 percent of the subscriptions of Part II members were payable in this manner. The balance of the subscription of each Part II member was payable in its own currency and was usable by IDA only with the agreement of the member. Both categories of subscriptions, however, carried the same voting rights.[29]

27. "Second Progress Report of the IDA Preparatory Committee" (SLC/0/60-40), Sept. 1, 1960, p. 7. His estimate was based on the assumption that IDA would make six to eight loans by the end of 1961 and would have committed about $400 million by June 30, 1962—assumptions that proved to be too optimistic.

28. Williams, "International Bank for Reconstruction and Development," p. 15. President Woods among other actions created a new post, that of "economic adviser to the president," who serves also as chairman of the Economic Committee.

29. See Chapter 12, below.

The Bank's executive directors are also the directors of IDA. After the Articles of Agreement of IDA were adopted, it proved possible—principally through calling the first two replenishments "contributions" instead of "capital subscriptions"—to obtain substantial resources from a small minority of members, the Part I countries, without reducing the voting strength of the Part II members. It also became possible for the Bank: (a) to transfer sizable sums from its net income to IDA, thereby making IDA slightly less dependent on governmental appropriations for its financial resources, and (b) after a minor amendment in the Bank's Articles of Agreement, to extend valuable loan assistance to IFC.

With the creation of IFC and IDA, the World Bank became the World Bank Group. The Group had another addition to the family in the mid-1960s —the International Centre for Settlement of Investment Disputes (ICSID). The president of the Bank in his personal capacity or the Bank as an institution had on various occasions been invited by governments or foreign investors to help settle disputes relating to investments. The experiences convinced the Bank that a permanent facility to deal with investment disputes between states and foreign investors could help promote mutual confidence and thereby stimulate the flow of private international capital into countries that wanted it. Again the executive directors and staff of the Bank, at the request of the board of governors, prepared an instrument, the Convention on the Settlement of Investment Disputes between States and Nationals of other States. The international organization created by the convention to carry out its provisions is ICSID. While legally correct, "international organization" erroneously suggests that there are meetings, messengers, flags, staff cars, elections, and other accoutrements of organizational life, which are not characteristic of ICSID.[30]

Further Evolution of the Bank and IDA

The desirability of helping governments identify and prepare projects that can be candidates for Bank or IDA financing—the Bank's entering wedge into the technical assistance business—has led it in several related directions. The Bank Group works closely with the United Nations Development Program (UNDP) and acts as the executing agency for a number of pre-investment studies financed by UNDP. It has entered into formal cooperative arrangements with FAO, Unesco, and WHO for developing projects for Bank/IDA consideration in the fields of agriculture, education, water supply, sanitation, and drainage. Informal arrangements for cooperation with other

30. See Chapter 11, below.

international organizations have also been made. Significantly, the Bank Group has gradually enlarged its own field staff. It maintains a permanent East African mission in Nairobi, a permanent West African mission in Abidjan, and resident staffs or representatives as of June 30, 1971, in India, Pakistan, Indonesia, and five other countries. (These are in addition to its office in Paris, which maintains a broad range of contacts with European governments, international organizations, and financial and academic institutions in Western Europe; its office in Tokyo for liaison with the Japanese government and the Japanese financial community; two offices in New York, staffed on a full-time basis only by secretaries, for facilitating liaison with the U.S. investment community and the United Nations; and a similarly staffed office in London, which sometimes serves as the scene for consultative group meetings and other gatherings.)

During the time when the Bank was acquiring its principal affiliates, it was operating in a climate of rising concessional assistance (grants and loans on favorable terms) from rich to poor countries. The official flow continued to increase from 1956 through 1963, but has moved erratically and, in real terms, only slightly upward since then. Meanwhile, the role of the United States, the principal aid supplier, has changed markedly. In terms of the net flow of official development assistance from members of the Development Assistance Committee of the Organisation for Economic Co-operation and Development, its proportion has dropped from more than 60 percent in 1956 to 45 percent in 1970. During the 1950s, the basic framework for U.S. foreign aid was the Mutual Security Act of 1951, as amended; and U.S. aid was justified primarily as a national security measure, needed to strengthen allies and to build up low-income countries so that they would be less vulnerable to communist invasion or takeover. When in early 1961 the Kennedy administration came into office, development itself was given a higher though by no means overriding priority, at least by the executive branch. Other donor nations followed suit, entered into intergovernmental discussions focused on development, and muffled their earlier rhetoric in favor of aid for self-serving reasons, such as winning markets for their exports and preserving historic ties with former colonies. Countries that did not already have overall development plans were encouraged to prepare them.

But weariness and disenchantment with aid soon took over in the United States, and the U.S. aid flow began to decline in the mid-1960s. No other large bilateral donor replaced the United States as financial and intellectual leader of the international development effort, and the multiplicity of badly coordinated bilateral and multilateral aid programs added to the general sense of confusion, ineffectiveness, and frustration.

Thus, when Robert S. McNamara became president of the World Bank and its affiliates in 1968, the time was ripe for filling the leadership vacuum that existed. During the latter part of Eugene Black's presidency, the Bank had played a key role in establishing the India and Pakistan consortia, providing chairmen for them, servicing them, and analyzing the development programs of those two countries. George Woods gave a strong impetus to the establishment of an analogous kind of coordinating mechanism, the consultative group, to rationalize the pattern of external assistance to other important developing countries.[31] Although the Bank/IDA contribution to the total flow of official development assistance continued to be minor (about 10 percent of the total), the Bank as an institution became steadily more prominent.

It seemed entirely appropriate that George Woods, president of the Bank, concerned about the declining priority for development assistance in some of the principal donor nations and the inadequacy of existing arrangements for assessing needs for funds and their availability, should propose a "grand assize" of the development effort in a 1967 speech in Stockholm. He suggested that an international group of experts in the field of development "study the consequences of 20 years of development assistance, assess the results, clarify the errors and propose the policies which will work better in the future."[32]

Woods's initiative was widely hailed. Some donor governments, however, harbored doubts about the merits of his proposal, and the soundings necessary before it could become a reality extended beyond Woods's term as president. His successor, McNamara, followed through by inviting Lester B. Pearson, former Prime Minister of Canada and winner of the Nobel Peace Prize, to set up a commission and undertake the "grand assize." At the September 1969 Bank-Fund meeting in Washington, Pearson's blue-ribbon international commission released its report.[33] The report took the form of a comprehensive, informative, readable book entitled *Partners in Development,* which contained more than ninety recommendations for strengthening and rationalizing the international development effort.

The Bank staff discovered thirty-three recommendations bearing on the work of the Bank Group. This, we hasten to add, was not because the Pearson Commission was hypercritical of the Bank, but rather because the com-

31. See Chapter 15, below.
32. George D. Woods, "Development—The Need for New Directions," address to the Swedish Bankers Association, Stockholm, Oct. 27, 1967, p. 12.
33. The commissioners were: Sir Edward Boyle (United Kingdom), Roberto de Oliveira Campos (Brazil), C. Douglas Dillon (United States), Wilfred Guth (Federal Republic of Germany), W. Arthur Lewis (Jamaica), Robert Marjolin (France), and Saburo Okita (Japan).

mission clearly considered the Bank Group the sturdiest reed on the development horizon. In a review of *Partners in Development,* the noted Canadian economist, Harry G. Johnson, said, somewhat hyperbolically, "From a cynical point of view, the World Bank has promoted eight nationally eminent men into eight world statesmen, and they have reciprocated by promoting the Bank into a major institution of world government."[34]

The Bank welcomed recommendations urging it to do a bit more of what it was already doing but was considerably less receptive to those affecting its organizational structure, its commitment to the project approach, and its established pattern of operations. President McNamara had committed himself to a substantially increased level of lending during the year preceding the release of the Pearson report—fiscal year 1969—and to a longer time frame than year-to-year planning could provide. A five-year program had been initiated, the objective of which was a level of lending by the Bank Group roughly twice that of the previous five-year period. Although the objective was not to make the Bank Group the largest single source of development assistance, the stepped-up Bank program, combined with a declining U.S. bilateral effort, had this effect, and the effect has increased the visibility and prominence of the Bank Group on the development horizon.

By September 1969, the Bank could aspire to a central role in promoting and coordinating international development programs. President McNamara, in his speech to the board of governors, took a few steps in this direction.

Our Country Economic Reports can and should become increasingly useful tools to all organizations working in the field of development. Beginning this year, therefore, we will organize a regular annual mission to each major developing country to report in detail on economic and social progress and on the prospects for the future. These missions will investigate all major sectors of the economy, and will seek to determine priorities in both investment and pre-investment activities. We will look to other relevant international organizations for assistance in their fields of specialization, and preliminary discussions have indicated that such cooperation will be willingly extended. We believe that the reports of these comprehensive missions, to be published on a regular twelve-month cycle, will be useful not only to the country itself and to the Bank, but to bilateral aid organizations and to the United Nations and its other agencies as well. They will provide an independent, objective, and wholly nonpartisan basis for evaluating progress in the Second Development Decade.[35]

He has also talked more than his predecessors did about the strategy of development, as well as its dimensions and the need for a more equitable

34. "Pearson's Grand Assize Fails: A Bleak Future for Foreign Aid," *The Round Table,* Vol. 60 (January 1970), pp. 24–25.
35. *Address to the Board of Governors,* Sept. 29, 1969, p. 22.

sharing of its fruits. He has established a Population Projects Department within the Bank, as well as a Special Projects Department, and has sought in other ways to adapt the organization and staff of the Bank Group to the requirements of the 1970s as he sees them.

It is too early to say whether the Bank, as it expands its program, will in fact be able to maintain the comprehensiveness and high quality forecast by McNamara. As for organizing additional consultative groups, important donor governments have not wanted to go as far and as fast as McNamara proposed.

The staff at the moment is also divided, as large staffs are prone to be. A modest number of activists welcome virtually all extensions of the frontiers of Bank activity and find the more frenetic atmosphere an overdue response to current needs. Another group is deeply distressed to see the institution "running off in all directions," setting itself up to make Jovian judgments about the overall development strategies of member countries, and submerging so cheerfully its basic role as financier of economic infrastructure. Many go about their business more or less as usual, touched but little by the winds that swirl around them. Still others feel that arriving more speedily at lending decisions, delegating more authority down the line, improving communication within the Bank Group, and other internal reforms are as vital to modernizing the agency as is broadening the range of its external concerns.[36]

The administrative style of the Bank is unconventional and is particularly disturbing to those nationals of countries other than the United States who have worked in governments in which the responsibilities of the various administrative units are clearly understood and firmly respected. To them, the Bank's style appears autocratic, quixotic, and distressingly disorderly.

The top executive of the Bank dominates the organization and encounters few internal checks and balances. The President's Council, about which more is said in Chapter 21, does not formulate policy—nor does any other group. What is not decided by the president tends to be left to the departments or divisions to arrange for themselves. Roles at every level are loosely defined. Individual initiative on the part of staff members is both expected and rewarded. By relying on people rather than procedures, the Bank derives a great advantage. But it also pays a price. As the organization continues to grow, more respect for lines of authority and more systematic policymaking machinery will in all probability be needed.

36. Although not in existence as of mid-1971, a staff association was in the making that would provide a recognized mechanism for consulting with management on conditions of work and service. In February 1972, the constitution of the Staff Association entered into force.

The question of how far the Bank has progressed on the road from bank to development-financing agency—and what is the difference between the two —will be discussed later. Suffice it to say here that the Bank has developed a staff and structure equipped to do very much more than borrow funds in the right markets at the right times, devote them to strengthening the economic infrastructure of creditworthy countries, and follow up its lending to insure repayment in full. It has created a fund (IDA) from which it can help countries that are unable to borrow on Bank terms. It has equipped itself with expertise on an ever-broader range of development questions. More-over, it has started to think in terms of five-year programs of country lending that will enable its clients, if they are made aware of the programs, to plan ahead with greater confidence.

The Bank Group can fill vacuums when its president wants to and its executive directors are not opposed. It remains independent of congresses and parliaments between triennial replenishments of IDA resources. For these reasons, and also because of the high quality of its professional staff, the Bank Group had managed by mid-1971 to become the most dynamic and probably the most respected promoter of development among major agencies in the development business.

Executive Directors and the Presidents They Elect

It is in the nature of things that relations between "management" and "board" will have their ups and downs. Management's objective is inevitably to translate its plans into action and to pursue its business with as much backing and as little "interference" as possible from its board of directors. The board, if it has any conscience at all, wants to be more than a rubber stamp; at least some of its members will want to alter certain policies or get into "operating details." Customary differences in point of view are usually submerged, however, and a common front formed when the institution is subjected to "attacks from the outside."

In the days of President Meyer, as was mentioned earlier, the board–management relationship was strained; the executive directors, under the leadership of the U.S. member of the board, were relatively powerful, though the Bank as an institution was weak and inexperienced. John J. McCloy made a different relationship with the executive directors a condition of his acceptance of the presidency. He and Garner were willing to let the executive directors know what they were doing, but not really to negotiate with them. They regarded the second U.S. executive director, Eugene Black, as part of management, but the other directors (if one can generalize about a group so diverse) had never felt so "out of it." Their resentment was considerable, but McCloy's presidency lasted only two years.

After McCloy's departure there was an immediate improvement in management–board relationships, not because Black differed fundamentally from McCloy in his convictions—their convictions were cut from the same cloth—but because of his personality and method of operation. Black had been a member of the board and knew how board members felt. During his presidency, most of the discussion with board members took place, not in formal meetings around the oval table in the flag-bedecked board room, but in informal consultations between Black and the principal directors or those concerned with particular questions. Without really giving the board as such any greater authority than it had had under McCloy, he managed to convey the feeling that its jurisdiction had been enlarged.

President Woods's relations became markedly less harmonious than Black's —with the staff as well as with the board—again primarily because of personality traits. Woods participated more aggressively in the discussions, sometimes interjecting sharp rejoinders and at other times engaging in long soliloquies. Meetings dragged on, to the point where everyone's patience was tried. Some critically important issues were decided during the contentious sessions, however. By the end of George Woods's regime, the Bank was engaged in a far broader range of developmental activities than at its beginning.

It should also be noted that the balance of power between president and board had been changed by the creation of IDA in the closing years of President Black's long reign. Until then, Black could in effect say to his board, "This is my money. I raised it in private capital markets. I can do what I want with it. If you don't approve, I'll resign and then what will you do for money?" However, IDA money was government money. The executive directors for Part I countries could, in effect, say to the president, "This is our money. You can't do as you please with it. You are not free to concentrate too much of it in India and Pakistan or elsewhere, and you will need our full cooperation to replenish the coffers when they become empty."

Their proprietary interest in the allocation of Bank Group resources could have plunged the directors promptly and deeply into development problems, including country requirements, country performance, and other matters. For reasons given in Chapter 12, however, involvement has been gradual and has taken place chiefly under President McNamara—a far more tactful board chairman than was Woods.

The executive directors are not a homogeneous group. Some are from the rich countries, in which the Bank raises its capital, some from the poor countries, in which it spends it. Originally twelve in number, there were twenty-one by 1971, of whom six had been appointed by the governments of France, Germany, India, Japan, the United Kingdom, and the United States; the other fifteen were elected and cast the votes of more than one member government.[37] Some, particularly in the early days, came to the position with international reputations and great influence at home. Some have been on the job for many years and have become respected elder statesmen within the group; others are neophytes. Some have developed pipelines into the institution and regard them as more informative and reliable sources than the presentations made at meetings. Others have themselves served as staff members or mission members before becoming executive directors.

Role in Selecting Presidents and Interpreting the Charter

Unlike most policy boards, the Bank's executive directors are on the premises virtually all the time. Their duties include selecting the president of the Bank, interpreting the Articles of Agreement, passing on all loans and bond issues, approving the annual budget, giving general guidance on matters of policy, and serving as links with the capitals of member governments. Their jobs can be sinecures or arduous assignments, depending on their interpretation of the role and its requirements.

The part they play in the selection of presidents has heretofore been minimal. Once it was conceded that the president should be a U.S. national, the task of finding a candidate acceptable at the highest levels of the U.S. government and in the U.S. financial community inevitably devolved upon the executive branch of the U.S. government. Presidents McCloy, Black, and Woods have played active roles in selecting their successors.[38] The executive directors at times have indicated unhappiness with the nominee and have privately grumbled about having had someone "forced down their throats." An opportunity to choose from a short list of nominees who were equally acceptable to the U.S. government would have been much appreciated but was

37. The Articles of Agreement, it will be recalled, provide for only five appointed executive directors. The situation as of June 30, 1971, was temporary, and it was expected that the executive director for India would subsequently become an elected rather than an appointed member.

38. Note, for example, the role of George Woods in the selection of Robert McNamara, as described by Henry L. Trewhitt in *McNamara: His Ordeal in the Pentagon* (Harper and Row, 1971), pp. 270–75. In an interview with the authors, Woods said that he wanted to establish retirement at the age of about sixty-five as a precedent for heads of the World Bank. As early as January 1967, therefore, he began a series of meetings with U.S. Secretary of the Treasury Henry H. Fowler and U.S. Executive Director of the Bank Livingston Merchant to consider candidates for the succession.

never given to them. They have played an important role in reelecting presidents and should be expected to play a more significant part in the selection of presidents in the future.

When it comes to interpreting the Articles of Agreement, the executive directors have had broad scope. They have been faced with questions of charter interpretation, and none of their interpretations has to date been appealed to the board of governors. Some questions have been dealt with formally; others have been settled implicitly. The Bank, for example, has spent considerable time, effort, and money on technical assistance although the Articles of Agreement make no mention of this form of aid. By authorizing the activity, the executive directors implicitly decided that the Bank had the power to provide technical assistance.[39] Similarly, in November 1951 they decided informally that nothing in the Articles of Agreement prevented the Bank from concerning itself in the Anglo-Iranian oil dispute. The executive directors also decided implicitly that it was within their powers to draft articles of agreement for the International Finance Corporation, the International Development Association, and the International Centre for Settlement of Investment Disputes and open them for signature and acceptance.

When the Bank makes a loan, the loan documents are approved by the Executive Directors, including the Executive Director appointed or elected by the member which is the borrower or guarantor. In submitting the loan documents to the Executive Directors, the President always includes in his report and recommendations a statement to the effect that he is satisfied that the loan proposal meets the requirements of the Articles of Agreement. The approval of the loan documents by the Executive Directors may therefore be taken to mean that the Directors, who also are the interpreting authority, are satisfied that the loan documents are within the scope of, and are consistent with, the Articles of Agreement.

Under these circumstances I think it quite appropriate to provide in the loan documents that neither the Bank, nor the borrower or guarantor may claim ... that the loan or guarantee agreement is invalid or unenforceable because of any provision of the Articles of Agreement.[40]

Other Functions

The directors are, of course, more interested in whether a loan *should* be made than whether it *can* be made. This has led to unhappiness about coming into the picture too late in the game. If management is dissatisfied with a proposal, the proposal never reaches the executive directors. If management

---

39. Aron Broches (general counsel of the IBRD), *International Legal Aspects of the Operations of the World Bank* (Leiden: A. W. Sijthoff, 1959), p. 337.
40. *Ibid.*, pp. 369–70.

favors it, negotiations may be so far advanced by the time it reaches the board that failure to endorse it will seem like a vote of no confidence in the president. One alternative used by the board has been to say, "All right this time, but not again, please." Another has been to institute procedures intended to inform the board of pending loans while they are still pending. The proportion of meeting time devoted to discussing policy papers, which can provide helpful guidelines for future lending, is currently being increased in relation to time spent discussing specific loans. On the whole, however, loan policy continues to be made on a case-by-case basis.

The board also passes on all bond issues. Individual board members have in some cases been the first to broach the possibility of an issue in a country they represent. The most notable case, perhaps, is the activity of the German director in the Bank's early borrowing in the Federal Republic of Germany.

The annual budget review used to give executive directors a chance to complain about the nationality composition of the staff, to urge greater representation from their country or region, and to recommend a reduction in Anglo-American representation. During the latter part of Woods's regime, executive directors increasingly used the budget review to raise questions about where the agency was going. The Canadians in particular pressed for program budgeting. McNamara has submitted with the budget a work program and lending program that have more and more become the focus of discussion.

Are executive directors simply representatives of governments, or are they, as is sometimes argued, members of a team that guides the Bank "objectively," with nothing more at heart than the welfare of humanity and the interests of the institution? In our view they are, in the final analysis, ambassadors of governments despite the fact that they are paid—indeed, well paid —by the Bank. Directors are appointed or elected for two-year terms. In the event of a conflict of interest, the appointed directors obviously must follow the instructions of their governments or resign. The remaining executive directors are sometimes in the position of representing governments with differing viewpoints on an issue. While on occasion expressing purely personal views, they too tend to give primacy to their responsibilities as representatives of governments. There is, of course, no law preventing governments from authorizing their ambassadors to rise above national interests and become spokesmen for a larger, international interest.

How actively should directors advance the interests of specific member governments? It is one thing to maintain that the Bank has too many North Americans or too few Africans on its staff, but quite another to lobby for the appointment of nationals of one's own government. Yet the line has at times been crossed—usually with little success from the point of view of the lobbyist.

Because executive directors have to sit in judgment on loan recommendations, it is generally agreed that they should not enter into loan negotiations. Nevertheless, some have shown great ingenuity in penetrating the gray area that surrounds formal negotiation—trying, for example, to have the Bank's work on a particular loan speeded up or given priority, asking that their country's negotiators be invited to Washington earlier than they would normally be, introducing them when they arrive to the counterparts with whom they will negotiate, and, on occasion, trying to eavesdrop on the negotiation while insisting that they are not crossing the boundary lines of propriety.

Governments sometimes consider it in their interest to oppose a proposed loan. The Polish coal loan of 1946–48 fell through largely because the U.S. government was not prepared to support it. In the 1960s, as the proportion of IDA's resources committed to India and Pakistan rose to almost three-fourths of the total, other member governments became increasingly uneasy and eventually forced through an understanding that the total credits to those two countries in any one year would be limited to no more than half of the total commitments of IDA funds for that year.[41] Latin American directors have complained unendingly that the Bank lends too little and too slowly to Latin America and shortchanges it with respect to IDA funds. Arab governments dislike loans to Israel and sometimes want to be recorded as opposed or abstaining when such loans are up for consideration.

The management and staff of the Bank tend to look to the executive directors to explain to home ministries what the Bank wants and to obtain support for it. Although, in the opinion of the Bank, executive directors are not always zealous enough in doing this, in the opinion of some national governments they are much too zealous. Some borrowers think of their executive directors more or less as captives of the Bank—paid generously by it, steeped in its club-like atmosphere, and out of touch with thinking at home.

The president of the Bank serves as chairman of the board of directors. Two of the present vice presidents (Sir Denis Rickett and Mohamed Shoaib) also have special responsibilities for keeping in touch with the executive directors. If management suspects that influential directors or member governments will object to a course of action, it tries to discover this through advance consultation and, if necessary, to defer the action. The secretary of the Bank, Morton M. Mendels, who has held the post since 1946, plays an important role as a link between board and management, enjoying the confi-

41. See Chapters 6 and 12, below.

dence of both. Formal votes are infrequent, but the secretary is sometimes asked to record a member government as dissenting or abstaining when a loan is under consideration.

One board of directors is enough. Presidents of the World Bank try to avoid acquiring what might in effect be two boards if they pressed too hard on issues that would open up the latent division between directors representing rich countries and those representing poor countries. McNamara in 1969, for example, would have liked to increase the 15 percent margin of preference that had been granted since 1962 to domestic as compared with foreign bidders on supplies for projects. No consensus could be reached, however, and he therefore decided not to insist on a decision.[42]

As a U.S. national, the president of the Bank should have (and to date has had) access to the highest levels of the U.S. government. To support him adequately and to provide responsible leadership within the board, the U.S. executive director also needs such access. Unfortunately, he has not always had it. The president of the Bank must speak as an international civil servant; and the absence of an authoritative spokesman for the United States, the largest stockholder, can operate as a handicap to the entire institution.

Very few board members qualify as experts in international development. When a loan is under consideration, the attention of the board tends to be concentrated on the project itself—its specific features and expected rate of return—although extensive economic documentation is available to the directors and may be reflected in the oral presentation by the staff. More directors are beginning to ask such questions as: What effect will the proposed loan have on income distribution in the borrowing country? Will it make the rich richer or benefit the needy? Can the executive directors get a clearer picture of the Bank Group's intentions with respect to country X before the board is presented with a loan or credit proposal that has already been studied to death? Would a more elaborate committee structure enable the board to delve more deeply into matters that concern it? Should the executive directors make field trips to form first-hand judgments about the effectiveness of Bank Group activity?

Broad issues have been discussed by the board during its consideration of policy papers and of the recommendations in the report of the Pearson Commission. Satisfying the understandable desire of those executive directors who want the board to play an increasingly significant role, without interfering too greatly with management's responsibilities, will not be easy.

Basically, the board can ask questions, raise problems, ratify proposals,

42. See Chapter 8, below.

and discourage initiatives for which governments may be unready. The board, particularly in the early days but also throughout its history, has included some men of real distinction, capable of creative pioneering activity. Under strong presidents, however, the board almost inevitably acts more as a brake than as an accelerator.[43]

Presidents and Their Presidencies

At the beginning of this chapter, we referred to the strong position of the president of the Bank (and, by implication, of its management) in influencing the evolution of the Bank and its affiliates. The Articles of Agreement of the Bank and Fund concerning the responsibilities of their respective chief administrative officers vis-à-vis executive directors, staff, and other international organizations were similar and did not presage the unique status attained over the years by the president of the Bank. The Fund's dealings, however, are primarily with central banks and ministries of finance in the highly sensitive area of monetary policy. This is a field in which key member nations remain notoriously reluctant to yield authority to an international secretariat without having the right at least to look constantly over the shoulders of those exercising the authority.

By contrast, the nature of most of the Bank's business—dealing with the private financial communities in rich countries in order to obtain resources with which to provide capital and technical assistance to poor countries—tends to make the president of the Bank a more independent, visible, and ubiquitous figure on the international horizon than is the managing director of the Fund. The insistence of most Bank presidents on exercising the full prerogatives of management, if not stretching them, also accounts for their strength.

43. During the years 1946–71, more than one hundred persons served as executive directors, and many of them influenced in significant fashion the history of the Bank Group. The names of all directors and alternates, as of the six dates for which organization charts are included in Appendix H, accompany those charts. At the risk of injustice to other equally influential executive directors, thirteen are mentioned here who, over the course of time, have affected notably the evolution of the Bank Group. Their home countries and periods of service as directors are also included: André van Campenhout (Belgium, 1960–present), Pieter Lieftinck (Netherlands, 1955–70), Luis Machado (Cuba, 1946–48, 1952–71), Jorge Mejía-Palacio (Colombia, 1954–68), René Larre (France, 1957–67), Louis Rasminsky (Canada, 1950–62), B. K. Nehru (India, 1949–54, 1958–62), Earl of Cromer (United Kingdom, 1959–61), Andrew N. Overby (United States, 1952–57), J. W. Beyen (Netherlands, 1946–52), Leon Baranski (Poland, 1946–50), Eugene R. Black (United States, 1947–49), and K. Varvaressos (Greece, 1946–48).

A new Bank president can do much to energize the institution and alter its course. But heads of international agencies, unlike prime ministers after an election, do not come into office with a popular mandate for a particular course of action. A World Bank president does not acquire a new team of vice presidents in the same way that a U.S. cabinet officer can usually acquire a fresh set of assistant secretaries shortly after taking office. He has few ambassadorships and honorific posts to which he can appoint people who might otherwise be obstructive. In short, he simply inherits a bureaucracy that is larger and more firmly wedded to its bureaucratic ways than when his predecessor took office. He may have to be autocratic in order to avoid being frustrated.

The terms of service of Bank presidents have ranged from six months for Eugene Meyer to thirteen years for Eugene Black. The five presidents to date have come to the Bank from different backgrounds and with different personalities. The international environment in which they have had to operate has changed drastically, due among other causes to the dramatic decline in the economic situation of Western Europe during the early postwar years, the subsequent, and equally dramatic, recovery of Western Europe and Japan, the waxing and waning of the cold war, the addition of sixty or more new sovereign states to international conference tables, the high importance they attach to development problems, and the growth and tapering off of bilateral development assistance. Each president accordingly has left his own mark on the institution he headed.

Tension with Directors under Meyer and McCloy

It is not our intention in this analytical history to dwell on personality differences among the Bank presidents, except where the differences had significant effects on the institutional evolution of the World Bank Group. If the Bank's most fundamental task during its first decade was to build a competent staff, obtain the confidence of private investors, and solidify its position in private capital markets, its early leaders, especially Eugene Black, were admirably suited to the task. George Martin, director of the Marketing Department of the Bank from 1950 through 1963, referred to Black in 1961 as "a master bond salesman," who

knew personally and was held in the highest esteem by every one of our underwriters, by every dealer throughout the country. . . .

If I had to say what in my opinion has made the World Bank as acceptable as it has been, I would say number one, it could never have gotten off the ground without the United States' 80 percent as a guarantee. Secondly, the management of the Bank as represented by Mr. Black. Thirdly was the sponsorship that now exists with the type of managers and the type of account which we have to sell our bonds. . . . They all dovetail. . . . And the outstanding thing, I believe, has been Mr. Black because of his integrity and the esteem in which he is held. . . .[44]

Black was also well equipped to establish a new relationship with his executive directors. Eugene Meyer, catapulted into the presidency at the twilight of his remarkable career, was not prepared to engage in guile or infighting with his board to resolve ambiguities in the charter concerning their respective roles. McCloy and Garner thought they should be busy building a bank. A columnist in the *Financial Times* of London welcomed their appointments when they were announced and, with respect to the executive directors, predicted that McCloy would not have much patience with "these chatterers" who have nothing to do but "sit around and give copious amateur advice."[45]

A more generous, after-the-fact interpretation has been provided by the secretary of the Bank:

Mr. McCloy was so completely wrapped up in the work of the Bank, in which he was acquitting himself extremely well, that he might have been guilty of scant reporting to the board; he might have been guilty of letting the board go by default once or twice. . . .

[Garner] certainly left the impression that in his mind the most efficient way for the board to operate was to agree to everything and thereby abbreviate meetings to the minimum time required. And, needless to say, not all board members behaved in this satisfactory manner. And the net result was that, while recommendations were approved, there was . . . an increasing restiveness. The board continued to be made up of men who had held high positions, who considered that their countries owned the Bank; if they were representatives of creditor countries, they felt they had a stake in the Bank; if they were representatives of borrowing countries, they felt the Bank existed for the purpose of lending money to their countries. . . . For people like this it was difficult to run a board meeting that would merely say "yes, yes, yes" to every item and then go home.[46]

Greater Harmony under Eugene Black

Relationships became explosively bad during McCloy's regime, but by the time he left, the position of management was so firmly established that his successor could adopt a more relaxed attitude without jeopardizing the preeminent position of management. Black and Garner (who continued as vice president to work tirelessly for competence and efficiency on the part of the staff) were the major builders of the Bank. From the moment that Black took over as president, the tone of board–management relations changed. He cul-

44. George Martin, "Oral History," pp. 23–24.
45. Quoted in the *New York Times,* March 4, 1947.
46. Morton M. Mendels, "Oral History," pp. 45–46.

tivated the board socially. He invited directors to his home for dinner. He took the board to Princeton University for a meeting with some of its faculty members; to Williamsburg, Virginia, for a tour of that beautifully reconstructed colonial capital; and to baseball games.[47] He had the ability to listen and, over time, to be converted. As a board, the directors exercised no more authority during his regime than they had before, but the atmosphere was markedly more cordial.

Black's attitude toward borrowers was also less standoffish than that of his predecessors. He wanted an intimate banker–client relationship with member countries. He played a major role in achieving a turn-around in the Bank's relations with Australia.[48] The speed with which the Bank provided a $100 million program loan to that country, moreover, helped get the Bank started on a more expansive vein. He was in no sense a risk-taker, but he gave the institution more momentum in the lending field than it had ever had. He took a lively personal interest in the establishment of the Economic Development Institute as a staff college for senior economic officials in less developed countries. His personality, his reputation for soundness, and his stature were vital attributes in securing a doubling of the capital subscriptions of the Bank in 1959.

He was at first strongly opposed to soft loans, for which there were vigorous advocates in the UN Economic and Social Council.

But the very fact that these loans are made on especially easy terms and are still called loans should make us suspicious. . . . In the end, although some loans will turn out well and be repaid, others will bring in their train, first, severe strain on the economy of the borrower and, finally, default. When this happens, there is likely to be ill will, rational and irrational, on both sides. The lender will resent the default on a loan made in good faith, the borrower will resent the years lost in abortive struggle to maintain payment on a debt, which he probably regarded in the first instance more as a promise of prosperity than a serious financial obligation. The effect of such defaults is to destroy credit generally and to wither the integrity of all orthodox lending. In my opinion, when a country has a choice between making loans or quasi-loans of this kind, it pays in the long run to choose grants.[49]

But in 1960 Black became president of IDA, a soft-loan fund, which calls its loans "credits."

The Bank's involvement in the mediation of international disputes of the

---

47. *Ibid.*, p. 66.
48. See Chapter 9, below.
49. IBRD, Address of Eugene R. Black to twelfth session of the Economic and Social Council, Press release (March 6, 1951), p. 7. At the next session of the General Assembly, Black more explicitly endorsed internationally administered grant aid. (UN General Assembly, Sixth Session, Second Committee, *Official Records,* 163rd meeting, Dec. 10, 1951, pp. 114–15.)

kind discussed in Chapter 18, below, was due in significant measure to Black's personal reputation. His success in winning the confidence of President Nasser of Egypt enabled the Bank to play a role in settling claims and counterclaims arising out of the nationalization of the Suez Canal. He and Vice President Iliff were instrumental in bringing India and Pakistan into agreement on plans for the development of the Indus River basin.

Black's economic views remained conservative, particularly with respect to Bank financing of government-owned enterprises, but the gap between his views and those of "liberals" in the development business narrowed during his presidency. His vaunted courtesy could be highly selective. He was no admirer of Latin America. He could be terribly stubborn. His shrewdness in appraising the other person's point of view, his talent for negotiation, and his avoidance of technical jargon and other forms of obfuscation nevertheless made him an exceedingly attractive principal spokesman.[50]

Renewed Tension under George Woods

Whereas Black brought to the Bank a mastery of bond marketing and of ways of adding to the Bank's loanable resources—at a time when these attributes were badly needed—George Woods, also a member of the banking fraternity, brought to the World Bank Group, at an equally opportune moment, expertise in investment banking. He came from the chairmanship of the board of The First Boston Corporation, but had frequently given his time, without pay, to special missions undertaken for the Bank at the request of its management. He was consequently not unfamiliar with Bank procedures and personnel.

Woods was sixty-one years old when he became the top executive. He had a secure reputation in the U.S. investment banking community and appeared neither to want nor to need psychological dividends from his new position. As president, he got off to a good, energetic start. Though self-assured and rather gruff, he was imaginative and willing to stick his neck out to expedite the transformation of the Bank into a development financing agency. He came in with the reputation of being Black's choice, yet he worked hard to transform "Black's Bank" into "Woods's Bank."

He built up the economic staff of the Bank and thereby introduced more of a development focus into the Bank Group's operations. He succeeded also in bringing about a more constructive relationship between the Bank and the rest of the UN family. The India and Pakistan consortia antedated

50. For more on Black's personality, see Morris, *The Road to Huddersfield* pp. 56–61.

Woods's presidency, but the number of country coordinating groups grew significantly during his term.

Within seven months of the time when he took office, however, Woods underwent major surgery. Frustrated and often suffering from nervous exhaustion during the latter half of his tenure, he became progressively more irascible and undiplomatic. He hectored his board of directors into approving program loans for India and Pakistan and offended member governments by his tactics in trying to secure a second IDA replenishment sufficient to permit new lending commitments totaling $1 billion a year. He did not succeed; $1 billion a year may have been visionary at that stage of IDA's life. He got $400 million—a substantial increase from the previous $250 million—but many informed persons believe he could have gotten that much at least a year earlier than he did, thereby avoiding the critical shortage of IDA funds in 1968.[51]

Faced with a falling off of interest in less developed lands on the part of developed countries, Woods sought to build relations with church organizations as part of the effort to educate the public and enlarge the constituency for development. In an article in *Foreign Affairs* in January 1966, he made one of the most widely quoted statements about the financial requirements of less developed countries to appear during the first "development decade": "A preliminary study made by the World Bank staff . . . suggests that the developing countries could put to constructive use, over the next five years, some $3 to $4 billion more each year than is currently being made available to them."[52] His call in Stockholm a year later for a "grand assize" of the development effort by internationally respected figures was another effort on his part to maintain world interest in developmental progress and to make the Bank more of an intellectual leader in the field.

There were at least two great ironies about his administration. One of his principal objectives was to make the Bank more responsive to the needs of developing countries, especially in view of the large number of African nations joining the Bank during the first half of the 1960s. During the latter part of Woods's regime, however, his relations with India turned sour because of the Bank's toughness in demanding changes in that country's economic policy and its subsequent inability to deliver in full the assumed quid pro quo in aid. He wound up on bad terms, not only with the Bank's largest less developed member country, but with other borrowers as well.

The second irony was that at the beginning of his term, he was troubled by

51. See Chapter 12, below.
52. George D. Woods, "The Development Decade in the Balance," *Foreign Affairs*, Vol. 44 (January 1966), p. 214.

an excess of prosperity and was embarrassed that the Bank's reserves were approaching $1 billion. With encouragement from the United States and Germany, he therefore introduced the policy of transferring a portion of the Bank's surplus to IDA. Such transfers in the three-year period 1964–66 amounted to $200 million. By 1966, however, market conditions had become so tight that the Bank, for the first time, was threatened by a shortage of funds. Woods at first recommended that no transfer be made to IDA in fiscal year 1967. When this encountered objections, he shepherded through the board a recommendation to transfer a token $10 million and in the process incurred the double displeasure of the IDA Part I countries, which resented the action, and of the Part II countries, which were disappointed because the amount was insignificant.[53]

McNamara: A Different Type of President

Robert S. McNamara was the first president to come from a nonbanking background. He took office in 1968, at the age of fifty-two. He had been an assistant professor of business administration at Harvard University during the early 1940s before joining the Ford Motor Company, of which he became president in 1960. From 1961 to 1968, he was U.S. secretary of defense. He left with a reputation as the man who tamed the untamable joint chiefs of staff and exercised the firmest leadership ever provided to the sprawling U.S. Department of Defense. His association with the controversial Vietnam war, however, complicated his takeover at the Bank, and he obviously had to make a more self-conscious effort than did his predecessors to fit into the new environment.

Relations between the president of the Bank and the board of directors seem to follow a cyclical pattern, and it did not require great perspicacity on McNamara's part to ascertain that they were at a low point in the cycle when he arrived. An investment in improving them consequently ought to pay off. Although McNamara put the executive directors on a rigorous meeting schedule and has led them through their business at a brisker pace than any of his predecessors, he has been quick to understand the import of their questions and underlying concerns and sensitive to their opinions.

53. See Chapter 12, below. Regarding Woods's desire to initiate the transfer policy, David E. Lilienthal, a personal friend, reports a 1963 conversation with him in which Woods said, "Well, they have built up a surplus—they call it a reserve but it's a surplus that in a year or so will be a pretty dramatic figure of a billion dollars. Can't we relax and do some things with that surplus that are part of *development*? That's in the Bank's title, you know." *The Journals of David E. Lilienthal*, Vol. 5: *The Harvest Years, 1959–1963* (Harper & Row, 1971), p. 480, entry of June 20, 1963.

This is not to say that McNamara's willingness to discuss pending business with the executive directors has brought them peace of mind. Under McNamara, both long-term and short-term borrowing by the Bank have increased sharply, lending activity has been greatly accelerated, loans have been extended to countries and to sectors in which the Bank has not previously been active, and the policy of the Bank on interest rates has been redefined in unbankerlike fashion to permit from time to time a "negative spread" (loans at less than it costs the Bank to borrow in capital markets).[54]

On the staff side, the sharp increase in Bank/IDA activity under McNamara has meant a corresponding increase in the personnel of the projects departments and the Economics Department, further subdivision of area departments as their staffs also grow, and additions all along the line. The larger bureaucratic pyramid inevitably means that the man at the top is farther removed than before from the middle and lower levels. The expansion in nontraditional fields of activity for international financial assistance—agriculture, education, clean water supplies, family planning—has required a further strengthening of relations with other international agencies, a task to which McNamara brings none of the aversion congenital to some of his predecessors.

His most characteristic innovation perhaps has been in the field of forward planning; day-to-day administration is not his forte. The Bank is trying to establish five-year programs for itself, to look ahead at what it should be doing, country by country, and to organize itself for the job. Its work is being systematized and scheduled as never before and designed to serve a broader clientele. Having been reelected for a second five-year term, McNamara is expected to remain in office until at least 1978.

Three Perspectives

The Bank's organizational evolution can be viewed in at least three ways. In one sense it represents the buildup of a highly centralized institution, blessed with strong presidents, but entering an era in which more decentralization from the top downward, as well as from Washington outward, may be a prerequisite for the increased scope and tempo of operations to which it is committing itself.

The Bank's evolution may also be viewed as the development, rather rapidly, of an organization impressively qualified to assist in the financing of an

54. See Chapter 5, below.

important but limited range of development projects, primarily in the fields of electric power and transportation. A running battle has been in progress ever since between those who, in effect, have wanted the Bank to concentrate on doing what it has learned to do well and those who have wanted it to exercise leadership across the whole spectrum of development.

Finally, the organization can be appraised in the perspective of the dream of Franklin D. Roosevelt and certain other architects of the post–World War II system. Their hope was that autonomous agencies created to deal with recognizable "technical" problems in various functional fields—international trade, international finance, monetary policy, world health, and so forth— would acquire competence and authority and thereby build at the technical level ties that would facilitate international cooperation at the political level.

To these perspectives we shall return in Parts 2, 3, and 4 of this book, and particularly in the closing chapter, in which some organizational and institutional changes and adaptations appropriate to the post-1971 years are discussed.

PART TWO

The Bank as Borrower and Lender

CHAPTER FIVE

Financing the Bank

IT WAS POINTED OUT in Chapter 2 that the Bank's capitalization consisted of 2 percent to be paid in gold or dollars, 18 percent in the currencies of the member countries and usable for lending purposes only with the consent of the contributing country, and 80 percent as a guarantee fund. This capital structure had certain obvious merits. It sought to assure that every country— rich and poor—would participate in providing capital (the 2 percent portion); it recognized that countries temporarily impoverished and in balance-of-payments difficulties would be able to contribute usable capital later (the 18 percent); and it embodied the expectation that the mobilization of capital from other sources would be much more important than the use of the Bank's own assets (the 80 percent).

When the Bank opened for business on June 25, 1946, the member governments were advised that the balance of their 2 percent was due in sixty days. By the time of the first annual meeting of the governors of the Bank and the Fund in September of that year, $143 million had been paid in, out of a possible total of $153 million.[1] Members were also advised of an additional call of 3 percent of capital subscriptions, payable in their own currencies and due on or before November 25, 1946, and were notified that the Bank expected the remainder of the 18 percent subscription to be paid in by May 26, 1947. The member governments duly paid in their 18 percent contributions, but only the U.S. share of $571,500,000 could in fact be used for Bank lending. When the Bank anounced its first loan to France, in May 1947, it was committing more than one-third of the loanable funds held by the Bank as of June 1, 1947.

1. China, Czechoslovakia, Denmark, Greece, Norway, Poland, and Yugoslavia had been excused from 0.5 percent out of their 2 percent payment for a period of five years, under Article II, section 8(a) of the Articles of Agreement, which permitted postponement if a country's metropolitan territory had suffered from enemy occupation or hostility.

The financial history of the Bank falls into three fairly distinguishable periods. During the first ten years, apart from Canada's payment of a part of its subscription and a few small payments from other countries, the U.S. subscription was the only fully usable 18 percent payment. During this period also the Bank established its position in the U.S. capital market. Some 85 percent of the Bank bonds were denominated in dollars. Indeed, the Bank in these years could be described, not unfairly, as a "dollar bank." The second period, lasting from 1956 to perhaps 1962 or 1963, saw the release for Bank use of most of the 18 percent subscriptions from European contributors and some others. These were years in which the Bank succeeded increasingly in tapping funds from other markets. And in 1959 its authorized capital was doubled. The third period, which has continued until this writing, is in some ways the reverse of the first. Balance-of-payments difficulties in the United States have limited the Bank's access to its capital market, and a majority of the Bank's funds have been raised elsewhere. This chapter follows the Bank's search for funds from the beginning until the end of fiscal year 1971.

The Bank's loanable funds come from four different sources: capital subscriptions, earnings available for investment, the sale of its own securities, and participations and sales out of portfolio. The sales of Bank securities fall into two classes: sales, principally of long-term bonds, to private investors; and sales, mainly of short-term securities, to governments—usually central banks. Participations take place when a Bank loan is made and investors contract with the Bank for some part of the loan. They are not required to advance cash until loan disbursements are actually made. Portfolio sales are, as the name suggests, sales to investors of parts of loans already made by the Bank. This chapter considers in turn each source of loanable funds and its development over the first quarter century of the Bank's history. First, capital subscriptions are considered, along with net earnings and the equity position of the Bank. Then the activities of the Bank as a borrower are discussed. But before capital subscriptions are considered, a word must be said about why the Bank's guarantee of loans to governments by private investors, which was intended to stimulate foreign portfolio lending, never developed.

It will be recalled from Chapter 2 that the delegates at Bretton Woods thought of the Bank largely as an institution that would bridge the period until private investors, who had been leery of foreign lending after the experience of the 1920s, would resume the practice of buying the securities of foreign governments. The Bank could contribute by adding its guarantee to that of the borrowing government. John Maynard Keynes, in particular, was impressed by the potential usefulness of this function. He advised Harry White "not to offer the absurd proposition of debtor countries being responsible for international investment."[2] But these same debtor countries could, he thought, perform a useful function by participating in the guarantee necessary to attract private investors.

The primary purpose of the Bank guarantee was considered to be to put lenders in direct touch with borrowers or to bring borrowers into the market. In fact the Bank has never guaranteed either a foreign loan of a private investor or a public offering of a foreign government. Initially the reason given for not using the guarantee was that the Bank had still to test the market for its own securities. But after the successful sale of $250 million in Bank securities in July 1947, this reason was less tenable. The guarantee function never got off the ground for a number of other valid reasons:

1. The use of the guarantee would have added little or nothing to the international flow of financial resources since it competed directly with the Bank's own borrowing capacity. The limit to the Bank's guaranteeing capacity, which in the early years was set by the size of the U.S. capital contribution, was also the limit of the Bank's borrowing capacity.

2. The cost to most borrowers would have been higher if they followed the guarantee route rather than borrowing directly from the Bank. Guarantees were not very popular in the U.S. market, and the legal complications involved in such issues were serious.

3. Despite the common feature of a Bank guarantee, there is reason to believe that different borrowing countries would have had to pay substantially different interest rates on the money borrowed. This happens in the U.S. domestic market in the sale of housing bonds, despite the fact that those issued in different jurisdictions all have the same investment quality, since they all carry the same U.S. government guarantee. Nevertheless, the bonds of a well managed city sell at a lower yield than those of one less well managed. If a Dutch government loan guaranteed by the Bank sold at a lower yield than, say, one from Central America, this could reflect on the credit of the Bank.[3]

2. White's papers, quoted by Robert W. Oliver in "The Origin of the International Bank for Reconstruction and Development" (Ph.D. thesis, Princeton University, 1959), p. 425.

3. Oral History Project of Columbia University, interviews recorded in the summer of 1961 on the International Bank for Reconstruction and Development (cited hereinafter as "Oral History"). See interview of Davidson Sommers, p. 71. As the treasurer of the Bank put it (D. Crena de Iongh, "Oral History," p. 17), "The Bank guarantee should be considered to have a value of 100 percent and it would not be a very good thing for the Bank's credit if a bond of some small country with the guarantee of the Bank would be quoted in the market at a lower rate than bonds of a big country also guaranteed by the Bank. This would cast some shadow on the solvency of the Bank, and we all considered it would therefore be much better that . . . all the bonds issued should be bonds of the Bank."

Capital Subscriptions, Earnings, and Equity

The 2 percent subscriptions in gold or dollars have never presented much difficulty. The payments of $143 million from 38 countries in 1946 grew to $238.7 million from 116 countries as of June 30, 1971. The 18 percent subscriptions, however, involved a different and longer story. These subscriptions, according to the Articles of Agreement, "shall be loaned only with the approval in each case of the member whose currency is involved."[4] Furthermore, if such currency is loaned by the Bank and repaid, it cannot be loaned again or converted into another country's currency, except with the approval of the lending member.[5] And beyond this, each member government has the right to specify the terms under which its currency can be loaned. It might be limited to use for purchases in a particular country; and its use might be further limited to purchases of commodities that excluded the country's principal exports. Ecuador, for example, released the whole of its 18 percent to be used in Ecuador, but specified that none of its currency could be used for the procurement of cocoa, coffee, or bananas—the only products that that country exported in quantity. Since cocoa, coffee, and bananas were usually not needed in the construction of Bank projects, this was perhaps not a serious limitation. Some countries agreed to a release of their own currency for Bank lending only if the Bank consented to purchase an equivalent amount with a convertible currency, that is, dollars.

The 18 Percent Issue

Under the Articles of Agreement the Bank may only ask a member government to release its 18 percent subscription; it is entirely within the power of the member government to determine when that subscription will be released for Bank use, in what amounts, and under what conditions. But, as a senior Bank official put it, "the provision of the Articles which applies to every member, permitting the member to give its consent to the release, can be interpreted by implication to express an expectation that the member would give the release as soon as it could. That, at least, is the interpretation that we've given to the Articles within the Bank."[6]

This interpretation, however, was not very uniformly given by the members. The official quoted above noted that, as late as 1961, there were still perhaps a dozen countries that could have been expected, on the basis of

4. Article IV, section 2(a).
5. *Ibid.*, section 2(b).
6. S. R. Cope, "Oral History," p. 51. During the 1950s and early 1960s, Cope was one of the principal officers of the Bank engaged in 18 percent negotiations.

their balance-of-payments situation, to have released their 18 percent subscription but had in fact not done so.[7] It is fair to say, however, that in 1958, after the substantial movement in Western Europe toward convertibility, the problem was largely solved. By 1960, 80 percent of the 18 percent subscription had been released in usable form. But during the twelve years 1946–58 senior Bank officials had devoted a great deal of time and effort to negotiating with member countries for the release and use of their subscriptions.

The difficulties encountered by the Bank were the product not only of the wartime destruction of productive capacity in Western Europe, but of foreign exchange shortages and restrictions and disruptions of customary channels of trade. From 1946 to 1949 the United States not only was practically the sole source of Bank financing, but was almost the sole source of exports to be financed by Bank lending. The four reconstruction loans to Western European countries were used almost entirely for procurement within the United States. By 1950, however, under the impact of Marshall Plan assistance, industrial production in Western Europe was well on the way to recovery. And as a result of foreign exchange devaluation, firms in a number of these countries were in a position to become the lowest bidders in the international competition to sell various types of equipment. But with capital in short supply and balances of payments still in serious deficit, these countries were often unwilling to release their 18 percent subscriptions even for purchases within their own country; still less for procurement in other countries. A number of them refused to allow their exporters to sell in certain areas for payment other than in dollars. An internal Bank memorandum written in 1951 complained,

The Bank is sometimes unable to entertain apparently sound loan proposals because they involve large amounts of non-dollar currencies which are not available. While these currencies could be purchased with dollars, in many cases a borrower's ability to service dollar debt is less than its ability to service other foreign debt. This results in the Bank's lending neither the dollars nor the other currencies involved.

The United States had released all of its 18 percent portion ($571.5 million) by April 1947 for use in any country the Bank chose. By the end of 1949 Belgium had released $2 million (of its 18 percent subscription of $40.5 million), Canada $8 million (of $58.5 million), Denmark $0.1 million (of $12.24 million), and the United Kingdom $1.9 million (of $234 million). The scarcity of nondollar currencies was becoming a serious impediment to the Bank's lending program. A number of countries to which the Bank wanted to lend were considered to be definitely not creditworthy in terms of dollar repayment, though they were considered creditworthy for loans in various European currencies.

7. *Ibid.*

In February 1950, President Black presented a statement of the funds available for Bank lending (in millions of dollars):

I.	2 percent capital subscriptions	167.0
II.	18 percent subscriptions	595.5
III.	Borrowed funds	
	Swiss borrowing 4.0	
	U.S. borrowing 250.0	254.0
IV.	Surplus	20.3
	Total	1,036.8

Of this total, $896.5 million, that is, 85 percent, was from U.S. sources. "Unless," Black wrote, "some greater liberalization of the use of the nondollar 18 percent, or consent to the Bank's borrowing in their domestic markets, is conceded by the governments of the Bank's member states (other than the United States), the Bank will increasingly take on the pattern of a 'dollar bank.'"[8]

He went on to say, "Moreover, the fact that the United States has to all intents and purposes been the only member state of the Bank which has allowed the free use of its 18 percent capital subscription (or has permitted borrowings by the Bank in its domestic market) is one to which public opinion in the United States is becoming increasingly alive. I have met, and have tried to answer, this criticism on many occasions when addressing banking and other financial groups in the United States. But the present situation is difficult to explain away."

In the minds of the Bank's managers the situation was the less excusable in that a number of European countries had found themselves able to extend foreign credits on a bilateral basis while pleading an inability to release their capital subscriptions to the Bank. During this period of currency shortages and exchange restrictions the Bank did not relax its attention to economy and efficiency. But the situation did, on occasion, affect the choice of projects that the Bank was willing to finance. The Bank never told borrowers where they should buy, but it frequently did decide to finance the importation of goods for which the low bidder was likely to be a country whose 18 percent subscription had been released for internal procurement.[9] The Bank always insisted on providing the borrower with the currency needed (in line with the Articles of Agreement) rather than lending dollars for use in acquiring the needed currency. An additional reason for doing this was to avoid black

8. Memorandum to IBRD board of directors, Feb. 14, 1950.

9. Robert Cavanaugh, "Oral History," p. 8. Cavanaugh came to the Bank in 1947 as chief of the Finance Division in the Office of the Treasurer. He became treasurer in 1959 and left the service of the Bank in 1969.

market operations. If a borrower could use dollars to acquire the currency needed in the black market at a better rate than the official one, there would be a great temptation to do so.

Early in 1950 President Black appealed to governments (in the memorandum mentioned above) to release their 18 percent subscriptions. This failed to produce results, however, and as the Bank increased its lending to less developed countries whose normal trade channels were to Western Europe, the situation grew worse. An internal memorandum of February 1951 contained an estimate that of $420 million in Bank commitments (not disbursed) only $5.6 million could be met with inconvertible currencies—sterling $4 million, Swedish kroner $1.1 million, and French francs $0.5 million. At the same time loan negotiations were under way with Pakistan, Iraq, Yugoslavia, Iceland, and Finland, all of whose normal trade relations were with Western Europe. It was estimated that Western European countries could prove to be the low bidders on approximately $90 million of expenditures financed by these loans.

"This," the memorandum said, "together with the operations of the European Payments Union, which permits the use of Western European currencies interchangeably, calls for a review and reformation of the Bank's policy with regard to the use of 18 percent funds."

The United Kingdom and France were at this stage emerging as substantial European Payments Union (E.P.U.) creditors, while Germany and the Netherlands were heavy debtors. It was proposed that the United Kingdom, France, and perhaps Belgium be asked for a specified amount of 18 percent funds with the understanding that these funds might be disbursed in any E.P.U. country. This proposal also came to naught.

The situation looked bleak. An opportunity arose, however, in connection with proposed loans to Yugoslavia to nudge Western European governments on their 18 percent contribution. By 1950 the break between Yugoslavia and the Soviet Union was complete, and Yugoslavia was dotted with projects that were half or three-fourths finished and that had been started with Soviet and Eastern European assistance. The reserves of the Yugoslavian Central Bank were exhausted, and pre-war trade relations with Western European countries had not been reestablished. Tito was as much in need of political as of economic support, and the possibility emerged of securing both through the World Bank. A mission was dispatched by Yugoslavia in 1949 under the leadership of Dragoslav Avramović, an economist who later became a senior official in the Bank.

President Black saw in the situation an opportunity to tie Western European political interests in supporting Tito with their economic interests in resuming trade relations into a powerful argument for the release of 18 percent subscriptions. He announced to the executive directors that he would not consent to lending more than 12 million in dollars. "The position, therefore, is that unless the Western European countries concerned are able to concede the use by the Bank of their 18 percent capital subscriptions (or to allow the Bank to borrow in their domestic markets), it will not be possible for the Bank to make a loan to Yugoslavia at all." The possible adverse effects in the New York market of an exclusively dollar loan to Yugoslavia also affected the Bank's decision.[10]

It became a highly complex task to specify the projects to be financed, to find out where the equipment would come from, and to persuade governments to release their 18 percent to pay for it.[11] Nevertheless, the task was accomplished. Some twenty-five projects, in various stages of completion, were specified; four-fifths of the needed equipment was produced in Western Europe; and a dozen Western European countries released parts of their 18 percent subscriptions to finance the Yugoslav loans.

The practice of making special releases for specific purposes in specific countries became the pattern over the next few years. "It meant that a great deal of work was involved in getting a release because a case had to be made and sometimes argued with the country concerned. . . ."[12] The largest release was from the United Kingdom—£60 million ($168 million), agreed to in February 1953. It was to be used at the rate of £10 million a year and was restricted to borrowers within the Commonwealth. The greater part had to be spent inside the sterling area, though an undefined amount could be spent outside.[13] Convertible releases from France and Germany during this period were conditioned on an agreement that the Bank would buy an equivalent amount of their currency with convertible currencies. All of these releases required consultation with the releasing country on individual loans. This obviously involved a serious administrative burden.

The situation was exacerbated by the fact that authority to lend a local currency did not automatically give the Bank permission to relend the currency once the loan had been repaid. A letter from the treasurer of the Bank to the president in 1951 said, "It would appear that through 1955 we will have received at least $41 million of 18 percent currencies, which, at the present time, we have no authority to relend. If such authority is not received

10. A very small loan ($2.7 million) to Yugoslavia to encourage timber production and export had been made by the Bank in October 1949. See Chapter 6, below.
11. Martin Rosen, "Oral History," p. 67. Rosen was the head of two Bank teams that visited Yugoslavia in 1950. Later he became executive vice president of the International Finance Corporation. He left the Bank Group in 1969.
12. S. R. Cope, "Oral History," p. 46.
13. *Ibid.,* p. 47.

we will theoretically be forced to borrow an equal amount of funds to meet loan commitments."[14] The treasurer calculated that by 1955 the inability to relend would have cost the Bank over $3 million in interest charges.

In an attempt to avoid some of these restrictions the Bank proposed in 1955 to eleven European countries the formation of a pool of $50 million contributed from 18 percent subscriptions that could be used for Bank loans in any country so long as the loan involved expenditure in the area of the European Payments Union. A letter from Black to the governors of the Bank in their countries noted that,

although most of our Western European member governments have given some degree of release, to the whole or a substantial part, of their 18 percents for use by the Bank, restrictions of one kind or another have been attached to their releases to such an extent that, up to now, the Bank has found it possible to allocate only $135.4 million in its lending operations, and of this amount only $68 million has been disbursed. Of this amount of $135.4 million only $2.1 million has been given any degree of multilateral use and been available for disbursement outside the territory of the member country making the loan.

The Bank received a favorable response from all of the countries to which this appeal was addressed, except the United Kingdom. At the Bank-Fund meeting in September 1955, the U.K. governor, Mr. R. A. Butler, commented as follows on the pool proposal:

Our first responsibility is toward the Commonwealth, and at the end of 1952 we undertook to make a special effort to provide additional capital for worthwhile Commonwealth development. . . . I have had indeed to decide that it is not possible for us at present to embark on any new programme of releases from our sterling subscription to the Bank. We have indeed already undertaken to release up to £60 million by 1959 for loans to the Commonwealth, and this is as far as we can go at present.

In the meantime, however, the period of dollar shortages was coming to an end; international monetary reserves were more evenly distributed among countries; and trade channels were substantially reopened. Under these circumstances Western European countries were finding it progressively easier not only to release their 18 percent subscriptions but to give the release a multilateral application. In 1957 it was suggested to a staff committee of the Bank, which had been engaged primarily in allocating inconvertible European currencies to various loans, that all member governments be asked not only to release additional 18 percent funds, but to make these releases in a convertible form.[15] This time the result of the Bank's initiative was encouraging. Additional releases were secured amounting to $200 million and in a transferable form. Improvement in the balance of payments of member

14. Letter of July 8, 1951.
15. S. R. Cope, "Oral History," p. 50.

countries obviously had more to do with this than did the cogency of the Bank's arguments. The situation continued to improve, markedly assisted by a large step toward convertibility in 1958; and by 1960 the back of the problem had been broken. There were still countries able to release 18 percent subscriptions that had not done so, and to this day the Bank continues to maintain pressure for the release of subscriptions. But it had ceased to be an important activity.

In 1959 the Bank's capitalization was doubled. In this process the 18 percent became 9 percent. Since then the capitalization has been further increased as a result of the admission of new members, and total subscribed capital, as of June 30, 1971, was $23,871 million. Of this the 9 percent element amounted to $2,148.39 million. The Bank classifies these subscriptions as usable and nonusable, and the account stood as follows, as of June 30, 1971 (in millions of U.S. dollar equivalents):

On loan	1,683.60	
Usable by June 1, 1974	36.13	1,719.73
Not usable		428.66
		2,148.39

The nonusable currencies include not only subscriptions that have not been released but subscriptions that have been released for domestic procurement only and have not been used for this purpose. All the so-called Part I (high-income) countries of the International Development Association (IDA) have released their 9 percent for conversion into any currency, and a great many Part II (middle- and low-income) countries have also released a part of their subscriptions for this purpose. India, for example, which has at present a 9 percent subscription amounting to $81 million, has released $21.6 million for conversion into any currency and $50.4 million for purchases in India; $9 million has not been released. The 9 percent issue will not be completely solved until all the Bank members have attained that blissful state known as "self-sustaining growth." But it has already ceased to be an issue that seriously affects Bank lending policy. Whether this would continue to be true if the Bank asked for and received a large increase in capital subscriptions, including the 9 percent share, remains to be seen.

Increases in Authorized, Subscribed, and Usable Capital

The initial capital of the Bank authorized in the Articles of Agreement was $10 billion. On September 1, 1959, the authorized capital was increased to $21 billion. Of that increase $10 billion was to permit a doubling of capital subscriptions by existing members, while the additional $1 billion was to provide for the admission of new members and for increases in the subscriptions of existing members. The authorized capital was further increased for the latter purposes by $1 billion on December 31, 1963, and $2 billion on August 25, 1965. It was again increased by $3 billion on December 31, 1970. On June 30, 1971, it stood at $27 billion.

As was noted above, and will be discussed further below, the capitalization was doubled in 1959 for the purpose of increasing the guarantee obligations of members (particularly of the United States) represented by the uncalled portions of their subscriptions to the Bank's capital, rather than obtaining funds from member governments for Bank operations. Accordingly it was agreed that members would not be required to pay in the 2 percent or 18 percent portions of their newly subscribed shares, and the board of governors adopted a resolution that the 2 percent and the 18 percent portions of the new shares would be called only when they were needed to meet obligations of the Bank arising out of its borrowings or guarantees. The 2 percent, therefore, became 1 percent, and the 18 percent became 9 percent of the total subscription. It should be noted, however, that the 1 percent and the 9 percent not required to be paid in still remained subject to call. In order to preserve parity of treatment as among members after the doubling of the subscribed capital, subsequent special increases in subscriptions, as well as subscriptions of new members, involved payment by the countries concerned of the 2 percent and 18 percent on one-half of their subscriptions, with no payments being required on the other half. Again, however, the unpaid portions of this other half remain subject to call.

The doubling of the capitalization in 1959, then, added nothing to the Bank's holding of loanable funds. Additions that were made before 1970 have come entirely from new members and from adjustments in the subscriptions of certain countries to bring their subscriptions into line with their improved position in the world economy. Upward adjustments have been made in the subscriptions of Canada, Germany, and Japan among others. The development over time in the Bank's capital structure is indicated in Table 5-1.

In 1970 the International Monetary Fund (IMF) raised its quotas by nearly $8 billion, and the Bank considered seriously whether it should not expand its capital by a similar amount, this time with increases in its paid-in capital as well as its authorized and subscribed capital. It was noted that because there had been no general increase in paid-in capital since 1946, the paid-in amount had kept pace neither with the subscribed capital nor with the volume of the Bank's business. An internal Bank memorandum pointed out that projections of the Bank's future operations indicated the enormous size

Table 5-1. *Capital Structure of the World Bank, 1950–71*
Millions of U.S. dollars

End of fiscal year	Authorized capital	Subscribed capital	Paid-in capital	Usable capital
1950	10,000	8,348	1,670	750
1955	10,000	9,028	1,803	942
1960	21,000	19,308	2,023	1,626
1965	22,000	21,669	2,166	1,763
1970	24,000	23,159	2,316	1,884
1971	27,000	23,871	2,387	1,935

Source: International Bank for Reconstruction and Development.

of the capital requirements of the developing countries over the next five years and beyond:

Our studies also have brought out the large increases in wealth which have taken place and continue to take place in the rich countries of the world. Our task of helping to link the two—the growing needs and the growing resources—in adequate volume is made more difficult by the constraints which the Bank's inadequate capital structure imposes on our operations.

The IMF's increase in quotas consisted of a "general" increase, applicable to all member countries except the Republic of China, and "selective" increases to be obtained from seventy-five countries, including all Part I countries of IDA except the United Kingdom. The size of the selective increases varied from country to country, depending on its changed circumstances in the world economy. The Bank for a time considered following the Fund's example, but in the end decided to opt only for the selective increases. This has added to the authorized capital $3 billion and, as of June 30, 1971, $700 million to the subscribed capital. On the assumption that all the Part I countries subscribe and pay in 10 percent of subscriptions (1 percent plus 9 percent) and that the Part II countries pay in 1 percent, the usable capital of the Bank will be increased by about $170 million.

The reason why the Bank decided against asking for a general increase was that at the same time it faced a need to ask for a replenishment of IDA funds. It was requesting $800 million a year for IDA from the same member countries that would have to make the major contribution to paid-in capital. This was judged to be too much of a burden. Since the Bank became a Bank Group with the addition of the IFC in 1956 and of IDA in 1960, something should be said about how these additions have affected the Bank's access to capital. The IFC can be quickly disposed of. Although it draws its capital contributions from those Bank members who want to join, the amount of these contributions is too small to be of any significance. The Bank has authorized the IFC to borrow from it up to four times the IFC's unimpaired subscribed capital and surplus. But to the extent that this authority is made use of, it must be regarded as a Bank investment in a particular type of project.

The relation of the Bank to IDA, however, is a different question. On the one hand, IDA has substantially expanded the creditworthiness of certain countries for Bank loans. Prior to the establishment of IDA a number of poor countries to which the Bank had loaned extensively were considered to have about reached the limits of their ability to absorb and service foreign loans on Bank terms. But with money available for a fifty-year term, at no interest and with a service charge of only 0.75 percent, the ability to service debt could substantially increase. This made it possible to offer various "blends" of loan terms, a device that is discussed in Chapter 7. On the other hand, the fact that the countries contributing to IDA are also the principal sources of Bank funds, either as capital subscribers or as markets for the sale of Bank securities, may have (and on occasion has had) some influence on the availability of funds for Bank lending. Since both Bank and IDA loans are generally untied, a country in balance-of-payments difficulties that has made a substantial contribution to IDA may be less willing to make an additional contribution to capital or to open its capital market for the sale of Bank securities. Furthermore, the transfer to IDA of Bank profits, a practice that developed in the 1960s, affects the size of the Bank's equity and at some future time might conceivably affect its position in capital markets. Thus IDA, while extending the possible scope of Bank lending, may at some stage exert an adverse influence on the Bank's sources of loanable funds.

The 80 Percent Guarantee Fund

As was noted in Chapter 1, the Bretton Woods delegates thought that the size of the proposed guarantee fund might permit the Bank to borrow two to three times its total. In fact, the limits to Bank borrowing, at least until well into the 1960s, were set by the amount of the U.S. share of this fund. By the fall of 1958 the spread between the volume of outstanding debt and the amount of the U.S. guarantee had narrowed to about $700 million, and the U.S. rating services had begun to sound an alarm. Several institutions holding World Bank bonds were becoming nervous, and a representative of the Bank was told by the president of Moody's Investors Service that if the spread approached zero, Moody's would have seriously to reconsider the rating of IBRD issues.[16] This development coincided with a sharp increase in

---

16. Memorandum by William L. Bennett, "The World Bank and the Investment Market" (1969; processed).

the level of lending in 1957–58 from between $300 million and $400 million a year to between $700 million and $800 million. As a result of this new situation the board of governors, at its annual meeting in October 1958, asked the executive directors promptly to "consider the question of enlarging the resources of the Bank through an increase in its authorized capital."[17]

The executive directors addressed themselves to the problem and in December 1958 reported the following recommendations to the board of governors:[18]

(a) There is a need for an increase in the authorized capital of the Bank;

(b) the size of the increase should be 100% of the presently authorized capital;

(c) the increase in capital should become effective when a minimum of $7,000,000,000 is subscribed; and

(d) cash payment of such subscriptions should not be required as an addition to the Bank's lendable funds.

In coming to these conclusions the executive directors expressed the following opinions:

The problem is of staggering dimensions. . . . In real terms the ability of the underdeveloped countries of the world to absorb capital has improved as the development process has gathered momentum.

The United States is the principal market for the Bank's obligations. While the Bank's dollar bonds offered in that market, particularly those of short term, are being purchased in increasing measure by investors outside the United States, United States institutional investors are the main source of the Bank's long-term funds. . . .

The Executive Directors consider it unfortunate that such a degree of reliance should appear to be placed upon the guarantee of one member of the Bank to the apparent exclusion of the guarantees of other members. But the fact remains that, today, this attitude does exist and great weight must be attached to it.[19]

The board of governors accepted these recommendations at its fourteenth annual meeting in 1959. As a result of the doubling of subscriptions, the size of the U.S. guarantee increased from $2,540 million to $5,080 million. If the 10 percent of the U.S. subscription that was left uncalled by the governors' resolution is added, the U.S. guarantee was increased to $5,715 million. The concern of investors and the rating services was thereby alleviated, and Bank securities continued to enjoy a prime credit standing. By the end of fiscal year 1971 the funded debt of the IBRD was nearer the amount of the

17. IBRD, *Thirteenth Annual Meeting of the Board of Governors, Summary Proceedings,* Resolution No. 125, October 1958.

18. IBRD, "Proposal for an Increase in the Authorized Capital of the Bank," Report of the Executive Directors to the Board of Governors, Dec. 22, 1958.

19. See *Ibid.,* pp. 3–4.

U.S. guarantee than in 1959.[20] In the meantime, however, a number of currencies of member countries have become stronger than the U.S. dollar. It is thus hard to believe that the size of the U.S. guarantee any longer has the same significance in capital markets that it had during the early years of the Bank's history. As is noted elsewhere, the Bank has plans for a large increase in borrowing in the 1970s. It seems altogether probable that other reputable guarantees added to that of the United States will prove more than enough to satisfy investors in the capital markets of the world.

The Bank's Reserves

It has been explained above that the large volume of authorized and subscribed capital yields a relatively small amount of usable funds, mainly because of the nature of the Bank's capital structure. However, earnings from the reserve funds add to the total volume. The sum of usable capital plus reserves may be called the Bank's equity capital. The sum stood at $3,504 million as of June 30, 1971.

The retained earnings of the Bank are held in two reserve funds, only one of which is available for lending. The special reserve, established in accordance with Article IV, section 6, of the Articles of Agreement has been expanded by a commission of 1 percent charged on the outstanding portion of loans. According to Article IV, section 4(a), this charge, to be made for ten years after the beginning of operations, might then be either decreased or increased, depending on how adequate the reserve was considered to be. When the ten-year period was nearing its end, the committee on financial policy of the executive directors felt that

there is no precedent which can usefully be relied upon in determining the appropriate size of Bank reserves. Both the risks assumed by the Bank, on the one hand, and the safeguards inherent in its capital structure on the other are different in character from those of other, more conventional financial institutions. Many more years of experience will be necessary before it can be determined whether our operations may result in a proportionately greater or smaller loss than the previous losses in this field. Consequently there is obvious room for a difference of opinion as to what the amount of reserves should be and therefore as to the most appropriate rate of commission.[21]

Recognizing that there was room for a difference of opinion, the executive directors nevertheless decided on August 9, 1955, by a divided vote, to con-

20. On June 30, 1971, the funded debt of the Bank stood at $5,441.2 million, as against a U.S. guarantee of $5,715 million.
21. Secretary's Report, R-897, July 7, 1955.

tinue the 1 percent commission charge.[22] The decision to drop the charge was made in fiscal 1964, for reasons considered below.

The rather perfunctory provision in the Articles of Agreement for the payment of dividends to member governments[23] failed to foresee that the Bank would be a profitable institution and that the proper use of its earnings would present some interesting questions. In fact the Bank already had net earnings of more than $3 million at the end of fiscal year 1948 and over $10 million in fiscal 1949 after allocation to the special reserve; and its net earnings have increased steadily since then. The board of governors in 1948 and 1949 approved the recommendations of the executive directors that these earnings be retained in a surplus account. The directors expressed the view that at this stage in the Bank's development, net income should not be distributed as dividends and that "the special reserve is not an adequate reserve against losses in the light of the nature of the Bank's business."[24]

On March 14, 1950, Poland withdrew from membership in the Bank, and the Bank paid Poland its share of net earnings from surplus in addition to returning the 2 percent contribution. The executive directors decided this should not happen again. By action of the executive directors and the board of governors a supplemental reserve was created, to which the net income in fiscal 1950 amounting to $13,641,094 was transferred, and to which all future net income would be transferred unless and until otherwise decided. Since then this reserve has grown rapidly. The supplemental reserve at the end of the fiscal years specified (in millions of U.S. dollars) amounted to:

1950	27
1955	122
1960	342
1965	743
1970	1,150
1971	1,254

In fiscal year 1964, early in the administration of President Woods, the income derived from loan commissions amounted to $33 million, and the net income of the Bank to $97 million. At that time the special reserve stood at $288 million and the supplemental reserve at $605 million, making total reserves of $893 million. There was some fear on the part of the Bank manage-

22. The executive directors representing Australia, Indonesia, and Pakistan dissented from this decision. The director from Japan stated that, while he supported the decision, he wanted to record that Burma and Ceylon, which he also represented, favored a reduction of the commission.

23. Article V, section 14(a) and (b).

24. IBRD, *Report of the Executive Directors to the Board of Governors,* July 27, 1950.

ment that reserves approaching $1 billion might be subject to political attack. Indeed it had already been suggested in the U.S. Congress that the Bank might consider assuming certain deficits of the United Nations organizations. Consequently two important steps were taken. First, the executive directors decided that it was no longer necessary to allocate 1 percent of gross loan charges to the special reserve. "The Bank will now consider all income from loan charges as part of its regular income; and net income will thereby be increased by the equivalent of what otherwise would have automatically gone into the Special Reserve."[25]

Second, it was decided that only $47 million of the net income of $97 million in fiscal 1964 should be transferred to the supplemental reserve and that the remaining $50 million be made available as a grant to IDA.[26] An important policy question was involved in this decision. While excessive reserves might open the Bank to criticism, the Bank could be damaged even more by a suspicion that the disposition of the Bank's net income (and possibly even of its accrued reserves) would be dictated by the needs of IDA rather than by the need to preserve the Bank in a sound position. Accordingly, when the executive directors recommended to the Bank's board of governors the transfer of $50 million, they concurrently recommended the following statement of policy:

Any transfers to the Association will be made only out of net income which (i) accrued during the fiscal year in respect of which the transfer is made and (ii) is not needed for allocation to reserves or otherwise required to be retained in the Bank's business and, accordingly, could prudently be distributed as dividends.[27]

The board of governors accepted both the recommendation for transfers to IDA and the conditions to be attached to such transfers at its annual meet-

25. IBRD/IDA, *Annual Report, 1963–64,* p. 15.

26. This decision involved a question of legal interpretation. Article V, section 14, of the Bank's charter provides that the board of governors shall determine annually "what part of the Bank's net income, after making provision for reserves, shall be allocated to surplus and what part, if any, shall be distributed." Paragraph (b) of the same section indicates that by distribution is meant the payment of a dividend. The question therefore was whether section 14 permitted the board of governors to transfer the Bank's net income, after making provision for reserves, to IDA, rather than allocating it to surplus or paying it out by way of a dividend. This matter was settled by a formal interpretation of the articles by the executive directors under Article IX by a decision rendered on July 30, 1964, to the effect that net income (after making provision for reserves) which is available for distribution may be transferred to IDA by way of a grant if the executive directors and the governors are of the opinion that such a grant would best serve the purposes of the Bank and the interests of its members.

27. IBRD/IDA, *Annual Report, 1963–64,* p. 16. This statement of policy is quoted in every prospectus the Bank issues.

ing in September 1964. Since then, transfers of net income to IDA have been made in every year, reaching a level of $100 million in fiscal 1969 and $110 million in fiscal 1971. The size of the Bank's net income has also led to grants for other purposes. The Economic Development Institute (EDI), established in 1955, was already supported largely by the Bank. But beginning in the 1960s, grants charged to the administrative budget were also made for feasibility studies, for the support of research in education, and for other purposes.

As was noted above, usable capital plus the accumulation in reserves may be called the "equity capital" of the Bank. Is the Bank's equity sufficient to maintain its credit standing in the event of possible losses? This is difficult to say, but there are two ratios that throw some light on the potential credit standing of the Bank, apart from the guarantee fund represented by its callable capital. These are the equity–debt ratio and the ratio of net income to interest on funded debt—the interest coverage ratio. Table 5-2 shows total Bank equity and funded debt, 1950–71, and the equity–debt ratio in that period.

Table 5-3, for the same years, shows changes in the interest coverage ratio.

Of course, compared with those of most commercial or savings banks, these ratios, particularly the ratios of equity to debt, indicate extreme conservatism and safety. But the loans made by the World Bank, particularly in the second half of its first quarter century, bear no very close resemblance to the loans made by any kind of private bank. As late as fiscal year 1957, $204 million out of total Bank loans in that year of $388 million went to developed countries. But by fiscal 1968, if one excepts loans to Greece, Spain, and Yugoslavia, all the loans made by the World Bank went to less developed countries. Indeed, applying the test of market-eligibility, discussed in Chap-

Table 5-2. *World Bank Equity, Funded Debt, and Equity–Debt Ratio, 1950–71*
Dollar amounts in millions

End of fiscal year	Equity	Funded debt	Equity–debt ratio
1950	$ 778	$ 261	2.98
1955	1,126	852	1.32
1960	2,132	2,124	1.00
1965	2,719	2,742	0.99
1970	3,361	4,612	0.73
1971	3,504	5,441	0.64

Source: International Bank for Reconstruction and Development.

Table 5-3. *World Bank Net Income, Interest on Funded Debt, and Interest Coverage Ratio, 1950–71*
Dollar amounts in millions

End of fiscal year	Net income before interest	Interest payment on funded debt	Interest coverage ratio
1950	$ 20	$ 7	2.86
1955	51	26	1.96
1960	135	76	1.78
1965	242	106	2.28
1970	455	234	1.88
1971	517	305	1.70

Source: International Bank for Reconstruction and Development.

ter 7, the Bank is precluded from lending to countries that can borrow on reasonable terms in the private capital markets of the world. Most developed countries are now in that position. Consequently, a set of ratios that might suggest a high degree of conservatism for another type of financial institution does not necessarily bear that interpretation when applied to the World Bank.

Of course in the eyes of investors, the security behind the Bank's debt rests largely on the callable capital contributed by countries capable of meeting this obligation. This security has greatly increased as member countries other than the United States have gained in economic strength. Table 5-4 traces the growth of the Bank's funded debt, the callable capital of Part I (that is, developed) countries, and the ratio of this callable capital to funded debt.

The size of the guarantee fund in relation even to a projected rapid increase in funded debt makes it highly unlikely, if not impossible, that the purchaser of a Bank security will suffer loss. But the IBRD would be extremely loath

Table 5-4. *World Bank Funded Debt, Callable Capital of Part I Countries, and Ratio of Callable Capital to Funded Debt, 1950–71*
Dollar amounts in millions

End of fiscal year	Funded debt	Callable capital of Part I countries	Ratio of callable capital to funded debt
1950	$ 261	$ 5,217	19.99
1955	852	5,761	6.76
1960	2,124	13,455	6.49
1965	2,742	14,071	5.13
1970	4,612	14,613	3.51
1971	5,441	15,090	2.77

Source: International Bank for Reconstruction and Development.

to see this guarantee invoked, as would potential investors. The Bank, it is true, wants to make loans that promote development, but it is sufficiently like other banks to want to see these loans repaid.[28] While a default of $100 million or so would be taken in stride, really massive defaults or heavy losses to the Bank from debt renegotiation could seriously damage the credit of the institution in capital markets and increase the interest it would have to pay on borrowing regardless of the size of the guarantee fund.

There is, furthermore, the effect on the average cost of money to the Bank and, consequently on its profits, of the declining ratio of equity to outstanding debt. Debt cannot continue to increase rapidly while the Bank's equity increases slowly, without eventual adverse consequences on the Bank's earnings and credit standing. Much depends on how successful the Bank Group is, in conjunction with other aid suppliers and borrowing member countries themselves, in promoting growth in the less developed world. We venture the opinion, however, that, if the Bank is to continue to finance its loans principally by borrowing, it must, in the light of projected increases in the scale of borrowing, expand its equity in the not too distant future by a sizable increase in paid-in capital. Needless to say, such an increase, which would mean the acquisition of free money, would add substantially to the volume of Bank earnings.

The Bank as a Borrower

As we have repeatedly emphasized and, indeed, as its capital structure dictated, the chief source of the Bank's ability to lend is its ability to borrow. The Bank has engaged in long-term borrowing from capital markets and short-term borrowing from central banks and government agencies; it has induced certain investors to participate in its lending operations; and it has sold parts of its loan portfolio to others. We attempt in this section to cover systematically these various sources of funds, dealing first with the Bank in the U.S. capital market.

28. The Bank's attitude has been well expressed by one of its officials (see John de Wilde, "Oral History," p. 25):
The idea of the Bank has always been that while the loans made by our institution were in essence backed by the guarantees of the various member countries in terms of that portion of their capital subscriptions which was subject to call but had not in fact been called up, nevertheless a banking institution of this sort should never really have to invoke this guarantee. It should operate on the basis of its own credit standing. In other words it wanted to make loans under conditions which insured the repayment of these loans, so that it would never really have to call upon the member governments to cover any losses.

The Bank in the U.S. Capital Market[29]

It was clear from the start that whatever lending policy the Bank might want to pursue would be strictly conditioned by the necessity of finding U.S. investors who were willing to buy its securities or to accept its guarantee. As *The Economist* of London observed, a year after the founding of the Bank, "It should always have been evident that the main problem of the Bank would be to find not borrowers, but lenders prepared to accept reasonable terms."[30] The IBRD might later aspire to be a development institution, but first it had to become a bank, at least in the sense of an investment institution that the financial community would respect. And during its first years, this meant the U.S. financial community.

If the Bank had pursued the route of investment guarantees, it might have postponed for a while an approach to the market; but, for reasons explained above, the decision was against this course of action. If usable 18 percent contributions had been available from countries other than the United States, the Bank's position would have been stronger. But the institution had hardly opened its doors when requests for large loans came in from various European countries, and these were followed in the autumn of 1946 by a request from Chile for $40 million. Consequently the directors and the management turned their attention very soon to the problem of selling Bank securities.

Two kinds of obstacles confronted this venture. The first was the very low esteem in which foreign portfolio investment was held in the U.S. investing community as a result of the debacle of the 1920s. The second was the fact that the IBRD was a peculiar institution, in fact *sui generis*, whose securities did not fit into any of the categories that would under state laws make them automatically eligible for purchase by institutional investors. Furthermore, there continued to exist in the minds of the U.S. banking community, as an aftermath of the Bretton Woods debate, a suspicion that the Bank would turn out to be a political institution run in the interests of governments rather than on the basis of sound investment principles.

During the 1920s U.S. investors had purchased more than $11 billion in foreign government securities. At the end of World War II, well over a third of this investment was still in default. Of course U.S. investors were not the only ones who had engaged in this spree. But the mania for foreign portfolio

---

29. The authors wish to acknowledge assistance in preparing this section from memoranda written by two Bank officials: William L. Bennett, "The World Bank and the Investment Market" (1969; processed), and Harold Graves, "Notes Based on Interviews with R. W. Cavanaugh" (1968; processed).

30. "Bretton Woods in Practice," *The Economist*, Vol. 152 (March 8, 1947), p. 339.

investment took deeper hold in the United States than elsewhere, and U.S. investing institutions were less experienced than their foreign counterparts. The story of the foreign investment splurge of the 1920s has been told too frequently to bear repeating. It has been well summed up by Sir James Arthur Salter.[31] Until 1920, he points out, there was no mechanism for interesting the U.S. investor in foreign bonds. But during the 1920s a system was developed, based on thousands of local agents working on commission for a small number of large issuing houses in New York and Chicago. The development of this system, Sir Arthur remarks wryly, "was a remarkable achievement in organization."

It was at the other end of the operation, that of the examination of the character and purposes of the loan, the capacity of the borrower and the likelihood of the money being used productively, that the system was defective. There was too much competition and too little caution in negotiating the loans. The more prudent bankers were embarrassed by the competing offers of less responsible issuing houses, who were content to sell the bonds, take their substantial commissions, and leave the consequences to be borne by the investors.[32]

This experience was, of course, much in the minds of the Bretton Woods delegates and lay behind the provisions in the Articles of Agreement that were designed to assure that foreign loans would be made to finance only carefully selected productive projects with the security of the Bank's capital subscriptions behind each loan. But to most U.S. investors the Bank was, at the outset, just another device for channeling hard-earned U.S. savings into the pockets of foreigners of doubtful probity. "Now that international lending is in the air," said the *New York Herald Tribune*, referring to the Savannah conference, "with grossly exaggerated promises being made about the beneficial effects of a vast outpouring of American funds in intergovernmental loans, it seems timely to take a look at the record. . . . The record is far from brilliant."[33] It would require a great effort on the part of government

31. *Foreign Investment*, Essays in International Finance, No. 12 (International Finance Section, Princeton University, February 1951).

32. *Ibid.*, p. 15. Cleona Lewis, in *America's Stake in International Investment* (Brookings Institution, 1938, p. 377), gives some interesting examples of competition among U.S. and European investment houses. "At one time, according to testimony before the Senate Committee on Finance investigating the sale of foreign securities in the United States, there were 29 representatives of American financial houses in Colombia alone trying to negotiate loans for the national government, for the departments, and for other possible borrowers. Some 36 houses, most of them American, competed for a city of Budapest loan and 14 for a loan to the city of Belgrade. A Bavarian hamlet, discovered by American agents to be in need of about $125,000, was urged and finally persuaded to borrow 3 million dollars in the American market." Cited by Oliver, in "The Origin of the International Bank for Reconstruction and Development," p. 124.

33. George Wanders, "The Week in Finance," *New York Herald Tribune,* March 18, 1946.

and bank officials to correct these impressions and to establish in the minds of the investing public some understanding of the conditions under which the Bank proposed to borrow and to lend.

As a matter of fact, attention was directed to this problem very early in the Bank's history. Indeed, there had been some examination of the possible eligibility of Bank securities for U.S. investment before the Bretton Woods conference. Immediately after the Articles of Agreement became effective, early in 1946, the U.S. National Advisory Council on International Monetary and Financial Problems (NAC), an interdepartmental committee of the federal government, established working groups to look into the question of eligibility. "Staff members of the NAC agencies and of the Securities and Exchange Commission began a series of exploratory meetings with selected representatives of commercial banks (January 29, 1946), investment bankers (January 29, 1946), and insurance companies (January 28, 1946, February 5, 1946)."[34]

At this stage there appeared to be a substantial interest in forthcoming Bank securities. The Investment Bankers Association of America established in February 1946 a foreign investment committee, whose primary task was to examine the quality of prospective IBRD bonds.[35] The legal adviser on foreign investments of the U.S. Securities and Exchange Commission asked, in an article in the *Commercial and Financial Chronicle*, "Who may be expected to buy the direct or guaranteed bonds of the International Bank?" and found the answer not at all disturbing. Commercial banks that were members of the Federal Reserve System were permitted to purchase bonds of any one issue up to 10 percent of their capital and surplus, and this presumably signified a potential market of $600 million. Some 80 percent of trust funds were free of the restrictions of the "eligible list." Much the same situation existed for charitable and educational institutions. He concluded that "there should, therefore, be a healthy appetite for the new Bank's securities."[36]

On the other hand, the most important institutional investors were likely to be insurance companies and savings banks, for which state laws usually specified an eligibility list. It had been hoped that the activities of the NAC and the SEC in the investment community would have led to requests for changes in state legislation and administrative rulings favorable to investment in IBRD securities. Most state authorities, however, decided to defer action

34. Henry J. Bitterman, "Early Bank Bond Issues" (Nov. 29, 1966; processed), p. 4. The following few pages draw heavily on this memorandum.
35. *Ibid.*, p. 7.
36. Walter C. Louchheim, Jr., "The Marketing of World Bank Bonds," *Commercial and Financial Chronicle* (March 28, 1946).

until the Bank was in operation. As soon as he was appointed the U.S. director, Emilio G. Collado took the lead in the campaign for state legislation; and the New York law of March 1946, authorizing savings banks in that state to invest in Bank securities, was in part the result of his efforts.[37] This was important since many states follow the New York example, but the results were not forthcoming until the following year.

This then was the situation when the Bank opened its doors in June 1946, under the presidency of Eugene Meyer. It was expected in the financial community that the IBRD would soon proceed to a security issue, and although several sour notes had been struck in financial commentaries on the Bank, there appeared to be substantial interest in investing circles. But as months passed without any action and as evidence accumulated of sharp differences of opinion within the Bank, this interest declined. The executive directors, under the leadership of the U.S. director, favored an early issue and a large one. President Meyer was more cautious.

The Dutch director, J. W. Beyen, addressing the annual convention of the New York State Savings Banks Association in Quebec in October, explained the operations of the Bank and announced that it was preparing to borrow $1.5 billion to $2 billion during 1947. This statement was promptly repudiated by President Meyer. Headlines in the financial press following this episode included "Investment Groups Reported Bewildered by the Lack of Information," and "World Bank Seen off to Bad Start."[38] Despite this imbroglio, the U.S. director and the management of the Bank continued attempts to woo the investment community. Collado spoke to the Investment Bankers Association on December 3, 1946, and summarized the existing situation with respect to the eligibility of Bank bonds.[39] Meyer's address on December 13, at the annual meeting of the Life Insurance Association of America, emphasized the fact that the Bank now had five formal requests for loans, all of which were under serious consideration.[40]

But late in November, as was noted in Chapter 3, the Wisconsin State Banking Commission had voted unanimously to refuse to permit the purchase of Bank securities by any state banks, savings banks, or trust companies in Wisconsin.[41] On December 4, President Meyer announced his impending resignation from the Bank. Vice President Harold Smith died unexpectedly in January of the following year. In the ensuing interregnum

37. Bitterman, "Early Bank Bond Issues," p. 6.
38. *New York Herald Tribune,* Oct. 27 and 28, 1946.
39. Published as a pamphlet by the IBRD.
40. Published as a pamphlet by the IBRD.
41. *New York Herald Tribune,* Nov. 28, 1946.

the prestige of the Bank fell to an all-time low. Some of the savings banks in New York began agitating to have the securities the Bank was to issue removed from the list of those the mutual savings banks of New York might purchase.[42] When Eugene Black was asked, "What was the condition of the Bank's credit when you arrived in March 1947?," his reply was, "It didn't have any."[43]

The appointment of John McCloy as president, Robert Garner as vice president, and Eugene Black as U.S. executive director was accepted by the U.S. financial community as an indication that the Bank would now be in safe banking hands. It was interpreted by British observers as a vindication of the U.K. position at Savannah. "Twelve Executive Directors working 'in continuous session' . . . created almost insuperable administrative problems," observed *The Economist*.[44] Both inferences were substantially correct. The Bank was now in the hands of management that enjoyed the confidence of Wall Street, and, as we saw in Chapter 3, management no longer had to share its operational authority with the executive directors.

There was still much to be done before the Bank could market its first security issues. Certain members of the investment community professed to be uncertain whether the U.S. 80 percent subscription could be drawn on regardless of the action of other capital subscribers. On April 2, 1947, the executive directors in a series of interpretive decisions attempted to cover all contingencies.[45] The United States or any other member was indeed liable, regardless of the action of other governments. The consent of the National Advisory Council to an issue of Bank securities had to be obtained, but this was granted as a matter of course. Since in 1947 IBRD bonds were not in the category of exempt securities, special permission was required of the U.S. Securities and Exchange Commission. A general exemption would require legislation, and although this was considered, it was rejected in favor of a special exemption for the two issues contemplated in July. This was forthcoming by a decision of the SEC on June 18, 1947.

It was important that the member banks of the Federal Reserve System be encouraged to purchase IBRD securities. The comptroller of the currency was persuaded to issue a statement on May 29, 1947, "that national banks may purchase the debentures of the International Bank for Reconstruction and Development up to the full legal limit of ten per cent of their capital and

42. "World Bank Seen Facing New Blow," *New York Times,* Feb. 2, 1947.

43. Eugene Black, "Oral History," p. 7.

44. "Bretton Woods in Practice," *The Economist,* Vol. 152 (March 8, 1947).

45. These decisions were published in IBRD, *Second Annual Report, 1946–1947,* p. 39.

surplus."[46] Not much could be done in the time available to change state legislation that set limits on investments open to insurance companies, savings banks, and trust funds. In many cases, however, limits depended on administrative rulings by state officials. In other cases the legal department of the Bank made its own interpretation of state legislation. When the "Memorandum with Regard to the Legality of the Bonds for Investment by Commercial Banks, Savings Banks, Insurance Companies and Trustees in Certain Jurisdictions" was prepared in connection with the first two bond issues in July, a considerable number of investing institutions were found to be qualified to invest in Bank securities.[47]

By far the most difficult and time-consuming task, however, was to inform the investment community of the nature of the International Bank and its securities. After the decision had been made in early April 1947 to issue securities in July, McCloy, Garner, and Black were almost continually on the road, speaking to banking and insurance conventions and to almost any group of prospective buyers who were willing to listen. Shortly after the new team had taken office, E. Fleetwood Dunstan, vice president in charge of investment portfolio for the Bankers Trust Company, was appointed marketing director. In April he was put in charge of a New York office located in the Federal Reserve Bank in New York. For the purpose of selling the first bond issue his small staff was supplemented by a sizable group of volunteers from a number of leading investment banking and brokerage houses.[48] This combination of efforts succeeded in a remarkably short time in changing the attitudes of the investment community from one of near-apathy to something approaching enthusiasm.

In considering ways of distributing its securities, the Bank had several options open to it. Ideally it would have preferred to sell its bonds through competitive bidding. Under this method the Bank would have taken no risk if the issue were not fully sold, and presumably would have secured the best possible price. However, since the Bank's securities were as yet unknown and unseasoned, it was feared that competition would be less than active. As a

46. U.S. Treasury Department, Press release, cited in Bitterman, "Early Bank Bond Issues," p. 12.

47. The memorandum gives information for each state and the District of Columbia. It is prepared for every IBRD security issue in the United States, and an examination of the dossiers of subsequent issues makes clear the Bank's progress in expanding the list of qualified investors.

48. Bennett, "The World Bank and the Investment Market." "This group worked for about a month to six weeks on a voluntary basis; they occupied an enormous room on one of the Fed's upper floors. They sat at a long table and spent most of their time on the telephone urging the purchase of World Bank bonds, the first issues of which were scheduled for July 15, 1947."

second choice the Bank would have preferred a negotiated underwriting, which again would have shifted the risk. But under these circumstances, it was clear that investment firms would be willing to underwrite a Bank issue only at a cost higher than the Bank was willing to pay.

Two other possible methods of marketing were left: to make an offering through a sponsoring group (which would lend its name to the issue and administer the sale, but undertake no risk); or sell through an agency arrangement, in which the offering would be made through a large number of dealers, each acting as an agent for the Bank. On reflection, it did not seem advisable and perhaps not possible at this early stage in the life of the Bank to sell under a sponsorship arrangement. In addition, it seemed desirable to enlist the selling power of the largest possible number of securities dealers by inviting them to take a direct part in the offering and thereby to spread the sale of Bank bonds as widely as possible. The decision thus was made to sell through an agency arrangement.

This was a gigantic undertaking. The Bank got in touch with some 2,650 security dealers, and more than 1,700 participated in the sale of the Bank's two issues of July 15, 1947. These were $100 million in 2.25 percent, ten-year bonds, and $150 million in 3 percent, twenty-five-year bonds. Both were offered to agents at 100 on July 11. Both issues were heavily oversubscribed. The long-term bonds quickly were quoted at 103, and the ten-year issues at 101.5. The financial press commented in admiring terms, "The premiums paid last week ranged roughly from 1 to 3 points, which indicated that the Bank officials had gauged their offering terms with shrewd precision. The judgment and high efficiency displayed in this transaction have gained immense prestige for the Bank."[49]

Although the Bank's first security issues experienced various ups and downs in the market during the ensuing months, in May 1948 one of the leading financial writers felt able to say, "Bonds of the International Bank for Reconstruction and Development have come of age. Last week, after 10 months of seasoning in the most uncertain and convulsive bond market in two decades, the Bank's obligation could be said to have passed two major tests—that of comparative market performance and that of acceptability for legal investment in the Nation's major institutional investment centers."[50]

Both the executive directors and the Bank's staff had thought the first issues were too small. Many felt that the Bank should be borrowing and lending a billion dollars a year. Even the U.S. director, Eugene Black, in testimony

49. George Wanders, "The Week in Finance," *New York Herald Tribune,* July 21, 1947.
50. Paul Heffernan, *New York Times,* May 24, 1948.

before a congressional committee a year later, said that the Bank might soon attain a lending rate of $500 million a year.[51] In fact, after the four loans to European governments, the Bank's business, for reasons explained elsewhere, developed slowly.

Access to the U.S. bond market, and the interest rates a borrower might have to pay, were strongly influenced by the judgment of the various rating services. The Federal Reserve System's examiners require that a bond be rated at a minimum of *A* if it is to be held suitable for bank investment. Many state banking and insurance companies require a minimum rating of *BAA* or *A* for a bond to be eligible for institutional and trust investment in the juris-dictions. In some instances they must have this rating from at least two of the three services.

The IBRD has enjoyed the favor of the rating services from its first issues, and its position has steadily improved. The 1947 issues were rated *AA* by Fitch Investors Service and *A* by Standard and Poor's Corporation. Moody's Investors Service, the bellwether of the group, had never before rated a finan-cial institution, but in 1950 it made an exception for the IBRD, and the Bank's third issue enjoyed an *A* rating from Moody's, an *A*1 rating from Standard and Poors, and an *AA* rating from Fitch. Moody's rating was soon improved to *AA*, but it took the Bank nearly ten more years to acquire *AAA* status. Since the mid-1950s Bank securities have been given a triple *A* rating by all three services.

The Bank turned to the U.S. market again in 1950 with an issue of $100 million in 2 percent serial bonds with maturities varying from three to twelve years. This time it experimented with competitive bidding without notable success. In 1951 two issues of $50 million and $100 million were sold under the sponsorship of investment houses. The sponsorship method, however, did not satisfy the Bank's management since it did not give the sponsors a direct stake in the success of the particular issue at hand or of the bonds of the Bank in general. The management therefore decided to turn permanently to the method of underwriting on the basis of a negotiated price and chose two firms as continuing managers of the underwriting syndicate. One of these firms, Morgan Stanley and Company, was the most prestigious investment banking house in the country; and the other, the First Boston Corporation, was an aggressive, rapidly growing organization, which subsequently became the largest investment bank in the world.[52]

---

51. *International Bank for Reconstruction and Development Securities,* Hearings before the House Committee on Interstate and Foreign Commerce, 80 Cong. 2 sess. (1948), p. 67.

52. As was noted in Chapter 3, George D. Woods, chairman of the board of the First Boston Corporation, in 1963 became president of the World Bank.

From this time on, the IBRD was in the U.S. market nearly every year with one or more issues, and Bank securities became great favorites with the investment community. The yield on the first issue of U.S. dollar bonds was about 0.75 percent higher than on U.S. government bonds of comparable maturity. By 1952 this spread had narrowed to about 0.25 percent. Since then IBRD bonds have carried about the same yield as triple *A*–rated public utilities.

The development of a market for Bank securities in other than dollar denominations is discussed later in this chapter. Here it should be noted, however, that interest in IBRD dollar securities was evinced very early by individuals and institutional investors outside the United States. In fact the very first issues of Bank securities in 1947 were bought by investors in Canada, Latin America, Europe, and Asia. European banks began to buy bonds from the IBRD's dollar issues as early as 1950. These were mainly for other accounts, particularly insurance companies and trust funds. A few central banks also soon began to buy from the U.S. issues, and these purchases foreshadowed the later issues, which were designed specifically for central banks. The IBRD noted with satisfaction in 1954 that of the $221 million in new issues sold during the previous year, $96 million had been purchased outside the United States, including $50 million in dollar bonds. "For the first time, banking firms outside the United States participated as underwriters of Bank issues denominated in United States dollars."[53]

By the end of the first decade of operations, the IBRD had clearly established a highly respectable standing not only in the U.S. capital market but, as was indicated by the extensive sale outside the United States of both dollar and nondollar securities, in the capital markets of the world. It may be useful in considering both early and later periods of the Bank's history to reflect on the reasons for this high credit standing and on the changing nature of these reasons over time. In the early sales of Bank securities great emphasis was placed on the U.S. 80 percent subscription as a guarantee against loss. When the capital of the Bank was doubled in 1959, the doubling of the U.S. 80 percent was the primary objective. Since then, as was indicated above, the relative importance of the U.S. guarantee has lessened, and that of the other high-income country guarantees has increased.

The Bank in its early operations took the position that its credit standing would also be directly dependent on the character of its loans. The *Second Annual Report* states,

The Bank can secure the funds it needs from private investors only if it can convince them that its loans will be sound business risks. To be sure, investors in the Bank's securities have the guarantee afforded by the uncalled 80%. . . . How-

53. IBRD, *Ninth Annual Report, 1953–1954,* p. 40.

ever, despite this guarantee, it will not be possible for the Bank to sell its securities in the market in the amounts needed to carry out its objectives unless investors have confidence that their funds will be used only for economically sound and productive purposes.[54]

Moreover, at least some of the Bank's managerial personnel saw a beneficial reciprocal relationship between lending and borrowing policy. If sound loans were made, the Bank's position in capital markets would be improved. On the other hand, because the Bank was dependent on the bond market, it had to exercise unusual care in seeing that its loans *were* sound.[55]

In the early years of the Bank a sound loan meant not only that the project was carefully appraised but that, whenever possible, the project would produce earnings that would help repay the loan. The early lending of the IBRD in developing countries was overwhelmingly directed toward capital infrastructure, that is, railways, communication facilities, power plants, port facilities, and the like. While the need for this type of investment was undoubtedly great, a more searching examination of the development process might have suggested a wider range of activities, including education, urban development, and other areas in which the Bank only later showed an interest. At least some Bank officials, however, felt that to lend extensively in the "social field" would produce an adverse reaction in the financial community.[56]

This concern with opinion in the investment community affected more than the character of Bank loans. As we note in Chapter 5, the Bank refused to lend to Chile until that country had made an effort to settle its defaulted foreign debt. "Our efforts to sell bonds of the World Bank would be hindered if we were trying to sell bonds to people who held defaulted Chilean bonds, if we were to make a loan to Chile."[57] And as we have already reported, concern for investor opinion affected even the personnel policies of the Bank.

Although the investment community is still concerned with the effectiveness of Bank project lending, successive managements have been able to defend the view that the primary test of a lending program is what happens in the economy as a whole. Indeed, one test of whether the Bank can be considered to be a development institution might be the extent to which its lending policy looks beyond project viability toward consequences for the development of the economy. In any case Presidents Woods and McNamara have been able to extend the scope of Bank lending in the areas of agriculture, edu-

54. IBRD, *Second Annual Report, 1946–1947*, p. 15.
55. Robert Garner, "Oral History," p. 45.
56. Robert Cavanaugh, "Oral History," p. 63.
57. Garner, "Oral History," p. 14.

cation, urban development, and family planning without any noticeable repercussions in capital markets. However, the fact that the Bank has in recent
years found itself able to take a broader view of development lending must
in large part be attributed to the very strong position that the Bank management established early in the capital markets of the world.

We have dwelt at length on the Bank's early cultivation of the U.S. capital
market, which the Bank's management considered essential to the emergence
of the IBRD as a strong financial institution. The period since the mid-1950s
has been characterized by: (1) a decline in the relative importance of the
U.S. market as a source of Bank borrowing, (2) sharply rising interest rates,
(3) difficulties because of the adverse U.S. balance of payments in securing
the consent of the U.S. government to sales of Bank securities in the U.S.
market, and (4) with the advent of the McNamara administration, a sharp
rise in the volume of Bank borrowing in all markets.

Although the relative importance of the U.S. market as a source of long-
term Bank borrowing has declined, the volume of sales of dollar securities
has continued to increase at persistently higher interest rates. Table 5-5 shows
the amount of long-term dollar security issues of the Bank, together with
their interest rates and maturity.

The small, $5 million issue in 1962 was for a sale to a syndicate of Aus-
trian banks. All the other issues except one, which was for a private sale of
$120 million to the Deutsche Bundesbank, were underwritten by Morgan

Table 5-5. *World Bank Long-Term Dollar Security Issues,
Interest Rate, and Maturity, 1958–71*

Year of issue	Amount of issue (millions of U.S. dollars)	Interest rate (percent)	Maturity (number of years)
1958	150	4¼	21
1958	100	4½	15
1960	125	5	25
1960	120	4½	12
1962	100	4½	20
1962	5	4½	15
1965	200	4½	25
1966	175	5⅜	25
1967	250	5⅜	25
1967	150	5⅞	26
1968	150	6½	26
1969	265	6⅜	26
1970	200	8⅝	25
1971	—	—	—

Source: International Bank for Reconstruction and Development.

Stanley and the First Boston Corporation. It will be noted that there were no long-term sales between 1962 and 1965. During this period George Woods became president of the Bank, and the absence of sales represents in part his view that the cash holdings of the Bank were too large. In part it reflects increasing difficulty, for balance-of-payments reasons, in securing the consent of the U.S. Treasury to sales in the American market.

Concern in government quarters for the U.S. balance of payments had, of course, surfaced much earlier. Heavy gold losses in 1958 led to a decision in 1959 to tie U.S. bilateral assistance to procurement in the United States. The outflow of gold, however, was not stemmed. In the three years 1958, 1959, and 1960 gold losses, plus the increase in short-term liabilities of the United States, averaged $3.5 billion a year. When President John F. Kennedy came into office in January 1961, he lost no time in warning Congress that "this [deficit in the balance of payments and loss of gold] means that the United States must in the decades ahead, much more than at any time in the past, take its balance of payments into account when formulating its economic policies and conducting its economic affairs." The economic policies of the United States, of course, included policy with respect to contributions to IDA, to increases in the paid-in capital of the Bank, and to permission to sell securities in the U.S. market.

So far as the Bank's relations with the U.S. government were concerned, the crunch came in 1964 and 1965 and was concerned mainly with the IDA replenishment, as will be shown in Chapter 12. But access of the Bank to the U.S. capital market was also involved. When the Bank sought permission to borrow in 1965, the strength of the Treasury's opposition became obvious. That the secretary of the treasury was not alone in his opposition is suggested by the fact that in 1965 Senator Dirksen was seriously considering an amendment to the Foreign Assistance Act of that year that would have made Treasury approval of IBRD borrowing contingent on agreement by the Congress. The senator was persuaded not to introduce his amendment. But in no year after 1965 could it be taken for granted that the Treasury would consent to the sale of Bank securities in the U.S. market, as it had been before 1962. When President McNamara received permission for the Bank to sell $250 million in long-term securities in the U.S. market in 1968, he informed the secretary of the treasury that the Bank had plans for heavy borrowing in the years ahead and was assured that the permission granted in 1968 was without prejudice to further requests in 1969. But he committed the Bank, in fiscal 1970 and each fiscal year thereafter, to use its best efforts to see that the amount of new borrowings outside the United States would equal new borrowings in the United States, in each case net of repayments on previous borrowings.[58] Since borrowing outside the United States on a cumulative basis had long since reached 50 percent of total borrowing, this was perhaps not a particularly restrictive commitment.

That the United States should be concerned with the balance-of-payments effects of contributions to IDA is understandable. According to IBRD calculations, in the period from the inception of IDA to the end of fiscal year 1971, the estimated net loss to the U.S. balance of payments from operations of IDA amounted to $275 million.[59] This was a result in large part of the fact that IDA expenditures were concentrated in India and Pakistan, whose normal trade relations are with Western Europe. On the other hand, according to IBRD calculations, by conforming to requirements set by the U.S. Treasury, the Bank itself has been a consistent and heavy net contributor to U.S. foreign exchange earnings by a margin that dwarfs the net loss resulting from IDA operations.[60] There is, of course, a substantial lag between the time of the U.S. contribution to the IBRD in the form of capital subscriptions and security purchases and the time of the main return flows in the form of purchases of goods in the United States resulting from Bank loans abroad and of interest payments to U.S. investors. But this lag could be judged to offset the net long-term positive effect only in a period of extreme concern for immediate balance-of-payments considerations. We do not think that, over time, balance-of-payments difficulties should be a serious impediment to Bank borrowing in the U.S. market, though temporary disruptions could well occur.

58. See letter from George D. Woods to Henry H. Fowler (secretary of the U.S. treasury), March 11, 1968; and letter from Robert S. McNamara to Fowler, July 25, 1968.

59. IBRD, Treasurer's Department, Finance Division.

60. The estimated IBRD effects on the U.S. balance of payments from the inception of IBRD through calendar year 1970, are as follows (in millions of U.S. dollars):

IBRD-financed goods bought in the U.S.	3,455		
Interest paid by IBRD to U.S. bondholders	801		
Interest paid by IBRD to U.S. loan holders	164		
IBRD administrative expenses in the U.S. (including bond issuance cost)	350		
Total paid by IBRD to the U.S.		4,770	
U.S. payment of 1 percent subscription	64		
U.S. payment of 9 percent subscription	571		
IBRD bonds sold in the U.S., net of redemptions	1,841		
Net IBRD loan sales in the U.S.	128		
Investment income earned by the IBRD in the U.S.	838		
Total received by IBRD from the U.S.		3,442	
Net paid by IBRD to the U.S.			1,328
IBRD long-term investment in the U.S.			1,534
IBRD contribution to U.S. balance of payments			2,862

The rate of Bank lending was sharply increased with the advent of the McNamara regime. In his maiden address to the board of governors in September 1968, the president proposed to double the 1964–68 rate within the next five years, and by fiscal year 1971 this goal appeared to be within easy reach. Of course, the increase in commitments required a commensurate increase in Bank borrowing, though with some delay. Prior to fiscal 1969 the Bank had never borrowed more than $800 million gross in a single year from all sources. In fiscal year 1969 gross borrowing rose to $1.224 billion; in fiscal 1970 it amounted to $735 million; and in fiscal 1971 it increased again to $1.3 billion. Projections within the Bank foresee a borrowing rate that may rise to $2 billion by 1975. Although there was some grumbling in financial circles over the rate at which Bank lending and borrowing were increased, no serious difficulties have been encountered in raising the money required. The U.S. market in most years now supplies less than half of this money, and this, from the point of view of the Bank as an international institution, must be considered a desirable state of affairs.

Bank Borrowing outside the United States

As has been pointed out above, the Bank during the first ten years of its existence was close to being a dollar bank. Of the first $1 billion in Bank securities offered for sale, $835 million were denominated in dollars and only $165 million in other currencies. This does not mean, however, that all the dollar securities were sold in the United States. As early as 1951 the Bank noted that investors outside the United States were buying "substantial" amounts of dollar bonds, and it estimated that $39 million of these bonds were held by such investors, including the central banks of ten member countries.[61] In 1953, the managers of the Bank's U.S. dollar issues for the first time included European banks as underwriters and members of selling groups; and of the $175 million of dollar bonds offered in that year, about $50 million were sold to buyers in Europe.[62] In 1955 all Bank bonds issued were sold outside the United States, and by the end of fiscal year 1969, 60 percent of the IBRD's funded debt was held in other countries.[63]

The first nondollar issue was a private placement of 2.5 percent Swiss franc serial bonds of 17 million francs (about $4 million), dated April 1, 1948. It was sold to the Bank for International Settlements. The BIS had a positive desire to be useful, arising partly from a wish to counter the feeling

61. IBRD, *Sixth Annual Report, 1950–1951*, p. 44.
62. IBRD, *Ninth Annual Report, 1953–1954*, p. 40.
63. The figure at the end of fiscal 1971 was 62 percent.

that it was no longer a necessary institution. This was followed soon by another private issue in Switzerland of 28.5 million Swiss francs, in which the
BIS joined with the three leading Swiss commercial banks. The proceeds of
the issues were used principally for procurement in Western Europe of equipment financed by loans to the Netherlands and Yugoslavia.

The first public offering outside the United States was a £5 million issue
of 3.5 percent, twenty-year stock sold in the United Kingdom in fiscal 1951
through a syndicate of six banking houses headed by Baring Brothers and
Company, Ltd. As an indication of certain differences between U.S. and U.K.
investment practices, when a member of the Bank staff suggested that the
prospectus should carry a full description of the borrowing institution, the
suggestion was waved aside with the assurance that the name of Baring was
all that was needed. Although the IBRD had hoped to have an annual issue
in London, the next sale of securities was not until fiscal 1955. There have
been only three sterling issues in the history of the Bank prior to fiscal 1972.

The Bank was able to float its first issue of bonds in the Netherlands in
1954. This was an offering of fifteen-year bonds in the amount of 40 million
florins (equivalent to 10.5 million U.S. dollars). The issue was undertaken
by an underwriting group of fourteen banks headed by the Netherlands Trading Company (Nederlandsche Handel-Maatschappij).

At the time of the issues in the United Kingdom and the Netherlands
neither country had released a significant portion of its 18 percent subscription. The question that naturally arises is why, if these countries permitted
the sale of Bank securities in currencies that could be used for procurement
domestically, they could not release their 18 percent subscriptions for the
same purpose. The Bank wrestled with this problem and came to the conclusion that

where conditions are favorable, there are obvious long-term advantages in establishing the Bank's credit in the financial markets and in familiarizing local investors with its securities—even before all 18% funds are released. Such operations
are important steps in building future markets, which should become increasingly
useful as sources of investment funds.[64]

This building for the future was also deemed to justify paying, in Europe,
a substantially higher rate of interest than was customary at that time on
borrowing in the United States. Perhaps also the Bank's management wanted
to exorcise, at least to some extent, the specter of the IBRD as a "dollar
bank."

During its first ten years the Bank sold three issues of $15 million, $25
million, and $15 million, denominated in Canadian dollars; two issues each

64. IBRD, *Sixth Annual Report, 1950–1951*, p. 43.

of 40 million florins (about $11 million) in the Netherlands, two issues of £5 million each in the United Kingdom, and six public issues of 50 million Swiss francs in Switzerland. The only country besides the United States in which the Bank could regularly visit the capital market was Switzerland, and then only for small amounts. The Bank sold fairly sizable issues denominated in German marks in 1959 and 1960, but not until 1965 did it became a regular and large long-term borrower in the German market.

The fact that the Bank never during its first quarter century borrowed in the French market deserves a word of comment. In 1965 the Bank came close to floating an issue in the French market. According to former President George Woods, he and Finance Minister Valery Giscard d'Estaing had wanted the Bank to be the first international institution to sell bonds in France, but the Coal and Steel Community came in with an issue that froze out the Bank.[65] All things considered, it does not seem likely that France will be a major source of Bank borrowing, at least not in the near future.

All countries set limits on access to their capital markets by foreign borrowers—sometimes for balance-of-payments reasons and sometimes to conserve savings for domestic use. Until 1963 the United States was probably the capital market of the world that was most hospitable to foreign borrowing, but the imposition of the interest equalization tax changed that dramatically. Even Switzerland, which is the largest foreign lender in the world in proportion to the size of its capital market, limits foreign borrowing in order to conserve savings for domestic use. Switzerland has been unwilling to allow the Bank more than one issue of modest size each year. In most other countries the limitations have been much more drastic. Foreign borrowers are rarely admitted to the Swedish market except in the case of occasional Norwegian and Danish bond issues, and the sale of an IBRD issue in 1967 was an exceptional occurrence. Access to the Italian market is tightly controlled. The IBRD issue in 1961 was a somewhat special case. There was a small issue in Belgium in 1959—500 million Belgian francs (equivalent to $10 million) in ten-year bonds. The issue matured in 1969, and the Bank at the end of fiscal 1971 had no Belgian franc obligations. After early issues in the Netherlands in 1954 and 1955 the Bank returned to the Dutch market for small amounts in 1961, 1962, and 1968. In 1971 two issues of 60 million guilders each ($16.6 million) were sold, the first with a fifteen-year maturity and the second an intermediate security with a five-year maturity.

Since 1959 Germany has been by far the most important European source of Bank borrowing. In the years after 1967 the large surplus in the German balance of payments led the government to encourage the export of capital,

65. Conversation with George D. Woods, Dec. 16, 1969.

and the Bank was a highly favored instrument. In 1968 the Bank borrowed more on long term in Germany than in the United States. Most of the final sale of bonds in Germany is to individuals and to the banking system, though mortgage banks are the only institutional investors not legally entitled to invest in the IBRD.

The Bank has never given as much attention to the systematic expansion of the legal eligibility for investment in IBRD securities in other countries as in the U.S. and Canadian markets. One reason for this is that in other countries usually only one jurisdiction is involved, while in Canada and the United States there are many jurisdictions. But further, the Bank issues in the United States have generally been so large that the full potentiality of investors has had to be tapped. In most European markets this was not so. Then too the underwriters in Europe were usually larger in relation to their markets than were those in the United States, and their knowledge of these markets was probably greater. Finally, the regulations in most European issues markets appear to be less detailed and complicated than in the United States. On occasion, the Bank has pressed for the inclusion as potential purchasers of investing institutions that are precluded by existing law or administrative regulation from buying securities. In Switzerland, for example, the Bank has tried for years, so far without success, to make Bank securities eligible for purchase by life insurance companies for the investment of their legal reserves. But in general the IBRD has been content to let this burden be carried by its underwriters and distributors.

The Bank borrowed in the Middle East for the first time in 1968. A private placement amounting to $15 million of twenty-six-year, 6.5 percent bonds was undertaken with the Saudi Arabian Monetary Agency (the central bank) in May of that year. Later an additional $15 million for Saudi Arabia was added to the U.S. dollar offering of September 1968. The Bank sold its first public offering in a Middle Eastern market in Kuwait in August 1968. It would have been possible to place these bonds privately with the Kuwait Fund for Arab Economic Development, but the director of the organization was interested in beginning to develop a capital market in Kuwait in competition with the Lebanese market. Consequently the sizable issue of 15 million Kuwaiti dinars ($42 million) was bought by sheikhs, Kuwaiti banks, and the Ministry of Finance. In August 1969, the executive directors approved a ten-year issue of 10 million Libyan pounds, to carry 7.25 percent interest. But before arrangements could be completed, there was a change of government in Libya. This issue was later renegotiated into an intermediate-term (five-year) loan at a higher rate of interest and represented one of a number of initiatives by the Bank to tap such markets around the world.

The Bank's first borrowings in Japan, which are discussed below, took the form of short-term securities sold to the Bank of Japan. In the spring of 1971, however, the Bank negotiated a public issue of 11 billion yen ($30.6 million) in ten-year bonds. The cost to the Bank was 8.06 percent. Japan may well become an important future source to the IBRD of both short-term and long-term capital.

Short-term and Intermediate-term Borrowing

Beginning in 1953 the Bank had established a large, growing, and relatively stable market for short-term bonds and notes in the central banks of the world. The first issue designed specifically for this market, and the first dollar issue designed for sale entirely outside the United States, was one in 1956 of $75 million in two-year bonds, of which $52 million were sold to sixteen central banks (with the Bundesbank alone taking $17.5 million) and the rest to private purchasers. There were six other issues in which private purchasers were allowed to participate before 1958. From that time on, private buyers were excluded. A sufficient level of demand had been established in central banks, and by excluding private accounts, the Bank avoided paying a higher interest rate and also avoided some trouble in allocation. By 1966 this market was so well developed that the Bank increased its offerings to two issues a year with an annual volume of over $200 million. These issues have invariably been two-year dollar bonds placed directly by the IBRD with central banks, other governmental institutions, and international organizations. Recent issues have been large. So have been the numbers of purchasers. Shown below are the sales (in thousands of U.S. dollars) of two-year bonds designed primarily for central banks.

Issue	Amount
5.8 percent of 1968, September 15	144,500
6¾ percent of 1969, March 15	192,650
8 percent of 1969, September 15	175,000
8⅛ percent of 1970, March 15	174,500
7⅞ percent of 1970, September 15	175,000
5.20 percent of 1971, March 15	200,000

The issue of March 15, 1971, was sold to central banks and government institutions in sixty-seven countries and one international organization. The requirements of individual central banks for short-term IBRD securities vary, of course, from year to year. However, this is substantially offset by the changing number of participants; as some drop out, others increase their holdings. In the opinion of the Bank management, borrowing from central banks constitutes a relatively predictable source of funds.

In addition to these regular Bank issues of two-year bonds, the IBRD has been a large and persistent seller of short-term securities to the German Bundesbank. In 1970 the Bank borrowed in Japan for the first time. Two issues of serial bonds of 36 billion yen each ($100 million), which were to mature in 1973–75, were sold to the Bank of Japan at a price yielding 7.14 percent. In announcing these loans, "the Bank of Japan stated that it had decided to extend them on the basis of recent developments in Japan's balance of payments which had added materially to the country's monetary reserves."[66] The Bank of Japan made two more purchases of 36 billion yen in short-term and intermediate-term serial bonds in the spring of 1971 at a price to yield 7.43 percent and an additional purchase of 7 billion yen ($19.4 million) somewhat later. These short-term and intermediate-term purchases, plus the ten-year bond issues mentioned above and prepayment purchases from the Bank's portfolio (which are discussed below), mean that Japan accounted for an addition to the Bank's loanable funds of about $600 million in fiscal years 1970 and 1971.

The Bank also undertook intermediate-term borrowing in the United States for the first time in 1971 with an issue of $200 million in five-year notes with a 6.5 percent coupon and priced at par. This issue was quickly sold out and foreshadows further attempts to tap intermediate-term capital in the United States and in other markets.

The increasing proportion of Bank funds borrowed at short term has changed somewhat the relation of the average life of World Bank loans to the average life of the Bank's funded debt. As of June 30, 1968, this ratio stood at 9.98 years to 9.58 years; on June 30, 1971, it was 10.89 years to 8.47 years. While in principle it is not sound for an institution to lend at long term and borrow at short term, the discrepancy shown by these figures is not particularly significant for the Bank, though questions have been raised by various executive directors. The Bank's equity must be considered to be part of its revolving funds, and in any case the important question is how liquid does the IBRD need to be in the light of uncertainties concerning its cash flows.[67]

66. World Bank/IDA, *Annual Report, 1970*, p. 35. The *Report* continues:
    The Bank of Japan added that further factors influencing its decision regarding the loans were "the great contribution toward the development of the Japanese economy" made by the World Bank, and a desire on the part of Japan to "help the World Bank's activities and thereby strengthen international monetary cooperation."

67. The liquidity position of the Bank has to do with its volume of cash and realizable assets in relation to the difference between projected cash inflows and cash outflows. As an internal Bank memorandum observes, "The need to hold liquidity results from the possibility of divergences between actual and projected cash flows." The principal sources of possible differences between actual and projected flows are, "Firstly, disbursements are subject to variations. . . . Secondly, repayments and interest payments on loans receivable are subject to the risk of default or rescheduling. Thirdly, the Bank's access to the world's capital markets cannot be forecast with certainty."

The increase in short-term and medium-term borrowing, together with the projected rapid expansion of loan disbursements, led in the spring of 1971 to a reexamination of the Bank's liquidity position. The relation between the Bank's liquid assets and its estimated cash flows will henceforth be under continuous review.

Participations and Sales from Portfolio

As was noted above, participations take place at the time when a Bank loan is made and when investors buy from the Bank some part of the loan.[68] Portfolio sales are, as the name suggests, sales to investors of parts of loans from the Bank's established portfolio. In either case they represent sources of loan funds that, in effect, substitute for additional bond issues. That such sales are a far from negligible source is seen when the total of Bank loans to date is compared with the share taken up by outsiders. Total Bank loans signed to the end of fiscal year 1971, net of cancellations, refundings, and exchange adjustments, amounted to $16.1 billion. Outside participation in these loans, at the same date, totaled $2.4 billion.

The first sales from portfolio were made with the Bank's guarantee; they could scarcely have been made otherwise. The last sale from portfolio with a Bank guarantee was made in fiscal 1956. In the meantime, however, sales without guarantee had grown to sizable proportions. The development of participations and sales from portfolio was a strong interest of President Black—so strong indeed that this came to be known as the "Black Market." At its high point in 1961–62, outside participation in Bank loans yielded $319 million, which may be compared with total Bank loan commitments in the same year of $882 million and disbursements of $485 million. Black regarded such participation as a device for interesting investors in the purchase of foreign government securities. In addition, participations and sales from portfolios served to calm any fears the investment community might have that the IBRD was competing with private interests for business. As a former general counsel put it, "Any time anybody has accused us of doing something that they might have done, we've just said, 'Our whole portfolio is for sale, you can take it all over.' "[69]

68. Participations should be distinguished from joint and parallel financing in which the Bank shares a loan either with a private investor or with another provider of public assistance. Participation means purchasing some part of a loan already negotiated by the Bank. Joint financing between the Bank and private investors is discussed in Chapter 11, and in Chapter 15 joint and parallel financing involving the participation of other public bodies or programs are discussed.

69. Davidson Sommers, "Oral History," p. 72.

The principal purchasers of Bank loans have been commercial banks, insurance companies and other institutional investors, and central banks. Commercial banks have frequently used these purchases as a means of seeking new clients or of accommodating existing ones. Insurance companies have usually made purchases for investment purposes. Central banks have made nearly half the purchases. Central banks on a number of occasions have purchased, from Bank portfolio, loans to their own countries as a device for prepaying these loans. The initial Bank loan to France was retired in that way. And, of sales from portfolio of $169.8 million in 1970, $162.5 million represented purchases by the Bank of Japan in prepayment of Bank loans to Japan.

U.S. purchasers, in general, have preferred to participate in the Bank's loans at the time they are made, at least in part for the sake of publicity when the Bank announces the loan. European institutions, on the other hand, generally have a preference for buying from portfolio. Early in the Bank's history the reason was partly procedural; purchasing institutions had to obtain government licenses, and this took time. Apart from that, however, European institutions were reluctant to commit funds that might not be drawn down for two or three years; and some of them, far from being interested in publicity, were averse to it.[70] As Table 5-6 indicates, participations and portfolio sales of loans outside the United States have been nearly two and one-half times the volume inside; and sales to banks, including central banks, have quite overshadowed sales to other types of purchasers.

Table 5-7 shows a substantial decline in purchases of Bank loans following the high point reached in 1961–62. The reasons for this, in approximate order of importance, are: (1) the considerable rise in interest rates in recent years; (2) the restraint on sales arising from the Bank's decision not to act contrary to the purposes of the U.S. interest equalization tax; (3) a suspected decline in the quality of paper held by the Bank; and (4) changes in the attitude of the Bank management toward portfolio sales. As interest rates have risen, the attractiveness of longer-term borrowers' obligations held by the IBRD has declined, and the Bank has been loath to sell out of portfolio at a sizable discount, even though sales at a discount would not have involved a higher price for money than would have had to be paid on new issues. Although purchases of Bank loans are exempt from the interest equalization tax, the Bank, on its own decision, ceased after 1963 to make sales to U.S. investors of the securities of countries whose obligations otherwise would be subject to the tax. Selling from portfolio had been a very important function of the Bank's New York office before 1963 but was discontinued by 1967.

70. From interviews with R. W. Cavanaugh.

Table 5-6. *Participations in and Portfolio Sales of World Bank Loans, Cumulative to June 30, 1971*[a]

Type of purchaser	Number of purchasers	Amount of purchases (millions of U.S. dollar equivalents)
Purchasers inside the United States	**150**	**692.2**
Private banks	119	524.3
Private insurance companies	18	100.1
Other private purchasers	13	67.8
Purchasers outside the United States	**383**	**1,681.0**
Private banks	135	448.4
Private insurance companies	52	32.3
Other private purchasers	166	69.6
Public purchasers	30	1,130.9
Central banks and governmental organizations	(25)	(964.6)
International organizations	(5)	(166.2)
Total	**533**	**2,373.3**

Source: IBRD, Treasurer's Department, Securities Division. Prepared on the basis of registered owners. Amounts are rounded and may not add to totals.
  a. Including funds not called.

The European office of the Bank, on the other hand, was active in selling out of portfolio until 1969, when it was deterred by prevailing high interest rates.

As the Bank has moved from lending to developed countries to concentrating its loans in the less developed world, the quality of the portfolios, as judged in the capital markets of the world, has declined. The guarantees of the governments of most of the less developed countries are not regarded with the same respect as the guarantees of most Western European governments, even though the Bank to date has not experienced a default. Finally, changes in Bank management have had some effect on efforts to enlist outside participation. President Black, as was mentioned above, was very eager to enlarge this market; Presidents Woods and McNamara were less interested in doing so. In part, this was because the objectives the Bank had in mind in opening up the market in the first place had already been achieved. The nature of the Bank's portfolio was now well known, investors had become familiar with foreign borrowing governments under the Bank's tutelage, and there was no disposition to regard the Bank as taking away business that properly belonged to private investment houses.

In conclusion it should be emphasized that participation in and portfolio sales of loans have been an important source of Bank financing, accounting for nearly 15 percent of total outside funds attracted.

Table 5-7. *Outside Participation in World Bank Loans*
U.S. dollars

Fiscal year	With guarantee	Without guarantee	Total
All loans before fiscal 1952	28,549,000	4,468,496	33,017,496
1952	12,950,001	10,409,191	23,359,192
1953	8,304,145	6,330,820	14,634,965
1954	7,940,698	25,865,768	33,806,466
1955	783,500	98,393,636	99,177,136
1956	10,476,500	61,690,626	72,167,126
1957	. . .	56,894,751	56,894,751
1958	. . .	86,999,875	86,999,875
1959	. . .	148,435,519	148,435,519
1960	. . .	242,561,031	242,561,031
1961	. . .	202,132,415	202,132,415
1962	. . .	318,807,746	318,807,746
1963	. . .	273,321,774	273,321,774
1964	. . .	173,272,432	173,272,432
1965	. . .	106,166,332	106,166,332
1966	. . .	81,860,507	81,860,507
1967	. . .	68,585,455	68,585,455
1968	. . .	107,436,317	107,436,317
1969	. . .	34,698,430	34,698,430
1970	. . .	172,427,202	172,427,202
1971	. . .	23,529,208	23,529,208
Total	69,003,844	2,304,287,531	2,373,291,375

Source: IBRD, Information and Public Affairs Department.

Summary and Conclusions

Although the sale of its own securities in capital markets continues to be by far the most important source of loanable funds, the World Bank has become significantly less circumscribed in its lending policy by attitudes in the financial community than it was during the first ten years of its existence. In part this is because of the cautious policies pursued by the Bank's management during these ten years. In part it is the result of an escape from excessive dependence on the New York market brought about by the development of borrowing capacity in other markets around the world. But also it is partly the result of a growing realization by investors in Bank securities that not only the character of specific loan projects but the effects on the development of borrowers' economies should govern lending policy.

The security behind Bank borrowing is basically the capacity of members of the Bank to honor their 90 percent subscriptions, and this has increased greatly since the early years, when only the U.S. guarantee was considered to be valid. But the Bank would be exceedingly loath, and rightly so, to see this guarantee invoked. Any serious encroachment, through debt repudiation or renegotiation, on the equity of the Bank would be damaging to its position as a borrower. The Bank's equity can be considered to be that part of the paid-in capital that is usable, plus accumulations of reserves. Since the Bank first opened its doors its usable capital has been increased only by the release of the membership's 18 percent subscriptions and by the addition of new members. The doubling of the authorized capital in 1959 was not intended to add to usable capital. In the meantime the volume of Bank lending and borrowing has increased tremendously. The Bank considered asking for a large increase in authorized, subscribed, and paid-in capital in 1970, but the coincidence of a need to replenish IDA's capital led to the decision to scale it down. It must be recognized that IDA to some extent competes with the Bank for loanable capital, while at the same time the Bank's equity is diminished by transfers of earnings to IDA. On the other hand, if it were not for the availability of IDA money, the creditworthiness of many less developed countries for Bank borrowing would be seriously diminished. If the Bank Group is going to continue to grow as a set of development institutions, additional funds must be available from sources other than the Bank. This means from IDA replenishments, increases in the paid-in capital of the Bank, and retained earnings. If IDA funds are greatly increased and Bank earnings continue to be transferred to IDA, the result may be a large increase in the creditworthiness of less developed countries for Bank lending with very little increase in the equity behind Bank borrowing.

During its first decade, the Bank's borrowing was overwhelmingly in dollar-denominated issues. This plus the fact that the U.S. subscription was practically the only usable 18 percent subscription gave the World Bank the coloration of a "dollar bank." Even during this period, however, Bank securities were sold in large volume outside the United States, and toward the end of the Bank's first quarter century well over 60 percent of the Bank's funded debt was held in other countries. The percentage of short-term and medium-term debt held outside the United States was even larger.

The rapid development of borrowing at short and medium term has been a striking feature of Bank financing during recent years. This increased reliance on short-term money has been the product of (1) a rapid expansion in Bank lending, (2) high interest rates inhibiting the sale of long-term securities, particularly in the United States, (3) a belief on the part of management that interest rates must decline, and (4) a desire to accumulate sizable cash reserves. Bank profits for a time benefited substantially from this borrowing since accumulated cash was available for deposit at short term in commercial banks at high rates.

While the ratio of the average life of the Bank's outstanding debt to the average life of its outstanding loans has declined slightly, this does not appear to be a matter of any considerable importance. What is important in the short run is the volume of liquid assets the Bank needs to hold in view of the possibility that disbursements and borrowings will diverge from projected levels. In the long run it is important that the Bank's equity increase in some reasonable relation to its outstanding indebtedness.

CHAPTER SIX

The Bank as a Supplier of Capital, 1947–1952

DURING ITS FIRST five years of lending, the World Bank was not a major supplier of capital either for reconstruction or for development. Nevertheless, by June 30, 1952, it had made sixty-eight loans totaling the equivalent of $1.4 billion. More than 35 percent of the loan total was accounted for by the four European reconstruction loans approved between May 9 and August 28, 1947, for France, the Netherlands, Denmark, and Luxembourg. This means that the average size of the other sixty-four loans was about $14 million. They included, however, loans to all continents for a modest variety of undertakings. Disbursements (which tend to lag slightly behind commitments for reconstruction loans and far behind for development loans) amounted to some $875 million. The Bank's operating policies and procedures had become clear enough and firm enough in the minds of its management to permit describing them in some detail.

Under its Articles of Agreement, the Bank was expected to finance only those productive projects for which other financing was not available on reasonable terms. Surveying the field during its formative period, the management concluded that private capital would be most readily available to the low-income countries for the development of export products, such as tin, rubber, and petroleum. It hoped that light manufacturing industries, such as textiles, which required smaller amounts of capital and which had traditionally been private enterprise activities, would continue to be financed privately. The Bank management was opposed to financing government-owned industries.

150

This "conviction of the management" was based, according to Vice President Robert Garner, on three grounds. "We believed in private enterprise in those fields in which it could operate. . . . We felt that governments had so many things to do that were purely in their sphere that they shouldn't divert resources to other things, and . . . most governments are incapable of running industrial enterprises effectively."[1] The conviction was severely criticized by directors who were interested in World Bank financing for government-owned steel mills and other industrial undertakings. But the view of management was that,

if these countries are really going to develop, they could own transport, they could own power. They could have other infrastructure projects, but the only way they were really going to increase the production of goods and have people have more and get more jobs and raise the standard of living and build up the country was through the development of private enterprise and agriculture.[2]

Costly equipment from abroad, it was clear, would be required for electric power plants, transportation and communication systems, and other basic facilities that were no longer attractive to private capital, although they could be regarded as prerequisites for the attraction of private capital to industry, agriculture, and the services. Public utilities had attracted private capital to less developed countries in pre–World War II days, but it would have been unrealistic to expect them to continue to do so on any appreciable scale after the war. The investment was too large, the return to the investor too small, and the prospect of government intervention too great. Projects to develop electric power and transport facilities were accordingly considered especially appropriate for Bank financing.

At the same time, the Bank was led to eschew certain fields traditionally open to public investment, even in the highly developed free enterprise economies: namely, sanitation, education, and health facilities. Investments in these so-called "social overhead" fields were widely considered to be as fundamental to development as are investments in hydroelectric sites, railroads, highways, and "economic overhead" programs. The contribution of social overhead projects to increased production, however, is less measurable and direct than that of power plants, and they can be completed without large outlays of scarce foreign exchange. Financing them, moreover, might open

1. Oral History Project of Columbia University, interviews recorded in the summer of 1961 on the International Bank for Reconstruction and Development (cited hereinafter as "Oral History"). See interview of Robert L. Garner, p. 49. The Bank's official policy was less categorical, and in its first five years it did help to finance some state-owned enterprises, primarily in France and Finland.

2. *Ibid.*, p. 50.

the door to vastly increased demands for loans and raise hackles anew in Wall Street about the "soundness" of the Bank's management. It therefore seemed prudent to the management during the first postwar decade to consider as unsuitable in normal circumstances World Bank financing of projects for eliminating malaria, reducing illiteracy, building vocational schools, or establishing clinics. Yet the crying need for such projects and the paucity of domestic resources to finance them helped in later years to fan the flames for grants and soft loans to supplement the lending then being done by the World Bank on close-to-commercial terms.

One of the principal self-assigned jobs of a bureaucracy is to prove to itself and others that it is engaged in a rational, professional, genuinely significant undertaking. Whatever the reasons are that first push an agency into a particular pattern of activity, the bureaucracy can be relied on to give a cosmic twist to the rationale for that activity. The Bank was set up to help complete specific productive projects rather than to make general purpose loans, to finance only the foreign exchange costs of those projects, to secure a guarantee of repayment from the government of the country in which the project was to be located, and to finance only activities for which other financing was believed to be unavailable. These requirements, along with the practical necessity of concerning itself only with projects large enough to justify review and appraisal by a global agency with headquarters in Washington, D.C., practically assured a heavy concentration by the Bank on power plants, railroad lines, highway networks, and similar physical facilities. It was the availability of financing for such undertakings that stimulated philosophizing about the vital role of economic infrastructure in the development process, rather than the reverse.

The Bank became the leading proponent of the view that investment in transportation and communication facilities, port developments, power projects, and other public utilities was a precondition for the development of the rest of the economy.[3] The United Nations Educational, Scientific, and Cultural Organization (Unesco) of course considered investment in education to be the major precondition, while the Food and Agriculture Organization (FAO) thought that investment in agriculture was.

The Bank's philosophy with respect to various other needs of less developed countries and lending policies appropriate thereto was set forth in bits and pieces in its first four annual reports. Then in the fifth report, the agency summarized with considerable frankness its major operational policies, including in virtually every case not only the policy, but the rationale for it,

3. See Chapter 14, below.

thereby enabling the Bank to respond in a positive way to the increasingly vocal critics of specific policies.[4]

These policies were, of course, the product of a series of interacting factors, including clear and unambiguous provisions in the Articles of Agreement; interpretations and elaborations of provisions that gave only general guidance or could be construed in more than one way; genius and bias on the part of early leaders; pressure from the rapidly changing world in which those leaders lived; and the gradual accumulation of experience—in other words, trial and error. Information concerning some of the specific loans made or not made during the Bank's formative years will illustrate this process.

Early Lending

Not much space will be devoted here to the early reconstruction loans. They were mentioned in Chapter 3 and are discussed again in the analysis of program lending and local expenditure financing in Chapter 9. It should be remembered, however, that when the working party on the 1947 loan to France first met, nobody really knew where to begin, what kinds of questions to ask, and what sort of investigation to make. Neither the project approach nor the elements in analyzing creditworthiness had been developed. "The economic report on France . . . laid its stress not on financial resources or specific export prospects, but on the French 'collective will to recover.' "[5]

President McCloy's recommendation to the executive directors concerning the prospects for repayment of the 1947 loan to the Netherlands used language reminiscent of the promotional literature put out by travel agencies:

The Dutch people are skilled and hard-working. . . . The Government of the country rests on solid democratic principles and has given proof of stability and wise administration.

The Netherlands have never defaulted on their internal or external debt and have in fact redeemed some of their debts before maturity. . . . The excellence of their debt record, together with their long tradition as a trading and commercial nation make the Netherlands a good credit risk.[6]

The dispatch of a mission to France appeared unnecessary; the French mission in Washington was large enough and well enough informed to answer

4. International Bank for Reconstruction and Development, *Fifth Annual Report, 1949–1950,* pp. 7–17.

5. Richard H. Demuth, "A Look Backward," in *The First Fifteen Years,* IBRD, Personnel Division (June 1961), p. 7.

6. Recommendations of the President to the Executive Directors on the Netherlands loan application, R-121, Aug. 6, 1947, p. 8.

most of the Bank's questions. Nor was a mission sent to the Netherlands during loan negotiations, though one was sent to Denmark. If France as an old and responsible hand in international capital markets had ever expected a more favorable rate of interest from the Bank than would be available to newcomers, those hopes had been dashed by the Bank's decision of November 1946 to treat all borrowers alike at any given time with respect to rates of interest. What kind of collateral should the World Bank seek? The security to be provided by a government, it was decided, would be a pledge of its full faith and credit plus a promise that no future creditor would be able to obtain specific security unless the Bank were secured pari passu. This was the so-called negative pledge, which was to become a characteristic feature of the Bank's loan agreements.

The question of subsequent supervision—how to assure that Bank loans financed only the goods they were intended to finance and that the goods purchased reached the proper locations—presented itself in a different light in the case of general-purpose reconstruction loans involving 100 thousand or more purchases of items needed throughout the economy than for specific-purpose project loans involving equipment for a particular site. To would-be borrowers the idea that the Bank would itself want to check on the receipt and use of Bank-financed goods was an unwelcome departure from the practices of pre-war international finance. It was, however, a logical extension of requirements of the Lend-Lease Administration and the United Nations Relief and Rehabilitation Administration. Despite the distress it caused the French negotiating team, a small "supervision office" was subsequently set up in Paris. Similar offices to supervise the other reconstruction loans were established in The Hague and Copenhagen, and so-called "end-use supervision" became an accepted feature of lending by the World Bank.

In deciding that its Western European borrowers were satisfactory credit risks, the management of the Bank showed commendable courage. The assessment of repayment prospects, a basic activity to which the Bank perforce has devoted a great deal of time and energy, is not an exact science. It involves subjective as well as objective considerations. Political and psychological risks and uncertainties must be weighed along with economic and financial data (which may have the appearance of precision but in fact be irrelevant or highly inaccurate). Creditworthiness has consequently been a matter of controversy both within the Bank and between the Bank and its borrowers.

Should applicants already in default on outstanding debt be regarded ipso facto as poor risks and potential recidivists? This issue presented itself in connection with the Bank's very first loan to a less developed country.

The First Development Loan (Chile)

When McCloy, Black, and Garner came to the World Bank, the $40 million loan application from Chile was part of their inheritance. It included hydroelectric, forestry, harbor, urban and suburban transport, and railway projects. It raised a number of difficult questions and had been discussed at numerous working party and loan committee meetings. What were the Bank's obligations with respect to Chile's wish that its projects be considered as a package? How adequate were the technical and economic justifications and supporting data? Should Chile's defaults on outstanding pre–World War II bond issues disqualify it as a borrower from the World Bank?

In connection with the Chilean loan application, the executive directors had already approved a progress report which had addressed itself to the first and third of these issues. They had readily agreed that, in a loan application comprised of several independent projects, the staff of the Bank should be free to consider the projects separately on their individual merits. As for outstanding debts, the board had agreed that the Bank must take these into account, should give careful consideration to the attitude of the applicant and its desire to meet its obligations, but should not become an intermediary between the applicant and the holders of its foreign bonds and should not consider defaults of themselves to be a bar to Bank lending.[7] The staff thereafter concerned itself primarily with the many technical aspects of the Chilean loan application. The Chilean proposal, according to Simon Aldewereld, had arrived

in a book handsomely bound in black morocco leather, and I remember that one of the senior people in the Bank . . . expressed a belief that we would be able to make a loan for the project in about a week. But when we opened the book, we found that what we had was really more of an idea about a project, not a project sufficiently prepared that its needs for finance, equipment and manpower resources could be accurately forecast.

We found it necessary to visit Chile several times to get information about the project and its economic setting . . . . [Before the loan was finally made], members of the Bank staff had made suggestions about the financial plan, had contributed to the economic analysis of the scheme, had advised on changes of engineering and had helped study measures for improving the organization of the company which was to carry out the scheme.[8]

The debt issue grew to be a major problem after McCloy became the Bank's second president. Until 1931 Chile for more than a hundred years had

7. Secretary's Report, R-55, approved by the executive directors Dec. 10, 1946.
8. S. Aldewereld, *The Challenge of Development Aid,* address to the Swedish International Development Authority, Stockholm, May 6, 1966, p. 5.

never failed to meet its foreign indebtedness. In 1931, though, it suspended service on its foreign debt and continued the suspension until 1935—hardly surprising in view of the fact that debt service obligations at the depth of the Great Depression exceeded in absolute terms the total value of Chile's exports. A catastrophic earthquake in 1939 interrupted the repayment arrangements that had been made. As of December 31, 1945, the equivalent of nearly $300 million in dollar, sterling, and Swiss franc bonds issued between 1885 and 1930 (and bearing interest at rates of 4.5 to 8 percent) was in default. Unscrupulous lenders as well as major disasters (the Great Depression and the earthquake) were in large measure responsible for the situation.

The Export-Import Bank of Washington had already loaned Chile more than $75 million since 1939 for steel mill equipment, railway equipment, and other items needed for its economic development program and indeed had received repayments totaling $13 million. Yet when the Chilean delegation came to see Black soon after he had become U.S. executive director, to ask whether he would support the loan application that had been so strongly supported by his predecessor, he told them he would be unwilling to do so until they had made a settlement on their debt. "We never stated what the settlement was to be," said Black. "We just said it would have to be a settlement that was approved by the bond-holders' committee. We had to be satisfied that the defaulting country had the will to settle and was prepared to make a reasonable settlement."[9]

Garner and McCloy took the same line. Emilio Collado, the former U.S. executive director, who subsequently served briefly as a consultant to the Bank, wrote a long memorandum to McCloy in April 1947 that reiterated his own "strong personal conviction, having followed the Chilean debt situation for more than 10 years in my official capacities in the Government of the United States and being fully aware of the development of U.S. Government policy in this respect, that there is nothing in the Chilean debt situation which should prejudice the granting by the International Bank of development loans in the moderate amounts now under discussion."[10]

Vice President Garner, however, a few weeks later told the Chilean negotiators that "the most difficult policy problem facing the Bank is where borrowers are in default on previous debt. . . . The present management

9. Eugene R. Black, "Oral History," p. 5. Black always recognized that bondholders' conditions could be unreasonable, in which event it would be absurd for the Bank to require settlements satisfactory to them. What he sought was not a settlement at any cost, but a reasonable offer by the defaulting country to settle.

10. Office memorandum of April 8, 1947, from Collado to McCloy. It was clear by then that the first loan to Chile, if made, would be for much less than $40 million.

does not see how the Bank can make loans in the face of widespread dissatisfaction in financial and investment circles to whom the Bank must sell its own bonds. The principle applies, of course, not only to Chile but equally to all potential borrowers."[11]

The Bank announced two loans to Chile on the day after the settlement between Chile and its foreign bondholders had been reached. The first was a twenty-year $13.5 million loan at 4.5 percent interest to the Corporación de Fomento de la Producción, a government corporation for development, and the Empresa Nacional de Electricidad SA for power plant equipment; the second, a six-and-a-half-year, $2.5 million loan at 3.75 percent to the Fomento for the import of agricultural machinery. Both loans were guaranteed by the Republic of Chile.

The Bank's press release also reported that Chile had for several months been conducting negotiations with groups representing foreign bondholders in the United States, Great Britain, and Switzerland.

These negotiations culminated in the public announcement on March 24, 1948 by the Chilean Government of the basis of an offer of a new debt readjustment plan. The Foreign Bondholders Protective Council, Inc. of the United States have stated that this plan, when approved by the Chilean congress, will be recommended to bondholders. It is understood that similar arrangements have been made with the Council of Foreign Bondholders of Great Britain and the Association Suisse des Banquiers.[12]

The policy of not lending to countries in default on outstanding loans made the Bank vulnerable to the charge of being a bill collector for Wall Street, unsympathetic to the dilemmas of poor countries. The policy was applied even-handedly throughout the world (Greece, Yugoslavia, and elsewhere), but the initial victims were mostly in Latin America (Brazil, Peru, Bolivia, Ecuador, Costa Rica) because of the relatively high proportion of Latin American nations to total Bank membership at the time and the number of defaulters in that region. The Latin Americans

initially got pretty mad at us because we talked about defaulted debt. They regarded this as past, the sins of their fathers. . . . The world did throw a depression at them, and why should they have to be bothering about that now? . . .

There was a conference . . . in Santiago, and I was sent there. . . . The President of Chile delivered a stinging attack on the Bank. He said that Chile went to the Bank with her desperate needs for development, and did he receive a sympathetic reception? No, he did not. Did anybody try to understand their aspirations? No, they did not. . . . The Bank started talking to them immediately about $170

11. Notes in Bank files on meeting of May 21, 1947, of Garner and Burland (for the Bank) with Pedregal, Vergara, Santa Cruz, and Levine (for Chile).
12. IBRD, Press release, (March 25, 1948).

million or so worth of debt which had been in default since the depression. Is this helping Chile? But because there was nobody else to whom they could turn, they settled the debt. [They got a loan for $16 million.] Is this a quid pro quo for our sacrifices?[13]

Despite Chile's initial annoyance, some of those who had been most annoyed—according to the management of the Bank—later became proud of having reached a settlement and grateful to the Bank for having pushed the government so vigorously in this direction.

For subsequent supervision of the Chilean loans, the establishment of an office in Santiago similar to those set up in Europe to supervise the general purpose loans would have been inappropriate. The alternatives of stationing a Bank man at each project site or relying entirely on written reports were rejected in favor of a compromise solution: reports of various kinds at specified intervals from borrowers to Bank headquarters, plus periodic visits to project sites by members of the Bank staff to check the accuracy of the reports and discuss current and emerging problems. For project loans,

we had to keep informed about progress on all aspects of the project, whether they were financed with our money or not. We had to keep track of the placing of orders, of any delay in manufacture or delivery of equipment, and progress . . . in training men who were going to use that equipment, and at the same time keep ourselves informed of the financial aspects of all these different things.[14]

Early Lending to Other Latin American Countries

It became clear that electric power projects, especially in Latin America, were in a more advanced stage of study and planning than other types of projects. As a consequence, Bank loans during the years immediately following the four reconstruction loans were predominantly for power development. The technical staff of the Bank was small, and judgment as to the suitability of the first four projects in Latin America rested largely on technical data submitted by prospective borrowers. The Bank's principal emphasis was on prospects for repayment.

After a long period of unsettled relations with foreign investors, Mexico had, in the Bank's view, made a decent effort to reestablish her external credit

13. Harold Larsen, "Oral History," p. 16. (Larsen was accompanying Eugene Black.) An Associated Press dispatch of February 21, 1951, from Santiago, carried in the *New York Journal of Commerce* and elsewhere, makes it clear that the speech in question was President Gabriel Gonzalez Videla's welcoming speech to delegates to the twelfth session of the UN Economic and Social Council. The dispatch reported that Chile's president "demanded that the World Bank relax its strict policies in granting aid to underdeveloped countries" and alleged that "the World Bank showed 'a notorious tendency' to ignore requests for loans toward economic development."

14. Hugh B. Ripman, "Oral History," pp. 5–6.

and attract foreign capital. "The Bank therefore concluded that, while investment in Mexico was not free from risks, the situation was such as to justify the financing requested."[15] The technical report of the Bank's engineering adviser, M. J. Madigan, on the two power projects in Mexico for which $34.1 million was loaned in January 1949 read as follows:

I visited Mexico several times during the last year, and made inspections of the properties of the Mexican Light and Power Company and the Federal Electricity Commission. I checked over the proposed programs of expansion and am satisfied that they are reasonable and in line with good engineering practice. The staffs of both the Mexican Light and Power Company and the Commission are competent and I feel sure can carry out the program proposed.

The first loan ($24.1 million) was made to finance the purchase by the Federal Electricity Commission of equipment for completing new power-generating stations and transmission lines. The second loan ($10 million) was made to enable an official financing institution, Nacional Financiera, and the Federal Electricity Commission to finance a loan to the Mexican Light and Power Company for part of the cost of equipment needed in carrying out a program for the expansion of electric power generating and distributing facilities. A reorganization of the capital structure of "Mexlight" (a private corporation) was made a condition for further assistance from the Bank.[16]

15. IBRD, *Fourth Annual Report, 1948–1949,* p. 18. In addition to other sins, Mexico in its 1947 application to the Bank for help on a series of projects (of which the electric power proposals were judged most fundamental and most nearly ready for financing) had distressed the management of the Bank by presupposing the availability of Bank financing for substantial local currency requirements as well as for foreign exchange. In July 1948, it put itself in the bad graces of the International Monetary Fund by suspending a fixed parity for the peso and commencing to operate on a fluctuating exchange rate on the ground that the government did not wish to establish a new par value until it became clearer what that value should be. Although the new par value was not fixed until June 1949, the Bank management was willing to proceed with its initial loans on the basis of the October 1948 announcement by the Mexican minister of finance that his government intended "to balance the budget, to limit public works, to maintain credit restrictions, and to fix a new parity for the peso in consultation with the International Monetary Fund."

16. Mexlight had applied to the Bank for a long-term loan considerably larger than the $10 million, one-year loan obtained on January 6, 1949. However, in a letter dated December 31, 1948, President McCloy had informed Mexlight of the Bank's intention to negotiate a long-term loan of approximately $26 million for the purpose of refunding the short-term loan and financing further foreign exchange expenditures by Mexlight, provided that during 1949 Mexlight completed a reorganization satisfactory to the Bank. (Secretary's Report, R-202, Jan. 3, 1949: Proposed Loans to Nacional Financiera and Comisión Federal de Electricidad, Report and Recommendations of the President to the Executive Directors.) The $26 million loan to Mexlight was approved on April 28, 1950. In August 1950, the U.S. Export-Import Bank, to the distress of the World Bank, extended the $150 million line of credit to Mexico discussed in Chapter 15, below.

Although it did not become an established policy of the Bank to include rate covenants in loan agreements until some years later, the Bank in 1949 did obtain an assurance from the Mexican government in connection with its first loans to the Mexican Light and Power Company that the latter would be authorized to charge reasonable rates—by which the Bank meant rates sufficient to provide a reasonable rate of return to the company. The assurances were not very productive of results, and this influenced the later decision of the Bank to ask Mexico to cooperate in a study of Mexico's long-term power requirements and of a system of rate regulation that might be incorporated into law.[17]

Thus began a relationship with the power sector in Mexico that was to lead by June 30, 1971, to the approval of ten loans totaling approximately $600 million for expansion of the Mexican power system and to make the total net amount of Bank loans to Mexico as of mid-1971 ($1.053 billion) larger than that to any other member nation. (We are speaking here of Bank loans, not Bank loans plus IDA credits. On the latter basis, India and Pakistan rank first and second.)

Three weeks after announcing its first loans to Mexico, the Bank announced the loan of $75 million to the Brazilian Traction Light and Power Company, Ltd., a Canadian corporation, to finance most of the foreign exchange costs of an expansion of the hydroelectric power and telephone facilities of the company's Brazilian subsidiaries. It was a complex loan, in the negotiation of which the Bank's lawyers played a prominent role. It was also the first loan to include nondollar currencies in significant amounts.[18]

Shortly thereafter, work began on an ambitious development program for Brazil under the aegis of a Joint Brazil–United States Economic Development Commission, of which the U.S. member, J. Burke Knapp, was a high-ranking Bank economist who had been given a leave of absence to serve in that capacity. The bulk of the external finance to carry out the development program prepared by the commission was expected to come from the World Bank.

Brazil soon found itself in serious financial trouble, however, which led the Bank to question its creditworthiness and go slow on lending. This in turn led Brazil to allege that the Bank had defaulted on a commitment to it. A

17. See Chapter 8, below.
18. According to a Mexican economist who was a World Bank official at the time and participated in the studies and negotiations, "The Bank negotiated with the company even before it consulted the Brazilian Government, which was to guarantee the credit." Victor L. Urquidi, *The Challenge of Development in Latin America* (Praeger, 1964) p. 57.

tension built up that affected the Bank's relations with Brazil for many years and contributed to another tension of the 1950s—between the World Bank and the Export-Import Bank of the United States. Nevertheless, by mid-1971, Brazil had borrowed almost $1 billion from the Bank and ranked (after Mexico and India) as its third largest borrower.[19]

The power loan in late 1949 to an autonomous government agency in El Salvador (the Comisión Ejecutiva Hidroeléctrica del Rio Lempa) had several noteworthy features. It became one of the handful of World Bank projects that provided the basis for a series of stimulating generalizations by Albert O. Hirschman about the differential developmental effects of specific types of projects.[20] The feature that will be commented on at this point, however, is the type of technical assistance the Bank gave in financing the local-currency costs of the project. Although it appeared that sufficient capital funds were available in El Salvador, the limited local capital market provided no means for readily mobilizing such funds for investment.

At the request of the Salvadorean authorities the Bank made available the services of its Director of Marketing to advise and assist in the creation and distribution of a local bond issue in the amount of . . . $5,240,000. The issue was fully subscribed within a few days. Investors included financial institutions, business enterprises and individuals. A broad distribution of the bonds among individual investors was facilitated by a group of local commercial banks who underwrote a portion of the issue for redistribution to their clients.[21]

El Salvador also appears to be an example of a country that strenuously resisted the Bank's insistence on increasing its power rates but subsequently changed its attitude. In the first loan to El Salvador there was no rate covenant, and rather than increase rates, the government made funds available to the government-owned power company on concessionary terms to meet the company's operating deficits and its requirements for expansion. In its next power loan to El Salvador, the Bank obtained a rate covenant providing for a return of 8 percent on assets in operation. When another loan was subsequently applied for, the Bank indicated that it might agree to a lower rate of return, but the company asked that the 8 percent figure remain unchanged since it found that the covenant enabled it to operate without a government subsidy.

Another Latin American member, Colombia, submitted an application in July 1948 for a loan of $78 million. The application merely listed the

19. For more on the Bank and Brazil, see especially Chapter 19, below.
20. See Albert O. Hirschman, *Development Projects Observed* (Brookings Institution, 1967).
21. IBRD, *Fifth Annual Report, 1949–1950,* p. 25.

amounts desired for broad categories of investments, such as railroads, high-ways, power plants, agricultural equipment, and ports. In submitting this kind of shopping list, Colombia was by no means unique. The Europeans had submitted what were essentially shopping lists, and many of the initial applications from less developed countries were based on no more than "the existence, within the same national borders, of a desert and a waterfall and a fervent desire to marry the two, whatever the impediments."[22]

The Bank almost immediately sent a mission to review Colombia's fiscal and economic position. The mission "stressed the importance of balancing the national budget and of action to comply with recommendations of the International Monetary Fund with respect to reorganization of the country's foreign exchange controls and establishment of a new par value for its currency."[23] Legislation designed to accomplish these ends and authorizing the Colombian government to guarantee Bank loans was enacted. In late 1948 the Bank sent an "operational mission" to the country to select some specific projects for which the Bank might consider loans. The mission report recommended loans for a soda ash plant, three hydroelectric projects, and an agricultural machinery project.

Referring to that report, McCloy informed the Colombian ambassador in Washington that the Bank was prepared in principle to proceed with loans for the agricultural machinery and one of the hydroelectric projects (La Insula). The exact amount of the loan would depend on the receipt of further information. McCloy's letter also mentioned the organization of an economic survey mission to assist Colombia in preparing a comprehensive development program.[24] Except for loans for agricultural machinery and the hydro-electric project, all further borrowing should be postponed until after the economic survey mission had produced a report that would indicate priorities among projects worthy of consideration.

The Colombian ambassador promptly informed the Bank that his government did not want to postpone consideration of the other projects that the operational mission had commended to the Bank. The Bank acceded to Colombia's desire to keep the dialogue alive but insisted on the need for more data. The result was approval of a small loan ($5 million) in mid-1949 for the importation of agricultural machinery, and approval in late 1950 of two small power loans and in early 1951 of a highway construction and rehabilitation loan.[25]

22. "The International Bank," *The Times* (London), Feb. 4, 1949.
23. IBRD, *Fourth Annual Report, 1948–1949*, p. 20.
24. See Chapter 10, below.
25. See also Chapter 19, below.

In addition to the light the Colombian case sheds on the evolution of the Bank's project appraisal and negotiating techniques, the Bank's willingness to regard the loan for agricultural machinery as a specific project is noteworthy. Along with the similar earlier loan to Chile for agricultural machinery and the Bank's first Asian loan—to India in 1949 for railway rehabilitation—it was offered as proof that in project lending

the Bank has not dedicated itself solely to the financing of what might be called a single monumental affair. For example, in the case of India the Bank's loan for the rehabilitation of the railways did not involve a specific project in the monumental sense, but did involve a project providing for the purchase of equipment for the rehabilitation of the Indian railways. The Bank was prepared to regard that as a specific project.

In Colombia the Bank financed the importation of a quantity of agricultural machinery. It was prepared to regard that also as a specific project, although the amount of agricultural machinery, the importation of which the Bank financed, was only a part of the total amount of agricultural equipment which Colombia imported.[26]

First Loans in Asia and the Middle East

In contrast to the rather superficial technical appraisals that preceded some of the early power loans to Latin America, a much more adequate appraisal was made by a member of the Bank's staff in connection with a carefully prepared power project for India announced in April 1950. This project called for the financing of a portion of the cost of the first stage of a long-range scheme to develop the resources of the Damodar Valley. His technical report reached the Bank's board of directors along with the loan documents. It appraised technical aspects of the project and in addition, the market for power, the cost of production, and the financial aspects and organization of the government corporation that would construct and operate the enterprise. It reported that the corporation lacked a chief engineer and that its technical staff was weak. As a consequence, the Bank made it a condition of the loan that a chief engineer be appointed and a board of consultants formed to supervise the construction of the project.

The first Bank loans for agriculture, as has already been indicated, were small ones for the importation of tractors and agricultural equipment into Chile, Colombia, and India and (not previously mentioned) for grain storage facilities in Turkey. The first loan for irrigation—$18 million to Thailand in

26. W. A. B. Iliff, "Lending Policies and Procedures of the International Bank," in IBRD, Fifth Annual Meeting of the Board of Governors, *Summary Proceedings*, Nov. 30, 1950, p. 38.

1950—included some navigational benefits, but its main justification was that an assured water supply would be provided to a large rice-producing area in the central plain of Thailand.

Iraq, the first Middle Eastern country to obtain a World Bank loan, was added to the list of borrowers in mid-1950, when a flood control project, important for the protection of Baghdad, was approved. According to Raymond A. Wheeler, who had come to the Bank on March 1, 1949, to fill the newly created post of engineering adviser and who had lived in Baghdad during World War II, the city had long suffered from damaging floods.

The Bank made a loan for the construction of works to give permanent protection to the city of Baghdad and the surrounding area by the construction of a dam across the Tigris River, about 50 miles above Baghdad, at which point excess flood waters were diverted through the canal [an inlet channel which was part of the works] to a large uninhabited and barren depression called Wadi-Tharthar. Besides the benefit provided by these works in protecting the city of Baghdad from the flood overflows, there is another important benefit resulting from them in that the severe dust storms that originated in the Wadi-Tharthar will be prevented.[27]

Iraq's creditworthiness was based entirely on its oil resources. Because of the narrow base of this cornucopia-shaped source of revenue, the Bank wanted security for its loan and felt justified in turning to oil royalties. The loan agreement accordingly provided that Iraq would assign to the Bank its right to receive oil royalties from its concessions to certain petroleum companies. The Bank agreed, however, that Iraq could continue to receive royalties directly from the companies so long as it made principal and interest payments to the Bank on schedule.[28]

As far as the oil companies were concerned, principally the Iraq Petroleum Company, Ltd., this was the worst of both worlds. If they refused to pay the Bank when asked to, they would be in legal trouble for violating an agreement. If they consented, they would be denying the government of Iraq royalties it would otherwise receive and jeopardizing their future relations with that country. This was the first (and only) case of a demand by the Bank for security from *a government* that was enforceable against a third party. Fortu-

27. Raymond A. Wheeler, "Oral History," pp. 3–4. At the Bank, Wheeler had succeeded Michael J. Madigan, whose firm had been employed by the Bank as its consultant on engineering activities. The diversionary canal has been used several times, and Baghdad has had no serious flood damage since completion of the project. As of mid-1971, however, Wadi-Tharthar was nearly full and in danger of becoming useless unless an exit were constructed.

28. 155, United Nations *Treaty Series,* pp. 298, 330, 332. "International Bank for Reconstruction and Development and Iraq," Loan Agreement, Article VIII, section 11, and Indenture of Assignment, Article II, sections 1–3.

nately, despite the initial uneasiness of both the borrowing government and the petroleum companies, the venture ended without mishap. The loan was repaid ahead of schedule.

Ethiopia

In September 1950, three months after signing the loan agreement with Iraq, the Bank announced two loans to Ethiopia (its first in Africa): $5 million for a road program and $2 million in foreign exchange for a new development bank. Ethiopia's original application, received in late 1949, had been modest compared with those of some of the other early borrowers—$25 million for fifteen projects, including transportation, communications, agricultural development, improvement of water supplies, and assorted industrial undertakings in such fields as meat packing, textiles, chemicals, leather, and ceramics.

The Bank sent a mission, which concluded that priority should be given to highway improvement, the development of telecommunications, and the establishment of an industrial and agricultural development bank. The mission noted that in the 1930s, during the Italian occupation of Ethiopia, Italy had spent very large sums of money

to build a pretty grandiose road system, but for lack of maintenance the highway system was practically impassable. Large sections were washed out, and it was impossible to go from one city to another and be sure of when you were going to arrive. This impressed us with the need for having an organization that could not only build highways but could maintain them and carry out a sensible highway program. So we suggested the establishment of what has since become the Imperial Highway Authority.[29]

The first telecommunications loan to Ethiopia was made in early 1951. Telephone and telegraph services in Ethiopia at the time were poor, even by the standards of other less developed nations that were then members of the Bank. The system had been built in the years 1936–41, in part with military equipment of inadequate capacity, which, moreover, had been poorly maintained. Ethiopia wanted $1.5 million to replace and rehabilitate equipment that was on the verge of breakdown and to begin a program of expansion.

The telephones were then under the administration of the government. They had no idea even what their gross receipts were on telephones, much less any of

29. Orvis A. Schmidt, "Oral History," p. 14. "In consultation with the Bank, the Government has selected for the Authority a management of experienced administrators and technicians from the United States Bureau of Public Roads. An important function of the Authority is to train Ethiopian personnel in highway work." IBRD, *Sixth Annual Report, 1950–1951*, p. 18.

the other facts that were needed. So again we suggested that some type of telephone organization be set up, to which they agreed, and we then hired and paid for . . . a group of experts to go in and in effect prepare the project—prepare the engineering plans and the program that would be carried out with our loan to bring the telephone system back into operation and keep it that way. Again, you had to make a management contract. . . . In this case, they did it with the Swedish telephone authority.[30]

The loan agreement provided that, before the loan could become effective (that is, before disbursements from loan proceeds would be permitted), the government would establish a telecommunications authority having a charter satisfactory to the Bank and arrange for a management that would also be satisfactory to that institution. The Bank, which had discovered a penchant in Latin America and elsewhere for generous governmental use of publicly owned facilities without a "proper" allocation of charges, provided further in the loan agreement with Ethiopia that the Ethiopian government would pay for its use of the facilities of the telecommunications authority.[31]

Development Finance Companies: An Innovation

The Bank's support for, and willingness to finance as specific projects, private development banks or development finance companies in Mexico and Turkey, as well as Ethiopia, may well be the most innovational activity in development financing during the Bank's early years. These facilities to meet the needs for long-term financing in moderate amounts on the part of private industry in less developed countries grew primarily out of a visit to Turkey by Bank Vice President Garner in the spring of 1949. As Garner well knew, those who were most likely to invigorate the climate for private enterprise in less developed countries were the ones who wanted to establish privately owned manufacturing or processing plants. At the same time they were least likely to seek Bank financing for fear that the governmental guarantee of repayment of both principal and interest required by the Bank would subject them to closer scrutiny and interference from their own government than would otherwise be the case. Governments, for their part, would be reluctant to criticize this hesitancy because a lack of proposals from the private sector

30. Schmidt, "Oral History," p. 15.

31. The telecommunications board got off to a slow and faltering start. Its autonomy was seriously threatened several times. But twenty years later, after three more loans, persistent prodding from the Bank, and steady support from the Swedish Telephone Authority, the corporation was operating efficiently and profitably under Ethiopian management and was expanding telecommunication facilities at a rate of 12 percent a year without government subsidization.

would relieve the government of charges of favoritism for having guaranteed the borrowings of particular private groups within its borders.

Thus, partly because of the government-guarantee requirement, partly because of the inability of the Bank to make equity investments, and partly because of the impracticability of using the resources of a large international agency to investigate applications for small loans, the Bank was ill equipped to assist small and medium-sized private undertakings. A local institution that could carry out the necessary financial and technical investigations and make loans to, or equity investments in, private domestic enterprises provided an answer to these difficulties. In Istanbul the institution was the Industrial Development Bank of Turkey. The Turkish financial community subscribed equity capital, the Central Bank of Turkey provided additional capital on a loan basis, and the World Bank in October 1950 provided a $9 million loan, as well as the technical assistance necessary to launch the Industrial Development Bank.

More will be said later about the care and feeding of these institutions and the contributions they have made to development. There are by now some forty that have been assisted financially or technically by the World Bank Group. The objective here has simply been to illustrate the flexibility of the specific project concept, even during the Bank's early years of lending.[32]

Other Early Lending

The Bank's forays into the field of program lending for development included a series of loans to Australia that began with $100 million in 1950, $70 million to Belgium and the Belgian Congo in 1951 to assist in financing the first two years of a ten-year development program for the Congo, and modest loans in 1951 and 1953 to the Cassa per il Mezzogiorno for the development of southern Italy. They illustrate another breakthrough in the Bank's conception of development financing. Though the Bank found itself legally and administratively able to engage in this type of financing during its formative years, program lending was not destined to become an important activity during the Bank's first quarter century.[33]

In collaboration with the UN Economic Commission for Europe (ECE) and the Food and Agriculture Organization of the UN, and as a contribution to the restoration of East–West trade in Europe at a time when far stronger forces were working against it, the Bank spent a good deal of time and energy between 1947 and 1949 negotiating a complicated timber loan, which proved

32. See Chapter 11, below.
33. See Chapter 9, below.

to be a precedent for nothing whatsoever. Softwood and pitprops were needed for coal mines, and Western Europe's demand for coal was urgent. The timber committee of the ECE concluded that five timber exporting countries—Austria, Czechoslovakia, Finland, Poland, and Yugoslavia—could substantially increase their production and exports of sawed softwood and pitprops if certain equipment could be obtained from Western Europe and the United States. But how would the Eastern European borrowers get the dollars to repay the Bank for American-made equipment?

Representatives of the Bank came to Geneva in 1948 to help work out practical arrangements. By the summer of 1949, the project appeared to be shaping up as follows: The Bank would make loans to the timber exporting countries to finance the dollar purchases of equipment (approximately $8 million all together); equipment from Western Europe would be obtained by other agreements between the countries involved; the timber exporting countries would agree to export larger quantities of timber at reasonable prices, provided the necessary equipment were obtained; and the Western European timber importers would enter into timber payments agreements with the borrowers, under which the importing countries would pay dollars to the Bank for a sufficient part of the timber imported by them to assure repayment of the loans.

Austria and Poland in due course advised the Bank that they did not need loans for this purpose. Czechoslovakia withdrew its application after the communist coup of February 1948 because of difficulty in working out payments agreements with the importing countries. Yugoslavia, on the other hand, had ruptured its relations with the Soviet Union in 1948 and was desperately eager to develop its trade with the West. In October 1949, the Federal People's Republic of Yugoslavia received its first loan from the Bank—$2.7 million at 3 percent to be repaid in full by September 30, 1951. A loan of $2.3 million was made to Finland at the same time, and on the same terms.

These were the only truly short-term loans ever made by the Bank. They were consequently the first loans to be repaid in full. Though successful in a technical sense, the time and effort that went into their negotiation were probably out of proportion to the benefits obtained by any of the parties involved.

In the less developed world the Bank found lending for electric power development and transportation most congenial. The lending for railway rehabilitation and expansion in India that began in 1949 continued during the 1950s and 1960s and as of mid-1971 had resulted in more than $600 million in loans and credits. Thailand's railway system was also in bad shape at the close of World War II. During the war the country had been occupied by the Japanese, and its rail system became the primary bombing target of the allies. Twenty-eight bridges, including the three largest in the country, twenty-two principal stations, almost all the repair shops, 50 percent of the rolling stock, and much other equipment had been completely destroyed or lost. Postwar efforts to revitalize the system had been hampered by poor organization and by shortages of funds, material, and trained personnel.

The railways were run as one of the government departments; their accounts and finances were inextricably mingled with those of the government as a whole. The director general of the railways reported to the minister of communications and received instructions also from other cabinet members. The staff was subject to civil service regulations and was poorly paid. Procurement of equipment and materials was a long and complicated process.

The consultant retained by the Bank to appraise the project proposed by Thailand early in 1950 thought it would be impossible for the railway as it was then organized to operate efficiently or economically. He recommended that it be reconstituted as an autonomous entity and run on commercial principles, with its employees not under civil service.

As part of the project agreement, the government promised to establish an autonomous agency that would be responsible for the management, operation, maintenance, and development of the railways. The State Railways of Thailand was established in June 1951, and the first loan administration report (May 1953) said that railway finances were on a sounder basis and earnings had risen by virtue of a 20 percent increase in passenger fares and a 100 or 200 percent increase in freight rates. Furthermore, a modern accounting system had been established, and the consulting firm that had been chosen to design the workshops at Makkasan had submitted its report to the government.[34]

Ports as well as railways became beneficiaries of Bank loans to the transport sector. Frequently the Bank prescribed as a condition of the loan a remedy similar to its prescription for the railways—establishment of an autonomous port authority, such as Thai Port (for Bangkok). As might be expected, road programs and highway development were also considered "naturals" for Bank loans in cases where they appeared to make economic sense.[35]

Early Nonlending

The loan negotiations mentioned in the section above normally culminated in what at this point in our narrative can be called a happy ending: the signature of a loan agreement. The amount of the loan may have been much

34. For more on the Bank and Thailand, see Chapter 19, below.
35. See Chapter 20, below, for a retrospective look at the Bank Group's work in the transport sector.

smaller than that requested by the borrower. The negotiations may have been longer-lasting, more strenuous, and more comprehensive and demanding than the borrower expected. Nevertheless, a project or program was launched and a relationship established that could, and in most cases would, lead to further loans when both parties understood each other better.

Not all the negotiations followed this pattern. Among the exceptions were the large reconstruction loans for Poland and Czechoslovakia, referred to in Chapter 3, and the loans asked for by Iran and the Philippines.

Poland and Czechoslovakia

The Polish government first approached the Bank in the autumn of 1946 with a request for $600 million. The Bank's resources at the time were obviously inadequate for a reconstruction loan of that size. It was thought, however, that one in the neighborhood of $125 million for rehabilitation of the Polish coal industry might be possible. Since coal was desperately needed for the reconstruction of Western Europe, Poland, by increasing its exports, could earn the foreign exchange with which to pay interest and principal on a loan. In the spring of 1947, therefore, Poland submitted a memorandum requesting a coal loan in the amount of $128.5 million.

Bank officials naturally wondered whether Poland's relations with Russia were such that Poland might find itself unable to devote the necessary resources to repaying a loan from an institution toward which the USSR was hostile. They considered the risk worth taking and negotiated in good faith. An IBRD fact-finding group went to Poland in the summer of 1947 and concluded that a $45 million, rather short-term loan could quickly result in a substantial increase in coal output. The Polish government was clearly unhappy about this considerable comedown from the $600 million asked for a year earlier. The Polish government tried to nudge the figure back toward $125 million, and it stoutly resisted the idea that it should repay in full within a short span of time.

Negotiations continued. McCloy himself visited Warsaw and returned impressed with the potentialities of the Polish coal industry and eager to make a loan. By mid-1948, however, it had become clear to the Bank management that its largest stockholder, the United States government, would not grant export licenses for mining machinery to Poland and would instruct its executive director to vote against the loan if it were presented to the board for approval. Poland and Czechoslovakia, initially profoundly interested in participating in the Marshall Plan, had not been free to do so, and relations between them and the United States were growing progressively more strained.

As soon as Eugene Black, the U.S. executive director, became aware that he would have to vote against the coal loan to Poland, he conveyed that information to McCloy, who relayed the message to the Polish executive director, Leon Baranski. It was decided that the loan would not be presented to the board, and negotiations were suspended. The Bank, said the *Third Annual Report,*

is not unmindful of the importance of the economic development of its member countries in Europe which are not participants in ERP [the European Recovery Program, formal title of the Marshall Plan]. . . .

The Bank is fully cognizant of the injunction in its Articles of Agreement that its decisions shall be based only on economic considerations. Political tensions and uncertainties in or among its member countries, however, have a direct effect on economic and financial conditions in those countries and upon their credit position.[36]

Unable to obtain a loan and unable to participate constructively in the work of the Bank, Poland withdrew from the institution in 1950.

Negotiations with Czechoslovakia followed a parallel course. An application in the summer of 1946 for a reconstruction loan of $350 million was followed by prolonged and serious negotiations about a considerably smaller sum, but no loan agreement resulted. In addition, there was irreconcilable disagreement regarding payment of the unpaid 0.5 percent of the 2 percent capital subscription due the Bank from Czechoslovakia in gold or dollars. The executive directors in August 1951 ruled that Czechoslovakia was liable for the unpaid portion under Article II, section 8(a)(i) of the Articles of Agreement, according to which the payment was mandatory five years after the Bank began operations. Czechoslovakia maintained that the appropriate clause was Article II, section 8(a)(ii), in which no time period is specified. Czechoslovakia lost and was suspended from membership as of December 31, 1953. Its membership was formally terminated at the close of 1954.[37]

Iran and the Philippines

The long-drawn-out efforts of Iran to negotiate a loan represent another chapter in the chronicle of early loans that the Bank did not make. In 1946 Iran applied informally for a loan of $250 million for reconstruction and development. Negotiations dragged on for two or three years, with the Bank

---

36. IBRD, *Third Annual Report, 1947–1948*, p. 14.

37. As is usual in such cases, the argument was not simply a legal one and was complicated by grievances Czechoslovakia and the United States had against each other, grievances which may belong in a history of the cold war but need not be analyzed here.

requesting detailed economic and technical data that the Iranians were unable to supply. As a result of urging by the Bank, Iran established a Plan Organization as an autonomous agency of its government and hired a New York firm, Overseas Consultants, Incorporated (OCI), to assist in drawing up a development plan.

There were conflicting views as to whether Iran would need foreign aid for its development plan. OCI reported that revenues from oil exports could finance the bulk of public projects, although foreign financing would be needed in the private sector. This view was shared by the governor of the Bank of Iran. Other Iranian officials were eager to obtain World Bank financing, however, and in 1949 the Iranian government submitted a list of projects totaling $36 million to test the Bank's reaction. The Bank again indicated its willingness to lend to Iran when properly prepared projects were presented and also made clear that loans would be contingent upon broad-gauged economic reforms.

Vice President Garner visited Iran, the Bank seconded a staff member to the Plan Organization and sent an economic mission to the country. Meanwhile, relations between OCI and the government of Iran on the one hand, and between OCI and the Bank on the other, were becoming strained. Various Iranian officials objected to the transfer of power from the ministries to the Plan Organization and complained about OCI's fees. The Bank worried about the absence of an economist or financial expert on the OCI staff in Teheran and feared that OCI's efforts would not culminate in "finance-ready" projects. In January 1951 the contract between Iran and OCI was terminated, with OCI expressing frustration over the lack of accomplishment and charging that the Bank's failure to begin loan operations was an obstacle to the launching of the Plan.[38]

No concrete action emanated from the Bank's 1949 mission until August 1950, when the U.S. Export-Import Bank sent a mission to Iran. Within a matter of days the World Bank wired Teheran that it was prepared to lend $3 million to finance improvements at Khorramshahr Port (one of the projects on the $36 million list), but that discussions for further loans would be contingent upon economic reforms in Iran and the continued independence of the Plan Organization. When the Export-Import Bank announced a $25 million loan to Iran in the autumn of 1950, the Bank informed the U.S. State Department that it would not consider any loans beyond the $3 million port loan until a ceiling was placed on Export-Import Bank loans to Iran.

38. Overseas Consultants, Inc., "Overseas Consultants Withdraw from Iran," Press release (Jan. 24, 1951).

Later that year Iran turned down the $3 million loan for port improvement on grounds that it was politically unsupportable because the amount was too small. (Moreover, negotiations had dragged on for so long that the government had purchased all of the necessary equipment, and most of the port rehabilitation had been completed.) Iran then attempted to negotiate loans for two cement plants, which had also been on its list of projects. Negotiations again dragged on, with the Bank expressing doubts about the viability of the cement plants and insisting that essential economic reforms be implemented. The dispute over nationalization of the Anglo-Iranian Oil Company then intervened.[39] As the Bank's annual report for 1950–51 delicately phrased it, "Events in Iran since March 1951 have made it necessary for the Bank to wait until the situation has clarified sufficiently to enable the Bank to make a re-assessment of Iran's position."[40] When the Bank's report was being discussed at the UN Economic and Social Council in 1952, the Iranian delegate said, "This attitude of the Bank saddens us and causes us deep regret."[41] Not until January 1957 did the Bank make its first loan to Iran.

The failure of the Bank and the Philippines to enter into an early loan agreement appears to have been due in part to a conflict between the eagerness of the Philippines to get on with the physical job of reconstruction and development as rapidly as possible and the Bank's more measured, cautious pace and its emphasis on fundamental reforms in economic policy. The Philippines first approached the Bank for a loan in 1947, when they inquired about the possibility of financing for construction of a shipyard as part of a project for rehabilitating the Philippine coastal fleet. The government was also interested in loans for war-damaged infrastructure. The Bank sent a fact-finding mission (which the Philippine Republic hoped, and the Manila press rumored, would turn into a loan-negotiating mission).

The result of the mission was a letter to the government, in which the Bank stated that the country's reserve position was strong and that world markets were favorable for Philippine exports. Therefore, the Bank recommended that the Philippines spend a couple of years planning the most effective means for conserving foreign exchange, for channeling savings into capital investment, and for establishing priorities and drawing up projects. Then the government could apply for a Bank loan. The Bank was aware, however, of the

39. See Chapter 18, below.
40. IBRD, *Sixth Annual Report, 1950–1951*, p. 22.
41. English translation in the Bank files of the statement in French forwarded to President Black, June 25, 1952, by the Iranian delegation to the United Nations in New York. Iran, however, was also a source of despair and discouragement to the Bank; see George B. Baldwin, *Planning and Development in Iran* (Johns Hopkins Press, 1967).

Philippines' need for technical assistance in undertaking economic studies and project preparation, and it offered to help the government find technical consultants.

In the same letter the Bank suggested that the Philippine government might send a mission to Washington to discuss technical assistance priorities. This resulted in a technical mission from the Philippines, which, for several weeks during the summer of 1948, attended seminars in Washington on numerous topics, ranging from balance-of-payments problems to mineral resources to transport requirements. Again, the Phillippines hoped that the seminars would result in loan negotiations. (Much to the irritation of the Bank, the press in Manila frequently reported that a loan agreement was about to be signed.) But the Bank insisted that it wanted only to discuss Philippine development plans and needs. (Staff Loan Committee meetings stressed that while the Philippines was solvent at the time, many fiscal, economic, and monetary reforms were urgently needed before the Bank could consider extending a loan.)

In the summer of 1948 the Philippines submitted an application for loans for three hydroelectric projects and a chemical fertilizer plant. In November of that year President McCloy reportedly told the Philippine government that the Bank would consider a loan of up to $15 million for one or two hydroelectric projects, depending on the results of engineering and geological studies. Finally, in the summer of 1949, the Bank decided that the Philippine economy was in serious trouble—that balance-of-payments trends were not favorable and that the government was not instituting much-needed economic reforms—and refused to make the loan. By 1950 the Philippine government, no longer trying to obtain a Bank loan, applied to the United States, from which it was already receiving rehabilitation grants, for $250 million for its development plan. Relations between the Bank and the Philippines remained strained for years, with the Bank taking the position that, since the United States was financing that country's development plan, there was no place for Bank financing.[42]

Other Nonlending

Abortive on a much smaller scale was the first negotiation for a loan for the development of the colonial territories of a member country, namely the on-again, off-again discussions of the late 1940s between the Bank and the

42. During the Marshall Plan period (July 1, 1948–June 30, 1952), the Philippines received $588 million in economic aid from the United States, of which $530 million took the form of grants. The Philippines received its first Bank loan—to the National Power Corporation—in 1957, and a consultative group was organized by the Bank on its behalf in 1971.

Colonial Development Corporation (CDC) of the United Kingdom regarding a possible dollar loan for the purchase of equipment to be used in various dependent U.K. overseas territories. The Bank in 1948 had hopes of getting the United Kingdom, France, Belgium, and Portugal—the principal colonial powers in Africa—to collaborate in the development of that continent through such novel concepts as building roads that would connect with each other and ports designed to serve more than one territory. Orvis Schmidt and P. F. Craig-Martin were sent to Europe to discuss development planning for the colonies. The idea of planning on a continental scale proved premature, but a number of specific projects were suggested, and by autumn 1948 a sizable loan for the CDC was under discussion. This was whittled down by the usual process to a proposed $5 million.

In October 1949, representatives of the corporation came to Washington for negotiations, but problems arose on several issues. These included the negative pledge expected by the Bank, the complications the United Kingdom foresaw in entering into covenants whereby it would be guaranteeing performance by the colonies on various nonfinancial obligations under the loan contract, the possibility that the Bank might sell off a portion of the CDC loan without the prior consent of the corporation, the amount of end-use supervision, and other matters. Although progress was made in resolving these difficulties, the chairman of the corporation informed the Bank in late 1949 that

the terms of the loan, as worked out with his negotiators . . . were not acceptable. . . . Although expressing his appreciation that the Bank had exerted every effort to meet the Corporation's point of view, he stated that the Corporation did not desire to proceed further with the loan because "the Bank's requirements, especially the proposed non-financial covenants, are not reconcilable with the principles and methods by which this Corporation operates."[43]

The Colonial Development Corporation probably felt under much less pressure to modify its principles and swallow unpalatable procedures for a mere $5 million than did the typical borrower in the low-income world. The breakdown of negotiations made for bad relations between the Bank, on the one hand, and the British, on the other, for several years.[44]

Poland and Czechoslovakia were nonborrowers whose cases had heavy political overtones. The special case of the CDC was of a somewhat different

43. IBRD, *Fifth Annual Report, 1949–1950*, p. 32.

44. Lord Reith, who succeeded Lord Trefgarne as chairman of the CDC, however, was impressed by the caution the Bank had shown in the CDC negotiations. When in 1956 he was given an opportunity to associate the CDC with the Bank, he put £15 million into the Kariba hydroelectric power project (in what was then the Federation of Rhodesia and Nyasaland) almost entirely on the basis of the Bank's appraisal of that project.

type. Iran and the Philippines offer extreme examples of the more usual situation: the technically deficient project proposal. Such proposals were frequently deficient in ways that would in due course be remedied, but sometimes they were so hopelessly unrealistic or misconceived that a loan of any size or shape for the project would be out of the question. Or the member government may have been deemed not worthy of credit because it was pursuing "unsound" policies or had not yet conformed to some basic requirement of the Bank. Missions had been sent to Bolivia and Peru in 1948, for example, but "in each case the Bank emphasized that a necessary prerequisite of any loans would be a willingness on the Government's part to adopt certain measures to strengthen the country's financial position."[45] The result was a loan to Peru for port development in 1952, but none to Bolivia until 1964, when two IDA credits for power projects were approved. Ecuador in late 1950 seemed to be moving ahead satisfactorily in the queue of would-be borrowers. The Bank, though it expressed concern "at the continuing default in the service of Ecuador's external bonds," hoped "that an equitable solution of this problem" would be found during the coming year.[46] Additional reasons for concern emerged, and not until early 1954 did Ecuador receive its first loan—$8.5 million for highways. Nations that wanted Bank financing for government-owned development banks, publicly owned steel mills, municipal water systems, or aid to education were destined to wait still longer.

Lending, 1947–52, Classified by Purpose and Area

The preceding sections of this chapter have emphasized the way in which the Bank extended its lending to Latin America, Asia, the Middle East, and Africa and was prevented from lending to Poland or Czechoslovakia. It would be a mistake to infer, however, that the Bank abruptly withdrew from the so-called developed areas after the four reconstruction loans to Western Europe in 1947. Another $200 million in loans that were not classified as reconstruction loans had been made to European nations by June 30, 1952 —more than the total amount loaned to Asia and the Middle East or to Africa. Some of these were to underdeveloped European nations—for example, Iceland, Turkey, and Yugoslavia—or to underdeveloped regions of European nations, such as southern Italy. But several loans were made to

45. IBRD, *Fourth Annual Report, 1948–1949*, p. 23.
46. IBRD, *Fifth Annual Report, 1949–1950*, p. 26.

developed European countries. Table 6-1 summarizes Bank lending through June 30, 1952, by purpose and area.[47]

Electric power alone accounted for almost half of total project lending.[48] There were Bank-financed power projects, for the most part still under construction, in Australia, Belgium, Finland, Iceland, India, South Africa, Southern Rhodesia, Turkey, Yugoslavia, and a half dozen Latin American nations. More than three-fourths of the Bank's lending in the western hemisphere was for electric power.

Transportation was the other major claimant on Bank lending. Highway construction was being financed in Colombia, Ethiopia, and Nicaragua; railway rehabilitation in Australia, Brazil, India, Pakistan, Thailand, and South Africa; and port development in Peru, South Africa, Thailand, and Turkey. Loans for railroads far exceeded loans for all other types of transportation.

Agricultural lending was primarily for irrigation and flood control and for the importation of farm machinery. In 1950 a well publicized agricultural machinery loan was made to India to enable the Central Tractor Organization of the government to clear large areas of land in central India of a deep-rooted weed called "kans grass" and to develop methods of clearing jungle land in northern India for cultivation.[49] In 1952 Pakistan obtained an agricultural loan to help reclaim 660,000 acres of waste land in the Thal Desert in the northeast section of West Pakistan. Other agricultural loans helped to finance the mechanization of farming in Australia, Chile, Colombia, Nicaragua, and Paraguay, as well as irrigation in the Middle East and other regions, and grain storage in Nicaragua and Turkey.

Lending to industry was confined entirely to Europe and Australia.

Basic Policies: A Preview

The way in which the Bank began lending for different activities in different regions of the world and a few of the issues that arose in specific loan negotiations have been described above. With this as background, we indicate in a preliminary way below how certain policies appeared to be shaping up

47. The table is from the Bank's *Seventh Annual Report, 1951–1952,* which has also been drawn on heavily for the narrative portion of this section.

48. By total project lending, we mean total lending ($1,382 million) minus reconstruction loans ($497 million) and loans for general development plans ($80 million, of which $10 million was for southern Italy and $70 million for the then Belgian Congo).

49. The loan proved rather unsuccessful in achieving its primary objective of freeing for cultivation the areas covered by kans grass but was quite successful in training tractor operators and maintenance personnel.

Table 6-1. *World Bank Loans as of June 30, 1952, by Purpose and Area*
Millions of U.S. dollars

Purpose	Africa	Asia and the Middle East	Australia	Europe	Western Hemisphere	Total
Reconstruction loans[a]	...	...	...	**497**	...	**497**
Other loans, total	**125**	**129**	**100**	**202**	**329**	**885**
Electric power[b]	58	19	27	34	253	391
Transportation						
Railroads[c]	18	63	14	1	12	108
Shipping[d]	...	...	...	12	...	12
Airlines[e]	...	...	...	7	...	7
Roads[f]	5	...	6	...	20	31
Ports[g]	1	4	...	13	3	21
Subtotal	24	67	20	33	35	179
Communications[h]	1	...	...	...	24	25
Agriculture and Forestry						
Mechanization[i]	...	...	29	2	12	43
Irrigation and flood control[j]	...	31	10	13	1	55
Land improvement[k]	...	12	5	1	2	20
Grain storage[l]	...	...	...	4	1	5
Timber production[m]	...	...	...	5	...	5
Subtotal	...	43	44	25	16	128
Industry						
Manufacturing machinery	...	...	6	53	...	59
Mining equipment	...	...	3	8	...	11
Subtotal	...	...	9	61	...	70

General development						
Development banks	2	...	...	9	1	12
General development plans	40	...	...	40	...	80
Subtotal	42	...	...	49	1	92
Total, all loans	**125**	**129**	**100**	**699**	**329**	**1,382**

Source: IBRD, *Seventh Annual Report, 1951–1952*, p. 9.
a. To France, Netherlands, Denmark, and Luxembourg.
b. For machinery, equipment, and construction materials.
c. For locomotives, rolling stock, rails, and shop supplies.
d. For vessels and marine equipment.
e. For planes and spare parts.
f. For building machinery and equipment.
g. For docks, loading and dredging machinery, and harbor craft.
h. For telephone and telegraph equipment and supplies.
i. For general farm machinery, and equipment.
j. For construction equipment, and materials.
k. For machinery equipment, and construction materials.
l. For construction materials.
m. For machinery and vehicles.

179

after the Bank had gained several years' experience as a lender. In later chapters major policies are analyzed in more detail.

Creditworthiness and Repayment Prospects

The World Bank had to satisfy itself that, under prevailing market conditions, its borrowers would be unable to obtain loans elsewhere on terms that "in the opinion of the Bank" were reasonable. It was also enjoined to act "prudently in the interests both of the particular member in whose territories the project is located and of the members as a whole."[50] Thus, while the Bank's appraisals of creditworthiness ought to be more lenient than those of the private financial community, nothing in the Bank's charter encourages it to be bold.

In the early years, the prime preoccupation of the Bank's management was to prove the creditworthiness of the Bank itself in order to build up its own standing in the financial community. McCloy, Black, and Garner assumed, not without reason, that Bank loans to countries that were already in default on foreign loans might be disquieting to purchasers and potential purchasers of World Bank bonds. The Bank, moreover, was interested not only in its own standing in private capital markets but also in helping to establish conditions under which member governments would be able to borrow in the market on their own sooner than would otherwise be possible—and with cleaner hands. "Existing defaults are the most obvious obstacle to the restoration of credit," said its *Second Annual Report*. Clear evidence of a borrower's willingness to settle outstanding debts was thus made a prerequisite for loans. The Bank's pressure on debtors to settle overdue pre–World War II debts could have had the effect of making bondholders more demanding, but the various settlements reached seem, on the whole, to have represented reasonable compromises.

As time went on, the emphasis on *willingness* to repay decreased, and the analysis of creditworthiness was devoted increasingly to *capacity* to repay—a type of analysis destined to give more prominence to the work of the economists on the Bank's staff.

While numerous non-economic elements may seriously influence the *willingness* to service external debt . . . , the *capacity* to do so ultimately rests on two economic factors. In the first place, the debtor country's economy must be able to do without an amount of domestic income and savings equivalent to the debt service. Secondly, the debtor country must be in a position to convert such segregated savings into the required foreign exchange. And if debt service is increasing, there

50. IBRD, Articles of Agreement, Article III, section 4.

must also be an increase in both the capacity to save and the capacity to transfer savings. . . .

The analysis of change in debt-servicing capacity over time therefore requires an examination of the performance of debtor countries in both the field of income and savings and the field of foreign trade.[51]

As economists would be the first to admit, shifting the spotlight from psychological to economic aspects of creditworthiness may be more consistent with Article III, section 4(v), of the Articles of Agreement, but it does not eliminate the need for judgment. A vigorous case was made by Bank economists such as Paul Rosenstein-Rodan that creditworthiness should mean the ability to meet interest charges on a given (and gradually rising) level of foreign debt rather than the ability to repay principal as well as interest on *all* outstanding foreign debt. To include amortization schedules in calculations of creditworthiness was to assume that borrowers would in due course reduce to zero their net outstanding debt rather than roll it over. Credit prospects would seem particularly bleak if the amortization of substantial amounts of short-term foreign debt at relatively high rates of interest were included in the calculations.

The counterargument of other economists to Rosenstein-Rodan and his supporters was that amortization, being a fixed obligation, introduced rigidities into the situation that could cause difficulties. No country could count on always being able to borrow enough to cover amortization on existing debt plus its needs for additional capital. There are limits to the amount of gross borrowing that can be undertaken by any single country, and this sets limits to the external debt service burden that can be incurred without running into balance-of-payments difficulties.

As far as the Bank's management was concerned, debts were debts, and a conception of international lending that was based on anything other than their full repayment seemed immoral. Creditworthiness, according to the management, should be judged by conservative standards.

In 1949, for example, there was a long discussion at a board meeting as to whether it was "safe" to lend $100 million to India. Some board members expressed misgivings about lending that much, but the board decided in the end to go to $100 million, though not much beyond that amount. (By June 30, 1971, Bank loans to India added up to the equivalent of more than $1 billion and IDA credits to $1.5 billion; of the total of $2.5 billion, more than $450 million had been repaid.)

Those seeking an economic index of creditworthiness soon focused on

51. Dragoslav Avramović, assisted by Ravi Gulhati, *Debt Servicing Capacity and Postwar Growth in International Indebtedness* (Johns Hopkins Press, 1958), pp. 57, 59.

the so-called debt service ratio—the proportion of a country's earnings from exports of goods and services that is absorbed by interest and amortization payments on public and publicly guaranteed foreign debt. Like gross national product as an index of development, the debt service ratio is a somewhat simplistic measure which has nevertheless "shown strange powers of survival."[52] It is a seemingly straightforward and readily understandable relationship. It can be computed on what appears to be a firm statistical basis. Moreover, economic analysts who are well aware of its imperfections as a comprehensive indicator of debt servicing capacity have failed to suggest an equally useful alternative. *Faute de mieux*, international lending institutions have therefore leaned heavily upon it.[53]

But when they are leaning, what levels of debt service ratio should they regard as warning signals? A nation with debt service obligations amounting to 40 percent or more of its estimated export earnings during the ensuing three years obviously has a difficult short-term problem, if not a long-term problem. But what about ratios that are substantially below 40 percent? Should 10, 15, or 20 percent be regarded as "critical" and, if so, why?[54]

Foreign exchange is one of the scarcest . . . inputs for the developing debtor countries both over the short-run and over a longer period. The debt service is a continuing charge against this scarce resource. It is an indicator, . . . an incomplete one, of the strength of the temptation to default. As an indicator of temptation, the debt service ratio does not explicitly take into account the disadvantages of default in terms of reduction of borrowing facilities or deterioration of the terms on which it would be possible for the country to borrow after default. Implicitly, however, both the borrowers and the lenders presumably tend to compare the size of debt service liabilities with that of the likely capital inflow. In this sense the debt service ratio is a convenient yardstick of the "sacrifice" or "benefit foregone" of maintaining service. As long as debt service is low, it clearly does not "pay" to default; if it becomes very high, then it is natural to compare the gain from default with prospective capital inflow. But the question again arises: what is "low" and what is "high"? And whatever "low" and "high" may be, are they the same for everybody and under all circumstances?[55]

So long as inconvertibility among major currencies was a feature of the world economy (as it was during the early postwar years), the Bank felt that it had to concern itself not with foreign exchange earnings and obligations in total but specifically with dollar creditworthiness, Swiss franc creditworthiness, or sterling creditworthiness. As inconvertibility became less of a barrier

52. Dragoslav Avramović and others, *Economic Growth and External Debt* (Johns Hopkins Press, 1964), p. 38.
53. *Ibid.*
54. *Ibid.*, p. 39.
55. *Ibid.*, p. 42.

and the Bank began to turn its attention more seriously to the long-term problems of less developed countries, it became increasingly aware that, in the words of Avramović, "the significance of the debt service ratio for long-run analysis of debt servicing capacity is virtually nil."[56] The presence or absence of creditworthiness was not primarily a balance-of-payments problem, but a development problem that involved rate of growth, use of resources, level of savings, and so forth.[57]

The Specific Project Provision

The review of operational policies in the Bank's *Fifth Annual Report* admitted that there had been considerable criticism of the provision in the Articles of Agreement requiring that, except in special circumstances, Bank loans be for specific projects of reconstruction or development. The Bank's retort, already cited in Chapter 2, above, was that the provision required only that, before loans were granted, there be agreement both as to the types of goods and services to be procured and the uses to which they would be put.

In reply to the criticism that the specific project approach meant that the Bank examined the merits of particular projects in isolation, without reference to the overall needs of the borrowing country, the Bank asserted that it did "precisely the opposite." It sought to determine appropriate investment priorities in the borrowing nation and then to adapt its program of financial assistance to meet the priority needs.[58] Indeed, as the *Fifth Annual Report*

56. *Ibid.*, p. 42.
57. We say more about creditworthiness in Chapter 13 and elsewhere in this study. It can be, and at different times in the Bank's history has been, appraised in at least three different overlapping ways. (1) It can be judged on the basis of political and psychological factors—whether the country's past record with respect to foreign debts augurs well for the future, whether the country is considered politically stable and likely to remain so, and whether the prospects for maintaining its independence and freedom from foreign domination are good. (2) The claims of debt service, current and future, on export earnings can be studied, and figures in excess of 10 or 15 percent can be viewed as signs of reduced creditworthiness. (3) Attention can be riveted more firmly on the long-term outlook for self-sustaining growth (with a viable balance of payments) and on social and economic indicators of progress toward that goal.
58. See the discussion above on Ethiopia. Similarly, in Nicaragua,
in our early lending . . . we started with highways, went along simultaneously with farm machinery for clearing and bringing into production the land that would be opened up by the new roads, set up a development bank for agricultural lending to help the farmers finance the purchase of equipment . . . set up grain storage silos so that the new crops could be dried, cleaned and stored. . . . In our lending to a . . . country, we would have in mind a series of projects to be carried out over a fairly short period which complemented and reinforced each other.
Orvis A. Schmidt, "Oral History," p. 21.

said, "the Bank would prefer to go further, wherever that is feasible, and base its financing on a national development program, provided that it is properly worked out in terms of the projects by which the objectives of the program are to be attained."[59]

Interest Rates, Grace Periods, and Security for Loans

The main element in the interest rate charged by the Bank during the period covered by this chapter was the cost at which the Bank could borrow in the market plus a margin sufficient, along with income from capital, to cover the Bank's operating expenses and yield a modest amount for a reserve against contingencies. In addition, the Bank charged a uniform commission —1 percent a year—on the outstanding amounts of all loans, whether they were made from borrowed funds or from paid-in capital.

Normally the full interest rate on loans was not charged until the proceeds were disbursed. A commitment charge, however, began on the effective date of the loan and applied to the undisbursed portion of the loan, on the theory that the Bank deserved to be compensated for the cost of holding funds at the borrower's disposal. It was also argued that the charge—then 1.5 percent —would encourage the borrower to draw down the proceeds of the loan without unnecessary delay.[60] By comparison with the high interest rates prevalent in later years, the combined interest and other charges made by the Bank during the years 1947–52—from 3 to 4.75 percent—were much more favorable to borrowers than they were thought to be at the time. Moreover, the borrower was usually given a grace period of two to five years before the first installment of principal became due. In the Bank's early lending operations the length of the grace period was usually determined by the time believed necessary to bring the project into operation.

Where the borrower was a government, the negative pledge mentioned earlier in this chapter was regarded as sufficient security. If the borrower was a private company, the Bank asked for security, usually in the form of mortgages on real property. A principal reason for the Bank's demand for security in such cases was, and is, to protect the guarantor (the government) rather than the Bank. If the borrower fails to pay, the Bank expects the guarantor to pay. The Bank therefore tries to set up the loan in such a way as to

---

59. IBRD, *Fifth Annual Report, 1949–1950*, p. 8.
60. For a note on the merits of the case for a commitment charge, see Chapter 7, below.

minimize the likelihood of default and to put the guarantor in the strongest possible position as a creditor.[61]

Selection and Analysis of Projects

In theory at least, the Bank approached the question of which projects to finance by determining first "the important goals of a proper investment program" in the country in question and then gauging "the relative productivity of the various projects by the extent of their contribution to those goals." It recognized that, by financing only "good" projects, it might be releasing resources that the borrower could devote to "bad" projects, but it did not regard this "as in any way relieving it from the obligation of satisfying itself that the particular projects it finances are economically and technically sound and are of a high priority nature."[62]

The Bank preferred informal exploratory discussions with prospective borrowers before formal loan requests were filed. The actual process of investigation usually fell into two stages (which in some cases could proceed more or less concurrently).

The first stage is a general examination of the economy of the borrowing country with a view to determining (a) the approximate amount of additional external debt the country can afford to service and the rate at which it can effectively absorb such debt, (b) the general order of priority of the projects under consideration from the standpoint of their contribution to the country's development, and (c) the appropriateness of the government's economic and financial policies to further the development process. Where the proposed project is in a country to which the Bank has not previously made a loan, this first stage frequently requires intensive study of the country's agricultural, industrial and mineral resources, of its manpower, transport and power situation, of the state of its external trade and balance of payments, and of the condition of its internal finances, particularly its budget and currency position.[63]

Satisfaction of this encyclopedic interest of the Bank usually required the dispatch of a mission to the country. On the basis of the mission's report, the Bank tried to make at least a provisional judgment as to the amount of additional foreign debt the country could safely assume and of the projects that merited priority consideration.

In the second phase of the Bank's investigation, the particular project or projects proposed for financing were examined in detail. Only if the second

61. A. Broches, *International Legal Aspects of the Operations of the World Bank* (Leiden: A. W. Sijthoff, 1959), p. 358.

62. IBRD, *Fifth Annual Report, 1949–1950,* p. 9.

63. *Ibid.,* pp. 11–12.

phase of the investigation resulted in a favorable report on the project or projects (as submitted or subsequently modified) did the Bank advise the borrower of its willingness to enter into formal negotiations for a loan. The Bank, in other words, did not want to be in the position of turning down formal applications for loans. It deliberately set up its procedures so that the principal difficulties would be ironed out before so-called formal negotiations began.

The early literature of the Bank is full of references to "sound" economic policies, "sound" fiscal and monetary policies, and "sound" policies of various other kinds, with the clear implication that the distinction between sound and unsound policies is as obvious as the distinction between day and night. Some policies are unsound by every known test of experience. A prudent investor has no business lending other people's money to pursuers of such policies, and a lending institution with a conscience will do its utmost to turn sinners into saints. The distinction is not always perfectly clear, however, and, in such cases, those to whom it *is* crystal clear seem irritatingly doctrinaire.

In any event, the Bank's examination of general economic conditions in the borrowing country "not infrequently" revealed practices or policies which, in its view, affected the financial and monetary stability of the borrowing nation so adversely as to endanger the productive purposes and repayment prospects of any Bank lending. "In such cases, it is the policy of the Bank to require, as a condition precedent to Bank financing, that the borrowing country institute measures designed to restore stability to its economy."[64] The word "institute" was selected deliberately to avoid the implication that all necessary steps had to be completed *before* lending could begin. What was desired was concrete evidence that appropriate steps were being taken. With that evidence in hand, the Bank proclaimed its willingness to make the loan "concurrently with the execution of the measures adopted."[65]

Procurement and End-use Supervision

The Articles of Agreement prohibit loans the proceeds of which are available for expenditure only in a designated country (tied loans) but require the Bank to make certain that its funds are used exclusively "for the purposes for which the loan was granted, with due attention to considerations of economy and efficiency."[66] Certain requirements concerning end-use

64. *Ibid.,* pp. 12–13.
65. *Ibid.,* p. 13.
66. IBRD, Articles of Agreement, Article III, section 5(b).

supervision—techniques to ensure that Bank-financed supplies and equipment are used for the purposes and at the sites for which they have been procured—follow logically and directly from the charter. However, "due attention to considerations of economy and efficiency" does not axiomatically require procurement through international competitive bidding. Indeed, during the Bank's early days, when the only undestroyed industrial complex was that of the United States, the idea of establishing a procedure for soliciting bids on a more or less global basis could be attacked as visionary or academic. Nevertheless, beginning in about 1951 it was gradually introduced, largely through the efforts of Raymond A. Wheeler, and remains one of the Bank's proudest procedural achievements.

Initially there were no restrictions on the location of bidders and nothing to prevent suppliers in nonmember countries from submitting bids. It was decided in 1956, however, that it should not be required that international competitive bidding extend beyond sources within member countries of the Bank and the one nonmember country that was providing capital to the Bank, namely, Switzerland.

The objective of international competitive bidding, as it has evolved, has been twofold: (a) to serve the interests of both the Bank and the borrower by obtaining goods in the lowest-cost market consistent with satisfactory performance, and (b) to give all member countries a fair chance to supply goods financed by Bank loans. In pursuit of the objective, the Bank has not only advised but, when it had any doubt about the borrower's capability, required the borrower to employ a qualified consultant, or consulting firm, to assist in preparing specifications, in determining the qualifications of bidders, and in analyzing the relative merits of bids that are submitted.

Borrowing countries are inclined to feel that the bidding procedure should allow a sizable margin of preference for local suppliers in order to help develop domestic industry and save foreign exchange. Other member governments tend to feel that the bidding procedure is unfair if the margin of preference for domestic suppliers is at all great and thereby reduces opportunities for qualified foreign suppliers to obtain orders. Major subscribers of Bank capital also tend to regard the procedure as somehow unfair or insufficiently responsive to "political realities" if their own share in total procurement falls signficantly below the share of their subscriptions in the total capital resources of the Bank. Though the reason may be an inability to compete on a cost basis with other suppliers of comparable equipment, or the absence of adequate maintenance and service facilities for its equipment in the borrowing nation, a country contributing, say, 40 percent of the capital resources of an international lending institution and "getting back" only 25 percent of the institution's business will be unhappy about the workings of the procurement system.

The Bank recognized almost from the beginning that circumstances would arise in which international competitive bidding would be inappropriate. Initially, however, it tended to think of such circumstances as requiring concessions to a borrower's longstanding familiarity with particular types of equipment (British-made, French-made, and so on), or to the borrower's need for accessible maintenance and service facilities, rather than as requiring margins of preference for suppliers in the borrowing nations.[67]

Establishing an equitable system of international procurement for equipment and supplies is difficult enough. Establishing and monitoring such a system for procuring the services of consultants, where price competition is not a formal requirement of the Bank (and is, in fact, discouraged by that institution), is still more complicated. The Bank must approve the borrower's choice. To avoid a disillusioning climax to the procedure, the Bank has asked borrowers to present their "final" list of possible consultants before they invite the consultants to submit proposals. The Bank can thus satisfy itself that the firms on the list are, to the best of its knowledge, qualified to perform the work expected of them. Over the years the Bank has built up an extensive file of information on consultant firms in member countries and Switzerland.

General Wheeler promptly established the policy that the Bank would not accept a project appraisal from a source that might be selling equipment or services to the project or engaging in construction work for it. Applied to consultant services, this has meant, for example, that consulting engineering firms which combine their consulting functions with those of contracting (or which are associated with, affiliates of, or owned by contractors) are acceptable to the Bank only if they will disqualify themselves and their associates for work in any other capacity than as consultants on the particular project. In the case of consulting engineering affiliates of manufacturers, safeguards are employed to ensure not only that affiliates will be disqualified from future bidding but that the specifications they help design will be impartially drawn and will permit compliance on a competitive basis.

Expenditure of the proceeds of a World Bank loan has from the beginning been a cooperative undertaking, involving the Bank as well as the borrower. The borrower makes the purchases, and the Bank satisfies itself as to their legality and makes the necessary disbursements. The Bank can reimburse the borrower for its expenditures, it can make advances in order that the borrower may make its payments, or it can pay suppliers directly on behalf of

67. For more on the preference question, see Chapter 8, below.

the borrower. It can also reimburse commercial banks for payments under letters of credit and may, on payment of a special commission, undertake to do so unconditionally. Reports received from the commercial banks then become the basis for payment. Copies of contracts or purchase orders, invoices, evidence of shipping or engineer certificates, and independent proof of payment are normally required.

Since its very first loan, moreover, the Bank has been involved in checking the arrival of Bank-financed goods in the borrowing country and their use on projects. Because the Bank does not finance the total cost of a project, the successful completion of the project depends not only on the timely arrival at the project site of purchases financed by the Bank, but on a host of other factors as well. The Bank therefore insisted on being kept informed of the progress of the project as a whole and began on a case-by-case basis to design appropriate progress reporting systems for approved projects. The wealth of information demanded by the Bank continued to give rise to complaints by borrowers, particularly first-time borrowers. "The information requested by the Bank," said the *Fifth Annual Report* blandly, "is no more, and is usually much less, than that required by the borrower itself for the efficient control of its own operations. The Bank supplements its study of this data by occasional field investigations by members of its staff."[68] Some of the borrowers later expressed appreciation for the introduction of systems that helped them keep track of what they themselves were doing and could readily be used on a wider basis within the borrowing country.

Summary

The concept of the Bank as an institution with which prospective borrowers could file loan applications that loan officers in Washington could approve or disapprove, almost without leaving their desks, evaporated quickly. Prolonged negotiations, elaborate field investigations, and technical assistance in helping less developed countries select and prepare investment projects became commonplace.

Although the Bank was becoming increasingly preoccupied with the problems of borrowers in the less developed world, it continued through June 30, 1952, and beyond, to be active also in Europe and Australia.

The Bank recognized that investments of many kinds were needed for development but frequently implied that one kind was more essential than any other. The relative ease with which it could finance electric power, trans-

68. IBRD, *Fifth Annual Report, 1949–1950,* p. 16.

portation, and economic infrastructure projects—in reality the result of circumstance—made it an exponent of the thesis that public utility projects,
accompanied by financial stability and the encouragement of private investment, could do more than almost anything else to trigger development.

A corollary doctrine was that autonomous authorities comparable to the
Tennessee Valley Authority in the United States were needed to staff and
operate the projects and insulate them from the vagaries of domestic politics.
Whatever the merits of this particular institutional arrangement may be, the
Bank's affection for it illustrated its concern (almost from the time it began
lending) with institution-building—one of the central preoccupations of
agencies, national and international, dedicated to promoting development in
the low-income world.

The difficulties of reaching decisions solely on the basis of economic considerations, without reference to the political character of the member country concerned, were enormous in an intensely political world, as the Bank
discovered in dealing with the applications of Poland and Czechoslovakia for
large reconstruction loans.

The statutory requirement for government guarantees of loans to nongov-
ernmental borrowers was recognized as a handicap in lending for industrial
development. The Bank's stimulation of privately owned national development banks or finance companies to provide such loans was a partial answer,
to be supplemented at a later date by the establishment of the International
Finance Corporation.

The amount of time it took to process loan proposals, the interrogations
involved, and the elaborate documentation required by the Bank at all stages
of lending gave rise to understandable impatience among borrowers. The
Bank for its part wanted to be sure that its clients were creditworthy, that the
projects it financed were technically sound and of high priority, and that service payments on loans would not be jeopardized by the emergence of conditions which, with an early warning system, might have been foreseen and
corrected. A broader purpose of the visiting missions and the flow of documentation was to establish and maintain a continuing relationship with borrowers that would, the Bank hoped, facilitate later lending to those same
borrowers.

CHAPTER SEVEN

The Bank Group as a Supplier of Capital, 1952–1971

CHAPTER SIX initiated the discussion of the World Bank as a supplier of capital, described and analyzed a number of early Bank loans, and discussed the evolution of the Bank's lending policy during the first five years of its existence. This chapter returns to the subject of the Bank as a supplier of capital, covering the period 1952 to 1971. We shall be concerned with (1) the expansion of Bank loans and International Development Association (IDA) credits (the investments of the International Finance Corporation [IFC] are considered in Chapter 11); (2) the geographical and functional distribution of lending; (3) the relative share of the Bank Group in the total volume of development assistance, including that from bilateral suppliers and from other international agencies; (4) the terms of Bank and IDA lending; (5) the growth of interest payments and repayments of principal and its consequences for the net transfer of capital; (6) the rapidly increasing debt burden of the less developed world to the Bank Group and other lenders; and (7) the growing problem of debt renegotiation. This chapter will also introduce the discussion of Bank lending policy in Chapters 8 and 9.

The Growth of Bank and IDA Lending

As Table 7-1 shows, the Bank's annual lending commitments have increased tenfold since 1947. This growth has not been a steady year-to-year expansion but has proceeded from one level to another. The first two years

191

Table 7-1. *World Bank Loans and IDA Credits by Fiscal Years through June 30, 1971*
Gross commitments in millions of U.S. dollars

Fiscal year	World Bank loans		IDA credits		Total amount of loans and credits
	Number	Amount	Number	Amount	
1947	1	$ 250.0			$ 250.0
1948	5	263.0			263.0
1949	10	137.1			137.1
1950	12	166.3			166.3
1951	21	297.1			297.1
1952	19	298.6			298.6
1953	10	178.6			178.6
1954	26	323.7			323.7
1955	20	409.6			409.6
1956	26	396.0			396.0
1957	20	387.9			387.9
1958	34	710.8			710.8
1959	30	703.1			703.1
1960	31	658.7			658.7
1961	27	609.9	4	$ 101.0	710.9
1962	29	882.3	18	134.1	1,016.4
1963	28	448.7	17	260.1	708.8
1964	37	809.8	18	283.2	1,093.0
1965	38	1,023.3	20	309.1	1,332.4
1966	37	839.2	12	284.1	1,123.3
1967	46	876.8	20	353.5	1,230.3
1968	44	847.0	18	106.6	953.6
1969	84	1,399.2	38	385.0	1,784.2
1970	70	1,680.4	56	605.6	2,286.0
1971	78	1,896.4	53	584.0	2,480.4
Total	783	$16,493.5	274	$3,406.3	$19,899.8

Source: IBRD, Information and Public Affairs Department.

were dominated by the four reconstruction loans to Europe. Then after a temporary decline in its total commitments the Bank loaned at an annual rate of $300 million to $400 million until fiscal year 1958. For the next ten years the level of commitments hovered around $700 million to $800 million, with the figures in 1965 exceeding $1 billion for the first time. Beginning in fiscal 1969 the volume of Bank lending moved to a quite new level. IDA credits have moved steadily upward since 1961, except for the low figure in 1968 occasioned by delay in the second replenishment. In fiscal 1971, IDA credits accounted for approximately 24 percent of total Bank Group lending.

IDA, which is discussed in detail in Chapter 12, began operations in fiscal

1961. The level and rate of increase in IDA lending are determined principally by the amount of funding Part I countries are willing to undertake and by the share of its profits the Bank is willing to transfer to IDA. The initial subscriptions, of which approximately $750 million was fully usable, were intended to be committed by IDA over a period of five years. IDA in fact committed these funds over a period of three years, that is, at an annual rate of $250 million instead of the contemplated $150 million. The second replenishment, scheduled for 1967 but delayed until 1968, provided $400 million a year; and the third replenishment, which had been agreed upon but was not yet ratified in 1971, proposes $800 million. In every year but one since 1964, the Bank has added to these funds, by transfer from its own profits, amounts varying from $50 million to $110 million.[1] The rate of Bank lending is limited by the creditworthiness of potential borrowers and by the rate at which viable projects can be brought forward—not by a shortage of loanable funds. However, this is definitely not true of IDA, whose funds must be strictly rationed. Since the number of loans and credits in the period 1952–71 was large, we do not attempt, as we did in Chapter 6, to discuss particular loans but are concerned here primarily with the distribution of Bank lending to particular countries and areas.

Geographical Distribution of Bank Group Loans and Credits

The geographical distribution of Bank loans is determined by the ability of member countries to borrow on their own credit in the capital markets of the world, by their access to other multilateral and bilateral sources of funds, by considerations of creditworthiness, by the rate at which feasible projects are brought to the attention of the Bank, and by the Bank's judgment of the economic performance of member countries. The Bank had practically ceased to lend to developed countries by 1968. Its last loan to Japan was in 1966. In general, the developed countries of the world are capable of borrowing in capital markets on their own credit. (To use an inelegant phrase that was current in the Bank for a short time, they are "market eligible.") However, there are still a number of countries which, although they are able to borrow on their own credit in capital markets, are considered unable to borrow in sufficient volume to meet their needs. Thus, since 1967 the Bank has continued to lend in small volume to such countries as Iceland, Ireland, Israel, Finland, and New Zealand, which are judged to be in this situation.

1. In fiscal year 1968 the Bank transferred only $10 million.

To be creditworthy a country must give promise of an ability to service foreign debt and to repay Bank loans in convertible currency. There are a few poor member countries which are judged not to be creditworthy for any amount of Bank borrowing and which therefore qualify only for IDA credits. Some of the newly independent African countries belong in this category. There is a smaller group of countries whose per capita incomes are low enough to qualify them for IDA assistance but which also are judged to have some limited capacity to service debt on Bank terms.[2] India, which has been by far the largest borrower from the Bank Group, had by June 30, 1971, borrowed $1,051 million from the Bank and $1,507 million from IDA. The largest group of less developed countries has borrowed only from the Bank. These tend to be countries, mainly in Latin America or southern Europe, whose per capita incomes are not low enough to meet the IDA income qualification, or countries rich in oil or minerals that have a large capacity to service debt even though their per capita incomes may be low. Of the seventy-three less developed member countries that have borrowed from the Bank Group during the period ending June 30, 1971, twenty-two have received financing only from IDA, thirty-three only from the Bank, three only from IFC, and fifteen from both the Bank and IDA. The fact that some less developed countries have borrowed only from the Bank, however, does not mean that they are creditworthy for unlimited amounts.

A member country may be creditworthy on Bank terms, or IDA terms, or both and still find it difficult to present viable projects considered to be ready for financing. The scarcity of prepared projects is one reason for the low level of lending in various African countries. The Bank has also complained frequently of the neglect of project preparation by governments in Southern Asia. Mexico, on the other hand, has become the largest borrower from the Bank in part because it started early (the first IBRD loan to Mexico was made in 1949) and in part because it has succeeded in presenting a continuous flow of feasible projects and sector programs.

Finally, the geographical distribution of Bank loans has been influenced to some extent by Bank judgments of member country "performance." In a few cases the IBRD has refused to lend because of a repudiation of, or default of payments on, international debt. The pros and cons of this aspect of Bank policy were discussed in Chapter 6. We return to the subject in Chapter 11 and consider also the Bank's attitude toward expropriation without adequate compensation. But in addition the IBRD has conditioned its lend-

2. For more on per capita income and its relation to eligibility for IDA credits, see Chapter 12, below.

ing, to some extent at least, on a member country's performance in managing its own economic resources. The meaning of "performance" is discussed in some detail in Chapter 13. For now it may be said that the aspects of performance that may occasion a change in the volume of Bank lending to a particular country have mainly to do with the possible effect on creditworthiness of the government's policies.

As Table 7-2 shows, the ten largest borrowers from the Bank Group have accounted for nearly 50 percent of total Bank/IDA lending, as of June 30, 1971.

Only two of the ten largest borrowers are classified as Part I countries of IDA—Japan and Australia. Japan was a heavy borrower from the Bank beginning in 1953; the last Bank loan to Japan was made in 1966. Since then, as was noted in Chapter 5, Japan has become a large lender to the Bank. Approximately $325 million of Australia's total borrowing took the form of quasi-program loans, which will be discussed in Chapter 9. The Bank's last loan to Australia was in 1962.

Of the less developed countries on the list of the ten largest borrowers, two (India and Brazil) merit special attention. With neither of these countries has the Bank's relationship been consistently smooth. Lending to India developed slowly. Doubts were expressed concerning that country's creditworthiness for loans on Bank terms, and prior to 1956 only a little more than $125 million had been committed to it, mainly for the rehabilitation of the Indian railways. A favorable Bank report on Indian prospects in 1956 opened the door somewhat, but not until the formation of the India Consortium in 1958 did the Bank begin lending on a large scale. The appearance of IDA

Table 7-2. *Total Amounts Borrowed by the Ten Largest Borrowers from the Bank Group, to June 30, 1971*
Millions of U.S. dollars

Country	World Bank loans	IDA credits	Total
India	1,051	1,507	2,558
Pakistan	633	497	1,130
Mexico	1,053	...	1,053
Brazil	998	...	998
Colombia	872	19	891
Japan	857	...	857
Iran	612	...	612
Yugoslavia	565	...	565
Argentina	509	...	509
Australia	418	...	418

Source: IBRD, Information Office and Public Affairs Department.

on the scene in 1960 greatly increased the level of Bank Group commitments to India.

The early years of India's Third Plan (1961–62 to 1965–66) marked a high point in favorable relations with the Bank-led consortium. Members of the consortium pledged well over $1 billion a year in development assistance, with the Bank Group accounting for some 20 percent of the total. This favorable situation, however, was short-lived. A Bank mission in 1962 reported that growth in national income during the first year of India's Third Plan was disappointingly small, though it noted that, "The task which India is attempting in the field of economic development is incomparably more difficult than any which has faced the more developed economies of the West. . . ."[3] Subsequent reports were increasingly critical of the management of the Indian economy; and in 1964 the Bank decided, with the not very enthusiastic acquiescence of the Indian government, to undertake a comprehensive study of the country's economy. This study, which appeared in ten large mimeographed volumes, found many things wrong.[4]

Although the Bank mission recommended a great many changes in development policies, major attention was devoted to the need for reform of balance-of-payments policies, simplification of the elaborate system of controls over imports, and intensification of efforts to increase agricultural output. It was suggested that if the Indian government were willing to take these and other steps, a substantial increase in development assistance would be justified. The president of the Bank (Woods) accepted the analysis and appointed as negotiators Bernard Bell and André de Lattre, who carried these views to New Delhi in the summer of 1965. They intimated that without substantial changes in balance-of-payments and import policies, no increase in assistance for the Fourth Plan could be expected, and possibly a reduction should be anticipated. When the Indian representatives came to Washington in September 1965, they found the Fund agreeing that devaluation and import liberalization were essential. The United States, by far the largest provider of bilateral development assistance to India, lined up with the Bank and Fund and pressed in particular for reform in agricultural policies.

India's economic position was weak. A devastating drought in 1965 had severely reduced food grain production; and the 1965 war with Pakistan, though short, had been costly. A continuation of the drought in 1966 made India extremely dependent on U.S. food shipments. Negotiations for change in agricultural policies were relatively easy. The Indian minister of food,

3. "Current Economic Position and Prospects of India," AS91a, p. iv.
4. "IBRD Economic Mission to India 1964–65."

Subramaniam, was fully convinced of the need for change. Changes in the Indian exchange rate and import and export policies required greater study and consultation. India devalued the rupee by 36 percent in June 1966, an action followed by a political crisis. In expectation of devaluation and import liberalization the president of the Bank was committed to try to persuade consortium members to provide $900 million a year in commodity assistance in addition to project assistance and food imports. The consortium did in fact provide the additional assistance although it became increasingly difficult to sustain this level. The Bank made a sizable contribution in program credits, which are discussed in Chapter 9.

As we note in Chapter 13, the Indian case was perhaps the most striking example of attempts by the Bank to use "leverage" to bring about changes in a borrowing government's "performance." It did not leave the Bank's relations with India unscathed. Although, as the figures cited above indicate, the Bank Group has continued to lend heavily to India, that country is viewed by many on the Bank's staff as a peculiarly difficult borrower, and opinions in India of the Bank Group are not uniformly flattering.[5]

In contrast to the case of India, the Bank's early views of Brazil as a potential borrower were extremely optimistic. Between 1947 and 1954 the Bank loaned some $200 million, chiefly for electric power and railway transport. The creation of the Joint Brazil–United States Economic Development Commission in 1951, charged with preparing projects for a five-year development program, promised a large flow of bankable projects. In fact, the report of the joint commission in December 1954 proposed some forty-one projects, with a foreign exchange cost of $387 million. But in the meantime the Bank's relations with Brazil had taken a turn for the worse. Confronted with a foreign exchange crisis in 1951, the Vargas government abruptly decided to stop the transfer of earnings on foreign investment and the repatriation of capital. From that date on, relations between the Bank and the Brazilian government deteriorated.

There were many aspects of Brazilian government policy that the Bank felt jeopardized Brazil's creditworthiness for Bank loans. It would have liked to use the promise of development lending as leverage to bring about changes in policy. But the Bank considered that its position had been seriously undermined by an Export-Import Bank loan to Brazil of $300 million in 1953 to cover the repayment of commercial debt to U.S. exporters. This was regarded as a "bail out," which could have the effect only of lessening the pressure on the Brazilian government for needed changes in policy.

5. The Bank's relations with India are discussed in greater detail at various points in this study, including Chapters 12–14 and 19.

The Bank made very few loans to Brazil in the period 1954–59 and none at all from 1960 to 1965. During the late 1950s the rate of inflation in Brazil increased, and a stabilization program worked out with the International Monetary Fund (IMF) in 1958 was repudiated in 1959. Inflation became rampant, and the Bank withdrew entirely from Brazil. It did not begin lending to that country again until 1965. Since then Brazil has become one of the Bank's largest borrowers.[6]

The Bank's relations with other large borrowers have not been accompanied by such perturbations, although the course has not always run smoothly. But it must be said that, in the early 1960s, Bank/IDA lending presented a rather anomalous geographic pattern for a development institution. No loans were made to Brazil, Indonesia, or Ghana, and one of the Bank's largest borrowers was a developed country—Japan. However, this situation had improved substantially by the early 1970s. In fiscal years 1970 and 1971, 60 percent of Bank/IDA lending went to twelve countries, all Part II members of IDA. They were (in order of size of borrowing): India, $511 million; Brazil, $365 million; Colombia, $281 million; Mexico, $222 million; Iran, $213 million; Argentina, $211 million; Yugoslavia, $188 million; Indonesia, $176 million; Korea, $146 million; Pakistan, $144 million; Spain, $140 million; and Nigeria, $133 million. During that period the Bank/IDA made loans to seventy-five countries, about 35 percent of the total being to Asian countries, approximately 20 percent to Africa, about 30 percent to Latin America and the Caribbean, and most of the remaining 12 percent to Europe.

It would have to be said, however, that Bank Group lending has not done much to correct the very uneven distribution of assistance resulting from bilateral assistance programs. The distribution of bilateral assistance has been influenced mainly by the former colonial interests of metropolitan donors and by commercial and political considerations. In addition, there has obviously been at work what may be described as a "large-country syndrome." Relatively small amounts of assistance to a country the size of Uganda can produce substantial per capita receipts. This has been particularly evident in the small countries making up the French-speaking area of Africa. On the other hand, even the very large assistance flows to countries like India, Pakistan, and Indonesia have a very low per capita yield.

Lending by multilateral institutions has done little or nothing to correct this imbalance. In fact the countries that were at the top of the list of Bank/IDA borrowers, noted on page 195, were in most cases toward the bottom of

6. For more on the Bank and Brazil, see Chapter 19, below.

the same list in terms of per capita borrowing. Receipts per capita for these countries were: India ($4.67), Pakistan ($8.28), Mexico ($20.46), Brazil ($10.69), Colombia ($40.87), Japan ($8.24), Iran ($21.19), Yugoslavia ($27.20), Argentina ($21.55), and Australia ($32.63).

It may come as a surprise that the top ten receivers of Bank/IDA assistance on a per capita basis as of June 30, 1971, were: Iceland ($150.00), Cyprus ($76.16), the People's Republic of the Congo ($70.63), Botswana ($68.50), Mauritania ($63.08), Finland ($58.88), Israel ($51.50), Singapore ($49.32), Costa Rica ($47.62), and Trinidad and Tobago ($46.82). Only two countries on the list have a population of 3 million or more—Finland (4.7 million) and Israel (3.0 million). Iceland boasts a population of 200,000. Thus it is evident that, as a recipient of bilateral and multilateral assistance, the worst thing that can happen to a country, next to being poor, is to be large.

Distribution of Bank Group Lending among Economic Sectors

As was noted in Chapter 6, the Bank's early development loans to less developed countries were overwhelmingly concentrated in the areas of transportation and power. Table 7-3 reveals that, while Bank Group lending to less developed countries has broadened substantially, transportation and power still absorb close to 50 percent of IBRD financing in these countries.

The amounts shown in the table represent for fiscal years 1960 to 1971, inclusive, $13,338 million in Bank loans and IDA credits and $545 million in IFC investments. The IFC investments were, of course, entirely in the private sector and were made mainly for the financing of industrial activities. Although Bank and IDA projects are subject to similar tests of productivity, there are substantial differences in areas of financing—the result in large part of differences in country requirements. Power loans, which loom so large in Bank financing, have been of minor importance to IDA. On the other hand, social services represent a much larger fraction of IDA than of Bank financing. Agriculture in recent years has been a heavy claimant on both Bank and IDA funds. And IDA credits for industry have been practically limited to the financing of what are designated in Table 7-3 as maintenance imports. These are the industrial import credits to India and Pakistan that are discussed in Chapter 9 as "program loans." In describing the distribution of financing among economic sectors we give no further consideration at this point to differences among the Bank, IDA, and IFC, but treat the flow of funds from the Bank Group as a whole.

Table 7-3. *Distribution of Bank Group Lending to Less Developed Countries, by Sectors, 1960–71*

Gross commitments expressed in millions of U.S. dollars

Sector	Fiscal years									
	1960		1965		1970		1961–70		1971	
	Amount	*Percent*	*Amount*	*Percent*	*Amount*	*Percent*	*Amount*	*Percent*	*Amount*	*Percent*
Economic										
Agriculture	46	9	167	15	423	18	1,689	15	428	18
Industry	118	22	119	10	403	18	1,842	16	248	11
Transportation	200	38	422	37	664	29	3,364	29	625	27
Communications	...	...	33	3	85	4	362	3	196	8
Power	165	31	335	30	529	23	3,011	26	480	20
Tourism	...	...	...	...	1	...	18	...	10	0
Subtotal	529	100	1,076	95	2,105	92	10,286	89	1,987	84
Social										
Education	...	...	30	3	80	3	326	3	100	4
Health	...	...	...	...	...	...	...	...	...	...
Water supply	...	...	27	2	33	2	250	2	154	7
Family planning	...	...	...	...	2	...	2	...	8	0
Subtotal	...	...	57	5	115	5	578	5	262	11
Maintenance imports	...	...	...	...	75	3	655	6	25	1
Special and other	...	...	...	...	3	...	5	...	85	4
Total	529	100	1,133	100	2,298	100	11,524	100	2,359	100

Source: IBRD, Economic Program Department.

Although the share of Bank Group financing that is directed toward public utilities, transportation, power, and communications has declined over time, it is still large, and there is every reason to believe that it will continue to be large. Chapter 6 emphasized certain characteristics of the Bank's structure that favor this type of investment: the early emphasis on the financing of the foreign exchange costs of particular projects; the need for a guarantee from the government of the country in which projects were located; the limitation of financing to activities for which other sources of finance were unavailable; and the practical necessity of dealing with projects large enough to justify review and appraisal in Washington. These influences are still important. But there are other considerations.

During the first decade of the Bank's existence there was a tremendous shortage of investment in energy and transportation in both high- and low-income countries. Power outages and shortages were chronic and severe in most of the countries of Latin America and in the most important industrial centers of Asia. The condition of the railways and highways was having a disastrous effect on economic activity in many less developed countries; the Federation of Rhodesia could not get its minerals to ports for shipment to other countries; Brazil was importing potatoes from the Netherlands because this was easier than bringing food to Rio de Janeiro from one hundred miles inland; deliveries by the Indian railway system, one of the world's largest, were not merely hours but weeks late. The Bank in its early lending policy was responding to a series of emergency situations.

Continued heavy Bank lending in the public utility area after emergency situations had been taken care of reflects to some extent the large part transport and power requirements play in the total need for investment, especially public investment. Investment in transportation facilities of all kinds typically accounts for 15 to 25 percent of total investment, and investments in electric power typically lie in the range of 10 to 15 percent. Their share in public investment is, of course, much larger. Furthermore, at early stages of development the growth of needs for investment in these two areas tends to outpace the rate of growth of national income. The reason traditionally offered by the Bank in defense of its heavy lending in the area of economic overhead capital has been stated many times and was recently repeated in the annual report for 1969. "The existence of an adequate public service infrastructure is an essential precondition for sustained economic growth."[7]

The fact that the Bank was involved in loans for transportation and power and has continued to lend actively in this field has facilitated the continuing

7. World Bank/International Development Association, *Annual Report, 1969*, p. 13.

relationship between the Bank Group and borrowing institutions. The Bank's first power loan to Mexico was made in 1949, and since that time more than $600 million has been committed, in a series of loans, to the Mexican power sector. From 1951 to the end of fiscal year 1971, the Bank Group has financed eighteen power projects in Colombia. The Bank's first loan to the Indian Railways was made in 1950, and since then the Bank and IDA have extended thirteen loans and credits totaling some $640.4 million. This continuing relationship has made possible "the evolution at the staff level of a genuinely common effort by lender and borrower together"[8] and accounts for the major successes of the Bank Group in institution-building—those in the fields of power and transportation.

Some development specialists have criticized the heavy concentration of Bank Group lending in the area of public utilities. As we have noted, however, the capital requirements of this area, and particularly the needs for foreign exchange, are very large. The willingness of the Bank Group to undertake this type of financing has made it possible for borrowing countries to use their own resources for other purposes, including education.[9] Since lending by the Bank Group never, until very recently, accounted for more than 10 percent of official development assistance to less developed countries, there were other sources of finance for other requirements. And finally *if* it is true that an institution has particular capabilities for particular types of financing and other sources of finance are available for other needs, there is some merit in institutional specialization. If a legitimate criticism is to be made of the sectoral distribution of Bank Group financing, it is not that too much was loaned in the public utility field but that the Bank was too slow in overcoming what were thought to be obstacles in the area of agricultural and industrial financing.

After power and transportation the next largest field for Bank Group financing has been industry, which in Bank terminology includes manufactur-

8. World Bank/IDA, *Annual Report, 1971*, p. 18.

9. Oral History Project of Columbia University, interviews recorded in the summer of 1961 on the International Bank for Reconstruction and Development (cited hereinafter as "Oral History"). See interviews with John de Wilde, Harold Larsen, and Gerald Alter. Larsen, speaking in 1961, justifies the Bank's neglect of education and other sectors on two grounds: (1) Bank funds are substitutable for government funds, and (2) the Bank can deal more effectively with overhead capital projects. In his words,

I recall specifically that in one of my missions to a Latin American country, the Minister of Finance requested specific finance for housing and for hospitals. I asked him what his own Government's investments were and he said they were putting it into power and roads. These were satisfactorily taken care of, but he was short of money for these other purposes. We pointed out to him that we would finance the roads or power which would release his money for financing the social sector. He very quickly granted the point.

ing and mining. If all types of industrial financing are included, some 20 percent of Bank Group funds have gone into this area. These types include loans or credits from the Bank or IDA to finance particular manufacturing or mining projects; Bank Group lending to financial intermediaries (mainly development finance companies) for reinvestment in industrial enterprises; IFC investments; and program loans for the financing of industrial imports. Nearly half of total Bank Group industrial lending has been to development finance companies, whose activities, along with those of the IFC, are discussed in Chapter 11. Since Bank Group financing of industrial activity has been directed overwhelmingly to the private sector, a discussion of the Bank's views of the role of private industry in the development process is also postponed to Chapter 11. Program financing of industrial imports is considered in Chapter 9.

Bank Group lending in the field of agriculture was very slow to develop. In the period before 1963 less than 9 percent of total lending was directed to this area. Many potential agricultural projects had a high local expenditure component, and the strictures of the Articles of Agreement against lending for local expenditures discouraged financing such projects. Agriculture was neglected in most of the less developed countries, and agricultural ministries and institutions were among the least effective. Moreover, the Bank shared the conventional prejudice that agriculture was not the best route to development. Early Bank loans tended to concentrate on financing imports of agricultural equipment or of large-scale irrigation works and land clearance projects that were in the nature of overhead capital. The Bank still finances projects of this sort, but with the great expansion in lending during the past few years, the emphasis has been increasingly on smaller-scale, directly productive activity, such as agricultural credit, improved seeds, livestock improvement, palm oil production, and so on.[10]

Bank Group lending to the agricultural sector received a considerable impetus during President Woods's administration. Woods initiated the relationship between the Bank and the Food and Agriculture Organization of the UN (FAO) in identifying and preparing agricultural projects, in spite of considerable opposition among the Bank staff. The relations between the World Bank and the FAO are discussed in Chapter 17. But the real change of views on the role of agriculture in economic development, both within the Bank and outside, took place during the second half of the 1960s, partly as a result of the catastrophic drought years in the Indian subcontinent and partly because of the demonstrated effectiveness of new seed strains and new methods of

10. See Chapter 20, below.

cultivation. These factors quickly made themselves felt in Bank Group lending. Bank/IDA agricultural financing commitments for 1965–71 are shown in Table 7-4.

Table 7-4. *World Bank/IDA Commitments for Agricultural Financing, Fiscal Years 1965–71*
Millions of U.S. dollars

Fiscal year	World Bank	International Development Association	Total
1965	78.20	88.34	166.54
1966	120.70	31.70	152.40
1967	61.40	25.60	87.00
1968	145.30	27.20	172.50
1969	278.20	89.10	367.30
1970	186.80	226.08	412.88
1971	191.00	228.10	419.10

Source: International Bank for Reconstruction and Development.

In fiscal years 1969 through 1971, the Bank and IDA loaned as much for agricultural purposes as they had in the previous two decades and for a much wider variety of projects. In fiscal 1971, the Bank undertook for the first time the financing of agricultural research. A $12.7 million loan to Spain was designed to finance the reorganization of agricultural research for the whole country. One-fourth of these funds was allocated for "technical assistance, including the international recruitment of research specialists and consultants and 200 overseas training fellowships for Spanish scientists."[11] The Bank also took the initiative, in cooperation with the FAO and the United Nations Development Program (UNDP), in sponsoring a consultative group to advance international agricultural research.

The Bank Group's first loan for educational purposes was an IDA credit to Tunisia in 1962. Again, however, it was President Woods who stimulated an expansion of lending in this field. The Educational Projects Division was established in 1963, and a relationship was worked out with the United Nations Educational, Scientific and Cultural Organization (Unesco) in 1964 for the cooperative selection and preparation of educational projects.[12] The Bank Group's educational lending policy, approved by the board of directors in

11. World Bank/International Development Association, *Annual Report, 1971*, p. 7.
12. See Chapter 17, below, for a discussion of this relationship.

1963, had recommended that attention be concentrated on vocational and technical education and training and on general secondary education. Other categories were to be considered only under special circumstances.

These limitations on Bank Group lending in the educational field were dropped at the suggestion of President McNamara, and educational financing along with agriculture has been among the most rapidly growing sectors of Bank Group financing in recent years.[13] In fiscal 1971, Bank loans for educational projects amounted to $68.2 million and IDA credits to $32.4 million, for a total of $100.6 million. This was three times as high as the average level of lending for the five years ending in 1968.

Bank lending in the field of tourism did not begin until 1970, with a loan of $10 million for tourist hotels in Morocco. A Tourism Projects Department had been established in 1969. Until 1970 all the Bank Group's financing in this sector had been provided by the IFC and IBRD–assisted development finance companies. Since tourist receipts account for a large fraction of needed foreign exchange earnings in a number of less developed countries, this may well become a sizable area of financing, although the Bank foresees certain difficulties.[14]

Apart from education the Bank Group has made only a beginning in the areas characterized as "social" investment in Table 7-3. Although President McNamara has been a world spokesman for the cause of population planning, the Bank Group had made, by the end of fiscal 1971, only three small loans in the area of health and family planning. This figure, however, does not adequately reflect the extent of the Bank's involvement in this area. It has been actively engaged in technical assistance, and a number of loans and credits were ready for commitment in fiscal 1972. A Population Projects Department was established in 1971. The relation of urban investment to eco-

13. In 1970 President McNamara recommended, and the executive directors accepted, a restatement of the proper scope of Bank Group lending in this area:
We should broaden the scope of projects considered . . . and we should determine priorities and select projects on the basis of a thorough examination of the education system as a whole rather than by a priori designated areas of eligibility which may not relate to the particular country.
World Bank/IDA, *Annual Report, 1971*, p. 15.
14. . . . helter-skelter development [of tourism] can degrade or destroy important cultural assets, including many on which its own viability rests. Displays of alien affluence in the midst of local poverty can be disruptive. With adequate foresight and planning, however, the worst of such ills can be avoided and the benefits of tourism further increased. In some cases tourism projects can bring positive environmental improvements. A case in point is the project in Yugoslavia, which would not be justifiable, even in purely economic terms, if steps were not taken to assure that water off the beaches would be safe for swimming.
Ibid., p. 28.

nomic development is another field of recent Bank concern, but apart from a few recent loans for water supply and sewage, which are better grouped with capital infrastructure than with social investment, the Bank Group to date has done little in this field. Still it is clear that in recent years the Bank Group has increasingly directed its investments toward what may be called human resource development.

It is not our purpose here to discuss the relation of the Bank Group's sectoral allocation of financing, and changes over time in that allocation, to its changing conception of the development process and its role therein. That is reserved for Chapter 14. It should be emphasized, however, that "the creation of economic capacity," which in the early years was the Bank's principal objective, "is only permissive," as far as economic development is concerned. "Effective utilization and augmentation require attitudes, abilities, and incentives that cannot be taken for granted in most underdeveloped economies."[15] Furthermore, investments differ greatly in their capacity to generate productive attitudes and capabilities. At one end of the scale are power plants and cement mills, where the contribution is mainly in the form of additional capital equipment and institution building. At the other end is investment in education, in communication, and in part in agriculture. In the field of transportation, road construction is thought to be particularly productive in developing human capabilities since it encourages small-scale entrepreneurship in trucking and personnel transportation.[16]

The Bank in its early years leaned rather heavily to the view that the provision of viable capacity was its primary, if not sole, purpose. In recent years, however, the effect of different types of investment on human capabilities and attitudes has come very much to the fore. Needless to say, this enlarged consideration of the relation of investment to development greatly complicates the processes of project selection, appraisal, and supervision.

15. George W. Wilson, Barbara R. Bergmann, Leon V. Hirsch, and Martin S. Klein, *The Impact of Highway Investment on Development* (Brookings Institution, 1966), p. 195.

16. *General Problems of Transportation in Latin America* (Pan American Union, 1963). The Pan American Union study argues that road transportation is

a medium that can be organized into small companies, thereby helping to create . . . a group of entrepreneurs worthy of consideration. In this connection, the carrier with small resources is distinguished from the small tradesman in that, whereas the latter is concerned only with the use of working capital, the former, because he is using fixed capital, has to cope with the more complex problems relating to depreciation, obsolescence, and maintenance. That is why the small carrier has been assigned considerable importance as a future industrial entrepreneur.

Quoted in Wilson and others, *The Impact of Highway Investment . . .* , p. 201.

Share of Bank Group in Total Official Development Assistance

The activities of the Bank Group both as a development lender and, in the case of IDA, as a competitor for funds have been influenced significantly by the coexistence of bilateral assistance programs. Various aspects of the relationship between the Bank and bilateral development programs are discussed in Chapter 15. Here we are concerned with the quantitative importance of multilateral assistance flows in general, and those from the Bank Group in particular, in comparison with the total flow of financial resources to less developed countries. The principal multilateral assistance agencies, in addition to the Bank Group, are the Inter-American Development Bank, the Asian Development Bank, the African Development Bank, institutions of the European Economic Community, and the United Nations agencies. In 1969, commitments of the Bank Group were slightly more than 50 percent of total multilateral commitments (see Table 7-5), and with the rapid growth in Bank Group commitments after 1969, this share has substantially increased.

Data on foreign assistance flows are collected by both the Development Assistance Committee (DAC) of the Organisation for Economic Co-operation and Development (OECD) and the United Nations. The DAC figures are somewhat more complete and are used in the following discussion.[17] These figures, however, exclude contributions to the less developed countries from private voluntary agencies, financial flows from socialist countries, and assistance flows among less developed countries. Disbursements from the socialist countries averaged less than 5 percent of DAC official disbursements during the 1960s, and assistance flows among less developed countries have been minimal. Contributions from private voluntary agencies, on the other hand, have been relatively important. They are estimated to have been $840 million in the form of grants in 1970.[18]

17. The DAC distinguishes between official development assistance (ODA) and total official flows. ODA includes (1) bilateral grants and grant-like flows, (2) bilateral loans on concessional terms, and (3) contributions to multilateral organizations. Total official flows includes ODA from governments as well as ODA from multilateral organizations and other official flows. Net disbursements of ODA from governments in 1970 amounted to $6,808 million, while net disbursements of total official flows were $8,070 million (estimated). The concepts underlying the recording of the flow of financial resources to developing countries by the DAC are set out in Edwin M. Martin, *Development Assistance: Efforts and Policies of the Members of the Development Assistance Committee, 1969 Review* (Paris: OECD, 1969), Annex 1.

18. OECD, *Development Assistance, 1971 Review*, p. 39.

Table 7-5. *Total Assistance Commitments of Multilateral Agencies, 1969*
Amounts in millions of U.S. dollars

Agency	Commitments	Percent
Bank Group	1,650	52.6
Inter-American Development Bank	862	27.5
African Development Bank	8	0.3
Asian Development Bank	98	3.1
European Economic Community	202	6.4
United Nations agencies	316	10.1
Total	3,136	100.0

Sources: Organisation for Economic Co-operation and Development, and World Bank.

As Table 7-6 indicates, the share of the Bank Group (including the IFC) in net commitments and gross disbursements from DAC countries to less developed countries moved upward from 7 percent in 1960 to an average of 10 to 12 percent in the years 1961 to 1968. The Bank Group's share in commitments increased sharply in 1969 and 1970, but this was not yet reflected in gross and net disbursements.

Financial flows from the developed to the less developed world, as recorded by the DAC, are a dubious mixture. They include the provision of surplus agricultural products, loans on terms approaching those in capital

Table 7-6. *Share of Bank Group in Total Official Flows Received by Developing Countries from DAC Countries and Multilateral Agencies, Calendar Years 1960–70*
Amounts in millions of U.S. dollars

	Net commitments			Gross disbursements			Net disbursements		
	Total	Bank Group	Per-cent	Total	Bank Group	Per-cent	Total	Bank Group	Per-cent
1960	7,550ᵃ	538	7	5,205	354	7	4,648	257	6
1961	8,336ᵃ	722	9	6,291	330	5	5,643	206	4
1962	8,468	719	8	6,589	452	7	5,868	312	5
1963	8,023	860	11	7,161	579	8	6,304	430	7
1964	10,077	1,021	10	7,285	627	9	6,308	461	7
1965	8,567	1,034	12	7,853	770	10	6,738	583	9
1966	9,477	1,114	12	8,338	867	10	6,935	657	9
1967	10,060	670	7	8,755	954	11	7,345	717	10
1968	10,259	1,223	12	8,979	851	9	7,251	607	8
1969	10,739	1,706	16	9,363	979	10	7,418	690	9
1970	12,435ᵃ	2,215	18	10,100ᵃ	1,050	10	8,070ᵃ	738	9

Sources: Organisation for Economic Co-operation and Development and World Bank.
a. Partial estimates.

markets, grants for both capital and technical assistance, budgetary support for dependent overseas territories, and government-guaranteed suppliers' credits. The share of the Bank Group in the total outstanding public debt of less developed countries is substantially larger than its share in total official flows, as may be seen from the earlier tables in this chapter.[19] This is likely to be important in relation to the potential role of the Bank in debt renegotiation. On the other hand, the Bank's terms are substantially harder than the average bilateral terms on long-term transfers and very much harder than the average terms on total bilateral flows. Nor is this difference fully compensated for by the very soft terms of IDA lending, since IDA credits in the decade of the 1960s accounted for not more than 25 percent of total Bank Group lending. An offsetting factor of importance to less developed countries is the fact that Bank Group transfers are untied while almost all bilateral assistance is tied to procurement in the donor countries.

Table 7-7 shows estimates for 1968 of the Bank Group's share in total assistance flows from DAC countries, taking account of the grant element[20] in financial flows and the effect of aid-tying. Again it should be said that the Bank Group's share of total long-term lending, translated into grant-equivalents and adjusted for the effect of tying, would be substantially larger than the 6.5 percent indicated here as the share of total assistance flows so corrected. Furthermore, the figures for 1968 are abnormally low because of the delay in IDA replenishment noted above. Even so it must be recognized that, in the later years of the 1960s the Bank Group's share (however it is measured) of the total flow of official funds to the less developed world was a minor one. The rapid growth of Bank lending after 1968 and the anticipated doubling of IDA funds in 1972, together with the reduction in U.S. bilateral assistance, may be expected to change this situation substantially in the course of the next few years.

19. In a study ("The External Debt of Developing Countries") presented by the IBRD to the board of governors at its annual meeting in September 1971, an examination of the external public debt of eighty less developed countries indicates that, as of December 31, 1969, loans and credits extended by the Bank and IDA accounted for about 16 percent.

20. The "grant element" of a loan is the difference between the amount of the loan and the present value of the expected payments by the debtor (interest and principal) during the course of the loan. It is intended to represent the amount of the "concession" from market terms, the "true assistance" element of the loan. A commonly used discount rate in determining the present value of future payments is the rate used in calculating the grant-equivalent of Official Development Assistance commitments in Table 7-7: 10 percent. Using this discount rate, the grant-equivalent of a 7 percent, thirty-year, typical Bank loan with a ten-year grace period is 26 percent. The grant-equivalent of the normal IDA credit with a fifty-year maturity, a ten-year grace period, and a 0.75 percent service charge is 86.4 percent.

Table 7-7. *Percentage Distribution of Official Development Assistance, by Source, 1968*

Sources	Official Development Assistance commitments (1)		Grant-equivalent of Col. (1) (2)		Col. (2) adjusted for tied aid (3)	
Bilateral aid						
United States	39.7		44.8		41.9	
France	13.7		15.3		16.2	
United Kingdom	5.4		5.9		6.0	
Germany	5.1		4.8		4.9	
Other DAC countries	13.7		14.7		15.0	
Total bilateral aid		77.5		85.5		84.0
Multilateral aid						
World Bank/IDA	13.5		5.9		6.5	
Other agencies	9.0		8.6		9.5	
Total multilateral aid		22.5		14.5		16.0
Total, all sources		100.0		100.0		100.0

Source: IBRD, Economics Department, June 16, 1970. Figures are rounded and may not add to totals.

Note: No good data exist either for the extra costs imposed by tying, which may well vary significantly among donor countries, or for the proportion of commitments in 1968 that were tied. In computing the figures in Col. 3 of this table, it was assumed that 20 percent could be taken as a generally applicable round figure for the former, while the proportion of disbursements in 1968 that were tied was taken as an indicator of the proportion of tied commitments.

The data for total and ODA commitments for DAC countries in 1967 and 1968 are analyzed in greater detail in an article by P. D. Henderson, "The Distribution of Official Development Assistance Commitments by Recipient Countries and by Sources," *Bulletin of the Oxford University Institute of Economics and Statistics*, Vol. 33 (February 1971). See, in particular, Table 4. This table does not attempt an estimate of the effect of tying but, according to Henderson, "The extent of tying ... appears to be greatest in the case of Canada, Japan, and the United States" (p. 10).

Terms of Bank Group Lending

The only limitation placed by the Articles of Agreement on the terms of Bank lending was that during the first ten years of its existence a commission of "not less than one percent per annum and not greater than one and one-half percent per annum ... shall be charged on the outstanding portion of any ... loan."[21] At the end of that period the commission might be reduced if the accumulated reserve were judged by the Bank to be sufficient.[22] Otherwise, "the terms and conditions of interest and amortization payments, maturity

21. Article IV, section 4(a).

22. The executive directors initially set the commission charge at 1 percent, and it remained at that rate until it was discontinued on July 1, 1964, when the "Special Reserve" into which it was paid had reached $289 million.

and dates of payment of each loan shall be determined by the Bank."[23] The only directives relating to terms contained in the Articles of Agreement of IDA are the provisions in Article I that the terms of financing shall be "more flexible and bear less heavily on the balance of payments than those of conventional loans," and the broad language of Article V, which, as interpreted by the executive directors,

permit[s] the Association to carry out the directive of Article I, in the case of loans made from its freely convertible resources, in any number of ways: for example, by providing for lenient terms of repayment (such as loans repayable in foreign exchange with long maturities or long periods of grace or both, or loans repayable wholly or partly in local currency), by lending free of interest or at a low rate of interest, or by some combination of the foregoing.[24]

Although the Bank was free to set its own terms, the need to acquire the bulk of its new funds from capital markets dictated that interest on its loans be governed largely by its own borrowing rate. From the time the Bank opened its doors until 1964 the interest rate charged to all borrowers was 1.25 percentage points above the estimated cost of borrowing.

Beginning in 1965, the Bank for a time made a distinction between member countries that were able to borrow abroad on their own credit and those not able to do so. Those in the first group, the market-eligible countries, were expected to pay an interest charge that was 0.5 to 1 percent above the standard charge, depending on the length of the loan.[25] The only such loans ever made were to Japan and Italy, and the practice was discontinued in 1967. Indeed, in that year the standard rate was reduced to 0.375 percent above the estimated borrowing rate. As interest rates at which the Bank borrowed continued to rise, the executive directors decided not to increase the lending rate proportionately. This soon produced a "negative spread" between the borrowing and lending rates, which has continued to be a feature of Bank lending policy up to the present writing. The lending rate for most of calendar year 1970 was 7.25 percent. The weighted cost of Bank borrowing during the same period was 8.07 percent. This meant a negative spread of about 0.8

23. Article IV, section 4(a).

24. IDA, Articles of Agreement and accompanying report of the executive directors of the IBRD (Jan. 26, 1960). Par. 16 of the report.

25. During the year, the Bank considered whether it was justified in continuing to make loans to more developed countries, able to cover the bulk of their requirements for external capital from market sources, at the same interest rate as it charged . . . its less developed members. As a result of this consideration, the Bank decided that it would charge such countries rates of interest roughly comparable to those they pay when borrowing in the market. These rates would be up to one per cent higher than the Bank's standard interest rate, which remained at 5½% during the year. Pursuant to this policy, a 25-year loan of $75 million for an expressway in Japan carried an interest charge of 6½%, while 6¼% was charged on a 15-year $100 million loan for industrial projects in Italy.
IBRD/IDA, Annual Report, 1964–65, pp. 10 and 12.

percent. Obviously the maintenance of the negative spread cannot continue indefinitely without seriously reducing net income.

Shortly after IDA was established, the executive directors established terms for IDA project credits, from which they have never departed: fifty-year maturities, ten-year grace periods, and a 0.75 percent service charge. For countries able to borrow both from the Bank and from IDA the possibility exists of establishing terms intermediate between those of the two institutions by "blending" loans from both. There were fifteen such member borrowers in 1971. "Hard blend" countries are those that borrow predominantly from the Bank. "Soft blend" countries are those favored by IDA.

The terms on which the Bank or IDA lend, and even the combinations permitted by a blending of Bank loans and IDA credits, do not allow a very flexible response to the great variety of development needs and balance-of-payments difficulties presented by potential member borrowers. Furthermore, this lack of flexibility has tended to be increased by various policy decisions of the executive directors. The terms on which the Bank and IDA lend take no account of differences in risk either among borrowing countries or among different types of projects. It was decided that to charge one borrower more than another because of a presumed greater incidence of risk would be inappropriate for an international lending institution. If a member is creditworthy, it can borrow on customary Bank terms; if it is judged not to be creditworthy, the Bank will refuse to lend. The advent of IDA, of course, created a great difference in the terms on which different member countries can borrow. But there is the same equality of terms among "IDA countries" as there is among "Bank countries." Among different types of projects there can be, and are, differences in the length of grace periods and the maturity of Bank loans—justified in part by differences in the length of construction and pay-out periods—but no difference in interest charges on Bank loans.[26] The IDA terms are the same regardless of the nature of the project or the program.

The lending philosophy of the Bank has also contemplated from the beginning that loans to a member borrower would be repaid whether or not the Bank continued to lend to that country. During the early discussions of proposals for a Bank, prior to Bretton Woods, Keynes professed to believe that after the war an international lender could expect to be repaid only so long as he was prepared to continue financing repayment of past loans by the commitment of new ones. This was certainly not the view of his Bretton Woods colleagues nor of the management of the Bank when it took office.

---

26. Beginning in 1969, Bank loans for some industrial projects have carried a premium interest rate of 1.5–2 percent above the standard lending rate, the premium being payable in local currency. The premium is waived, however, to the extent that the borrowing government charges the enterprise a fee for guaranteeing the loan.

As was noted in Chapter 6, attempts by Bank economists to persuade the management that creditworthiness should be judged on the basis of the ability of a borrower to pay interest charges, and that normal procedure should be to "roll over" debt when it came due, were doomed to failure. International lending based on any other conception than that "debts are debts" was considered as not only financially irresponsible but immoral.

The decision of the executive directors in 1964 to reserve IDA credits for poor countries imposed another element of rigidity on Bank Group lending. There are a number of less developed countries that can meet neither IDA's income tests nor the Bank's creditworthiness criteria. And those that can meet only the Bank's criteria could generally do so to a much greater degree if they were entitled to "blended" Bank-IDA lending. The reasons for the income test are obviously cogent, but it does impose additional inflexibility on Bank Group lending.

Bank lending policy has, of course, been frequently discussed by the executive directors, and suggestions have been made for increasing its flexibility. At various times directors have proposed that, instead of being transferred to IDA, profits should be used to subsidize Bank loans. Latin American directors have consistently argued against the IDA income test and in favor of greater emphasis on the balance-of-payments considerations mentioned in the Articles of Agreement. Others have felt that IDA should depart from its flat 0.75 percent service charge and adopt a range of interest rates. Some have argued against the Bank's continued use of commitment charges on the undisbursed portion of loans.[27] But these and other critiques and proposals have been consistently rejected.

Nor has the Bank been more receptive to outside suggestions for changes in the types and terms of Bank lending. At the first United Nations Conference on Trade and Development (UNCTAD) in 1964 two proposals that could affect its lending policy were referred to the Bank for study. One of these, advanced by David Horowitz, governor of the Bank of Israel and head of the Israeli delegation to the conference, suggested that the difference between the cost of Bank borrowing and a lending rate to less developed countries of, say, 1 percent be subsidized by an interest-equalization fund maintained by annual appropriations from the industrialized countries. This, Mr. Horowitz felt, would make possible a large expansion in soft lending by the

27. Commitment charges are believed by some to be useful in encouraging timely disbursement of loans. There seems to be little evidence to support this view. It is also argued that commitment fees compensate the lender for the lower returns on moneys that he is obliged to hold in highly liquid form awaiting disbursement. This is ordinarily true, but there have been periods of high short-term interest rates when earnings on investments of liquid assets have accounted for a sizable fraction of the Bank's profits.

Bank, IDA, or some other international institution at a relatively small cost to contributing members, at least in the early years of the program. The second proposal, sponsored initially by Sweden and the United Kingdom, led to a resolution requesting the World Bank to study the feasibility of a scheme that "should aim to deal with problems arising from adverse movements in export proceeds which prove to be of a nature or duration which cannot be dealt with by short-term balance of payments support." An "adverse movement" was defined as a "shortfall from reasonable expectations," and the purpose of the proposed scheme would be "to provide longer term assistance to developing countries which would help them to avoid disruption of their development programs."[28] It was understood that, if a feasible scheme could be worked out, the Bank Group would be the principal source of finance.

The staff of the Bank undertook a careful study of the Horowitz proposal and presented its report in February 1965.[29] As originally proposed by Mr. Horowitz, the scheme contemplated raising $2 billion a year over a ten-year period, but was later modified by him into a proposal for raising $3 billion over a five-year period. Although the Bank staff made no recommendation for or against the proposal, so many difficulties were underlined in the report that the scheme was not carried further. The bonds to be issued by the borrowing authority would need to be guaranteed jointly and possibly individually by the Part I countries of IDA, in proportion to their IMF quotas. These governments would have to agree to open their markets on a regular basis to the sales of the proposed securities. And if soft loans to less developed countries were to have long maturities, it would be necessary for Part I countries to commit themselves to payments into the interest equalization fund for periods of similar length. If all these commitments were made and if, as the proposal suggested, borrowing operations were conducted "to the extent feasible in those countries which, at the time, had a balance of payments surplus," it seemed very doubtful to the staff, and to their advisers from various financial centers, that money could be raised in this amount. And if it were raised by the Bank or IDA, it was thought that the effect on the terms of the Bank's own borrowing would inevitably be adverse.[30]

28. Resolution A IV.18 on Supplementary Financial Measures, adopted at the First UNCTAD Conference by 106 votes to 0, with 10 abstentions.

29. IBRD, "The Horowitz Proposal," a staff report (February 1965). This did not purport to represent the views of the executive directors.

30. It was not clear from the proposal whether the moneys to be raised would be in addition to IDA contributions or a replacement for them. If they were merely to replace IDA contributions, the gains would not have been great since the second IDA replenishment brought the contributed amounts up to $400 million a year, to which the Bank added substantially by transferring profits.

The resolution on what has come to be called supplementary finance was subjected to intensive study in the Bank, and in December 1965 a report entitled "Study on Supplementary Financial Measures" was transmitted to the secretary-general of the United Nations with a letter from President Woods stating, "I believe that the scheme forms the basis for a feasible solution to a problem of major importance and that it is worthy of the most careful consideration by all governments." The letter went on to say, "In accordance with past practice in similar cases, this study does not purport to represent the views of the Executive Directors of the Bank, or of the governments which appointed or elected them."

The scheme in question was predicated on the assumption that it would be supplementary to, and not a substitute for, already existing forms of aid. The international agency designated to administer the program (presumably IDA) would establish for each participating developing country, in cooperation with its planning authorities, realistic projections of export earnings for the country's development planning period. In addition, the agency and the cooperating country would agree on a development program, including performance targets and a "policy package." Short-falls in export earnings below projected levels would be compensated only to the extent that they arose from causes other than the country's own poor performance and threatened to disrupt the development program. The study estimated that $1.5 billion to $2 billion would be required for an initial five-year experimental period.

There is no doubt that unexpected short-falls of export earnings can seriously disrupt development programs and have done so in the past, and that longer-term financing, over and above the short-term "compensatory financing" facilities provided by the IMF, could make a useful contribution to development.[31] But whatever one thinks of the merits of the scheme outlined above, it foundered for lack of financing. Discussions by members of the Bank's management with representatives of those governments that would have had to bear the brunt of the financing revealed little disposition to take on the burden. And as it became clear that any substantial contribution to supplementary finance would probably be at the expense of IDA replenish-

31. As N. M. Perera, minister of finance of Ceylon, reported at the 1970 meeting of the boards of governors of the Bank and the Fund, his country had lost $170 million in export earnings between 1965 and 1969 from the fall in tea prices alone. This he estimated was about equal to the total amount of aid provided Ceylon during the same period. He went on to say, "Had the kind of scheme of supplementary financing advocated within UNCTAD and formulated by the Bank staff in 1965 been in existence over this period, Ceylon would surely have been entitled to draw on it for much of what she received, and aid in any meaningful sense would in fact have had to exceed the amounts received on this account." IBRD, Press release, (Sept. 23, 1970), p. 2.

ment, the Bank tended to lose what enthusiasm it might have had for the scheme. Although the second UNCTAD conference in 1968 urged the IBRD to persevere in its search for a workable scheme, President McNamara informed the UN Trade and Development Board in August 1970 that he saw little point in pursuing this matter unless and until possible sources of financing became more visible.[32]

The second UNCTAD conference, January–March 1968, also suggested a study by the IBRD, in consultation with the IMF and the secretary-general of UNCTAD, of possible improvements in the techniques of lending. "In particular the study should take into account the possibility of postponing or waiving interest and amortization payments in years of foreign exchange stringency."[33] Although this suggestion for possible improvements in the techniques of lending was formulated with other lenders as well as the Bank in mind, it would, of course, also enable the Bank to increase its lending flexibility. What the proposers had specifically in mind was the so-called "bisque" clause of the Anglo-American Financial Agreement of 1946, which provided a waiver of the 2 percent interest payment in any year in which the United Kingdom's "foreign exchange income was not sufficient to meet its pre-war level of imports adjusted to current prices."[34]

It is fairly clear from the way the proposal was formed that "improvement in techniques of lending" was intended to mean "better" or "softer" terms. This could be accomplished by various changes designed to increase the "grant element" of loans, but not only by such changes. For a borrower it would be better if the payment of interest and principal could be postponed during a period of severe balance-of-payments difficulty, even though such postponement might add little to the grant element.[35] A Bank staff study makes it clear that, so far as the grant element of loans is concerned, interest rates and charges are of overwhelming importance.[36] Changes in the length of grace periods and maturities have relatively little influence at any but very

32. McNamara's statement, however, did not dispose of the matter. At the tenth session of the UNCTAD Trade and Development Board (Geneva, Aug. 26–Sept. 18, 1970) the position of the IBRD was severely criticized. A declaration of the UNCTAD board, which achieved a fair consensus among the delegates, expressed the hope that the Bank would give further consideration to supplementary finance and would, in the meantime, pursue its efforts to work out a discretionary scheme.

33. TD/L37, Annex I, 29 (11).

34. When the U.K. asked for a waiver in 1956, the formula was found to be unworkable. Consequently the agreement was amended in 1957 to allow the U.K. to postpone payments of up to seven installments of principal and interest until the end of the period of amortization.

35. In fact the Bank's Articles of Agreement (Article IV, section 4[c]) provide for such a contingency, though this particular provision has never been invoked.

36. IBRD, "Possible Improvements in Techniques of Lending" (April 1970; processed).

low rates of interest. On the other hand, the lengthening of grace periods and maturities may be of considerable interest to borrowers if it permits productive processes and export earning capacity to be well established before payments and repayments begin. The conclusions of the staff study on improvements in techniques of lending were not intended to apply specifically to Bank lending policy, though the Bank was not excluded. It is doubtful, however, whether the operations of the Bank Group have been or will be much affected by the study. In particular there is no evidence that acceptance of a bisque clause or similar arrangements involving postponement or waiver of interest or principal charges has found, or will find, favor in Bank lending policy.

There have been other proposals from outside the Bank for changes in lending policy, but none of these has met with much enthusiasm. In the meantime, however, as the Bank lending rate has increased from the 4 to 5 percent on early loans to 7.25 percent in 1970 and 1971, and as IDA funds, despite a considerable increase, have had to be strictly rationed, the Bank's ability to respond to the needs of its less developed members has been called into question. As a senior official of the Bank put it,

It is doubtful that anyone at Bretton Woods seriously contemplated the extent to which countries would again build up intolerable levels of debt long before their needs for external capital were met or would have such limited savings capacity and growth potential that they would have no creditworthiness for borrowing in the first place.[37]

The Bank's answer to this problem was IDA, but in view of the limitations to IDA financing this was at best a very incomplete answer.[38]

Repayments from Borrowers and Their Effect on Net Lending and Net Capital Transfers of the Bank Group

Net lending is normally defined as gross disbursement minus repayment of principal. If one is concerned with the net transfer of funds, however, it is necessary to deduct also payments of interest and other charges. As was noted in Table 7-6, gross disbursements of the Bank Group in 1968 on loans to developing countries amounted to 9 percent of total gross disbursements of official flows from DAC countries and multilateral agencies. Net disbursements amounted to 8 percent of total net disbursements. The Bank Group, despite the "soft" money of IDA, lends on somewhat harder terms than the average terms of bilateral assistance programs. Needless to say, the figures

37. J. H. Williams, "International Bank for Reconstruction and Development" (paper delivered to the Fourth Maxwell Institute on the United Nations, Bretton Woods, New Hampshire, Aug. 27–Sept. 1, 1967; processed), p. 7.
38. For our recommendations on terms of loans, see Chapter 21.

for the "hard-lending" Bank (Table 7-8) show a very different relationship between gross and net lending and capital transfers than the figures for the "soft-lending" IDA (Table 7-9).

Certain aspects of Table 7-8 are worthy of comment. Net Bank lending to developed countries had become negative by 1964, and net transfers had become negative as early as 1961. This is as it should be. As was indicated above, the Bank has undertaken few commitments to developed countries since 1967. From now on a reverse net flow of funds can be expected until loans to developed countries have been amortized. Although gross disbursements to less developed countries have increased steadily, there has been no substantial increase in net lending since 1963; and it was in that year that net capital transfers to less developed countries also reached a maximum. Taking both groups of borrowers together, net transfers of funds from the Bank to all its members reached a very low level in 1969 and was negative in 1970. This situation, however, will change rather substantially over the next few years with the very large expansion of Bank lending.

Since IDA credits are extended with a ten-year grace period, there has been to date no difference between gross and net lending. The small charges reflect the 0.75 percent a year service payments. The decline in IDA disbursements in 1969 and 1970 was the result of a delay in consummating the second replenishment.

When the figures on Bank and IDA lending are combined, they reveal that net lending reached a high point of $786 million in 1967, while net transfers reached a high point of $495 million in the same year. These amounts will increase, at least for a few years, with the large expansion of Bank lending, but loans at 7.25 percent, even though maturities are long, lead rather quickly to large reverse flows. Sizable replenishment of IDA funds could improve the situation over a much longer period.

The contrast between gross disbursements for the Bank Group of over $1 billion in 1968 and net transfers of $415 million (not to mention net transfers of $269 million in 1969 and $96 million in 1970) presents a rather somber picture that has not escaped the attention of the Bank's management. There are only three ways in which this picture could be improved. The first is through a continuous and sizable increase in gross Bank lending. This could raise net lending and net transfer but only for a limited time. If the Bretton Woods conception of the Bank's role were correct, this would be sufficient. In the course of time any borrowing country well embarked on the process of development should expect to become a net exporter of capital. But for many less developed countries this at best is a long-term prospect. Second, the relation between gross and net transfers could be changed by

Table 7-8. *Flow of World Bank Funds, by Type of Flow and Country Group, Fiscal Years 1947–70*
Millions of U.S. dollars

Type of flow	Cumulative through 1959	1960	1961	1962	1963	1964	1965	1966	1967	1968	1969	1970
Developing countries												
1. Disbursements	1,799.30	365.90	274.20	368.80	475.30	464.20	511.41	551.54	598.46	609.64	653.77	745.99
2. Repayments	219.37	93.67	115.99	133.31	146.03	161.80	179.01	200.72	229.95	237.44	276.82	306.32
3. Net lending (1–2)	1,579.93	272.23	158.21	235.49	329.27	302.40	332.40	350.82	368.51	372.20	376.95	439.67
4. Charges	275.25	83.15	101.71	111.95	130.29	153.61	167.23	185.41	205.49	225.46	249.52	285.26
5. Net transfer (3–4)	1,304.68	189.08	56.50	123.54	198.98	148.79	165.17	165.41	163.02	146.74	127.43	154.41
Developed countries (earlier borrowers)												
1. Disbursements	1,578.00	178.00	124.30	116.60	145.10	94.70	94.32	116.88	191.98	162.31	108.27	8.35
2. Repayments	281.47	64.46	74.77	92.35	97.45	105.58	120.71	217.13	116.54	120.19	125.70	135.73
3. Net lending (1–2)	1,296.53	113.54	49.53	24.25	47.65	−10.88	−26.39	−10.25	75.44	42.12	−17.43	−127.38
4. Charges	376.47	59.98	64.40	70.92	74.76	76.28	76.58	76.64	79.21	84.24	86.86	85.88
5. Net transfer (3–4)	920.06	53.56	−14.87	−46.67	−27.11	−87.16	−102.97	−86.89	−3.77	−42.12	−104.29	−213.26
Total												
1. Disbursements	3,377.30	543.90	398.50	485.40	620.40	558.90	605.73	668.42	790.44	771.95	762.04	754.34
2. Repayments	500.84	158.13	190.76	225.66	243.48	267.38	299.72	327.85	346.49	357.63	402.52	442.05
3. Net lending (1–2)	2,876.46	385.77	207.74	259.74	376.92	291.52	306.01	340.57	443.95	414.32	359.52	312.29
4. Charges	651.72	143.13	166.11	182.87	205.05	229.89	243.81	262.05	284.70	309.70	336.38	371.14
5. Net transfer (3–4)	2,224.74	242.64	41.63	76.87	171.87	61.63	62.20	78.52	159.25	104.62	23.14	−58.85

Source: IBRD, Programming and Budgeting Department, Aug. 5, 1971.

219

Table 7-9. Flow of IDA Funds to Developing Countries, by Type of Flow, Fiscal Years 1962-70
Millions of U.S. dollars

Type of flow	1962	1963	1964	1965	1966	1967	1968	1969	1970
1. Disbursements	12.20	56.20	124.10	222.20	266.90	342.09	318.82	255.79	143.35
2. Repayments	...	...	...	...	...	...	...	0.06	0.13
3. Net lending (1–2)	12.20	56.20	124.10	222.20	266.90	342.09	318.82	255.73	143.22
4. Charges	...	0.14	0.77	1.77	3.58	5.36	8.13	10.21	12.11
5. Net transfer (3–4)	12.20	56.06	123.33	220.43	263.32	336.73	310.69	245.52	131.11

Source: IBRD, Programming and Budgeting Department, Aug. 5, 1971.

softening the terms of lending. For the Bank Group this could be done, under existing policies, only by increasing IDA credits as a percentage of total operations. This is probably the only route that offers long-term promise for the Bank Group as an important development institution. Third, this relation could be changed ex post through debt renegotiation. We therefore turn now to a consideration of the debt position of less developed countries and the existing and potential role of the Bank in debt renegotiation.

The Burden of Debt and the Problem of Debt Rescheduling

The IBRD had begun as early as 1956, with increasing emphasis in the 1960s, to stress the problem created by the growing volume of external debt among less developed member countries. The Articles of Agreement of IDA recognized the necessity for softer terms of lending for countries whose creditworthiness for Bank loans was in jeopardy. Beginning in 1964 the Bank's annual reports have presented data on outstanding debt and debt service charges. The report for 1963–64 noted that "the heavy debt burden that weighs on an increasing number of its member countries has been a continuing concern of the World Bank Group."[39] Given its dependence on capital markets and the shortage of IDA funds, there was little the Bank Group could do to ease that burden other than to extend the length of grace periods and loan maturities. This was done in a number of loan agreements in the 1960s. Under the presidency of George Woods the problem of external debt became a central preoccupation of the Bank. It lay behind the proposal for a second IDA replenishment of $1 billion a year. In fact only $400 million was realized and this only after substantial delay. This preoccupation was also heavily emphasized in President Woods' 1967 speech in Stockholm proposing the "grand assize," later undertaken by the [Pearson] Commission on International Development. Both the seriousness of the problem and the Bank's emphasis on its seriousness have increased during the McNamara regime; and at the 1970 meeting of the boards of governors in Copenhagen approval was given to studies by the Bank and Fund on the present magnitude of the problem.

39. IBRD/IDA, *Annual Report, 1963–1964*, p. 8. A study by Dragoslav Avramović and other Bank officials (*Economic Growth and External Debt* [Johns Hopkins Press, 1964]) presented the material the IBRD had begun systematically to collect on external debt and debt service charges and noted that the external debt of less developed countries had increased, on the average, at an annual rate of 15 percent a year between 1955 and 1962 (p. 101).

The Bank was, of course, not the only institution seized of this matter. The Development Assistance Committee of the OECD since 1963 has had the debt problem under continuous review, and in 1965 and again in 1969 the DAC made specific recommendations to its members to improve the terms of lending and expand the percentage of assistance taking the form of grants.

Despite these efforts, the average terms of bilateral assistance programs became more rather than less severe during the period 1964–68, and improvement since then has been slight.[40] The international lending agencies, dependent on capital markets, have seen their own lending rates pushed upward under the influence of tight money. The total external public debt of less developed countries stood at approximately $60 billion at the end of 1969, and this debt has continued to grow at the rate of 14 percent a year.[41] Debt service payments grew at the same rate in the period 1956–69, though the annual rate from 1960 to 1969 fell to 9 percent. Over the decade of the 1960s this was substantially above the rates of growth both of GNP and of export earnings in the less developed world.

The Bank estimated that debt service payments by less developed countries amounted to about $5 billion in 1969.[42] This represented approximately 33 percent of the total gross inflow of external funds to the less developed nations. Debt service payments represented about 12 percent of total export earnings of less developed countries in the mid-1960s. Ten years earlier the figure had been 6 percent.[43] There is, of course, a large variation among the less developed countries in the seriousness of their debt problems. Oil-rich countries and a few others face no difficulties. Some less developed countries have problems that are amenable to solutions involving changes only in their own domestic policies. Although the debt burdens of some others have been growing rapidly, their export earnings, and hence their ability to service debt, have been growing even more rapidly. South Korea and Taiwan are conspicuous examples. But there still remain a number of less developed countries, members of the IBRD, that will not be able to manage their foreign debt problems without some kind of external assistance.

These countries tend to fall into two groups depending on the structure of

40. The Report of the Commission on International Development [the Pearson Commission] said: "The average interest rate on loans from the members of the DAC has increased from 3.1 per cent in 1964 to 3.3 per cent in 1968, and average maturity of loans has declined from 28.4 years to 24.8 years. . . . As a result, the average concessional value of the loans as expressed in the grant element [using a 10 percent discount rate] declined from 54 per cent to 48 per cent, between 1964 and 1968." (*Partners in Development* [Praeger, 1969], p. 163.)

41. World Bank/IDA, *Annual Report, 1971*, p. 50.

42. *Ibid.*

43. OECD, *Development Assistance, 1967 Review*, p. 73.

their external debt. For the first group the main debt burden is occasioned by short-term borrowing, guaranteed and unguaranteed, from private sources. Suppliers' credits are frequently the principal component. In such cases relief may be provided by spreading repayment over a relatively short period. Typically the rescheduling is accompanied by borrowing from the IMF and involves commitments on the part of the borrower with respect to monetary and fiscal measures and limits on further short-term debt. All creditors tend to be treated equally. Most of the rescheduling exercises that have been undertaken since 1957 have been of this type. The primary objective of such debt refinancing, the Pearson Commission observed, "has been to 'bail out' the borrower by providing strictly short-run accommodation. The emphasis has usually been placed on speedy resumption of debt service payments rather than on re-establishing [a] financial framework for orderly growth."[44]

If the debt crisis is the result merely of a bunching of maturities, usually short-term, or a temporary short-fall of export earnings, a stretchout of the period of repayment may be sufficient. But operations of this sort have frequently resulted in a need for repeated reschedulings. Table 7-10 shows debt reschedulings that took place between 1957 and 1969. Argentina went through four such operations in eight years and Indonesia three debt reschedulings in three years.

The second group of debt problems now coming to the fore is of a rather different kind. These problems are not the result of a bunching of maturities, a temporary decline in export earnings, or debt mismanagement in any obvious sense. They are the product of the accumulation of long-term debt in quantities and on terms that exceed prospective ability to repay. The large increase in bilateral and multilateral development assistance flows in the 1960s had begun by 1970 to generate unmanageable demands for reverse flows. Grace periods began to expire, and loan terms, as we have pointed out above, became increasingly onerous. This creates a situation that cannot be managed by a temporary postponement of service charges. Furthermore, development assistance has been provided on terms that vary greatly among bilateral and multilateral lenders. A question of equitable burden-sharing among creditor countries arises, which is generally not the case in the typical rescheduling of short-term private debt.

A World Bank report prepared for the board of governors in 1971 suggested that over the next five years some twelve countries might fall in the first category of debt problems and perhaps four in the second category. The first group includes several Latin American countries, as well as Iran, the Ivory

44. *Partners in Development*, pp. 156–57.

Table 7-10. *Debt Reschedulings, 1957–1969*

Country	Years in which payments deferred	Institutional arrangement
Argentina	1957	Paris Club
	1961–62	Paris Club
	1963–64	Paris Club
	1965	Paris Club
Brazil	1961–65	The Hague Club
	1964–65	The Hague Club
Chile	1965–66	Paris Club
Turkey	1958–63	OEEC Auspices
	1964–67	OECD Donor Consortium
	1968	OECD Donor Consortium
Indonesia	1966–67	Donor Consortium
	1968	Donor Consortium
	1969	Donor Consortium
India	1968	Donor Consortium under IBRD leadership
Ghana	1966–68	IMF Auspices
	1969–70	IMF Auspices
	1969–72	IMF Auspices
Peru	1968–69	U.K. Auspices
Liberia	1963	Bilateral
United Arab Republic	1967–68	Bilateral[a]
Yugoslavia	1965–66	Bilateral

Source: Charles R. Frank, Jr., *Debt and Terms of Aid* (Overseas Development Council, 1970), p. 27. Frank notes that "A number of countries not included in this table rescheduled some very short-term debt (less than one year maturity)." The Paris and Hague Clubs were groups of creditors who met in Paris and in the Hague.

a. Rescheduled arrears with major creditors except the United States.

Coast, Korea, the Philippines, and Tunisia, but represents about one-third of the total debt of developing countries. "A common characteristic of these countries is that they have undertaken a significant amount of short-term borrowing in the past and therefore are vulnerable to temporary debt servicing difficulties resulting from unexpected fluctuations in foreign exchange availabilities."[45]

The second group, according to the Bank report, includes Ceylon, Ghana, India, and Pakistan, which account for about one-fifth of total debt, and would have included Indonesia prior to the debt negotiations of 1966–68 and 1970. "Essentially, these are countries which have accumulated such large amounts of debt in the past, and whose development is likely to be such a prolonged process, that they are likely to encounter serious and protracted debt service difficulties unless large amounts of external assistance are available to them."[46]

The rescheduling of Indian debt in 1968 and Indonesian debt in 1970 will

45. IBRD, "External Debt Study" (R71–178), July 14, 1971.
46. *Ibid.,* p. 6.

need at some stage to be reviewed. In the Indian case the objective of the consortium was a reduction of debt service charges to about 20 percent of export earnings. This necessitated a rescheduling on very favorable terms of 25 percent of debt due in 1968, but this percentage will inevitably increase over time. The burden-sharing arrangement worked out by the Bank discriminated, as it should, rather sharply in favor of soft lenders.[47] The Indonesian rescheduling of April 1970 provided for a repayment of outstanding principal ($900 million) over a thirty-year period. No new moratorium interest was to be paid on the principal, and the interest that was already due on the rescheduled debt was not to be repaid until the second half of the thirty-year period.[48]

It is inevitable that the Bank as well as the Fund will become deeply immersed in debt renegotiation exercises in the 1970s. Not only is the Bank one of the largest capital lenders, but the complexity of the burden-sharing operation is such that the services of an international institution are likely to be indispensable. The Pearson Commission's analysis of the debt problems confronting less developed countries led to a recommendation that "debt relief operations avoid the need for repeated reschedulings and seek to reestablish a realistic basis for development finance." The commission went on to say, "The World Bank and the IMF, as important providers of long-term and short-term finance, respectively, must of course participate in rescheduling discussions."[49]

In the debt renegotiations that have taken place to this writing, the Bank has not renegotiated its own debt except in the case of India. Nor does it plan to do so. A staff study approved by the executive directors in 1971 states the Bank's position as follows:

The Bank Group has considerable flexibility in the determination of maturities and grace periods on Bank lending and in the blend of Bank/IDA resources provided to individual countries and will use this flexibility in appropriate ways to assist countries faced with debt servicing difficulties. It will thereby reduce the burden of relief to be shared by other creditors while helping to provide the debtor country with the resources necessary to continue its economic develop-

47. See Charles R. Frank, *Debt and Terms of Aid* (Overseas Development Council, 1970), pp. 27–28.
48. World Bank/IDA, *Annual Report, 1970*, p. 52. Further flexibility was introduced into the agreement under a provision for additional relief through an option to defer part of the principal repayments due during the first eight years. Provision was also made for a limited review of these arrangements any time after 1980 in the light of Indonesia's economic situation at that time.
The Bank cautions, however, that the Indonesian rescheduling terms should not be taken as a precedent. "Indonesia's economy was prostrate . . . and drastic measures were required."
49. *Partners in Development,* p. 157.

ment. Since the Bank's direct participation in debt rescheduling would have an adverse effect on both the volume and cost of capital available to it, such action is not planned in the future.[50]

The Bank's assessment of the prospective debt position of less developed countries in the 1970s seems to us on the whole to be a rather optimistic one, depending as it does on the assumption that the volume of development assistance will increase substantially. If the assumption is correct, the Bank may well be able to maintain its preferred position in debt renegotiation. Whether the Bank will be able, if this assumption is not fulfilled, to maintain this position intact while participating actively in debt renegotiations that cut deeply into other creditor positions remains to be seen.[51] But in any case the Bank will necessarily find itself involved in burden-sharing negotiations that substantially extend the boundaries of the field of economic diplomacy it has occupied to date.

Summary and Conclusions

Although lending by the Bank Group has increased ten-fold from the $250-million-a-year level of its early reconstruction loans, the increase has not been steady and continuous. After a slow beginning, development loans attained an annual level of $300 million to $400 million, which persisted until fiscal year 1958. At this time, bilateral development assistance programs had not yet emerged on a massive scale, and Bank lending was divided between developed and less developed countries. Loan commitments moved to a new level of $700 million in 1958 and over the next decade varied, with one or two exceptional years, around $700 million to $800 million a year. A major increase in Bank Group lending during this period came from the expansion of IDA credits beginning in fiscal 1961. These were years that saw a great expansion in bilateral assistance and increasing activity of the Bank as a co-ordinator of assistance flows through consortia and consultative groups. Although bilateral development assistance tended to level off after 1967, Bank lending beginning in 1968 has moved to a decidedly higher plateau. And

50. IBRD, "External Debt Study," p. 11.

51. At a meeting of the executive directors, in a committee of the whole, to discuss recommendations of the Pearson Commission (August 4, 1970), one director noted that the Bank had hitherto sought and been accorded the status of preferred creditor in rescheduling and suggested that in the interests of a more comprehensive approach it might be time for the Bank to reconsider its position in this respect. President McNamara emphatically rejected this suggestion. While the capital markets' attitude toward Bank bond issues had not been disturbed by the "negative spread" between the Bank's lending rate and the rate at which it currently borrowed, by transfers of part of its net income to IDA, or by the extension of its lending into such fields as agriculture or education, a major rescheduling of the Bank loans would, he was sure, have a disastrous effect.

after the hiatus resulting from a delay in the second replenishment, so has that of IDA. Furthermore, since the Bank, with a few exceptions, ceased lending to developed countries after 1967, almost the total flow of Bank Group funds is now to the less developed world. It can be said with some truth that since 1950 the World Bank has been transformed from a banking institution that finances viable projects in a number of its member countries into a development institution that transfers resources on a large scale, though still mainly on a project basis, from the developed to the less developed world.

The sharp diminution of lending to developed countries after 1967 and the acceptance in 1964 of an income test for IDA credits has, of course, had a considerable influence on the geographical distribution of Bank Group financing. Within the area now open to Bank lending, the distribution of funds, on a per capita basis, has been decidedly uneven. Considering the terms on which the Bank was established, this could hardly be otherwise. The IBRD lends for viable projects in creditworthy countries whose overall performance suggests that they will continue to be creditworthy. Since the creditworthiness of a sizable number of Bank member countries has been increased by the flow of bilateral assistance, it is probable that Bank lending has tended to increase rather than decrease the disparities in total development assistance received on a per capita basis—disparities that are inherent in the nature of bilateral programs.

The share of the World Bank in the total flow of official financial resources to the less developed world has never been very large and, at least until very recently, has shown no disposition to increase. On a gross basis it has amounted to 10 to 12 percent, and on a net basis has been even less, since the average terms of Bank Group lending are somewhat harder than those of bilateral programs. A translation of these flows to a grant basis lowers the Bank Group share even further. On the other hand, since Bank Group loans and credits are untied, they are worth substantially more, dollar for dollar—perhaps 20 percent more—than bilateral assistance. The Bank Group's share in long-term lending is substantially greater, of course, than its share in the total flow of financial resources. And it is possible if not probable that, considering a potential shift of development assistance from bilateral to multilateral channels, the Bank Group's share in both long-term and total flows will become very much larger in the 1970s.

There has always been a wide gap between the terms on which the Bank could and did lend and the variety of needs of its member borrowers for external financing. Until 1964 the Bank's lending rate was determined by the average cost of money on the markets in which the Bank borrowed, plus a 1.25 percent spread. During the period of extremely high interest costs the

Bank has loaned on terms slightly below its average cost of borrowing, but what is significant about Bank terms is the continuous increase in hardness from 4.5 percent in the late 1940s to 5.5 percent in the late 1950s to 7 percent in the late 1960s. The appearance on the scene of IDA introduced greater flexibility into Bank Group lending, but the persistent shortage of IDA funds and the introduction in 1964 of the IDA income test has greatly limited this flexibility. The blending of Bank and IDA terms is limited to countries that qualify for IDA financing, and in these countries the shortage of IDA money has seriously restricted action. Despite the relative rigidity of Bank Group terms, there has never been much receptivity to suggestions for increased flexibility emanating either from within or from outside the institution. The fact is that the Bank will probably respond more flexibly to the needs of its members only if IDA resources are substantially increased.

Although Bank Group commitments and disbursements have continued to increase, net lending—and particularly net transfers—reveal a rather different picture. Net transfers of capital from the Bank reached a very low figure in fiscal year 1969 and were negative in fiscal 1970. While IDA credits tell a different story, combined Bank Group net lending reached a high point of $786 million in fiscal 1967 and net transfers a high point of $495 million in the same year. However, net lending and net transfers began to increase again in 1971 with the large expansion of Bank lending and will continue to increase with the expansion of IDA funds.

The large reverse flows of debt service charges to the Bank are part of the serious debt situation in which many less developed countries now find themselves. The total external public debt of less developed countries stood at $60 billion by the end of 1969, and unguaranteed private external debt would add several billions more. Debt service payments by 1970 were approaching 40 percent of the total flow of funds to the less developed world. While many countries still had easily manageable debts, some four or five faced problems that were becoming unmanageable. The debt rescheduling exercises of the 1950s and early 1960s involved short-term debt only, and the rescheduling involved only short-term postponements usually accompanied by IMF assistance and under IMF auspices. But by 1965 long-term public debt was also involved, and the rescheduling of debt in India in 1968 and in Indonesia in 1970 appears to foreshadow a series of operations in the 1970s that will involve a long-term postponement, a scaling down, and perhaps a cancellation of service payments and also a difficult task of apportioning the burden among creditors. Debt renegotiation has become part of development assistance policy, and it is inevitable that the Bank, as well as the Fund, will become deeply involved.

CHAPTER EIGHT

Project Lending and
Project Appraisal

THE GROWTH OF Bank Group operations in terms of geographic scope and functional diversification has been brought out in earlier chapters of this study. In this and the following chapter, we focus more directly and analytically on the developmental objectives of Bank Group lending. For purposes of exposition, the discussion distinguishes project lending (treated in this chapter) from program lending (discussed in Chapter 9).

So-called "local expenditure financing"—providing foreign exchange to cover local expenditures on goods and services that can be obtained in the borrowing country and therefore need not be imported—may be project-oriented *and* program-oriented. In other words, such financing may help make possible the undertaking of specific high priority projects, and it can also provide the foreign exchange needed for an overall development program. The main discussion of local expenditure financing is reserved for Chapter 9. Here our primary concern is with the selection and appraisal of projects.

The Bank and the International Development Association (IDA), from their beginnings until June 30, 1971, granted 1,057 loans and credits. According to Bank terminology, only 4 of these were for reconstruction—the loans in 1947 and 1948 to France, the Netherlands, Denmark, and Luxembourg. The remaining 1,053 are classified as development loans. If some 26 loans that the Bank classifies as nonproject or program loans are subtracted, this leaves 1,027 loans or credits committed for what are called "projects." But these projects are a mixed bag indeed. As a commentator on Bank project lending observes, "the Bank usually has interpreted the references to projects in its Articles to mean a proposal for a capital investment to develop facilities to provide goods or services." But, as he goes on to say,

projects in this sense can vary widely in size, character, and complexity. They can consist of an investment to build something entirely new, quite specific, and virtually a unit in itself such as [a] Peruvian cement plant . . . or the Volta hydroelectric scheme in Ghana . . . or of investments for the expansion or improvement of existing facilities such as the installation of additional generators in an existing power plant or the several expansions of the Indian Iron and Steel Company . . . or of a much more generalized investment involving a great many facilities and activities such as the modernization of the Spanish railways. . . ."[1]

If a "program loan" is defined as a loan to finance the importation of raw materials, intermediate products, and equipment related to a national development program, and "project loans" are limited to the financing of specific and independent productive installations, a clear distinction can be drawn between project and program lending. In practice the distinction is far from

---

1. John A. King, Jr., *Economic Development Projects and Their Appraisal* (Johns Hopkins Press, 1967), pp. 3–4. This is one of the few illuminating studies that have been made of Bank project lending. Another is *Development Projects Observed* by Albert O. Hirschman (Brookings Institution, 1967). King is an IBRD official, and his study was undertaken under the auspices of the Bank's Economic Development Institute. It includes a survey of some twenty-nine Bank and IDA loans and credits.

King makes no attempt to assess the results of these loans though considerable information is provided concerning the difficulties encountered. His study is, however, an invaluable compendium of Bank practice with respect to project lending and, indeed, is used as a textbook in the indoctrination of young officials in project work. The authors have drawn heavily on this source in describing IBRD project lending practice.

The Hirschman study was based on eleven projects, for which the author was given full access to IBRD material and which he pursued by inquiry on the ground in the borrowing countries. While the IBRD may have hoped to get from this study a systematic appraisal, project by project, of the developmental consequences of its loans, it got instead a perceptive and imaginative analysis of a number of significant relationships between project investment and development that are not ordinarily taken into account by project appraisers. The analysis is flavored by Professor Hirschman's well known propensity for subtle paradox. This study does not lend itself to use as a manual for the instruction of would-be project appraisers, but the insights it provides could be neglected by such appraisers only at considerable cost.

There are, of course, many other studies that comment on various aspects of Bank project lending. A book by George W. Wilson, Barbara R. Bergmann, Leon V. Hirsch, and Martin S. Klein, *The Impact of Highway Investment on Development* (Brookings Institution, 1966), analyzes the results of a number of IBRD highway loans in Central and South America. Hans A. Adler ("Economic Evaluation of Transport Projects") and A. Robert Sadove and Gary Fromm ("Financing Transport Investment") in Gary Fromm (ed.), *Transport Investment and Economic Development* (Brookings Institution, 1965), draw heavily on Bank lending experience. Judith Tendler, *Electric Power in Brazil* (Harvard University Press, 1968), deals with IBRD lending for power development in Brazil. However, a comprehensive comparison of expectations and realization with respect to IBRD project loans, or an analysis of their consequences for development, is still to be made.

clear. Numerous IDA credits to the Indian railways have financed a great variety of imports—from finished items, such as rolling stock, rails, and signaling equipment, to nonferrous metal imports for the production in India of locomotives and rolling stock. A Bank loan financed imports of equipment for several dozen Indian coal mines, with the allocation among them primarily in the hands of an Indian government agency. The first Bank loan in the field of agriculture, and many subsequent ones as well, were for the importation of various types of agricultural equipment with the ultimate destination unspecified. A large part of the Bank's industrial lending has been to privately controlled development banks or development corporations. In these cases the Bank is financing the importation of equipment for enterprises to which the borrowing development corporation may decide to lend. Much the same can be said of IDA lending to agricultural credit associations. Thus, project lending as conceived by the Bank Group is very different from the financing of isolated, free standing capital installations.

On the other hand, it is not quite correct to describe the financing that the Bank calls "program lending" as providing imports for national development programs without regard to the specific installations in which these imports are to be used. The first IDA industrial import credit to India in 1964, which is classified as a program loan, not only specified the imports of materials, components, and equipment to be financed but also specified the firms in three capital goods–producing industries that were to be licensed to receive these imports. Was this a project or a program loan? Although later industrial import credits (which are discussed in Chapter 9) were not so specific as to use, they *were* related to particular segments of the Indian economy rather than to the general development program. The term "sector loans" has never come into common use in the Bank Group, but increasingly project loans and credits tend to embrace groups of interrelated installations and activities within specific sectors of the economy.

Although project and program lending shade into each other, they do in fact present different problems and opportunities to development lenders and contribute differently to the development process in the borrowing countries. The distinction is not merely semantic. If the lender wants not only to specify the imports to be financed but to follow them through to final use, he had better confine himself to financing the directly traceable foreign exchange costs of identifiable projects. Expanding this financing to some part of local expenditures may give the lender more control over the project but at the expense of losing control of the use of the foreign exchange equivalent of the local expenditures.

Whether a lender can limit himself to project lending while effectively promoting the development of the borrowing country depends greatly on how much capital from all sources is to be transferred to that country and on the share of the particular lender in the total transfer. In the 1950s, when development assistance from all sources was relatively small, bilateral assistance programs, as well as the IBRD, favored project lending. It is still favored in many bilateral programs. But for reasons discussed at some length in Chapter 9, massive transfers of capital tend to outrun the capabilities of project lending. Bilateral assistance programs, which have accounted in recent years for 80 to 90 percent of concessional transfers, have inevitably shifted to program lending. Even the Bank and IDA, as indicated above, have extended program loans and credits. Moreover, these institutions have been able to concentrate in the project field to the degree they have largely because other assistance suppliers have been willing to finance the general imports needed to make projects viable. Whether this situation will persist remains to be seen. In any case, and for whatever reason, the Bank has been able to specialize in project lending and, apart from the first four reconstruction loans and a few other loans to be discussed in Chapter 9, has achieved its reputation mainly as a project lender.

An evaluation of the Bank and IDA as project lending agencies encounters a series of difficulties, however, which are discussed at greater length in Chapters 19 and 20. Briefly, (a) projects are frequently not the independent, free standing capital installations to which traditional cost-benefit analysis was designed to apply but are rather an interrelated set of investment and technical assistance activities of considerable complexity; (b) even if all Bank and IDA projects *were* independent and free standing capital installations, an assessment of their probable economic consequences in countries that are in the process of development faces exceptional difficulties; and (c) there have not been many systematic attempts to compare project results with project expectations, let alone to assess their consequence in the development process. What the reader may expect from this chapter then is substantially less than an evaluation of the contribution of Bank and IDA project lending to the economic development of borrowing countries. The accent is rather on what the Bank Group has done in this area and how project techniques have developed over time.

Project Selection and Preparation

Before project selection is discussed, the question must first be considered whether a member is eligible to borrow from the Bank or IDA. If the country is able to obtain the proposed loan on reasonable terms in the private capital market, it should not resort to the Bank. Japan, for example, which had been a heavy borrower from the Bank up to 1967, now has ample access to private capital markets. In the second place, since the Bank expects to be paid back, the borrower must be creditworthy for borrowing on Bank terms. We have already discussed the concept of creditworthiness in Chapter 6. But third, even if a country is judged to be creditworthy by current tests, it may become ineligible to borrow if it is pursuing policies that may endanger (a) its future creditworthiness or (b) its contribution to the financing of Bank-supported projects. A country receiving IDA credits must meet certain tests, which are fully described in Chapter 12.

At the eleventh annual meeting of the board of governors in September 1956, President Black dealt forcefully with the suggestion

that the Bank should not make it a condition of loans that borrowing countries should change their policies in regard to such matters as unbalanced budgets and inadequate power rates. We have made no secret of the fact that we sometimes refuse to lend to countries which are pursuing unsound policies or to borrowers who, because of governmental restrictions on rates, are unable to maintain a sound financial position. . . . When we lend, we want our money to contribute to the growth of local savings and to stimulate their application to productive purposes. We do not think it is the Bank's role to help governments postpone the difficult decisions needed to mobilize local resources.[2]

We shall postpone until Chapter 13 ("Leverage and Performance") a rounded consideration of attempts by the Bank to influence a borrower's policies and practices, but here it should be pointed out that the Bank has, on a number of occasions, refused to, or ceased to, lend to a member country because of policies of the country that are considered to affect adversely its creditworthiness or its domestic contributions to development.

When both the eligibility of a member country for Bank or IDA borrowing and the approximate amount for which it is eligible have been determined, the process of project selection can begin. In the ordinary course of dealings between borrowers and lenders in market economies it is the borrower who identifies the need for investment and works out a proposed use of funds; the lender "appraises" the project and decides whether or not to provide the funds. Sometimes in the course of making the early development loans discussed in Chapter 6 the Bank found itself in this sort of relationship with its borrowers. The first power loans to Brazil and Mexico, for example, were to foreign owned companies—the Brazilian Traction, Power and Light Company and the Mexican Power and Light Company—both of which had

2. International Bank for Reconstruction and Development, Annual Meeting of the Board of Governors (Sept. 24–28, 1956), *Summary Proceedings.* Comments of President Eugene Black on discussion of annual report, p. 13.

the technical and financial competence to work out presentable projects. But early in its history the IBRD began to lend for projects that were not competently presented, and as less developed countries became more important borrowers from the Bank Group, the number of such projects increased. Consequently the IBRD found itself working both sides of the street. It would help a potential borrower locate a promising investment, help to prepare a feasible project, and then appraise the result of its own efforts.[3]

It is customary in the Bank Group to distinguish project identification from project preparation and from project appraisal; and indeed a particular loan may be granted only after missions have been sent to identify, prepare, and appraise the project. But these activities have a way of merging into each other, and the Bank is usually very much involved in all three.[4] "Project identification," according to the Bank's operational memorandum, "is the preliminary determination of the nature and size of potential projects and the establishment of the prima facie priority of such projects in a country's development."[5] Since identification is not oriented primarily toward the physical characteristics of the project but rather toward its position in the hierarchy of possible projects, the leadership of the various types of missions concerned with identification is usually in the hands of a country specialist from one of the area departments of the Bank. But since identification also implies something about the feasibility of a specific installation, technicians, who are either members of the Bank's staff or consultants, are invariably included in such missions. A considerable portion of the time of the Bank's technical staff is, in fact, devoted to project identification. This is part of the Bank's technical assistance to borrowers, treated in greater detail in Chapter 10.

Project preparation, in the Bank's lexicon, "consists of the steps needed to bring a project to the point at which a determination can be made whether and how it can be carried out effectively and at a cost comparing favorably

3. The Bank's fourth annual report (1948–49), discusses the rapidly expanding technical assistance work in this area (pp. 10–12).

4. These three stages, plus project supervision, are described by Warren C. Baum in "The Project Cycle," *Finance and Development,* Vol. 7 (June 1970). Baum at that time was associate director of projects.

5. IBRD, Operational memorandum 7.02 (Aug. 22, 1966). According to Baum ("The Project Cycle," p. 4),

there are essentially three tests involved in the identification of a project. The first is whether the sector of the economy into which the project falls, and the project itself, are of high priority for development and are so recognized in the government's development plans. The second is whether, on prima facie grounds, the project seems to be feasible; that is, whether a technical solution to the problem to which the project is addressed can be found at a cost commensurate with the benefits to be expected. And the third test is whether the government is willing to support the project by financial and other means.

with the contribution it would be expected to make to development."[6] Preparation normally involves not only a technical feasibility study but also a consideration of the proposed management and organization of the project, its commercial and financial aspects, and changes in government policy that may be needed to make the enterprise successful. Identification and preparation are intended to make the project ready for appraisal.

Project appraisal is clearly a function of the Bank as a lender. Project preparation, perhaps more than identification, might be considered to be the responsibility of the borrower. So it is; but nevertheless the Bank usually participates actively as an adviser. IBRD technicians do not design projects, but they advise borrowers on the choice of consultants who do. Furthermore, the Bank specifies the information it will need concerning the project, including the list of materials and equipment to be financed; and in general it participates more or less actively in the shaping of the project. Of course the degree of Bank participation varies with the ability of the borrower to perform these tasks, and it also varies among different areas of Bank lending. In certain of the newer sectors in which the Bank has made loans, such as education and some aspects of agriculture, collaboration is apt to be closer than it is in more traditional fields.

Project Appraisal

It might be thought that, at this stage, with a project identified and prepared, the only thing left for the Bank to do would be to say yes or no. Sometimes it happens this way though not very frequently. Appraisal missions more usually find themselves suggesting changes of one sort or another, and sometimes what started out as an appraisal mission turns out to have the task of preparation or even of identification. In theory the IBRD, up to the point of appraisal, acts only as an adviser to the borrower; it then puts on the hat of a lender and disposes of the application. Early in the history of Bank project lending this "arm's length" relationship in fact existed. It was asserted that if the Bank had helped in the preparation of a project, it could not then objectively appraise its own work. But this long ago gave way to a more incestuous relationship. As Baum puts it,

Experience has demonstrated that we do not get enough good projects to appraise unless we are involved intimately in their identification and preparation. The result is that, instead of having an invisible dividing line, with identification and preparation of projects on one side and appraisal and supervision on the other,

6. Operational memorandum 7.02.

there is a continuing cycle in which the Bank is closely engaged at all stages. One of the benefits of this change of attitude is that, through better preparation, fewer projects are rejected at the appraisal stage, although the final version of the project may be quite different from its original conception.[7]

Two consequences of the Bank's practice in project lending should be noted. It is a very lengthy process and may take several years from the initiation of the search for projects to the final commitment of the loan. This is a frequent source of complaint by borrowing governments and is one reason why many of them prefer quickly disbursed program loans.[8] The Bank's answer is that projects usually involve long-term investments, and it is worth devoting the time necessary to anticipate the difficulties a particular project is likely to face and to shape it into a viable entity. While this is true, it also means that it is extremely difficult, if not impossible, by a proper phasing of projects, to provide in any year the flow of external assistance that an assessment of external financing requirements may show to be needed. Second, the close and prolonged relationship between the staff of the Bank and representatives of the borrowers through the various stages of the project cycle means that by the time a project has met the tests of appraisal, the Bank is all but committed. While no loan can be made until the executive directors approve, a project loan recommended by the president and staff of the Bank has never been rejected.

As we have noted, the early applications for project loans came in the main from prospective borrowers who were capable of presenting relatively complete proposals.[9] This was fortunate since the Bank was in no position to undertake serious appraisal. Negotiations were in the hands of loan officers supported by a minimum of technical expertise. Initially the Loan Department had no technical staff, and a memorandum by Vice President Robert L. Garner, dated March 24, 1947, advised that in acquiring engineering and technical competence the staff should be kept small. The situation was not substantially improved until 1949, when Lieutenant General R. A. Wheeler,

7. Baum, "The Project Cycle," p. 6.

8. This is also a matter frequently discussed by the executive directors. A staff paper circulated to the directors on September 4, 1970 (Sec. M 70-427) stated that the "median processing time" between the departure of the first appraisal mission and board approval for project loans or credits was 9.6 months in fiscal year 1969 and 8 months in fiscal year 1970. But the time elapsing between the first consideration of a project by the Bank staff and the departure of the first appraisal mission is normally a multiple of the "median processing time."

9. The authors are greatly indebted to A. D. Spottswood for preparing a long and useful background memorandum on Bank lending practice. Mr. Spottswood was employed as an engineer in 1947 in what was then the Loan Department and participated in the project work of the Bank until his retirement in 1969.

retired former chief of engineers of the U.S. Army, was brought to the Bank on a permanent basis to organize the engineering staff. And only after 1952, when the Technical Operations Department was formed, could the Bank be said to be equipped for serious project appraisal.

At that stage, however, the techniques of project appraisal were not at all sophisticated. Early power projects were approved if the yield promised to exceed the often artificially low rates at which many governmental agencies could borrow, with no attention being paid to the opportunity cost of capital. These artificial rates inevitably favored hydroelectric projects, with their high investment costs and low operating costs, as against thermal plants, with low investment and higher operating costs. Indeed in the early hydropower loans the possibility of a thermal alternative was rarely investigated. The Bank's lending for large irrigation and land projects usually proceeded on the basis of a highly subjective estimate of gross benefits compared with expected costs, without the detailed study of projected land use, cropping patterns, distances to market, and anticipated prices that has characterized recent appraisals in the agricultural field.

The extremely low interest rates at which governments in many of the less developed countries borrowed to finance projects in the public sector and the meager financial rates of return typically earned by public power enterprises, as well as the difficulties of comparing costs and benefits generated at different periods of time by long-lived projects, led to a number of changes in the 1950s in the Bank's techniques of project selection and approval. These changes included (1) the introduction of electric power rate covenants that aimed to achieve an adequate rate of earnings as a condition of approval of power loans, (2) a search for the "real" or "equilibrium" or "opportunity" cost of capital as the proper indicator of what rate of return should be expected from investments, and (3) the introduction of the so-called "discounted cash flow" method of finding the present value of costs incurred and benefits received at different points in time. All of these changes occurred first in the appraisal of power projects and later spread to projects in other sectors. The introduction of rate covenants came first.

The Bank had from the beginning insisted that loan agreements contain covenants stating the obligations of the borrower to administer the loan properly. These covenants are "boilerplate" in any loan agreement. The Bank, as we mentioned in Chapter 6, first turned its attention to power rates in 1949, when it received assurances from the Mexican government in connection with its first power loan that the government would grant reasonable rates to the Mexican Power and Light Company. It was soon discovered that something more than these assurances would be necessary. Of the twenty-one power loans made by the Bank between January 1, 1953, and January 1, 1956, eleven were accompanied by specific rate covenants. There was, however, considerable difference of opinion in the Bank concerning the propriety of such covenants and initially a substantial amount of resistance from borrowers who felt that their sovereignty was being infringed. The experience with power loans (discussed in Chapter 6) suggests, however, the favorable change in attitude that typically occurred.

During the 1950s, in Latin America in particular, the unwillingness of governments to raise power rates in the face of persistent inflation was putting private power operations in jeopardy and necessitating continuous subsidy to public operations. The Bank was much concerned with this situation. In 1953 the president persuaded the Mexican government to undertake with the Bank a joint study of Mexico's long-term power needs and of a system of rate regulation that might be incorporated into law. This study had a considerable effect on rate regulation in Mexico. In the same year the Bank commissioned a study of the Latin American electric power industry by David F. Cavers, then associate dean of the Harvard Law School, and others.[10] In the meantime the Bank was formulating its own policy with respect to power rates. It was stated succinctly in a letter to the government of India in August 1957, in connection with the Koyna hydroelectric project, from W. A. B. Iliff, then vice president of the Bank:

In its appraisal of public power undertakings in developing countries, the Bank considers that an appropriate test of the adequacy of the power rates is whether the projected earnings are sufficient:
(a) To meet all operating, maintenance and administrative expenses, including tax, interest charges and depreciation calculated on a realistic basis.
(b) To create a surplus out of which
(i) to make suitable provision for the repayment of all loans and advances, insofar as this is not covered by depreciation, and in addition,
(ii) to set aside a reasonable sum for investment in the expansion of the enterprise.

From this time forward, rate covenants regularly accompanied the Bank's power loans. They also became a part of loans for port and telecommunications facilities and railways, and recently the Bank has begun to concern itself with road-user charges, urban water rates, and irrigation charges. Since power and port facilities are monopolies, little difficulty has been encountered in prescribing charges designed not only to cover their properly calculated

10. This study was later published. David F. Cavers and James R. Nelson, *Electric Power Regulation in Latin America* (Johns Hopkins Press, 1959).

costs but to finance expected expansion, though there has frequently been resistance from borrowers. Railways present a different problem; there is usually little need for an expansion of railway investment, but the Bank generally insists on rates capable of generating a positive return. The rate covenant attached to a recent loan to the East African Railways anticipates a 7 percent return. Rate covenants attached to loans for telecommunications facilities, urban waterworks, irrigation projects, and roads vary widely.

Until recently public utility rate policies pursued by the IBRD have been concerned primarily with financial objectives rather than with the optimum use of resources. This means that the Bank has paid a great deal of attention to the level of rates but very little to their structure. The financial autonomy of an enterprise, whether public or private, has been considered as conducive to its administrative autonomy, and the Bank has always favored a maximum degree of administrative independence for entities engaged in commercial operations. Various elements in the Bank have also favored the use of rate policy as a means of generating domestic savings through the financing of public utility expansion. This view, together with an interest in the structure of utility rates, raises delicate questions concerning the degree to which it is justifiable for the Bank to intervene in domestic economic affairs. If a country is to increase its savings rate, whether this is to be accomplished through higher utility rates, taxation, or some other policy might be considered the country's own decision to make. Again, if it is agreed that rates should be high enough to cover costs, it might, perhaps, be left to domestic authorities to determine how the overall costs should be divided between residential and industrial users. On the other hand, if the Bank is to be concerned with all aspects of development performance, it obviously has a legitimate interest in both the level and the structure of utility rates.

Whatever one's view on these matters, it should be emphasized that the Bank's interest that power rates be adequate to cover costs, including a proper charge for capital, has had a profound effect on the administration of public utility properties not only in Latin America but throughout the area of Bank lending. The inclusion of rate covenants in power loans to India has had a significant influence on rate policies both of the central government and of the states. A Bank loan to India in 1965 to finance transmission equipment for the interconnection of the power facilities of sixteen state electricity boards provided for a revision of rate levels to achieve a return of 11 percent on assets in operation, with the understanding that 3 percent would be available to finance expansion.[11]

11. This loan is discussed in greater detail in Chapter 13.

Innovations in Project Appraisal

Certain other innovations have been introduced in the Bank's appraisal procedure for electric power projects. In the late 1950s the use of an "accounting" or "shadow" price of capital began to replace the nominal or monetary cost of capital in comparing hydro-power and thermal-power possibilities. And at approximately the same time, less satisfactory methods of calculating rates of return gave way to the discounted cash flows technique. Once applied in the power area, these innovations spread to other sectors of Bank lending.

The consequences of using rates of interest that represent the cost of government borrowing in comparing hydro and thermal opportunities were brought to the attention of the Bank's project appraisers in a memorandum entitled "Cost of Capital in the Choice Between Hydro and Thermal Power," by Robert Sadove, then of the Economics Department.[12] Sadove pointed out that since the cost of capital accounts for 80 to 85 percent of the unit cost of power in a hydro station, compared with approximately 40 percent in a thermal station, it makes a great deal of difference how much the investment is expected to earn. The Bank's practice in making hydro–thermal comparisons on government-owned power facilities had been to use the government's borrowing rate, which in some eighteen to twenty Bank-financed installations had averaged about 4.5 percent. But the rate used in calculations concerning Bank-financed private power plants had averaged about 9 percent. Furthermore, it was pointed out that the estimated yield on a number of Bank-financed projects outside the power area typically ranged between 12 and 16 percent.

The conclusion was that the rates at which governments normally borrowed in less developed countries tended to be substantially below the "real" cost or value of capital in these countries. Government borrowing was typically subject to a set of institutional influences that produced an artificially low rate. But what was the appropriate rate? It was thought that this might be approximated by observing rates paid by other prime borrowers or the returns expected from investment in other than power projects. The memorandum pointed out that the rates of interest paid by the Austrian government on two government-owned hydro-power projects were 4.1 percent and 5.5 percent,

12. IBRD, Report EC-53a (Jan. 17, 1957). Of course the concept of "shadow" or "accounting" prices was a familiar one in the literature of economic development and had in fact been expounded concisely and with apt illustrations by Jan Tinbergen in *Design of Development*, which was written in 1955 and published for the Bank's Economic Development Institute by the Johns Hopkins Press in 1958.

"whereas interest in that country normally seems to be 9% to 9½%."[13] It was also observed that "representative returns in the private sector are not usually below 15%."[14] These facts were discussed in the Staff Loan Committee, and their acceptance substantially changed Bank practice, as is described below.

At about the same time, improved methods of measuring benefits received and costs incurred at different points in time were introduced into Bank practice. The evaluation of prospective costs and benefits in early Bank projects followed procedures customarily used at that time in the private investment community, with little attempt being made to standardize methods among projects. In general, the expected value of gross benefits was compared with expected gross costs over the anticipated life of the project, and the resulting average annual net benefits were related to the proposed volume of investment. No efforts were made to find the present value of benefits anticipated or costs expected at different points in time. And, as we have indicated above, estimates of gross benefits and costs, at least in the evaluation of early agricultural projects, were highly subjective. The discounted cash flow technique of estimating anticipated rates of return on investment was not generally used in the private sector of Western economies until the mid-1950s, and it was several years later before the Bank began to use these techniques. The impetus came from the Economics Department and the Economic Development Institute (EDI) rather than from the department of the Bank specifically concerned with project appraisal. The discounted cash flow technique was used in evaluating power projects in the late 1950s but not until 1961 in appraising agricultural projects.

"The discounted cash flow method provides us with a tool for comparing different inflows and outflows by expressing them, through the known rate of discount, in terms of a single figure which takes account of the total amounts of income and expenditure, the pattern in which they are spread out over time, and the life span of the project."[15] Ideally, the "known rate of discount" is the opportunity cost of capital in the economy. If this is not known, a "single figure" can be found by calculating the rate that will equalize the present value of expected benefits and expected costs, that is, the internal rate of return. If an evaluator were presented with a series of well prepared projects, a comparison of their internal rates of return would indicate a different ordering

13. Sadove, "Cost of Capital in the Choice Between Hydro and Thermal Power," p. 6.

14. *Ibid.*, p. 7.

15. Organisation for Economic Co-operation and Development, *Manual of Industrial Project Analysis in Developing Countries,* Development Centre Studies, Vol. 1 (Paris: OECD, 1968), p. 116.

than would follow from a discounting of net benefits by a single discount rate representing the opportunity cost of capital, and the latter procedure would have to be preferred. In fact, neither the Bank nor any other external lender is customarily presented with a series of well prepared projects from which priority investment decisions can be made. In practice, projects are evaluated one by one, or at best a choice is offered among two or three closely related versions of what is essentially the same project. Consequently current Bank and IDA practice is to calculate an internal rate of return, which, if it seems to be on the low side, is then compared with some notional figure presumed to approximate the opportunity cost of capital to the economy in question.

As we have indicated above, the search for the cost of capital to the economy has led the Bank to examine the returns to investment in private power projects, in large-scale manufacturing installations, and in other uses. It might be thought that, since the area departments of the Bank are concerned with country analysis, it would be their job to estimate the cost of capital to the economy. But representatives of the Bank's technical departments testify that the area departments tend to be unresponsive to appeals for such estimates. It is perhaps remarkable how frequently 10 percent turns out to be the opportunity cost of capital no matter what economy is involved or what the year of estimate.[16] In general, if Bank projects promise an internal rate of economic return of 10 percent—or even better of 12 percent—they are considered acceptable.

The conclusion was accepted by the Bank in the late 1950s that, in appraising power projects, it would be preferable to substitute for the nominal rates at which governments borrowed at home and abroad, an "accounting"

16. It might be interesting, though perhaps not very useful, to trace the history of the 10 percent figure as the appropriate cost of capital in evaluating projects in less developed countries. Jan Tinbergen uses this figure in his *Design of Development,* p. 86. It is borrowed from him by the Economic Commission for Latin America, *Manual on Development Projects* (UN publication, E/CN 12/426), p. 235. It is used in the "Report of the Energy Survey of India Committee" (June 1964) and in numerous other studies. On the other hand, various other reports "break new ground" by suggesting 12 percent, based on as much or as little evidence. See, for example, "India Coal Transport Study," undertaken for the Indian government and financed in part by the Bank (June 1, 1964; processed). The Bank's most recent pronouncement on this cloudy subject (IBRD, Operational memorandum 2.21 [March 1, 1971]), after referring obliquely to various direct and indirect ways of arriving at a reasonable estimate of capital's approximate opportunity cost, goes on to say,

In most countries the OCC [Opportunity Cost of Capital] will fall within a range of approximately 8 to 14 percent. When projects can show Internal Economic Returns of 14 percent or higher it is not necessary to estimate the OCC for comparison purposes; at rates below 14 percent specific reference to the OCC should normally be made. There may occasionally be countries whose OCC falls outside the range cited, or sectors for which the normal country rate may not be appropriate; such cases would represent exceptions calling for special justification.

or "shadow" price in less developed economies that might depart from the "real" values of the inputs or outputs under consideration. A 1957 memorandum to the Staff Loan Committee advocating the use of an accounting price for capital also noted that

an initial determination in favor of thermal rather than hydro power may be altered if the element of foreign exchange expenditures on imported fuel is brought into consideration. A country's balance of payments position may be such that it will be prepared to pay a substantial premium for the solution which minimizes foreign exchange outlays.[17]

In fact, weighing the cost of domestic as against foreign sources of fuel in power generation is by no means unusual, and the relevance of a shadow rate of foreign exchange in making such comparisons has frequently been noted in Bank studies.[18] At the same time there is very little evidence that a shadow rate of exchange, at least until recently, has ever been used in Bank appraisals of power projects.[19] This may have been because until 1967 no economist was ever employed in the technical division of the Bank that is concerned with appraising power projects. In other areas of project lending, however, shadow rates for foreign exchange and labor inputs have been used frequently, if not systematically.

It is extremely difficult, however, to present an adequate account of the evolution of Bank practice with respect to the use of shadow prices for inputs and outputs in appraising projects. As we have said, shadow prices for capital (the opportunity cost of capital) were used in the appraisal of power projects as early as 1957 or 1958, but this use filtered only gradually to other project divisions. Until recently, shadow prices of foreign exchange were not applied in the appraisal of power projects, even in situations that called for their application. When shadow foreign exchange rates were used, moreover, their use at times did not appear explicitly in project evaluation reports because of the implied suggestion that the country in which the project was located should revise its exchange rate. Occasionally one finds evidence in project evaluation reports of the use of shadow wage rates, but this practice cannot have been very systematic. An operational policy memorandum issued in 1971 notes that the Bank has in the past made rather limited use of shadow prices in its project work but then specifies the situations in which such prices should be used in the future.

Shadow prices are values assumed for important cost or benefit elements when market prices are seriously distorted and do not reflect real scarcities in the econ-

17. IBRD, Memorandum SLC/0/878 (Jan. 2, 1957), p. 3.
18. For example, the "India Coal Transport Study," cited in note 16, above.
19. From a conversation with David Knox, June 4, 1970. Knox was the first economist employed in the public utilities division. He is currently director of the Transportation Projects Department.

omy. However, because of differing concepts as to what shadow prices should represent, plus difficulties in their measurement, the Bank has made rather limited use of them in its project work.[20]

Currently adjustments are usually made for subsidies, taxes, and other "artificial" influences on prices. The world market price of a product frequently is substituted for the domestic price.[21] It is certainly true that the Bank Group increasingly attempts systematically to allow for price distortions in evaluating projects. It is probably true that these corrections are more frequently used in calculating an economic rate of return for projects with a defined technology than in choosing among possible technologies.[22]

20. IBRD, Operational policy memorandum 2.21 (March 31, 1971). The memorandum goes on to say:

> The principal role of a project calculation made with shadow prices is to see whether the project looks significantly more or less attractive for the economy than it does when economic tests are made with actual prices. If a project scores unacceptably low marks when shadow prices are used, despite acceptable scores with actual prices, the Bank would normally decline to finance it. Conversely, a project with an unacceptable score when market prices are used may look acceptable when shadow prices are used. Revenue earning projects cannot live on "shadow prices." The Bank will finance such projects only if it is appropriate and feasible through the introduction of protection, subsidies, or devaluation, to bridge the gap between an unfavorable financial analysis based on market prices and a favorable economic analysis based on shadow prices.

21. The proposals of Little and Mirrlees for a complete substitution of world market prices for domestic prices in project evaluation and their suggested techniques for converting the domestic prices of nontraded inputs and outputs into world market price equivalents, although actively discussed in the Bank, have not, as of this writing, been accepted. See Ian Little and James Mirrlees, *Manual of Industrial Project Analysis in Developing Countries,* Vol. 2. *Social Cost-Benefit Analysis* (Paris: Organisation for Economic Co-operation and Development, 1969). For the views of one Bank official on these proposals, see George B. Baldwin, "A Layman's Guide to Little/Mirrlees," *Finance and Development,* Vol. 9 (March 1972).

22. Economists on the Bank's staff and, increasingly, executive directors have raised questions regarding labor saving techniques on Bank-financed projects, particularly road construction projects. The technical departments of the Bank are certainly aware of the advisability of using labor, which is in surplus, and economizing capital, which is in short supply in most of the less developed countries, when costs can thereby be reduced and standards maintained. It would have to be said, however, that there has been no very persistent pressure to bring this about and, until recently, no systematic study of the possibility of using alternative techniques. In 1965, in response to urging by the executive directors, a report based on Bank Group experience was prepared on the "Substitution of Labor for Equipment in Road Construction" (TO-477). This report was rather perfunctory and inconclusive. It was not until later that the Bank initiated a series of professional studies of this subject. The results of these studies began to appear only in 1971.

A critic of agricultural lending policy charged the Bank in 1971 with neglect of labor-intensive techniques and an "unwavering focus on the rate of return." To this a Bank staff member replied: "The problem is with the difficulty of preparing and executing highly labor-intensive projects. If we could overcome this difficulty, the rate of return calculations (using appropriate shadow prices) would come in very handily." (Papers prepared for the president's 1971 address to the World Bank's board of governors.)

Price distortions in the economies of borrowing countries not only complicate the calculation of an economic rate of return to be expected from Bank-financed projects, but also a determination of what inputs into the project should be procured locally and what ones should be imported from abroad.[23] The IBRD has two interests of central importance to be served by this choice: (a) to minimize the cost of the project by procuring inputs from lowest-cost sources, and (b) to encourage the development of borrowing countries by assisting their industries in producing inputs for Bank projects. Unfortunately these interests are frequently in conflict. Furthermore, even among the capital exporting countries (which are the normal suppliers of imported inputs to a project), tariffs, subsidies, and other commercial devices may give "artificial" advantages or disadvantages to countries competing for Bank-financed imports. The Bank has wrestled with these impediments to "fair" competitive bidding in a number of contexts, but so far as commercial policies affecting capital exporting countries are concerned, it has usually decided to accept the existing trading and protective systems of member countries.[24]

23. The authors have relied heavily in this discussion of what is called in the Bank "domestic preference policy" on a memorandum from Warren C. Baum and Gregory B. Votaw to Robert S. McNamara, "Domestic Preference Policy: Alternative Approaches" (Oct. 13, 1969).

24. An interesting paper, "Two Types of Bank Policy," written in 1960 by Bank economist Hugh Collier, cites a number of cases in which the Bank's interest in competitive bidding has clashed with existing trade restrictions. In the 1950s a Bank working party was established to consider the Bank's policy with respect to Commonwealth preference and other trade preference systems. "Did not such systems mean that some suppliers would have an advantage over others"? The working party concluded that preferences were only one of many methods whereby countries attempted to obtain advantages for their exporters, and the Bank could not hope to deal with all of them. "Moreover, preferences were a matter of concern to GATT, and those with complaints should refer them to GATT."

Shortly afterward a similar question arose with respect to shipping charges. Should the Bank finance freight charges if the borrowing country insisted on using its own ships? Again a working party was appointed, some members of which felt that the Bank could not square financing higher freight charges with its policy of competitive bidding. But again the Bank decided it would do nothing about this practice. "The decision was taken largely for the simple reason that there was nothing the Bank could usefully do about the matter anyway."

As was indicated in the text, the question of reconsidering preferences and protection emerged in particularly difficult form in connection with local procurement. Here the Bank has straddled the issue. Until 1962 it ignored the question, and the 1960 paper by Collier suggests that it should have continued to ignore it. But when producers in less developed countries began, on a significant scale, to bid on equipment to be supplied to Bank-financed projects in their own countries behind protective barriers that included quantitive restrictions on imports, as well as very high tariffs, the Bank decided it would have to limit the degree of protection to be allowed if competitive bidding were to mean anything.

When the Bank first undertook to finance domestic inputs, this practice was limited to developed countries. In the first place these borrowers, being already industrialized, were capable of producing capital equipment in competition with outside suppliers. Second, the level of protection offered to domestic suppliers was generally low and consequently impinged to only a small extent on fair competitive bidding. As will be reported in Chapter 9, the first local expenditure financing in a less developed country involved the domestic procurement of inputs to an electric power facility in Mexico in 1958. But, as less developed countries industrialized further, this problem began to arise frequently. The Bank was interested in promoting industrialization, and it recognized that industrialization was difficult without some degree of protection of industrial "infants." However, it wanted to make sure that the infants it encouraged by its procurement policies had some reasonable chance of growing into industries that would eventually be capable of standing on their own feet. After much discussion in the Bank's staff and board of directors, it was decided in 1962 that local producers should be entitled to a maximum level of protection of 15 percent in bidding on Bank projects. Henceforth either the existing tariff rate or 15 percent, whichever was lower, would be accepted.

This policy had the merit of simplicity, which was important, and it proved to be acceptable to capital exporting countries, which have the dominant voice in IBRD policymaking. Any other merit, however, is difficult to discern. What needs to be protected is the domestic value added segment of output. If value added domestically is only 10 percent of the total value of the product and the imported inputs are duty free, a nominal tariff of 15 percent can mean an effective tariff of 150 percent. Or the effective tariff can well be negative if the duty on imported inputs exceeds 15 percent. Furthermore, commercial policy in less developed countries frequently embraces import prohibitions and quantitative restrictions, export taxes and subsidies, and a wide range of nominal tariffs. Domestic currencies are often overvalued, and exchange rate policy may decree a variety of rates for different types of imports. Under these circumstances it is difficult to calculate the level of effective protection enjoyed by a particular domestic product.[25] By the same token it is equally difficult to translate the significance of a 15 percent rate of nominal protection into its equivalent in effective protection of value added.

25. Although systematic treatment of the difference between nominal and effective tariff rates and their trade consequences is fairly recent, a sizable literature on this subject has already developed. A consultant to the Bank, Bela Balassa, has been an important contributor. See in particular his *The Structure of Protection in Developing Countries* (Johns Hopkins Press, 1971).

Even if the problem of calculating effective rates is solved, it by no means follows that a rate appropriate for encouraging a promising industrial infant in one country is also appropriate in another. Less developed countries come in various sizes, shapes, and degrees of modernization. A level of effective protection that may be adequate, if extended over a given period of time, to make a particular kind of industrial processing in one country competitive in world markets may be quite inadequate to serve the same purpose in another.

Prolonged study and reflection concerning this range of problems in the Bank has not succeeded in moving the analysis forward. *Some* interference with existing systems of protection is necessary if Bank projects are to enjoy the benefits of international competition. Quantitative restrictions on imports from low cost bidders must be removed, and excessively high taxes on these imports must be reduced if foreign bidders are to have a chance. On the other hand, there is a widespread complaint in less developed countries that the 15 percent level is far too low to provide adequate protection of infant industries, and thus local bidders are in effect excluded from Bank financing. A proposal by the president to the executive directors in 1969 that the nominal level of permissible protection be raised to 25 percent met with a negative reaction from the representatives of the rich and also of some of the poor countries. It appeared to the rich countries that such a change would limit their opportunities for exports. The proposal did not appeal to a number of the less developed countries because it seemed inadequate. Although *some* interference with existing commercial practices is necessary if international competitive bidding is to be effective, the kind of intervention that would produce a satisfactory compromise between the two objectives of keeping the costs of projects low, while at the same time encouraging promising domestic industries, has so far eluded the Bank Group and, for that matter, everyone else.

Economic and Financial Rates of Return

In its evaluation of projects the Bank undertakes both an economic and a financial analysis. Each yields an expected rate of return. In some cases both the economic and the financial return are judged to be adequate, and in some cases both are judged to be inadequate. When the calculated economic return diverges from the calculated financial return, which is not uncommon, it is because either (a) the economic analysis uses shadow prices while the financial analysis does not, or (b) a significant fraction of the expected benefits or of the anticipated costs to the economy cannot be captured by, or are not incurred by, the project itself. Earlier in this chapter we discussed briefly the circumstances in which shadow prices are used in the economic evaluation of projects, and we shall refer below, again briefly, to the consideration of external benefits and costs in project appraisals. Here a word needs to be said about the task of financial analysis, which has always played an important role in the Bank's project appraisal and which is by no means limited to the calculation of an expected rate of return.

"The emphasis of financial analysis is on the cash-flow of private and public sector funds related to a project and its effect on resource use, especially on investment in future periods."[26] One of the most common and most persistent difficulties encountered in the financing of public sector projects is in assuring that the obligations of the government or public agency with respect to domestic currency financing are met during the period of construction and the first years of operation before the project has become an income-earning property. It is a function of financial analysis to discern the sources, the timing, and the uses of such funds. When the property has begun to generate income, will the income be adequate to cover operating costs, depreciation, and interest charges and, if necessary, provide funds for expansion? Will the cash flow furthermore be adequate to meet charges as they occur? The insistence that an examination of the financial viability of projects be an essential part of project appraisal stems from a lack of experience in less developed countries, particularly in the public sector, in the planning and management of financial flows. Furthermore, since governments in many of these countries frequently encounter great difficulties in raising revenue for investment, financial analysis may well have to be concerned with how the project entity may be made to generate funds for its own expansion.

A very large fraction of Bank-financed projects is revenue producing, and the Bank has shown a strong predilection for forms of organization that make possible the use of these revenues for the project itself. But increasingly the Bank and IDA finance nonrevenue-producing projects in fields such as road transportation, education, and family planning.[27] Here the focus of financial analysis is on the revenue position of the relevant government departments or agencies, for example, highway departments, ministries of education, and

26. Sadove and Fromm, "Financing Transport Development," in Fromm (ed.), *Transport Investment and Economic Development*, p. 238.

27. Two kinds of projects fall in this category: (a) projects yielding services that cannot be sold and therefore generate no revenue (for example, educational projects); and (b) projects generating revenue but not to a separate entity with financial autonomy (for example, irrigation projects).

so on. This may involve an examination of specific tax proposals, such as highway user charges or gasoline taxes, or even of the fiscal position of the government as a whole. Such an examination may cause conditions relating to broad fiscal measures to be attached to loans for specific projects. This question will be considered in Chapter 13, where we discuss leverage and performance. Here we only reemphasize that financial analysis is an essential part of project evaluation.

Any particular investment is inevitably embedded in a matrix of surrounding economic and other activities which it influences and by which it in turn is influenced. A feeder road network introduced into an agricultural area that has heretofore enjoyed only primitive means of transport will not only reduce travel time and travel costs but, in so doing, may well change cropping patterns in the area and influence production techniques. These in turn could require alterations and adjustments in the proposed feeder road network. There are ways of handling such relationships in evaluating projects through systems analysis, and increasingly the Bank has equipped itself to deal with them. Projects in the form of independent installations are giving way to sets of interdependent capital-using activities. The capital requirements of the entire power sector are considered rather than those of a single power plant. The evaluation of road networks or of complementary rail and road facilities is replacing that of isolated road or rail projects. The financing of a refinery may be considered only if the refinery is part of a petro-chemical complex. In extending the area of project evaluation to include interrelated activities the Bank moves in the direction of dealing with those costs and benefits to the economy that are external to individual investments but may be made internal to a group of investments considered together.

But the external influence of a sizable investment project in a less developed country may extend far beyond changes in the pattern of current economic activities. Skilled workers trained at the expense of one enterprise may become available to other enterprises at no training cost to the latter. As we noted earlier in this chapter, the financing of road projects may give entrepreneurial experience to bus and truck operators that can be used elsewhere in the economy. The motivations and values of peasants who are introduced to manufacturing practices are subject to changes that are likely to influence the development process significantly. And the political consequences of various types of investment may seriously affect this process. In 1969 and 1970 IDA extended a number of credits to India and Pakistan for the importation of tractors. The possible political consequences of such financing was the subject of vigorous discussion not only by the staff of the Bank but also among the executive directors.[28] In view of these possible influences that are external to the project itself, to what extent can they and should they be taken into account by project appraisers?

Hirschman has made the most extensive effort to date to evaluate Bank techniques of project appraisal. While finding the indirect or "side" effects of project lending to be of great importance, he considers that these "effects are so varied as to escape detection by one or even several criteria *uniformly applied to all projects.*" It is Hirschman's view, based on a study of some eleven World Bank project loans, that,

upon inspection, each project turns out to represent a *unique constellation* of experiences and consequences, of direct and indirect effects. This uniqueness in turn results from the varied interplay between the structural characteristics of projects, on the one hand, and the social and political environment, on the other.[29]

An examination of the cases analyzed by Hirschman tends to support the view that in a number of instances the "side" effects of projects turned out, on the basis of hindsight, to be of substantial importance. But it also suggests that in many instances it would have been impossible for even the most perspicacious project appraiser to have taken them into account in advance of the decision to invest. What the post-mortems show is that projects with an expected life of twenty-five or fifty years or more tend to develop a life of their own, unforeseen and unforeseeable by the project appraiser. This does not eliminate the value, indeed the necessity, of project appraisal using whatever facts and techniques of analysis and forecasting may be available, nor indeed does Hirschman deny this. But it does tend to moderate one's confidence in the validity of long-term forecasts. As Keynes once remarked, if capitalists foresaw all the uncertainties to which their investments would be subjected, they would probably not have invested in the first place. He attributed their behavior largely to the possession of an unusual endowment of

28. On the one hand, it was argued that the expansion of capital intensive technologies would occasion severe labor displacement; that the already sizable income gap between large farmers and small ones would increase; and that the effect of increased efficiency of production in areas susceptible to the green revolution would be to lower the prices of goods produced by poverty-stricken small units that are incapable of enjoying the benefits of this revolution. It was suggested that the "green" revolution might well turn "red." On the other hand, it was said that in areas of proposed tractor use there was a shortage rather than an abundance of labor; that, with appropriate institutional changes, mechanization would be made available to the small farmer; that the optimum degree of intensity of cultivation simply could not be attained with bullock power; and finally, that mechanization was inevitable in southern Asia in any case, whether or not the Bank participated in its financing.

29. Hirschman, *Development Projects Observed*, p. 186.

"animal spirits." Since the Bank is using other people's money for the most part, so much animal spirit is perhaps not required to make an investment decision. What is required is a certain amount of faith in the development prospects of a country—a faith that transcends the expectations that can with certainty be associated with particular projects.

As we have already noted, early appraisals of Bank projects were principally in the hands of engineers and financial analysts. The central task of the engineer is to determine what quantities of raw materials, labor, fuel, and equipment fed into properly designed installations will produce the desired output over the lifetime of the installation. The engineers are assisted in determining the scale and location of the installation by commercial studies of the volume and geographical distribution of prospective demand for the output. The financial analysts, as was emphasized above, are concerned not only with the calculation of an expected rate of return based on projected market prices for inputs and outputs but also with sources of finance and cash flows. The economist's role in project evaluation is to assist the comparison of the proposed capital investment with alternative uses of capital in a given sector of the economy or the economy as a whole. As the Bank has extended its interest from particular projects to the characteristics of the development process in the economies of borrowing countries, the role of economic analysis has tended to become more important.

The emergence from the investment process of an enterprise or institution earning the expected rate of return and making its expected contribution to the economy presupposes capable management and an organization giving management adequate scope. Project appraisals by the Bank Group have always paid close attention to questions of management and organization. After considering these questions briefly, we turn to the final stage of the project cycle—end-use supervision or, in current Bank terminology, "project supervision."

Although an examination of the qualifications of existing or proposed management personnel has always been an essential element in project appraisal, the Bank has traditionally avoided taking any direct responsibility for providing management. It considers itself a project financier, not a project manager. On the other hand, it has rather frequently required borrowers, as a condition for receiving loans, to employ managers or management consultants from outside and has assisted them in selecting these individuals or firms. However, the Bank has usually limited its role to that of finder and has insisted that the borrower, subject to consultation with the Bank, make the final selection. One reason is the fear that a Bank-selected executive would have conflicting loyalties. The results have not always been successful. On a number of occasions managers or consultants recommended by the Bank have created problems for borrowers about which the latter have been reluctant to complain for fear of harming their general relations with the Bank.

A Bank operational memorandum observes, with respect to Bank-recommended managers and consultants, "The role is sometimes a delicate one, and their aim should always be to hand over as soon as practicable to those who have formal responsibility."[30]

This is a difficult role to play. The consultant walks a tight rope between performing a purely advisory function, with the local executive making the decisions and taking the responsibility, and assuming the executive function himself. The first course of action may provide excellent training opportunities, but the second course may be necessary if the enterprise is to succeed. The concentration of Bank lending in countries of meager development and its expansion into areas requiring increasing amounts of technical assistance, seem currently to be moving the Bank toward greater managerial responsibility, at least for certain types of projects.

The Bank and IDA, in fact, have tended for a number of years to assume greater managerial responsibility in some fields of lending than in others—for example, in agriculture, particularly livestock projects, and development finance companies. In 1966 the Agricultural Development Advisory Service was established in eastern Africa to recruit experienced expatriate civil servants for secondment to governments in the region. Initially those employed by the Service worked on project identification and preparation, but most of them were later assigned as project managers. In 1967 President Woods authorized the employment of up to ten executives at headquarters to be seconded by the Bank to borrowers as project managers. All were assigned to livestock projects. The IBRD has taken an active interest in providing competent management to industrial finance companies since it began to lend in this area. In 1966 a working party, organized to survey experience in the field of management assistance, concluded that the Bank would have to play a more active role in the future than it had in the past.[31] The activities of the Bank Group in the field of management are further discussed in Chapter 10 on technical assistance.

It is impossible even for efficient management to function effectively in a setting that seriously limits its scope of action. In its lending for public sector projects the Bank has, from the beginning, paid close attention to the form of organization within which the project was expected to operate, and it has frequently conditioned its loans on the willingness of the borrower to make

30. IBRD, Operational memorandum 5.04 (May 31, 1970), par. 15.
31. "Bank Assistance in Project Management" (December 1968; processed).

organizational changes. When projects in the private sector are being financed, public policies affecting the operation of the enterprises have come under close scrutiny. In the eyes of a considerable number of executive directors and senior Bank officials a principal argument in favor of the Bank's project approach is the potential contribution of project lending to the creation of viable economic institutions and enterprises, which are so frequently lacking in less developed countries.

Effectively functioning organizations, however, do not spring into being overnight, and in most of the situations in which the Bank has contributed significantly to organizational development, it has made multiple loans to the borrowing entity over a considerable period of time. Organizational changes that are made as a condition of a first loan are consolidated and extended in connection with second and subsequent loans.

We discussed in Chapter 6 the Bank's role in reorganizing railway operations in Thailand and in improving the organization and management of the Imperial Board of Telecommunications in Ethiopia. In both cases these entities were the recipients of a number of loans or credits that engaged the interest of the Bank Group over a considerable period of time. These were two of many examples that could be cited of the Bank's concern with problems of organization.

As we noted above in discussing the financial aspects of project appraisal, the Bank has, so far as possible, used its influence to assure that the income of public revenue-producing entities be kept separate from other government revenues and be used, when needed, for the expansion of the organization's own facilities. One of the main reasons for this insistence is the belief that financial autonomy is a necessary condition for administratve autonomy. At times the Bank's predilection for administrative and financial independence of revenue-producing public agencies, it is alleged, has been incompatible with the political power structure and governing mores of the borrowing country. There is a certain amount of truth in this allegation. As Hirschman points out, an autonomous agency established in part to avoid political contamination may in a multi-community society become the enclave of one community and anathema to the others. This was apparently what happened to the Nigerian railways, which were organized into an independent corporation, at Bank insistence, in 1955 and fell under the almost complete domination of the Ibo community after independence.[32] One of the results was refusal to use the railway, and sabotage, by the other communities. The reverse problem, also cited by Hirschman, appears when the attempt to avoid

32. Hirschman, *Development Projects Observed*, pp. 140–53 and 156.

political contamination leads to the formation of an organization so isolated that it loses all political support. This seems to have been the fate of the Damodar Valley Corporation, "when it was locked in battle with the state of West Bengal over its irrigation and power programs and was unable to obtain the backing of the central government."[33]

No doubt both of these examples are to the point though it is not clear that the administration of the Nigerian railways or the Damodar power and water facilities by regular government departments would have avoided other difficulties even more serious. The quasi-independent public corporation is obviously not a panacea capable of protecting revenue-producing public enterprises from all the effects of nepotism, corruption, political interference, and incompetence that beset governments in some less developed countries or, for that matter, in some developed countries also. In fact, given a choice between financing an enterprise run by a government department in the political tradition of such departments and one administered by a newly formed public corporation, a careful investor would, in many cases, not lend at all. But the Bank and IDA are development institutions and are expected to take chances a sober investor would eschew. And in taking chances they have to make choices. On the record as a whole they have not shown themselves to be misguided in exhibiting a strong preference for the quasi-autonomous agency to manage public sector enterprises.

Project Supervision

To complete the so-called "project cycle," a word needs to be said about project supervision. As we have noted earlier, a sizable portion of the time of the technical personnel of the Bank is employed in this activity.[34] The term "end-use" was borrowed from the lend-lease dictionary. When Wilfrid Baumgartner, the French negotiator of the Bank's first reconstruction loan, was confronted with the multiplicity of conditions (expressed in legal language) expected to cover the use made of imports financed by the loan, he is reported to have thrown up his hands and suggested that the Bank merely be assured of the right of end-use inspection, "which is a term we all understand."

33. *Ibid.*, p. 157.
34. A committee appointed in 1963 to review end-use policies and procedures of the Bank noted in its report in July 1964 to the senior staff (SSM: A/64–66) that from 35 to 40 percent of the time of the staff of the Technical Operations Department was spent on end-use supervision. Later information suggests that this was an overestimate, and certainly in 1971 the figure, though still large, was substantially lower.

A loan by the Bank or a credit from IDA normally specifies not only the imports to be financed by foreign exchange but the inputs to the project expected to be financed from local currency sources. The first step in project supervision is the supervision of procurement. A 1964 report on end-use policies and procedures states:

As far as the substance of procurement supervision is concerned, a considerable amount of work could be eliminated if the Bank were willing to take the consequences of not checking in detail the action of its borrowers and their suppliers. But the Committee believes that the amount of money involved in procurement, the nature of the various interests affected and the opportunities for improprieties are too great to permit the Bank to shy away from this responsibility. As long as the Bank continues its basic policy of requiring international competition, it would be unwise to curtail the supervision of procurement in any substantial way.[35]

Supervision of construction is perhaps the centerpiece of end-use activities, and more is involved than merely overseeing the carrying out of a designed plan of operations. Unforeseen difficulties may arise in the course of construction, or changes may be made at the last moment in various aspects of project design. It is the task of a supervisory mission to help the borrower work out desired modifications and estimate their impact on project cost. Nor are the functions of such missions limited to purely engineering aspects. The borrower is committed to a certain level of local-cost financing, and project supervision may involve applying substantial pressure on governments to assure that this financing is forthcoming. And other conditions apply to the period of construction whose fulfillment will need to be supervised.

Project supervision, moreover, is by no means completed when the last brick is in place and the installation is ready for operation. The loan agreement may well have included provisions related to management and organization. To see such provisions implemented is the task of supervisory missions. Recent Bank loans to port authorities contain the following typical financial covenants:

Except as the Bank shall otherwise agree, the Borrower shall take all necessary measures (including but not limited to adjustments of tariffs) as shall be required to provide the Borrower at all times with net operating revenue sufficient to ensure a rate of return of not less than x percent on the Borrower's net fixed assets in operation.

Except as the Bank shall otherwise agree, the Borrower shall not incur any debt [unless certain financial operating ratios are achieved].[36]

35. IBRD, "Report on End-Use Policies and Procedures of the Bank and the Association" (July 8, 1964; processed), p. iii.
36. For example, see the covenants in the $12.5 million Bank loan for Bangkok port improvement, in July 1970. (702-TH).

Provisions such as these in loan agreements assure that the task of project supervision will continue long after the construction period is over. This effect, moreover, is reinforced by the practice of making multiple loans to the same entity to permit it to modify and expand a set of related activities. A succession of preparation, appraisal, and supervision missions may well maintain a continuing relationship between lender and borrower in connection with these activities for a period of fifteen to twenty years. In the Bank's view, this relationship should not be irksome because "both partners are striving to make a common venture successful and good supervision does not consist merely in finding fault but in ensuring that project objectives are attained at the least cost and in the least time."[37]

After considerable experimentation the Bank early came to the conclusion that project supervision can best be managed by periodic missions plus systematic reporting. Although a resident representative would be on the job continuously, the danger has been considered too great that he might become closely involved with management. On the other hand, to limit the relationship to reporting would be clearly inadequate. The Bank wants to maintain some sort of arm's-length relationship with its borrowers, though, as we have seen in connection with other aspects of the project cycle, the length of these arms has tended to shorten. Borrowers sometimes complain of the "hit and run" character of Bank missions, which quarter themselves in leading hostelries of nearby cities and inundate ministries with requests for data. However, it is not certain that they would prefer to have a resident representative breathing down their necks. And it *is* clear that the Bank could not content itself with long-range correspondence. The supervisory mission, therefore, has appeared to be on the whole the most workable alternative. However, the division of authority between Washington and the field on various aspects of the project cycle may be in process of change, as we observe in Chapter 21.

The complex and changing relationships between the area and technical departments of the Bank are discussed elsewhere in this book, but it should be emphasized here that sensible project lending demands a skillful interweaving of country, sector, and project analysis. The relationship between area and project departments bears some resemblance to the relationship between planning commissions and development departments in borrowing countries. Effective planning requires the preparation of feasible projects, but economically justified projects cannot be selected without a survey being made of the resources available and the general order of priority of their use. This interweaving of macro- and micro-analysis requires a continuous give

37. King, *Economic Development Projects and Their Appraisal*, p. 15.

and take between planners and project appraisers, and the same kind of relationship must exist between the area and projects departments of the Bank if lending programs are to promote economic development.

Summary and Conclusions

There has been a very substantial advance in the sophistication of project analysis since the time when the Bank depended almost entirely on engineering and financial expertise and concentrated its lending heavily in the areas of electric power and rail transport. This is evident not only in its appraisal of specific projects but in its relation of specific projects to the development process in various borrowing countries. The Bank's country analyses are used extensively by regional development banks and bilateral assistance programs. Its advice on project preparation is widely sought, and its techniques of project appraisal and supervision are models of painstaking care.

At the same time it cannot be said that the Bank has been an outstanding leader in applying new techniques of project appraisal or analysis of development processes.[38] It came rather slowly to the use of the discounted cash flow technique of calculating rates of return; and its methods of correcting for price distortions in the economies of its borrowers, at least until recently, have been neither systematic nor comprehensive. Whether the Bank's appraisers have taken possible "side effects" of project development as fully into account as they should have is difficult to say. Certainly hindsight has revealed many unforeseen consequences, as is inevitable. The IBRD's lending has increasingly embraced interrelated investment-oriented activities, inviting a systems type of analysis; and between its consultants and its staff the Bank has begun to meet these requirements. Not until 1968, however, were computer facilities installed. The Bank has rarely applied linear programming techniques to discover optimum combinations of inputs for particular projects.[39] The gap is large between academically contrived growth models and dynamic project appraisals and the techniques used by the Bank, and it pre-

38. See Oral History Project of Columbia University (interviews recorded in the summer of 1961 on the International Bank for Reconstruction and Development), interview of P. N. Rosenstein-Rodan.

39. Linear programming was applied to an analysis of water and other inputs in the Bank's impressive study of investment in the huge Indus Basin project. It has also been applied in connection with a few other large-scale projects. That this technique has not been more widely used is sometimes attributed by Bank officials to the fact that a project usually takes such a variety of shapes in the process of coming into being that linear programming or other types of systems analysis are impracticable.

sumably will continue to be. However, Bank practice as of 1971 appears to be superior to that of other project lenders.

The Bank has perhaps been less venturesome than some other project lenders, at least until recently, in exploring new avenues of investment. A justification for caution in the early years was the assumption that the eyes of the capital markets of the world were fastened not only on the Bank's financial position and the creditworthiness of its borrowers but on the outlook for future income from specific projects. Until well into the 1960s electric power and transportation were the overwhelmingly favorite fields of endeavor; and Bank lending for industrial projects has been handicapped by some fairly doctrinaire predilections in favor of private enterprise. Not until 1968 was lending to publicly controlled development corporations permitted. Before the mid-1960s agricultural loans absorbed a very small fraction of Bank and IDA resources, and lending in the field of education was not begun until 1962. This situation, it is true, has changed markedly in the last few years. Industry, agriculture, and education are now among the most rapidly growing areas of lending, and the Bank Group has developed an interest in tourism, urban development, and population planning. Looking at the record as a whole, however, it would have to be said that, at least until recent years, project lending by the Bank in some respects has been based on a narrower concept of the development process than has the project lending of either the Inter-American Development Bank or the U.S. Agency for International Development.

Considering the very large numbers of projects financed by the Bank over the years, there have been relatively few technical failures. Bank projects have generally produced what they were expected to produce. That neither the Bank nor IDA has as yet suffered a financial loss is, of course, more the result of the creditworthiness of borrowers and of government guarantees than of the uniform viability of projects. It might perhaps be argued that an innovating institution should have made more mistakes. Considering the financial structure of the Bank, however, any appreciable increase in the number of mistakes, particularly if some were major mistakes, would probably have affected adversely its ability to finance even the relatively riskless projects.

A more common criticism, and one more difficult to dispose of, is that the Bank's practice of supervising construction, as well as the operation of projects in their early years, tends to deprive borrowers of learning opportunities. It is said, for example, that the activities of foreign firms in the planning and construction of a sizable Bank-financed road network in West Pakistan were so all-embracing as to deprive the West Pakistan public works department of any share in the responsibility. Whether it is true in this particular case, it raises a question that we have encountered before in discussing technical assistance activities. Is it better to emphasize the learning process at the expense of possible mistakes or to make sure that the operation is well done, even though done by outsiders? There is no single answer to this question, but it is probably true that the Bank, perhaps with excessive zeal for the correct technical solution, has not in its project lending contributed as much to the education of its borrowers as it should have.

The IBRD has not, at least until recently, paid enough attention to the ecological or environmental effects of the projects it has financed. Needless to say, it has not been alone in this neglect. Nor is it subject, even now, to any considerable pressure from its borrowers to remedy this deficiency. Public officials and businessmen in less developed countries tend to be willing to accept dirtier rather than cleaner air, and more rather than less stream pollution, since these effects in their minds are necessary concomitants of the desired industrialization. The campaign to protect the environment is still limited largely to the developed world. Still, there are ways of limiting adverse environmental effects without slowing industrialization, and the costs of such procedures are worth investigating. The IBRD has recently employed specialists to work on this problem.

Perhaps the most serious criticism of IBRD project lending is its failure to assess adequately the developmental consequences of its loans. End-use supervision falls short of dealing with this question. Although the commission that reported in 1964 on project supervision recommended that a number of case studies be made of "the question whether the economic results of its projects are in line with those forecast during appraisal, and if not, why not," not much has been done until very recently to implement this recommendation. Yet a careful study of the economic consequences of a selected series of Bank project loans could clearly contribute much both to an understanding of the development process and to an improvement of Bank project lending.

Finally, it must be said that, although legitimate criticism can be levied here and there at project selection and development, the Bank's high standing as a project lender is fully deserved.

CHAPTER NINE

Program Lending and Local Expenditure Financing

As was pointed out in Chapter 8, the IBRD's conception of projects and project lending has been fairly broad and flexible within the limits set by identifiable expansions of productive capacity and the financing of imports relatable to this expansion. Under the Articles of Agreement the financing of imports that may add to production, but not necessarily to capital investment, is justifiable only in "exceptional circumstances." Similarly, the financing of local expenditures, even though undertaken for the purpose of capital investment, needs the covering cloak of "exceptional circumstances."[1] What the exceptional circumstances are that would justify the financing of local expenditures or the making of what have come to be called "program loans" has been a perennial issue in discussions of Bank lending policy. From the time the Bank began operations there has been a division of opinion among the staff, among the executive directors, and within management on the extent to which the project provisions and local expenditure provisions of the Articles of Agreement of the Bank and of IDA do or should limit Bank Group lending. There is still division on this question.

The lending policy of the Bank and IDA, as circumscribed either by their Articles of Agreement or by the Bank's interpretation of these Articles, has been subject to a great deal of outside criticism. It has frequently been stated or implied that until the IBRD shows itself willing to move substantially further in the direction of local expenditure financing and program lending

1. International Bank for Reconstruction and Development, Articles of Agreement, Article IV, section 3(b) and (c).

260

than it has to date, it can hardly be called a development institution, nor will it be in an effective position to act as a leader or coordinator of the development efforts of others. The group of experts appointed by the secretary-general of the United Nations in 1949 to report on "National and International Measures for Full Employment" recommended that the World Bank make loans for "general development purposes not only in special circumstances but generally." In commenting on this recommendation at the ensuing meeting of the United Nations Economic and Social Council, President Black stated that a loan for general purposes "really means a loan for a purpose or purposes unknown."

As a leader in various consortia and consultative groups, the Bank has frequently found itself exhorting bilateral assistance providers to increase their program lending although it has shown little disposition to follow its own advice. This attitude has generated a great deal of grumbling and complaining, particularly in the U.S. Agency for International Development.

The Pearson Commission, which was initiated and financed by the Bank, recommended with respect to local expenditure financing that "aid-givers should remove regulations which limit or prevent contributions to the local costs of projects and make a greater effort to encourage local procurement wherever economically justified."[2]

With respect to program lending, the Pearson Commission made two recommendations, one directed specifically to IDA.

Aid-givers should adapt the forms of aid to the needs and level of development of the receiving country and recognize the great value, in many cases, of more program aid.

IDA should undertake program lending wherever appropriate, seeking, if necessary, statutory change to make this possible.[3]

In the extensive debate in the United States in 1969 and 1970 concerning U.S. development assistance policy, proposals to shift assistance from bilateral to multilateral channels frequently raised the question whether the Bank was willing to undertake more program lending. The Bank has been resistant to outside suggestions that, in general, it embrace a more flexible lending policy and, in particular, undertake more program lending.

At the end of our discussion of the development of Bank policy on program loans and the financing of local expenditure we will comment on the effect of that policy on the Bank Group's position as a development institution. But before the historical evolution of Bank policy is discussed, some-

2. *Partners in Development*, Report of the Commission on International Development, Lester B. Pearson, chairman (Praeger, 1969), p. 190.
3. *Ibid.*

thing should be said about the meaning of "local expenditure financing" and "program lending," and their relation to each other.

Any capital investment is likely to require imported equipment, materials, and subassemblies to be financed through the expenditure of foreign exchange. It will also require inputs of domestic materials and labor, which will be financed in local currency. The less developed a country is, the larger the foreign exchange component for a particular type of capital installation is likely to be. As higher stages of development are reached, particularly as the size of the industrial sector increases, a country will find itself capable of producing domestically some of the capital goods it formerly imported, and consequently the percentage of the total cost of a particular installation that will require foreign exchange financing will tend to decrease. In this case some part of the capital transfer may have to take the form of imports that are not necessarily related to specific projects. These imports can be financed by including in project loans an amount of foreign exchange in excess of the import requirements of the project itself and available for general imports; or they may be financed by program loans covering the foreign exchange costs of a given volume of imports specified in more or less detail and related to a development program rather than to specific capital projects. Which method is preferable depends on circumstances to be discussed later.

The conditions under which the Bank may undertake local expenditure financing are specified in Article IV, section 3, of the Articles of Agreement. Paragraph b of that section states that "the Bank may, in exceptional circumstances when local currency required for the purposes of the loan cannot be raised by the borrower on reasonable terms, provide the borrower as part of the loan with an appropriate amount of that currency."

The only domestic currencies owned by the Bank are the unconverted 18 percent contributions of members, or borrowings from these members, and paragraph b has been interpreted to refer only to a loan to a country from that country's 18 percent contribution or from the Bank's borrowings in that currency. Any country in control of its own currency would not need to borrow it from the Bank or any other outsider. It could borrow from its own central bank or print the money it needed. However, some members of the Bank do not control the overall quantity of the money they use. Liberia and Panama, for example, use U.S. dollars. The only loan the Bank has ever made in the currency of the borrower was in connection with the Kariba Dam project in what was then the Federation of Rhodesia and Nyasaland. The Bank supplied the borrower with sterling from the U.K. 18 percent contribution, to be used for purchases in the United Kingdom. This was in fact the currency of the borrower. This type of local currency lending, however, is too infrequent and unimportant to concern us further.

The local expenditure lending that *is* important is that which provides foreign exchange in excess of the quantity needed to finance the import requirements of a project. Article IV, section 3(c), deals with that subject in language of less than perfect clarity:

The Bank, if the project gives rise indirectly to an increased need for foreign exchange by the member in whose territories the project is located, may in exceptional circumstances provide the borrower as part of the loan with an appropriate amount of gold or foreign exchange not in excess of the borrower's local expenditure in connection with the purpose of the loan.

This might be interpreted as justifying local expenditure financing only in an amount sufficient to cover the indirect as well as the direct foreign exchange costs of a project, for example, imported materials or subassemblies for equipment produced locally for the project. The Bank has, in fact, interpreted the language more broadly and, in so doing, has distinguished three different types of situations in which local expenditure financing may be justified.[4]

Countries that are chronically short of foreign exchange have a strong inducement to present to foreign lenders projects for which the import component is high. These may not be, at least in the eyes of the lender, the highest priority projects. Typically the foreign exchange component of agricultural and educational projects, for example, tends to be low, though their potential contribution to development may be large. Consequently, the "financing of local expenditures is justified when the financing of foreign expenditures only would not enable the Bank to assist in the financing of the highest priority projects."[5]

For those components of a product that are suitable for international competitive bidding, a local supplier who takes into account the applicable preference margin, discussed in Chapter 8, may be the lowest bidder. Since the Bank wants to encourage local procurement whenever it is economically justified, it has shown itself willing for its project loans to cover the total cost of such procurement. This procedure will normally provide the borrower with free foreign exchange, which can be used to cover the cost of imports that are not necessarily connected with the project.

Both of the above justifications of local expenditure financing involve what might be called "project considerations," which affect either the choice of the project or the choice of suppliers for a project. But the IBRD is also

4. Local expenditure financing, by our definition, which is also the Bank's, does not include indirect foreign exchange costs that are directly traceable to a project. For example, if a domestic producer of equipment for a Bank-financed project requires imported materials to produce this equipment, we call the financing of such imports "foreign exchange financing" rather than "local expenditure financing."

5. IBRD, Staff paper, Sec M 68-436 (Nov. 29, 1968).

willing to finance local costs, that is, to supply foreign exchange above and beyond the import requirement of a project in order to meet the foreign exchange needs of a development program. The financing of local costs, however, whether project or program oriented, is subject to the overriding condition that "the borrowing country has a suitable development program and is making an adequate development effort."[6]

The Bank Group's program lending is subject to the same conditions. Strictly speaking, a program loan has two characteristics: (a) it is designed to finance a particular kind of foreign exchange deficit—a deficit arising from planned foreign exchange expenditures in excess of the foreign exchange prospectively available for a national development program; and (b) the imports to be financed are not earmarked for specific capital installations. The Bank's actual practice is somewhat looser than this. After referring to twenty-two "program loans" undertaken by the Bank Group, an operational memorandum goes on to say,

Most of these loans have taken the form of the provision of foreign exchange to enable commodities which are important to development to be imported instead of the provision of capital to particular borrowers. The commodities may be limited to imported goods used in particular sectors or areas or may cover part of the needs of a development program for the whole economy.[7]

6. IBRD, Operational memorandum 2.03 (June 9, 1969), "Foreign Exchange Loans for Local Expenditure."

7. IBRD, Operational memorandum 2.07 (May 20, 1969) lists, in Annex A, some twenty-two program loans or credits that had been committed by the end of calendar year 1968. Sixteen of these were Bank loans, and six were IDA credits.

The Bank loans listed in the memorandum (which total $1,055.5 million) include: reconstruction loans to France, the Netherlands, Denmark, and Luxembourg (1946–48), amounting to $497 million; five loans to Australia (1951–57), totaling $308.5 million; one loan of $70 million in 1951–52 to Belgium; two totaling $20 million (1952–54) to Italy (Cassa per il Mezzogiorno); two loans to Norway (1954–55), totaling $50 million; one of $75 million to Iran in 1957; and in 1962, a loan to India of $35 million.

India received four IDA credits in the years 1964–69, totaling $405 million, and in 1966–67 Pakistan was granted two credits for a total of $50 million.

This list omits a program loan of $40 million to the Belgian Congo in 1952, which was guaranteed by the Belgian government, and wrongly classifies a 1962 Bank loan to India. This was a loan to a development finance company (the ICICI). Such loans the Bank normally considers to be project loans.

Between December 31, 1968, and the end of fiscal year 1971, IDA extended two more industrial import credits to India. In fiscal 1971 IDA extended a $25 million credit to Pakistan, after a devastating hurricane, "to help the Government carry out a large rehabilitation program," and the Bank made an $80 million loan to Nigeria "to help the Government carry out its plans for post-war economic rehabilitation" (World Bank/International Development Association, *Annual Report, 1971*, pp. 28–29), and indeed all four of these additional loans and credits conform to the Bank's conception of program loans. Thus by the end of fiscal year 1971, the Bank Group had extended some twenty-six program loans or credits.

Some of these Bank "program loans" would be called sector loans by other foreign assistance agencies. And, as we noted in Chapter 8, certain of the industrial import loans to India (which are included in the program category) come close to being project oriented in the sense that particular uses and users are specified. In recent years the term "program loan" has lost favor in the Bank to the less precise term "non-project loan." But regardless of the designation, we are concerned in this chapter with the financing of imports that are not specifically directed to particular capital installations. According to the operational memorandum cited above, important characteristics of such financing are that it enables "a larger amount of external aid to be made available to a country than might be possible if aid were limited to the direct foreign exchange cost of projects"; and it is "a method by which external aid can be provided rapidly. . . ."[8]

Although the term "program lending" was not in common use when the Bank opened its doors, there is no doubt that the first four reconstruction loans made by the Bank were program loans. The French applied in 1946 for a loan of $500 million and specified a number of commodities whose imports were to be financed, which were grouped in the following categories: equipment, $106 million; energy, $180 million; and raw materials, $214 million.

Included in the energy category were $120 million for coal and $60 million for petroleum imports. Although the total commitment of the Bank on this loan was scaled down to $250 million, the share of the total for each commodity category was unchanged. These commodities were to be a part of the required imports for the first year of a "development plan."

The discussion by the executive directors turned on two questions. What is a project? How far beyond the confines of a project can "special circumstances" carry Bank lending policy? One director stated that "the pipeline kind of loan" is enough to justify the title "project." The chairman felt that the French application contemplated a more specific kind of project, the "Monnet Plan." Another director said that although the French loan is not for a special project, it is for a "general project," that is, the implementation of the French development plan.[9]

If the French application did not constitute a project, how far could "special circumstances" justify an extension of Bank lending policy? Some directors felt that the term "special circumstances" was broad enough to include straight balance-of-payments support, irrespective of the character of the balance-of-payments deficit. But the sense of the meeting appears to have been expressed by the Polish representative. A loan

8. IBRD, Operational memorandum 2.07 (May 20, 1969), p. 1.
9. IBRD, Meeting of Executive Directors, *Transcript of Proceedings* (May 9, 1947).

must always be controlled by the Bank as in the case of the French loan. Countries will want to buy things. They may not construct a bridge; or a railway; but they need to import raw materials, in order to make their industries work—that's a general project. But I don't think we shall ever grant a loan to any country for general purposes to be determined by the country itself.[10]

This indeed has been the policy of the executive directors. There was no intention, as the Bretton Woods discussion made clear, to create an institution that would undertake loans for the poorly specified purposes that characterized international lending in the 1920s. The imports financed by the French loan were specified, but of course it proved impossible to follow these imports through to their end use, that is, to determine whether imported coal was used in generating energy for the production of capital rather than consumers' goods. This is characteristic of program loans and, perhaps more so, of local expenditure financing. The effect of such loans on the economic activities of the borrower can be determined, if at all, only by a more aggregative type of analysis.[11]

Subsequent discussion by the executive directors on the later reconstruction loans reveals a maturing of judgment both on the nature of the special circumstances that might justify Bank lending and on the kind of evidence of productive use the Bank should seek in connection with program loans. In recommending a loan of $195 million to the Netherlands, President McCloy stated that "the foreign exchange needs of the Netherlands in order to restore its economy are of such a general nature and the plan of the Netherlands for the restoration of its economy is consequently also of such a general and flexible character as to constitute special circumstances warranting the Bank in making the loan on the terms and conditions proposed."[12]

The kind of evidence the Bank intended to consider in determining that the imports financed by a program loan were appropriately used is indicated in the president's statement on the Danish reconstruction loan of $40 million.

The Danish Government's chief contribution to the execution of the Reconstruction Program, apart from certain foreign borrowing, consists in restricting domestic consumption, granting priority in the allocation of critical materials to the production of capital goods, channeling savings to investment through taxation policy, and applying selective and quantitative controls over imports—all with the object of encouraging the extraordinary capital formation required for reconstruction

10. *Ibid.*

11. Of course, strictly speaking this is true also of a project loan since the loan permits the borrowing government to use its own foreign exchange for other purposes.

12. IBRD, Recommendation of the President to the Executive Directors (Aug. 6, 1947).

and modernization of its productive resources and of putting right its balance of payments on current international account.[13]

In other words, the justification of a program loan lies in the use the borrowing country makes of its own, as well as of borrowed, foreign resources. The borrowing country must have a "suitable development program" and make an "adequate development effort."

The four reconstruction loans had not raised the local expenditure issue; the proceeds of these loans were earmarked exclusively for specific imports. An application in 1949 from Belgium raised the local expenditure question for the first time in operational form.[14] Belgium wanted a loan to finance not only the imports of equipment associated with particular projects but additional foreign exchange that might be added to its reserves or might finance the import of unspecified commodities. Discussion of this application by the executive directors' committee on financial policy resulted in a consensus on the following propositions:

The "exceptional circumstances" clause of Article IV, section 3(c), was at issue:

"Exceptional circumstances" would have to be defined case by case; "Financing a local expenditure in Belgium would make it difficult to avoid similar financing in many other member countries"; and "The power to make local currency expenditure loans should be exercised cautiously, if at all."[15]

This discussion of the Belgian application led in subsequent meetings of the finance committee to a report, accepted by the executive directors, which defined the major lines of Bank policy on local expenditure financing, at least

13. IBRD, Recommendation of the President to the Executive Directors (Aug. 20, 1947).

14. The first indication of staff discussion of the local currency issue the authors have been able to discover is a typewritten memorandum dated June 9, 1948. This memo distinguished the problem of supplying a country with its own currency from the question of supplying foreign exchange beyond the import requirements of a particular project. It said that "the essential purpose of such a loan is not to enable the borrower to meet expenses payable in local currency but rather to prevent the payment of such expenses from causing undue inflation in the country in which the project is located."

15. IBRD, Memorandum of Meeting of the Committee on Financial Policy of the Executive Directors (March 10, 1949). The U.S. director, Eugene Black,
> stated that a local expenditure loan to Belgium would have a favorable reception in the market because of Belgium's strong economic position. On the other hand, there was some doubt as to the reaction of the market to loans for local currency expenditure in other countries. So far the Bank's policy had been to make loans only for import requirements, and it was doubtful whether the market would understand a change in this policy. The U.S. market had had rather bad experience from 1920 on with loans for local expenditure.

until 1964, when the subject was reexamined. The report, after citing a number of conditions that would have to be met, concluded that,

as a matter of sound loan policy, the Bank may, in appropriate circumstances and on appropriate conditions, make a loan for the purpose of providing local currency for the financing of a reconstruction or development project in the territories of a member and that, in connection with such a loan, the Bank may permit the foreign exchange proceeds of the loan to be added to the monetary reserves of the member.[16]

The considerations governing local expenditure lending are more clearly stated in the Bank's fifth annual report.

In general, the Bank's policy may be summarized by saying that local expenditures may be financed if the following conditions are satisfied: (a) if the project to be financed is of such economic urgency that the country's ability to undertake foreign borrowing—which is more or less limited in all cases—is better utilized in financing this project than in financing the direct foreign exchange costs of alternative projects; (b) if the local currency costs of the project cannot reasonably be met out of available domestic resources; and (c) if it is apparent that, unless foreign exchange is made available to the borrowing country to be employed for the import of either consumer goods or raw materials, the local currency expenditures involved in the project will lead to inflationary pressures.[17]

Condition (a) clearly relates to what we have earlier called a project consideration, that is, a consideration bearing on the choice of the project. Conditions (b) and (c), however, relate to the need to supplement domestic savings with foreign savings, that is, to the savings and import requirements of a development program. How much local expenditure financing the Bank was willing to undertake would become clear only in subsequent lending operations.

The Belgian application more or less coincided with a rather active dissatisfaction in the economic staff concerning the slowness with which Bank lending was developing. In fiscal year 1947–48 the Bank committed $251 million, of which all but $16 million was for reconstruction loans to the Netherlands and Denmark. The $16 million represented two loans to Chile. In 1948–49, total commitments fell to $135.25 million. In the annual report for that year it was stated, rather apologetically, that "the Bank cannot and should not be expected to provide the answer to all or even a major part of the world's financial ills."[18]

Certain economists in the Bank, however, took the position that the low volume of Bank lending was the result of Bank policy rather than of a short-

16. IBRD, Report R-221 (March 31, 1949). Submitted to the executive directors and accepted April 5, 1949.

17. IBRD, *Fifth Annual Report, 1949–1950*, p. 11.

18. IBRD, *Fourth Annual Report, 1948–1949*, p. 5.

age either of loanable funds or of feasible capital projects. If the IBRD were interested in promoting development through a transfer of capital, the option of program loans was available in special circumstances. And if the Bank were willing to finance local costs, its choice of projects could be widened.

A memorandum of March 29, 1949, from Leonard Rist to President McCloy, pointed out that

a transfer of capital cannot take place in any form other than a transfer of goods and services. The category of goods is irrelevant. Whether a country imports grains, motor cars, cranes, turbines or pig iron, it does add to its overall resources. . . .

There is no doubt that Britain or France could never have invested as much as they did in 1947 and 1948 had it not been for the considerable import of consumer goods, including food, which they received through the means of loans, grants and sales of foreign assets.

Of course, Rist goes on, it is necessary to make sure that the transfer will add to investment. "This involves an examination of the overall investment policy of the country."

Assuming that the above conditions are met, there does not seem to be any economic reason why a transfer of capital involving consumers goods as well as capital goods could not be financed by the Bank.[19]

A note on "Local Currency Loans" by P. N. Rosenstein-Rodan concludes that "if the country is creditworthy and if the project is sound, such loans should only be denied under exceptional circumstances." Local currency lending should be the rule rather than the exception. He goes on to say,

In our opinion the exclusion of local currency loans narrows the scope of the Bank's activity and eliminates, *a priori*, more than half of investment projects which could otherwise be submitted and classified as sound projects for Bank financing. The scarcity of well prepared bankable projects is thus largely created by the Bank policy of excluding local currency loans.[20]

Whether because of these arguments or for other reasons, the IBRD undertook in the 1950s a series of loans of a type it has been loath to consider in recent years. The lending in question included two loans to Belgium and the Belgian Congo for $70 million in September 1951, two loans totaling $20 million to the Italian Cassa per il Mezzogiorno in 1952 and 1954, five loans to Australia between 1951 and 1957 totaling $308.5 million, and two loans

19. The discussion between the economists and the Bank management during this period recalls the controversy of the 1890s, participated in by Eugen von Böhm-Bawerk, J. B. Clark, Frank W. Taussig, and others, concerning the nature of capital and capital goods.
20. Dated Jan. 13, 1950.

to Norway for $50 million in 1954–55. It should be noted that all these loans were either to, or guaranteed by, developed countries.

The loan to Belgium was for $30 million, and the loan to the Congo, guaranteed by the Belgian government, was for $40 million. Both loans were intended to finance part of the first two years' expenditure of a ten-year Congo development program. This was the first lending to a colony that the Bank had undertaken, but it was shortly to be followed by a number of colonial loans, all guaranteed by metropolitan governments. It was a program loan in the sense that it was intended to meet the foreign exchange requirements of a development program. But no attempt was made to specify the imports needed to carry out this program. In the term then current in the Bank this was described as an "impact loan." What was intended to be financed was the foreign exchange "impact" of expenditures in local currencies in Belgium and the Congo relating to the development program. As it was explained to the executive directors by staff members who had worked on the loan negotiations, the Bank's economists had used "the best figures that are available [concerning] the economic impact on Belgium and on the Belgian Congo of the execution of the plan. The consequence of that estimation is that we have no list of goods, as we have had in most loans which we have made, because what we are really financing is a wide range of production and consumer goods, and it would be quite impossible to attempt to draw any sort of list to which we could tie the borrowers specifically."[21]

The Bank exercised no detailed supervision over the particular projects on which expenditures were made within the context of the development program. The disbursement of both loans was based on the reported expenditures of the Office d'Exploitation des Transports Coloniaux (OTRACO), a public organization which administered the larger part of the transport network of the Congo. Thus the Bank had the opportunity and the responsibility of following these expenditures closely and of getting "an insight into the development not only of the OTRACO program itself, but an insight into the development of the whole plan." If the expenditures on the program slow down, "we will slow down in our disbursements so as to keep pace with the progress of the program which is the real basis for this loan."[22]

Although there was a lively discussion among the directors, there seems to have been no objection to this type of loan. Indeed the sense of the meeting appears to have been that it marked a desirable increase in the flexibility of

21. IBRD, Special Meeting of the Executive Directors, *Transcript of Proceedings* (Sept. 13, 1951).
22. *Ibid.*

Bank lending. The intervention in the discussion by a Latin American representative is of some interest. "Latin America will always back loans of this nature and is very pleased with this first experience. . . ." The Bank, in fact, has never made a program loan to a Latin American member country.

The second set of impact loans made by the Bank were the two loans of $10 million each to the Cassa per il Mezzogiorno in 1952 and 1954. After this the term "impact loan" disappeared from the Bank's lexicon. So also, except for minor aberrations, did the practice of making program loans without reaching an agreement with the borrower as to what imports were to be financed. The loans to Belgium and the Belgian Congo and to Italy mark the closest approach to what one director declared the Bank would never do, that is "grant a loan to any country for general purposes to be determined by the country itself." The Italian loans did not go quite this far, but they came close. Although the loans to Belgium and the Congo had been approved without difficulty, the loans to Italy excited considerable controversy.[23]

The Cassa was a public corporation established and financed by the Italian government to advance the development of southern Italy. It operated through hundreds of contractors, who engaged in particular projects and who were, of course, paid in lire. The dollars provided by the Bank loans were sold by the Cassa to the Italian government for lire. The dollars then disappeared from the Bank's purview and were used by the government for current imports and additions to its monetary reserves. The lire were credited to a special account by the Cassa and used for projects in the selection and supervision of which the Bank played a role. This role, however, was rather tenuous. Disbursement of the loan was to be proportional to the Cassa's expenditures on the development program. But as the responsible staff officer said to the executive directors,

We cannot supervise the plan through the disbursement procedure. We will supervise the plan through the normal means of receiving progress reports, going over these and having a look at the development once in a while, but, most particularly, by close contact with the Italian Government and with the Cassa, and every indication has been given us of a cordial welcome when we go.[24]

23. According to Leonard Rist, this controversy "was a little acrimonious, I think it will be fair to say." He goes on to say, "It took some time for some of us to accept the idea that what a foreign loan finances is imports in general, and that there is an element of substitutability among them." (Oral History Project of Columbia University, interviews recorded in the summer of 1961 on the International Bank for Reconstruction and Development [cited hereinafter as "Oral History"]. Quotation is from interview of Rist, p. 51.)
24. IBRD, Special Meeting of Executive Directors, *Transcript of Proceedings* (Oct 10, 1951).

Again the directors offered no objection to the first Italian loan. Indeed one of the most prominent among them remarked,

I am quite sure that we all feel great satisfaction that the solution has been found to make it possible for us to participate in a very important and interesting scheme without being hampered in that by misunderstood orthodoxies about what we should or shouldn't do. . . . I see this control on the spending of the counterpart lire more as a form of cooperation between the Cassa and ourselves than as a sort of supervision.[25]

The only difference the second Italian loan introduced was the dropping of the special account for projects in which the Bank had some rights of supervision and selection. The Bank's only role now was to receive reports about, and to inspect from time to time, the progress of the general development program. But, as is suggested above, these Italian loans probably represented the furthest the Bank has been able to advance (retreat) from orthodoxy, and the advance (retreat) was of relatively short duration.

The Australian loans were in some respects *sui generis*. The U.S. secretary of state at the time the first loan was negotiated (Dean Acheson) had this to contribute. After remarking that many prime ministers came to Washington in that period for financial assistance, he said,

The only successful visit that comes to mind is one by Robert Menzies, Prime Minister of Australia, who slipped into town hardly noticed and in a day and a half was gone again with a loan of two hundred fifty million dollars from the World Bank for Australia's great water and power development. But Bob Menzies knew the ropes as well as or better than we did ourselves.[26]

Mr. Menzies, however, had something more going for him than a knowledge of the ropes. The Australian member of the board of directors at that time (the early 1950s) heartily disapproved of the Bank and all its works. He disliked the relationship between the management and the executive directors, he disapproved of the cumbersomeness of Bank operations and the slowness with which lending operations were developing. Consequently he advised the Australian delegation about to depart for Washington to try to negotiate dollar financing that it should go to the U.S. Export-Import Bank and stay away from the IBRD. However, since it was recently established U.S. policy that countries seeking to borrow should first approach the IBRD unless special U.S. interests were involved, the Australian mission found it necessary to approach the Bank. It did so, however, with a set of "impossible conditions," hoping and expecting to be turned down.[27] This was to be a balance-of-pay-

25. *Ibid.*
26. Dean Acheson, *Present at the Creation: My Years in the State Department* (Norton, 1969), p. 502.
27. Davidson Sommers in his contribution to the "Oral History" (pp. 29–31) gives a graphic picture of these negotiations.

ments loan; there was to be no examination of projects; "as a matter of fact we've only got three weeks, and then we're going home."

Although the Australian delegation may have thought the conditions unacceptable, the president of the Bank (Black) thought otherwise. The Australians had brought with them a carefully considered list of imports requiring dollar financing; there was no doubt that Australia was creditworthy; it was important to nail down the recently announced U.S. policy that the Bank should be the preferred lender in the absence of special U.S. interests; and it was important that the Bank establish good relations with Australia. The visiting mission had asked for a loan of $100 million to cover dollar import requirements for a two-year period. The Bank staff suggested $50 million pending the visit of a Bank staff mission to Australia to obtain additional information. The Australians, however, would have none of that, and President Black put the loan through within three weeks of the mission's arrival. During the discussion of this loan in the board of directors an Asian director remarked, perhaps a trifle plaintively, "I should like to express the hope that these more liberal attitudes—if I may say so, these intelligent liberal attitudes—will be followed in the consideration by this Board of other loans, loan applications, and also in the administration of loans already granted."[28]

By the time of the second and subsequent loans to Australia, the Bank was able to dispatch missions that acquired substantially more detailed information on the imports to be financed and the uses to which these imports would be put. But the Australians resisted all efforts to "projectize" borrowings from the Bank. Speaking of the first loan, a former general counsel and vice president of the Bank observed: "From that time on the Australians were staunch supporters of the Bank, although they used this precedent to make us continue to make loans to them for a long time that we wouldn't make to anybody else."[29]

The remaining program loans undertaken by the Bank require only brief mention. In 1954 and 1955 the Bank made two loans of $25 million each to Norway "to help meet the anticipated strain on the balance of payments in the next few years. The strain comes partly from a high rate of investment, particularly in shipping."[30] These loans were in fact rather similar to the Australian loans. Norway was a creditworthy country, and her investment program as a whole was judged to be sound. The imports to be financed were specified to only a limited extent. The chief difference from the first Austra-

28. IBRD, Special Meeting of Executive Directors, *Transcript of Proceedings* (Aug. 22, 1950).

29. Sommers, "Oral History," p. 32.

30. IBRD, Two Hundred and Fifty-First Regular Meeting of Executive Directors, *Transcript of Proceedings* (April 8, 1954).

lian loan was that, in this case, the Bank had an opportunity to send an investigatory mission to the borrower in advance of the loan. To the question from a director as to why the Bank had not loaned for projects, the answer was given, "the problem we were faced with was to find a means of disbursement for Norway so that Norway could draw down the money of the loan quickly."[31]

The World Bank in 1957 made a loan of $75 million to Iran to cover foreign exchange expenditures under Iran's Seven Year Development Plan. This was the first program loan to a less developed country ever made by the Bank, and until a so-called rehabilitation loan was made to Nigeria in 1971, it was also the last made by the Bank as distinguished from the International Development Association (IDA). Expenditures under the loan were in the hands of the Plan Organization, an agency funded mainly by an allocation of a percentage of Iran's oil revenues. The Plan Organization had embarked on a series of development expenditures that exceeded its current revenues, and the purpose of the loan was to cover the deficiency for a period during which the increasing oil revenues of Iran would again permit a matching of revenues and expenditures. In explaining to the executive directors why the Bank proposed in this case to depart so far from its tradition of project lending, the staff representative said:

The development program covered a large number of activities, few of which were expected to form conveniently-sized Bank projects or to be sufficiently prepared from a technical standpoint.

Taking into account the time likely to be needed by the Bank for an adequate appraisal of the potential projects and the fact that such larger sized projects in the aggregate probably would not add up to the amount needed by the Plan Organization, the project approach did not appear to offer a practical method of dealing with the situation in Iran, at any rate for the time being.[32]

This loan specified in detail neither the imports to be financed nor the uses to which these imports would be put. On the other hand, the Bank proposed to use the "leverage" stemming from this loan to bring about certain changes in Iranian practice. The loan agreement set forth expenditure limits which the Plan Organization was not to exceed. The Bank also accepted an invitation from the Plan Organization to provide a sizable group of technicians who not only assisted in project preparation but kept the Bank informed on the progress of the development program.

Most of the remaining loans of the Bank Group that have been considered

31. *Ibid.*
32. IBRD, Meeting of Executive Directors, *Transcript of Proceedings* (Jan. 18, 1957).

to fall within the program category have taken the form of IDA industrial import credits. Before turning to this subject, however, it is necessary to retrace our steps and consider the development of Bank policy in the field of local expenditure financing.

Development of Bank Policy on Local Expenditure Financing

We left this subject earlier at the point where the executive directors had accepted a policy directive on local currency lending in 1949 (R-221), a policy that is stated more fully in the *Fifth Annual Report, 1949–1950*. We had noted that certain economists in the Bank, dissatisfied with what they considered to be the slow rate of development of Bank lending, were extolling the merits of "impact loans" and urging more local expenditure financing. The predominant sentiment in the Bank, however, was for limiting local expenditure financing to developed countries.

An operational memorandum in 1953 on local expenditure financing emphasized two types of justification:[33]

(b) The borrowing country's imports include so few capital goods of the type required for projects, that, if the Bank limited itself to loans of the normal kind, the amounts that the country could expect to borrow from the Bank would be less than could be justified on creditworthy grounds. . . .

(e) There is no reasonable expectation that the required funds can be raised locally without undesirable consequences.

Countries whose investment projects require limited imports of capital equipment tend to be developed countries with a sizable industrial sector.

The operational memorandum stated at the conclusion that

the size of the loan will be determined by the Bank's judgment of what share of the local expenditures the Bank considers it reasonable to finance, rather than by an estimate of the "impact" on the country's foreign exchange resources, of the local expenditure on the project or program.

Impact loans were out. But the meaning the statement intended to give to the term "reasonable" is far from clear. What is evident from the record, however, is that the local currency component of certain Bank loans was large. A power loan of $25 million to Austria in 1954, for example, involved a direct foreign exchange expenditure of only $2.9 million. The total estimated cost

33. IBRD, Operational memorandum 1.22 (Dec. 4, 1953).

of the project was $115 million. The president's report on this loan (March 9, 1954) said:

The greater part of the expenditure on the project will be incurred in Austria, as relatively little imported equipment is needed. Consequently, if the loan were confined to financing imports, it would provide only an insignificant proportion of the capital needed. These needs cannot wholly be met by raising funds locally, because of the general shortage of capital in Austria. In these circumstances it is, in my opinion, appropriate to extend a loan in foreign exchange to cover part of the expenditure in local currencies which cannot otherwise be raised.

It has been estimated that from its beginning until the end of 1963, the Bank made forty-nine loans containing some element of local expenditure financing.[34] Most of these loans were to developed countries. But toward the end of the period this situation began to change as manufacturing capacity in a number of the less developed countries continued to increase. A power loan to Mexico in 1958 focused attention on this problem. Penstocks for hydroelectric projects had been included in the list of imported goods to be financed by the loan, but it appeared that these could be produced locally at competitive costs. A task force was established to consider the question. It came to the conclusion that while it should continue to be the Bank's policy to include in its financing only goods that the borrowing country normally imported from abroad, the Bank should be prepared to finance the procurement of such goods locally if it turned out that local producers could supply them competitively. This conclusion was embodied in a statement to the executive directors by the director of the Department of Operations–Western Hemisphere.[35] The statement pointed out that to do otherwise would place the borrower in the awkward position of not knowing how much of the loan could be used before all orders were placed.

The Mexican case raised the question: "When is a bid from a domestic producer who enjoys tariff protection to be considered competitive"? We have discussed this question at some length in Chapter 8, and there is no need to repeat that discussion here. But it should be pointed out that, even after this question had been raised in connection with the Mexican loan, the Bank continued to lend for local procurement in developed countries without any extensive inquiry into the question of tariff protection.[36] The problem

34. FPC/64-4 (May 1, 1964), "Foreign Exchange Loans for Local Expenditure," Appendix, p. 4.

35. R58-103 (Sept. 16, 1958).

36. A memorandum from the Department of Operations, Europe, March 24, 1964 (File Policies and Procedures, General, Vol. IV), pointed out that between 1961 and 1964 the Bank had made four loans to Yugoslavia. "In all these cases the direct import

of the degree of preference to be permitted a domestic supplier apparently was raised only in connection with loans to less developed member countries.

By the time IDA was established in 1960, the Bank had had considerable experience with local expenditure lending and had found it a useful tool. The Articles of Agreement of IDA simply state that "the Association, in special cases, may make foreign exchange available for local expenditures."[37] Although there is no logical reason why the practice of the Bank with respect to local expenditure financing should be any different from that of IDA, a general feeling was created by differences in the language of the Articles of Agreement of the Bank and IDA that "IDA can be more liberal than the Bank in financing local expenditure and this seems to have been reflected in IDA's practice."[38]

During the years following the formation of IDA, questions concerning the appropriate limits of local expenditure lending continued to arise in connection with both Bank and IDA loans and became a subject for frequent discussion in the Financial Policy Committee. Consequently in 1964, the staff was asked to undertake a thorough review of past and current practice and policy. The result was a memorandum ("Foreign Exchange Loans for Local Expenditures") presented by President Woods to the financial policy committee. This memorandum not only tabulated the available information on all Bank and IDA loans having a local expenditure content but analyzed the relation of local expenditure lending to the international transfer of capital.[39]

---

requirements were quite small, generally less than one-third of the amount of the loan. Disbursement was permitted against total expenditure, domestic and foreign, despite the existence of high tariffs protecting domestic producers."

The same memorandum calls attention to a number of other loans financing local procurement that were made with little discussion of the tariff question. Of the loans cited, one was to Australia; three were to Austria; one to Iceland; and a long series was to Japan. In a number of these cases, "the Bank considered the tariff question, described the situation in loan documents, but took no action."

On the loans to Japan made between 1953 and 1966, total disbursements amounted to $857 million, of which more than $720 million was used to purchase goods and services in Japan.

37. Article V, section 2(e).

38. FPC/64-4 (May 1, 1964), Appendix, p. 5. In Annex D of this report, covering the period from the beginning of IDA to the end of 1963, it is shown that

in those cases where IDA has made local expenditure loans the proportion of the total cost of the project which has been covered by the IDA credit has averaged about 48 percent whereas the corresponding figure for the Bank is about 35 percent. Out of 42 credits made by IDA since May 1961, 22 have included some local expenditure financing, whereas over the same period the Bank made 84 loans of which only 17 involved any local expenditure.

39. FPC/64-4 (May 1, 1964).

There is no economic significance in the distinction between financing the imports required for a project and financing the local expenditure. Both accomplish the purpose of moving real resources from one country to another and both serve the purpose of assisting in financing economic development.

[However] care must be taken to conserve borrowing capacity by ensuring that borrowing countries make the maximum effort to encourage savings and reserve their external borrowing capacity for projects of high priority. . . .

The Bank must therefore make difficult judgments regarding the capacity of countries to mobilize domestic sources of financing. While it would be a mistake to encourage a country to resort needlessly to external financing of local expenditures, it would equally be a mistake to frustrate a development program by artificially limiting the Bank's contribution to the foreign exchange content in the case of development projects for which the borrower is unable to mobilize sufficient resources to meet the local expenditure.[40]

The discussion of this report in the Financial Policy Committee led to a series of conclusions presented by President Woods to the executive directors on June 16, 1964. These conclusions, the president said, were not revolutionary and indeed represented no radical departure from the practice the Bank had followed since 1949. A reexamination of the problem had become necessary primarily because the Bank was now undertaking financing in new nations, primarily in Africa, where on occasion it had appeared to finance the total costs of projects. A second consideration had to do with the fact that a number of less developed countries had now developed a considerable capacity to produce their own equipment. However,

1. There is no intention to abandon the project approach in favor of program financing. He [Woods] agrees with M. Larre [France] that the Bank's insistence on the project approach is one of the bases of its strong reputation with major sources of finance.

2. There is no intention to begin the financing of balance of payments deficits, recognizing that the line to be drawn is a tenuous one. The criterion will be: is the project sound on its merits and is it of high priority? . . .

3. On the question of preferences, the Bank faces a certain dilemma. It wants to preserve international competitive bidding but it also wants to give the less developed countries "a leg up."

This is where the matter stood during the remainder of the Woods administration. During this period a substantial part of both Bank loans and IDA credits represented local expenditure financing.[41] Although the emphasis

40. *Ibid.*, p. 9.
41. During the period beginning with fiscal year 1961–62 and ending with fiscal 1967–68, the Bank disbursed $3,271.1 million on loan commitments made during this period. Of these disbursements, 71.6 percent represented foreign expenditures, 27.2 percent were local expenditures, and 1.2 percent were undetermined.
During the same period IDA disbursed $1,342.5 million of the credits signed in these

remained on the selection of high priority projects, local expenditure lending continued to be an important device for meeting a part of the general import requirements of the borrowers' development programs.[42] The executive directors evidenced no particular objection to this practice. Indeed local expenditure financing, which according to the Bank's charter was justified only in "exceptional circumstances," and according to the Articles of Agreement of IDA only "in special cases," had become a customary aspect of Bank lending practice.

When Robert McNamara became president of the Bank, a number of aspects of Bank policy were brought up for reexamination, including in particular program lending and local expenditure financing. The president asked for staff memoranda on these subjects, and the results of staff cogitation were presented to the executive directors in the form of a memorandum on "Foreign Exchange Loans for Local Currency Expenditures" (July 30, 1968), and a memorandum on "Program Lending" (November 5, 1968). In presenting the memorandum on local currency expenditures, the president remarked, "The major evolution in the recommendations compared to the 1964 statement is that they attempt to spell out more clearly the various cases where the financing of local currency expenditures by the World Bank and IDA would be permissible and useful in securing a more efficient use of resources in our member countries."

The first of the two memoranda was favorably received by the executive directors, who suggested no change in its recommendations. Indeed these

---

years. Of this total, 82.8 percent represented foreign expenditures and 13.9 percent local expenditures; while 3.3 percent was undetermined. Memorandum on "Foreign Exchange Loans for Local Currency Expenditures," presented by the president to the executive directors (June 30, 1968), Annex II.

The rather surprisingly low percentage of IDA local currency lending is in large part accounted for by the fact that India and Pakistan (by far the largest borrowers from IDA) were supplied with sizable "import credits" for specified industrial imports, which in other countries would have been financed by local currency lending.

42. How this objective was seen by at least some of the operating personnel of the Bank is indicated in a memorandum from Roger Chaufournier (then deputy director of the Western Hemisphere Department) to J. Burke Knapp (vice president), dated October 24, 1968. In Peru

we financed 60 percent of project cost, on the average, regardless of the foreign exchange content, in order to maintain a sufficient flow of foreign exchange to the country. In Paraguay we used the technique of varying percentages of disbursements over time, disbursing 80 percent of the project cost the first year when the resource requirements were greatest. At the other end of the spectrum there is the case of Venezuela, where the Bank made the conscious decision to finance less than the foreign exchange cost of a highway project, because the *overall* requirement of the economy did not justify the amount of lending which would otherwise have been appropriate on narrow project grounds.

recommendations represented no change in the Bank's practice, though the practice was perhaps stated more clearly than in previous documents.[43] But though fair sailing was encountered on the subject of local expenditure financing, this was certainly not true of the memorandum on program lending. The preparation of this memo had laid bare a considerable division of opinion in the staff of the Bank, and the discussion by the executive directors revealed at least as great a division. The preparation of the memorandum had been undertaken initially by a group of staff officers who favored an expansion of program lending. But the persistent gnawing of the critics had produced a paper which, while extolling the merits of program lending, ended with a set of recommendations that did little more than endorse existing Bank policy.[44]

The executive directors were not long in perceiving the considerable difference between the elephant promised by the paper and the mouse delivered by the conclusions. While the ensuing discussion indicated considerable support for judicious program lending, the vociferousness of the opposition succeeded, in the end, in extracting from the management of the Bank a commitment that it would henceforth bring to the attention of the executive directors any proposal to undertake a program loan early in its conception. All in all, this episode represented a setback for those elements in the Bank favoring program lending.[45]

43. After stating that the analysis of the paper applied equally to financing by the Bank and by IDA, the memorandum proposed the following recommendations:

(a) If indirect foreign costs can be identified clearly, the Bank should consider financing local expenditures equivalent to such costs to the extent necessary;

(b) If it is uncertain whether specific project costs will be foreign or local, the Bank should provide financing in a manner which will not discriminate against local suppliers;

(c) If a project appears desirable on all grounds except that it has too small a foreign exchange component to justify Bank participation, then the Bank should stand ready to consider supplementing its lending through financing of some local costs; and

(d) If, on the basis of careful appraisal of a country's overall development program and of the country's own efforts to finance the program, the Bank judges that the financial requirements of the program will exceed the limits of available local savings and expected foreign exchange resources, the Bank should be prepared to finance local costs of certain high priority projects.

44. The critical conclusion of the memorandum (p. 9) was the following:

Investment projects or sector loans [including the financing of local expenditures] are likely to remain the predominant type of lending for an indefinite period in the future. Proposals for program lending will be presented to the Directors whenever special circumstances make it necessary to achieve the Bank's and IDA's objectives, but it is not anticipated that during the next twelve months "special circumstances" will require program lending in more than two or three countries, and even there such program lending will be supplementary to project and sector lending.

45. IBRD, Sec M 69-1, memorandum on "Discussion on Program Lending at Meet-

An opportunity arose some two years later to rejoin the issue on program lending and local expenditure financing. This was in connection with the recommendations of the Pearson Commission (in *Partners in Development*), referred to earlier in this chapter. The papers prepared for submission by the president to the executive directors on the recommendation of the commission make clear the preference in the Bank for local expenditure financing. "Where the country's justifiable external capital needs for its investment program exceed the foreign exchange requirements of high-priority projects, the Bank's . . . preference should be to provide assistance in the form of specific project financing with a substantial local currency expenditure component." At the same time the definition of "exceptional circumstances" that might justify program lending was somewhat broadened. Such circumstances may arise when:

(a) A borrowing country presents a development program, with supporting economic and financial policies, which is judged to provide a satisfactory basis for external assistance in a given amount.

(b) The needed transfer of resources from external lenders in support of the development program cannot be achieved effectively and expeditiously by the financing of investment projects, including justifiable local currency expenditures in connection therewith.

(c) Other external lenders are not prepared to fill this gap by non-project lending.[46]

President McNamara considered that if these standards were applied, the Bank Group might, in fiscal 1972 and 1973, "find it appropriate to extend program loans or credits to perhaps four or five countries, and that this form of assistance might amount to some 7 to 10 percent of our total lending commitments." But he also indicated that these estimates were speculative and represented only his "best guess."[47]

There is no doubt that the dislike for program lending on the part of a number of executive directors has been strongly influenced by the IDA experience with import credits to India and Pakistan, to which we now turn.

---

ing of the Executive Directors" (Dec. 3, 1968). The chairman (Vice President Knapp), in summing up the discussion, said that there was logic in the idea that, in the field of program lending, where they [the staff] had not the guidance of their established criteria for project lending, they should keep in touch with the Executive Directors before embarking on firm negotiations, and he would report the proposal that the Board be given a "preview" of program loans to the President.

46. IBRD, President's Memorandum to the Executive Directors (Dec. 15, 1970).

47. *Ibid.*

Industrial Import Credits

As was indicated earlier in this chapter, the IDA industrial import credits
to India and to Pakistan have been classified as program loans. Since discussion among the Bank's staff and in the board of directors centered on the
credits to India, we shall concentrate on these. The commitments are shown
in Table 9-1.

Consideration of these credits inevitably involves us in questions that are
examined at length in later chapters. IDA credits to India and Pakistan, committed before the end of the period of the first replenishment, in 1968,
amounted to 72.5 percent of total IDA funds. Concentration of such a large
amount in two countries inevitably provoked opposition and raised questions
concerning IDA policy, which are considered in Chapter 12. The credits to
both India and Pakistan were committed within the framework of consortium
arrangements. The fact that, in consortia, the Bank is acting with and for
others expands in certain respects its influence on borrowing governments.
In other respects it constitutes a serious constraint. These questions are considered in Chapter 15. Finally, the Bank undertook, particularly in connection with the credits committed in 1966, to bring substantial pressure on the
Indian government to change important domestic policies. In fact, in the
Indian case, probably the Bank went further than in any other case in using
"leverage" to try to improve macroeconomic "performance." This question
is discussed in further detail in Chapter 13. While some consideration of these
questions can hardly be avoided here, a fuller discussion is postponed until
later.

The first Indian credit was designed to make materials, components, and

Table 9-1. *IDA Credits to India for*
Industrial Imports, 1964–70

Credits	Amount (in millions of U.S. dollars)	Year in which approved by executive directors of IDA
First	90	1964
Second	100	1965
Third	150	1966
Fourth	65	1966
Fifth	125	1969
Sixth	75	1970

Source: International Development Association.

balancing equipment available for the manufacture of road transport equipment, machine tools, and heavy electrical apparatus—all capital goods–producing industries. In preparation for this credit a sizable group of Bank engineers and consultants had spent two months in India examining firms in these industries and selecting a number of efficient producers. The Indian government agreed to take such steps as were necessary to assure that the IDA-financed imports were in addition to, and not a replacement for, imports normally scheduled for these industries. The government also agreed to undertake certain measures simplifying import controls and assuring greater continuity of imports. The Bank was not able to specify sources of supply or insist on competitive bidding, but, as was explained by a staff member, "we have satisfied ourselves that the firms that will benefit under the credit do indeed procure their materials from the best source whenever and to the extent that untied foreign exchange is available."[48] The Bank could not, in general, trace specific inputs to specific outputs, but "follow-up procedures should insure that the effects of the credit would be measured." At least, "the credit has opened opportunities for a further exchange of views between the government and the Bank on the future development of the industries covered by the credit."[49]

In introducing this credit, President Woods said:

The present proposal would represent a further evolution of Bank/IDA lending policy. In the past in India loans such as those to the Railways financed materials, parts, components and sub-assemblies for incorporation in capital goods required for the development of rail transport, and the Bank Loan of August 9, 1961, provided a flow of equipment and spare parts for the expansion of production in the private coal industry.[50]

The recommendations of the president described this as a credit for an "industrial imports project." But earlier, in a general statement on Bank financial policy that dealt with, among other things, Bank lending policy, he had come out rather strongly for what he called maintenance import loans. "We should be prepared, in addition to our normal project loans, to make available, in appropriate cases, long-term financing for the import of components and spare parts for industry generally or for some particular segment of industry of special importance to the given economy."[51]

48. IDA, Meeting of Executive Directors, *Transcript of Proceedings* (June 4, 1964).
49. *Ibid.*
50. IBRD, Report and Recommendations of the President to the Executive Directors on a Proposed Development Credit for an Industrial Imports Project (May 28, 1964), P-376, p. 1.
51. FPC 63-8 (July 18, 1963). The statement continues:
What I have in mind here is that, in some of our less developed member countries,

Whether this particular credit was properly called a project loan or a program loan was perhaps of little importance except to the executive directors, to some of whom the term "program loan" was highly suspect. In fact it was passed by the executive directors with little discussion and no disapproval. The credit illustrates one of the shadowy boundaries between project and program loans; how closely must inputs be traced to outputs in order to justify the term "project financing"? By this test, subsequent industrial import credits to India departed increasingly from the project category and approached straight program lending.

The second industrial import credit was committed during the final year of India's Third Five-Year Plan (1960–65) and was regarded by both the management and the executive directors as the fulfillment of an implied promise to see this plan through. In introducing the proposed credit, a staff official referred back to the Bank's appraisal of this plan in 1960.

Chances of reaching the industrial output targets in the Third Plan will depend more on the availability of (so-called) "maintenance imports," fuel, and power than on the new capacity created during the next five years. This underlies the need for more flexible foreign aid policies. . . . All subsequent economic missions (from the Bank) have come to the same conclusion but with increasing emphasis on the "maintenance import" requirements.[52]

The credit added certain branches of the construction industry and wires and cables to the list of industries whose maintenance imports were to be financed. Otherwise, the conditions of the first credit were maintained. One director wondered whether the Bank could not introduce some kind of competitive bidding procedure. Another director, habitually opposed to program lending, was able to convince himself that this was in the nature of a project loan. "The special utilization for special groups of goods is clearly indicated in the report. This is not a free loan for whatever the country would like to purchase abroad."[53] The president perhaps encouraged this line of thought by reflecting on how far the Bank had come from the time when a project was exemplified by a power plant. Again there was no real opposition to the credit, partly perhaps because the directors regarded it as a quasi-commit-

---

the expansion, modernization and maintenance of industrial undertakings is hampered not so much by unavailability or insufficiency of industrial credit or capital as by a foreign exchange shortage. Where the growth of industry is so impeded, the Bank should, I believe, be prepared to consider making a long-term loan to the government, the proceeds of which would be sold against local currency to industrial enterprises for the purchase of imported equipment or parts required to increase their production.

52. IDA, Meeting of Executive Directors, *Transcript of Proceedings* (Aug. 10, 1965).

53. *Ibid.*

ment to Third Plan financing, and partly because the wolf of program lending still appeared to wear the sheep's clothing of project lending.

These trappings, however, had mainly disappeared with the third and fourth credits, and so had the sweet reasonableness that had characterized the earlier discussions by the executive directors. These credits, totaling $215 million, must be considered together. They constituted the Bank's proposed contribution to a total of $900 million in commodity assistance from consortium members to India, to permit and induce a series of important changes in Indian economic policies. The changes most relevant to this proposed commodity assistance were a sharp devaluation of the rupee, announced in June 1966, and an extensive liberalization of Indian import policies. These events are discussed at greater length in Chapter 13. In presenting the credits to the directors, the staff made an effort to describe them as a continuation of what had gone before. "Although it is proposed to increase substantially the number of industries, we would still expect more than half the proceeds of the proposed credit to be used in the same capital equipment–producing sectors as were covered."[54] Concerning the new industries to be supplied with IDA-financed imports,

There has been no effort to make a detailed appraisal even in the major firms in these industries. . . . We see no reason to believe that companies benefiting under the proposed new credit are, taken as a group, significantly less efficient than companies whose affairs are quite well known to us as a result of previous credits.[55]

Opposition to the credit was voiced by a number of directors, including those from Latin America, on the ground that it absorbed 52 percent of one year's IDA contributions from governments for one country. "This should call for a review of the management's policy with regard to the size and proportion of the distribution of IDA funds." Furthermore, a commitment of this size and proportion to India "whose development plans have not been particularly successful" may well have adverse effects on the second IDA replenishment currently under negotiation.[56]

But there was also objection to the character of the loan. "In this case," said one director, "even more than in the preceding cases of industrial import loans, we are pushing forward almost to an unlimited extent away from the project concept, and approaching—well, we've almost reached it, I think—the balance of payments concept."[57] Furthermore, the Bank was using

54. IDA, Meeting of Executive Directors, *Transcript of Proceedings* (Aug. 18, 1966).
55. *Ibid.*
56. *Ibid.*
57. *Ibid.*

fifty-year money to finance current imports, such as tires and tubes, pesticides, and fertilizers. "We are doing here the job of the Monetary Fund, which has the responsibility of financing short-term balance-of-payments deficits. The Bank has no such responsibility."[58]

In the end, the two credits were approved, but notice was given that any further import credits for India would have hard sledding. In fact this turned out to be an understatement.

The fifth industrial imports credit to India was brought before the executive directors under conditions that could hardly have been more forbidding. This credit had been intended to finance imports in the fiscal year 1967–68. In fact it was not brought before the board until June 18, 1968, and even then not for final action. The delay was the result of a failure of the U.S. Congress to vote the U.S. share of the second IDA replenishment. The fifth import credit had been negotiated by the retiring president of the Bank, George Woods, subject to approval by the executive directors, as a part of the arrangement under which India undertook changes in its balance-of-payments policies. He therefore regarded this credit as a moral commitment of the Bank, and so did the Indian government. Treating it as such, the government of India had gone ahead with its import policy, with the result that by the time the credit was presented to the board, India had for several months been importing commodities at the rate of $10 million to $12 million a month, which it expected would be financed retroactively by IDA.

When the fifth credit was presented to the executive directors, the new president, Robert McNamara, had been in office only eight weeks. After a careful study of the situation he came to the conclusion that IDA indeed had a moral commitment to honor this credit. He decided to bring the matter before the board, even though IDA funds were still not available, in order to be able to assure the Indian government that its import program would eventually be financed. McNamara presented this view to the board in strong language. Referring to the remarks of one of the directors, he said,

The points that he has made that, in effect, this Board has had full knowledge of the way the Bank has been operating with the members of the Consortium, and has in the past approved certain policies with respect to India, which, in turn, had led India to act in certain ways—quite contrary to the expressions of opinion some of you have made here, this morning ... is absolutely basic. ... Are you prepared, today, to direct India to change its basic economic plan?[59]

58. IDA, Meeting of Executive Directors, *Transcript of Proceedings* (Dec. 22, 1966).
59. IDA, Meeting of Executive Directors, *Transcript of Proceedings* (June 18, 1968).

This view eventually carried the day but only after an acrid debate, in which several issues were inextricably mixed. India and Pakistan were getting too large a share of IDA funds; IDA was being asked to finance retroactively an expenditure that the executive directors had never agreed to; this was balance-of-payments support pure and simple with no touch of project lending; neither the Bank nor IDA was faced with even a moral commitment since, until the executive directors acted, there could be no commitment of any sort. In the end the executive directors did accept the moral commitment but only after it was understood that the credit would not be brought to the board for action until (1) IDA had adequate funds and (2) the executive directors had had an opportunity to discuss thoroughly the subject of program lending. In concluding the discussion one director remarked that when this credit was reconsidered for action, thought should be given to ensuring that it was the last credit of its kind.[60]

The promised discussion by the executive directors of a paper on program lending was held on December 3, 1968, with (as was indicated earlier) inconclusive results. The fifth Indian industrial import credit was presented for action by the executive directors on January 14, 1969. Although the United States had still not met its commitment to the second IDA replenishment, the generous action of other countries had provided sufficient funds. In presenting the credit for action the Bank's staff representative said,

The problem which confronts us is . . . that India's total requirements for non-food aid considerably exceed its requirements for imports of capital goods. . . . The needs of the Indian economy, of course, for external assistance could be satisfactorily met by credits of a different type more directly associated with projects, provided that they are made in significant amounts of local expenditure. . . . It is our intent to move in this direction, but there's no pipeline of such credits, and one cannot be built up for a number of years. Consequently, whether or not this type of credit can in general be appropriate, I think there is a strong argument for continuing with such credits until appropriate projects can be substituted.[61]

The sixth and, at this writing, the last industrial import credit for India was approved on April 21, 1970, in the amount of $75 million. The discussion revealed the customary division of opinion among the executive directors. These opinions tended to fall into three groups. The first group espoused the view that the Bank and IDA had been established as project lending agencies, had achieved distinction in this area, and should confine their activities to it. Technical assistance could best be extended through project lending, and to depart from such lending was to move toward "mere" balance-of-payments

60. *Ibid.*
61. IDA, Meeting of Executive Directors, *Transcript of Proceedings* (Jan. 14, 1969).

support, which in any case was the function of the International Monetary
Fund (IMF). The second group took the position that while there was a case
for program lending, the continued extension of import credits to India permitted and encouraged a delay in preparing and presenting projects, always a
weak point in Indian planning. This view was shared by a number of staff
members who felt that a more generous provision of local currency financing
not only would provide the government with the free foreign exchange it
needed but would enlist its support in breaking bottlenecks in the development of projects.[62] The third group not only was favorably disposed toward
program lending but considered India a legitimate claimant. A greater contribution could be made to development by assuring the full use of existing
capacity than by financing new capacity.

President McNamara summed up the discussion in a way that foreshadowed the conclusions of the 1971 policy paper on "Program Lending and
Local Expenditure Financing," discussed above. He said that when a country like India needed more foreign exchange for development than could be
provided through specific project lending, import lending was justified. He
agreed, however, that the possibilities of specific project financing should
be fully explored before resort was made to import credits.[63]

We offered the opinion, earlier in this chapter, that the Bank's apparently
growing dislike for program lending had been fed by its experience with industrial import credits to India and Pakistan. There is no doubt that in the
Bank's discussion of these credits the merits and demerits of program lending
were too often confused by irrelevant but real issues, such as the share of the
two countries in IDA lending, the imminence of discussions of IDA's second
replenishment, the relations of the Bank to other members of the consortia,
and the appropriate role of management vis-à-vis the executive directors.
Over and beyond these sources of confusion there was a gnawing doubt among
the staff and among the directors as to whether the industrial import credits
to India were accomplishing the purposes for which they were designed. Still,
what seems to have emerged from the long discussion of program lending
is the conclusion that such lending is a possibility to be considered seriously
and not to be treated as a last resort. Whether this advance is enough to per-

62. Shortly before this board discussion, a $35 million IDA credit for the Kadana
irrigation project in India had been approved (February 20, 1970). The credit had a
local expenditure component of 90 percent, and this provision of free foreign exchange
had been accepted by the executive directors without hesitation. Although the project
had been started in 1954, progress (involving cooperation between the central government and the state government of Gujarat) had been slow. The size of the local expenditure component in this credit was expected to energize both governments.
63. SSM/A/70-13 (April 24, 1970).

mit the Bank Group to play the role it would like to play of supplier of capital and technical assistance and coordinator of development efforts remains to be seen.

Summary and Conclusions

In summing up and appraising IBRD policy with respect to program lending and local currency financing there are two central questions to be considered. The first looks at the problem from the point of view of the borrower —a developing country. If resources are to be supplied from the outside, in what form (capital goods and project-oriented *or* commodities and program-oriented) and in what proportions should these resources be provided? The second looks at the problem from the point of view of the Bank. If some part of the need is for commodity assistance and the Bank wants to participate in providing this sort of assistance, should it do so through local expenditure financing or through program lending?

Before plunging into a discussion of these questions it seems advisable to restate our understanding of terms and review Bank practice briefly. By "local expenditure financing" we mean project lending in excess of the foreign exchange expenditures that are directly traceable to the project. Obviously the terms "directly" and "traceable" require a rather arbitrary interpretation.[64] A certain amount of local cost financing may be undertaken for reasons relating to the selection or management of a project; other local cost financing is designed to help finance a sector or country development program. But whether project-oriented, or sector- or country-oriented, it provides "free" foreign exchange, over whose use the lender has little or no control.

As for program loans, it will have to be frankly admitted that there is no definition of the term that can cover all the loans and credits committed by the Bank and IDA that have been called program loans. The four reconstruction loans and the loans to Australia specified the imports to be financed, at least in broad categories, but did not follow these imports through to eventual outputs. In the loans to Belgium, the Belgian Congo, and Italy no attempt was made to discover or control the uses to which the foreign exchange provided by the loan was put. The early import credits to India specified not only the imports to be financed but the industries, and even the firms, that were to use

---

64. The interpretation requires selecting some cut-off point. We do not seek to follow foreign exchange expenditures beyond the first round of suppliers to a project. Nor do we include the foreign exchange impact of any change in aggregate income or income distribution deriving from expenditures on the project.

these imports. The later credits, however, traced the use of imports much less closely. The only term that could pretend to encompass this variety is the negative one, "non-project." They were all non-project loans in the sense that (1) they were not intended to finance identifiable increases in productive capacity, and (2) the imports financed could not be traced through to final output in any precise fashion. One would be tempted to cast aside the term "program loan" were it not for one important consideration. The deficit in the balance of payments that a program loan is designed to finance is a planned deficit, a programmed deficit, and not an accidental one. A development program, insofar as it calls for supplementing domestic savings with a transfer of resources from abroad, raises the question of how these resources are to be transferred. They may be transferred either in the form of capital goods earmarked for specific projects or in the form of imports of goods and services that are not so earmarked. Program loans are one means for accomplishing this commodity transfer.

The other principal means is local expenditure financing, and it is clear on the record that generally this has been the preferred method for the Bank Group. In the Kadana irrigation project credit, referred to above, the more than 90 percent of the $35 million that was earmarked for local currency expenditure was "justified on country economic grounds."[65] Although it was made clear by Bank officials in the board's discussion that "country economic grounds" meant the provision of foreign exchange for non-project-oriented imports, this somehow seemed to some directors less reprehensible than program lending.

The objection was frequently raised in discussions among executive directors in connection with the industrial import credits to India that these represented "balance-of-payments" support. So indeed they did (as do also project and sector loans) in the sense that they supplied foreign exchange that would not have been available in the absence of the loan. A program lender must certainly try to distinguish a programmed deficit from other kinds of deficits. But so also must a project lender. The Bank has rather frequently curtailed its project lending—or even stopped lending altogether—to a country whose fiscal, monetary, and foreign exchange policies adversely affect domestic savings and foreign exchange earnings. To evaluate a multi-year lending program, even if it consists entirely of projects, inevitably involves the Bank in the same kind of analysis of country performance as does a program loan.

The point is sometimes made in meetings of the executive directors that program lending finances quick disbursing imports to meet temporary balance-

65. IBRD, Report PA-27a (Jan. 21, 1970), Kadana Irrigation Project (India), p. ii.

of-payments difficulties, which are the proper province of the International Monetary Fund. It is true that program loans are more quickly disbursed than are project loans. But it does not follow that such imports are necessarily required for only a limited period of time. To bring developing countries to a capability of self-sustaining growth is a long-term process. There is a case for program lending if (a) donor agencies are willing to provide a substantial volume of foreign assistance; (b) this volume exceeds the requirements of some recipient countries for imports directly related to specific projects; and (c) lenders are unable or unwilling to provide sufficient local expenditure financing to cover maintenance import requirements. When the case for program lending is valid, its validity is quite independent of considerations connected with the timing of disbursements.

It is sometimes said that program lending tends to lead to undesirable intervention into sensitive areas of the development policy of the borrowing country. The Bank has by now succeeded in establishing a position with respect to the supervision and management of projects that is generally accepted, though not quite without cavil. The performance that affects the productivity of program loans, however, is sector or country performance, rather than project performance. But concern with sector or country performance is not attached exclusively to program lending. The question as to what steps the Bank may find it desirable to take in an attempt to improve country performance is independent of the type of loan, given a lending program of any considerable size. The most that can be said is that program loans, dollar for dollar, give a lender more "leverage" than do project loans, if the lender wants to use such leverage. Situations involving this issue are discussed in Chapter 13.

The objections to program lending sketched above, though frequently encountered in the Bank, raise a set of false issues. There are some important reasons, however, for preferring to supply foreign exchange for a development program through local expenditure lending. A too easy resort to program lending may accentuate a fault that is common to the planning efforts of many developing countries—a neglect of preinvestment activity and project preparation. The Bank prides itself on building institutions; and this generally involves a long-term association with a borrower and a willingness to lubricate the partnership with a generous contribution (through local expenditure financing) to the partner's general development requirements for foreign exchange. If the Bank is convinced of the solidity of a borrower's development program, it may prefer to help that program by providing, via local expenditure financing, what is really free foreign exchange rather than to undertake a program loan to cover the costs of specified imports. Finally, if program loans are necessary, there is some reason for the Bank with its untied funds to concentrate on projects and leave program lending to the tied funds of bilateral programs. Tying is likely to be less disadvantageous to borrowers if the tied funds are available for a wide variety of imports, as in the case of program loans. It should be noted also that lending institutions other than the Bank have concentrated on project lending while still making a sizable contribution to borrowers in free foreign exchange through local expenditure financing.[66]

Whether the Bank's contribution to the non-project foreign exchange requirements of borrowing member countries can and should be limited to financing local expenditures for particular investment projects appears to depend on:

(a) what share of the official capital transfers to these countries needs to be in commodities that are not associated with particular investment projects;

(b) what part of this share is likely to be provided by other assistance providers; and

(c) what role the Bank wants to play in coordinating total official capital transfers to its member countries.

The share of official capital transfers to a borrowing country that can most appropriately be made in the form of non-project commodity imports will depend mainly on the relation of total external assistance flows to the level of investment, the relation of total imports to gross national product, and the commodity composition of domestic production and therefore of imports.

If external assistance, from the Bank Group and other sources, constitutes a *small fraction* of gross investment, it will normally not be difficult to apply this assistance entirely to project financing. Either the recipient country's own savings and foreign exchange earnings will be large enough to take care of the major part of its investment requirements and their import components (as in the case of Mexico, for example), or absorptive capacity for any kind of foreign investment will be small (as it is in many African countries). Where external assistance accounts for a *larger proportion* of gross investment, it may be more difficult to balance an expansion of productive capacity with the inputs, many of them imported, that are needed for full capacity operations. But if the term "projects" is defined liberally, as the Bank has in practice defined it, and particularly if project lending covers a part of local

66. Local expenditure financing accounted for 64.4 percent of the disbursements of the Inter-American Development Bank's fund for special operations in the period ending September 30, 1969. Disbursements totaled $306 million. During the period of its operations, 82.3 percent of the $410.3 million of disbursements of the social progress trust fund represented local expenditure financing.

expenditure costs, it may nevertheless be possible to limit external assistance to project financing.

Whether a developing country's needs for imported inputs can be met more effectively by program loans or by financing some of the local currency expenditures of projects depends very much on what share of total investment is to be covered by external assistance. When the Bank has had a choice, it has usually followed the local expenditure route. But if external assistance accounts for a large fraction of total investment, it is extremely difficult, through financing local expenditures on projects, to assemble and phase the foreign exchange expenditures required for a proper flow of maintenance imports.

Foreign assistance in recent years has averaged about 15 percent of gross investment for the developing world as a whole. But in many countries it is substantially larger. In India it has averaged about 25 percent of gross investment and in Pakistan about 40 percent; in other countries it has been even higher. For these countries particularly it has been difficult to provide the amount of external capital needed for investment purposes through project loans exclusively, even with a sizable local expenditure component.

A second consideration bearing on the merits of project as against program lending in any given country has to do with the relation of the volume of imports to gross national product. In countries where imports are a small fraction of GNP, while foreign assistance accounts for a large fraction of these imports (again as in India), the suppliers of development finance, including the Bank Group, have considerably less choice in what they can finance than they do when imports are larger. When the difference to be financed between gross investment and domestic savings represents 2 percent of gross national product, there is much more freedom in selecting the items to be financed if imports amount to 20 percent of GNP than if they amount to only 6 percent. To oversimplify, in the first situation foreign assistance finances one out of ten items imported as against one out of three in the second. In economies of the latter type, an appropriate level of foreign assistance cannot be provided through financing the foreign exchange requirements of projects alone; such financing has to be supplemented either by program loans or by the financing of some local currency expenditures of projects.

Another important factor affecting the usefulness of a program lending component in foreign assistance is the structure of the recipient country's economy and its relationship to the composition of imports. In general the more developed an economy and the larger its industrial sector, the less dependent it is on project imports. Several developing countries now have substantial capacity for producing inputs for capital investment. These same countries, however, may be short of raw materials, petroleum products, fertilizers, and supplementary equipment needed to obtain full production from the capital equipment they can produce. While the Bank's broad definition of projects and its willingness, where necessary, to provide substantial financing of local expenditures enable it to take care of some part of these import requirements, it is not likely to prove feasible, at all times in all such countries, to provide an adequate level of assistance without some program lending component.

Among countries that have been recipients of sizable Bank loans perhaps India and Brazil conform most closely to the characteristics discussed above. But in eight or ten countries among those receiving the largest amounts of foreign assistance much less than half of official aid is in the form of imports of capital goods.

The Bank has been able to limit its program lending in recent years in part because certain bilateral assistance providers have been willing to play a large role in financing commodity imports. The U.S. Agency for International Development has been a conspicuous program lender, but if bilateral assistance declines and, in particular, if there is a strong shift in the provision of economic development assistance from bilateral to multilateral channels (including the Bank and IDA), the Bank Group may well have to reconsider its current practice.

Finally, if the Bank Group should in the course of time become a more important coordinator of assistance flows from various sources than it is at present, it may find it increasingly difficult to prescribe program lending to others while reserving project lending for itself, even though it asserts its comparative advantage as a project lender.

CHAPTER TEN

The Bank and IDA as Sources
of Technical Assistance

SINCE THE WORLD BANK'S first loan to Chile in the spring of 1948, its capital has generally been available only for doing specific things in specific ways—ways that have often been unfamiliar and have had to be learned. Though the Bank is fundamentally an investment agency and its charter does not mention technical assistance as such, it has, as we have already noted, taken the position that it can and should furnish technical assistance, provided such help is related to its lending operations, past, present, or future.[1] Within this self-imposed limitation, Bank-financed and Bank-sponsored technical assistance has increased steadily over the years—probably at a rate more rapid than that at which total disbursements for Bank loans and International Development Association (IDA) credits have been increasing.

The problem of measurement is complicated by the fact that, on the whole, technical assistance from the Bank Group is whatever the Bank says it is. Nevertheless, for purposes of discussion and analysis, four categories of Bank-sponsored technical assistance can be distinguished: (a) technical assistance that is not connected with an immediate investment project—for example, technical assistance to a ministry to improve its general functioning; (b) technical assistance related to the preinvestment stage of an investment project or program—for example, assistance in project identification or project preparation, feasibility studies, and sector studies; (c) technical assistance

1. This position is consistent with the general attitude of the Bank that activities in furtherance of its purposes, and particularly those ancillary to its principal operations, and not inconsistent with any other provisions of the Articles of Agreement, may be undertaken. The Articles of Agreement of the International Development Association (Article V, section 5[v]) specifically authorize IDA to provide technical assistance.

that is connected with a specific loan or credit and is identifiable as a type of technical assistance—for example, inclusion in a loan of funds for the employment of foreign consultants to help launch the project; and (d) technical assistance that is inextricably interwoven with the making or supervising of a Bank loan or IDA credit and therefore is not separately identifiable.

If the familiar analogy of the iceberg were invoked in connection with the Bank's technical assistance activities, category (d), which is going to get the shortest shrift in this chapter, would represent the submerged, invisible nine-tenths of the iceberg. The Bank quickly decided that it should not simply accept or reject loan proposals. It felt impelled to suggest modifications of certain technical aspects of proposed projects, to recommend specific administrative or organizational arrangements for carrying out the work, and to advise on the financial plan, including the mobilization of local capital. Many examples have already been cited in this study; two more are given below.

Early in the Bank's history, a Latin American member requested a sizable railway loan, primarily to finance the purchase of some large, speedy, and highly efficient locomotives. The Bank's investigation showed that locomotives as heavy as those requested could not be borne by the country's railway tracks and roadbed. Moreover, if the locomotives did manage to cross the bridges without crashing into the waters below and traveled at the speeds expected of them, they would derail themselves on the curves. Instead of rejecting the loan proposal, the Bank helped the borrower choose a different type of locomotive.[2]

More recently the water supply system of the rapidly growing capital city of a member government in the Caribbean region needed to be expanded and modernized. It was estimated that the system the government preferred would have cost more than $40 million, would have required resettling several thousand persons, and would have taken a long time to complete. After investigation by the Bank, a $9 million project was devised that could be completed more promptly and should meet adequately the capital city's needs for the medium-term future.

Moving from the inextricably interwoven technical assistance of the Bank Group to the extricably interwoven—category (c), above—it is relatively easy for the Bank to include with the capital assistance for a development project the funding for identifiable types of technical assistance. During the three fiscal years 1969–71, an average of more than $40 million a year was included in regular Bank loans and IDA credits for such technical assistance

2. Cited by Geoffrey M. Wilson, vice president of the Bank and IDA, in *Technical Assistance Activities of the World Bank*. Address before the Institute of Banking and Financial Studies, Paris (June 4, 1964).

—for experts and consultants from abroad to provide management or technical services during the early stages of the project, for studies designed to identify additional projects in the same sector that might be suitable for Bank Group financing, and for overseas training for nationals of the borrowing countries, who would later replace the experts from abroad.

Technical assistance that is indirectly related to lending—categories (a) and (b) above—includes help in preparing country development programs, establishing development priorities, organizing and administering planning machinery, and training nationals of less developed countries to administer programs and prepare projects that merit external financing. The objective in such cases is to establish a factual foundation, an economic environment, and an institutional framework conducive to development and—more self-serving perhaps, but also obviously related to the promotion of orderly growth and development—to assure a full pipeline of projects suitable for financing by the Bank Group.

For more than a decade, the reports of the Bank's general survey missions, beginning with the influential report on Colombia in 1950, were regarded by the Bank as its most notable venture in this type of technical assistance. The comprehensive survey mission, which was expected to produce a report that would serve as the basis for a national development program in the country surveyed, fell into disuse in the mid-1960s. A lineal descendant survives, however, in the extensive program of country economic reporting in which the Bank is currently engaged.

Less ambitious than country programming but at least as valuable as a prelude to capital investment are sector and feasibility studies. Sector studies may be, and often are, financed by the Bank out of its administrative funds rather than through loans or credits. For relevant engineering and/or feasibility studies, the Bank or IDA may provide a loan or credit simply and solely for the study. In fact, however, the Bank has made only two such loans—one to Guinea in 1966 for the engineering of a railway and port project and one to Tunisia in 1969 for some road engineering; IDA has extended about a dozen such credits. The more usual method is the "piggyback" operation, whereby the loan for a given project includes funds for feasibility studies or detailed engineering of subsequent projects.

Since 1959, the chosen instrument of the United Nations for financing preinvestment studies has been the UN Special Fund, which was combined in 1966 with the UN Expanded Programme of Technical Assistance to become the United Nations Development Program (UNDP). The UNDP, hoping to obviate the build-up of a big bureaucracy of its own, decided to work through "executing agencies," that is, through the United Nations itself and other agencies in the UN system, such as the World Health Organization (WHO) and the International Labour Organisation (ILO). By mid-1971, the Bank had served as executing agency for eighty-eight UNDP-financed projects costing more than $75 million. The Bank, in turn, normally uses private consulting firms or governmental or quasi-governmental agencies in member countries to make the studies for which it is the executing agency. The Bank then supervises the work of the consultants.

The Bank customarily acts as executing agency for the UNDP only for preinvestment studies in which the Bank Group is interested. These include studies of everything from tourism for the islands of Bali and Fiji to water and power development in East Pakistan, usually on the assumption that they may lead to later investment by the Bank, IDA, or the International Finance Corporation (IFC). Until mid-1969, the Bank itself had been willing to provide grant financing for preinvestment studies that for one reason or another could not be financed by the UNDP. However, in 1965 and again in 1969, the UNDP simplified its procedures for handling the type of preinvestment study that had previously given rise to Bank grants and made it possible for the Bank virtually to retire from the business of making grants for technical assistance.

Until the UN Special Fund was created, the Bank's relationship to the rest of the UN economic and social system was ceremonial, pro forma, and non-operational. The technical assistance provided by the regular UN agencies was small-scale and seldom investment-oriented. The launching of the Special Fund significantly increased the volume of funds available for investment-oriented technical assistance and enabled the Bank as well as the other agencies to draw on those funds. One of the results has been to strengthen the relationship between the Bank and the rest of the UN family and give it operational content.

Through its cooperative arrangements with the Food and Agriculture Organization of the UN (FAO) and the United Nations Educational, Scientific and Cultural Organization (Unesco), the Bank has uncovered a number of new opportunities for investment in agriculture and education. It has also been able, with a small additional technical assistance investment of its own, to transform into bankable projects a number of studies for which the FAO and Unesco were the executing agencies and the UNDP the principal financier.[3] Within the Bank, overall responsibility for liaison with the UN family and for technical assistance policy is vested in the Development Services Department.

3. As is noted in Chapter 17, below, the Bank in 1971 entered into a similar cooperative arrangement with the World Health Organization (WHO) to facilitate Bank Group lending in the fields of water supply, sewage disposal, and storm drainage.

The Bank's staff college, the Economic Development Institute (EDI), which has now been providing training in the field of economic development in Washington for more than fifteen years, can logically be regarded as Bank-sponsored technical assistance. The "permanent missions" in eastern and western Africa, the resident staff in Indonesia, and some of the resident representation in other countries may be regarded as further forms of technical assistance. The Agricultural Development Service, which is attached to the mission in Nairobi, is clearly a response to Africa's need for technical assistance as perceived by the Bank.

In summary, the Bank during its first quarter century has engaged in a variety of noteworthy activities which, in our view, can most appropriately be discussed in this chapter on technical assistance.

Assistance in Development Programming

In tracing the evolution of IBRD assistance to member countries in development programming, the historian quickly discovers that all roads lead not to Rome but to Bogotá. The Bank's first comprehensive economic survey mission arrived in Bogotá in July 1949. Less than four months later the last mission member departed, and by mid-1950 the mission had produced a 642-page report, *The Basis of a Development Program for Colombia.*[4]

This was not, let us make clear, either the first mission sent out by the Bank, or even its first mission to Colombia. The management and staff of the IBRD had already proven themselves a ubiquitous lot, eager to amass information and quick to give advice. Missions, consultants, and advisers from Washington had been forerunners, concomitants, and aftermaths of all of the Bank's development lending. Those missions confirmed the inadequacy of development programming efforts in most cases and noted the absence of government agencies charged with designing an overall framework for development and appraising project proposals in the light of that framework. It was against this background that the Bank organized the general survey mission to Colombia. That effort, in turn, set the pattern for two dozen other missions to survey the development potentialities and problems of member countries and to make recommendations designed to help their governments formulate long-term development programs.

The government of Colombia, of course, asked for the mission, but the Bank, especially Vice President Robert L. Garner, had a great deal to do with

---

4. Published for the Bank by the Johns Hopkins Press, 1950.

stimulating the request. Colombia was among the most advanced of the Bank's less developed members, a potential showcase for a carefully worked-out investment program, though Colombian officials had told the Bank management frankly that regional rivalries made agreement on an overall development strategy and program exceedingly difficult. The nation was divided into several separate regions, with a widespread tendency among its citizens to give regional loyalties precedence over national loyalty. The Bank's recommendations on priorities, it was hoped, would help overcome this tendency.

Within the Bank, below the management level, there was opposition from some who said that, if the Bank helped a country draw up a development program, it would be morally committed to financing at least a portion of the program and should therefore be wary of such commitments. Refusal to help, on the other hand, might mean only that some other international agency would organize the mission. The FAO, for example, had sent a mission of twelve experts to Greece in 1946, presumably to study agriculture, fisheries, and related activities. Illustrative of both the catholic nature of the interests of the FAO and the inherent difficulty of dealing only with the sector covered by its charter, the report emphasized that agricultural development in Greece could not occur without parallel developments in other sectors. Its eighty-nine recommendations therefore dealt with industrialization, taxation, and public administration, as well as with irrigation and more narrowly agricultural issues. And, to the great indignation of the Bank, the recommendations included some advice on what that institution might usefully do.[5]

The Bank had been even more distressed by the affirmative response of the UN secretary-general in the summer of 1948 to the request of the government of Haiti for a team to assist in planning the economic development of that country.[6] By the close of 1948, various agencies were issuing mission reports and recommending priorities for domestic and foreign investment. Meanwhile, the Bank was being severely criticized for the slow pace of its development lending.

The Bank's fourteen-man mission to Colombia took much longer to organize than the three or four months it spent in Colombia. The chief of the mission was Lauchlin Currie, an economic consultant in New York who had earlier been a White House assistant to Presidents Roosevelt and Truman. The mission included several members of the Bank staff, a member of the

5. Food and Agriculture Organization, *Report of the FAO Mission for Greece* (March 1947).

6. The mission to Haiti involved not only the United Nations, but also WHO, Unesco, FAO, and the International Monetary Fund. See UN Mission of Technical Assistance to the Republic of Haiti, *Mission to Haiti* (July 1949).

staff of the IMF, experts nominated by the FAO and the WHO, and consultants recruited by the Bank for the mission. The cost of the mission was shared by the Bank and the Colombian government.

After its field work, the mission spent a year preparing a comprehensive report. The legal position of the Bank was that this report, and reports of later survey missions, were the responsibility of the mission chief. The Bank did not necessarily approve the recommendations; it merely presented the report as work done by a competent and serious group, whose conclusions deserved careful consideration by the government of the country surveyed. Though the Bank thus reserved its legal position, it was aware that it could not completely escape responsibility for the content of mission reports, and for that reason it reviewed draft reports of survey missions in painstaking detail, often pressing for substantial revisions prior to their release.

To return to the prototype case, the Bank suggested upon completion of the Colombian report that the government set up a nonpartisan citizens' committee to review the report and make recommendations for government action. An economic development committee was accordingly set up, and for the first time in years members of the two principal political parties in Colombia found themselves working together. They sat for months, helped and encouraged by a member of the Bank's staff and two consultants who had been members of the mission. The Economic Development Committee, said the Bank's sixth annual report (1950–1951),

has submitted a number of recommendations which were adopted by the Government and translated into positive action. Inflation was checked, new regulations relaxing foreign-exchange controls were enacted, and the highway program mentioned below was adopted. The Government also reorganized the Banco de la República and announced a more liberal policy regarding the import and export of capital. Upon completion of its work, the Committee will submit plans for a comprehensive development program to the Government. In the meantime, a number of United Nations and United States experts have been invited to render special assistance in various fields and are now working in Colombia.[7]

Most significantly, the Bank, which had intended to await completion of the overall program before making additional loans, decided to support immediately a three-year highway rehabilitation project. All the evidence indicated that rehabilitation of the existing trunk highway system would be a key part of the overall program. Therefore, in April 1951 a loan of $16.5 million was made by the Bank to finance the foreign-exchange costs of the necessary work. By this act the Bank demonstrated that its technical assistance could quickly, or relatively quickly, bring in its train capital assistance—as well as

7. P. 35.

a handsome adornment for the bookshelves of development specialists.[8] Since 1951 five additional highway development loans have been made to Colombia.

Two dozen more general survey missions were dispatched by the Bank, half of them during the years 1950–54 and the remainder in the period 1955–64: Turkey, Nicaragua, Guatemala, and Cuba (1950); Iraq, Ceylon, and Surinam (1951); Jamaica (1952); British Guiana and Nigeria (1953); Malaya and Syria (1954); Jordan (1955); Italian Somaliland (1956); Thailand (1957); Libya (1958); Tanganyika and Venezuela (1959); Uganda (1960); Spain and Kenya (1961); the Territory of Papua and New Guinea, and Kuwait (1962); and Morocco (1964).[9] A number of these missions were sent at the request of the ruling colonial power, before the area surveyed

8. IBRD, Fifth Annual Meeting of the Board of Governors (Sept. 6–14, 1950), *Summary Proceedings*, statement on "Technical Assistance Activities of the International Bank," p. 49:

> It is this combination of technical and financial aid which is the new aspect of the Bank's program and the one which gives the most promise that the program may be effective. The Bank recognizes that when it sends out such a mission it assumes a moral obligation to help, with its financial resources, in the development of the country concerned, provided that that country does its own part in formulating and carrying forward a properly balanced development program.

9. In Mexico the government and the World Bank agreed to establish a joint working party, consisting of two Mexican and two Bank economists, to assess the major long-term trends in the Mexican economy, with particular reference to Mexico's ability to absorb additional foreign investment. Because of this special arrangement, *The Economic Development of Mexico* (1953), although quite influential, is not regarded by the Bank as the report of a general survey mission. In the case of regular survey mission reports, arrangements were normally made for translating the report, where necessary, into the language of the country and publishing it there. With two exceptions, noted below, an English version of each report was published by the Johns Hopkins Press. The titles and dates of publication of the English texts, in the order of their publication, are: *The Basis of a Development Program for Colombia* (1950), *The Economy of Turkey* (1951), *Report on Cuba* (1951), *The Economic Development of Iraq* (1952), *Surinam: Recommendations for a Ten Year Development Program* (1952), *The Economic Development of Jamaica* (1952), *The Economic Development of Nicaragua* (1953), *The Economic Development of Ceylon* (1953), *The Economic Development of British Guiana* (1953), *The Economic Development of Nigeria* (1955), *The Economic Development of Malaya* (1955), *The Economic Development of Syria* (1955), *The Economic Development of Jordan* (1957), *A Public Development Program for Thailand* (1959), *The Economic Development of Libya* (1960), *The Economic Development of Tanganyika* (1961), *The Economic Development of Venezuela* (1961), *The Economic Development of Uganda* (1962), *The Economic Development of Spain* (1963), *The Economic Development of Kenya* (1963), *The Economic Development of the Territory of Papua and New Guinea* (1965), *The Economic Development of Kuwait* (1965), and *The Economic Development of Morocco* (1966). The two exceptions are: *The Economic Development of Guatemala*, published by the IBRD in 1951, and "The Economy of the Trust Territory of Somaliland," issued by the IBRD in 1957 as a mimeographed report.

achieved independence. The membership of the mission to Colombia had been predominantly Anglo Saxon, but later missions tended to be more international. Moreover, prior to their release, draft reports of the later missions were discussed in greater detail with the governments responsible for the areas surveyed; and most of the missions managed to have their say in fewer than the 642 pages required by the mission to Colombia. It became customary for either the mission chief, or the chief economist, or both, to be selected from among the regular members of the Bank staff, in order that the specialized knowledge accumulated by the Bank would be available to the survey group and that there would be continuity between the work of the mission and the subsequent activities of the Bank.

A review of the first fifteen published reports referred to them—justifiably, in our view—as "the largest single collection of information extant on the problems and characteristics of underdeveloped economies. A careful reader of these reports is impressed with the wealth of detail and the obviously painstaking care with which the material has been assembled."[10] Basically, however, this particular reviewer was exceedingly, perhaps excessively, critical of the missions for trying to do too much and actually doing too little.[11] The objective of the exercise, however, was not to win high marks from development economists, but to put forward a set of recommendations that were tailored to the area and could be taken to heart by the appropriate political authorities. No formula guaranteed success.

To Turkey, the second country to ask for a mission, the wrong kind was sent. It was headed by an American businessman whose understanding of development problems was inadequate, and it got into trouble. Its report was eventually written by the regular staff of the Bank rather than by the mission. The 1954 mission to Syria was headed by Pieter Lieftinck, a former finance minister of the Netherlands, whose associations with the Bank as an executive director and in various other important capacities covered all of the Bank's first twenty-five years. Lending plans for three of the survey team's recommended projects reached a fairly advanced stage but came to naught as Syria grew increasingly anti-Western and unwilling to accept various well established

10. Frederick T. Moore, "The World Bank and Its Economic Missions," *Review of Economics and Statistics*, Vol. 42 (February 1960), p. 81.

11. "Their reports are replete with data on almost every conceivable aspect of economic activity; the reader feels inundated with statistics. And to what purpose? Most of the statistics are never used again. They are obviously meant to be purely illustrative and descriptive. For the most part they do not contribute to an understanding of the critical development problems in the economy, and they are not used in setting up a program or in checking its internal consistency sector by sector, and finally specifying the implications of alternative programs." *Ibid.*, pp. 89–90.

Bank policies. (Not until December 1963 did Syria allow itself to become indebted to the Bank Group.)

In Iraq too, the general survey mission was frustrated by political upheavals that occurred not long after the report was submitted. Some of its recommendations, however, were subsequently carried out with assistance from the Soviet Union and Eastern European countries. In Libya, the mission's solemn strictures, though well directed, were undermined by a happier event—an underestimation of the vastness of the country's oil resources and of the speed with which revenues therefrom would accrue to the Libyan government.

Other reports were influential, resulting (like the Colombia report) in the creation of new national bodies for programming and planning, or in strengthening machinery already in existence, as well as focusing attention on the need for a coordinated long-term approach to development problems. Nicaragua accepted the Bank's recommendations as the basis for its future economic policy, organized a national economic council to coordinate government policies and supervise the execution of a development program, and took various other development-oriented actions. In Jamaica a development program covering the years 1955–60 was drawn up on the basis of the Bank's report. Similarly, in Malaya the mission report was used as the basis of discussion in drawing up a long-term development program, and various specific recommendations, such as the establishment of a central bank and changes in the education program, were put into effect. Nigeria adopted federal and regional development programs and reorganized development institutions along lines suggested by the Bank mission.[12] The report on Uganda served as the basis for that country's early development programming.

General survey missions tended either to precede or to be accompanied by the setting up of planning offices in member countries. Once such offices were established, governments wanted resident advisers or short-term specialists to work with their planning officials rather than a team to supply the makings of a development plan. The Bank in 1962 established the post of adviser on planning organization in the headquarters office to provide member countries with advice on setting up machinery for formulating and implementing development programs. Such advice continues to be solicited. During the fiscal

12. These and other examples will be found in IBRD, *Policies and Operations of the World Bank, IFC and IDA* (amended to June 30, 1963), pp. 72–74. The government of Nigeria, eager to make the report on that country available for public discussion, issued a version printed locally (with the Bank's approval) only three weeks after receiving the final text and about six months before the version printed by the Johns Hopkins Press became available.

year ending June 30, 1971, staff members of the Bank visited nine countries to review their development planning and policymaking machinery and advise on technical assistance needs. In addition, previously initiated secondments of planning advisers to the governments of Ethiopia and Mauritius were extended.[13]

After the mid-1960s, the comprehensive survey by an "independent" mission was more or less abandoned. Development planning, thanks to other agencies as well as to the Bank, had been made respectable in both the less developed and the more developed portions of the world. The obvious candidates had been surveyed, and interest in bulky overall reports was dwindling. Their very comprehensiveness meant that they were a long time in gestation, with release sometimes delayed until two years after the study began. Moreover, the Bank had long been experimenting with specialized missions of different kinds—missions organized in 1950 and 1951, in conjunction with the FAO, to Chile, Uruguay, and Peru to prepare recommendations on agricultural development, and missions to make other types of sector and feasibility studies.

Country Economic Reporting: 1965 and After

Although the comprehensive economic survey mission is supposed to have died quietly in the mid-1960s, its spiritual heir is alive today in the program of country economic reporting initiated earlier in the Bank's history but vastly expanded under President Robert S. McNamara. Whereas the survey reports were one-time affairs, designed to provide a basis for a national development program, the economic reports are expected to be revised and updated in ways that permit regular reviews of development performance. And whereas the survey missions produced bulky books for which the mission director was formally responsible, the economic missions aim at more succinct documents for which the Bank itself assumes responsibility. In both instances, the Bank has been aware that hesitation on its part might cause leadership of the venture to be assumed by some other international agency.

The objective of country economic reporting has been to obtain, for each member country, an inventory of development progress and problems which could later be updated and expanded. McNamara, when he became president, proposed a major enlargement of this effort. His program, first outlined

13. World Bank/International Development Association, *Annual Report, 1971,* p. 31.

in his 1969 address to the board of governors, was elaborated upon in his speech to the Columbia University conference on international economic development in February 1970:

To provide a solid foundation for consultation and action by both developed and developing nations, in the whole field of development strategy and administration of aid, we plan a new and expanded program of Country Economic Missions. These will be regularly scheduled, thoroughly staffed, comprehensive missions whose mandate will be to assist the member government to draw up an overall development strategy which will include every major sector of the economy, and every relevant aspect of the nation's social framework. . . .

Our own Bank staff on the mission will be looking into not only the traditional problems of economic growth, but the other facets of development as well: questions of population increase, urbanization, land reform, income distribution, public health, environmental preservation, and all the related issues. Once the mission is completed, we will promptly produce for use by all of the parties concerned a thorough Economic Report which will serve as a profile of the country's progress and of its overall development plan.

The non-Bank staff on such missions would consist of personnel from FAO, Unesco, WHO, ILO, UNDP, and other sources. McNamara's program contemplated annual reports on the larger member countries and reports every two or three years on the others. "The essential point is that they will be comprehensive in scope, regular in schedule, and will form the basis for strategic rather than tactical development financing."

Questions promptly arose as to whether the program was overly ambitious. Could the Bank assemble the competence to diagnose "every relevant aspect of a nation's social framework" and prescribe or evaluate strategies for dealing with them? Were such reports really needed on an annual, biennial, or triennial basis? How much of a burden and disruption would the missions be in the host countries? How valuable as technical assistance? How costly to the Bank? How important to bilateral aid givers and other international agencies? The Bank's position, of course, is that missions are not sent unless they are wanted. If they are wanted and are sent, a smaller mission usually makes a return trip to discuss the draft of the findings and recommendations. The report is then addressed to the government of the country concerned, but copies go also to the Bank's executive directors, to aid-giving governments, and to other international agencies. Though McNamara's initial proposal has been scaled down and his concept modified, the volume of economic reporting by the Bank has increased substantially during his presidency.

The substantive content of the Bank's country economic reports, and of its country program papers and notes, is commented on in Chapter 14, below. The point to be underscored here is that one of the aims of the Bank's current reporting system is to provide a basis for decisions regarding technical as well as financial assistance to a country. Moreover, the economic reports themselves, by virtue of the problems they highlight and the solutions toward which they point, constitute technical assistance to member countries in an amount which, though not readily quantifiable, is judged by the Bank to be "substantial."[14]

Assistance in Project Identification and Preparation

Since the terms "sector study," "institutional study," and "feasibility study" are not necessarily self-explanatory, it may be useful to define them.[15]

A "sector study" is an analysis of a sector of the economy with a view to preparing a coordinated investment program for that sector and selecting priority projects within it. The sector may be broadly or narrowly defined; the Colombia transport study undertaken in 1961 covered roads, railways, airlines, river transport, and ports, whereas the Peru highway study, as its name indicates, was limited to roads. Geographically, the study may be countrywide, as was the survey of the electric power needs and potential of Argentina, or it may be limited to a province or region. Or, like the Central American telecommunications study, it may cover several countries. The study may be concerned both with setting policy for the sector and with the institutional arrangements for carrying out the policy proposed.

Although it is more frequently one part of a sector study, the "institutional study" may be undertaken as an independent task. It usually calls for examining the organization and capability of an institution—a power or highway authority, or a port commission—that is expected to perform a function within a particular sector. A "feasibility study" determines whether a project that has already been identified is in reality technically feasible and economically justified.

The Bank normally becomes involved in sector, institutional, and feasibility studies only if they are likely to lead to Bank-financed or IDA-financed investment projects. This means that the Bank does not usually undertake such studies in countries where, in the Bank's own somewhat stuffy language, "there is at the time no prospect of Bank or IDA operations because of un-

14. *Ibid.*

15. This section draws liberally on a "Review of Completed Sector and Feasibility Studies," circulated for internal IBRD use by John A. King, Jr., of the Development Services Department in January 1968.

satisfactory economic policy or performance or the failure to honor international obligations."[16]

Involvement in project identification and preparation is a way of building up the Bank Group's pipeline. The initial position of the Bank was that preparation of a project was the responsibility of the borrower; if the Bank became involved, it could not thereafter be sufficiently objective in appraising the project. Though buttressed by logic, this position soon gave way to the pressure of events. "Experience has demonstrated that we do not get enough good projects to appraise unless we are involved intimately in their identification and preparation."[17]

UNDP-financed and Bank-financed Preinvestment Studies

When the Bank undertakes preinvestment studies, it may do so on its own or as executing agency for the UNDP. The first study undertaken by the Bank as executing agency was the aforementioned Argentine power survey, which began in May 1959 and was completed in June 1960. The actual work was done by consulting engineering firms and was supervised by a two-man steering committee consisting of a representative from the Argentine government and one from the Bank.

By June 30, 1971, the Bank had been named executing agency for eighty-eight studies financed by the UNDP, of which forty-three had been completed and forty-five were in progress. Sixty of the eighty-eight projects had been approved since January 1, 1967. In terms of sectors, transport work was predominant, accounting for $51 million of the total of $77 million obtained from the UNDP. Public utilities ($11 million) ran second. Agriculture and planning and advisory studies were the only other sectors to account for more than $3 million. Geographically, Africa accounted for $30 million, Asia and the Pacific for $24 million, and the Western Hemisphere for nearly $20 million of the $77 million total.

Though it had previously done similar work as part of its lending program, the Bank's own program of technical assistance *grants* for sector and feasibility studies, including institutional studies, did not begin until 1961. It was in part a response to requests for studies too small to be considered by the UNDP, in part a response to requests that were believed to be too urgent to await processing and approval under the procedures of the UNDP at that

16. IBRD, Operational memorandum 7.03 (Sept. 30, 1969).
17. Warren C. Baum, "The Project Cycle," *Finance and Development,* Vol. 7 (June 1970), p. 6.

time, and in part a way of keeping in bounds a Bank surplus that was mounting at an almost embarrassing rate. Of the $14.7 million allocated between January 1, 1961, and June 30, 1969 (there were no Bank-financed grants in fiscal 1970 or 1971), more than 75 percent was allocated during the years 1963–65, when the UNDP was more ponderous and inflexible than it was later. These were also the years when the first three grants were made from the Bank to IDA, and the Bank soon convinced itself that making contributions to IDA, formally approved by the Bank's board of governors, was a more orderly way of using its surplus than doling out grants for sector and feasibility studies.[18]

The pattern of Bank-financed sector and feasibility studies paralleled that of UNDP-financed studies for which the Bank was executing agency. Thirty of the Bank's forty-five grants, accounting for $8.6 million, were for transport studies, and six, accounting for $3.5 million, were in public utilities. Agriculture, with $1.6 million, accounted for most of the remainder. Geographically, the Western Hemisphere came first. South Asia was a close second. Between them, they accounted for $8.0 million of the total of $14.7 million for Bank-financed sector and feasibility studies. Forty-three of the forty-five projects undertaken had been completed by mid-1971.

In carrying out both Bank-financed and UNDP-financed sector and feasibility studies, the Bank usually works through subcontractors, in contrast to the normal practice of the FAO and the other specialized agencies that also act as executing agents for UNDP-financed studies. The subcontractors may be either private consulting firms or government agencies. Use of consultants, in the Bank's view, tends to provide teams of higher quality. It focuses responsibility, permits the assignment of professionals to a short-term task without interrupting their normal career activity, saves time in mobilizing the team, simplifies finding replacements for ill or unsatisfactory members, and provides the additional resources of the consultant's head office for supporting and strengthening the study.

The Bank maintains extensive files on the capabilities and experience of consultant firms that have indicated an interest in undertaking studies.[19] Such firms are classified so that the Bank can identify those that are independent as against those that are associated with, or owned by, contractors

18. Early in fiscal 1972, the Bank made a $200,000 technical assistance grant to help finance a team of planning and technical experts who would work as part of the central organization for economic policymaking and planning in one of its newest member countries, the Yemen Arab Republic. (In this case, the Bank's grant was matched by the grant of an equal amount by the Kuwait Fund for Arab Economic Development.)

19. See IBRD brochure, *Uses of Consultants by the World Bank and Its Borrowers* (September 1966).

or manufacturers. The latter, to be acceptable during the preinvestment stage, must avoid conflict-of-interest problems by agreeing to disqualify themselves and their associates from participating in any construction activities or in supplying equipment for projects growing out of the feasibility studies they have undertaken.

The selection of appropriate consultants is, of course, critical to the success of a study. Initially the Bank relied heavily on already established engineering consultant firms. Because many of them were set up to design and supervise construction projects, they often lacked a staff capable of handling the nonengineering aspects of a study, the most important of which in those days were assumed to be the economic aspects. But the character of such firms has changed significantly over the years, partly as a result of the Bank's interest in building up their capabilities in nonengineering fields, particularly their economic competence. In addition, an impressive array of economic, educational, management, and other specialized consulting services has become available.

At the preinvestment stage, those environmental aspects of projects that might have a direct impact on the economic and financial success of the project itself have regularly been considered—for example, problems of waterlogging and salinity in irrigation projects, watershed and erosion control in hydroelectric and multipurpose river development schemes, and pasture development and animal disease problems in livestock projects. This, however, has not been true of environmental aspects external to the project, such as the increased incidence of water-borne disease resulting from projects that change the pattern of water distribution and use. Only recently and rarely have broad environmental, political, sociological, and other facets that are external to the project been seriously considered at the project preparation stage.[20]

Given the complexity of sector and feasibility studies and the limitations of consultant firms, the Bank's role as overseer of the consultant services being rendered is also critically important to the success of the undertaking. In general, investment projects, which constitute the principal raison d'être

20. The following rationale, given in the World Bank/IDA annual report for 1971 (p. 23), for the Bank's interest in the improvement of municipal water and sewerage facilities would have been dismissed as unpersuasive and unacceptable a few years ago:

A major reason why the Bank Group has tried to encourage the development of this sector is that its benefits are so pervasive. It is generally accepted that the financial returns accruing to water and sewerage authorities considerably understate the true benefits to the community, by no means all of which are readily apparent or easily quantifiable. Environmental improvement, a valuable end in itself, can also result in additional financial benefits by improving the community's productive capacity through raising or safeguarding the level of public health.

of the World Bank, have been more closely and expertly supervised than have sector and feasibility studies. As the Bank has gained more experience with the latter type of study, however, it has increased its supervisory competence. Supervision of sector and feasibility studies is the responsibility of the projects departments. In the transportation and agriculture projects departments, technical assistance sections or units have been created to concentrate on overseeing sector and feasibility studies.[21]

The most obvious tests of success for such studies are (a) whether they result in subsequent capital investment by the Bank Group or by others, (b) whether they prevent misinvestment, and (c) whether they result in transferring needed skills to the host country or in creating or strengthening an institution important to its economy. On the first test, which of course begs the question whether the ensuing capital investment is itself successful, the program of preinvestment studies can be regarded as a success.

As of June 30, 1971, forty-three UNDP-financed studies had been completed. Of these, twenty-six had resulted in Bank Group investment, seven were in the post-1971 lending program of the Bank or IDA, and four projects had led to investment by other multilateral or private lenders. Three projects were directed not toward investment but toward developing conditions that could promote or facilitate investment—for example, financing advisers to the Planning Commission of Pakistan. Two completed studies were without scheduled follow-up investment as of the end of the 1971 fiscal year, and one study had been terminated because the project it contemplated was found to be economically unfeasible.

The total amount of follow-up investment by the Bank Group on projects executed for the UNDP (at a cost of $32.6 million to the UNDP) exceeded $1 billion. Inasmuch as the Bank Group finances only part of the costs of a project, and in four of these cases paved the way for other external investment without making any investment of its own, the total investment growing out of the forty-three completed sector and feasibility studies must have been substantially higher than $1 billion.

The study mentioned above that was terminated because it was economically unfeasible was a survey of coal deposits in the Cauca Valley in Colombia. Since the deposits were quickly found to be uneconomic for exploitation, the UNDP-financed study may be regarded as having prevented the misin-

21. Though both sector and feasibility studies are preinvestment undertakings, they are not twins. A number of the Bank's current sector studies are not assigned to subcontractors but are undertaken directly by the Bank, using a mixture of regular Bank staff and temporary consultants—with the costs of the studies charged to the administrative expenses of the Bank.

vestment which might have occurred if the preparatory survey had not been made.

Success in institution-building and skill-transfer is harder to measure, though, as King says, "it can be argued that providing a country with a local capability for keeping a sector program in power or transport up-to-date in the light of changing needs or for making its own feasibility studies . . . is considerably more important than providing it with a specific sector or feasibility study."[22] It is doubtful whether the program has been as successful in training and institution-building as it has in filling the pipeline of investment projects—if for no other reason than that the transfer of skills and managerial competence almost inevitably takes longer than the time allocated for the study. The natural tendency of both the consultant firms and the Bank has been to regard preparation of an acceptable report as the main job and to consider all other responsibilities as secondary. Moreover, practitioners are not necessarily good teachers, and the consultants most likely to produce a good study may not be particularly effective in training counterparts who approach the task from different cultural backgrounds.

The Bank has frequently been criticized by borrowers—deservedly in our view—for excessive concern with the viability of projects and insufficient concern with the transfer of skills. The Bank could on occasion require its consultants to employ local personnel, or more local personnel than it has in the past, on sector and feasibility studies. In other ways too, it could seek to expand the role of the borrowing nation in shaping projects for Bank or IDA financing.

Division of Labor between Bank and UNDP

Since the need for a feasibility study is often uncovered by the Bank, which can finance the study through a grant, loan, or credit if it so desires, what are the mechanics for reaching a division of labor between the Bank and the UNDP in this field? If the study is initially proposed by or to the Bank, the Bank gives the UNDP a "right of first refusal." If the UNDP agrees to provide a grant to cover the financing of the proposed study, it normally designates the Bank as the executing agency. Only if the UNDP declines does the Bank consider financing the study.[23]

---

22. King, "Review of Completed Sector and Feasibility Studies," p. 15.
23. Why might the UNDP refuse to finance a feasibility study? It might do so because it lacked the requisite funds, or felt it was already overcommitted in the country in question, or foresaw other difficulties.

As was indicated earlier, the Bank had been willing to finance through grants small preinvestment studies (usually ones costing $200,000 or less), but simplified UNDP procedures adopted in mid-1969 have made grant financing by the Bank for small preinvestment studies a rarity since then. Larger preinvestment studies not undertaken by the UNDP can be financed by special IDA credits or by including their cost in a regular Bank loan or IDA credit.

Just as the Bank gives the UNDP the right of first refusal, so the UNDP gives the Bank (and other participating agencies) a chance to comment on all requests for UNDP assistance. If, as happens occasionally, the study has been proposed to the UNDP by the government of a less developed country without the Bank's prior knowledge, but the Bank believes the study might pave the way for an investment project financed by the Bank Group, the Bank may be given the opportunity to become the executing agency. Even if the Bank does not want to be the executing agency, it may note its "special interest" and ask the UNDP to instruct the executing agency to consult the Bank in working out the plan for the study. The Bank has most frequently indicated a special interest in studies for which the FAO has been the executing agency.

When the Bank serves as executing agency for the UNDP, it draws up the "plan of operations" for the study in consultation with the host government, negotiates the terms of reference with the government, employs the consultants, supervises the field work, and reviews the consultants' report. It also submits to UNDP a confidential assessment of their work.

In a very real sense, the Bank has been a savior of the UNDP insofar as the latter's true preinvestment activities are concerned. The UNDP makes grants to establish or strengthen training institutions and to finance other work that does not have as its immediate objective the preparation of a proposal for capital investment. With respect to the UNDP's preinvestment work, however, the amount of follow-up investment generated by its projects, other than those for which the Bank has been executing agency, has been extremely modest. The reason appears to be that the Bank is by definition investment-oriented while the other executing agencies have tended, on the whole, to be technical-assistance-oriented. This has led their project teams until recently (they normally do not use consultant firms) to produce preinvestment studies rich in technical detail but, unfortunately, "almost totally devoid of the financial data and analyses that are needed for [an] investment decision."[24]

24. K. W. Taylor, "The Pre-Investment Function in the International Development System," *International Development Review*, Vol. 12 (No. 2, 1970), p. 4.

Cooperative Arrangements with FAO and Unesco

In 1963, the Bank and IDA decided to increase their activities in the fields of agriculture and education. To assist member governments in identifying and preparing projects in these fields, the Bank subsequently entered into agreements with the FAO and Unesco for jointly financed cooperative programs. Under the agreements, the Bank has had access to the expertise and experience of the other two specialized agencies, the agencies have acquired a financial partner, and the number of agricultural and educational projects presented for financing has increased. Project appraisal and supervision continue to be responsibilities of the Bank, but FAO and Unesco staff members frequently participate in these activities and on occasion provide technical assistance in carrying out projects.[25]

Under the memorandum of understanding between the Bank and the FAO, the Bank finances 75 percent and the FAO 25 percent of the cooperative program's budget, which during the fiscal year ended June 30, 1971, supported some fifty man-years of investment specialists' time, compared with eight man-years when the joint program was started. In relation to the UNDP, this "unusual but highly efficient procedure" produces much of the follow-up investment resulting from UNDP projects for which the FAO has served as executing agency.

The project identification and feasibility reports prepared in this way are submitted exclusively to the IBRD for appraisal and are normally not made available to other sources of financing, such as the regional development banks with which FAO has similar but parallel co-operative arrangements, unless and until the IBRD has taken a decision on financing. The high level of professional competence and performance of the FAO/IBRD Cooperative Programme is attested [to] by the large number of IBRD loans and IDA credits which have been made to date on the basis of its reports. . . . There is . . . no question regarding the efficiency of this arrangement, but only regarding the policy implications of a process in which the cream of the investment potential of an increasing number of UNDP pre-investment projects, for which large sums of money have been contributed on a multilateral basis, is being skimmed off for the exclusive use of one source of financing.[26]

25. IBRD, *The World Bank, IDA and IFC: Policies and Operations* (June 1969), p. 46.

26. Taylor, "The Pre-Investment Function in the International Development System," p. 5. The "one source of financing" is, however, a specialized agency of the United Nations, whereas the regional banks are not. Moreover, the decision as to who finances the follow-up investment project is made by the borrower, not by the international agencies. According to World Bank sources, there have been changes in financing agency as between the World Bank and the Inter-American Development Bank, almost at the last moment. These include switches in favor of the IDB on projects identified under the FAO/World Bank cooperative program.

The IBRD's arrangements with Unesco, which provided thirty man-years of professional staff time in fiscal year 1971, compared with eight in 1964, are open to the same compliments and criticisms. The original agreement covered education projects but gave Unesco sole responsibility for the field of educational planning. On education projects, Unesco was to assume responsibility for initial project identification, for assisting in project preparation, and for evaluating projects to determine whether they were meeting the educational objectives that were originally sought. To exercise its responsibility the Bank found that it had to make its own investigations to a greater extent than had been expected. It also became much more concerned with stimulating and assisting planning that would give rise to educational systems suited to contemporary needs.[27]

Educational planning in less developed countries seemed to be dedicated primarily to determining how many teachers, classrooms, and buildings would be required to accommodate a given increase of students. This planning appeared to the Bank to be insufficiently concerned with establishing educational objectives and studying alternative paths to those objectives. One corrective device available to the Bank was to include in a Bank loan or IDA credit for the construction of educational facilities, or other work in the education sector, the financing for technical assistance that would be needed in planning a subsequent phase of the educational program of the borrowing country. This device has been used.

In addition, in fiscal 1971 the Bank-Unesco agreement was expanded to provide Unesco with additional budgetary support *from* the Bank for technical support *to* the Bank—and *through* the Bank, to member countries—in educational planning and sector studies. Cooperation was thereby extended to cover the full span from sector studies through system planning to the preparation of specific educational projects for final evaluation and consideration by the Bank.[28]

Technical Assistance Incorporated in Loans and Credits

Economic survey missions and preinvestment missions, eager to produce the studies demanded of them within the time limits imposed on them, are not the ideal mechanisms for patiently training local personnel and building durable institutions in low-income countries. The regular loan and credit operations of the Bank Group, particularly the series of loans within the same

27. Harold Graves, Internal memorandum on the Bank's activities in the education sector (Nov. 5, 1969).
28. See also Chapter 17, below.

sector of the borrower's economy, offer a more suitable means of contributing to these objectives.

The Bank can incorporate various kinds of technical assistance in a capital assistance project; and the volume of technical assistance financed by the Bank in this manner substantially exceeds the volume financed by it in other ways. Some of the loan-incorporated technical assistance—helping the borrower select appropriate equipment, prepare tenders for international bidding, or use progress reports as a tool of management—is inextricably embedded in international lending as practiced by the Bank Group. Some is readily identifiable, for example, the salary of a foreign consultant or the cost of investigating the feasibility of a second investment project in the same sector.

The practice of including funds for the employment of foreign managers or specialists in the host country began early in IBRD lending. In institution-building, the Bank's most characteristic prescription also manifested itself at an early date. We have mentioned in earlier chapters its preference for, and sponsorship of, relatively autonomous "authorities" to set rates, hire and fire personnel, and operate utility systems, transport systems, and other segments of a nation's infrastructure. That preference has become legendary.[29] Examples include: the Damodar Valley Corporation in India, the Cauca Valley Corporation in Colombia, and the Imperial Telecommunications Board in Ethiopia. The practice of including in a loan some funds for the foreign training of local personnel to replace the foreign managers, and funds required for the identification and preparation of additional investment projects in the same sector of the economy, developed more slowly but has been a feature of Bank lending for some years.

Only since fiscal year 1969, however, has the Bank tried to keep records on the amount of technical assistance included in its regular loans and credits. The sum was approximately $40 million in that year and nearly $50 million in fiscal 1971. The breakdown of the total amount of technical assistance included in IBRD loans and IDA credits for fiscal years 1969 through 1971 was as follows (in millions of U.S. dollars):[30]

	1969	1970	1971
For experts and consultants	28.9	23.0	40.0
For feasibility studies	9.1	15.3	5.2
For overseas training	1.5	2.2	4.4
Total	39.5	40.4	49.6

29. See Chapters 6 and 8, above, and 19 and 20, below.

30. World Bank/IDA, annual reports, 1969–71. Details may not add to totals due to rounding.

Illustrations can be found in almost every category of Bank loan or IDA credit. The $19 million to the Cameroon for road work, which was approved in fiscal 1970, included $289,200 for feasibility studies. The $5 million committed for the agricultural development bank of Afghanistan permits the expenditure of $378,000 to employ foreign experts and consultants and $278,000 for the overseas training of local personnel. The $35 million approved in fiscal 1970 for a port development project in East Africa includes $420,000 for feasibility studies. A Bank loan of $12.7 million in 1971 to help finance a reorganization of agricultural research in Spain—the Bank Group's first loan in any field that can be classified as primarily for research—includes $276,000 for internationally recruited experts and consultants serving in Spain and $2.3 million in fellowships for two hundred Spanish scientists to study abroad.

Lending for livestock improvement, after a long period of trial and error, appears finally to have come into its own. The "one invariable characteristic" of Bank/IDA assistance in this field, and in several others as well, is that finance is tied inseparably to the acceptance and effective use of technical services. This tie is maintained at every stage and every level, although the Bank's direct involvement in providing the technical service component is normally confined to assistance in assuring sound project management, plus aid when necessary in recruiting outside consultants or specialist staff.[31]

The Bank's first foray into the livestock field began in the early 1950s in Uruguay with a livestock- and pasture-improvement project, to implement the 1951 report of the Bank/FAO mission to that country. The mission's report advocated dividing pastures with fences, planting trees on permanent grasslands, introducing legumes, using increased amounts of lime and phosphate, controlling animal diseases, improving irrigation, transportation, storage, and marketing, and so on—the comprehensive program par excellence.[32]

Valuable experiments were undertaken by a few progressive and wealthy landowners, but nothing much happened in Uruguay's stagnant livestock economy until 1960, when long drawn-out negotiations between the Bank and the Uruguayan government culminated in a $7 million loan. By that time the project was essentially a pilot program, the scope of which had been re-

31. Donald J. Pryor, "Livestock: The Recognition of a Stepchild," *Finance and Development,* Vol. 7 (September 1970), p. 21.

32. For more on the "comprehensive program whose many components are given equal emphasis and are pronounced to be interrelated," see Albert O. Hirschman, *Development Projects Observed* (Brookings Institution, 1967), p. 23.

duced to four principal measures. However, the active work of the administering agency and its technical advisers from abroad

centered almost wholly on pasture improvement for two good reasons: (1) progress in this area clearly conditions advances in subdivision and in fodder conservation, and probably also in disease control; (2) while the general principles of natural grassland improvement were well known, there remained great areas of technological ignorance about the precise manner of applying those principles in Uruguay.[33]

Reducing technological ignorance required time; disbursements under the loan were consequently slow during the early years. By 1964, the administering agency, the Honorary Livestock Commission, had completed the necessary experiments and more or less knew which methods would be most reliable in different regions of the country. It was decided that the pilot phase could be concluded and the program applied over a much wider area. In 1965, therefore, the Bank granted a new loan of $12.7 million for the next phase.[34]

The next phase placed heavy emphasis on the development of techniques for extending necessary credits to individual ranchers. Thereafter, the system could be adapted to the needs of other countries. The great bulk of the Bank/IDA funds for livestock projects, totaling some $350 million as of June 30, 1971, has been committed since 1967.

Public financial institutions in the borrowing countries—agricultural and livestock banks or their equivalent—usually administer the program. On the advice of the World Bank and as a condition of its lending, qualified technicians are employed by the administering institution to help ranchers work out detailed investment plans that will justify loans to them, advise them on technical and management questions, and visit them regularly to assure proper execution of the plan. In a few countries such as Mexico, technicians with all the necessary qualifications can be recruited locally, but in most of the countries in which livestock projects are in operation, foreign specialists obtained with the advice and assistance of the Bank head the technical staffs.[35]

33. *Ibid.*, p. 40.

34. *Ibid.*, p. 41. Hirschman summarizes the experiments that were undertaken during the pilot phase, draws some interesting conclusions about the kinds of projects whose course is most likely to be marked by technological uncertainty, and mentions as one of the effects thereof the greater attractiveness to developers of infrastructure investments as compared with those in agriculture. He also describes changes in the attitudes of participating landowners during the pre-1967 life of the Uruguayan project. (See pp. 41–43, 45, 150–51.) By 1970, meat exports from Uruguay had reached 153,000 metric tons, valued at $88 million, as compared with 69,000 metric tons, valued at $27.4 million, in 1961.

35. Pryor, "Livestock: The Recognition of a Stepchild," p. 22.

Lest our description of the Bank's promotion of livestock improvement sound too idyllic, we hasten to add that the program has also been severely criticized, principally on the ground that the direct beneficiaries tend to be ranchers who are already fairly affluent, while vast numbers of landless peasants remain landless.[36] The criticism is thus directed at the Bank's priorities and values rather than its techniques. Few would deny that its support for agricultural and industrial credit institutions in developing countries illustrates well its ability to integrate technical and financial assistance. Both technical and financial aid have been required to launch such institutions, and those institutions, in turn, have made technical assistance an important ingredient of the financial assistance they provide.[37]

The Bank has consistently stressed the need for good management of the projects it finances and has made a practice of obtaining specific undertakings with respect to management from its borrowers. Where it has thought that adequate local management would not be available, it has insisted that qualified foreign firms or specialists be employed to manage the project, at least during its initial stages, and that arrangements be made for training local personnel. Although the Bank has helped in various ways to find individuals and organizations qualified for such work, it has with few exceptions avoided taking direct responsibility for providing managers for projects it finances.

One set of exceptions—the hiring by the Bank of managers for certain livestock projects in Latin America—has already been cited. A second breach of the Bank's self-imposed limits on the provision of management was the establishment of the Agricultural Development Service in eastern Africa in 1966. The Service is comprised of men with managerial experience (primarily former agricultural officers and administrators of the colonial powers) selected by the Bank and available for seconding on a reimbursable basis to agricultural projects in eastern Africa. The Bank assures them of employment between project assignments. The projects in question are normally Bank-financed or IDA-financed, but need not be.

36. See Chapter 14, below.
37. "Our assistance to these institutions [industrial development banks] has not been confined to loans; we have also helped them at their request, in their recruitment and other problems. . . . We believe strongly that, in proper circumstances and properly organized and managed, these institutions can make a significant contribution to development . . . not only by providing long-term industrial financing—a type of financing frequently heretofore unavailable—but also by establishing new standards of investigation and supervision and thereby creating confidence among local investors in the enterprises financed. And they can contribute significantly, too, by serving as a link to foreign enterprise, skill and capital." Address by Eugene R. Black, president of IBRD, before the 25th session of the Economic and Social Council of the UN (April 17, 1958). For more on industrial development banks, see also Chapter 11, below.

It is noteworthy that, to date at least, the Bank's willingness to assume some responsibility for providing qualified managers for livestock projects in Latin America and agricultural undertakings in eastern Africa does not appear to have had any harmful consequences. The Bank's tradition of specifying in a loan contract that the project manager must be "satisfactory" to the Bank, coupled with the Bank's willingness to "nominate" managers, enabled it to live with the illusion that it did not provide management. Crossing the illusory line, it was feared, would weaken the borrower's sense of responsibility for making a success of the project, subject the manager to dual loyalties, or get the Bank into trouble, legally or morally, if the management proved deficient or the project ran into stormy weather.

If there is a need for foreign managers, there is also, almost by definition, a need to train local personnel to replace them. While the foreign managers should be expected to help train successors, more formal arrangements, including foreign training for potential successors, may be needed. The sums included in Bank and IDA project loans and credits for overseas training are modest, amounting to less than 10 percent of those included in fiscal years 1969 through 1971 for the employment of experts and consultants. This is due in part to a wholesome skepticism about the value of foreign as opposed to local training and, in part, to a feeling within the Bank that its expertise is in the design and execution of projects and selection of equipment; it should leave training to others—to other specialized agencies of the United Nations and to bilateral programs. These sources, the Bank might add, can provide the training on a grant basis and save the less developed country the costs of loan assistance for the purpose.[38]

Permanent Missions, Impermanent Missions, and Development Advisory Services

Throughout its history the Bank, as we have said, has been headquarters-centered. Although its practice has been to rely on visiting missions rather than resident missions, posts for resident representatives or advisers have been part of the table of organization since the 1940s. At first, the principal objec-

38. "The UNDP also has a high ratio of experts to training. This I think stems partly from the fact that it is much easier to do it yourself than to train someone else to do it. ... I suspect that recruitment policies play a considerable role. It is relatively easy to identify an expert from the record. It is not at all easy to identify somebody who is capable of communicating effectively and training someone to do the job." Letter from Anne Winslow, Carnegie Endowment for International Peace, to Robert E. Asher (Dec. 16, 1970).

tive was to serve directly the interests of the member country—for example, by responding to its request (which was sometimes an inspired request) for a readily accessible source of advice on development policy. Annual reports for the years 1946–60 convey the impression that the stationing of members of the Bank staff as advisers in the capitals of member governments, particularly in the Western Hemisphere, was growing steadily. Subsequent reports indicate a fall-off in this practice. However, there was an increase in field representation established at the initiative of the Bank and designed to serve more directly its own interests by giving it a set of eyes and ears closer to the member country than Washington, D.C. (In the latter case, the interests of the host government are presumed also to be served, though indirectly rather than directly, and its agreement remains a prerequisite to the establishment of the mission.)[39]

Resident representatives stationed by the Bank are responsible solely to the Bank. Even though their duties may include advisory services to the local government, there is no ambiguity about "whose men" they are. A seconded adviser assigned to the service of a member country, on the other hand, is expected to serve that country in accordance with his best professional judgment and not to report to the Bank or receive instructions from the Bank on the substance of his advice to the government.

In the early 1960s, when country development programming was still a major form of Bank-sponsored technical assistance, the Bank established a development advisory service (DAS) to fill two functions. First it was to serve as an elite corps, comprised mostly of development generalists with wide experience and established reputations, but containing also some younger men of exceptional ability and promise, who could be seconded to member governments to advise on the preparation and execution of national development programs. The second function was to provide a reservoir for mature

39. Two quotations from Bank documents will illustrate the difference between host country–oriented and Bank-oriented missions:

In May 1954 the Government [of Ecuador] created an Economic Planning and Coordination Board along lines suggested by the Bank. At the request of the Government the Bank is assisting in organizing the work of the Board and in recruiting its technical staff. The Bank has also agreed to station a representative in Ecuador to assist the Board in formulating a long-range development program.

IBRD, *Ninth Annual Report, 1953–1954*, p. 33.

Where the Bank is actively concerned in following the planning and implementation of the development program as a whole—for example, when the Bank is acting as leader of a consortium or consultative group—resident representation may be necessary to enable the Bank to gain adequate insight into the program, to anticipate and adjust to problems arising in its execution, and to establish proper rapport with the national authorities.

IBRD, Operational memorandum 7.04 (Sept. 30, 1969), p. 2.

talent of a kind the Bank might find difficult to recruit for regular staff positions but was almost certain to need.

We've been concentrating on short-term experts, short-term missions, survey missions, and similar kinds of advisers going out for short periods of time. We've always known that wasn't the whole answer or even a major part of the answer . . . there just is a tremendous need for more people available on a full-time basis, particularly for long-term resident assignments.

When we tried to find these people outside the Bank, we ran into the problem that nobody wants to leave his occupation and career for two years with no assurance of re-employment . . . and . . . to get the kind of people we wanted we had to offer a career service.

Finally we have decided to establish . . . a new foreign service which we are calling the Development Advisory Service, which is largely an administrative gimmick designed to enable us to get in high-level people without their worrying what their position is vis-à-vis the economic adviser and the area department director, etc., and with their positions and salaries and so forth depending on their professional qualifications, not on their particular positions in the administrative hierarchy. . . .

What we want to do is to give a satisfying career in the whole field of development, with perhaps two-thirds of the total time spent in resident assignments abroad.[40]

The DAS was established in January 1962, and during the four years in which it functioned, twenty-five people were appointed to it. In providing technical assistance to the Bank, it was eminently successful; a number of the recruits moved into key posts in the Bank. It was less successful in providing technical assistance to member governments, for reasons common to most such efforts: inadequate prior analysis of what the government really wanted or needed; failure of governments to assign adequate counterpart personnel to work with the advisers; inflexibility on the part of some of the advisers; and so on.

By the end of four years, moreover, the basic character of the Bank's technical assistance and advisory activities had changed, and they had become more closely enmeshed in its lending operations. The DAS as a separate organizational entity, a distinct corps of "expert talent," was therefore terminated.

In particular, the demand for advice on development planning and policies through general survey missions or seconded advisers did not grow as expected, largely because the Bank was providing more of this kind of advice through its regular economic missions and consultations with governments. In addition, we found that where such a demand existed, we could sometimes meet it through

40. Oral History Project of Columbia University, interviews recorded in the summer of 1961 on the International Bank for Reconstruction and Development (cited hereinafter as "Oral History"). Quotation is from interview of Richard H. Demuth, pp. 79–81.

contractual arrangements such as that with the Harvard Development Advisory Service for Pakistan. At the same time it was becoming apparent that assistance in project identification and preparation was a more urgent need in most countries than the provision of development planning or policy advice, and one which the Bank is more peculiarly qualified to meet. The second development was that the Bank recruitment policy became much more flexible and based on a longer term perspective of Bank requirements. We felt that we no longer needed, as we had in 1962, a separate group of budgeted posts, without line responsibilities, in order to meet the demand for mature and experienced officers.[41]

The shortage of well prepared projects from African countries having become, in the Bank's view, particularly critical, the Bank in 1965 established "permanent missions" in eastern Africa (at Nairobi) and in western Africa (at Abidjan), primarily to assist governments in those areas in identifying and preparing projects for Bank Group financing, especially in the agricultural and transport sectors. Mission personnel are available also to advise governments on policy issues and practical problems arising in connection with Bank-financed projects. Attached administratively to the Bank's Nairobi office is the previously mentioned Agricultural Development Service, formed early in 1966 to provide experienced managerial personnel for agricultural and rural development projects in eastern Africa.[42]

As was reported in Chapter 4, the Bank also maintains resident representatives or teams in certain other countries. The most important, at present, in the technical assistance context is the team which has been in Indonesia since 1968. The mission's first assignment is to advise Indonesian authorities on questions of economic policy and administration. Its second is to help Indonesia's planning organization and other government agencies with the coordination and use of technical assistance, "including studies to identify and prepare projects, the selection of consultants, the framing of terms of reference, and related matters."[43]

The first IDA technical assistance credit to Indonesia, for $2 million approved in 1968, appears to have been a way of giving the mission a drawing account for useful work. It was earmarked for preinvestment and feasibility studies; but in contrast to normal Bank procedure, the specific studies to

41. Letter from Richard H. Demuth to Edgar O. Edwards of the Ford Foundation (Dec. 14, 1970).
42. See David Gordon, "The World Bank's Mission in Eastern Africa," in *Finance and Development*, Vol. 5 (March 1968). Gordon was chief of the Bank's permanent mission in eastern Africa at the time he wrote the article.
43. IBRD, *The World Bank, IDA and IFC: Policies and Operations* (June 1969), p. 47. Indonesia had withdrawn from the Bank in 1965 and been readmitted in 1967. Prior to the dispatch of the mission, which was headed by Bernard R. Bell, the Bank Group had made no investments in Indonesia.

which the proceeds would be devoted were not known at the time the credit was approved. Part of it was used for the detailed engineering of an irrigation project for which IDA subsequently lent $18.5 million. A second technical assistance credit of $4 million was approved in 1970 to finance studies and preparatory work "needed to bring a wide range of projects to a stage at which they can be implemented"—projects "which will be selected by the Indonesian Government in association with the World Bank's Resident Staff in Djakarta."[44] The Djakarta mission has assisted the Indonesians in arranging aid from non–Bank Group sources, as well as from the Bank Group, and has been concerned with a much wider range of technical assistance to the host government than merely help in preparing proposals for investment projects. The major role played by the Bank in institution-building in Indonesia during the post-Sukarno years is widely recognized.

The Economic Development Institute

The Bank's most durable venture in technical assistance that is not connected with any immediate loan or credit proposal is the Economic Development Institute (EDI), established in the mid-1950s, principally to provide training for officials concerned with development programs and projects in the low-income countries. The EDI offers a series of courses designed to give participants a perspective on the general process of development and a working knowledge of techniques useful in handling the particular problems that confront them in their work.

Origins and Establishment

It owes its origin to several streams of thought that had been gathering momentum in the Bank during the early 1950s. One was the growing belief at the Bank that the relatively low level of economic management in the countries with which it dealt constituted a major impediment to development; the Bank ought to do more than it had been doing to raise that level, specifically by training key people in the governments of less developed countries. Another was the feeling of staff members, such as Paul Rosenstein-Rodan (the imaginative economist who is generally regarded as the godfather of the EDI), that the Bank should become substantially more involved than it was in economic research on development questions. Staff members, it was said,

44. IDA, Press release (Sept. 11, 1970).

did not have close enough contact with people in academic and other institutions, national and international, who were studying development problems.

Related to the view that the Bank might learn something from outsiders who were studying the development process was the feeling of others on the staff that their institution, willy-nilly, was accumulating knowledge, practical experience, and insights that it had an obligation to share. The Bank management was not particularly hospitable to basic research as a function of its regular economic staff, but felt that an institute, established by and closely linked to the Bank, could become a leading center for research on development.

As has been pointed out by William Diamond, one of the original faculty members of the EDI, there is no necessary connection between these streams of thought.[45] However, support gradually emerged for an institute that could to some extent fill both the training and the research needs. President Eugene Black became enthusiastic about the idea, provided something practical could be worked out. The possibility of Harvard University or the Massachusetts Institute of Technology setting up the center in Washington and operating it was investigated but the two institutions rejected the opportunity.

In the summer of 1952, the management obtained the concurrence of the executive directors in a proposal to explore the idea of an economic development institute to be organized by the Bank and to explore the willingness of private foundations to share in its costs. (It was assumed that the approval of the executive directors for a Bank-operated facility would be more easily obtained if they could be told that one or more private foundations had enough faith in the undertaking to help finance it during its first few years.) A "Preliminary Proposal for an Economic Development Institute," which foreshadowed very well the agency that later emerged, was then prepared by the Bank staff as a basis for discussions with government agencies, educational institutions, and private foundations.

The interest of the Rockefeller Foundation having been elicited, A. K. Cairncross, a distinguished economist then on the faculty of the University of Glasgow, was invited in 1954 to come to Washington to study the situation in more detail and ascertain what, if anything, the Bank could and should do that no other institution could be expected to do equally well. Cairncross, after interviewing a large number of people, argued that the Bank's special advantage was its close and intimate contact with the day-to-day problems of development. Use of the Bank's staff and the Bank's documentation would lend a realism to research and training that no other institution could provide.

45. "Oral History," p. 4.

His recommendations for bringing small groups of relatively senior officials from less developed countries to Washington contemplated that they would live together and work together for about six months in an exciting, mind-stretching exercise. "The fellows should be housed together, in or near Washington, and they should eat, sleep, and study at the place selected."[46]

The Ford Foundation joined the Rockefeller Foundation in providing half of the budget for the first three years, and Professor Cairncross was prevailed upon to become the first director of the EDI.[47]

The Bank solved temporarily the next problem (finding quarters for the institute), by renting a large old house in northwest Washington owned by Mrs. Eugene Meyer, wife of the first president of the Bank. But the house proved to be too small and ill arranged to serve as sleeping and working quarters; the necessary doubling up in bedrooms and sharing of bathroom facilities by a number of people became sore points. The net result for the first class (January–June 1956) was an exciting time intellectually and, too often, a miserable time in terms of personal relationships and personal comfort. Since late 1956, the Bank has made it possible for participants to live in greater privacy in hotels or apartments accessible to the EDI.[48]

The big worry at the beginning was: would the participants be competent enough to warrant the expenditure involved? On the whole, the caliber of participants from less developed countries has been high. They have for the most part been mid-career or senior officials, some of whom have previously studied economics and some of whom have not, but all of whom have borne important responsibilities for development planning and promotion in their homelands.

Curriculum, Faculty, and Fellows

Until 1962, the EDI offered only a six-months general course, given once a year, in the formulation and administration of policies, programs, and projects related to economic development. As the Bank's overall interest in project preparation and sector planning increased, the EDI increased the

46. A. K. Cairncross, "Economic Development Institute," memorandum (Aug. 19, 1954), p. 18.

47. He subsequently was named economic adviser to the British government and in 1967 became Sir Alec Cairncross.

48. Since the mid-1960s, the Bank has partially achieved the objective of keeping the group together by housing all of them in one apartment building—at first in one leased for their exclusive use and more recently in one occupied also by participants in the institute operated by the International Monetary Fund. EDI classes are held in an EDI wing at the Bank's headquarters.

project content of its curriculum, adding shorter courses of two or three months' duration dealing with the preparation and evaluation of projects, either generally or in especially important sectors, such as industry and agriculture, and recently, transportation and education. The first course in French was offered in 1962 and the first Spanish course in 1963. The French and Spanish courses, which have always been of less than six months' duration, have gradually become project courses.

The number of participants selected for a course is normally limited to twenty-five. The chief requirement is that the nominees be concerned in their jobs with matters of economic policy or with the preparation and appraisal of projects in the fields in which project courses are offered. The government, through the central bank, planning office, or other nominating agency, is expected to assure the institute that the candidate will be given a leave of absence at full pay for the duration of the course; also that he intends to return to government employment and will be placed in his former position or in another of comparable or greater responsibility at the end of the course. Until 1966, governments also had to pay a sizable tuition fee for each participant, which served as a further indication of the serious intent of the agency making the nomination.

About six months before a course begins, announcements of the course are sent to agencies (in less developed member countries of the Bank) that engage in activities relevant to the course—for example, departments of agriculture for agriculture courses. These agencies, directly or through a central coordinating mechanism, nominate candidates. Actual selection is by an admissions committee composed of senior officials of the Bank.

The Bank grossly underestimated the demand for EDI courses. When the institute was founded, it was thought that demand would decline and permit the phasing out of the operation before very many years. To date, that assumption has been unwarranted; the number of nominations received per course has recently been running at more than four times the number of places available.[49]

As is explained in Chapter 14, on the Bank's conception of the development process, the Bank has views as to what constitutes good development policy, but the views have never been monolithically held within the institution. The courses of the EDI are devoted to discussion and the pooling of experience rather than to indoctrination or formal instruction. Attention is

49. The EDI pays the traveling expenses of the participants and, in the case of the general development course, though not for the shorter projects courses, the traveling expenses of the participant's wife. In addition to the housing accommodations, each participant receives a per diem allowance to cover meals and some incidental expenses.

concentrated on actual situations and on policies concerned with those sectors of the economy—agriculture, industry, transportation, education, and so forth—that are considered of special importance to development. Considerable use is made of case studies drawn from the actual experience of the Bank. The normal concerns of economists with resource mobilization and allocation and returns on investment tend to be emphasized more heavily than the social and cultural aspects of development.

Though the initial worry centered around the character and quality of the participants the EDI would attract, recruitment of an adequate teaching staff has proved to be at least as great a problem. The institute has a full-time teaching staff comprised of personnel transferred for periods of two years or more from other departments of the Bank, plus several persons from universities, government agencies, or research centers. In addition to the full-time faculty, staff members of various departments of the World Bank Group frequently conduct sessions on subjects on which they have particular knowledge or experience. Outsiders are also invited in to give lectures or attend specific sessions.

The outstanding character and intellect of Cairncross, as well as of his first faculty, which included some of the best people at the Bank, gave the EDI international respectability from the beginning. His successors in the directorship have been Michael L. Hoffman (1957–61), John H. Adler (1962–67), and K. S. Krishnaswamy (1967–72). Other senior personnel on the regular staff of the Bank who have served as faculty members of the EDI include Hans A. Adler, George B. Baldwin, William Diamond, Benjamin B. King, the late Samuel Lipkowitz, and Albert Waterston. Distinguished outsiders include Sir Arthur Gaitskell (U.K.), Just Faaland (the Christian Michelsen Institute, Norway), Nurul Islam (Pakistan Institute of Development Economics), Mahbub ul Haq (Pakistan Planning Commission; now a member of the Bank staff), Arnold C. Harberger (University of Chicago), Bagicha S. Minhas (New Delhi), and W. Brian Reddaway (Cambridge University).

Nevertheless, it was apparent by the mid-1960s that the average quality of the teaching staff had deteriorated by comparison with that of the early halcyon years of the institute. With rare exceptions, teaching stints at the EDI did not become highly prized portions of a Bank official's career, nor was an occasional lecture at EDI a high priority activity for officials in operational jobs. The institute expanded rapidly and until a few years ago was perennially shorthanded. The teaching staff found itself hard pressed to do more than prepare for classes and teach them. Opportunities to reflect on one's experience and to put the reflections on paper were lacking. More time is now available for writing, but this has not resulted in more writing, either of case studies and materials particularly suitable for EDI use, or of more academic and theoretical research on the development process.

It may seem odd that an institution as large as the Bank should find it difficult to release two or three outstanding people each year for assignment to the EDI. But it must be remembered that outstanding people are outstandingly valuable, that the Bank's own workload has been increasing, that it has regarded international lending as its real mission, and that assigning productive, fully occupied officials to periods of teaching and quiet reflection requires sacrificing obvious short-term benefits for uncertain long-term ones. The virtues of the long view are easier to preach than to practice.

If top management would make it crystal clear that assignment to the EDI is a normal, desirable part of the career of a Bank official that would be appropriately rewarded, it could help overcome the view that such an assignment, like a field post with the Bank, is a dignified form of exile from the mainstream. Since Eugene Black's departure, however, Bank presidents have not shown intense interest in the EDI. Nevertheless, the EDI continues to fill creditably a role that is in certain respects unique.

The EDI's project courses have no real counterpart in the universities, are obviously related to the Bank's lending activities, and can and do make use of case histories accumulated by the Bank. The general development course, it has been argued, is more nearly "university stuff." With more universities now offering courses on economic growth and macroeconomics, is it necessary for the EDI to do so? Examination reveals an important difference in approach and emphasis; the EDI (in our view) is better equipped to meet the needs of mid-career economic administrators from less developed countries, whose jobs require some understanding of the workings of the economy as a whole, of the relationship of the various sectors thereto, and of the role of project appraisal in sector development.

Participants who complete the courses given in Washington by the EDI receive certificates as Fellows of the Institute. By June 30, 1971, more than thirteen hundred officials had attended EDI courses. Implausible friendships between Taiwanese and Yugoslavs, Indians and Pakistanis, and Israelis and Arabs have been formed.

Some prominent alumni have languished in jail as a result of political upheavals or personal peccadillos, and some are living as exiles in foreign lands. Some have served as prime ministers or ministers of finance or planning. A preponderant number occupy responsible posts in their countries and are putting to good use the training they have received. So infiltrated with strategically placed EDI alumni are the governments of certain less developed member countries that some representatives of the new left profess to see in the situation evidence of neo-imperialism, of a system whereby the Bank can influence or dominate policymaking in the interest of something more sinister than sensible use of available resources by member countries. Others have asked whether there are enough alumni in most governments to make any real difference in domestic standards of development administration.

If consideration is limited to fellows of the sixteen general development courses given between 1956 and 1971, twelve member countries (six of which are in Asia) have ten or more fellows. If, however, fellows of project courses are included, twenty-one countries have twenty or more fellows, and, more significantly perhaps, the twenty countries having ten to nineteen fellows include some quite small countries.[50]

The total number of participants in EDI courses in Washington—about two hundred in 1970–71—is expected to rise to three hundred by 1976. The general development course in Washington is expected to be retained, but its duration has been reduced from six months to eighteen weeks. The number of courses specializing in particular sectors will be increased. The EDI has for some years experimented with courses overseas, usually project-oriented courses, and envisages an enlargement of these overseas activities during the 1970s.

EDI Publications and Library Service

The first EDI publication, *Development Banks*, by William Diamond, was based on notes used by Mr. Diamond for discussions in EDI seminars.[51] The institute's second publication, *The Design of Development,* by Jan Tinbergen, who a decade later won the Nobel Prize in economics, was actually prepared in 1955, before the EDI was established. It was written in response to a request from the then economic director of the World Bank, Leonard Rist. The paper was later used at the EDI, however, as a basis for discussions of development policies and of problems of programming and project appraisal. It raised the question of "shadow pricing" and appeared to deserve a better fate than mimeographing. Accordingly, it was published by the EDI.[52] After its publication, Tinbergen came to the institute as a guest lecturer.

50. See EDI, *Directory of Fellows* (July 1971). The twenty-one countries with twenty or more fellows are: Argentina, Bolivia, Brazil, Chile, Colombia, Ecuador, Ghana, India, Indonesia, Iran, Korea, Malaysia, Nigeria, Pakistan, Philippines, Spain, Taiwan, Thailand, Turkey, United Arab Republic, and Yugoslavia.

51. Johns Hopkins Press, 1957. The same press published for the Bank two years later *Problems and Practices of Development Banks* by Shirley Boskey, though the latter was not an EDI publication.

52. Johns Hopkins Press, 1958. For more on shadow pricing, see Chapter 8, above.

The sixth publication of the EDI, *Development Planning: Lessons of Experience*, by Albert Waterston, though larger (706 pages) than its five predecessors combined, has become the institute's best seller.[53] Mr. Waterston, during his first teaching assignment at the EDI, probed the experience of many countries to assess the efficiency and effectiveness of their planning organizations. In cooperation with others, he had described in three earlier EDI monographs the planning machinery of Morocco, Yugoslavia, and Pakistan. Lessons from the experience of these countries and of many others were brought together in *Development Planning*, which reached rather gloomy conclusions about the efficacy and appropriateness of conventional macroeconomic planning as then practiced in the less developed countries, largely on the recommendation of experts from the more developed countries.

The only new book published by the EDI since 1965 is *Economic Development Projects and Their Appraisal*, by John A. King, Jr. (1967). The fall-off in publications based on the work of the EDI staff, however, appears to have been counterbalanced by an increase in publications resulting from the work of the regular economic staff of the Bank and consultants to the economics department.

In 1960, with financial help from the Rockefeller Foundation, the EDI began a useful service to countries where materials on economic development were virtually unavailable—the provision of small libraries comprised of books, articles, and reference materials useful to practitioners in the field of economic development. Supplementary materials are distributed annually.

Bank policies can be and are criticized in EDI courses, but it is doubtful whether many have been modified as a result. Cost–benefit analysis may be the exception that proves the rule. The EDI on occasion brings to Washington university economists and others whose views on development policy differ drastically from those prevailing at the Bank, and members of the Bank staff have opportunities to hear them, meet with them, and agree or disagree with what they say. The central purpose of the EDI, however, is not the education of the Bank staff but the training of officials in less developed countries, particularly in techniques of project preparation and appraisal.

In Summary

Good advice is rare, and good advice that is listened to is even rarer. But the Bank provides a powerful amplifier—the prospect of capital assistance to finance its recommendations. Because of this, Bank advice has at times

53. Johns Hopkins Press, 1965. A revised fourth edition was published in 1971.

been followed when advice that is just as good, or better, from agencies less affluent than the Bank has been ignored. If the acceptability of the Bank's advice is enhanced, so also is the responsibility for seeing that it is of superior quality. The Bank's technical assistance tends to be high-cost assistance. Its studies are comprehensive and carefully reviewed, its personnel are not deployed in villages and barrios, its own specialists and those financed through its efforts are well paid. On the whole, however, Bank-furnished technical assistance appears to us to be of high quality, though a full-scale appraisal of this especially hard-to-measure form of aid is beyond the scope of this chapter.

In the technical assistance efforts of the post-World War II era, two radically different approaches are discernible. One approach regards technical assistance primarily as a way of overcoming a less developed country's shortage of high-level skills. The function of technical assistance then becomes twofold.

It can help fill gaps between the skill requirements implicit in development programmes and the domestic stock of skills. But it is also needed to strengthen and supplement a country's capacity to produce new skills via its education system. . . . Technical assistance may be directed towards both an immediate increase in the stock of skills, by providing "experts" who will do operational jobs, and towards swelling the flow, by adding to facilities and building institutions for education and training.[54]

Opposed to this is the grass-roots approach espoused by experts such as David E. Lilienthal, former chairman of the Tennessee Valley Authority and now chairman of the private Development and Resources Corporation. He stresses "the almost unlimited latent capacity of the average man" and criticizes the other approach as based, consciously or unconsciously, on creating an elite corps in the developing countries—a literate, educated minority capable of directing modified forms of institutions that have "worked" elsewhere. He and those who share his view stress the need for popular participation in the selection and execution of a wide variety of projects. They argue that truly indigenous institutions will then be created and that, if substantial local participation in planning and execution will jeopardize the physical work, it is questionable whether the project is worth undertaking at all. When responsibility is vested in the average man, *"change can come quickly*—far more quickly than the tired and disillusioned ask us to believe."[55]

54. Angus Maddison, *Foreign Skills and Technical Assistance in Economic Development* (Paris: Development Centre of the Organisation for Economic Co-operation and Development, 1965), pp. 12–13.

55. David E. Lilienthal, "The Road to Change," *International Development Review,* Vol. 6 (December 1964), p. 10. See also Richard V. Gilbert, "The Works Programme in East Pakistan," *International Labour Review,* Vol. 89 (March 1964).

Both approaches are probably necessary and valid, and not always as distinguishable from each other in practice as in theory. Nevertheless, it seems fair to say that the Bank's technical assistance efforts, with their emphasis on careful planning and efficient, businesslike execution of a limited number of investment projects, exemplify the elitist more than the grass-roots approach.

Specifically, Bank-inspired technical assistance has traveled two paths, one inextricably linked to lending and the other extricably linked. During the 1950s, influenced in all probability by the prevailing view that technical assistance was not really technical assistance unless it was divorced from capital assistance, the Bank publicized more heavily technical assistance that was not directly related to immediate requests for project financing. It publicized its country survey missions, its resident advisers, its help in mobilizing domestic capital for development, and its EDI. A number of countries, including some that were not yet fully independent, were given a framework for thinking about development problems and an opportunity to send key officials abroad for the general development course offered by the EDI.

By the mid-1960s, less developed countries had become less interested in advice on overall policies and planning. An urgent need, however, and one the Bank considered itself well qualified to help meet, was for assistance in project identification and preparation. The Bank had pioneered in techniques of project appraisal and could by 1962 add "projects courses" to the EDI's offerings and emphasize, more than it ever had before, the need for sector programs and feasibility studies.

With the establishment of the UNDP, a free source of funds for preinvestment studies became available to the less developed countries. Ironically, the regular technical assistance agencies of the UN were poorly equipped to serve as executing agencies for the UNDP and produce preinvestment surveys replete with cost-benefit data, market information, estimates of capital requirements, rates of return on capital, and other details essential for making investment decisions. The Bank's cooperation was vital in making a success of the UNDP. In the process of collaborating, the Bank significantly strengthened its own position in the hierarchy of international development machinery and lengthened the pipeline of projects suitable for Bank or IDA investment.

Though the Bank considered itself peculiarly well equipped for the micro-level function of assisting in project identification and preparation, it had no false modesty about its ability to assist at the macro level in judging the economic performance of developing countries. It has therefore taken the lead in building a new program of comprehensive economic reports on member countries.

The Bank-furnished technical assistance one tends to talk about is, of course, that which can most readily be isolated for analysis. The bulk of the

Bank's technical assistance, it should not be forgotten, is firmly embedded in its regular loan and credit operations. The Bank began life in the less developed world in the 1940s as a financier of specific projects. The bulk of its technical assistance evolved out of its interest in finding and financing projects that it could regard as technically sound, economically viable, and of high priority for the development of the borrowing country. The Bank's sponsorship of development programming was not the beginning of its technical assistance activity as much as it was a further reflection of its interest in financing "good" projects—by ensuring a better economic-policy setting for, and relationship between, potential investment projects within a less developed country. Its institution-building began early and can best be judged by studying the industrial finance corporations, agricultural credit banks, power authorities, and so forth that were created as concomitants of its investment projects.

In summary, the Bank and IDA have sought to contribute, to almost every lending operation in which they have become engaged, something more than financing. Not all of the "something more" has been technical assistance, but much of it, including a portion of what borrowers may have regarded as administrative harassment, has been technical assistance. The close supervision of lending that characterizes Bank Group operations, the heavy injection of solicited and unsolicited advice, have helped to produce a record remarkably free of corruption. Given the prevalence of corruption in the less developed world as well as elsewhere, the Bank Group's virtually scandal-free record is no mean achievement.

CHAPTER ELEVEN

The Bank Group
and the Private Investor

THE ARTICLES OF AGREEMENT of the International Bank for Reconstruction and Development (IBRD) set as one of the institution's principal objectives the promotion and encouragement of private investment for productive purposes.[1] The relationship with private investors has been fundamental to the Bank, generating the largest part of its financial resources, markedly influencing some of its policies and operations, and inspiring many of its activities, including the creation of its first affiliate, the International Finance Corporation (IFC). The Bank Group has operated through many channels and has used a number of devices in encouraging and promoting private investment. To help bring relevant activities into focus, our discussion is divided into three parts.

The first covers the Bank Group's work in promoting private international capital flows. Here the Bank has insisted that borrowers make reasonable efforts to settle outstanding government debt that is in default, and it has tried to discourage the expropriation of private investment without adequate compensation; it has used its guarantee functions to stimulate foreign private investment and has engaged in parallel financing with private investors; the Bank was instrumental in establishing the International Centre for Settlement of Investment Disputes (ICSID); and it has actively concerned itself with schemes for the international insurance of foreign private investments.

The second focus in this chapter is Bank Group financing of private enterprise. The Bank Group has channeled some 20 percent or more of its total investment into the financing of private enterprise. Approximately nine-

---

1. Article I(ii).

tenths of this has been directed into industry, which, in Bank terminology, includes manufacturing and mining. As we have already pointed out, there are four principal types of Bank Group industrial financing: loans for industrial projects by the Bank or IDA; IFC investments; Bank Group investment in financial intermediaries, such as development banks and development finance companies; and program loans for financing industrial imports.[2] Since industrial project loans and industrial import financing have been discussed earlier in this book, this chapter considers in particular the two remaining channels of industrial financing: IFC investments and Bank Group financing of development finance companies. In recent years there has been a rapid increase in Bank Group financing of private enterprise in agriculture—through agricultural credit institutions, loans for livestock improvement, and other farm activities. Investment in private tourist facilities has also come to the fore.

Third, we deal in this chapter with the Bank Group's efforts to encourage the mobilization of domestic capital. It has offered advice and assistance to member governments on ways and means of raising capital and has participated actively in the initiation and development of local capital markets.

Since nine-tenths of the Bank Group's financing of private enterprise has been directed toward the industrial sector, this chapter concludes with a discussion of some aspects of Bank Group policy toward industrial development.

Promoting Private International Capital Flows

From the beginning and through most of the first quarter century of its existence, the Bank saw itself dealing with only a minor part of total development finance; the major part would have to come from private investors. Consequently the "climate" for foreign private investment became a serious concern. This climate was obviously relevant to both portfolio and private direct investment.

Defaulted Debt and Expropriation

As we noted in Chapter 6, the Bank concluded early that a settlement of government defaulted debt was essential to a resumption of the flow of foreign private portfolio investment, as well as to the sale of its own securities, and made it a condition for receipt of a Bank loan that a reasonable attempt be made to negotiate such a settlement. This problem was confined largely to

2. See Chapters 8 and 9, above.

Latin American members since, in the less developed world, they were virtually the only nations that had been independent long enough to borrow on their own credit.

While the back of the problem was broken by the mid-1950s, the last of the cases that had existed when the Bank was founded were not settled until many years later. One of these was the external government debt of Greece, which was a cause of disagreement between the government and the Bank and was highly publicized in Greece for nearly a decade. The government finally reached an agreement concerning the defaulted U.S. dollar portion of the debt in 1962; an agreement with holders of the defaulted sterling debt was reached in 1964,[3] although it was not implemented until after still further delay. Finally, one of the oldest defaults of all was resolved in 1966. With the help of Luis Machado, the Latin American executive director concerned, a settlement of the external debt of Guatemala finally was arrived at after a bondholder had won a test case in the highest Guatemalan court. The settlement involved payment on bonds originally issued in 1829, nearly a century and a half before.

The Bank's concern for defaulted public debt did not particularly endear the institution to debtor countries, especially those in Latin America. True, the Bank's position had a certain logic: in order to lend, the Bank itself had to borrow in the market; and how could it borrow on behalf of prospective clients who had failed to pay back existing debt?

On the other hand, some of the debt was superannuated, had been issued on unrealistic terms, and was in the hands of speculators rather than investors. Despite the Bank's sincere assurances of its own impartiality, it could not altogether avoid the appearance of being a debt collector for particularly prosperous citizens of rich countries, and Latin American political leaders found it all the easier to attack the institution as an instrument of imperialist North American capitalism. Nor, despite the hopes of the Bank, was the debt settlement followed by a revival of portfolio investment; even in the Bank's own portfolio, the obligations of its Latin American borrowers remained less attractive to international investors than securities issued or guaranteed by European governments.

Nevertheless, the effort was not wasted. The Bank's unflinching rectitude on the question of defaults and expropriations commended the bonds of the Bank itself to the financial community, especially in the United States and Germany, and earned the Bank the warm support of influential financial journalists and commentators in North America and Western Europe.

3. IBRD, Press release (July 16, 1964).

The Bank has followed a parallel policy of not lending to governments that expropriate private property without making arrangements for adequate compensation. As the "Blue Book" states it,

The Bank is charged, under its Articles of Agreement, to encourage international investment. It has, therefore, a direct interest in the creation and maintenance of satisfactory relations between member countries and their external creditors. Accordingly, the normal practice is to inform governments who are involved in such disputes that the Bank or IDA will not assist them unless and until they make appropriate efforts to reach a fair and equitable setlement.[4]

Expropriations without arrangements for adequate compensation (frequently in addition to other considerations) were a bar to Bank/IDA loans that otherwise might have been made in Algeria (after 1964), in Indonesia (during the Sukarno regime), in Iraq (in the mid-1960s), in the United Arab Republic (throughout most of the 1960s), and in the Democratic Republic of the Congo (between 1961 and 1969).[5]

Nationalization of foreign properties in 1970 and 1971, particularly in Latin America, has brought this issue to the fore again in a form that may presage difficulty for the Bank. In 1970 the Bolivian government nationalized the property of the International Metals Processing Company, and in the spring of 1971, the government of Guyana nationalized the Demerara Bauxite Company, a wholly owned subsidiary of the Aluminium Company of Canada. Bank loans and IDA credits to both these countries were pending at the time of expropriation. The executive directors considered that negotiations directed toward equitable settlement were in train and approved the loans. But the U.S. director abstained. The possibility arises that what the Bank considers reasonable efforts to assure equitable treatment may not be so regarded by one or more of the Bank's members. The question of compensation for the expropriated International Petroleum Company in Peru has not yet been settled as of this writing, and a number of cases loom on the horizon in Chile and in other parts of the world. It would be convenient if the Bank Group could avoid confrontation with its member governments, particularly those on whom it is dependent for financial support. This could be done if judgment on equitable compensation could be referred to another international body. This was the thought behind the formation of ICSID. Un-

4. IBRD, *The World Bank, IDA and IFC, Policies and Operations* (June 1969), p. 31.

5. The IFC was to some degree independent in this respect. In April 1962, before the final settlement of the Greek debt, the IFC made an investment in a fertilizer company in Greece, apparently on the principle that the private sector should not be penalized for shortcomings of the government.

fortunately, a number of Bank members, including all its Latin American members, have not seen fit to join the Centre.[6]

Settlement of Investment Disputes

As early as 1947, the Bank suggested that a body of technical experts might be established who would recommend equitable settlements of defaulted debt and declared that it would be "willing and anxious," by providing staff or otherwise, to contribute to the success of such a project.[7] Nothing came of this suggestion, but near the end of President Black's administration, it emerged again in somewhat more elaborate form.

This came about virtually as a matter of self-defense. Requests were being made with increasing frequency for the Bank or its president to mediate disputes between investors and governments. The Bank had attempted such a mediation in 1951, following the expropriation of the Anglo-Iranian Oil Company.[8] The president of the Bank, acting in a personal capacity, in 1958 had assisted in a settlement for the expropriation by the Egyptian government of the Suez Canal Company, in 1959 for that government's expropriation or sequestration of certain properties owned by British nationals, and in 1962 for the resumption of service on certain bonds of the city of Tokyo that were held by international investors.

By 1960, it seemed that a systematic way should be found to deal with requests for such mediation; and the Bank's board of governors authorized a study of the matter in 1962. At this time, a number of ideas for nurturing the courage of private capital were in the air. One that was particularly endorsed by the German banking community was that governments should adopt a code of conduct which would ensure the fair treatment of foreign investors. This proposal was taken up by the Organisation for Economic Co-operation and Development (OECD) but did not lead to the adoption of a multilateral convention. Another, then being discussed in OECD, was for a multilateral system for guaranteeing international investments against nonbusiness risks.

The Bank's solution was more modest than either of these. It created ICSID, to which contending parties could have recourse on an entirely voluntary basis. The executive directors gave final approval in 1965 for the submission to governments of an international convention creating ICSID; on Octo-

6. For further discussion of the Bank's views on nationalization and expropriation of private investment, see Chapter 21.
7. IBRD, *Second Annual Report, 1946–1947*, p. 13.
8. See Chapter 18, below.

ber 14, 1966, it came into being with its office at the headquarters of the World Bank.[9]

The Centre provides facilities for, but does not itself engage in, conciliation and arbitration. This is undertaken by conciliation commissions and arbitral tribunals, whose members are drawn from panels maintained at the Centre. The administrative machinery consists of a secretary-general, who maintains offices at the Bank, and an administrative council, on which each contracting state has one vote. The council is chaired by the president of the Bank. As of June 30, 1971, the convention had been signed by sixty-six states and ratified by sixty-two.

The convention is not concerned with all conflicts of interest between foreign investors and host governments but only with legal disputes arising directly out of an investment. The facilities of ICSID are not available for disputes between individuals, between states, or between a citizen of a state and his own government. The consent of both parties is necessary if a suit is to be submitted, but once it is submitted, the case cannot be withdrawn unilaterally.

The inaugural meeting of the administrative council of the Centre was held February 2, 1967, at which time the general counsel of the Bank, Aron Broches, was elected secretary-general of the new organization. Some members had been named to the panels of conciliators and arbitrators by the time of the first annual report (1966/1967). These panels, however, have had little to do; as of June 30, 1971, no dispute had been brought to the Centre. This does not mean, however, that ICSID has been without effect. As its third annual report notes, "While no cases have been brought to the Centre, the number of instruments—including investment contracts, bilateral investment treaties, and national legislation—containing provisions for the conciliation and arbitration of future disputes pursuant to the Convention on the Settlement of Investment Disputes between States and Nationals of Other States is increasing, and additional States have taken steps to become parties to the Convention."[10] And the fourth annual report says that "a number of interna-

9. See Shirley Boskey and Piero Sella, "Settling Investment Disputes," *Finance and Development*, Vol. 2 (September 1965). The following account in the text parallels closely the above-mentioned article and the introduction to Volume I of the official ICSID history. See also Aron Broches, "Development of International Law by the International Bank for Reconstruction and Development," *Proceedings of the American Society of International Law* (April 1965), p. 33, for an account of the role of the Bank's executive directors and board of governors in drafting and approving the ICSID convention. ICSID, *Rules and Regulations* (January 1, 1968), contains a full account of ICSID procedures. See also the annual reports of ICSID, beginning in 1966/67.

10. 1968/1969, p. 3.

tional investors now routinely include in such instruments provision for the submission of disputes to the Centre."[11]

Latin American member countries have never been willing to adhere to ICSID or, for that matter, to any form of international arbitration, preferring to rely on their own legal machinery for settling disputes between the state and foreign investors. Spokesmen for the Latin American position frequently express the view that the existence of international machinery tends to lessen national concern for effective settlement. This has not been the prevailing view outside Latin America, and most of the less developed countries in Asia and Africa are now members of the convention. While it would be difficult to demonstrate that foreign private investment in Asia and Africa has been encouraged by adherence to the convention, and discouraged in Latin America because those countries failed to adhere, ICSID must be regarded as part of the broad set of institutional arrangements among states that lessen the risks involved in international trade and investment. And the World Bank is primarily responsible for its existence.

Guarantees and Combined Operations

The Articles of Agreement of the IBRD do not mention, let alone distinguish between, developed and developing countries. The Bank has concerned itself with encouraging the flow of private capital to both. According to the Articles, the Bank's principal instrument for this purpose was to have been the guaranteeing of "loans and other investments made by private investors" through the usual investment channels.[12] As was pointed out in Chapter 5, the Bank never engaged in underwriting new issues. But it did use a related device to overcome the qualms of private investors about international investment. It sold, with its guarantee, the obligations received from borrowers in connection with its own loans.

When the Bank loaned $16 million to Belgium in March 1949, arrangements had already been made for the whole loan to be taken up (with the Bank's guarantee) by private investment institutions. The Bank loan did not provide capital. It simply gave the Bank occasion to guarantee the credit of the borrower.

The Bank thereafter continued to sell parts of loans from its portfolio with its guarantee. But the practice dwindled as the Bank itself began to be more active in offering its own bonds to the public, since it was thought that the

11. 1969/1970, p. 3. Furthermore, as was reported in Chapter 4, above, a dispute has now been referred to the Centre.
12. Article I(ii).

market for the Bank's obligations would be confused if securities of too many different kinds bearing the Bank's name were outstanding. The use of the guarantee was ended altogether in 1955.

In the meantime, the Bank had invented a device, short of a guarantee, to support direct borrowing from private investors by member governments. This was to engage in a joint financing with the investment market on behalf of an individual borrower. The first such operation was undertaken in December 1954 on behalf of Belgium, which was seeking funds to improve its internal waterways and the Port of Antwerp. Belgium's total borrowing was $50 million, of which private investors took $30 million at maturities of ten years or less. The Bank took the long end of the transaction. It made Belgium a fifteen-year loan of $20 million, on which repayment did not begin until after the final maturity of the bonds sold to private purchasers.[13]

The Bank's intention was not only to provide funds, but to enhance the attractiveness of the market offering. By providing part of the capital needed, the Bank did indeed lighten the pressures that otherwise would have been exerted on the market; by taking the longer maturities, the Bank made it possible for Belgium to offer shorter and less speculative maturities to private investors; and by making its loan, the Bank certified both the credit of the borrower and the soundness of the purpose for which funds were sought.

Beginning with the Belgian transaction, the Bank engaged in fifteen combined operations with the market. The last occurred in 1960; after that, most of the borrowers who had benefited did not find it necessary any longer to rely on Bank assistance, or indeed to borrow abroad at all. The total of these transactions amounted to $562 million. Private investors accounted for more than half the total, as is shown in Table 11-1.

Investment Insurance

While, for reasons cited in Chapter 5, the Bank early decided not to guarantee the service of loans made by others, the staff nevertheless continued to mull over possible uses of the Bank's guarantee powers. In 1948 an internal memorandum put forward the idea that the Bank should insure private investors against certain types of risk: in the case of investments approved jointly by the Bank and by a cooperating government, the Bank would make good any losses occasioned by the failure of the government to observe pledges against nontransferability of earnings, confiscation, discriminatory

13. IBRD, Press release (Dec. 15, 1954).

Table 11-1. *Joint Operations of the World Bank and the Private Investment Market, 1954–60*
Thousands of U.S. dollars

Year	Country	World Bank loan	Bond or note issue	Total financing
1954	Belgium	20,000	30,000	50,000
1955	Norway	25,000	15,000	40,000
1955	South Africa	25,200	25,000	50,200
1956	Australia (Qantas Airline)	9,230	17,770	27,000
1957	Air India International	5,600	11,200	16,800
1957	Belgium	10,000	30,000	40,000
1957	South Africa	25,000	35,000	60,000
1958	Federation of Rhodesia and Nyasaland	19,000	6,000	25,000
1958	South Africa	25,000	25,000	50,000
1958	Austria	25,000	25,000	50,000
1959	Japan	10,000	30,000	40,000
1959	Denmark	20,000	20,000	40,000
1959	Italy (Cassa per il Mezzogiorno)	20,000	30,000	50,000
1960	Japan Development Bank and Kawasaki Steel Corporation	6,000	4,000	10,000
1960	Japan Development Bank and Sumitomo Metal Industries	7,000	5,800	12,800
Total		252,030	309,770	561,800

Source: IBRD, Treasurer's Department.

government regulations, and the like.[14] This idea made no headway; but later many capital-exporting countries adopted schemes to insure the foreign investments of their nationals against noncommercial risks, including the risks of nationalization without adequate compensation and of inability to repatriate capital or earnings.[15] In the 1950s a number of plans were put forward for international insurance, and some of these suggested the Bank as an appropriate agency for administration. The Bank's initial reaction was adverse. Memoranda from the general counsel of the Bank pointed out a number of technical difficulties, particularly those connected with settling investors' claims and "recourse claims" of the insurance agency against host states, and concluded that a multilateral insurance scheme was "a rather unpromising

14. "Proposed Plan for Guaranteeing Foreign Private Investments against Transfer Risks and Certain Other Risks" (March 3, 1948; processed).
15. This discussion of the Bank's relation to international insurance schemes draws largely on a memorandum by Shirley Boskey, "The Bank and Investment Insurance" (Sept. 29, 1970).

proposal for the Bank to become actively associated with."[16] The Bank was especially concerned about a possibility, naturally appealing to investors who wanted to engage the Bank's interest, that it might find itself using its lending power as a bargaining weapon when embroiled in pressing for the settlement of claims.

The nationalizations in Cuba, the Congo, and Indonesia, however, impressed the Bank with the "political" risks confronting foreign investors, and, urged by the Development Assistance Group of OEEC, it decided in the spring of 1961 to undertake a study "without preconceptions" of the usefulness of the various proposals that had been put forward. This study was submitted in 1962 to the Development Assistance Committee (DAC), successor to the OEEC Group. Although the pros and cons were discussed, the study reached no positive conclusions and did not mention the possibility of the Bank as the executive agency. In 1964, the first United Nations Conference on Trade and Development (UNCTAD) invited the Bank to pursue its studies in consultation with both the less and the more developed countries. The Bank promised to do so as soon as it had heard from OECD. That organization finally responded in June 1965 with a report in the form of articles of agreement for a proposed International Investment Guarantee Corporation, to be affiliated in some way with the Bank.

The Bank then decided to proceed with its study, and the executive directors, sitting as a committee of the whole, discussed the principal issues involved in a multilateral scheme, using the OECD outline as a point of departure. In the light of these discussions, the staff in November 1966 prepared draft articles of agreement for an International Investment Insurance Agency.

Despite the existence of a number of national schemes, there appeared to be a function for an international agency in providing coverage for (a) investments originating in a country that lacked a national scheme or to be made in a country to which a national scheme did not extend; (b) investments made by international consortia; and (c) some forms of investments and some types of risks that were not covered by a particular national scheme. There remained also the possibility of reinsuring with the multilateral scheme risks that were covered under a national scheme. In September 1969, the Pearson Commission strongly recommended that an international insurance scheme be affiliated with the Bank.[17]

As of June 30, 1971, all the principal capital-exporting countries except Germany favored some such scheme, although with varying degrees of fervor.

16. Aron Broches, Memoranda of April 14 and April 26, 1961.
17. *Partners in Development: Report of the Commission on International Development,* Lester B. Pearson, chairman (Praeger, 1969), p. 109.

It appeared that if an international insurance plan were to come into being, it would have some relationship with the Bank, but not one that would involve the Bank in the settlement of disputes that might arise. But there were still a number of issues to be resolved, the most critical being those concerning the sharing of losses and of the administrative expenses of the administering agency. Under the original OECD proposal, countries in which investments were made would not be expected to share losses, but they would be expected to contribute to administrative expenses. Since executive directors from less developed countries appeared to indicate an unwillingness to share either losses or administrative expenses, both the Bank's first draft of articles of agreement and a second one in 1968 assumed that *no* financial contribution would be made by the developing countries.

When the executive directors were reassembled in March 1970 as a committee of the whole, however, a number of directors from capital-exporting countries indicated that their governments considered it important that the developing countries share *both* administrative expenses and losses from the scheme; and at least one developed country made it clear that its participation was contingent on such an arrangement.

Bank Group Financing of Private Industrial Enterprise

Since industrial project and program lending have been treated elsewhere, we limit ourselves here to a discussion of the IFC and of Bank Group financing of development finance companies.

Formation of the International Finance Corporation

Although the first suggestions for an IFC date back to 1948, the corporation did not come into being until 1956. This long gestation period gave evidence of hesitation, and in some cases hostility, among officials and private groups whose cooperation was necessary. Governments of industrialized countries for a time did not see clearly a need for the corporation. The private financial community, particularly in the United States, thought it might intrude on private business. Both sides were a little uncertain about the ambivalent character of the proposed institution, which was to invest public funds in the private sector. When the IFC finally was created, it was considerably weaker than its inventors had intended. Not until 1970 did it finally begin to operate with the resources and the powers originally envisaged.

The idea for an IFC was born out of interaction between ideas circulating among the staff of the Bank and in the U.S. government in the late 1940s. In the spring of 1948, the members and staff of the U.S. National Advisory Council on International Monetary and Financial Problems (NAC) were considering whether the administration should ask the Congress to add $500 million to the lending authority of the Export-Import Bank. Eugene Black, then U.S. executive director of the World Bank, vigorously opposed the idea and stated his opposition in a letter to U.S. Treasury Secretary John Snyder, chairman of the NAC. Not only did the Eximbank have plenty of lending authority left, but to extend it further would be to prejudice, perhaps fatally, the prospects of the World Bank in the field of development lending. There were other things the Eximbank might do. Specifically Black suggested that a subsidiary be created "to do equity financing in Latin America."

In January of the following year President Truman announced his Point Four program of technical assistance, which started speculation in the staff of the World Bank about the new program's implications for development lending. A memorandum was prepared for President McCloy by Richard Demuth suggesting that although Point Four would begin with technical assistance, this might well be followed by transfers of capital. In that event, the memorandum said, a new "international development corporation," established as a subsidiary of the World Bank, "would probably be the best mechanism of productive investment of the funds provided."[18]

Both Black's proposal and the idea presented to McCloy were considered within the U.S. government. Neither was adopted, for the time being, despite the best efforts of McCloy to win support for the new Bank subsidiary. To tell the truth, there was even some opposition among the Bank staff. The Bank itself was not fully seasoned, and it was thought dangerous to embark on a new experiment in a difficult field. But Black, when he succeeded McCloy as president of the Bank in the summer of 1949, continued to be interested. And Garner, the vice president of the Bank and a fervent advocate of private enterprise, was enthusiastic. If honors are to be awarded to the prime movers of the IFC, the laurels should appropriately be shared by Garner and his assistant, Demuth.

The future IFC received an assist in 1950 from President Truman's Advisory Board on International Development. The President asked the chairman of the board, Nelson Rockefeller, to consider specifically what might be done in underdeveloped countries and to recommend "desirable plans to accomplish with maximum dispatch and effectiveness the broad objectives and

18. Memorandum to McCloy from Demuth, "The International Bank and 'Point IV'" (March 1, 1949).

policies of the Point Four program" for international economic develop-ment.[19] To Rockefeller and his staff, who were looking for concrete sugges-tions, the idea of an international development corporation was an attractive one. The group's report, published in March 1951, recommended that the United States take the initiative in creating an international finance corpora-tion, as an affiliate of the International Bank, with authority to make loans in local and foreign currencies to private enterprise without the requirement of government guarantees and also to participate with private investors in making nonvoting equity investments in local currencies. The authorized capital suggested was $400 million, of which one-third would be paid in initially, and the remaining two-thirds would be subject to call.[20]

The idea also met with favor in certain quarters in the United Nations. In May 1951 a group of experts appointed by UN Secretary-General Trygve Lie commended the Rockefeller proposal for study. After the Bank suggested subtly that it would not be averse to undertaking the study itself, it was asked by the Economic and Social Council to do so.

Lodging in the United Nations the question of creating the IFC proved to be, in at least two respects, a crucial factor in bringing the corporation into being. The habitual reluctance of ECOSOC and the General Assembly to kill off any initiative that even remotely promised an advantage to the majority of the UN membership kept the proposal active; and during this period ECOSOC generated schemes for financing economic development, such as the United Nations Economic Development Administration (UNEDA) and the Special United Nations Fund for Economic Development (SUNFED), which were so repugnant to conservative secretaries of the U.S. Treasury that, by comparison, the notion of an IFC came in time to seem to them positively attractive.

This approval, however, was a long time in coming, and in the meantime it became clear that there was some U.S. opposition to the IFC outside the U.S. government. A sketch of the proposed organization, prepared in the Bank,[21] was discussed by Bank representatives in banking circles in Western Europe and the United States. In general, the reaction in Europe was favor-able. But in the United States, although opinion in certain quarters was favor-able, in others serious questions were raised. It was argued that it was wrong in principle to use government funds to acquire shares of ownership in private enterprises; that the investments of the corporation would be riskier than was

19. *Partners in Progress: a Report to the President by the International Develop-ment Advisory Board* (March 1951), pp. 89–90.
20. *Ibid.*, pp. 84–85.
21. Internal staff memorandum (Oct. 15, 1951).

suitable for funds raised from taxpayers; that the World Bank itself was not yet sufficiently experienced in its own business to take on another line of activity; and that it would be difficult to find, let alone keep, the kind of staff required, since their skills could find greater rewards elsewhere.

The proposal met with opposition even in the Bank. The first discussion of the idea in a meeting of the executive directors, early in January 1952, failed to reveal any enthusiasm for the idea. A European director commonly recognized as the intellectual leader of the board questioned the need. The U.S. director remained silent. A director representing several Latin American countries—later to be in the vanguard of support for the IFC—remarked that among Latin American entrepreneurs, foreign capital was not considered to be in short supply in the private sector.

Despite these objections and lack of enthusiasm in certain quarters, President Black transmitted a staff report to the secretary-general of the United Nations at the end of 1952 and, for information, to the member governments of the Bank. The report concluded that, taken all together, existing institutions did not "adequately meet the need for stimulating private international investment." The IFC might fill the gap in a number of ways. First, it would provide funds "to enable private investors, both domestic and foreign, to undertake promising projects which are now held back by lack of adequate capital." Second, it could bring promising opportunities to the attention of foreign investors; and third, by its own participation it could encourage the participation of others who might be held back by lack of confidence. In addition, the spreading activities and growing experience of the corporation would enable it to play a useful role in settling differences between governments and investors and would equip it to give helpful advice on the development of local capital markets.[22]

Truman's advisory board, chaired by Nelson Rockefeller, had recommended a capital of $400 million and had suggested that the finance corporation might open for business with a paid-in capital of $135 million. The Bank report expressed the view that, as countries joined, operations might begin before that sum had been reached.

The Bank staff report was discussed by the Economic and Social Council in June 1952. Delegations from less developed countries lined up behind the IFC almost unanimously. But the U.S. delegate turned a cold shoulder. The IFC, he said, might simply finance ventures that otherwise would be financed by existing institutions, without adding to the total amount of finance avail-

22. IBRD, "Report on the Proposal for an International Finance Corporation" (April 29, 1952).

able.[23] In the end, the council simply noted that the Bank was continuing its study and asked for further progress reports.

The Bank's 1954 report went to a United Nations that was increasingly dissatisfied with existing institutions for the financing of economic development. The SUNFED proposal had already been formulated, and both it and the 1954 IFC status report were on the ECOSOC agenda; both proposals were strongly supported by representatives of the less developed world. Luis Machado, then governor representing Cuba, strongly supported the IFC in a speech at the annual meeting of the governors of the Bank and Fund in September 1954.[24] Although U.S. spokesmen at the United Nations held their ground against both ideas, the pressure on the U.S. delegation was heavy and was felt as far away as Washington.

In the end, the U.S. government capitulated, taking up the least costly of the proposals it was being importuned to accept. The Bank was invited to submit more information about its ideas for an IFC, and after it had done so, an understanding was reached in meetings between the Bank's president, vice president, and general counsel, on the one hand, and Treasury Secretary George Humphrey and Under Secretary Randolph Burgess, on the other. On November 11, a few days before a conference at Rio de Janeiro was to begin, Secretary Humphrey, in his capacity as chairman of the NAC, announced that the administration would ask congressional approval for U.S. participation in the corporation.

The Bank, however, paid a substantial price for this victory. In the second status report, the staff itself had suggested that the IFC might begin its operations with as little as $100 million; and according to Mr. Humphrey's announcement, this was the level at which the corporation was to be capitalized (rather than the $400 million level recommended by the Rockefeller group). The secretary also pronounced firmly against any equity financing by the IFC. The effect of either of these concessions on the operations of the IFC would have been serious; the two combined were deeply to prejudice the corporation's chance of success.

Yet it was within the framework of these limitations that the Bank's board of directors set about the task of preparing articles of agreement for the IFC. These articles envisaged an institution with an authorized capital stock of

23. B. E. Matecki, *Establishment of the International Finance Corporation and United States Policy* (Praeger, 1957), p. 106.

24. Machado has been connected with the Bank since its beginning. He was present at both Bretton Woods and Savannah, was one of the first group of directors elected to the Bank, and with the exception of a four-year period, continued as a director until 1971.

$100 million, fully paid in and entirely in U.S. dollars; with membership open to any member of the IBRD; intended to finance new or expanding private enterprises, but not necessarily precluded from investing in enterprises in which governments held an interest; prohibited from investing in capital stock; able to lend without government guarantee; and charged with revolving its funds "by selling its investments to private investors whenever it can appropriately do so on satisfactory terms."[25]

The Articles of Agreement had decreed that a minimum of thirty countries, with capital subscriptions totaling at least $75 million, would need to accept membership to bring the corporation into being. This requirement was met on July 20, 1956, when thirty-one countries had taken up membership with a capital contribution of $78,366,000. The inaugural meeting of the board of directors was held on July 24, with Robert L. Garner, who had served as vice president of the Bank, in the chair as president of the new IFC. By the time of the second meeting of the board of governors of the corporation, held in conjunction with the annual meeting of the governors of the World Bank in September 1957, there were fifty-one members, whose capital subscriptions totaled $92 million.

Mr. Garner's appointment as president of the new institution felicitously served two purposes. It brought to this post a man whose devotion to private enterprise no one could doubt. And it removed from the management of the Bank an officer whose strength manifestly did not lie in the conduct of negotiations with member governments, particularly with less developed member governments.

The International Finance Corporation in Operation

The IFC opened its doors in 1956 heavily handicapped. The authorized capital, instead of being the $400 million or $500 million contemplated by its promoters, was a meager $100 million. And the corporation was denied the right to make equity investments. There were, moreover, other difficulties that combined to make the first five years of IFC operations extremely frustrating. Some were inherent in the Articles of Agreement, and others were the product of managerial decisions.

The Articles specify that the IFC is to invest in private projects, and only

25. Articles of Agreement of the International Finance Corporation, July 20, 1956 (Article III, section 3[vi]).

The purpose of the Corporation [as set out in Article I] is to further economic development by encouraging the growth of productive private enterprise in member countries, particularly in the less developed areas, thus supplementing the activities of the International Bank for Reconstruction and Development.

"in cases where sufficient private capital is not available on reasonable terms."[26] This meant that the IFC had a quite difficult assignment to begin with: it had to deal with private projects which were not sufficiently attractive to obtain all the private capital needed, but which nevertheless had some prospect of being "productive." The position was like that of the farm hand thanking the farmer for the bottle of whiskey he had been given: "If it had been any better, you wouldn't have given it to me, and if it had been worse, I couldn't have drunk it."

The situation with respect to the availability of private investment, moreover, had changed substantially between the time when the IFC was first conceived and the time when it finally got into operation. An investment corporation with U.S. dollars to offer was a glittering idea in 1949; it was less so after the arrival of convertibility of European currencies. The availability of capital, moreover, had markedly increased, and by 1956, for example, entrepreneurs in the sterling area had little difficulty in finding financing in London for promising ventures.

To this situation the IFC itself added other difficulties. It could have been regarded as a pilot operation, to be enlarged if and when its usefulness had been demonstrated. Instead Garner preferred to treat the initial $100 million capital as all that would ever be available. A $10 million investment was considered to be out of the question since this would have required committing 10 percent of the total of IFC capital. Early in the history of the corporation, therefore, a limit of $2 million was set on individual IFC investments.

The IFC, in short, had to find investment projects that were marginal to begin with, that were relatively small (and perhaps more likely to have deficiencies of management and other capabilities), that could survive the rigors of the IFC's careful technical examination, and that would emerge (because of the ban on equity investment by the corporation) in forms that were often unfamiliar in less developed countries. There was always a danger that the IFC would be approached to finance only the weakest ventures that had absolutely no other alternative; and this served to increase the management's obsession with technical investigations, security, and the highest possible returns. As a result, the IFC soon became known far and wide as a difficult and demanding investment partner; and this made it still harder to find business.

These problems were discussed within the IFC with increasing intensity. By 1960 it was being argued with great persuasiveness that the corporation had no future unless it could change its policies in important respects; and it

26. Article I(i).

was apparent that without such changes a number of senior officers would leave. Under this pressure, two major issues were resolved. In February 1961 it was announced that an amendment to the Articles would be sought in order to remove the ban on equity investment; and in 1961, in the last months of Mr. Garner's administration, the IFC began consistently to break through the $2 million limitation on individual commitments.

This eased the corporation's difficulties but still left the fundamental problem that the IFC in the nature of things would be dealing with proposals that, on their merits, were marginal. When, in October 1961, Martin Rosen succeeded Mr. Garner as chief executive officer of the IFC (with the title of executive vice president), he largely escaped from this limitation by adopting the concept that the corporation was a "special situations bank." Mere lack of private capital was no longer an indispensable prerequisite for IFC participation in the financing of a project. Other considerations might also apply, such as the need for the IFC's expertise in negotiating with the governments of particular host countries or the desirability of IFC participation as a shield against possible government intervention. During the Rosen regime many investments were justified on these and similar nonfinancial grounds.

As may be seen from Table 11-2, during the five-year period of Garner's presidency (1956–61) the IFC made forty-five investment commitments involving planned outlays of $58 million. In the next five years investments averaged about $20 million a year, not a very large figure for a World Bank affiliate. This rate approximately doubled in the years 1966–68 and doubled again after McNamara became president in 1968.

The authority to undertake equity financing plus the transfer to the IFC in 1962 of the responsibility for development finance companies (DFCs) concentrated attention in the IFC on the organizing and financing of these companies. Between 1962 and 1966, the IFC made a series of equity investments in DFCs and accepted invitations to be represented on the boards of ten of the companies. At the time, it was thought that the development finance companies would constitute a kind of intelligence and referral network for the IFC, bringing in business that would be too expensive and time-consuming for the corporation to recruit for itself. There were indeed a number of cases in which the IFC joined with a DFC in joint financing of investments. But on the whole, the IFC failed to encourage cooperation, and the DFCs turned out to be competitors of the corporation, taking the business for themselves instead of referring it to the IFC.

Although development finance companies were a fruitful field for equity investment by the corporation, its major financing was directed toward basic manufacturing industry. As Table 11-3 indicates, mining and public utilities were also areas of IFC concern, and in 1966, with its financing of the Kenya Hotel Properties, it made its first investment in tourism.

IFC investment in an enterprise typically includes both equity and debt financing. The corporation, however, avoids being the largest shareholder in an enterprise, generally limiting itself to less than 25 percent of the total equity. It is forbidden by its charter from assuming any management responsibility. The flexibility of the IFC's investment capabilities was of considerable advantage in helping to put together new enterprises, which was Vice President Rosen's particular forte. "IFC funds are available for local currency expenditures and for foreign exchange costs of projects: they may be used to meet working capital requirements as well as to purchase fixed assets. The actual terms of an investment can be tailored closely to the needs of an available situation: for example, in a mixed loan and equity investment, part of the loan interest due IFC may be made payable in the form of shares."[27] The flexibility of IFC lending also facilitated sales from portfolio. A combination of loan and equity tends to be more salable than either is by itself. This also had a bearing on the resources and profitability of the IFC; the more it could sell, the more resources it had, and the more quickly it could realize profits. Consequently the corporation devoted a great deal of time to the questions of participations and sales. Therefore, although the volume of investment during the Rosen period (1961–69) was not large, the IFC's impact on the promotion and financing of new enterprises was greater than the data might suggest.

The Articles of Agreement of the IFC adjure the corporation to make a profit and to promote economic development. Otherwise they say nothing about investment criteria. Article III, section 3(v), directs the IFC to invest its funds on "terms and conditions normally obtained by private investors for similar financing." And paragraph (vi) of the same section states that "the Corporation shall seek to revolve its funds by selling its investments to private investors whenever it can appropriately do so on satisfactory terms." Obviously the salability of the corporation's investments will depend primarily on their profitability. On the other hand, Article I states that, "the Corporation shall: (1) in association with private investors, assist in financing the establishment, improvement and expansion of productive private enterprises which would contribute to the development of its member countries. . . ."

It is doubtful whether the founders of the IFC were deeply concerned with the possibility of conflict between high profitability and significant contribution to development. This possibility, however, has come to the fore in recent

27. International Finance Corporation, *Annual Report, 1965–66,* p. 9.

Table 11-2. *Commitments and Disbursements of the International Finance Corporation, Fiscal Years 1957–71*
Amounts in U.S. dollars

Fiscal year	Number of commitments, including supplemental commitments	Operational investments	Standby and underwriting commitments	Total commitments	Disbursements
1957	1	2,000,000	...	2,000,000	...
1958	8	8,710,000	...	8,710,000	3,317,000
1959	14	10,565,000	...	10,565,000	6,560,000
1960	14	23,747,000	...	23,747,000	12,825,273
1961	10	6,159,000	...	6,159,000	10,378,563
1962	10	18,397,420	2,942,500	21,339,920	11,876,176
1963	12	12,939,005	5,111,357	18,050,362	15,914,726
1964	18	18,251,441	2,549,708	20,801,149	15,584,141
1965	16	19,689,811	5,952,779	25,642,590	16,262,799
1966	21	26,848,349	8,497,973	35,346,322	21,841,002
1967	14	49,014,779	8,501	49,023,280	25,423,655
1968	16	41,400,133	9,020,000	50,420,133	33,086,915
1969	27	87,779,133	5,086,383	92,865,516	33,404,670
1970	29	107,951,394	3,896,648	111,848,042	85,270,482
1971	24	94,282,984	7,013,423	101,296,407	72,002,525
Gross commitments, net of exchange adjustments	234	527,735,449	50,079,272	577,814,721	
Cancellations and terminations		33,495,286	234,321	33,729,607	
Net commitments and disbursements		494,240,163	49,844,951	544,085,114	363,747,927

Source: IBRD, Treasurer's Department.

Table 11-3. *Commitments of the International Finance Corporation Classified by Purpose, to June 30, 1971*
Expressed in U.S. dollars

Purpose	Amount		
Development finance companies			53,174,705
Money and capital market institutions			702,702
Industry			
Manufacturing			
Cement and other construction materials	71,518,521		
Pulp and paper products	69,780,290		
Textiles and fibers	60,044,510		
Fertilizer	56,597,249		
Iron and steel	54,618,502		
Chemicals and petrochemical products	35,751,916		
Machinery	34,449,345		
Food and food processing	24,160,978		
Other manufacturing	36,498,845		
Subtotal		443,420,156	
Nonmanufacturing			
Mining	36,744,015		
Utilities and printing and publishing	23,500,000		
Tourism	20,273,143		
Subtotal		80,517,158	523,937,314
Total, all purposes			577,814,721

Source: IBRD, Treasurer's Department.

years in connection with the industrial financing undertaken both by the IFC and by Bank Group–financed industrial development companies. We shall have an occasion to discuss this conflict presently. The Pearson Commission, after surveying IFC activities, concluded that, "In practice profitability has been the principal investment criterion. This is clearly a necessary criterion for any agency which would stimulate the growth of the private sector, but it is not a sufficient criterion for an agency purporting to be concerned with economic development."[28] If the pursuit of development criteria means taking account of differences between the market and equilibrium prices of in-

28. *Partners in Development*, pp. 114–15. The report comments on IFC investment practice as follows: "Many of the projects in which it has participated have certainly benefited the host country, but others have contributed only marginally, if at all, to economic development. In particular, they have often been in sectors subsidized by very high effective tariff protection. In very few cases are investments preceded by an analysis of their impact on the economy as a whole" (p. 114). The report, however, supplies no particulars.

puts and outputs, it is true that, until 1969 at least, this did not enter seriously into IFC calculations. However, it is not quite fair to say that the corporation ignored all other considerations save profitability. In general it eschewed investment in enterprises whose profits depended on an exorbitant degree of protection even though it was guided by no very sophisticated analysis of the development process. Its investment behavior was inevitably influenced by the development policies of the countries in which it invested, and it has been disinclined, at least until recently, to question the validity of these policies.

The IFC has benefited in at least two important respects from its association with the World Bank Group. It has had available to it the country economic studies and the country expertise of the large and experienced Bank staff. And since it was free of taxes and dividend obligations, it has been able to spend much more time and effort on particular investment prospects than would have been possible for a private investment bank. On the other hand, it has received much less benefit than would have been possible from a more cooperative association. Very few projects have been suggested to the IFC by a Bank mission. And in general, the staff of the Bank and IDA are uninterested in the activities of the IFC. Projects come to the attention of the corporation either through the central office in Washington or through the activities of staff members on temporary assignment overseas. The IFC has never had more than one staff member permanently assigned abroad, an officer representing the corporation in Europe. It seems probable that if the investment targets announced in 1969 and 1970 are to be met, the IFC will have to station permanent staff members in at least some of the overseas areas of potential investment.

As we have indicated, the future of the IFC in the early 1960s looked busy. The corporation had been given the authority to invest in equities and had broken through the $2 million investment limits. The development finance function of the Bank had been transferred to the IFC in 1962. In 1965 President Woods transferred the industrial projects division of the Technical Operations Department of the Bank to the IFC. He was at that time very interested in the promotion and financing of fertilizer enterprises in India and elsewhere, bringing foreign capital and expertise together with local entrepreneurship. Rosen was the only individual in the Bank Group whom Woods believed capable of putting together deals of this kind. In the end these projects did not materialize on the scale hoped for, but in any case the IFC was now in charge of work on industrial projects. With this responsibility and with development finance companies under its wing, the IFC was able to say in its *Tenth Annual Report (1965–66)*, "Within the World Bank Group—the

Bank, the International Development Association and IFC itself—the Corporation's status has changed: it has become the main instrument for dealing with private enterprise, regardless of which member of the Group is to provide the financing."[29]

Although the investment rate of the IFC increased steadily during the Rosen administration, it remained on a relatively small scale. The evidence suggests that this scale of operations suited Rosen's style and interests. Testimony is unanimous that he was a first-rate investment promoter and highly skilled in putting together workable combinations of foreign and domestic capital, expertise, and entrepreneurship. It is also unanimously agreed that he wanted to keep all important decisions in his own hands. This would have been impossible with a large-scale IFC. Rosen accepted without enthusiasm the Bank line of credit that was extended to the IFC in 1966, and it became for him an important objective not to use it, partly because he feared that to use it would subject the corporation to an increasing degree of Bank control.[30] This position led him to put extra emphasis on inviting other investors into IFC ventures and on selling participations in enterprises that were already launched.

The rapid growth of Bank lending to development finance companies had raised doubts by 1968 as to whether this activity could any longer be seen as appropriate for the IFC. Furthermore, Bank policy was changed in June 1968 to permit lending to publicly controlled finance companies, which diluted to some extent the justification of private enterprise affiliation with the IFC. In 1969 President McNamara transferred these activities to the Bank. In the same year the industrial projects work, which had been transferred to the IFC in 1965, was returned to the Bank for reasons to be considered below. The IFC was left with the financing of the type of enterprises in the private sector it had originally been organized to undertake.

Martin Rosen resigned as executive vice president of the IFC in October 1969, and his place was taken by William S. Gaud, former head of the U.S. Agency for International Development. Gaud came into office determined to increase substantially the rate of investment of the IFC and to make it a development institution in fact as well as in principle. These objectives have been strongly supported by President McNamara. It is too early to try to

29. P. 7.

30. Additional resources for the IFC could have been provided by capital contributions from members or by sale of the corporation's own securities, which was authorized by the Articles of Agreement. But it was feared that a request for capital contributions would endanger IDA subscriptions and that attempts to sell IFC securities might interfere with the Bank's own marketing operations. Consequently the Bank chose the course of lending to the IFC.

assess the results of these efforts, but something can be said here about changes contemplated in types of investment, and more will be said later about planned changes in investment criteria.[31]

Some of the modifications sought by the new administration of the IFC are emphasized in the corporation's statement of general policies, published in January 1970. It is proposed to continue the lower limit of $1 million on investments, with $20 million to be considered ordinarily as the upper limit. Less insistence is to be placed on shaping investments with resale as the objective. This implies some relaxation of corporation policy with respect to straight loans. The IFC should consider lending to regional development finance companies, such as the Atlantic Community Development Group for Latin America (ADELA) and the Private Investment Company for Asia (PICA), provided they follow policies generally consistent with those of the IFC. In June 1970 the IFC made a $10 million loan to ADELA. There is no intention, however, of converting the IFC into a lending institution. Its primary purpose is still to be the mobilization of capital for new enterprises and the expansion of existing ones. The 1970 statement of general policies heavily stresses identifying and promoting projects; assisting the development of capital markets; and giving counsel to developing countries on measures likely to create a climate conducive to the growth of private investment. These tasks are unlikely to be performed effectively unless permanent representation abroad is established, and this appears to be the intention of the new administration. The older IFC was sometimes characterized by Rosen as a "special situations investment bank." This term is not favorably regarded by the new executive vice president. In his view it is and must be a development institution, or it is nothing.

IFC investments exceeded $100 million for the first time in fiscal 1970, and a target of $150 million in 1973 has been set. Investments in fiscal 1971, however, fell short of the 1970 total, and there is some doubt whether the 1973 target can be attained. The fact is that IFC is now operating in a different environment than existed in the mid-1950s. Development finance companies have proliferated in most of the less developed world and, financed by low-cost money from the Bank Group and other sources, compete directly with the IFC. Regional finance companies, such as ADELA, have come into the field. And in a number of countries private enterprises, in some of which the IFC is interested, have been taken over by governments. There is prob-

31. International Finance Corporation, *General Policies* (January 1970). Gaud also revealed some of his thinking in an interview published in *Finance and Development* Vol. 7 (March 1970). Before assuming office he had been asked by McNamara to undertake a survey of the operations of the Bank in the field of industry.

ably still plenty of room for the IFC to maneuver but only if it seeks business more aggressively than it has in the past.

It needs to be said finally that the climate for foreign private investment has chilled appreciably in a number of countries in which the IFC has traditionally been interested. In others, although investment in new manufacturing areas is encouraged, particularly if it brings with it needed technical knowledge and expertise, investment and company formation in industries already cultivated by local entrepreneurial talent are not particularly welcome. If the IFC is to fulfill its development function, it will have to adapt to this situation. There is still a large and important role to be played in helping to organize the transfer of technology through participation in company promotion and investment, and the IFC is well equipped to undertake this task.

The Bank Group and Development Finance Companies

Prior to the formation of the IFC, Bank financing of relatively small-scale private enterprise was undertaken through loans to commercial and investment banks and development finance companies. The relatively small foreign exchange requirements of each enterprise and its distance from Washington argued for the use of financial intermediaries. As required by the IBRD's charter, the loans to intermediaries were guaranteed by governments, and the finance companies channeled the funds to the enterprises to be financed. In 1949 a loan of $15 million was made to the Herstelbank of the Netherlands, the proceeds of which were made available to twenty-four Dutch corporations in a number of industries for the importation of equipment. In 1949, $12.5 million was lent to the Bank of Finland, $10 million of which was earmarked for woodworking industries. In 1950, $10 million was loaned to a consortium of eight Mexican banks and the Nacional Financiera.[32]

The Bank soon discovered, however, that, apart from well established investment banks in the developed countries, institutions prepared to undertake long- and medium-term financing of private enterprise were lacking. If

---

32. This loan expired June 30, 1952, with only $556,000 having been disbursed. The disappointing results of this experiment can be traced to several causes. First, the line of credit became effective at a time when the foreign-exchange holdings in Mexico were increasing rapidly, and the Mexican banks did not feel the need for this credit; private capital from abroad became more readily available, and the Bank's line of credit became correspondingly less attractive. Second, the requirements of Mexican law regarding loans for private industry are both strict and complex, and have made the practical operation of the line of credit difficult. Third, potential borrowers under the line of credit were reluctant to assume any part of the foreign-exchange risk involved.
IBRD, *Seventh Annual Report, 1951–1952*, pp. 32–33.

360 THE WORLD BANK SINCE BRETTON WOODS

this kind of lending were to be undertaken in most of the less developed world, the IBRD would have to participate in bringing such institutions into being. The first operation of this sort consisted of a $2 million loan in 1950 for the new, government-controlled Development Bank of Ethiopia. This was the first and, until 1970, the last loan the Bank made to a government-controlled development bank. Also in 1950, the IBRD made a loan of $9 million to the newly created Industrial Development Bank of Turkey. This bank was established with technical assistance from the World Bank, as was noted in Chapter 6, above, and the arrangements worked out in this instance served to a considerable extent as a pattern for future involvement in development finance companies. The authorized capital of Turkish lira (TL) 12,500,000 (about $4.5 million) was subscribed by some eighteen private institutions, and the Turkish government provided a low-interest loan of the same amount. The debt–equity ratio of the new institution was then three to one, a ratio favored for such companies by the IBRD. The Turkish venture was followed by Bank participation in the formation of the Industrial Credit and Investment Corporation of India (ICICI), to which a loan of $10 million was made in 1955, and by Bank participation in forming the Pakistan Industrial Credit and Investment Corporation (PICIC) in 1957, accompanied by a loan of $4.2 million. Still, in the period before fiscal year 1960, despite its interest in financing private enterprise, the Bank had made only six relatively small loans to development finance companies.

This situation changed rapidly beginning in the early 1960s, and the Bank was soon joined in this financing by the IFC and, in a few instances, by IDA. Altogether the Bank Group, as of June 30, 1971, had loaned to and invested in development finance companies nearly $1.4 billion, which constitutes just under 50 percent of total Bank Group industrial financing, including IDA industrial import credits. (See Table 11-4.)

Before 1962 most of the Bank's promotional work on development finance companies (DFCs) had been carried out by special consultants.[33] The appraisal of such companies in preparation for loans and credits was done by the staff of the Industry Division of the Technical Operations Department. No one in that division devoted full time to DFCs, though two or three had specialized in the area.[34] In January 1962, the work was transferred to a Development Finance Company Division of the IFC, and the staff was put on a full-time basis. The sizable Bank lending program in this field dates from

33. George D. Woods, later president of the Bank, was the chief consultant in the organization of ICICI, PICIC, and the Private Development Corporation of the Philippines.
34. William Diamond, "The Work of the Development Finance Companies Department," IBRD memorandum (July 26, 1968).

Table 11-4. *Bank Group Assistance to Development Finance Companies,*
Fiscal Years 1951–71
Millions of U.S. dollars

| Fiscal | | | IFC | |
year	Bank	IDA	Shares	Loans
1951	7.0			
1952	...			
1953	...			
1954	9.0			
1955	10.0			
1956	...			
1957	...			
1958	13.5			
1959	...			
1960	34.2			
1961	35.0			
1962	27.0	5.0	4.00	
1963	80.0	5.0	2.47	
1964	17.5	...	5.51	
1965	79.0	15.0	0.05	
1966	100.0	...	1.52	
1967	50.0	...	0.34	
1968	159.0	...	0.70	7.5
1969	193.0	...	3.02	8.0
1970	191.0	25.0	3.49	12.0
1971	253.0	...	1.49	5.0
Total	1,258.2	50.0	22.59	32.5

Source: IBRD, Controller's Department.

this period. The first head of the division was Abdel Galeel El Emary, but after a few months he transferred to the World Bank staff, and his place was taken by William Diamond, the Bank's principal authority on development finance companies and the director of work in this area since his appointment.[35] In 1968 a separate Department of Development Finance Companies

35. The IBRD has become an authority on development finance companies as well as a principal lender to and investor in these institutions. Three books and a substantial number of articles on development finance companies have been contributed by Bank officials. The books, all published by the Johns Hopkins Press, are: William Diamond, *Development Banks* (Economic Development Institute, IBRD, 1957); Shirley Boskey, *Problems and Practices of Development Banks* (IBRD, 1959); and William Diamond (ed.), *Development Finance Companies: Aspects of Policy and Operations* (IBRD, 1968). The latter volume consists of essays written by IFC officials after a conference in 1965, to which officials of the twenty-one DFCs that had received Bank loans at that time were invited.

was established in the Bank, largely because Bank and IDA financing had come to dwarf the equity investments of the IFC in these companies.

The development finance companies in which the Bank Group has invested have certain characteristics distinguishing them from most of the development banks that were in existence in less developed countries before the IBRD began operating in the field. The development banks, which were created in considerable numbers in the 1920s and 1930s, were mainly government-controlled banks established to undertake public investment. The corporate form was a matter of government organization representing an alternative to operating through a government department. The DFCs in which the Bank Group was interested were all established to promote the expansion of private enterprise. Until 1970, they (with one exception) were all set up as shareholder-owned-and-controlled companies. As Diamond puts it, "these two facts imposed on each of the institutions the necessity of operating on the basis of financial, economic and technical criteria rather than on the basis of political criteria." They all had "the task of resisting governmental pressure, yet being sufficiently responsive to governmental policy to justify the official financial support without which most companies would not have the resources to do the job."[36] The two objectives of operating as a private development bank while responding adequately to government interests and pressures usually involved a delicate balancing act, the results of which we shall consider presently.

An appraisal of the contribution of DFCs to economic development, and of the Bank's role in promoting this contribution, needs to take into account (1) their relative success in channeling investment and entrepreneurship into financially viable enterprises; (2) their success in mobilizing savings and contributing to the creation of functioning capital markets; and (3) the social costs and benefits of DFC investments as compared to possible alternatives. In summarizing the evidence relevant to these issues we would have to say that the success of DFCs, in cooperation with the Bank Group, has been much greater in channeling investment and entrepreneurship into financially viable enterprises than it has been in mobilizing domestic savings and contributing to the development of capital markets. Development finance companies, at least until recently, have paid little or no attention to social costs and benefits. Within the limits set by government priorities and administrative controls, they have tended to finance those enterprises that promised the highest profitability by the private market test.

As of June 30, 1971, the Bank Group was associated with thirty-two pre-

36. Diamond (ed.), *Development Finance Companies*, pp. 2–3.

dominantly privately controlled development companies and seven publicly controlled companies. The Bank Group's association with publicly controlled companies, except for the early Ethiopian venture, dates from June 15, 1968.[37]

The most difficult financing for a DFC to raise is private share capital. Finance companies have tended on the whole not to be very profitable, and the subscriptions of both domestic and foreign shareholders have frequently been motivated more by considerations of good will, self-defense, and a desire for information about profitable investment opportunities than by anticipated profits from DFC shares. The larger part of domestic capital for most of these companies has come from government contributions, mainly in the form of low interest loans. Under these circumstances it is an open question whether such DFCs can be said to be privately controlled. As an IFC official has put it,

Most of the development finance companies associated with the World Bank have been sponsored, and initially all have been financed or otherwise supported by their governments. This fact places upon them a responsibility—even if their own objectives did not—to behave in the public interest as well as in the interests of their own stockholders. It also exposes them to the dangers of political pressures, which could severely inhibit their ability to act either in the interests of the general public or of their shareholders.[38]

Despite such misgivings as these dangers might generate, the Bank Group, at least until the change of policy toward government-controlled companies in 1968, felt that private companies had substantial advantages over government-controlled companies in the promotion of private enterprise. This is still probably the predominant opinion in the Bank. A privately controlled DFC is much more likely to look for and acquire competent and experienced business management. Indeed the IBRD has been instrumental in finding the management for a number of the DFCs with which it has been associated. It is important both for its own profitability and for the development of a capital market that a development finance company dispose of its portfolio and reinvest as rapidly as is feasible. It may be taken for granted that a private

---

37. The ICICI of India started out as a privately controlled company but, because of nationalizations of shareholding enterprises, was by 1969 a corporation whose shares were largely in the hands of state enterprises.

38. P. M. Mathew, "Relations between Governments and Development Finance Companies," in Diamond (ed.), *Development Finance Companies*, p. 91. In summarizing the discussion that gave rise to this paper Mathew says, "Underlying the discussion was the uneasy feeling that, in the words of one participant, most development finance companies were 'basically quasi-governmental institutions' since, directly or indirectly, they received a substantial part of their resources from government." (P. 92.)

company will sell when it finds a more profitable use for its capital. A government company, on the other hand, will frequently find itself under severe pressure from the public and the legislature both to keep its profitable ventures and to subsidize foundering enterprises. Although privately controlled DFCs have certainly been influenced in their investment decisions by governments to which they owe so much of their financing, they are better able to resist improper political pressures than their government counterparts.

In some cases, the World Bank family has been able to play a part in maintaining the independence of a development finance company. An IFC subscription to share capital, sometimes accompanied by its presence on the board of directors and almost always involving an intimate relationship, has on occasion provided a shield against government pressure. No less important has been the World Bank's insistence on operational independence as a condition for a Bank loan.[39]

The Bank Group has not as yet had a great deal of experience in lending to government-controlled DFCs although, as of June 30, 1971, eight loans had been made to such companies.[40] In the opinion of the director of the concerned department, it is more difficult to appraise a government DFC than a private one (particularly to reach judgments on managerial efficiency) and much more time-consuming. If and when private companies financed by publicly controlled DFCs become nationalized, as has happened in a few cases, the World Bank may be confronted with the problem whether to lend to public DFCs that are engaged predominantly in financing publicly owned rather than private enterprise.

Since an extensive literature is available on development banks and development finance companies, it is unnecessary to describe in any detail their principal activities. It should be noted, however, that the DFCs with which the Bank Group is associated perform a wide range of functions. At a minimum such a company may limit itself to appraising a project and suggesting a few changes before investing. At the opposite extreme a DFC may generate the idea of a project, arrange for the financing, organize the company, and, possibly for a time, manage it.[41] A number of the finance companies with which the Bank Group has been associated have actively engaged not only in financing projects but in providing technical assistance. Since such expertise is scarce in less developed countries, it has been necessary for the Bank Group to lend a helping hand. It seems probable that more technical assistance has had to be provided per dollar of lending to DFCs than for any other

39. *Ibid.*, pp. 106–07.
40. The IFC is prevented by its charter from investing in public enterprises, including publicly controlled development finance companies.
41. E. T. Kuiper, "The Promotional Role of a Development Finance Company," in Diamond (ed.), *Development Finance Companies*, pp. 7–8.

type of project with which the Bank Group has been concerned. The appraisal and follow up work is extensive. Frequently the Bank Group has had to find managers and other top personnel. The IFC has placed a number of people on the boards of directors of companies in which it has a share interest. Executives of DFCs are brought to Washington for extensive training periods, and a great deal of information and written advice is provided to these companies.

In its early association with development finance companies the Bank insisted on approving all proposed investments in which foreign exchange provided by the Bank was to be used. The extent to which the Bank continued to exercise this control depended on its experience with the company. In general, the Bank now begins its relations with a DFC by allowing it to commit Bank funds for an individual project up to some limit, say $50,000, without prior approval from the Bank. As the Bank's confidence in the company grows, the limit is raised to a point where usually very few projects need to be submitted for prior approval. In any case, approval does not involve the Bank Group in anything as important as an appraisal mission. It basically means examining the prospectus and related papers to note apparent anomalies.

When one considers that the Bank Group has loaned nearly $1.5 billion to development finance companies, that this is only a part (though frequently a large part) of the investible funds of these companies, and that the investments of the DFCs are, in turn, only a fraction (usually small) of the total investment in the industrial enterprises they finance, it is obvious that the leverage potential of Bank Group participation in private industrialization has been large. The Bank Group's record in bringing financially viable private enterprises into being is impressive. In the judgment of one of the most knowledgeable men in the business, James Raj,

On the whole, the operations with the development finance companies have been useful and successful. Nearly all of these banks have helped to initiate enterprises that could not otherwise exist. Nearly all have served as a focal point for introducing foreign investors to their countries and prompting these investors to begin serious explorations.[42]

With respect to the development of local capital markets, however, neither the Bank Group in general nor development finance companies and the IFC in particular, have been anywhere near as successful.

42. Statement by Raj to Harold Graves (March 30, 1970). James Raj was a high official in the ICICI, later the managing director of the Nigerian Industrial Development Bank and, until his retirement in 1969, vice president of the IFC.

Mobilizing Domestic Capital for Investment

Although the Bank was charged by its Articles of Agreement with encouraging international investment, the fact soon had to be faced that domestic investment, or the scarcity of it, was of even greater concern. After all, the Bank's foreign exchange loans were only supplemental to domestic investments. At an early date, especially in the power sector, Bank-financed projects began to encounter difficulties on the side of domestic finance. Persistent inflation eroded the value of the domestic currency originally provided; governments were slow to authorize rate increases or to provide more funds; and the local capital market, if any, was not adequate to make up the deficiency. The Bank's response in a few cases was to encourage private investors to invest in securities issued by specific development enterprises. In 1949, for example, the Bank was able to assist El Salvador in financing a hydroelectric project on the Lempa River by advising on the issue and sale of bonds to local banks, financial institutions, and business enterprises heretofore unaccustomed to purchasing such securities. In 1952, the Bank helped to accomplish something of a tour de force—inducing investors in a less developed country to put their money in a privately controlled public utility, the Cukurova Power Company of Turkey.

In actual loan discussions with individual member governments, the Bank sought to improve the general climate for private investment.

For one thing [a staff document explained in 1954] . . . the influence of the Bank has frequently been exerted to encourage borrowing countries to adopt economic and financial policies conducive to development, such as measures to achieve economic and monetary stability. . . . Moreover, the Bank takes into account . . . the willingness of the borrowing country to provide fair treatment to investors. . . . It adheres rigidly to the principle that it will not finance projects for which private capital is available on reasonable terms. . . . And through its technical assistance . . . the Bank has often had occasion to point out the role which private investment, foreign as well as domestic, can perform in strengthening the economy of the country.[43]

Discrimination by member governments against what the Bank's management considered to be reasonable interests and possibilities of private entrepreneurs was likely to affect adversely the Bank's opinion of its clients and, on occasion, has affected its lending policy. The words of a general survey mission, while written independently, nevertheless indicated the Bank's early attitude: "The primary responsibility for progress in the improvement

43. *The International Bank for Reconstruction and Development, 1946–1953* (Johns Hopkins Press, 1954), p. 112.

of industrial organization and standards is, of course, that of private enterprise. . . . It was not, of course, within the mission's province to recommend action by private enterprise. Our recommendations are necessarily limited to government action."[44] And, as President Black said to the board of governors in 1957, "What government does not already have its hands full without reaching out into new fields? What government has so much foreign exchange that it can afford to bar a responsible foreign investor? There is no ideological argument here. Just common sense."[45] One reason, however, why governments reached "into new fields" was that institutions were lacking that could channel domestic savings effectively into private enterprises in which savers could have confidence. In many, if not most, less developed countries these were among the least developed institutions. When we speak of capital markets, we include not only the institutions that mobilize and invest savings but the laws governing the behavior of lenders and borrowers and the organization and practices of business firms participating in the market. As Diamond puts it,

The institutions include savings banks, commercial banks, stock exchanges, issue houses, etc. The laws concern security liability and business organization. The practices involve the techniques and traditions of enterprise and finance. These elements are no less important to economic development than capital and production techniques. Their underdevelopment can be an important obstacle to economic growth. In the face of this intricate network of problems, it is small wonder that in the past government securities have generally been the first securities to be marketed in most countries and that in some underdeveloped countries today the government is the most important single institution for generating and mobilizing savings.[46]

In many less developed countries the chief obstacle to capital formation is not a lack of savings capacity but the absence of investment incentives that would induce saving. In such countries a tradition of family owned and controlled enterprises may inhibit the issue of securities available to the public. Even if securities are issued, there is frequently a failure to disclose relevant information, and the information that is disclosed lacks credibility. Adequate accounting, auditing, and reporting practices are essential to the inducement of outside investment in private enterprises. Although short-term lending facilities are available almost everywhere, capital markets in many less developed countries lack institutions experienced in medium- and long-term lend-

44. *The Economic Development of Malaya*, report of a mission organized by the IBRD (Johns Hopkins Press, 1955), p. 122.

45. IBRD, Annual Meeting of the Board of Governors, *Summary Proceedings* (September 1957), p. 10.

46. Diamond, *Development Banks*, pp. 15–16.

ing. The kinds of investments that are available to potential investors are sometimes ill adapted to the investors' requirements. One of the most serious deficiencies is the absence of such institutions as security exchanges that could assure investors a satisfactory degree of liquidity. The efficiency of a capital market is to be judged by the extent to which it can make potential savings actual and direct these savings toward investment opportunities at minimum cost. Recent studies have illustrated the substantial variations known to exist in the efficiency of capital markets in developed countries.[47] And there is no doubt that capital markets in most less developed countries are inefficient both in generating savings and in transferring these savings to appropriate investment opportunities. This is a serious handicap to economic development.

The Bank has, first and last, undertaken a substantial amount of study of the organization, functioning, and deficiencies of capital markets in the less developed world. For a few years it supported a capital markets unit that produced a series of surveys of capital markets in particular countries.[48] The IBRD has also undertaken, at the request of Colombia, Peru, Tunisia, Pakistan, Chile, and other governments, studies leading to recommendations for improving capital markets. As was noted above, the Bank has frequently provided technical assistance to governments that are concerned with generating local savings for investment in public sector projects. It has also responded in a number of cases to requests for technical assistance in putting some part of the machinery of a capital market in place. In 1965, for example, a consultant was sent to Pakistan to help the government develop a securities exchange in Karachi. These studies and these efforts, however, have tended to be somewhat isolated from the regular work of the Bank.

In view of the importance of capital markets for the development process, it might have been supposed that country economic reports would pay a great deal of attention to this aspect of the economy. This has rarely been true. Country economic reports are prepared under the direction of staff members who are more concerned with Bank Group lending to governments than with institutions in the private sector. Representatives of the IFC are rarely included in Bank missions.

Except for technical assistance from the Bank or IDA, most of the activity concerned with developing capital markets has come from the IFC and Bank Group–financed DFCs. The IFC helps in the financing of enterprises with

47. Organisation for Economic Co-operation and Development, *Capital Markets Study* (Paris, March 1967). See Chapter 5, above.

48. The capital markets unit was headed in the years 1959–61 by a distinguished economist, the late Antonin Basch, author of *Financing Economic Development* (Macmillan, 1964).

which it is concerned "through stand-by and other underwriting arrangements in support of public offerings or private placement of shares, debentures and other corporate securities."[49] It has made a contribution by introducing types of securities with which local capital markets were unfamiliar. In the process of putting together new firms or expanding old ones it has helped to mobilize local investment. And in selling off its own holdings it has helped to enlarge the size of the market.

The development finance companies financed by the Bank Group have engaged in similar activities, chiefly with money supplied by governments or borrowed from the IBRD. The Industrial and Mining Development Bank of Iran, to which the World Bank Group had committed $205 million by the end of 1971, helped to create a capital market in Iran and played an important role in establishing the Tehran stock exchange. As we have noted above, private capital contributions to Bank-financed DFCs have usually been small. Nor have these companies, once established, ordinarily sought to raise private capital by issuing their own securities. The large Indian ICICI did not issue its first debt security until 1966. The Pakistan Industrial Credit and Investment Corporation (PICIC), which has been in existence since 1957, has yet to issue such a security. Turkey's development bank (TSKB) established in 1950, has never issued a security, and in 1970 the contribution from private sources stood at 4.4 percent of the funds available to the Turkish bank. The main contribution of DFCs to mobilizing domestic capital has come from their underwriting of the sale of securities of companies in which they have been interested, from entering into standby arrangements, and from the selling off of participations. These companies, as we have noted above, have been more successful in channeling available funds into investment opportunities than in mobilizing new savings. In the opinion of the Bank's chief authority on DFCs, a recitation of their activities makes the DFC contribution to the development of capital markets seem larger than in fact it has been.

Since 1968, however, the Bank Group, and particularly the IFC, has increasingly turned its attention to ways of assisting the development of local capital markets. The borrowing and lending rates of the development finance companies financed by the Bank Group have come under close scrutiny both by management and by the board of directors.[50] Member governments, in subsidizing these companies, have frequently insisted on lending terms that are substantially below the real cost of capital. Consequently the profit

49. IFC, *General Policies* (1971), p. 8.
50. President's memorandum, "Policies of the World Bank Group towards Development Finance Companies," R68-204 (Nov. 1, 1968). "Interest Rates Charged by Development Finance Companies and Terms of Government Loans to Such Companies," Sec M70-149 (April 8, 1970).

record of DFCs has been adversely affected, making it difficult for them to attract new equity capital. Moreover, DFCs, frequently because of government influence, have been loath to pay interest rates high enough to permit the sale of their own debt issues. The contribution of DFCs to the mobilization of savings, by both equity issues and debt, has therefore been much less than might have been expected. The attention of the Bank Group has now been focused on this problem. Since investment in DFCs was, by 1971, approaching $1.5 billion and growing at the rate of $250 million a year, the IBRD appears to be in a position to bring substantial influence to bear on DFC policies.

There are, of course, many kinds of investment companies other than DFCs, and the IFC indicated in its 1971 report on *General Policies* that it stood ready to finance any or all of these if they are "well managed, contribute to the development of the countries in which they are doing business and follow policies generally consistent with those of IFC."[51] An expansion of the kinds of investing institutions to which the IFC is willing to lend implies an expansion in the technical assistance the IFC is willing to make available to advise on capital market problems. In 1971 such an expansion was well under way. At the request of the Korean government, the IFC dispatched a three-man mission in November 1970 to review the Korean capital market situation and make recommendations. A similar mission was sent to the Republic of China in February 1971, and a number of other governments have asked for technical assistance in improving the functioning of their capital markets.

The Bank Group in 1970 assigned the primary function of capital market assistance to IFC. A memorandum from Gaud to McNamara (June 8, 1970) noted that "today this is everyone's business and no one's responsibility" and proposed the establishment of a capital markets unit somewhere in the Bank Group. The president decided to establish this in the IFC, and on March 25, 1971, a new capital markets department was announced.[52] It seems reason-

---

51. In his interview with representatives of *Finance and Development* (March 1970), Gaud mentions mutual funds, savings and loan associations, credit unions, and insurance companies as financial institutions that might merit IFC support.

52. International Finance Corporation, Press release (March 25, 1971). The IFC administrative circular (March 25, 1971) states:

> The primary task of the Capital Markets Department is to assist in the establishment and operation of sound institutions to channel private savings into productive private investments. It will also concern itself with the institutional and policy framework which affects such institutions. The Department will advise developing countries on programs and policy measures designed to broaden and diversify the scope of existing capital markets and, in this connection, will give particular attention to defining areas and possibilities for early and effective action.

able to suppose that the Bank Group's contribution to effective functioning of local capital markets may be substantially greater in the future than it has been in the past.

Industrialization and Development

As we have noted, 90 percent or more of the Bank Group's financing of private activity has been directed toward the industrial sector, which in Bank terminology includes manufacture and mining. A more complete discussion of the Bank's conception of the development process and its role therein is postponed until Chapter 14. But here a few words need to be said specifically about the development within the Bank Group of views concerning industrialization. During the long period of the Black administration these views were comparatively clear-cut. Although industrialization was definitely considered to be an essential part of the development process, the Bank felt it should play a relatively small role in direct industrial financing. It was the view of management that, on the whole, enough private capital was available for small- and medium-scale undertakings.[53] These funds might be supplemented by Bank lending to financial intermediaries. But, as we have seen, Bank loans to industrial development banks and finance companies in the 1950s were few and small. And when the IFC came into being, its initial limitations made any sizable contribution to industrial financing impossible. The Bank was unwilling, for reasons discussed above, to lend for public sector industrial projects. Consequently the proper role for the Bank was considered to be the financing of undertakings that are not attractive to private capital (that is, infrastructure) and, in the field of industry, projects (for example, steel in India and Japan) that are so large that not all the necessary capital could be raised from local private sources. In fact, prior to 1965 the major part of the Bank's direct financing of industrial enterprises was in developed countries. Japan and Australia were particularly large borrowers.

The few industrial projects that the Bank was willing to finance in the public sector during the 1950s were all intended at some stage to be transferred to private control. Two of the largest were in Pakistan. The Karnaphuli Paper Company in East Pakistan had been founded under government ownership in 1954. In the following year, in connection with a loan to the company and in pursuance of the stated policy of the government itself, the Bank persuaded the Pakistan Industrial Development Corporation to offer a majority of the firm's shares to the public. As an inducement to the public to

---

53. IBRD, *Third Annual Report, 1947–1948*, p. 18.

subscribe, the Bank let it be known in advance that a loan was probably in the offing. As it happened, 70 percent of the enterprise passed into private hands. By far the most elaborate exercise of this sort involved a loan in 1954 to the Sui Gas Transmission Company, also in Pakistan.

Not content with refusing to finance industrial projects in the public sector, the Bank attempted, as was noted above, to restrain the activities of its member borrowers in this area. It cannot be said, however, that it was uniformly successful in this. Turkey's relations with the Bank, for example, which for a time almost broke down altogether, were not improved by the Bank's efforts to reduce state intervention in the industrial sector. Nor were the Bank's relations with Brazil improved by its recommendations to that country that it permit foreign companies to prospect for oil.

The best publicized case of this kind, however, was that of India. Ever since his first visit to India in 1952, President Black had been vexed by what he considered India's doctrinaire and unrealistic discrimination against private capital and its unjustifiable preference for industrializing through investment in the public sector. In 1956 he used the occasion of a report to the Bank on economic policies in India to write to the newly appointed minister of finance, T. T. Krishnamachari.

Once again, I wish to emphasize my conviction that India's interest lies in giving private enterprise, both Indian and foreign, every encouragement to make its maximum contribution to the development of the economy, particularly in the industrial field. . . . I have the distinct impression that the potentialities of private enterprise are commonly underestimated in India and that its operations are subjected to unnecessary restrictions. Above all, in a country which is short of capital, and with limited resources of managerial talent, it is important that the respective roles of public and private enterprise should be fixed entirely on a basis which will ensure the most effective contribution of each to development, and not by any theoretical concept of the role that each should play.

I see a tendency toward this latter approach in your Industrial Policy Resolution of last April, which reserves to the State exclusive responsibility for new undertakings in a large number of industries, including oil, coal and other minerals.[54]

Although Black's letter went on to say some pleasant things about the Bank's relations with India, these were excluded when the letter fell into the hands of an enterprising journalist and appeared in the *Financial Times* of London and *Capital*, a weekly published in Calcutta. What was left was a bleak and unfriendly document, from which the inference could be drawn in India that the Bank was making a shift of government policy toward the private sector an important condition for further Bank lending.

54. IBRD, "Some Observations of the IBRD Mission on Economic Programmes and Policies in India" (June 30, 1956; processed).

Publication of the letter provoked a wide outcry. The New Delhi correspondent of *The Times* of London declared that conditions suggested in the letter, "although ostensibly economic only, are fiercely political."[55] Indian newspapers commented sharply that "to draw the red herring of ideology across the trail of India's economic and financial policies is as mistaken as it is mischievous,"[56] declared that "India will . . . little tolerate blackmail,"[57] and denounced the "hidden threat"[58] and "humiliating conditions"[59] of Mr. Black's letter.

Under cover of this barrage, Krishnamachari in his reply to Black's letter was able to sound a note of wise reasonableness.

I am aware that your views and ours about private and public enterprise do not altogether coincide though the differences are not quite as great as seem to appear in public debate. We are, of course, not convinced that the motive of private profit is the only one which can ensure efficient operation of an industry; nor do we believe that private enterprise is inherently superior to state enterprise.

The result of this exchange was to make it appear, at least to Indian eyes, that it was the Bank that was doctrinaire, while the Indian government was wisely pragmatic. A more objective observer, on the other hand, might well conclude that, to a certain extent, doctrine held both parties in thrall. In any case this was one of a number of incidents that, over time, have ruffled relations between the Bank and India. In view of the volume of Bank Group lending to India, however, it must be supposed that these differences were not too serious.

It seems doubtful that, on balance, the early efforts of the Bank to influence policies in member countries concerning the relation of public and private sector activities bore much fruit.

The arrival of George Woods at the beginning of 1963 brought to the presidency of the Bank an investment banker with long experience in problems of industrial financing and close association with private industrialists, both inside and outside the United States. In his first address to the board of governors of the World Bank Group, he proclaimed his intention of expanding the Group's assistance to industry and of making it "more versatile" than it had previously been.[60] This initiative quickly became evident in increased Bank lending to development finance companies, lending which reached

55. *The Times* (London), Oct. 11, 1956.
56. *The Hindustan Standard* (Calcutta), Oct. 11, 1956.
57. *The Free Press Journal* (Bombay), Oct. 13, 1956.
58. *Vyapar* (Bombay), Oct. 13, 1956.
59. *Jana Satta* (Bombay), Oct. 11, 1956.
60. IBRD, Annual Meeting of the Board of Governors, *Summary Proceedings* (1963), pp. 11–12.

$100 million for the first time in 1966 and amounted to $159 million in 1968, the last year of the Woods administration. Total commitments of the IFC grew from $18 million in 1962–63 to over $50 million in 1967–68 and reached $92 million in the following year.

Woods also favored the use of IDA credits for the financing of equipment, parts, and raw materials for industrial production. The so-called industrial import credits to India and Pakistan were undertaken under his initiative, and although they later came under attack in the board of directors, as we noted in Chapter 9, they constituted for a period a substantial fraction of the Bank Group's industrial financing. "We should be prepared," he maintained, "in addition to our normal project loans, to make available, in appropriate cases, long-term financing for the import of components and spare parts for industry generally or for some particular segment of industry of special importance to the given economy."[61]

The Bank's strict policy against lending for industrial projects in the public sector was, as we have indicated above, also modified in the Woods regime although the restriction against lending to publicly controlled development finance companies continued until 1968. The change in attitude toward public sector projects was associated with President Woods's ambition to stimulate the production of chemical fertilizers, which in many of the Bank's member countries were produced mainly in the public sector. The increased use of fertilizers was "the most promising single way to bring about a decisive improvement in food production. . . ."[62] In India alone, he calculated "a capital investment on the order of $2–3 billion in fertilizer plants would help produce, over a 10-year period, a $30 billion increase in the output of food grains."[63]

To bring foreign capital and technology together with local initiative, materials, and markets for the purpose of fertilizer production proved, however, more difficult than was anticipated. Although the Bank Group did in fact finance a number of fertilizer projects, only one (during the Woods administration) was in the public sector.[64] Over all, the Woods administration saw a

61. FPC 63-8 (July 18, 1963), p. 13. Quoted in Chapter 9.
62. Address to the Board of Governors, IBRD (Sept. 27, 1966), p. 8.
63. Address to the Economic and Social Council of the United Nations (Nov. 13, 1967), p. 6.
64. This was a financing of $30 million for the Congo Potash Company. The company was owned, to the extent of 85 percent, by two French companies, including Potasses d'Alsace, which in turn were owned by the French government. The government of the Congo received a 15 percent participation by way of compensation for the mineral concession that it had granted to the company. Ironically, as if to confirm the premonitions of Woods's predecessors, the company's operations soon encountered serious difficulties.

very large increase not only in the volume of industrial financing but in the percentage of total Bank Group financing that was allocated to this area.

This trend was continued and accelerated during the McNamara regime. We have already mentioned the many changes in organization and policy that have affected industrial lending since 1968. The IFC division dealing with loans to development finance companies was established as a separate department of the Bank, and the restriction against lending to publicly controlled DFCs was lifted. The industrial projects division of the IFC was transferred to the Bank as a new department. Of the eleven industrial projects under consideration by this department on June 30, 1971, ten were in the public sector. The IFC under new management has introduced many changes in policy and has established, as we have noted, a Capital Markets Department. And changes in Bank policy in 1971 in the direction of a somewhat more relaxed attitude toward program lending seem likely to increase the share of Bank Group financing that is directed toward the industrial sector.

It cannot be said, however, that even with these changes the Bank Group has as yet been able to develop a persuasive doctrine of industrial development or to coordinate effectively the many instruments it has at hand to promote industrial development. The contrast between Bank lending in transportation, electric power, education, and to some extent in agriculture (where the choice of projects is based on in-depth sectoral studies) and the relatively ad hoc character of industrial financing is striking. This is recognized, at this writing, by the management and staff of the Bank.[65]

Industrial lending by the Bank Group, following policies generally favored by borrowing governments, has for the most part been directed toward import replacement. Nevertheless, a case can be made for the proposition that so far as direct financing by the Bank is concerned, considerations of comparative advantage have not been completely ignored. The projects so financed have generally been large enterprises relying heavily on domestic materials that have a sizable domestic value added component in their total costs. Mining enterprises financed by the Bank have almost invariably been earners of foreign exchange. In the manufacturing field, iron and steel, chemicals, fertilizers, pulp and paper, and cement have been favored areas. Until the late 1960s, however, in IFC investments and Bank loans to development finance companies, which together constitute well over half of total Bank financing of industrial enterprises, very little attention has been paid to com-

65. See, for example, World Bank, *Industry*, Sector Working Paper (April 1972), especially pp. 22–25.

parative advantage and developmental consequences. Prospective enterprise profit has generally been identified with prospective contribution to national economic growth. The Bank Group has, of course, frequently attempted to influence policies in borrowing countries in a way designed to bring prices into closer touch with real costs. In particular, interest rates, foreign exchange rates, and commercial policies have been matters of concern. But in the evaluation of projects for IFC or DFC investment little attention has been paid to anything except prospective profits.

It is now well publicized that in many, if not in most, less developed countries government policies favoring import substitution during the last two decades have brought industrial development at an excessively high cost. A long series of studies has documented the propositions that, as a result of extremely high protection of domestic industry, (1) industrialization has contributed much less to economic growth than the national income figures on domestic value added would suggest and (2) the possibilities of export earnings have been seriously diminished.[66] The Bank Group turned its attention vigorously to this problem in the mid-1960s, and since then a long series of studies has begun to have an effect on industrial lending policies. The elaborate Bank study of the Indian economy in 1964–65 highlighted the distortions brought about in Indian industry by excessive tariffs, import restrictions, exchange rate policy, and government control.[67] A series of studies begun in 1965 revealed the high cost of import substitution in automotive industries, the manufacturing of heavy electrical equipment, and heavy manufacturing equipment in a number of less developed countries.[68] An extensive examination of growth strategies of a number of semi-industrial countries, under the

66. See, in particular, Ian Little, Tibor Scitovsky, and Maurice Scott, *Industry and Trade in Some Developing Countries; a Comparative Study* (published for the Development Centre of the OECD by the Oxford University Press, London, 1971). This volume was based on country studies (separately published) of India, Pakistan, Argentina, Brazil, the Philippines, Taiwan, and Mexico. See also Bela Balassa and associates, *The Structure of Protection in Developing Countries* (Johns Hopkins Press, 1971). This book draws on country studies of trade and development in Argentina, Brazil, Chile, Mexico, Korea, Western Malaysia, Pakistan, the Philippines, and Taiwan.

67. IBRD, Economic Mission to India, 1964–65, "Report to the President of the IBRD and the IDA on India's Economic Development Effort." 14 vols. (1965; processed).

68. These studies were initiated under the direction of Barend de Vries. Two have been published: Jack Baranson, *Automotive Industries in Developing Countries*, Occasional Paper No. 8 (IBRD, 1967); and Ayhan Cilingiroglu, *Manufacture of Heavy Electrical Equipment in Developing Countries*, Occasional Paper No. 9 (IBRD, 1967). A third paper by Bertil Walstedt, "Heavy Manufacturing Equipment in Developing Countries," has been processed. A side issue in these studies was that of how much concession should be allowed by the Bank in procurement in less developed countries.

direction of Bela Balassa, has centered attention on the relation of trade policies to export performance and economic growth.[69] The Bank's country studies now usually pay explicit attention to the direction as well as the volume of industrial investment.[70]

The effect of these investigations on Bank Group industrial financing began to be felt toward the end of the 1960s, particularly on the investment policies of the IFC and on loans to DFCs. As we have noted, the management of the Bank and the board of directors have shown increasing concern that DFCs financed by the Bank borrow and lend at rates approaching the real cost of capital. A calculation of effective as well as of nominal rates of protection has come to be a part of the appraisal of projects for IFC investments. In the period before William Gaud took over the administration, the IFC was without the services of a professional economist. Now an evaluation of the economic (that is, the developmental) prospects of a project receives as much attention as do the technical, financial, and managerial aspects. A similar trend is visible in the Bank's lending policy toward development finance companies. However, there is still a large gap between the enunciation of principles and their application to project evaluation and to the industrial investment policies of the IFC and of the numerous DFCs financed by the Bank.[71] Furthermore, it must be said that to date the Bank's analysis of the problems and possibilities of the industrial sector of borrowing members has lagged behind the standards set in various other sectors of Bank lending. Nor has the Bank Group yet succeeded in coordinating effectively the many lending and technical assistance instruments at its disposal in the industrial field.

69. Bela Balassa and associates, *The Structure of Protection in Developing Countries* (Johns Hopkins Press, 1971).

70. Special studies of industrial strategy in a number of Bank member countries have paid particular attention to considerations of comparative advantage. See in particular D. Avramović, "Industrialization of Pakistan," 3 vols. (IBRD, March 10, 1970; processed); Avramović, "Industrialization of Iran—the Record, the Problems and the Prospects" (IBRD, May 18, 1970; processed); and L. Walinsky and H. Hughes, "Industrial Policies and Manufacturing Industries in Brazil" (IBRD, Dec. 19, 1969; processed).

71. The sector working paper for industry, cited above, after stating that the calculation of an economic rate of return "can shed light not only on the contribution of the project to domestic product but also on the protection and balance of payments implications of an investment" goes on to say, "There are several difficult problems in estimating the economic rate of return, however, which need careful attention and require the exercise of judgment. These center around the identification of appropriate long term international prices for project outputs and inputs, the measurement of external economies and diseconomies, the estimation of shadow prices for the primary factors, and the rate at which project efficiency will improve over time." P. 33.

Summary and Conclusions

The Bank Group has been involved in private investment and private enterprise through a multifaceted set of activities difficult to reduce to orderly exposition. So far as portfolio investors in the capital-exporting countries are concerned, the Bank has offered a channel to foreign investment through the purchase of Bank bonds and participations in Bank loans. The funds thus invested have gone into all the areas of activity that are financed by the Bank under government guarantee—at first mainly into capital infrastructure but later into a wider range of activities. The sale of IFC investments has included both debt and equity securities. But the Bank has also facilitated direct foreign private investment by bringing its influence to bear on member government policies and practices and by the creation of ICSID.

So far as the promotion of private investment and private enterprise in capital importing countries is concerned, the Bank Group has done much more than lend to and invest in private ventures. The financing of capital infrastructure in the areas of transportation, energy, and communication has paved the way for private agricultural and industrial development. Technical assistance, as well as money for development finance companies, has helped launch and expand large numbers of industrial enterprises. The IFC has been a promoter and organizer as well as a financier of business firms. And Bank Group influence on policies in borrowing countries has frequently succeeded in removing obstacles to domestic as well as foreign private investment.

But the Bank Group has also been an important provider of capital to private enterprise. It has done so through government guaranteed loans to large privately controlled enterprises; through program loans financing the imports of industrial materials, parts, and equipment; through loans and investments in development finance companies; and through nonguaranteed financing by the IFC of private enterprises.

Apart from a few early loans to private power companies and a small amount of financing of agricultural and tourist enterprises, Bank Group financing of private enterprise has concentrated in the area of manufacturing and mining. Although the Bank's management has always considered industrialization to be an essential element in the development process, in the earlier years it was less concerned with Bank investment in this area than with providing an appropriate environment for growth. This attitude changed over time, and along with this change came increased concern for the direction of industrial investment. The financing of profitable import-substituting industry by IFC and Bank-financed development finance companies, without much regard for the relation of domestic to international prices, was, by the late 1960s, beginning to give way to a more discriminating policy of industrial financing. There has also been a change in the Bank Group's attitude toward government control of industrial enterprises. While the Bank Group has made a substantial contribution to industrial development in a number of member countries, it needs to be said that, to date, industrial lending has lagged somewhat behind other areas of Bank lending in the sophistication of project evaluation and sector analysis and in the coordination of available development instrumentalities.

CHAPTER TWELVE

The International Development Association

THE INTERNATIONAL DEVELOPMENT ASSOCIATION (IDA), the soft loan affiliate of the World Bank, came into being in 1960. Its creation and subsequent expansion can be explained in various ways. The IDA can be viewed as a significant indirect result of the vigorous campaign of the less developed countries for a sizable fund, under United Nations control, to provide grants and long-term, low-interest loans for economic and social development. IDA is not under UN control, it does not make grants, and it operates by weighted voting. Yet it stands as living proof that the "international power structure" is responsive to persistent peaceful pressure.

The IDA confirms one's faith in the ability of bureaucracies to remain afloat, to unfurl fresh sail, and to benefit from prevailing winds. The outlook in 1960 for an agency equipped only to make loans at close-to-commercial rates of interest to countries unable to borrow elsewhere would have been bleak indeed. The Western Europeans and the Australians were becoming too creditworthy to borrow from the Bank. The Japanese were still large borrowers but obviously not destined to remain so. Among the less developed countries, on the other hand, India, Pakistan, and some other major borrowers were piling up external debt so rapidly as to call into question their continued creditworthiness for loans on Bank terms. The creditworthiness of newly independent countries in Africa for interest-bearing loans was also questionable. IDA, in short, had to be invented to keep the Bank preeminent, or at least eminent, in the growing complex of multilateral agencies attempting to facilitate international development.

As an international organization affiliated with the World Bank, IDA is an elaborate fiction. Called an "association" and possessed of Articles of

Agreement, officers, governmental members galore, and all the trappings of other international agencies, it is as yet simply a fund administered by the World Bank. Its aim is to finance the same types of projects as does the Bank, selected according to the same standards, but on terms that place a lighter burden on the balance of payments of the borrowing country. The result has been to broaden substantially the range of nations with which the Bank Group deals and to increase the amount of financing it provides.

Finally, the creation of IDA can be viewed as a watershed, or major landmark, in the evolution of the World Bank Group. It marks the as yet incomplete transformation of an institution that at first resembled a bank into something that by mid-1971 more nearly resembled an institution for financing and promoting development. There is no widely accepted definition of the term "development agency" that can be cited to illuminate the transformation we have in mind. The essence of the difference between a bank and a development agency, however, is the greater concern of the latter with development goals, strategy, and performance, with meeting the most pressing developmental needs as well as with financing good projects, and with rationing its resources to take all claims upon them properly into account.

The validity of these different ways of looking at the IDA should be easier to judge after the following more detailed report on its origins and creation, the use and first three replenishments of its resources, and the policy issues raised during the course of its first ten years.

Prehistory of IDA (1949–59)

The World Bank, it will be recalled, got off to a slow and stumbling start. Nothing in its first four or five years indicated that it would cut an impressive swath in the field of development.

Even if the Bank had gotten off to a speedier and smoother start, the range within which it apparently would confine its assistance—the provision of loans at close-to-commercial rates of interest to cover the foreign exchange costs of productive projects narrowly defined—seemed to the less developed countries to ignore their equally urgent need for funds to finance so-called non-self-liquidating projects, "low-yielding and slow-yielding projects" in such fields as health, education, and housing.[1] In the United Nations, more-

---

1. The Bank's early favorites—electric power projects—can also be thought of as low-yielding and slow-yielding. The returns are calculable, however, and accrue to the agency that supplies the service. Highway projects other than toll roads are non-self-liquidating, but not until April 1951 did the Bank approve its first loan for highway work (in Colombia).

over, the less developed countries for the first time in history had numerous platforms from which to launch pleas for corrective action. The platforms included two short-lived bodies, the Subcommission on Economic Development and the Economic and Employment Commission of the Economic and Social Council (ECOSOC) and four more permanent organs, the Economic Committee of the Economic and Social Council, ECOSOC itself, the Economic and Financial Committee of the General Assembly, and the Assembly itself.

In the United Nations

A March 1949 report of the Subcommission on Economic Development noted that the World Bank had said it was prepared to expand its activities in financing economic development projects.

Nevertheless, on a realistic assessment it cannot be assumed that the Bank could, in the foreseeable future, be able to make a significant contribution to the massive investments required for economic development involved over a long period. Moreover, even if the finance available through the Bank could be increased beyond present expectations, the Sub-Commission is of the opinion that the terms on which it would be available under the policy established by the Bank limit the effectiveness of this financing to under-developed countries. There are fields and types of investment required for economic development which can neither satisfy the preconditions required by the Bank, nor carry the interest charges involved, nor be liquidated within the period required. . . .

It is for these reasons that the Sub-Commission extended its consideration of international finance beyond the activities of the Bank, and discussed the possibilities of opening up new sources of international finance under United Nations auspices.[2]

The subcommission "took note" of the statement presented by its Indian chairman, V. K. R. V. Rao, and annexed to its report Mr. Rao's suggestion for a new international organization to be called the United Nations Economic Development Administration (UNEDA). It would be financed by contributions from member governments (in their own currencies) and would perform a variety of developmental functions. Financial assistance from UNEDA would "normally take the form of loans and not grants, though terms of repayment will be liberal and the interest charged may be only nominal."

The American expert on the subcommission, Emilio G. Collado, who had

2. UN Economic and Social Council, Report of the Third Session of the Sub-Commission on Economic Development, Doc. E/CN.1/65 (April 12, 1949), paragraphs 38 and 40.

previously served as the first U.S. executive director of the Bank, found himself "unable to concur" in certain paragraphs of the subcommission's report. His government, he said, "should look primarily to American private enterprise" and "should rely fundamentally on the International Bank for Reconstruction and Development for financing or collaborating in financing closely circumscribed types of project basic to development not readily susceptible of implementation by purely private financing."[3]

The Bank also reacted negatively to the Rao proposal and suggested that the functions proposed for UNEDA either came within the Bank's terms of reference or did not need to be performed. "Since loans made by the Bank are on terms which are not designed to make any substantial profit, it is clear that any greater liberality in the terms of UNEDA loans would amount simply to disguised inter-governmental grants."[4]

The cold water poured on the proposal by respectable sources of cold water was not enough to drown it. UNEDA resurfaced as an International Development Authority, as a Special United Nations Fund for Economic Development (SUNFED), and under other aliases before achieving any real-life identity. The desire of the less developed countries for access to capital on easier terms than those of the World Bank began to take on the proportions of a campaign at the Economic and Social Council in 1950.[5]

From 1950 until at least 1960, "financing economic development" was the most passionately debated economic issue in the United Nations. The less developed countries, led primarily by Chile, India, and Yugoslavia, showed extraordinary ingenuity in keeping the issue alive and inching forward toward their goal. Their campaign splashed over from United Nations channels into other channels and back again, creating waves and ripples in Washington; in European, Asian, and Latin American capitals; in World Bank circles; and among special commissions and committees, national and international. The developed countries, led by an increasingly isolated United States, at first opposed, then postponed, and eventually deflected the campaign. The World Bank, a major beneficiary of the diversionary tactic, gradually shifted its position on soft loans 180 degrees.

3. From footnote to paragraph 28 of the subcommission's report.
4. UN Secretariat, Department of Economic Affairs, *Methods of Financing Economic Development in Under-Developed Countries* (1949), p. 143. For more on the Bank's reaction to UNEDA, see Chapter 14, below.
5. See, for example, John G. Hadwen and Johan Kaufmann, *How United Nations Decisions Are Made* (Leiden: A. W. Sijthoff, 1960), pp. 85–111; James H. Weaver, *The International Development Association: A New Approach to Foreign Aid* (Praeger, 1965); Robert E. Asher and others, *The United Nations and Promotion of the General Welfare* (Brookings Institution, 1957), pp. 626–39.

In March 1951, the U.S. International Development Advisory Board, of which Nelson A. Rockefeller was chairman, reported to President Truman the existence of

many projects of basic importance to the development of underdeveloped countries that cannot be financed entirely on a loan basis. Our considered judgment is that *such public works can be most effectively financed and developed through a well-managed international agency. . . . The Advisory Board recommends the prompt creation of a new International Development Authority in which all the free nations will be invited to participate.*[6]

The Rockefeller board suggested that the proposed International Development Authority be set up with grant funds initially totaling not more than half a billion dollars, that it have its own board of directors, and that it operate under a management contract with the World Bank. This idea, it said, had been discussed with officials of the World Bank. "We believe that the International Bank would give sympathetic consideration to making its management facilities available to the new Development Authority which we are recommending."[7]

At the time the Rockefeller report appeared, a group of experts appointed by the secretary-general of the United Nations was winding up an assignment to prepare proposals for ECOSOC on the economic development of underdeveloped countries. The experts were extremely critical of the World Bank, which they said "has not adequately realized that it is an agency charged by the United Nations with the duty of promoting economic development." The Bank, by making its bond issues acceptable in capital markets, had been "highly successful" in eliminating fears that it would not be able to borrow enough to lend on the required scale. It still, however, "attaches excessive importance to the foreign currency aspects of development. . . . The Bank puts the cart of foreign exchange difficulties before the horse of economic development."[8]

Having picked up from the Rockefeller report the idea for an International

---

6. *Partners in Progress: a Report to the President by the International Development Advisory Board* (March 1951), pp. 72–73. The IDAB report was the second in a long series of postwar reports on U.S. foreign economic policy. The first, prepared under the direction of Gordon Gray (a special assistant to the President), appeared in late 1950, while the United Nations General Assembly was debating the financing of economic development. The Gray report recommended U.S. grants for economic development as well as for technical assistance.

7. *Ibid.*, p. 73.

8. UN Department of Economic Affairs, *Measures for the Economic Development of Under-Developed Countries* (May 1951), pp. 82–83. The experts were Alberto Baltra Cortez, D. R. Gadgil, George Hakim, W. Arthur Lewis, and Theodore W. Schultz.

Finance Corporation and commended it to the UN for study, the experts also urged that the United Nations establish an International Development Authority capable of making grants-in-aid in amounts that would increase rapidly to a level of about $3 billion a year. The UN group then considered whether an additional institution should be created to make loans at very low rates of interest, "such as one-half of 1 percent, for investment in social capital. . . ." It concluded (as had the Rockefeller group) that this was unnecessary because the same purpose could be served by combining a loan from the International Bank with a grant from the International Development Authority in cases where an undertaking, "desirable on social grounds, could not meet the full burden of loan finance."[9]

Nevertheless, from 1951 on, advocacy of grant aid for economic development was combined in the United Nations with advocacy of soft loans. As armament expenditures in the United States and elsewhere mounted, the prospects for a large grant-in-aid fund grew dimmer, and soft loans began to emerge as an alternative for which the developed countries might settle. A Chilean proposal that would have required the Economic and Social Council to prepare a blueprint for the establishment, as soon as circumstances permitted, of a special fund for grants-in-aid and long-term, low-interest loans was rejected by the council in the summer of 1951, but was accepted by the General Assembly in January 1952. A committee was appointed, and in the spring of 1953 it issued its report on a Special United Nations Fund for Economic Development.[10]

The Bank's management initially was infinitely more opposed to soft loans than to grants. It steadfastly maintained that the major impediment to an expanded flow of public finance was the dearth of adequately prepared project proposals for financing on Bank terms. Yet it also recognized publicly the existence of capital requirements for education, health, sanitation, and other purposes indispensable for development that were, in its view, inappropriate for Bank loans. At the UN Economic and Social Council in 1951, Eugene Black made the strongly anti-soft-loan, moderately pro-grant-aid statement quoted in Chapter 4. In a similar vein, he reported to his board of governors at their 1951 meeting his opinion that the Bank would be able

to meet all the capital needs of economic development in our member states, to the extent that those needs ought properly to be met on a long-term loan basis. . . .

That is not to say that there may not be other useful instruments in the field of

9. *Ibid.*, p. 86.
10. UN Department of Economic Affairs, *Report on a Special United Nations Fund for Economic Development,* by a Committee Appointed by the Secretary-General, Doc. E/2381 (Nov. 18, 1953).

providing capital, on an international basis, for economic growth. . . . Under present world conditions, it does not appear likely that any significant amount of grant capital will be provided on a truly international basis; but the idea has merits that might well be considered in a later and happier day.[11]

Long before it resulted in the establishment in 1966 of the capital-less UN Capital Development Fund, the pressure for SUNFED produced tangential results that were more important than the ultimate direct result. The 1956 decision of the Bank's board of governors to establish an International Finance Corporation can, as was noted in Chapter 11, be attributed in part to a desire of the Bank's principal stockholders to respond in concrete fashion to the mounting pressure in the United Nations for new types of development finance. The establishment of the United Nations Special Fund in October 1958 to finance preinvestment work was even more clearly a response. And Black said in an interview with Weaver that IDA "was really an idea to offset the urge for SUNFED."[12]

In the U.S. Government and the World Bank

In 1954, the United States adopted Public Law 480, the *Agricultural Trade Development and Assistance Act*. Title I of the act authorized the U.S. government to sell surplus agricultural commodities, accept inconvertible local currencies in exchange, and make loans and grants for economic development from its local currency holdings. P.L. 480 sales were neither the first nor the last source of U.S.-owned local currency accumulations, but they became by far the largest source. The U.S. Development Loan Fund, established in 1957, made its loans in dollars but was authorized to accept foreign currencies in repayment of those loans and to use the repayments for additional lending.

As American holdings of inconvertible foreign currencies mounted, confusion concerning the economic value and political significance of these holdings also mounted. They could properly be characterized as accumulations of "funny money," but large numbers of people took them seriously. For reasons that need not be gone into here, a search began for ways to draw down the holdings or transfer them to other hands.

In this atmosphere Senator A. S. Mike Monroney of Oklahoma in February 1958 announced his intention to introduce into the U.S. Senate within

---

11. *Summary Proceedings* of the 1951 Meeting of the Board of Governors of the International Bank for Reconstruction and Development (IBRD, 1951), p. 6. Quoted in Weaver, *The International Development Association*, pp. 19–20.

12. Weaver, *The International Development Association*, p. 28.

the ensuing forty-eight hours a resolution saying, "It is the sense of the Senate that consideration should be given to the establishment of an International Development Association, in cooperation with the International Bank for Reconstruction and Development." He envisaged a competently managed nonpolitical agency to which the United States could transfer substantial quantities of local currency holdings. With these and other resources, the agency would make long-term loans at low rates of interest and repayable in local currencies to supplement World Bank loans. Monroney's grasp of international economics was not profound, but he was a humanitarian and a skillful politician.

As soon as his announcement was released, Eugene Black decided to endorse the idea publicly. In a story that began on the front page of the *New York Times*, Black commented at some length on the proposal, emphasizing that "the general concept outlined by Senator Monroney seems to be one that the Bank should be willing to explore."[13]

By mid-summer a revised version of the Monroney resolution had obtained support in the executive branch of the U.S. government and had been adopted by a better than 2-to-1 vote in the Senate. Robert B. Anderson, the U.S. secretary of the treasury, together with C. Douglas Dillon, under secretary of state for economic affairs, began exploring the subject informally with other members of the World Bank. In the other major developed countries, enthusiasm for an IDA in mid-1958 was well below the infectious level. Ludwig Erhard, economic minister of the Federal Republic of Germany,

felt that the Monroney Resolution was a wooly-headed idea which would undermine the World Bank. His fear was that the debtor countries would have a choice between the IBRD and the IDA and that soft loans would sweep the whole interest structure away. The Central Bank of Germany was strongly opposed to IDA based on the non-revolving character of the IDA fund—it would require continuous replenishment by member governments. . . . There was a fear that IDA would destroy the trust which the Bank enjoyed in the capital markets.[14]

Nevertheless, Anderson announced to the board of governors in New Delhi in 1958 that the U.S. government was making its own study of the feasibility and desirability of an IDA and expressed the hope that other countries

13. *New York Times*, Feb. 24, 1958. See also International Bank for Reconstruction and Development, *Thirteenth Annual Report, 1957–1958*, p. 6.

14. Weaver, *The International Development Association*, p. 90. See also James Patrick Sewell, *Functionalism and World Politics: A Study Based on United Nations Programs for Financing Economic Development* (Princeton University Press, 1966), pp. 223–24. (Before the end of 1958, however, Erhard had indicated that he was prepared to support the creation of an IDA.)

would at the same time give thought to the matter.[15] After New Delhi, Anderson continued his explorations with other governments, stressing the growing need of the less developed countries for soft loans and the specter of SUNFED under UN auspices if IDA were not set up as an affiliate of the Bank.

Because of the discussion in Chapter 7, we have not stressed in this chapter the mounting debt burden of the less developed countries, the role of the Bank in calling attention to the problem, and the limited role for the Bank if it continued to be authorized to make loans only at conventional rates of interest to creditworthy countries unable to borrow in the private market. Undoubtedly, however, the most compelling argument for a new international facility was the outlook for the developing world if there were no soft loans and/or grant aid.

Countries such as India and Pakistan would find it next to impossible to squeeze more out of their domestic economies and consequently would probably have to lower their development sights considerably. The newly independent African nations, whose credit had not yet been established and whose domestic resources were often extremely limited, would be in a bad way. Countries with the most glowing export prospects would tend to get the most development assistance.

Once the validity of this line of argument was conceded and the question shifted to the auspices for a soft loan facility, the rich countries that would have to provide the resources held all the cards. As between the UN proper and the World Bank, the preference of the major contributors was clear. In a letter dated July 31, 1959, the U.S. secretary of the treasury proposed to the president of the World Bank that the Bank's executive directors prepare, for submission to member governments, draft articles of agreement for an International Development Association. He included some proposed guidelines for the use of the executive directors. In forwarding Secretary Anderson's letter to member governments of the Bank, President Black said,

I am fully in accord with the suggestion of the Governor for the United States that our meeting in September should be the occasion for taking action looking toward its consideration and, as I would hope, toward the establishment of an International Development Association.

Loaded applecarts are never upset at annual meetings of the board of governors. A number of important and relevant points were made during

15. Robert B. Anderson (the U.S. governor), address of October 6, 1958, to the boards of governors of the IBRD and the IMF. A significant part of Black's address of October 7 to the boards was also devoted to paving the way for IDA. On October 9, alternate U.S. Governor Dillon spelled out in more detail than Anderson the current state of U.S. thinking with respect to an IDA.

the discussion, however, and on October 1, 1959, the governors unanimously agreed to a resolution instructing the executive directors to formulate articles of agreement for an IDA.[16]

IDA Articles of Agreement

The executive directors of the Bank were in reality waiting with open arms for the instructions issued by their board of governors in October 1959. The IDA concept had by then been debated for ten years, during the course of which governments had been softened up, to a greater degree than they themselves realized, for the final compromises that would be necessary in order to launch the enterprise. In May 1959, the U.S. executive director had sent his fellow directors a memorandum outlining his government's current thinking on the major points of substance to be considered in establishing an IDA—size, purpose, structure, voting rights, replenishment arrangements, currencies to be subscribed, use of currencies subscribed, and so forth. The executive directors had had the experience of negotiating articles of agreement for the International Finance Corporation.

Eugene Black chaired the negotiating sessions, and by late January 1960 a highly flexible charter was distributed to governments for approval. By September 24, 1960, enough governments had accepted membership to bring the IDA into being. As is often the case, a number of knotty issues were postponed rather than resolved during the negotiations.

The instructions of the board of governors implied that IDA would have its own Articles of Agreement. But this was a political rather than a legal necessity. Authority to make soft loans and/or grants could have been obtained by amending the Bank's charter. Amending the Bank's existing Articles of Agreement, however, was judged too hazardous a procedure.

It would have made much more sense simply to amend the Bank charter to confer upon the Bank new functions. But . . . to amend the Bank's charter in that respect might open discussions of the Bank charter, invite more amendments, etc., etc., and it [IDA] was therefore set up as a completely new and separate organization even though under the same top management.

Another consideration was to emphasize to the world, especially to the inves-

16. Since members of the Bank staff (most notably Davidson Sommers and Richard H. Demuth) had worked informally with U.S. Treasury personnel on the proposed guidelines, as well as with representatives of other governments, the guidelines came as no surprise to the Bank. The American-proposed guidelines, and the views of the developed and underdeveloped countries as expressed during the 1959 "debate," are summarized by Weaver in *The International Development Association*, pp. 93–98.

tors in Bank bonds, the completely different financial status of the two institutions.[17]

Consequently, within a few days after the close of the 1959 annual meeting, President Black formally proposed to the executive directors that, after a preliminary discussion among them of the important questions raised by the proposal for an IDA, the staff prepare a draft charter reflecting that discussion and that this be followed by detailed consideration of each of the draft charter's provisions. As a basis for the preliminary discussion, he attached to his procedural proposal a staff memorandum entitled, "Principal Points for Consideration in Connection with Proposed International Development Association."[18]

Principal Issues

The main issues that arose during the negotiation of the IDA Articles of Agreement were: the amount of its authorized capital; the shares to be contributed by members and the form they would take; the role (if any) for inconvertible currencies that might be contributed to IDA or received by IDA in repayment of hard-currency loans; whether the organization should make grants or soft loans and, in the latter event, how the requisite degree of softness should be obtained; and the kinds of activity which should be financed.

The United States had proposed that the authorized capital for the first five years be $1 billion, a figure that the Bank management, the governments of India, Ghana, several European countries, and certain other members considered low. The U.S. view prevailed, and the articles provided for initial subscriptions that would aggregate $1 billion, if all the then-members of the Bank became original members of IDA.

Should the subscriptions of members be proportional to their subscriptions of Bank capital? This was a hard fought issue. The Benelux countries in particular, but also the United Kingdom and South Africa, felt that a formula based on gross national product or some other current measure of ability to

17. Oral History Project of Columbia University, interviews recorded in the summer of 1961 on the International Bank for Reconstruction and Development (cited hereinafter as "Oral History"). Quotation here is from interview of J. Burke Knapp, p. 34. As a former director of the Bank's European office said in a memorandum to the authors of this study, "A great deal of trouble was taken by the European office at the time the IDA started to dissociate IDA from the Bank and therefore to avoid any possibility that the existence of IDA would make Bank bonds less attractive." At headquarters, the IDA annual report, published since 1964 as part of a joint Bank/IDA report, was published separately for IDA's first three years.
18. Document IDA/R59-1 (Oct. 9, 1959).

pay would be fairer to them than the Bretton Woods formula, which was designed before the breakup of colonial empires and even then was more appropriate for the International Monetary Fund (IMF) than for the Bank. Nevertheless, a formula based on about 5 percent of subscriptions to the IBRD as of the end of 1959 was adopted. (The United Kingdom became an original member, but the Netherlands waited until June 30, 1961, to deposit its instrument of ratification, and Belgium-Luxembourg held off until 1963.)

How much of each subscription should be paid in gold or fully convertible currencies and over what period of time? Should the charter distinguish among members on the basis of levels of industrialization, capacity to make contributions in convertible currency, or per capita income? If so, what classes of subscribers should be created, and which members should be assigned to each class? The decisions that emerged incorporated concessions to numerous vigorously expressed points of view.

Although there was intermittent support for at least three categories of members, the final decision, as reported in Chapter 4, above, was for two categories: Part I to include the richer countries and Part II the less affluent countries. What was the basis for assignment to Part I or Part II?

Well, this presented the Bank with an interesting and rather difficult question. A large number of economic criteria were made available by the Bank, the amount of capital exported by the country, the gross national product of the country, and various other things of that sort. These were reviewed by the Board of Directors. But in the ultimate analysis, the management of the Bank was invited to present a list of those countries which, in their opinion, and based on the background of the World Bank, should be in category I and those which should be in category II. The management presented this list, and the various executive directors who were negotiating the charter discussed it and agreed that this was an adequate list.[19]

In allocating members to Part I or Part II, the Bank staff relied primarily on per capita income figures. Most cases were fairly obvious, but a few were not. Spain said it was flattered to be asked to be in Part I but did not feel it belonged there. Finland accepted Part I status. Japan as a capital exporter was put in Part I despite its then modest level of per capita income. Israel, a massive capital importer, was placed in Part II; so were Iceland, Ireland, and Yugoslavia.[20]

Subscriptions were divided into a 10 percent component to be paid by all members in gold or convertible currency, and a 90 percent component. For

19. T. Graydon Upton, executive director for the United States, to the Committee on Foreign Relations of the United States Senate, March 18, 1960, in Hearings on S. 3074 to provide for the participation of the United States in the International Development Association, 86 Cong. 2 sess., pp. 22–23.

20. Weaver, *The International Development Association,* pp. 108–09.

Part I countries, the 90 percent component was also payable in gold or convertible currency, in five equal annual installments. Part II countries, however, were legally obligated to make only the 10 percent component available on a freely convertible basis. The 10 percent component too could be paid in installments—half of it (5 percent) the first year and 1.25 percent each year for the following four years.[21]

The Bank's general pattern of voting rights was followed. Each member of IDA was given a minimum of 500 votes, plus one vote for each $5,000 of initial subscription. Since the Bank pattern had given each member a minimum of 250 votes (plus one additional vote for each $100,000 of capital stock subscribed by it), the effect of the deviation was to give the less developed countries a slightly stronger voice in IDA than they had in the Bank after the doubling of the Bank's capital stock in 1959.

Had all sixty-eight members of the Bank promptly joined IDA, its usable resources on the basis of initial subscriptions (nominally totaling $1 billion) would have been $786.7 million, comprised of $763 million from the seventeen Part I countries and $23.7 million (10 percent of $237 million) from the fifty-one Part II countries. This would have permitted disbursements totaling $150 million to $160 million annually.

It will be recalled that, for some members of the U.S. Congress, one of the most attractive features of the IDA proposal was "the possibility it offered of facilitating the constructive use of some of the currencies of other countries ('local currencies') owned by the United States."[22] During the negotiation of the charter, however, no enthusiasm was shown by other countries for making IDA a recipient of inconvertible currencies. Largely in deference to the United States, the charter expressly authorizes IDA to enter into arrangements, "on such terms and conditions . . . as may be agreed upon, to receive from any member, in addition to the amounts payable . . . on account of its initial or any additional subscription, supplementary resources in the currency of another member, provided . . . that the member whose currency is

21. Thus, the subscriptions of Part I countries were payable in full in gold or convertible currencies, 23 percent of the total (18 percent plus 5 percent) during the first year, and 19.25 percent (18 percent plus 1.25 percent) during each of the next four years. Part II countries would get voting rights based on their full subscriptions, though they would be required to pay in only the 10 percent component in gold or convertible currencies—5 percent the first year and 1.25 percent during each of the next four years. The balance of the subscriptions of Part II members, as we said in Chapter 4, was payable in the member's own currency and usable by IDA only with the agreement of the member.

22. Quotation is from the *Special Report of the National Advisory Council* [on International Monetary and Financial Problems] *on the Proposed International Development Association,* 86 Cong. 2 sess., House Doc. No. 345, p. 8.

involved agrees to the use of such currency as supplementary resources and to the terms and conditions governing such use."[23]

This provision has remained a dead letter. The existence of sizable holdings of U.S.-owned local currencies unquestionably hastened the creation of IDA but has had no effect on its operations. The same is true for the idea of IDA loans repayable in local currencies. There was more sympathy among executive directors for this type of soft loan, and the charter did not foreclose it; but no use has been made of the provision authorizing such loans. In these respects, the IDA that came off the drawing board is as different from Senator Monroney's initial concept as the automobile is from the oxcart.[24]

While the charter had to be reasonably specific regarding the volume and character of IDA's initial resources, it could be vaguer concerning the use of those resources. In the interests of flexibility, which became a kind of watchword during the negotiations, a number of operational issues were "decided" only in very general terms. The Latin Americans, for example, were especially eager for an IDA that would finance "social" projects. The long-standing controversy concerning so-called non-self-liquidating projects was resolved by authorizing the financing of

any project which is of high developmental priority, that is, which will make an important contribution to the development of the area or areas concerned, whether or not the project is revenue-producing or directly productive. Thus projects such as water supply, sanitation, pilot housing and the like are eligible for financing, although it is expected that a major part of the Association's financing is likely to be for projects of the type financed by the Bank.[25]

Concerning project versus program financing, the charter, to the disappointment of India and some other nations, specified that

financing shall normally be in support of specific projects. The words "specific projects" are intended to include, as in the Bank's practice, such proposals as a railway program, an agricultural credit program, or a group of related projects forming part of a development program. [Article V] Section 1(b) permits the

23. Article III, section 2(a).
24. During the evolution of the Articles of Agreement of IDA, the original notions about this being a local currency institution were largely changed. The management of the Bank took a very dim view of the idea of lending foreign exchange against repayment of local currency. We didn't want to have the responsibility of administering these local currency funds, and in fact we were inclined to denounce it as almost a dishonest device. . . . And we were even more alarmed at the prospect of having to take over a pot of Indian rupees or other local currencies from the United States Government and be responsible for their administration.
Knapp, "Oral History," pp. 29–30.
25. Articles of Agreement of the IDA and Accompanying Report of the Executive Directors of the IBRD (Jan. 26, 1960), par. 14 of the report.

Association to provide financing for other than specific projects in special circumstances.[26]

The most important objective of the founders was to provide a multilateral source of development finance that would bear less heavily on the balance of payments of low-income countries than do conventional loans. From this point of view, grants would of course be ideal. Spokesmen for high-income countries, such as the United Kingdom, France, Canada, and the Netherlands, argued as eloquently as did spokesmen for low-income countries that IDA should have the authority to make grants. But the United States, intensely aware of the congressional preference for loans no matter how soft, disagreed. The charter provided that financing out of initial subscriptions would take the form of loans.[27]

The technique for making the loans sufficiently soft was not specified. Loans repayable in local currency, as we have already noted, were not precluded, but the Bank staff had also focused the attention of the executive directors on alternative devices, such as loans repayable in foreign exchange with long maturities, or long periods of grace, or both, and free of interest or carrying a very low rate of interest. Similarly, the staff had foreseen the complications that might arise if funds loaned to governments on especially favorable terms were reloaned without a change in terms to entities in the borrowing country that were capable of paying normal interest rates in local currency. To meet the problem, the two-step loan, which subsequently became IDA policy, had been suggested.[28]

The Nordic nations had wanted an IDA open to a broader membership than just the members of the World Bank; membership in the Bank, however, was made a prerequisite for membership in the IDA. Unlike the International Finance Corporation (IFC) of 1956–61, IDA was not to have a

26. *Ibid.*, par. 15.

27. A compromise provision of the charter, however, authorizes IDA to make grants from subsequently subscribed funds if the authorization for the subscription expressly permits financing on a grant basis or to make grants from donated funds if the arrangements under which the funds were donated expressly authorize such financing. (Article V, section 2[a] i and ii, which to date have remained dormant.)

28. The policy and its rationale were described in somewhat doctrinaire language in IDA's *Annual Report for 1961–62*, pp. 6–7. The statement began: "If the proceeds of an IDA credit were passed on to the agency executing a revenue-producing project at the concessionary terms obtained by the borrowing government itself, the effect would be to give the project a substantial financial subsidy. This was no part of IDA's purposes, and would encourage the waste and misdirection of scarce investment funds. IDA therefore requires that the borrowing government, if it re-lends the proceeds of an IDA credit for investment in a revenue-producing project, will do so on terms which will impose on the agency executing the project the normal financial discipline with regard to the fixing of rates and charges to consumers."

separate president; the president of the Bank would serve as president of the IDA.[29] A governmental guarantee of a loan to an entity other than a member country was made discretionary, not mandatory as in the Bank's charter.[30] IDA was authorized to provide financing to public international or regional organizations, as well as to governments and public or private entities in the territories of member governments. IDA was expressly authorized to provide technical assistance and advisory services, and these it could offer on a grant basis.

Governmental Approval of the IDA Charter

None of the executive directors opposed the charter that emerged from their October 1959–January 1960 sessions; but the directors for the Netherlands and Belgium found themselves unable to support it, primarily because of the "unreasonably high" subscriptions fixed for them, but also for other reasons. The Netherlands government considered as "too rigid" the provisions on membership, which excluded countries not members of the Bank; on voting power, which excluded equal partnership of the less developed countries; on forms and terms of investment financing, which excluded grants; and on the "all-or-nothing" replenishment requirement, under which members would not be obligated to subscribe but, if they did, would have to subscribe an amount sufficient to maintain their relative voting power. The Netherlands, moreover, remained concerned about the monetary and commercial implications of the use of so-called local currencies for international investment purposes and about the absence of an explicit provision requiring IDA to apply the same standards as the Bank to international debtors willfully in default on their obligations.[31]

The key to governmental approval of the IDA charter was assumed to be the United States. The congressional hearings there went smoothly, with Secretary of the Treasury Anderson, Under Secretary of State Dillon, Senator Monroney, John J. McCloy, chairman of the Chase Manhattan Bank and

---

29. Similarly, the board of governors and the executive directors of IDA would be those who held the same positions in the Bank and would serve ex officio in IDA.

30. As of June 30, 1972, however, IDA credits had been made available without governmental guarantee to only three areas, which, at the time of the credits, were the so-called High Commission Territories in Southern Africa: Bechuanaland, Swaziland, and Basutoland. They were already slated for independence and are now, as Botswana, Swaziland, and Lesotho, members of IDA in their own right.

31. IDA/60-7 (Jan. 29, 1960), p. 3. In the United Nations, the Netherlands had become a strong supporter of SUNFED, which would presumably be even more "flexible" than IDA.

a former president of the World Bank, and others all testifying in favor of U.S. membership.[32] Congressional approval for U.S. participation was obtained by mid-year, thus assuring IDA of $320 million of the $650 million needed to bring the Articles of Agreement into force. By September 24, 1960, the charter had been signed on behalf of eight Part I governments, whose subscriptions aggregated $597.4 million, and seven Part II governments, with subscriptions amounting to $88.8 million, for a total of $686.2 million.

Use of IDA Resources

Reminiscing in 1961, when IDA was not only still an infant, but a rather puny one, Vice President Knapp confirmed that

the management of the Bank was very chary about having IDA created with resources as small as a billion dollars. I think generally in the Bank it is felt that IDA will stand or fall in accordance with whether that proves to be simply a starting mark or whether it remains only on that scale.

It isn't just that we wanted to have more money. . . . What we were concerned about particularly—and what we're still very much concerned about—is the fact that if the resources are that small, there's a very perplexing and difficult and burdensome problem of having to make a reasonable allocation. . . . In the case of the Bank, we never had to ration money. We always claimed—and I think it's true —that we've always been able to raise all the money for the Bank that was required to finance bankable projects brought forward by countries with adequate creditworthiness. But in the case of IDA, while maintaining project standards, we are taking a very much more liberal view of creditworthiness standards. Again, there are huge demands, and the rationing of money is a very heavy responsibility to place upon the management. And, what's more, it inevitably takes us into a realm of political judgments. . . .[33]

In other words, so long as the Bank can market enough bonds to raise the money it needs, financing a Bank project in Country X will not deprive any other member country of Bank funds. Financing an IDA project in Country X, however, reduces the amount of IDA funds available for expenditure elsewhere. As will be brought out in the next section of this chapter, IDA's

32. Mr. McCloy explained that when he was president of the World Bank (1947–49), "it was absolutely essential to fight a vigorous battle against so-called soft loans. . . . But I have come to feel that now . . . there may be a place for the so-called soft loans. . . . The fact that a loan is called 'soft' does not mean that it will not be repaid. . . . In many cases, the IDA will make loans that will be repaid in hard currencies, perhaps over a longer period than the normal operations of the bank, and with low interest rates and a considerable moratorium before repayment begins." Hearings on S. 3074, 86 Cong. 2 sess. (March 2, 1960), pp. 52–53.

33. Knapp, "Oral History," pp. 31–32.

resources have been replenished several times, each time on a scale enabling its annual level of commitments to exceed substantially the level before that replenishment. Nevertheless, demand has always exceeded supply, and IDA has been unable to escape the rationing problem.

Since IDA's resources, by and large, have been devoted to the financing of activities that are also eligible for Bank financing, the story of the use of those resources will be found primarily in other chapters of this study—most of which deal with IDA credits as well as Bank loans. Here we discuss only a few special problems concerning the use of IDA resources, initial and subsequent—problems related to the overall distribution of its resources and the terms on which they are made available.

It was clear from the Articles of Agreement that IDA was to have "a more benign personality than the Bank."[34] It was also clear that the additional benignity should manifest itself in two principal ways. The terms of its loans (or credits, as they were to be called) should be easier than the Bank's terms, which then required interest of about 6 percent on loans averaging fifteen to twenty years in length. Furthermore, IDA did not need to concentrate to the same extent as the Bank on electric power and transportation; it could also interest itself in projects of a more social character. What, in fact, did it do?

IDA Credits During Early Years

Because IDA was grafted onto a functioning organization, its initial financing could be devoted to projects already in the Bank's pipeline, provided the projects were located in appropriate Part II countries. In May 1961 IDA announced its first development credit—$9 million to Honduras to help carry out a program of highway development and maintenance.

Specifically, the program included the bulk of the financing for a sixty-two-mile extension of the Western Highway of Honduras (from its terminus at Santa Rosa de Copan to the border of El Salvador), the construction of some feeder roads, the continuation of a highway maintenance program, and a highway planning survey. The highway extension was to traverse a region which, though one of the most populous in Honduras, was still not accessible by road. Products moved out mainly by mule and to a limited extent by air transport. Honduras was among the least developed countries in Latin America and had the highest proportion of rural population of any nation in the Western Hemisphere. Its per capita income, though not shockingly low by

34. Geoffrey M. Wilson, vice president of the Bank and IDA, Address before the Institute of Banking and Financial Studies (Paris, June 4, 1964).

Asian or African standards, was nevertheless one of the lowest in Latin America. The gains of the preceding decade—those that had not been offset by a population growth rate of more than 3 percent a year—had accrued largely to commercial agriculture and to the urban sector. The 80 percent of the population that lived on the land, on an income below $100 per person per year, had benefited but little.

The Bank had already made two highway and two electric power loans to Honduras. Preliminary engineering studies for the new highway extension had been financed by the Bank's highway maintenance loan of 1955. Design studies had been financed by the Bank's highway construction loan of 1958. Detailed plans for the proposed extension had been completed in 1959. In short, in terms of the country and sector being dealt with, and the preparation of the project to be financed, there was nothing novel about the first IDA credit.

The provisions of the loan agreement consequently followed the normal pattern of loan agreements, with one major and several minor deviations. The major deviation concerned the terms of the credit. It was for fifty years and interest-free but bore a service charge of 0.75 percent annually on the amounts withdrawn and outstanding. Like Bank loans, it was repayable in foreign exchange, but amortization was to begin only after a ten-year grace period. Thereafter, 1 percent of the principal would be repayable for ten years and 3 percent repayable annually for the final thirty years. The service charge was intended to meet IDA's administrative costs.[35]

Spurred by the approaching end of its first fiscal year, IDA in June 1961 extended three more development credits on the same fifty-year terms as the credit to Honduras. The effect was to raise to $101 million the level of IDA activity during 1960–61 and to extend its operations beyond Latin America to Africa and Asia as well.

---

35. The fifty-year, interest-free loan, which was to become the standard for project credits from IDA, was not conceived with Honduras in mind. It had been recommended by a staff preparatory committee as generally preferable to loans repayable in local currency and other arrangements for lightening the burden on the borrower's balance of payments. Whereas the duration of Bank loans and the length of the grace period varied with the nature of the project being financed, it was recommended that the maturity and grace period of IDA loans should, with few exceptions, be uniform.

On the first Honduran credit, the minor deviations from the Bank's standard loan procedure included the absence of a provision for a negative pledge on the borrower's assets and of a requirement that the borrower deliver bonds to IDA. Of interest also is the fact that part of the remaining cost of the project, for which IDA promised to provide the equivalent of $9 million, was by advance agreement to take the form of a loan of $2.25 million and a technical assistance grant of $250,000 from the newly established Inter-American Development Bank.

The second credit was for $13 million to Sudan for the Roseires Dam project on the Blue Nile. Extended in conjunction with a Bank loan of $19.5 million, the credit is noteworthy as the first joint IDA–World Bank operation. The third and largest credit was to India in the amount of $60 million, to cover half the cost of improvements to the national highways during the first three and a half years of India's newly begun third five-year plan. The fourth credit ($19 million for the foreign-exchange costs of road improvements in Chile, one of the richest Part II countries) was again extended jointly with a World Bank loan. Joint operations permit the blending of assistance in such fashion as to enable the Bank Group to charge, on its overall investment in a project (or a country), any rate of interest between the 0.75 percent service charge of IDA and the market rate of the Bank—so long as it has sufficient IDA resources to combine with the funds raised by the Bank in capital markets.

Although the inability of IDA to extend grant aid was regarded by many as a major defect, the technique popularized during the late 1960s for measuring the grant-equivalent of loans at less than market rates of interest enables one to see in retrospect that straight IDA assistance comes very close to being grant aid. As was explained in Chapter 7, the concessionary element in the standard IDA credit, at a 10 percent discount rate, is equal to 86.4 percent of the credit; a $1 million credit, in other words, is equivalent to a grant of $864,000. (It would be exceedingly difficult, however, for a donor to parlay an $864,000 grant into a fifty-year relationship with the recipient. Proponents of grant aid are probably justified in considering a loan that, in economic terms, is 86 percent grant to be a far cry, psychologically and politically, from 100 percent grant aid.)

In the second year of IDA operations—the fiscal year ending June 30, 1962—its level of activity stepped up to eighteen credits, totaling $134 million. These included six credits to India, three to Pakistan, and four to Taiwan. The purposes for which these credits were extended involved no radical departures from Bank practice, except in the case of credits of $2 million and $4.4 million, respectively, to finance municipal water supply systems in Amman, Jordan, and Taipei, Taiwan. A total of $260 million was committed during the third year, with the result that by mid-1963 IDA credits totaling $495 million had been extended to eighteen different countries.

The third fiscal year brought at least one long-contemplated departure from traditional Bank practice—the approval of an IDA credit for education. In addressing the UN Economic and Social Council in April 1960, the president of the Bank had indicated that IDA, if and when it came into existence, would enter the field of educational financing, especially to meet the needs of the new countries of Africa. Twelve months later Tunisia submitted the first application for IDA funds for education. A credit in the amount of $5 million to finance the construction of six new secondary schools was approved in September 1962.

Shortly thereafter—in January 1963—the Philippines applied for an IDA credit to expand the College of Agriculture of the University of the Philippines at Los Baños. On the basis of its financial and economic situation, however, the Philippines was not regarded as eligible for an IDA credit. The Projects Department of the Bank prepared a memorandum arguing that educational development was a field suitable for the Bank. The management agreed that the Bank, in principle, could finance the Los Baños project. In June, the government of the Philippines, after some demurral, said that it would be willing to accept a Bank loan rather than an IDA credit. Late in October 1964, the Bank loan for the project was signed.

As had long been known, India and Pakistan alone could easily have absorbed all of IDA's resources. The concept of an allocation system (that is, a system under which a country or region could acquire an implicit right to a particular share of IDA's funds) had been rejected by the staff preparatory committee that had been put to work as soon as the executive directors had completed the drafting of the IDA charter. In lieu of allocations, a system of unannounced "limitations" was recommended, with a view to giving priority to poorer countries in the Part II category and to countries which, for reasons beyond their control, were unable to finance a satisfactory rate of development through the use of their own resources plus those borrowed from abroad on conventional terms. The policy of avoiding an allocation system while striving for an equitable and politically realistic distribution of available funds was described with semantic artistry in IDA's first annual report:

> IDA has no policy of allocating its funds in advance. An effort is being made, however, to assure wide geographic distribution of development credits, taking into account the priority which should be given to the poorer countries. At the same time, it probably will be necessary to observe a limit on credits for some countries which could quickly present enough suitable projects to absorb a disproportionate amount of IDA funds.[36]

The Allocation Problem

The allocation problem and its half sister, the eligibility problem, were to remain issues for IDA throughout the period covered by this study. Pre-IDA analysis of creditworthiness was more or less stood on its head by the advent

36. International Development Association, *First Annual Report, 1960–1961,* pp. 4–5.

of IDA. Until then, economists wrote their economic reports to demonstrate that countries *were* creditworthy and thus qualified for Bank loans. In 1961, the desire was to show that countries were *not* creditworthy and thus they qualified for IDA credits. If, in this vein, assessments of creditworthiness become too conservative, "then we will give IDA credits where we might give Bank loans and so draw on painful grant money rather than on relatively painless borrowed money."[37]

Credits to India and Pakistan represented such a sizable fraction of total credits during the early IDA years that the global organization began to be referred to in private as the "India-Pakistan Development Association." Credits to these two countries absorbed more than 70 percent of all IDA credits during the period 1960–65. Because of their large populations, their receipts on a per capita basis were not nearly so far out of line, and if extreme poverty added to a country's entitlement to IDA resources, the concentration on India and Pakistan could easily be justified. Nevertheless, it gave rise to a great deal of grumbling, and in March 1968, the executive directors agreed that India's share in future IDA commitments should be reduced from the then prevailing level of 51 percent to 40 percent, and that of Pakistan from 19 percent to 12.5 percent of total commitments. Although the new ceilings have been observed, India and Pakistan together have accounted for 60 percent of total IDA commitments of $3.4 billion during the period between IDA's first credit and June 30, 1971.

Both the Bank and IDA were more active during the second half of the 1960s than during the first half, with IDA's level rising somewhat more rapidly, so that it accounted for more than one-fourth of the combined Bank-IDA level during the years 1966–70. Throughout this section we are discussing *new loans and credits* (net of cancellations), not *net transfers of resources* (which take into account reverse flows from earlier loans and are discussed in the last section of this chapter).

The modest decrease in the proportion of IDA commitments to India and Pakistan during 1966–70, as compared with 1961–65, facilitated a rise in the absolute level of credits to Africa from about $125 million to $460 million, or from about 10 percent to more than 25 percent of total credits. By contrast, Africa's share in total Bank loans—also about 10 percent during 1961–65—rose to only 15 percent in 1966–70. The level of IDA credits to nations in the Western Hemisphere—more than 8 percent of total IDA credits in 1961–65—shrank to 3 percent during 1966–70. Bank lending to Western Hemisphere nations, however, was larger, absolutely and proportionately, in 1966–70 than in 1961–65.

---

37. J. P. Hayes, Internal memorandum (Nov. 20, 1961).

Differences between IDA and the Bank with respect to type of project financed are to some extent explained by IDA's concentration on South Asia. Almost one-fourth of IDA's resources during 1961–70 were devoted to program lending (principally to India and Pakistan), as compared to less than 1 percent of the Bank's resources. A further 20 to 25 percent of IDA resources has been devoted to projects in the agricultural sector, as compared to 10 percent of the Bank's, with the Bank's agricultural commitments more heavily concentrated than IDA's in the years 1966–70. During both halves of the decade IDA devoted a larger proportion of its resources than the Bank did to financing educational projects. As might be expected, IDA has lagged far behind the Bank in proportion of resources devoted to electric power projects and to industry.[38]

The distribution of IDA resources represents the reconciliation in practice of various not wholly consistent policy objectives, such as favoring the neediest countries, favoring countries suffering from balance-of-payments difficulties not of their own making, requiring projects to yield economic and financial returns similar to those expected of Bank-financed projects, and requiring the borrowing nations to pursue reasonably sensible macroeconomic policies. Because no reconciliation will satisfy everyone, the proceedings of the annual Bank–Fund meetings and meetings of IDA's executive directors contain a good deal of criticism.

IDA's Articles of Agreement do not mention the per capita income of a country as a criterion, but IDA has tended to limit its credits to those countries with per capita incomes of less than $300 a year and, in fact, to assist primarily those with per capita incomes below $100. Eager to get into business, IDA during the first two years extended credits to four Latin American countries—Chile, Colombia, Costa Rica, and Nicaragua—which, though their per capita incomes were in the $250 to $500 range, had finance-ready projects. After a discussion of lending policy by the executive directors in 1964, IDA concentrated its lending activities on countries with per capita incomes of $250 or less. A further discussion in 1968 produced a consensus that there should be no rigid ceilings and that some exceptions for countries in the $250 to $300 range should be permitted.

The resulting modest role of IDA in Latin America has been a source of unending complaint from spokesmen for Latin American members. One of their executive directors once remarked at a board meeting that Latin American governments should be classified as Part III members of IDA, since they

---

38. For details, see Appendix Tables E-4 and E-5 on Bank loans and IDA credits by purpose and area for 1961–65, 1966–70 and January–June 1971.

were neither donors nor recipients. Insult, in their view, has been added to injury by authorizations for the transfer of $485 million to IDA during the period 1964–71 from Bank net income in excess of reserve requirements.[39] As they see it, they are paying higher rates of interest on Bank loans than would otherwise be necessary in order to build up profits, which are then transferred to an affiliate from which they derive almost no direct benefit.

Malaysia and Thailand have argued that IDA policies should not penalize prudence, and Taiwan (in 1964) urged that credits not be refused to a country whose balance of payments has temporarily become favorable. France has pressed strongly for more IDA assistance to French-speaking Africa, and African nations generally have argued persistently in favor of more IDA credits for their continent. Practically all less developed member countries other than India and Pakistan have at some time advocated a "fairer" distribution of funds or distribution on a wider geographic basis.

The Bank staff has kept IDA policy under almost continuous review and has conducted special reviews in 1963 (before the first replenishment became effective), in 1968, and in 1970.[40] The lending criteria used by IDA, as the 1968 review said, were better adapted to avoiding a waste of IDA funds than to relating positively the amount and type of IDA assistance to the long-term development needs of the country. If a particular borrower was poorer, less creditworthy, performing better, and had a more attractive project than another borrower, the implied priority was obvious. In the more common case, in which the four criteria did not all point in the same direction, the priority necessarily became ambiguous.

In the very early years, as we have indicated, the emphasis on good projects and the desire to get on with the job tended to favor countries that were ready with projects of a familiar type. India and Pakistan may have benefited additionally because of the existence of the consortia described in Chapter 15; the Bank's leadership in establishing these entities made the Bank Group eager to render them effective. Very few credits could be made to African nations during IDA's first few years, partly because many did not join IDA until 1962 or 1963.

The poverty criterion used by IDA during the 1960s took no account officially of differences among countries below about $300 a year in per capita income. However, for India and Pakistan (IDA's largest borrowers) a spe-

39. See the section on Replenishment of IDA Resources, below.
40. "IDA Lending Policy," Report no. EC-119b (Nov. 26, 1963); "Report of the Working Group on IDA Policies" (May 24, 1968); president's memorandum of July 16, 1968, to executive directors; and president's memorandum of June 17, 1970, in response to the Pearson Commission's recommendations.

cific amount of IDA resources has been set aside as part of the Bank Group's contribution to the aid consortia. Elsewhere, countries that received an unusually high volume of credits per capita have subsequently been temporarily barred from further credits. This implied ceiling on IDA credits per capita has had its main impact on small countries. Finally, when periodic reviews of IDA allocations have taken place, particularly those in anticipation of replenishments, apparent discrepancies have been revealed and a special effort made to remedy them—for example, by extending IDA credits to poor member countries to which credits had not yet been extended.

With respect to the economic performance of member countries, IDA, like the Bank, has found it exceedingly difficult to establish objective standards and in fact has relied largely on ad hoc judgments to assess the extent to which performance should influence the granting or withholding of credits.[41] The performance criterion has been applied primarily to macroeconomic performance, especially in the field of public savings; and short-run considerations appear to have played an unduly prominent part. Constraints on performance differ widely from country to country, and different standards have therefore been used for different countries.

The project test has meant that IDA projects have been judged by the same standards as Bank projects. For a considerable time, this excluded from IDA assistance such countries as Nepal and Upper Volta, which could not prepare projects of the requisite standard, though the countries were probably eligible on grounds of poverty, creditworthiness, and performance. The Bank's permanent missions in eastern and western Africa were established to assist in project preparation and its Agricultural Development Service to assist in project management in Africa.[42] The project test, it has been suggested, may also have penalized certain smaller and poorer countries by forcing IDA activity into the pattern of Bank-financed projects when greater emphasis on exploring obstacles to economic development in those countries might have unearthed other loan possibilities.

In the allocation of IDA resources, problems of creditworthiness arise in two totally different ways. First, there is the problem of how IDA should

41. See Chapter 13, in which we interpret the Bank Group's position to be that, despite difficulties in judging performance, borrowing from IDA necessitates a more searching review of overall performance than does borrowing on Bank terms.

42. As evidence of the Bank Group's growing interest in technical assistance, IDA since 1966 has extended a small number of project preparation credits, usually for amounts of $1 million or less, with ten-year rather than fifty-year maturities, and two-year grace periods. Such project preparation credits are intended to be refinanced through a long-term credit for the project itself in those cases in which the project goes forward under Bank Group financing.

treat a country which is poor in terms of income per capita but which has no apparent shortage of foreign exchange. Second, there is the opposite case of a country which is relatively well off in terms of income but which faces a critical shortage of foreign exchange.

In fact, few if any extremely poor countries have been denied IDA assistance simply because they have not exhausted their creditworthiness for conventional lending. With respect to the less poor Part II countries, during most of the life of IDA there has been a tendency for decisions to be influenced by comparatively short-term liquidity problems. The fact that a country will encounter difficulties in servicing its foreign debt in the next five years or that its debt service ratio will reach a burdensome level within the foreseeable future has been accepted as indicating a lack of creditworthiness. For countries retaining some ability to finance loans on conventional terms, IDA and Bank assistance could be blended.

The obvious shortcomings of the criteria used earlier for allocating IDA resources led the 1968 working group to search for alternative methods of (a) giving appropriate weight to the moral commitment of the international community to do something about extreme poverty, as reflected in gross inequalities in income levels among nations, and (b) ensuring that IDA credits would be efficiently and effectively utilized. The formula and guidelines they proposed, however, were not commended to the executive directors by management and therefore acquired no official status. The most important change resulting from discussion at the executive director level was the backing given to greater help to the poorer countries, particularly in Africa, in project preparation. The decision to reduce the India-Pakistan share of total commitments in order to permit a broader geographic distribution of credits, and to apply less rigidly the $250 ceiling on per capita income in a country, have already been mentioned. Later a ceiling was also put on IDA credits to Indonesia.

The Pearson Commission in its 1969 report, *Partners in Development*, urged that IDA employ its resources to offset inequities in the distribution of bilateral development assistance.[43] It had noted that the existing distribution of bilateral aid had for political and historical reasons been extremely uneven and appeared to bear little relationship to need, performance, poverty, or other economic criteria.

The commission's proposal implied a sharper break with past practice than the staff and executive directors of the IDA were prepared to endorse. It

---

43. *Partners in Development,* Report of the Commission on International Development, Lester B. Pearson, chairman (Praeger, 1969), p. 230.

would have meant greater concentration on a small group of countries, although the pressure of member governments during most of IDA's lifetime had been for a broader distribution. It could also involve a kind of negation of bilateral efforts. Would the major contributors to IDA, which were also the main sources of bilateral development assistance, be willing to increase their contributions to IDA if the principal criterion for allocating IDA credits were to offset the collective results of their own development assistance policies?

The idea that IDA funds should be directed toward countries receiving unduly small amounts of aid from other sources was recognized as meritorious. Securing greater equity in the overall distribution of aid was consequently accepted as an additional criterion in reaching judgments on the allocation of IDA funds.

Replenishment of IDA Resources

As everyone connected with the operation must have known, the level of IDA activity permitted by the initial subscriptions was too low to be meaningful in a worldwide sense. Today, a decade later, IDA is expected (if we ignore price increases) to operate at more than five times its initial level—that is, at approximately $900 million a year for the three-year period that began July 1, 1971. This still rather modest level has been reached as the result of three replenishment exercises involving extensive intergovernmental negotiations, the transfer to IDA of a substantial sum in IBRD profits, and some special supplementary contributions.

Uneventful Course of First Replenishment

The first replenishment was comparatively uneventful. The United States took the lead; the crucial discussions were not held under Bank Group auspices. Representatives of the United States, the United Kingdom, Germany, France, and Italy met several times in Paris in late 1962 and early 1963 and concluded that it would be easier to persuade parliaments to appropriate funds for a three-year period than for the five-year period proposed by Eugene Black, as president of the Bank and IDA. The amount they agreed on was $250 million a year. The most significant feature of the first replenishment was that the $250 million was to be provided entirely by Part I countries, with no contributions from Part II countries—an idea proposed by the staff when IDA was still on the drawing board but then rejected by the United States as unsalable politically.

The controversial issues having been settled elsewhere, the executive directors were able to prepare a report (dated September 9, 1963) to the board of governors "based on the understanding that 17 governments are prepared, subject to legislative or other necessary approval, to make a total of $750 million in freely usable funds available to IDA . . . for commitment in new development credits over a period extending to at least June 30, 1966."[44] The first installment on the new resources would not be due until November 1965.

The replenishment, it was agreed, should take the form of supplemental contributions rather than increases in subscriptions. Increased subscriptions from Part I but not Part II countries would involve adjustments of voting rights and other complications. For Belgium and Luxembourg, however, which were not yet members of IDA and had not previously subscribed any capital, the replenishment contributions would be divided equally between an initial subscription and an additional contribution.

The deadline by which governments were to notify IDA that they would act to replenish its resources, originally March 1, 1964, had to be extended to June 30 when it became apparent that the legislation authorizing the U.S. contribution ($312 million) would not be passed by March 1. On the second time around, the U.S. House of Representatives acted favorably on the measure, and the requirement imposed by IDA's executive directors—readiness to act on the part of twelve of the prospective contributing members, whose contributions aggregated at least $600 million—could be met.

The executive directors were not unaware of the anomaly in seeking IDA funds from member governments while the Bank itself was piling up profits at an almost indecent rate. At their request, the staff of the Bank in 1963 prepared a paper in which it was proposed that a portion of the Bank's earnings be channeled to IDA, either by a direct transfer or by declaring a Bank dividend, which the dividend receivers would take into account in determining their contributions to IDA. A majority of the directors considered dividends to be inappropriate. Eugene Black, who had been opposed to transfers of Bank surpluses to IDA (largely because of a personal commitment made to the financial community at the time IDA was formed that there would be no financial connection between the Bank and IDA), had been succeeded in the presidency by George Woods as of January 1, 1963. Woods had no similar commitment to honor and was convinced that the Bank could easily survive such adverse repercussions on the financial community as transfers might have.

Accordingly IDA's resources have been increased by transfers represent-

44. IDA, Press release (Sept. 13, 1963).

ing a portion of the IBRD's net annual income for each fiscal year since 1964.[45] With two exceptions—1964, when the amount was $50 million, and 1967, when it dropped to a token $10 million—the transfers have been in the amount of $75 million or $100 million. Total transfers authorized as of June 30, 1971, amounted to the equivalent of $485 million. (An additional $110 million was authorized for the period ending June 30, 1972.) Since the IBRD's net income will probably remain high during the 1970s and its reserve position strong, this source of IDA funds should remain available for the foreseeable future.

A special supplementary contribution of $5.8 million to IDA's resources was approved by the Swedish Parliament in May 1962, thereby setting a precedent which at first only Sweden followed. The contribution was in freely convertible Swedish kronor, was not tied to Swedish exports, and gave Sweden no additional voting rights. It was followed by six additional special supplementary contributions from Sweden, totaling $49.5 million, between 1963 and mid-1971.

Switzerland, which is not a member of the Bank and therefore is not eligible for membership in IDA, decided in 1966 to make a $12 million loan to IDA, payable in three equal annual installments beginning in mid-1968. The terms of the Swiss loan were better than IDA's own terms. The Swiss loan was repayable in fifty years, interest-free, and *without* a service charge (because the Swiss would not incur the administrative expenses that the 0.75 percent charge was intended to cover).

Troubled Course of Second Replenishment

Whereas the first IDA replenishment took less than two years to negotiate, the second took nearly four years and was a touch-and-go affair almost from the start. George Woods was well into his presidency by the time the governors authorized the start of negotiations (September 1965). He was convinced that the less developed countries could put to constructive use substantially more capital than they were then getting, and he was eager to catapult IDA from its $250-million-a-year level of operations to a much higher level. The total he sought, "a good round figure to put forward," was $1 billion a year.[46] Woods also considered it more appropriate for the Bank

45. The actions have been authorized by Resolution No. 208, adopted by the board of governors of the Bank on September 10, 1964. The policy is that transfers to IDA should not exceed the amounts that the Bank might otherwise have declared as dividends.

46. Interview with George Woods by the authors, Oct. 17, 1972.

president to take the lead in the negotiations than for a major multilateral agency to sit in the wings while others occupied the center of the stage.[47]

On July 14, 1966, therefore, Mr. Woods proposed that the Part I members replenish IDA's resources on the scale of $1 billion a year for a three-year period, a scale he considered well within the capabilities of the industrialized nations. It became apparent during the 1966 annual meeting that the United States attached considerable importance to avoiding negative effects on its balance of payments from the proposed replenishment; the statistics showed that U.S. contributions to IDA accounted for about 40 percent of total contributions, but IDA-financed procurement in the United States had been less than 20 percent of total IDA-financed procurement. The question of safeguards for countries with balance-of-payments difficulties thus became a major stumbling block to completion of the negotiations.

Mr. Woods decided to concentrate first on discussions with the United States, both because of its balance-of-payments and budgetary problems and because it was the only major contributor that favored the billion-dollar level. He intended to follow up these discussions with similar discussions with the German, British, and French governments—a procedure which led *The Economist* to comment that "Mr. Woods apparently believes in multilateral giving but bilateral asking."[48] If his negotiations with the United States had been short and sweet, his decision as to procedure might have been vindicated. It was April 1967, however, before he consulted any Part I countries other than the United States, and their irritation at being left in the dark for so long was a factor in delaying completion of the replenishment for another two years.

During the remaining months of 1967 and early 1968, four multilateral meetings of representatives of Part I countries took place in European capitals, and a working party on balance-of-payments safeguards met in Washington under the chairmanship of J. Burke Knapp, vice president of the Bank. Bilateral consultations with major European contributors were held between these meetings. President Woods made three visits to European capitals, and consultations with the U.S. government continued in Washington. The main issues included the balance-of-payments safeguards, the aggregate amount of the replenishment, and the share of the total to be contributed by each participating member country. Other issues were also raised, including the possibility of greater control by the donor countries over IDA's management

47. The following brief history of the second IDA replenishment draws extensively on an internal memorandum on the subject (dated September 2, 1969) by Barbara Eschenbach.

48. *The Economist,* Vol. 224 (London, Sept. 30, 1967), p. 1210.

and lending policies, the geographical distribution of IDA credits, and the question whether the replenishment should take the form of loans or additional subscriptions, rather than contributions.

It became clear that the level of operations proposed by President Woods was far in excess of what would be obtainable and that the tied aid arrangements favored by the United States were generally objectionable. European nations that only a few years earlier had been at least as zealous as the United States in protecting their balances of payments, that had been extremely reluctant to release their 18 percent subscriptions to the Bank, and that still continued to tie their bilateral aid, rose in righteous wrath at the U.S. proposal to permit countries in balance-of-payments difficulties to tie some or all of their IDA contributions.

Replenishment was becoming increasingly urgent, and Woods in early 1968 accepted defeat. On amounts, he proposed to the executive directors representing Part I countries that they replenish at a constant annual rate of $400 million for three years—a figure beyond which the members of the European Economic Community simply would not go. On balance-of-payments protection, Woods accepted an ad hoc arrangement that would help the United States, the only nation that requested safeguards, but skirted the issue of tied aid in future IDA operations.

Basically the latter arrangement gave the United States so-called "end-of-queue" treatment. As was subsequently spelled out in a procedural memorandum, the United States would not have to contribute on a pro rata basis until July 1, 1971, at the earliest. Until then, the United States would contribute only the portion of its share that represented identifiable IDA procurement in the United States; a postponement period of three years would be granted for the deferred amounts. Meanwhile, the majority of Part I member countries would compensate for the deferred U.S. amounts, namely the difference between the U.S. pro rata share for each payment period (its absolute ceiling regardless of the amount of procurement in the United States) and the amount put up by the United States to cover actual procurement in the United States.

The burden-sharing problem was also resolved in ad hoc fashion. A few countries decided that they could participate in the second replenishment only if their proportionate shares were below their shares of the first replenishment. The resultant deficit (from the desired $1.2 billion for three years) could not be offset by the addition of Belgium and Luxembourg as Part I countries, plus the Swiss loan. Five countries—Canada, Denmark, Finland, the Netherlands, and Sweden—therefore offered supplementary contributions totaling $17.5 million to close the remaining gap.

For the replenishment to come into force, a minimum of twelve nations would have to notify IDA by June 30, 1968, that they would contribute at least $950 million of the proposed $1.2 billion. This meant that the agreement could not come into being unless the U.S. government enacted the legislation enabling it to make its contribution of $480 million. The troubled course of the necessary legislation need not be traced here. Suffice it to say that not until July 23, 1969, did the United States deposit its formal notification of acceptance. Meanwhile, IDA was on thin ice, saved by the willingness of Canada and most other Part I countries to put some or all of their contributions at IDA's disposal, even though the replenishment was not at the time legally effective and ratification by the largest contributor was not assured.

The delay in completing the second replenishment had both political and economic repercussions. IDA commitments, which had been rising fairly steadily between 1961 and 1967, dropped from $354 million in fiscal year 1967 to $107 million in fiscal 1968. Because disbursements lag behind commitments, the direct economic repercussions showed up primarily in declining expenditures in 1969 and 1970 ($256 million and $143 million, as compared with $319 million in 1968). During the period of stringency, moreover, a number of transactions took the form of Bank loans that, if IDA funds had been available, would have been IDA credits.

The political repercussions included not only the additional strain on relations among the principal contributors and between Mr. Woods and those contributors, but also the added complications that the delay introduced into such major IDA operations as the $125 million credit of January 1969 to enable India to continue industrial imports at the rate of $10 million to $15 million a month, effective January 1, 1968, the closing date for disbursements under a preceding credit.[49] Had the second IDA replenishment exercise been completed by mid-1967, consideration of an IDA credit to India to cover certain 1968 imports would have avoided completely the problem of retroactivity—of a credit for expenditures already made but not authorized in advance by the board. But by January 1969 it was possible for an executive director opposed to the loan to add to his earlier arguments that the board was approving a loan for something already "imported, eaten, and paid for."

Third and Largest Replenishment

The third and largest replenishment exercise, thanks to good preparatory work by Vice President Sir Denis Rickett and others, got off to a handsome start. President McNamara began discussions with Part I members in Decem-

49. For details see Chapter 9, above.

ber 1969. By June 1970, agreement had been reached on the proposals to be made by the executive directors. They were calculated to enable IDA to operate at an annual level of more than $900 million.

Until the third replenishment, all resources except the initial subscriptions had been made available in the form of contributions that did not carry voting rights. Because the additional contributions were in many cases in proportions different from those fixed for initial subscriptions, the relative voting power of nearly all Part I members was not in proportion to the total amounts contributed by them. And the differences in some cases were substantial.

To rectify the situation, it was agreed that the resources provided by Part I members would be represented partly by subscriptions carrying voting rights and partly by contributions not carrying voting rights. The subscription and the voting rights carried with it for each member would be calculated so that the proportion of its votes (excluding its five hundred membership votes) to the total of all Part I votes (also excluding membership votes) would be equal to its proportionate share of the total resources made available by Part I members from initial subscriptions, first and second replenishment contributions, supplementary contributions, and funds provided to the third replenishment. Conferring additional votes on Part I members would increase their voting power in relation to that of Part II members unless the latter also made additional subscriptions that were sufficient to permit them to maintain their relative voting power. The small additional balancing sum required of Part II members was made payable entirely in their own currencies.[50]

Three Part II countries—Ireland, Spain, and Yugoslavia—agreed to make contributions (in usable form) totaling $10 million. Switzerland again agreed to participate in the exercise by lending the equivalent of more than $30 million, subject to the approval of its parliament, on the same terms as those of its earlier $12 million loan.[51]

The target date for the replenishment to become effective was June 30, 1971, by which time at least twelve Part I countries, pledging not less than $1.9 billion, were to notify IDA formally that they would make their specified

50. IDA, "Report of the Executive Directors to the Board of Governors on Additions to IDA Resources: Third Replenishment" (July 21, 1970).
51. Iceland, a Part II member of IDA with a high per capita income, notified the association late in 1971 that it wanted to be regarded as a Part I member and to participate as such in the third replenishment. The amount involved for the third replenishment was only $450,000. The case is interesting because the IDA Articles of Agreement do not expressly cover changes of status, and Iceland is the first country to have made such a request. The change of status was accomplished by an exchange of letters between Iceland and IDA and was approved by the executive directors on November 5, 1971.

contributions. Although it had been hoped that this time the United States would complete the necessary action with respect to its share ($960 million) within the allotted period, it again failed to do so. The deadline for final action had to be extended several times, and once more a package of advance contributions from other sources had to be put together in order for IDA to function without interruption.

Table 12-1 summarizes, by source, the total amount ($3,343 million) that had become available to IDA for commitment from its establishment to June 30, 1971. When and if the third replenishment is finally completed, the total will become $5,773 million.

Adequacy of IDA Structure

The Bank has not been quick to foresee the impact that a growing IDA would and should have on the Bank Group's personnel needs, organizational structure, operational policies, and relations with member governments.

As was reported in Chapter 4, the Bank's director of administration estimated in September 1960, shortly before IDA began operations, that committing $400 million in IDA funds by June 30, 1962, would require eight additional staff members for the area departments and another eleven in what was then called the Technical Operations Department. This guess turned out to be ludicrously low. Many more people were needed because of the larger range of countries IDA brought into the Bank/IDA scope, the new types of projects to be financed, the increased need for help in project preparation and identification, and the greater concern with the overall economic performance of borrowers. The solution was to add the necessary personnel but maintain the organizational structure developed for Bank lending.

The Bank's staff thus also serves IDA, and the Bank each year charges IDA a management fee. The projects departments claim that when they are appraising a proposed project, particularly if it is from a "blend country," which receives both Bank loans and IDA credits, they often do not know whether the activity will later be financed out of Bank funds or IDA funds. Moreover, if they did know, their appraisal would be unaffected. According to the Pearson Commission,

IDA is now in effect the World Bank operating according to a special set of instructions for the management of a special fund. . . . The Executive Boards and the staff of the two organizations are identical. The operational policies of IDA are almost indistinguishable from those of the Bank, with the exception that loans

Table 12-1. *Resources Available for Commitment by IDA,*
as of June 30, 1971
Millions of U.S. dollars

Source of funds	Amount	
Initial subscriptions[a]		
Part I countries	751.3	
Part II countries	44.6[b]	
Subtotal		795.9
First replenishment[c]		
Part I countries	744.7	
Subtotal		744.7
Second replenishment[d]		
Part I countries (regular contributions)	1,170.5	
Supplementary contributions (Canada, Denmark, Finland, Netherlands, Norway, Sweden)	18.8	
Swiss loan	12.1	
Subtotal		1,201.4
Special supplementary contributions[e]		
Sweden	49.5	
Denmark	15.0	
Subtotal		64.5
Contribution from a nonmember (New Zealand)		5.6
Transfers from World Bank		485.0
Net income and repayments		46.1
Total funds available to June 30, 1971		3,343.2
Less: development credits signed to June 30, 1971		3,340.4
Available for further commitment		2.8
Proposed third replenishment[f]		
18 Part I countries[g]	2,398.1	
3 Part II countries (Ireland, Spain, Yugoslavia)	10.5	
Swiss loan	31.8	
Total, third replenishment[h]		2,440.4

Source: IBRD, Controller's Department.

a. For the first five years (1960–64).

b. Includes the 10 percent portion of the subscriptions of Part II members payable in gold or convertible currency ($26.3 million) and that part of the 90 percent portion of the subscriptions of Part II members released on a convertible basis, plus the releases on a nonconvertible basis that were actually used.

c. For 1965–68.

d. Intended for the three-year period beginning July 1, 1968, but because of delays, not available until Aug. 22, 1969. Therefore, two annual installments were collected during 1969 and the final payment in November 1970.

e. Excludes the supplementary contributions mentioned as part of the second replenishment (as well as Sweden and Denmark's initial capital subscriptions and their "regular" replenishment contributions). Includes in the case of Sweden, seven special supplementary contributions—three before 1965, and one in each of the years 1965, 1966, 1967, and 1968.

f. Proposed for three years beginning July 1, 1971.

g. Part I countries as of June 30, 1971, were: Australia, Austria, Belgium, Canada, Denmark, Finland, France, Germany, Italy, Japan, Kuwait, Luxembourg, Netherlands, Norway, South Africa, Sweden, the United Kingdom, and the United States. (In November 1971 Iceland became a Part I country.)

h. Exclusive of transfers from the World Bank and repayments on previous credits during the third replenishment commitment period.

on IDA's concessional terms are only available to countries below a certain income level. The criteria for worthwhile projects are, at least in principle, the same. . . .

IDA's attachment to the World Bank has undoubtedly been a highly efficient arrangement. It has guaranteed to contributors that soft lending has been done with the same thorough attention to the careful use of funds that has characterized the Bank's ordinary business. On the other hand, the availability of a soft-loan window has broadened the scope for action of the World Bank as a development institution.[52]

At the same time that the Bank has exercised a restraining influence on IDA, IDA has been a liberating influence on the Bank. The Bank's unwillingness during the 1950s to lend for certain types of projects—education, water supply, housing, and similar non–self-liquidating ventures—helped to build up the pressure for an IDA. But after IDA came into being, the illogic of a policy whereby a less creditworthy country would have access to Bank Group assistance for a wider range of projects than would a fully creditworthy country was finally recognized in the Philippine education case mentioned above. The Bank then found it possible to make loans for the same types of projects as IDA. Similarly the Bank, though unable to meet IDA's lending terms, also found it possible in certain cases to make loans for considerably longer terms—with final maturities as distant as thirty years—and with longer grace periods (seven to ten years) than it made before 1960.

The Pearson Commission, reporting when IDA was still at the $400-million-a-year level, questioned whether IDA's organizational structure would be suitable for the substantially enlarged IDA, which it favored.

The World Bank, which borrows in the private capital markets, must always maintain the highest credit standing. This consideration has naturally shaped the operating principles and procedures of the Bank. The sources of IDA's funds are different, and so, in practice, are many of its activities. Country programming will undoubtedly become more prominent in IDA, and so will such techniques as nonproject lending, local cost-financing, and debt relief. Over time, it is to be expected that such innovations will require organizational change. *Therefore, we recommend that the President of the World Bank undertake a review of the need for organizational change of the International Development Association as its functions increase.*[53]

The commission did not indicate what kind of organizational change might be desirable, and it clearly was concerned primarily with IDA's policies. President McNamara, properly primed by his staff, disagreed unequivocally with the commission recommendation. The source of funds, he told his board of governors, is irrelevant. What contributes most to the development

52. *Partners in Development*, p. 223.
53. *Ibid.*, p. 226.

of the borrowing country should be "the decisive factor" in both Bank and IDA operations.

If the Bank were in fact subordinating the development interest of its borrowers to other considerations, the proper solution . . . would be to change the Bank's policies—not to reorganize IDA. Any policy which can be justified for IDA as consistent with its development function can . . . be equally justified for the Bank, and the Bank should adopt it.[54]

In terms of logic, the president's point of view has much to commend it. If one wants to transform the Bank as well as IDA into a development financing institution, it is better to treat them as Siamese twins than to split off IDA and organize it to facilitate non-project lending and local expenditure financing, to apply new criteria for allocating resources, and to supply more assistance to very poor and very small countries that lack projects to feed into the pipeline. Historically, the Bank has been a project-financing institution, concerned about its image in private capital markets, fearful that the image might be tarnished by program lending or lending for activities not directly productive, and under no real compulsion to reach judgments about overall development strategy. There are executive directors and staff members who would prefer to keep it that way, and to the extent that they have influence, the transformation of an integrated Bank/IDA into something else may be retarded.

The relationship of the president to his board of directors was destined to change in any event—the 1970s are not the 1950s—but the rate of change has been accelerated by the establishment and expansion of IDA. It was pointed out in Chapter 4 that, until the advent of IDA, the president of the World Bank could exercise great freedom in allocating available resources because he had raised those resources in private capital markets and could raise more when more "good" projects were presented for financing. By and large, allocation was not a problem.

When IDA entered the picture, allocation became a problem because every IDA project that was approved reduced the balance available for commitment to other projects. The resources were contributed by governments, and governments (through their executive directors) gradually became more interested in eligibility criteria, economic performance, development strategy, and the means proposed for stimulating previously neglected sectors of the economy. The full impact of the board of directors' growing interest in development policy became most apparent only toward the end of the 1960s. For

54. Robert S. McNamara, Address to the Board of Governors, Copenhagen (Sept. 21, 1970).

most of IDA's first decade, representatives of the treasuries, ministries of finance, and central banks of Part I countries were their principal spokesmen. They tended to be more interested in financial policy than in development policy. During the protracted negotiations for the second replenishment, however, aid ministries became more actively involved. With the third replenishment, IDA will be disposing of enough of each Part I country's aid resources to make the aid ministry intensely interested in IDA policies.

IDA in Perspective

At the beginning of this chapter we suggested several different ways of looking at the creation and operation of IDA as an affiliate of the World Bank. Each of these perspectives has some validity, but no one of them alone will suffice.

IDA represents a triumph for the persevering campaign of the less developed countries, waged principally in the United Nations, for a multilateral source of investment funds at rates far below those charged by the Bank—rates that in fact approach grant aid. Without IDA, 1818 H Street would not be a significant source of financial assistance to the very poor countries of the world, especially those with per capita incomes below $100, nor to other poor countries lacking the capacity to service loans on World Bank terms. The range of countries that would be dealt with by the Bank Group if there were no IDA would be significantly smaller. Similarly, the Bank's involvement in aid coordination and development strategy would not have attained its present proportions.

The Pearson Commission, as we have seen, was not uncritical of IDA. It concluded, however, that IDA should continue to handle at least the share of multilateral finance it had handled during 1965–67, and perhaps more.

The great demand for concessional development finance and the interest in greater internationalization of the aid system converge on IDA. It has a proven record, and it is impossible to imagine the successful creation at this time of another agency with greater capacity to combine the disbursement of soft money on a global scale with committed leadership in aid strategy though, as we have said, the regional development banks perform similar functions at the regional level and commend themselves to the attention of donors for similar reasons.[55]

55. *Partners in Development*, p. 223. The commission estimated that in 1965–67 more than 40 percent of the official contributions of the members of the Development Assistance Committee of the OECD to multilateral agencies went to IDA.

The most important fact to us at the moment is that without a further increase in the volume of IDA credits and in their proportion to total loans and credits from the Bank Group to less developed countries, the Group's *net* transfer of resources to those countries will probably become negative or negligible. When Bank and IDA resources are combined, capital transfers net of principal repayments and interest and commitment charges reached a high point of $500 million in 1967, more than three-fifths of which was accounted for by IDA. The story on net transfers from each institution during the fiscal years 1962–71 is summarized in Table 12-2.

Even at the lower levels in fiscal 1969 and 1970, net transfers from IDA during the five most recent years total $1,246 million, as compared with $849 million in Bank transfers. When the depressing effects of the delay in completing the second IDA replenishment have been overcome and the third replenishment begins to be reflected in disbursements, net transfers of IDA funds should rise substantially above their 1967 high. Net transfers from the Bank may be increased by larger gross disbursements on Bank loans during the first half of the 1970s. In the longer run, it is hard to escape the conclusion that the Bank Group's future financial contribution to the less developed world is dependent on further rises in the level of IDA activity, though its role as coordinator of development assistance, appraiser of development performance, and mediator between less developed and more developed countries need not parallel its financial role.

Putting all IDA project assistance on a uniform fifty-year basis may have been justified initially. The terms of IDA credits now seem unnecessarily inflexible. Accordingly, in Chapter 21 we endorse the recommendation of Escott Reid of Canada for what would in effect be three types of IDA loans: thirty-, forty-, and fifty-year credits.

The system for obtaining IDA replenishments is precarious enough to raise the question whether a more automatic procedure can be devised that is also politically palatable. To date, replenishments have been set up so that they

Table 12-2. *Net Transfers from the World Bank and IDA to Less Developed Countries, Fiscal Years 1962–71*
Millions of dollars

Source	1962	1963	1964	1965	1966	1967	1968	1969	1970	1971
Bank	124	199	149	165	165	163	147	127	154	258
IDA	12	56	123	220	263	337	311	246	131	221
Total	136	255	272	385	428	500	458	373	285	479

Source: IBRD, Economics Department. For more details, see Tables 7-8 and 7-9, above.

could not technically come into force without the U.S. contribution, and the United States has been late three out of three times. The United States and the United Kingdom together provide more than half the funds and, with Germany, Canada, France, and Japan, more than 80 percent of the total. Although replenishment at five-year intervals was originally contemplated, the three-year cycle is becoming habitual, meaning that before the wounds of one round have healed, the next round is under way. Even when it is successful, the system discourages planning on a time scale appropriate to a development financing agency. In Chapter 21, therefore, we return to the question of the length of the replenishment cycle and discuss also some alternative sources of financing for IDA.

CHAPTER THIRTEEN

Leverage and Performance

AT VARIOUS POINTS in the preceding chapters we have had occasion to note that the Bank, in connection with project or program loans and local expenditure financing, has attempted to influence borrowers to make effective use of their own as well as of Bank-provided resources and to take steps the Bank felt would further the process of development. The Bank and the International Development Association (IDA) in financing particular projects not only have been closely concerned with methods of procurement and construction but have tried to influence the choice of management and the character of the organization within which management was expected to function. Rate covenants have specified pricing policies to be followed by power companies, railways, and port organizations. Financial covenants have set limits to borrowing by enterprises and have indicated how the accounts were to be kept. Supplementary letters have set out the Bank's expectations with respect to the behavior of agencies of the borrowing governments on matters less formal than those covered by loan covenants. Letters of intent have been requested of ministers of finance on the provision of local funds necessary to the completion of projects. Oral understandings have been reached concerning the reciprocal obligations of lender and borrower. And managements, at both higher and lower levels, of Bank-financed projects have frequently been subject to advice, solicited and unsolicited, from technical personnel engaged in country or project missions. The Bank has usually made no bones about the behavior it expects from borrowers.[1]

Although conditions attached to a project loan are usually limited to matters affecting the viability of the project itself, this is not invariably so. Adequate financing of local expenditure costs by the borrower may not be forth-

1. See, for example, the quote in Chapter 8 from President Eugene Black's September 1956 statement to the board of governors.

420

coming without new taxes or changes in the composition of government expenditures; and when this is necessary, the Bank has not hesitated to concern itself with questions of fiscal policy. The growing practice of lending for interrelated activities has increased the Bank's interest in those policies of the borrower that affect broad sectors of its economy. The appropriate relationship of road and rail in the transport sector and changes in crops, inputs, and techniques of cultivation to be associated with large-scale irrigation or land clearance schemes are examples. Furthermore, the Bank has repeatedly indicated that it is interested in good performance not only at the level of projects and sectors but in the economy as a whole. To quote from an operational memorandum:

> Inefficiencies and waste anywhere in the economy reduce or offset the effectiveness of even the best projects, and if serious enough would impair the country's ability to service debt, including debt to the Bank. Bank and IDA lending thus involves an examination of past performance in borrowing countries.[2]

"Leverage," in this context, is one of a number of terms designed to indicate the existence of, and degree of, influence exercised by a lender on the behavior of a borrower. Variants of the term—of differing degrees of acceptability—are bargaining power, "arm twisting," and intervention. Leverage can be exercised by advice and persuasion, strengthened perhaps by the expectation of reward or punishment, and by conditions attached to the loan that must be fulfilled before or during the process of financing. If development lending and borrowing were activities in which the lender and borrower always saw eye to eye, with respect to both the objective to be attained and the means to attain it, there would be no occasion for using leverage. The relation between the Bank and a borrowing member country is sometimes described as if this indeed were a fact. Both, it is said, are engaged in a mutual effort to promote the development of the member country. Although there is actually a high degree of mutuality, there can be strong differences of opinion concerning both development priorities and the means of advancing them. Leverage is exercised when the borrower is persuaded or induced, as a condition of receiving a loan, to do something he would not otherwise have done.

Needless to say the use of leverage can be the source of considerable friction between lender and borrower. On more than one occasion a member country has broken off relations with the Bank on the ground that the requests or demands of the Bank amounted to an infringement of its sovereignty; and on other occasions the Bank has taken the initiative and stopped

2. International Bank for Reconstruction and Development, Operational memorandum 4.01 (April 14, 1965).

the loan on the ground that its advice was being ignored. Moreover, this is a relationship in which *how* things are done is almost as important as *what* is done. The Bank and IDA have rather frequently been charged with arrogance. High level officials in borrowing governments do not always relish receiving advice from Bank staff members of obviously junior status. Nor is the animus always limited to junior staff members. On one occasion a former president of the Bank was referred to by a former minister of finance as "India's public enemy number one." Another president, Eugene Black, has coined the phrase "development diplomacy" to embrace, among other things, the relationship between development lenders and borrowers. As with other types of diplomacy, one of the objectives to be sought is to serve the interest of the sovereign (in this case the Bank) with as little damage as possible to relations between the Bank and its members. *Suaviter in modo*, though a worthy objective, is not always realized in Bank operations.

The term "performance" or "economic performance," as used both within and outside the Bank, confuses two rather different things: (a) the behavior of various indicators that reflect the rate and character of a country's development; and (b) the actions of individual institutions and governments that are assumed to influence this behavior. According to the first conception, good performance is indicated by the favorable behavior, say, of per capita income, of export earnings, of marginal savings rates, and of other variables. According to the second, good performance is indicated by specified types of action in the field of monetary policy, changes in tax rates or administration, the installation of an approved system of managerial accounting in public enterprises, and so on.

Current usage in the U.S. Agency for International Development (AID) tends to identify performance with the behavior of various development indicators and to characterize the action assumed to influence these indicators as "self-help" measures. This seems to us awkward terminology. We should prefer to give performance an action connotation and equate good performance with good management in whatever context performance standards are to be applied—that is, at the level of an enterprise, a sector, or the economy as a whole.

The Bank, or any other development lender, can try to influence performance directly by conditioning its loans on specific actions it wants to see taken, or indirectly, by varying its volume of lending with the behavior of certain development indicators in the hope that the borrowing country may be induced to take steps to improve this behavior. The Bank has, in fact, followed both courses. On occasion it has declared a country ineligible for Bank lending on the ground that the rate of inflation was excessively high, or the trend of export earnings was downward, or government revenues were inadequate, leaving it to the borrowing country, if it so desired, to improve the behavior of these indicators, by whatever steps it chose to take. It has also, particularly in Latin America, pursued a policy of "graduated response," varying the volume of its lending according to the relative success of stabilization programs or the rate of increase of export earnings. There are some who feel strongly that this is the only kind of intervention a development lender is justified in undertaking. Any attempt to influence directly the policies or practices of a borrowing country, they feel, is unwarranted interference in its internal affairs.

However that may be, the Bank does in fact attempt to influence performance directly. This is conspicuously so at the project level, where the IBRD actively concerns itself with the choice of managerial personnel, price policy, financial management, and other matters. It is true also of sectoral lending programs, and not infrequently the Bank or IDA has conditioned its loans or credits on specific changes in overall economic policy.

It would be convenient, not only for the Bank but for everyone concerned with the development process, if good performance in terms of a specified set of policy actions were uniformly accompanied by the favorable behavior of a set of development indicators. But such is not the case. This is primarily because the constraints on performance, as well as on management, differ widely among countries. The principal constraints are imposed by a country's endowment of natural and human resources, by the susceptibility of its economy to external influences, and by the political and cultural milieu within which decisions are made.

The natural resource endowment of Pakistan limits the scope of developmental activities in ways that Iran's does not. The shortage of educated and technically trained manpower in various African countries constitutes a handicap to growth not easily overcome by even the most astute managerial performance at the top. Possibly, over time, external assistance can lessen these constraints by natural resource surveys or by education and training programs. Over the not-so-short run, however, they are real limitations to performance.

Development management is also constrained by external circumstances that are beyond its control. An adverse trend in the external terms of trade can impose limits on the effective use of domestic resources. This is a recurring difficulty in Latin America.

Management of resource use takes place within a cultural and political milieu that can seriously constrain management performance. Parliamentary and civil service constraints on the management of public sector enterprises in India can thwart even first rate administrative talent. Perhaps external pressure from the Bank or from bilateral aid sources can do something about this, but if so, the proper focus of attention is on the constraints and not on the internal management. The cultural environment of traditional agriculture imposes serious limits on the rate of dissemination of modernizing techniques. A judgment on performance needs to take these limits into account. At the national level there are wide differences in the capacity of governments to put into effect economically necessary but politically unpopular policies. As both the International Monetary Fund (IMF) and the Bank have discovered, strong governments are hard to find and, when found, may prove short-lived, precisely because popular support for them has evaporated.

These observations appear to lead to the conclusions that:

a. Similar behavior of development indicators in two or more countries may hide serious differences between the countries in the level of managerial performance, and vice versa; and

b. A judgment on the managerial performance of an enterprise, a sector, or the economy as a whole will need to take account not only of the behavior of the development indicators but also of the constraints under which management operates.

It is perhaps unnecessary to emphasize that the provision of external resources can, under the best of circumstances, make only a partial contribution to development. The main determinants have to do with how effectively a country generates and uses its own resources, together with those received from abroad; hence the Bank's interest in performance. Nor is the Bank alone in this interest. The IMF "conditions" access to drawing rights or standby arrangements on adequate performance in the area of stabilization policies. And accepted doctrine in the U.S. Agency for International Development holds that the "inducement effect" of assistance on policies in the receiving countries can have a greater effect on development than the mere transfer of resources has. In considering the possibilities of influence from the point of view of Bank lending policy, we are concerned in this chapter with the following questions:

1. What are the sources of Bank influence or "leverage"?
2. What aspects of performance has the Bank tried to influence?
3. How successful have these efforts been?

Sources of Bank Influence or Leverage

When Polonius offered his son the sage advice, "Neither a borrower nor a lender be," he had in mind, on the one hand, the possibility that a borrower may be subjected to lender influence and, on the other, the question (of concern also to the Bank) of the borrower's creditworthiness. Here we are concerned not with creditworthiness but rather with the influence of a lender on a borrower. In a world in which countries seeking development are short of domestic savings or foreign exchange, or both, access to an external source of capital is decidedly more than a matter of convenience. If access to this source is thought to depend, at least to some extent, on performance, the potential lender can have an influence on domestic policies in the borrowing country without attaching conditions to the loan and even without offering advice. The borrower may do what he thinks the lender will expect him to do. This is certainly one of the main sources of Bank influence. It is worthwhile to take certain types of action in order to stay in the good graces of the Bank, particularly since this probably means also being in the good graces of the IMF and other external suppliers of capital.

Obviously the extent to which a borrower will be willing to take action to put himself in the good graces of the Bank will depend on a number of things. It will depend on how serious is his need for external funds. For example, in the early 1960s, Ceylon was unwilling to take action desired by the Bank, and also by the Fund, but as its foreign reserves continued to melt, Ceylon became increasingly willing. It will depend on the volume of potential borrowing in relation to the borrower's development program or import requirements. Bank lending to Brazil in relation to both these magnitudes has been considered too small to be taken into account by the Brazilian government in shaping macroeconomic policies. But if Bank lending were joined to other external capital flows, perhaps through a consultative group, the volume might be large enough. It will depend on the terms on which external resources are available. IDA dollars are worth more than Bank dollars. In many countries a loan with a substantial local expenditure component is worth more to the borrowing country than a loan of similar magnitude that covers only foreign exchange costs; and similarly, program dollars may be worth more than project dollars. And, as was suggested above, the fact that lenders may consult with each other or act in concert is also a powerful consideration.

The various elements that may increase or diminish Bank leverage will be examined below. Here it needs to be emphasized that the Bank can and does exert influence—not by attaching conditions to loans, not even by offering advice, but merely by being a potential lender known to be interested in questions of economic performance. In the view of some, this is the only role the Bank should play, that is, to form judgments as to whether a country's performance makes it eligible or ineligible for Bank lending and to shape lending programs accordingly. Others, however, attach great importance to the technical assistance operations of the Bank, which essentially means giving advice.

A great deal of the Bank's technical assistance is directly related to lending for specific projects. So far as this advice is concerned with the location and construction of a facility it is generally accepted without cavil by the borrowing country, which recognizes the Bank, together with its recommended consultants, as a valuable repository of scarce techniques. Complaints of intervention may arise if the Bank interests itself in a broader range of considerations, such as price or investment policies or the choice of managerial personnel. These complaints may grow if interests and policies affecting a whole sector of the economy, such as agriculture or transportation, are involved. And of course the area of macroeconomic policy is even more sensitive. Still, if all that is being offered is advice, with no suggestion of a connection between the acceptance or rejection of the advice and the ability of the country to borrow, there is not likely to be much resentment. Nor is the advice likely to be of much influence.

It is advice connected with money or the promise of money that usually becomes effective.[3] That this is so cannot be doubted by anyone who has observed the relative effectiveness of identical advice when it is offered by Unesco or the Food and Agriculture Organization (FAO) and when it is offered by the Bank. Unesco had been providing sensible advice on educational planning for years before the Bank entered the field of educational lending. Sometimes some parts of this advice were accepted. But there was a notable increase in attention given to educational planning when it became clear that projects fitting into a sensible program of educational development had some chance of being financed. A favorite phrase in the Bank is "establishing a dialogue" between the Bank and government officials in borrowing countries on matters of economic performance. Such a dialogue, however, needs to be lubricated by lending operations and very easily becomes a monologue in the absence of these operations.

Early in 1968 what appear to have been useful discussions on Portuguese development policies took place between a Bank team and representatives of the Portuguese government. Later in the year the Economic Committee of the Bank decided that, although Portugal for various reasons was not eligible for Bank lending, it might be desirable to provide assistance in the form of continuing discussions in various areas of development policy. It proved difficult, however, to pursue this dialogue in the absence of prospective Bank lending.

3. It should be noted, however, that in 1961 Kuwait asked for, and received, a comprehensive survey mission, which completed its work in 1963. The Kuwaiti must have wanted advice since there was no prospect that they would ask for money.

A beginning had been made in the late 1960s in establishing Bank relations with the Democratic Republic of the Congo (now Zaire), and it was
reported by experienced Bank representatives that the government of the
Congo Republic had great confidence in the wisdom and objectivity of Bank
advice. But although the Congo could certainly have used sensible advice,
with or without external funds, the same representatives were of the opinion
that it would be useless to try to influence broad development policies in the
Congo without an accompanying Bank lending program.

Some twenty-five Bank economic survey missions have by now made their
reports on particular countries. Many of these reports offer advice on development programs and policies. Occasionally the advice is taken seriously,
and the results become visible in a development program. When this does
happen it is usually quite obviously because Bank support of the development
program is expected. But perhaps enough has been said here and in Chapter
10 to support the contention that advice is listened to more intently if it
comes from a source capable of supplying funds—even if the provision of
funds is not deliberately conditioned on acceptance of the advice.

It may, of course, be so conditioned, and there can be no doubt that, under
certain circumstances, these conditions add to Bank leverage. The amount
and character of Bank leverage would appear to depend on (a) how valuable
what the Bank has to offer is to the borrowing country; (b) how closely related the nature and terms of the loan are to the conditions the country is
asked to accept; and (c) what support there is in the borrowing country for
the conditions the Bank attempts to attach to its loans. We have already
mentioned briefly most of the considerations affecting (a), that is, the urgency of a country's need for external funds, the volume of assistance in view,
and the terms and conditions under which it is offered. But that discussion
must be expanded somewhat.

A country that has little interest in development will presumably have little
need for external funds and will offer poor prospects for the exercise of Bank
leverage. This is said to have been the situation in Portugal in the late 1960s.
The director of the European and Middle East Department stated to the Economic Committee in March 1967 that "it is not so much foreign capital that
Portugal needs as a development program." On the other hand, Portugal
clearly wanted very much to continue borrowing from the Bank, and certain
elements in the government wanted the Bank's assistance in bringing about
changes in development policy.

That the volume of lending in relation to requirements is relevant to leverage does not need to be argued extensively. It is difficult, if not impossible,
to attach far-reaching, non-project conditions to a project loan. On the other

hand, if a project loan promises to be part of a broader lending program that is sizable in relation to requirements, it may be possible for the Bank to negotiate changes in a country's sectoral or even its macroeconomic policies. A $26 million Brazilian highway loan in 1968 was accompanied by fairly explicit commitments from the Brazilian government for far-reaching reforms in the transportation sector. Bank leverage in this case, however, was augmented by Brazil's expectations of substantial additional financing of transportation projects, which would cover, moreover, a sizable fraction of local costs.

The doctrine of "graduated response," now in favor in the western hemisphere departments of the Bank, is an explicit recognition of the relation of the proposed volume of lending to leverage. This was applied to a Latin American country in 1970, and lending at the rate of $50 million a year was suggested at the existing level of performance; an increase of $100 million a year would be granted if sectoral performance were improved in certain specific respects; and lending would be increased by another $50 million a year if adequate performance in the area of stabilization policy were achieved.

If assistance providers act together, merging their funds in an attempt to effect certain changes in performance, leverage may be substantially increased. However, this "ganging up" of creditors can provoke resentment in the borrowing country, making the effective exercise of influence difficult. Although a consultative group was not formed for Costa Rica, the Bank, the Fund, and the U.S. Agency for International Development (AID) acted closely together in evaluating the proposed public investment program for 1965–68, provoking the charge that an "unholy alliance" of capital suppliers was threatening Costa Rican sovereignty. On the other hand, the government of Ceylon seems to have welcomed the opportunity of dealing with the aid group as a unit through the mediation of the Bank, and this also seems to be the attitude of the Colombian government in dealing with the Bank-led consultative group. In both these countries leverage was definitely increased by joining Bank funds with those of other capital suppliers. Such joint action, moreover, makes it possible to blend program and project lending to fit the requirements of the borrowing country.

Whether leverage is increased by joint action depends very much on whether the various lenders see eye to eye on the uses to which leverage is to be put. The consultative group for Peru was not a success in 1966 and 1967 partly because various members had different objectives. The Bank and the Fund were ready to act together, but the United States had business and political objectives in view, such as protecting the interests of a U.S. oil company and limiting Peruvian military expenditures, that militated against effective joint action. The European members of the consultative group were not interested in Peruvian performance but rather in providing what turned out to be an excessively large volume of suppliers' credits.

The possibilities of, and limitations to, generating leverage through consultative groups and consortia is a subject in itself and is touched on in other chapters. Certain of these groups have a core of insiders interested in using leverage to improve performance and a fringe of outsiders who evince no such interest. And the existence of the outsiders may or may not enhance the leverage the insiders are trying to exercise. In the large consortia organized to finance development in India and Pakistan the members most openly concerned with efforts to influence performance have been the Bank and AID.[4] In the consultative group for Colombia it has been the Bank, the Fund, and AID. The only point to be emphasized here is that under certain circumstances—but not all—joint action by potential lenders can increase leverage.

Bank Group Lending—Terms and Leverage

As we have emphasized, the value of external assistance to a borrower depends not only on its volume but also on the terms on which it is provided and the degree of flexibility the form of lending permits. Although the IBRD's operational memorandum 4.01 of April 14, 1965, states that "consideration of the economic performance of a country is equally necessary for the Bank and for IDA," a number of arguments are advanced in Bank papers for paying particular attention to performance in countries receiving IDA credits. These countries are the very poor countries, and therefore the difference between good and bad performance is of greater significance to the well-being of the population; IDA funds involve greater sacrifice on the part of the contributing countries, and therefore there is a particular need to scrutinize their use; IDA funds are rationed, and consequently the case for an IDA allocation must be airtight; and so on. Whatever the merit of these arguments, it is a fact that a given volume of IDA credits carries greater leverage than an equivalent volume of Bank lending, and considerable evidence exists that the Bank tries to use this leverage.

Loans or credits in excess of the direct and indirect foreign exchange cost of a project provide "free foreign exchange" that can be flexibly used to increase reserves or cover the cost of imports that are not related to the project, but are possibly related to a development program. Increasingly the Bank

4. This was conspicuously true in the early years of the consortia. In later years the United Kingdom, Germany, and Canada have also shown considerable interest in performance.

has shown itself willing to undertake local expenditure financing of specific projects in order to provide foreign exchange for a borrower's development program. As we saw in Chapter 9, such financing can, under certain circumstances, substitute effectively for program lending. A recommendation from the president on "Foreign Exchange Loans for Local Currency Expenditures," accepted by the board of directors in 1968, observed that,

in attempting to exercise a beneficial influence on policy in macroeconomic matters, the Bank has a stronger bargaining position if it is reasonably free to vary the proportion of project costs it will finance than if it is tied to financing the predetermined proportion set arbitrarily by the identifiable foreign cost component. Moreover, an unwillingness to finance local costs could effectively exclude the Bank from operations in some countries, so that a dialogue could not even be begun.[5]

Program loans can provide foreign exchange for commodity imports, and, to the extent that program dollars are worth more to a borrowing country than project dollars, such loans offer the possibility of increased leverage. The leverage associated with program lending by AID and drawing rights from the IMF has been used extensively in attempts to influence macroeconomic policy in borrowing countries. A common practice has been to release these loans in quarterly or semiannual tranches, based on an assessment of performance during the previous period. Without examining the effectiveness of this use of leverage, or the possibility of politically adverse side effects, there is no denying that the balance-of-payments support afforded by such loans directly affects the macroeconomic policy choices open to the borrowing country. Efforts by the lender to influence these policy choices, while they may be resented, are not likely to be considered totally irrelevant to the purposes of the loan.

The Bank Group, as we noted in Chapter 9, has made a series of program loans and credits. But for a number of reasons the leverage provided by these loans and credits has not been widely used to try to influence macroeconomic policy. With the exception of a loan to Iran in 1957, all the Bank program loans, until the loan to Nigeria in 1971, were made to developed member countries whose general economic policies were presumably acceptable to the Bank. In the case of Iran the Bank did try to exert influence on the borrower's development policy, and from 1957 to approximately 1964 the Bank played an active role both in helping to shape the investment program of the Plan Organization and in advising on monetary and fiscal policy. For much of this time the Bank maintained a resident representative in Iran, who was actively consulted on matters of domestic economic policy, and a group of

5. Sec M68-436 (Nov. 29, 1968).

technicians selected by the Bank assisted the Plan Organization in the selection and preparation of projects. The leverage provided by the program loan was augmented, moreover, by an active program of project lending directed mainly toward large-scale hydroelectric and irrigation facilities.

IDA, as we have said in earlier chapters, has extended large program credits to India and Pakistan, but the leverage associated with these credits either has been used to influence sectoral rather than macroeconomic policies or has been subsumed under the blanket of the larger consortium operations in which the Bank was not only a leading participant but the chief negotiator with respect to general performance considerations. In sum, while the Bank and IDA have not in fact been able to exert much influence on macroeconomic policies through program lending, except through participating in consortia, it remains true that in many countries program dollars are considered to be worth more than project dollars, a fact that the Bank Group may well take into account if it becomes a more active program lender.

In Bank practice, project loans are increasingly regarded as part of a relatively long-term lending program. While project conditions are attached to individual loans, the lending program as a whole has much broader leverage implications. Here the Bank's leverage lies in its ability to declare a country eligible or ineligible for Bank loans and to "graduate" its loans according to its judgment of performance past or prospective—in other words, to reward a country for its past performance or to induce good performance in the future. It is the view of some members of the Bank staff that the ability to graduate the level of lending in accordance with the borrower's performance gives the Bank as much leverage in the area of macroeconomic policies as might accompany program lending. It should be remembered, however, that projects have long gestation periods, and it may be difficult to introduce a stop-and-go policy that any borrower will take seriously. While this is a fact of some importance, it must also be recognized that, as the volume and relative importance of Bank Group lending to a member country increases and, along with this increase, the scope, the local expenditure component, and the time horizon of lending programs expand, leverage tends to come from the lending program as a whole, as well as from the individual projects that compose the program.

Political Requirements for Leverage

An indispensable source of leverage is the support the Bank may enjoy within the borrowing country for the changes in development policies, practices, or institutions it seeks to accomplish. It is a commonplace that attempts by external suppliers of capital to buy changes in economic policies and practices are likely to fail if the government in the borrowing country is convinced that the proposed changes are inimical to the country's interest or to the interest of those in power. If by chance such changes are brought about, they are likely to be frustrated by evasion, noncompliance, and the opening up of effective loopholes. At the other extreme is the situation in which a government is convinced that what the external lender suggests is in the country's interest and should be undertaken whether or not financing is made available. As Hirschman puts it, "paradoxically, therefore, program aid is fully effective only when it does not achieve anything—when, that is, no *quid pro quo* (in the sense of a policy that would not have been undertaken in the absence of aid) is exacted as the price of aid."[6]

All the real cases of attempted use of leverage with which we are familiar fall between these extremes. Someone—the government, the executive branch of the government, the prime minister, or other important public officials—has to be convinced that proposed changes are desirable, either with or without external financial assistance, or that these changes will become possible and desirable if financing is provided. At the same time, since changes in macroeconomic policy will inevitably affect certain elements in the community adversely and these elements may be represented in government, there may well be political opposition. In the typical case involving the use of leverage the Bank is likely to find itself supporting the executive branch of the government against opposition elements in the parliament, or the prime minister and minister of finance against spending ministries or even the interests of a particular ministry against the rest of the government. How much influence the Bank can exercise depends largely on the amount and character of the political support behind proposed projects.

Consider the case of import liberalization in Pakistan in 1964 and 1965. The minister of finance and the planning commission convinced the president that a certain measure of import liberalization was economically desirable and would be politically feasible, given the external financing of an adequate flow of commodity imports. Both AID and the Bank urged these steps, and most of the financing was provided by the former. At the same time the proposed changes in import policy were opposed by the head of the central bank, who feared a deterioration in Pakistan's balance of payments, and by established importers, who would lose the financial advantage of their import quotas. Insofar as the Bank exercised influence, it did so by supporting the posi-

6. Albert O. Hirschman and Richard M. Bird, *Foreign Aid—A Critique and a Proposal*, Essays in International Finance, No. 69 (International Finance Section, Princeton University, July 1968), p. 8.

tion of the Ministry of Finance against other elements inside and outside the government.

The insistence of the Bank on increased public savings in the Philippines in 1967 as a condition of further lending amounted, in effect, to support of President Marcos in his attempt to wring further tax legislation from the Philippine congress. In this case the President used the Bank's insistence as a powerful argument for such legislation. The leverage of the Indian communications loans, from 1964 to the present, has been used to support the interests of the Ministry of Posts and Telegraphs in the introduction of commercial accounting and modern management practices against the Ministry of Finance and other elements in the Indian government that want to maintain established practices. In this case the Ministry of Posts and Telegraphs, without Bank support, would have been unable to accomplish much. That they could not accomplish more attests to the political strength of the forces arrayed against them. The relative failure of the Bank to accomplish more in the area of transport coordination in India results in part from the impotence of the Road Wings in the Ministry of Transport in relation to the very great political influence exerted by the Ministry of Railways. In Spain, on the other hand, the Bank was able to induce large changes in railway administration and transport coordination by supporting, with financial assistance and advice, the Ministry of Transport against opposing elements in the government.

The conditions attached to the Brazilian livestock loan in 1967 committed the Brazilian government to eliminating existing controls on the pricing, marketing, and export of livestock. At the time there was division within the government on the desirability of controlling food prices. In essence the Bank's support was behind the minister of economy and the director of the Central Bank, who favored a market determination of food prices, and against the head of the National Supply Agency (Sunab), who favored a continuation of price control and state trading. Occasionally the Bank bets on the wrong horse and sometimes backs wrong or questionable policies. In Peru substantial support was given to the public sector development program espoused by President Belaúnde in 1965 in the expectation that he had sufficient political strength to get the required internal financing from the Peruvian Congress. This proved impossible, with the result that the fiscal conditions on which the Bank lending program in Peru was based were not fulfilled.

In sum, the ability of the Bank, or of any other external lender, to influence development policy in a borrowing country depends very much on the political support that can be generated for the lender's proposals. If the support is complete, both inside and outside the government, no leverage is involved. In the typical case, however, the Bank finds itself supporting certain elements in the government or in the community against others. This is all but inevitable if the proposed policy changes are macroeconomic, and it is usually true if what is involved are changes in broad sectoral policies. Changes in fiscal and monetary policy affect the distribution of income; devaluation or changes in tariff rates benefit some to the disadvantage of others. Usually the various interests enjoy some form of political representation, and consequently the proposed policy changes become a matter of intragovernmental debate. An extreme example of the internal debate that may come from efforts by outside lenders to influence domestic policy is (as we noted in Chapter 7) that of the Bank negotiations with India in 1965–66. Here the leverage was great (several hundred million dollars a year in balance-of-payments assistance), the policy changes requested were extensive, and the division of opinion in India on the wisdom of the proposed changes was marked.

Certain areas of domestic policy are much more sensitive to suggestions of external influence than are others. In these areas the leverage of the Bank, or any other external lender, is apt to be slight. This raises the question of what kind of performance the Bank has attempted and should attempt to promote.

Project and Sector Performance

The Bank is predominantly a project lender, and the leverage it has used has taken the form mainly of conditions attached to particular projects or of threats or promises either to withhold or to grant project loans or to reduce or raise the level of such lending. Here we are concerned first with conditions attached to project loans and then with those aspects of country performance that the Bank/IDA may try to influence by varying its level of commitments to particular borrowers. The conditions the Bank expects the borrower to comply with are embodied in covenants written into the loan agreement or project agreement; in supplementary letters or in letters of intent from the borrower to the Bank; and in memoranda of understanding or agreed minutes of negotiating meetings. These different forms in which the borrower's obligations are expressed have different legal standing and are given different degrees of publicity. Only violations of covenants in the loan or project agreement are subject to the Bank's legal sanctions and only printed loan and project agreements are registered with the United Nations as international agreements. Supplementary letters or letters of intent and memoranda of understanding are ordinarily not published. No legal action lies against infringement of the provisions contained in these documents. But this does not mean that such infringement is treated lightly. The real leverage of the Bank lies in the continuing need of its borrowers for funds and its own disposition to meet those needs.

The principal legal sanctions the Bank could use would be to accelerate the maturity of a loan or to cancel or suspend disbursements. Acceleration of maturity, which means that the borrower would be obligated to repay principal and interest immediately, has never been used.[7] On a few occasions loans have been canceled, though sometimes they have been reinstated on somewhat different terms. Suspension of disbursements has been more frequent.

Conditions written into loan agreements range from general conditions that are contained in all, or almost all, loan agreements down to very specific obligations tailored to the nature of the project. Practically all loan agreements contain a covenant to the effect that "the Borrower will carry out the Project with due diligence," the so-called negative pledge clause, which binds the borrower to put no other financial obligations ahead of those to the Bank; and various other covenants relating to the procurement of goods, the provision of adequate local expenditure financing, the acquisition of land, and so on. From here the conditions become more specific in relation to the characteristics of particular projects. They may include provisions concerning highway maintenance, subsidy provisions, marketing arrangements for agricultural projects, covenants regarding the selection of managerial personnel and consultants, and covenants relating to electricity rates, highway tolls, water charges, and port duties.

In the main the Legal Department of the Bank favors general as against specific provisions, and it has succeeded in reducing the scope of supplementary letters in favor of incorporating provisions as covenants in published loan agreements. On the whole, though, the number and specificity of loan covenants have tended to increase. The technical departments of the Bank greatly prefer covenants like "the borrower agrees to complete x miles of road" by a particular date, to covenants requiring the borrower to "proceed

7. "The Bank, at its option, may by notice to the borrower and the Guarantor declare the principal of the Loan and of all Bonds then outstanding to be due and payable immediately together with interest and other charges thereon. . . ." *General Conditions Applicable to Loan and Guarantee Agreements* (Jan. 31, 1969), Article VII, section 7.01.

with due diligence." And in general the technical departments have had their way. In some instances the specificity of loan covenants has tended to work against the Bank because more general language aimed at achieving a result rather than specifying the methods to be used would have given the Bank greater rights. In many other instances the specificity of loan covenants has led to a large number of technical violations by borrowers.

There are also differences in approach and emphasis between the area and the projects departments. In general the projects departments are concerned primarily with the viability of the project and with the conditions they deem necessary to viability, without much regard for the sensibilities of the borrower. The area departments, on the other hand, are concerned primarily with relations between the Bank and the borrowing country over the whole range of the Bank Group's activities and seek to avoid what they consider unnecessary irritation. Perhaps the most abrasive conditions in loan agreements are those requiring the borrower to secure the Bank's approval of the choice of management for the project. It tends to be the view in area departments that such conditions are often ineffectual and are bound to cause political problems. The technical departments, on the other hand, tend to feel that such provisions, at a minimum, cause the borrower to use greater care in selecting managerial personnel.

Most of the conditions attached to project loans can be said to be directly and appropriately related to the success of the project and thus seldom meet with objection from borrowers. On the other hand, borrowers sometimes feel that conditions obligating them to employ foreign engineering, management, or financial consultants are an imposition when local talent is available and, furthermore, that such conditions deprive them of an opportunity to learn by doing. It can be argued that price covenants governing electricity rates, road-use charges, water rates, port duties, and the like go beyond conditions that affect the viability of the project, particularly if the charges include an element designed to provide for the financing of expansions. There are, after all, alternative ways of financing, including government subsidy. Still, these and other conditions are legitimately associated with project viability— certainly in the view of the Bank and also in the view of most borrowers.

As we have said, however, the Bank has tried increasingly to use the leverage of project lending to bring about changes in sectoral policies. The Bank has some inhibitions about attaching sectoral conditions to project loans or IDA credits and about making lending for a particular project dependent on a satisfactory prior understanding about sectoral policies; but on occasion both of these have been done. When sectoral conditions have been applied, it is usually in connection with repeated loans to a single borrower over a period of years or with loans to related projects. We have noted elsewhere the not altogether successful attempts in the course of some thirteen Bank loans and IDA credits to the Indian railways to bring about fairer road–rail competition through reductions in road user charges and less restrictive licensing of road vehicles. Loans for related agricultural projects have sometimes been conditioned on the elimination of price controls on particular crops or on the removal of impediments to export. Attempts to attach broader general policy conditions to project loans have been limited largely to fiscal proposals designed to facilitate the local expenditure contribution to Bank/IDA–financed projects.

Perhaps the most deliberate, persistent, and successful attempts by the Bank/IDA to use the leverage of project lending to bring about significant changes in the borrower's policies have been the rate conditions attached to electric power loans. As we noted in Chapter 8, rate policies in Latin America and southern Asia have been revolutionized, partly as the result of Bank influence. The $70 million power transmission loan to India[8] in 1965 offers a good example of Bank persistence and of some of the difficulties encountered. The borrower was the Indian government, and the beneficiaries were a large number of state electricity boards. At the time of the loan the rate of return on the investments of these boards was extraordinarily low, averaging less than 3 percent. A primary condition of the loan was that the government of India would obtain from each of the participating boards an agreement, endorsed by the state concerned, that the board "shall undertake all steps necessary to earn, at the earliest possible date, and to maintain thereafter, a reasonable return on its capital base." This was spelled out in a supplementary letter as meaning a total return of 11 percent—including a 6 percent interest payment on borrowing, a 3 percent rate of profit, a contribution of 0.5 percent to general reserves, and the electricity duty of 1.5 percent.

Returns of this magnitude had already been recommended by the government's Energy Survey Committee; and in 1964 a report of the Power Tariff Committee, composed of representatives of the central and state governments, suggested the precise figures the Bank later adopted. There was thus no question of forcing on the government a course of action it was not prepared to accept. What the loan did was to add the leverage of the Bank to that of the central government vis-à-vis the state electricity boards. At frequent intervals the Bank sent officials to India to assess progress and to meet in New Delhi with representatives of the state boards. That the task required pressure is indicated by the fact that as of the closing date for disbursements

8. A twenty-year loan at 5.5 percent interest.

(June 30, 1968), only $19.3 million of the $70 million Bank loan had been spent.

The government of India asked for an extension of the time limit along with certain other changes. The president of the Bank, after considering this request, recommended to the executive directors that the Bank "continue disbursements under the Loan, but without postponing the closing date, until January 1969, in the expectation that by then all reasonable steps will have been taken by the Boards to improve their rates of return and that agreements will have been reached with them on revised financial undertakings."[9]

The final stage was reached in March 1969, when the following recommendations of the president were accepted by the executive directors:

a. Disbursements under the Loan shall continue until May 15, 1969, by which date satisfactory revised financial undertakings signed by the Boards, endorsed by their State Governments, and revised in the manner outlined above, should have been received by the Bank.

b. The undisbursed portion of the Loan applicable to any Board which fails to submit satisfactory revised financial undertakings [shall] be cancelled; and

c. The closing date for the balance of the loan [shall] be postponed until December 31, 1970.[10]

The leverage exercised by the Bank in this case was embodied in an effectiveness condition that tailored disbursement to performance by the state electricity boards. There was small chance that the results, such as they were, would have been forthcoming, even though favored by the government of India, without the use of Bank leverage.

As we emphasized in discussing leverage earlier in this chapter, the Bank or any other foreign lender finds it difficult, if not impossible, to impose conditions on a borrower unless some elements in the borrowing country consider it to be in the country's interest to meet these conditions. In the case of Ceylon, the Bank over a long period of time has found itself supported by, and supporting, one political party that espoused orthodox economic and financial policies acceptable to the Bank, while having unfavorable relations with another. As a result the Bank's relations with Ceylon have involved periods of little activity as well as periods of extensive activity. These relations are relevant here because of the light they throw on possible political reactions to conditions attached to a project loan.

The loan in question involved joint Bank and IDA financing for the Mahaweli Ganga irrigation project recommended to the executive directors in January 1970. It was proposed that the Bank lend $14.5 million and that

9. R68-137 (July 25, 1968).
10. R69-48 (March 10, 1969).

a similar amount be provided by an IDA credit. The terms and conditions of the loan had been worked out with representatives of the government of Prime Minister Dudley Senanayake. The conditions were not more stringent than those of other Bank loans of a similar nature, but when the government put the proposal before parliament, it aroused a storm of opposition, which ended only when the party headed by Mrs. Bandaranaike walked out without voting on the bill. Thereafter the loan, or rather the conditions attached to it, became an issue in a bitter election campaign that culminated in the national vote of May 27, 1970.

In negotiating the loan the Bank's representatives had received assurances from the government of Ceylon that included, among others, undertakings to employ consultants acceptable to the Bank Group, to transfer certain power assets to the Ceylon Electricity Board on terms and conditions acceptable to the Bank Group, and to raise water charges to not less than forty rupees per acre per year. The conditions of the financing were that no disbursements would be made until after, among other things,

the enactment and coming into force of legislation acceptable to the Bank establishing the Board and defining its powers;

the setting up of an organization structure for the Board, acceptable to the Bank, and the filling of senior positions on the Board's staff; and

the appointment of a general manager and deputy general managers satisfactory to the Bank Group.

It was not the project itself to which the opposition objected—indeed, this project had been suggested by a previous Bandaranaike government—but to certain of the conditions. Among these provisions were some, like the negative pledge clause, that are found in all Bank loan agreements. This indicated a lack of familiarity on the part of the opposition with typical Bank practice, an unfamiliarity for which the Bank itself was not altogether free of blame.[11] But the assurances given by the government of Ceylon that drew the greatest fire were the agreement to employ consultants acceptable to the Bank Group and the agreement to raise water charges. The opposition held that perfectly competent professionals were available in Ceylon and consequently there was no need to employ foreign consultants. Raising water rates ran counter to the egalitarian principles of Mrs. Bandaranaike's party.

---

11. A senior staff officer of the Bank, thoroughly familiar with Ceylon and with this particular loan, reported to the authors that,

(a) the IBRD (myself included) had very little contact with the opposition. We foolishly isolated ourselves;

(b) many so-called standard provisions of our agreements are misunderstood, and there is no good authoritative primer in which they are explained to newcomers (including new governments).

The conditions that would defer disbursement under the loan until legislation was enacted, administrative changes effected, and managers appointed that were approved by the Bank were denounced root and branch as infringements of Ceylonese sovereignty.

The result of the May election was an overwhelming victory for the party of Mrs. Bandaranaike. In a parliament of roughly 150 her party now held 90 seats and her coalition 120. The party of Mr. Senanayake was reduced to 20 seats. This political event drastically changed, at least for a time, the relations of the Bank with Ceylon. Of three outstanding loans negotiated with the previous government one was canceled outright, and the other two, including the Mahaweli project loan, were denounced as unacceptable and were to be renegotiated. It is difficult to understand the situation in 1970 without some knowledge of what had gone before.

The Bank had made loans to Ceylon in 1954, 1958, and 1961. The last loan of $15 million was made at a time when Ceylon's foreign exchange situation was becoming highly unfavorable. Shortly after this, it was decided, early in the period of a previous Bandaranaike government, that Ceylon was no longer creditworthy, and the Bank withdrew. From 1961 to 1965 Ceylon was in continuous budgetary deficit, borrowing from the Central Bank to subsidize public services and the sale of consumer goods. Imports of raw materials and equipment for industrial use were curtailed to sustain consumer goods imports. Nevertheless, at the annual meeting of the Bank and Fund in 1964 representatives from Ceylon indicated that their government wished to resume serious discussions with the Bank. They were told that until a satisfactory stabilization program was worked out with the IMF, the question could not be pursued further. The IMF was in fact approached, but before negotiations could be completed the Bandaranaike government was defeated in the House, and elections were called. The then opposition party, under the leadership of Senanayake, came to power in March 1965.

By this time the economic crisis was acute, and reserves were exhausted. The United States and the United Kingdom asked the Bank to organize an aid group, and the Bank, with some reluctance, agreed on condition that Ceylon work out a stabilization agreement with the IMF before the aid group had its first meeting. The government of Ceylon proceeded to negotiate a standby arrangement with the Fund, and the first meeting of the aid group was held in August 1965. During the five years the Senanayake administration was in office, the aid group channeled a substantial amount of program assistance to Ceylon, and the Bank began to resume project lending. Using the leverage of the aid group, the Bank persuaded the government to take a number of politically difficult steps—notably, reducing the subsidized rice ration, increasing charges for municipal bus services, and (in 1967) devaluing the rupee. Although the economy of Ceylon took some significant steps forward during this time, this progress, as the elections of 1970 indicated, did not greatly influence popular opinion.[12] It is against this historical background of the withdrawal of the Bank during the previous Bandaranaike government and the extensive support (accompanied by onerous conditions) given to the Senanayake government that the political reaction to the conditions attached to the Mahaweli project loan must be viewed. It must be noted, however, that despite the tense relations between the Bank and the incoming Bandaranaike government, it became possible in the course of the following year to compromise differences and reestablish effective cooperation.

Since the Bank's relations with each of its borrowing members has unique features, it is difficult to draw lessons of general applicability from this example. But it does seem to show that loan conditions that may be perfectly acceptable in one country can become the source of political turmoil in another; that these political reactions can be seriously exacerbated if the Bank works with one political party to the exclusion of its opposition; and that there is probably a trade-off between conditions thought necessary to the viability of a project and conditions that permit satisfactory relations between the Bank and its borrowers. It seems clear, moreover, that this trade-off will vary substantially among countries and within a particular country over time.

We turn now to a discussion of efforts by the Bank/IDA to influence country performance.

Country Performance

Early in this chapter a distinction was drawn between the behavior of economic variables that are considered to indicate the state or rate of progress of the development process, and performance in the sense of various management activities or policies. It was pointed out that although the Bank, or another external lender, might under certain circumstances influence man-

12. Although the gross national product in Ceylon grew at a more rapid rate during this period than during the previous one, the balance-of-payments position was hardly better at the end than at the beginning of the Senanayake government.

In 1969 exports and aid receipts were 266 million rupees below balance-of-payments estimates, and imports exceeded the import budget by 131 million rupees. The deficit from these accounts totaled 397 million rupees, of which 84 million was covered by larger-than-expected receipts from current invisibles, suppliers' credits, and bilateral transactions. The balance, 313 million rupees, was financed by short-term foreign bank borrowing and virtual depletion of convertible reserves.

agerial performance directly, its influence on the behavior of economic indicators must necessarily be indirect. It was also emphasized that the relationship between a specific managerial action and the behavior of the indicators the action is intended to influence is frequently not well understood and varies substantially among different economies as well as in the same economy over time.

The Bank, in general, as is true of any lender trying to influence the development process in a borrowing country, has a choice between bestowing rewards after the event or trying to induce the event by setting conditions for the granting of the loan. And if rewards are to be conferred, the lender can base its decision on development results as measured by various indicators, leaving it to the borrowing countries to pursue whatever policies they consider conducive to these results; or the lender can base its decision on management performance, or on some combination of results and practices. There is, in the view of some, a marked difference between rewarding performance and inducing performance by setting conditions. A former AID official, Charles E. Lindblom, has said that,

> although the United States and other lenders would be mistaken if they tried to buy the policies they like in India by making aid contingent on India's accepting their advice, at the same time they will do well to make clear that the attractiveness of lending to India—the prospect that it will pay off either to India or to the lender—depends on Indian policy. . . .
>
> The distinction between trying to buy, with aid, the policies we like and coming more generously to the assistance of policies that promise growth is a fine one; but it is a genuine one.[13]

If we ignore the pejorative connotation of the word "buy," and perhaps substitute for it "induce," the distinction tends to become even finer. And if the emphasis is on policies, profound insight is needed to discover a perceptible difference between a set of policies that if followed is known to be capable of generating lending and lending on condition that this same set of policies is followed. There *is*, however, a distinction between lending on the basis of approved behavior of development indicators, leaving it to the borrower to approach this behavior by whatever policies he sees fit, and lending that tries to reward specific policies or induce their adoption. The Bank has governed its lending operations by judgments both of the significance of development indicators and of the effect of particular policies; and with respect to policies it has on occasion rewarded and on other occasions attempted to induce their adoption.

13. C. E. Lindblom, "Has India an Economic Future?" *Foreign Affairs*, Vol. 44 (January 1966), p. 250.

The development indicators commonly taken into account in Bank analysis include various measures of (a) the rate of growth of national and per capita income, (b) rates of growth of factor inputs, particularly domestic savings rates and public sector savings rates, (c) rates of growth of output and investment in various sectors, (d) putative measures of efficiency of resource use, such as sectoral and aggregate capital–output ratios, and (e) various indicators of external viability. Unemployment rates have not, at least until recently, occupied an important place in Bank assessments of development prospects, though in a number of less developed countries the social and political implications of rising unemployment may seriously affect these prospects. Since there is no tested theory of the growth process that would suggest the relative importance of the indicators mentioned above and relate them to each other and to an accepted definition of what economic development means, the indicators are at best partial tests, with "good" behavior of one indicator frequently accompanied by "poor" behavior of another.

There is a strong a priori case for tailoring Bank lending to an assessment of "results" as measured by various development indicators, leaving it to the borrowing country to attain the results considered desirable by whatever mix of policy actions seems under the circumstances to be economically and politically feasible. After all, there is usually a fairly wide range of alternative means of accomplishing a particular economic result, and an external judgment on what might be the optimum set of measures in particular circumstances is apt to be rather subjective. The rate of growth of national or per capita income is commonly considered to be the best single measure of economic development, and it is obvious from a casual inspection of recent economic history that given rates of growth can be, and have been, attained by very different combinations of partial development indicators. There is, for example, a wide range of variation in the relations of investment rates and growth rates. In Argentina in the 1950s, a very high rate of domestic saving and investment was accompanied by a very low rate of growth of national income. In Ghana from 1960 to 1966, gross domestic savings averaged over 20 percent of GNP, yet the rate of growth of real national income was very low. On the other hand, in the Philippines, GNP rose at a relatively satisfactory rate during most of the decade of the 1960s while domestic savings and total investment have been relatively small in relation to GNP. If the rate of growth of real GNP in a country is, and for some time has been, considered satisfactory—say 6 percent or above—there is much to be said for letting well enough alone.

If actual growth rates are manifestly less than potential and desirable rates, a search for reasons is called for. Obviously many possibilities open up. Domestic savings may be inadequate. Public savings may not be enough to cover the investment costs of necessary infrastructure or the local currency cost of such infrastructure if it is assumed that external sources will cover the foreign exchange financing. Educational and training programs may feed insufficient technical and managerial inputs into the economy. Inadequate rates of growth of output in particular sectors, for example agriculture, may generate bottlenecks. Factor inputs in particular industries and sectors may yield low outputs because of managerial weaknesses, uneconomical plant size, poor location of particular facilities, or other reasons. Undervaluation of foreign exchange savings or earnings may impair external viability. These and other factors are considered in country studies and form the background for Bank lending policy.

Putting aside the burden created by the inadequacy of statistics and other types of information, which in most less developed countries is fairly heavy, there are three other difficulties encountered in determining whether the actual growth in a particular country is close to, or far removed from, the potential rate; that is, whether overall performance merits or does not merit Bank lending. The first of these has to do with possible discrepancies between growth or development measured by the rate of increase in real national or per capita income and other considerations that political leadership needs to and should take into account. The second is concerned with the constraints on action to promote development, which vary greatly from country to country. The third has to do with a lack of a growth theory or growth models capable of specifying the necessary and sufficient conditions of development with enough precision and in enough detail to make possible an assessment of the probable effect of small variations in growth-related variables.

Presumably the primary objective of both development lenders and borrowers is the attainment within some time period of a state of self-sustaining growth. "Self-sustaining growth" should mean not only an end of the need to borrow abroad on concessional terms but also the maintenance and adaptation internally of conditions necessary to the growth process. Among the most important of these conditions is a certain degree of political stability. But maintaining political stability may require government action that works against maximizing the average rate of growth of national income over a specified time period. The fact that more profitable economic opportunities were available in West than in East Pakistan should not necessarily have led to the conclusion that public and private investment should be concentrated in West Pakistan. A government may not be able to tolerate the kind of income distribution that would maximize domestic savings and, through domestic savings, the growth rate. Clearly a number of governments in the postwar period have gone so far in the direction of protecting low-income groups through taxation and welfare measures as seriously to endanger growth prospects. But there is a problem of balancing considerations of economic growth against considerations of political and social stability that any government must take into account. Recent studies have concluded that under present conditions in Brazil and Colombia (and perhaps also in other Latin American countries) a growth rate of national income of at least 8 percent a year is required to prevent the already high rate of unemployment from becoming higher. The political consequences of increasing unemployment may be such that measures to enlarge employment opportunities will be desirable, even at the expense of some reduction in the potential growth rate. Obviously, strong governments can go further than can weak governments in ignoring, or suppressing, political opposition to some of the consequences of economic growth. But all governments have to take these considerations into account. Consequently they also have to be taken into account by any lender concerned with promoting self-sustaining growth.

Creditworthiness as a Criterion of Performance

Earlier in this chapter we emphasized some of the constraints that make it difficult to judge whether the behavior of development indicators has the same significance with respect to performance in one country as it has in another. An oil- or mineral-rich country may find it easier to expand export earnings than one not so blessed. Savings rates are likely to be influenced by increases in per capita income and in the relative size of the business sector. An increase in agricultural productivity is apt to be easier to achieve in areas dominated by large or medium-sized farms that produce for the market than in areas characterized by small-scale subsistence farming. If a major objective of external lenders is to reward or induce performance that brings the actual pace of development of a borrower closer to potential, existing constraints need to be taken into account. By grouping countries at similar stages of development, and with similar per capita incomes and natural resource endowments, attempts have been made to judge (from the behavior of economic indicators) the character of managerial performance. If one country shows average or marginal rates of saving that are substantially higher than those of other countries in the same group, or more rapidly growing export earnings, or a lower aggregate or sectoral capital–output ratio, is this persuasive evidence of superior managerial performance? It would be rash to draw such conclusions without a thoroughgoing examination of the constraints affecting the management of the economy. Even with such an examination, conclusions are apt to include a strong subjective element.

But even assuming that we have a clear-cut idea of what the significant trade-offs are among the various objectives embraced in the notion of self-sustaining growth and a satisfactory appraisal of the limitations under which the management of the economy operates, can we form a judgment, based on the behavior of various development indicators, that the development process is proceeding as well as can be expected under existing circumstances? A third difficulty in making such a judgment has to do with the lack of an adequate growth theory or set of testable hypotheses relating the behavior of relevant variables to an acceptable concept of what development means. This is an area currently occupied by the constructors of growth models or planning models. Despite the fact that these constructions have thrown a good deal of light on interrelationships in the economy and promise in the future to throw more, they are at present either so aggregative as to conceal most of what we really need to know; or if they are disaggregated, they depend, in order to be calculable, on a series of more or less arbitrary constraints and assumed relationships. It is fair to conclude that an increase in the rate of investment will be followed, with some time lag, by an increase in output if there is no increase in the aggregate capital–output ratio. But for this to happen, what new investment will be needed, and how will it have to be allocated among various sectors in the economy? What substitution between capital and labor inputs will be required? And what are the implications for foreign trade or external assistance? It is possible to give quantitative answers to each of these and to other relevant questions but only if it can be assumed that other quantities in the system behave in the expected way. This is not to say that we know nothing about the growth process but only that the possibilities of substitution and adaptation in the system are such that a fairly wide range of variation in the behavior of particular indicators is permissible and is compatible with the attainment of a particular development objective.

What this amounts to in practical terms is that by examining development indicators one may be able to detect gross "inadequacies and inconsistencies" that are incompatible with the growth process but not much more than this. It may be possible, for example, to determine that the rate of public saving is inadequate to finance the necessary infrastructure and that without a private market for public debt, efforts to provide this infrastructure by borrowing can only be inflationary. It has certainly seemed possible to conclude that, in recent years, the lagging growth rate of agricultural output in a number of less developed countries has been a serious bottleneck to overall development. An examination of current rates of growth in export earnings will throw light on the question of what imports of capital equipment a country will be able to finance in the near future from its own resources. But beyond this type of judgment on crude deficiencies in the growth process, it is not possible to proceed far.

Still this may be far enough to permit a determination of a useful direction for Bank lending. If acceptable lending policy means devising the highest priority uses of investment funds—with full recognition of the relative claims of the various sectors, of alternative technologies, of project versus program lending, within the context of a projected optimum growth process—the choice would encounter all the difficulties mentioned above. But if it merely means choosing technically and economically viable projects within a sector that is "crudely deficient" in relation to other sectors, this does not present such serious difficulties. Bank lending has, in the main, been of this sort.

It follows, moreover, from what has been said above, that the criteria used by the Bank in assessing the development policies of borrowing member countries have the same rough and ready characteristics that pertain to Bank lending policy. An examination of these criteria reveals a heavy emphasis on indicators and policies relating to creditworthiness and, furthermore, to creditworthiness judged on a not very long-term basis. Indeed, so large has creditworthiness loomed in the Bank's calculations, it is doubtful whether, given a viable project in a country judged to be creditworthy by traditional standards, Bank lending policy looks beyond the project to any other development indicators or aspects of development policy. The few situations that have come to our attention in which it could plausibly be argued that the Bank has looked beyond established creditworthiness and project viability to overall development considerations turn out, on examination, to be somewhat less-than-convincing examples. Four of these cases involve recent Bank lending policy in the Philippines, in Portugal, in Venezuela, and in Jamaica.

In 1966 the president of the Bank informed the President of the Philippines that he saw "serious difficulties in the way of future lending for Government projects in the Philippines" because of poor economic performance. By commonly accepted economic indicators the Philippines was a creditworthy country. But a low level of public savings precluded the public infrastructure investment that was deemed necessary to facilitate a satisfactory rate of economic growth. In the words of the Bank's communication, there is an "apparent lack of an adequate revenue base to enable the Government to finance the peso expenditures associated with any major increase in development outlays. This results from the fact that for years the Congress has failed to approve new revenue measures."

This would appear to be a case in which the Bank refused to continue lending to a creditworthy country whose real national income had been increasing in recent years at a rate of 5 to 6 percent a year, because of a judgment that an unsatisfactory rate of expansion of public investment was frustrating the attainment of a higher growth rate. This conclusion, however, is complicated by the fact that the Bank encountered serious difficulties in executing its own projects because of governmental inefficiencies, particularly in the Department of Public Works and Communications. If Bank projects in the Philippines had been effectively managed and carried out, there is some doubt whether the Bank would still have withheld lending on the ground that inadequate macroeconomic performance was slowing development.

Portugal in 1967 was an eminently creditworthy country; indeed one of the aspects of Portuguese performance criticized by the Bank was the maintenance of what was considered an unduly high ratio of reserves to imports. Nevertheless, the Bank refused in that year to undertake further lending in Portugal primarily because of the absence of a "dynamic and flexible approach to development." At the same time there was no doubt that Portugal had viable economic projects that it had presented to the Bank for financing. This then appears to be a situation in which the Bank refused to lend for viable economic projects in a creditworthy country because of poor overall performance—in this case, a failure to produce a "dynamic" development program.

Again, however, there are elements that modify this picture. Portugal, in addition to being creditworthy, was also at least marginally "market eligible," that is, capable of borrowing in capital markets and thus not necessarily dependent on Bank financing. Furthermore, there is more than a suspicion that a UN resolution of September 1966, which appealed to the Bank and Fund to refrain "from granting any financial assistance to . . . Portugal" had the effect of intensifying the Bank's search for aspects of development performance that might justify a refusal to lend.[14] Altogether it is difficult to conclude that the Bank's judgment of performance in Portugal should be accepted as indicative of the type of performance that, in another country, would make that country ineligible for Bank loans.

Venezuela is another creditworthy country in which, despite the existence of viable projects, the Bank is alleged to have withheld lending because of poor overall performance. The Venezuelan development program for 1965–68 was surveyed by a Bank mission, which concluded (a) that the country would need to borrow from abroad $270 million to finance the program, and (b) that Venezuela was creditworthy for this amount of borrowing. These conclusions were reviewed at a meeting of the Economic Committee and were

14. This UN resolution (A/AC. 109/L. 330) gave the Bank considerable difficulty. It was obviously based on political considerations. Yet Article IV, section 10, of the Bank's charter clearly states, "The Bank and its officers shall not interfere in the political affairs of any member; nor shall they be influenced in their decisions by the political character of the member or members concerned." This issue is discussed further in Chapter 17, below.

accepted, but the committee "also agreed that the additional fiscal efforts by the Government, proposed by the Bank Mission, should be made and that a decision on the Bank lending program therefore be postponed until Government decisions on the size of the investment program—especially for 1966—and the measures needed to finance it, have been taken."[15] Discussion with the director of the Western Hemisphere Department confirmed that the Bank had indeed withheld lending because of dissatisfaction with Venezuela's own financial effort.

Jamaica may present a somewhat similar example. A Bank mission had no difficulty in concluding that Jamaica was creditworthy. Indeed, "the over-all outlook for the balance of payments during the next five years is quite favorable." Nevertheless, the recent performance of the Jamaican economy was in certain respects considered to be unfavorable, and it is said by responsible officials that inadequate performance has led to a slowdown of Bank lending. The inadequate performance chiefly complained of had to do with "inadequate preparation and implementation of public investment projects, absence of realistic financing plans and the pursuit of inadequate or unsuitable programs particularly with regard to the agricultural sector." The inadequate preparation of projects was said to have produced "infrastructural bottlenecks in transport, power and water supply...."[16]

An examination of these and other cases in which the Bank is alleged to have withheld lending to a creditworthy country because of dissatisfaction with overall performance suggests that the principal cause of dissatisfaction was an inadequate savings-investment effort on the part of the borrowing country. And in all these cases there is some doubt whether the principal cause of Bank action was not inadequate project preparation and failure to provide necessary local expenditure financing for Bank projects rather than poor macroeconomic policy. In any case it seems reasonable to conclude that, given viable projects in a creditworthy country, the Bank's inquiry into overall performance is not apt to probe more deeply than to question whether public savings are adequate to meet the local expenditure costs of what are considered to be desirable infrastructure investments.

This is certainly not true in countries where the financial risk of lending is thought to be considerable, and particularly it is not true in countries to which IDA credits are extended. Latin American countries are mainly Bank countries, though small IDA credits have been given to some of them. Creditworthiness, however, is frequently in doubt, and the examination of overall

15. EC/M/65-29 (Aug. 16, 1965).
16. See Draft Report, "Current Economic Position and Prospects of Jamaica" (Oct. 2, 1968).

performance in Latin America has focused sharply on policies affecting creditworthiness. Also, in general, the Bank's position seems to be that borrowing from IDA not only justifies but demands a more searching inquiry into overall performance than seems necessary for borrowers on harder terms.

As was noted in Chapter 6, above, the Bank's studies of creditworthiness, undertaken largely under the direction of Dragoslav Avramović, have properly distinguished the short-term external liquidity problem from the long-term debt service problem.[17] It is recognized that a country with good prospects of long-term external viability may nevertheless find itself in difficulty in the short run because of a bunching of debt maturities, a failure of export crops, a lack of responsiveness of its exchange rate to the rate of internal inflation, and for other reasons. This is an area of operations occupied mainly by the IMF, though the Bank and other lenders can assist by consolidating short-term debt and undertaking new lending with adequate grace periods and long-term maturities. If the problem is indeed short-term, these measures together with appropriate changes in monetary, fiscal, and foreign exchange policies, in response to conditions negotiated with the IMF, may be enough to overcome the difficulty. In this case and if indeed the long-term prospects of external viability are good, the Bank would normally and rightly accept the policy recommendations of the Fund and might give these recommendations its support by conditioning its own lending on the implementation of these proposals by the borrowing country.[18]

Over the longer term it is held that a country can meet its debt service charges if (a) its marginal rate of return on investment is higher than the international borrowing rate and (b) the rate of domestic saving becomes sufficiently high at some point to meet domestic investment requirements and yield a surplus for debt service. How long a period is required to attain external viability will depend on the terms of external lending, what happens to the marginal productivity of investment, and what happens to the rate of domestic savings. These conclusions are correct, and the analysis leading to them is illuminating, but it is based on some formidable assumptions. In particular,

The rates of return which have to be compared with the rate of interest in order to determine whether or not borrowing is advantageous can only be validly calculated on the basis of prices which reflect the true opportunity cost of all products and factors of production. Among other conditions, the rate of return can only

17. D. Avramović and associates, IBRD, Economic Department, *Economic Growth and External Debt* (Johns Hopkins Press, 1964).

18. The relation between Bank and Fund policies is discussed further in Chapter 16.

be validly computed at prices which are consistent with a viable balance of payments—i.e., at correct "shadow prices" of foreign exchange. It may therefore be misleading to say that, because the rate of return on an investment is 7 per cent, therefore this investment can be financed by borrowing externally at 6 per cent without danger to the balance of payments. Rather, it is necessary first to determine the conditions in which the balance of payments will remain viable, given prospective external debt service obligations and capital inflow; for it is only on the basis of such conditions and the "shadow prices" derived from such conditions, that it is possible validly to calculate a rate of return on investment so as to show whether borrowing is advantageous or not.[19]

In fact the situation is even more difficult than this. A valid calculation of the rate of return on investment that is expected to be productive over time will depend not only on prices that reflect current opportunity costs but also on prices (including interest rates and foreign exchange rates) that are expected to reflect changing opportunity costs over time. If these assumptions are granted, it can be shown that there is no incompatibility between actions and policies that are optimal with respect to economic growth and actions and policies that are optimal with respect to the attainment and maintenance of external viability. The performance the Bank should like to see in the interests of putting its money to good use is the same performance the Bank should like to see in the interests of getting paid back. If returns on investment are properly calculated, there is no trade-off, at least no long-term trade-off, between a higher rate of growth and a better balance of payments. Export activities form a sector like any other, for example, agriculture or electric power, in the sense that an optimum rate of growth of national income requires a sectoral rate of growth consistent with that optimum.

The fact that it is impossible to calculate current opportunity costs of products and factors (including interest and exchange rates), taking full account of interdependencies, let alone attempt to predict the time-paths of such costs and prices, does not destroy the validity of the proposition that partial corrections of existing costs and prices that are reasonably made in the interests of promoting economic development can also contribute to an improvement of a country's external position, that is, to creditworthiness. It is on these partial measures that the Bank's criteria of country performance have inevitably focused.

Elements of country performance are considered extensively in country studies, in the recommendations emanating from the area departments responsible for these countries, in the Bank's Economic Committee, and by the

19. Avramović, *Economic Growth and External Debt*, p. 165.

Bank's top management.[20] In general the examination of country performance is more comprehensive in country studies than in the consideration of particular loans and credits. This consideration, it is fair to say, has become concerned increasingly with the social aspects of development. But in general, as the discussion moves toward a final recommendation, attention tends to focus on considerations of creditworthiness.

In February 1967, of the less developed countries whose eligibility for Bank/IDA lending was questioned, that of three was held to be contingent on the outcome of pending discussions. In the case of three others eligibility was considered to be limited because of unsatisfactory performance. The remaining seven countries fell in a category, noted in a May 1968 report of the working group on IDA policies, where behavior had been contrary to accepted international morality, or where political conditions were so unsettled that productive use of IDA funds could not be expected.

In Ghana under Nkrumah or in Indonesia under Sukarno it required no very subtle analysis to discover that economic management was such as to render these countries ineligible for Bank/IDA financing. In the six countries where eligibility was either limited or contingent, the performance complained of had to do with policies endangering creditworthiness.

Creditworthiness in the medium-term context favored by the Bank can be adversely affected by a wide range of policies hampering export earnings, inducing a flight of capital, directing imports toward nonproductive uses, and discouraging foreign private investment. This range of policy issues the Bank has had primarily in mind in attempting to use the leverage of its lending policy to improve performance. It may be useful to mention some examples.

The Bank, before 1965, had been a persistent but relatively unimportant lender to Peru and had shown no particular interest in country performance. In that year a major economic mission concluded that Peru deserved sub-

20. The process by which the Bank makes decisions on country lending programs and the conditions, if any, to be attached thereto, has gone through a considerable evolution. Early in the Bank's history the critical questions were: is the project viable, and is the country eligible for Bank lending? There was little or no connection between the decisions on these issues. In the course of time, however, individual projects began to be considered in relation to a lending program the level of which might be varied according to judgments of development prospects in a particular country. The establishment of this relationship was the responsibility of area departments, and their recommendations were adjudicated in the Staff Loan Committee before going to top management and the board of directors. In the first years of the McNamara regime these procedures were substantially altered. The area departments were asked to formulate for each country in which the Bank was engaged a five-year lending program in which proposed projects are related to longer-term development objectives. The programs go through a series of scrutinies, ending up in an examination, at least once a year, by the president's review committee.

stantial external support "provided the Government pursued suitable fiscal policies."[21] In January of the following year the Loan Committee accepted recommendations for a lending program of $130 million for 1966 and 1967. It was stated that "the possibility of lending such a substantial amount over a sufficiently long-time period gave the Bank the required leverage to ensure that the Peruvian Government would adopt the recent Bank Economic Mission's recommendations, which had already been accepted in principle."[22] This acceptance was reflected in a "Memorandum of Understanding on the Financial Policies of the Government of Peru." The memorandum stated in very general terms the government's intention to raise new tax revenues, to curtail borrowing from the central bank and to limit commitments for short-term suppliers' credits. The proposed lending would be conditional on progress in implementing the memorandum of understanding.

Sufficient progress was made in early 1966 in negotiations between the Bank and Peruvian authorities and between the United States and Peru to justify the formation of a consultative group. This group held its first and (as of this writing) last meeting in Paris in July 1966. Beginning in the autumn of that year the economic situation in Peru progressively disintegrated. Borrowing from the central bank and the rate of inflation increased; Parliament refused to vote tax increases; the balance of payments worsened rapidly; and by August 1, 1967, the banking system had lost $140 million in reserves, partially as a result of a flight of capital. Peru's external public debt had increased from $580 million at the end of 1964 to about $900 million at the end of 1966. Meanwhile the purchase by Peru of $20 million worth of Mystères planes from France had led to a cancellation of a proposed $40 million in program loans from the U.S. Agency for International Development. Under these circumstances the Bank stopped lending to Peru and called off the second meeting of the consultative group. This brief account does less than justice to a complex situation in which not only the Bank and AID, but also the IMF, the IDB, and European suppliers were involved. But the central point is that the Bank's decision to increase lending was based on expected changes in Peruvian policies that would increase creditworthiness and on the condition that such changes were realized. When in fact these changes were not realized, the Bank ceased to lend.

Bank lending in Chile has never at any time been sufficiently large, in relation to financing from other sources, to permit any considerable influence on general economic policy. The Bank has tried to influence policies in certain sectors, notably transportation and agriculture. For the rest, judgments

21. WH-155a (Dec. 28, 1965).
22. EC/M/66-2 (Jan. 6, 1966).

on performance relate to the question whether the Bank should increase or decrease the amount of its lending to Chile. The areas of performance of particular relevance to these decisions have had to do with policies affecting creditworthiness. In June 1967 a proposed loan of $11.6 million for a highway maintenance project was presented to the Loan Committee, and four other proposed loans in transportation and education were in various stages of preparation. The Bank's five-year program contemplated a lending rate of $35 million a year in Chile. In connection with the highway loan the Bank asked for and received from the minister of finance written assurance concerning the government's intention with respect to exchange rate policy and external debt management, but this action by the Bank must be viewed as only additional support for pressure already applied by the AID and the Fund.

Deterioration in Chilean economic performance beginning in 1967, and leading to very uncertain balance-of-payments prospects over the next two or three years, stimulated the Economic Committee to consider, in August 1968, "what specific performance tests, and what possible additional economic policy conditions, apart from exchange rate flexibility and external debt management, should be applied in deciding on the level and composition of further lending in Chile in 1969. . . ."[23]

Discussion revealed that, in the opinion of the Western Hemisphere Department a liquidity crisis might be avoided by further emergency aid from the United States, including P.L. 480 shipments made necessary by the drought, and by some rescheduling of short- and medium-term debt. In the light of these circumstances the Economic Committee agreed to accept a recommendation to continue lending, beyond the highway maintenance loan, provided Chile maintained its flexible exchange rate policy, continued limitations on short- and medium-term external debt, and took "action in the area of fiscal, income and monetary policy which could reasonably be expected (a) to keep the rate of inflation down to not more than 30–40 percent a year without resort to additional physical controls, and (b) to ensure that at least 60–70 percent of public investment will be financed out of public savings."[24]

Although the Bank's attention in Chile was focused primarily on considerations affecting creditworthiness, it must be said that the fact that the Frei government had introduced various reforms that could favorably affect Chile's long-term development prospects appears to have predisposed the Bank to take a lenient view toward these considerations.

The Bank's concern for creditworthiness in Latin American economies

23. EC/O/68-81 (Aug. 16, 1968).
24. *Ibid.*

has inevitably centered on policies affecting the rate of inflation and on the effects of inflation on the balance of payments. Country performance, therefore, has been judged mainly in terms of monetary and fiscal policy, exchange rate policy, and policies affecting the structure of imports and exports. On the other hand, in southern Asia (or at least in India and Pakistan), although considerations of creditworthiness have also tended to shape judgments of country performance, inflationary policies have not been the central issue. For most of the period in which the Bank/IDA have operated in India and Pakistan, price levels have been relatively stable under the influence of conservative monetary and fiscal policies. Creditworthiness has been judged to be adversely affected by the slow growth of exports, by a neglect of agricultural output that threatened to cause an unnecessarily heavy use of scarce foreign exchange for the importation of foodstuffs, and by industrial policies that paid little attention to considerations of comparative advantage. Studies of country performance in India and Pakistan and discussions in the Economic Committee have thus stressed exchange rates that substantially overvalued the rupee, the lack of adequate agricultural price incentives and of necessary agricultural inputs, and import controls and foreign exchange licensing practices that hampered a market determination of the direction of industrial development.

We have already mentioned the successful efforts of the Bank, in conjunction with AID, to persuade Pakistan to liberalize its import policies in 1965. As was noted in Chapter 7, the Bank made serious efforts in the mid-1960s to influence economic performance in India. The aspects of performance at issue were primarily balance-of-payments policies, controls over imports, and the relative stress to be put on agricultural output. It was the view of the Bank that poor performance in these areas not only handicapped growth but seriously endangered creditworthiness for further borrowing. Although the Bank, using the leverage of the India Consortium, tried to bring about changes in development priorities and policies that would probably not have taken place, at least at that time, without this leverage, there were some rather serious political side effects that have influenced the relations between the Bank and the government of India in the years since 1966.[25]

The Indian case represents perhaps the strongest attempt the Bank has ever made to use its own leverage, and the leverage of consortium associates, to induce changes in aggregative economic policies in a borrowing country.

---

25. Some sense of the reaction in India is given by this quotation from an article "Indian Economy and the World Bank Role," *The Hindu* (New Delhi, Aug. 22, 1964). "There is a feeling in New Delhi that the World Bank's attitude to India has latterly stiffened. Conversely, it is a belief that our feeling of helplessness has emboldened the Bank to raise questions which in different circumstances it may not have done."

In our opinion, these steps were necessary and became feasible because of a substantial increase in program assistance. To corroborate this view, however, would require an argument too lengthy to be undertaken here. Whether desirable changes in Indian economic policies could have been accomplished with less political fallout is difficult for outside observers to say.

Résumé

We have perhaps said enough to substantiate the point that the aspects of country performance of particular interest to the Bank have been closely related to considerations of creditworthiness. It has been argued above that, in the long run and on the basis of certain assumptions concerning the behavior of prices in the economic system, there need be no incompatibility between conditions favoring creditworthiness and those favoring economic growth. External viability of the economy indeed is necessary to the attainment of self-sustaining growth. In the shorter run, however, actions and policies needed to sustain the ability of an economy to service external debt may indeed be incompatible with the structural changes needed for long-term economic development.

If external assistance in larger volume were available on more favorable terms, a developing country might be able to take the steps needed to modernize its economy while still maintaining service on external debt. If assistance is in short supply, a choice may have to be made between maintaining external viability and policies conducive to long-term development. Bank lending policy, in fact, recognizes this necessity. As we have indicated above, the willingness of AID to expand program lending in Chile and offer P.L. 480 support predisposed the Bank to take a relaxed view of Chile's short-run balance-of-payments difficulties and to look with favor on the longer-term promise of the Frei government's development policies. As things are, the Bank is more or less compelled by its own financial position to lay heavy emphasis, in judging country performance, on relatively short-term considerations affecting creditworthiness. IDA funds are limited and have to be rationed. Bank funds are unlimited only so long as borrowing countries can fulfill their debt service obligations on terms determined largely by the state of world capital markets. The considerations of creditworthiness that loom large in the Bank's assessment of country performance tend to impinge rather clearly on the considerations taken into account by the IMF in recommending stabilization measures. We shall have occasion later to consider the views of the Fund and the Bank on stabilization and growth in Chapter 16, which discusses the relationship between these two agencies.

CHAPTER FOURTEEN

The Bank's Conception of the Development Process and Its Role Therein

THE AUTHORS HAVE FREQUENTLY referred in the preceding chapters to views within the Bank Group on the developmental requirements of member countries and the Bank's contribution toward meeting these requirements; to limitations imposed by the Articles of Agreement and by administrative decisions on various courses of Bank action; to various effects the way in which the Bank is organized has on the way development problems are envisaged; and to changes that have taken place as new presidents have come into office. From time to time the Bank as a bank has been contrasted with the Bank as a development organization. Now we will pull these scattered remarks together and try to trace the evolution of the Bank's thinking about the nature of the development process and the Bank Group's relation to that process.

To speak of the views of the Bank or Bank Group at any stage in this evolution is, of course, to ignore, or at least to minimize, the differences of views that have always existed among individual directors, and within the management and staff of the Bank. The Bank has never been a monolithic institution; and as the size of its professional staff has increased, it has tended to become less so. Nevertheless, there has been and is a set of views that may fairly be said to characterize the thinking of Bank representatives at different points in time on how development comes about and how it can be assisted.

These views have been influenced by thinking about the process of eco-

457

nomic development outside the Bank but even more by changes in its own lending experience. The gradual shift of attention and interest from developed to less developed countries was, of course, of profound significance. As late as 1957, 52.7 percent of Bank financing was still directed to what were later called Part I countries of IDA. By 1968, this had been reduced to zero. Since the less developed world presents a wide spectrum of developmental situations, the Bank's experience and its thinking about development have broadened with its membership. Early financing in Latin America brought the IBRD face to face with problems of inflation and the relation of stabilization policies to economic growth. Fiscal, monetary, and foreign exchange policies became tests of the "performance" of borrowing countries, particularly in Latin America, and this experience has helped to shape the Bank's views of the development process. In southern Asia, where in many member countries inflation has not been a serious problem, other considerations affecting development have come to the fore. In India and Pakistan the failure of factor prices to reflect factor scarcities, and in general the discrepancy between prices and opportunity costs, have assumed priority in the Bank's thinking. Later, experience in Africa focused attention on the importance of education, training, and human resource development. Although the Bank has tended to deal with member countries independently, without trying to compare or contrast them with each other, and usually without crystallizing experience into explicit hypotheses regarding the development process, it is still possible to trace a certain evolution in Bank thought.

The Early Period

After an initial period, when the Bank thought of itself as a temporary institution bridging the gap until international capital markets would revive (or at least tried to give that impression to the financial community), it generated some fairly firm ideas as to what development was about and how an international lending institution could contribute. One will, however, look in vain in the Bank files, both current and old, for any evidence of accepted theories of development or models of the development process. The Bank's conception of how countries develop can be seen in the views expressed on how development can be promoted and in the actions taken. Stripped to its essentials, the early Bank conception of development requirements might be stated as follows. A primary condition for the release of private initiative and investment, both domestic and foreign, is that there be an adequate complement of public overhead capital: railways, roads, power plants, port installations, and communications facilities. This capital is customarily provided by the public sector, which must be developed systematically, with due attention to the progressive elimination of bottlenecks. Hence the need for planning and programming public sector investment. Given an adequate capital infrastructure and a satisfactory climate for private investment, both domestic and foreign, it can reasonably be expected that production will expand.

A satisfactory climate for private investment requires a politically stable government pursuing sound monetary and fiscal policies. A government interested in economic development will recognize, moreover, that the public and private sectors have different, though equally important, roles to play. If governments undertake to mobilize the domestic savings required to cover the large local currency cost of the necessary capital infrastructure, they will have their hands full without seeking to divert scarce public resources into activities the private sector can perform better. In the main these activities lie in the areas of agriculture, industry, commerce, and financial and personal services. In these areas the market is generally a better guide to the allocation of resources than governmental controls would be. This picture of the Bank's conception of the development process is, to be sure, a caricature, but like all caricatures it is intended to bring out and emphasize the essential features of the subject under study.[1]

Given this picture of development requirements, it was clear how the Bank could best undertake development assistance: first and foremost, by helping to meet the large foreign exchange requirements for capital infrastructure through project loans and by providing, if necessary, technical assistance in the selection and preparation of projects; second, by emphasizing priorities in the selection of projects and assisting member countries to frame sensible public sector development programs with priority considerations in mind; third, by attempting to influence borrowing countries to adopt development policies designed to promote the mobilization of foreign and domestic capital and its allocation through market forces to its most productive uses. One deficiency of the Bank as a development institution was considered by the management to be its inability to assist the private sector more directly by lending to private enterprise without government guarantee and by making equity investments. The need for the equivalent of an International Finance Corporation (IFC) was emphasized by Bank management

1. One of the most complete statements of the Bank's early views on development is presented in Robert L. Garner's valedictory address on his retirement as president of the International Finance Corporation. Meeting of the Board of Governors, Vienna (Sept. 21, 1961).

as early as 1948, and the Bank very early sought to satisfy part of this need by lending directly to development finance companies, which in turn financed private enterprise. But despite the absence, until 1956, of an IFC, there was no doubt in the minds of Bank management that it was a development institution equipped to make a sizable contribution to satisfying the requirements of its less developed member countries. The fact that the Bank was dependent on capital markets for the bulk of its funds was to the management an asset rather than a liability. As we noted in Chapter 5, it was in their view fortunate that the Bank was substantially dependent on the bond market since it meant that the Bank was limited to the kind of lending that, because it had to be productive, would "build confidence in the Bank." Furthermore, dependence on the market meant independence from the political pressure of donor governments.

That an adequate economic infrastructure is a necessary precondition of economic development has been a leading tenet of Bank philosophy almost from the beginning of its operations. As the sixth annual report put it,

It is only natural that, except for the early reconstruction loans, the Bank's lending operations have been concentrated in the field of basic utilities. An adequate supply of power, communications and transportation facilities is a precondition for the most productive application of private savings in new enterprises. It is also the first step in the gradual industrialization and diversification of the underdeveloped countries. These basic facilities require large initial capital outlays, which, because of the low level of savings and the inadequate development of savings institutions, often cannot be financed wholly by the countries themselves. Moreover, most of the machinery and equipment used in the construction of these facilities must be imported. Therefore the resources of the Bank are called upon to provide the foreign exchange necessary for the building of these vitally important facilities.[2]

Despite the recognized need for investment in infrastructure as a precondition to economic development, Bank lending increased very slowly. The *Fourth Annual Report, 1948–1949* reads like a defense of the Bank's caution, and the defense consists of a discovery of how very undeveloped "less developed countries" are. "Money alone is no solution. . . . Perhaps the most striking single lesson which the Bank has learned in the course of its

2. International Bank for Reconstruction and Development, *Sixth Annual Report, 1950–1951*, p. 14. This was also the Bank's view twenty years later. (See IBRD, *100 Questions and Answers* [March 1970], p. 39.) To the question "Why has so large a proportion of the Bank's lending been for the development of transportation and electric power?" the answer was given: "An improvement in basic services such as transportation and electric power has been a primary prerequisite for faster economic growth throughout the developing world. . . . Although much has been achieved, the need for further investment is still pressing."

operations is how limited is the capacity of the underdeveloped countries to absorb capital quickly for really productive purposes."

The reasons for this are many.

Of fundamental importance is the low level of education and health prevailing in most underdeveloped countries. . . . Without requiring any large expenditure of money, technical help in such matters as training teachers and doctors, establishing and operating schools of many different kinds, improving sanitary and public health facilities and eradicating such wide-spread and debilitating diseases as malaria, can do as much, in the long run, as any other single factor towards creating the conditions necessary for accelerated economic progress, particularly in the under-populated countries.[3]

It should be noted that these development requirements could, in the opinion of the Bank, be handled effectively by providing technical assistance and that very little investment would be needed.

A second important set of limiting factors is political in character. In some underdeveloped countries, frequent changes in government result in economic and financial insecurity and prevent the consistency of policy and continuity of administration that are so important for development. . . . Certainly no amount of external aid, technical or financial, can replace the essential will and determination on the part of the government of the country concerned to adopt the often difficult and politically unpopular economic and financial measures necessary to create a favorable environment for development.[4]

Then there was the question of social structure, with its extremes of wealth and poverty. "In such cases, strong vested interests often resist any changes which would alter their position." But, "on the other hand, attempts to reorganize the social order often go to the other extreme and result in policies and measures which make productive investment so hazardous as to frighten away both local and foreign capital."[5]

These and other considerations explained the "gap which exists between the concept of development potentialities, on the one hand, and the formulation of practical propositions designed for the realization of those potentialities, on the other."[6] In other words, that explains the low volume of Bank lending. But, as we noted in earlier chapters, there were some, both inside and outside the Bank, who thought that the Bank could lend much more and lend it effectively if it did not confine itself to the financing of the foreign exchange costs of a limited range of projects. Pressure inside the Bank did for a time lead to some program lending and local expenditure financing,

3. IBRD, *Fourth Annual Report, 1948–1949*, p. 8.
4. *Ibid.*
5. *Ibid.*, pp. 8–9.
6. *Ibid.*, p. 9.

but so far as program loans by the Bank were concerned, this was a temporary aberration. The Bank's first program loan was to the Congo in 1951, and its last (until a loan to Nigeria in 1971) was to Iran in 1957. During this period, moreover, the major flow of program funds was to developed countries, principally Australia, rather than to less developed countries. Until a power loan in Mexico in 1958, local expenditure financing was reserved entirely for projects in developed countries. Thus during the first ten or twelve years of the Bank's existence its capital contributions to the less developed world consisted of a relatively small annual flow of funds devoted almost entirely to the financing of the foreign exchange costs of specific projects, three-fourths of which were in the area of public utilities.

This, in the opinion of the IBRD management, was about what could be expected of a soundly managed international development institution. The ability of less developed countries to absorb external funds and to use them effectively must be judged to be extremely limited. "It must be emphasized that it is only the amount of productive investment which takes place, and not the mere availability of money, which is important."[7] The early pressure for a greatly expanded flow of development assistance provided on easier terms, as we noted in Chapter 12, came not from the Bank but from other UN agencies and from bilateral sources.[8]

The attitude of the Bank management toward competing official lending institutions, whether bilateral or multilateral, was negative. Such institutions might increase the flow of funds to the less developed world but were un-

7. *Ibid.,* p. 8.

8. A report by a group of experts appointed by the secretary-general of the United Nations (*Measures for the Economic Development of Underdeveloped Countries,* May 3, 1951 [E/1986 ST/ECA/10]), estimated that to raise per capita incomes in the less developed world by 2 percent a year would require annual capital assistance of $10 billion, as against an existing flow that "does not exceed $1.5 billion and is probably nearer to $1 billion."

This was the first of many analyses that have tried to estimate the "gap" between requirements and availabilities of foreign assistance if less developed countries were to attain some target growth rate. The IBRD has never been favorably disposed toward such efforts. Nor was the group of experts, which included W. Arthur Lewis, Theodore W. Schultz, D. R. Gadgil, George Hakim, and Alberto Baltra Cortez, favorably impressed by the Bank's efforts.

The Bank has been lending to the underdeveloped countries at a rate well below $300 million annually, and expects not to exceed this figure in the next few years. In view of the need of the underdeveloped countries for capital, the Bank cannot be said to be meeting the challenge of the circumstances. (P. 83.)

The Bank should set itself a target of at least $1 billion a year, to be reached in five years. "If it shows no signs of reaching this target," the whole question of a proper international lending agency should be reviewed." (P. 84.)

likely to add to productive investment.⁹ In President Black's view, international transfers of capital ought to take the form either of loans for sound projects at close-to-commercial rates or outright grants. The resources of the Bank were considered to be more than adequate for financing sound projects. Soft loans were "fuzzy loans," which had no place in international development finance. Still, Bank lending had moved up to a new and higher plateau by 1958, and the Bank had come to recognize the need for a larger volume of Bank financing and of financing on easier terms. By this time the IBRD was moving into a rather different conception of the development process and development requirements, which we shall consider presently.

9. As will be seen in Chapter 15, the IBRD was in its early years engaged in a competitive struggle with the U.S. Export-Import Bank. In the opinion of the IBRD, Eximbank lending should be limited to purposes that concerned either the political and security interests of the United States, such as the financing of the procurement of strategic materials, or to the financing of U.S. foreign trade. Long-term development lending was the prerogative of the IBRD; the supposed lack of bankable projects in the less developed world made additional development financing agencies unnecessary.

The Bank applauded the announcement in 1949 of President Truman's Point Four program of technical assistance, and at that stage the management, at least, considered this the proper role, and perhaps the only proper role, for bilateral development assistance. The so-called Gray Report (*Report to the President on Foreign Economic Policies* [1950]) urged that the United States undertake capital assistance to less developed countries. And when the U.S. bilateral program expanded from technical assistance to capital transfers in the early 1950s, primarily on a grant basis, the Bank argued that while the quality of the program could be improved, it nevertheless deserved citizen support and should be enlarged. In its more realistic moments the Bank was aware that the existence of the U.S. bilateral program shielded it from requests for loans it would have been unwilling to make and that such economic improvement as the bilateral program helped to achieve would make its own life easier. The Bank had little to say about other bilateral lending programs apart from complaints about the excessive amount of short-term export financing contained in some of these programs.

The Bank in a report to the UN Department of Economic Affairs in 1949 on *Methods of Financing Economic Development in Under-developed Countries* stated frankly, "It is quite clear that there are capital requirements for health, sanitation, education and similar purposes which are indispensable for economic development and cannot readily be expected to yield a direct return." The report then went on to say,

The Bank is aware that unofficial proposals have been advanced in some quarters that additional funds should be made available to finance development by way of grants. It is not possible for the Bank at the present stage to evaluate the merits of such proposals. The decision on them is a matter for the governments of those countries in a position to provide such additional funds.

It is probably true to say that in the early 1950s the Bank's management disapproved of the provision of capital assistance on soft terms. Technical assistance on a grant basis was the preferred method. If capital assistance was required on terms softer than those of the Bank, it should, like technical assistance, be provided on a grant basis. Soft loans presupposed a lending agency, and the Bank was chary of the appearance of other development lending agencies.

In the period before the mid-1950s, not only was the absorptive capacity of less developed countries for sound project lending considered meager, but even a relatively small flow of funds could be justified as a contribution to development only if borrowing countries followed sensible development policies. This meant in general settling outstanding external debt obligations, pursuing conservative monetary and fiscal policies, generating enough public savings to cover the local currency costs of necessary capital infrastructure, providing a hospitable climate for foreign and domestic private investment, and recognizing the management's boundary line between activities appropriate to the public sector and those appropriate to the private sector.

As we noted in Chapter 6, the question of external debt obligations came to the fore in the Bank's very first project loan—to Chile in 1948. The Bank made it a condition of the loan that Chile make a reasonable effort to come to terms with its foreign bondholders. This has continued to be Bank policy ever since, its latest application having been in Guatemala in 1968. A similar policy governed Bank lending to member countries that expropriated foreign private investments. The Bank would refuse to lend unless and until appropriate efforts had been made to reach a fair and equitable settlement.

The Bank's early dealings in Latin America, moreover, brought it face to face with the relation of stabilization policies to development. The first survey mission to Colombia (in 1949) stressed the importance of balancing the national budget and of taking action to comply with recommendations of the International Monetary Fund (IMF) with respect to reorganization of the country's foreign exchange controls and establishment of a new par value for its currency. An adequate stabilization policy was as necessary a condition for development in the view of the Bank as it was in the view of the Fund. Without such a policy, domestic savings and foreign investment would be impaired, the price system would be unable to perform its essential function with respect to resource allocation, and creditworthiness for Bank lending would suffer. In 1954 the Bank sharply reduced lending to Brazil because of policies thought to be conducive to inflation and balance-of-payments difficulties, and the Brazilian action served notice to other potential borrowers in Latin America and elsewhere that adequate stabilization measures would be considered a condition of Bank lending.

The IBRD has from the beginning of its lending to less developed member countries emphasized the importance of generating public savings to cover the local currency cost of capital infrastructure. As we noted in Chapter 8, the Bank in its project evaluation has always stressed heavily the financial analysis of the sources and uses of domestic funds required by the project. In the case of revenue-producing projects, it has insisted on pricing policies capable of generating revenues to finance expansion of the project. In the case of nonrevenue-producing projects, the revenue position of relevant government departments and agencies has been examined, and the Bank has frequently found itself suggesting new taxes and various other fiscal measures. A primary condition of lending for local expenditures has always been that the borrowing country must show that it has made an adequate fiscal effort to raise revenue and is unable to go further without causing adverse economic consequences. A local currency component is not to be considered unless, in the words of an operational memorandum, "the borrowing country has a suitable development program and is making an adequate development effort."[10] This has long been Bank policy, though, as we have noted, in recent years it is a policy sometimes honored in the breach.

A member country's record with respect to total savings, of course, is always noted in country reports prepared by the Bank, but it is the record with respect to public savings—particularly public savings related to the local currency costs of Bank projects—that affects the decision as to whether the Bank should lend or not lend. It has been argued in certain quarters that the Bank's emphasis on public savings generated by tax increases has been self-defeating since tax increases have usually been followed by increases in current government expenditures rather than investment and possibly also by a decline in private savings.[11] Whether or not this is so, it is a fact that the Bank's conception of good development performance on the part of the borrower has assigned a high place to public savings.

As we have emphasized, a primary concern in the Bank's financing of transportation, power, port installations, and communications facilities has been to provide the framework needed for the expansion of private enterprise, the real motive power behind economic development. Foreign private investment should have an important role to play in the development process, and it was early stated that "one of the principal objectives of the Bank, therefore, is to help to create conditions which will encourage a steady and substantial stream of private investment, particularly equity investment, flowing into its underdeveloped member countries."[12] But the stimulation of

10. IBRD, Operational memorandum 2.03 (June 9, 1969).
11. Stanley Please, "Saving Through Taxation—Reality or Mirage?" *Finance and Development*, Vol. 4 (March 1967). See also "The Please Effect Revisited," paper prepared for a seminar held at the U.S. Agency for International Development (processed; April 2, 1970). In 1970 Please was chief of the IBRD's Division of Domestic Finance for Developing Countries.
12. IBRD, *Third Annual Report, 1947–1948*, p. 20.

domestic private savings and enterprise must be considered of even greater importance in the development process. As the Bank pointed out in its 1949 report to the UN Department of Economic Affairs on methods of financing economic development, private foreign equity investors were likely to be interested only in certain lines of activity, mainly in the exploitation of raw materials or in production for foreign markets.[13] Whereas other bodies established by the United Nations were advising less developed countries to industrialize and, in particular, to concentrate on heavy industry, the IBRD itself favored the development of light industry.[14] This was not an area of primary interest to foreign investors but one that must depend mainly on domestic private enterprise and the generation of domestic savings. It was clearly important then that governments interested in development take the steps necessary to encourage domestic savings and investment in the private sector.

If private investment and private enterprise were to accomplish the development task they were capable of performing, it was thought desirable that a clear distinction be drawn between economic activities appropriate to the public sector and those that could better be undertaken by private enterprise. There was not much of a positive character that the Bank could do about this except to criticize UN or other reports advocating heavy industrial projects in the public sector and to look with disapproval on member countries, such as India, which appeared to be following this advice. But the IBRD could at least refuse to lend for any such purpose. This refusal sprang from a sincere conviction on the part of the Bank management that, regardless of the cultural background and the politico-economic structure of the potential borrowing country, industrial enterprises are better managed in the private sector and that, with the serious arrears in economic and social overhead capital confronting less developed countries, governments would have enough to do managing a public sector that did not include industrial enterprises. The very few publicly controlled industrial projects the Bank financed in its early years were all designed to be turned over to private control at a specified stage.

These then were the main lines a country must follow if it sought development. The appropriate role of the Bank as a development institution was

13. UN Department of Economic Affairs, *Methods of Financing Economic Development in Under-Developed Countries,* "Submission from the IBRD," Sales No. 1949 II. B.4.

14. See Memorandum from the IBRD to the Economic and Employment Commission of the UN. Doc E/CN. 1/71 (1949).

clearly indicated. There were people both inside and outside the Bank, as we have indicated, who found this role inadequate.

As was noted above, one may search in vain in the Bank's archives for anything approaching a systematic account of a "normal" development process, or for the principal variants from such a norm that the Bank has encountered in its experience, or for models illuminating the relationship among the main variables that would need to be taken into account in assessing development prospects. One would have thought that the systematic attention given by the Bank Group over long periods of time to the development of member countries might have led, through country comparisons, to a grouping of these countries into significant development cases or models for use in formulating development strategies. After all, the burgeoning literature on economic development was full, if not of accepted theories or tested hypotheses, at least of promising suggestions of alternative models and structural differences that might be expected to appear at different stages of development. There are labor-surplus economies and export-oriented economies, as well as characteristic differences in structure of production between small economies and large economies at similar per capita income levels and among economies of similar size at different per capita income levels. In fact the only grouping of developing economies that has emerged from Bank experience is the product of administrative organization rather than of politico-economic analysis.

The administrative organization of the Bank may, in fact, be partially responsible for its early lack of attention to development analysis. The technical departments have the primary task of shaping and appraising projects, and this does not usually take them very far into the relationship of the particular project to the development process. The area departments, on the other hand, tend to look, in the large, at the countries confided to their care. Their analysis deals mainly in aggregates: growth rates of gross national product, import requirements, growth rates of export earnings, savings rates, government tax revenues, and the like. With the technical departments concentrating on projects and the area departments skating on the rather thin ice of their aggregates, there is a danger that certain essential elements of the development process—concerned with the relative rates and characteristics of sectoral growth, the development of capital markets, and various institutional changes—will be lost from sight. Presumably it should have been the task of the Economics Department to probe more deeply into the development process, make needed comparisons, and illuminate relationships that are difficult for operating departments to take into account. But at least until the mid-1960s, Economics was a small, undermanned department, and although its growth in recent years has been notable, it has had the usual difficulties of a research staff in making its influence on operations felt.[15]

If the Bank Group were taxed with its failure to produce anything like a theory of development or even a systematic analysis of major permutations and combinations, it would no doubt reply that it is an operating institution concerned with lending and technical assistance and not primarily with research. This is, of course, true. Yet it would not perhaps be expecting too much to consider that the Bank, as the principal international development agency with long experience in most of the less developed countries of the world, should also be a leader in development thought. In fact, as Rosenstein-Rodan noted in 1961, the Bank has in general been a follower and at times a rather reluctant follower.[16]

It required a good deal of outside criticism and pressure to persuade the Bank that the absorptive capacity of less developed countries for external assistance could not be satisfied by a trickle of loans limited to the financing of the foreign exchange costs of specific projects. The Bank was slow to realize that well considered projects, financed from whatever source, could increase rather than diminish the creditworthiness of a country for subsequent lending. As we noted in Chapter 8, certain of the Bank's techniques of project appraisal, such as discounted cash flow, were adopted long after they had become standard practice in the business world. The use of shadow prices in project evaluation has come slowly and haltingly, and it is still applied unsystematically in the various technical departments. Various types of system analysis applicable to related clusters of investments have only recently come into use. Bank management, moreover, has been reluctant to accept the proposition that certain types of current expenditure, for example, government subsidies to encourage the introduction of spraying equipment, can make as large a contribution to development as investment in capital equipment.

Although the Bank Group has greatly expanded the scope of its lending in recent years, it was slow to break away from its early devotion to capital infrastructure. Manpower analysis and techniques of manpower planning had developed extensively in the outside world before the Bank showed any great

15. Speaking of the situation as it existed in the early 1960s, John de Wilde, acting director of the Economic Staff during that period, reported to one of the authors that there had never been a research program in the proper sense of the word. Members of the Economic Staff were detached with little notice to serve on overseas missions and when at home were rarely employed in research of basic significance for an understanding of development processes.

16. From interview of Paul Rosenstein-Rodan, Oral History Project of Columbia University, interviews recorded in the summer of 1961 on the International Bank for Reconstruction and Development (cited hereinafter as "Oral History").

interest in human resource development. It required several years of academic discussion of the difference between nominal and effective tariffs and of the complex effects on the level of protection of tariffs on inputs and outputs, and of overvalued currencies and quantitative restrictions, before the IBRD took a serious interest in the relation of these considerations to appropriate channels of industrialization. The IBRD has only recently showed a concern for the effects of its lending policies on income distribution and, through income distribution, on social development and political stability. And now after several years of public concern for the ecological consequences of economic expansion, the Bank is taking a somewhat belated interest in this problem. In some ways the regional banks and various bilateral assistance programs have been more venturesome and experimental in their lending programs than has the World Bank.

While all this is true, it is by no means the whole story. The Bank's principal contributions to an analysis of development processes are in its country studies and reports. Naturally these vary in depth and comprehensiveness, depending on the extent of the Bank's involvement. In countries where the Bank Group limited its lending to a project or two every other year, the economic reports tend to be perfunctory and not very illuminating. In others, visited frequently by project, sector, and country missions, the economic reports are substantial pieces of analysis. And despite various deficiencies they are the best surveys available country by country of development prospects and problems. As such, they are used extensively by consortia and consultative groups, by regional banks, by the U.S. Agency for International Development (AID) and U.K. Ministry of Overseas Development, and by other bilateral and multilateral assistance agencies. The Bank may not be a leader in development thought, but it has become a leader among development institutions in applying the available techniques to an analysis of the development problems of particular countries.

Later Developments

The growth of experience in the less developed world, outside pressures, and the initiation of bilateral assistance programs of various kinds had, by the mid-1950s, begun to enlarge the Bank's conception of development requirements and what it could do to satisfy them. During the next decade the Bank became the Bank Group with the addition of the International Finance Corporation and the International Development Association (IDA). The volume of Bank lending moved to a higher plateau, and the membership was enlarged, particularly by the addition of newly independent African countries. Changes in IBRD thinking, begun during the Black administration, were carried on into the administration of President Woods and developed further. Again, if we may attempt a sketch of the new elements in the Bank's thinking, in about 1965, certain ones seem predominant.

The Bank was by then convinced that opportunities for the effective use of external assistance were very much larger than had been conceived earlier; that in many less developed countries the growth process was likely to be of such long duration as to preclude exclusive dependence on financing on normal Bank terms; and that creditworthiness for Bank lending would inevitably increase as member countries developed economically, with the help of external funds from other sources. The Bank also became aware that domestic policies conducive to development embraced more than adequate stabilization measures, plus the public savings necessary to finance the local currency cost of capital infrastructure, and a favorable climate for domestic and foreign private investment. Experience, particularly in Africa, opened the Bank's eyes to the importance of human resource development and the necessity of lending to cover not only foreign exchange costs but certain local currency costs as well. This was accompanied by a considerable expansion of lending in other sectors, including industry and agriculture. Finally the sharp distinction between roles appropriate to the public sector and those appropriate to the private sector began to be softened. These changes are described largely in terms of Bank action, but this action was in response to wider perceptions of what the development process was all about.

As we have noted, the Bank tended to justify the low volume of lending in early years on the grounds of the limited capacity of less developed countries to absorb capital for "really productive purposes." This ability could be increased by providing technical assistance for project preparation, but at best the expansion of absorptive capacity would be a slow process. Furthermore, Bank management in the early years tended to think of a member country's ability to service debt, including debt to the Bank, in rather static terms. Undue attention was paid to current debt service ratios, and it was thought that ability to service debt might easily be "exhausted" by further borrowing. The management tended to be alarmed by a ratio of debt service to export earnings of 10 percent, and in the days of early lending to Mexico feared that Mexico's recent $150 million line of credit from the Export-Import Bank might exhaust its creditworthiness. Later when a commitment of around $250 million was being considered to finance projects in Brazil proposed by the joint Brazilian-American development commission, the suggestion that certain of these might be financed by the Export-Import Bank was rejected, in part on the grounds that this might reduce Brazil's capacity to service debt to the Bank.[17] Only gradually did the Bank management come to realize that creditworthiness was essentially a function of growth and that absorptive capacity increased with absorption.

As we have several times noted, the Bank had recognized very early that development required something more than the provision of capital. The low level of education and health in many less developed countries was a serious handicap. Technical assistance was required, but it was thought that this could be provided on a grant basis without generating larger requirements for capital assistance than the Bank could meet. Pressure from UN agencies and commissions and the Bank's own experience in southern Asia led management to feel that, in certain parts of the world at least, development was likely to be a slower process, requiring more assistance on easier terms, than had been envisaged. The Bank was never willing to accept the premises of the "gap analysis" that an inflow of capital would more or less automatically produce an increase in national output through a calculable marginal capital–output ratio, but it did come to see that a greatly increased volume of external assistance could be used effectively. As we noted in Chapter 12, the Bank espoused IDA in large part to avoid capital-dispensing agencies that would be competitive and, as it believed, politically vulnerable, such as SUNFED, proposed for UN administration; but by the time IDA was established, the Bank management was itself convinced of the need for a much larger flow of external assistance on much easier terms.

If Latin America had focused the Bank's attention on development problems in the early 1950s, it was India and to a lesser extent Pakistan that came to the center of the stage in the late 1950s and early 1960s. The Bank's views on the relation of adequate stabilization measures to development were shaped in Latin America. Southern Asia posed a wider range of questions, and India became probably the most studied country among the Bank's membership. The Bank's first loan to India was in 1949, and at that stage there was serious doubt in the minds of management whether India could be considered creditworthy for more than a small amount. But beginning in 1956, and for a few years thereafter, India became a favored borrower. India absorbed more than half of IDA's funds after 1960, and the availability of IDA money was judged to increase India's creditworthiness for Bank lending. These favorable views were, however, dissipated in the early 1960s as it became clear that at the current rate of growth of GNP, and particularly of

---

17. The same line of thought prevailed in the Bank's early relations with India. The suggestion of a 1956 Bank mission to India that India might be creditworthy for $700 million of Bank lending marked a distinct change.

export earnings, India would continue to be dependent on massive external assistance for the indefinite future. A number of Bank missions, culminating in the large Bell mission in 1964–65, sought the reasons for this slow rate of growth, and these investigations helped to shape the Bank's views on the nature of the development process.

Since Bank lending to India is discussed at many points in this study, it is unnecessary here to do more than emphasize the highlights. The Indian experience reinforced the Bank's views on the importance of balanced growth, in the sense that attainment of a given rate of growth of national output required appropriate growth rates in the important sectors of the economy. The agricultural and export sectors of the Indian economy were conspicuous laggards, and the Bank attributed a large part of India's poor performance to their deficiencies. These and other deficiencies were, in a deeper sense, thought to be attributable largely to the failure of the price system to provide the right signals and the proper incentives for larger production. Food price controls held down farm incomes and made it unprofitable to increase fertilizer and other inputs needed to increase agricultural output. An overvalued rupee plus a high degree of protection for domestic manufactures deprived producers of incentives to export. Artificially low interest rates, particularly to public sector enterprises, stimulated large-scale installations and capital-intensive technologies—at the expense of more efficient scales and fuller employment. A multitude of controls increased the cost of road transport and prevented the development of an economic relationship of road and rail transport. Of course pricing deficiencies, and in particular faulty exchange and interest rates, had always been taken into account by the Bank in analyzing handicaps to development, but lending experience in southern Asia moved these considerations several notches upward in the appraisal of development priorities.

An enlargement of the scope of Bank lending during the Woods administration, with increased emphasis on industry, agriculture, and education, was probably more the result of a change in the Bank's conception of its proper role than a change in its conception of development requirements. But earlier beliefs that, given the proper climate for investment, unassisted private savings and private enterprise could be expected to provide the necessary inputs for industrial expansion (apart from very large-scale enterprise), gave way to a broader concern for these aspects of development. The rapid growth of Bank lending to development finance companies did not begin until the 1960s. Along with this lending, technical assistance began to be provided to these companies in forming new enterprises and developing capital markets. In the agricultural sector also, the Bank, assisted by IDA funds, broadened its range of concerns from large-scale government-sponsored irrigation and land clearance projects to institutional arrangements designed to change cropping patterns and provide increased inputs of use to individual farmers. Educational lending developed slowly, but, largely under the influence of lending experience in newly affiliated African member countries, human resource development gained added emphasis. The expansion of the scope of Bank Group lending was then, at least in part, a reflection of a broader conception of the development process.

Finally, not until the 1960s did changes in the Bank's views on the proper role of public- and private-sector enterprise become perceptible. Again it was experience in lending to African countries, where private enterprise was all but nonexistent, plus the need in Asia for government participation if fertilizer production was to be rapidly expanded, that altered Bank views. What came to be the Bank's concern in industrial enterprises was not the locus of ownership but rather the effectiveness and independence from political pressure of the management, whatever the ownership. But not until 1968, as we have noted earlier, was the Bank willing to countenance public ownership and control of Bank-financed development finance companies.

More Recent Views

It may be that at this writing the Bank is in the process of moving to a rather different level of understanding of the development process and of the measurement of development, but it is too early to pronounce with certainty on these matters. The indications are that there will be (a) some broadening of the scope of Bank lending and changes in the emphasis given to various development policies; (b) changes in the Bank's time horizon and in certain directions of research; and (c) an expansion, expressed largely through pronouncements of the president, in what the Bank should understand to be the meaning of development.

Under President McNamara the IBRD not only has followed the initiative of President Woods in greatly expanding lending in the areas of industry, agriculture, and education but also is exploring new fields in population planning, urbanization, unemployment, and export-oriented industrialization. It is true that lending for population-planning activities has to date been minimal, but the president of the Bank has become a world spokesman for the proposition that without adequate population planning the prospects for growth in per capita income in many less developed countries are illusory. Loans and credits for urban development have up to now been limited to the financing of a few water and sewage installations, but the role of urban investment in national development is now under active investigation, and increased lending in this area can be expected. The threat to development of the rising tide of unemployment in the Third World was the theme of the president's address to the board of governors in September 1971. As we noted in Chapter 8, the Bank is now engaged for the first time in its history in a serious study of the effects on costs of substituting labor for capital in various installations and activities. In the course of time the results of these investigations will no doubt affect project evaluation and lending policy. And, as we noted in Chapter 11, a new interest in the effects of tariff structures, overvalued currencies, and exchange controls on the direction of industrial development is evident in lending to development finance companies and in the operation of the IFC. These changes in Bank practice are the result of evolving views concerning development priorities.

The initiation of five-year lending programs for all member countries to which the Bank customarily lends inevitably leads to a more thorough consideration of the relation of the financing of particular projects to the development process. This, together with the large expansion of Bank lending and a commensurate increase in the number of Bank missions visiting the principal borrowing countries, has tended to produce more knowledgeable and penetrating country economic reports.[18] Since 1969 these reports, together with estimates from projects departments of lending possibilities, and evaluations from area departments of relevant political and social factors, have been distilled into country program papers for consideration by the president of the Bank after review by the Economic Committee. These papers are intended to derive, from Bank Group perception of country problems, prospects, and potential, a coordinated plan of action for Bank Group activities, both financial and advisory. The analysis is expected to cover essentially four subjects at both macroeconomic and sector levels: (a) development objectives, (b) obstacles and problems, (c) solutions, and (d) the Bank Group contribution.

This kind of country analysis, subjected to critical scrutiny by the various area and technical departments and to review by the Economic Committee, can hardly fail in the course of time to lead to generalizations of broader application than to particular economies. If the Bank also continues a program recently begun of evaluating the developmental consequences of particular

18. In his address to the board of governors of the Bank and Fund (Sept. 29, 1969), quoted in Chapter 4, and in his February 1970 speech, quoted in Chapter 10, President McNamara announced an expansion of the program of country economic reporting and promised publication on a regular basis.

loans rather than contenting itself with an "end-use" inspection of whether the money was properly spent, the Bank may well be in process of becoming, if not a leader of developmental thought, at least the main repository of what has in fact been learned.[19]

It must be said that to date the Bank, like most other investigators and practitioners, has tended to assess economic development very much in terms of the rate of increase in per capita national product and of indicators directly relevant to this increase. To be sure, very early in the Bank's annual reports, as we have mentioned earlier in this chapter, it was noted that of "fundamental importance is the level of education and health"; that political stability and the will of the government to promote development are essential; that wide extremes of wealth and poverty may lead vested interests to resist change; and that "the problem of making necessary adjustments in traditional social relationships without destroying the stability essential to development" is a serious and relevant problem. But though these considerations have been mentioned in annual reports and frequently also in country economic studies, it cannot be said that they have greatly affected decisions to lend or not to lend. The Bank has rarely enquired in making a loan what the consequences are likely to be for income distribution, the political power of vested interests, or the stability of particular governments.

This may be in process of change. As President McNamara has stated eloquently on a number of occasions, an adequate rate of growth of GNP is a necessary but not sufficient condition of successful development.

We have made a start at broadening the concept of development beyond the simple limits of economic growth. The emerging nations need, and are determined to achieve, greater economic advance. But . . . we believe economic progress remains precarious and sterile without corresponding social improvement. Fully human development demands attention to both. We intend, in the Bank, to give attention to both.[20]

McNamara has spelled out in some detail the objectives he deems essential in bringing about social transformation and improvement in the quality of human life. First and foremost are adequate family planning, improved nutrition, an increase in literacy, management of the growing problem of unemployment, reasonable programs of urban development, and a much wider sharing of the benefits of agricultural and industrial development. Concern with these questions is already apparent in the Bank's country studies.

19. In 1970 the Bank began an assessment in Colombia of the consequences for development of its total lending program in that country. This assessment, about which we have more to say in Chapter 19, is in our view outstanding.

20. Robert S. McNamara, Address to the Board of Governors, Copenhagen (Sept. 21, 1970).

At this point, however, a serious question arises concerning the relevance of these considerations to the Bank's objectives. At bottom is an issue concerning the significance of gross national product, or GNP per capita, as a measure of development. A growth of GNP could have either or both of two meanings. It could signify an increase in the economic resources available to satisfy a society's wants, that is, an increase in capacity. Or it could mean an increase in welfare or economic welfare, that is, an increase in the level of want satisfaction. Most economic analysis puts no great faith in GNP as a measure of welfare or even of economic welfare. At best it is accepted as a measure, and a not too satisfactory one, of a capacity to dispose of economic resources. This distinction is important to the Bank's operations and is developed further in the appendix to this chapter.

If income redistribution, urban or regional development, or reduction of the power of vested interests are considered relevant to the growth of GNP as a measure of the capacity to use resources, it can be argued that they should be taken into account by the Bank. If they are to be considered as essential inputs to the growth of GNP, there is presumably no incompatibility between, say, a proposed redistribution of income and the growth of economic capacity over time. And assuming that the Bank can persuade a borrowing government that this is so, there should be no objection to the Bank's efforts to do so. On the other hand, if income redistribution is to be considered a welfare objective, independent of the growth of GNP and perhaps incompatible with such growth, a different set of considerations emerges. The Bank is vulnerable whenever it tries to substitute its own judgment of how economic capacity is to be used in the public interest for the judgment of borrowing member governments. It is one thing to broaden the scope of inputs that are taken into account in a lending program; it is quite another to redefine for the borrower the objectives of public policy. It is not altogether clear that the Bank in recent pronouncements has observed this distinction.

Even if the Bank limits itself to a broadening of the inputs that could be taken into account in promoting development, there are formidable areas of ignorance and severe resistances to be overcome in borrowing countries.

In his Copenhagen speech the president of the Bank addressed himself to the question of what needs to be known.

We do not want simply to say that rising unemployment is a "bad thing," and something must be done about it. We want to know its scale, its causes, its impact and the range of policies and options which are open to governments, international agencies and the private sector to deal with it.

We do not want simply to sense that the "green revolution" requires a comparable social revolution in the organization and education of the small farmer.

We want to know what evidence or working models are available on methods of cooperative enterprise, of decentralized credit systems, of smaller-scale technology, and of price and market guarantees.

We do not want simply to deplore over-rapid urbanization in the primary cities. We want the most accurate and careful studies of internal migration, town-formation, decentralized urbanism and regional balance.[21]

These are formidable research requirements. And if we add to them what would need to be known about political and social structures in order to gauge "options open to governments" and to estimate the probable responses of interest groups to various proposals in the area of social change, it would have to be said that the Bank is at present not very well equipped to deal with these questions. The economics of development is not a very well understood subject, and the politics and sociology of development are even less so.[22]

But over and beyond this is the question of the reaction of borrowing countries to attempts on the part of the Bank to shape projects in the direction of particular social consequences. One or two examples from recent Bank experience may illustrate the nature of the problem. In 1969, IDA extended sizable credits to India and to Pakistan to finance the importation of tractors. As we noted in Chapter 8, opinion in the Bank was divided on the merits of these credits. It could be argued that they served the interests mainly of large, well-to-do farmers and would tend to replace techniques of production that were decidedly more labor-intensive, thus creating undesirable employment effects. Although it was held in rebuttal that tractors could also serve the interests of small farmers through cooperatives and local credit arrangements, no firm program to bring this about was suggested. On the whole, moreover, it seemed doubtful whether the governments of India and Pakistan could be dissuaded from importing tractors, whatever action the Bank took.

In 1970 the Bank made loans to two Latin American countries for livestock development. In both cases an objection was raised in the board of directors that these loans were made to comparatively affluent farmers, while the vast majority of cultivators in these countries, who were certainly not affluent, were neglected. A director from Latin America, in response to this objection, said that he was surprised to see it suggested that the Bank should be concerned with redistributing income; he had understood that the purpose of the Bank was to promote economic development, in which case it was appropriate to finance those who were capable of assisting such development.

There is no doubt that during the last few years the Bank has greatly ex-

21. *Ibid.*
22. See the appendix to this chapter, "A Note on the Meaning of Economic Development."

panded its conception of development requirements and of the social and political considerations that may be relevant to economic growth. It may, however, face a dilemma in choosing between the objective of a rapid expansion of lending and an adequate appraisal of these considerations. But beyond this is the question whether, if income redistribution, fuller employment, relief of depressed areas, and other possible social objectives run counter to economic growth, the Bank is in a position to substitute its judgment concerning appropriate public policy for that of the borrowing member country.

The membership of the Bank embraces a wide spectrum of social structure and political organization, ranging from tribally oriented or militarily controlled governments, on the one hand, to those approximating democratic societies, on the other. The IBRD has paid little attention to the political configuration of borrowing governments, provided they followed economic policies conducive to creditworthiness. Indeed it was strictly forbidden by the Articles of Agreement to do so.[23] A result has been that on more than one occasion the Bank has found itself reducing the level of lending to governments newly turned democratic because of unsatisfactory fiscal, monetary, or foreign exchange policies or increasing the level of lending to militarily controlled governments with a capacity to enforce economic austerity.

This, of course, is anathema to left-wing critics and to some others who are not particularly radical, and it is the basis of charges that the Bank is a reactionary and imperialist institution and will remain so unless and until it confines its assistance to the poorest countries of the world and, in particular, to those attempting to escape from "political and economic colonialism." The directors and management of the Bank Group had occasion to become acquainted with these views at the annual meeting in Copenhagen in 1970 through both a document that was distributed[24] and rather raucous oral exposition.

As one reviews the history of the Bank, taking into account the predominant ideology of the directors representing countries having a majority of the votes (and for much of the first twenty-five years, the ideology of management as well), one must in all fairness concede a measure of validity to the left-wing criticism. The way in which this ideology has been shaped conforms in significant degree to the interests and conventional wisdom of its principal

23. Article IV, section 10.

24. "World Bank Report." A translation of the Danish original, prepared for the World Bank Group in 1970 by a number of Danish anti-imperialist organizations (processed). A more moderate but still severely critical account of Bank lending policy, particularly in Latin America, is presented in Teresa Hayter, *Aid As Imperialism* (Penguin Books, 1971).

stockholders. International competitive bidding, reluctance to accord preferences to local suppliers, emphasis on financing foreign exchange costs, insistence on a predominant use of foreign consultants, attitudes toward public sector industries, assertion of the right to approve project managers—all proclaim the Bank to be a Western capitalist institution. Such an institution can contribute and, we believe, *has* contributed to the development of the less developed world. But increasingly the Bank has found itself in conflict with its less developed member countries on the issues noted above and on others. Although it has to a certain extent adapted its policies and practices, this adaptation has been limited by the concern of those member countries that supply not only most of the capital but most of the management and senior technicians as well.

Summary and Conclusions

The IBRD has, in the course of its evolution, moved from early reconstruction loans to exclusive concern with development lending and from lending for projects in developed countries to the financing of projects exclusively in the less developed world. It has supplemented its financing of capital requirements with technical assistance at the project, sector, and national levels. The Bank, joined by the IFC and the IDA, has become a Bank Group more capable of responding flexibly to the needs of its members. It has substantially broadened the scope of its lending and, through participation in consortia and consultative groups, has become a coordinator of assistance flows from other sources. In the course of this evolution the Bank Group has assumed the role of principal spokesman to rich countries for the needs of the less developed world for external assistance.

An observer noting these changes could conclude that in becoming less of a Bank the IBRD has become more of a development institution. This is true, but the changes in Bank policies and practices have been accompanied by a continuing change in the conceptions of Bank management concerning the nature of developmental requirements and what the IBRD could do about them. Management, even in the early stages, conceived of the Bank as a development institution doing all or most of the things that could practically be done by an external agency to promote development. If the IBRD now casts its net more widely, it is because management's conception of the development process and requirements has changed rather than because the early managers thought of themselves as bankers while their successors considered themselves to be developers.

Although the evolution of the Bank's thinking about the development process cannot easily be divided into periods, it is possible to distinguish, at least roughly, two stages—the first covering the period to the mid-1950s and the second from then to the McNamara administration. The IBRD may now be entering a third stage. During the first stage the Bank thought of less developed countries as having a very limited absorptive capacity for external financing of productive projects. The financing that was required should be limited rather closely to the foreign exchange costs of capital infrastructure. Even this amount of financing could be used productively only if the borrowing countries programmed their public investment carefully. But given an adequate provision of transport, power, port, and communications facilities, private investment, both domestic and foreign, could be expected to generate development, provided the borrowing governments followed sensible economic policies. This meant, in particular, conservative monetary and foreign exchange policies and budgetary practices capable of generating the public savings required to finance the local currency cost of capital infrastructure. In addition it was necessary, in order to assure a flow of external private investment, to settle arrears on existing foreign debt, and, if foreign enterprises were expropriated, to negotiate equitable compensation.

The second stage was introduced by a gradual realization on the part of the Bank that the external requirements of the less developed world were much larger than had been contemplated earlier and that in many countries repayment could not be expected unless financing were provided on much easier terms. The Bank, reinforced by the IFC and IDA, expanded its own lending but found this dwarfed by the greatly increased outflow of bilateral assistance. The Bank assumed during this period an important role as a leading coordinator of foreign assistance and as spokesman for the assistance requirements of the less developed world. The scope of lending was extended, with greater emphasis on education, industry, and agriculture. The Bank Group substantially increased the volume of its local expenditure financing and, through IDA, of program lending. But development still meant to the Bank Group an increase in GNP, and the Bank's concern with country performance was rather closely limited to policies and practices affected by the rate of growth of GNP.

The McNamara administration has been characterized by a greatly increased volume of Bank Group lending and by an expanded scope of considerations thought to be relevant to the development process: notably family planning, urbanization, and unemployment. What may mark this as a third stage in the Bank's development thinking is the suggestion that there may be more to the development process than a satisfactory rate of growth of GNP. There is talk in the corridors of the Bank, in the president's speeches, and even in the board of directors of income redistribution, of the social and political aspects of development, and of human resource development, not as devices for facilitating economic growth but as desirable ends in themselves. To date, these considerations have not been translated in any very impressive fashion into the Bank lending program, and there are obviously formidable obstacles facing any attempt to go very far in this direction. So long as the Bank remains an organization in which member countries have some influence on decision-making, it is going to be difficult to subject country programs to the kind of critical scrutiny such a lending program would require.

Appendix

A Note on the Meaning of Economic Development

When economists began, after the Second World War, to turn their attention to the problems of less developed countries, there was a rather natural tendency to identify economic development with a demonstrated capacity to sustain a "satisfactory" rate of increase in the gross national product, or perhaps of per capita GNP. Indeed it was asserted in certain quarters that if an economy had sustained such a rate for as much as two or three decades, it could safely be assumed that the process of economic development was well under way. Expositions of the conditions necessary to economic development ranged from simple Harrod-Domar type models (which emphasized the rate of saving and a marginal capital–output ratio and compressed all the influences bearing on the effective use of inputs into one figure) to more complex analyses of the relationships of various growth indicators. The indicators, however, tended to be limited to quantitatively measurable economic magnitudes considered to be directly relevant to the rate of growth of GNP.

From here the discussion of development tended to move in two different but subtly interrelated directions. The first led toward a broader conception of the inputs needed to promote growth of per capita GNP. The second moved toward a broader conception of output, that is, toward a consideration of elements other than the rate of growth of per capita GNP that would need to be taken into account for a deeper understanding of development. Inevitably this broadening of the scope of inputs that needed to be taken into account and of outputs that constituted development tended to produce a complex means–ends relationship, in which it was frequently difficult to disentangle inputs from outputs. Political stability, for example, could be considered a necessary condition, that is, an input, for development; but it could also be regarded as an output, that is, as an essential aspect of the meaning of development. A fairer distribution of income, since it would contribute to political stability, could be thought of at the same time as a condition of development and as an essential aspect of the concept of development. But despite these difficulties, it is useful to distinguish between broad conceptions of inputs and outputs in tracing the expansion of development analysis.

On the input side the early emphasis on capital investment gave way to a consideration of additional factors. An examination of human resource inputs suggested an analysis of manpower requirements, proceeding from certain target rates of growth to a calculation of the types and quantities of labor needed to attain these rates. The necessary labor inputs required education and training, and it was noted that investment in human resource development might yield returns as large as, or larger than, investment in physical capital. But whether the human resource inputs were approached through an analysis of manpower requirements or of anticipated rates of return to investment in human resources, the basis of the calculation was a growth rate of GNP. Reflection on the contribution of education to economic development led to an examination of other "nonconventional" inputs—technological innovations, improvements in the functioning of factor and product markets, and so on; and estimates were attempted of the relative contribution of conventional inputs—land, labor, and capital—as against the totality of unconventional inputs. Up to this point the analysis of inputs, broadly defined, was embraced within the normal boundaries of economics.

But now it was pointed out that behind these economic inputs, conventional and unconventional, lay more fundamental influences having to do with the social and ethnic structures of the society, social values, individual motivations, and various political factors. Entrepreneurship was an essential requirement for development, and it was noted that in many less developed countries entrepreneurs tended to come in unusual concentrations from certain elements of the population. In India certain castes and in Pakistan and Malaysia certain communities produced far more than their share. In other countries elements of the population that, for one reason or other, were declassé—the Chinese in Indonesia, for example—also produced more than their share. The social and ethnic structure of a population might well have something to do with the rate of growth of GNP. This rate of growth would also depend on how high a value the population placed on material well-being in comparison with other values. There were obviously large differences among countries in this respect, and the reasons for these differences lay deeply buried in the culture. Differences in personal need to achieve, whatever the values of the society, were also evident in different populations. And various political considerations, such as the extent of participation in local and national decision-making, clearly had a bearing. But despite the variety of these noneconomic inputs, they were all considered to be possible explanations of differences in observed rates of growth of GNP.

Of course it was recognized that gross national product per capita stood for a number of other things; it was a generalized measure of a certain way of life. Numerous studies made it clear that there were remarkable similarities in consumption patterns among countries with similar per capita incomes. As per capita income increased, one could rather confidently expect an increase in literacy, in the number of hospital beds per thousand of population, and in the general level of social services. The growth of per capita GNP was put forward simply as the best measure of a changing life style. And changes in the life style associated with increases in per capita GNP were commonly thought of as economic development, or simply development.

When one turns, however, from a consideration of inputs to a consideration of outputs, from a concern with the conditions of development to the meaning of development, a different set of questions is brought into focus. As we have noted, an increase in per capita GNP is generally accompanied by fairly predictable changes in the pattern of private and public consumption, as well as fairly predictable changes in productive activities: savings, the length of the workweek, the structure of employment, and so on. These changes may or may not have any particular welfare significance, and most economists have been content to leave it at that. A growth in per capita income, they note, can provide a *capacity* for making a material contribution to individual or social preferences, whether or not this is in fact the result.[25] But others have insisted that development depends not only on an increase in capacity but on how the increased capacity is used. And changes in the pattern of consumption and economic activities associated with increases in GNP make, at best, only a partial contribution. Other factors are involved, such as income distribution, public participation in decision-making, the spatial distribution of the population, ecological considerations, and so on. Furthermore, the pursuit of some of these values may well be at the expense

25. Something of this sort seems to have been in Keynes's mind when he offered a toast at the dinner of the Royal Economic Society in 1945. "I give you the toast of the Royal Economic Society, of economics and economists, who are the trustees not of civilization but of the possibility of civilization."

of a growth in per capita GNP. But how are these welfare-generating components to be combined, and who is going to measure the trade-offs among them? What is this deeper meaning of development as an output? Is it the output of a process to which there are many complex inputs? An increase in inputs, if effectively used, must by definition increase output, however it is measured. But an increase in one dimension of a multi-valued output may or may not be compatible with an increase in other dimensions.

As we have noted in this chapter, it is thought in some circles that the Bank has made a beginning "at broadening the concept of development beyond the simple limits of economic growth." It is not quite clear, however, whether in discussing the elements that need to be taken into account—family planning, literacy, unemployment, reasonable urban development, a wider sharing of the benefits of industrial development—what is involved is merely a broadening of the consideration of inputs needed for growth, or alternatively, a broadening of the meaning of development itself. And if the latter is meant, and if introducing considerations other than economic growth means a slowing down of growth, it is not clear whether this involves decisions for the Bank to make rather than the government of the borrowing country.

Hollis Chenery offers the following definition: "Economic development is the set of structural changes required to sustain the growth of output and to respond to the preferences of society."[26] It is not quite clear from the definition whether growth of output is one, but only one, indicator of social preference or whether it stands by itself as a condition necessary to the satisfaction of whatever social preferences the society may manifest.

There are other writers who seem to have acquired some degree of conviction concerning the objectives, other than growth, that need to be taken into account in assessing development. After criticizing growth of gross domestic product as a measure of development, the author of a recent contribution to the *International Development Review* suggests that *"national development is the continuous process whereby the people of a nation learn how to use effectively the available human and material resources so as to attain what they believe to be a better life."*[27] He then proceeds to develop this notion in a manner that suggests that he knows what the people want.

Development policies . . . would concentrate on people-oriented projects rather than on material structures (the edifice complex). Motivating larger food production and effective control of population growth would become much more important than contributions of material resources which the LDC may not be able to use effectively because of inadequate knowhow.

26. Hollis Chenery, "The Developing Economy" (unpublished manuscript).
27. William M. Blaisdell, "Defining 'National Development': A Proposal," *International Development Review*, Vol. 12 (June 1970), p. 40.

Reflection on these and other contributions to defining the meaning of development raises a number of questions.

If development means something more than self-sustaining growth of GNP, or GNP per capita, is there at least a rough consensus on what these other elements are and how their weight should be assessed in relation to economic growth? The answer to this question would seem to be "no." However vague the concept of economic aspects of development may be, it is infinitely clearer than the concepts of political and social aspects of development.

Whether or not there is such a consensus, is it appropriate for an external financing agency to substitute its own views on the nature of development for those of a borrowing country? Again the answer would seem to be "no." It is difficult enough for such an agency to persuade a borrower to take relevant inputs into account without entering into, or attempting to replace, the political process by means of which social preferences get defined.

If an essential element of development is an increasing ability by society to respond to social preferences, what is "the society," and how does its preference function get expressed? Who are "the people," and how do we know what they want? It seems worthwhile to pause for a moment on these questions since answers to them reflect very much both the limitations on the Bank's sphere of action and a particular kind of criticism frequently leveled at the Bank's operations.

The proximate source of the policies that define the scope of the public and private sectors, that affect the accumulation of savings and allocate investment in the public sector, and that initiate whatever set of controls limit or stimulate activities in the private sector is government—but government acting within a set of beliefs, values, institutions, and social groupings that are the product of evolutionary processes in the society. The beginning of an answer to the questions "who are the people?" and "how do social preferences get expressed?" may be discovered through speculation concerning the extent to which government can shape, or is inevitably shaped by, the society of which it is a part. In the relatively stable Western democracies of the nineteenth and twentieth centuries, there can be little doubt that governments were shaped by their societies and that social preferences, to the extent that they fell within the scope of government influence, were at least approximately expressed by government.[28] In these societies, changes in economic and social structures, in wants, and in values tend to be reflected, albeit be-

28. "The main feature of British history since the seventeenth century has been the remoulding of a State by a powerful Society." See George Unwin, *Studies in Economic History* (London: Macmillan, 1927), p. 28.

latedly, in government organization and public policies. If any external agency, say the World Bank, were trying through its lending policy to promote development (defined in terms of response to society's preferences) in these countries, it could presumably rely on established government policies as a roughly adequate guide to these preferences.

At the other extremes there are countries whose governments, using the tools of repression and terror, may be able to a considerable extent to reshape societies.[29] Of course, in Marxian theory, government is merely the icing on the cake, an element of superstructure that rests on a social structure whose framework is essentially the economic mode of production. Governments will fall with the societies that support them and rise in a different form with the new society generated in "the womb of the old." But the state as a "monopoly of violence," to use Lenin's phrase, may retard the disappearance of the old society and, under the guise of the dictatorship of the proletariat, serve to eliminate any impediments to the development of the new. Whatever the role of the state in Marxian theory, in practice, Communist governments have shown themselves to have substantial influence in reshaping the societies of which they are a part. Authoritarian governments of other types, including dictatorships of the right, have also managed to reshape in significant ways the societies they claim to represent. Of course, there are limitations to what they can do, but the contrast between the interaction of government and society in, say, the United Kingdom and that in the Soviet Union or Paraguay is clear enough for any observer.

The less developed countries that are members of the Bank tend to fall between the extremes. In some of the least developed of them, society scarcely exists except in tribal form. In others, divided by a social dualism between a modernized and a traditional sector, government may reflect the preference of one to the disadvantage of the other. There are no doubt member countries in which an elite governs with little concern for the welfare of the masses. And there are member countries approaching the type in which the acts of government appear to reflect relatively well the preferences of society. To draw from this welter of experiences a generalized concept of development that lays heavy stress on adequate response to social preference is a difficult task indeed. Perhaps after all it is better to think of *economic* development in terms of a capacity—of a sustained capacity—to provide material assistance toward the realization of whatever set of social preferences is expressed by governments.

29. Occasionally this may be done without much overt oppression. Witness Kemal Ataturk's Turkey, Bourguiba's Tunisia, or the operations of the Mexican Revolutionary Party and of Japanese governments during the Meiji period.

This, at least, is the most practical way for the Bank to think about development. Since it is an agency under the control of governments and is in any case forbidden by its Articles of Agreement to let its lending policy be influenced by political structures, it cannot look behind governments for some indication of social preferences not capable of expression by them. The Bank's project appraisals in some sectors attempt an estimate of the project's potential contribution to GNP, that is, a calculation by less than satisfactory means of a social rate of return. The Bank's technical assistance to planning bodies assumes that the objective of the exercise is to increase the rate of growth. And the Bank's attempts to use its leverage to influence domestic policies of borrowing countries make the same assumption. Insofar as income redistribution, effects on employment, urbanization, or other factors that may affect political stability are taken into account, they are, and should be, regarded as inputs related to an output of GNP rather than outputs representing an aspect of development not embraced within the meaning of GNP. This may be an inadequate concept of economic development, but it seems to be the only one appropriate to the Bank and perhaps the only generalized concept to which, for the time being, definite meaning can be attached.

PART THREE

The Bank in the Realm of International Diplomacy

CHAPTER FIFTEEN

The Bank Group and Bilateral Development Finance

IN PART I OF THIS STUDY we dealt with the origins of the Bank, its establishment, and its organizational evolution into the Bank Group of today. In Part II we analyzed the operations of the Bank Group as borrower, lender, and promoter of development. Here in Part III we turn from the Bank Group as such to its "foreign relations." Specifically, we focus in this chapter on the Bank Group as competitor and coordinator of bilateral development finance. The next two chapters deal with the Bank as part of a burgeoning family of multilateral agencies, economic and political, global and regional, with which a modus vivendi has had to be sought. Finally, the Bank's role as mediator in certain international disputes involving its member governments is analyzed.

The share of the Bank Group in the total flow of official development assistance has traditionally been small. Whether in terms of net commitments, of gross disbursements, or of net disbursements, it amounted to about 10 percent of the total flow from members of the Development Assistance Committee (DAC) of the Organisation for Economic Co-operation and Development (OECD) over the years 1965–68. Before 1965, it tended to be below 10 percent. Since 1968, the Bank Group's share in total commitments has turned sharply upward.[1]

During most of the life of the World Bank, the U.S. bilateral assistance program was overwhelmingly the largest and most far-flung—larger in dollar terms than the programs of all other countries combined. Ever since the Colombo Plan was initiated by the Commonwealth foreign ministers in 1950,

1. See Chapter 7, above.

491

however—and before that if one includes colonial development schemes—
other bilateral programs have also been in operation. The French program,
for example, though smaller in absolute size than that of the United States,
has been large enough to be very important in Africa and for many years
has been larger in relation to the gross national product of France than the
American program has been to the GNP of the United States.

Gradually, development assistance extended bilaterally has become a feature of the foreign policies of most of the high-income countries, many of the
middle-income countries, and some of the low-income countries. In most
Western industrialized nations, foreign aid has become institutionalized
through the establishment of a bureau or department or ministry in the central government to which policymaking and operational responsibilities have
been assigned. Much of the development assistance available from these institutions is tied to sources of supply in the donor nation. Each donor nation,
moreover, has other special legal and procedural requirements with which
aid-receivers have to comply.

Side by side with the proliferation of development agencies, there has been
a proliferation of national export-import banks, suppliers' credit facilities,
and other machinery useful in the development of the low-income world but
not designed with that as its primary objective. Most such institutions have
as their underlying objectives to build markets for the exports of domestic
suppliers in the industrialized country in which they are located and to provide credit terms at least as favorable as those provided by their major commercial rivals abroad.

In this competitive, rapidly changing international environment the World
Bank has had to carve out a suitable niche for itself. The job has required
more than a broad charter and professions of high esteem from member governments. An international agency has to meet a recognized need, preferably
in a way that is recognizably superior to that of relevant national agencies. It
has to have financial and intellectual muscles to flex. It must have political
sense about when to flex them and when to beat a strategic retreat.

This chapter deals with a number of overlapping challenges to the Bank
arising from the ebb and flow of bilateral finance. Treated first are the relationships of the Bank to programs of the U.S. government, with emphasis on
the recurrent tension with the Export-Import Bank in contrast to good relationships with the Economic Cooperation Administration (ECA) and its
successor agencies and with the shortlived Development Loan Fund (DLF).

Other bilateral programs, even those of major powers, have never dwarfed
the activities of the Bank. Conflicts with specific programs have been rare.
However, the general problem of the terms of aid—the relative plethora of

suppliers' credits and hard loans, coupled with the insufficiency and maldistribution of grants and soft loans—has long been a source of concern to the Bank. The debt burdens of the less developed countries and the problem of debt-rescheduling have been discussed in Chapter 7. In this chapter we call attention to problems associated with coordinating the flow of finance from multiple sources. Countries such as Canada, the Netherlands, and Sweden have been more than willing to lean on the Bank for help in deciding where to put their development aid and how to use it most effectively. Major powers —France, Germany, Great Britain, and Japan—though not unwilling, have been less tractable.

Nevertheless, as the number of providers and receivers of assistance grew in the 1950s, the need for greater coordination of aid efforts became increasingly apparent. Though very much a donors' club, the DAC, since its establishment in 1961, has evolved into an important permanent forum for the exchange of information on the policies and practices of its member nations. Simultaneously, the Bank has experimented with two major types of coordinating devices, one country-focused and the other project- or sector-focused.

The country-focused mechanism is the consortium or consultative group. As of June 30, 1971, the Bank was chairing fifteen or sixteen such groups and participating in several others. No two were alike. A large portion of this chapter is therefore devoted to analyzing the Bank's experience with these dissimilar structures for reviewing the requirements and performance of designated countries in Asia, Africa, and Latin America.

The project- or sector-focused effort goes by the name of "joint financing"; that is, at least one external source of finance other than the Bank Group is associated in funding a large investment project or sector development program. No great ingenuity is required if the complementary source of finance takes the form of grants or soft loans available for expenditure anywhere in the world. The problem, however, is not just to channel additional funds to high-priority undertakings but also to extract the economic benefits of untied aid from aid that is, in fact, tied. The latter requires winning acceptance of arrangements whereby funds available only for procurement within a restricted geographic area (or for a limited range of goods) will nevertheless be used to finance contracts won on the basis of international competitive bidding. Ideally the award procedure should take into consideration not only cash prices but credit terms, because the latter obviously affect the real cost of the equipment and services being purchased.

Given the reluctance of national governments to abandon machinery that is believed to serve their special commercial or foreign policy interests, bilateral agencies are not about to fade away. And the less developed countries would suffer if they did, since the opportunity to shop among different sources of finance serves as a protection against excessive dependence on any single source. The question is how far governments will be willing to accord a global multilateral agency such as the World Bank, which represents both rich and poor countries, a position of *primus inter pares,* assuring it of both substantial resources of its own and a major role in channeling other resources to points where they are most needed.

The Bank and U.S. Government Programs

Until about 1958, when the Bank took the initiative in convening what later became known as the India Consortium, its principal problems in relationships with bilateral assistance programs were with agencies of the U.S. government, especially the Export-Import Bank of the United States. That there should have been problems may seem odd in light of the prominent U.S. role in establishing the World Bank and providing its resources and leadership, and in light of the friendly personal relationships between Bank presidents and upper echelon officials of the U.S. government. A moment's reflection will make it plain, however, that periodic tension and conflict were almost inevitable.

By 1946 the Export-Import Bank, familiarly known as the Eximbank, had been in business for a dozen years. Agencies that are in business like to stay in business. This agency, moreover, had a good record, particularly during the Second World War and the difficult months preceding the first long-term development lending by the World Bank. The Export-Import Bank believed it had a unique role to play and that countries should be free to come to either the Eximbank or the World Bank for financing, using the latter only when other sources of finance proved unavailable on reasonable terms. It totally rejected the concept that the World Bank should be *the* banker rather than *a* banker for member countries.

The World Bank recognized that its resources were limited until its credit was fully established in capital markets, and the world's principal currencies became convertible. It willingly bowed out of any major role in financing European reconstruction after courageously making the half billion dollars in reconstruction loans described earlier in this study. (This withdrawal from the competition was undoubtedly a factor in the friendly relations between Marshall Plan officials and World Bank leaders.)

But the World Bank did have grounds for thinking of itself as the chosen instrument of the international community for long-term lending for development—as a standard-setter for an international financial morality whose norms would not be undermined by agencies of its own member governments; as an authoritative source of information on would-be borrowers' credit-worthiness; and as the means by which creditworthy borrowers would be able to purchase from the lowest-cost sources of supply.

In February 1946, the U.S. National Advisory Council on International Monetary and Financial Problems (NAC) prepared a statement on the foreign loan policy of the U.S. government, which the President of the United States fully endorsed and transmitted to the Congress. The objective of the United States, it said, was to assist in creating, through reconstruction and "sound economic development," an international economic environment free from warring economic blocs and from barriers obstructing the flow of international trade and capital.

The International Bank will be the principal agency to make foreign loans for reconstruction and development which private capital cannot furnish on reasonable terms. It provides a means by which the risks as well as the benefits from international lending will be shared by all of its members. It is expected that the International Bank will begin lending operations in the latter half of 1946 and that during the calendar year 1947 the International Bank will assume the primary responsibility for meeting the world's international capital requirements that cannot be met by private investors on their own account and risk.[2]

During the period January 1946–June 1947, meeting the most urgent foreign needs, the NAC thought, would require loan commitments of approximately $3.25 billion by the Eximbank, exclusive of a proposed credit of $3.75 billion to Great Britain. Between 1934 and 1939, the Eximbank had operated on a limited scale, its activities for the most part confined to short- and medium-term credits to finance the export of specific products or commodities. From 1939 to the end of the Second World War, the Eximbank had extended a number of direct long-term loans to Latin American countries and to countries on other continents. In 1945, in anticipation of the needs of war-torn nations for emergency assistance from the United States, the Eximbank (by legislation signed on the same day as the Bretton Woods Agreements Act) saw its lending authority raised to $3.5 billion. Between September 1945 and late 1946, the great bulk of the lending of the Export-Import Bank consisted of large long-term credits to the governments of France, Belgium, the Netherlands, Greece, Poland, Norway, Denmark, and Finland.

In Latin America, as of the end of 1947, the Eximbank had extended

2. *Report of the U.S. National Advisory Council on International Monetary and Financial Problems,* H. Doc. 497, 79 Cong. 2 sess. (1946), p. 17.

credit authorizations of about $1.1 billion. In April 1948, President Truman asked the Congress for an increase of $500 million in the lending authority of the Eximbank, saying in his message that "this increased lending authority would place the bank in a position to assist in meeting essential requirements for the financing of economic development in the other American Republics. It would permit the bank to make loans for well-planned development projects which are economically justified and to cooperate most effectively with private funds."

William McChesney Martin, Jr., then president of the Export-Import Bank, assured the Latin Americans that "the existing close cooperation between the Export-Import Bank and the International Bank will continue in order to ensure that the latter institution will have every opportunity to discharge its functions as the principal intergovernmental source of development credits."[3]

Tension between World Bank and Eximbank, 1948–52

It is true that periodic meetings between top officials of the World Bank and of the Eximbank to discuss mutual problems—meetings that continued with decreasing frequency through the early 1950s—had begun in January 1948. Any implication, however, that relations were entirely harmonious or that the management of the World Bank viewed with equanimity the proposed increase in the Eximbank's lending authority was for public relations purposes only. President John J. McCloy and U.S. Executive Director Black were strongly opposed to the increase.

In a long letter dated March 8, 1948, Eugene Black as executive director of the World Bank representing the United States, told John W. Snyder, U.S. secretary of the treasury and chairman of the NAC, of his "increasing concern that the potential contribution of the International Bank to the development of Latin America has been underestimated in many quarters, with the result that proposals are being advanced for further United States financial assistance to Latin America of a type which would cut directly across the bows of the Bank at a very critical stage in its history." Some of the development projects of Latin American members that the World Bank had for some time been considering were "about ready for financing."

3. Remarks before Committee 4 of the Ninth International Conference of American States, Bogotá, Colombia, April 16, 1948. The immediately preceding quote from President Truman's message is given in the opening paragraph of William McC. Martin's statement.

If, particularly just at this time, the United States should offer to make available to the Latin American countries financial assistance duplicating that available from the Bank, but on easier terms, it seems obvious that the Bank's prestige would be seriously undermined and its future efficacy greatly impaired.

The then uncommitted funds of the Eximbank—some $500 million—appeared to Black sufficient for situations in which the United States,

for political reasons or otherwise, should desire to make a long-term Latin American development loan which the International Bank is either unwilling or unable to make. However, I am convinced that the Eximbank should not, as a matter of policy, make such long-term development loans except under the most exceptional circumstances.

This continued to be the line of the World Bank. Although the Marshall Plan was launched in 1948, the increase in the Eximbank's lending authority was still pending in December of that year when, in a conversation with President Truman, John J. McCloy expressed some general thoughts on the lending policies of the U.S. government and how the IBRD fitted in with them. Truman invited him to prepare a memorandum on the subject. In January 1949, McCloy sent Secretary of the Treasury Snyder a lengthy draft that he had prepared as an expression of his own views. It was not a statement approved by the Bank's executive directors. McCloy suggested that it might be distributed to the members of the NAC and/or that Snyder might want to take up some of the points in it with President Truman.

The principal point was the by then familiar one that the World Bank should be regarded by the United States as the main public source of loans for long-term international investment.

The arguments usually advanced by those who advocate a resumption by the United States Government of the lending functions which are now the responsibility of the International Bank are that the Bank does not have sufficient resources to make the necessary loans, that the Bank's management has followed too "tough" a policy with respect to granting loans and as a result has accomplished little, and that the Bank's loan charges are too high. In my opinion none of these arguments is well-founded.

The Bank's interest charges on long-term loans were then 4.5 percent, as compared with charges of 3.5 percent on Eximbank loans and 2.5 percent on loans negotiated by the Economic Cooperation Administration (ECA).[4] The difference between the two banks was due largely to the 1 percent commission the World Bank was required to charge by its Articles of Agreement. No prospective borrower, said McCloy, would go to the Bank

---

4. Most ECA transactions were grants. See the section, below, on Relations with U.S. Agencies Other Than Eximbank for an account of the change in U.S. policy that was made after the end of the Marshall Plan.

for funds at 4.5 percent if it could secure them from the United States at 3.5 percent or less. Some countries that had begun negotiations with the World Bank had abandoned or delayed their negotiations when they had seen that there was a chance of getting the desired financing from the ECA or the Eximbank. McCloy considered it a fundamental mistake

to think that if the United States should make substantial additional funds available for long-term reconstruction and development loans, such loans would simply supplement International Bank investments. In fact, they would supplant International Bank loans and would in all probability force the International Bank largely to curtail, or perhaps even to suspend, its operations.

Both the World Bank and the Eximbank continued to operate. Each institution suspected the other of "stealing" its clients, concealing information on pending negotiations, and engaging in other forms of unfair competition. To some extent both were right, and borrowers were not above playing the two agencies off against each other.

The annex to Black's letter of March 8, 1948, to John Snyder mentions that a few weeks earlier the chairman of the board of the Mexican Light and Power Company, Ltd. had called to discuss his company's development plans, "in connection with which an application had been under consideration by the Export-Import Bank. Due to the proposed 20-year repayment involved [that is, to the fact that it was a long-term loan], it seemed that the application might more properly be dealt with by the International Bank and it was submitted to this Bank for study on 18 February."

Early in 1949, the World Bank and the Eximbank made a joint review and appraisal of Mexico's ability to assume and service external debt. Both institutions had recently made loans to Mexico, and both had received applications for new loans. In August 1950, the Eximbank with no prior notice to the World Bank (according to Bank sources), announced that it was opening a $150 million line of credit in favor of Mexico, for the financing of projects to be determined later. The management of the World Bank, with its then quite conservative standards of creditworthiness, did not recognize that the investment of an additional $150 million could increase Mexico's debt servicing capacity. It concluded that the existence of the line of credit from the Eximbank left almost no scope for IBRD lending.

Consequently, when in 1951 the Federal Electricity Commission of Mexico requested a loan to finance power projects, the Bank said that it could consider a loan only if Mexico were willing to forgo the use of an equivalent amount of the Eximbank credit. To the irritation of the Eximbank, the Mexican government agreed to this condition. The president of the World Bank, moreover, informed the Mexican authorities that the Bank welcomed opportunities to deal with Mexico but that, if Mexico wished to deal with two banks for development loans, the World Bank would not be one of them.

Eugene Black felt strongly that member governments should regard the World Bank as the only bank to which they would turn for advice on development programming and long-term loans for "sound" projects. He said this on a number of occasions in off-the-record conversations during the years 1949–55. Reminiscing in 1961, however, he said equally firmly that there had never been any competition between the World Bank and the Eximbank.

Our quarrel . . . was not with the Eximbank as a bank, but the fact that we felt they might be doing things that would jeopardize the credit of a country. Or we thought that they might be willing to lend money to a country that we'd turned down because it wasn't following the proper policies. That would be, so to speak, pulling the rug out from under us in trying to get the country to put their affairs in shape. [Readers of Chapter 6 of this study will recall the Bank's unwillingness to make loans to members in default on pre-World War II bonds at a time when the Eximbank was extending credits and receiving repayments without requiring borrowers to reach settlements with bondholders' committees.] But our real concern was that every time the Eximbank made a loan, it was adding to the debt of the country, and those loans were going to rank *pari passu* with ours. . . . Now it may have been that we felt in the early days that certain countries had a limited amount of credit, and if the country went and tried to get all the money they could from the World Bank and all the money they could from the Eximbank, they might get more than they ought to get.[5]

The position of Mexico, Brazil, Chile, and other governments was basically that they ought to get as much credit as they could and use whatever source would be best, from their point of view, in a given situation. They respected the growing expertise of the World Bank in certain fields, but on the whole considered it slow, nosy, costly, and inflexible. Gradually an unofficial division of labor emerged.

Over the three years 1948–50, although the volume of development loans made by the two institutions—$575 million by the Eximbank and $525 million by the World Bank—was about the same, the types of loans were not.

If only those loans clearly specified as to purpose are compared, IBRD loans of $245 million for power installations far exceeded the $15 million of Export-Import Bank power loans, as did the IBRD communication loans of $25 million compared to the $5 million of corresponding Export-Import Bank loans. The $140 million lent for manufacturing and mining by the Export-Import Bank, on the other hand, exceeded the $65 million of corresponding IBRD loans; and

5. Oral History Project of Columbia University, interviews recorded in the summer of 1961 on the International Bank for Reconstruction and Development (cited hereinafter as "Oral History"). Quotation is from interview of Eugene R. Black, p. 30.

the Export-Import Bank's loans of $150 million for agriculture and forestry and $175 million for transport also exceeded the corresponding $100 million and $90 million of IBRD loans.

If the miscellaneous Export-Import Bank development loans are assumed to have been utilized in roughly the same proportions as the other development loans, only about half of these loans represented investments in basic utilities such as power, transportation, communications, irrigation and flood control. Corresponding IBRD loans accounted for three-fourths of its development loans. . . .

The operations of the two Banks during the three years 1948–50 differ even more distinctly as to the countries to which these loans were made. . . . $235 million of the Export-Import Bank's development loans were lent to countries which are not IBRD members.[6]

As a general rule, Eximbank credits were available only to finance the purchase of materials and equipment produced or manufactured in the United States and of technical services of American firms and individuals. In 1951, the lending authority of the Eximbank was raised to $4.5 billion.[7]

Competition in Lending to Japan

In August 1952, Japan joined the World Bank and shortly thereafter received a World Bank mission, which made an appraisal of the prospects of the Japanese economy. It found them not very bright.[8] But, as was correctly reported in a subsequently published Japanese book, this mission had no direct relationship to Japan's first World Bank loan, the circumstances of which "produced a strange feeling upon the Japanese side."[9] Japan had been negotiating for months with the Eximbank, which was about to agree to two loans totaling roughly $40 million for financing (without governmental guarantee) generating equipment for two steam power plants owned by private Japanese companies. The equipment was to be supplied by the Westinghouse Electric Company and the General Electric Company.

Eugene Black felt strongly that the proposed loans were inappropriate for the Eximbank but were within the competence of the World Bank. He told some members of the board of the Eximbank that, if they made the loans, his own desire (which he believed would be shared by his board of directors) would be that no World Bank loans be made to Japan. The directors of the

6. Mervyn L. Weiner, "The Lending Policies of the Export-Import Bank," Paper E-228 (Aug. 7, 1952), a report prepared for use within the World Bank.

7. Public Law 158, 82 Cong., approved Oct. 3, 1951.

8. IBRD, "Japan: Economic Situation and Prospects" (June 18, 1953; processed).

9. Eiji Ozaka, *The World Bank* (Tokyo: Research Association of Japan on International Problems, 1969). We draw here on an unauthorized but professional translation of Chapter 6, "World Bank Loans to Japan," pp. 40–51.

Eximbank felt equally strongly that the $40 million power loans to Japan should be made by the Eximbank and—for political reasons—should be made quickly. Mr. Black reiterated his opposition to high officials at the U.S. Treasury and State Departments. Before long, he was informed that the Eximbank stood ready to cancel the loans on the assumption that they would be made quickly by the World Bank. He relayed this information to the Japanese ambassador in Washington, who was taken aback by the change of plan.

Black, however, was prepared to move rapidly. The Bank's commitment to international competitive bidding nevertheless raised a major problem. Both Westinghouse and General Electric had already done a lot of technical work in preparation for the orders, were certain to get the business if the financing were provided by the Eximbank, and were equally certain to register their sense of betrayal to the newly installed Republican administration in Washington if the World Bank permitted the equipment to be obtained elsewhere. Fortunately, the World Bank's commitment to international competitive bidding was not ironclad; it had recognized that it would not use this procedure in all circumstances.[10] The proposed Japanese loan, in Black's view, represented an "exceptional circumstance."

The Japanese government proved willing to guarantee the loan, which was then made by the World Bank to the Japan Development Bank for re-lending to the private power companies. Thus began, "with some commotion," the long and fruitful relationship whereby Japan became one of the largest borrowers from the World Bank and ultimately a substantial lender to that institution.

Harmony with the Eximbank, from whose jaws the electric power loans had been snatched, was not so easily achieved. If the project had not been speedily approved by the World Bank, and if the equipment had not been obtained from American suppliers, the Eximbank would have had reason to feel doubly aggrieved. Yet the willingness of the World Bank to abbreviate its investigation of creditworthiness, expedite its project appraisal, and dispense with competitive bidding enabled the Eximbank to grumble at length about the international agency's alleged sacrifice of principle to expediency.[11]

10. See R. A. Wheeler, Engineering Adviser to the Loan Director, "International Bidding," IBRD, *Sixth Annual Meeting of the Board of Governors, Summary Proceedings* (Nov. 30, 1951), p. 30.

11. Although the World Bank elbowed its way into the picture, it did not elbow out the Eximbank. Between October 1953 and July 1966, the World Bank made thirty-one loans, totaling $857 million, to Japan. Between March 1956 and November 1969, Eximbank loans to Japan, repayable in U.S. dollars, totaled $886 million.

Reduced Tension with Eximbank after 1953–54

The financing by the Eximbank of the Asunción water supply system in Paraguay in 1954 gave the World Bank a renewed opportunity to grumble about the U.S. agency. Paraguay had requested a loan for this purpose from the World Bank in 1953 and had been turned down. The Bank regarded the project as providing an amenity (uncontaminated water in sufficient quantity) rather than an increase in output. It felt that the waterworks project should be postponed until Paraguay could afford to finance it from domestic resources. In late 1953, the Paraguayan government, having been visited by U.S. Senator Homer E. Capehart and given assurances that the Eximbank would finance the project, shelved its plan for mobilizing the necessary domestic resources. The World Bank estimated that Paraguay could service only an additional $7 million in external debt—the amount of the Eximbank loan—and dropped from its agenda consideration of loans to Paraguay for various other purposes that the Bank regarded as more productive than the waterworks project.

We referred obliquely to the fact that in January 1953, Eisenhower succeeded Truman as President of the United States. The change of administrations had brought into office a new, economy-minded secretary of the treasury, before whom Black could press his claims for a further clarification of World Bank–Eximbank roles. In effect, Black could say, "If you wish to economize, why not clip the wings of your Eximbank, which overlaps what we, the World Bank, should be doing"? The secretary of the treasury was sympathetic.[12]

On April 30, 1953, President Eisenhower sent to Congress a plan for reorganizing the Eximbank, ostensibly for the purpose of simplifying its structure by providing for a managing director at its head instead of a board. Equally important was the administration's desire to reduce the Eximbank's autonomy and make it more subservient to the U.S. Treasury.[13]

This led to an outcry from U.S. manufacturers and exporters, especially

12. See Chapter 9, above, for our account of the Bank's first loan to Australia in 1953, after an Australian delegation that expected to deal with the Eximbank was shunted to the World Bank upon arrival in Washington.

13. The Export-Import Bank "under the reorganization effective June 30 was left with bookkeeping rather than policy functions and was put in charge of a managing director, in effect a $17,500 per year errand-boy as far as policy was concerned. Immediately the Latin Americans were told that hereafter they were to look to the World Bank for development financing." Simon G. Hanson, "The End of the Good-Neighbor Policy," *Inter-American Economic Affairs*, Vol. 7 (Autumn 1953), pp. 21–22.

as they began to feel the pinch of a "rolling readjustment" in the American economy. Statements began to be issued by American industrialists favoring the Export-Import Bank over the World Bank because the Eximbank's loans were tied to U.S. exports. In response to these expressions of opinion, Senator Capehart, chairman of the Senate Committee on Banking and Currency, launched an inquiry into the activities of the two banks, particularly in Latin America.

Described as "one of the highest-powered, highest-pressure salesmen this country has ever produced," Capehart, accompanied by a sizable entourage, visited a number of Latin American countries.[14] He also conducted extensive public hearings in Washington.[15] In due course a law was passed, with widespread support in both houses of Congress, that reversed the 1953 change in the status of the Export-Import Bank and reestablished it even more firmly as an independent agency of the U.S. government.[16] Although the Eximbank at the time had more than $1 billion in unused lending authority, the Congress, to emphasize its desire for a stepped-up level of Eximbank activity, increased its lending authority by $500 million—in other words, to $5 billion. As Senator Homer E. Capehart said on the floor of the Senate in mid-1954,

The intent of the bill is that the Export-Import Bank shall adopt a more aggressive policy, become more active, and make more loans of all types than it has been making during the past 12 months. It is not desired that the bank make any bad loans, but it is the intention of the bill that the bank shall become a more aggressive and active banking institution. We are particularly interested in helping American exporters, and lending money on long-time terms to so-called backward countries.[17]

There is no need to trace in comparable detail the post-1954 relationships of the World Bank and the Eximbank. With all prospect that either institution would win a total victory over the other eliminated, each has developed more than enough business to keep itself usefully occupied. Though conflict has not been eliminated, relationships during the 1960s can be classified as good.[18]

14. *Fortune* (February 1941), pp. 63–64.
15. See *Study of Export-Import Bank and World Bank,* Hearings before the Senate Committee on Banking and Currency, 83 Cong. 2 sess., on S. Res. 25; and *Study of Latin American Countries,* Interim Report of the Senate Committee on Banking and Currency, 83 Cong. 2 sess., S. Rept. 1082 (March 1954).
16. Public Law 570, 83 Cong. 2 sess. (1954); 68 Stat. 677.
17. July 6, 1954. The Eximbank's lending authority was subsequently raised to $7 billion, then to $9 billion, $13.5 billion, and as of this writing, $20 billion.
18. For reference to a 1970 flare-up, see the discussion below on joint and parallel financing.

In retrospect, it is evident that the ability of the less developed countries to put capital to productive use was underestimated, and their capacity to service foreign debt was less limited than the management of the World Bank thought in the late 1940s and early 1950s. Moreover, the concept that McCloy and Black brought with them from their experience as private investment bankers, or with investment bankers—that a client should have but one banker and that banker's advice should be followed—was with rare exceptions unsalable. The clients of the World Bank were sovereign governments resistant to the idea that they should become the wards of any single guardian. Nor was the U.S. government prepared to support the concept. By and large the Eximbank was able to maintain its position that clients should be free to patronize either the Eximbank or the World Bank, without the latter being in a position to veto a proposed loan on the ground that the country was borrowing too much or not getting proper credit terms or on the ground that the loan should be made by the global institution rather than the U.S. government institution.

Relations with U.S. Agencies Other Than Eximbank

During the Marshall Plan period (1948–52), more than 80 percent of American bilateral aid was in the form of grants. As the initial administering agency, the Economic Cooperation Administration, was superseded by the Mutual Security Agency, the Foreign Operations Administration, the International Cooperation Administration, and the Agency for International Development, a growing proportion of U.S. aid was provided on a loan basis. From 1958 to 1961, the United States operated an independent government corporation—the Development Loan Fund (DLF)—established over the opposition of the Export-Import Bank to provide investment capital on flexible terms to less developed countries. With this U.S. institution, the World Bank was able to cooperate closely. That the relationship with the DLF was more harmonious than that with the Eximbank was due not only to the difference in personalities—Robert L. Garner of the IBRD and Herbert Gaston of the Eximbank, who did much of the negotiating, were testier men than their successors—but also to differences in scope.

A joint operation between the World Bank and the Eximbank, for example, would almost inevitably have meant that the Eximbank would finance the equipment to be purchased in the United States while the World Bank financed non-dollar procurement for the project. This seemingly logical division of labor, however, would have reduced the share of World Bank funds spent in the U.S. market, would have alienated U.S. industry by making it feel that it was failing to get business from the World Bank commensurate with the American contribution to the capital resources of the Bank, and thus would have complicated the subsequent marketing of Bank bonds in the United States. Joint operations with the DLF, however, did not need to follow this course because the DLF pursued more liberal policies than the Eximbank with respect to both the terms of its loans and the types of expenditures it financed. Specifically, it frequently financed local currency expenditures, thereby permitting what J. Burke Knapp of the World Bank has called "a natural marriage of convenience," in which the World Bank financed the foreign exchange expenditures of a project in, say, Latin America and the DLF financed a portion of the local currency expenditures.[19]

Collaboration of this type was not infrequent, and in such cases the DLF usually delegated to the World Bank authority to represent its interests in the administration of the loans—in supervising the launching of the project, in receiving progress reports after the project came into being, and so on. The liberal procurement policies of the DLF, however, rapidly became less so as concern about the deteriorating U.S. balance of payments mounted. The DLF was abolished as a separate agency in 1961, and under the new Agency for International Development (AID) the trend with respect to both loans and grants under the U.S. bilateral program during the 1960s was toward tying expenditures to American sources of supply. Business groups that were dependent on Eximbank financing continued to be critical of the World Bank's procurement practices. Moreover, the Bank's habit of skimming off "good projects," and financing primarily their foreign exchange costs, all too frequently put the large U.S. aid program in the unglamorous role of residual supplier of assistance, thereby exacerbating the public relations problems of the AID. Nevertheless, the prestige of the World Bank remained high in the United States, and the U.S. government during the 1960s became a major supporter of aid coordination under the auspices of the World Bank.[20]

The Bank and Other Bilateral Programs

Where bilateral programs are modest in absolute size, the political expectations tied to them tend to be correspondingly modest. With little hope of independently achieving a major political impact through their develop-

19. J. Burke Knapp, "Oral History," p. 48.
20. See the section on Consortia and Consultative Groups, below.

ment assistance programs and with little justification for building up sizable administrative structures, Canada, the Netherlands, the Scandinavian countries, and other middle powers can turn cheerfully to the World Bank Group for guidance. The major powers—France, Germany, Great Britain, Japan— like the United States, are more ambivalent. In specific export sectors and in specific regions of the world, they may have independent national objectives that make them less than eager to be coordinated or constrained. At the same time, they may seek a low political profile and recognize that one way to achieve it is to operate within a multilateral framework.

The Colombo Plan was one of the earliest such frameworks. According to the communiqué issued with the first report, which included the development programs prepared by the Commonwealth countries of south and southeast Asia, the Colombo Plan was a cooperative venture "to enable members to help one another through bilateral arrangements for assistance, both capital and technical."[21] Much of its work consisted of publicizing the capital and technical assistance needs of the area. It was not a Marshall Plan for Asia. It established no machinery comparable to the Organisation for European Economic Co-operation in Paris, and it could look to no major source of finance, such as the ECA in Washington. We mention it primarily for two reasons: (a) the World Bank was involved as a friend-at-court by both sides almost from the beginning, and (b) it gave rise to a by-now-almost-forgotten forerunner of what, in the era of consortia and consultative groups, are termed aid-coordinating groups at the country level.

At the first Colombo Plan meeting, the Indian delegation suggested to the governments of Canada, Australia, and New Zealand that they consult the Bank with regard to projects on which to spend their Colombo Plan contributions. The Indian delegation added that the Bank had received information on India that was confidential, but that its government had no objection to the Bank's passing on any necessary information to contributing countries. The contributing countries welcomed the suggestion, pointing out that they did not know in detail the development and financial problems of India, Pakistan, and the other countries of the region.

The Canadian government, in particular, followed up through its executive director the invitation to consult with the Bank and coordinate its bilateral assistance with Bank lending in the area. The Bank, as it had made clear to both contributing and recipient countries, was eager to be consulted. Still adhering to a rather narrow definition of the activities for which it could

21. For a contemporary account see, for example, Antonin Basch, "The Colombo Plan: A Case of Regional Economic Cooperation," *International Organization,* Vol. 9 (February 1955), pp. 1–18.

make loans and not yet fully convinced that grant aid to poor countries could improve their creditworthiness for loans, it was somewhat fearful that, under the Colombo Plan, grants might be given for projects that were eligible for loans.[22]

Pakistan's minister of economic affairs, commerce, and education, Fazlur Rahman, told World Bank President Eugene Black that he was concerned about the possibility of discussions between the Bank and the donors on investment projects in Pakistan, without Pakistan's knowledge. Mr. Black informed him that if a donor consulted the Bank on Pakistan, it would be only fair for the government of Pakistan to be fully informed of the questions raised and the Bank's viewpoint on them, so that Pakistan could express its own views. Conversely, Pakistan should keep the Bank informed of the progress of its discussions with donor countries, so that the Bank would have full knowledge of the projects Pakistan hoped to have financed by grants. "It was agreed that only such a triangular relationship would allow the Bank to play its role as banker of Pakistan, while leaving full freedom of decision to the three parties involved."[23]

The Bank was accepted by all concerned as a participant in the Colombo Plan. In 1953 Eugene Black made another suggestion to Pakistan, which was acted upon—that Chaudhri Mohammad Ali, the then minister of finance and economic affairs, set up a committee in Karachi, comprised of representatives of countries giving development aid to Pakistan and representatives of the World Bank, to ensure proper coordination in the utilization of loans and grant aid received from various sources. At a meeting in Karachi in October 1953, attended also by the resident representative of the United Nations, it was agreed that the proposed coordinating committee would be set up. We call attention to the action, not because of its intrinsic importance —it soon lapsed—but as an early example of coordinating mechanisms that were to become more widespread in the 1960s.

The proliferation of bilateral sources of finance during the late 1950s, although it rarely resulted in conflicts with specific agencies of the capital-exporting countries, did give rise to some general problems of concern to the Bank. These included the indiscriminate extension of suppliers' credits, the growing debt burden of the less developed countries, and the odd distribution of official development assistance in relation to need, economic per-

22. Staff Loan Committee records for January–February 1952.
23. Memorandum of conversation, February 4, 1952, in Bank files. The term "banker of Pakistan" is noteworthy in light of the discussion earlier in this chapter of relations between the World Bank and the Export-Import Bank of the United States.

formance, or other "rational" criteria. All three of these problems are discussed elsewhere in this study and will receive only passing mention here.

Suppliers' credits required that equipment be bought from the country that gave the credit. Moreover, said Eugene Black,

the terms, particularly the length of them, were not proper. Often they [the suppliers] might make a loan of three or four years just to build a hydroelectric power plant. . . . By the time the plant was built, the loan would come due, and the borrower had had no chance to establish any earnings to pay the loan off. I pointed out the danger of that. As a matter of fact, we set up a system where we kept a record of all those debts, and we supplied this record to the capital-exporting countries, just to show them what was happening, because if they didn't watch out, they [were] going to build up a top-heavy short-term indebtedness, which . . . would create a very serious problem, which has happened in a good many countries.[24]

Argentina, Brazil, and Turkey are examples of countries in which it happened. Excessive short-term debt was, of course, only an acute manifestation of the more general tendency of the capital-hungry poor countries to take on, over time, a larger external debt than they could safely carry. The published work of Bank officials during the late 1950s and thereafter made it clear that the foreign debt of the low-income countries had begun to climb at an alarming rate.[25] The Bank became the principal source of debt statistics for the international community, and ultimately, as we reported in Chapter 7, it became involved in debt-rescheduling exercises for certain countries.

Though its members have been willing to have the Bank play an important role in debt-rescheduling, they have not responded enthusiastically to the Pearson Commission recommendation that the Bank's soft-loan affiliate, the International Development Association (IDA), allocate its resources in such a way as to offset the most serious imbalances created by the allocation of bilateral aid. Because bilateral development assistance has been used as an instrument of foreign policy, its distribution to date has been determined more by political, historic, and commercial considerations than by economic and technical findings concerning the need, or stage of development, or absorptive capacity, or creditworthiness of potential recipients. For reasons brought out in Chapter 12, the Pearson Commission's recommendation for

24. "Oral History," p. 32.

25. See Dragoslav Avramović, assisted by Ravi Gulhati, *Debt Servicing Capacity and Postwar Growth in International Indebtedness* (Johns Hopkins Press, 1958); Avramović and Gulhati, *Debt Servicing Problems of Low-Income Countries, 1956–1958* (Johns Hopkins Press, 1960); Dragoslav Avramović and associates, *Economic Growth and External Debt* (Johns Hopkins Press, 1964); World Bank/IDA, *Annual Report, 1971*, pp. 50–56.

rationalizing through IDA the present "irrational" distribution of aid is likely to be carried out gingerly if at all.

The nation that has been most willing to turn to the Bank for guidance in distributing its bilateral aid is Sweden. Virtually all Swedish capital assistance is given through, or in parallel financing with, multilateral agencies. Its seven unrestricted special contributions to IDA have been merged with, and placed under the control of, the Bank Group to the same extent as "regular" subscriptions and contributions to IDA. Denmark, a member, and New Zealand, which is not a member, have also made special contributions to IDA in the form of grants. Switzerland, another nonmember, has made its contribution in the form of fifty-year interest-free loans.[26]

Many projects have been financed jointly by IDA and Sweden since early 1966, when Sweden's initiative in utilizing the Bank Group's appraisal services and in promoting joint financing resulted in an untied twenty-year loan from Sweden to Pakistan, at 2 percent interest, to supplement an IDA credit to that country. In most later instances, Swedish assistance has been available on the same terms as IDA assistance. Increasingly, however, Sweden has been developing views of its own on where its aid should go and for what purposes.

The willingness of Canada to turn to the Bank for guidance in distributing its bilateral aid has already been noted. A later entrant into the development assistance field, the Netherlands, hesitated for some years to embark on a bilateral program.

Being a small country, the Netherlands had not sufficient financial means at its disposal to give extensive bilateral assistance to underdeveloped countries. So only a very limited number of such countries could be considered for such assistance, and that might affect our relations with other countries adversely, since our country is far less trammelled than for instance the United Kingdom is, with its Commonwealth or France with its "Community." There is therefore a danger that if the Netherlands should arbitrarily decide to give bilateral assistance to a few countries, we should be subjected to political and economic pressure to induce us to give assistance beyond our financial capacity.[27]

The World Bank's ability to organize consortia and consultative groups "has greatly aided the Netherlands Government in finding a solution for the problem of how properly to allocate our limited resources for bilateral aid. We have chosen to lean heavily upon the policies of the Bank with respect to both the selection of beneficiaries and the distribution of our aid among them,

26. See Chapter 12, above.
27. "Netherlands Policy for Aid to Developing Countries," memorandum from the minister of foreign affairs to the chairman of the second chamber, August 4, 1962, p. 4 (of English copy at Netherlands Embassy, Washington, D.C.).

restricting ourselves to those countries for which the Bank has organized consortia or consultative groups and is sharing financing."[28]

The Netherlands, in addition, is the first and only member government to have made a loan to the International Finance Corporation—$5 million in 1971. Because the funds available to the IFC for equity investments are more limited than those for lending, the Dutch agreed to make their loan on terms that permit it to be used by the IFC for equity investments.

Consortia and Consultative Groups

Consortia and consultative groups provide a forum for the coordination of development assistance programs and policies with respect to the country on whose behalf the group is organized. Coordination, to the extent that it is achieved, results from the exchange of information and views, not from the right of any participant to direct the actions of other participants.

The groups are country-focused, but not country-anchored. They generally meet in Paris or Washington, rather than in the capital of the "recipient" country, though they are occasionally supplemented by coordinating groups at the country level, which do meet in the capital cities. Both consortia and consultative groups began as "donors' clubs," since the recipient countries were not full-fledged members. But the participation of receiving countries has increased with the passage of time, and recently the formal distinction between "member" and "recipient" has been quietly dropped. All are now "participants." In terms of actual aid agreements, the recipient negotiates with each donor or lender bilaterally and not with the consortium or consultative group as a whole.

In the early days of their history (1958 to about 1963), the principal membership of these aid groups typically included the Bank, Canada, France, Germany, Italy, Japan, the United Kingdom, and the United States. The

28. Statement by S. Posthuma, managing director, De Nederlandsche Bank N.V. and alternate governor of the World Bank for the Netherlands, at 1963 meeting of the board of governors. IBRD, Press release (Oct. 2, 1963). See also *Development Assistance Efforts and Policies of the Netherlands* (The Hague: Ministry of Foreign Affairs, 1968), p. 28 of English version. The more recent statement makes it clear that capital assistance from the Netherlands is not limited exclusively to countries for which the World Bank has organized consortia or consultative groups. Countries for which the same function has been performed by the OECD or the Inter-American Development Bank are also eligible. So are Indonesia (for which there is an aid-coordinating group, chaired by the Netherlands) and overseas parts of the Kingdom of the Netherlands. The Dutch policy, it is said, has helped the Netherlands avoid setting up "costly aid administration machinery."

International Monetary Fund generally sent an observer. Membership expanded during the 1960s as the smaller European countries (the Scandinavian countries, the Netherlands, Belgium, Austria, Switzerland, Finland, and Spain), and occasionally others (for example, Australia, India, Kuwait, and Taiwan), joined some of the clubs. Like the IMF, the United Nations Development Program is at present a participant in all Bank-sponsored coordinating groups. The membership in June 1971 of both Bank-sponsored and other aid-coordination groups in which the Bank was a participant is shown in Table 15-1.

The distinction between a consortium and a consultative group was at first considerably sharper than it has been since the mid-1960s. The original distinction was that a consortium devoted much of its attention to securing "pledges" of sufficient amounts of aid to meet targets specified in the recipient's development plan. (India and Pakistan are the only two countries for which the Bank has organized consortia.) The consultative groups were developed in the wake of negative reactions on the part of the donors (including the Bank) to the pledging sessions of consortia. The most important feature of the first consultative groups, as defined, was that they were *not* to be concerned with fund raising.

While the distinction has faded, it cannot yet be said that there is no difference between consortia and consultative groups. Although the consortia no longer convene pledging sessions to fill foreign exchange gaps, the principal donors usually come prepared to state in fairly specific terms their intentions or commitments with respect to aid for the ensuing year. At the very least, countries not prepared to speak up at the meeting are expected to advise the recipient and the Bank as soon as a decision has been made. This may or may not happen in connection with consultative group meetings. Typically, at the latter, the Bank and three or four countries outline in rather general terms their assistance plans while the remaining participants make noncommittal statements of good intentions.

The Bank's resident missions in India and Pakistan have been involved in consortium activities; resident missions of comparable strength have not been functioning in most of the areas served by consultative groups. The Bank at the request of the Indian government put a rescheduling of India's foreign debt on the agenda of the India Consortium. The consortium for Pakistan had been sympathetic to a similar effort, but the civil strife in that country in 1971 ruptured the operations of the consortium.

In summary, the two Bank-chaired consortia appear to have more to them than do most of the consultative groups. This is due mainly to the extent and nature of donor involvement in India and Pakistan—but partly to the fact

Table 15-1. Bank-Sponsored and Other Aid Coordination Groups in Which the Bank Participates, 1971

Group	Australia	Austria	Belgium	Canada	China	Denmark	Finland	France	Germany	India	Israel	Italy	Japan	Kuwait	Luxembourg	Netherlands	New Zealand	Norway	Spain	Sweden	Switzerland	United Kingdom	United States	Yugoslavia	AfDB[a]	AsDB[a]	CIAP[a]	DAC/OECD[a]	EIB[a]	EEC[a]	IMF[a]	UNDP[a]	IDB[a]
Bank-sponsored consortia																																	
India	X	X	X	X				X	X			X	X			X				X	X	X	X			P		O			P	P	P
Pakistan	X	X	X	X				X	X			X	X			X				X	O	X	X			P		O			P	P	P
Bank-sponsored Consultative groups																																	
Colombia			X	X		X		X	X			X	X			X			X		O	X	X				P	O			P	P	P
Congo (K)			X	X				X	X			X	X			O					O	O	X		P			O	P	P	P	P	
East Africa			X	X			X	X	X			X				X		X		X	X	X	X	X	P			O			P	P	
Ethiopia				O			X	X	X		O	X				O				X	O	X	X		P			O			P	P	
Ghana		O	X	X		X		X	X			X	X			O				X	O	X	X		P			O			P	P	
Korea		O	X	X	X	X		X	X			X	X			O					O	X	X			P		O			P	P	
Malaysia	X	X	X	X		X		X	X			X	X			O	X				X	X	X			P		O			P	P	
Morocco			X	X				X	X			X	X	X		X		O	O		X	X	X		P			O		P	P	P	
Nigeria			X	X				X	X			X	X			O	O			X	O	X	X		P			O			P	P	
Philippines		X	O	O				X	O			X	X			O	O	O	X		O	O	X			P		O			P	P	
Thailand	X		X	X				X	X	O		X	X			O		X		X	X	X	X			P		O			P	P	
Tunisia			X	X				X	X			X	X			X				X	O	X	X		P			O	P	P	P	P	
Other Bank-sponsored groups																																	
Ceylon	X		X	X		O		X	X	O		O	X			X				O	O	X	X			P		O			P	P	
Other groups in which Bank participates																																	
Indonesia[b]		O	X	X		O		X	X	O		X	X			X	O	O		X	O	X	X			P		O			P	P	
Turkey[c]	X	O	X	X		O		X	X	O		X	X		X	X		X	X	X	X	X	X					O	P	P	P	P	

Source: IBRD, Policies and Operations: The World Bank, IDA, and IFC (June 1971), p. 43. Groups in which the Bank did not consider itself to be active as of June 1971 are not listed.

Note: X = member; O = observer; P = participating international agency.

a. See glossary, pp. xx–xxiii, above.
b. Intergovernmental group for Indonesia, sponsored by the Netherlands.
c. OECD-sponsored consortium.

THE BANK GROUP AND BILATERAL FINANCE 513

that the consortia have been in existence longer, that one of their original purposes was fund raising, that "finance-ready" (or almost ready) projects have more frequently been available in both India and Pakistan, and that IDA funds have been heavily concentrated in these two countries. Nonetheless, consortia–consultative group distinctions have been blurred considerably, so that the consultative group for Colombia, which also has finance-ready projects put before it, and the Intergovernmental Group for Indonesia may well have as much substance as the two consortia.

While, in principle, all parties concerned are committed to the economic development of the recipient country, the various participants approach consortia and consultative groups from different standpoints. The recipient is hoping for the largest possible amount of aid with the fewest possible strings attached. The bilateral donors stress constraints on the amounts they can supply and the need for good development performance on the part of the aid-receiver. Some of them really do not have much in the way of a foreign aid program and are interested primarily in commercial opportunities for contractors and exporters in their own country. Former colonial powers may be looking for others to help pick up the tab in cases where the recipient is an ex-colony. Similarly, the United States may promote the "burden-sharing" idea in countries where it has been the major or almost sole contributor. In addition, the United States has been suspected of trying to use the consortia and consultative groups to persuade the Bank and other donors to set criteria and performance standards that the United States wants to have generalized but would hesitate to employ on its own.

The Bank as organizer and chairman of these groups serves as a middle man, and the middle man's lot is not necessarily a happy one. As friend in court to the recipient, the Bank finds itself constantly seeking more aid and better terms from other donors. As a donor and development counselor, the Bank takes a keen interest in the recipients' performance and frequently becomes a pacesetter in terms of performance standards to be observed by the aid receiver. As was brought out in our earlier discussion of leverage and performance, the Bank as chairman of an aid-coordinating group may find its power and influence enhanced by virtue of the fact that it is acting on behalf of others and not just on its own. The reverse is also true. It may become a lightning rod for resentment on the part of the recipient because of the pressure it has helped mobilize, particularly if policy changes are made by the recipient but the quid pro quo in aid fails to materialize. Whether the Bank's own leverage is increased depends heavily on whether the donors see eye to eye on the uses to which aid should be put and on the receptivity of key elements in the recipient government to the recommendations that emerge from the group. If a powerful donor differs with the Bank on major issues, the Bank's position in the group may be seriously undermined.

Each consortium and consultative group has had a unique history; generalizations are possible only with the greatest circumspection.

The India Consortium

The first consortium, the one for India, was not organized initially for the purpose of mobilizing and coordinating external financing for India's five-year development plans. Rather, it was originally conceived as a temporary rescue operation that came into being in 1958, after it had become apparent that India's rapidly shrinking holdings of foreign exchange would be wholly insufficient to finance the second five-year plan, which was then under way.[29] Until 1961, the meetings were officially referred to as "meetings on India's foreign exchange situation." B. K. Nehru, who was appointed India's commissioner-general for economic affairs in Washington to lead the operations from the Indian side, describes the task as India saw it.

It was decided that this immediate rescue operation should not be handled through diplomatic channels in order to avoid any political flavour being brought into it but should be regarded as a simple banking operation. The World Bank was our international banker. We were to go to it and place our difficulties before it, tell it that we wanted a large loan and ask it to raise the finance for us from whatever sources it thought proper in a manner similar to what a commercial concern would do *vis-a-vis* its own bankers, if it got into financial difficulties. . . .

It was . . . demanded by me and agreed to by him [Mr. Black] that we would not directly ask any government to help us and we would not even be present at any meetings the World Bank might arrange of governments who it thought would be willing to finance us. Mr. Black demanded and I agreed that we would explain to governments what our difficulties were, but that would be the limit of our activity.

The first meeting of what subsequently became the Aid-India Consortium was held in Washington in August 1958 and agreed to give us to the last cent the money we said we would need which was over a billion dollars. There were no political conditions attached nor any economic ones beyond our undertaking to complete the (reduced) Plan as presented to the World Bank.[30]

While the meetings for the next year or two tended to have an ad hoc

29. India's first five-year plan covered the years 1951–56 and the second the years 1956–61. For more on these and later plans, see the section on India in Chapter 19, below.

30. B. K. Nehru, "The Way We Looked for Money Abroad," in Vadilal Dagli (ed.), *Two Decades of Indo-U.S. Relations* (Bombay: Vora and Company, 1969), pp. 20–21.

character, with no formal indications to bilateral donors that a permanent multilateral aid group was coming into being, the Indian government was drawing up its third five-year plan on the assumption that extensive foreign aid would be made available, and India and the Bank were seeking to pave the way for the formation of a group under Bank auspices that would provide the necessary external financing. B. K. Nehru's office devoted a great deal of effort to drumming up support for the concept of a positive long-term commitment to India's third five-year plan.

In early 1960, Eugene Black suggested the "mission of the three wise men" —a six-week trip by three well known bankers (Hermann J. Abs of Germany, Sir Oliver Franks of the United Kingdom, and Allan Sproul of the United States) to study at first hand economic conditions in India and Pakistan.

In making this suggestion, which was prompted by the terms of a resolution introduced into the United States Senate by Senators John F. Kennedy and John Sherman Cooper, and passed unanimously by that body, I was guided by the conviction that visits by prominent members of the business and financial communities of the industrially developed countries would help to achieve a wider understanding of the problems confronting the less developed areas of the world.[31]

The result was that in September 1960, the "meeting on India's foreign-exchange situation," held in Paris for the first time, was devoted to India's third five-year plan. The word "consortium" began to be used in connection with the meetings. A pattern took shape of holding two meetings a year, the first to discuss the Indian economic situation and the second to raise money for its development plan. These latter meetings were known as "pledging sessions."

The pledging sessions were serious affairs, during which it was sought to produce the full amount that the development plan specified for that year. On more than one occasion in the early 1960s, the meeting was adjourned temporarily because the donors had not come up with sufficient pledges to meet requirements; delegates were sent back to try to coax more money from their governments. Before the temporary adjournment, the United States tried on occasion to induce other governments to increase their contributions by holding out a carrot: the United States would increase its pledge if other consortium members (including the Bank/IDA) would match the increase. This bargaining tactic, though not unsuccessful, was eventually dropped as

---

31. From Black's foreword to *Bankers' Mission to India and Pakistan, February–March 1960* (IBRD, 1960). The Mission's report took the form of a joint letter from the three bankers to the president of the World Bank. It was printed by the IBRD under the foregoing title and was well publicized. This mission was followed by a Bank staff mission to appraise in more detail India's third five-year plan.

the compulsory character of the pledging sessions faded away by the mid-1960s.[32]

There had always been quite a bit of dissatisfaction on the part of most donors (including the Bank) with certain of India's economic policies and overall development strategies. As the early 1960s slipped by and the Indian economy was not performing up to expectations, the exasperation of the donors continued—but so did the pledges. In September 1965, war broke out between India and Pakistan. The United States stopped aid to both countries, and the India Consortium did not meet for eighteen months. After the cessation of hostilities, when the future of the consortia for both countries was in doubt, a news item appeared in the *Times of India* that indirectly indicated the ways in which the Bank's position in a consortium could be constrained or severely put to the test:

> The new Finance Minister is unlikely to adopt Mr. T. T. Krishnamachari's proposal for disbanding the Aid-India Club and to negotiate foreign assistance bilaterally. . . .
>
> Mr. Krishnamachari's main reason for opposing the machinery of the club was that the sponsors—the World Bank—were peculiarly susceptible to pressures by the U.S. Not only did the views of the American administration influence thinking in the bank . . . but Wall Street, which provided a great deal of the bank's loan funds, too was a factor. . . .
>
> Whatever pressures the U.S. may have exercised on the World Bank in recent months, the latter did not falter in its commitments to this country. . . .
>
> In fact, the bank appears to be responding . . . to our supplementary request for an IDA loan of $60 million for the purchase of fertilizer. In the past, it has regularly turned down such applications. . . .
>
> The U.S. has certainly pressured Japan and West Germany in the matter of pledged aid, but even these countries have unfrozen their assistance.[33]

As a price for new pledges from the consortium (including the Bank/IDA), India in 1966 agreed to several basic changes in economic policy, most notably a liberalization of imports.[34] Since 1966, discussion of India's performance with respect to these policy changes in particular and overall performance in general has constituted an important aspect of consortium meetings. The Indian delegation clearly is not delighted to receive the advice heaped upon it and has been known to give advice itself on occasion. For example, at the 1970 meetings, the chief Indian delegate pointed out that it

32. Another example of the compulsory nature of the early fund-raising efforts was the $30 million "entrance fee" paid in the form of aid by France in 1961 as a condition of consortium membership.

33. *Times of India* (New Delhi), January 8, 1966. T. T. Krishnamachari was the former minister of finance.

34. See Chapter 13, above.

was very difficult to continue with the import liberalization program, so heartily "recommended" by the consortium and by the Bank in particular, if the Bank/IDA was not willing to make available the program loans necessary to cover the import program.

Despite strains, the consortium has continued to function. Negotiations for rescheduling India's external debts, first undertaken within the consortium framework in 1968, appeared at the beginning of the second development decade as one of the principal problems facing the group. In what appears to be an effort to reach out in new directions, another area to which the consortium has recently turned its attention is family planning. The consortium has also engaged in extensive discussion of aid-tying. Although proposals have been made that the consortium "go it alone" on untying aid (that is, that consortium members as a group untie their aid to India), the disposition in 1969 and 1970 was to await the outcome of DAC negotiations on the problem. At the June 1971 meeting, considerable attention was given to problems associated with the sudden influx of millions of refugees from East Pakistan.

The Pakistan Consortium

The consortium for Pakistan was formed in 1960, primarily because, given the post-World War II political history of the subcontinent, it was inconceivable that a consortium should be formed for India without parallel action for Pakistan. In the Pakistan Consortium, however, the relationship between recipient and donors is reported to have been more informal and less touchy during the 1960s than the corresponding relationship in the India Consortium.[35]

Pakistani officials did not think that their national sovereignty was infringed when their economic policies and development strategy were discussed within the consortium. Something akin to a feeling of "thinking this through together" characterized the discussions at meetings and when Pakistani officials were in contact with the Bank and consortium representatives between meetings. In describing the consortium's modus operandi, White said:

This close connection between the Planning Commission and the consortium was symptomatic of a more fundamental aspect of the whole relationship between Pakistan and the aid-givers. In Pakistan, the boundary line between the givers and receivers of aid became a fluid one. When necessary, the Planning Commis-

35. For an excellent account of the consortium's first five years, see John White, *Pledged to Development: A Study of International Consortia and the Strategy of Aid* (London: Overseas Development Institute, Ltd., 1967), pp. 57–89.

sion and the Finance Ministry could seek the alliance of the consortium in persuading other departments to accept a change in policy. On other occasions, the World Bank, the USA, or some other member of the consortium could seek the alliance of the Government of Pakistan in order to impress its own view on the consortium as a whole.[36]

With respect to the relationship between the Bank and the bilateral members, White noted:

In shaping the consortium's response to the needs of Pakistan, the World Bank played a crucial role as advocate and agent. Throughout the period of the second plan, the World Bank maintained an exceptionally strong and explicit position concerning the terms of aid appropriate to Pakistan's prospects. . . . It was aided in this endeavor by the United States, which provided a large proportion of the funds needed to give reality to the World Bank's initiatives.[37]

The consortium followed the Indian pattern of two meetings a year—one concerned with economic analysis and the second devoted to pledging. Without warning, Pakistan in 1961 revised its development targets and asked for a much larger amount of aid than it had been expected to request. The Pakistan Planning Commission agreed to document its request; at the January 1962 meeting, the consortium accepted its case. The result was overpledging. At the end of the period covered by the pledges made at the consortium's June 1961 and January 1962 meetings, $100 million in uncommitted funds was still available because of the absence of fully prepared projects to which resources could be assigned. This produced a two-fold effect: (1) It gave "pledging," particularly the "gap-filling" variety, a bad name in the minds of the Bank and most of the bilateral participants. While the consortium continued to hold pledging sessions for several years, the "gap-filling" aspect of it faded away, and "pledging" came to mean basically, announcing one's contribution. Eventually, the practice of holding a separate annual meeting for this purpose disappeared. (2) The second result of the over-pledging was that it shifted the emphasis within the consortium to development performance.

The next watershed in the history of the Pakistan Consortium was the war with India in 1965. As was noted earlier, the United States discontinued aid to both countries, and the future of the consortia was in doubt. President Woods, however, was willing to continue the venture if the other parties concerned wanted it, provided the emphasis was on performance, on removing bottlenecks in the economy, on expediting project preparation and completion, and the like. One of the chief economic policies that the Bank, the

36. *Ibid.,* pp. 59–60.
37. *Ibid.,* p. 85.

United States, and the United Kingdom wanted Pakistan to adopt was an extensive import liberalization program. This was made possible primarily by commodity assistance from the United States, but the Bank too eventually agreed to give Pakistan a relatively small IDA credit for program lending (which was called a loan for "industrial imports") in order to facilitate liberalization of import procedures.

After 1966, the consortium for Pakistan, like that for India, reduced its financial assistance (particularly in the program lending area). This forced both countries to cut back their development plans. In 1968, an agreement was negotiated within the framework of the Pakistan Consortium for financing the construction of the huge dam on the Indus River at Tarbela.[38] Despite cutbacks in aid levels and the hardening of terms in recent years, the attitude of Pakistan with respect to the consortium appears to have been tempered by recognition of the fact that Pakistan, through 1970, had been less severely hit by aid cutbacks than had many less developed countries. There was also a conviction that, over the years, Pakistan had received more aid through the consortium than it would have received without it. A rescheduling of its external debt was under consideration when in 1971 Pakistan unilaterally declared a moratorium on service payments to other governments. A political crisis that resulted in the death of a shockingly large number of East Pakistani and the pell-mell flight to India of millions of others had paralyzed the economy. Though divided on what they should do bilaterally, the aid-providers agreed that, for the time being, consortium meetings would be futile. The consortium, in other words, is in limbo as of this writing.[39]

Consultative Groups

Antipathy toward the concept of the consortium, and toward pledging sessions in particular, replaced sympathy in the minds of most of the bilateral donors and within Bank circles after the experience of the 1962 pledging session of the Pakistan Consortium. Yet many of the less developed countries for obvious reasons liked the idea of a consortium and wanted one to be formed on their behalf. In 1962, the Bank received requests from Nigeria,

38. See World Bank/IDA, *Annual Report, 1968*, pp. 20–22, and Chapter 19, below.
39. As an addendum to the above discussion of consortia, we remind readers that the OECD in the early 1960s formed consortia for two of its members, Greece and Turkey. The Bank joined both groups. Greece's need for external assistance on concessional terms was by then limited, however, and the Greek Consortium never really got off the ground. The Turkey Consortium encountered heavy weather in its first three years but has been functioning reasonably successfully since about 1965. (For more on the Turkey Consortium, see White, *Pledged to Development*, pp. 90–167.)

Tunisia, Colombia, and Sudan, each of which wanted a consortium focused on pledging. The only major aid donor sympathetic to increasing the number of consortia was the United States, which under President Kennedy was attempting to reorient its foreign aid program.[40] The United Kingdom also felt that some kind of coordinating mechanism among donors was necessary. By mid-1963, the Bank had agreed to establish for each of the four applicants the less formal coordinating mechanism which came to be known as the "consultative group."

In addition to prodding from the United States, the United Kingdom, and potential recipients, the activities of the Development Assistance Committee of the OECD and its predecessor, the Development Assistance Group, probably spurred the Bank. The DAG and DAC were expected by their members to increase the effectiveness of bilateral assistance programs and to play some kind of coordinating role. The United States in 1962 proposed that the DAC select one country in each region of the world and then consider both the development program and the needs of each country selected as well as the policies and aid programs of DAC members vis-à-vis that country. The country selected for Latin America was Colombia, which appeared to be making comparatively good economic progress.

Why not . . . form a group within the DAC which, without any specific commitment to funds, could discuss needs and programs and contribute to mutual understanding of problems and prospects? . . .

No such group was formed. . . . Many donors regarded the proposal for a co-ordinating group as only one small step removed from a financial commitment. Authorship of the suggestion in the United States seemed to be a tip-off to an American hope for increased, non-American contributions. The proposal, moreover, met the undisguised hostility of the World Bank. Its involvement with Colombia had been long and extensive, and it clearly regarded the proposed DAC consultative group as intrusive. In addition, the Bank probably felt that the work of the DAC would not only duplicate its own work on Colombian problems but might lead to recommendations from the DAC on the lending policies of the Bank itself. . . . The Colombian case therefore was compromised: the DAC was allowed to hold a meeting or two, the subject was effectively referred back to the World Bank, the Bank organized its own consultative group, and there the matter rested.[41]

The Colombian case may not be the only one in which the DAC's interest in a particular developing country, as manifested in the holding of meetings to discuss the country's development program and needs, stimulated the interest of the Bank in forming a consultative group. The DAC held a country

40. White, *Pledged to Development*, p. 43.

41. Seymour J. Rubin, *The Conscience of the Rich Nations: The Development Assistance Committee and the Common Aid Effort* (Harper and Row, published for the Council on Foreign Relations, 1966), pp. 89–91.

meeting on Thailand and in early 1963 established a coordinating group in Bangkok to improve technical assistance to Thailand. (It was worthy of note that Thai officials participated fully in these meetings.) Subsequently, in 1965, an informal consultative group on Thailand, followed later by a more formal one, was organized by the Bank. The DAC held meetings on East Africa in Paris in 1963 and in Nairobi in 1964 to discuss needs for financial help in meeting local costs and, later, for technical assistance. The Bank organized a consultative group for East Africa (Kenya, Tanzania, Uganda, and the East African Community) in 1968. While it is not fair to conclude that the Bank would not have formed these groups had it not been spurred by DAC activities—there seems to have been genuine confusion and uncertainty in the early 1960s concerning the appropriate roles of DAC and the Bank in aid coordination—it is apparent that the Bank was not initially a true leader in the formation of consultative groups.

Early Consultative Group Meetings

The topics under discussion and the quality and tone of the early consultative group meetings sponsored by the Bank reflected a lack of enthusiasm on the part of most bilateral donors and the Bank with respect to the new enterprise. The primary responsibility for preparation for the meetings was thrust upon a staff loan officer, who was expected to carry this in addition to his regular workload. The meetings consisted of a discussion of the recipient's economy or development plan, with some bilateral members and the Bank describing their current aid activities in the country. In the early years, meetings usually included "private" sessions of donors only, as well as sessions at which recipients were invited to state their cases and answer questions. Meetings for Tunisia and Nigeria were held every few months during the first three years of the groups' existence. The Sudan group barely got under way before it became inactive, due to domestic political upheaval and fundamental foreign policy changes. With so little being attempted by the consultative groups in Africa, the fact that little was accomplished should not have been surprising.

This state of affairs was not accepted lightly by either the Tunisians or the Nigerians. In the first place, despite repeated efforts by members of the Bank staff to impress upon the recipients the concept that there was to be no pledging or fund-raising, both countries seemed to feel that these functions *ought* to be the primary responsibility of the group. The divergence in viewpoints of the donors and recipients as to purpose was painfully clear at the meeting for Tunisia in October 1962, when the chief Tunisian delegate referred in his prepared statement to "filling the gap" with respect to foreign exchange requirements for the country's plan. He was immediately "corrected" by the Belgian, German, and Italian delegations, which insisted that the group existed strictly for purposes of exchange of information.

Nigeria tried every tactic it could think of to pump life and substance into its group. The government established the position of Commissioner General for Economic Affairs, attached to the Nigerian embassy in Washington, to serve as a link between the consultative group and the Nigerian government. The commissioner (Chief S. O. Adebo) requested that a secretariat be established for the group but was turned down. He asked to attend the meetings and was placated by being invited to one individual session. He did succeed, before civil war broke out in Nigeria, in bringing about a ten-day visit to that country by Bank President George Woods.[42]

While two of the African consultative groups were not performing very satisfactorily and one (Sudan) was not functioning at all, the experience with the consultative group for Colombia was more positive. Owing to its weakened balance-of-payments position, the price Colombia had to pay to get the group formed was devaluation. Shortly after devaluation, the United States came forth with a large program loan that gave the consultative group a sense of accomplishment. In addition, according to White, "one reason for the early success of the Colombia group was that coordination in the financing of projects was what was most urgently needed. This was relatively easy to achieve, once the appropriate mechanism had been established."[43]

42. The utter disillusionment of the Nigerians was expressed in a letter dated April 7, 1965, from Chief Adebo to the director of the African Department of the Bank, A. G. El Emary:

I have been in recent correspondence with my government concerning the performance of the Consultative Group of countries which, under the guidance of the World Bank, are *supposed* to be helping Nigeria with the financing of its current development plan.

I use the term "supposed" advisedly in the preceding paragraph. Not all the countries named have shown the degree of keenness to provide us with financial assistance that they displayed in raising our expectations when we sounded them out in the course of preparation of our plan. Some of the countries have given us valuable help, but a great deal of this has seemed to us to result more from bilateral promotion conducted outside the Group framework than from deliberations or other action within that framework. . . .

I have my own ideas as to the weaknesses of the present arrangements. Some of them seem to me to be attributable to the members of the Group, and some to the nature of our own governmental machinery in Nigeria. I also [feel] that . . . the Bank's own organization for looking after the Consultative Group could be improved.

The letter goes on to request that a high level Bank official come to Lagos to review with Nigerian officials the arrangements for the group. The Bank's response to this was the above-mentioned visit to Nigeria by President Woods.

43. *Pledged to Development,* p. 44.

1964 Review

By 1964, it was generally recognized that the consultative groups, with the possible exception of the Colombia group, were not functioning satisfactorily. The Bank set up a working party to review the problem and to make recommendations for improving the consultative mechanism. In the next annual report the broad conclusions of the working party were summarized:

> During the fiscal year, the Bank carried out an intensive review of the work of the groups it has organized, canvassing informally the views of major capital-exporting countries as well as of the developing countries for which consultative groups have been formed. Its conclusion was that there continues to be a pressing need for effective arrangements to coordinate aid, and that the organization and administration of consultative groups is an appropriate and important function for the Bank to assume. At the same time, it was recognized that each consultative group requires a high degree of staff support in the maintenance of liaison and the preparation and exchange of information concerning the recipient country's economic position, performance, problems and capital requirements.[44]

The guidelines issued by the working party dealt with the purposes of, operating procedures for, and criteria for the establishment of consultative groups. The guidelines also included suggestions regarding the functions that the Bank might fulfill with respect to the groups. Among these were: (1) comprehensive reporting on the country's development possibilities, problems, and performance in greater depth than was usual for Bank loans; (2) recommendations concerning appropriate types and terms of aid; (3) assistance to the recipient in drawing up a development plan; (4) project identification and feasibility studies; (5) advice to recipients and donors as to which sectors and projects deserved priority for external financing.

The more activist role envisioned for the Bank as manager and chief sponsor of consultative groups had a number of implications. In very concrete terms, an increase in personnel would be required for the expanded staff work that each group would entail; one loan officer could no longer do all of the work in his spare time. The Bank, in the course of its almost continuous review of the recipient's plans and policies, its general economic analysis, and its work on project identification and preparation would become more deeply involved in the affairs of the recipient government than formerly. The Bank would also be in more frequent contact with the donors during the intervals between actual meetings of the various groups. A senior official in the Development Services Department, Michael L. Hoffman, was assigned responsibility for overseeing all aspects of the Bank's work on aid coordina-

---

44. IBRD/IDA, *Annual Report, 1964–65*, p. 12.

tion; operational responsibility for the management of the individual groups remained with the area departments.[45]

Post-1965 Meetings

The Bank was eager to show results from its more energetic policies and expanded efforts. The consultative group meeting for Nigeria held in Paris in February 1966 to discuss Nigeria's "revised development plan" was notably more successful than any previous meeting of this group, despite the fact that a military coup d'état had very recently occurred in Nigeria.

In the presentation by the Nigerian delegation, a theme was introduced that was to come up at virtually every meeting of every consultative group in which it had not already arisen—a plea for more non-project aid. The Bank's standard response was to endorse in principle the need for non-project aid, to point out that the Bank's charter permitted it to give non-project aid only in "special circumstances," and to urge the bilateral donors to provide this type of assistance. The United States and the United Kingdom had been giving non-project aid and were expected to continue to do so. Finally,

At the end of the meeting the World Bank declared its intention of committing up to $100m [million] in new loans in the coming year. Several participants subsequently made the comment that if the World Bank had made this declaration earlier in the meeting, other countries would have followed suit with similar promises, which would in effect have had the status of voluntary pledges.

This was a remarkable meeting in several ways, and certainly very different from its predecessors. The willingness to think in terms of a "gap," the recognition of the need for international discipline in export credits, the specific recommendation on the terms of lending; these were all new features.[46]

In the eyes of the Bank, the meeting of the consultative group for Tunisia held in Paris in March 1967 also showed marked improvement.[47] In addition to contributing to the improvement in the functioning of two of the existing groups, the Bank in 1965 and 1966 established new consultative groups for Ceylon, Malaysia, South Korea, and Thailand.[48] The formation of groups for Thailand and Malaysia represented a new departure in the history of aid-coordinating groups. This was the first time a consortium or con-

45. Michael Hoffman is also the author of a lucid, informative article, "The Coordination of Aid," in *Effective Aid* (London: Overseas Development Institute, Ltd., 1967), pp. 65–83.

46. White, *Pledged to Development*, p. 55.

47. IBRD, Internal memorandum from M. L. Hoffman to George Woods, March 20, 1967.

48. The group organized on behalf of Ceylon as a rescue operation is called the "Aid Group for Ceylon" and technically is not classified as a consultative group.

sultative group had been formed, not to deal with a current crisis, but in anticipation of future needs.[49]

After its burst of activity with respect to consultative groups in the mid-1960s, the Bank's pace slackened. Between 1967 and 1970, consultative groups under Bank chairmanship were formed only for Morocco and East Africa. In addition, in 1970 the Bank took over responsibility for the Ghana group, which was formed initially under the auspices of the International Monetary Fund to deal with Ghana's urgent and serious balance-of-payments problems in the aftermath of the fall of the Nkrumah regime.

The Sudan group has remained inactive. (Sudan does not maintain diplomatic relations with most of the donors.) As of mid-1971, however, it had not been officially disbanded. The group established for Peru in 1966 was, as reported in Chapter 13, above, also unsuccessful and consigned to the inactive list.[50] The group for Nigeria, due to civil war there, was dormant between the February 1966 meeting, which had ended on a note of such promise, and the spring of 1971. Despite high hopes in 1967 both for the consultative group and for the Tunisian economy, by 1970 the economic development policies of the government had boomeranged. The Bank was faced with the choice either of pulling out on performance grounds or of remaining in Tunisia in order to help the country through a very difficult period. Apparently because of the Tunisian government's determination to alter its economic policies, the Bank has chosen the latter course.

The Colombia consultative group, which enjoyed the distinction of being regarded as successful at the very start, has not enjoyed smooth sailing throughout its course. In the mid-1960s, according to White,

The Colombian Government produced an improvement in policy, and the group produced an increase in aid. Then the policy deteriorated again and the increase in aid slowed down, amid a certain amount of recrimination over which was the cause of which.[51]

In 1967, the Colombian economy was not in good shape—foreign exchange reserves were being drawn down rapidly, exports were sluggish, and inflation seemed out of control. Colombia dealt with these problems with some success, and at the January 1969 consultative group meeting, the Colombian delegation referred to the "greatly stepped-up flow" of aid.

The focal point of the Colombia consultative group meetings is a project list, which usually carries the endorsement of the Bank. Projects suitable for joint or bilateral financing are identified. The complex business of nego-

49. White, *Pledged to Development*, p. 56.
50. It was revived in February 1972.
51. *Pledged to Development*, p. 44.

tiating joint financing arrangements has not been a function of the consultative group, as such, but the difference is formal: the same people get together the next day to discuss joint financing.[52]

In 1967 the Netherlands formed the Intergovernmental Group on Indonesia after the collapse of the Sukarno regime. The first order of business was to draw up a stabilization program to deal with the desperate balance-of-payments situation and the virtual collapse of the Indonesian economy. In late 1969 the group began to focus its attention more on the development program and on arranging for its financing. A great deal of the preparation and economic analysis for the group is undertaken by the Bank. Much of the external assistance required is for program loans, and it is the Bank and the Fund that set forth the estimates for both program and project lending and make recommendations concerning the terms of aid. The group is more reminiscent of what a consortium used to be than of a consultative group in that, while the minutes of meetings do not itemize the commitments or offers made by various donors, by the end of each meeting the delegates invariably conclude that the targets will be met.

Guyana formed an aid-coordinating group (the Aid Donors Conference) on its own behalf. The first meeting was in 1967 and was held, not in Paris or Washington, but in Georgetown, the capital of Guyana. With the prime minister of the receiving country in the chair, there has been a tendency for the shoe to be on the other foot. The donors get more prodding on amounts and terms of aid, and the emphasis on the recipient's performance is less heavy. Honduras, like Guyana, has sponsored its own aid group. In both cases, the Bank's participation has been limited.

The Recommendations of the Pearson Commission

With the role of the consortia watered down in terms of their original fund-raising function, with some consultative groups in a moribund state, others functioning satisfactorily, and still others struggling to get under way, and with each group's meeting different from the last, the Pearson Commission came out firmly in October 1969 with recommendations that the number of consultative groups be greatly expanded and the consultative process strengthened.[53]

President McNamara, welcoming most of the commission's advice with respect to consultative groups, recommended to the Bank's executive direc-

---

52. For more on joint and parallel financing of projects, see the next section of this chapter.

53. *Partners in Development,* Report of the Commission on International Development, Lester B. Pearson, chairman (Praeger, 1969), pp. 129–31.

tors in February 1970 that the Bank take the initiative in forming such groups for most, if not all, of the twenty large countries for which no coordinating machinery existed, and possibly for other countries as well. He also recommended, in the spirit of the commission's report, that existing consultative groups be strengthened by more frequent meetings, by the coordination of major technical assistance requirements, and by focusing on overall development strategy.

The president's proposal for forming new groups ran into considerable opposition from the executive directors. Several European countries, most notably France and Germany, strongly opposed the formation of numerous new groups on the grounds that, as major donor countries, they would be expected to join and would be under pressure to establish an aid program for the recipient or increase present levels of assistance. Some of the potential beneficiaries—among them Argentina, Brazil, and Chile—had no interest in having aid-coordinating groups formed on their behalf. Because of this opposition and the Bank's own recognition of the mixed results of existing aid coordination efforts, new consultative groups were established in 1971 for only three countries (the Philippines, Zaire, and Ethiopia) instead of for some fifteen or twenty countries.

Although this would appear to represent a setback—or at least not much of an advance—for supporters of aid coordination under Bank sponsorship, it may be that supporters have endowed this particular mechanism with greater virtues than it has. Some of the economic reports for meetings have been excellent, but others have been inadequate. The mechanism is useful only if the country is already receiving, or is likely soon to receive, significant amounts of aid from several different sources willing to engage in a more coordinated effort. The chief coordinator probably needs chips to put into the game; if its contribution is dwarfed by aid from other sources, or if it is unable to deliver types of aid considered essential, its position may be weakened. Expertise, persuasion, and publicity can do much but will not always succeed in covering up the conflicts of purpose that characterize the different efforts. After all, the principal reason for a bilateral development assistance program is the donor's desire for the opportunity to use it as an instrument of, or an expression of, its own foreign policy. This tends to produce a commitment to development per se, or development along lines promulgated by international institutions, that is more ambiguous than the commitment of the international institutions themselves.

The effectiveness of these coordinating groups depends heavily also on the political, social, economic, and administrative situation of the recipient country. The two Bank-sponsored consortia were in limbo for at least a year and a half after the India–Pakistan War in 1965, and the future of the Pakistan

Consortium in the wake of the 1971 civil war was again in doubt. The consultative group for Nigeria felt it had no choice but to bow out when civil war erupted in that country. Political pressures in Tunisia resulted in economic policies that set back the country's development prospects in spite of the policy prescriptions of the Bank on behalf of the consultative group for Tunisia.

To a recipient country one of the most valuable unexpected benefits of establishing a consultative group is often the improved internal coordination resulting from the need to prepare reports and position papers for meetings of the group. Beyond this, the country can hope for a slight increase in foreign aid or less "slippage" than might have occurred in the wake of shrinking bilateral programs, an improvement in the terms of aid from some sources for some loans, and perhaps more joint financing of projects than it might otherwise obtain. In recent years the Bank on various occasions has suggested that aid coordination as carried out at present—by officials from the capitals of donor countries who normally concentrate on reviewing the performance of the recipient country and its need for external resources—could usefully be supplemented by setting up local coordinating groups in the capitals of recipient countries to discuss related matters, including individual technical assistance and preinvestment projects and specific details of investment projects.

From the point of view of the smaller bilateral donors, the economic analysis, preinvestment surveys, and recommendations on project and sector priorities provided by the Bank (whose competence in these areas is highly respected) are of considerable benefit. From the standpoint of the Bank, the consultative groups represent an opportunity to improve the terms, the continuity, and the flow of external assistance, and to improve the development performance of the recipient more than would otherwise be feasible. Within the ranks of the Bank, there are those who feel strongly that the payoff has not been worth the effort, that the Bank risks compromising its independence and integrity by sponsoring such clubs, or that the Bank simply should not be in the aid-coordination business. But their views are more than counterbalanced by the views of Presidents Woods and McNamara, who have espoused and strongly supported a leading role for the Bank in this field.

Joint and Parallel Financing

As readers of this book will already have noted, World Bank Group financing never covers the full cost of a project. Consequently financing is always jointly provided, involving as a minimum one member of the Bank

Group and a local source of finance. The Bank or IDA meets some or all of the foreign exchange costs of the project, and the borrower assumes responsibility for some or all of the local currency costs.[54] In accordance with Bank terminology, however, we shall use the term "joint financing" to cover cases involving at least one institutional source (other than the World Bank Group) outside the country in which the project is located, and such institutional sources will be called "co-lenders," even though they may be providing funds on a grant basis or investing in shares.

The principal sources of funds for joint operations are: (a) individuals or institutions subscribing to market issues or private placements of bonds, (b) institutional investors associating themselves in the financing of a particular project by participating in a Bank loan, (c) national aid agencies or export financing agencies, and (d) international aid agencies. Complications most often arise with category (c)—the national aid and export financing agencies —although touchy questions of prestige may arise when other international agencies join in financing a project or program.

The simplest method of joint financing is through a Bank loan for a specific project, accompanied by a public bond issue for general capital purposes. Examples include the foreign borrowings by Austria, Belgium, Italy, and Norway, in conjunction with Bank loans to those countries.[55] The sale of participations in previously negotiated Bank loans is also a straightforward operation. In such cases, the investor does not normally negotiate with the borrower and is only remotely identified with the project.

Arrangements involving national aid and export-financing agencies, particularly the latter, have been more difficult. With a few notable exceptions, such as the Swedish International Development Agency, most national agencies still tie the funds they provide to purchases from their own countries. The Bank has devoted many man-hours to the quest for arrangements that will have the practical effect of untying tied aid. If this is to be done through joint financing, credit offers must be obtained from the countries likely to win orders under a system of international competitive bidding. Each country must agree to finance all, or a stipulated fraction, of the orders it receives. If international competitive bidding is to be open to all Bank members, credit offers will have to be available from all the countries that are likely to be competitive.

The Bank's interest in working out joint financing arrangements normally springs from a desire to help a member country obtain additional development finance on reasonable terms for priority undertakings. The Bank may

54. For financial arrangements under the IFC, see Chapter 11, above.
55. See Chapter 11, above.

also on occasion want to limit its investment in a particular country or project, or to supplement its scarce IDA resources with other funds available on a soft-loan or grant basis. Co-lenders may wish to take advantage of the Bank's work on project appraisal and loan administration in order to help ensure that their own funds finance "good" projects as well as exports from the co-financing country.

Interlocking covenants in the Bank loan can make co-lenders more confident that their loans will be repaid on schedule. The fact that their funds finance equipment and supplies whose prices are set by international competitive bidding can protect them from charges that their prices are excessive. In the case of important projects, such as the Volta River power and aluminum project in Ghana, or the modernization of a major sector of the economy, such as the power or transport sector, numerous parties may wish, for reasons of prestige as well as for export promotion, to be identified with the venture.

The $1.2 billion Indus Basin Development Fund, set up in 1960 to finance the construction of irrigation and other works in Pakistan, represents one way of associating others in the financing of a program too large for the Bank to undertake on its own. It involved contributions from eight governments to a fund under Bank management and supervision but, for various reasons, did not constitute a precedent that could be widely used.[56]

Large projects or programs give rise to many contracts for equipment and supplies. Arrangements whereby the individual contracts are financed partly by the Bank and partly by the co-lender or lenders constitute "joint financing" in the strictest sense of the term. Arrangements whereby the Bank provides all the external finance for certain contracts or separable facilities of the project (or program) and the co-lenders provide all the external finance for other contracts or other facilities, represent the kind of joint financing that the Bank calls "parallel financing."

In true joint financing, in contrast with parallel financing, the Bank and the participating countries agree on the cost-sharing formula and the minimum terms of export credits. Each participating country, for example, may agree to finance half the cost of orders placed with suppliers in that country and to offer a minimum maturity of ten years from delivery of the equipment, while the Bank finances the remaining half of the cost out of its longer-term loan. All equipment is procured on the basis of international competitive bidding open to all Bank member countries and Switzerland. Orders placed

---

56. For more on the financing of the development of the Indus River Basin, see Chapter 18, below.

in member countries other than those participating as co-lenders are financed wholly by the Bank. This means that the Bank's share in the external costs of the total project is almost inevitably larger than the cost-sharing formula implies.

While in joint financing the same goods are financed in part by the Bank and in part by the co-lenders, in parallel financing the Bank and the co-lenders finance separate lists of goods. In parallel financing, the bidding *on the goods financed by the Bank* is open to all Bank members and to Switzerland. The bidding *on goods financed by co-lenders,* however, is restricted to suppliers able to arrange financing on the minimum stated terms. The co-lenders finance the orders placed in their countries.

Experiments and Compromises

In the Niger Dam project in Nigeria in 1964, extensive competitive bidding for major works had already taken place before the Bank loan was signed. The amounts from other lenders that could be utilized on the project were known, and the Bank loan could cover the external financing still needed for the project, after taking into account usable financing from other lenders. The result was a Bank loan of $82 million and tied loans of $59.6 million from Italy, the Netherlands, the United States, and the United Kingdom, and a grant of $1.7 million from Canada. But how should the financing be handled for large projects for which competitive bidding is still in the future and the amounts that will have to be put up by the Bank and the co-lenders are therefore not yet known?

An organized effort to involve national aid and export promotion agencies at the pre-bidding stage began in 1964–65 with a series of exploratory discussions by the Bank staff with government officials of aid-giving countries and representatives of private financing institutions. The pilot project was a Mexican power project costing $309 million, for which a Bank loan of $110 million was made in December 1965. Arrangements for joint financing in the amount of about $35 million were made with Canada, France, Italy, Japan, and Switzerland. The arrangements provided that contracts potentially subject to joint financing would be awarded on the basis of cash prices (that is, without taking credit terms into account). Moreover, the Bank would finance two-thirds and joint lenders one-third of the amount of the contract.

Following this experience, discussions with governments and private financing institutions were continued under the auspices of an ad hoc group consisting of member countries of the consultative group for Colombia and those interested in joint financing of projects in both Colombia and Mexico.

In October 1967, agreement in principle was reached on joint financing for three projects in Colombia and one in Mexico, all smaller than the initial pilot project.[57] The general formula for joint financing of these Colombian and Mexican projects—a Bogotá water supply project, a Bogotá power supply project, a power interconnection project for Colombia, and a second project in Mexico's power sector—was that half would be supplied by the Bank and half by the supplying countries in the case of contracts for the Colombian projects, and two-thirds by the Bank, one-third by the supplying countries in the case of contracts for the Mexican project. This formula applied only to individual orders for imported goods of at least $200,000, and totaling for each individual project at least $1 million in any one supplying country. The goods to be imported for the project under joint financing arrangements would be procured on the basis of international competitive bidding in accordance with practices usually followed for Bank projects. Other features of the formula included a minimum maturity period of ten years for joint loans and an agreement that the Bank would finance 100 percent of the imports that were not eligible for joint financing under the formula, as well as of goods procured in countries not participating in the joint financing arrangement.

When the Bank finances an agreed fraction of the cost of every one of the hundreds of contracts for foreign supplies and equipment awarded under a large project, it assumes a much heavier burden of administrative work than when it alone finances certain contracts while co-lenders finance others. Co-lenders also add to their workload and reduce their freedom of action. Nevertheless, some projects are not readily divisible into Bank and non-Bank portions. And some borrowers prefer joint financing, as do some of the lenders (France, for example).

Parallel financing—under which bidding is limited to suppliers in countries that are willing to agree in advance to put up finance—appeared as of mid-1971 to be more acceptable to the United States, or at least to its Export-Import Bank. When tension between the World Bank and the Export-Import Bank of the United States flared up again in 1970–71 over the financing of a huge expansion of the Brazilian steel industry, parallel financing provided an answer. Since 1941, when the Eximbank had financed the building of the Volta Redonda plant near Rio de Janeiro, it had taken "a fierce proprietary interest in Brazil's steel industry."[58] However, as Brazil began to see in other sectors the price saving attainable through international competitive bidding, it began wanting the same advantages for its steel industry. Accordingly, it

---

57. IBRD, Sec M 69-541, Dec. 12, 1969, p. 22.

58. "World Bank Craves a Slice of Exim's Pie," *Business Week* (Feb. 13, 1971), p. 28.

stunned the Eximbank, from which it already had a preliminary commitment for a $120 million loan, with a request for joint financing to be arranged by the World Bank. The Eximbank objected strenuously.[59]

The final compromise was a parallel arrangement whereby the financing of equipment purchases for the $1.3 billion expansion of the Brazilian steel industry would be divided between loans from the World Bank and the Inter-American Development Bank (IDB) and "suppliers' credits" (a generic term encompassing loans from the Eximbank and similar sources of credit). All equipment would be procured through international competitive bidding, but only the World Bank and the IDB-financed portions would be subject to the Bank's procurement procedures and supervision. The contemplated World Bank portion—$180 million—was to take the form of loans to three separate steel companies.

Numerous financing arrangements intrinsically as complex as the foregoing have been worked out with less tension and publicity. The foreign exchange costs (equivalent to $68 million) of an $84 million fertilizer plant in Sumatra are being provided by IDA ($30 million), the "soft-loan window" of the Asian Development Bank ($10 million), the U.S. Agency for International Development ($20 million), and the Overseas Economic Cooperation Fund of Japan ($8 million). The equipment and services financed by the international agencies will be procured by competitive bidding; the U.S. and Japanese contributions will be tied to procurement in those countries.[60] Operations with aid agencies, generally speaking, are easier to organize and execute than are operations with the more commercially minded export-financing institutions.

Operations with French, German, and British Agencies

Particularly noteworthy is the extent of joint financing between the Bank/IDA and French lending agencies in formerly French areas of Africa. In the early 1960s more than 95 percent of French bilateral aid was going to countries in the franc zone. France, as we have noted, was a reluctant dragon

59. There was more at stake than specific steel equipment sales at a time when U.S. industry was particularly eager to bolster its exports. Under an aggressive new president, the Eximbank could reassert its view, long shared by segments of U.S. industry, that the international agency should not finance commercial or self-liquidating ventures that could be financed with "traditional" Eximbank support. The article in *Business Week*, quoted above, said that the Eximbank had to date enjoyed "a virtual monopoly in financing nuclear power plants overseas," a monopoly that might be challenged by the World Bank. The timing of the article—early 1971, when Congress was expected to vote on the third and largest replenishment of IDA resources—seemed well selected to induce cautious behavior on the part of the World Bank.

60. IDA, Press release (June 4, 1970).

when the formation of new consortia and consultative groups was proposed —usually for countries for which France had not previously been providing aid. Nevertheless, there was considerable sentiment in France for a selective extension of bilateral aid beyond the area of traditional concentration, and for a broader sharing of responsibility for assistance within the area both with fellow members of the European Economic Community and with multilateral agencies.[61]

To joint financing operations with the Bank and IDA in African nations, the French agencies (such as the Fonds d'Aide et de Coopération [FAC] and the Caisse Centrale de Coopération Economique [CCCE]) have taken a cooperative and flexible approach. France has provided both grant and loan aid. Although a number of the projects involve total costs of less than $10 million, the list also includes some very large undertakings involving total costs in excess of $100 million—for example, the Miferma iron ore project in Mauritania, agreed on in 1960, which is financed by loans from the Bank, the CCCE, and the French Treasury, as well as by share capital.

Joint financing operations between the Bank/IDA and Germany are fewer in number than those with France, and most of them are of more recent date. Both France and Germany, moreover, participate indirectly in the Bank/IDA's joint operations with two institutions of the European Economic Community—the European Development Fund and the European Investment Bank (EIB).

Though the United Kingdom has been heavily involved in some of the joint financing operations embracing the Bank/IDA and co-lenders from several countries—for example, the Indus Basin and the Tarbela Projects—it has not been very heavily involved in Bank/IDA operations in which it is the only bilateral participant.

The World Bank, to the best of our knowledge, has never been willing to defer to a regional bank for project supervision and administration, and the regional institutions do not always want to be coordinated by the World Bank. In the financing of the Keban project in Turkey, in which the European Investment Bank and four countries, as well as the World Bank, participated, the EIB was unwilling to accept a position subordinate to the IBRD, and the project was divided into two parts.

In summary, joint financing has been a feature of Bank operations for quite a few years, but the number of such operations and the amounts involved have increased since 1968, due both to greater efforts on the part of

61. See, for example, Ministère d'Etat Chargé de la Réforme Administrative, *La Politique de Coopération avec les Pays en Voie de Développement* (Paris, 1963), especially pp. 75–79. The document is better known as the Jeanneney Report.

the Bank to bring bilateral financing into Bank Group undertakings and to an increased desire on the part of national aid and export-financing agencies to become associated with projects appraised and partly financed by the Bank Group.

A Retrospective View

Born into an environment in which it tended to be dwarfed by national agencies of the U.S. government, the International Bank for Reconstruction and Development soon withdrew from the field of reconstruction in Europe. To obtain a firm toehold in the area of project financing in less developed countries it had to slug it out at times with the Export-Import Bank of the United States. This required battling on two fronts: at the highest levels of the U.S. government, and with would-be borrowers accustomed to dealing with the United States on a bilateral basis.

A number of member countries—Mexico, Iran, Japan, and others—were quietly informed by the president of the World Bank that the international agency should be more than *a* banker to their country, it should be *the* banker. This was a pretentious position to take vis-à-vis sovereign governments, but it probably helped convince them that it would be advantageous to enter into relationships with the World Bank. Having discovered some of those advantages—a review of each project proposal in terms of its priority and contribution to the development of the host country, a thorough appraisal of the technical and financial aspects of all proposals, and a great concern for their balance-of-payments effects—most member countries promptly concluded that they would not give a monopoly position to any agency. They would deal with the World Bank, the Export-Import Bank of the United States, the Kreditanstalt für Wiederaufbau, and any other potential sources of credit.

Moreover, it became apparent that the World Bank's initial estimates of the creditworthiness of borrowers were too cautious. The willingness of other lenders to be more venturesome helped pave the way for more realistic estimates of the capacity of less developed countries to put external capital to productive use. Crises could and did result from the bunch-up of short-term suppliers' credits, from the assumption of excessive amounts of medium- and long-term credit at commercial or close-to-commercial rates of interest, and from the pursuit of unwise policies. Fortunately the proliferation of export-financing machinery in the industrialized countries was accompanied for some years by an increase in the number of national agencies providing soft loans and grants.

By the late 1950s this opened up, or opened wider, an important new area for the exercise of leadership by the World Bank Group—the development of country-focused and project-focused coordinating mechanisms. The India Consortium came into being in 1958 as a temporary rescue operation rather than as a quasi-permanent piece of machinery. It was followed inevitably by a consortium to mobilize aid for Pakistan's development programs and, equally inevitably, by hesitation on the part of most aid donors to become parties to additional arrangements that could involve pledging sessions or commitments to meet the foreign exchange gaps of particular low-income countries.

The Bank's response was the more informal club called "the consultative group." Under Bank auspices, such groups were established for fifteen countries between 1962 and June 30, 1971. Although donor countries (in consortia as well as consultative groups) wanted to steer clear of commitments regarding levels of aid, receivers tended to feel that the job of the club should be to produce more aid, or aid on better terms, than would otherwise be forthcoming. Despite this divergence of views (and the modest list of achievements attributable to coordinating groups), consortia and consultative groups represent important half-way houses in the effort to rationalize the administration of development assistance at the country level.

Arrangements for associating other external sources of finance with the World Bank Group in financing specific projects or sector programs—joint and parallel financing—have also resulted in a great deal of extra work for the staff of the Bank. The main advantages of such operations are that they provide a means whereby funds from other sources are channeled into high priority projects, that those sources need not be anonymous and can seek credit for what they have done, that capital goods can be purchased from the more efficient suppliers, that project execution is likely to be more effective, and that by relying on the World Bank, other international and national agencies (particularly those in some of the smaller aid-giving countries) can avoid having to build up large staffs for project appraisal and supervision.

Tied aid produces less real assistance per dollar than does aid that is expended on the basis of international competitive bidding. The extra work for the Bank that is attributable to joint operations stems principally from the effort to make more efficient use of tied aid and, if possible, to use it as efficiently as untied aid. Joint or parallel financing operations can be undertaken in countries for which coordinating groups have been established, as has been done in Colombia, where the consultative group has had a voice both in developing the ground rules for such financing and in the selection of projects. On the other hand, the Bank has sponsored multiple financing of the expansion of the Mexican power industry, although Mexico as a country is the focus of neither a consortium nor a consultative group. Parallel financing, which is simpler than joint financing, is now preferred by most donors. The fact that the availability of export credit is expanding more rapidly than that of development assistance on concessional terms is, however, bound to create problems for most of the less developed countries.

The further growth of joint and parallel financing arrangements would be facilitated by a lengthening and standardizing of credit terms from export-financing agencies. While it is obvious that grant aid is the best bargain for a less developed country, considerable skill may be required to array the multiplicity of loan and credit terms in ways that permit intelligent choices to be made. Nonpartisan analysis by an international secretariat can be helpful to all concerned. Some of the less developed countries, moreover, are by now able to produce capital equipment on an internationally competitive basis but can hardly afford to offer credit terms as generous as those available from already industrialized nations. Under parallel financing, India can be assured of an opportunity to bid on equipment for Brazil that will be purchased through Bank financing but not on equipment whose purchase will be financed through tied bilateral funding—unless India has already made a credit offer in anticipation of becoming a supplier. Only when all bilateral finance is untied will all potential suppliers of equipment be on an equal footing.

In this chapter on the Bank and bilateral sources of finance, it has been noted more or less in passing that other international agencies as well as the Bank have taken part in the operations described. Although the Bank has emerged as a principal coordinator of bilateral development assistance, it is not alone in the field. The evolution of the Bank's relations with other international agencies, global and regional, is analyzed in the next two chapters of this book.

CHAPTER SIXTEEN

The World Bank and the International Monetary Fund

VARIOUS ASPECTS OF the relation between the World Bank and the International Monetary Fund (IMF) have been noted in earlier chapters. These institutions are frequently called the Bretton Woods twins, but, as we observed in Chapter 2, in the eyes of their parents they were by no means identical twins or even equal. The decision to create the Bank as a separate institution was made only at the last moment; the primary attention of the delegates was on the Fund. Indeed a number of sections of the Articles of Agreement of the Bank were lifted bodily from those of the Fund, and very few of the participants and observers at Bretton Woods and Savannah doubted that the IMF would be the premier organization. In Chapters 3 and 4 we discussed the different relationships that have developed between the management and the governing boards of these two institutions and the reasons therefor. The centerpiece of the Fund is the board of executive directors. As the official history of the IMF puts it, "the focus throughout [this volume] is on the Board of Executive Directors, but without neglecting the work of the Governors on the one hand and that of the staff on the other."[1] A history of the Bank, on the other hand, must necessarily concentrate on management and staff, though, in so doing, we hope we have also done justice to the governing boards.

Chapter 7 considered some aspects of the relationship between the Bank and the Fund in the increasingly important area of debt renegotiation. As the example of Ghana since the fall of Nkrumah indicates, the Fund may take

1. J. Keith Horsefield, *Chronicle*, Vol. 1 of Horsefield (ed.), *The International Monetary Fund, 1945–1965: Twenty Years of International Monetary Coöperation* (International Monetary Fund, 1969), p. xi.

the leadership in negotiation connected with the consideration of short-term debt and the provision of temporary financing required for the stabilization program, while the Bank may take over as the head of a group of creditors and capital suppliers concerned with longer-run problems. In Chapters 13 and 15 we referred to the use of Bank leverage to support stabilization conditions negotiated by the Fund and touched on Bank–Fund relationships in consortia and consultative groups. Here we propose to trace the development of the institutional relationship between the Bank and the Fund, to consider some of the interconnections between short-term stabilization policies and longer-term growth policies, and to speculate on what the relation between these two institutions might be. Before plunging into this subject, however, a few words should be said about certain characteristics of the Fund.

The International Monetary Fund

The IMF is two things. It is, as its name suggests, a fund that is available to countries having balance-of-payments difficulties. It represents also an agreement by the participating countries to behave circumspectly in their handling of such difficulties. Fund resources are available to member countries either through an exercise of drawing rights (that is, purchase by the Fund of a member country's domestic currency) or, beginning in 1952, through the consummation of a standby agreement.[2] Before 1961 no country was permitted to draw on Fund resources for more than 200 percent of its quota. Since then a number of countries have been allowed to exceed these limits, and by 1966 five countries had drawn more than 225 percent of their quotas. Still, access to Fund resources is strictly limited, and although the resources have been substantially increased by actions taken in 1958, 1966, and 1970, the amount available to any particular country is small in relation both to possible foreign exchange requirements and to the external financing that may be available from other sources.[3] Furthermore, Fund financing

2. A standby arrangement permits a drawing from the Fund of up to a specified amount within a specified period. An extension of the period can be negotiated.

3. The total of Fund subscriptions and quotas was set, in the Articles of Agreement, at $8,800 million. Subscriptions payable in gold were set at the smaller of the following two magnitudes: (a) 25 percent of a country's quota, or (b) 10 percent of its official holdings of gold and U.S. dollars. The remainder of a country's subscription was payable in its own currency. The total of subscriptions and quotas was increased in 1958, 1966, and 1970, and on June 30, 1971, stood at $28,477,810,000. This does not include Special Drawing Rights (SDRs). The net cumulative allocation of SDRs was $6,363,286,600 as of the same date.

is available only on a short- or medium-term basis—three to five years. As a senior official of the IMF has said,

One of the cardinal rules governing access to the Fund's resources is that such assistance must be repaid within five years at the outside. The significance of this rule is two-fold. It has the practical effect of ensuring the revolving character of the Fund's capital. Repayment to the Fund within a relatively short time also serves to verify that the Fund's assistance had been sought to deal with temporary, as distinct from fundamental, balance of payments difficulties.[4]

As we noted above, the "Articles" constitute an agreement among member countries to behave circumspectly, that is, to take into account the interests of other trading and investing countries in handling their balance-of-payments difficulties. But suppose countries do not behave circumspectly? Should access to the Fund then be denied? Or, alternatively, when access is permitted, what steps should the Fund be entitled to take to "persuade" or "induce" or "compel" proper behavior? This was an issue that badly divided American and British negotiators at Bretton Woods and Savannah, and it was not until the late 1950s, when Fund resources began to be heavily engaged, that a firm policy emerged. The report of the managing director (Per Jacobsson) in 1957 summarized the different "degrees of conditionality" which had been developed by the IMF and which continue to be Fund policy to date.

Access to the gold tranche is almost automatic; and requests for drawings within the next 25 per cent (the so-called "first credit tranche") are also treated liberally but, even so, such requests will be approved only if the country asking for assistance can show that it is making reasonable efforts to solve its own problems. For drawings beyond that tranche (i.e., beyond the first 50 per cent of the quota), substantial justification is required. . . . [Justification includes the presentation by the borrowing country of] "well-balanced and adequate programs which are aimed at establishing or maintaining the enduring stability of the currencies concerned at realistic rates of exchange."[5]

Increasingly the Fund has turned toward standby arrangements as against drawing rights both because the former are better adapted to the requirements of stabilization programs and because they offer more effective opportunities for using influence. As an IMF policy document puts it, under standby arrangements,

drawings on the Fund are usually phased between two or more periods, and may be made only while certain specific conditions are being observed. If these

4. E. Walter Robichek, "IMF Financial Programs" (Dec. 7, 1965; processed).

5. Per Jacobsson, *International Monetary Problems, 1957–63* (International Monetary Fund, 1964), p. 20. A review of policy on the use of Fund resources undertaken by the executive directors in 1968 concluded that "stand-by arrangements that did not go beyond the first credit tranche would in future not include phasing [that is, timing of drawing rights] or performance clauses." IMF, *Annual Report, 1969*, p. 37.

conditions are not satisfied, drawings may be resumed only after new understandings are reached. This type of stand-by arrangement provides greater assurance of the proper use of Fund resources than are immediate drawings granted
on the basis only of the member's declaration that it intends to follow certain
practices. It strengthens the hands of the authorities to implement more energetically policies designed to establish or maintain the monetary stability and liberal
payments system required to facilitate economic growth. At the same time it
strengthens the confidence of other lenders in the ability of the country to promote these objectives, thus leading to the provision of further resources for meeting both immediate and longer term needs.[6]

What the Fund is engaged in, through consultation, advice, and persuasion, is a financial programming operation designed to bring into balance
externally the supply and demand for foreign exchange with the smallest
feasible resort to restrictions on trade and payments and internally to bring
into balance the supply and demand for credit by noninflationary methods
and with an eye to the investment and output decisions on which the continued growth of the economy depends. The principal instrument relied on
to achieve external balance is the exchange rate—in words hallowed by Fund
usage, a "realistic rate of exchange." The principal instrument internally is
the credit ceiling, used to achieve, through control of the quantity of money,
an "enduring stability of the currency." But there are all sorts of combinations and permutations connected with the use of these basic instruments,
and the Fund must necessarily concern itself, in the area of fiscal policy, with
government expenditures, the tax structure and tax rates, and the price policies of public enterprises; in the area of income policy, with wage rates and
price controls; and with many aspects of capital and foreign exchange
markets.[7] Inevitably the Fund is involved in highly sensitive areas of public
decision-making.

The Fund, even more than the Bank, is a technical assistance agency, and
a large portion of the time of its staff is spent in advising finance ministers
and central bankers on matters of common concern. Frequently this advice
is accepted without cavil. Indeed it is not unusual for finance ministers to
welcome the support of the Fund against the spending ministries in their own
governments. As Jacobsson said in presenting the 1961 Report to the
Board of Governors, "It is precisely when this identity of interest is fully
realized that the programs which are supported by Fund assistance can be
carried out in a spirit of mutual confidence and the desired success achieved."[8]

6. "Policies on the Use of Fund Resources." International Monetary Fund, document SM/66/14 (Jan. 24, 1966; processed).
7. The IMF annual report for 1966 (pp. 21–27) contains a sophisticated account
of the kinds of stabilization problems encountered by the Fund and the various instruments used in dealing with them.
8. See Jacobsson, *International Monetary Problems, 1957–63*, p. 251.

Frequently, however, representatives of the Fund and the member country do not see precisely eye to eye, at least not at the beginning. In such circumstances the arguments of the Fund's representatives gain a certain weight because of the fact that access by the member country to needed foreign exchange depends on agreement. Officials of the IMF are quite naturally allergic to the use of such obnoxious words and phrases as "leverage," "strings," "bargaining power," and "arm twisting." They like to think—and perhaps this is the typical situation—that the Fund is there only in order to make possible the adoption of policies and practices that, in the short run, would be impossible for a member country without access to the Fund. Nevertheless, the very terms "conditions" and "conditionality" suggest a bargain, an exchange of quid pro quo, and what a member country agrees to do is often rather different from what it would choose to do if access to the Fund were available without strings. Furthermore, as we have noted above, even if ministers of finance and central bankers require no persuasion, they are frequently glad to have the leverage supplied by the Fund to bring colleagues in their own governments into line.

The financial resources of the IMF that are available to a less developed country are, however, relatively small as compared to what are frequently its financial needs. If to these resources can be added the financial support of other capital suppliers, two consequences may follow. The leverage of the Fund can be increased substantially, and the IMF, on the basis of these additional resources, may be able to take a broader view than would otherwise be possible of the conditions needed to overcome balance-of-payments difficulties. One major purpose of a stabilization exercise is to induce a country to take the necessary steps to bring its international payments into balance within a reasonable period of time. The necessary steps and the timing of these steps may be very much affected by the amounts of foreign exchange, over and above its current export earnings, to which the country may expect to have access.

The practice of making compliance with Fund policies a condition of access to capital from other quarters began in the early 1950s. U.S. Treasury officials became increasingly restive at what they considered "bail-out" operations (particularly in Latin America) that involved the use of U.S. public funds to meet balance-of-payments crises, which frequently had been brought about by excessive short-term borrowings from private sources. They thus began to insist on compliance. There were, at least initially, some misgivings on the part of IMF officials concerning this practice. Some officials questioned whether use by the U.S. government of Fund conditions as a guide to its lending policies might not injure the Fund's "image" as an international institution. But whatever the strength of these misgivings, they appear to have been temporary. Per Jacobsson, while managing director of the Fund, welcomed such support. Speaking in 1958 on the subject of the "International Liquidity Problem," he referred to IMF activities in promoting monetary discipline:

> Its action in this respect is enhanced by the fact that in several instances American aid has not been given before an agreement has been reached with the Fund. Since monetary discipline is exerted by changes in fiscal and credit policies, it would be politically difficult for the American authorities to try to exert a direct influence—there could easily be accusations of dollar diplomacy. But once an agreement is reached with the Fund, the American authorities can demand the observance of the provisions in such an agreement. From the point of view of the Fund, also, a combination with the lending activities of other agencies is very useful. A country will often need funds of various kinds—in addition to the short-term funds furnished by the International Monetary Fund, it may need long-term capital also. In all this work the Fund maintains close contact with the World Bank.[9]

It soon became customary for European creditors, New York bankers, and the World Bank, in special situations, to make negotiation of and compliance with Fund agreements a condition of lending. Renegotiation of short-term debt with representatives of the groups of creditors known as the Paris or Hague "clubs" usually turned on conditions considered satisfactory by the IMF. Under these circumstances, a commitment of resources by creditors and capital suppliers that was three or four times the size of Fund drawings could depend on compliance with Fund agreements. Financial resources in the form of immediately available foreign exchange or a close substitute, such as quick-disbursing program loans, can contribute more to the effective solution of a stabilization crisis than can project lending. Although, as Per Jacobsson says in the passage quoted above, a country in balance-of-payments difficulties may need long-term capital also, the most effective contribution the Bank could make to the short-term problem would be program lending or local expenditure financing.

Increasingly the Bank and the Fund have come to support each other in dealing with the balance-of-payments problems of member governments both inside and outside of consortia and consultative groups. The "performance standards" of the IMF are inevitably concerned with short-term stabilization measures and policies. As we said in Chapter 13, the country performance standards given main emphasis by the Bank are concerned primarily with

---

9. *Ibid.*, p. 63. Whatever may have been the situation in 1958, U.S. authorities later showed little hestitation in bringing influence to bear in connection with bilateral foreign aid programs.

creditworthiness and relate to very much the same range of issues. How the longer-run considerations of growth and development fare in the preoccupations of the Bank and the Fund we shall consider below, after a brief look at the development of institutional relationships.

Institutional Relationships

It will be remembered that the Articles of Agreement of the Bank provide that, to become a member of that institution, a country must be a member of the Fund. And it was certainly the belief of the founding fathers that the two institutions should work closely together.[10] Their boards of governors meet jointly in annual Bank–Fund or Fund–Bank meetings. A number of Bank executive directors or their alternates have, moreover, also been simultaneously directors or alternates of the Fund. Furthermore, the Bank and the Fund have lived cheek-by-jowl throughout their active existence. After a few months in temporary quarters each institution occupied a separate floor of the same building at 1818 H Street in Washington, D.C. Later the Fund moved into a new building next door, leaving 1818 occupied wholly by the Bank. As both the Bank and the Fund expanded, they moved into two new buildings in the same block. In view of these facts it might have been thought that the connection between these two institutions was extremely close. But apart from some tentative approaches early in their history and increasing contacts in recent years, both organizations have been all too independent of each other. On the administrative side, although there has been increasing use of joint services, early decisions in the direction of separateness have been difficult to overcome.[11] On the substantive side, each institution main-

10. "Currency stabilization cannot be completely separated from the provision of long-term international credits. The two institutions designed to deal with these problems will find that cooperation between them is essential." U.S. Treasury Department, "Questions and Answers" [concerning the proposed World Bank]. IMF Records Office (June 10, 1944; processed).

11. In 1971 the following common services were administered by the Bank and were jointly financed: telephone services, language laboratory assistance, joint language training programs, secretarial services for joint office at the United Nations, credit union space, Paris office, interpreter services, parking, cash cage, computer services.

The following common services were administered by the Fund: joint general library, joint law library, the publications *Finance and Development* and *Direction of Trade*, liaison office, Concordia Apartments for housing fellows of the Bank's EDI and of the IMF Institute.

Annual meetings are administered in alternate years by the Bank and the Fund.

tains its own statistical services; the training program of the Bank and the Fund are operated by each independently, and although about 90 percent of the Fund's country studies are relevant to the work of the Bank and vice versa, joint use of personnel on country missions is infrequent, and jointly sponsored missions are unknown. In recent years the heavy overlap of research and responsibility has begun to be recognized, but there is still a long way to go.

The reasons for this partial estrangement are numerous. The Bank and Fund followed different courses of development, and at various stages of this development the prestige of one institution tended to overshadow the other. The two sets of Articles of Agreement foreshadowed a difference in the relationship of each institution with its member countries, and, as was noted in earlier chapters, the Bank management established a different relationship with its executive directors than was attained by the management of the Fund. Personality conflicts loomed rather large at certain stages. And, perhaps most important, during the 1950s both the Bank and the Fund held conceptions of their appropriate roles and functions that left little room for cooperation.

At a very early stage, in fact, before the two institutions were fully in operation, a "Report of a Joint Standing Committee on Provisional Procedure for Liaison between Fund and Bank on Financial Assistance to Members" was accepted by the executive directors of the Fund on November 12, 1946, and by the executive directors of the Bank on November 15. This joint committee agreed "that Fund and Bank activities are complementary in many respects and that it was essential that a procedure should be quickly prepared in order to ensure that there should be close collaboration on financial assistance to members, with due regard to the respective responsibilities of the two institutions."[12] By the spring of 1947 an elaborate system of liaison had been established.[13] For the preparation of the Bank's first loan

12. IBRD Files, R-37, 1946. The work of this committee is noted in Horsefield, *Chronicle*, p. 145.

13. Memorandum, M. M. Mendels, secretary of the Bank, to R. H. Demuth, April 23, 1947:

At present there are various liaison channels between the Bank and the Fund:

(a) The President of the Bank and the Managing Director of the Fund on major questions;

(b) The Joint Standing Committee of the Fund and Bank Executive Directors on financial assistance to Members;

(c) Departmental working liaison; for example, the two Research Departments, the two Legal Departments, the Bank's Treasurer with the Fund's Director of Operations and the Fund's Comptroller.

(d) The Secretaries.

—to France—the Fund made available the services of two of its experts. A Fund representative also accompanied the Bank mission to negotiate the program loan to Denmark. The Bank's first survey mission to Colombia in 1949 was joined by an expert from the Fund.

These early years, when both institutions considered their functions to be to an important extent complementary, were not, however, followed by the degree of collaboration that might have been expected therefrom. In 1950 both the Bank and the Fund were engaged in negotiations with the government of Guatemala, and the directors of the Fund feared the possibility of a serious divergence of advice. As a consequence the deputy managing director of the Fund (Overby) drafted a detailed memorandum suggesting closer working relations between the two institutions. These suggestions were received rather coolly by the management of the Bank, and nothing came of them.[14] At the seventh annual meeting of the board of governors of the Fund and Bank (1952), the governor from the United Kingdom suggested to the Committee on Finance and Organization that the possibility of closer liaison be examined. As a result of his initiative, the president of the Bank and the managing director of the Fund appointed a joint committee. The areas of possible collaboration examined by the committee were (a) the collection and compilation of basic economic data, (b) the uses of technical manpower on Bank and Fund missions, and (c) administrative services. The committee reported that the only area offering promise of joint action was (c), but that, since total expenditure on administrative services was small and the manpower of both agencies fully engaged, the promise was not sufficient to justify action. "As regards the other two categories," the IMF history reports, "the committee was even more cautious."[15] Collaboration might be advanced by frequent and regular meetings of the heads of operational departments, general counsels, secretaries, and the heads of research departments. But joint missions and joint research were not to be thought of.

Some notion of the attitude of the Fund toward collaboration at this period—and the Bank was fully as reserved—is given in the IMF history's discussion of a Bank request for personnel for two Bank missions that was received by the Fund directors.[16] The first involved a mission to Burma, and the request was granted only after assurance had been given by the managing director that "the independence of the staff member would be safeguarded, and that his views would be reflected in the mission's report." The second request was for an expert for a Bank mission to Nigeria. The U.S. repre-

14. IMF files EBM/571, Item 9.
15. Horsefield, *Chronicle*, p. 341.
16. *Ibid.*, p. 342.

sentative on the Fund board wanted to be assured that, if this were done, "each such request would be dealt with ad hoc, so as to avoid the possibility that on some future occasion a Bank mission might cover some important monetary or exchange problem in its report without this report having been reviewed by the Fund Board." This assurance was also given.

Although there were occasional discussions in the Bank staff in the 1950s concerning the desirability of closer relations with the Fund, little if anything was done about it.[17] No Bank official was asked during this period to serve on a Fund mission, and very few Fund experts were asked to serve on Bank missions. The Fund occasionally complained of encroachment by the Bank in areas of Fund engagement,[18] and the Bank sometimes complained of a failure to be informed and of conflicting advice to member governments.[19] On the whole, however, the relationship between the two institutions could be characterized as one of reserved neutrality. This did not prevent close collaboration between individuals on the Bank and Fund staffs, but these contacts were on a personal rather than an institutional basis.

The shift from an early period of close association to a later period of rather distant reserve was in part the result of the disparate rates of development of the Bank and Fund. The Bank was in business by 1947 with the first of its four reconstruction loans. And although project lending started slowly, it grew steadily. The Fund, on the other hand, was nearly moribund in the years before 1952. What saved it was the beginning in that year of the compulsory Article XIV discussions. These brought the staff of the IMF into

17. An Iliff–Brenner Report in 1953 (*Report of Bank–Fund Committee on Joint Services and Joint Missions*) recommended that periodic meetings be held between the heads of corresponding departments to help coordinate work programs, but the attempts made to follow this recommendation were sporadic. A memorandum to the Staff Loan Committee in 1959 considered various situations in which a joint Bank–Fund approach might be desirable, but the discussion indicated a consensus that any such approach should definitely be on an ad hoc basis and that no attempt should be made to establish general standards.

18. The Bank's first mission to Spain, in 1958, concluded that what Spain needed first was a stabilization program. When this view was communicated to the deputy managing director of the Fund, the Bank representatives were told in no uncertain terms that it was the responsibility of the Fund to decide when and if Spain needed such a program.

19. A rather sharp letter from Black to Jacobsson, June 18, 1957, complains of the failure of Fund personnel to inform Bank personnel on actions proposed in Colombia and goes on to say, "Furthermore, and even more directly related to the proposed Fund actions, our people have long been extremely skeptical about the wisdom of Colombia undertaking new fixed obligations to fund its commercial backlog. It is well known to your staff that we have repeatedly advised the Colombian Government against this sort of action." A little later a similar case of divergent advice occurred in Paraguay.

at least annual contact with most of its members and paved the way for the provision of much-needed technical assistance in the areas of monetary, fiscal, and exchange policies. But although the Fund was actively engaged in technical assistance operations, the drawing on its financial resources by member countries proceeded slowly, as is indicated in Table 16-1.

Table 16-1. *Summary of International Monetary Fund Transactions, Fiscal Years 1948–57*
Thousands of U.S. dollars

Fiscal year (ending April 30)	Total purchases by members	Total standby arrangements in force at end of fiscal years
1948	606,245	...
1949	119,438	...
1950	51,800	...
1951	28,000	...
1952	46,250	...
1953	66,125	55,000
1954	231,290	112,500
1955	48,750	112,500
1956	38,750	97,500
1957	1,114,047	1,212,280

Source: International Monetary Fund, annual reports.

The relatively large drawing in 1948, $300 million of which was by the United Kingdom, reflected an aberration on the part of the Fund management since it would be difficult to justify most of that drawing as short-term balance-of-payments support. This aberration, however, was short-lived, and the IMF executive directors immediately returned to the position from which they have never since departed that the resources of the Fund are available to deal only with temporary rather than with structural balance-of-payments disequilibrium. The very large increase in 1957 marks the Suez crisis and represents mainly support of the United Kingdom and France. It may be said that only after 1956 was the Fund really in business.

During its first ten years the IMF ran an annual deficit. In the same period the profits of the Bank continually increased and totaled $184 million by the end of fiscal year 1955. This difference caught the attention of financial communities around the world, and it must be said that various members of the Bank's management displayed a too obvious satisfaction with the relative success of their institution. It was during this period also that Eugene Black emerged as a prominent spokesman on international financial matters and became the dominant figure at Bank–Fund meetings. None of these developments inspired a cordiality in relationships.

The relative prestige of the two institutions began to change after 1956. The sizable assistance from the Fund to Britain and France in 1957 was followed by a substantial increase in the use by others of Fund resources. Moreover, 1956 witnessed the emergence on the scene of a very active and articulate managing director of the Fund, Per Jacobsson. Henceforth, although Bank–Fund collaboration did not notably increase, the relationship became in a sense a rivalry between more equal participants.

That collaboration was not more effective during the 1950s and early 1960s was also in large part the result of a rather narrow conception by both institutions of their proper role in international economic relations. Despite a few ventures in unconventional directions, the Bank adhered closely to project lending, and, as we have said, these projects tended to be large capital-intensive installations in the field of economic overhead. If a country was adjudged to be creditworthy and the project viable, the loan was made. If the country was not creditworthy, a loan was not made no matter how viable the project. The fitting of individual projects into a longer-term lending program came slowly, and even more slowly came an awareness of the complex relationship between stabilization and growth policies. Although the Fund never quite espoused the doctrine often attributed to it that stabilization is a necessary and sufficient condition for economic growth, its management often talked as if it did. In a background paper, for example, prepared in 1960 for a Development Assistance Group meeting in Paris, Per Jacobsson asserted that fifteen years of Fund experience made one conclusion evident:

> That conclusion is that monetary stability is an essential condition, and indeed the only reliable basis, for sustained growth. Monetary stability increases the resources that can be made available for development in two ways. In the first place, it increases the long-term flow of genuine domestic savings. In the second place, it stimulates the inflow of capital from abroad, as countries, by demonstrating their ability to run their domestic financial affairs completely, appear more creditworthy to foreign sources of capital.
>
> At least as important is the fact that monetary stability creates a climate for the proper allocation of resources saved in the economy or contributed by foreign capital.[20]

---

20. Jacobsson, *International Monetary Problems, 1957–63,* pp. 117–18. This statement might appear to go fairly far toward expressing the view that stabilization is not only a necessary but a sufficient condition for growth. But the same Per Jacobsson rarely let pass the occasion of his annual report without urging developed countries to channel at least 1 percent of their GNP into loans and grants to promote the development of less developed countries.

The Fund's heavy emphasis on monetary stability as a condition of economic growth and the Bank's view of its role as that of a project lender, especially for economic overhead projects, meant that the interconnections between stability and growth and the opportunities they offered for fruitful collaboration tended to be ignored.

Although the Bank and the Fund had a common interest in short-term stabilization measures as a means of increasing creditworthiness, their approaches tended to be independent. As Jacobsson noted above, one of the important advantages of monetary stability was the improvement of a country's creditworthiness. And views were expressed by members of the Bank staff that the "Bank might be even more interested than the Fund in a diligent search for stabilization measures outside the field of investment if only to minimize the cutback that might be necessary in the size of the investment program."[21] But situations in which the relations of stabilization measures to creditworthiness were jointly explored were exceedingly rare.

Changes in the top management of both the Bank and the Fund in 1963 offered the possibility of establishing new relationships between the Bretton Woods twins. George Woods became president of the Bank and Pierre-Paul Schweitzer, managing director of the Fund. Furthermore, by this time the stature of the Fund, which had been increased by large and growing financial and technical assistance relations with less developed countries and by the movement to the center of the stage of the problem of international liquidity, was fully equal to that of the Bank.

The Woods regime, as we have related elsewhere, was marked by the development of closer relations between the Bank and other United Nations agencies and by stronger efforts to assume leadership in assistance relationships between the developed and the less developed world. These efforts did not leave relations between the Bank and the Fund undisturbed. Before Schweitzer took office as managing director, he was visited in Paris by Woods, who wanted to promote cooperation. And in fact since 1963, however effective or ineffective staff cooperation may have been, relations at the top have been close and amicable. It has not been easy, however, to reverse practices and attitudes developed during two decades of competitive independence. In 1964 the IMF established a Fiscal Policy Division, one of a number of steps suggesting a greater interest in the relation of stabilization policy to economic development. The relations established in 1966 between this division and a similar unit in the Bank represent the high point to date in Bank–

21. Memorandum of W. Gilmartin to M. M. Rosen, "Bank–Fund Collaboration" (Jan. 23, 1959).

Fund collaboration. It was recognized that technical assistance in the fiscal field belongs to the Fund, and it was agreed that the staff of the division would be increased to permit the attachment of IMF fiscal experts to Bank missions. There is in the fiscal field a relatively free exchange of information between the two institutions, as well as fairly effective coordination of research and an exchange of personnel. At about the same time the Economic Committee of the Bank began to invite Fund personnel to participate in the discussion of country reports and country program papers.

In 1965 discussions took place between senior officials of the Bank and Fund in an attempt to define areas of interest and responsibility. These discussions produced two documents which, after much revision on both sides, ultimately emerged as joint statements by the president of the Bank and the managing director of the Fund and were considered by the boards of directors of both institutions. The first was a memorandum dated January 19, 1966, which dealt mainly with procedures. The second, dated December 9, 1966, set out the primary interests of the Bank and the Fund and was designed to assure, as far as possible, a consistent view on advice to be given to member countries. The second document generated a Bank operational memorandum entitled "Bank/Fund Collaboration," which guided the staff of the Bank until the memorandum was revised in the spring of 1970.[22] It was not the purpose of the operational memorandum to draw sharp lines of jurisdiction but rather "to emphasize how large is the area of common interest." It insisted, in fact, that no aspect of the "structure and progress" of member countries should be ignored by either institution. Within this range of common interest it is important that there be consistency in the advice given to member countries. "To this end, staff members of both institutions should be guided by the following paragraphs":

As between the two institutions, the Bank is recognized as having primary responsibility for the composition and appropriateness of development programs and project evaluation, including development priorities. On those matters, the Fund, and particularly the field missions of the Fund, should inform themselves of the established views and positions of the Bank and adopt those views as the working basis for their own work. . . .

As between the two institutions, the Fund is recognized as having primary responsibility for exchange and restrictive systems, for adjustment of temporary balance of payments disequilibrium and for evaluating and assisting members to work out stabilization programs as a sound basis for economic advance.

The specification of particular areas of competence and responsibility for one institution did not prevent the staff of the other from having independent

22. IBRD, Operational memorandum 9.01 (Jan. 12, 1967).

and divergent views in these areas. But the Bank was ostensibly prevented from presenting its views to a member government in the area of Fund responsibility without the prior consent of the Fund, and vice versa. This, in fact, is a directive that seems from time to time to be honored in the breach.

The active discussion of Bank–Fund relationships in the years 1965–67 and the resultant directives might be thought to mark an entirely new chapter in this history of collaboration. But the language of the agreements was very general, and the directives left substantial room for maneuvering. A senior official of the Bank commented on an early version to the effect that "the statement is vague enough to be innocuous and leaves the staff of both institutions reasonably free to act in accordance with the needs of particular situations." Another senior official said to the authors that it was remarkable, in view of the seriousness of the discussion, how little progress was made in resolving difficulties. Still these discussions and the formal agreements between top management, ratified by boards of directors, did serve to indicate to the staffs of both institutions that earlier attitudes of suspicion and reserve might well be modified if not abandoned. Since the mid-1960s, collaboration between the Bank and Fund on matters of common interest has depended largely on the personalities of officials holding parallel positions in the respective institutions. Relationships have been particularly close in the Latin American area, partly because problems of inflation have been of acute concern to both the Bank and the Fund. They have been on occasion relatively reserved in other areas. But in general, under both Woods and McNamara, collaboration has become substantially more effective.

Bank–Fund relationships were again subject to extended discussion in the spring of 1970, largely as the result of a recommendation of the Pearson Commission. The commission urged that "the World Bank and the IMF, in countries where both operate, adopt procedures for preparing unified country assessments and assuring consistent policy advice."[23] The president of the Bank, on February 18, 1970, distributed to the board of directors a memorandum prepared jointly with the managing director of the Fund on "Further Steps for Collaboration between the IMF and the IBRD." This

---

23. *Partners in Development,* Report of the Commission on International Development, Lester B. Pearson, chairman (Praeger, 1969), p. 220. Of course, the report notes,

> the two institutions have somewhat different functions which require some differences in priorities, but we believe that measures should be taken to ensure that differences are resolved at headquarters so that it is not left to the recipient to calculate whose advice he can ignore at lesser cost. . . . The two institutions have different expertise to contribute and the low-income countries are entitled to a fully integrated view in terms of development objectives, and investment and growth policies which take into account monetary, fiscal, and exchange rate issues.

memorandum was devoted largely to procedural changes designed to avoid duplication of effort and to assure that Bank and Fund appraisals and policy recommendations were broadly consistent. The memorandum provided for joint consultations before the departure of a Bank or Fund mission, debriefing after the return of a mission, the circulation of draft documents, the coordination of technical assistance, and collaboration in the field.

The Board had no difficulty in accepting the recommendations in the joint statement, but it was pointed out that this did not meet the Pearson recommendation that the Bank and Fund should prepare unified country assessments and assure consistent policy advice. As one director said, this would be completely impractical and would indeed assume a complete integration of the boards of the two institutions.[24] This appeared to be the view of the other directors also.

Even without the introduction of unified country assessments, the Bank and the Fund have moved closer together. But there is still much unnecessary duplication of effort, particularly in the collection of data of common interest; collaboration, except in the area of fiscal policy, is sometimes largely formal; and the question of satisfactory relationships of stabilization policies and growth policies, which should be of central concern to both organizations, remains on the periphery of attention.[25]

24. Verbatim report of the executive directors, Aug. 13, 1970.
25. The initiation by the IMF in 1967 of Special Drawing Rights (SDRs) and various proposals to "link" these rights with assistance to less developed countries may at some time in the future add another dimension to relations between the Fund and the Bank. This could happen if some part of the newly created SDRs were transferred, say, to IDA to be used for development credits. The primary purpose of the creation of SDRs is to provide an orderly increase in global reserves, and the allocation to various member countries is on the basis of their Fund quotas. If any reallocation of SDRs were to take place, either through Fund action or through the action of recipient countries, the costs would be borne by countries disposing of less than their quota shares, which, to reestablish these shares, would have to earn SDRs or their equivalent in convertible currencies by exporting real resources. The beneficiaries, of course, would be those countries, presumably less developed countries, which would have more than their quota shares to be used either for increasing imports or augmenting their own reserves.
Proposals for linking international credit creation with development assistance go back at least to the "Stamp Plan" (see Maxwell Stamp, "The Fund and the Future," *Lloyds Bank Review* [October 1958]) and since 1967 have been the subject of vigorous debate—by, among others, two groups of experts appointed by UNCTAD, the Subcommittee on International Exchange and Payments of the U.S. Congress Joint Economic Committee, and the Inter American Committee on the Alliance for Progress. Needless to say, the subject has been under close scrutiny by the staff of the Fund and by its executive directors. It seems unnecessary for us to enter into this debate here, but we say more about a possible link between SDRs and development assistance in Chapter 21.

It might be thought that the annual meetings of the boards of governors of the Bank and the Fund would be an effective instrument for promoting collaboration. These are meetings of substantial importance in financial circles, bringing together not only members of the governing boards and senior staff members of the two organizations but also leading members of financial communities throughout the noncommunist world. But although these meetings serve a useful purpose as a sounding board for the views of central bankers, finance ministers, the president of the Bank, and the managing director of the Fund and also provide an opportunity for personal contacts and much conviviality, the subject of Bank–Fund collaboration is rarely addressed.

Stabilization and Growth

There is no doubt that, over time, the Bank and the Fund have influenced each other's policies. The Fund has directed the Bank's attention to the developmental consequences of stabilization measures. Indeed the Bank has generally accepted the Fund proposition that stabilization is a necessary though not sufficient condition for growth. Furthermore, the Bank has frequently thrown its weight behind conditions proposed by the Fund. In Ceylon in 1965, in the United Arab Republic in 1964, and on many occasions in Latin America, agreement with the Fund has been a condition of Bank lending.[26] The Bank and the Fund both participate in a number of consultative groups and consortia, and although there have been complaints within the Bank that in some of the group meetings, Fund representatives limit their participation to admonitions against inflation, in others the Fund has participated actively in shaping policy recommendations.

On the other hand, although there is general agreement in the Bank that stabilization is important, there is not always agreement that the Fund's stabilization proposals are appropriate, and there is some evidence that over time the Bank's views may have influenced the Fund's views. In general the Bank does not appear to be as allergic to inflation as the Fund so long as there are appropriate changes in critically important prices. Of decisive importance are exchange and interest rates and, of somewhat less importance, public utility rates and food prices. In a number of Latin American inflations the Bank has favored a flexible or fluctuating exchange rate as the course of

26. In recent years, however, the Bank has refrained from insisting on compliance with Fund conditions as a requirement for lending, at least in Latin America.

action best designed to maintain continuously proper incentives to export and *dis*incentives to import. This was the principal condition of Bank lending in Chile in the latter part of the 1960s. In Brazil in 1967–68 the Bank favored a flexible exchange rate policy as against the Fund's initial recommendation of a sharp devaluation. The same divergence of views existed with respect to Argentina in the late 1960s. In the case of Brazil the policy of the government turned, in fact, toward a floating exchange rate. There is some evidence that in recent years the Fund, at least in Latin America, has shown increasing tolerance for exchange rate flexibility, though whether this owes anything to the influence of the Bank, it is impossible to say.

Exchange rate policy is undoubtedly the substantive area that has caused the Bank and the Fund the greatest difficulty. The Fund some time ago recognized, though grudgingly, that the Bank had a legitimate interest in this area and could appropriately discuss the problem in country reports. Shadow rates of exchange have for a long time been used by the Bank in appraising projects; the rate of exchange clearly affects the allocation of resources among sectors of an economy and consequently the pattern of economic growth; rates of exchange, by influencing export earnings and import expenditures, bear directly on considerations of creditworthiness. On the other hand, it has been recognized in several statements of relations between the Bank and the Fund that the Fund has primary responsibility in the field of exchange rate policy, a field in which the Bank is expected not to present its views to member governments without the consent of the Fund.[27] Although this understanding has been violated on a number of occasions, with a resulting protest from the managing director of the Fund, these violations are exceptional. Discussions of exchange rate policy in the Bank's country reports are cleared with the Fund, and in general there is a pooling of views of Bank and Fund staff members on aspects of exchange rate policy of interest to both organizations. It is understood that the actual negotiation of changes in exchange rates is a prerogative of the Fund and must be conducted in strict confidence.

The Fund's influence on interest rates is mainly through recommendations affecting the quantity of money, particularly those relating to credit ceilings. The Bank has approached this problem more directly. As we emphasized in Chapter 8 on Project Lending, the Bank has frequently used shadow rates of interest in evaluating projects. In inflationary situations the Bank has frequently attempted to condition its loans to credit institutions by insisting that these institutions lend at a positive real rate of interest, that is, a rate in excess of the rate of inflation. Sometimes it has failed in such attempts. In 1968,

27. IBRD, Operational memorandum 9.01 (May 31, 1970).

for example, a proposed Bank loan to an agricultural credit agency in Brazil was conditioned on the agency's charging a positive real rate of interest on its loans to farmers. The Ministry of Finance refused to accept this condition on the ground that farmers would not borrow at interest rates calculated on the basis of an index representing all prices when the prices of their own products have been from time to time subject to control. Under these circumstances who is to say whether the farmers or the minister of finance were wrong?

As we have seen in previous chapters, the conditions the Bank attached to power loans in inflationary situations in Latin America have had a very significant influence on electricity rates. In part the Bank's concern has arisen from the conviction that financial viability is a necessary condition for administrative independence. But more important has been a concern for public savings and a fear of the inflationary consequences of continuous government subsidy of public utility enterprises. At various stages government subsidies to the railways in Brazil have approached 2 percent of GNP. The principal condition attached to the large transportation lending program in Brazil proposed in 1968 was a sharp increase in railway rates. The Bank's main interest in the price of food grains and other agricultural products is that adequate incentives for agricultural output be provided. In inflationary situations in Latin America and in southern Asia, attempts to control food prices in the interests of urban labor have frequently tended to impede economic growth.

The Bank has taken a somewhat more lenient attitude toward inflation than the Fund, provided that a borrower was willing to adjust the critical prices discussed above. But of course the Fund is interested also in the price adjustments even though the priorities assigned to them and the measures proposed to bring them about may be different. Even when there is no difference in the analyses on which the Bank and Fund act, there may be a difference in behavior since the Fund feels frequently that it is the only force for monetary and fiscal restraint among a group of spending interests, including the Bank.

The principal difficulty in Bank–Fund collaboration is not that there are sharp differences in the analyses and prescriptions of the two institutions but that both take a relatively short-term view of their responsibilities toward members. The Fund, of course, can claim that it was established to deal primarily with short-term balance-of-payments difficulties. But it has described itself, for many years at least, as a development institution, and, to the extent that the Fund's own resources have been augmented on many occasions by the lending power of the World Bank, regional banks, and bilateral assistance programs, it should perhaps have been able to take a somewhat broader view of its opportunities and responsibilities. The Bank has no such defense. It was established to finance development, and development is a long-term process. To be sure, the Bank expects its loans to be repaid, which focuses attention on creditworthiness; but creditworthiness, as we have said, depends in the long run on growth.

Neither the Bank nor the Fund, of course, in emphasizing the importance of stabilization policies, is concerned exclusively with the short-run consequences of these policies. Both institutions emphasize the importance of increased domestic savings and recommend tax measures to expand public investment rather than public consumption, perhaps without always having in mind the effect of these measures on private savings. Both have attempted to correct price distortions in the economy, particularly interest rates, exchange rates, public utility rates, and agricultural prices, which have long-term as well as short-term consequences. The Bank's lending policy attempts to correct sectoral imbalances by financing projects in obvious bottleneck areas. All of these may be said to promote economic development.

If the Bank and the Fund have not moved further away from relatively short-term considerations, it may be the result of an overemphasis on stabilization as a necessary, though not sufficient, condition of growth—to the neglect of the equally important proposition that, in many situations, growth is a necessary, though not sufficient, condition for effective stabilization. If this reciprocal relationship between stability and growth has been neglected, this neglect is not chargeable exclusively to the Bank and the Fund. This is a relatively underdeveloped area in economic analysis despite the fact that many medium-term development plans have been wrecked by stabilization difficulties and many stabilization plans have foundered on a too rapid expansion of development expenditure. Still the neglect of this relationship in economic analysis offers little excuse for the failure of the Bank and the Fund to give the problem a central position in their own research activity.

The different concerns of the Fund and the Bank resemble in some respects the different concerns of ministries of finance and of planning commissions, and as the Bank moves increasingly into the preparation of five-year lending programs, the resemblance tends to become closer. Finance ministries should, but usually do not, take due account, in formulating their short-term revenue and expenditure policies, of the consequences for the planning commission's development targets. Planning commissions should, but usually do not, shape their investment proposals with full regard for the financial limitations as seen by the ministry of finance. Failures to establish effective integration of short- and long-term planning dot the development horizon of the less developed countries and are not unknown in the developed world. Clearly a satisfactory reconciliation of short- and longer-term objectives is not an easy task. Nor is it easy to satisfy the different obligations of the Fund and Bank without a greater integration, or at least coordination, of the policies advocated by the two organizations. A greater degree of coordination and integration has, in fact, in recent years characterized the activities of the Bank and the Fund. In general the staff of each organization is now well briefed with respect to the problems of specific countries. They both participate in presentations to consortia and consultative groups. Although cooperation in the fiscal area is somewhat better organized than elsewhere, earlier attitudes of suspicion and overt hostility are giving way to more open dealing in other fields of common interest. Furthermore, it is inevitable that, in dealing with the knotty and increasingly important problems of debt renegotiation and rescheduling, the staffs of the Bank and Fund will have to work closely together. Cooperation will be further strengthened if a tie is ever established between the issuance of Special Drawing Rights and development finance through the instrumentality of IDA.

Still, if the Bank and Fund are to work together effectively and fulfill the expectations of the Bretton Woods founders, a good deal remains to be done. There continues to exist a sizable overlap in the fact-gathering activities of the two institutions, which a coordination of statistical work could overcome. The cordial atmosphere that characterizes relationships at the top of the two organizations has not yet penetrated uniformly to lower levels. A joint study needs to be made of the relationships of stabilization and growth policies and of how, in countries of concern to both the Bank and the Fund, the particular responsibilities of each institution can be exercised with due regard for the interests of the other. What is required in Bank–Fund dealings with member countries is a single set of policy recommendations covering both short- and long-term issues. This is not likely to come about without an acceptance, despite the objections of some of the executive directors, of the Pearson Commission recommendation that "the World Bank and the IMF, in countries where both operate, should adopt procedures for preparing unified country assessments."

CHAPTER SEVENTEEN

The Bank Group and Other International Organizations

ON NOVEMBER 15, 1947, the International Bank for Reconstruction and Development reluctantly and warily, but formally and officially, became part of the network known as the "United Nations system." The legal agreement confirming its status as a specialized agency was more nearly a declaration of independence from the global organization than of cooperation with it. The Bank, as we reported in Chapter 3, for some years went to considerable pains to keep its relationship with the United Nations as well as with the other specialized agencies at a long arm's length.

The creation of the UN Special Fund in late 1957 marked a major turning point in Bank–United Nations relations. The turn was not a hairpin curve. Relations had been growing more cordial for several years before the General Assembly decided to establish a fund under UN auspices to provide grants for "preinvestment" projects—not because member governments had long perceived the need for this kind of fund, but because they could not agree on the more ambitious step of establishing an institution to provide capital for investment projects on terms more lenient than those of the Bank. The Special Fund provided a new kind of technical assistance, and the Bank played a constructive behind-the-scenes role in moving it from the drawing board to the operational phase. Like other specialized agencies, the Bank became an executing agency for the Special Fund, but at the policy level its relationship was unique.

The arrangements whereby specialized agencies of the United Nations

Note. This chapter deals with the Bank Group's relations with multilateral organizations other than the International Monetary Fund. Bank–Fund relations were the subject of Chapter 16.

became executing agencies of the Special Fund (financed by the latter to perform agreed functions) may have served as partial precedents for the cooperative arrangements negotiated by the Bank in 1964 whereby the Food and Agriculture Organization of the United Nations (FAO) and the United Nations Educational, Scientific, and Cultural Organization (Unesco) became, in a sense, executing agencies of the Bank in project identification and preparation. The Bank had decided independently to expand its lending in agriculture and education and, rather than relying entirely on its own staff, to collaborate closely with the appropriate functional agencies of the United Nations in these sectors. The experience with FAO and Unesco led, in turn, to a similar cooperative agreement in 1971 with the World Health Organization (WHO) for work in the fields of water supply and sewerage.

In this chapter, we shall analyze in more detail the interacting processes whereby the Bank moved from an isolated and peripheral position in the United Nations system to a more central role, while the system itself moved from research, discussion, and small-scale technical assistance to active participation in promoting development at local, national, and regional levels. At the same time, we shall try to bear in mind that the United Nations system is also a nonsystem. It lacks any real general staff. Each of the dozen or so specialized agencies has its own charter, membership, governing council, and rules of procedure. Organizations such as the United Nations Conference on Trade and Development (UNCTAD) and the United Nations Industrial Development Organization (UNIDO) function very much like specialized agencies but are organizations of the General Assembly. The Bank and the Fund, which are specialized agencies, function quite differently from other such agencies. The Bank itself has acquired affiliates, which have formal and informal relationships with other international bodies. Moreover, conflicts can arise between the Bank Group and the United Nations that show the tensions inherent in the simultaneous pursuit of functional and political, or governmental, approaches to world order. Witness the apparent impasse over the appropriate treatment of Portugal and South Africa because of their colonial and apartheid policies.

The proliferation of international machinery since the close of World War II has not been confined to machinery within the UN system or to agencies with jurisdictions that do not overlap those of the Bank. From the Bank's point of view, the most important international development body totally outside the UN system is the Development Assistance Committee (DAC) of the Organisation for Economic Co-operation and Development (OECD) in Paris. The relationship of the Bank with OECD/DAC has on the whole been harmonious and fruitful, though the Bank has opposed (and has not been alone in opposing) the assumption of operational functions by OECD in the field of development.

While the Bank Group remains the only public international source of investment finance that is virtually world wide in scope, it no longer enjoys a monopoly position on any continent. Accordingly, we devote a section of this chapter to the relations of the World Bank Group with the Inter-American, Asian, and African development banks, and with certain other regional development financing institutions. The regional banks, unlike the World Bank, are not formally linked to the United Nations.

Pre-1958 Relations with the United Nations

After the unhappy experience of negotiating the agreement whereby the Bank became a specialized agency of the United Nations, the attitude of the Bank was "even though we're married, we can still sleep in separate rooms and live our own lives." The attitude of the UN was "you have married into a patriarchy in which the General Assembly is the *pater familias;* it will address you directly and through the machinery of its Economic and Social Council; pay attention when it does."

The Economic and Social Council (ECOSOC), its commissions and subcommissions, and the early expert groups appointed by the UN secretary-general at the request of ECOSOC tended to be severely critical of the Bank. As has been noted in earlier chapters, they felt that the Bank's level of lending for development was far too low, its loan terms too hard, its project approach too narrow, and its procedures too rigid. The Bank reciprocated by regarding the UN and its subsidiaries as busybody empire-builders or do-gooders, blind to the realities of international finance, bent on jeopardizing the Bank's standing on Wall Street, agitating for more development finance than could be used productively, and sending out survey missions that should have been organized by the Bank and would have been better if they had been.

ECOSOC's subcommission on employment and economic stability considered the Bank in 1949 "a useful but a minor addition to existing financial machinery at a time when world uncertainty makes venture capital extremely unventuresome."[1] A high official of the Bank considered some jealousy on the part of the UN inevitable because it was natural for the UN to think it

1. UN Subcommission on Employment and Economic Stability, *Report of the Third Session,* Doc. E/CN. 1/66 (April 26, 1949), par. 32.

"too bad that all this money was wasted on us when they had the really intelligent ideas as to how to use it."[2]

Noneconomic as well as economic questions were made more complicated by mutual suspicion. Article 102 of the United Nations Charter, for example, plainly requires that every treaty and international agreement entered into by any member of the UN be registered with the secretariat and published by it; unless it is so registered, it cannot be invoked before any organ of the UN (including the World Court). With the approval of the Bank's executive directors, however, its general counsel, Chester A. McLain, in late 1946 notified the UN legal department that he did not believe that the Bank's loan and guarantee agreements, being technical and financial in character, required registration.

In early 1948, the secretary of the Bank offered to *file* and *record* the agreements, but not to *register* them. The UN secretariat, however, refused to accept the documents for filing and recording. It advised the Bank that loan and guarantee agreements with members of the UN were subject to registration and not eligible for filing and recording. By May 1951 other specialized agencies and many member governments had registered agreements of various kinds, including many of a technical and financial nature. Discussions between the UN secretariat and the Bank were therefore reopened.

A reasonably clear and simple procedure was worked out and became effective in 1952. Basically it provided that the Bank would register loan and guarantee agreements between the Bank and states that are members of the United Nations. It would submit, for filing and recording, agreements with states not members of the UN. The Bank would neither register nor file letters exchanged with borrowers that concerned conditions to be satisfied prior to the coming into force of loans, and various other subsidiary loan documents. The procedure, in the view of the Bank's general counsel, offered various advantages and safeguards and "no substantial disadvantages."[3]

To date, the World Bank and IDA are the only international lending agencies that publish their loan agreements and, in addition, register them with

2. Oral History Project of Columbia University, interviews recorded in the summer of 1961 on the International Bank for Reconstruction and Development (cited hereinafter as "Oral History"). Quotation is from interview of Davidson Sommers, p. 9.

3. Memorandum of May 15, 1952, from Davidson Sommers (successor to Chester McLain as general counsel) to Eugene Black, "Registration of Bank's Loan and Guarantee Agreements under the United Nations Charter." See also A. Broches and Shirley Boskey, "Theory and Practice of Treaty Registration, with Particular Reference to Agreements of the International Bank," *Netherlands International Law Review* (Issue 2–3, 1957), pp. 28–34.

the United Nations. UN registration and subsequent publication in the United Nations Treaty Series has the political advantage of putting it clearly on record that Bank and IDA agreements are open covenants and underscores their character as treaties in the broad sense of the term. In view of the substantial trouble and expense to which the United Nations has been put in order to include loan and guarantee agreements of the Bank Group in its treaty series, it may by now regret its earlier insistence on including them. The Bank, for its part, has fully overcome its original misgivings. According to Aron Broches—the Bank's present general counsel and an early proponent of registration—registration helps cure the tendency of negotiators to relegate politically sensitive obligations to "side letters." If these letters are intended to be binding, the Bank will include them in the registration documents, and they will eventually be published along with the principal agreement.

The General Assembly at first devoted considerable time and energy to reviewing the activities of the various specialized agencies but soon left this responsibility to its Economic and Social Council. ECOSOC was willing to talk at length about the work of the agencies—the annual report of the president of the World Bank continues to be one of the high points on its agenda —but ECOSOC was and is ill equipped to exercise substantive or administrative coordination. In 1946, "desirous of discharging effectively its responsibility . . . to coordinate the activities of the specialized agencies," it requested the UN secretary-general to establish as a standing committee the Administrative Committee on Coordination (ACC), consisting of the secretary-general as chairman and the heads of the specialized agencies as members.[4]

World Bank participation in the ACC was riskless because its basic agreement with the UN exempted the Bank from budgetary control and protected it from other types of coordination. Furthermore, the other specialized agencies were almost as determined as the Bank was to resist coordination. The ACC, though it owes its existence to an ECOSOC resolution, is in reality an interagency committee whose members are responsible to their own organizations. It meets twice a year in closed sessions.

The committee is not without substantive accomplishments, but its chief value has probably been the opportunity it has provided for the top execu-

4. For information on ECOSOC–ACC relations, see Martin Hill, "The Administrative Committee on Co-ordination," in Evan Luard (ed.), *The Evolution of International Organizations* (Praeger, 1966). See also George A. Codding, Jr., "The Relationship of the League and the United Nations with the Independent Agencies: A Comparison," *Annals of International Studies* (Geneva, 1970).

tives of the major units in the UN system, whose offices are in different cities, to get to know each other and learn more about each other's work. Though differences between the structure and organization of the Bank and Fund and that of other specialized agencies place extra constraints on their interagency relationships, considerable cooperation and some coordination have evolved within the system as a result of the interchanges of view.

The structural and organizational differences to which we refer extend beyond the Bank's budgetary autonomy and include the absence of Communist countries (other than Yugoslavia) from its membership roster, its system of weighted voting, its ties to finance ministries and treasuries rather than to foreign offices or to functional ministries (such as agriculture and labor departments), and its greater freedom to hire personnel without reference to their country of origin. The effect of these features of the Bank is a different balance of power within the organization between the more and the less developed countries, an ability (during its early years at least) to pay higher salaries to its staff, and an ability to say "no" to more governments without jeopardizing the reelection of the chief executive or the adoption of his budget. These in turn have encouraged the Bank to consider itself more competent, more independent, more nonpolitical, and better equipped than other agencies to promote the true welfare of its clients.

Until the Expanded Program of Technical Assistance (EPTA) was established in 1950, the Bank could also feel that the principal function of the UN and the other specialized agencies was to convene conferences, collect figures, and set standards, whereas it (the Bank) had an operational function, a job to do—in short, loans to make. The launching of EPTA gave the entire UN system an operational role. It carried employees of the international agencies to the most faraway communities, enabling them to touch in a direct way the daily lives of large numbers of ordinary people.

At the top of the EPTA pyramid were two pieces of machinery. The Technical Assistance Committee was an intergovernmental organ, a committee of ECOSOC, responsible for reviewing the annual program submitted to it by the Technical Assistance Board (TAB) and for certain other duties. TAB was an interagency body composed of representatives of the secretariats of the participating agencies plus an executive chairman appointed by the UN secretary-general after consultation with the participating agencies.[5] In-

5. The participating agencies included the UN Technical Assistance Administration (UNTAA), which is the organization within the UN secretariat established to administer technical assistance in fields not covered by other agencies or falling positively within the scope of the United Nations—public administration, for example. Next to the FAO, the UNTAA was the largest claimant for EPTA funds during the early life of the program.

tended to be an integrating and coordinating body, it promptly devoted itself to preserving the autonomy of the participating agencies.

The Bank was not a participating agency in the sense of receiving allocations from EPTA to finance technical assistance projects. As we said in Chapter 10, it developed a technical assistance program of its own. It was, however, a nonvoting member of TAB. As an "observer," it played a passive role and continued to regard itself primarily as a financier of investment projects.

Near the base of the EPTA pyramid were the resident representatives selected by the executive chairman of TAB, in consultation with the heads of the participating agencies, to represent EPTA and provide a measure of coordination at the country level. Their efforts were resisted by the Food and Agriculture Organization, the World Health Organization, and most of the other participating agencies, as moves toward centralization of the UN system. The Bank wanted nothing to do with the resident representatives ("res-reps," as they were called), and because it was not a recipient of EPTA funds, it could succeed admirably in this uncooperative aim.

Although the Bank did not "join" the UN until 1958, when it helped to bring the United Nations Special Fund into being, the distance between it and the UN began shrinking before then. Dag Hammarskjöld succeeded Trygve Lie as UN secretary-general in 1953 and consciously cultivated an improved relationship with Eugene Black. In contrast to McCloy and Garner, Black was at least outwardly friendly to the UN (though not above grumbling privately to his colleagues). He was also aware that the Bank's reputation on Wall Street was by then secure enough to withstand the apparent stigma of better relations with the UN. David Owen, the UN's first under-secretary-general for economic affairs, became the full-time executive chairman of the Technical Assistance Board. In 1955 Philippe de Seynes became under-secretary-general for economic and social affairs. He had had no role in negotiating the basic agreement between the Bank and the UN or sending the 1948 survey mission to Haiti or selecting the experts who had made well publicized reports on development that included severe criticism of the Bank. The Bank staff found de Seynes, a French national, easier to deal with than Owen.

By the mid-1950s, moreover, the Russians had huffed and puffed as much as they could about the departure of Poland and Czechoslovakia as members of the Bank, and most of the governments represented at General Assembly and ECOSOC sessions were fed up with Cold War debates. To Latin America, Asia, and Africa, getting on with the job of economic development was infinitely more important. The steam they generated at UN meetings in favor of new sources of development finance helped build up pressure for the International Finance Corporation, which was established in 1956 as an affiliate of the World Bank.

Moreover, in 1956, war had broken out in the Middle East. Divisive in innumerable more important ways, it did provide a fresh opportunity for collaboration between the Bank and the UN at the staff level. Hammarskjöld had been given two monumental jobs—to establish the United Nations Emergency Force in the area and to clear the Suez Canal of the forty-eight ships, tugs, barges, and bridges sunk or scuttled in that waterway. To organize and expedite clearance of the canal, he asked Black to put at the disposal of the United Nations the former engineering adviser to the Bank, Lieutenant General R. A. Wheeler, and another Bank consultant. Black concurred, the clearance was brilliantly executed, and "it was a source of gratification to the Bank that Lt. General Wheeler and Mr. Connors should have been so prominently associated with the operation. Also at the request of the United Nations, the Bank acted as its fiscal agent for the funds contributed by various governments towards the cost of the clearance of the Canal."[6]

Thus the stage for more lasting cooperation between the Bank and the rest of the UN system had been well set by late 1957, when the General Assembly established the UN Special Fund.

Post-1958 Relations with UN Development Machinery

Commenting in 1970 on the Bank's relations with other international institutions, President McNamara said,

Next only to the IMF [International Monetary Fund], our closest institutional relationships are with the UNDP [United Nations Development Program, the result of a 1966 "merger" of the UN Special Fund and the Expanded Program of Technical Assistance]. Since the establishment of the Special Fund, a principal function of the UNDP has been the financing of preinvestment studies. The principal function of the World Bank Group is the financing of investment projects. Preinvestment and investment are, of course, two stages of a single economic process. UNDP feasibility studies, for example, even when their findings are favorable, are fully useful only if the projects studied can ultimately be

6. IBRD, *Twelfth Annual Report, 1956–1957*, p. 26. Mr. Black, in one of his several successful forays into the realm of international diplomacy, was also instrumental in bringing about the 1958 financial settlement between the United Arab Republic and the Suez Canal Company resulting from nationalization of the Canal by the UAR in 1956. For a lively account of how Hammarskjöld came to request Wheeler's services and what Wheeler accomplished, see Joseph P. Lash, *Dag Hammarskjöld: Custodian of the Brushfire Peace* (Doubleday and Company, 1961), pp. 94–97.

financed and, conversely, investment projects proposed to the Bank can be properly appraised and funded only if satisfactory feasibility studies of these projects have previously been made.[7]

If preinvestment and investment are but stages of a single economic process—and few would dispute this—one might question the Solomonesque wisdom of the international community in assigning them to separate multilateral agencies with different memberships, financial policies, and administrative practices. The decision reflected a political compromise resulting from the long campaign of the less developed countries to establish a capital development fund under UN auspices.[8] The United Nations Special Fund would, in deference to the less developed countries, be clearly differentiated from technical assistance. In deference to the United States in particular and the other developed countries to a lesser extent, it would be equally clearly differentiated from capital assistance.

At the ECOSOC session in the summer of 1957, a resolution had been adopted by a vote of fifteen to three (with the United States, the United Kingdom, and Canada opposed) urging the General Assembly to establish a Special United Nations Fund for Economic Development (SUNFED). The United States fully expected the General Assembly in the fall to vote for SUNFED by a big majority, leaving the U.S. delegation isolated in opposition, unless a constructive alternative were found. The alternative proposed by the United States and modified during debate was the Special Fund, which the General Assembly decided on December 14, 1957, to establish.[9]

Relations with Special Fund, UNDP, and UNCTAD

Even before December 14, there had been discussion within the Bank, and between the Bank and the UN, regarding the Bank's role in the proposed UN Special Fund. The outcome of these discussions was an agreement early in 1958 to give the Bank a special position vis-à-vis the Special Fund that would distinguish it from the other specialized agencies and recognize the symbiotic relationship between investment and preinvestment. The device agreed on was a Consultative Board, consisting of the UN secretary-general, the president of the World Bank, and the executive chairman of the Technical Assistance Board, which was to meet periodically with and advise the managing director of the Special Fund. At the time, it was not clear who the

7. Robert S. McNamara, Address before the Economic and Social Council, Nov. 13, 1970.
8. See Chapter 12, above; also John G. Hadwen and Johan Kaufmann, *How United Nations Decisions Are Made* (Leiden: A. W. Sijthoff, 1960).
9. GA Res. 1219 (XII).

managing director would be, but it was agreed that in the selection process the Bank would be consulted de facto, if not de jure, and also that the Bank would undertake some projects for the Special Fund.

The ECOSOC meeting in the summer of 1958 rejected a USSR proposal to exclude the Bank from the Consultative Board. The Special Fund became operational on January 1, 1959, with Paul G. Hoffman as its managing director and an eighteen-nation Governing Council to provide general policy guidance.[10] The Bank loaned staff to Hoffman to help launch the Special Fund.

The Consultative Board provided a mechanism whereby project proposals could be circulated for comment. Like the ACC, it meets at the head-of-agency level. Eugene Black and his successors on the board have played an active role in advising the managing director of the Special Fund (later the administrator of the UNDP) in the examination and appraisal of proposed projects and programs.[11] At the operating level, as we noted in Chapter 10, the Bank was better equipped than any other specialized agency to serve as an executing agency for the UN Special Fund in carrying out preinvestment studies.

The management and staff of the Special Fund, eager to build up the field offices, which were headed by resident representatives, into effective coordinating centers for all technical and preinvestment assistance provided by the UN system, encountered considerable resistance from the technical assistance agencies, which has only gradually been overcome. The Bank, though it invented and promulgated the term "aid coordination groups" to describe the consortia and consultative groups that it heads, resists coordination by the United Nations. Its position has been "cooperation, *si;* coordination, *no.*" Virtually everyone underscores the desirability of coordinating technical and financial assistance to a given country, but no agency wishes to be coordinated by another.

To return to the late 1950s, the International Development Association

10. Hoffman had earlier been administrator of the U.S. agency for dispensing Marshall Plan assistance. He was also an intellectual father of the Special Fund, having spelled out a role for it in an article, "Blueprint for Foreign Aid," which appeared in the *New York Times Magazine* on February 17, 1957. The article was unusually influential because it appeared while Hoffman was serving as a member of the U.S. delegation to a General Assembly session and because it revealed more clearly than any previous publication of comparable stature an apparent major gap in the investment process—the need for better international arrangements to finance and execute preinvestment studies.

The Governing Council has several times been enlarged, and when the UNDP was created in 1966 by a merger of the Special Fund with EPTA, the managing director of the Special Fund became administrator of the UNDP.

11. The Consultative Board was expanded in 1966 to include the heads of other participating and executing agencies and was re-christened the Inter-Agency Consultative Board.

(IDA), like the Special Fund, owes its existence in large measure to prolonged agitation within the UN for a capital development fund. Unlike the Special Fund, however, IDA was not created as part of the UN. As soon as it became clear that IDA would be set up as an affiliate of the World Bank—and before it became equally clear that it would simply be a fund administered by the Bank—Dag Hammarskjöld, the then secretary-general of the UN, began urging Bank President Eugene Black to agree to a special institutional link between IDA and the UN. As a possibility, he suggested that the Consultative Board of the United Nations Special Fund be used for the purpose of coordinating the activities of IDA with those carried out under related programs within the UN family.

President Black politely but firmly rejected this suggestion. "In my judgment," he said, "the formal institutional links between IDA and the United Nations and other specialized agencies should follow the same pattern as has been established in the case of the Bank, although clearly the creation of IDA will intensify the need for close cooperation at the working level."[12] His letter did not end the exchange of views. For our purposes, however, it is sufficient to say that the IDA agreement with the UN, approved in early 1961, established on a formal basis (and included IDA in) the Liaison Committee, which had been operating on an informal basis for several years. The purpose of the Liaison Committee, which predated the Special Fund, was to permit an informal exchange of information between the Bank and the UN as a whole rather than between the Bank and the Special Fund or its successor, the UNDP. The committee had been, and was expected to continue, meeting at the working rather than the head-of-agency level and to achieve the formidable feat of assuring coordination through consultation. Despite an apparently binding requirement for four meetings a year, the liaison committee is now inactive.[13]

By the time UNCTAD I, the mammoth, contentious United Nations Conference on Trade and Development, met in Geneva in the spring of 1964, the less developed countries had become a major political force in the UN.

---

12. Letter of October 23, 1959, to Dag Hammarskjöld.
13. The relevant provision of the UN/IDA agreement—Article II—reads:
There is hereby created a Liaison Committee composed of the Secretary-General of the United Nations and the President of the Bank and the Association, which the Executive Chairman of the United Nations Technical Assistance Board and the Managing Director of the United Nations Special Fund, or their representatives, shall be invited to join as full participants. Through this Liaison Committee, which shall meet periodically and not less often than four times a year, the participants shall keep each other fully informed, and shall consult each other as required, on their current programmes and future plans in areas of common interest and concern thereby assuring coordination of their technical assistance and other development activities.

In economic forums the North–South struggle had virtually replaced the East–West conflict. George Woods had become president of the Bank. He saw in UNCTAD an opportunity to exhibit a thoroughly cooperative attitude on relations with other international agencies.

The Bank, he said in his address to that group, intended to participate "actively and affirmatively" in UNCTAD's deliberations. It had embarked on a "program of critical self-analysis," the first consequence of which had been a decision to expand the scope of its financing. Building infrastructure was not an end in itself, and the Bank had concluded that it should now greatly increase its assistance to agricultural and industrial production. Because investment requirements for the contemplated types of agricultural work called primarily for local currency expenditures, he was recommending to his executive directors that they show a greater willingness to help finance such expenditures. Part of the broadened assistance to industry would take the form of program loans or, as Woods phrased it, "long-term financing for programs to import individual pieces of equipment, components and spare parts in cases where existing industrial capacity is not fully used because there is a lack of foreign exchange with which to buy such equipment from abroad."

Lending for educational purposes would also be expanded. Through longer grace periods and longer-term loans, the terms of Bank financing were becoming more flexible. Finally, technical assistance and training activities, particularly those involving project identification and preparation, would be "greatly enlarged." All in all, this was heady music with which to launch the conference and was well calculated to prepare the delegates, who numbered more than two thousand, to turn to the Bank for certain of the follow-up studies they later requested.[14]

The follow-up studies themselves—an analysis of the Horowitz proposal for increasing the level of capital transfers by subsidizing interest rates, and a study transmitted to the UN secretary-general in December 1965 under the not-very-informative title "Study on Supplementary Financial Measures"—were discussed in Chapter 8, above. They proved to be somewhat of a let-down for the less developed countries; neither has as yet produced any noticeable change in international lending policies. There is, however, no statute of limitations on ideas.[15]

14. The conference met from March 23 to June 16, 1964. Woods's address was delivered on March 25.
15. The Bank was also urged by UNCTAD I to get on with its study of an international investment guarantee system, but the real impetus in this case came from the OECD. The most memorable achievement of UNCTAD II, held in New Delhi in 1968, is probably the agreement in favor of the early establishment of a generalized system of tariff preferences for less developed countries in the markets of industralized countries—an agreement only partially implemented as of this writing.

Relations with FAO, Unesco, and WHO

George Woods's announcement at UNCTAD I of the Bank's intention to expand its lending in the fields of agriculture and education made it clear that this would be done in cooperation with the appropriate specialized agencies in these fields, namely the FAO and Unesco. In retrospect, this course of action appears normal and self-evident. At the time, however, most people in the Bank felt that the "normal" way for it to expand its lending in a new field would be to hire the necessary experts and proceed with the same independence it had shown in the fields of electric power and transportation. Woods, recognizing the nature of the decision taken by the international community when it established a series of funtional agencies, firmly overruled the proponents of independence and chose the more difficult path of collaboration, at least at the preinvestment stage. Woods, in short, strengthened the Bank's links with the rest of the UN family and forged a few new ones.

Nevertheless, the establishment of UNCTAD further distorted the functional approach to international community adopted by the architects of the post–World War II system. The less developed countries, by bringing into being a new agency for the comprehensive review of trade, aid, and financial questions related to development, also raised new problems concerning the division of labor and the coordination of effort within the UN system. For the poor countries, however, "the primary concern has not been organizational neatness or financial responsibility, but immediate results. If traditional UN bodies were inadequate to meet their needs, new ones had to be created in which they would have greater control."[16]

In the eyes of the World Bank, the cooperative arrangements with FAO and Unesco have been successful. They have helped pave the way for increased investment by the Bank Group in agriculture and education while preserving and strengthening functional specialization within the UN family. The level of developmental competence in two important branches of the family has been raised as a result of the emphasis on "practical, investment-oriented" activities. At present, the FAO staff is concerned with one phase or another of project preparation for about 40 percent of the agricultural projects in the Bank's pipeline. The Bank offers comments on terms of reference and plans of operation for those UNDP projects for which FAO is the executing agency and which are most likely to result in investment—with a view to making them more attractive for Bank financing if and when they reach the project appraisal stage. Bank representatives also meet periodically with

16. Gardner, "The United Nations Conference on Trade and Development," in Richard N. Gardner and Max F. Millikan (eds.), *The Global Partnership: International Agencies and Economic Development* (Praeger, 1968), p. 121.

FAO and UNDP representatives to review the progress of various preinvestment studies in the agricultural sector.

The arrangement with Unesco is similar. Its Educational Financing Division is devoted exclusively to Bank work. In 1969–71 the division assisted borrowers in identifying about two-thirds, and preparing four-fifths of the educational projects undertaken by the Bank. "In the original agreement no provision was made for cost-sharing or other cooperation with respect to services that are closely related to project identification and preparation, such as educational planning."[17] The consequence, in the Bank's view, was that whereas Unesco's Educational Financing Division had become a reasonably effective unit, its Planning Division suffered from neglect and lack of budgetary support. During 1971, therefore, the Cooperative Program was expanded to provide services made available by Unesco's Division of Educational Planning and Administration and by its Department of School and Higher Education. These services will include the provision of educational country profiles intended to increase the Bank's knowledge of requirements in this sector.

From the Bank's point of view, its financing of 75 percent of the budgets of the cooperative programs with FAO and Unesco is proof of its willingness to back with hard cash public professions of cooperation. Some observers, however, are uneasy about the Bank's "buying into" other functional agencies and thereby increasing its leverage within the UN system. According to Sir Robert Jackson, the Bank's "arrangements with FAO and UNESCO constitute a new pre-investment axis. . . . There is . . . a very real danger that the centre of gravity for pre-investment work could be pulled away from UNDP to IBRD."[18] We take the more relaxed view that the separation of responsibilities for preinvestment and investment was a historical accident rather than a blueprint for efficient organization. The present "cooperative arrangements" bear watching, but, to date at least, they seem sensible from the point of view of development promotion because they have brought to the attention of an agency that is able and willing to provide financing more good investment projects than would otherwise have been financed.

We confess to some surprise, however, at the course of the Bank's own administrative expenditures for agriculture and education since the 1963–64 decisions to rely heavily on FAO and Unesco. The administrative budget of the Agriculture Projects Department in the Bank/IDA in fiscal 1971 was

17. World Bank, *Education,* Sector Working Paper (September 1971), p. 17.
18. Sir Robert Jackson, "A Study of the Capacity of the United Nations Development System" (Geneva: United Nations, 1969), Vol. 1, pp. 20–21. "The Jackson Report."

almost four times as great as the Bank's contribution to the Cooperative Program with FAO; the budget of the Education Projects Department was about three times the size of the Bank's contribution to the Cooperative Program with Unesco. Obviously, the Bank has been increasing its own stable of specialists in these sectors more rapidly than have the units in FAO and Unesco that are financed by the joint programs. The main reason is that the cooperative arrangements cover only project identification and preparation—functions that were originally considered the responsibility of the borrower. They convey no monopoly position in those phases of the project cycle to which they apply; and they do not apply to appraisal and supervision, responsibilities that would be harder both for the Bank to share and for the cooperating agencies to assume. It has therefore become easy for some of the Bank staff to think of the other agencies as adjuncts employed by the Bank to help the borrower rather than as full partners of the Bank in a joint venture.[19]

A cooperative agreement with the World Health Organization, similar to the agreements with FAO and Unesco, was negotiated in early 1971 for work in the fields of water supply, sewerage, and storm drainage. This would seem to indicate that the specialized agencies themselves may be less uneasy about the consequences of a financial link to the World Bank than are Sir Robert Jackson and like-minded critics.

As of mid-1971, the Bank was not organically linked to FAO's industrial counterpart in the UN system, the United Nations Industrial Development Organization (UNIDO), which began functioning in 1967. But UNIDO, in the opinion of the Industrial Projects Department of the Bank, was still young and, like World Bank bonds in the 1940s, unseasoned. Accordingly, the Bank's desire was for ad hoc cooperation.[20] There has been talk of a formal agreement with the International Labour Organisation (ILO), which could effectively reflect the Bank's growing concern with the employment dimension of development. But entering into an arrangement with the ILO would obviously be more difficult than entering into arrangements with agencies whose work is confined to recognizable economic sectors.

19. "There is a large separate staff in the FAO *working full time for the Bank* on the identification and preparation of projects, with costs shared between the two institutions. The United Nations Educational, Scientific and Cultural Organization (UNESCO) *performs similar services for the Bank* in the field of education." Warren C. Baum, "The Project Cycle," *Finance and Development*, Vol. 7 (June 1970), p. 4. (Emphasis has been added.) The FAO, it should be noted, has never been able to recruit personnel for all of the posts authorized under the joint program and at times has had difficulty in raising its 25 percent of the shared budget.

20. By mid-1972, however, discussions with a view to establishing a formal cooperative arrangement had begun.

The most recent development in collaboration among the Bank, FAO, and UNDP is their joint sponsorship of a new kind of consultative group, the Consultative Group on International Agricultural Research. Its origins lie in two long-established and successful international research institutes, the International Rice Research Institute in the Philippines and the International Maize and Wheat Improvement Centre in Mexico, which developed the high-yielding varieties of rice, wheat, and corn that are at the heart of the so-called green revolution. The institutes had been made possible primarily by the Rockefeller and Ford Foundations, which, having brilliantly demonstrated the value of the type of sustained international research exemplified by these institutes, were nevertheless unwilling to increase their subsidies to them. Yet an expansion of those institutes and the creation of new ones seemed to be needed to help less developed countries improve the quality of their agricultural output.

In 1968, the director-general of the FAO proposed that the international community, building on the experience of the previously established centers, examine ways and means of expanding research in cereals to areas not yet affected by the present technology and of organizing comparable research efforts for other major crops and for agricultural problems. After the usual meetings at various levels and places, French and German misgivings were overcome, and the Consultative Group on International Agricultural Research was established in 1971. It is "the only consultative mechanism which has been established to consider, not the problems and external assistance needs of a particular country, but the research priorities in an important sector and the means for financing research efforts to meet agreed priority needs."[21]

Conflicting Recommendations from Experts

All arrangements for the promotion of development have been subjected to critical scrutiny within the last few years, and we have had occasion earlier in this book to mention by name some of the commission, committee, and task force reports summarizing the results of such scrutiny. A genuinely international approach to the promotion of development in the low-income

---

21. Richard H. Demuth, "The International Agricultural Research Consultative Group," *International Development Review*, Vol. 13 (September 1971), p. 46. The secretariat of the group is provided by the Bank, while the FAO provides the secretariat for the technical advisory committee of distinguished scientists responsible for advising the group on gaps in agricultural research and priorities for filling them. The membership of the consultative group as of June 30, 1971, consisted only of developed countries, international institutions, and American foundations, but invitations to participate were expected to be issued to a small number of less developed countries.

world, it is widely agreed, requires a considerable restructuring of the present complex of competing, inadequately financed, more or less autonomous agencies—most of which were not designed for the specific purpose of promoting development.

It is not our purpose here to evaluate the reports but rather to note that they recommend mutually inconsistent changes in the system. Just as a male infant learns how to behave like a boy almost from birth and without being told and a female child learns what is expected of her as a girl, so the Pearson, Jackson, Tinbergen, and Prebisch reports provide predictably different answers to the problem of restructuring the international machinery. Authored by persons of unimpeachable integrity and great objectivity, who could not possibly be bought, the various reports come up, *mirabile dictu,* with organizational pyramids that give top place to the agency that put the particular study group into orbit.[22] As was first noted by Arthur E. Goldschmidt, the Pearson report is clearly IBRD-centered, the Jackson report UNDP-centered, and the Tinbergen report ECOSOC-centered. The Prebisch report gives center stage to regional machinery, specifically the Inter-American Development Bank and the Inter-American Committee on the Alliance for Progress.[23]

The recommendations of the experts, moreover, are being acted upon. The Bank is expanding its program of country economic reports, increasing the number of consultative groups that it chairs, adding slightly to its field staff, and in other respects preparing to fill the vacuum created by the lowered profile of the United States. Meanwhile the UNDP has moved toward fulfillment of the Jackson recommendation that country programs of technical and preinvestment assistance be prepared by the government and the UNDP "resrep," assisted by other international agency personnel, with the World Bank "closely associated with the process."[24] The Bank is being invited to participate in country programming exercises being undertaken by the UNDP.

22. Robert E. Asher, "Development Assistance in DD II: The Recommendations of Perkins, Pearson, Peterson, Prebisch, and Others," *International Organization,* Vol. 25 (Winter 1971), p. 109 (Brookings Reprint 208).

23. The Pearson, Jackson, and Tinbergen reports are global in scope, whereas the Prebisch report is regional. Their formal titles are, respectively: *Partners in Development,* Report of the Commission on International Development, Lester B. Pearson, Chairman (Praeger, 1969); Jackson, "A Study of the Capacity of the United Nations Development System" (Geneva: United Nations, 1969); *Towards Accelerated Development: Proposals for the Second United Nations Development Decade* (UN Document ST/ECA/128 [the Tinbergen Report], United Nations, 1970); Raul Prebisch, "Change and Development: Latin America's Great Task," Report submitted to the Inter-American Development Bank (1970; processed).

24. Jackson, "A Study of the Capacity of the United Nations Development System," Vol. 1, p. 21.

Conversely, the Bank has agreed to involve UNDP resreps in its expanded program of country economic reports. They are expected to contribute to the analysis of what is sometimes called "the preinvestment sector," though it is obviously not a sector in the sense that agriculture, industry, or transport are. The Bank has now made it a point to include in every Bank-sponsored consortium or consultative group the UNDP resrep for the country in question.

The current expansion of country studies and programs, under various auspices, should result in better forward programming of both capital assistance and technical assistance. Genuine integration of these two different forms of foreign aid, however, remains difficult. The UNDP would surely wish to include in its country programs all feasibility studies commended to it by the Bank as likely to lead to investment. Whether the indicative planning figures used by UNDP—the aggregate resources the country might expect to receive from UNDP over the three-to-five-year period covered by the country program—or the administrator's program reserve fund will be large enough to permit this was not clear as of June 30, 1971.

What seems clear to us is that the Bank has performed well as executing agency for the UNDP. As was pointed out in Chapter 10, it has been responsible for much of the follow-up investment resulting from preinvestment studies financed by the UNDP. Relations at both headquarters and country levels are outwardly good. Beneath the surface, a somewhat unequal struggle for leadership of the international development effort goes on. As in all such struggles, each party moves in two directions at once—in some respects toward closer cooperation and in other respects toward greater independence.

The Bank and the Organisation for Economic Co-operation and Development

President McNamara, in his 1970 address to the Economic and Social Council, quoted above, mentioned the Development Assistance Committee of the OECD, "which, although not a UN organization, is playing an increasingly important role in coordination of the development assistance policies of the major capital-exporting countries. The Bank maintains very close contact with the work of the DAC."[25]

25. Address of November 13, 1970. The OECD, in the words of Seymour J. Rubin, "rose, in October 1961, from the warm ashes of the OEEC," the organization of European Marshall Plan beneficiaries. The successor organization includes, in addition, the United States, Canada, and Japan as full members.

Relations have been cordial, in part perhaps because the DAC has not acquired major operational functions. The few cases in which less-than-amicable feelings have been exhibited have involved situations in which the DAC appeared to be acquiring an operational role—for example, when it experimented with the formation of aid-coordinating groups.[26] When the OECD Development Centre was first proposed in 1961, the Bank opposed it on the grounds that the center would serve no new purpose, that it would compound existing confusion as to which agency should do what, and that it would compete for European personnel with the Bank's development advisory service.[27] Though there was also little enthusiasm among government delegations for the project, the center was nevertheless established in Paris in 1963. It has convened "field seminars" in developing countries and produced some high quality research. We are unaware of any tension between the center and the Bank since the center was created.

The Bank (specifically George Woods and Dragoslav Avramović) played a vital role in the early 1960s in alerting OECD to the need for improving the terms of aid. On various other occasions the DAC has nudged the Bank in directions that can only be considered desirable. Though known as a rich nations' club, the DAC has pleaded the case for reorienting aid-coordinating groups more toward the needs of the recipient country, for example, by establishing criteria governing aid to a particular recipient.[28] In terms of equality between recipient and donors, the DAC led the way when it invited Thai officials to all sessions of its country meeting on Thailand in 1962. It urged that consultative groups meet at least once every two years and that prompter burial services be held for those that were dead. The OECD, as was reported in Chapter 11, provided much of the impetus for the Bank's work on multilateral investment insurance.

26. See Chapter 15, above.

27. The proposal for an OECD Development Centre appeared first in President Kennedy's speech of May 17, 1961, before the Canadian Parliament in Ottawa. It had not previously been widely discussed within the U.S. government and therefore took by surprise not only other members of the OECD but also most of the people in Washington concerned with OECD affairs.

28. The [aid-coordinating] groups have also been slow to become involved in the co-ordination of attitudes toward recipient development policies or in seeking agreement on criteria governing aid to a particular recipient. The question of harmonisation of terms is a key example. Whereas the DAC attempts to establish general principles and criteria for the harmonisation of terms, actual harmonisation can only be applied on a case-by-case basis. . . . The Bank has, on occasion, indicated what it considered to be an appropriate range of terms in individual cases, but has seldom pressed the question of harmonisation so far as to assume a leadership role in urging specific terms in specific cases.
Edwin M. Martin, *Development Assistance: Efforts and Policies of the Members of the Development Assistance Committee, 1969 Review* (Paris: OECD, 1969), p. 197.

In the field of data gathering, there is good cooperation. The OECD produces the best available information on the flow of financial resources from DAC countries to developing countries and makes sophisticated analyses of the data. The Bank collects information from its less developed member countries on their external debt and debt-servicing obligations. The Bank and OECD make an effort to reconcile the figures from donors with those from receivers, and on tables in the Bank's annual reports "Source: World Bank and OECD" is a familiar tag line.

On matters that clearly fall into the category of policy issues of a general character for donor countries the Bank has often been willing to take a back seat and encourage the DAC to exercise leadership. Such matters include aid terms, burden-sharing, and reviews of the performance of donor countries.[29] On the question of untying aid, the DAC has for some years provided the main forum, with the Bank playing a supportive role not only through active preparation for and attendance at meetings on the subject, but also by seeing that discussions of tying in Bank-sponsored consortia and consultative groups are coordinated with the work of the DAC.

The Bank and Regional Development Banks

The establishment of a series of regional development banks between 1959 and 1970 is at once a tribute and a rebuke to the World Bank: a tribute in the sense that it could not have happened without the example previously set by the World Bank of probity, technical and economic competence, and ability to raise funds in capital markets and put them to productive use in low-income countries; a rebuke in the sense that, had the World Bank been as popular in those countries as it thought it was, their desire for regional banks would have been weaker. Other factors also influenced the decision: the feeling of the less developed countries that the more spigots from which funds might flow, the larger the total flow would be; the iron law of international organization that prohibits establishing machinery in one region without establishing, sooner or later, comparable machinery in other regions; and the determination of the less developed countries to have a larger say in affairs affecting them than they had in the early postwar years.

29. On overall financial flows (as well as on terms of aid) each member of the DAC wants to appear in the best possible light in relation to the targets set. The result is that the published data probably exaggerate considerably the volume of aid supplied to less developed countries.

The Inter-American Development Bank

The concept of a regional development bank appears to have originated in Latin America, where proposals for establishing some sort of regional bank were first aired in the late nineteenth century.[30] Although execution of the idea was deferred by two world wars, in the early 1950s the Latin Americans began pressing hard for a regional bank when it seemed apparent to them that total capital flows from all sources and the amounts, terms, provisos, and purposes of World Bank loans for their region were inadequate. They had long disliked the Bank's policy of refusing to lend unless reasonable efforts were made by member governments to settle defaults on their outstanding foreign bonds. Additionally, they felt that certain of their countries could no longer borrow on conventional Bank terms (IDA was not yet a reality, and it was of little use to Latin America when it came into being); that the Bank was not interested in making loans to promote regional integration; and that the Bank was insufficiently interested in covering local currency expenditures as well as foreign exchange costs in its project loans. The Eisenhower administration, which had opposed the establishment of a Latin American bank, underwent a sudden change of heart in the late 1950s, and the Inter-American Development Bank (IDB), with official U.S. assistance, began operations in December 1959.

Before the IDB was launched, there was opposition to its establishment on the part of many senior World Bank officials who felt that the new institution would duplicate the Bank's work and that the two institutions would compete for funds, projects, and staff.[31] Moreover, many World Bank officials were convinced that the regional bank would operate under lower standards and, in accordance with Gresham's law, would ease the World Bank out of Latin America. Although these misgivings were privately held and the Bank officially greeted the new institution in 1959 politely and with expressions of its desire for cooperation, the true attitude of many (though not all) of the Bank's senior people was known by IDB officials and executive directors. Thus, relationships between the two institutions, while offi-

---

30. Manmohan Singh, *Regional Development Banks,* Carnegie Endowment for International Peace, International Conciliation Series, No. 576 (January 1970), p. 21. See also Chapter 2, above.

31. This objection contrasted with the Bank's position on the abortive attempt in the late 1950s to form an Arab Development Bank. The Bank supported that proposal on the grounds that it would tap new sources of development funds, namely, money from oil-rich countries.

cially correct, were clouded from the start by dissatisfaction on the part of the new institution with the past performance of the older one and by suspicion on the part of the older one about the future performance of a new rival.

The Bank, however, provided the IDB with samples of the documentation it used, with the country economic reports it prepared for nations in the region, and with lists of projects under consideration or approved. The IDB from the beginning kept the Bank abreast of its activities by sending it periodic lists of loan approvals, technical assistance studies undertaken, and so on. Staff liaison was facilitated by the fact that IDB headquarters was located in Washington. Informal liaison in the early days was so effective that meetings of the Inter-American Development Assistance Coordinating Group (comprised of representatives of the IDB, the World Bank, and the U.S. Agency for International Development) were discontinued after a few sessions because they seemed unnecessary.

An implicit division of labor between the two banks prevailed in the early 1960s. As of 1960, roughly 90 percent of World Bank loans in Latin America had been for power and transport. IBRD lending in these fields continued (with some branching out), while the IDB was eager to lend in fields such as agriculture, industry, housing, water supply, and education, which it felt the World Bank had neglected.

Moreover, the IDB was *not* proving to be an irresponsible lender. World Bank Vice President Knapp in 1961 said:

> The Inter-American Bank's capital is set up very much like the World Bank's. ... So far [the IDB] has been ... conservative in its transactions, no doubt reflecting the desire in their mind to build up their reputation as a banking institution and to establish ... credit. And from our point of view it's a great safeguard that that sort of motivation exists.[32]

Finally, the Bank Group and the IDB, after an unbelievable amount of effort, succeeded in negotiating several joint financing operations, the first being a highway project in Honduras, which also received the first IDA credit. There were, of course, exceptions to this determined, rather labored cooperation—notably, unhappiness on the part of the Bank with IDB lending on "soft" terms to countries that the Bank thought could afford harder (IBRD) terms, some questionable IDB loans, and some competition between the two banks for good projects. Jacob Kaplan asserts that "Bank loans to Mexico and Venezuela increased remarkably after the Inter-American Development Bank came into being, which suggested to some a desire to cap-

32. J. Burke Knapp, "Oral History," pp. 54–55.

ture from a new competitor the best available projects in the two Latin American countries whose debt-service prospects are much the strongest."[33]

By 1968 it was apparent that the earlier implicit division of labor was breaking down. The IDB, with increased resources, was expanding its lending in the transportation and power fields while the World Bank was increasing its lending in the social fields. The growing overlap between the two banks was recognized in a joint Bank–IDB staff meeting held in July 1969. The IDB's annual loan commitments had about reached the level of Bank commitments for Latin America, and no solution to the division-of-labor problem came out of the meeting.

In a thoughtful memorandum to McNamara on Bank–IDB relations in August 1969, Gerald Alter, then director of the Western Hemisphere Department of the IBRD, pointed to the friction between the two banks arising from the disintegration of the previous division of labor. Alter emphasized that the IDB did not generally undermine the role the Bank saw for itself as maintainer of standards, promoter of improvements in policy, or builder of institutions. He noted that when the Bank made it plain to the IDB that the latter's willingness to lend for a particular project would undermine what the Bank was trying to do, the IDB was usually cooperative. Conflict arose when the Bank had not clearly defined in advance the specific improvements in policies and institutions it was seeking. Alter went on to suggest that the Bank's newly installed system of program planning should help in this area because when a project was included by the Bank in a country program, the policy objectives would be stated.

Nevertheless, tension between the staffs of the two Banks flared up again in September 1969, when IDB President Felipe Herrera, in a strongly worded letter to McNamara, complained about improper interference by IBRD staff in plans for a highway loan for Paraguay, which the IDB had been studying for four years and which it regarded as one of its best transport projects. The Paraguayan project was not an outstandingly good one, but McNamara's response was temperate and included a relatively successful effort to restore IDB–Bank relations to a more positive footing.

In an effort to strengthen the country review process under the Inter-American Committee on the Alliance for Progress (CIAP), the Bank in June 1970 arranged with the IDB and CIAP to conduct an experiment in coordinated use of country economic analyses, with Chile as a test case. The Bank was to distribute its draft economic report on Chile to CIAP and through CIAP to other agencies (including the IDB and AID). The agencies receiv-

33. Jacob J. Kaplan, *The Challenge of Foreign Aid: Policies, Problems, and Possibilities* (Praeger, 1967), p. 363. Cited by Judith Tendler in "Foreign Aid: A Study in Atypical Bureaucracy," unpublished manuscript, December 1970.

ing the report were to make written comments. After the report was revised in the light of these comments, CIAP would circulate it, together with its own analysis of certain questions, as a paper that would serve as the basis for discussion at CIAP's next country review of Chile. This experiment carried out the spirit of the Pearson Commission report, which recommended that the Bank and regional banks take the lead in expanding the CIAP country review process and providing the analytic and reporting services needed.[34]

By mid-1971, the efforts to establish a more fruitful relationship among the Bank, CIAP, and IDB appeared to have succeeded, with the World Bank emphasizing the strengthening of CIAP as a policy review body for development programs in Latin America which could rely basically on country economic reports prepared by the World Bank. The annual review of operations in the common member countries was reportedly thorough and satisfactory to both banks. The Bank had proposed (and the IDB had accepted) a joint review of Latin American steel projects from the standpoint of regional integration (a standpoint which, in the past, the Bank had been accused of ignoring). By August 1970, the schedules of IBRD mission reports and CIAP reviews had been coordinated for eight countries in the CIAP review cycle, and CIAP had resumed inviting Bank representatives to its plenary sessions and had extended invitations also to IDB staff.[35]

European Investment Bank and European Development Fund

In 1958 two financial institutions were established within the framework of the European Economic Community: the European Development Fund, which has provided grant aid in substantial volume to French-speaking African nations, and the European Investment Bank, which seeks to promote balanced growth within the Community through loans and guarantees for projects in, for example, southern Italy. The European Investment Bank (EIB) has also made loans to Greece, Turkey, and African countries associated with the Community.

Within the World Bank there was opposition to the establishment of the EIB. As in the case of the Inter-American Development Bank, the opposition was not publicly expressed, but neither was it a closely held secret. Since the EIB's establishment, however, the World Bank's relations with it have been

---

34. See *Partners in Development*, pp. 130–31.
35. The plan for a general Bank–IDB review of Latin American steel projects was not carried out but was transformed into specific joint lending and project appraisal for the steel expansion program in Brazil mentioned in Chapter 15, above, and possibly for an expansion of production in Mexico.

what in French would be called "correct"—not warm, but certainly not hostile. Relations with the European Development Fund went through an initial period of awkwardness. A top-level drive for a viable working relationship was made by the World Bank in 1970. Roger Chaufournier, director of the Western Africa Department, worked hard at this, and it has been followed by more or less formalized semiannual consultation between the two institutions on operations, as well as by increasingly frequent working level collaboration.

Both European institutions have participated over the years in joint ventures with the Bank, IDA, or IFC. The volume of Bank Group business with the European Development Fund has become quite substantial.

African Development Bank

The African Development Bank (AfDB), established in 1964 under the impetus of the UN Economic Commission for Africa, has had a difficult time carving out a proper niche for itself. It is wholly owned by its African members. As yet, it has very modest resources at its disposal, and these are available only for lending on conventional terms. Although Africa's need for grants and soft loans is considerably more obvious than its need for a small supplementary source of hard loans, the AfDB—unlike the IDB and the Asian Development Bank—does not, as of this writing, have soft-loan funds at its disposal. "The absence of developed countries from its membership has greatly limited the financial resources at its disposal—clearly illustrating the inverse relationship between the developing countries' desire to control regional institutions and the actual financial viability of such institutions."[36]

In the planning stages, the World Bank lent one of its senior officials, Abdel El Emary, to the organizers, and he played an important role in launching the regional bank. Nevertheless, relations soon grew strained, due in part to the personality of AfDB's first president, in part to lack of clarity within AfDB as to what it ought to do, given its modest resources, and in part to an understandable fear that in any collaborative undertakings the AfDB would be overshadowed by the senior institution.

The World Bank, moreover, was not notably sensitive to the AfDB's political need for projects that could fly the AfDB flag or to certain other niceties of the situation. A proposal from within the staff that the World Bank choose a good African project from its pipeline and transfer it to the AfDB for execution was vetoed by President Woods as being a kindness over and above the call of duty. An alternative proposal that the AfDB pick up as its first loan a portion of a regional project appraised by the Bank encountered such

36. Singh, *Regional Development Banks*, p. 68.

delay and ambivalence on the AfDB's part that the World Bank's executive directors approved full financing of the undertaking by the World Bank, with a proviso for canceling a portion if and when that portion was approved as an AfDB project. This seemingly efficient procedure not only made the AfDB a junior partner but appeared to put pressure on it to become one. The president of the AfDB asked the World Bank to second some high-level talent to the AfDB and was understandably unhappy with the counter-proposal from Washington: "Send some of your people here and we will train them at headquarters." George Woods visited Abidjan, the headquarters of AfDB, in 1965 and met the first president of the AfDB, but under circumstances that only exacerbated existing tension.

As time passed and the African bank still had not effectively begun operations, the World Bank made a more determined effort to help it. The offer of staff training was sweetened by the World Bank's volunteering to pay travel expenses and a stipend to trainees, but it still was not accepted. In 1967 the African Development Bank, the Economic Commission for Africa, the UNDP, and the World Bank agreed to work in concert in preparing preinvestment studies for certain kinds of regional projects.[37] McNamara visited the AfDB offices in 1969 and ordered the Bank's permanent mission in Abidjan to offer every possible assistance short of actual project appraisal. The World Bank tried hard to find projects suitable for joint financing and to be quite flexible about the arrangements. Finally, in 1970, it succeeded. An electricity generation and transmission project for Malawi was set up by the Bank as two projects—a $5.3 million IDA credit primarily to cover the foreign exchange costs of new hydroelectric and thermal generating facilities and a $3 million loan from AfDB to finance distribution and transmission facilities. With its own newly elected president in charge, the AfDB also accepted the Bank's offer of staff training for two of its top officers and accepted the Bank's invitation to join an appraisal mission for a telecommunications project in Ghana.

Asian Development Bank

When the idea of an Asian Development Bank (AsDB) was first being considered by the UN Economic Commission for Asia and the Far East, the World Bank was at least as unenthusiastic as it had been about competition in other regions. Since the AsDB's establishment in 1966, however, with a charter consciously modeled on that of the World Bank, relations between the two institutions have been amicable. Eugene Black, a few years after

---

37. Their discussions referred specifically to projects that were in the transport, power, and telecommunications sectors and affected more than one African country.

stepping down from the presidency of the World Bank, served as adviser to the preparatory committee of the AsDB. At U.S. President Lyndon Johnson's request, and somewhat to his own surprise, Black traveled extensively in Europe as well as Asia pleading the cause of the Asian Bank in high political and financial circles. The AsDB's first president and vice-president had previously served as executive directors of the World Bank, and they sought and received advice and guidance from their former colleagues. A further factor in the smoothness of the relationship between the AsDB and the IBRD is that the latter by 1965 had resigned itself to the fact that regional banks were inevitable and, furthermore, not much of a threat to the global institution.

The World Bank extended the same offers of cooperation (staff training, joint financing, and joint project appraisal) to the Asian Bank that it had extended to the AfDB. While the proposal to train some AsDB staff at the Economic Development Institute of the World Bank was the only offer accepted readily by the AsDB (this regional bank was as wary as the other regional banks of being overshadowed by the World Bank in a joint financing operation), the World Bank has demonstrated its willingness to be helpful in various ways. These have included assigning an agricultural specialist to the steering committee of a comprehensive AsDB agricultural survey, assigning another member of the IBRD staff to participate in a study of the economy of Southeast Asia in the 1970s, and assigning a senior staff officer to the steering committee of a regional transport survey. In addition, there is a regular exchange of country studies, and members of World Bank missions to Asian nations regularly visit AsDB headquarters in Manila. The World Bank has invited the AsDB to send observers to consortia and consultative group meetings for various nations in Asia and by 1969 had passed along several small projects to the Asian Bank for financing. While articles have occasionally appeared in the Asian press charging that the World Bank has skimmed off the cream among projects and left the dregs for the regional bank, official complaints do not appear to have been registered to this effect.

World Bank/Regional Bank Relations Summarized

Initially the Bank felt threatened by newcomers on the scene. The Bank was already doing the job that needed to be done, and in its view new multilateral lending agencies would be competing with it for the same projects and the same funds. Furthermore, a regional bank would surely operate under lower standards, have a less capable staff, and be more politically motivated than the simon-pure World Bank. As the 1960s rolled along and the proliferation of regional development banks became inevitable, the Bank's misgivings faded. Its public stance in any event was to welcome the new institutions and usually to offer some real assistance to them in getting started (for example, legal advice pertaining to articles of agreement and loan procedures, advice on administrative matters, exchange of information on projects, offers of staff training, cooperation on compilation of data on external debt, and so on). The differences among the Latin American, African, and Asian development banks are at least as significant as the differences between them and the World Bank—due to differences in resources at their disposal, in voice given to countries outside the region, and in sense of regional identity and solidarity within the area served. The only regional bank in the less developed world that has given the IBRD almost no cause for worry has been the Asian Development Bank, because the World Bank's staff considers the AsDB "just like us"—but too small to constitute a threat. The AsDB regards itself as more sensitive than the World Bank to the needs of the Asian region. The AsDB, AfDB, and IDB are, of course, more heavily staffed by nationals of borrowing countries than is the World Bank.

The future of regional banks depends heavily on the kinds of compromises reached with respect to control. As John White suggests:

Developing countries see regional banks as a means of exercising greater control over the distribution of resources to themselves. Developed countries see regional banks as a way of making their own control of resources less explicit, while retaining an effective influence over the use to which the resources are put and over the pattern of economic relations which they promote. More simply, developed countries see regional banks as a way of making their own position as aid-givers less embarrassing, while developing countries see regional banks as a way of embarrassing the aid-givers more effectively.[38]

Relations between the World Bank and regional banks might be tidier if clear lines could be drawn between the types of projects financed by each. Except for the normally keener desire of regional institutions to promote regional integration, a logical division of labor would at present be difficult to arrive at and almost impossible to enforce.[39]

Beyond Economics: Portugal and South Africa

The story of the Bank's relationship with other international agencies, as we have reported it, could lead the reader to believe that the cycle is quite predictable: mutual suspicion at the beginning, some published statements

---

38. John White, *Regional Development Banks* (London: Overseas Development Institute, Ltd., 1970, and New York: Praeger, 1972), p. 191.
39. See also Chapter 21, below.

and agreements to make it appear that all is well, occasional tension during the early years over alleged violations of the agreements, gradual recognition that there is room for both agencies and much to be gained from genuine co-operation, and smooth sailing thereafter. However true this may be for relationships among the so-called functional agencies, the international system is not limited to functional machinery. The United Nations itself is an over-arching exception. The General Assembly of the United Nations,

in its efforts to penalize Portugal and the Republic of South Africa for their colonial and apartheid policies . . . has called upon the specialized agencies to deny to those states the benefits of membership in their respective organizations. The International Bank for Reconstruction and Development (IBRD) has refused to do so on the ground that it is a nonpolitical, functional organization without authority to impose sanctions upon members for conduct unrelated to its purposes. The pointed exchange of views between the United Nations and the World Bank on this question illustrates the serious problem of the proper relationship between the United Nations and the specialized agencies and exposes one of the difficulties of the functionalist strategy for world order.[40]

The dispute began in 1961 and for several years related only to Portugal. In 1965 a special committee of the General Assembly bearing the mouth-filling title, Special Committee on the Situation with Regard to the Implementation of the Declaration on the Granting of Independence to Colonial Countries and Peoples, passed a resolution containing stronger language than that of earlier resolutions. Specifically, the committee appealed

to all the specialized agencies of the United Nations, and in particular the International Bank for Reconstruction and Development and the International Monetary Fund . . . to refrain from granting Portugal any financial, economic or technical assistance so long as the Portuguese Government fails to renounce its colonial policy, which constitutes a flagrant violation of the provisions of the Charter of the United Nations.[41]

The General Assembly later in the year "included a similar but somewhat watered-down provision" in a resolution it passed. Having long been agitated about apartheid in South Africa, it also passed a resolution on South Africa. Both were promptly forwarded to the Bank.[42]

Because loans for both countries were under consideration, President Woods in March 1966 circulated copies of the resolutions to the Bank's executive directors. At the same time he reminded them of the provision in

---

40. Samuel A. Bleicher, "UN v. IBRD: A Dilemma of Functionalism," *International Organization*, Vol. 24 (Winter 1970), p. 31. This section draws heavily on Bleicher's excellent, well footnoted article.

41. UN Doc. A/AC.109/124 and Corr. 1 (June 10, 1965).

42. Bleicher, "UN v. IBRD," p. 32.

the Bank's Articles of Agreement that economic considerations alone were relevant to their decisions.

Therefore, I propose to continue to treat requests for loans from these countries in the same manner as applications from other members. . . .

I am aware that the situation in Africa could affect the economic development, foreign trade and finances of Portugal and South Africa. It will therefore be necessary, in reviewing the economic condition and prospects of these countries, to take account of the situation as it develops.

In June 1966, the Bank approved a $10 million loan to Portugal, raising the total of Bank loans approved for that country to $57.5 million. In September 1966, it approved a $20 million loan to South Africa, thus raising its total lending to the Republic of South Africa to $241.8 million, of which $196.8 million represented pre-1960 lending and had been substantially repaid.

At the General Assembly in the fall of 1966, the Soviet Union alleged that the Bank was disdainful of the UN. In an effort to be cooperative, the Bank's general counsel, Aron Broches, appeared at the November 28 meeting of the appropriate committee of the General Assembly and explained the lending policies of the Bank. In December, the president of the Bank and the secretary-general of the UN conferred and agreed on early consultations between the two organizations. Exchanges of legal views continued for some time thereafter without a reconciliation of differences.

The UN argued that Article IV, section 10, of the Bank's Articles of Agreement was intended to prohibit interference in the *internal* political affairs of its members and to prohibit discrimination against any member country because of the political character of the government of that country. In the view of the UN, however, the section did not oblige the Bank to disregard the *international* conduct of a member country and the repercussions of such conduct on international peace and security.

The Bank argued that

there is no justification for imparting to the term "political," as the Secretariat memorandum does, the qualification "internal." The prohibition against interference "in the political affairs of any member" is not limited to interference in the member's *internal* political affairs but extends as well to the relations of a member with other states, *i.e.,* its *external* political affairs. Just as the Bank is precluded in making decisions on loans or guarantees from interfering in the domestic political activities of a member government, so it is precluded from interfering or attempting to interfere with the foreign policy of that government. . . .

The Bank may and does take into consideration, and is influenced in its lending decisions by, the economic effects which stem from the political character of a member and from the censures and condemnations of that member by United Nations organs.[43]

The Bank throughout its presentations stressed its functional character. In transmitting the above-cited memorandum to the United Nations, the Bank's general counsel wrote:

I should like to add that, in my opinion, the prohibition contained in express terms in Section 10 of Article IV of the Articles of Agreement of the Bank is no more than a reflection of the technical and functional character of the Bank as it is established under its Articles of Agreement.

The purposes of the Bank set forth in Article I of the Articles of Agreement are limited and the Bank must be guided in the exercise of its functions by those purposes alone. The member governments of the Bank have not deemed it appropriate to grant the Bank a larger function in the international community, and the characterization of the Bank as a financial and economic agency and not a political one was explicitly recognized by the United Nations in its Relationship Agreement with the Bank.

The upshot was an exchange of letters between President Woods and Secretary-General U Thant in August 1967, in which they said in effect, "It's too bad we can't agree, but let's be friends."[44]

43. Comments of the Legal Department of the Bank (May 4, 1967) on UN Secretariat Memorandum of March 3, 1967, pp. 6–7. Professor Bleicher suggests that the legal contentions of the two organizations can be boiled down to two questions: (1) *must* the Bank comply with the call of the General Assembly, and (2) *may* the Bank comply? He concludes that the answer to the first question is clearly no and says that the Bank could have rested its case there. But the Bank chose to go further and demonstrate that it was not legally *permitted* under its charter to consider UN recommendations of this type. Here the Bank, in Bleicher's view, was on shakier ground.

44. Letter, George Woods to U Thant, August 18, 1967:

My dear Secretary-General:

The Legal Counsel of the United Nations has, as you know, sent us a paper containing a closely reasoned legal argument why the World Bank should take certain actions under the General Assembly's requests for the withholding of economic assistance to Portugal and South Africa. The Bank's General Counsel has replied with legal arguments to show that, under the terms of its Agreement with the United Nations, the Bank is not obligated to comply with such requests and, indeed, under the terms of its own Articles of Agreement, is not free to do so. The Legal Counsel of the United Nations has since written that he continues to adhere to his original views, to which the United Nations organs concerned will doubtless give great weight. However, the Executive Directors of the Bank who, as you know, are responsible for interpreting the Articles of Agreement, having carefully considered all the arguments advanced, have although with some dissents, endorsed the position taken by the Bank's General Counsel. It seems to me unlikely that additional legal argumentation would change the situation.

In the circumstances, I should like at this point to leave legal argumentation aside and to assure you—and through you the various United Nations organs concerned—that the World Bank is keenly aware and proud of being part of the United Nations family. Its earnest desire is to cooperate with the United Nations by all legitimate means and, to the extent consistent with its Articles of Agreement, to avoid any action that might run counter to the fulfillment of the great purposes of

The proper role of the Bank in assisting in the enforcement of UN decisions is regarded by Bleicher as the crucial policy question underlying the dispute. The functionalist strategy of international organization, succinctly recapitulated by Bleicher, is built upon four basic assumptions: (1) cooperation between states for specific welfare-oriented benefits is possible in situations in which political cooperation is impossible; (2) successful cooperation on a nonpolitical basis through functional international organizations will breed habits of cooperation leading to the multiplication and expansion of functional machinery; (3) the satisfaction of human needs by these organizations will engender a gradual transfer of loyalties away from national units to international organizations; (4) the growing scope and effectiveness of the network of functional agencies will ultimately lead to an integrated world community capable of supporting a strengthened international organization or government of general competence.[45] From another perspective, namely,

what might be called a "governmental" approach to international organization, world order depends primarily upon the creation of worldwide expectations of the effectiveness of United Nations decisions as a means of controlling unilateral threats or use of force and universally condemned social or economic policies. The greater the range of resources that the United Nations can mobilize for rewarding approved policies and punishing unacceptable conduct, the greater will be the probability and expectation of success. National governments almost universally have constitutional authority to impose sanctions on uncooperative segments of the community by withdrawing or threatening to withdraw any one or more of the multitude of varieties of assistance, both economic and noneconomic, which it [sic] supplies. . . . The United Nations in its efforts to impose sanctions upon Portugal and South Africa is unable to control the analogous resources allocated by international organizations because of the independence of the specialized agencies. To the extent that they carry their political neutrality to the extreme of refusing to support the United Nations in enforcing its most crucial decisions the functionalist experiment is pursued at the expense of weakening the United Nations, and the agencies' fear of entanglement with a collapsing United Nations may turn into a self-fulfilling prophecy.[46]

---

the United Nations. I give you this assurance in the hope that it may be helpful in dissipating any misunderstanding of the Bank's attitude.

Secretary-General U Thant's reply to George Woods, dated August 23, 1967, welcomed "the assurance you have been good enough to convey to me . . . of the Bank's desire to co-operate with the United Nations by all legitimate means. . . . In view of the differences which exist regarding the interpretation of the basic texts, I share your feeling that additional legal argumentation would not be productive at this stage. . . ."

45. Bleicher, "UN v. IBRD: A Dilemma of Functionalism," pp. 42–43.

46. *Ibid,* pp. 44–45. Whether the efforts of the United Nations to impose sanctions on Portugal and South Africa really represent, as Bleicher implies, "its most crucial decisions" is of course arguable.

Although the Bank has made no formal concessions to this type of reasoning, the fact is that no loans have been made to Portugal or South Africa from 1966 to this writing. However, if the countries concerned had been more obvious candidates for Bank Group assistance, or if Portugal and South Africa should again qualify on economic grounds, the problem would re-arise in a more difficult form.[47] Meanwhile, the Bank has tried to be coopera-tive. Before making loans to Botswana and Zambia, it required them to con-sult the United Nations regarding the applicability of the Security Council resolutions on Southern Rhodesia to their special circumstances.[48]

Because of the weighted voting procedures of the World Bank and differ-ences between Bank and UN membership, divergences of policy are possible even if all governments belonging to both organizations remain consistent in the positions they take in the respective policymaking organs of the two agencies. It is an oft-noted fact, however, that national governments that pound the conference tables for better coordination among international agencies are themselves lamentably uncoordinated in what they espouse in the different international organizations to which they belong. Many of the governments that have voted for anti-Bank resolutions in the United Nations have in board meetings of the Bank supported the positions to which the United Nations took exception.

Some Concluding Thoughts

As international machinery has proliferated and the separate paths initially allocated to each agency have criss-crossed and grown more crowded, inter-agency relations have become more complex. There is no dearth of coordi-nators. Indeed, the competition for that role has never been keener. In the development field, the Bank Group is clearly the candidate of the Pearson Commission and must by any standard be considered a front runner. Our purpose in this chapter, however, has not been to elect a coordinator, but to sketch the evolution of the Bank's relationship with various organs and agen-cies, some of which are parts of the United Nations proper, some of which are loosely connected with the UN, and some of which are totally outside of the UN framework.

47. See also Chapter 13, above.
48. The Security Council resolutions impose sanctions on Southern Rhodesia. There is no procedure for obtaining exemptions from the provisions of the resolutions but, by informing the Council in advance of their need for economic relations with Southern Rhodesia in order to complete the projects, the Bank's borrowers were able to prevent adverse reactions from the Council.

Relations with the Organisation for Economic Co-operation and Development and its Development Assistance Committee have usually been amicable at all levels, primarily because the OECD and the DAC are not engaged in development financing operations, but also because the OECD/DAC and the Bank feel that they "speak the same language." The fact that the DAC is a donors' club may help to facilitate communication.

Relations with the United Nations have not been as intimate and for most purposes have not needed to be. The Bank has been about as loyal a member of the UN family as the other specialized agencies, even though its financial independence has made it, comparatively speaking, a man of means—with all that that implies in terms of relations with impoverished relatives. The General Assembly and ECOSOC were severely critical of the Bank during the first postwar decade, but in the process helped to create a climate suitable for the establishment of the IFC and IDA as affiliates of the Bank.

The Bank was only peripherally involved in the UN Expanded Program of Technical Assistance and during most of its life has been busily and usefully expanding its own program of technical assistance. Its aloofness toward the UN, which had been moderating for several years, disappeared almost entirely when a companion organization to EPTA, the Special Fund, was set up in the late 1950s to provide preinvestment assistance under UN auspices. (EPTA and the Special Fund were "federated" in 1966 to become the UN Development Program [UNDP].)

The decision to assign two stages (preinvestment and investment) of a single process to different multilateral agencies represented a political compromise with the advantages and disadvantages that such compromises often have. It highlighted a function that the international community had barely been aware of, it took some of the steam out of the drive for a capital development fund within the UN, and it gave the UNDP new leverage for coordinating portions of the work of the specialized agencies.

The assignment of the preinvestment function to an autonomous agency within the United Nations may, however, have inflated preinvestment work into a mystique well beyond its intrinsic importance in the investment process. It certainly has made the UN family (specifically the UNDP) possessive about the function. Many UN members wanted a capital development fund under UN auspices but had to settle, for the time being at least, for a new kind of technical assistance; the dichotomy between preinvestment and investment created by that historical accident has been raised to the level of immutable doctrine.[49] Because UNDP assistance—amounting at present to

---

49. While the extension of UN services toward the provision of capital has been checked by the rejection of SUNFED and by the weakness of the CDF [Capital Development Fund], the extension of IBRD's services both to preinvestment and some

about $250 million annually for technical assistance and preinvestment work —is available on a grant basis, the present organizational situation helps to sanctify a division between grant and loan aid, based not on the economic situation of the nation that is host to a project but on the portion of the investment process financed by the respective agencies.

The parceling out of responsibilities among numerous international agencies may also help to explain why the Bank, in accordance with the same principle that leads industrial corporations to seek vertical integration, has tried to assure itself of a stable supply of investment projects by financing important segments of the work of FAO, Unesco, and WHO.[50]

The establishment of regional banks in the less developed world was greeted by the World Bank with trepidation. Yet it is almost certainly true that, because of their existence, more funds have been raised for development than would otherwise have become available and more persons from less developed countries have gained experience in the management and operation of development banks. We have seen no substantial evidence that allegedly lower standards employed by some regional banks have harmed the cause of development, hampered the sale of World Bank bonds, or made it more difficult for the World Bank to operate in countries served by the regional banks while maintaining its own eligibility and performance criteria. The fact that borrowers have a stronger voice in the non-European regional banks than in the World Bank leads some analysts in the northern hemisphere to conclude that the decisions of regional banks must be less objective and more "political." But analysts in the southern hemisphere may be equally justified in concluding that institutions controlled by lenders—the control sanctioned by history—will be "objective" in favor of the sources of funds.

---

forms of technical assistance has been considerable. Although, by agreement, collision and duplication have been avoided, the tendency is clearly present. . . . It remains true that a more rational distribution of resources would be obtained if multilateral technical assistance and pre-investment work were channelled through the body set up for the purpose [that is, the UNDP].
Jackson, *A Study of the Capacity of the United Nations Development System,* Vol. 2, pp. 17–18.

These reasons and other experience [previously cited by the author] confirm the soundness of the original concept of pre-investment as an independent, specialized, multilateral function designed to facilitate capital investment of all types and from all sources, thereby serving as fully as possible the pre-investment needs of the developing countries and the international development system.
K. W. Taylor, "The Pre-Investment Function in the International Development System" (Carnegie Endowment for International Peace, Occasional Paper No. 8, 1970), p. 43.

50. "The Bank, in sum, moved somewhat in the direction of 'backward vertical integration' in order to increase its control over the supply of projects submitted to it." Judith Tendler, "Foreign Aid: A Study in Atypical Bureaucracy" (unpublished manuscript, December 1970), pp. 107–08.

The probability of collisions when functional approaches to world order are pursued by one part of the international system and other approaches by other parts is illustrated by the UN–Bank clash on Portugal and the Republic of South Africa. In this instance, the Bank was put on the defensive. But the fact that collisions can occur does not invalidate a major justification for the functional approach to international cooperation: the many possibilities of constructive cooperation among members in specific economic or technical situations while broader political cooperation remains impossible. Thus the Bank can lend to member countries resources obtained from other members that do not recognize the governments of the borrowers, it can associate borrowers that do not deal with each other in a scheme such as the development of the Indus River Basin, and it can promote international cooperation in many other situations by treating as a technical, economic issue a problem that in any other context would inevitably become a harder-to-solve political problem.

Collisions between international agencies can also occur because member governments are inconsistent in the positions they take in the two agencies or because the chief executives of the agencies fail to exhibit the good sense that George Woods and U Thant showed when, after fruitless interagency exchanges of legal opinions on Portugal and South Africa, they agreed to disagree. In the specific dispute, moreover, an outcome satisfactory to the protagonists, in fact if not in principle, has been possible because the Bank up until the time of this writing has been able to find good technical and economic reasons for not making loans to Portugal and South Africa.

Despite well known deficiencies in the present arrangements for international cooperation, Presidents Woods and McNamara, more than any of their predecessors, have seen the Bank Group as an integral part of an emerging international system; they have consequently sought to improve the effectiveness of the system as well as of the Bank Group.

In order to keep the whole question of Bank relations with other international agencies in perspective, it may be useful in conclusion, to underscore a point made by John White in his study of regional development banks: for most international institutions, other international agencies are part of the environment in which they operate, but only a minor part. "The relations of multilateral development agencies with each other as a class are less important than their relations both with the developed countries which provide bilaterally the bulk of world aid and with those other countries the development of which both multilateral aid and bilateral aid are intended to promote."[51]

51. White, *Regional Development Banks,* p. 17.

CHAPTER EIGHTEEN

The Bank as International Mediator: Three Episodes

BY HAROLD N. GRAVES, JR.

ON MAY 1, 1951, the Shah of Iran signed a law nationalizing the oil industry in Iran and on the next day signed another statute specifying how nationalization was to be carried out. The second statute directed the government to dispossess the "former" Anglo-Iranian Oil Company "forthwith."[1] It thereby brought to its final crisis the long-disputed oil question in Iran.

The oil nationalization also, incidentally, served to thrust the World Bank onto the stage of world politics. It was the first of three such instances that will be recounted in this chapter, the others being the dispute between India and Pakistan over waters of the Indus River system and the projected financing of a gigantic new dam on the Nile River in Egypt. The actions of the Bank have not infrequently given rise to political issues within individual member countries. But in these three cases, where the political issues already existed, the Bank's role was of wide international interest; and what the Bank did, or attempted to do, was of immediate and topical concern in the foreign offices of the world's leading nations.

Iran: Oil

The Anglo-Persian Oil Company (as it was called until 1927) was formed by predominantly British interests in 1909 to develop and operate a concession granted in 1901. Using the profits from its Iranian production, the com-

---

1. Nasrollah Saifpour Fatemi, *Oil Diplomacy: Powderkeg in Iran* (Whittier Books, 1954), pp. 342–43.

595

pany had found its way into world markets by 1920 and was beginning to develop oil resources outside Iran.[2] By the time of the May 1951 law, the Anglo-Iranian Oil Company (AIOC) had an imposing share of the global market for crude petroleum and petroleum products. Its refinery on the island of Abadan, on the western border of Iran, was the largest in the world.[3]

From the company's earliest days, its operations had been considered to be vital to Britain. The oil fields and refinery in Iran were the chief source of petroleum and petroleum products within the British sphere of influence—an assured source of supply to Britain's navy and merchant fleet. At the time of nationalization, the U.K. government owned more than half the shares of the company.

The business of AIOC was conducted on commercial, not diplomatic, principles, and there was intermittent friction with the government of Iran from the outset. The government presented its first complaint before the company was a year old.

In 1947 a sensation was caused in Tehran by publication of the fact that, because of a limitation on dividends by AIOC, the British government in the previous year had received revenue in taxes from the company (about £15 million) that was twice as great as the Iranian government's income from royalties and its share of net profits. Action against the AIOC concession became the rallying cry of an intensive propaganda campaign waged by political and religious groups cooperating in the National Front. On October 22, the Majlis passed a resolution directing the government of Iran to enter into discussions with the company with a view to securing Iran's national rights in her natural resources.[4]

In July 1949, negotiations finally resulted in a proposed supplemental agreement to the 1933 concession—offering a complicated, sliding-scale formula to increase the government's share of profits beyond the 20 percent to which it had been entitled. The agreement was subject, however, to ratification by the Majlis, and an Oil Commission composed of members of the Majlis began to study the matter. In the face of opposition from the com-

2. A detailed account of the company's early history is included in *Persian Oil: A Study in Power Politics*, by L. P. Elwell-Sutton (London: Lawrence and Wishart, Ltd., 1955). An account more sympathetic to the company is given in Laurence Lockhart, "The Causes of the Anglo-Persian Oil Dispute," *Royal Central Asian Journal*, Vol. 40, (June 1953), pp. 134–50.

3. International Bank for Reconstruction and Development, "Review of the International Bank's Negotiations Concerning the Iranian Oil Problem" (April 3, 1952; processed).

4. Elwell-Sutton, *Persian Oil*, p. 119.

mission, as well as a rising clamor by the National Front for nationalization of the oil industry, the government suddenly withdrew the proposed agreement from consideration at the end of 1950.

In February 1951, AIOC offered a 50–50 profit-sharing arrangement to Tehran. Events, however, already had swept past the point of no return. Under new instructions from the Majlis, the Oil Commission started preparing a report "setting out a line of policy for the government." Among other things, the commission asked the prime minister, General Ali Razmara, to prepare an opinion on the question of nationalization. After canvassing the ministries concerned, the general published the conclusions of his experts. They said that nationalization would be both illegal and impractical: The AIOC concession could not legally be canceled; the costs of compensation for expropriation would be £300 million or more; there were not enough Iranian technicians and financial experts to operate the industry; Iran would lose heavily in prestige abroad; it would be unwise to antagonize the British.[5]

Razmara's report was published on March 3, 1951. Nevertheless, on March 6, the commission approved the principles of nationalization. On March 7, on his way to attend a funeral, the general was assassinated by a Muslim fanatic, and in less than two months nationalization was law.

Attempts to stay the full effect of nationalization failed. The company applied to the president of the International Court of Justice for an arbitration proceeding, and the court subsequently issued a standstill order; but the Iranian government already had denied that the court had jurisdiction.

In June an AIOC delegation went to Tehran to repeat the company's earlier offer of a fifty-fifty profit-sharing arrangement, but to no effect. In August, after the Tehran authorities had been persuaded, through the intercession of roving U.S. Ambassador W. Averell Harriman, to receive British government representatives, the visit of the Lord Privy Seal, Richard Stokes, likewise was unsuccessful. In the following month, with Iranian troops occupying the Abadan refinery and British warships in the vicinity, the British government took the last step; it appealed to the United Nations Security Council to pass a resolution calling for the resumption of negotiations between the parties to the oil dispute.[6]

5. *Ibid.,* pp. 206–07.
6. Alan W. Ford, *The Anglo-Iranian Oil Dispute, 1951–1952* (University of California Press, Los Angeles, 1954), pp. 124–26. The Security Council proceedings were adjourned in October 1951 without action, and in the summer of 1952, the International Court decided that it did not have jurisdiction. The legal issues are extensively reviewed in Ford's book (pp. 124–53 and 164–212).

First Encounter

Onto this treacherous terrain, the World Bank ventured in November 1951. The occasion was the visit to the United States of Dr. Mohammed Mossadegh, the Iranian prime minister and leader of the National Front, who had come to speak about the British resolution before the Security Council. Concurrently, he engaged in conversations with U.S. Assistant Secretary of State George McGhee, who was continuing American efforts to mediate the oil question.

The idea of involving the Bank came from a diplomat from a country friendly to both Britain and Iran, Amjad Ali, Pakistan's minister of economic affairs in Washington. The thought struck him that since both Britain and Iran were members of the Bank, and the Bank had some expertise in technical and financial matters, the Bank might in some way be able to act as an honest broker between the parties to the dispute. Amjad Ali's idea was pursued by the Pakistani ambassador in Washington, A. H. Ispahani. After preliminary soundings with the Bank's management and Mossadegh, on November 10 the ambassador escorted Vice President Garner of the Bank to Mossadegh's rooms at the Shoreham Hotel in Washington for a face-to-face discussion with the Iranian premier. Garner said that of course he did not know whether the Bank could help solve a controversy where others had failed, but that it was willing to try. He explained that in broad outline, the Bank's approach might include the following points:

• The Bank would act as trustee for resumed oil operations in Iran during an interim period, giving time for the negotiation of a permanent settlement between the parties.

• The Bank would designate a person or organization to operate the properties and sell the oil. This person or organization would not be British.

• The Bank would find the funds that would be necessary to bring the properties back into operation.

• The oil would be marketed through established channels.

• The proceeds from the sale of oil would be divided into three parts. One part would go to Iran, one part would go to the company, and one part would be put into escrow, to be distributed under the terms of the final settlement.[7]

The essence of the proposal [the Bank later explained] was its interim character. The arrangement would be for a short period only. The Bank would be acting as a neutral institution of which both parties were members and not in its own interest. The sum to be put into escrow would be large enough to cover,

7. IBRD, Staff memorandum, Nov. 10, 1951.

so to speak, the area of disagreement. This sum would be held undistributed pending a final settlement. Thus neither party would have to compromise any legal rights in order to permit an immediate resumption of the flow of oil and the revenue accruing therefrom, and an atmosphere could be created in which negotiations for a permanent settlement could proceed.[8]

Dr. Mossadegh's comments were few, and they did not suggest flat opposition to any of Garner's suggestions. The meeting ended on a high note. Dr. Mossadegh remarked that if the Bank were able to accomplish something in this difficult matter, it would be doing a service not only to Iran but to humanity.

The discussion had begun on a note of practicality: when Garner explained that he had not come to play the role of a judge between the parties, Dr. Mossadegh replied in truthful jest, "Well, if you were a judge, I might not be interested in talking to you, because I couldn't get any money out of a judge."[9]

Consultation

Steps were taken immediately to inform the British authorities of the encounter with Dr. Mossadegh. With the assistance of Chester McLain, the Bank's former general counsel, and Walter J. Levy, an independent American oil expert who had been in Tehran with Harriman, meetings were soon begun in the Bank to expand Garner's ideas. A two-page memorandum took form, tentatively outlining the type of proposal the management would be prepared to recommend to the executive directors of the Bank.

The memorandum repeated, and added to, the main points made earlier: "Upon the request of both parties," the Bank would act as trustee pending final settlement. The trusteeship would continue for two years or until a final settlement was reached, whichever was earlier; if the settlement was not reached in two years, the trusteeship would automatically be extended from year to year, subject to cancellation "by any party" on six months' notice. Clauses were included that indicated a responsiveness to Iran's financial problems: not only would the Bank try to obtain, or would itself provide, funds needed for the resumption of oil operations in Iran, the Bank also

---

8. IBRD, "Review of the International Bank's Negotiations Concerning the Iranian Oil Problem."

9. As quoted by Garner in a meeting of the Bank's executive directors, November 23, 1951. Three days later, after the Garner interview, the U.S. Department of State announced the failure of its efforts to mediate the oil question. Within twenty-four hours, the prime minister appealed to President Truman for a U.S. loan of $120 million.

would try to work out arrangements for the provision of funds to meet the Iranian government's need for revenues pending the resumption of income from oil.

For the distribution of the proceeds from oil sales, the memorandum proposed a method that would avoid the implication that the company enjoyed equal rights with the government of Iran. The division would be into two parts rather than three. The Iranian government would receive half. The other half would be used for expenses and for an escrow account, which the Bank would dispose of according to the terms of the final settlement. No current payments would be made to AIOC, but "the purchaser" (that is, the company) would profit through being able to buy the oil at an attractive discount.

The Bank was proposing, in effect, to work toward its objectives through an activity that was very different from its normal operations. Whether it could legitimately concern itself with the Anglo-Iranian matter was therefore a question. At an informal meeting of the executive directors on November 23, 1951, Aron Broches, at that time assistant general counsel of the Bank, argued that the Bank could properly proceed. The Bank, he pointed out, was not an institution with strictly limited powers, the suggested operations were such as to further its general objectives, and there was nothing in the Articles of Agreement to forbid action along the lines discussed. The directors had no difficulty in accepting these views. Several of them observed that the case at hand was sufficiently important to two of the Bank's member governments to be worthy of the Bank's best efforts.

Immediately thereafter, Garner flew to Rome, where a meeting of the North Atlantic Council of the NATO countries was taking place. There he talked with Sir Anthony Eden, the British foreign secretary, and also met with Dean Acheson, the U.S. secretary of state; John W. Snyder, the secretary of the treasury; and Harriman. "All of them," Garner later recalled, "gave us encouragement."[10]

Discussions already had begun in London on November 19, 1951, between members of the Bank staff and senior British officials. Sir Roger Makins, then deputy under-secretary of state for foreign affairs, had agreed at the outset that the Bank's approach seemed sufficiently practicable to warrant further development. A week later AIOC indicated that it also was willing for the Bank to proceed.

The London conferees accepted the principle that the Bank would have

10. Oral History Project of Columbia University, interviews recorded in the summer of 1961 on the International Bank for Reconstruction and Development (cited hereinafter as "Oral History"). Quotation is from interview of Robert L. Garner, p. 66.

complete freedom in implementing the arrangements for interim operation of the oil properties. This would be necessary in any case, Garner thought, but it might have the additional advantage of showing the Iranians that the interim arrangements were not simply a facade for the restoration of AIOC. It had been assumed in the Bank that the bulk of the technicians needed at Abadan would in fact have to be supplied by AIOC, and the London talks confirmed that this manpower would be available. On the other hand, the Bank was quite aware that it lacked an important piece of information: it had no idea what Dr. Mossadegh might think about readmitting British technicians to Iran.

It was clearly not the role of the British participants in the London discussions to offer proposals. On the government side, the chief concern, stressed by the foreign secretary, was that nothing in the Bank's approach should prejudice the case then pending before the International Court. It was left up to the Bank to decide whether it could see a feasible basis for an interim arrangement and, if it was decided to proceed, to determine how and when the proposals would be presented to the government of Iran.

Garner left London feeling encouraged. Solid progress, he felt, had been made in the discussions. But one of the conditions mentioned to the Bank's executive directors had not been met—that the Bank be asked to proceed by *both* parties. It did not have a clear-cut request from the government of Iran.

Formulating an Approach

Three weeks had now passed since the opening conversation between Garner and Mossadegh. For Mossadegh, the perspective was one of urgency. His government had a more and more pressing need for revenue. Even more than revenue from oil, there was need from a political point of view to press beyond mere interim arrangements and to make the principle of nationalization an operating reality.

Early in December, a message was dispatched through Pakistani diplomatic channels to Mossadegh, informing him that Garner had been in London for conversations parallel to his talk with the prime minister and that the British had thought the matter merited further exploration by the Bank. When would be a convenient time for a visit by Garner to Tehran?

The reply came quickly. It would be desirable to arrive within the next ten days. Under the nationalization law of May 2, 1951, Iranian oil could be sold only to customers who had been buying it in 1950. In view of expressions of interest from other sources, preparations were now being made to amend the law in this respect; but if Garner or his representative could arrive by December 16, the amendment would be withheld.

The Bank could not act that quickly. Garner replied that he did not think a well considered plan could be prepared by that date, and Tehran's answer was that the government could not delay its action in favor of potential new customers. Garner then assured Mossadegh that the Bank wanted, at the earliest possible moment, to make a proposal that would have the support of its executive directors. In order to do that, it appeared desirable for the Bank to send a team to see the oil fields and refinery and to obtain any information that would be helpful. The prime minister's answer, on December 20, was that Iran's need was "desperate." After December 26, 1951, the Iranians would sell oil to anyone who wished to buy it; but in Tehran's view this need not stand in the way of a visit from the Bank, for the Bank later would simply deliver oil to the customers according to whatever purchase agreements had been signed.

Preparations went forward for a reconnaissance in Iran, to be carried out by two men, Hector Prud'homme and Torkild Rieber. Prud'homme, the leader of the mission, was the Bank's loan officer for Iranian matters. Rieber was a personal acquaintance to whom Garner had turned.[11]

The terms of reference drawn up for Prud'homme and Rieber were brief. The team was to examine the state of the oil installations, which no outsider had seen since the departure of the last AIOC employees in October. The two men also were to carry a letter from Garner to Mossadegh outlining the basis on which the Bank was prepared to work out specific arrangements for the interim operation of the oil industry, and to glean whatever useful evidence they could about the attitude of Iranian officials on the oil question.

The letter to the prime minister, dated December 28, 1951, was one of twins; the other was addressed to Sir Oliver Franks, the British ambassador in Washington. The text stated most of the principles that the Bank had expounded all along, beginning with Garner's first talk with Dr. Mossadegh. Its principal points were:

• The interim oil operations would be conducted under a neutral top executive group selected by, and responsible to, the Bank. The Bank would

11. Prud'homme was an investment banker with earlier experience in the U.S. diplomatic service. He was controlled in manner and sensitive in his relations with other people; his conversations with Mossadegh were conducted in French. "Cap" Rieber could be called on without raising the conflict-of-interest issue that might have arisen if Garner had turned to one of the major oil companies for an expert. A Norwegian-born American, Rieber had risen from seaman to tanker captain to chairman of the Texas Oil Company; after leaving Texaco, he became president of a smaller, independent concern, the Barber Oil Company. He was practical, perceptive, vigorous, and bluntly outspoken.

be free to hire and discharge such other personnel as it considered necessary for efficient operations, "without being restricted in the choice of nationalities."

- The Bank would be given all authority necessary to carry out the interim arrangement.
- The Bank would undertake to see that funds were made available for resuming oil operations.
- The Bank would make a bulk export contract for the sale of oil through established British distribution channels.

In addition to these familiar points, the letter made two other points that departed from earlier ideas. One, in recognition of the concern expressed by the Foreign Office, was simply that:

- The interim arrangement would be "without prejudice to the legal rights of the interested parties."

In the other, the Bank reverted to a three-way, rather than a two-way, division of the proceeds of oil sales:

- One part would go to Iran and one part to the bulk buyer; the remainder would be held by the Bank in trust.

Reversion to this formula reflected a difficulty that would have been encountered in a two-part division between the Iranians and the Bank, with the company getting its share through being able to purchase oil at a discount. To get agreement on the principle of a two-part formula, it first would have been necessary to agree on a specific price and discount, and this would have complicated the main question, which was whether Iran would agree in principle to work toward an arrangement involving the Bank in the oil issue.

Finally, the letter asked for "confirmation that the principles outlined . . . are acceptable to your Government as a basis for discussions."

The omens, not all of which were known in Washington at the time, were not propitious. When he talked to the Majlis on December 11, Mossadegh confirmed that he had indeed discussed the oil question with the Bank. Unless the Bank agreed with Iranian views on the pricing of oil, he said, "it would not be advisable for our country that they [the Bank] should bring in money . . . and add another misfortune to those we are suffering from." A fortnight later, an American news agency reported that the prime minister had told a press conference that the plan of settling the oil dispute through the World Bank was unacceptable for two reasons: Iran would not agree to sell oil to Britain at less than world prices, and Iran would not agree to the rehiring of oil technicians from AIOC. Three days before the arrival of Prud'homme and Rieber in Tehran, there was a riot in the capital protesting the intervention of the Bank.

Second Encounter

Prud'homme and Rieber arrived at Tehran airport on New Year's Eve. They were met by Hossein Pirnia, under-secretary of the Ministry of Finance, which had oversight of the oil concession. His thoughts were running far beyond interim arrangements. He spoke of the possibility of creating an Iranian producing and refining agency and of creating an international organization for distributing oil—the latter a process, Rieber cautioned, that would take a long time.

The next morning, the World Bank team saw the prime minister. He was cordial and in good humor; Prud'homme recalled later that "we laughed a good deal about various things." But the overall effect on the Bank team was one of shock. When the prime minister settled down to business, he summed up the situation as follows: (1) The Bank would provide funds to resume the oil operation. This had been agreed in Washington, the prime minister said. (2) The Bank would hold back a certain part of oil revenues against possible claims by AIOC. This also had been agreed. (3) No British nationals and no AIOC technicians would be reemployed. This had been agreed. (4) There would have to be agreement about the price of oil. On this point the Bank had made no suggestion.

When Mossadegh pronounced his third point, the Bank team could scarcely believe him. Did the prime minister, Rieber asked, really mean that there could be *no* British employees at the working level? The answer, Mossadegh said, was yes.

The gap in ideas between Washington and Tehran yawned still wider when Mossadegh explained his own thoughts on price and commercial arrangements. There would be no discount and no cash payments to the British at all. The Iranians would deliver oil to the British in lieu of compensation, at a valuation equivalent to a world market price or regionally posted price (neither of which had customarily been used by AIOC). To other customers, a commercial discount would be offered. At the end of this interview, and after a further talk with Under-Secretary Pirnia, the Bank team concluded that unless the Iranian position could be changed, the Bank's own approach (as outlined in the still undelivered letter from Garner to Mossadegh) would be irrelevant.

On the next day Prud'homme and Rieber made a round of calls. Diplomatic secretaries in the Pakistan embassy (in the temporary absence of the ambassador) expressed amazement that the Bank had believed it would be possible for British technicians to return to the oil operation; in fact, this was a political impossibility, and there must have been a grievous misunderstanding in Washington on this point.[12]

The World Bank representatives also shared their trouble with the U.S. ambassador in Tehran, Mr. Loy Henderson. After discussion with him, Prud'homme decided it would be wise, in order to avoid prejudice to future negotiations, to eliminate language from Garner's letter that suggested a role for British technicians, or indeed any British role, in an interim operation. The middle page of the letter was retyped. The new text, instead of speaking of the sale of oil through established *British* channels, spoke simply of established channels. And in the stipulation that the Bank would be free to hire and fire such operational personnel as it saw fit, *without being restricted in the choice of nationalities,* this final clause was deleted. At the end of the day, the new text was given to Pirnia for delivery to the prime minister. The Bank's views, divergent from those of Mossadegh, were now irrevocably on the record.

It was a troubled Pirnia who came to see the Bank team at their hotel in the suburbs of Tehran the next morning. Prime Minister Mossadegh had been angry, and the question had arisen of asking the Bank mission to leave Iran. The letter was unfortunate, said Pirnia. Its tone smacked of British high-handedness. The suggestion of a three-way split of oil revenues, putting the Iranian government on the same footing as an ex-concessionaire, was totally unacceptable.

Late in the afternoon, Pirnia delivered the prime minister's formal reply to the Garner letter. The reply—which had been released to the press four hours earlier—asked questions and raised objections; to the issues already raised *viva voce* in Tehran, it added a third: "The International Bank should keep . . . in mind that any intervention on its part in the exploitation of the oil resources in Iran should be regarded as a delegation of authority from the Iranian Government; in other words, the Bank should act on behalf of the Iranian Government and carry out its orders and give its accounts to the said Government. . . . It is impossible for the Iranian Government to accept any other undertakings with the Bank." In a report to Washington, Prud'homme summed up the march of events succinctly: "We almost got thrown out."

Once again the American ambassador offered counsel. At his suggestion, the Bank representatives held their ground. Prud'homme wrote the prime minister a note, observing that time for study would be needed before Garner

12. When Mr. Garner told Dr. Mossadegh that the Bank's idea was to arrange for the oil operation to be run by an organization that was not British, did the prime minister assume that such an organization would not include any British staff?

could reply and suggesting that it might expedite later discussions if the Bank team could visit the oil installations in the interval. He also asked that the team have an early opportunity to "chat" with the prime minister.

The chat, on the next day, lasted for ninety minutes. Mossadegh stressed Iran's need for money, in the form of either American aid or a World Bank loan. He indicated agreement with the idea, expressed earlier by Pirnia, of a separate distributing organization to be formed with the help of the Bank. He cordially agreed to a visit to the oil fields, in the belief that a first-hand report to the outside world on this subject would be helpful. The refinery and the oil fields, far from being sabotaged as had been rumored, were found to be in excellent condition, brightwork burnished and every item in place.

On January 7, 1952, the British ambassador responded to Garner's letter of December 28, saying that the principles described in it were "generally acceptable" to the British government. Two days later, a communiqué issued after wide-ranging talks between President Truman and the visiting British prime minister, Winston Churchill, included a sentence on the oil question: "We both hope that the initiative taken by the International Bank for Reconstruction and Development will lead to a solution of the Iranian oil problem acceptable to all the interests concerned."

But Mossadegh, in his answer to Garner, already had declared that the British, since they had not taken advantage of the opportunity to buy oil, no longer could be considered to be any more "concerned" than anyone else. On other points, his views remained unchanged. When Prud'homme and Rieber, before starting home, had a parting interview with the prime minister, the latter reviewed the long history of the oil question, summarized again the four points of his first talk with the Bank team, and reiterated that Garner's letter was simply another British proposal and the Bank itself nothing but a phonograph playing the British record over and over.

Withdrawal and Return: Third Encounter

Dr. Mossadegh's vigorous rejection of Garner's letter, written after such careful consultations in London, took the Bank's management by surprise. Nevertheless, the outlook was not considered to be totally discouraging. The impression lingered from Mossadegh's discussions with the State Department in Washington that if accommodation could be reached on all other counts, a compromise on the question of British technicians was possible. The facts also suggested that the material basis for Iranian obduracy was weakening. A study showed that the world output of crude oil had not declined in the second half of 1951, despite the closing down of the Iranian fields. Refinery output was down only 0.2 percent, and refinery construction in progress would be adequate to replace the capacity of Abadan by 1953.

In the light of these and other considerations the Bank's executive directors agreed that it was time to try actual negotiations in Tehran. (The previous Prud'homme-Rieber trip had been a fact-finding mission.) Mossadegh, no doubt hoping for a decisive upturn in his favor, telegraphed that he would be "delighted" to receive the vice president of the Bank. A five-man team set out for the Iranian capital. In addition to Garner, Prud'homme, and Rieber, it consisted of Samuel Lipkowitz, an industrial economist on the Bank's staff, and Ellsworth Clark, a member of the Bank's legal staff (later to become an assistant general counsel), who preceded the main group as an advance party of one.

On February 12 the group had a first meeting with Mossadegh. He again said that the return of British technicians to Tehran was out of the question; later it might be permitted, but the attitude of the Iranian people made it impossible now; and anyway, if the British came back, that would provoke Soviet pressure for an entrée into northern Iran. In vain, Garner and his colleagues pressed the point that it would be impossible to find enough technicians elsewhere. (It was estimated that at least two thousand would be needed.) In vain they argued that Iran was in danger of permanently losing its markets for oil.

At the end of three hours of discussion, Mossadegh remained unmoved. A breakdown in the talks was averted only at the last minute by the intervention of Khalil Talleghani, minister of agriculture and secretary to the Cabinet. He tactfully suggested that the point about technicians be set aside and that the visitors turn to other issues.

Seven days of intense and earnest talk followed. On the third of these days, work began on an aide-mémoire, stating the respective positions of the two sides. On the fourth day, at the suggestion of Transport and Information Minister Bousheri, two members of the Iranian Senate joined the discussions. They seemed anxious that agreement be reached and persuaded Garner, who had intended to leave the following night, to stay another forty-eight hours.

Mr. Garner suggested a two-part distribution of income and an attractive discount to the bulk purchaser of oil. Mossadegh countered by suggesting a smaller discount and prices for refined oil that would not have been competitive in the world market. No further progress was made, and the Iranians continued to say that on this score the Bank was simply putting forth the British proposals all over again.

The larger question of Iranian government finances continued to haunt Mossadegh. If British technicians were allowed to return, he had gravely explained at one point in the discussions, his government would fall; and if oil operations were not resumed, a financial crisis might ensue that also would topple his government. As between the two issues, he would prefer to go out on the latter. But when he pressed Garner several times on the question of budgetary support from the Bank, he found that the Bank's attitude on this question had changed since November.

Iran's financial need was now seen as a lever that could force Mossadegh toward agreement. On the question of budgetary support, he found Garner as unyielding as he himself had been on the matter of technicians. For the present, there could be no question of Bank funds for anything but the resumption of oil operations; help for the Iranian budget might be found after an interim arrangement had been made for oil operations, but not before.

Work on the aide-mémoire, nevertheless, inched forward. During six days of drafting, discussing, and re-drafting, virtually every paragraph became a ground for contest. On the Iranian side, the procedures became more formidable, ultimately drawing in not only members of the Parliamentary Oil Commission but also the Cabinet to consider the document.

Some agreement was reached on lesser points, but on major points there was no meeting of the minds. Agreement could be reached only on language that discreetly expressed or blandly concealed unresolved questions, especially about the employment of British nationals, the pricing of oil, and the distribution of oil income. At the end, it proved impossible to agree even on how to disagree.

On February 19, 1952, the last day of talks, the Iranians proposed that a phrase be inserted indicating that the Bank would manage the oil operations "for the account of Iran." When the aide-mémoire came forward for signature by Garner and the prime minister, the Bank vice president took exception to this language and refused to sign. What was now being put forward seemed to Garner and his colleagues clearly to imply that the Bank was to be considered as acting as agent for Iran alone. The prime minister said he could not delete the phrase without consulting the Cabinet. He himself appeared to be uncertain about the meaning of the new language. Several hours of discussion failed to resolve the matter.

In the end, all was anticlimax. With the members of the Oil Commission and the Cabinet gathered for the occasion, the signing of the aide-mémoire did not take place. Some of the senators present were visibly dismayed, but after all, said Garner, it was the substance of the discussions that mattered, and an aide-mémoire, while it would have been helpful, was not indispensable. He and the Bank would continue to exert their best efforts toward an interim solution.

Finally, a joint communiqué was issued to the press. It indicated that discussions had taken place "in an atmosphere of cordiality and goodwill," that "a frank exchange of views" had clarified the respective positions of the Iranian government and the Bank, and that the matter would be pursued further.[13]

A month later, following further fruitless discussion in London and Tehran and a postmortem in Washington, the Bank rang down the curtain on the Iranian matter. On April 3, 1952, it published a summary account of the negotiations, together with a press release, which said that the Bank had informed Iran and the United Kingdom "that it stands ready, as in the past, to assist in working out any practicable suggestion which offers a reasonable prospect of success."[14]

Retrospect

Rieber returned to Iran as oil adviser to the government, and the settlement of the oil question in 1954 bore some traces of the earlier discussions in which he had participated. Nevertheless, the Bank's first experiment in the field of international mediation had not achieved its objective.

In retrospect, it is easy to say that there never was a real chance that the Bank's efforts to mediate the oil matter would succeed. The British would have been perfectly content with an arrangement that would restore the flow of oil and of revenues to both parties, but Mossadegh and his colleagues never showed any serious interest in such an arrangement. They wanted to press on quickly to a final settlement, and it was necessary from their point of view that even interim measures should contain elements of something more than a pro forma recognition of oil nationalization—the very action, as the British saw it, on which a verdict was being sought in international courts of law and public opinion.

The Bank had no lever powerful enough to change the position of either party. Neither side, in fact, seems to have been convinced that the discussions with the Bank constituted the principal action. However unrealistically, the British continued to look toward the International Court of Justice and the Iranians toward the possibility of an American loan for a solution to their

13. *New York Times,* Feb. 20, 1952, p. 4.
14. IBRD, Press release (April 3, 1952).

problems. It was only after these two possibilities had disappeared and Dr. Mossadegh himself had vanished from the Iranian political scene that the steps leading to a settlement finally began.

India and Pakistan: Water

The mediation between India and Pakistan of the question of dividing and developing the waters of the Indus River system was the longest the Bank ever undertook. Nine years passed between the Bank's first initiatives and the final signing of the Indus Waters Treaty in 1960. The settlement was literally a vital achievement, bringing life-giving water to the farms of the Indus Valley more copiously than ever before and fending off the possibility of a disastrous war, over the issue of water for irrigation, between the two nations into which some 475 million people of the Indian subcontinent were divided in 1947.

The Indus River rises high in the Himalayas. Before it finally flows into the Arabian Sea, far to the south, it has covered 1,800 miles—a distance as great as that from New York to Denver or from Rome to Baghdad. As the river flows southward, it is fed from the east by the waters of five other rivers: the Jhelum, the Chenab, the Ravi, the Sutlej, and the Beas. Without these rivers the lower reaches of the Indus Valley would be a desert to rival the Sahara.

In fact, however, when the Bank was mediating the question, the valley was supporting no less than fifty million people. What made this possible was that the rivers then fed—as they still do today—the largest irrigation system in the world. It was a system that had taken a century to develop. It comprised almost 34,000 miles of main canals and tributaries, with a total capacity greater than the annual flow of the Nile and watering some twenty-five million acres of land, four-fifths of it in Pakistan.[15]

There was no water storage anywhere in the system, and while irrigation capacity could be increased by the construction of new canals, the water had to be taken as it ran. Within a given canal capacity, what was taken upstream could not be used below, and each use established downstream meant that less water could be taken above. Particularly after 1920, there was increasing competition for water, especially between the provincial governments of the Punjab, upstream, and Sind, downstream.

15. Neil Bass, "The Role of the World Bank in the Indus Basin Water Agreement between India and Pakistan," paper presented at a seminar on international river basins at the University of British Columbia in Canada, Sept. 13, 1961.

The partition of the subcontinent into India and Pakistan in 1947 abruptly cut the irrigation system in two. In the former province of Punjab, itself now divided in two, the new political boundary created problems. The border crossed and recrossed the Central Bari Doab Canal, separating it from the controlling headworks on the Ravi River at Madhoput in the Indian state of East Punjab. The Dipalpur Canal similarly was put in the Pakistani state of West Punjab, while the controlling headworks on the Sutlej River were at Ferozepore in East Punjab. The problem was solved temporarily by an agreement signed by a Punjab Partition Committee, continuing the pre-partition flow of water through March 31, 1948, and leaving it to the Punjab governments to come to a new agreement in the meantime.

Neither government, however, made any move toward a new arrangement. At the end of the stipulated period, the authorities of East Punjab promptly stopped the flow of water from the Upper Bari Doab Canal. In the ensuing clamor of protest, the question of the Indus waters for the first time was handed up to the two national governments for consideration. There were meetings in New Delhi; the flow of water was resumed on April 30; and in the Indian capital on May 4, 1948, a new agreement was signed by Prime Minister Nehru for India and by Finance Minister Ghulam Mohammed for Pakistan.

Pakistan later contended that the May 4 document had been signed under duress. Since India, as the upstream power, had the physical capability to divert water from Pakistan, the Pakistani indeed had no feasible alternative to some form of agreement. The arrangment of May 4 did in fact abolish the status quo on the rivers. It laid down the principle that India would increase its withdrawals and use of the waters of the eastern tributaries—but would do so gradually, so that Pakistan could replace the water by contriving to tap alternative sources.

The May 4 arrangement had no time limit, but it specified that further meetings would be held. In meetings at New Delhi and Karachi in 1949, Pakistan pressed for the recognition and protection of uses already established downstream (which would have negated the May 4 provision for the gradual transfer of some water to India) and also wanted, in the event that negotiations failed, a final adjudication by the International Court of Justice. When India stood firm on the principles of May 4, Pakistan in November stated that the document could no longer be considered to be in force. Correspondence between the two prime ministers during the following year failed to resolve the question. For the time being, the rivers continued to be shared as before, but each government was preparing works for new uses of the waters.

Enter the Bank

Now a *deus ex machina* appeared in the person of David E. Lilienthal, a distinguished American recently retired from public service. He was the former chairman of the U.S. Atomic Energy Commission and had been chairman of the world-famous Tennessee Valley Authority (TVA). As a private citizen, Lilienthal visited the Indus Valley in 1951, and in an article published that summer he suggested a formula for dealing with the Indus matter.

The whole Indus system [he said] must be developed as a unit . . . as is the TVA system. . . . Jointly financed (perhaps with World Bank help) an Indus Engineering Corporation, with representation by technical men of India, Pakistan and the World Bank, can readily work out an operating scheme. . . . Once the scheme is designed, the works can be operated by an Indo-Pakistan Agency, or by a supranational international agency such as the Schuman Plan provided in Europe, or by some special corporation like the Port of New York Authority.[16]

The Lilienthal proposal immediately caught the notice of the World Bank management. The Bank had stumbled over the Indus question already; in 1949, Pakistan had cited the water controversy in objecting to Bank consideration of an Indian request for financing part of the Bakhra-Nangal multipurpose scheme on the Jhelum River; and India, only a few weeks before the Lilienthal article appeared, had given the same reason for objecting to a Pakistani request for financing a barrage at Kotri on the Indus.

Not only did the Indus issue stand in the way of constructive action by the Bank on the subcontinent, it was cause for concern in a wider sense. With two of the Bank's potentially largest customers so bitterly opposed, the world's investors might regard the Bank's own prospects with a skepticism that would cripple its ability to raise money through borrowing.[17]

On September 8, 1951, after soundings had been taken with the British and American governments, President Black addressed letters to the prime ministers of India and Pakistan.

Since the Bank's name has now been publicly mentioned in this connection [he wrote], I should like to ask you whether you are disposed to look with favor upon Mr. Lilienthal's proposal. If so . . . I should be most happy to recommend that the Bank lend its good offices in such directions as might be considered appropriate by the two governments, make available qualified members of its staff and consider any financing proposals that might develop as a result of joint planning.

16. David E. Lilienthal, "Another 'Korea' in the Making?" *Collier's* (Aug. 4, 1951).

17. Eugene R. Black, "The Indus: A Moral for Nations," *New York Times,* Dec. 11, 1960.

The response from Pakistan was a warm acceptance: Here at last was the chance of a third-party mediation that might rescue Pakistan from its unhappy position as the downstream supplicant for water. On September 25, Prime Minister Liaquat Ali Khan wrote to Black that,

Pakistan is prepared to enter into an agreement . . . on the bases proposed by Mr. Lilienthal for a settlement of the waters dispute. . . . The constructive program envisaged by Mr. Lilienthal would be greatly facilitated were the Bank to exercise its tendered good offices. Indeed, without the aid of good offices such as you have tendered, little, if any, progress toward a constructive solution could be anticipated.

Prime Minister Nehru's reply, dated the same day, was more reserved. Any settlement would have to take into account the May 1948 agreement, of which he sent a copy with his letter. Nor did he think that the joint agency suggested by Mr. Lilienthal was a practical possibility, for the present at least. But he welcomed the idea of the development of the Indus system as a single unit, along with the association of the Bank with a joint technical survey on which a development program could be based.

The Bank staff then turned to the question of how to proceed. On November 8, Black addressed another letter to Prime Minister Nehru and the prime minister of Pakistan (then Khwaja Nazimuddin, following the assassination of Liaquat Ali Khan). He restated the principles of the Lilienthal proposal: (a) that there was enough water in the Indus system to continue existing uses and to meet the future needs of both countries; (b) that the Indus waters should be cooperatively developed as a unit; and (c) that the problem of water development should be solved on a functional and not a political plane, "without regard to past negotiations and past claims." He proposed that engineers designated by the two countries, assisted by a Bank engineer, should jointly prepare a comprehensive long-range plan for the development of the water resources of the Indus Basin.

This formulation was not accepted. Prime Minister Nehru was out on the hustings in a general election campaign and did not reply to Black's letter until January 1952. Then he took exception to two of Lilienthal's principles: (1) while cooperative development of the Indus system was desirable, it was nevertheless necessary to take into account the fact that the area had been divided into two political units; and (2) with respect to past negotiations, the existence of the May 1948 agreement could not be ignored. Happily, the prime minister noted, Black was coming to India the following month, and the Indus matter could be discussed then.

In February, Black made a long-planned visit to the subcontinent. In discussions with the two prime ministers, he tried to work out a statement on which the cooperative work of engineers could be based. What finally emerged was agreement on the main point: Engineers from the two countries *would* meet to formulate a plan. As Black summed it up in a letter to the prime ministers in March 1952, the objective would be to draw up "specific engineering measures by which the supplies [of water] effectively available to each country will be increased substantially beyond what they have ever been." While the work was in progress, a standstill agreement would be in effect: Neither side would take any action to diminish the water available to the other for existing uses.

There were no common terms of reference, and each side explicitly was left free to withdraw at any time. Both parties had to defer their ambitions on major points. Pakistan put aside its desire that the matter be arbitrated or that the work be conducted under a neutral chairman; India put aside the idea of reducing supplies to the Central Bari Doab and Dipalpur Canals in order to increase her own water uses, as she had been entitled to do under the May 1948 arrangement. But these were not considered, by India and the Bank at least, to be serious drawbacks, since it was expected that a final solution would be reached in six months or so.[18]

The Work Begins . . . and Ends

The problem to be taken up by the working party of engineers was one of enormous complexity. The Indus, the tributaries reaching it through Indian territory, and the canals drawing water from the rivers formed an intricate network of interdependent flows.

The contributions of the rivers to the total flow, in an average year, are shown in Table 18-1. Not only did the flow differ from river to river, but there were major fluctuations from year to year. There were major seasonal variations in the rivers and in the system as a whole. There were many local variations arising from seepage and evaporation. For six months, from October through March, the waters were low. In the next three months, as the run-off from the melting Himalayan snows began to race toward the south, the flow was four times greater, and from July through September the flow was seven times greater than in the period of low water.

The need for water, on the other hand, never ceased. Throughout the valley, crops were grown both during the summer season (*kharif*) and the

18. For some of these and many other details, it has been possible to draw on a manuscript "Indus Waters Treaty: An Exercise in International Mediation," by N. D. Gulhati, to be published in 1973 by Allied Publishers, New Delhi. The author was a member of the Indian engineering delegation during the whole of the Indus negotiations and was the Indian representative during most of them.

winter season (*rabi*). Meeting the water requirement called for the coordinated management of an intricate system with many interdependent variables of rivers, canals, and crop needs. To study the development of the system required an immensely comprehensive and specific knowledge of the behavior of the many parts of the irrigation network—not merely in broad terms of rivers and seasons, but in details of small segments of the system and periods as brief as ten days.

The individuals chosen to prepare the joint plan for developing the Indus waters held their inaugural meeting in Washington on May 6, 1952. The Pakistan designee was Mohammed Abdul Hamid, the chief engineer of Punjab; the Indian designee was A. N. Khosla, chairman of the Central Water and Power Commission of India. Each was assisted by additional engineers, and each had legal counsel standing by. The Bank designee was Lieutenant General Raymond A. Wheeler, engineering adviser to the Bank, a man of great personal charm and sagacity as well as high engineering and administrative competence.

Notions about how to proceed differed sharply between the two delegations. After a nine-thousand-mile trip through the Indus basin by the working party, and after more months of fact gathering, the engineering delegations met once more in Washington on September 1, 1953. They could not agree on how to begin. After three weeks, the idea of joint planning was abandoned, and it was agreed that each side would present a plan of its own by early October.

The Indian delegation at that time presented a plan for the basin as a whole, the first such plan ever to be prepared. The Pakistan plan, on the other hand, did not suggest any development on the Indian side; Engineer

Table 18-1. *Contributions of Rivers to Total Flow of Water in India and Pakistan*

River	Water flow in millions of acre-feet[a]	Percent of total
Indus	90.0	53.5
Jhelum	23.0	13.6
Chenab	23.0	13.6
Sutlej	13.5	8.0
Beas	12.7	7.5
Ravi	6.4	3.8

Source: Derived from Gulhati, "Indus Waters Treaty."
a. An acre-foot of water is the amount required to cover an area of one acre to a depth of one foot.

Hamid held that the undeveloped areas in India were outside the Indus Basin and therefore were not entitled to water from the Indus system.

The Pakistan designee based his plan on an uninterrupted flow from existing sources. The Indian designee held fast to the 1948 document: Pakistan should meet some of her existing uses by tapping alternative sources. As for sharing additional waters made available by new development, the Pakistan designee wanted them divided in the same proportion as the existing flow, with Pakistan therefore receiving the major part. The Indian designee argued that the shares should be equal. India claimed all the flow from the eastern rivers (Ravi, Sutlej, and Beas); Pakistan wanted 30 percent of it. Pakistan claimed all the flow from the western rivers (Indus, Chenab, and Jhelum); India wanted 7 percent of that flow.

The two sides did agree that the system could be developed to a point where the usable flow of water would be about 120 million acre-feet a year. But the two plans were more than 12 million acre-feet apart on the distribution of the flow. The Indian plan would have allotted Pakistan 90 million acre-feet; the Pakistan plan claimed 102.5 million. The Pakistan plan would have allowed India 15.5 million acre-feet; the Indian designee wanted at least 29 million.

Faced with the prospect of a permanent deadlock, General Wheeler in mid-December began preparing a proposal to be offered by the Bank. The two sides tacitly welcomed this initiative, and the plan was presented to them separately on February 5, 1954.[19]

The Bank proposal was almost startlingly simple. Under it, the entire flow of the western rivers would be reserved for Pakistan, and the entire flow of the eastern rivers would be reserved, in principle, for India. During a transition period of five years, however, India would continue to supply from its sources withdrawals needed for Pakistan's existing uses then being met by water based on the eastern rivers. In the meantime, Pakistan would construct the works needed to tap alternative sources of supply, and the cost of these works in Pakistan would be borne by India.

As it happened, the resulting shares of water (calculated at 22 million acre-feet for India and 97 for Pakistan) would halve the difference between the shares proposed by the two sides. The division would meet the historic uses of both sides; it would leave each free to construct storage for generating new supplies; and neither side would be dependent on the other for the operation of any works governing the flow of water.

19. The text of the Bank proposal was made public in Appendix I to an IBRD press release of December 10, 1954.

The proposal, for the time being, left some questions unanswered—especially the extent and cost of the replacement works for which India was to be financially liable. But the Bank argued strongly that the plan was "simple, workable, and fair," and in a letter to the prime ministers on February 8, 1954, President Black urged that the two governments accept the proposal in principle without delay.

Instead, for more than six months the negotiations hovered on the verge of collapse. The Pakistani delegation was thunderstruck by the Bank's proposal and quickly began preparing to return to Karachi—an action from which it was dissuaded only by the intervention of President Black himself. Giving an oral critique of the proposal in mid-March, the Pakistan designee declared that no plan that failed to allocate to Pakistan some of the waters of the eastern rivers could be considered workable. A letter from Pakistan Prime Minister Mohammed Ali in mid-May said that the best hope of reaching agreement was through the Bank, but asserted that the division of waters now proposed was unfair.

The Bank countered with pressure on Pakistan: in conversations with Foreign Minister Zafrulla Khan in Washington, the management declared that if the negotiations were not resumed, the reasons would have to be made public, and Pakistan would have to bear the blame.

Ultimately each side agreed to proceed, under terms of reference set out by Black in a letter of August 13, 1954. By September 30, 1955, he proposed, a comprehensive scheme would be drawn up on the basis of the Bank proposal. From the flow waters of the western rivers, the scheme would aim to cover the actual amounts of water that customarily had been used in Pakistan and in Jammu and Kashmir before partition, and to make additional water available for the requirements of irrigation schemes in the Thal and at Kotri in Pakistan. Out of any water remaining, the scheme would try to meet, to the extent possible, the requirements of Sukkur and Gudu and of future development in the State of Jammu and Kashmir. After nearly three years of effort by the Bank, it at last seemed possible for negotiations to proceed on an agreed basis.

The Work Resumes (1954–57)

When the negotiators gathered in Washington on December 6, 1954, it was with a somewhat revised cast of principal characters. There was a new Pakistan designee: G. Mueenuddin, who was an alumnus of the former Indian civil service, one of the most senior members of the civil service in Pakistan, and a top official of the Ministry of Industries; and who was more willing to communicate his views to Karachi and had greater influence there than his predecessor had had. The Indian designee was N. D. Gulhati; an engineer, studious, precise, and tenacious, he had been de facto designee since illness had forced his predecessor, A. N. Khosla, to return to India the year before.

The Bank representative was William A. B. Iliff, assistant to the president (and vice president from 1956), who was the senior Briton in the Bank. He was named as a result of urging from Zafrulla Khan in the previous summer that the Bank carry out its mission through a member of the management rather than through the purely technical team headed by General Wheeler. General Wheeler himself continued to be the Bank's senior engineer concerned with the Indus question; and the Bank also retained an American engineering consulting firm (Knappen, Tippetts, Abbet and McCarthy) to gather and analyze data for which it previously had relied on India and Pakistan.

Before work on a comprehensive plan could proceed, more urgent business intervened. The Indian government had decided that, since the Indus matter had dragged on for an unforeseen length of time, New Delhi would no longer be bound by the standstill agreement of 1952 with the Bank. In May 1954, it notified the government of Pakistan that in July it would open the Bakhra Canal, making use of water from the Sutlej River.

By common consent, the first business of the new negotiators in Washington at the end of 1954 was to work out further arrangements, designated as "transitional," for Indian withdrawals from the eastern rivers. This necessitated an updating of knowledge of new works on the Indian side and of the extent to which replacement works had been completed on the Pakistan side; and a Bank team, headed by Mr. Iliff and accompanied by Indian and Pakistan engineers, visited the subcontinent in March and April 1955 to make an on-the-spot inspection. After bargaining on both sides—and a warning from Iliff that he would recommend an end to the Bank's good offices unless an understanding was achieved—an "ad hoc agreement" on transitional arrangements, outlined by the Bank Group, was reached in June.[20]

The agreement was the first formal document that the two governments had signed concerning the Indus matter since May 1948. It covered the *kharif* crop season, from April through September 1955. More importantly it confirmed the essence of the 1948 arrangements, including the principle that Indian withdrawals would not proceed faster than Pakistan's ability to replace them. The document also provided (as did subsequent agreements) that

20. IBRD, "Indus Waters Agreement between the Government of India and the Government of Pakistan for *Ad Hoc* Transitional Arrangements for 1955," June 21, 1955.

each side would appoint a special commissioner to supervise the execution of the agreement.

Despite mutual suspicion and recrimination, two further ad hoc agreements were negotiated to cover the period to March 31, 1957.[21] In the meantime, no progress had been made in formulating a comprehensive plan. Early in 1955, the Bank Group had tried to get the two sides to cooperate with the Bank in putting together, step by step, a "preliminary trial plan" that would not have been binding on either side, but it had not succeeded.

It was clear by now that Pakistan would never agree to any plan that did not provide for new, developmental uses. In August 1955, the Bank's consultants therefore were asked by the Bank to prepare both a minimum plan to meet historic uses and an "optimum plan" that would allow for development and make maximum use of the potential of the rivers. Toward the end of 1955, the consultants presented their findings, adding a major complication to the Indus question: for either plan, flow water would be insufficient, and in either case, storage works would be necessary.

Storage works would call for added expenditures. India could not be asked to bear the cost of developmental works in Pakistan, and Pakistan could not afford to. On March 13, 1956, the Bank quietly called a meeting of representatives of Australia, Canada, New Zealand, the United Kingdom, and the United States, at which Iliff floated the idea that help through government grants ultimately might be necessary. As if to underline the gravity of the issue, a twelve-hour shooting affray broke out on the night of March 18 on the Indo-Pakistan frontier between Pakistan border police and Indian troops that had been brought in to help repair the damage done to the canal at Ferozepore by the floods of the previous October.

On May 21, the Bank sent an aide-mémoire to both sides. It confirmed that the Bank proposal would have to be modified by providing storage on the western rivers and proposed that work be continued to develop a plan that would include storage. If by March 1957 there seemed to be no reasonable prospect of a settlement, said the aide-mémoire, the Bank management would have to consider whether to continue its good offices.

India replied that work could go ahead only if Pakistan now accepted unconditionally the allocation of the eastern rivers to India, as had been proposed by the Bank. The prime minister of Pakistan (Chaudhri Mohammad

---

21. The "Indus Waters Agreement between the Government of India and the Government of Pakistan for *Ad Hoc* Transitional Arrangements for Rabi, 1955–56," Oct. 31, 1955; and the "Indus Waters Agreement between the Government of India and the Government of Pakistan for *Ad Hoc* Transitional Arrangements for the Period from April 1, 1956, to March 31, 1957," Sept. 24, 1956.

Ali), in a meeting with Iliff in London in June, angrily stated that the Bank proposal was political and not technical and put a stamp of morality on the "illegal contention" that India was entitled to the exclusive use of all the water flowing through her territory.

The Bank was not diverted by the contentions of either side. In a letter of July 30, 1956, Iliff recommended that the governments simply agree to continue their efforts to work out a settlement on the basis of the Bank's proposal, as modified by the aide-mémoire. After an interval of more than a month, the governments agreed to continue. When fall and winter passed without result, Black asked the two sides to continue their work until September 1957; and in April, acceptances were forthcoming, despite Prime Minister Nehru's expression of serious concern at the lack of progress.

Plans put forward from the two sides nevertheless remained far apart. A proposal to extend the deadline by one year to September 30, 1958, was rejected by India. Said the Indian representative in Washington, "We would not agree to continue much longer a situation in which Pakistan was free to develop new uses on the Western Rivers while India was limited to increasing her use of water by the pace at which Pakistan proceeded with replacement works."[22] Finally, a three-month extension to the end of 1957 was agreed upon.

Cutting the Gordian Knot

As the year 1958 began, the Indus negotiations were at a standstill, and there seemed to be no prospect that they could be moved forward. There was no agreement in effect concerning transitional arrangements, nor even concerning the continuation of cooperative work in Washington. The Pakistan plan provided 6 million acre-feet of storage; the Indian concept, while more generous than before, still held the requirement to be only 1.5 million to 2.5 million. The difference in cost was wide: $700 million under the Pakistan plan, $80 million for the Indian approach.

The Bank cast about for a new basis of agreement. The idea of storage on the Indus itself, with link canals provided for transferring water so stored to the eastern rivers, was put aside as too expensive. Storage on the Jhelum, Pakistan had argued, was not an alternative; the work already going ahead at Mangla was needed for new development rather than for replacement. Iliff turned to a third possibility, based on a transaction that would take place on the Indian side of the border. This was to intercept the waters of the Chenab, one of the western rivers, at Marhu and tunnel them to the Ravi, an eastern

22. Gulhati, "Indus Waters Treaty."

river; an equivalent amount of water would be delivered to Pakistan at Ferozepore on the Sutlej.

Iliff took the idea to the subcontinent in January 1958. The authorities in New Delhi found it unacceptable. In Karachi, Iliff was unable to obtain any reaction at all; Prime Minister Feroz Khan Noon was attending a Baghdad Pact meeting in Ankara. When the prime minister finally was able to consider the proposal, he found the idea of putting control works on the Indian side of the border utterly repugnant. To fend it off, on March 8 he sent a cable to Washington that created the possibility of putting the negotiations on an entirely new footing: he proposed that the Indian financial liability, instead of being related to actual replacement works, should be limited to what the Marhu tunnel scheme, the most economical solution, would have cost.

In April the parties were asked to come to Rome, where Iliff was engaged in mediating the dispute between Egypt and the dispossessed shareholders of the Suez Canal Company. (See the discussion on page 641, below.) It was agreed that Pakistan would prepare a plan providing for substantial works in Pakistan, which would include four link canals, storage on three tributaries of the Jhelum, and the Mangla Dam already under construction. Another new idea, resulting from Noon's proposal to limit India's financial liability, was brought into the open. The March 1956 meeting with potential aid-givers had taken place without the knowledge of India and Pakistan, but now Iliff specified that a large supplement to the financial contribution to India would be sought to support the new scheme.

The Pakistan plan, when it emerged in July, was grandiose in its proportions and unacceptable to India. The proposal, however, did represent signal progress in one respect: it was the first to be put forward from Pakistan that was based entirely on the Bank proposal that Pakistan should take the waters of the western rivers but make no demands for waters of the eastern rivers. In fact, a new willingness to agree now became evident in Karachi. On his way back from the annual meeting of the Bank's board of governors, held in New Delhi in 1958, President Black had stopped in Karachi and had met Field Marshal Ayub, who had just become martial law administrator and was soon to assume the presidency of Pakistan. The two men had hit it off famously. Not long after their meeting, Mueenuddin addressed a note to the Bank saying that his government accepted "without condition or reservation" the principles of the Bank proposal as amended by the aide-mémoire of 1956.

The Bank had discovered early in 1959 that the U.S. authorities would be willing to make a large contribution to the cost of works in Pakistan. On March 26, the Bank followed up by sending a formal memorandum to the governments of Australia, Canada, the United Kingdom, and the United

States, indicating the reason for, and the nature of, the external financial requirements of the Indus scheme. The reactions were favorable: In addition, New Zealand soon came forward with an offer of assistance, while Germany was added to the list of "friendly governments" after a discussion between Black and Economics Minister Erhard in June.

Concurrently the engineering teams had gone ahead to negotiate a new ad hoc agreement. The enterprise had been initiated by Mueenuddin. He saw a new agreement as advantageous in soliciting financial support for an Indus scheme and necessary in view of the fact that India's Bakhra reservoir was to receive a considerable amount of water during *kharif* 1959. A document outlining ad hoc arrangements for *rabi* 1958–59 and *kharif* 1959 was signed on April 17. Under it, Pakistan agreed to run the replacement canals (Marala–Ravi and Balloki–Suleimanke) at 80 percent of capacity during *kharif*. The parties thereby brought themselves close to a final agreement—but another year and a half was required to achieve it.

The Final Phase

Encouraged by the trend of events, Black and Iliff journeyed to the subcontinent in May 1959 with the draft of final heads of agreement of an Indus Waters Treaty. It provided that a system of works, for both replacement and development, would be built in Pakistan—with the advice of the Bank, but without the participation or agreement of India. This removed a troublesome issue, since it became unnecessary for an agreement to mention the Mangla Dam, which was being built on disputed territory.

A second matter covered by the heads of agreement was the length of the transition period during which the replacement works would be completed and Indian withdrawals from the eastern rivers would gradually rise to their final level. The period was set at ten years—midway between the five years the Indians thought necessary and the fifteen the Pakistanis wanted; the period would end in 1969 or 1970, depending on when the treaty was signed. Allowance was made for extensions of up to three years, with reductions in the Indian contribution for each year's extension. Outside the heads of agreement an offer was made to India to make it easier for it to accept the proposed transitional period: Since the new canals in Rajasthan would need water before 1969 or 1970, the Bank would arrange for financial assistance to help India build a storage dam on the Beas River to enhance the supply; the United States would provide $33 million, and the Bank would lend $23 million.

The heads of agreement further envisioned the establishment of an Indus Basin Development Commission with five members—two named by India, two by Pakistan, and a neutral chairman—to resolve questions arising under the treaty. Finally, it was specified that an ad hoc sum would be fixed as the Indian financial contribution toward the cost of replacement works.

After amendments and revisions in New Delhi, the heads of agreement were accepted by the Indian government. The first firm understanding to be reached under the new outline fixed the Indian financial contribution at £62.5 million (the equivalent at that time of $175 million), a figure agreed to on May 14 by Iliff and B. K. Nehru (the Indian economic commissioner in Washington and formerly an executive director of the Bank) and ratified the next day at the last of three meetings between Prime Minister Nehru and President Black. The whole arrangement, the prime minister declared, represented "the final Indian position and cannot be further modified in favor of Pakistan."

In Karachi, Black and Iliff obtained the Pakistan government's acceptance of the heads of agreement also and took up the matter of the works to be built in Pakistan. On May 18, Black handed President Ayub a memorandum asking that Pakistan adopt a system of works, including storage at Tarbela on the Indus as well as Mangla on the Jhelum, but amended from earlier proposals so as not to cost more than the equivalent of $838 million (the costs as estimated by the Bank's consultants).

Now it remained to agree in detail to what already had been agreed to *en large*. After intensive discussions in London and Washington, a draft of an Indus Waters Treaty was sent by the Bank to the governments in January 1960 for their comments. The draft consisted of a preamble and eleven articles, and for almost every one of its provisions, there was a history of demands and counter-demands.[23] It was agreed that an Indus Commission, consisting of one representative from each side, would be created to settle any question that might arise under the treaty. If the commissioners could not agree, a third party (who could be the secretary-general of the United Nations) might arbitrate. But on the chief issues of the Indus controversy, disagreement persisted.

The schedule of water transfers during the transitional period was left to be worked out and to be expressed in an annex to the treaty. It was accepted that India could use some of the waters of the western rivers, but the actual amounts of water to be used and of storage to be provided were left for another annex. As yet unresolved (and ultimately settled outside the treaty) were financial claims and counter-claims arising out of the arrangements of May 1948—mainly seigniorage charges by India for water delivered to Pak-

23. *Ibid.*

istan, against which Pakistan had opposed claims for the expense of operating the replacement works so that India could enjoy the use of the eastern rivers. In addition, Pakistan wanted, and India opposed (but finally accepted), a *force majeure* clause, which would extend the transition period (and thereby postpone Indian withdrawals) if for some extraordinary reason beyond the control of Pakistan the necessary financial support from friendly governments was not forthcoming.

After almost two months of deadlock, the Bank made public the financial plan that had been worked out for financing the Indus scheme by grants from friendly governments and World Bank loans, observing that the support of the donors "would, of course, be contingent on the ratification of the Waters Treaty now under negotiation."[24] The amount of financing proposed to cover the cost of replacement and development works in Pakistan (and the cost of the Beas Dam in India) was $747 million[25]—a long step from President Black's modest undertaking, more than eight years before, "to consider any financing proposal that might develop from joint planning." The Bank management meanwhile had been negotiating an agreement by friendly governments and the Bank to establish an Indus Basin Development Fund, which was approved by the Bank's executive directors on April 26.[26]

In May, following discussions in London with President Ayub and members of his Cabinet, Iliff was able to obtain Pakistan's agreement to Indian uses of western waters already accepted by Gulhati. India would be allowed to impound 3 million acre-feet on tributaries of the western rivers and 0.6 million on the Chenab itself and would be permitted to irrigate 70,000 acres from the Indus River, 400,000 from the Jhelum, and 231,000 from the Chenab.

But there was still no progress on the main issue, which was the schedule of water transfers during the transition period. The problem was a hard one for both sides: A solution required that Pakistan irrevocably commit itself to a schedule for constructing and putting replacement works into operation; and both sides had to agree on how to share the deficit in water supply that, until the completion of the Mangla Dam, could be expected to mark *rabi* and early *kharif*.

As summer approached, in a last attack on the question, the Bank management began to apply heavier and heavier pressure. In June 1960, Iliff summoned the heads of both delegations and told them that he felt the only

24. IBRD, Press release (March 1, 1960).

25. Aloys Arthur Michel, *The Indus Rivers* (Yale University Press, 1967), p. 251.

26. A somewhat amended and final version of the agreement was approved by the executive directors on September 8, 1960. See IBRD, "Indus Basin Development Fund Agreement," p. 22, and "Annexures," September 19, 1960.

way to reach a settlement was for the Bank to offer its own proposal on transitional arrangements; if either side rejected the proposal (and it must have been obvious by then that Pakistan would accept), the negotiations would end. Gulhati demurred, and the suggestion was withdrawn within a few days—only to be renewed by the Pakistan government itself, so that it was necessary for the Bank to inform the authorities at the highest level in New Delhi of the situation. Then the Bank's most authoritative voice stated a drastic position: In conferences at the end of June and early in July, President Black informed Gulhati that the Bank had exhausted its possibilities as good officer and could not continue the negotiations any further. He therefore asked Gulhati to forward the Bank's most recent proposal to New Delhi with a recommendation that it be accepted.

Gulhati stood his ground. The Bank's recent formulations, he said, would cut India's use of the eastern rivers below the levels permitted when the heads of agreement of the proposed treaty had been accepted in 1959. India, said Gulhati, could not accept such a slowing down of the development of water uses in Rajasthan, nor could it permit the Bank to impose such a burdensome restriction on the use of Indian waters in Indian territory.

Black, Gulhati later recalled, yielded "gracefully and magnanimously." Characteristically, however, he was able to get as much as he gave: Gulhati agreed that within ten days, India would present rock-bottom proposals, to which Iliff, without indicating their source, would try to obtain Pakistan's agreement. To Nehru and Ayub, Black now sent messages that "a breakdown of these negotiations, no matter where the fault might lie, when so much already has been accomplished, would be an international disaster of the first magnitude." From Nehru, he particularly solicited "another manifestation of generosity and magnanimity on the part of India."

Ayub responded that Pakistan was still quite willing for the Bank to put forward a proposal of its own on the transitional period. Nehru, professing surprise that still more was being asked of India beyond the "heavy sacrifice" already accepted under the heads of agreement of the proposed treaty, nevertheless agreed to give Gulhati new and more liberal instructions.

On July 14, 1960, Gulhati offered a new proposal. The Bank team now began further negotiations with the Indian delegation, trying to work out transitional arrangements that the Bank would consider fair to Pakistan and India would consider acceptable. By early August, the work had advanced as far as it could within the scope of Gulhati's instructions. In a letter of August 5, Black made one final appeal to Nehru for further concessions. Iliff carried the letter to New Delhi and on August 11 was told by Nehru that India would accept the transitional arrangements as modified by the Bank.

More drafting ensued in Washington, followed by acceptance of the entire text of the treaty, by India on September 6 and by Pakistan on September 10.

In accordance with his long-standing wish, Nehru journeyed to Karachi to sign the treaty. On the evening of September 19, in a huge tent specially pitched for the occasion and made gay with colored lights, Iliff and the representatives of the donor governments first signed the Indus Development Fund Agreement; then Ayub and Nehru at long last signed the Indus Waters Treaty, 1960.

Sequel

The Bank's lengthiest negotiation was over. In a sense, its success was due to sheer longevity: The longer the negotiations continued, the more difficult it became for either side to take the responsibility for breaking them off, and the more sensitive the parties became to intermittent Bank threats that if the negotiations were broken off, the Bank would have to allocate the blame before the court of world opinion. But there were other factors: The Bank's doggedness and ingenuity in keeping the negotiations alive; the Bank's ability to find and provide finance for the physical works needed to carry out an Indus agreement; the fact that for India, the Indus matter was not a question of life or death but left room for maneuver and concession; and the circumstance that, toward the end, Pakistan had a government sufficiently strong to risk the domestic political consequences of an agreement. More compelling than any of these perhaps was the fact that, in the view of reasonable men, there was no acceptable alternative to a settlement.

The Bank, and later the International Development Association (IDA), continued to be deeply involved in the development of the Indus Waters. On the same day as the signing of the Indus Waters Treaty 1960, the Bank made a loan of $90 million (including $10 million for the capitalization of interest) toward the cost of the Mangla Dam—this being the only project ever presented to the executive directors without a paper providing an economic justification. In 1962 the Bank reported to the parties to the 1960 agreement that it would not be possible to finance from the resources of the Indus Basin Development Fund the construction of the whole system contemplated by the agreement. After intensive, prolonged discussion and negotiations among the Bank, the contributing governments, and Pakistan, a new financial plan, the details of which need not be spelled out here, was negotiated. A further step toward financing the Indus works was taken in June 1966, when IDA extended a loan to India for equipment needed to carry out the Beas River project, on the Indian side of the frontier and outside the framework of the Indus Waters Treaty itself.

Finally, the Tarbela Development Fund was set up in May 1968 to supplement the amounts available for the Tarbela Dam from the Indus Development Fund. The Bank and the governments of Canada, France, Italy, the United Kingdom, and the United States agreed to provide the equivalent of $174 million to the new fund, and Pakistan agreed to provide rupees to meet the local costs, estimated at $335.5 million. In the meantime, the estimate of the total cost of the Tarbela Dam had risen to the equivalent of $827.5 million.[27]

By 1968, the only other commitment undertaken by the Bank at the time of the Indus negotiations also had been discharged. In his meeting with Pakistan Prime Minister Chaudhri Mohammad Ali in London in June 1956, Iliff had offered to have the Bank, quite apart from the negotiations, organize a study to serve as the basis of the long-range development of the Indus waters. This offer was revived and confirmed in an understanding between President Woods and President Ayub in November 1963.

The study was carried out by several firms of consulting engineers and a group of Bank staff members directed by Dr. P. Lieftinck, an executive director of the Bank and former finance minister of the Netherlands. The study was in two parts. The first part, completed in early 1965, dealt with the proposal for building the Tarbela Dam; it found the project to be technically feasible and economically justified.

The second part, submitted to the Pakistan and other governments participating in the financing of the Indus development in August 1967, outlined a comprehensive program for using West Pakistan's water and power resources to provide the government with a basis for development planning in these sectors within the framework of successive five-year plans. It was perhaps the most detailed and sophisticated analysis ever made of valley development in a developing country.[28]

Egypt: The High Dam

Among all the episodes in the life of the Bank, that which most clearly affected the course of history was the effort to negotiate finance for the construction of the High Dam near the northernmost cataract of the Nile. In July 1956, withdrawal of American and British offers to join the Bank in

---

27. IBRD, Press release (May 2, 1968).
28. Pieter Lieftinck, A. Robert Sadove, and Thomas C. Creyke, *Water and Power Resources of West Pakistan: A Study in Sector Planning,* 3 vols. (Johns Hopkins Press, 1969).

financing the dam was followed within a week by a counterblow from Egyptian Prime Minister Gamal Abdel Nasser: he nationalized the properties of the foreign-owned Suez Canal Company. The sequel, before the year was out, was military action against Egypt by the armed forces of France, Israel, and the United Kingdom.

Egypt and the great river flowing through it had fascinated outsiders at least since the time of Herodotus. The highest officials of the Bank were equally under its spell. President Black believed that a constructive relationship with Egypt was the key to mitigating the distrust of the Bank by the Arab states and opening the way for an active role for the Bank in financing economic development in the Middle East.

A scheme for Nile development, which aroused wide interest, was the so-called "century storage" scheme, based on the extremes of high and low water as measured over a span of a hundred years. Its urgent objective was to make more water available for Egyptian agriculture and so to keep farm production from falling behind the inexorable competition of population growth. As developed in the Egyptian Ministry of Public Works, it would have been based on works at the main sources of the White and Blue Niles—Lakes Victoria, Albert, and Tana. Victoria and Tana would have been reservoirs, and Albert would have served to regulate the volume of water flowing to Egypt. In addition, a channel three hundred kilometers long would have detoured the White Nile past the swamps of the southern Sudan, where half the river's flow is lost through evaporation and seepage; and smaller reservoirs would have provided short-term storage further downstream. The plan would have considerably increased the flow of water to Egypt, and it had other advantages too. The principal works, however, would have had to be constructed outside Egypt, in Ethiopia and the Sudan.

In 1948, another scheme was proposed to serve the same objectives. Its author was Adrian Daninos, an Alexandrian of Greek descent. This was the scheme of the High Dam—so called to distinguish it from the Aswan Dam that already existed near the First Cataract of tht Nile.[29] On July 30, 1952, four days after King Farouk was sent into exile, Daninos submitted his proposal to the Army officers who were the new rulers of Egypt. They adopted it and in November retained a German engineering combine, the Hochtief and Dortmunder Union, to draw up specific plans.

In January 1953, Egyptian Finance Minister Abdel Galeel El Emary wrote to President Black asking that the Bank consider financing the High

29. For a good account of schemes to develop the Nile, and of the final evolution of the High Dam, see Tom Little, *High Dam at Aswan* (John Day, 1965), pp. 5–35.

Dam. A few days later, Daninos himself visited Mr. Black in Washington to speak well of the new government and to promote the dam.

In the following month Black visited Egypt in the course of a tour of Bank member countries in the Middle East. He was taken to the site of the dam, where he was much impressed by what he was told of the promise the project gave of water for Egyptian agriculture and power for Egyptian industry.

Black was also impressed by the difficulties. It was possible that the Egyptian government might not be constitutionally authorized to enter into loan contracts. The cost seemed overwhelming—$200 million in foreign exchange for the reservoir alone and at least twice that much when power and other elements were added in. And while the High Dam certainly seemed the right *kind* of thing to do, it was not clear whether this was the right project.

The Bank's watchword therefore was caution. Soon after Mr. Black's return, the Bank made an offer to the Egyptians to arrange for an engineering study of the High Dam scheme, financed by $200,000, which the U.S. Foreign Operations Administration (as the American foreign aid agency was then called) was willing to provide. The scheme would depend on Egypt's reaching agreement with the Sudan, and perhaps other upstream countries also, about sharing the waters of the Nile; the Bank therefore indicated to the Egyptians that it could not make any final decision until a comprehensive study was made of Nile development as a whole. Within the Bank, it looked as if as much as three years would be needed to prepare the project to a point where a decision about financing could be made.

The Egyptians were not willing to accept the delays implied in the Bank's offers of technical assistance. They simply commissioned their German consultants to proceed with engineering studies of the High Dam scheme. In Cairo the suspicion grew that the Bank was procrastinating for political reasons, reflecting the displeasure of the United Kingdom, the Bank's second-largest shareholder, over Egyptian pressure to end the longtime occupation of the Suez Canal Zone by British troops.

In January 1954, a Bank deputation visited Cairo and labored hard to dispel Egyptian fears, but without notable success.[30] Six months later, while lunching with Black, the Egyptian ambassador in Washington, Ahmed Hussein, reported that "certain quarters" in Egypt feared that the United States was influencing the Bank to conduct its business in such a way as to encourage political concessions to the United Kingdom.

---

30. It consisted of Mohamed Shoaib of Pakistan, who represented Egypt on the Bank's Board of Executive Directors, and Dorsey Stephens, the Bank's representative in the Middle East, whose office was in Beirut.

The Bank Proceeds

Black did indeed think that the Bank could not make loans to Egypt so long as the Canal Zone dispute continued. But the thought sprang from Mr. Black's own desire for the Bank to preserve its reputation for prudence and propriety. In Britain, the High Dam proposal did not engage the interest of the top echelons until 1955, a year later.[31]

Early in 1954, the Bank concluded that an aide-mémoire stating its position to the Egyptian government might clarify the situation. After five months of relatively desultory drafting and revision, such a document was handed to Ambassador Hussein on June 22. It was friendly but uncompromising in tone: The president of the Bank, it recalled, already had indicated (on his visit to Egypt) an interest in participating in Egyptian development within the limits of Egyptian capacity to service Bank loans and in circumstances where the Egyptian government "under its own law and practice" could contract external financial obligations.

As for the High Dam scheme itself, the Bank was prepared to study it. The Bank could not, however, rest on the recommendation of the German combine or even on the review by the international panel of experts; it would have to make up its mind on the basis of its own investigation. On only one point did the Bank back down: It no longer spoke of a full-scale examination of Nile Valley development, but simply mentioned that a desk study would have to be done.

In mid-September, part of the Egyptian reaction was communicated privately to Mr. Black. The Egyptian government reacted with some asperity to any questioning of its constitutional powers. After all, the United Kingdom had settled the Suez Canal question with the Egyptian authorities in July, and this had involved both political and financial commitments on the part of Egypt. Why should the Bank be any more difficult than the British?

But matters did move forward decisively. The government's formal reply was handed to the Bank on September 24. At the same time, a top-level Egyptian delegation, headed by Mr. El Emary (now the former minister of finance), arrived for specific discussions.[32] The response to the aide-mémoire asked for "a thorough and expeditious examination" of the High Dam proposal. It expressed the hope that the Bank would undertake to organize the financing of the High Dam project and to participate in the financing itself.

31. See Harold Macmillan, *Tides of Fortune: 1945–55* (Harper & Row, 1969), pp. 657–58.

32. Mr. El Emary later became governor of the Bank of Egypt and still later an officer of the World Bank.

In the discussions, Mr. El Emary stressed that Egypt wished to regard the Bank as the only channel for outside funds for the dam, looking for the Bank both to provide and to recruit the necessary external finance.

The Bank reacted promptly. In the next few weeks, an agricultural and a financial expert borrowed from other organizations went to Egypt to consult on the fertilizer project. Egyptian engineers visited Washington in October; the next month the Bank sent two engineers to Cairo to begin appraising the High Dam project.[33] They were followed early in the year by a Bank economist, John C. de Wilde, who began a long and painstaking examination of the Egyptian economy, the prospective costs and benefits of the High Dam project, and the capacity of Egypt to service external debt. An agronomist came from the Netherlands to study the Egyptian government's choice of areas to be served by irrigation water from the Aswan reservoir and the possible cropping patterns in those areas.

In October, fortune at last seemed to be smiling on the Aswan enterprise. The head of the Bank's Department of Operations for Asia and the Middle East reported to Black with evident relief that "the Bank's relations with Egypt . . . seem to have entered into a more active and favorable phase." Davidson Sommers, the Bank's general counsel, examined the constitutional question and tentatively concluded that legal objections to an Egyptian loan might be outweighed by "the wish to maintain good relations between Egypt and the Bank, together with the unlikeliness of a future repudiation by Egypt of her obligations to the Bank. . . ." The U.S. Foreign Operations Administration expressed a desire that the United States be associated with the Aswan High Dam in view of the project's great popularity in Egypt.[34]

At the beginning of December, an international panel of experts retained by the Egyptian government submitted its report.[35] The experts concluded that it would be practical and safe to build a high, rockfill dam with a clay core 6.5 miles upstream from the existing Aswan Dam.

The High Dam, in the estimation of the experts, would take at least ten years to build. It would be one of the largest man-made structures of all time—5,000 meters wide at the crest of the dam, 111 meters high, and 1,300 meters thick at the base. The volume of materials needed would amount to

33. Gail Hathaway, borrowed from the office of the chief of engineers of the United States Army, and Neil Bass of the Bank's own staff. Mr. Hathaway later became engineering adviser to the Bank.

34. Mr. Black had already, after his return from Egypt, acquainted President Eisenhower with the project.

35. The panel consisted of Mr. André Coyne (France), Dr. Max Preuss (Germany), Mr. I. C. Steele (United States), Dr. Lorenz G. Straub (United States), and Dr. Karl Terzaghi (United States).

44 million cubic meters (seventeen times as large as the Great Pyramid of Cheops). The dam would create a reservoir with a capacity of 130 billion cubic meters—four times the size of any man-made reservoir in existence. Its primary purpose would be to store, for irrigation purposes, virtually all the run-off from the annual flood of the Nile.

When the irrigation aspects of the project were in full operation, some fifteen to eighteen years after the beginning of construction, the country's agricultural income would be increased by about 45 percent. That would, however, only keep abreast of the population growth that might be expected to occur in the meantime. It would arrest the decline in the amount of cultivable land per head in Egypt but would not turn the trend around.

The project, however, included another developmental component—a power station that initially would be equipped with 720,000 kilowatts of generating capacity and transmission lines that would carry the power five hundred miles to Cairo. Ultimately, its capacity could be doubled, which would allow it to generate as much as half of the total power that Egyptian industry might require by 1973.

The Bank's consultant, Gail Hathaway, made his own report to the Bank early in April 1955. To achieve the purposes in view, he concluded, there was no alternative to the High Dam scheme as developed by the German engineers and accepted by the international panel. He confirmed that, as Bank officials already had learned from conversations with the Egyptians, it would be necessary to determine Sudan's share in the natural flow of Nile waters and to recognize Sudan's right to build control works needed for using the flow effectively. It also would be necessary for Egypt to indemnify the Sudan for the flooding of Sudanese territory, which would require the resettlement of some 12,500 people.

The Bank Agrees to Negotiate

The Bank's study of the economic and financial aspects of the High Dam project continued into the summer. Finally at the end of August the Bank reached a favorable conclusion and so informed the Egyptian government in a memorandum. The memorandum stated three major conclusions about the project, (1) that it was "technically sound," (2) that it was "economically sound" (although the Bank was not happy about some areas tentatively chosen for irrigation), and (3) that it was of such a size that it would impose on Egypt the need for strict fiscal discipline.

The demands of the High Dam scheme, said the memorandum, "would require a rigid limitation on the Government's commitments to other projects" in order to avoid inflation, which would imperil the financing of the project. An investment program should be drafted for the years during which the dam would be under construction, estimating financial resources and allocating them by broad categories of expenditure. The Bank thought that the High Dam scheme would require government expenditures of nearly 300 million Egyptian pounds; in addition, another 100 million pounds would be needed for other planned projects. The total, the Bank believed, was greater than the resources that would be available, and thus it would be necessary to consider whether some expenditures already planned could be deferred until after the completion of the dam.

For its part, the Bank was prepared to give immediate assistance in the three matters (apart from the Sudanese question) that it considered most urgent: in helping to draw up an investment program, in planning the procedures to be followed in organizing, planning, and carrying out the High Dam scheme, and in developing procedures for determining which irrigation areas promised the highest agricultural output. In response to the Bank's invitation, an Egyptian delegation came to Washington in November to discuss the High Dam. The group was led by Abdel Moneim El Kaissouny, the minister of economy, and included representatives of the High Dam Authority, the agency established by the Egyptian government to plan and execute the High Dam project.

Talks began in a meeting with President Black and members of the Bank staff on November 21, 1955. Black opened by repeating, in effect, the concerns expressed in the August memorandum. He was able to say further that the Bank calculated Egypt's borrowing capacity at some $200 million, compared with the $400 million of foreign exchange needed for the project. He had been informed that the United States and British governments both wished to help and that their assistance would take the form of grants. The Bank, said Black, understood the urgent wish of the Egyptian government to announce the start of the project. On the other hand, the Bank was not well disposed to the idea, favored in Egypt, that the government should proceed directly toward awarding a contract for the project to a consortium of English, French, and German firms, which the Hochtief and Dortmunder Union had formed for the purpose. This matter could be further explored during the stay of the delegation.

The Egyptians continued to feel a sense of urgency. They wanted work to start no later than July 1957, at the beginning of the period of low water, when it would be easiest to divert the Nile from its channel and begin work on the foundations of the dam. To meet that deadline, it would be necessary to sign the civil works contract by July 1956, and the High Dam Authority wanted to begin negotiating this contract on a cost-plus-fee basis with the Hochtief group.

The Bank was adamantly opposed; it insisted that the civil works contract be awarded on the basis of international competition. If negotiations were restricted to the Hochtief group, the Authority would not have the benefit of more economical methods of project execution that might be devised by other contractors.[36] In any case, it was the policy of the Bank, as an international institution, to require international competition.

It was too early, the Bank continued to argue, to place a contract for all the civil works; not enough planning and designing had been done for that. Perhaps the project could be broken into two phases. In the first phase, the flow of the Nile would be diverted by means of cofferdams and tunnels, and the foundation work would be done for the High Dam. In the second, the dam would be completed. It would be practical to set a deadline of July 1956 for contracting the first phase, and the remainder could be contracted after further preparation. A tentative suggestion was made from the Bank side that the contract for the first phase might be let, after all, to the Hochtief Consortium, and the second phase might be done on a competitive basis.

After taking counsel with Dr. Terzaghi, a member of the international panel, the Egyptians returned to the talks, agreeing that it would be feasible to divide the civil works in two. But a day later (December 6, 1955), the Bank was informed that even if it were willing to relax its own rule, competition for the contract would still be necessary, since the U.S. International Cooperation Administration (as the U.S. foreign aid agency was then called) would not make its funds available otherwise.

By mutual consent, the technical talks came to an end at this point. It had been agreed that every effort should be made to begin construction by July 1957, that it was desirable to do the work on the basis of cost-plus-fixed-fee contractual arrangements, and that the civil works for the project could be carried out in two phases. Whether the civil works contract would be let on a competitive basis was not agreed, but it was clear that it would have to be in order to obtain financing.

Concurrently, the Bank resolved the constitutional question: An internal memorandum from the legal staff, although conceding that a loan to the transitional government of Egypt would depart from earlier practice, said "that the present Government of Egypt is the actual Government of Egypt, is generally recognized as such by members of the Bank, and is acting as such in the Bank and other international organizations."

---

36. As was later demonstrated, ironically, when Russian engineers developed a more economical scheme for carrying out the civil works.

In the meantime, Black was holding conversations with American and British representatives about participating in the project. The two agreed to propose to their governments—subject, in the case of the United States, to legislative approval—that they provide a total of $70 million to cover the foreign exchange costs of the first phase of the project—$54.6 million from the United States and £5.5 million from the United Kingdom. Beyond that, the two governments "would be prepared to consider sympathetically in the light of then existing circumstances further support toward financing the later stages to supplement World Bank financing."[37]

The proposals of the two governments were based on the following conditions: that the Bank would agree to participate in the foreign exchange financing of the project in an amount equivalent to $200 million; that the Bank would supervise the disbursement of the funds provided by the governments; that Egypt would allocate its resources in such a way as to ensure that the project would be completed; and that the contractor, supplies, and equipment for the first phase of the project would be chosen on the basis of international competition.

The offers also were contingent on the strict conditions (1) that the Egyptian government and the Bank would agree on, and periodically review, an Egyptian investment program giving priority to the project, (2) that the government would not incur obligations in excess of amounts Egypt and the Bank agreed were prudent, and (3) that the organization, execution, and administration of the High Dam scheme would be carried out in accordance with understandings between the government of Egypt and the Bank. In addition, it was necessary that agreement concerning the use of Nile waters be reached with the Sudan.

Black reported to his executive directors on December 16, 1955, that the High Dam discussions had been concluded, and that aides-mémoire concerning the American and British proposals had been given to Kaissouny. He obtained approval of a procedure that would move the Bank toward a commitment on the dam: He would give Kaissouny a letter to the prime minister of Egypt, indicating the Bank's conditions for participating in the financing of the dam and stating that the Bank would agree to the financing. The letter would be unsigned. When the Bank had been informed that the American and British proposals, together with the Bank's conditions, were acceptaale to the government of Egypt, Black would take the matter back to the executive directors and ask that they approve his signing the letter and the commitment it expressed.

37. Press announcement issued through the U.S. Department of State, Dec. 17, 1955.

The next day, bearing the American and British aides-mémoire and Black's unsigned letter, Kaissouny left for Cairo. The next news out of the Egyptian capital was discouraging. Nasser and the Egyptian press were angrily criticizing the offers of financing for the dam.[38] Black resolved to go to Cairo to see what could be done to recoup the situation.

At the end of the previous September, the British government had learned that the Egyptians had agreed to exchange cotton for military supplies from the Soviet Union.[39] In October, the Egyptian ambassador in Washington, on leaving an interview at the State Department, had told newspaper reporters that the Soviet Union had offered to provide finance for the High Dam. These maneuvers had simply heightened the desire of the Western powers to associate themselves with the dam.

This was still their mood when Black and members of the Bank staff left for Cairo. John Foster Dulles telephoned to say that he felt that financing the dam was "one of the most important things facing the U.S. government," and to offer all possible help to Mr. Black in his mission. In London, where Mr. Black stopped en route to Cairo, Prime Minister Eden was equally encouraging. "What Mr. Dulles and Mr. Eden were really saying," Mr. Black concluded, ". . . was that . . . they hoped . . . that I would realize the importance of this and would not be too inflexible in working this out."[40]

In Cairo, Black met with a courteous reception. Ten days of negotiations, led on the Egyptian side chiefly by Dr. Kaissouny, produced agreement that was "substantial," as a press communiqué said, but only partial. A crucial disagreement remained.

As set out in the aides-mémoire, the American and British commitment was firm only for the first phase of the project. Kaissouny had expressed anxiety about this during his talks in Washington. Later, Nasser declared that the arrangement was a "trap. . . . It appeared that we were to . . . begin building the projected dam. . . . And then we should be stopped halfway through. . . ."[41]

In his talks with Black, the premier attempted to delete from the Bank's new draft letter any mention of the aides-mémoire. This would have turned the Bank's conditional offer of financing into an independent and absolute commitment. Black refused.[42]

Black urged Nasser to accept the terms of the American and British offers.

38. Kennett Love, *Suez, the Twice-Fought War* (McGraw-Hill, 1969), p. 311.
39. Humphrey Trevelyan, *The Middle East in Revolution* (Gambit, 1970), p. 30.
40. Dulles Oral History Collection, Dulles Memorial Library, Princeton University.
41. Quoted in Love, *Suez, the Twice-Fought War*, p. 311.
42. Trevelyan, *The Middle East in Revolution*, p. 51.

The prime minister did not agree. Near the end of February 1956, through a spokesman, a statement of his objections was made orally to the British ambassador,[43] and messages went to Washington and London. They asked for a stronger commitment for American and British financing of the later stages of the High Dam scheme.[44]

On Black's return, a technical report on the High Dam project was prepared and sent to the executive directors at the end of February. Although it was labeled "preliminary," this 35,000-word paper was the most comprehensive project analysis that had ever been submitted to the board. Table 18-2 shows expenditures proposed in the report for the High Dam project. Benefits from the project, the report observed, would begin before the scheme was completed. The cofferdams would permit some controlled irrigation after the fifth year, and there would be benefits for flood control and navigation thereafter. Power generation and transmission might begin in the sixth year. Benefits would rise as the project progressed. At completion, the annual economic return would amount to an estimated 28.5 percent of the investment. If indirect effects, especially the stimulation of the economy by rising agricultural income, were taken into account, the economic rate of return might be as high as 35 or 40 percent.

Even as the Bank staff was presenting the virtues of the High Dam project, the ardor of the Bank's prospective partners had begun to cool. At the end of January, when Prime Minister Eden visited Washington a few days after Black had passed through London en route to Cairo, he seemed less enthusiastic about the High Dam than the World Bank president had thought he was. Premier Nasser's Arab nationalism and Egyptian support for restive elements in Algeria, Iraq, and Jordan had been a source of continuing irritation. In conversations with President Eisenhower and Secretary Dulles, Eden and Foreign Secretary Selwyn Lloyd "agreed that the future of our policy in the Middle East depended to a considerable extent on Nasser. . . . The Americans thought that the present talks about the Aswan Dam with Mr. Black might indicate his state of mind. If his attitude on this and other matters was that he would not cooperate, we would both have to reconsider our policy towards him."[45]

Not only did Premier Nasser decline the terms of the American and British aides-mémoire, but Arab nationalist activities supported by Cairo, and especially propaganda against the regimes in Jordan and in Iraq (the lone Arab

43. *Ibid.,* p. 52.
44. *Mutual Security Appropriations for 1957,* Hearings before the Appropriations Committee of the United States Senate, 84 Cong. 2 sess. (1956), p. 24.
45. Sir Anthony Eden, *Full Circle* (Houghton Mifflin, 1960), p. 374.

Table 18-2. *Proposed Expenditures on Egyptian High Dam Project, in Foreign Exchange and Local Currency*
In millions of U.S. dollar equivalents

Purpose	Foreign exchange expenditures	Local currency expenditures	Total
The dam and civil works	149	167	316
Power equipment and transmission facilities	126	39	165
Irrigation and related facilities	72	225	297
Indemnities and resettlement	6	23	29
Interest during construction (on external and internal borrowings)	37	83	120
Other expenditures (on reclamation and housing)	—	393	393
Total, all purposes	390	930	1,320

Source: IBRD, Technical report on High Dam project.

signatory to the Baghdad Pact sponsored by the United Kingdom and the United States), grew more intense. On March 1, 1956, British prestige in the Middle East suffered a severe blow. The King of Jordan dismissed Lieutenant-General Sir John Bagot Glubb, British chief of staff of the Arab legion, and his senior British officers. As Anthony Nutting, then British minister of state for foreign affairs, later recalled, "For Eden . . . this was the last straw. . . . This reverse, he insisted, was Nasser's doing. . . . Nasser was our Enemy No. 1 in the Middle East and he would not rest until he had destroyed all our friends and eliminated the last vestiges of our influence. . . . Nasser must therefore be . . . destroyed."[46]

American attitudes also had begun to change. Black had received a hint of this immediately after his negotiations in Cairo. On his way home, he had a rendezvous at the Rome airport with Henry Byroade, the U.S. ambassador to Egypt, who had been in Washington during Black's stay in the Egyptian capital. The ambassador, himself a convert to the Aswan scheme, indicated that pressures in the State Department for an early resolution of the High Dam affair were diminished because of congressional opposition.[47] In March 1956, when the foreign aid bill for the fiscal year 1957 was presented to a House Subcommittee on Appropriations, no congressman defended the Aswan Dam financing against attack; the aid administrator, John Hollister, pleaded in mitigation that the funds from the 1956 appropriation that might have been made available for the Dam were now destined for use elsewhere.[48]

46. Anthony Nutting, *No End of a Lesson* (Clarkson N. Potter, Inc., 1967), p. 27.
47. Interview with Mr. Black (Oct. 9, 1970).
48. As early as January, Senators Morse and Neuberger of Oregon had attacked

In the middle of May, Premier Nasser hit Americans on a particularly sensitive nerve: The Egyptian government gave diplomatic recognition to the Chinese Communist regime in Peking. When Secretary Dulles appeared in closed session before the Senate Appropriations Committee on June 19, 1956, under questioning he assured the committee that with respect to the Aswan scheme "there is no commitment of any kind."

Insistence on finance for the dam clearly would have caused a destructive debate on the administration's foreign aid legislation then wending its way through congressional committees. The administration itself had gnawing doubts about the proposal. Aid to the Aswan scheme did not seem to promise any less unruly deportment by Premier Nasser; in the upper echelons of the State Department, it was thought likely that association with the project, with its massive complexity and its requirement for severe fiscal discipline over more than a decade, would in the end be a cause of friction rather than of friendship between Egypt and the donor nations.[49]

By the time of Dulles's testimony before the Senate Appropriations Committee, the possibility of British and American aid for the High Dam was, for all practical intents and purposes, dead. But the corpse was very lifelike. The negative attitude of the governments was not publicly declared and seems not to have been fully divulged even to the Bank; there apparently was some hope that Nasser himself would conclude the affair by publicly rejecting the Western offers.[50] Early in April, however, Premier Nasser had told a correspondent of the *New York Times* that in spite of a Russian offer in "very general" terms to finance the dam, he was still looking to the Bank and to the Western powers for help.[51] As late as July 6, the press spokesman of the Department of State said that funds for the High Dam would be available in the foreign aid appropriation for the fiscal year 1957 and that the offer to assist in the project "still stands."[52]

One last event gave the illusion of life to the scheme for financing the dam. When President Black suggested that he might explore the situation in Cairo

---

the administration for backing the High Dam while refusing to help finance the Hell's Canyon Dam in their section of the country. (Love, *Suez: the Twice-Fought War,* p. 310.) In the Senate some legislators opposed aid to Egypt because of that country's neutralist policy; others feared that the High Dam would increase cotton production in Egypt to the detriment of U.S. cotton.

49. See the recollections of Robert R. Bowie, then director of the Policy Planning Staff of the Department of State, in the Dulles Oral History Collection.

50. Trevelyan, *The Middle East in Revolution,* p. 54.

51. *New York Times,* April 2, 1956.

52. United Press dispatch distributed by the Washington City News Service, July 6, 1956.

on his way back from a journey he had planned to Iran and Saudi Arabia, the State Department agreed that a stopover might be useful. In a meeting on June 20 (the day after Dulles's testimony before the Senate Appropriations Committee), Black found the prime minister "rather surprised and hurt that he had gotten no answer to his suggested changes in the terms of the grants. . . . I tried to explain to Mr. Nasser . . . [that he should] accept the terms of the American and British grants . . . so that we could start work on building the Aswan Dam."[53] The next day, Black told a newspaper correspondent that the Bank was "fully prepared" to do its part in financing the dam.[54]

On his return to Washington a few days later, Black went straight from National Airport to a meeting with Secretary Dulles, Under Secretary Herbert C. Hoover, Jr., and Robert D. Murphy, deputy under secretary for political affairs, where he reported his conversation with Nasser. The diplomats began listing the difficulties of their position, and Dulles speculated that perhaps the Aswan scheme was beyond the capacity of the Egyptians to carry out. Black said that if it were decided not to finance the dam, this would in a sense be a relief to the Bank, since collaboration with the Egyptians and the construction of the project itself promised to be long and arduous. But, he added, it was certain that if the American offer were withdrawn, the Egyptian reaction would be extreme. Mr. Dulles made no rejoinder; he simply left the room and did not return.

Apart from Black, at least one other person had a driving desire to see the Aswan scheme financed from the West. That was Ahmed Hussein, the Egyptian ambassador in Washington. Home for lengthy consultations, he talked to Premier Nasser about the dam early in July. The prime minister, by that time, had concluded that there was no longer any hope of Western financing,[55] but he agreed that the ambassador, on his return to Washington, could inform the State Department that Egypt was now willing to accept the terms of the aides-mémoire.

When the ambassador delivered this message to Secretary Dulles on July 19, 1956, he was informed that the American government had decided that it was not feasible "in present circumstances" to participate in the Aswan scheme.[56] That scheme had depended on "Egyptian readiness and ability to concentrate its economic resources upon this vast construction program." Since the time of the December 1955 offer, agreement had not been reached with other countries concerning Nile water rights, and the ability of Egypt to

53. Eugene Black, Dulles Oral History Collection.

53. Eugene Black, Dulles Oral History Collection.
54. *New York Times,* June 22, 1956.
55. Love, *Suez, the Twice-Fought War,* p. 321. See also Trevelyan, *The Middle East in Revolution,* p. 54.
56. U.S. State Department, Press release No. 401, July 19, 1956.

devote adequate resources to assure the project's success had become "more uncertain." On the following day the British Parliament was informed that the British offer also had been withdrawn. The Bank's offer (which, in any case, had never been formalized) lapsed, since the Bank no longer had any financial partners for the Aswan scheme.[57]

The dramatic sequel is well known. On July 26, 1956, Premier Nasser announced that the government was taking over the property and operations of the Suez Canal Company. On October 29, after a series of border incidents, Israeli troops invaded Egypt, and on December 2, British and French military action against Egypt began—ostensibly for the purpose of protecting the Canal Zone but, in the opinion of many observers, actually for the purpose of overturning Premier Nasser.

Postscript

In the end, from having been a prominent actor in an affair that attracted world-wide attention, the Bank emerged from the High Dam adventure with a wider reputation and enhanced prestige. Black's faithfulness to the cause of the dam won him, after further reflection by Premier Nasser, the confidence of the government of Egypt. At the instigation of UN Secretary-General Dag Hammarskjöld, and at the request of the parties, Black, in 1958, lent the good offices of the Bank to negotiations for settling the claims arising from the expropriation of the Suez Canal Company.[58] A year later, acting in a personal capacity, he helped arrange compensation by the Egyptian government for enterprises and individuals whose property had been sequestered or expropriated as a consequence of the Suez "incident" of 1956.[59] These

57. The State Department did not inform the World Bank of its position regarding the dam until an hour or so after Ambassador Hussein had seen Secretary Dulles. Then a telephone call was made to W. A. B. (later Sir William) Iliff, vice president of the Bank, since Black was away from Washington at the time. Sir William later recalled (in an interview on June 10, 1970) that the statement read to him was represented as being essentially the same as the statement that was handed to Ambassador Hussein after Secretary Dulles had paraphrased it orally. This statement imputed to the World Bank an unfavorable judgment concerning Egypt's capacity to carry out the Aswan project. At Sir William's insistence, the imputation was deleted from the statement given to the press. But it would have been contained in the text given to the ambassador and no doubt circulated through other diplomatic channels. This would help explain why the impression was long widespread in Europe and the Middle East that it was the Bank, rather than the United States, that was responsible for the collapse of the scheme for financing the dam.

58. Interview with Sir William Iliff, June 10, 1970. The negotiations were conducted for the Bank by W. A. B. Iliff, vice president, assisted by George D. Woods, chairman of The First Boston Corporation and later president of the World Bank. See *New York Times*, April 30, 1958; also IBRD, *Thirteenth Annual Report, 1957–1958*, p. 6.

59. *The Times* (London), Feb. 28, 1959; *New York Times*, March 1, 1959.

settlements helped restore Egypt to international financial respectability. They opened the way at the end of 1959 for the Bank to lend the Suez Canal Authority $56.5 million to improve the canal, and for participation in that financing by nine private banks of the United States and Japan.

In retrospect, it is hard to escape the conclusion that, once Premier Nasser refused to accept the tripartite offers of December 1955, there was only the slightest chance of making the High Dam a cooperative venture among Egypt, the World Bank, Britain, and the United States. Despite Black's very considerable persuasive powers, the Egyptian leader took no initiative of his own to negotiate the question of the aides-mémoire until he had concluded that the offers they expressed were no longer in effect.

The Western powers also took a passive attitude; they did not go beyond permitting Black to explore the matter in January and again in June, by which time, it appears, the Western offers were already moribund beyond any real hope of resuscitation. The Bank's experience, however, yielded no evidence that Egyptian Prime Minister Nasser was thinking actively of obtaining Soviet finance for the Aswan scheme prior to the withdrawal of the Western offers; and after that withdrawal, seventeen months elapsed before the signing of the agreement for Soviet financing of phase one of the construction of the dam.

Ironically, it was a consideration raised by the Bank for purely technical reasons—the splitting of finance for the project into two phases—that proved to be the non-negotiable point. To Premier Nasser, the conditional character of the offers of finance for phase two apparently looked like a device by which the Western powers could exert pressure for Egyptian participation in a settlement of Arab-Israeli tensions; and they may have thought of it as potentially useful in this regard. Significantly, the two-part division of the work was accepted in the later financing by the Soviet Union, whose Middle East policy was not equally suspect to Cairo. Whether or not the Bank's technical point was a critical factor, it finally became clear that the Bank's influence could not be decisive: Black's active and positive interest in the development of Egypt could not stand against tides of great-power politics that were running the other way.

Conclusion

The story of the High Dam emphasizes once more the fact that each of the three episodes of Bank history considered in this chapter was essentially political in character, although in each the Bank intended to act strictly on the plane of economics and finance. All three cases, because they were political, were outside the normal stream of the Bank's activity and expertise. It is not surprising, in the circumstances, that in retrospect the Bank appears to have approached them with some naiveté.

The Bank was not well informed about the issues of the Iranian and Indus cases before it offered to try to resolve them, and it was further handicapped by its own limitations. In the 1950s the Bank still clearly bore the stamp, in its staff and in its outlook, of its creation by the high-income countries. Particularly in the Iranian oil matter, although it made a conscientious and determined effort to be impartial, it did not escape bias, in this case favoring the interests of the United Kingdom.

It may be worth noting that the Bank's intervention succeeded in the Indus matter, where there was a dispute between two developing countries, whereas it failed in the Iranian oil and High Dam cases, where there was opposition between developing and developed countries. In the first instance, the contestants were relatively equal; in the other two, they clearly were not. Moreover, in the first case, the great powers both supported the intervention of the Bank but refrained from intervention themselves. In the Iranian and High Dam episodes, however, the great powers were themselves protagonists; whatever chance the Bank might have had to succeed on a technical plane was destroyed by the action of the great powers on a political plane.

In all three cases, there was the factor of money, which might have been expected to exert an important influence, particularly on developing countries. In the Iranian case, however, the Bank's management denied itself this useful instrument. In the High Dam case, it was the Bank's failure to influence the developed countries that was crucial, and here money could not have been a factor. But in the Indus case, which involved two needy nations, the availability of finance, although by itself not sufficient, was a necessary condition of agreement on the Indus Waters Treaty 1960.

Finally, let it be recognized that the Bank, when it intervened in these three cases, engaged in activity of a kind not foreseen by the Bretton Woods Charter and, in doing so, acted imaginatively and constructively. The history of international mediations is far from being studded with successes. For the Bank to have succeeded in even one of these three tortuous and difficult negotiations can be considered a distinct contribution.

PART FOUR

The Bank in Retrospect
and Prospect

CHAPTER NINETEEN

Beginnings of a Balance Sheet: Five Country Vignettes

THE READER WHO HAS worked his way to this point in our study may be tempted to say, "So what? The Bank by mid-1971 had made nearly eight hundred loans, and the IDA had extended nearly three hundred credits. The loans and credits totaled nearly $20 billion, and more than $13 billion had been disbursed. The net commitments of the International Finance Corporation (IFC) exceeded $500 million, and the Bank Group had provided technical assistance in substantial volume. But is the world as a whole, and the less developed portion of it in particular, any better off because there has been a World Bank?"

We believe that the answer is yes. But the reader is also entitled to ask for evidence supporting our judgment and some indication as to whether the benefits justify the costs. Although evidence is scattered throughout the earlier chapters, our objective has been to analyze the Bank's policies and their evolution rather than to make a systematic appraisal of its lending operations. Had we attempted the latter, we would inevitably have found ourselves on more treacherous terrain, both because of the scarcity of "hard" data and the difficulty of interpreting such data as can be adduced.

The promotion of development, as has been said *ad nauseam,* must be the mission of the less developed countries themselves. To claim that the Bank Group is responsible for any considerable fraction of the remarkable rate of growth attained by the low-income countries as a whole since World War II would be quite unwarranted. The Bank Group has never had the resources or personnel to be more than a facilitator, often only a minor facilitator compared with the aid agencies of its richer member governments.

647

The total volume of Bank Group disbursements in a year, even at the $1.2 billion level attained in fiscal year 1971, amounted to less than 0.5 percent of the gross national product and perhaps 3 percent of total investment in its less developed member countries. Although one cannot credibly claim that the Bank Group has decisively influenced the overall rate of development, it has had observable impacts both on the methods of fostering economic and social change and on the changes wrought in particular places at particular times.

A serious shortcoming of the Bank, however, and of virtually all other development agencies as well, has been their failure until quite recently to evaluate their own performance in the countries in which they have been operating at least as critically as they evaluate the performance of their clients. The Bank has thought of itself—and still does—principally as a project lender. Beyond such elementary questions as whether the road that was supposed to have been built has actually been built according to specifications and is functioning more or less as anticipated, the standards for judging projects are open to dispute. What appears successful to one group because of seemingly favorable economic effects—the provision of electricity to a substantial number of users at a reasonable cost from an unsubsidized enterprise, or the improvement of livestock farming in a region in which it had been grossly inefficient—may appear to others a failure because of seemingly unfavorable social or political effects, such as increasing regional disparities in income, making the rich richer while bypassing the poor, or helping to keep a "bad" government in power.

In a country like Mexico, which has made excellent economic progress and has received substantial assistance from the Bank, some believe that the progress was due almost exclusively to Mexico's firm adherence to policies it considered appropriate rather than to the regular flow of loans and advice. There are other countries in which economic, social, or political progress remains hard to detect, despite Herculean efforts by the Bank. The lesson is, of course, that development takes place when there is a will to develop and a forward-looking, development-minded government in power. The Bank can ally itself with the development-minded elements in the country and reinforce their efforts. But the Bank's biggest handicap is its inability to guarantee that development-minded officials will come into power or remain in power.

If one is convinced that in most low-income countries immediate, wholesale shake-ups of society—in other words, revolutions—are necessary before real progress can occur, he will probably consider the Bank counter-revolutionary, meaning that, in his view, the institution is worse than useless. However, one who harbors grave doubts about the efficacy of revolutions in bringing about the great leap forward that serves as their justification will look more kindly on efforts to move ahead one step at a time, in collaboration with governments that may be less than heroic but better than contemptible. A series of steps, individually modest and sometimes barely perceptible, cumulatively can bring about in a relatively short span of time a restructuring of society that will be favorable to broad-based, humane programs of development.

Usually the question is not evolution versus revolution, but whether a particular action will expedite or delay orderly evolution. Will foreign exchange for this project make it easier for the government to postpone fundamental reforms that are overdue and would otherwise have to be made? Will it help a corrupt or despotic government stay in power? Can it contribute to the establishment of an institution that will be effective and appropriate for the nation and the sector in which the institution is to be planted? Under the best of circumstances, judgments will differ.

A final complication in our case is that we have had neither the time nor the resources to do the field work that would enable us to verify all our conclusions as to the effects, positive and negative, of Bank operations in specific countries and sectors.

We devote this chapter nevertheless to brief reports on five countries that together account for close to one-third of total Bank loans and IDA credits during the years 1946–71: Colombia, Brazil, Pakistan, India, and Thailand. Our primary focus is the impact of the Bank Group in each of these countries. Relationships, however, are by definition two-way affairs; a secondary focus, relevant for this history, is the impact of the country and its problems on the Bank Group.

We begin with Colombia. Except for 1957 and 1965, the Bank has made at least one loan to that country in every year since 1949. Colombia was the first country to have its economy studied by a Bank-sponsored general survey mission. It was the first Bank member to have that variant of the consortium known as the consultative group established on its behalf. It was also a first in various other respects.

The Bank and Colombia

Although Colombia does not rank among the top ten member countries in per capita receipts of Bank/IDA assistance, it is the only country with a population in excess of five million to rank among the top fifteen. With a population of twenty-two million, Colombia as of June 30, 1971, had received forty-nine loans and credits, totaling almost $900 million, since the signing of the first agricultural machinery loan in August 1949. Of that total, $524 million had been disbursed.

Both in the 1950s and in the 1960s, the Bank Group accounted for about one-third of all loans from international and foreign governmental agencies to Colombia. It maintained resident representation in Bogotá during most of these years. It has dispatched innumerable missions to Colombia, gained a wealth of experience there, and provided advice as well as information on Colombia to the members of the consultative group that it organized on that country's behalf. Small wonder then that, when an Operations Evaluation Division was created within the Bank's Programming and Budgeting Department in September 1970, Colombia was chosen as the subject for the first major study of the overall impact of the Bank on development. With the cooperation of the Colombian government, an admirably frank, comprehensive, penetrating report covering operations through December 31, 1970, was prepared.[1]

Although both IDA and the IFC have invested in Colombia, Bank Group activity there means loans from the Bank itself. The IFC has been active in Colombia since 1959 and has made many investments there, but its commitments total less than $20 million. The IDA extended a $19.5 million credit for highways to Colombia in 1961, the first year of that agency's operations. All other Bank Group operations have taken the form of Bank loans. Of the $750 million committed by the Bank/IDA through December 31, 1970, $294 million was for electric power and $136 million for highways.[2] The electric power and highway projects that the Bank helped finance have had a real impact on Colombia's development—eliminating bottlenecks, facilitating economic integration in a nation where regional loyalties have

1. We acknowledge with gratitude our debt to the evaluation team headed by Christopher Willoughby, but take upon ourselves responsibility for the judgments expressed in this section.

Late in May 1971, several loan agreements were signed, which account for about $150 million of the total of $900 million that had been committed to Colombia by the Bank Group as of June 30, 1971. The agreements involved water supply for Bogotá and Palmira, assistance to industry in various areas through five development finance companies, telecommunications, and land colonization. Except to illustrate the types of activity for which the Bank is now lending, they can have had no developmental impact during the period covered by our analytical history, and we ignore them in the balance of this section.

2. Of the balance, $62.5 million was for development finance companies, $54 million for railway rehabilitation, $41 million for the Atlantic Railroad, $35 million for livestock credit, $32.5 million for water supply, $30 million for the Paz del Rio steel mill, and smaller amounts for agricultural credit, education, and miscellaneous activities.

long been strong, improving the efficiency of construction and maintenance in the power and transport sectors, and strengthening their administration.

Power and Transport Loans

The Bank's power loans have gone to six of Colombia's seven largest cities, but have been heavily concentrated in three of them—Bogotá, Cali, and Medellín. Similarly, the Bank's highway financing has been concentrated entirely on trunk routes, mainly between the major cities, which are capitals of their respective regions. Highway financing, in addition to the contribution it has made to the gradual integration of the country by linking its major cities, has helped make agriculture more efficient.

Frequent landslides have hindered and delayed highway construction, and cost overruns have been substantial. However, the roads built appear to have been well worth building and to have yielded high returns, even after taking into account the delays and cost overruns. The average rate of return in terms of cost savings (excluding time savings) to road users is estimated to be 25 percent, which is very high. On some highways, vehicle operating costs have declined by 50 percent or more during the twenty-year period. Highway maintenance has been poor, but is improving. It remains expensive and inadequate, however, despite repeated efforts by the Bank to improve the situation. There is considerable evidence of underinvestment in feeder roads, and the design standards for highways built with Bank assistance in the 1960s may have been too high.

Although the Bank can be accused of overinvesting in trunk highways and in power facilities for urban areas, it is not clear that the resources that theoretically would have been freed by lower investments in these fields could have been spent more effectively by other Colombian agencies. At a minimum, strenuous institution-building efforts in the other fields would have been necessary.

The Bank has helped to install about half of the power-generating capacity in Colombia today. Large backlogs of electricity demand had built up in the major cities after the financial crisis and the sharp decline in coffee prices during the second half of the 1950s. Colombia's own foreign-exchange earnings would not have permitted importation of the equipment needed. The Bank made it possible for the various companies responsible for power supply in the cities to expand sooner and with plants of larger size at a lower unit cost than would otherwise have been possible. The electric power companies that received assistance from the Bank were strong compared to most public and quasi-public agencies in Colombia.

As for utility tariffs, the Bank for fifteen years confined itself to negotiating, with each of the companies to which it made loans, tariff covenants designed to ensure coverage of debt service and some contribution to the costs of future expansion. In the early 1960s, when inflation was rapid and the government was reluctant to approve increases in rate schedules, the covenants proved inadequate. The resultant peso shortages delayed the completion of projects. In the second half of the 1960s, the Bank was able to revert to an idea put forward in 1950 in the influential report of its general survey mission to Colombia—establishment of a public utility regulatory commission. Such a commission (the Junta Nacional de Tarifas) was finally established in 1968 and has since then made a beginning at raising utility tariffs to what the Bank regards as more adequate levels.

The other major institutional contribution of the Bank in the electric power sector has been the establishment of the Interconnection Company in 1968. It followed five years of sustained effort on the part of the Bank to overcome the companies' distrust of each other and their desire to keep for themselves the benefits of their favorable power sites.

Establishment of the Colombian National Railways as an autonomous institution was a condition of the Bank's first railway loan in 1952. The payoff on the Bank's railroad investments in Colombia, however, has been poor compared to the rate of return on its highway and electric power investments. The Atlantic Railroad Project cost about twice the amount originally expected and, in financial terms, is the most important single project in which the Bank has been involved in Colombia. Despite its low rate of return (apparently less than 5 percent), it is almost certainly better than the two schemes the Colombian authorities had under consideration at the time the project was chosen. Had more attention been devoted to planning and promoting the development of the region through which the railroad passes, there might have been more freight to haul and a better rate of return. Shortfalls in demands for goods and services, construction and investment delays, cost overruns, and service of poor quality have also contributed to low yields on the Bank's investments in railway rehabilitation in the 1960s, yields that are below the opportunity costs of capital in Colombia.

Other Bank Group Assistance to Colombia

In industrial development the Bank had argued strongly but unsuccessfully against the original Paz del Rio steel mill plan in 1950–51. Later, when called on for help, the Bank insisted on a management assistance contract that provided for the employment of foreign consultants (which the steel company did not want), had a hand in shaping the expansion program of 1963, and invested $30 million in expansion of the mill. The result is still one of the smallest integrated steel mills in the world, from which economic benefits, though rising, have to date been very modest.

The Bank has also contributed to industrial development through its loans in 1959 and subsequent years to the Banco de la República for use by private development finance companies (corporaciones financieras), which in turn invest in manufacturing industries. The Bank's affiliate, the IFC, has taken equity participations in each of the five financieras established with Bank Group help, and these financieras have become by far the most important institutional sources of equity finance in Colombia for private industry. The Bank played a role in 1962–63 in helping Colombians establish the Private Investment Fund (PIF) as an official entity to obtain credits from abroad and channel them to projects in the private sector. The Bank helped raise foreign funds for the PIF but did not itself provide any.

Other assistance from the Bank to the private sector included loans to the Agricultural Bank for livestock improvement work and to the Institute for Agrarian Reform (INCORA), an autonomous body established in 1961 to provide credit to farmers. INCORA has undertaken a variety of projects, among them land reclamation, land acquisition and subsequent subdivision, colonization, and consolidation of uneconomic small holdings. On the whole, medium- and large-scale producers appear to have been the principal beneficiaries of the agricultural and industrial credits the Bank Group helped to make possible.

Considering not just the private sector, but the Bank's overall contribution to the mobilization of resources for development in Colombia, it can be termed a major contribution. The Bank has on occasion made its electric power and other loans conditional on specific steps by the borrowers to charge "more adequate," meaning higher, prices for the services rendered. By helping to strengthen and make more efficient the major government spending agencies, of which the Ministry of Public Works is the largest but by no means the most efficient, the Bank may have helped indirectly to overcome the national reluctance to pay taxes. The Bank played an important role in raising funds for Colombian development among members of the consultative group. Reference was made earlier in this study to the Bank's preparatory work for the group's meetings, its role in arranging for the joint financing of specific projects by several foreign agencies, its regular circulation of lists of finance-ready development projects to the group's participants, and the reliance of those participants on the Bank's assessments of creditworthiness. During the 1960s the countries and agencies participating in the consultative group committed over $2 billion in loans for Colombian development.

The availability of foreign credit on a fairly generous scale has enabled Colombia to expand the size of its development program; foreign credit, however, does not appear to have been a substitute for a reasonable effort to raise funds through taxation. National government revenues, mainly taxes, doubled in real terms over the years 1950–63 and almost doubled again in the very much briefer period 1963–70. The number of income-tax payers increased from fewer than 100,000 in 1950 to well over a million in 1970.

In the early 1950s the Bank had rejected overtures for the financing of education and municipal water supplies. By the late 1960s, however, the Bank was active in both fields. It is too early to assess its contribution, but the Bank appears to have helped imaginatively in developing the projects selected. They look promising.

In negotiations with Colombia on macroeconomic policy, the Bank's emphasis in the 1960s was primarily on matters affecting public expenditures, especially the size of the government surplus on current account, the investment budget, the foreign exchange rate, the growth of minor exports, and some matters of sector policy, such as the rate policy on public utilities. Colombia's record in macroeconomic terms has been respectable. Gross national product, having grown at an average annual rate of almost 5 percent in real terms for twenty years and at better than 6 percent annually in the period 1968–70, stood in 1970 at more than 2.5 times the 1950 level. Population growth has been rapid too—better than 3 percent a year—so that the improvement per person in gross national product has been modest. Primary and secondary school enrollment has quadrupled. Investment has grown at an average rate of only 4 percent for the period as a whole but at more than 13 percent a year from 1965 through 1970. Service obligations on foreign debt stand at nearly ten times their 1950 level and will rise further, but due to successful export efforts the debt service ratio has been falling and was less than 12 percent in 1969.

Coffee, the principal foreign exchange earner, which accounted for over 70 percent of exports in the early 1950s, accounted for a little over 40 percent in the late 1960s. Exports of other goods and services have grown at an average annual rate of 7.7 percent. Trade is less heavily oriented toward the United States, and exports of manufactures, which earned $2 million to $3 million in the early 1950s, brought in $70 million or more a year in foreign exchange during the late 1960s.

Despite the progress made, unemployment and underemployment in Colombia remain explosively high, and the poorest 60 percent of the population receive a smaller percentage of total national income than in almost any other less developed country. As a corollary, the highest 20 percent of the population appear to receive a larger proportion of total national income than in other less developed countries.

Every major economic report on Colombia by the Bank, including the economic survey published in 1950, has indicated that the country's greatest economic problem is widespread poverty in rural areas. It directly affects between one-fourth and one-third of the population, despite massive migration over the years into the towns. Rural areas contain the bulk of the lower half of income earners in Colombia. Based on impressions and on such data as are available, one would conclude that the rural poor have become worse off relatively in terms of income, and absolutely in such important respects as housing and nutrition.

Until quite recently the Bank has not been concerned in an operational way with the impact of its loans and advice on income distribution and social justice. It has assumed that it should make its contribution to development mainly by transferring resources to borrowers in the power and transport sectors and through intermediaries for the private sector. It has considered the private sector to be the most dynamic and efficient element in the Colombian economy. It believed poverty could best be attacked indirectly by fostering more rapid growth of medium- and large-scale manufacturing and commercialized agriculture. It adhered to its project approach, distinguishing rather sharply until recently between "economic" projects of a "productive" character, which it could finance, and "social" projects, which it preferred not to finance. It not only eschewed program loans but provided very little foreign exchange to cover the local currency costs of Bank-supported projects. Although elsewhere in this study we make a general case in favor of more program lending by the Bank, we are not prepared to say that the Bank's impact on Colombian development would have been notably more favorable (except perhaps in the years 1957–59) if a sizable fraction of its lending had taken the form of program loans.

Summary

In summary, the Bank concentrated its loans in Colombia rather heavily on urban and urban-oriented projects. It played a crucial role in eliminating major bottlenecks in the power and transport sectors and helped to create and improve institutions dealing with those sectors. Through its involvement in those sectors it provided a basis for industrial growth. It also helped to meet the huge investment needs resulting from rapid urbanization; and, indeed, in the process it may have added somewhat to the speed with which Colombia was urbanizing. It eased balance-of-payments problems through the transfer of its own resources and through the active role it played in bringing in foreign exchange from others. The economic reports of the Bank have provided a good framework for discussions of overall economic policy within the consultative group.[3] The fact that a consultative group exists means that there are other external sources of funds to which Colombia can turn for help in financing activities that the World Bank is not prepared to finance. The Bank does appear to have had a significant impact on fiscal policy; Colombia's growing tax income is vitally important for the further development of the nation.

The corporaciones financieras, steadfastly supported by the Bank Group as a means of promoting efficient industrial development, have helped large rather than small enterprises. The Bank Group did not ask them to do differently, and it was probably economically rational for them to do what they did—whether or not it was wise for the Bank to have made it so easy for them to follow that course and thereby risk worsening the distribution of income within the country. The Bank did not address itself explicitly to the problem of rural poverty. It did nothing to encourage land reform despite the extremely small size of the vast majority of farms. Similarly it took no direct action to finance feeder roads and other rural infrastructure. Its interest in education is of recent vintage, and as of the end of 1970, it was not active in the fields of health and housing.

With the clairvoyance of hindsight, one can be both appreciative and critical of the Bank's role in Colombia. It has known, at least since the comprehensive report in 1950 of its general survey mission, that poverty in the countryside and the maldistribution of income constitute explosive elements —not only in Colombia but in other Latin American nations as well. Yet the Bank has waited until almost the eleventh hour to address itself with any directness to those problems. The alternatives, however, were not as self-evident in the 1950s as they may appear to be in the 1970s. Furthermore, the Bank was not the government of Colombia. It could only nudge the government, and it did so, chiefly in the direction of completing physical links between isolated regions of the country, mobilizing financial resources for development, and creating or improving the competence of agencies having

---

3. See, for example, *Economic Growth of Colombia: Problems and Prospects*, report of a mission, headed by Dragoslav Avramović, sent to Colombia by the World Bank in 1970 (Johns Hopkins University Press, 1972). However, this report, which includes more than 250 tables in the text and 39 in the statistical annex, omits any explicit treatment of the sensitive subject of income distribution.

developmental roles to play. If these were not top-priority requirements, they were not far down on the list.

The Bank and Brazil

The Bank's relations with Brazil, its third largest borrower as of June 30, 1971, have been very warm, very cold, and tepid. Until 1952, Brazil was considered a thoroughly promising candidate for Bank lending. Then certain policies followed by the Brazilian government were considered by the Bank to jeopardize Brazil's creditworthiness. The Bank tried to use the leverage of its proposed loans to modify those policies, but this led to an estrangement with the Brazilian government. Lending declined in 1953 and 1954 and was nil in 1955–57. It was substantial, however, in 1958. From 1959 to 1965, inflation was rampant in Brazil, and between June 1959 and February 1965 the Bank made no loans.[4]

The fall of the Goulart government in March 1964, however, marked the beginning of another change in policy. With inflation gradually being brought under control and the Bank becoming more confident of Brazil's ability to manage its balance of payments, the period since February 1965 has seen a rising trend in Bank lending and a considerable increase in the influence of the Bank on Brazilian development policy, particularly in the power, transport, and agricultural sectors.

The Pre-1953 Period

Brazil was one of the first less developed countries to be visited by a president of the Bank (McCloy in 1949). In the same year, a Bank mission to Brazil headed by Richard H. Demuth received a very favorable impression

4. Bank loans to Brazil through June 30, 1971, totaled $1,023.5 million. IFC commitments amounting to $50.9 million were made to various industries in Brazil during the years 1957–59 and 1966–70. Bank lending by years, with the sectors to which loans were made in descending order according to the volume received by the sector, shows the ups and downs of Bank/Brazil relations and the exclusive concentration of Bank lending in the power and transport sectors until 1967. (Amounts in millions of U.S. dollars.)

1949	75.0	(electric power)	1965	79.5	(power)
1950	15.0	(electric power)	1966	149.6	(power)
1951	15.0	(electric power)	1967	40.0	(agriculture)
1952	37.5	(power and railways)	1968	96.9	(power, roads, industry)
1953	32.8	(power, railways, roads)	1969	No loans	
1954	18.8	(power)	1970	205.0	(roads, power, industry)
1955–57	No loans		1971	160.4	(power, ports, water
1958	86.4	(power)	(first half)		supply, pollution
1959	11.6	(power)			control, education)
1960–64	No loans				

of lending opportunities there. Eugene Black visited Brazil in 1951 and was much impressed.

During the period 1949–53, the Bank's lending to Brazil was heavily concentrated in the electric power sector, although two sizable railway loans and a small road loan were made. Primarily Brazil served as guarantor for a series of power loans to private companies, the largest of which was to the Canadian-owned Brazilian Light and Power Company. Private ownership of power and other public utilities, however, was on its way out in Brazil.

In 1946, publicly owned electricity-generating plants accounted for only 6 percent of total power generation, but by the end of 1953, 50 percent of the generating capacity under construction was in the public sector. Brazil's three leading railway lines were nationalized in 1945, and its coastal shipping had been nationalized before then. Petrobras, the government-controlled monopoly for petroleum exploration and production, was established in 1948. This movement of enterprises from the private to the public sector had a bearing on the Bank's attitude toward Brazil, particularly as the deficits incurred in the operation of the publicly owned power installations, railways, and other utilities became responsible in large measure for the inflation Brazil experienced during the 1950s.

The year 1951 saw the formation of the Joint Brazil–United States Economic Development Commission. It was charged with outlining priorities for a five-year development program for Brazil and preparing projects for inclusion in the program. The Bank was brought into the discussions at an early stage and showed itself eager to finance the foreign exchange costs of viable projects. A position had recently been established with the U.S. government that the Bank was to be looked to as the primary source of finance for overseas development projects guaranteed by the borrowing government, and the Bank did not want to see this position weakened.[5]

Encouraged by this agreement, President Black was moved to venture the opinion that over the next five years the Bank might well put $250 million into Brazilian projects. At a meeting between Vice President Garner of the Bank and representatives of the Brazilian government in April 1951 it was agreed that $300 million over the next five years was an appropriate planning figure. Of course these statements and estimates were carefully safeguarded. Well prepared projects would need to be presented, and Brazil's creditworthiness would have to be maintained. But it is clear from the record that the Brazilian government considered it had a "moral commitment" from the Bank for financing in the amount of $250 million to $300 million. In fact

5. See Chapter 15, above.

on June 19, 1951, the leader of the majority in the Brazilian Chamber of Deputies announced in the Chamber that Brazil had obtained a loan of $300 million from the International Bank.

The American member of the joint commission was Francis Truslow Adams. Unfortunately, Mr. Adams died en route to Brazil. After some canvassing of the situation, the U.S. Department of State persuaded President Black to release one of his senior staff members, J. Burke Knapp, a U.S. national who had formerly worked in the Department of State, to take Adams's place. The Brazilians, not surprisingly, interpreted this appointment as assurance that the IBRD intended to finance the foreign exchange costs of projects recommended by the joint commission. Knapp left for Brazil in the autumn of 1951 on a year's leave of absence. When he returned, he assumed the position of director of the Bank's Western Hemisphere Department with the rather delicate task of helping appraise the projects which, as a member of the joint commission, he had approved for presentation to the Bank.

When plans for the joint commission were being discussed in late 1950 and early 1951, the economic prospects in Brazil, both short-term and long-term, looked favorable. Brazil had come out of the war with large foreign exchange reserves, coffee prices were high, and the country was industrializing rapidly. In 1951, however, the situation changed and became progressively worse. Brazil had a foreign trade deficit of $250 million in 1951, and this increased to $600 million in 1952. Foreign exchange requirements were covered mainly by suppliers' credits, and by the end of 1952 Brazil had accumulated a short-term foreign debt of $1.3 billion. During this period, inflation accelerated, and Brazil's foreign exchange rate became increasingly untenable.

Confronted with a foreign exchange crisis, the Vargas government rather suddenly decided, in late 1951, to stop the transfer of earnings on foreign investment and the repatriation of capital and, over a weekend, put the necessary decrees into effect. According to some observers it might have been possible, given conciliatory responses from the Bank and the U.S. government, to work out a satisfactory modification of Brazilian policy. But both the Bank and the U.S. Department of State sent sharp, far-from-conciliatory notes of protest. From then on, the relations between the IBRD and the Brazilian government changed from "a partnership arrangement" for the joint consideration of development projects to rather suspicious arm's length dealings.

Although the Brazilian minister of finance, Horacio Lafer, assured President Black in January 1952 that he would give earnest attention to the working out of a fair and satisfactory solution to the remittance problem, the Bank decided that, apart from two projects already far advanced, it would make no further loans to Brazil until this problem had been solved. Otherwise, despite continued representations from Brazilian officials, the Bank refused to go beyond sending technicians to study projects that might be considered for financing once the remittance question had been dealt with. By December 15 the Brazilian Congress had enacted legislation, which went into effect in January 1953, creating a limited free market for foreign exchange that would permit the inflow and outflow of capital and earnings as well as the acquisition of foreign exchange for tourism. The Brazilian government believed that the way had now been cleared for Bank financing of the five-year development program. It was mistaken.

The Years 1953–59

The Bank now said that, although it was ready to finance five relatively small projects, it would not contemplate further lending until it had an opportunity to reconsider the long-term prospects of the Brazilian economy. In preparing for this reconsideration it sent one of its senior economists, Harold Larsen, to study the situation. His report, made available to the Bank in April 1953, was pessimistic.[6] The Brazilian government, sensing increasing difficulties in dealing with the Bank, began to turn to the U.S. government for support. In March 1953 the Eximbank announced a loan of $300 million to Brazil (payable in three years) for the repayment of commercial debts to American exporters. In the same month the State Department inquired what the Bank would think of a proposal that the United States find financing for the Brazilian railways, provided a satisfactory railway reorganization bill were passed.

The Bank thought less than nothing of this proposal and said so. Furthermore, it regarded the $300 million Eximbank loan as a "bail out" which could have the effect only of lessening the pressure on the Brazilian government for needed changes in policy. Subject to periodic assessments of creditworthiness, the Bank announced its intention to move step by step with the Brazilian government in carrying out a railway rehabilitation program. It was essential for the Brazilians to show convincing progress in the direction of reorganizing the top structure of the federal railways and carrying out the

6. "I came back and said, 'This is not a case of miscalculation. This is built into the Brazilian economy. They will always have balance-of-payments difficulties as long as they continue these domestic policies.'" Oral History Project of Columbia University, interviews recorded in the summer of 1961 on the International Bank for Reconstruction and Development (cited hereinafter as "Oral History"). Quotation is from interview of Harold Larsen, p. 10.

necessary reforms in management and operating procedures. Any suggestions that the U.S. government might be willing to provide financing would simply undercut the Bank's efforts to improve the economic situation in Brazil. It was intimated by the Bank's management that if the time should ever come when the U.S. government felt obliged to move into Brazil with large development loans, the Bank would have to withdraw completely from operations there.

In the meantime, the joint commission was coming to the end of its labors. It managed to produce an excellent analysis of the Brazilian economy and came up with some forty-one projects considered to be of high priority, worthy of being financed, and requiring nearly $400 million in foreign exchange.[7] But the Bank wasn't interested. As its president told a succession of Brazilian finance ministers—Lafer in 1953, Aranha in 1954, and Gudin in 1955—there could be no further discussion of loans until the Bank and the Brazilian government had sat down together for a full consideration of Brazil's economic prospects.

In October 1953 Brazil had taken a substantial further step toward devaluing its currency and introducing greater exchange rate flexibility. A multiple exchange rate system was introduced, and a foreign exchange auction created. The Bank mission sent to Brazil in 1954 found that

the overimportation of 1951 and 1952 was brought under control in 1953, and the principal commercial backlogs have been funded or otherwise regularized. The exchange system has been drastically revised with resultant de facto devaluation of the cruzeiro. The measures taken are at present effectively restraining imports and are permitting the movement of high-cost "problem" exports into world markets.[8]

But apparently this was not enough.

What did the Bank want of Brazil as conditions of lending? This is not entirely clear since the government of Brazil could never be induced to "sit down" with the Bank for a discussion that might make these conditions explicit. Knapp, reviewing the Bank's relations with Brazil some years later, mentions control of inflation, balancing the budget, restricting credit to the private sector, changing the exchange rate, and exercising some austerity in import programs as steps the Bank desired to see taken.[9] In the Bank, as Knapp noted, Brazil was considered to be "one of two or three classic cases

7. See its three-hundred-page report, *The Development of Brazil*, published in 1954 in the United States by the Government Printing Office, for the Institute of Inter-American Affairs, Foreign Operations Administration.

8. "Current Economic Conditions and Prospects of Brazil," W.H. 23-0 (July 8, 1954), p. 1.

9. J. Burke Knapp, "Oral History," p. 8.

of how inflation leads to balance of payments disequilibrium and hence to destroying a country's creditworthiness."[10] In addition, but related to the stabilization measures, the Bank wanted a thoroughgoing reform of the railway administration. The Brazilian railways were a major source of persistent government deficits.

The formation of Petrobras was considered by the Bank to have been a serious mistake, as was the continued exclusion of foreign oil companies from exploration. Oil constituted 20 percent by value of Brazil's imports, and the possibility of replacing these imports with domestically produced oil should, in the view of Bank management, have led the Brazilian government to encourage all possible efforts to discover and exploit domestic sources.

It was an impressive list of domestic policies that the Bank wanted to see remedied, but it was never clearly specified what particular action by the Brazilian government would elicit what response from the Bank. The Bank ceased lending to Brazil in 1954 on the ground that the country was not creditworthy and, with a few exceptions in 1958 and 1959, did not resume lending until 1965.

Faced with this decision on the part of the Bank, Brazil turned increasingly to the U.S. government. Eventually the Export-Import Bank took over a large share of the financing of projects recommended by the joint commission. The United States attempted to condition these loans by insisting that Brazil follow the recommendations of the International Monetary Fund (IMF). The attempt met with indifferent success.

As one looks back on the relations of the Bank and Brazil in the 1950s from the vantage point of 1971, it seems clear that the Bank seriously overestimated its capacity to influence macroeconomic policies. Furthermore, its judgment of creditworthiness seems to have been rather static and limited. Brazil's gross national product grew at the rate of 6.8 percent a year in real terms in the 1950s. And although the rate of inflation continued at 15 to 20 percent until 1959 and foreign exchange policies left much to be desired, Brazil would hardly have been judged not creditworthy by present standards.

From 1959 to 1971

Although Brazil during the 1950s would probably have been judged creditworthy by today's standards, there is no doubt that the policies subsequently followed, together with the political instability of the early 1960s, made it eminently noncreditworthy. Kubitschek's expenditures on Brasilia during the

10. *Ibid.*, p. 9.

last years of his regime, added to government deficits from other sources, were turning a persistent into a rampant inflation. The IMF worked out a stabilization program in 1958, but the Brazilian government repudiated it in 1959. In 1960 Kubitschek was succeeded in the presidency by Janio Quadros, who lasted less than a year. Goulart came in March 1961 and was ousted by the military government of Castelo Branco in April 1964. The effect of Brazil's skyrocketing inflation on its balance of payments was catastrophic. In 1953, debt service charges had been 13 percent of merchandise exports; in 1960 they were 44 percent. The Hague Club of Brazilian creditors rescheduled debt in 1961 and again in 1964. Debt to the World Bank was not rescheduled, nor did the Bank make any loans to Brazil during this period. Shortly before the overthrow of the Goulart regime, however, President Woods had indicated to Brazil that the Bank would be willing to make certain power loans in the hope that disbursements on those loans would offset amortization payments from Brazil to the Bank, which were then becoming due.

Although the Bank made no new commitments to Brazil during this period, disbursements amounted to $26 million. It is interesting that, in the years 1964–67, when external assistance could be, and indeed was, helpful to Brazil's stabilization effort, net disbursements from World Bank loans were a negative $30 million and from the Eximbank a negative $119 million. Project lending with its long hiatus between commitments and disbursements cannot contribute much to short-term balance-of-payments requirements.

The government of Castelo Branco, which took over after a military coup in April 1964, initiated a stabilization program under the economic leadership of Minister of Finance Bulhoes and Minister of Planning and Economic Coordination Campos. The increase in the cost of living in Guanabara state was brought down from an annual rate of 100 percent in the last quarter of the Goulart government to about 25 percent by 1967.[11] The Bank resumed lending to Brazil with a $22.5 million power loan in February 1965 and followed this with a number of other power loans. But Bank financing was not limited to power. In the eighteen-month period ending June 30, 1971, some $365 million was committed for industrial expansion, water supply, pollution control, roads, ports, and education.[12]

The large volume of lending in the field of transportation (railways, roads,

---

11. In 1967 General Costa e Silva was inaugurated as president. In August 1969, after instituting dictatorial rule, he suffered a stroke. A military triumvirate took over and later named General Emilio Garrastazú Médici president.

12. For information on the "parallel financing" of Brazil's steel expansion program, see Chapter 15, above.

and ports) followed an extensive transportation survey begun in 1965, for which the Bank made a grant of $1.5 million to Brazil to cover half the foreign exchange cost of the first phase.[13] Transportation investment over the next four years, financed by the Brazilian government, U.S. AID, the Eximbank, the Inter-American Development Bank, and the World Bank, was guided largely by the recommendations of this survey. Another effect of the transport survey was that a large number of young Brazilians were trained in transport planning and project evaluation, with the result that the growth of domestic consulting services was stimulated.

Furthermore, Brazil in two memoranda of understanding that were worked out with the World Bank in 1965 and 1967 agreed to undertake certain policy actions in the transport field, the most important being to limit highway construction until master plans had been completed, to close certain uneconomic railway lines, to cease building certain new lines, and to rationalize port operations and investment. Although the assurances given were not always carried through in full, the Bank has been able, in connection with subsequent loans and a persistent dialogue, to have a good deal of influence on railway, highway, and port administration in Brazil.

World Bank advice to the minister of finance had something to do with Brazil's acceptance of a flexible exchange rate policy, but most of the Bank's influence on Brazilian policy has been at the sectoral level. A livestock loan of $40 million in 1967 specified in considerable detail how the project was to be operated, and in the main these conditions were observed. With considerably less success, the Bank has also, in connection with loans to agricultural and industrial credit agencies, tried to insist that these agencies lend at a positive real rate of interest.

The Twenty-five-year Period as a Whole

Brazil at first seemed to be an ideal candidate for Bank lending—a charter member of the institution, a major less developed country, rich in resources, and creditworthy for several hundred million dollars even by the Bank's conservative standards. Although the price of coffee skyrocketed during the Korean war, Brazil exhausted its reserves and went heavily into debt in the early 1950s. Just when the country hoped to obtain the fruits of the work that had gone into preparing its development program, the Bank began to question its creditworthiness and to resist financing projects emanating from

13. The second phase, begun in 1967, although it was also carried out under the supervision of the Bank, was financed mainly by the U.S. Agency for International Development (AID) and the United Nations Development Program (UNDP).

the Joint Brazil–United States Economic Development Commission, on which a prominent member of the Bank's staff—on leave, it is true—had served as the top U.S. member.

Brazil alleged that the Bank defaulted on a commitment to help it. A tension built up that affected the Bank's relationship with that country for a dozen years and influenced its policy throughout Latin America. In the process, the Bank revealed a great deal about what it believed domestic economic policies should be in a country that is seeking development and attempted to use the leverage of its lending program to move Brazil in this direction. The attempt failed, in part because Brazil was too big and independent to be treated like an unruly child and in part because of the existence of an alternative source of finance (the U.S. government).

Rampant inflation in Brazil began to be brought under control in the mid-1960s, and Bank lending to Brazil has been increasing since then. The Bank has grown wiser about the economic policies that a developing country such as Brazil can reasonably be expected to follow. Brazil has grown wiser about economic policies and priorities and how to implement them. Beginning with the power and transport sectors, and now spilling over into other sectors, the Bank has had an impact on resource allocation. It has helped Brazil adopt a flexible exchange rate policy and, through parallel financing, has improved Brazil's ability to mobilize and maximize external resources for development. It has, in its view, observed the shadowy boundary line that separates economics from politics and has based its decisions solely on economic considerations, as required by its Articles of Agreement. Brazil can absorb large sums via the project route, and the Bank expects to continue lending to Brazil at a substantial level.

The Bank in the Subcontinent

India and Pakistan, as every reader of this study must know by now, were the two largest receivers of Bank Group assistance during the years 1947–71.[14] Both are wretchedly poor countries. Relations between them have been notoriously bad. Because each nation has been hypercritical of any action that could be construed as showing favoritism toward (or as strengthening)

14. From 1947 to 1971, Pakistan consisted of an east wing and a west wing, separated by more than a thousand miles of Indian territory. It split into two countries in late 1971, when the former east wing became Bangladesh. Unless otherwise noted, Pakistan in this chapter means the Pakistan of 1947–71.

its neighbor, aid agencies have felt some compulsion to pursue parallel courses of action in the two countries.

Thus the Bank's railway and agriculture loans to India in 1949 were followed by railway and agriculture loans to Pakistan in 1952. Establishment of the Industrial Credit and Investment Corporation of India (ICICI) as a development finance company in 1955 was followed in 1957 by the establishment of the Pakistan Industrial Credit and Investment Corporation (PICIC). When suggestions were made for a mission of "three wise men" to study economic conditions in India at first hand and thereby—it was hoped —encourage outside support for India's third five-year plan, it was almost unthinkable that the wise men would visit India and ignore Pakistan. The result was the 1960 report to the then president of the World Bank, Eugene Black, entitled *Bankers' Mission to India and Pakistan*.[15]

When IDA came into being as an affiliate of the Bank in 1960, either India or Pakistan alone could have absorbed all its resources. A rationing system had to be adopted that not only limited the proportion of the total that could go to the subcontinent but also divided that total among the rival claimants. The establishment of what later became the India Consortium was followed inevitably by the establishment of a Pakistan Consortium, and these remain the only consortia organized and chaired by the Bank. Resident missions were stationed in each country. Program loans (industrial imports projects) for one country required program loans for the other. In short, sauce for the goose had to serve as sauce for the gander, and India and Pakistan together became the pilot areas for any number of new initiatives in the field of development assistance.

The consequence is a great temptation to compare development performance in the two areas. Since one of the authors has already succumbed to that temptation, we resist it here and confine ourselves instead to commenting briefly on Bank Group activity, first in Pakistan, and then in India.[16]

Pakistan until the 1958 Coup

The break-up in late 1971 of the uneasy amalgamation that had for twenty-four years been known as Pakistan raises acutely embarrassing questions for the Bank and other would-be developers. Was it a miracle that Pakistan held together as long as it did? Was the Bank Group justified in in-

15. See Chapter 12, above.
16. See Edward S. Mason, *Economic Development in India and Pakistan*, Occasional Papers in International Affairs, no. 13 (Harvard University, Center for International Affairs, September 1966).

vesting $1.13 billion in Bank loans and IDA credits, plus $28 million in IFC commitments, in the two wings of the fledgling nation? How relevant and how timely was the Bank's advice on economic policy? Why did Pakistan appear to be soaring during the first half of the 1960s and to be almost a model of good developmental behavior? When the fall from grace began, how hard should the Bank or the members of the Bank-chaired consortium have pressed Pakistan to carry out policies to which some of the outsiders attached importance and to which the government paid lip service?

Few countries have celebrated their independence under conditions as inauspicious as did Pakistan. The partition of the subcontinent had given rise to widespread strife between Moslems and Hindus, uprooting millions of them and taking a staggering toll in human life. The commerce and industry of the Sind, where Karachi, the capital of the new Islamic nation, was located, had been largely in the hands of non-Moslems. The industrial installations of the country as a whole consisted almost entirely of fourteen aging cotton textile mills. East Pakistan embraced two-thirds of the population of Bengal but without its capital, Calcutta, which was also the locus of the managerial competence and entrepreneurial experience of the eastern area. The two wings differed sharply in climatic conditions and natural resources, but in neither respect could either wing boast. An overwhelming majority of the nation's seventy-five million people eked out a highly precarious living from traditional agriculture.

Pakistan's economic performance during the 1950s ranked somewhere between poor and miserable. Gross national product rose at an average annual rate of about 2.5 percent. Since population was also growing at about that rate, average income per person remained unchanged. Agricultural output increased at an average annual rate of 1.3 percent for the country as a whole and probably declined in East Pakistan. The price of raw jute fell in 1952 to one-third of its level at the peak of the Korean boom, and Pakistan's export earnings during the 1950s were sluggish. The one bright spot was the industrial sector, where domestic production, mainly of highly protected consumer goods, yielded a 15-percent-a-year increase in large-scale industrial output. A major reason for Pakistan's poor economic performance was that it lacked a government able and willing to get on with the task of development. Between 1953, when the Planning Commission was established, and 1958, when General Ayub Khan came to power in a bloodless revolution, there were five governments, each headed by a different prime minister. None gave high priority to development.

It was during this period that the Bank became involved. Its first loan—$27.2 million in 1952—was for the rehabilitation, improvement, and modernization of the overworked, undermaintained, largely obsolete railway systems in the two wings. Further loans to the railways were made in 1957 and 1959. In the late 1950s separate boards were established for each wing, and subsequent loans could be made specifically for the Pakistan Western Railways or the Pakistan Eastern Railways.

In agriculture the main problem in West Pakistan is scarcity of water and the need for irrigation, whereas in East Pakistan it is an excess of water and the need to control the flow during the monsoon period. The Bank's only commitment in the agricultural sector in Pakistan in the 1950s was the small loan in 1952, mentioned in Chapter 6. It financed the import of tractors and machinery to help reclaim 660,000 acres of wasteland in the Thal desert between the Indus and Jhelum rivers. The Bank opposed investment in heavy industry and initially even discouraged the establishment of jute processing mills.

The total installed capacity for the generation of electric power in 1947, when Pakistan became independent, was a mere 114,000 kilowatts. The Bank's growing expertise in financing power development could, it seemed, be put to good use in Pakistan. In 1952 one of the world's largest natural gas fields was discovered in West Pakistan at Sui in the Baluchistan desert, more than three hundred miles north of Karachi and two hundred to five hundred miles south of the other logical areas of consumption. In June 1954, having satisfied itself on the viability and priority of the project, the Bank agreed to make a loan of $14 million to meet the foreign exchange costs of constructing a pipeline from Sui to Karachi. The pipeline was completed during the summer of 1955. The initial gas connection was with the Karachi Electric Supply Corporation (KESC), which became and remains the Sui Gas Transmission Company's largest customer. Other industrial buyers, however, quickly followed, and the availability of natural gas unquestionably helped to stimulate industrial production in Pakistan. Further Bank loans for expanding the gas transmission system followed in the 1960s.

In addition to its help in financing construction of the pipeline, the World Bank encouraged the utilization of Sui gas through its various loans to the KESC for an electric power expansion program. The first of these, in 1955, permitted the KESC to double its generating capacity and partially relieve the acute power shortage in rapidly growing Karachi. Almost all of West Pakistan's imports and exports were passing through Karachi, which was its only port; and the Bank, also in 1955, made its first loan for rehabilitation and modernization of port facilities.

A World Bank mission led by George D. Woods, then chairman of the First Boston Corporation, visited Pakistan in 1956 to explore the possibilities of setting up a privately owned institution specializing in the provision of industrial credit. The result was the incorporation in 1957 of the PICIC, to which by June 30, 1971, the Bank had committed $184 million in loans and the IFC about a half million dollars in share capital. The Bank actively assisted in securing competent management for the PICIC, helped teach the staff the techniques of project analysis, trained PICIC personnel in project evaluation courses offered by the Bank's Economic Development Institute in Washington, and enabled them also to work for short periods in operating departments of the Bank and IFC. The PICIC became a strong, influential institution, regarded by the Bank as one of the best managed industrial finance companies that it has had a role in launching. The PICIC, however, has been helpful primarily to large enterprises.[17]

While the Bank was addressing itself with some success to certain obvious shortages and economic deficiencies in Pakistan, the performance of the country as a whole left much to be desired. Vice President J. Burke Knapp visited West Pakistan in early 1958. He was "very well received and had a wonderful opportunity to see the country." Nevertheless, the visit left him "deeply disturbed" and "wondering very seriously how far we ought to go ahead there after the second KESC loan, which will bring our total investment in the country to around $125 million." The political situation was extremely uncertain. The government was preoccupied with difficult problems with India, Kashmir being one. The food situation was getting desperate, but Knapp found "no real sign of an attack" on it. "I assume that we continue to regard West Pakistan power development as top priority, although I note it would be better if we could do more in East Pakistan."[18]

A Bank economic report shortly thereafter made it plain that Pakistan was in for several years of economic trouble. Underlying the nation's economic difficulties, it argued, was the large budget deficit aggravated by large defense expenditures and financed by inflationary means. The most pressing development problems were in the agricultural sector. The report recommended remedies to the budgetary and agricultural crises but did not discuss the likelihood that Pakistan could be persuaded to adopt those remedies.[19]

17. Another agency, the Pakistan Industrial Development Corporation, had as one of its main objectives the establishment of small industries. It received a credit of $6.5 million from IDA in 1962 to set up industrial estates for small and medium-sized private enterprises in West Pakistan near Lahore and a $20 million credit in 1970 to finance larger industries in both wings.

18. The quoted material is from J. Burke Knapp, letter of January 24, 1958, to Joseph Rucinski, director of operations, South Asia and Middle East, in Washington.

19. This paragraph is based on an internal memorandum of August 27, 1958, from R. F. Skillings to S. R. Cope, "SLC Papers on Pakistan."

A New Era for Pakistan?

The breakdown of parliamentary politics paved the way for the 1958 coup by General Ayub Khan, head of the Pakistan army, who promptly declared martial law. Soon after his coup, he began to introduce a system of "basic democracy," resting on locally elected village councils. A new era seemed to be dawning. A program to involve the people themselves in planning and executing development projects began in 1959 when an Academy for Village Development was established, at Comilla in East Pakistan, to train officers of the government concerned with rural development. Shortly afterward

it was assigned responsibility for directing all aspects of development work in the Comilla headquarters Thana, including agricultural extension, co-operation, education, local works and rural administration. . . . It is directed by Akhtar Hameed Khan, a great teacher and organiser, combining with many saintly qualities an illuminating intelligence and a tough pragmatism and objectivity. He assembled a faculty of great capability. . . .

The Academy launched a four-pronged attack to produce a revolutionary change in agricultural methods and village organisation without a revolutionary change in government authority or land tenure.[20]

During the winter of 1961–62, it conducted a local program of public works employing the unemployed and underemployed of the area on small local projects, such as village roads, drainage, and irrigation. The results were so encouraging that when a serious flood hit East Pakistan in the latter part of 1962, and the president of Pakistan promised 100 million rupees ($21 million) for a flood relief program, the director of the Comilla Academy and the secretary for basic democracies decided that the time was ripe for expanding the Comilla Works Program to all of East Pakistan, both the rural and urban areas. In January 1963, the U.S. Agency for International Development made available the necessary 100 million rupees out of local currency, which had been received through the sale of surplus American wheat. For the next ten weeks, the people of the province put on an amazing demonstration of the vitality of the grass roots of East Pakistan. In May 1963, the president of Pakistan acclaimed the experiment and announced that the program in East Pakistan would be doubled in 1963–64 and a program in West Pakistan would be initiated.

The adoption of an export bonus scheme in 1959 marked the beginning of an intensive campaign to expand export earnings. In Pakistan, between 1960 and 1965, GNP increased at an average annual rate of 5.5 percent,

20. Richard V. Gilbert, "The Works Programme in East Pakistan," *International Labour Review*, Vol. 89 (March 1964), p. 217.

agricultural output at 3.5 percent, export earnings at 7 percent, and large-scale industrial output at 13 percent. Pakistan was on the way to becoming a success story.

Or was it? Influential circles in East Pakistan felt exploited and expressed grievances, which were not withheld from the Bank. At the request of Mohamed Shoaib (then minister of finance in Pakistan), David L. Gordon, resident representative of the Bank and confidential adviser to the minister of finance, prepared a long memorandum in 1961 on economic relations between East and West Pakistan, in which he summarized and analyzed the deeply held feeling of east wing intellectuals that their region was being exploited. Shoaib distributed copies to members of the cabinet, and Gordon sent a copy to the Bank in Washington. The argument of the east wing intellectuals in brief was that:

• The east wing had been poorer than the west at the time of independence, and the gap had widened since then.

• The gap had been aggravated by financial transfers from the east wing to the west—resulting from higher levels of government spending and government-assisted investment in the west, the use of eastern foreign exchange earnings to finance western imports, and the relatively high prices of west wing industrial products sold in the east.

• Equity required a faster rate of development and rise of living standards in the east than in the west in order eventually to equalize the levels.

• The principal means to this end should be a steep increase in the east wing's share of public expenditures.[21]

The level of development outlays, for a variety of reasons, continued to be much higher in the west than the east, with most development funds derived from foreign aid. Pakistan's overvalued currency distorted the terms of trade between the two wings, to the disadvantage of the east, and exaggerated the investment contribution that Pakistan was making to its own development in relation to the foreign contribution. The government was as preoccupied with defense as with development, and Pakistan's defense potential was concentrated mainly in the west. The Bank's most important contribution to defusing tension between India and Pakistan was the landmark Indus Waters Treaty signed in 1960.[22] The engineering concept behind the treaty involved the creation of an enormous system of "link" canals for transferring water from the Indus, Jhelum, and Chenab Rivers to meet the irrigation requirements of the eastern portions of West Pakistan, which had

21. David L. Gordon, Memorandum (Dec. 2, 1961), pp. 1–2.
22. See Chapter 18, above.

previously been served by the Beas, Ravi, and Sutlej Rivers. The waters of the latter three rivers were allocated to India.

Execution of the concept required large sums of money, in both foreign exchange and rupees. The Bank performed admirably in mobilizing the necessary resources. Pakistan nevertheless felt, understandably enough, that aid received for the Indus works was basically not development assistance but compensation for the loss of irrigation facilities rendered useless by the diversion of water from the three eastern branches of the Indus to India. Developmental features, however, certainly included the new electric power facilities. The mammoth Mangla Dam on the Jhelum River, completed at an estimated cost of $600 million, provided the hydroelectric power potential for an enormous increase in the capacity of West Pakistan's northern grid. The Tarbela Dam on the Indus, when complete, will be the largest dam of its kind in the world and the keystone in a program for meeting West Pakistan's need for additional water and electric power.[23]

Despite the high drama and awe-inspiring character of these undertakings, their numerous direct benefits, and their contribution to the rationalization and modernization of the policies and procedures of the Water and Power Development Authority of West Pakistan, they raise troublesome questions. Have the benefits been too concentrated to warrant the priority accorded to the projects? Has the provision of the local currency counterpart represented too large a claim on Pakistan's modest domestic resources for development? Have the projects served as magnets for a disproportionate share of Pakistan's foreign aid?

The East Pakistan Water and Power Development Authority was also addicted to big projects. However, it would be wrong to imply that no attention was being paid during the 1960s to development in other sectors or to development at the grass roots. The first agricultural assistance from the Bank Group after the small 1952 loan was a remarkably successful IDA credit in 1962 that helped finance the installation of some seven hundred electrically operated tubewells and pumping plants in West Pakistan. Then, following a joint FAO/Bank study, the IDA in 1965 granted the government of Pakistan a further $27 million credit for re-lending to the Agricultural Development Bank, which in turn could make loans directly to farmers. The beneficiaries of these efforts turned out to be large farmers. Agricultural output, particularly of cotton and rice in West Pakistan, grew during the first half of the 1960s and was in substantial measure responsible for the coun-

23. See Chapter 18, above, for more on the special study of the water and power resources of West Pakistan carried out during the years 1964–67 by a World Bank team. The first part of that study, completed in 1965, dealt with the proposal for the Tarbela Dam.

try's increased export earnings. Bank officials worked closely with Pakistani colleagues and in various speeches and publications expressed satisfaction with the way things were going.[24]

Tension Followed by Tragedy

The war with India in 1965 over the Rann of Kutch and Kashmir served as a setback to international cooperation, but it was soon over. The future of the Bank-organized consortium, which had functioned effectively since 1960, was jeopardized. As was reported in Chapter 15, however, the consortium was continued, though members began finding much to be uneasy about.

Pakistan's defense budget had become a major constraint on its developmental efforts. Those efforts appeared to be making small numbers of industrialists and large farmers fabulously rich but to be bypassing the vast majority of the population. Despite the demonstrated success of the Comilla approach to integrated rural development in East Pakistan, support for it was feeble. As of 1969, it was still confined largely to the Comilla district. Corruption in Pakistan was said to be widespread. Riots broke out, and in March 1969 Ayub turned the country over to the head of the army, Yahya Khan, who declared martial law. He threw out the old constitution and promised a new one after the 1970 elections. The latter were the first direct general elections in Pakistan's history. The Awami League's sweeping victory in East Pakistan set the stage for the bloody civil war unleashed there by Yahya Khan and the subsequent breakup of Pakistan—after yet another war with India—into Pakistan and Bangladesh. On May 1, 1971, Pakistan unilaterally declared a moratorium on its external debt payments to bilateral creditors, and there the matter stands as of this writing.

Religious hostilities, regional antagonisms, and forces virtually beyond control may have rendered the outcome inevitable. Yet gnawing doubts persist. Even if the tide could not have been turned, could the Bank and the members of the Bank-sponsored consortium have acquitted themselves more impressively?

---

24. The close cooperation between the World Bank and Pakistan has not been limited to creditor–debtor relations. Bank experts have collaborated intimately with their Pakistani colleagues all through the First and Second Five-Year Plans and in the preparation of the Third Plan. The Bank also helped to finance continuing assistance by the Development Advisory Service of Harvard University to Pakistan's Planning Commission and the Provincial Planning Departments. . . .

The satisfactory achievements under Pakistan's Second Five-Year Plan (1960/61–1964/65) were largely due to agricultural improvement. . . . The Third Plan puts even stronger emphasis on agricultural development, which the Plan describes as "the sine qua non for the development of the country's economy."

"The World Bank and Pakistan" (IBRD, Information release, January 1968, pp. 2 and 11).

Although the Bank made it clear that Pakistan's creditworthiness dissolved when Yahya Khan's soldiers went on their rampage in East Pakistan in March 1971, the Bank Group had provided considerable assistance of a fairly diversified nature during the second half of the 1960s. The Bank's initial efforts in Pakistan were directed toward breaking bottlenecks in the power and transport sectors. It favored the kind of projects it was best at, and these were generally large, engineering-type undertakings. It usually selected those promising the highest rates of return, and they tended to be in West Pakistan. In evaluating an ongoing activity such as the PICIC, the Bank concerned itself more with the efficiency of the management and with the rate of return on PICIC investments than with the geographic concentration of those investments or the size and type of industrial activity being assisted.

The Bank kept a watchful eye on the macroeconomic indicators, particularly on increases in GNP. Its advice on liberalizing the network of import controls and giving the price system a chance to work was good. It supported devaluation of the overvalued rupee. It often took sympathetic note of objectives such as rural development and regional balance, but until the late 1960s it was far from vigorous in their pursuit. It did not actively support the Comilla approach to rural development when the potentialities of that approach were first being demonstrated. Nor at the June 1965 meeting of the consortium, when Pakistan's draft five-year plan for 1965–70 was under discussion, did it support or encourage the drive for social justice envisaged by the planners in their chapter on "Economic Problems and Policies."[25] The drive implied a considerable expansion of the public sector and a predominant share of total investment in East Pakistan. Three years later, in May 1968, I.P.M. Cargill of the Bank was able to report to the consortium that a team had been set up by the Bank to make a comprehensive study of agriculture and water resources in East Pakistan. When in the same year the forward-looking socio-economic objectives of Pakistan's proposed fourth five-year plan were presented to the consortium, they were not vigorously

25. "One of the most complex problems is the worsening income distribution in the country. . . . A substantial part of capital formation has originated in a few big industrial families and, on the basis of their growing economic power, these families have been able to pre-empt the credit facilities available from commercial banks and specialised financial institutions. This has tended to inhibit the process of broadening the base of ownership of industrial capital as well as raised a vociferous demand for better distribution of incomes. Continuation of generous tax concessions by the Government and widespread prevalence of tax evasion, have enabled these accumulations to grow. . . .

"Another serious problem is that of unemployment. . . .

"It is quite clear on the eve of the Third Plan that the conflict between economic dynamism and social justice has become fairly sharp." Pakistan Planning Commission, *The Third Five Year Plan (1965–70)* (May 1965), pp. 117–18.

backed by that body. Nevertheless, the fourth plan (1970–75) seemed to indicate a determination on Pakistan's part to act.

But Pakistan's planners were never in political control, and the country from the beginning had been dominated by West Pakistan. Despite the fine words in the plan, the more meaningful cue—the 1970–71 budget—reconfirmed the old bias toward West Pakistan.

By mid-1970, the Bank's team produced an action report for East Pakistan, which was of immense promise and included a major rural development program.[26] When East Pakistan was hit by a devastating cyclone in November 1970, World Bank missions in the area helped the government prepare in record time a reconstruction program for the cyclone-affected coastal areas; an IDA credit of $25 million to finance certain parts of the program was approved on January 13, 1971. But no disbursements were made because, before they could be, the separation of the two wings had become a reality.

In retrospect, it is unfortunate that the strategy of development that the Bank had arrived at by mid-1970 did not dominate its thinking five years earlier. The development strategy for East Pakistan urged upon the Bank by its resident representative in Pakistan in August 1970 nevertheless can be of use in Bangladesh as well as elsewhere. The strategy, he said, should emphasize "projects and methods that make maximum use of unskilled and underemployed labor and, especially in rural districts, permit of decentralized administration relying heavily on local initiative and responsibility. The comprehensive approach to rural development pioneered by the Comilla Academy—including cooperative organization, rural works, and locally-managed irrigation schemes . . ." embodied these principles. Therefore, that approach "should be widely extended."[27]

India and Its Achievements in the 1950s

No country has been studied more by the World Bank than India, and it is no exaggeration to say that India has influenced the Bank as much as the Bank has influenced India.[28]

26. International Bank for Reconstruction and Development, "Proposals for an Action Program, East Pakistan Agriculture and Water Development," Report No. PS-2a (July 17, 1970).

27. David L. Gordon, "Development Strategy for East Pakistan," typewritten memorandum of Aug. 15, 1970.

28. In view of the many earlier references in this study to Bank Group relations with, and operations in, India, we shall be highly selective in what we say in this section. See Chapter 7 for a thumbnail sketch of the evolution of lending relations; Chapter 9 for an analysis of the six industrial import credits of 1964–70; Chapter 11 for strains caused by differences of view concerning the role of private enterprise, espe-

Bank lending to India, though it began early, grew slowly and averaged only $20 million a year during the period 1949–55. India still had a large accumulation of sterling balances on which she could draw. The establishment in 1958 of the Aid-India Group (later known as the India Consortium) marked the beginning of lending on a larger scale. The years 1958–62 probably represented the high point in cordial relations between India and the Bank Group. By June 30, 1971, loans and credits to India added up to more than $2.5 billion, accounting for almost half of all credits extended by IDA and one-sixteenth of all Bank lending. But India has a population of some 550 million—one-sixth that of the entire world. Its receipts on a per capita basis have consequently been exceedingly modest—far below those of the other countries discussed in this chapter.[29] India, moreover, has never been a *tabula rasa* patiently awaiting outside advice on development priorities or strategy before deciding on a course of action. Since obtaining its independence in 1947, India has had a government able and willing to assign a high priority to economic development and has been a repository of strongly held ideas on what needed to be done.

Its Planning Commission began life under the chairmanship of the prime minister, who took this duty seriously. India's drive for development evoked admiration at home and abroad. The rate of increase in the gross national product averaged slightly over 3 percent a year in real terms during the first half of the 1950s and slightly less than 4 percent during the second half—a record substantially better than that of most of southern Asia. Tax receipts rose. Total savings, public and private, increased during the 1950s from 5 or 6 percent of national income to about 8 percent.

The index of industrial production rose at a rate of about 7 percent a year. Agricultural output grew much more slowly; the increase, moreover, was due principally to an expansion of the area under cultivation and a growth in farm employment rather than to improved productivity. India was laying the basis, particularly during the period of its second five-year plan (1956–

---

cially in industrial development; Chapter 12 for India's role in developing the IDA concept and India's heavy claim on IDA resources; Chapter 13 for the Bank's efforts to use the leverage of loans and credits to obtain policy changes at project, sector, or national levels in India; Chapter 14 for the important ways in which its experience in India influenced the Bank's conception of development; Chapter 15 for a brief history of the India Consortium; and Chapter 18 for the Bank's role in working out the Indus Waters Treaty. Consult the index to this book ("India") for numerous other references.

29. According to the Economic and Social Data Division of the Bank, per capita receipts of Bank/IDA assistance in India through June 30, 1971, amounted to $4.67, compared with $40.87 for Colombia, $10.69 for Brazil, $10.53 for Thailand, and $8.28 for Pakistan.

61), for heavy industry. The core of that plan was a large expansion in iron- and steel-making facilities, heavy engineering, heavy electrical equipment, and chemical plants. This involved sizable investments in coal and iron ore mining as well as in railways and electric power. The Bank, during the second half of the 1950s, made more of the same kinds of loans it had made during the first half—for railway modernization, electric power, iron and steel, port development (Calcutta and Madras), and, through the ICICI, for private in- dustry generally.

Requirements for foreign aid during the first five-year plan period (1951– 56) turned out to be smaller than expected—because of export sales attribut- able to the Korean war, good weather, and failure to launch all of the im- port-intensive industrial undertakings adumbrated in the plan.

The second plan encountered balance-of-payments difficulties almost from the outset and had to be pared drastically at midterm. As was reported in Chapter 15, the Bank, at India's request, organized an international rescue operation in 1958. The rescue team supplied the billion dollars needed to complete financing of the plan and in due course became the India Consor- tium.

"Encouraged by our experience during the second plan," said I. G. Patel in his Lal Bahadur Shastri memorial lectures on foreign aid, "we wanted the Consortium to assess and underwrite in advance our requirements of foreign exchange during the third plan period as a whole so that we could embark on the plan with full confidence." To facilitate this, the Bank and the Indian government arranged for the 1960 mission of three prominent members of the international financial community. The "three wise men"—Sir Oliver Franks of the United Kingdom, Hermann Abs of Germany, and Allan Sproul of the United States—prepared the report, which Patel describes, in words not usually applied to the handiwork of bankers, as "one of the most heart- warming documents in the annals of international relations."[30]

The Difficult 1960s

Though substantial amounts of foreign aid were mobilized during the third plan period, the World Bank became increasingly critical of the management of the Indian economy. A characteristic feature of a development program

---

30. I. G. Patel, *Foreign Aid* (New Delhi: Allied Publishers Private, Ltd., 1968), p. 14. (Patel in 1968 was special secretary in India's Ministry of Finance.) The Bank- ers' mission was followed, at a more technical level, by a World Bank mission headed by Michael L. Hoffman, which also gave a general endorsement to the third five-year plan, including its emphasis on industry. A further factor in the warm relations be- tween the Bank and India *circa* 1960 was the completion that year, after long Bank involvement, of the Indus Waters Treaty.

centered on heavy industry is the long gestation period between initial investment and operation at full capacity of the new facilities. Thus, impressive results in the period covered by the third five-year plan (1961–66) could hardly
have been expected. Nevertheless, during the first four years of the period,
the overall growth rate averaged 4.3 percent—better than the average during
the second plan period, but disappointing because it was below the high
targets that had been set. The steel industry appeared to be staggering under
a heavy burden of governmental controls. Agriculture performed poorly even
before the catastrophic weather conditions of 1965–67.

Since India by the early 1960s was by far the largest borrower from the
Bank Group and since the Bank was responsible to the consortium for reporting on the state of the economy, the Bank in 1964 proposed that a new
in-depth study be undertaken of the reasons for the unsatisfactory performance of the economy. This proposal was not particularly well received by
the Indian government. After considerable negotiation, it was decided that
the study would go forward on the understanding that its primary purpose
was to inform the president of the Bank on the condition of the Indian economy and that the report would be available only to the Bank and the government of India. The assessment was said to be needed in order to guide the
Bank in proposing consortium financing for the fourth five-year plan, which
was scheduled to begin April 1, 1966 (but was later postponed).

The Bank, it will be recalled from Chapter 7, received a critical, ten-
volume report from the mission headed by Bernard R. Bell. President Woods
accepted the analysis, sent Bell and André de Lattre to negotiate with various
members of the Indian government, and played an active role himself in 1965
and 1966. The three aspects of performance that were considered most damaging to India's creditworthiness and prospects for economic growth were
exchange rate policy, administrative controls over imports, and the relative
neglect of agriculture.

Through the consortium, a pressure group formed, which India was in a
weak position to resist.[31] The Bank's third and fourth import credits in
August and December 1966, totaling $215 million, constituted its proposed
contribution to $900 million in commodity assistance from consortium mem-
bers to permit and induce certain changes in economic policy. India agreed

31. In addition to economic difficulties, there had been a sharp upsurge in defense
expenditures, brief wars with China in 1962 and with Pakistan in 1965, the death of
Jawaharlal Nehru in 1964, and the death of his successor as prime minister, Lal
Bahadur Shastri, in January 1966, a few hours after he had signed the Tashkent accord
with Pakistan. Shastri was succeeded by Mrs. Indira Gandhi, who was promptly faced
with a power struggle within the Congress party.

to liberalize its import controls. At about the same time, India, after consulting the IMF, devalued the rupee by 36 percent. The 1966 credits represent, in our view, the Bank's most significant attempt to use the leverage of its lending to modify macroeconomic policies in a major member country.[32] The benefits of the policy modifications made in India in 1966 have been obscured by some historical accidents, such as India's drought-induced recession, a sharp decline in U.S. aid (which amounted to a virtual "freeze" during a critical period), and the protracted negotiations for the second IDA replenishment with resultant serious delays in making available to India its fifth and sixth IDA credits for industrial imports.

Some participants and observers argue that Bank influence was decisive in bringing about policy changes that would not otherwise have occurred when they did. Others, equally well informed, are more skeptical and point to pressure exercised independently by the United States or suggest that devaluation became necessary because of the obvious and inescapable weakness of the rupee. The Indian government, in our view, would surely have been more hesitant to liberalize imports or make other changes in economic policy when it did, if it had not been for the promise by the Bank to raise $900 million annually in program aid. The Bank raised the promised sum in 1966 but was never afterward able to approach this figure, with the result that relations between the Bank and India for the next few years were visibly tarnished.

The relative neglect of India's huge agricultural sector had become a source of distress to the Bank before the series of bad monsoons in the 1960s. Some believe that Sir John Crawford, the eminent Australian who was a member of the Bell mission to India, was highly influential in stimulating the adoption of the new technology that produced the green revolution. Others think the process was already under way and that he observed, publicized, and perhaps expedited it. Certainly C. S. Subramaniam, India's minister of food and agriculture, was fully aware of the need for change. The Bank in general pressed for adequate price incentives for agricultural producers and high priority for the inputs they needed (including fertilizers). It continued its traditional support for large flood control and irrigation schemes but at

32. In indicating that the Bank went further here than elsewhere in exercising leverage, we are referring to the leverage on overall economic policy associated (correctly or incorrectly) with non-project or program lending, not to the leverage on a specific enterprise associated with project lending or the leverage on sector policy associated with a series of loans to enterprises within a single sector of the economy. (See Chapter 13, above.) In Brazil in the 1950s, the Bank wanted fundamental changes in economic policies, but negotiations never reached the stage of spelling out which specific changes would induce what levels and types of project loans from the Bank.

the same time experimented with other approaches to agricultural development—agricultural credit projects, for example.

India operated on the basis of annual plans in 1967, 1968, and 1969. Agriculture led the contribution to income growth with record outputs of food grains in 1967-68 and 1969-70. (This reflected good weather as well as better agricultural practices.) The fourth five-year plan (1969-70–1973-74) speaks

of the spirit of self-reliance and postulates a declining net resource transfer. It is visualized that by the end of the Fifth Plan (1978/79), the economy should generate a surplus of resources sufficient to cover interest charges on the foreign debt. This is an admirable perspective from the standpoint of self-reliance but one that forecloses the option of (a) raising total income faster than 5.7% per annum and (b) allowing per capita private consumption to increase faster than 2.6% per annum. The choice of the planners is probably based on a shrewd judgment regarding the outlook for foreign aid.[33]

Twenty-five percent of all Bank/IDA assistance to India through June 30, 1971—by far the largest amount lent by the Bank Group to any single enterprise anywhere—went to the railway system. To some extent these were program loans dressed up as project lending. The strings attached to the railway loans and credits, however, tended to relate to railway administration and operation and to railway–highway competition—in short, to the transport sector, not to overall economic policy. Deflecting Indian planners from their commitment to railway development has been difficult. Until after June 30, 1971, few in the Bank believed that the effort could be termed successful. But the Bank's own views of what to do about the world's ailing railways have jelled slowly. As of early 1972, these views were finding greater acceptance in India; there was a greater willingness to abandon obsolete railway lines, to concentrate on the long-haul, bulk traffic for which railways are the most efficient form of transport, and to let highways carry what they can best carry.

The Bank's dedicated efforts to persuade India to do less to discourage the private sector, and more to encourage it, have had marginal effects that we consider beneficial. Exchanges of views over the years have blunted the orthodoxies of both parties to the debate, while earning the Bank a reputa-

33. Ravi I. Gulhati, "The Question of India's External Debt," *India Quarterly*, Vol. 28 (January–March 1972), p. 10. The net transfer of foreign resources in 1968–69, he points out, was one-half that in the preceding year, and it declined sharply once again in 1969-70. The reference to "foreclosure" of growth in excess of 5.7 percent a year overall and 2.6 percent per capita should not be taken as gospel; economic forecasting is not that exact a science. Nevertheless, it does seem clear that a continued decline in net aid will contribute to a lower rate of growth than a country as poor as India ought to achieve during the 1970s.

tion in India for conservatism that has been hard to dispel. The Bank's work on a proposal for a fertilizer plant in Cochin, Kerala, led to a much-improved process and therefore a better, more useful project. The Cochin plant, incidentally, was the first publicly owned industrial establishment in India to receive direct Bank or IDA financing.

The ICICI—a privately managed development finance company headquartered in Bombay that was launched with substantial technical assistance from the World Bank and has received more than $200 million in Bank loans since 1955—is generally considered to have done a good job. It has helped introduce modern management techniques to its industrial clients, provided them with finance (predominantly in the form of loans but including also some equity investments and underwriting), and contributed to the development of a capital market in India. The Bank's affiliate, the IFC, has made eleven investments in India, mostly in joint ventures. In dollar terms, three-fourths of its commitment total is in the fertilizer industry.

The Bank has been acutely conscious of the importance of family planning in India and has helped to arrange a consortium meeting on the subject. But Indian planners and bilateral donors are also acutely conscious of the problem. No loans or credits for family planning had been extended to India by the Bank Group as of the close of the 1971 fiscal year.

Bank reports challenging the priority accorded to investment in atomic power may have delayed and/or reduced—but not prevented—the commitment of non-Bank resources to such projects. Bank loans and IDA credits for the expansion of electricity-generating capacity have facilitated industrialization, especially in the area served by the Damodar Valley Corporation and in the Bombay-Poona region. Bank activity in the power sector probably contributed also to improvements in financial practices and to some mobilization of savings through higher rates.

India's Influence on the Bank

In introducing this section we suggested that India had influenced the Bank as much as the Bank had influenced India. This applies particularly to the Bank's conception of the development process—of the role of government in the process, of the need for grants, soft loans, and program assistance, and of the degree to which solidly based growth depends on rural development, which in turn depends on a great deal more than the opportunity for farmers to benefit from government investment in irrigation and flood control.

In the eyes of the Bank's management, India (because of its obvious needs and limited creditworthiness) offered the clearest justification for the creation of IDA as its soft-loan affiliate; without IDA, the Bank could not have continued to be heavily involved in India. The Bank's views on non-project or program lending to less developed countries have been shaped substantially by its experience during the 1960s in India. India's ability to produce capital equipment has been instrumental in securing changes in Bank policy on international competitive bidding in order to permit a margin of preference for domestic suppliers of goods.

The India Consortium represented not only the Bank's maiden effort in the coordination of aid from multiple sources, but probably also its major effort. India offers the only example of debt-relief negotiations in which an adjustment of service on outstanding World Bank loans has been part of the package. The Bank's June 1969 loan to India for growing seeds of high-yielding varieties of food grains represented the Bank Group's first financing anywhere of seed production, a key component of the green revolution. India's progress toward achieving economic self-sufficiency in food grains within the space of a few short years has done much to highlight for the Bank (and for the world as a whole) the so-called "second-generation" problems of the green revolution. Economic self-sufficiency in food, however, is not the same as nutritional self-sufficiency. The Bank's current interest in malnutrition is a function largely of the scope of the problem in India, despite some ingenious efforts in that country to compensate for widespread protein deficiencies.

The Swings of the Pendulum in Retrospect

Underlying the history of Bank relations with India has been the broad trend of "fashionable" thinking about the subcontinent. As it gradually became involved, the Bank—like other external sources of assistance—was appalled by India's poverty, dazzled by its size and by the prestige of being active there, and impressed by the articulateness of its political leaders and top-level civil servants and by the high priority they accorded to economic development. The Bank conceived of its task as seeing that India's five-year plans got support, especially since India's needs for investment in infrastructure (railways, electric power, irrigation) matched the Bank's availabilities and expertise.

A decade later the mood had changed to one of disenchantment—with planning, with India, with infrastructure. The importance of investment in agriculture, education, and human resource development was becoming apparent. What had previously been viewed as technical excellence in India was characterized as doctrinaire arrogance. Partly as a result of the overblown expectations of an earlier period, India was seen as a bottomless pit, absorbing vast amounts of aid with little or no visible result. In order that more IDA funds could be allocated elsewhere, ceilings were clapped on IDA assistance to India. Specific "quids" began to be demanded for every "quo," with both sides at different times failing to deliver as expected.

The pendulum as of this writing appears to be slowly swinging back toward midpoint as the Bank and India arrive at a more mature view of what each can do. India has survived without abandoning democratic procedures and without a procession of military dictators. The distribution of the fruits of two decades of productivity increases has been less skewed in favor of the rich in India than in most of the low-income world. Nevertheless, a major question in India, as well as elsewhere in the developing countries, is whether the rates of growth attained have reduced the appalling poverty of the lowest third on the income ladder. Though India in early 1972 was more united and self-confident than at any time in the previous two decades, it faced problems of staggering magnitude, to the solution of which the Bank's contribution would necessarily be modest.

The Bank and Thailand

Thailand, like Colombia, is a medium-sized, long-independent, potentially rich country, in the development of which the Bank Group has been intimately involved for more than two decades.[34] By Bank Group, we mean here the Bank and the IFC. No credits have been extended to Thailand by the Bank's soft-loan affiliate, the IDA. Indeed, the country's financial position appeared so favorable in 1967 that further Bank lending seemed unnecessary. The government, however, valued so highly the Bank's technical assistance and certain disciplinary features of its lending that it went to unusual lengths to keep the Bank in the picture. As is described below, it went through the motions of borrowing from the Bank, for the sake of the corollary benefits of following Bank-prescribed policies and procedures, but arranged to buy back immediately the bulk of the Bank's lending during the years 1967–68, leaving the Bank as financier of only a fraction of the foreign-exchange costs of agreed projects. On the basis of macroeconomic indicators, Thai-

---

34. Its population in mid-1971 was about thirty-seven million; its area approximately two hundred thousand square miles. The Bank's first loans to Thailand, made in October 1950, were also the Bank's first loans in Southeast Asia.

land's development record since the close of World War II has been excellent. GNP has risen by more than 6.5 percent a year.

As of June 30, 1971, the Bank had made twenty-two loans to Thailand totaling $394 million. Ten loans for transportation accounted for half of this total.[35] Five loans totaling $75 million had been made for flood control and irrigation. One loan, the Bank's largest single investment in the country, was for the Yanhee multipurpose project on the Ping River—$66 million for power, flood control, and irrigation. Four loans totaling $64.1 million were for electric power. A loan of $6 million for education and one of $2.5 million to the Industrial Finance Corporation of Thailand complete the list. The IFC's commitments as of June 30, 1971, amounted to $22.8 million, of which $22.1 million was in the Siam Cement Group Companies.

Lending, in other words, has been heavily weighted toward basic infrastructure. There has been little lending for industrial development and education and none for agricultural credit. This has been due in part to Thailand's own assessment of its priorities. Its infrastructure had been badly neglected during World War II and urgently needed investment. The government has been relying on the private sector as an engine of growth and has envisaged its own role as one of supporting private initiative by providing power, transport, and flood control facilities rather than becoming directly involved in financing private sector activities. This philosophy of development seemed to the World Bank eminently sound during most of the period under review.

During the 1950s, industry was of minor importance in the Thai economy. By the mid-1960s, when the industrial sector began to expand quite rapidly, there was no great shortage of foreign exchange for imports. Suppliers' credits, moreover, were readily available. Because the Thai government cannot guarantee loans to the private sector, World Bank assistance to the sector has been negligible. The government-supported Industrial Finance Corporation of Thailand, which has received technical assistance and a small loan from the World Bank, has been a weak and unenterprising institution, quite incapable of competing with commercial banks.

Agricultural credit had traditionally been provided by the rice traders. It appeared to involve only short-term requirements for domestic currency and therefore not to be a field for World Bank involvement. The production and export of rice, moreover, was believed to be expanding satisfactorily.

In education, the small volume of Bank lending can be attributed in part

35. For *roads:* four loans totaling $123 million; for *railways:* three loans totaling $37 million; for *ports:* three loans totaling $20.3 million.

to the Bank's own delay in entering the field. It is also attributable in part to feelings by Thai authorities that foreign loans would bring with them unwelcome influences on the cultural and social life of Thailand and that borrowing for projects having indirect and immeasurable returns would run counter to sound fiscal policy.

Toward the end of the 1960s, government attitudes and policies toward the private sector and toward educational development began to change. If the use of suppliers' credits goes unchecked and U.S. expenditures in Southeast Asia decline, Thailand could well face serious debt-servicing problems in the early 1980s. The country's reserves are falling, and longer-term capital for the private sector is needed. In education, there is still a marked preference for grant or IDA-type assistance, rather than World Bank loans, but the 1960s virtually ended Thailand's cultural isolation. In agriculture, Thailand's current priority is to diversify out of rice (because of marketing and price difficulties to which the green revolution has contributed) into other crops. The development of the latter can be handicapped by the high cost of unofficial credit from traditional sources.

The Bank's activities in Thailand over the past twenty years may be considered under three rubrics: (a) the project-financing work of the Bank, (b) the institution-building activities, and (c) the Bank's influence on Thailand's economic policies.

Project Financing

With regard to project financing, the greater part of Bank involvement, it will be recalled, has been in irrigation and flood control, electric power, and transportation. In irrigation and flood control, there has been an extensive effort by Thailand, with the support of the Bank, to improve the system in the central plain served by the Chao Phya River and its four northern tributaries, the Ping, Wang, Yom, and Nan.

The Chao Phya has been, and is still, the life stream of the Thai people. From the ancient city of Ayudhaya in the river's central valley, the Thai nation consolidated, developed its civilization, flowered, and spread. And the annual flood and ebb of the river across its flanking plains, crisscrossed by the dikes and canals of an elementary irrigation system, allowed the growth of one of the great rice bowls of Asia, traditionally providing a surplus for export. For generations, too, the river and its tributaries, and their flanking and interconnecting canals, have formed the country's main routes for commerce—a flourishing central trading highway linking the province with the town, and the town with other trading nations abroad.

For all their bounty, however, the Chao Phya and its principal tributaries are, in their natural state, capricious rivers.[36]

In the early 1950s, the Bank began helping the Thai government to overcome the river system's capriciousness. The first step was a diversion dam on the main Chao Phya at Chainat, which by 1957 was softening the brunt of floods and allowing a wider diffusion of the Chao Phya waters into canals, old and new, on the central plain. Subsequently a large storage dam was built for both irrigation and power on the Ping River at Yanhee.[37] Completed in 1964, it rises five hundred feet above the river bed and creates a reservoir capable of storing twelve billion cubic meters of water. Another large storage dam financed in part by the Bank—the Phasom Dam and reservoir—on another northern tributary, the Nan, is nearing completion. This comprehensive improvement of the irrigation and flood control system was appraised and undertaken in the expectation of a substantial increase in the productivity of the central plain. The construction of the major irrigation works was carried out effectively by the Royal Irrigation Department (RID) under the supervision of consulting engineers hired at the Bank's insistence in the 1950s and early 1960s.

The RID had for many years been designing and building flood dispersal works to improve transportation and to control the inundation around Bangkok during the rainy season, but it had little or no experience in all-weather irrigation. As a result, the RID's basic design for the central plain's water distribution system put the canals too low in the ground, thereby reducing the head and limiting the areas that could be irrigated in the dry season. As flood protection and dispersal schemes, the projects were successful. Rice yields have improved significantly, and farm output, formerly highly erratic, has stabilized over the years. The investment per hectare has been low.

From an irrigation standpoint, however, the productivity increase has been disappointing. The RID, the consultants, and the Bank apparently took too much for granted in expecting that the farmers of the central plain would, on their own initiative, take full advantage of these newly created facilities and themselves build the distribution systems that were needed at farm level. The kind of research and extension system necessary to explain the advantages of water control to the farmers and to develop the technology that would make the most of the new potentialities was lacking.

36. David Love, "Controlling the Chao Phya," *Finance and Development,* Vol. 4 (December 1967), pp. 237–38.

37. See "Yanhee (Thailand) Multipurpose Project," in Edwin M. Martin, *Development Assistance: Efforts and Policies of the Members of the Development Assistance Committee, 1968 Review* (Paris: Organisation for Economic Co-operation and Development, December 1968), pp. 199–207.

Moreover, because of the design deficiencies, the farmer had no assurance that water could or would be delivered regularly to his farm if he dug and maintained the necessary channels. In any event, the dry season in the central plain was the pleasant time when farmers could stand in pools and ditches behind the receding flood, netting minnows with which to flavor their rice. It is also clear in retrospect that, when the projects were being appraised, information on the suitability of the soils of the central plain for irrigated farming during the dry season was inadequate. Most of the soils proved to be heavy clays suitable only for rice cultivation.

The second large area of development in which the Bank played an active part, electric power, was of course closely associated with the above-mentioned irrigation and flood control efforts, particularly in connection with the Yanhee project for construction of the Bhumiphol Dam. Power expansion and the Bank's contribution thereto have been positive factors in the rapid expansion of the Thai economy.[38] The way in which the expansion program was launched, however, has made it less efficient than it might have been. The electricity-generating capabilities of the Ping River, on which the Bhumiphol Dam was built, were substantially overestimated, and the forecasts of growth in demand for power were much too low. Taking into account the shortfall in the generating capabilities of the Bhumiphol Dam and the previously reported disappointments in the project's contribution to agricultural output, a current reassessment of this sizable multipurpose development effort would probably call into question its economic justification.

In transportation, the Bank's railway lending has been mainly for expanding and modernizing the system. In addition to financing the importation of equipment, the Bank can be said to have improved considerably the efficiency and the management of the railway system. There has been justifiable concern about the deteriorating financial position of the railway system despite its increased efficiency. Has the shift of traffic from the railways to the highways been inevitable? The railways have complained about unfair competition from especially privileged highway carriers, and the Bank on more than one occasion has sought government intervention to eliminate the special privileges. Its interventions have been unsuccessful. Even if they had been successful, it is doubtful whether they would have helped the financial position of the railways to any great extent.

When the Bank first became involved in highway development, Thailand's highway system was rudimentary, and the construction agency was inefficient

38. When the Yanhee project was under consideration, the per capita level of power consumption in Thailand was estimated to be only 9 kilowatt-hours, as compared with 20 in India and Ceylon, and 200 in Mexico.

and ridden with graft. Nevertheless, the Bank was able to insure that the projects it financed were carried out fairly efficiently and fairly honestly. It was also able to introduce a coordinated approach to highway development and a set of highway priorities. Feeder roads need substantial further development; and better coordination of different modes of transport, especially road and rail, is needed.

The port of Bangkok represents the third major area of Bank involvement in the transport sector. The port is undoubtedly better and more efficient because of World Bank involvement than it would otherwise be. Bangkok, forty miles up the Chao Phya river from the sea and with a shallow draft for ocean-going vessels, is a difficult port on a river requiring major dredging. The Bank has provided substantial technical assistance in improving both the operations and the physical setting of the port, as well as in expanding its capacity. A major question remains unresolved, however: Would it have been better to develop an alternative deep water port than to concentrate on expanding the capacity of Bangkok? The issue has been studied and debated since the late 1950s. At the time, the Bank probably helped tip the scales in favor of developing Bangkok and delaying consideration of an alternative. By the time the Bank was ready to consider sympathetically an alternative, it was too late. Strategic considerations concerning the build-up of the naval base at Sattaheep, and its possible use for commercial as well as military traffic, had become factors. If the Bank had taken a different view in the late 1950s and early 1960s and had pressed its view, decisions about further port development might not be as difficult as they have become.

Institution-Building

The execution of Bank-financed projects in Thailand, once a haphazard, catch-as-catch-can business, has become fairly effective. Some of the credit for this transformation is certainly due to the institution-building efforts of the Bank, especially in irrigation (the Royal Irrigation Department), in electric power (the Electricity Generating Authority of Thailand [EGAT], formerly the Yanhee Electricity Authority), in railways and ports (autonomous agencies created at the Bank's insistence), and in highways (the Highway Department of the Ministry of National Development). Among these, the Bank's influence was probably least in irrigation, because the RID was already an effective organization with a capable and farsighted director-general.[39] (As was previously noted, however, its effectiveness did not extend to the on-farm end of irrigation improvements.)

39. Xujati Kambhu, who in 1964 became deputy minister of national development.

The autonomous port and railway administrations for which the Bank served as midwife did not eliminate meddling in their affairs by others. Nevertheless, the amount of interference was far less than it would have been had these agencies remained a part of the regular civil service. Removing them from civil service routines and creating separate financial accounts for these institutions permitted substantial improvements in their organization and methods of operation.

Perhaps even more impressive has been the organization for the generation and wholesale distribution of electric power. In connection with its loan for the Yanhee multipurpose project, the Bank insisted that a separate authority be created. The Yanhee Electricity Authority, now EGAT, has evolved into a highly efficient organization. Less impressive have been the institutional improvements in retail power distribution in urban areas under the Metropolitan Electricity Authority and in rural areas under the Provincial Power Authority. In these two parts of the power sector, the Bank unfortunately has not become involved financially or as an institution-builder.

Substantial institutional improvement has also occurred in the Highway Department. Largely as a result of the Bank's technical assistance and training efforts, the disorganized and corrupt arrangements of the 1950s for highway construction have been reformed. The Highway Department is now one of the more effective branches of the Thai government.

The supreme tribute to the Bank's technical assistance work in Thailand has already been mentioned—the keen desire of the Thais in 1967, when their financial position was such that further Bank lending could not be justified, to maintain nominal financial participation by the Bank in order to obtain technical assistance in preparing, appraising, and carrying out specific development projects. More importantly, the policy reflected the desires of some persons in Thailand, mainly at technical and staff levels but presumably also some at the political level, to ensure a reasonable degree of honesty in the selection of contractors and suppliers, the disbursement of funds, and the management of roads and highways.

Influence on Macroeconomic Policy

Although in the early 1950s the Thai government envisaged its role in the promotion of development in very limited terms, some elements in the government saw the need for more active official efforts. They found increasing support from the prime minister as he became able, after the postwar political uncertainties, to consolidate his position. The development-minded elements in the government also gained substantial support for their efforts from the backing and guidance of the World Bank. Economic and technical missions visited Thailand in the early 1950s, and from 1956 until 1965 the Bank had maintained a resident representative in Bangkok. In addition, an economic mission of the Bank was in Thailand for about a year in 1958 to make a general survey of the economy and recommend priorities for public investment. There was a later resident mission in 1962–63 to assist the planning authorities.

The principal areas of Bank influence on broad economic policy have been in the management of external debt, in the domestic financial policies pursued by the government, and in the planning of development. In the first of these areas, Thailand, in connection with the Yanhee multipurpose loan, in effect bound itself to obtain the agreement of the Bank for any further net increase in its foreign debt during the construction period of the Yanhee project. In the light of Thailand's favorable external debt position at the time (September 1957), this restriction reflected undue concern on the part of the Bank. It was also an impractical condition for the Bank to supervise adequately without hampering justifiable borrowings on Thailand's part. The Bank exercised its authority in a liberal and sensible way, so that the legal restriction did not become the limitation it might have been. On the other hand, it did prove to be an effective device for centralizing and coordinating external borrowing in Thailand, enabling the financial authorities for the first time to scrutinize in advance the desirability of specific foreign borrowings by official agencies.

Regarding domestic financial policy, Thailand, in connection with the Yanhee loan, in effect undertook to observe an absolute annual limit on net additional government borrowing from the central bank. Like the limitation on foreign borrowing, this limitation seemed unnecessarily restrictive in the context of Thailand's financial circumstances. However, the Bank again followed a liberal line in the observance of the condition, and it agreed to exceptions.

The investment priorities recommended by the Bank's survey mission of 1958 probably could and would have been chosen by the Thais in any case. Nevertheless, there was really no organization in Thailand then for the formulation of a development program beyond each year's budget exercise. Hence this mission provided Thailand for the first time with a longer-term view of its development requirements. Public investment for the next three years followed very closely the recommendations of the mission. It was also on the recommendation of that mission that Thailand established its economic planning agency, the National Economic Development Board.

The chief exception to the Bank's broad approval of Thai economic policy in recent years has concerned the development of Thailand's poverty-stricken, restless Northeast. Though the Bank has felt for fifteen years that more should be done for the Northeast than the Thais were doing, the situation has not really changed except for the effects in that region of large military spending by the United States and some roads and other amenities resulting from a U.S.-sponsored rural improvement program. If the truth were told, however, the Bank, though it has emphasized the needs of the Northeast, has made few concrete proposals. A main objective of the 1962–63 resident mission was to contribute to the solution of the Northeast problem. That effort unfortunately was brought to a premature end by a helicopter accident in which members of the mission and their Thai associates were killed.

The National Economic Development Board has now completed its third five-year program. Its programs have not been influential, though they have played some role in determining priorities and coordinating investment in a longer-term framework than that of the budget. At the time the NEDB was created, some Thai officials thought it would be most effective as part of the Ministry of Finance, which at that time also included the budgeting function. The Bank disagreed and persuaded the government that the NEDB should be an independent agency, in a position to view objectively financial policies as well as investment priorities. The result was an NEDB isolated from government operations and less influential than it might have been.

During the 1960s the Bank felt no great need to reshape the Thai economy, which appeared to be enjoying rapid growth with financial stability. To an important extent, the good record was a product of external developments that are rapidly diminishing in importance—favorable markets for rice and large dollar inflows related to the U.S. war effort in Vietnam.

Thailand's two decades of remarkably rapid overall growth have been accompanied by population increases in excess of 3 percent a year, an inequitable sharing of the fruits of economic growth among income classes, insufficient attention to the development of its principal problem area (the northeast region), and a capital city bursting at the seams and illustrating graphically most of the ills of urban centers in the early 1970s. Despite the encouraging record of 1950–70, it would be folly to pretend that the medium-term outlook in Thailand is brilliant.

Postscript

The country vignettes in this chapter share some common features that tell a good deal about the strengths and weaknesses of the Bank as a development agency. The generalizations and broader inferences to be drawn from the specific experiences, however, are for the most part reserved for Chapter 20.

The picture we have conveyed here may be somewhat distorted because we limited ourselves to countries in which the Bank had been involved on a broad enough scale to have an impact in more than one sector and for enough years to permit perspective. This practically ruled out African members; the big surge of membership from that continent occurred during the first half of the 1960s. By then, the Bank and development specialists everywhere—thanks to an earlier period of trial and error—were more aware of the importance of investment in agriculture, in education, and in disadvantaged regions; the pattern of Bank Group investments in its newer members might consequently seem more in harmony with current thinking about the strategy of development.

The Bank's earlier concentration on economic infrastructure was not an aberration, however. In country after country at the end of World War II, railways existed but were paralyzed for lack of equipment. Electric power supplies were rationed. Blackouts were frequent. The absence of heavy industry was the most obvious symbol of underdevelopment. And the Tennessee Valley Authority was the most admired model for upgrading an entire region. Under those circumstances, what reception would have been given to a lending institution that said, "Your top priorities are not infrastructure, industrialization, or other activities requiring sizable amounts of foreign exchange. You need land reform, a different educational curriculum, a family planning program, and greater equality in the distribution of income"?

With rare exceptions, less developed countries that have had extensive relations with the Bank Group are infinitely better informed about themselves than before they joined the Bank, and far better equipped to deal effectively with whatever problems they regard as most urgent.

CHAPTER TWENTY

The Balance Sheet Continued: Sectoral and Overall Impact

THE COUNTRY VIGNETTES in Chapter 19 underscore the Bank's highly conservative initial estimates of the creditworthiness of its less developed member countries, its heavy emphasis until very recently on economic infrastructure (especially in the fields of electric power and transportation), and its tendency to overestimate the leverage on the policies of borrowers that was inherent in lending at the modest levels at which the Bank was prepared to lend. Although the Bank provided major assistance to borrowers in planning their public investment programs and in developing long-range perspectives, it tried at the same time to persuade them to give relatively free play to market forces and to rely on a strong private sector as a principal engine of growth.

Apart from its financing of large-scale irrigation projects and some encouragement of mechanization, the Bank was slow to become seriously interested in agricultural development. But the countries with which it was dealing were for the most part determined to give priority to industrialization and, until about 1960, would have resented external pressure to do otherwise.

If the Bank did not set the fashion, it fell readily into the pattern of measuring a country's developmental progress in terms of its relative price stability, and its increases in gross national product, rate of investment, savings rates or marginal savings rates, export earnings, and other conventional macroeconomic indicators. But before the Bank is criticized for its prolonged neglect of the social and civic dimensions of the development process, it should be recalled that the countries to which it was lending were, with few exceptions, not notably eager to provide arable land to the landless, to adopt labor-intensive methods of production, to correct regional disparities, to improve the distribution of income through progressive taxation or other means, or to honor in other ways the brave words in their constitutions.

The Bank Group, as we said in introducing the preceding chapter, concentrated nearly one-third of all its loans and credits during the years 1946–71 in the five countries discussed in that chapter. It has concentrated more than two-thirds of its resources in three sectors—transportation, electric power, and agriculture. In addition to such influence as it has had in countries and sectors in which it was heavily engaged, its standards and methods of operation have had some noteworthy across-the-board effects.

This chapter begins with a brief summary of some of these broader impacts. We include then some comments of an evaluational character on the Bank's approach to the transportation sector, which has been and is expected to continue to be, the largest claimant on Bank/IDA resources. We turn next to agriculture, which for long was a modest claimant but is expected to be the second largest during the five-year period ending June 30, 1976. After reviewing transportation and agriculture, we look at the power sector, which is scheduled to drop from second to third place as a claimant but to continue to bulk large in total lending. We close with a few comments on some of the Bank's other areas of concern, including education, telecommunication, and water supply and sewerage.

Overall Impact

Some of the Bank's impact on methods of promoting development is a result of the fact that it was itself a pilot project—the first international institution of its kind to be created. Precedents for its actions were few and far between, much underbrush had to be cleared away, and every height that was scaled revealed new obstacles in the path ahead. If the Bank was a cautious explorer, as concerned with keeping its supply lines open and protecting its rear as with sprinting boldly from hilltop to hilltop, it had plausible reasons for caution. Girding itself for the long pull has proved consistent with the nature of the development process.

Continuity as an Asset

Indeed one of the most important assets of the Bank, in our view, has been continuity. It has been "here to stay." The Bank is therefore relatively invulnerable to short-term political and economic winds and to sudden changes in fashion. It can plan ahead and enter into long-term partnerships for the development of vital sectors of the economies of member nations.

The reasons for this special source of strength are familiar. The Bank Group has a financial base that makes it substantially independent of the appropriation process. Reconstruction and development are its objectives; its relations with members can grow strained because of differences of view on how best to promote these objectives, but the strains need not be compounded by the numerous nondevelopmental considerations that enter into bilateral relationships. The Bank Group has members on every continent, at almost all points on the political spectrum. Though dominated by its larger shareholders, the smallest subscribers are also members and, as such, have some voice in policymaking—a voice that in their view (and ours) is too weak but nonetheless audible.

At the beginning, members could not be confident that they were dealing with a stable, quasi-permanent institution. But that soon changed. Before long, a member country that succeeded in engaging the Bank in its developmental efforts could usually count on a continuation and intensification of the relationship. There have, of course, been many exceptions to this generalization. Indonesia went so far as to withdraw from membership between 1965 and 1967. Brazil obtained loans in every year from 1949 through 1954, but relations were often strained, and no loans were obtained between March 1954 and January 1958 and none between June 1959 and February 1965. Iran and the Philippines, contrary to their desires, both had to wait until 1957 for their first loans but have since been frequent borrowers. On occasion, Turkey and the World Bank have virtually broken off diplomatic relations. In Ceylon in 1970, the conditions attached to a Bank loan became an issue in a bitterly fought election campaign.

Despite instances of temporary strain and the permanent underlying tension inherent in borrower–lender relationships, the Bank's relations with its borrowers have on the whole been harmonious, durable, and increasingly intimate. The extent and continuity of the Bank's involvement in Colombia— forty-nine loans and credits during the period 1949–71—helped make Colombia the first country in which the Bank, with the collaboration of the government of the country, made a comprehensive effort to evaluate the Bank's contribution to national development.[1] Japan's first loan from the Bank came in 1953 in lieu of a loan it had expected to obtain from the Export-Import Bank of the United States and in a manner that was somewhat of a shock to Japan. But during the years 1953–66 Japan was the Bank's

---

1. See Chapter 19, above.

biggest borrower. The cordial relationship established during its thirteen years as a borrower was a factor in its subsequent decision to become a lender to the Bank. The Bank's relationships with countries as different from Japan, and from each other, as Nicaragua and Yugoslavia have been constant and close.

A related consequence of the Bank's being "here to stay" and having considerable autonomy is that it has been able to obtain a remarkably competent staff, willing and eager to make service to the institution a career. In other chapters, we have been critical of certain attitudes of Bank personnel—tendencies toward arrogance, lack of empathy, unwarranted righteousness—but the Bank's staff, to invert Winston Churchill's phrase, has much to be immodest about. Its project appraisal techniques are the most thoroughgoing that have been applied and have served as a model for regional development banks, for national development finance companies, and for many other institutional investors. Its economic reports are the best available surveys of development problems and prospects. While their principal purpose is to facilitate dialogue between the Bank and the country covered by the report, they are also of great value to other international and regional development agencies and to the donor members of consortia and consultative groups. The smaller donors, in particular, would be unable to justify independent preparation of reports of comparable scope and reliability.

The Bank has one of the largest single groups of transport economists in the world and has probably amassed more information about transport conditions in developing countries than any other agency. The Bank's Development Finance Companies Department is also unique. Bank personnel in our view merit high marks for their part in launching competent national agencies to promote industrial development in India, Pakistan, Turkey, and a number of other countries. The Bank's resident mission in Indonesia, which normally includes nine or ten professionals, has added substantially to the number of persons in that country able to deal competently with problems of economic policy.

Strong Leadership

The Bank has been blessed with strong leadership. Presidents Meyer, Mc-Cloy, Black, Woods, and McNamara have been outstanding men by almost any standard. Each has benefited from policies initiated by his predecessor and has left his own indelible imprint on the institution. Eugene Meyer, who resigned as president before borrowing and lending actually began, initiated the practice of hiring first class personnel. John J. McCloy and Robert L.

Garner got the organization going. They put an end to the tug-of-war between president and executive directors for stewardship of the institution and established the tradition of executive leadership.

Eugene Black preserved the authority of the president while improving the relationship between the president and the board of directors. His principal achievement, however, was the establishment of the Bank's credit and its reputation for probity and high standards of performance. With the addition of the International Finance Corporation (IFC) and the International Development Association (IDA) as affiliates, the Bank during Black's presidency became the Bank Group. Through his services in mediating international disputes that could be labeled economic, most notably that concerning the division of the waters of the Indus River Basin between India and Pakistan (a task in which he was brilliantly aided by Vice President W. A. B. Iliff), Black emerged as an international statesman of the first order. His economic views remained conservative, and during his incumbency the proportion of Bank Group resources deployed for the financing of projects outside the electric power and transport sectors was small. Nevertheless, it was Black who started the Bank thinking about education, and it was during Black's regime that the Bank Group's first loan for education was made.

George D. Woods greatly expanded the Bank Group's activities in education, agriculture, and other nontraditional fields, and in the process he reaped the benefits of Black's cautious first steps. (Similarly, Woods promoted project identification and preparation, and his successor, Robert S. McNamara, benefited from the pipeline that Woods had started to fill.) Woods was imaginative, eager to speed the transformation of the Bank into something more nearly resembling a development financing agency, courageous, and either unaware of, or contemptuous of, the adage that "discretion is the better part of valor." He developed new and stronger relations between the Bank and other international agencies, encouraged the establishment of consultative groups to facilitate the coordination of external assistance (the India and Pakistan consortia were launched during Black's presidency), and initiated the grand assize that resulted in the publication of the Pearson Commission report, *Partners in Development,* eighteen months after McNamara became president.

McNamara has further broadened the range of activities eligible for Bank Group financing, deepened the Bank Group's concern with development strategy, doubled its lending, and almost doubled its staff. Under him, *country* lending programs for several years in the future have been developed, and the preparation of comprehensive country reports that emphasize social as well as economic and financial trends has been systematized. Commitments, not surprisingly, have risen more spectacularly than disbursements; some of the new program emphases are as yet barely reflected even in commitments, and the desire to respond to the increased absorptive capacity of the less developed nations by keeping the level of Bank lending high has created a conflict between engaging in tried-and-true, readily expandable types of lending and investing the extra man-hours needed to launch and supervise new, unfamiliar, inherently more difficult programs.

Our comments on the significance of all this for the future of the World Bank Group are reserved for the next chapter. The point here is simply that McNamara is clearly in the tradition of strong presidents, that he more than any of his predecessors has cultivated strength from among the low-income members as well as from the Bank's richer member governments—and has tried to make the Bank an integral part of a stronger international system. To the extent that the Bank's good record and reputation are attributable to the quality of its leadership—and we have no doubt that the extent is considerable—Meyer, McCloy, Black, Woods, and McNamara are entitled to share the laurels. They have been aided by competent vice presidents; J. Burke Knapp, vice president under three presidents and chairman of the Loan Committee, has provided invaluable continuity at the top.

There has also been more continuity at the executive directors' level than might be inferred from the fact that more than one hundred persons served as "E.D.s" during the years 1946–71. Though they are elected or appointed for two-year terms, re-elections and re-appointments are frequent, and a number of directors have remained in their posts for more than a decade. As we noted in Chapter 4, some of these, as well as others who served for much shorter periods, have influenced markedly the evolution of the Bank Group.

Some Consequences and Limitations of the Project Approach

The Bank has put development lending on a businesslike basis and made it respectable. The pattern and flow of international investment were ruptured beyond recognition by the Great Depression and the Second World War. Efforts to revive the flow under new auspices met with enormous suspicion. The Bank pioneered in raising capital in the markets of the developed countries (and later in oil-rich underdeveloped countries) for investment in productive projects in poor, underdeveloped countries. It has provided borrowers with an honorable alternative to bilateral assistance.

To help ensure effective use of the proceeds of its loans and to flag difficulties as they arise, the Bank has placed great emphasis on the close control of disbursements and the supervision of projects. Its arrangements for procurement on the basis of international competitive bidding are time-consuming and occasionally irritating to less developed countries that would like larger margins of preference for domestic suppliers of goods and services. They have, however, immensely broadened the sources of supply from which the less developed countries obtain imports. They have protected the Bank from charges of favoritism among potential suppliers. They have helped to expose the higher economic costs of tied aid. They have minimized the money outlay for goods and services that meet the specifications in the invitation to bid. The specifications may in a few instances—some highway loans, for example—have been unnecessarily exacting, but insistence on excellence is probably a forgivable sin.

The moral code for the Bank's top leadership is provided by the "laws of economics." A conscious effort is made to give the status of natural law to this flexible code.[2] "We ask a lot of questions," said Eugene Black,

and attach a lot of conditions to our loans. I need hardly say that we would never get away with this if we did not bend every effort to render the language of economics as morally antiseptic as the language the weather forecaster uses in giving tomorrow's prediction. We look on ourselves as technicians or artisans. Words like "savings" and "investment," "efficiency," and "productivity" are tools of our trade, and like good artisans we try to develop proper standards for their use.[3]

The Bank is primarily a project lending agency. Its project approach, combined with its concern for all aspects of the borrower's economic condition and prospects, may put it in the position of trying to reap one of the alleged benefits of program lending—an opportunity to influence the overall economic policy of the borrower—while adhering to the more modest lending totals and the more time-consuming procedures implicit in project lending. Although the Bank operates in countries in which corruption is widespread, Bank-financed projects have remained almost totally free of scandal. The Bank's painstaking procedures for the identification, preparation, appraisal, and supervision of projects account not only for the absence of corruption but also for the fact that, with few exceptions, its completed projects have done about what they set out to do and have resulted in rates of return in excess of the rates of interest paid.

The available statistics regarding physical changes in member countries

2. James Patrick Sewell, *Functionalism and World Politics* (Princeton University Press, 1966), p. 260.
3. *Ibid.*, p. 263. The quotation is from Eugene Black, "Newly Developing Nations: Economics and the Cold War," *General Electric Forum* (January–March, 1962), p. 35.

wrought with the help of Bank Group financing are impressive.[4] The summary in the footnote, moreover, does not include the output of the projects of development finance companies assisted by the Bank/IDA or of any of the plants to which the IFC has made commitments. It is incomplete in other respects, too; but the most complete list would answer at only a very superficial level the question "What has the Bank Group accomplished?" and would beg the question whether the roads should have been built, the generating capacity installed, the railroad track renewed, and so on.

Bank-financed projects have rarely turned out to be white elephants. A distinction should probably be made, however, between noble and ignoble failures. The latter would include railroads that find themselves without goods

4. In the five fiscal years 1967–71, Bank/IDA projects have provided, among other things, for the following:

Transportation

The construction or improvement of nearly 24,000 miles of road in Asia, Africa, Europe, and Central America; the engineering of 8,000 miles of roads; the installation or improvement of highway maintenance programs in thirteen countries.

Port improvements in eighteen countries through the construction of passenger and cargo buildings and the provision of new dredges, harbor craft, navigation aids, and other equipment.

The improvement of railroads in fifteen countries by providing 51,000 freight cars, 650 passenger cars, 850 diesel locomotives, and 3,750 miles of track renewal.

Public Utilities

The installation of 22,500 megawatts of electric power–generating capacity in forty-three countries; the extension of transmission lines in twenty-six countries; forty-three distribution systems in eight countries.

The improvement and installation of water supply systems in twenty-three cities.

The expansion of telephone exchanges and the installation of new subscribers' telephone lines in eighteen countries (four African, nine Asian, one European, three Central American, and one South American).

The installation of more than eight hundred miles of gas pipelines.

Agriculture

The irrigation of over four million acres in thirteen countries.

Flood protection and drainage of nearly 1.3 million acres and the reconstruction of many miles of canals.

Land development (cooperatives, plantations, mechanization) involving 1.5 million acres; the development of 6,400 ranches; the financing of six agricultural research centers in Spain and major assistance in launching the consultative group on international agricultural research; and the provision of agricultural credit in several countries.

Education

The construction, expansion, and/or equipping of about eight hundred general secondary and specialized training schools, one hundred teacher-training colleges, and fourteen agricultural universities.

Education projects (six African, three Asian, three European, six Central American, and three South American) to expand enrollment in general secondary schools by more than 300,000 pupils.

Industry

The financing of aluminum mining, refining, and smelting facilities in Brazil; fertilizer plants in India, Indonesia, and Pakistan; nickel mining in the Dominican Republic; potash mining in the Congo (Brazzaville); and bauxite mining in Guinea.

Source: Memorandum of Feb. 16, 1972, to authors from A. V. Urquhart, World Bank, Office of the Director, Projects.

to transport and mines that produce no minerals; the former would include the unsuccessful results of a more venturesome type of pioneering—for example, attempts to modify traditional agricultural practices in ways that increase the earnings and self-respect of those on the bottom rungs of the income ladder, or efforts to improve the educational system by financing proposals that look promising on paper and may even have worked as pilot projects elsewhere but do not produce encouraging results in their new surroundings. The Bank is responsible for few failures of either type.

Banks are understandably loath to underwrite investments that may turn sour, but development agencies have to be more venturesome. A frequent criticism of the World Bank as a development agency is that it has been too cautious, that it has skimmed off the cream of the crop and left the chancy projects to others, that for too long it concentrated too exclusively on power and transport expansion, and that until recently it was anything but bold in exploring new areas for investment. We consider the criticism relevant for the first fifteen years of Bank lending, but decreasingly so since about 1963. Industry, agriculture, and education are growing areas of Bank Group investment, and much research is being devoted to the development of new approaches in all areas, traditional as well as nontraditional.

Institution-Building

A further distinguishing feature of a development promotion agency, as contrasted with a commercial bank, should be the development agency's concern with institution-building—in other words, with establishing and strengthening mechanisms that permanently improve the country's capacity to cope with its problems. In this sense, the Bank has unquestionably been a development agency since its earliest days and is becoming more so. Institution-building has been emphasized increasingly at national, sector, and project levels. Many Bank officials assert that, in judging the impact of the agency, amounts loaned and immediate physical changes wrought are of secondary importance. The primary consideration, from the developmental point of view, should be the Bank's success in creating or improving institutions used by the borrowing country in planning and carrying out investments in the sectors to which loans and credits go.

The Bank's particular hallmark in institution-building has been its stress on the autonomous agency or authority, operated by highly qualified, expert managers who are insulated from domestic political pressures (but responsive, of course, to the nonpolitical pressures emanating from the Bank's own headquarters). The insulation consists in part of a rate structure or source of income enabling the authority to provide, without government subsidy, the service it is supposed to provide. The greatest successes of the Bank have been in the sectors—electric power and transportation—in which it has concentrated for the longest period of time.

In Mexico, a highly inefficient and fragmented power sector has been transformed into a strong national network since 1949, with the aid of ten World Bank loans. The Bank is convinced that it

was the stream of loans, rather than any single one, that helped create the opportunity for achieving important improvements. . . . Experience has demonstrated that continuity—in lending, in project development and supervision, in affecting needed policy changes—is critical for effective development of the power sector.[5]

Mexico's Comisión Federal de Electricidad has grown to the point where it is able to borrow internationally on its own credit—a state of bliss that can be over-rated but nevertheless represents a notable achievement. In earlier chapters we mentioned the Imperial Highway Authority in Ethiopia, the Honorary Livestock Commission in Uruguay, and the Electricity Generating Authority of Thailand as examples of successful institutions assisted by the Bank Group.

Initially, the Bank in trying to develop institutions capable of carrying out Bank-financed projects probably overemphasized the legal status of the agency and its need for protection from outside interference. Only gradually did the Bank become involved in strengthening the internal operations of such agencies, especially their planning functions, personnel policies, and management information systems.

The Bank's traditional emphasis on insulating the institutions from domestic politics can result in institutional behavior so at variance with dominant thinking in the borrowing country as to contribute to the downfall of the government of the country or reduce drastically the future independence of the agency. Insistence on a policy of operating without subsidy can result in injustices to elements in the community that are already disadvantaged. Concern for efficiency may put in the saddle foreign managers and consultants who deny local colleagues enough opportunity to exercise judgment or make mistakes or learn from experience. Instances of each of these follies can be cited and would prove that the Bank's record is far from perfect. We assert only that the record is more than creditable. Investments in the less developed countries have tended to be better planned and executed than they would have been without the Bank's none-too-gentle prodding. A fair amount of misinvestment has been prevented, and a sizable reservoir of competence has been created.

5. World Bank Group, *Profiles of Development* (September 1971), p. 9.

The Bank has long recognized the importance of training nationals of less developed countries. Its Economic Development Institute has improved the qualifications of more than 1,300 EDI Fellows. The Bank also includes provisions for on-the-site training in many of its projects. Here the results have been only moderately successful. As was hinted at in the preceding paragraph, foreign managers and consultants on Bank projects have tended to be more interested in completing their substantive assignments and meeting their deadlines than in training counterparts.

Encouragement of Private Investment and Enterprise

Institution-building embraces also such institutions as capital markets, price incentives, and greater reliance on tariffs and less on import licensing procedures. Helping a nation recognize the role of price policy in increasing its output of rice, fertilizer, or other needed products can be an important service. As we have noted throughout this history, and particularly in Chapter 11, the Bank's commitment to private enterprise as an instrument of development has been strong. The Articles of Agreement directed the Bank to promote and encourage "private investment for productive purposes," and the various presidents of the Bank have taken this directive seriously. The Bank has sought private capital through the sale of its securities in capital markets, through the sale of participations in its loans, and through the joint financing of projects with private investors. Concern for the reaction of capital markets to its lending policy has shaped the selection of projects—very strongly in the Bank's early years but somewhat less so thereafter.

The Bank's first affiliate, the IFC, is concerned exclusively with organizing and investing in private enterprise. It has come to be regarded as an honest broker between local and foreign investors. Not only has the Bank interested itself in the settlement of investment disputes, public and private, it has established the International Centre for Settlement of Investment Disputes (ICSID) as an additional affiliate and has formulated a scheme for international insurance of private foreign investment. It has financed private enterprise directly through the establishment of financial intermediaries, such as development finance companies, and through the import of industrial materials under loans that would be called program loans by lenders less committed to the project approach than is the World Bank. Beyond all this, it has been a spokesman in both developed and less developed countries for the role of private investment and private enterprise, domestic and foreign, in the development process.

The Bank, in short, has carried out energetically and perseveringly the injunction in its Articles of Agreement on the subject of private investment. Its pro-private-enterprise bias often irritated borrowers during the 1950s and early 1960s, including major clients, such as India, that were committed to other orthodoxies. But no ready-made ideology proved strong enough to survive intact the wholesale shocks of the development process. Orthodoxy of every kind has given way to more pragmatic approaches. As the 1970s began, the feeling was widespread that the world had learned far too little about how to promote development effectively and equitably. The search for new approaches was never more intense. Most of the new approaches have tried to reorient development strategy away from maximizing increases in the gross national product of a country and toward alleviating more directly the starkest manifestations of poverty—joblessness, homelessness, malnutrition.

Here we stand after two decades of development, trying to pick up the pieces, and we simply do not know whether problems associated with dire poverty have increased or decreased or what real impact the growth of GNP has made on them. We do know that the rate of growth, as measured by the increase in GNP, has been fairly respectable in the 1960's, especially by historical standards. We also know that some developing countries have achieved a fairly high rate of growth over a sustained period. . . . Has it resulted in a reduction in the worst forms of poverty—malnutrition, disease, illiteracy, shelterless population, squalid housing? Has it meant more employment and greater equality of opportunities? Has the character of development conformed to what the masses really wanted? We know so little in this field. There are only a few selected indices and they are rather disquieting.

This hot pursuit of GNP growth was not necessarily wrong; it only blurred our vision. It is no use pretending that it did not, for how else can we explain the worsening poverty in many developing countries? How else can we explain our . . . preoccupation . . . with endless refinements of statistical series concerning GNP, investment, saving, exports and imports; continuing fascination with growth models; and formulation of evaluation criteria primarily in terms of output increases? If eradication of poverty was the real objective, why did so little professional work go into determining the extent of unemployment, maldistribution of incomes, malnutrition, shelterless population or other forms of poverty?[6]

Public Assistance and Its Timing

While it has become commonplace to assert that the Bank is as much a source of technical assistance as of financial assistance and that its institution-building is more important than its lending, the amount, the direction, and the timing of its loans and credits are not irrelevant. Indeed the present tendency to imply that money matters only because it makes technical assis-

6. Mahbub ul Haq, "Employment in the 1970's: A New Perspective," *International Development Review*, Vol. 13, No. 4 (1971), pp. 10–11.

tance more acceptable may grossly underestimate the economic effects of a generous inflow of capital. The postwar economic records of Greece, Israel, Korea, Taiwan, and several other countries are due not to the niceties of project design and appraisal, but rather, it would seem, to the lubricating effects of sustained, large-scale, non-project assistance provided bilaterally in the form of commodity imports.

The timing of assistance is extremely important. The early reconstruction loans made in 1947 helped keep France, the Netherlands, Denmark, and Luxembourg afloat until the Marshall Plan became operative. The half billion dollars provided by the Bank was, of course, only a small fraction of the external finance needed for European recovery, but it came at a strategic moment. Moreover, the repayments, which began almost immediately, provided the Bank with a welcome source of income during the years in which it was solidifying its position in the capital markets of the world.

Somewhat similarly, the Bank cannot claim on the strength of its lending or technical assistance to have been a major influence in Central America during the 1960s, but it probably was in the 1950s, before the Inter-American Development Bank was established and while bilateral assistance to Central America was inconsequential. In India, Bank/IDA assistance at the same per capita level as Bank/IDA assistance to Nicaragua would have required an inflow of nearly $18 billion during the 1950s and 1960s, as compared with actual Bank/IDA commitments totaling $2.6 billion. Nevertheless, through its initiative in organizing in 1958 the rescue mission that later became the India Consortium, the Bank played an indispensable role in raising the sizable amount of foreign exchange needed to complete India's second five-year plan.

Having made the obvious point that the timing of assistance can be very important and the less obvious one that the Bank has on occasion come on stage at the strategic moment, it is only fair to add that the Bank's project approach, which has many advantages, drastically limits the agency's ability to provide a financial shot in the arm in response to sudden need. The gestation period for a Bank project is two to three years, and signature of the loan agreement may precede initial disbursements by another six months or more. This means that the Bank's economic impact during the critical period immediately following the overthrow of an Nkrumah in Ghana or a Sukarno in Indonesia may be nil.[7] Because of difficulty in obtaining long-term assistance

---

7. The speedy approval of a reconstruction loan in the wake of a cyclone that devastated East Pakistan in late 1970 is proof that this need not be so. All Bank members, moreover, are also members of the International Monetary Fund and entitled in certain circumstances to draw on that agency in the event of temporary balance-of-payments difficulties.

quickly, the country may rely excessively on short-term suppliers' credits for new plant and equipment and thus compound a foreign debt situation that is already close to intolerable. When in due course the Bank becomes involved, however, its combination of financial and technical assistance, made available through a series of loans in the same sector, can bring about a remarkable transformation of that sector within a period of time that, in the perspective of development, is brief—say, ten or fifteen years.

Transportation

Lending for transportation represents the largest single category of Bank/ IDA lending.[8] By June 30, 1971, total lending for railways, highways, ports, and pipelines exceeded $6 billion, of which 85 percent had taken the form of Bank loans and 15 percent was in IDA credits. The share of transportation in total lending rose from a modest 18 percent in the pre-1955 period to about 40 percent in the early 1960s. It represented about 30 percent during the period 1966–71. Despite all that has been said and written by Bank spokesmen about new areas of lending, the share of transportation in the total is not expected to drop by more than 2 or 3 percent in the next few years.

Within the transport sector, the trend has been away from railway lending toward lending for highway work. Until 1960, railway lending accounted for more than half of all Bank transport lending and amounted to twice that for highways. Since 1960, highway financing has been dominant. In the decade ended June 30, 1971, highway lending totaled $2.4 billion, as compared with $1.4 billion for railways. Investment in ports has been devoted primarily to the expansion of berthing capacity and has been modest—$626 million out of the $6.16 billion committed to the sector since the beginning of operations. Lending for pipelines and aviation has been still more modest. "Transportation," for our purposes, means road and rail transport.[9]

8. In this section we draw heavily on the excellent sector working paper, *Transportation,* published by the Bank in January 1972.

9. No loans have been made for the direct financing of bus or trucking companies. "There has been some indirect involvement in vehicle manufacture and assembly, however, via the general industrial import credits to India and in truck and bus company operations through financing of development finance companies. In addition, there was a specific IDA credit to Pakistan for truck assembly and import of buses and spares, and the International Finance Corporation . . . has made loans to and equity investments in vehicle manufacturing firms in Brazil and Yugoslavia." (*Ibid.,* p. 14.)

Although the level of Bank Group commitments in the transport sector is high in absolute terms, its current level of lending has been estimated to represent less than 4 percent of total public and private investment in the sector and less than 8 percent of public transport investment in the member countries now borrowing from it. The World Bank Group, however, is a major source of external finance; its lending in the transport field during the past five years is believed to be about equal to that of all other multilateral and official bilateral lenders combined. The fifteen areas in which Bank/IDA transport lending has exceeded $100 million—India, Japan, Pakistan, Yugoslavia, Spain, East Africa, Mexico, Argentina, Colombia, Thailand, Iran, Brazil, South Africa, Nigeria, and Peru—account for about two-thirds of all its transport lending. As we have already noted, highway lending has been concentrated heavily on paved roads of a relatively high standard; very little has been invested in feeder or access roads, though there are plans to increase such investment.

What the Bank describes as "project-associated sectoral reforms" are a major part of its business. They have "a longer lasting and wider impact on the economy and the sector" than most of the other investments financed internationally.[10]

In connection with Bank Group transport lending, railway, harbor and airport corporations or authorities have been set up as autonomous entities in an attempt to improve their efficiency. Systems to promote financial integrity and major accounting, costing and budgetary reforms have been undertaken. . . . Transport planning units have been created and staffed, and equipped with new investment and policy criteria. Highway authorities have been reorganized. Vehicle licensing and road transport regulation laws and practices have been reformed. Pricing policies and specific rates, fares and taxes have been changed, as have procurement and contracting policies and procedures. Policies with respect to hiring and firing of personnel and wages paid have been affected. Limitations have been placed on certain kinds of investments and debt. Individual managements have been appraised and agreements have been reached that borrowers would consult with the Bank on certain appointments. In some cases, the transport sector has been approached as a whole and the Bank has sought to set its lending for particular projects in the context of agreements on major policy decisions and performance criteria set out in memoranda of understanding related to the entire sector.[11]

The aim of the Bank's persistent, time-consuming efforts at reform is, of course, to create a policy and institutional framework that will enable the borrowing country to make efficient use of its transport resources. On the whole, the Bank has found it easier to make a positive impact through the

10. *Ibid.,* p. 20.
11. *Ibid.,* pp. 19–20.

creation or reinforcement of a single management agency—a national railway authority, for example—than to organize a comprehensive transport or transport planning agency that would serve as an umbrella for the various authorities, agencies, and ministries with operational responsibilities for different components of the transport sector. The Bank has tried in country after country to establish the umbrella-type agency, but success has been elusive.

Similarly, the Bank's appraisal of individual projects has been better and stronger than its analysis of intra-sectoral or inter-sectoral priorities. Its project appraisal techniques and analyses have been adopted by a number of countries and are serving them well.

For years, a basic policy prescription of the Bank for both railways and highways was that the price charged to the user should be such that "full costs" would be recovered through freight and passenger rates and from taxes paid by users. There was no precise consensus on what constituted "full costs," but the term was meant to include not only operating and maintenance costs, but depreciation charges and a return on the investment sufficient to finance expansion or renewal of the system. In theory the Bank ought to have made considerable headway in its efforts to persuade railroads to adopt a pricing system based on these principles because (a) with the passing of the colonial era, the Bank became the most accessible source of financing for railroads in less developed countries, and (b) railroads generally are managed by one authority in a country, meaning that the Bank could focus its efforts on a single entity.

In practice, however, the record has been spotty. The Bank has enjoyed some success in moving railways toward a cost-based pricing system, but attempts to persuade railways to recover "full costs" through tariffs have generally failed because the higher tariffs would often have resulted in the loss of highly prized categories of goods to road transport.

In road transport, most Asian and African governments already levied user charges sufficient to cover full costs by most definitions of that term. In Latin America, where road user charges are traditionally low, the Bank has had some success in persuading governments at least to increase these charges. Colombia, after years of prodding by the Bank, increased gasoline taxes in the late 1960s. Brazil, similarly stimulated, in January 1970 put into effect a new uniform road tax, which has greatly increased tax collections. By and large, however, road taxes are a visible irritant to large numbers of people. Political opposition consequently is heavy, and the Bank's favorite policy prescription has not yet been widely adopted in Latin America. The Bank has become more flexible in its view of what constitutes recovery of full costs and has surely been right in believing that financial viability is a valid target. Moreover, in our view as well as the Bank's, direct subsidies, which are open and aboveboard, are preferable to hidden subsidies resulting from uneconomic pricing policies.

Another important policy issue in transportation is the matter of inter-modal competition between existing road and rail facilities and the con-comitant question of new investment in either mode for facilities that parallel an existing highway or railroad. At first the Bank maintained that road–rail competition, though it might be an issue in certain specific instances, was not generally a fundamental issue because each mode would attract and carry its own "natural" traffic. Although the Bank over the years has favored inter-modal competition, the stumbling block to a coherent policy on the question has been that the Bank (in company with national governments, transport specialists, and almost everyone else) has not really known what to do about railroads.[12] In pressing for intermodal competition, the Bank for some time concentrated on persuading governments with heavy restrictions on motor transport to modify the restrictions so that road transport could compete with railroads. In some areas (for example, East Africa) the Bank has been suc-cessful; in others (for example, India) it has been much less successful.

Only recently has the Bank focused on the question of allowing or press-ing railroads to compete with the motor transport industry. Since the mid-1960s, it has increasingly emphasized the importance of railway rate policies that permit or induce the railroads to compete with trucking and has generally tried to persuade railroad authorities to adopt a more commercial outlook. The difficulties associated with developing practical criteria for rail invest-ments, the paucity of evaluations of past Bank investments, and the extremely high cost of investments in this field have given rise to almost continuous de-bate within the Bank and on the outside as to the wisdom of nearly every major investment decision on railway projects.

While the Bank Group has tended to select the least risky projects in all modes, it is also true that in its investment decisions the financial rate of return as a criterion has had decreasing influence. In the last decade a serious

---

12. The transport sector paper notes that typically the railway seeking Bank Group assistance was built in large part before the advent of a road transport industry. It was therefore built to serve all kinds of transport needs and is in a state of decline. "The strategy of Bank lending in the railway sector has been to help break or avoid this cycle of railway decline, where the railways have a proper economic role to play in the future development of member countries. While there may be a few projects involving new construction to serve captive demand, by far the majority of railway projects will require a continuation of that strategy. They will focus on rehabilitation, extensive reform, and retreat from over-extended systems. . . ." (*Ibid.*, p. 32.)

effort has been made to evaluate projects on the basis of economic as well as financial criteria and to take a developmental approach. Although good progress has been made in evaluating the economic costs and benefits of individual projects, the Bank's efforts to view potential transport investments within the context of a broader systems approach are in a fairly rudimentary stage. The Bank itself is acutely aware of this.

More important than better microeconomic techniques . . . is the need to refine the Bank's analysis of the developmental effects of transportation investment— the connection between investment and economic output. The major and undoubtedly justified effort to improve the Bank's ability to quantify the costs and benefits of transport investments has had the effect of directing the approach toward one of micro, or engineering, economic and financial analysis, where quantification is more feasible. It has probably also helped to account for the fact that such projects as low standard roads to open up areas of potential production, and similar promotional investments, have not figured large in the Bank's lending program. In short, while the Bank can be fairly satisfied with its assessment of individual projects, the analysis of intra-sectoral and, perhaps more important, inter-sectoral priorities within a development strategy remains weak. If the Bank is to be able to assess priorities in the transport sector rather than merely say "yes" or "no" to an investment proposal, it must go beyond the quantification of user savings and be able to define each project's dynamic effects on the economy as a whole. This is all the more important if transport lending is to go beyond serving established demand and reinforcing existing patterns of economic location and income, and to become more useful in helping to solve the serious problems of unemployment and geographic or sectoral income inequalities by generating new output.[13]

Although this is primarily a clarion call for the future, the Bank has begun to move toward such an approach through its sector-wide studies of transport in such countries as Brazil, Iran, and Mexico. The transport projects that wind up in the Bank's country programs are increasingly based on in-depth sector studies and are planned in relation to other projects in the country program. The scale on which this developmental thrust will be realized depends on many factors, including acceptance of the approach by member countries and by departments of the Bank other than the Transport Projects Department, and on the successful development of the data and complex tools required for a systems/developmental approach.

Agriculture

During the first postwar decade rapid industrialization was widely regarded as the key to economic growth and higher levels of living. By the mid-1960s, however, the secretary-general of the United Nations could, without

13. *Ibid.*, pp. 18–19.

being accused of seeking to keep the less developed countries in rustic sub-servience, warn that

unless production on the farms . . . begins to go up, there is no surplus for saving, no surplus to feed the towns, no surplus to keep pace with rising population and keep down costly imports of food, no agricultural raw materials to feed into in-dustry and, above all, no rise in farm income to provide an expanding market for the nascent industrial system. There is no conflict between the priorities of farming and industry, and the need to re-emphasize farming springs not from any desire to "keep developing economies dependent" but simply to counteract the glamour of factory chimneys which may all too often be smoking above products which no one in the community can afford to buy.[14]

The Bank Group has felt keenly the impact of this change in perception. It decided in 1963 to step up its support for agricultural development and to provide substantial assistance for project identification and preparation. As a consequence, Bank/IDA loans and credits for agricultural development be-tween mid-1963 and mid-1968 amounted to almost as much as during the preceding sixteen years—about $600 million. Between July 1, 1968, and June 30, 1971, another $1.2 billion was committed—a three-year total equal to the total of the preceding twenty-one years. The share of agriculture in total Bank Group lending rose from 8.5 percent during the years 1947–63 to almost 19 percent in 1968–71.[15]

The Bank Group has become the principal external contributor to agri-cultural investment in the less developed countries, providing in the year ended June 30, 1971, about 40 percent of all foreign financial assistance to agriculture. It expects its share to reach 50 percent by the mid-1970s. Be-cause the overwhelming bulk of agricultural investment comes from domestic sources, however, the Bank Group's share in total investment in agriculture in the less developed countries remains minute—probably between 1 and 2 percent as of this writing.[16]

About half of all Bank/IDA lending for agriculture has been for irriga-tion, drainage, and flood control. A number of the big dams have not resulted in the increases in irrigated farmland and agricultural output that had been forecast. As was brought out in our country vignettes and elsewhere in this study, it is one thing to collect water behind a dam and another thing to move it from behind the dam or from the main distributary canals to individual farm plots. Moreover, since irrigated farmland rarely constitutes more than

14. "The United Nations Development Decade at Mid-Point: An Appraisal by the Secretary-General," UN Document E/4071 (June 11, 1965), p. 32.

15. World Bank, *Agriculture,* Sector Working Paper (June 1972), p. 37. The figures for Bank/IDA investments refer to *direct* lending for agriculture. They exclude the indirect support provided by Bank Group investments in road transportation, agri-culture-related industries, educational facilities in rural areas, and rural electrification.

16. *Ibid.,* pp. 58–59.

a small fraction of all farmland, even successful irrigation projects raise disturbing issues of equity and priority. An evaluation by the Bank of irrigation projects in Mexico makes several relevant points.

The importance of irrigation in recent development experience in Mexico is hard to overestimate. Great reliance has been placed upon it as part of overall agricultural policy which has led to the development of serious social and economic inequities that have recently begun to prick the political conscience of the country. . . .

While the vast majority of the rural population eke out a meager living from small holdings . . . about 10 percent of farmers are located in the more prosperous irrigated districts. . . .

This raises the question of how benefits are distributed among farmer classes. . . . Private farmers able to mortgage and sell their land were greatly advantaged as compared to the *ejidatarios* who could only realize the increased value of their land in the form of improved yields through time; even this impact was constrained by a lack of production credits. On an even broader scale it might be speculated that the opportunities for government investment in irrigation have diverted attention from the urgent needs of the remaining 90 percent of Mexico's farmers.[17]

The Bank's livestock loans, as we have indicated earlier in this study, have earned valuable foreign exchange, but frequently they have benefited directly and primarily the relatively well-to-do ranchers in Latin America. Agricultural credit, largely for medium- and long-term loans, appears also to have helped principally medium- and high-income farmers.

In addition to the limitations inherent in the initial policy of concentrating on irrigation and commercial production for export, the Bank's agricultural lending has been constrained by various policy preferences, including an unwillingness to lend for short-term credit; a reluctance to finance undertakings involving large local-currency and small foreign-exchange expenditures, coupled with a few disputes concerning the conditions under which other-than-foreign-exchange costs would be met; a distaste for financing land reform; and ambivalence with respect to loans and credits to intermediary institutions that required financial subsidies from their governments to cover administrative costs or that lent to farmers on concessional terms.[18]

17. IBRD, Economics Department, "An Economic Evaluation of Irrigation Rehabilitation Projects in Mexico," Report No. EC-180 (September 1971), pp. i, 2, 25.

18. A 1964 policy paper signed by George Woods, which set forth the Bank's principal guidelines on agricultural lending for the balance of the 1960s, said "Farm credit institutions will normally not be able to build up an adequate staff and cover other administrative costs out of their earnings and will therefore often require a governmental subvention in some form. . . . We should regard such a subvention in appropriate cases as an advantage rather than a disadvantage so far as Bank/IDA financing is concerned." (IBRD, Memorandum, FPC/64-1, "Agriculture" [Jan. 17, 1964], p. 21.) However, Operational memorandum 2.61 of March 31, 1971, on agriculture indicates

When in the mid-1960s the problems of rural poverty moved into the foreground of development thinking, the cry went up for an "integrated approach," not just to agricultural development, but to general rural development. The Agriculture Projects Department, which had devoted much effort to breaking down broader proposals into narrower "Bank-type" projects, began to be criticized for not designing more comprehensive projects aimed at alleviating the plight of the rural poor. In point of fact, though most of its pre-1965 projects were focused on irrigation, livestock improvement, and commercial crop production for export, there had already been a series of loans for resettlement and colonization and several comprehensive regional development programs. They had met with mixed results.

What the Bank calls "integrated smallholder development programs" are relatively recent. Bank Group lending for them has involved considerable innovation. Two principal strategies have emerged. One strategy, illustrated by the successful smallholder tea project in Kenya, concentrates attention on a specific cash crop. The Kenya project provided credit and extension services for the tea plantings of smallholders scattered throughout the tea-growing zones of the country, together with tea-processing factories and access roads. Wider application of this strategy is limited by the disheartening market prospects for a number of cash crops.[19]

The second strategy, according to the Bank, is

to concentrate attention on the overall development of a specific geographical area which has a high potential and is of manageable size. The activities supported include production both for subsistence and for a marketable surplus, and such aspects as soil conservation, local marketing facilities for food surpluses, input supplies, roads and social services. Recent examples of such a strategy are the Lilongwe and Karonga projects in Malawi, the Wolamo project in Ethiopia and the Casamance project in Senegal.

The principal danger in this strategy is that too many scarce resources, particularly of trained manpower, may be concentrated on a small area. It may become difficult to apply the strategy on a large scale later because of budgetary and manpower constraints.[20]

Discussion of the Lilongwe project in Malawi began in early 1966, and agreement on a $6 million IDA credit was reached in early 1968. The project, which began to produce visible results in two years, embraced the consolida-

---

that "the operating policies of the intermediary institutions should result in financially viable operations such that neither the provision of agricultural credit nor its administration needs to be subsidized. Subsidization through low interest rates is usually regarded as an undesirable means of encouraging agricultural development . . . but it may be considered in special cases . . .; discrimination in interest rates between large and small farms is also generally undesirable" (p. 5).

19. *Ibid.,* p. 45.
20. *Ibid.,* p. 45. The Jengka Triangle project in Malaysia should also be mentioned.

tion and redistribution of land, the introduction of tubewells, fertilizer, and seed distribution, the provision of feeder roads and extension services, and the establishment of credit facilities and marketing outlets. Groundnuts, tobacco, and stallfed cattle were introduced; farmers also increased greatly their production of maize and beans, which had been their major crops before the project was launched.

The Bank's Agricultural Development Service (see Chapter 10, above) had helped prepare the project and has been heavily involved in day-to-day project management, including the establishment of local cooperative societies for handling credit and marketing, the provision of extension services, and the technical training of Africans for agricultural management and field work. Lilongwe—unlike the smallholder tea project in Kenya and several other Bank projects in eastern Africa—was not the outgrowth of an earlier British colonial project. Nevertheless, the cumulative experience of the ADS staff, many of whom had been in the colonial service and were familiar with past British successes and failures, is considered to be an important factor in the success of the Lilongwe project.

The 1971 appraisal report for a follow-up $7.25 million IDA credit for Lilongwe reported that the economic return for Phase I was above the original estimate, expenditures were within the cost estimates, and there were broad-based benefits. "Experience indicates," said the report,

that significant improvements in productivity can be obtained by an integrated package program consisting of soil conservation measures, improvements in rural infrastructure, a concentrated extension and credit effort, and land reorganization and registration of holdings. . . . The success in Malawi of the integrated project approach justifies what in 1968 was a departure from the usual type of Bank/IDA agricultural project.[21]

In the nations that were formerly a part of French West Africa, most Bank/IDA operations include arrangements with French agencies whereby the latter participate in project preparation, project management, and other aspects of the undertaking. The arrangements seem at present advantageous to all concerned. The situation could change, however, if relations between France and her former colonies grew strained and former French colonial experts now serving as project managers and technical advisers became less welcome in the area.

21. Lilongwe Agricultural Development Project, Phase II, Appraisal Report, Report No. PA-76a (April 16, 1971), p. 3. By early 1972, when the IDA announced approval of its fourth credit for rural development in Malawi, it said: "Providing services of this nature—all interconnected and integrated under a single project—has come to be regarded by the World Bank Group as a crucial strategy in attacking the problems of rural poverty that abound in many parts of Africa." IDA, Press release (Jan. 20, 1972).

Willingness to diversify its agricultural lending, to undertake comprehensive rural development programs, to intensify its own research, and to play the role it has played in launching the Consultative Group on International Agricultural Research described in Chapter 17 represent long steps forward for the Bank Group. A promising beginning has at last been made although many questions remain unresolved. If the Bank, at the threshold of its second quarter century, does not have all the answers, it appears at least to be seeking them earnestly and with full cognizance of their urgency.

Electric Power

In no sector has the Bank Group had a greater impact than in electric power. Its successes, by and large, are not the result of groping and pioneering followed by conceptual breakthroughs, but are due rather to the relative ease of transferring the technology of power generation from more developed to less developed countries if foreign exchange is made available for importing equipment. The Bank has been heavily involved in the power sector since its earliest days, has concentrated its financial and technical assistance on a small number of countries, and has made numerous loans to those countries.

Through June 30, 1971, Bank/IDA financing for electric power facilities in less developed member countries totaled $5.3 billion, or 27 percent of all Bank/IDA commitments. Through these loans, the Bank has been associated with the construction of about one-fifth of the estimated 100 million kilowatts of capacity now installed in forty-one less developed countries and with an additional 16 million kilowatts under construction in mid-1971. Four countries—Argentina, Brazil, Mexico, and Taiwan—account for more than 40 percent of the $2 billion committed during the fiscal years 1967–71.[22]

For the five-year period ending June 30, 1976, Bank/IDA lending for electric power is expected to rise in absolute terms but to drop to about 17 percent of total lending—below the proportion for agriculture, which it previously exceeded. A substantial increase in the number of borrowing countries is also planned—a matter of regret to some of the specialists in the Bank because it means a more scattered effort, with less opportunity for institution-building in the areas expected to receive only one or two loans rather than a series.

The Bank has approached investment in electric power largely from an engineering point of view and has evaluated proposed projects primarily in

22. World Bank, *Electric Power*, Sector Working Paper (December 1971), pp. 3 and 9. During the years 1967–71, the Bank appears to have provided more than 50 percent of all external public assistance to the power sector (p. 8).

financial terms. In the same vein, from the standpoint of institution-building, the projects of which the Bank is most proud are those in which the power company involved is run on sound financial lines and is well managed in terms of minimizing power losses and meeting demand with reliability. Within this context, the Bank has had considerable success in helping to establish or reorganize existing power companies or authorities and to inculcate in them planning capabilities, modern managerial procedures, and tariffs that aim at a reasonable rate of return on the investment. Brazil, India, Malaysia, Mexico, Thailand, and West Pakistan come to mind as examples.

As we have noted earlier, an agreement that tariffs will be set in such fashion as to produce a specified rate of return is usually part of the loan agreement or of the accompanying letters of understanding. These agreements normally do not produce the desired financial targets immediately, although the Bank usually succeeds in bringing the borrower closer to self-support. In some instances, loans have been delayed for as much as two years because of a tug-of-war between the Bank and the borrower over tariff increases. To date, the Bank has been concerned primarily with the total financial return from user charges, and the borrower's tariff structure has traditionally been ignored. Several studies of rate systems have recently been made, however, and the Bank apparently intends to bring this area within the scope of its discussions with borrowers.[23]

Another facet of Bank lending in the power sector, and another reason why its specialists prefer to concentrate Bank/IDA investments in selected countries, is the Bank's strong interest in establishing coordinated national power systems or, in large countries like Brazil, regional systems. In a number of countries the electric power sector, when the Bank made its first loan, was characterized by scattered generating plants and distribution facilities owned and operated by a variety of companies or public authorities. The Bank has often helped bring into being a coordinated national system, in which the various subsystems have been interconnected to achieve economies of scale.

The Bank pioneered in the mid-1950s with respect to methodology for comparing hydro with thermal plants and considers this issue in each loan appraisal in which it is relevant. The evaluation, however, is often made by consultants, who tend to use market rather than shadow (economic) prices in their calculations and thus weigh the case more heavily in financial than in economic terms.

23. "It is probably true that many developing countries could benefit from tariff structures which reflected more closely than at present the structure of system incremental costs. The problem will be considered further after results of the West Pakistan study are evaluated." (*Ibid.*, p. 14.)

The Bank's earliest objective was to overcome power shortages, particularly in urban centers. Later the emphasis shifted from eliminating shortages to obtaining policy and institutional reforms of the kinds we have already mentioned—"adequate tariffs," better techniques for evaluating the hydrothermal issue, and rationalization of the supply side. By its own standards, Bank lending in this sector has had clear positive effects.

On balance, however, the criteria used by the Bank until just a few years ago have been more appropriate for a financial institution than for an institution striving to make economic development its objective. One of the rules of thumb, for example, has been that power facilities should be built to meet demand. Loans, in other words, have customarily been made for projects in areas in which there is already great demand for power or in which forecast demand is highest. Until recently little thought has been given to whether facilities should be built where demand forecasts might be lower but the facility might make a greater contribution to the economic development of the country or provide service to a sector (agriculture, for example) or to a region to which the government attaches high priority.

Another aspect of Bank lending to which attention should be called is the strong emphasis on lending to companies engaged in power generation as compared to companies in power distribution. The practical justification is understandable. In the former case, substantial amounts of foreign exchange are required for plant expansion, and only a few companies or agencies in a country need be dealt with. In power distribution, Bank lending would be far from easy and might require lending to a number of distributing companies (or choosing among them), as well as providing more technical assistance and manpower training. The need for assistance in this area is demonstrated by the almost universal finding in project appraisal reports that the distribution system in the country should be strengthened.

Broadly speaking, appraisal reports on proposed power projects describe the power situation in the country or region and incorporate forecasts of demand translated into the number of kilowatt-hours the new facility will produce and sell, the resultant revenues, and the rate of return. A careful analysis of the borrower's present and future financial picture is a key component of the appraisal.[24]

While the Bank has approached lending for electric power largely in terms of building generating capacity to meet projected demand and has engaged

24. There are, of course, exceptions to the typical financial analysis approach. For example, *Water and Power Resources of West Pakistan* by Pieter Lieftinck, A. Robert Sadove, and Thomas C. Creyke (Johns Hopkins Press, 1968–69), a three-volume, Bank-financed study, contains extensive calculations of the *economic* benefits and costs of various projects.

in project planning and evaluation primarily from a combined engineering and financial approach, indications of interest in broadening its perspective have become increasingly evident. The sector paper touches on five areas of growing concern: "system planning, which encompasses market forecasting and the selection of least-cost alternatives; evaluation of the structure, as distinct from the level, of electricity tariffs; village electrification; nuclear power; and environmental problems."[25]

In the past, the Bank has not made loans explicitly for village electrification. Today it is investigating the possibilities for more active assistance in this field. In describing the Bank's research on the subject, the sector paper recognizes that the difficulties associated with identifying, quantifying, and calculating benefits and costs of rural electrification programs are simply one aspect of the general problem of evaluating the economic benefits of electric power projects.

Despite recognition of the inadequacies of the present framework for evaluation, there is detectable reluctance within the Bank to move away from its traditional approach and residual skepticism about the feasibility of evaluating power projects from the point of view of their developmental impact. This concern is understandable. The difficulties associated with measuring economic costs and benefits—including agreement on the shadow prices to be used in specific cases—are formidable. The Bank's traditional approach moreover has served well both the Bank and its member countries. Large amounts of additional generating capacity have been installed. The amount of capital made available to the less developed countries is sizable. Power company management in general, and financial management in particular, have been notably improved.

Other Sectors

In terms of the volume of resources committed and the duration of its involvement, the Bank's role in financing education projects is much more modest than its role in agriculture, transportation, or electric power. From the time of its entry into the field in September 1962 through June 30, 1971, the Bank/IDA approved education loans and credits to forty-two countries for a total amount equivalent to $431 million, of which 44 percent was committed to Africa. Projections for the five-year period ending June 30, 1976, envisage operations in sixty countries and total lending of about $800 million. In the parlance of the U.S. stock market, education is one of the Bank's

25. *Electric Power,* Sector Working Paper, p. 12.

"growth industries." The Bank expects to become, if it is not already, the largest outside financier of educational assistance to less developed countries.[26]

The Bank has concentrated on capital financing aimed at the middle reaches of the school system—in other words, on constructing and equipping secondary schools and such related facilities as student dormitories. Equipping education facilities has meant financing not only laboratory and workshop articles needed for teaching science and for vocational training, and providing books for libraries, but in at least two cases, financing livestock for agricultural schools. Almost one-fourth of the Bank's financial assistance has gone to university and postsecondary education, and virtually none of it directly to primary education. The technical assistance component in Bank lending has been quite small, with the Bank relying on other agencies (principally the United Nations Educational, Scientific and Cultural Organization) to provide the related technical assistance.

Nearly half of the additional student places that were provided through Bank projects in 1970 and 1971 were in the fields of technical education and teacher training. In substantive terms, the thrust of Bank-financed education projects has been to put practical and prevocational subjects on an equal basis with academic subjects in the general secondary education curriculum. The Bank believes it has made a successful start in twenty-one countries. Moreover,

science teaching has been strengthened and the ratio of science graduates to arts graduates will now be compatible with the market demand in countries such as Colombia and Uganda. The inclusion of curriculum reform studies in recent Kenya and Iran projects will hopefully lead to the practice of continuing reform. . . . The instructional television in the Ivory Coast project which is being introduced in the formal education system will be designed to constitute an integral part of the student's learning process as routine as the use of textbooks.[27]

In the telecommunication sector, the Bank's involvement dates back to 1949, but more than two-thirds of the nearly $600 million provided by the Bank and IDA was committed during the five-year period ending June 30, 1971. The World Bank is the principal multilateral source of finance for telephone systems in the less developed world, but not the principal source of external finance. Most of the foreign finance appears to have been provided by bilateral lending agencies and by suppliers in the industrialized countries.

26. World Bank, *Education,* Sector Working Paper (September 1971), pp. 14, 24, and 28.
27. *Ibid.,* p. 15.

The sector paper is doubtless right in pointing out that financing provided by suppliers is oriented toward the goods financed (usually switching equipment and microwave systems) rather than toward "projects as a whole or the efficient growth of communication systems and the fulfillment of their role in development."[28] The implication, also correct, is that the Bank focuses on the latter and can help poor countries avoid such consequences of the former as telephone exchanges that are completed but do not have cables to connect them to subscribers.

As in electric power and various other sectors, the Bank has helped to introduce better procurement practices into the telecommunication sector. International competitive bidding is said to have led to remarkable reductions in cost—"about 30% on average and much more in some cases."[29] In India, which is now able to manufacture its own telecommunication equipment at reasonable prices, the Bank in recent telecommunication loans has financed the foreign costs of imported raw materials and components used in making the equipment.

It takes some stretching of the English language to consider water supply and sewerage facilities as a "sector" of the economy, but the Bank does so, indicating awareness of the contribution to the inflation of terminology which it thereby makes by occasionally placing the word in quotation marks. Whether it is a sector or a type of project is immaterial for our purposes. This is an area in which the principal multilateral source of development finance is not the World Bank but the Inter-American Development Bank, which in the 1960s provided borrowers in its region with almost 2.5 times the amount lent by the Bank/IDA to all regions during the same period.

The World Bank, for reasons brought out earlier in this study, was slow to invest in better facilities (and institutions) for the collection, transmission, and distribution of potable water, and the collection, treatment, and disposal of liquid wastes. As of June 30, 1971, cumulative commitments of the Bank and IDA amounted to a modest $329 million, but more was lent in the 1971 fiscal year than in all the previous years. In summary, says the sector paper somewhat wistfully: "Investment in this sector would seem to be much more suited to the Bank Group's development objectives than the limited Bank involvement to date would indicate."[30]

All lending to date has been to urban areas; no rural water projects had

28. World Bank, *Telecommunication,* Sector Working Paper (November 1971), p. 16.

29. *Ibid.*

30. World Bank, *Water Supply and Sewerage,* Sector Working Paper (October 1971), p. 9.

been approved as of mid-1971. The Bank considers its concentration on urban areas justified for many of the same reasons that have justified its concentration of electric power investment in cities, plus at least one other reason: the public health effects will be greatest where population is densest. As in other sectors, institutional improvement is turning out to be much more difficult to achieve than engineering improvement. It is too early to speak of triumphs and failures. We believe that the Bank is headed in the right direction and will achieve a better urban–rural balance in its water-supply efforts than it did in areas of lending that it entered in the 1950s, before the role of agriculture and rural development generally were as widely appreciated.

If this study were undertaken a few years hence, some comments on the Bank's assistance in the field of family planning would certainly be in order. Since only three family planning projects (totaling $10 million) had been approved by the close of the 1971 fiscal year, it would be premature to say more at present than that the Bank has helped immensely to raise the priority assigned to this crucial problem.

The Legacy in Brief

We have not attempted in this chapter to comment on the Bank Group's impact on the industrial sector in less developed countries. In Chapter 11, however, we lamented the Bank's failure to have formulated as yet a convincing theory of industrial development or to have coordinated effectively the various instruments at its disposal for promoting industrial development. Additional "conclusions" not reiterated here are to be found in the closing sections of earlier chapters and in our final chapter, "At the Threshold of the Bank's Second Quarter Century."

There are recognized fields of development lending that the Bank has to date avoided. Housing, with some minor exceptions—such as student dormitories in educational projects—may be the most conspicuous example; the Inter-American Development Bank has lent extensively in this field. Public works projects, intended primarily to provide jobs for the unemployed and underemployed, are also examples; the U.S. AID has financed such projects in Pakistan, Morocco, Tunisia, and elsewhere. The Bank's financing of small-scale enterprise, even through financial intermediaries, has been extremely limited. Nor has the Bank shown much interest in financing export promotion schemes or international commodity agreements. We mention these, not because we want the Bank to finance every conceivable type of project, but because, from the point of view of development, some hitherto neglected fields may deserve a high enough priority to replace fields for which external finance has become less important.[31]

If this analytical history had been written from the standpoint of borrowers, certain shortcomings of the Bank would doubtless have been more heavily underscored: the limitations of its project approach, the length of time it takes to activate a project, the attitudes of some of its negotiators, the relative absence of nationals of less developed countries in important posts, and the Bank's confidence in outside consultants, some of whom may be no better qualified than some local personnel. We have tried to avoid writing from any particular standpoint in order to include various points of view—those of the Bank, of its principal stockholders, and of its major borrowers, as well as the views of the North American authors of this study.

Few would disagree, we suspect, with the conclusion that the Bank has had a significant and on the whole beneficial impact on the areas in which it has concentrated its lending. The concentration in certain sectors does not mean that its impact has been limited to those sectors. Because resources are to some extent interchangeable, borrowers have greater freedom than they otherwise would to devote to the development of other sectors resources not needed to complement Bank loans. Furthermore, the project appraisal techniques, purchasing procedures, and institution-building policies introduced by the Bank are also transferable to other sectors at the option of the borrowing country. Finally, advice on overall economic policy is by definition sector-free. As the Bank has amassed more information and more experience, and has become less of a Bank and more of a development agency, its advice has become more relevant and more useful both to the borrowing government and to others interested in assisting that government.

The World Bank, in summary, appears to have earned its right to play not just *a,* but *the* leading role in nurturing and coordinating the international development effort during the 1970s.

---

31. A theme of this study, to which we revert in Chapter 21, is the desirability of a better division of labor among international agencies.

CHAPTER TWENTY-ONE

At the Threshold of the Bank's Second Quarter Century

ALTHOUGH THEIR VISION of the future was inevitably imperfect, the Bretton Woods participants succeeded in creating two institutions that have managed to adapt to the postwar world surprisingly well. So far as the subject of our interest is concerned, the World Bank successfully negotiated the short transition from lending exclusively for reconstruction to lending for development as well, and the longer transition from a period of lending to both developed and less developed countries to all-but-exclusive lending to the latter. As it became clear that development in important parts of the world must inevitably be slower than expected and that creditworthiness for borrowing on Bank terms was limited, the International Development Association (IDA) was brought into being to lend on softer terms. The World Bank Group learned in the course of time that its potential contribution to development was not necessarily limited to financing the foreign exchange costs of capital infrastructure. Not only was the range of feasible projects increased substantially, but the meaning of "exceptional circumstances" justifying program lending and local expenditure financing was reinterpreted.

The Bank Group, moreover, achieved a predominant position among bilateral and other international programs as a coordinator of development assistance. And its earlier views on the peculiar merits of private enterprise in the development process have given way to broader conceptions. As we have noted from time to time, the Bank with increasing size has become increasingly bureaucratic, and the heavy hand of precedent has not been wholly absent. Still it faces its second quarter century as a lively and flexible institution with few signs of the creaking joints and blurred vision that are frequently expected in an aging bureaucracy.

Nevertheless, it has been clear for some time that the Bretton Woods world that for so long encapsulated the Bank and the Fund has been coming apart at the seams. The Fund, confronted with the breakdown of the world monetary order that was dependent on the dollar, will either become much more important as a center of monetary decision-making or will yield its place to other centers. And the Bank faces a future as murky in some ways as that confronting the Bretton Woods founders. Changes in the power and influence of various countries and blocs in relation to each other and to international institutions cannot fail to affect the organization and governance of the Bank. The voting strength of the United States has declined from 37 percent in 1946 to less than 25 percent in 1971. The European Community, with the accession of the United Kingdom, will rival the United States in economic weight, and in terms of foreign trade it will be substantially larger. Japan has become not only a world economic power but an important contributor to the Bank. It is possible that Romania or Hungary, or both, will become members. If the People's Republic of China joins the Fund and the Bank, it may be taken for granted that the Soviet Union and other countries of Eastern Europe will not be far behind. If all this happens, the Bank Group will be a very different set of institutions than it is now.

Even if "all this" does not happen and the Bank continues to be an international financial instrument, active primarily in the noncommunist world, how well supported and favored an instrument it will be is still unclear. The Bank, during the first decade of its existence, was essentially a "dollar bank," and the process of internationalization has been gradual. Not until 1957 was more borrowed outside the United States than inside. The initiative for the Bank's first affiliate, the International Finance Corporation (IFC), was primarily American, and the United States was also active in the creation of the Bank's second affiliate, the IDA. But from the mid-1960s U.S. support has wavered. The Bank has enjoyed only limited access to the New York capital market. Although the United States until recently has pressed for larger IDA resources, its deteriorating balance-of-payments position has conditioned the terms on which it was willing to contribute. Furthermore, the rapid decline in U.S. support of its own bilateral assistance program has tended to carry with it a more critical attitude toward international programs. The United States, of course, continues to exercise a large influence on Bank activities through its 25 percent command of votes, its 40 percent contribution to IDA, and the size and importance of its capital market. But increasingly it becomes a restraining rather than a stimulating influence. If the Bank is to continue to be an effective international financial instrument, the declining American influence must be compensated for by growing support from other quarters.

We take it for granted that the Bank Group will continue to lend exclusively, or nearly so, to the less developed world. But this world is also in process of change. Less developed member countries are increasingly able to manage their own economic affairs, and although their need for, and ability to use, development assistance increases rather than diminishes, their unwillingness to accept it on the former terms is becoming evident in many quarters. Furthermore they have created institutions, among them the United Nations Conference on Trade and Development (UNCTAD), which, if lacking in power, do not lack the ability to articulate their cause.

If the Bank is successfully to adapt itself to the kind of change foreshadowed at the threshold of its second quarter century, certain issues must be faced. If the Bank Group is to serve effectively all of its less developed members, including the poorest, a continuous expansion of IDA funds needs to be assured. If the Bank proper is to finance its loans principally by borrowing in the capital markets of the world, it still needs to pursue policies that command confidence in these markets.

The fact that the Bank depends primarily on capital markets rather than on governments for its funds is in many ways a source of strength and independence. The fact also that IDA financing is contributed by many governments rather than by one adds something to Bank Group maneuverability. Still it cannot be denied that dependence on capital markets and on legislative appropriations in the wealthy countries of the world limits, in some fairly important respects, the ability of the Bank Group to function as an effective financier of development. If this dependence were relaxed, the Bank's management would be freer, when member countries nationalize foreign properties, to adapt to this situation on the basis of its own judgment of the overall performance of the member country, without excessive concern for the reaction of legislatures and capital markets. The Bank might also be able to offer greater encouragement to industrial development in less developed countries by granting greater preference for local procurement without an exaggerated concern for the export prospects of its richer members. Less attention to what capital markets consider sound investments might permit a more relaxed attitude toward financing current costs or employment-expanding public works programs. And if the Bank could escape from the vagaries of capital markets, it would be possible to operate without so great an emphasis on liquidity.

It is, of course, possible to imagine the Bank evolving into a very different kind of international institution than it now is—an institution that succeeds in escaping from dependence on capital markets and on government contributions derived from taxation. If member governments were willing to double their paid-in capital contributions, the interest-free capital of the Bank would be increased from its 1971 level of $2,150 million to over $4 billion. This action plus various changes in terms of lending might be expected to double the net profits of the Bank. If something like $400 million were transferred annually from profits to surplus, by 1980 the equity of the Bank could approach $10 billion. This could for all practical purposes make the Bank independent of the short-term vagaries of capital markets. If, furthermore, the Bank Group could at the same time free itself from the triennial IDA replenishment exercise, by transfers of Special Drawing Rights (SDRs), some form of international taxation, or some of the revenue from international schemes to exploit the economic resources of the seabeds, the Bank Group's freedom of action would be enormously increased. It cannot be said that such an evolution is impossible, and for those who are interested in a more fruitful and less exacerbating assistance relationship between the developed and the less developed world it is, perhaps, an evolution devoutly to be wished for. At the same time, speculation on this course of development carries us farther into the Bank's second quarter century than the authors are willing to venture.

In this chapter we assume that certain fundamental characteristics of the Bank Group remain unchanged—that is, that it continues to lend predominantly, if not exclusively, to less developed member countries; that it continues to rely for financing of Bank loans principally on the sale of its own securities; that it continues as a soft lender on an increasing scale however its IDA funds are obtained; and that, except for IFC, it lends to governments on the basis of a government guarantee. In other words, we envision the Bank as being the principal international financial intermediary channeling private funds and public contributions from the developed to the less developed world but an institution heavily influenced by its developed country membership. The questions that concern us are how will such an institution adapt itself internally to changing membership and increased size, and how will it adapt itself externally to the changing world in which it is called upon to operate? We discuss these questions under the following headings: financial problems confronting the Bank, the scope and direction of Bank lending, the terms of Bank lending, the organization of the Bank, the Bank's role in the area of private investment, and the Bank as part of an emerging international system.

Financial Prospects

The most critical financial element for the future of the Bank Group as a development institution is the replenishment and increase of funds available to IDA. Without IDA the Bank could no doubt continue to lend exclusively to what may be called less developed countries, but these would be essentially middle-income countries, namely, most of Latin America, Iran, Malaysia, and a few other countries in Asia, and some Middle Eastern and African members. Commitments could proceed at a level of $2 billion to $2.5 billion a year and could even increase over time as the creditworthiness of these countries improved. The financial communities of the world would, no doubt, view the Bank as a highly successful institution with net profits of $200 million or more plowed annually into surplus rather than dissipated to IDA or other "unprofitable" uses. There would be no difficulty in selling the necessary quantity of Bank securities in capital markets. Moreover, such an institution could, at least for a time, accomplish a net transfer of financial resources from the developed to the less developed world, as early borrowers in Europe, Japan, Australia, and elsewhere paid off their loans and Bank lending to the less developed countries increased. Moreover, if Bank loans were accompanied by technical assistance and help in institution-building, the contribution of the IBRD to the development of the more economically advanced of the less developed countries could be considered respectable. But the Bank Group would either have to terminate lending in India, Pakistan, Indonesia, Ceylon, and most of its member countries in black Africa or assume far greater risks of default than it has ever before been willing to assume.

If the Bank Group is to continue as a development agency supplying assistance to those members who need it most, not only will IDA funds have to be replenished but these funds must constitute a reasonable percentage, say 35 to 40 percent, of total Bank Group lending. Both the Pearson Commission and the Peterson Commission recommended that IDA replenishments should reach $1 billion a year in 1972 and $1.5 billion by 1975. The Pearson Commission also recommended that the third replenishment should cover a five-year period, 1971–75.[1] These recommendations appear to have been overtaken by events. The agreement on the third replenishment was for a three-year period at the rate of $800 million a year. If the IBRD continues to transfer $100 million or so a year from profits, IDA credits for the period 1972–74 will total only a little more than $900 million a year. With Bank loans approaching $2 billion a year during the same period, Bank Group financing is definitely skewed in favor of the middle-income countries.

The Bank very much needs a large increase in IDA money if it is effec-

1. *Partners in Development*, Report of the Commission on International Development, Lester B. Pearson, chairman (Praeger, 1969), p. 224. *U.S. Foreign Assistance in the 1970s: A New Approach*, Report to the President from the Task Force on International Development, Rudolph A. Peterson, chairman, March 4, 1970, p. 24.

tively to serve the development requirements of its lower-income members. An increase, however, from the $800 million of the third replenishment to the $1.5 billion recommended in 1975 by the Pearson and Peterson commissions is difficult to envisage unless there is a marked shift in emphasis from bilateral to multilateral assistance, with the Bank Group a favored intermediary. It is possible, but not probable, that more generous legislative behavior would be encouraged by a change in replenishment procedure whereby high-income members would make their contributions in the form of fifty-year, no-interest loans (the form taken by the Swiss contributions to IDA) rather than of grants. In addition to the benefits it would derive from more IDA money, the Bank Group could benefit also by some degree of escape from the technical replenishment exercise and from the dependence of its lending policy on legislative whims. A five-year replenishment cycle might help on both counts. Beyond this, many suggestions have been offered for alternative sources of IDA financing.

The Pearson Commission recommended that bilateral donors commit half or more of interest payments due them on bilateral loans to less developed countries to subsidize interest rates on Bank loans. This could accomplish a purpose similar to that of the present practice of "blending" Bank loans and IDA credits. The "Horowitz Plan," which we discussed in Chapter 7, suggested that "soft money" be provided by borrowing in capital markets, with the Part I countries of IDA—the richer members—financing the difference between the borrowing rate and the terms on IDA credits. There have been many suggestions for an international tax on the consumption of some widely used commodity or a small tax on national incomes, the proceeds of which might be made available for development. It has also been suggested that the international exploitation of the resources of the seabeds could yield returns to be channeled into the development of poor countries, with IDA as one of the channels. None of these proposals, however, has evoked as much public interest either in rich or in poor countries as the use for development purposes of the SDRs issued by the International Monetary Fund (IMF). This has now become the prospective source of development funds most highly favored by many experts, by most members of UNCTAD, and by others. Nearly every speaker from a less developed country at the Bank–Fund meeting in 1971 recommended a tie between the issuing of SDRs and the provision of development finance, usually under the auspices of IDA.

We discussed the possibility of such a link in Chapter 16. There appeared to be a strong argument against inaugurating a tie between SDRs and the provision of development assistance unless and until SDRs had established a firm position as an acceptable reserve asset. If now a giant step is taken in monetary reorganization, replacing dollars, pounds, other reserve currencies, and possibly gold with SDRs, a different situation would be created. Such a replacement would not add to liquidity, but the fact that it is taken—if, indeed, it is taken—would itself set the stamp of approval on SDRs as a reserve asset. This would, however, settle one issue, only to raise a number of others. Would the non-reserve countries that now hold surplus short-term dollar and sterling securities on which they earn substantial rates of interest be willing to exchange them for SDRs that earn much lower rates? If so, the IMF could presumably use the difference between what it pays and what it receives to finance IDA. Will the developed countries consent at some stage to a distribution of SDRs that does not follow IMF quotas but gives a larger share to the less developed world? To do so would mean giving up a claim on real resources and would create fresh problems of burden-sharing. Would the United States and the United Kingdom, the principal reserve currency countries, be willing to "fund" the surplus dollars and sterling that non-reserve countries now hold and discharge this obligation over time by running export surpluses?[2] If so, how could it be assured that the claims on these export surpluses would be channeled to the less developed countries?

If a transfer of resources from the wealthy countries of the world to the poorer is to be considered a more or less permanent aspect of international relations, there are strong reasons for preferring a quasi-automatic allocation of newly created SDRs rather than the voting by parliaments of bilateral assistance programs or contributions to international agencies. And if this should come to pass, there are also strong reasons for making use of IDA's experience in accomplishing the resource transfer. The establishment of such a link would obviously encompass only a small part of the resource transfer that needs to be accomplished through bilateral and international assistance programs, but it would not be an insignificant part. If IDA were the preferred instrument, the problem of IDA financing would largely be solved.

Although there is much to be said for a link between the introduction of SDRs into the monetary system and development assistance, establishing such a link would require international agreement achieved in the face of formidable obstacles. It is our opinion that, although SDR creation and transfer may become a significant source of development finance by the end of the 1970s, it is not likely to be a substitute for current forms of IDA replenishment in the near future. If IDA replenishment is to be adequate, it would appear at this stage in the Bank's history that the leadership will need to

2. Such a proposal was, in fact, advanced by Anthony Barber, chancellor of the exchequer and governor of the Fund for the United Kingdom, at the annual Bank–Fund meeting, September 28, 1971.

come from outside the United States. What the next IDA replenishment will bring forth is anyone's guess, but it seems overly optimistic at this time to assume a figure of more than $1.2 billion a year for the period 1974 to 1977, rising perhaps to $1.5 billion by 1980. It is possible that, before the end of the decade, alternative sources of IDA financing may be found.

The volume of funds available for IDA and other concessional lending institutions will have a definite bearing not only on the allocation of loans among different member countries but also on the rate at which total Bank lending can increase. A strong case can be made for the proposition that the Bank should expand its activities as rapidly as it prudently can. What this rate of expansion might be will obviously be subject to a number of external and internal considerations: What volume of foreign exchange can less developed member countries be expected, over the next several years, to use effectively? What share of these foreign exchange requirements can reasonably be expected to be met by export earnings? Of the residual not covered by such earnings what share can be expected to be covered by grants and loans from other than Bank sources, and on what terms are the loans likely to be received? The resultant of such estimates might be considered to represent the requirements of creditworthy member countries for borrowing on Bank terms. The Bank has, in fact, undertaken calculations of this sort for planning purposes and has arrived at the conclusion that Bank lending commitments might increase from $1.9 billion in 1973 to $3.5 billion in 1978. This would mean an increase of about 10 percent a year in monetary magnitudes and 8 percent a year in real terms. While such calculations are no doubt useful and relevant, they serve principally to reinforce a judgment based on other considerations that such a rate of increase is practicable. If we accept this figure—and we do accept it for the purpose of considering the problems and prospects of an international financial institution of this size—can the Bank be expected to raise such an amount of money, and from what sources?

A careful study undertaken in the Bank toward the end of 1971 indicates that the projected volume of financing is feasible. It would require total gross borrowing of over $11 billion in fiscal years 1974–78, and net borrowing of $6.6 billion. This is about double the expected total for the fiscal years 1969–73. The principal sources are expected to continue to be central banks for short-term funds and the capital markets of the world for medium- and long-term borrowing. It is recognized that at some time toward the end of the decade the Bank will have to ask the board of governors to increase its capital, particularly the 90 percent guarantee fund. For reasons suggested in Chapter 5, it would be highly desirable to use that occasion to increase paid-in capital. It is also recognized that, so long as the Bank depends heavily on borrowing in capital markets, it will have to maintain a high degree of liquidity. The problem of financing the projected expansion of Bank lending does not seem to be serious so long as the credit standing of the Bank is maintained. Even gross borrowing of $11 billion over a five-year period, less whatever is raised from short-term borrowing from central banks, represents only a fraction of 1 percent of total long-term security sales on the capital markets of the world.

If then we accept the planning figures suggested above, the Bank Group might, toward the end of the 1970s, consist of the Bank, lending at the rate of $3.5 billion a year, an IDA, lending between $1 billion and $1.5 billion, and an IFC, investing about $200 million a year.[3] What staffing and management problems would such an organization confront? That would depend very much on the scope and direction of Bank lending, to which we now turn.

Scope and Direction of Bank Group Lending

The final years of the Bank's first quarter century witnessed some notable changes in the allocation of Bank Group lending among various economic sectors, the emergence of new types of projects, a further loosening of restrictions on local expenditure financing and program lending, and a broadening of the Bank's conception of factors relevant to development. A rapid expansion of lending in the fields of industry, agriculture, and education reduced the share in total lending of the traditional areas—transportation and electric power. Urban development, tourism, and family planning became areas of project lending.

The strictures of the Articles of Agreement on local expenditure financing had been sufficiently loosened to permit the choice of almost any project the Bank deemed worth financing, at least within the customary limits of Bank projects. Whether this loosening is sufficient to permit the financing of employment-creating public works projects when practically all inputs are of local origin is uncertain, although, as we noted in Chapter 9, the IDA credit for the Kadana irrigation project in India, committed in 1970, had a local currency component of 93 percent. Local expenditure financing rather than program lending had become the preferred method of contributing to the foreign exchange component of development programs sums over and be-

3. This relationship between Bank loans and IDA credits could hardly be considered satisfactory. It would imply heavy lending to countries such as Brazil, Venezuela, Mexico, and Iran and inadequate commitments to the poorer countries of the less developed world. Nevertheless, it is the pattern of lending that is likely to prevail if IDA replenishment cannot be supplemented from other sources.

yond those required to buy the imports needed on Bank-financed projects. At the same time, reinterpretation of the Articles of Agreement had provided more room for program lending, although the Bank's management has as yet shown no great disposition to take advantage of this reinterpretation.

If we are to take seriously the various pronouncements of management and discussions in the board of directors, there have also been significant changes in the Bank's conception of how the development process is to be promoted. It is not enough to transfer capital to an increasing range of viable projects, to contribute foreign exchange to development programs through local expenditure financing and program lending, and to assist in the building of institutions. If development is to be understood as a sustained increase in the capacity of member countries to satisfy social preferences, then a reduction of unemployment and underemployment, a more equitable distribution of income, and wider participation by the citizenry in decision-making may need to be considered as necessary inputs. To meet these requirements, however, a considerable expansion in the kinds of projects and policies the Bank is willing to finance and support, a much more careful examination of the income-distribution and employment-creating aspects of projects than has hitherto been undertaken, and, in all probability, a large expansion in technical assistance would appear to be necessary. It must be said that, to date, there continues to be a sizable gap between the public pronouncements of some of the Bank's spokesmen and its day-to-day practice.

So far as the scope and direction of lending are concerned, the Bank at the threshold of its second quarter century faces somewhat of a dilemma. Should it continue to expand the scope of its lending, trying to meet all the requirements of development that an external financing agency could conceivably be expected to meet, while paying increased attention to income distribution and employment? Or should the Bank be content with more limited horizons and continue to be a project lending agency specializing in types of projects in which it has achieved a well deserved reputation? Should it try to occupy some middle ground? What division of responsibility with regional development banks should be envisaged? How these questions are answered will affect very much the volume of Bank lending, the character of Bank loans, and the size and specialization of its staff.

As we reported in the previous section, the Bank's advance planning envisages approximately a doubling, in real terms, of Bank Group lending by 1980. This would mean that the Group would lend, in 1971 dollars, over $5 billion a year by the end of the decade. Assuming the availability of funds, this seems to be an attainable program, with the IBRD continuing to be predominantly a project lender if Bank lending is directed mainly to infrastructure and to large-scale industrial and agricultural projects (including financial intermediaries), and if present techniques of project appraisal are pursued with present consideration (or neglect) of income-redistribution, employment-creation, and other "social" effects. Even so, this rate of expansion would impose a heavy, but not unmanageable, recruitment problem. On the other hand, if the Bank attempts to enlarge substantially the scope of its lending to include employment-creating public works programs and small-scale industrial and agricultural projects while at the same time expanding the considerations needing to be taken into account in project selection and appraisal, the projected lending targets present greater difficulties. A movement in this direction would need to be accompanied by a recruitment program designed to bring to the Bank a rather different mix of professional competence than it now has. And, perhaps more important, the Bank would need to advance substantially its understanding of the development process in member countries.

The very rapid expansion of Bank Group lending in fiscal years 1969, 1970, and 1971, which saw roughly a doubling of commitments, placed a heavy strain on Bank staff, augmented as it was by a substantial number of new recruits. This pressure perhaps helps to explain the emerging gap between pronouncements of the Bank management on what needs to be done in project selection and appraisal and what, in fact, is being done. Fiscal years 1972 and 1973 are intended to be years of consolidation. Bank commitments in these years are expected to be $1,800 million and $1,900 million, which fall short of the $1,921 million committed in fiscal 1971.[4] Although some increase is expected in IDA credits, the pressure on the staff should be eased.

Beginning in fiscal year 1974, plans, as we have said, call for Bank lending to increase by about 8 percent a year in real terms. The rate of increase for the Bank Group as a whole would perhaps be slightly lower than this. Whether the IBRD can successfully recruit, organize, and train the staff needed to meet its projected lending program depends on the distribution of loans and credits among various economic sectors, on the types of projects financed in each sector, on the considerations that are brought to bear on project selection and supervision, and on how the tasks of the project cycle are divided among the Bank, member borrowers, and other international agencies. Certain influences being brought to bear on Bank Group lending would considerably increase the difficulties of recruitment, organization, and training. Other possible developments could substantially lessen these difficulties.

4. It should be noted, however, that the 1971 figure exceeded the target lending program by some $200 million.

Power, rail, and trunk road projects in general require smaller staff inputs per dollar lent than do industrial and agricultural projects and much less than projects in education, family planning, and urban development. Large projects in any sector economize staff time as compared with small projects. The large-scale irrigation and land clearance projects favored by the agricultural projects unit in the early years of the Bank required much smaller staff inputs per dollar lent than did later types of agricultural loans. Project selection and appraisal techniques focusing exclusively on considerations relating to a projected rate of return are less time-consuming than those that attempt an assessment of various side effects. Serious efforts to maximize the contribution of domestic inputs, for example, by breaking large road construction projects into small parcels manageable by local contractors, require sizable staff inputs for appraisal and supervision. A marked shift in Bank Group lending away from infrastructure projects toward a broader range of projects, away from large-scale projects toward smaller ones, and away from concentration on rates of return toward attempts to assess effects on employment and income distribution would all tend to increase staff requirements per dollar of financing.

On the other hand, there are certain potential influences on Bank Group lending that tend in the opposite direction. International competitive bidding makes enormous demands on staff time; the larger the local expenditure component in project financing, the smaller will staff requirements be per dollar of lending. Since there is a significant trend in Bank financing toward covering a larger share of local costs, staff requirements are to that extent lower. Program lending obviously requires a much smaller staff input per dollar than does project lending. Furthermore, as we have frequently noted, the ability of less developed member countries to manage their own economic affairs, including the selection and supervision of projects, continues to improve. It is not to be expected that the Bank will need indefinitely to immerse itself as deeply in all stages of the project cycle as it has in the past. One of the frequent criticisms of Bank practice emanating from less developed borrowers is that the Bank Group pays too much attention to the viability of a project and too little to providing experience for local people who will have to manage the project or design similar ones in the future. Finally, as we indicate in a later section of this chapter, the Bank could, if it wished, rely more heavily on other international agencies than it has to date.

There are, in fact, a series of trade-offs between an expansion of lending, and various changes in the scope and direction of lending, that might increase the Bank's effectiveness as a development agency. These alternatives need to be given a more careful examination than they have received to date.

Terms of Future Bank Group Lending

As we noted in Chapter 7, the terms of Bank Group lending show a certain lack of flexibility. The Bank lends to all creditworthy member borrowers at the same interest rates, with the maturity of its loans conceptually related to the life of projects. Maturities of twenty years are typical. IDA lends at a service charge of 0.75 percent, on fifty-year maturities with a ten-year grace period. Neither Bank nor IDA terms make any allowances for differences in credit- or IDA-worthiness among borrowers. The blending of Bank and IDA terms makes possible a substantial variation in average borrowing rates, but this is the only element of flexibility. Some fifteen countries borrow both from the Bank and from IDA. The Bank has, moreover, been resistant to suggestions from UNCTAD and other sources that might increase flexibility.

It is our view that the Bank might well reconsider its lending terms.[5] From 1965 to 1967 the Bank lent to two so-called "market eligible" member countries at 0.75 and 1 percent above its standard rate. These were countries able to meet some but not all of their external borrowing requirements in capital markets, and the Bank saw no reason why this deficiency should be met at less than market rates. By 1967 a sharp rise in the cost of Bank borrowing had led to a change in the relationship between these costs and standard lending rates. The "spread," which had been 1.5 percent, was reduced to 0.375 percent in 1967. Shortly afterward the special rate to market eligible countries was abandoned, and all member countries deemed creditworthy borrowed on the same terms. The continued rise in interest rates was not accompanied by a commensurate rise in Bank lending rates, and by 1969 the spread had become negative. In fiscal 1971 the weighted average cost of Bank borrowing was 8.07 percent against a lending rate of 7.25 percent, yielding a negative spread of about 0.80 percent.

Abandonment of the "market eligible rate" and continued lending at a negative spread have reduced Bank profits below what they might have been by an amount that in fiscal 1971 may have been as much as $40 million. These foregone profits could have been used to supplement IDA funds, to subsidize interest rates to some of the Bank's poorer borrowers who are nevertheless too rich to be eligible for IDA credits, or to increase the Bank's equity position. The chief financial problem of the Bank Group over the next decade will not be how to meet the borrowing requirements of its middle-

5. We have been influenced in these views by a number of suggestions made by Escott Reid in a series of unpublished papers on the future of the Bank. Reid is a former senior Bank official and a former Canadian high commissioner in India.

income members but how to meet the requirements of poor countries. Some transfer of income from its market eligible borrowers, and the upper tier of its middle-income members, to poorer countries could make a considerable contribution to meeting these requirements.

We suggest a return to the 1 percent spread (above the standard rate) for market eligible countries and a spread of at least 0.5 percent for the most creditworthy of the Bank's middle-income borrowers. If the weighted average of the Bank's borrowing rates was 6.5 percent, and its standard lending rate 7 percent, this would mean a lending rate of 8 percent to market eligible countries and 7.5 percent to other highly creditworthy borrowers. With a rate of price inflation of internationally traded goods of at least 2 percent a year in all countries whose currencies are lent by the Bank, this would mean lending rates in real terms of 6 and 5.5 percent and perhaps less. Such rates do not seem exorbitant. The additional profits generated by these lending rates could, as we have noted above, either be used to subsidize interest rates to the poorer Bank borrowers or be transferred to IDA.

The terms of lending, broadly defined, obviously include the terms on which existing debt may be renegotiated. As we said in Chapter 7, there is reason to believe that a number of less developed countries will face, over the next decade, serious problems of debt renegotiation. It remains to be seen whether the Bank, either as a lender or as a member of a creditor group organized to deal with renegotiation problems, will be able to follow the policy it has, with minor exceptions, maintained to date of refusing to alter the terms of its own loans.

Not only are Bank lending terms unnecessarily inflexible, but so are those of IDA. Although the 0.75 percent service charge has, since the beginning of IDA, meant that credits are provided at a negative real rate of interest, we do not suggest a change in this service charge. The fifty-year maturity of IDA credits, on the other hand, seems to us to have become indefensible. No one can foresee what is going to happen to a country's development and credit standing fifty years hence. The economic prospects of South Korea and Taiwan seemed highly suspect ten or twelve years ago, but their economic achievements since then have been spectacular. Nor is it necessary to assure a fifty-year time horizon to IDA borrowers in order to facilitate a long-term development strategy. We suggest that the maturity of IDA credits be changed from fifty to thirty years, leaving the ten-year grace period intact. The Bank or the borrower could then request a renegotiation of the credit at the end of twenty years and either shorten or extend the credit with an upper limit of fifty years. This suggestion is made by Escott Reid, who notes:

If IDA credits had a maturity of 30 years, 2½ percent might be repayable [annually] in the second decade and 7½ percent in the third decade. If, as a result of renegotiation, the loan was extended to a total length of 40 years, the annual repayments in the last years of the loan would be 3¾ percent; if extended to a total of 50 years, 2½ percent. This would in effect create three types of IDA loans: 30-year loans, 40-year loans, and 50-year loans.[6]

These suggested changes in the terms of Bank Group lending would make it possible to achieve a better adaptation to a borrowing country's ability to pay, accomplish a certain transfer of funds from the wealthier Bank borrowers to the less wealthy, and relieve the Bank of some of the onus of excessively long-term forecasting.

Organization and Administration of the Bank

As we noted earlier in this chapter, there have been significant changes in the relative economic weight of Bank members and in their importance as providers of finance since 1946. Although the United States is still by far the largest single contributor of funds to the Bank, IDA, and IFC, its predominance is no longer overwhelming. Furthermore, as we have emphasized, the leadership once provided by the United States appears to be faltering. The question therefore arises whether there should not be significant changes in the nationality composition of the Bank's top management. Will it for much longer be necessary, as it certainly appeared to be in 1946, that the president be a citizen of the United States? It seems clearly inappropriate that five of the nine top members of the Bank staff should still be Americans.

As it happens, the Bank will shortly be confronted with large changes in its top management. Of the nine officials mentioned above, five at the end of June 1972 will be facing retirement within three years. An opportunity therefore exists for a very considerable reshaping of the nationality structure of the Bank's top staff. Such a reshaping, moreover, could encourage other member countries to exercise more of the leadership formerly provided by the United States. It has been suggested that, in addition to substantial changes in the nationality composition of the staff, consideration should be given to locating the Bank's headquarters outside the United States, presumably in Western Europe. This would certainly facilitate the recruitment of non-Americans to the Bank staff. Such a transfer, however, hardly seems practicable considering the amount of the investment in its Washington headquarters, the fact that the New York capital market remains by far the largest

6. *Ibid.*

single source of Bank borrowing, and that the United States still contributes 40 percent of IDA funds.

As of January 1972, the less developed world was represented in top management by only one official, Mohamed Shoaib of Pakistan, a vice president. At the same time the votes of third world members amounted to 38 percent of the total. Would not the effectiveness of the Bank Group's relations with its principal borrowers be strengthened if they had greater representation in top management and a larger share of the votes? So far as adding more third world representatives to the senior staff is concerned, this would seem not only feasible but desirable. A marked increase in the voting strength of the borrowers as a group, however, would be a different matter. Some increase, taking account perhaps of member countries' populations, in addition to the economic considerations that now govern voting strength, might be possible. But so long as the Bank Group relies for its financing overwhelmingly on the contributions of developed country members and on the sale of securities in the capital markets of these countries, control by this membership seems inevitable. Any substantial lessening of this control would in all probability jeopardize the Bank's customary sources of finance.

As we said in Chapter 4, the Bank, in contrast to the Fund, very early became a management-dominated organization. It has continued, with some modification, to be so to the present time. This, plus the fact that the Bank Group, until recently at least, has contributed a relatively small share of the flow of development finance to the less developed world, has tended to generate a rather small amount of interest among member governments in providing the Bank with strong executive directors. This has not been true of the Fund, where the board of directors has a strong voice. Furthermore, the governors of the Bank and Fund, who head the delegations to the annual meetings, have generally been ministers of finance or central bankers. In most years, they have had a decidedly greater interest in the affairs of the Fund than in those of its sister organization. Although there have always been a few Bank directors of outstanding ability, persons appointed or elected to the board after the first few years of its existence tended, until recently, to be run-of-the-mill. The creation of IDA made some difference since the provision of financing was a matter of government action rather than of the sale of Bank securities on capital markets. The doubling of Bank Group lending under President McNamara has made a further difference. And if Bank Group lending doubles again before the end of the 1970s, and the institution becomes the principal source of loans to the less developed world and plays a prominent role in coordinating development assistance from all sources, it seems probable that the IBRD will receive more of the attention of member governments. If this does happen, it can hardly fail to affect the caliber of appointments to the board of directors and the degree of outside interest in Bank policy. Nevertheless, so long as the Bank remains predominantly a project lending institution, it seems inevitable that it will continue to be management-dominated. The selection, appraisal, and supervision of projects are not tasks for a board of directors. But increasingly the Bank is concerned with development policy and with quasi-diplomatic relations with member borrowers. An able board of directors could make a real contribution in these areas, and, in the process, the role of the board in the administration of the Bank might well be enhanced.

The IBRD has, almost from the beginning, been a highly centralized organization with decisions made in Washington rather than in the field, and made by the president and his close advisers without any considerable delegation of authority. It has operated more like a medium-sized family corporation under the direction of a strong president than like a large corporation or government ministry managed in accordance with well recognized principles of administration. The basic framework of the organization laid down in 1952, with its division of functions among the project departments (which are responsible for the appraisal and supervision of particular loans) and the area departments (which are responsible for country lending policies) remained unchanged for twenty years. This type of organization has the merit of providing certain necessary checks and balances. It works against undue concentration on project viability on the one hand and undue concern for country relationships on the other. It also has the effect of throwing all serious differences of opinion, that is, all important policy questions, into the lap of top management. The system worked fairly well when the volume of Bank lending was small and when a manageable number of loans could receive the scrutiny of the Staff Loan Committee on their way to consideration by the president and his board of directors. It appears to work less well with a Bank Group committing $2.5 billion a year to some seventy-five countries.

A further doubling of Bank Group lending will almost certainly call for significant changes both in internal organization and in relationships between Washington and the field. In fact, in January 1972 the decision was announced "to undertake a comprehensive study of the World Bank Group's organization and main operating procedures to assure that the Bank's structure is well suited to the projected scope and level of its activities."[7] An expansion of lending to particular countries, together with a broadening of the range of projects involved and the initiation of five-year country lending pro-

7. World Bank/IDA, Administrative circular (Jan. 7, 1972).

grams, substantially increases the importance of the work of area departments. Although the depth and sophistication of the Bank's country studies
have greatly increased in recent years, the area departments, as of early 1972,
are on the whole inadequately staffed to administer the kind of relationships
that are emerging between the Bank and its principal borrowers. With an
expansion of staff in all departments there is much to be said for a devolu-
tion of authority in country lending programs from the Bank's top management to a small number of strengthened area departments. As we have noted
in earlier chapters, the developmental analysis undertaken by the Bank has
always suffered to some extent from the fact that the area departments have
tended to concentrate on macroeconomic considerations, while the project
departments have been concerned principally with specific projects, to the
relative neglect of the area in between. The increased emphasis on sector
analysis in recent years has partially overcome this weakness. But analysis
of development problems and prospects in borrowing countries could certainly benefit from a closer relationship between country and project specialists.[8]

If the Bank were organized along area lines, with considerable authority
over country programs in the hands of directors of area departments, the
difficulties of maintaining consistency in Bank lending policy in different
areas would increase. Some inconsistency might be justified by real differences among areas—for example, most of South America is at a different
stage of development than most of Africa. Nevertheless, there will be need
for a strong central core that is concerned not only with the consistency problem but with other policy questions confronting the Bank. The pre-1972 organization of the Bank is weak in this respect. The president's council, established during the Woods regime, is not a body that discusses and formulates
policy. Rather, its members report on matters of current interest to themselves and top management. The president frequently makes ad hoc assignments to members of the council, which on occasion cut across the regular
channels of Bank communication. What appears to be needed is a strong

8. As this study is being prepared for the press, changes in the organization of the
Bank Group designed to strengthen area concentration and to bring about a closer
relationship between country and project specialists have been put in train.

On August 10, 1972, President McNamara announced, on the completion of the
first phase of the study of the Bank Group's organization and operating procedures, a
restructuring of the regional and technical departments, to go into effect October 1,
1972. The President stated that "regionalization of operations will both provide closer
integration of the area and project activities of the Bank and establish even more firmly
that the development of individual countries is the basis on which the Bank's program
is built."

policy group, limited in numbers and drawn from various departments of the Bank, whose function it is to discuss central policy questions and to act as a systematic means of communication between top management and the staff of the Bank. A frequent complaint is that at present the president and his chief advisers spend a great deal of time on matters of importance to them while the rest of the work of the Bank is governed by ad hoc decisions made by lower officials, who compromise their differences without much regard for policy consistency. As the Bank grows in size, it will presumably need to take on more of the formal bureaucratic trappings of a large corporation or a government ministry.

The Bank is a highly centralized institution, not only in its headquarters operations but also with respect to overseas activities. All stages of the project cycle are managed from Washington, and field operations are carried on by short-term missions. Except in one or two cases, country economic reports are prepared in Washington, again with the help of short-term missions to the field. Even in the countries and areas in which the Bank has permanent representatives, headquarters holds these representatives in most cases on a very short leash. The IBRD had, on June 30, 1971, eleven resident overseas missions, eight accredited to individual countries and two regional missions.[9] Establishment of two other country missions, in Ghana and Nepal, had been agreed upon. Most of the country missions are small—one- or two-man affairs—and their functions are limited to economic reporting and to preliminary project identification. The permanent regional missions in eastern and western Africa are concerned mainly with helping governments in the area identify and prepare projects, and their activities have substantially accelerated Bank lending in these areas. The missions in Pakistan, and particularly in India, have contributed substantially to the preparation of what are judged in the Bank to be exceptionally good economic reports. The resident mission in Indonesia encompasses by far the widest range of activities and enjoys the greatest degree of autonomy. It needs to be emphasized that all of these missions have been established on an ad hoc basis. The Bank to date has not indicated the specific conditions that justify resident missions and affect their size, their role, and their relations with Washington headquarters.

The planned increase in lending, the enlarged scope of project selection, the technical assistance and advisory role the Bank expects to play in con-

9. The individual country missions were in Afghanistan, the Democratic Republic of the Congo (Zaire), Colombia, Ethiopia, India, Indonesia, Nigeria, and Pakistan. The regional missions were in Nairobi (for eastern Africa) and Abidjan (for western Africa). The eleventh overseas mission, in Bangkok, was established to consider projects in the Mekong Valley.

nection with large borrowers, and the advisability of establishing closer relations with other UN agencies in the field and with bilateral assistance programs, all suggest that the Bank must soon develop a policy on overseas
representation. There is much to be said for strengthening and increasing the
number of overseas missions, for enlarging their functions, and for delegating
to them authority now exercised in Washington. To do this effectively, however, will present the Bank with a difficult set of problems. Moreover, resistance within headquarters to any substantial movement in this direction is
strong. The resistance would be less strong if internal reorganization were
completed before new policy on overseas missions is adopted. These missions
would presumably report to the heads of the relevant area departments. The
size of missions and the authority delegated to them could be expected to be a
matter of primary concern to area department heads.

It should be obvious that certain segments of Bank operations can be
more effectively performed in the field than in Washington, provided that
the field mission is well staffed—an important proviso. The range of activities
that can be effectively undertaken, however, depends on the size and qualifications of the field staff. Preponderant management opinion holds, wisely we
think, that resident missions should be fairly small.[10] Overseas personnel
can easily become too conspicuous. Furthermore, it is probable that a number of member borrowers will not want large Bank missions and may object
to as many as ten people. Some may not want any mission at all. A mission
with a membership of ten could help at some stages of the project cycle,
notably those of project identification and supervision, but would lack the
specialization necessary to take over a sizable part of the process.

The project departments in Washington have tended to hold that all stages
of the project are so interdependent that little can be delegated to the field,
but this view seems to be changing. A well staffed field mission can certainly
acquire a deeper understanding of development problems and prospects, in
particular the political and administrative limitations under which a government operates, than can short-term missions, no matter how well staffed they
are. This understanding, moreover, is essential to effective advice on sensitive
issues of development policy. Such advice, however, is not likely to be listened
to unless officials receiving the advice are sure that the adviser speaks with
the authority of the Bank. Thus a considerable delegation of responsibility
and authority is necessary for the fully effective operation of field missions.
Such delegation, with one or two exceptions, has not been Bank practice.

10. A report to the president of the Bank prepared in 1971 suggests ten to twelve
members as a maximum.

Well staffed field missions can substantially improve the lending operations of the Bank, and the need for such missions increases with the scale and scope of Bank lending. Nevertheless, the problems of recruitment and of change in administrative organization and procedures are formidable. An effective overseas staff must have not only professional competence, but the ability to live and work in a strange environment, sufficient diplomacy to deal in nonarrogant fashion with local officials and the representatives of other assistance agencies, and enough ability in jurisdictional infighting to assure that authority delegated to the field stays delegated.

These requirements imply a higher level of qualification than is usually demanded of Bank field staff. The Bank's record in selecting staff for foreign assignment is not one of uniform success. Although it has in general been adequately represented abroad, the selection process will need to be more rigorous if overseas missions are to accomplish what is coming to be expected of them. There are, moreover, the additional problems of fitting staff returning from the field into a proper promotion schedule and fitting field missions with added responsibility and authority into the Bank's traditional decision-making process. None of these difficulties is insuperable, and if they are overcome, the Bank can gain much from the increased numbers of staff members who will have had extensive experience in less developed countries. The difficulties are, however, sufficiently real to justify a cautious and experimental expansion in the size and numbers of overseas missions.

The Bank Group and the Private Sector

The structure and operations of the Bank have brought it into somewhat ambiguous relationships with the private sectors of both its developed and less developed member countries. On the one hand, the Bank is dependent on capital markets for the greater part of its funds; and the Bank Group as a whole has made close to 20 percent of its total commitments to private enterprise in borrowing countries. On the other hand, since over 80 percent of its total loans and investments has been directed to projects in the public sector, the staff of the Bank has inevitably been more concerned with the behavior and well-being of this sector than with the role of private enterprise in a country's development. On the whole, the trend in less developed member countries has been toward more rather than less government intervention in the economy. And changes in Bank policy foreshadow a decreasing rather than an increasing share of Bank Group commitments in the private sectors of its member countries. As Bank loans and IDA credits move increasingly toward the public sector, the Bank Group's management has attempted to build up the IFC as a strong protagonist and supporter of the role of private enterprise in the development process. If this effort is to be successful, the position of IFC within the Bank needs to be substantially strengthened, the Corporation must be effectively represented overseas as well as in Washington, and it must adapt its policies to changing attitudes in the less developed countries toward foreign private investment.

Increasing economic nationalism in less developed countries suggests that the terms on which foreign private investment will be permitted and encouraged in the future are likely to be substantially altered. Joint ventures, management contracts, and similar arrangements will increasingly take the place of complete foreign ownership. Furthermore, the areas of foreign investment are in process of change. Nationalizations and expropriations have been heavily concentrated in the fields of natural resources and banking and insurance. And in the rapidly growing manufacturing area it is not so much investment that is welcomed as investment accompanied by new technical, managerial, and marketing expertise.

The growing volume of nationalizations and expropriations will inevitably confront the Bank with a serious problem. On the one hand, its developed member countries and private investors will look to the Bank to stand squarely for prompt and equitable compensation. On the other hand, its less developed member borrowers will expect an attitude and behavior more responsive to their developmental difficulties. Whether the Bank will be able to adhere to its traditional policy in the face of increasing nationalizations and expropriations is a moot question. All in all, the Bank Group faces in the 1970s a rather different set of problems in the area of private investment than it did in 1946.

Certainly in the minds of most people, the Bank has the reputation of being a bastion of private enterprise. It usually comes as a surprise to the same people that over 80 percent of Bank Group commitments are to public sector enterprises. Furthermore this percentage, partly because of changes in Bank policy and partly because of an increase in the importance of the public sector in most of the borrowing countries, will inevitably increase. The Bank began to finance industrial enterprises in the public sector in the late 1960s, and in fiscal year 1971, of eleven industrial enterprises under consideration for Bank or IDA financing, ten were in the public sector. The shift in policy in 1968 permitting financing of government-controlled development finance companies has been followed by commitments to more publicly controlled companies than to privately controlled enterprises.

This predominant and growing concern with public sector investment has inevitably produced in the staff of the Bank an involvement in questions of government ownership, management, and policy that contrasts rather sharply with public impressions of the institution and frequently with official pronouncements from top management. Furthermore, it tends to handicap in certain respects the attainment of the Bank's objectives in the private sector. As we have noted, Bank missions rarely, if ever, turn up investment opportunities of interest to the IFC; IFC personnel are rarely, if ever, included in the membership of Bank missions; country economic reports are usually not very illuminating on the problems and prospects of the private sector; and in general the IFC tends to be regarded by most of the Bank staff as a relatively insignificant appendage, which indeed it has been. Although nine-tenths of the Bank's commitments in the private sector have been in manufacturing and mining, the industrial area has been less subject than almost any other area to the kind of sector analysis that could produce a sound lending strategy.

Beginning with the McNamara regime, attempts have been made to strengthen the IFC and to make it into the central instrument of Bank Group action in the field of private investment and private enterprise. A certain degree of success has attended these efforts. The Bank's concern with the development of capital markets in borrowing member countries is now centered in the IFC, and the Bank Group can and should make a substantially greater contribution in this area than it has in the past. The IFC, moreover, is now actively immersed in the Bank's attempt to move beyond ad hoc financing of industrial projects toward a more considered strategy of industrial development. But the IFC is still too loosely related to the central operations of the Bank to assure that the potential contribution to development of private investment and private enterprise is taken fully into account; it is still inadequately represented overseas; and its investment policies are still imperfectly adapted to changing views in less developed countries on acceptable forms of foreign investment.

If the IFC is to become the Bank Group's chosen instrument in the development of the private sector, it must become a central element in the Group rather than a lightly regarded appendage. IFC staff should frequently, if not regularly, be included in Bank economic missions. Country economic reports should invariably include sections dealing with the problems and prospects of the private sector. And the rotation of staff among various assignments in the Bank Group should include at least some IFC positions. All this would be helpful, but it may not be enough unless the executive vice president of the IFC also becomes a high official, perhaps a vice president, of the Bank itself, with authority over Bank personnel concerned with private sector matters. The first two heads of the IFC were anxious to maximize the distance between the Corporation and the Bank, and the personnel they recruited were frequently as disdainful of the "bureaucrats" in the Bank/IDA as these people were of them. This situation needs to be radically changed if the IFC is to become a development institution and a full and effective member of the Bank Group.

Through most of its existence the IFC has been relatively passive with respect to investment opportunities. These have either presented themselves at its doors in Washington or have, rather incidentally, been called to the attention of its personnel on their various travels. If the Corporation is to make its weight felt as a full-fledged member of the Bank Group, it must be more effectively represented in the areas where it is expected that investment opportunities can be found. There is something to be said for including an IFC representative in the Bank's regional missions. And certainly the promotion, as well as the appraisal, of investment opportunities should be the primary concern of a number of staff members.

The investment policy of the IFC increasingly takes into account considerations other than maximum profitability and may be expected to respond to host country demands that foreign private investment bring with it innovations and technical expertise. There is an important role for the IFC to play in bringing together local capital and entrepreneurship with foreign technical know-how and marketing connections. The Corporation has, of course, done this in the past, but on occasion its investments have resulted merely in adding one more establishment in industries that were already served by local enterprise. The receptivity of less developed countries to traditional types of foreign investment is in process of change, and the IFC has a leadership role to play in devising arrangements adapted to these changes.

One of the most difficult problems involving private foreign investment that the Bank will confront in the 1970s is a rethinking of its lending policy in member countries that have nationalized or expropriated foreign-owned properties. Early in its history the Bank acquired kudos in financial communities around the world for the firm stand it took on the importance of settling defaulted government debt. Financial communities and their governments are, in the 1970s, much more concerned with the stance the Bank will assume with respect to the obligations of its member governments toward private property owners. The Bank's policy on expropriations is similar to its policy on default. "The Bank will not lend for projects in a country if it considers that the position taken by that country with respect to alien owners of expropriated property is substantially affecting its international credit standing.

Nor will it appraise projects in such a country unless it has good grounds for believing that the obstacles to lending will soon be removed."[11]

This policy appears to be acceptable to at least the Bank's capital-exporting member countries, and it must be said that the IBRD is the only international lending institution that has attempted to formulate policy in this area. But, of course, the administration of this or any other general policy confronts difficulties when each case has unique features and usually surfaces on a sea made turbulent by the winds of economic nationalism. The primary issues on which the Bank's policy calls for judgment are whether the action taken by an expropriating country "is substantially affecting its international credit standing"; whether "reasonable efforts" are being made to arrive at a settlement; and whether such a settlement can be considered to be "equitable." None of these is an easy question to answer.

As we pointed out in Chapter 11, the Bank has, on a number of occasions, ceased lending, or has refused to lend, to a member country when expropriation was a factor to be considered. This happened in Algeria (after 1964), in Indonesia (during the Sukarno regime), in Iraq (in the mid-1960s), in the United Arab Republic (throughout most of the 1960s), and (from 1961 to 1969) in the Democratic Republic of the Congo (Zaire). But instances of nationalization and expropriation appear to be increasing, and a large number of recent expropriations have taken place in countries of special interest to the Bank's largest stockholder.[12] At the present writing the principal problem confronting the Bank in this area has to do with its lending policy in countries charged with expropriating property of U.S. citizens, but in the past other capital-exporting member countries have been involved, and it is probable they will also be involved in the future. As the Pearson Com-

---

11. IBRD, Operational policy memorandum 1.01 (March 31, 1971), p. 3.

Reasons for not proceeding with lending operations include:

(1) A denial of liability for compensation coupled with a refusal to submit the dispute to judicial or quasi-judicial determination.

(2) An admission of liability for compensation in general terms coupled with either an offer of compensation obviously inadequate in amount or terms of payment and not subject to negotiation, or else a failure to negotiate in good faith over such matters or to submit them to judicial or quasi-judicial determination.

(3) A failure, in the Bank's judgment, to make reasonable efforts to arrive at settlements.

(4) A failure to pay and, if required, to transfer abroad compensation in accordance with the terms of an agreed settlement, a judicial decree or an arbitral award.

12. A recent study by the U.S. Department of State reports: "Some 70 current situations involving nationalization, expropriation, or negotiated sale of assets of concerns with U.S. majority or minority interests have been identified in developing countries—16 in Chile alone." Bureau of Intelligence and Research, "Nationalization, Expropriation and Other Takings of United States and Certain Foreign Property Since 1960" (Nov. 30, 1971; processed).

mission observed, it is "unrealistic to expect governments of capital-exporting countries to remain passive when the property of their citizens is subject to discriminatory or confiscatory treatment by other countries."[13] Among the actions they tend to take is to try to influence the Bank to follow the same course of action they seek to pursue in their own bilateral programs.[14]

Confiscation of foreign properties or expropriation without adequate compensation can hardly fail to affect adversely the credit standing of the expropriating country and may possibly lower its creditworthiness for Bank lending. But there are considerable differences in policy among capital-exporting member countries, ranging from soft to hard line postures. Moreover, the gap in positions taken on this issue between developed, capital-exporting countries and less developed, capital-importing countries tends to be even larger.[15] Consequently the Bank finds it necessary to make its own judgments. It would be convenient if individual cases could be referred to the International Centre for Settlement of Investment Disputes, but, as we have noted, a substantial number of less developed member countries are not signatories of the convention.

There seems to be no point in attempting to reformulate the Bank's general policy. Any general statement founders on the rock of particular application. The Bank is to some extent protected in arriving at its own judgment by the

13. *Partners in Development*, p. 107.

14. On occasion they have attempted to persuade the Bank to take a sterner course of action than they themselves have been willing to follow.

A report to the president on investment disputes, made by a Bank staff committee and completed early in 1972, approved in general of Bank policy as stated in operational policy memorandum 101, cited above. The study, however, made a number of practical suggestions concerning the application of this policy. In particular it saw no need for action unless the claimant's government expressed a desire that the Bank concern itself with an expropriation. And it saw no reason why the Bank should refuse to lend when the claimant's government continued to lend to the expropriating country or did not object to the continuation of lending by other multilateral agencies.

15. In 1958 the UN General Assembly referred this problem to a Commission on Permanent Sovereignty. The resolution prepared by this commission and accepted by the UN General Assembly (Resolution 1803 [XVII]) stated that, in cases of expropriation,

the owner shall be paid appropriate compensation, in accordance with the rules in force in the state taking such measures in the exercise of its sovereignty and in accordance with international law. In any case when the question of compensation gives rise to a controversy, the national jurisdiction of the state taking such measures shall be exhausted. However upon agreement of sovereign states and other parties concerned, settlement of the dispute should be made through arbitration or international adjudication.

Under the terms of this resolution the "sovereign state" can decide whether or not to submit the case to arbitration and adjudication, and no machinery for such action is proposed. Furthermore, discussion in the commission revealed wide differences of opinion between developed and less developed members on what might constitute adequate compensation.

diversity of views among its executive directors. But there is no blinking the fact that this judgment must take into account the need to raise funds through the sale of Bank securities in capital markets and the contributions of Part I countries to IDA.

The Bank as Part of an Emerging International System

The Bank and its affiliates, as we have tried to make clear, have become an increasingly integral part of the complex of international machinery that has grown up since the close of World War II. While it is easy to exaggerate the extent to which the Bank Group's future depends on the future of the system as a whole—in other words, on the general climate for international cooperation in solving economic, social, and political problems—it is hard today to conceive of that future as completely independent of the outlook for the rest of the system.

Twenty-five years ago the management of the Bank not only did not need to think of its future as linked to the future of other international agencies, but it may have been justified in believing that visible ties to the United Nations or other international agencies would operate as a handicap. Independence was considered essential to obtain the desired reputation as a hard-headed, business-like, nonpolitical organization; to gain the confidence of the private investors who would provide the Bank with its loanable capital; and to attain a triple-A rating for its bonds. Once the Bank's credit was firmly established, this attitude changed gradually, influenced also during the 1950s by: (1) the development of cordial personal relationships between UN Secretary-General Dag Hammarskjöld and Bank President Eugene Black; (2) the formalizing of various ties between agencies without damage to the Bank's reputation; (3) the establishment of a UN Special Fund to provide, among other things, grants for preinvestment surveys and studies; and (4) the need to work out a modus vivendi with a newly created potential competitor of the World Bank—the Inter-American Development Bank. The change in attitude toward other agencies accelerated during the 1960s with the decision of President George Woods to enter into formal cooperative arrangements with FAO and Unesco and informal cooperation with UNCTAD; the spread of regional development banks to Africa and Asia, where the World Bank had previously been the only important multilateral lending agency; and the relative ease of collaboration by the Bank with the OECD and its Development Assistance Committee, as well as with the financial institutions of the European Economic Community.

The painless part of the journey has by now been completed. The road during the next decade is likely to be rockier and more tortuous for at least two reasons—the existence of increased nationalism within member governments and the reluctance of other international agencies to be less than full partners of the Bank. As for nationalism, it is evident everywhere, and the sense of international community that sustained the growth of international cooperation for twenty-five years has weakened markedly. This means a less expansionist climate for all parts of the international system, more disposition on the part of governments to calculate costs and benefits only in short-range terms, and louder demands for efficient, coordinated use of existing resources in lieu of increased resources for the agencies promoting development. Nevertheless, an agency such as the World Bank, which can raise at least part of its funds by selling bonds, may enjoy somewhat greater freedom than agencies totally dependent on appropriations. As for inter-agency collaboration, the cooperation of the Bank with other agencies has been more one-sided in the past than it can be or deserves to be in the future. The Bank has become a partner of various agencies without enabling those agencies to feel that they are full and equal partners of the Bank. They will expect more voice in country economic reporting, in evaluating development performance, and in the selection, appraisal, and supervision of investment projects.

We are aware, of course, that so long as the overwhelming bulk of development assistance is distributed bilaterally, the most rational multilateral arrangements cannot offset the irrationalities of competing bilateral efforts. But we would argue that better coordinated, more rational multilateral arrangements are to some unmeasurable extent a prerequisite for greater reliance on multilateral channels.

Whatever the general climate may be, the Bank will need to integrate its activities more closely with those of some international institutions than of others. Among the specialized agencies of the United Nations, the Bank's relations with the IMF—an agency of the same species as the Bank and about the only one it regards as an equal—will continue to be extremely important. The importance of this relationship will inevitably increase if, from the reorganization of the world monetary system under way at this writing, the Fund emerges as the chief arbiter of exchange relationships and of international liquidity. Cooperation between the Bank and the Fund became significantly closer during the 1960s, but, as we noted earlier, there is still some way to go. Acceptance of the Pearson Commission recommendation of joint country missions would not only assure that consistent advice was given to member countries but would substantially improve the economic reporting of both agencies and would effectively direct attention to the neglected relationship between stabilization and growth policies. And if at some stage a link is established between the creation of SDRs and development finance via the IDA, close cooperation between the two agencies would be almost inevitable.

As for specialized agencies other than the Fund, the Bank has already helped to make FAO and Unesco more development-oriented and investment-oriented than they were initially. The device has been the cooperative arrangement, now extended also to the World Health Organization, whereby certain units in those agencies receive 75 percent of their financing from the Bank to assist governments in project identification and preparation. The cooperation to date consists basically of the other agencies working on projects designated by, or agreed on with, the Bank in order to keep its project pipeline well filled. The agencies are not excluded from a role in project appraisal and supervision, but the Bank has specifically reserved to itself full responsibility in these two areas. The projects, as they come out of the Bank's pipeline, advance also, of course, the basic objectives of the agencies that helped identify and prepare them.

The rather modest role assigned to those agencies and the rapid rate at which the Bank has been building up its own staff of agricultural and educational specialists does little to prevent further disintegration of the concept of functional specialization within the UN family. In order to preserve and strengthen the concept—and avoid doing things that can be done elsewhere —it would seem desirable for the Bank to associate the relevant specialized agencies more actively and responsibly in project appraisal and project supervision.

As an executing agency for the United Nations Development Program (UNDP), the Bank, which is investment-oriented, has been far more successful than the other specialized agencies, which have tended to be technical assistance–oriented and to have had difficulty in providing preinvestment surveys that could serve as a basis for investment decisions. The Bank has also provided most of the follow-up investment that has resulted from UNDP-financed preinvestment surveys. The Bank has thus made a major contribution to the success of the UNDP.

But the present relationships between preinvestment and investment financing agencies are open to challenge because of the administrative split that they preserve between two stages of what is essentially a single economic process, the arbitrary division between grant and loan aid that they perpetuate, and the proportion of follow-up investment that is undertaken by the World Bank as compared with the regional banks. If more of the communist countries join the World Bank in the years to come, the principal difference between UNDP and World Bank membership will have disappeared and, with it, one of the more obvious present barriers to a merger of the pre-investment and investment functions.

Today a member government too rich to qualify for soft loans from IDA can nevertheless obtain grant financing from the UNDP. The UNDP is already a sizable though not a massive source of grant aid—providing nearly $250 million a year for preinvestment surveys and other forms of technical assistance. With the burgeoning interest in meeting the special needs of the least developed countries, in programming external assistance on a country rather than a project-by-project basis, and in adjusting the burden of debt service, the international community will surely scrutinize anew the current criteria for allocating grant aid and loan aid. The Bank Group can concentrate more IDA assistance on the very poor countries. It is not, however, within the power of the Bank to change eligibility for UNDP aid, although it is within the power of the member countries of the Bank to do so in the appropriate policymaking organ of the UNDP.

The regional development banks, which are not part of the UN system, have seldom served as executing agencies for the UNDP or provided any significant amount of follow-up investment. One of them, the African Development Bank, does not command the resources to be a significant source of investment funds. If there are going to be regional development banks—and it seems plain that there will be—strengthening them, bringing them more fully into the international system, and helping to develop a specialized role for them would appear to be to the advantage of the World Bank. This is in large measure recognized by the IBRD, which has already done a good deal to help build up the regional banks. The regional banks at present would probably oppose any formal or semi-formal division of labor. They fear that they would get the short end of the stick; the division would reflect current differences in resources and competence. Both the World Bank and the regional banks can brandish a convenient shield to protect their ever-broadening ranges of lending: "If member governments choose to come to us rather than to someone else for financing, it would be wrong for us to refuse them." This commendable respect for the wishes of member governments is not wholly convincing; no public agency needs to do everything it is asked to do.

The evolution of a division of labor will differ from region to region. We have no blueprint to offer and only a few suggestions to make. One is that the World Bank make a more strenuous effort to involve the regional banks in joint financing operations on terms that make them genuine partners rather than junior partners. Another is for the World Bank, which ought to decentralize in any case, to propose the delegation of certain functions to the regional banks—the preparation of certain country economic reports, lending for so-called regional integration projects, lending for the refinancing of export credits granted by less developed countries, and lending for types of projects (for example, feeder roads) that can best be supervised by an agency that is more at home in the region than the World Bank. The latter might even make the regional banks fiscal agents or provide them with a portion of the resources required to carry out functions assigned to them.

The regional banks might say that the industrialized countries that have their own export financing machinery and have never encouraged the World Bank to finance the equivalent of suppliers' credits for exports of capital goods from less developed countries are not about to agree that this is an ideal function for regional banks to undertake. And the World Bank could add that it cannot, for example, delegate country economic reporting if its executive directors and the consultative groups which it chairs believe the reports would then be too uncritical to serve as a basis for decisions.

We are trying here, however, to look beyond the immediate future. With the encouragement of its members, the World Bank has done an excellent job of building industrial development banks and more recently agricultural credit institutions at the national level. Though the challenge would be of a somewhat different nature, the World Bank is capable of doing equally well in strengthening lending institutions at the regional level.

The problem is substantially different insofar as the European Fund for Development and the European Investment Bank, particularly the former, are concerned. These instruments of the European Economic Community can hardly be said to need building up by the World Bank. When the United Kingdom and the countries now negotiating with the EEC join the Community, its financial institutions may be significantly enlarged with respect to both resources at their command and geographic area served. In that event, a majority of the principal contributors to IDA would have, in the enlarged European Fund for Development, an institution of their own that could use its resources for the advancement of virtually the same countries as are eligible for IDA assistance. The Europeans could choose to build the European Development Fund at the expense of the IDA unless persuaded that they had adequate representation at the upper levels of the Bank/IDA and that it was in any event advantageous from a long-term standpoint to strengthen institutions in which less developed as well as more developed countries (including Japan and the United States) were members and shareholders.

The international system for the promotion of development is, as Sir Robert Jackson has said, a non-system. Our suggestions for improving relations between different parts of the non-system should not be construed as a plan for creating a group of equals in which no one is *primus inter pares*. The World Bank Group is better equipped than any agency we know of, national or international, to wear, at the economic and financial level, the *primus-inter-pares* mantle. President McNamara has been gratifyingly aware of the need to strengthen the international development effort and to give it fresh leadership.

The dream of specialists and technocrats is that politicians will assure them the wherewithal to pursue their objectives but will never complicate the pursuit by introducing political considerations. This dream is destined to remain a reverie. Even if the implementation of agreed development strategies were delegated to managers and economists and technicians, the process of reaching agreement would continue to be essentially political. Neither the weighted voting system of the Bank nor the one-nation, one-vote system of the United Nations provides a satisfactory basis for obtaining necessary political guidance from the international community.

True international community, moreover, remains farther away than anyone can now see. Meanwhile, the most one can hope for is support of and tolerance for gradually improving, reasonably sensible, makeshift arrangements for facilitating economic and social development in the low-income world.

A Final Word

We have in general throughout this volume, and in this concluding chapter in particular, assumed that reasonably sensible arrangements will in fact be forthcoming. But no one reflecting, in the climate of 1972, on the relation between the developed and less developed world over all, and on the role of the World Bank in this relationship in particular, can discern much reason for optimism. The third IDA replenishment has proved as difficult to complete as the second, and obstacles to increased replenishment in the fourth round already loom on the horizon. It is becoming abundantly clear that if the Bank Group is to continue to assist development in its poorer member countries, some alternative to this triennial confrontation must be found.

Official development assistance from all sources, which it was hoped would in the UN's second development decade run at 0.7 percent of the developed countries' gross national product, was in 1971 approximately half that amount, and the future trend seems as likely to be downward as upward. This situation and prospect cannot help but have an adverse effect on development prospects and therefore on the creditworthiness of many countries for Bank borrowing. If the trend of official development assistance is indeed downward, the less developed world may presently find itself to be a capital exporter rather than a capital importer. If this situation does in fact impend, the borrowing countries will find themselves immersed in debt rescheduling exercises of a number and difficulty hitherto uncontemplated. The Bank may well find it impossible to collect from a number of important borrowers without committing an equivalent amount in new loans. While this situation would not be particularly alarming from the point of view of the Bank's credit standing, an institution limited to a zero net transfer of capital can hardly be characterized as a development institution.

The prospects, in our view, are not this bleak. As we pointed out earlier in this chapter, the Bank could play a useful role in assisting development in middle-income countries without IDA money. But it is well to recognize that if those member countries most in need of development are to be effectively assisted, the Bank Group not only needs a substantial increase in IDA funds but must continue to be a part of a larger international development effort in which the trend of official development assistance, the earnings of less developed countries from international trade, and, one hopes, their receipts of foreign private investment and technology as well, are clearly rising.

Appendixes

APPENDIX A

Articles of Agreement

A-1. Articles of Agreement
of the International Bank for Reconstruction and Development
(As amended effective December 17, 1965)

The Governments on whose behalf the present Agreement is signed agree as follows:

INTRODUCTORY ARTICLE

The International Bank for Reconstruction and Development is established and shall operate in accordance with the following provisions:

ARTICLE I. Purposes

The purposes of the Bank are:

(i) To assist in the reconstruction and development of territories of members by facilitating the investment of capital for productive purposes, including the restoration of economies destroyed or disrupted by war, the reconversion of productive facilities to peacetime needs and the encouragement of the development of productive facilities and resources in less developed countries.

(ii) To promote private foreign investment by means of guarantees or participations in loans and other investments made by private investors; and when private capital is not available on reasonable terms, to supplement private investment by providing, on suitable conditions, finance for productive purposes out of its own capital, funds raised by it and its other resources.

(iii) To promote the long-range balanced growth of international trade and the maintenance of equilibrium in balances of payments by encouraging international investment for the development of the productive resources of members, thereby assisting in raising productivity, the standard of living and conditions of labor in their territories.

(iv) To arrange the loans made or guaranteed by it in relation to international loans through other channels so that the more useful and urgent projects, large and small alike, will be dealt with first.

759

(v) To conduct its operations with due regard to the effect of international investment on business conditions in the territories of members and, in the immediate postwar years, to assist in bringing about a smooth transition from a wartime to a peacetime economy.

The Bank shall be guided in all its decisions by the purposes set forth above.

ARTICLE II. Membership in and Capital of the Bank

Section 1. *Membership*

(a) The original members of the Bank shall be those members of the International Monetary Fund which accept membership in the Bank before the date specified in Article XI, Section 2(e).

(b) Membership shall be open to other members of the Fund, at such times and in accordance with such terms as may be prescribed by the Bank.

Section 2. *Authorized capital*

(a) The authorized capital stock of the Bank shall be $10,000,000,000,[1] in terms of United States dollars of the weight and fineness in effect on July 1, 1944. The capital stock shall be divided into 100,000 shares having a par value of $100,000 each, which shall be available for subscription only by members.

(b) The capital stock may be increased when the Bank deems it advisable by a three-fourths majority of the total voting power.

Section 3. *Subscription of shares*

(a) Each member shall subscribe shares of the capital stock of the Bank. The minimum number of shares to be subscribed by the original members shall be those set forth in Schedule A. The minimum number of shares to be subscribed by other members shall be determined by the Bank, which shall reserve a sufficient portion of its capital stock for subscription by such members.

(b) The Bank shall prescribe rules laying down the conditions under which members may subscribe shares of the authorized capital stock of the Bank in addition to their minimum subscriptions.

(c) If the authorized capital stock of the Bank is increased, each member shall have a reasonable opportunity to subscribe, under such conditions as the Bank shall decide, a proportion of the increase of stock equivalent to the proportion which its stock theretofore subscribed bears to the total capital stock of the Bank, but no member shall be obligated to subscribe any part of the increased capital.

Section 4. *Issue price of shares*

Shares included in the minimum subscriptions of original members shall be issued at par. Other shares shall be issued at par unless the Bank by a majority of the total voting power decides in special circumstances to issue them on other terms.

Section 5. *Division and calls of subscribed capital*

The subscription of each member shall be divided into two parts as follows:

(i) twenty percent shall be paid or subject to call under Section 7 (i) of this Article as needed by the Bank for its operations;

---

1. As of August 25, 1965, the authorized capital stock of the Bank had been increased to $24 billion, divided into 240,000 shares having a par value of $100,000 each. As of December 31, 1970, it was increased to $27 billion.

(ii) the remaining eighty percent shall be subject to call by the Bank only when required to meet obligations of the Bank created under Article IV, Sections 1 (a) (ii) and (iii).

Calls on unpaid subscriptions shall be uniform on all shares.

Section 6.   *Limitation on liability*

Liability on shares shall be limited to the unpaid portion of the issue price of the shares.

Section 7   *Method of payment of subscriptions for shares*

Payment of subscriptions for shares shall be made in gold or United States dollars and in the currencies of the members as follows:

(i) under Section 5 (i) of this Article, two percent of the price of each share shall be payable in gold or United States dollars, and, when calls are made, the remaining eighteen percent shall be paid in the currency of the member;

(ii) when a call is made under Section 5 (ii) of this Article, payment may be made at the option of the member either in gold, in United States dollars or in the currency required to discharge the obligations of the Bank for the purpose for which the call is made;

(iii) when a member makes payments in any currency under (i) and (ii) above, such payments shall be made in amounts equal in value to the member's liability under the call. This liability shall be a proportionate part of the subscribed capital stock of the Bank as authorized and defined in Section 2 of this Article.

Section 8.   *Time of payment of subscriptions*

(a) The two percent payable on each share in gold or United States dollars under Section 7 (i) of this Article, shall be paid within sixty days of the date on which the Bank begins operations, provided that

(i) any original member of the Bank whose metropolitan territory has suffered from enemy occupation or hostilities during the present war shall be granted the right to postpone payment of one-half percent until five years after that date;

(ii) an original member who cannot make such a payment because it has not recovered possession of its gold reserves which are still seized or immobilized as a result of the war may postpone all payment until such date as the Bank shall decide.

(b) The remainder of the price of each share payable under Section 7 (i) of this Article shall be paid as and when called by the Bank, provided that

(i) the Bank shall, within one year of its beginning operations, call not less than eight percent of the price of the share in addition to the payment of two percent referred to in (a) above;

(ii) not more than five percent of the price of the share shall be called in any period of three months.

Section 9.   *Maintenance of value of certain currency holdings of the Bank*

(a) Whenever (i) the par value of a member's currency is reduced, or (ii) the foreign exchange value of a member's currency has, in the opinion of the Bank, depreciated to a significant extent within that member's territories, the member shall pay to the Bank within a reasonable time an additional amount of its own currency sufficient to maintain the value, as of the time of initial subscription, of the amount of the currency of such member which is held by the Bank and derived from currency originally paid in to the Bank by the member under Article II, Section 7 (i), from currency referred to in Article IV, Section 2 (b), or from any additional currency furnished under the provisions of the present paragraph, and which has not been repurchased by the member for gold or for the currency of any member which is acceptable to the Bank.

(b) Whenever the par value of a member's currency is increased, the Bank shall return to such member within a reasonable time an amount of that member's currency equal to the increase in the value of the amount of such currency described in (a) above.

(c) The provisions of the preceding paragraphs may be waived by the Bank when a uniform proportionate change in the par values of the currencies of all its members is made by the International Monetary Fund.

Section 10.   *Restriction on disposal of shares*

Shares shall not be pledged or encumbered in any manner whatever and they shall be transferable only to the Bank.

ARTICLE III. General Provisions Relating to Loans and Guarantees

Section 1.   *Use of resources*

(a) The resources and the facilities of the Bank shall be used exclusively for the benefit of members with equitable consideration to projects for development and projects for reconstruction alike.

(b) For the purpose of facilitating the restoration and reconstruction of the economy of members whose metropolitan territories have suffered great devastation from enemy occupation or hostilities, the Bank, in determining the conditions and terms of loans made to such members, shall pay special regard to lightening the financial burden and expediting the completion of such restoration and reconstruction.

Section 2.   *Dealings between members and the Bank*

Each member shall deal with the Bank only through its Treasury, central bank, stabilization fund or other similar fiscal agency, and the Bank shall deal with members only by or through the same agencies.

Section 3.   *Limitations on guarantees and borrowings of the Bank*

The total amount outstanding of guarantees, participations in loans and direct loans made by the Bank shall not be increased at any time, if by such increase the total would exceed one hundred percent of the unimpaired subscribed capital, reserves and surplus of the Bank.

Section 4.   *Conditions on which the Bank may guarantee or make loans*

The Bank may guarantee, participate in, or make loans to any member or any political sub-division thereof and any business, industrial, and agricultural enterprise in the territories of a member, subject to the following conditions:

(i)   When the member in whose territories the project is located is not itself the borrower, the member or the central bank or some comparable agency of the member which is acceptable to the Bank, fully guarantees the repayment of the principal and the payment of interest and other charges on the loan.

(ii) The Bank is satisfied that in the prevailing market conditions the borrower would be unable otherwise to obtain the loan under conditions which in the opinion of the Bank are reasonable for the borrower.

(iii) A competent committee, as provided for in Article V, Section 7, has submitted a written report recommending the project after a careful study of the merits of the proposal.

(iv) In the opinion of the Bank the rate of interest and other charges are reasonable and such rate, charges and the schedule for repayment of principal are appropriate to the project.

(v) In making or guaranteeing a loan, the Bank shall pay due regard to the prospects that the borrower, and, if the borrower is not a member, that the guarantor, will be in position to meet its obligations under the loan; and the Bank shall act prudently in the interests both of the particular member in whose territories the project is located and of the members as a whole.

(vi) In guaranteeing a loan made by other investors, the Bank receives suitable compensation for its risk.

(vii) Loans made or guaranteed by the Bank shall, except in special circumstances, be for the purpose of specific projects of reconstruction or development.

Section 5. *Use of loans guaranteed, participated in or made by the Bank*

(a) The Bank shall impose no conditions that the proceeds of a loan shall be spent in the territories of any particular member or members.

(b) The Bank shall make arrangements to ensure that the proceeds of any loan are used only for the purposes for which the loan was granted, with due attention to considerations of economy and efficiency and without regard to political or other non-economic influences or considerations.

(c) In the case of loans made by the Bank, it shall open an account in the name of the borrower and the amount of the loan shall be credited to this account in the currency or currencies in which the loan is made. The borrower shall be permitted by the Bank to draw on this account only to meet expenses in connection with the project as they are actually incurred.

Section 6. *Loans to the International Finance Corporation*[2]

(a) The Bank may make, participate in, or guarantee loans to the International Finance Corporation, an affiliate of the Bank, for use in its lending operations. The total amount outstanding of such loans, participations and guarantees shall not be increased if, at the time or as a result thereof, the aggregate amount of debt (including the guarantee of any debt) incurred by the said Corporation from any source and then outstanding shall exceed an amount equal to four times its unimpaired subscribed capital and surplus.

(b) The provisions of Article III, Sections 4 and 5(c) and of Article IV, Section 3 shall not apply to loans, participations and guarantees authorized by this Section.

2. Section added by amendment effective Dec. 17, 1965.

ARTICLE IV. Operations

Section 1. *Methods of making or facilitating loans*

(a) The Bank may make or facilitate loans which satisfy the general conditions of Article III in any of the following ways:

  (i) By making or participating in direct loans out of its own funds corresponding to its unimpaired paid-up capital and surplus and, subject to Section 6 of this Article, to its reserves.

  (ii) By making or participating in direct loans out of funds raised in the market of a member, or otherwise borrowed by the Bank.

  (iii) By guaranteeing in whole or in part loans made by private investors through the usual investment channels.

(b) The Bank may borrow funds under (a) (ii) above or guarantee loans under (a) (iii) above only with the approval of the member in whose markets the funds are raised and the member in whose currency the loan is denominated, and only if those members agree that the proceeds may be exchanged for the currency of any other member without restriction.

Section 2. *Availability and transferability of currencies*

(a) Currencies paid into the Bank under Article II, Section 7 (i), shall be loaned only with the approval in each case of the member whose currency is involved; provided, however, that if necessary, after the Bank's subscribed capital has been entirely called, such currencies shall, without restriction by the members whose currencies are offered, be used or exchanged for the currencies required to meet contractual payments of interest, other charges or amortization on the Bank's own borrowings, or to meet the Bank's liabilities with respect to such contractual payments on loans guaranteed by the Bank.

(b) Currencies received by the Bank from borrowers or guarantors in payment on account of principal of direct loans made with currencies referred to in (a) above shall be exchanged for the currencies of other members or reloaned only with the approval in each case of the members whose currencies are involved; provided, however, that if necessary, after the Bank's subscribed capital has been entirely called, such currencies shall, without restriction by the members whose currencies are offered, be used or exchanged for the currencies required to meet contractual payments of interest, other charges or amortization on the Bank's own borrowings, or to meet the Bank's liabilities with respect to such contractual payments on loans guaranteed by the Bank.

(c) Currencies received by the Bank from borrowers or guarantors in payment on account of principal of direct loans made by the Bank under Section 1 (a) (ii) of this Article, shall be held and used, without restriction by the members, to make amortization payments, or to anticipate payment of or repurchase part or all of the Bank's own obligations.

(d) All other currencies available to the Bank, including those raised in the market or otherwise borrowed under Section 1 (a) (ii) of this Article, those obtained by the sale of gold, those received as payments of interest and other charges for direct loans made under Sections 1 (a) (i) and (ii), and those received as payments of commissions and other charges under Section 1 (a) (iii), shall be used or exchanged for other currencies or gold required in the operations of the Bank without restriction by the members whose currencies are offered.

(e) Currencies raised in the markets of members by borrowers on loans guaranteed by the Bank under Section 1 (a) (iii) of this Article, shall also be used or exchanged for other currencies without restriction by such members.

Section 3.   *Provision of currencies for direct loans*

The following provisions shall apply to direct loans under Sections 1 (a) (i) and (ii) of this Article:

(a) The Bank shall furnish the borrower with such currencies of members, other than the member in whose territories the project is located, as are needed by the borrower for expenditures to be made in the territories of such other members to carry out the purposes of the loan.

(b) The Bank may, in exceptional circumstances when local currency required for the purposes of the loan cannot be raised by the borrower on reasonable terms, provide the borrower as part of the loan with an appropriate amount of that currency.

(c) The Bank, if the project gives rise indirectly to an increased need for foreign exchange by the member in whose territories the project is located, may in exceptional circumstances provide the borrower as part of the loan with an appropriate amount of gold or foreign exchange not in excess of the borrower's local expenditure in connection with the purposes of the loan.

(d) The Bank may, in exceptional circumstances, at the request of a member in whose territories a portion of the loan is spent, repurchase with gold or foreign exchange a part of that member's currency thus spent but in no case shall the part so repurchased exceed the amount by which the expenditure of the loan in those territories gives rise to an increased need for foreign exchange.

Section 4.   *Payment provisions for direct loans*

Loan contracts under Section 1 (a) (i) or (ii) of this Article shall be made in accordance with the following payment provisions:

(a) The terms and conditions of interest and amortization payments, maturity and dates of payment of each loan shall be determined by the Bank. The Bank shall also determine the rate and any other terms and conditions of commission to be charged in connection with such loan.

In the case of loans made under Section 1 (a) (ii) of this Article during the first ten years of the Bank's operations, this rate of commission shall be not less than one percent per annum and not greater than one and one-half percent per annum, and shall be charged on the outstanding portion of any such loan. At the end of this period of ten years, the rate of commission may be reduced by the Bank with respect both to the outstanding portions of loans already made and to future loans, if the reserves accumulated by the Bank under Section 6 of this Article and out of other earnings are considered by it sufficient to justify a reduction. In the case of future loans the Bank shall also have discretion to increase the rate of commission beyond the above limit, if experience indicates that an increase is advisable.

(b) All loan contracts shall stipulate the currency or currencies in which payments under the contract shall be made to the Bank. At the option of the borrower, however, such payments may be made in gold, or subject to the agreement of the Bank, in the currency of a member other than that prescribed in the contract.

    (i) In the case of loans made under Section 1 (a) (i) of this Article, the loan contracts shall provide that payments to the Bank of interest, other charges and amortization shall be made in the currency loaned, unless the member whose currency is loaned agrees that such payments shall be made in some other specified currency or currencies. These payments, subject to the provisions of Article II, Section 9 (c), shall be equivalent to the value of such contractual payments at the time the loans were made, in terms of a currency specified for the purpose by the Bank by a three-fourths majority of the total voting power.

    (ii) In the case of loans made under Section 1 (a) (ii) of this Article, the total amount outstanding and payable to the Bank in any one currency shall at no time exceed the total amount of the outstanding borrowings made by the Bank under Section 1 (a) (ii) and payable in the same currency.

  (c) If a member suffers from an acute exchange stringency, so that the service of any loan contracted by that member or guaranteed by it or by one of its agencies cannot be provided in the stipulated manner, the member concerned may apply to the Bank for a relaxation of the conditions of payment. If the Bank is satisfied that some relaxation is in the interests of the particular member and of the operations of the Bank and of its members as a whole, it may take action under either, or both, of the following paragraphs with respect to the whole, or part, of the annual service:

    (i) The Bank may, in its discretion, make arrangements with the member concerned to accept service payments on the loan in the member's currency for periods not to exceed three years upon appropriate terms regarding the use of such currency and the maintenance of its foreign exchange value; and for the repurchase of such currency on appropriate terms.

    (ii) The Bank may modify the terms of amortization or extend the life of the loan, or both.

Section 5.   *Guarantees*

  (a) In guaranteeing a loan placed through the usual investment channels, the Bank shall charge a guarantee commission payable periodically on the amount of the loan outstanding at a rate determined by the Bank. During the first ten years of the Bank's operations, this rate shall be not less than one percent per annum and not greater than one and one-half percent per annum. At the end of this period of ten years, the rate of commission may be reduced by the Bank with respect both to the outstanding portions of loans already guaranteed and to future loans if the reserves accumulated by the Bank under Section 6 of this Article and out of other earnings are considered by it sufficient to justify a reduction. In the case of future loans the Bank shall also have discretion to increase the rate of commission beyond the above limit, if experience indicates that an increase is advisable.

  (b) Guarantee commissions shall be paid directly to the Bank by the borrower.

  (c) Guarantees by the Bank shall provide that the Bank may terminate its liability with respect to interest if, upon default by the borrower and by the guarantor, if any, the Bank offers to purchase, at par and interest accrued to a date designated in the offer, the bonds or other obligations guaranteed.

(d) The Bank shall have power to determine any other terms and conditions of the guarantee.

Section 6. *Special reserve*

The amount of commissions received by the Bank under Sections 4 and 5 of this Article shall be set aside as a special reserve, which shall be kept available for meeting liabilities of the Bank in accordance with Section 7 of this Article. The special reserve shall be held in such liquid form, permitted under this Agreement, as the Executive Directors may decide.

Section 7. *Methods of meeting liabilities of the Bank in case of defaults*

In cases of default on loans made, participated in, or guaranteed by the Bank:

(a) The Bank shall make such arrangements as may be feasible to adjust the obligations under the loans, including arrangements under or analogous to those provided in Section 4 (c) of this Article.

(b) The payments in discharge of the Bank's liabilities on borrowings or guarantees under Section 1 (a) (ii) and (iii) of this Article shall be charged:

(i) first, against the special reserve provide in Section 6 of this Article.

(ii) then, to the extent necessary and at the discretion of the Bank, against the other reserves, surplus and capital available to the Bank.

(c) Whenever necessary to meet contractual payments of interest, other charges or amortization on the Bank's own borrowings, or to meet the Bank's liabilities with respect to similar payments on loans guaranteed by it, the Bank may call an appropriate amount of the unpaid subscriptions of members in accordance with Article II, Sections 5 and 7. Moreover, if it believes that a default may be of long duration, the Bank may call an additional amount of such unpaid subscriptions not to exceed in any one year one percent of the total subscriptions of the members for the following purposes:

(i) To redeem prior to maturity, or otherwise discharge its liability on, all or part of the outstanding principal of any loan guaranteed by it in respect of which the debtor is in default.

(ii) To repurchase, or otherwise discharge its liability on, all or part of its own outstanding borrowings.

Section 8. *Miscellaneous operations*

In addition to the operations specified elsewhere in this Agreement, the Bank shall have the power:

(i) To buy and sell securities it has issued and to buy and sell securities which it has guaranteed or in which it has invested, provided that the Bank shall obtain the approval of the member in whose territories the securities are to be bought or sold.

(ii) To guarantee securities in which it has invested for the purpose of facilitating their sale.

(iii) To borrow the currency of any member with the approval of that member.

(iv) To buy and sell such other securities as the Directors by a three-fourths majority of the total voting power may deem proper for the investment of all or part of the special reserve under Section 6 of this Article.

In exercising the powers conferred by this Section, the Bank may deal with any person, partnership, association, corporation or other legal entity in the territories of any member.

Section 9.   *Warning to be placed on securities*

Every security guaranteed or issued by the Bank shall bear on its face a conspicuous statement to the effect that it is not an obligation of any government unless expressly stated on the security.

Section 10.   *Political activity prohibited*

The Bank and its officers shall not interfere in the political affairs of any member; nor shall they be influenced in their decisions by the political character of the member or members concerned. Only economic considerations shall be relevant to their decisions, and these considerations shall be weighed impartially in order to achieve the purposes stated in Article I.

ARTICLE V. Organization and Management

Section 1.   *Structure of the Bank*

The Bank shall have a Board of Governors, Executive Directors, a President and such other officers and staff to perform such duties as the Bank may determine.

Section 2.   *Board of Governors*

(a) All the powers of the Bank shall be vested in the Board of Governors consisting of one governor and one alternate appointed by each member in such manner as it may determine. Each governor and each alternate shall serve for five years, subject to the pleasure of the member appointing him, and may be reappointed. No alternate may vote except in the absence of his principal. The Board shall select one of the governors as Chairman.

(b) The Board of Governors may delegate to the Executive Directors authority to exercise any powers of the Board, except the power to:

(i)   Admit new members and determine the conditions of their admission;

(ii)   Increase or decrease the capital stock;

(iii) Suspend a member;

(iv)   Decide appeals from interpretations of this Agreement given by the Executive Directors;

(v)   Make arrangements to cooperate with other international organizations (other than informal arrangements of a temporary and administrative character);

(vi)   Decide to suspend permanently the operations of the Bank and to distribute its assets;

(vii) Determine the distribution of the net income of the Bank.

(c) The Board of Governors shall hold an annual meeting and such other meetings as may be provided for by the Board or called by the Executive Directors. Meetings of the Board shall be called by the Directors whenever requested by five members or by members having one-quarter of the total voting power.

(d) A quorum for any meeting of the Board of Governors shall be a majority of the Governors, exercising not less than two-thirds of the total voting power.

(e) The Board of Governors may by regulation establish a procedure whereby the Executive Directors, when they deem such action to be in the best interests of the Bank, may obtain a vote of the Governors on a specific question without calling a meeting of the Board.

(f) The Board of Governors, and the Executive Directors to the extent authorized, may adopt such rules and regulations as may be necessary or appropriate to conduct the business of the Bank.

(g) Governors and alternates shall serve as such without compensation from the Bank, but the Bank shall pay them reasonable expenses incurred in attending meetings.

(h) The Board of Governors shall determine the remuneration to be paid to the Executive Directors and the salary and terms of the contract of service of the President.

Section 3.   *Voting*

(a) Each member shall have two hundred fifty votes plus one additional vote for each share of stock held.

(b) Except as otherwise specifically provided, all matters before the Bank shall be decided by a majority of the votes cast.

Section 4.   *Executive Directors*

(a) The Executive Directors shall be responsible for the conduct of the general operations of the Bank, and for this purpose, shall exercise all the powers delegated to them by the Board of Governors.

(b) There shall be twelve Executive Directors, who need not be governors, and of whom:

  (i) five shall be appointed, one by each of the five members having the largest number of shares;

  (ii) seven shall be elected according to Schedule B by all the Governors other than those appointed by the five members referred to in (i) above.

For the purpose of this paragraph, "members" means governments of countries whose names are set forth in Schedule A, whether they are original members or become members in accordance with Article II, Section 1 (b). When governments of other countries become members, the Board of Governors may, by a four-fifths majority of the total voting power, increase the total number of directors by increasing the number of directors to be elected.

Executive directors shall be appointed or elected every two years.

(c) Each executive director shall appoint an alternate with full power to act for him when he is not present. When the executive directors appointing them are present, alternates may participate in meetings but shall not vote.

(d) Directors shall continue in office until their successors are appointed or elected. If the office of an elected director becomes vacant more than ninety days before the end of his term, another director shall be elected for the remainder of the term by the governors who elected the former director. A majority of the votes cast shall be required for election. While the office remains vacant, the alternate of the former director shall exercise his powers, except that of appointing an alternate.

(e) The Executive Directors shall function in continuous session at the principal office of the Bank and shall meet as often as the business of the Bank may require.

(f) A quorum for any meeting of the Executive Directors shall be a majority of the Directors, exercising not less than one-half of the total voting power.

(g) Each appointed director shall be entitled to cast the number of votes allotted under Section 3 of this Article to the member appointing him. Each elected director shall be entitled to cast the number of votes which counted toward his election. All the votes which a director is entitled to cast shall be cast as a unit.

(h) The Board of Governors shall adopt regulations under which a member not entitled to appoint a director under (b) above may send a representative to attend any meeting of the Executive Directors when a request made by, or a matter particularly affecting, that member is under consideration.

(i) The Executive Directors may appoint such committees as they deem advisable. Membership of such committees need not be limited to governors or directors or their alternates.

Section 5.   *President and staff*

(a) The Executive Directors shall select a President who shall not be a governor or an executive director or an alternate for either. The President shall be Chairman of the Executive Directors, but shall have no vote except a deciding vote in case of an equal division. He may participate in meetings of the Board of Governors, but shall not vote at such meetings. The President shall cease to hold office when the Executive Directors so decide.

(b) The President shall be chief of the operating staff of the Bank and shall conduct, under the direction of the Executive Directors, the ordinary business of the Bank. Subject to the general control of the Executive Directors, he shall be responsible for the organization, appointment and dismissal of the officers and staff.

(c) The President, officers and staff of the Bank, in the discharge of their offices, owe their duty entirely to the Bank and to no other authority. Each member of the Bank shall respect the international character of this duty and shall refrain from all attempts to influence any of them in the discharge of their duties.

(d) In appointing the officers and staff the President shall, subject to the paramount importance of securing the highest standards of efficiency and of technical competence, pay due regard to the importance of recruiting personnel on as wide a geographical basis as possible.

Section 6.   *Advisory Council*

(a) There shall be an Advisory Council of not less than seven persons selected by the Board of Governors including representatives of banking, commercial, industrial, labor, and agricultural interests, and with as wide a national representation as possible. In those fields where specialized international organizations exist, the members of the Council representative of those fields shall be selected in agreement with such organizations. The Council shall advise the Bank on matters of general policy. The Council shall meet annually and on such other occasions as the Bank may request.

(b) Councilors shall serve for two years and may be reappointed. They shall be paid their reasonable expenses incurred on behalf of the Bank.

Section 7.   *Loan committees*

The committees required to report on loans under Article III, Section 4, shall be appointed by the Bank. Each such committee shall include an expert selected by the governor representing the member in whose territories the project is located and one or more members of the technical staff of the Bank.

Section 8.   *Relationship to other international organizations*

(a) The Bank, within the terms of this Agreement, shall cooperate with any general international organization and with public international organizations having specialized responsibilities in related fields. Any arrangements for such cooperation which would involve a modification of any provision of this Agreement may be effected only after amendment to this Agreement under Article VIII.

(b) In making decisions on applications for loans or guarantees relating to matters directly within the competence of any international organization of the types specified in the preceding paragraph and participated in primarily by members of the Bank, the Bank shall give consideration to the views and recommendations of such organization.

Section 9.   *Location of offices*

(a) The principal office of the Bank shall be located in the territory of the member holding the greatest number of shares.

(b) The Bank may establish agencies or branch offices in the territories of any member of the Bank.

Section 10.   *Regional offices and councils*

(a) The Bank may establish regional offices and determine the location of, and the areas to be covered by, each regional office.

(b) Each regional office shall be advised by a regional council representative of the entire area and selected in such manner as the Bank may decide.

Section 11.   *Depositories*

(a) Each member shall designate its central bank as a depository for all the Bank's holdings of its currency or, if it has no central bank, it shall designate such other institution as may be acceptable to the Bank.

(b) The Bank may hold other assets, including gold, in depositories designated by the five members having the largest number of shares and in such other designated depositories as the Bank may select. Initially, at least one-half of the gold holdings of the Bank shall be held in the depository designated by the member in whose territory the Bank has its principal office, and at least forty percent shall be held in the depositories designated by the remaining four members referred to above, each of such depositories to hold, initially, not less than the amount of gold paid on the shares of the member designating it. However, all transfers of gold by the Bank shall be made with due regard to the costs of transport and anticipated requirements of the Bank. In an emergency the Executive Directors may transfer all or any part of the Bank's gold holdings to any place where they can be adequately protected.

Section 12.   *Form of holdings of currency*

The Bank shall accept from any member, in place of any part of the member's currency, paid in to the Bank under Article II, Section 7 (i), or to meet amortization payments on loans made with such currency, and not needed by the Bank in its operations, notes or similar obligations issued by the Government of the member or the depository designated by such member, which shall be non-negotiable, non-interest-bearing and payable at their par value on demand by credit to the account of the Bank in the designated depository.

Section 13.   *Publication of reports and provision of information*

(a) The Bank shall publish an annual report containing an audited statement of its accounts and shall circulate to members at intervals of three months or less a summary statement of its financial position and a profit and loss statement showing the results of its operations.

(b) The Bank may publish such other reports as it deems desirable to carry out its purposes.

(c) Copies of all reports, statements and publications made under this section shall be distributed to members.

Section 14. *Allocation of net income*

(a) The Board of Governors shall determine annually what part of the Bank's net income, after making provision for reserves, shall be allocated to surplus and what part, if any, shall be distributed.

(b) If any part is distributed, up to two percent non-cumulative shall be paid, as a first charge against the distribution for any year, to each member on the basis of the average amount of the loans outstanding during the year made under Article IV, Section 1 (a) (i), out of currency corresponding to its subscription. If two percent is paid as a first charge, any balance remaining to be distributed shall be paid to all members in proportion to their shares. Payments to each member shall be made in its own currency, or if that currency is not available in other currency acceptable to the member. If such payments are made in currencies other than the member's own currency, the transfer of the currency and its use by the receiving member after payment shall be without restriction by the members.

ARTICLE VI. Withdrawal and Suspension of Membership:
Suspension of Operations

Section 1. *Right of members to withdraw*

Any member may withdraw from the Bank at any time by transmitting a notice in writing to the Bank at its principal office. Withdrawal shall become effective on the date such notice is received.

Section 2. *Suspension of membership*

If a member fails to fulfill any of its obligations to the Bank, the Bank may suspend its membership by decision of a majority of the Governors, exercising a majority of the total voting power. The member so suspended shall automatically cease to be a member one year from the date of its suspension unless a decision is taken by the same majority to restore the member to good standing.

While under suspension, a member shall not be entitled to exercise any rights under this Agreement, except the right of withdrawal, but shall remain subject to all obligations.

Section 3. *Cessation of membership in International Monetary Fund*

Any member which ceases to be a member of the International Monetary Fund shall automatically cease after three months to be a member of the Bank unless the Bank by three-fourths of the total voting power has agreed to allow it to remain a member.

Section 4. *Settlement of accounts with governments ceasing to be members*

(a) When a government ceases to be a member, it shall remain liable for its direct obligations to the Bank and for its contingent liabilities to the Bank so long as any part of the loans or guarantees contracted before it ceased to be a member are outstanding; but it shall cease to incur liabilities with respect to loans and guarantees entered into thereafter by the Bank and to share either in the income or the expenses of the Bank.

(b) At the time a government ceases to be a member, the Bank shall arrange for the repurchase of its shares as a part of the settlement of accounts with such government in accordance with the provisions of (c) and (d) below. For this purpose the repurchase price of the shares shall be the value shown by the books of the Bank on the day the government ceases to be a member.

(c) The payment for shares repurchased by the Bank under this section shall be governed by the following conditions:

(i) Any amount due to the government for its shares shall be withheld so long as the government, its central bank or any of its agencies remains liable, as borrower or guarantor, to the Bank and such amount may, at the option of the Bank, be applied on any such liability as it matures. No amount shall be withheld on account of the liability of the government resulting from its subscription for shares under Article II, Section 5 (ii). In any event, no amount due to a member for its shares shall be paid until six months after the date upon which the government ceases to be a member.

(ii) Payments for shares may be made from time to time, upon their surrender by the government, to the extent by which the amount due as the repurchase price in (b) above exceeds the aggregate of liabilities on loans and guarantees in (c) (i) above until the former member has received the full repurchase price.

(iii) Payments shall be made in the currency of the country receiving payment or at the option of the Bank in gold.

(iv) If losses are sustained by the Bank on any guarantees, participations in loans, or loans which were outstanding on the date when the government ceased to be a member, and the amount of such losses exceeds the amount of the reserve provided against losses on the date when the government ceased to be a member, such government shall be obligated to repay upon demand the amount by which the repurchase price of its shares would have been reduced, if the losses had been taken into account when the repurchase price was determined. In addition, the former member government shall remain liable on any call for unpaid subscriptions under Article II, Section 5 (ii), to the extent that it would have been required to respond if the impairment of capital had occurred and the call had been made at the time the repurchase price of its shares was determined.

(d) If the Bank suspends permanently its operations under Section 5 (b) of this Article, within six months of the date upon which any government ceases to be a member, all rights of such government shall be determined by the provisions of Section 5 of this Article.

Section 5.   *Suspension of operations and settlement of obligations*

(a) In an emergency the Executive Directors may suspend temporarily operations in respect of new loans and guarantees pending an opportunity for further consideration and action by the Board of Governors.

(b) The Bank may suspend permanently its operations in respect of new loans and guarantees by vote of a majority of the Governors, exercising a majority of the total voting power. After such suspension of operations the Bank shall forthwith cease all activities, except those incident to the orderly realization, conservation, and preservation of its assets and settlement of its obligations.

(c) The liability of all members for uncalled subscriptions to the capital stock of the Bank and in respect of the depreciation of their own currencies shall continue until all claims of creditors, including all contingent claims, shall have been discharged.

(d) All creditors holding direct claims shall be paid out of the assets of the Bank, and then out of payments to the Bank on calls on unpaid subscriptions. Before making any payments to creditors holding direct claims, the Executive Directors shall make such arrangements as are necessary, in their judgment, to insure a distribution to holders of contingent claims ratably with creditors holding direct claims.

(e) No distribution shall be made to members on account of their subscriptions to the capital stock of the Bank until
  (i) all liabilities to creditors have been discharged or provided for, and
  (ii) a majority of the Governors, exercising a majority of the total voting power, have decided to make a distribution.

(f) After a decision to make a distribution has been taken under (e) above, the Executive Directors may by a two-thirds majority vote make successive distributions of the assets of the Bank to members until all of the assets have been distributed. This distribution shall be subject to the prior settlement of all outstanding claims of the Bank against each member.

(g) Before any distribution of assets is made, the Executive Directors shall fix the proportionate share of each member according to the ratio of its shareholding to the total outstanding shares of the Bank.

(h) The Executive Directors shall value the assets to be distributed as at the date of distribution and then proceed to distribute in the following manner:
  (i) There shall be paid to each member in its own obligations or those of its official agencies or legal entities within its territories, insofar as they are available for distribution, an amount equivalent in value to its proportionate share of the total amount to be distributed.
  (ii) Any balance due to a member after payment has been made under (i) above shall be paid, in its own currency, insofar as it is held by the Bank, up to an amount equivalent in value to such balance.
  (iii) Any balance due to a member after payment has been made under (i) and (ii) above shall be paid in gold or currency acceptable to the member, insofar as they are held by the Bank, up to an amount equivalent in value to such balance.
  (iv) Any remaining assets held by the Bank after payments have been made to members under (i), (ii), and (iii) above shall be distributed *pro rata* among the members.

(i) Any member receiving assets distributed by the Bank in accordance with (h) above, shall enjoy the same rights with respect to such assets as the Bank enjoyed prior to their distribution.

ARTICLE VII. Status, Immunities and Privileges

Section 1. *Purposes of Article*

To enable the Bank to fulfill the functions with which it is entrusted, the status, immunities and privileges set forth in this Article shall be accorded to the Bank in the territories of each member.

Section 2. *Status of the Bank*

The Bank shall possess full juridical personality, and, in particular, the capacity:
   (i) to contract;
   (ii) to acquire and dispose of immovable and movable property;
   (iii) to institute legal proceedings.

Section 3. *Position of the Bank with regard to judicial process*

Actions may be brought against the Bank only in a court of competent juris- diction in the territories of a member in which the Bank has an office, has ap- pointed an agent for the purpose of accepting service or notice of process, or has issued or guaranteed securities. No actions shall, however, be brought by members or persons acting for or deriving claims from members. The property and assets of the Bank shall, wheresoever located and by whomsoever held, be immune from all forms of seizure, attachment or execution before the delivery of final judgment against the Bank.

Section 4. *Immunity of assets from seizure*

Property and assets of the Bank, wherever located and by whomsoever held, shall be immune from search, requisition, confiscation, expropriation or any other form of seizure by executive or legislative action.

Section 5. *Immunity of archives*

The archives of the Bank shall be inviolable.

Section 6. *Freedom of assets from restrictions*

To the extent necessary to carry out the operations provided for in this Agree- ment and subject to the provisions of this Agreement, all property and assets of the Bank shall be free from restrictions, regulations, controls and moratoria of any nature.

Section 7. *Privilege for communications*

The official communications of the Bank shall be accorded by each member the same treatment that it accords to the official communications of other members.

Section 8. *Immunities and privileges of officers and employees*

All governors, executive directors, alternates, officers and employees of the Bank
   (i) shall be immune from legal process with respect to acts performed by them in their official capacity except when the Bank waives this im- munity;
   (ii) not being local nationals, shall be accorded the same immunities from immigration restrictions, alien registration requirements and national service obligations and the same facilities as regards exchange restric- tions as are accorded by members to the representatives, officials, and employees of comparable rank of other members;

    (iii) shall be granted the same treatment in respect of travelling facilities as is accorded by members to representatives, officials and employees of comparable rank of other members.

Section 9.   *Immunities from taxation*

(a) The Bank, its assets, property, income and its operations and transactions authorized by this Agreement, shall be immune from all taxation and from all customs duties. The Bank shall also be immune from liability for the collection or payment of any tax or duty.

(b) No tax shall be levied on or in respect of salaries and emoluments paid by the Bank to executive directors, alternates, officials or employees of the Bank who are not local citizens, local subjects, or other local nationals.

(c) No taxation of any kind shall be levied on any obligation or security issued by the Bank (including any dividend or interest thereon) by whomsoever held—

    (i) which discriminates against such obligation or security solely because it is issued by the Bank; or

    (ii) if the sole jurisdictional basis for such taxation is the place or currency in which it is issued, made payable or paid, or the location of any office or place of business maintained by the Bank.

(d) No taxation of any kind shall be levied on any obligation or security guaranteed by the Bank (including any dividend or interest thereon) by whomsoever held—

    (i) which discriminates against such obligation or security solely because it is guaranteed by the Bank; or

    (ii) if the sole jurisdictional basis for such taxation is the location of any office or place of business maintained by the Bank.

Section 10.   *Application of Article*

Each member shall take such action as is necessary in its own territories for the purpose of making effective in terms of its own law the principles set forth in this Article and shall inform the Bank of the detailed action which it has taken.

Article VIII. Amendments

(a) Any proposal to introduce modifications in this Agreement, whether emanating from a member, a governor or the Executive Directors, shall be communicated to the Chairman of the Board of Governors who shall bring the proposal before the Board. If the proposed amendment is approved by the Board the Bank shall, by circular letter or telegram, ask all members whether they accept the proposed amendment. When three-fifths of the members, having four-fifths of the total voting power, have accepted the proposed amendments, the Bank shall certify the fact by formal communication addressed to all members.

(b) Notwithstanding (a) above, acceptance by all members is required in the case of any amendment modifying

    (i) the right to withdraw from the Bank provided in Article VI, Section 1;

    (ii) the right secured by Article II, Section 3 (c);

    (iii) the limitation on liability provided in Article II, Section 6.

(c) Amendments shall enter into force for all members three months after the date of the formal communication unless a shorter period is specified in the circular letter or telegram.

ARTICLE IX. Interpretation

(a) Any question of interpretation of the provisions of this Agreement arising between any member and the Bank or between any members of the Bank shall be submitted to the Executive Directors for their decision. If the question particularly affects any member not entitled to appoint an executive director, it shall be entitled to representation in accordance with Article V, Section 4 (h).

(b) In any case where the Executive Directors have given a decision under (a) above, any member may require that the question be referred to the Board of Governors, whose decision shall be final. Pending the result of the reference to the Board, the Bank may, so far as it deems necessary, act on the basis of the decision of the Executive Directors.

(c) Whenever a disagreement arises between the Bank and a country which has ceased to be a member, or between the Bank and any member during the permanent suspension of the Bank, such disagreement shall be submitted to arbitration by a tribunal of three arbitrators, one appointed by the Bank, another by the country involved and an umpire who, unless the parties otherwise agree, shall be appointed by the President of the Permanent Court of International Justice or such other authority as may have been prescribed by regulation adopted by the Bank. The umpire shall have full power to settle all questions of procedure in any case where the parties are in disagreement with respect thereto.

ARTICLE X. Approval Deemed Given

Whenever the approval of any member is required before any act may be done by the Bank, except in Article VIII, approval shall be deemed to have been given unless the member presents an objection within such reasonable period as the Bank may fix in notifying the member of the proposed act.

ARTICLE XI. Final Provisions

Section 1. *Entry into force*

This Agreement shall enter into force when it has been signed on behalf of governments whose minimum subscriptions comprise not less than sixty-five percent of the total subscriptions set forth in Schedule A and when the instruments referred to in Section 2 (a) of this Article have been deposited on their behalf, but in no event shall this Agreement enter into force before May 1, 1945.

Section 2. *Signature*

(a) Each government on whose behalf this Agreement is signed shall deposit with the Government of the United States of America an instrument setting forth that it has accepted this Agreement in accordance with its law and has taken all steps necessary to enable it to carry out all of its obligations under this Agreement.

(b) Each government shall become a member of the Bank as from the date of the deposit on its behalf of the instrument referred to in (a) above, except that no government shall become a member before this Agreement enters into force under Section 1 of this Article.

(c) The Government of the United States of America shall inform the governments of all countries whose names are set forth in Schedule A, and all governments whose membership is approved in accordance with Article II, Section 1 (b), of all signatures of this Agreement and of the deposit of all instruments referred to in (a) above.

(d) At the time this Agreement is signed on its behalf, each government shall transmit to the Government of the United States of America one one-hundredth of one percent of the price of each share in gold or United States dollars for the purpose of meeting administrative expenses of the Bank. This payment shall be credited on account of the payment to be made in accordance with Article II, Section 8 (a). The Government of the United States of America shall hold such funds in a special deposit account and shall transmit them to the Board of Governors of the Bank when the initial meeting has been called under Section 3 of this Article. If this Agreement has not come into force by December 31, 1945, the Government of the United States of America shall return such funds to the governments that transmitted them.

(e) This Agreement shall remain open for signature at Washington on behalf of the governments of the countries whose names are set forth in Schedule A until December 31, 1945.

(f) After December 31, 1945, this Agreement shall be open for signature on behalf of the government of any country whose membership has been approved in accordance with Article II, Section 1 (b).

(g) By their signature of this Agreement, all governments accept it both on their own behalf and in respect of all their colonies, overseas territories, all territories under their protection, suzerainty, or authority and all territories in respect of which they exercise a mandate.

(h) In the case of governments whose metropolitan territories have been under enemy occupation, the deposit of the instrument referred to in (a) above may be delayed until one hundred and eighty days after the date on which these territories have been liberated. If, however, it is not deposited by any such government before the expiration of this period, the signature affixed on behalf of that government shall become void and the portion of its subscription paid under (d) above shall be returned to it.

(i) Paragraphs (d) and (h) shall come into force with regard to each signatory government as from the date of its signature.

Section 3.   *Inauguration of the Bank*

(a) As soon as this Agreement enters into force under Section 1 of this Article, each member shall appoint a governor and the member to whom the largest number of shares is allocated in Schedule A shall call the first meeting of the Board of Governors.

(b) At the first meeting of the Board of Governors, arrangements shall be made for the selection of provisional executive directors. The governments of the five countries, to which the largest number of shares are allocated in Schedule A, shall appoint provisional executive directors. If one or more of such governments have not become members, the executive directorships which they would be entitled to fill shall remain vacant until they become members, or until January 1, 1946, whichever is the earlier. Seven provisional executive directors shall be elected in accordance with the provisions of Schedule B and shall remain in office until the date of the first regular election of executive directors which shall be held as soon as practicable after January 1, 1946.

(c) The Board of Governors may delegate to the provisional executive directors any powers except those which may not be delegated to the Executive Directors.

(d) The Bank shall notify members when it is ready to commence operations.

DONE at Washington, in a single copy which shall remain deposited in the archives of the Government of the United States of America, which shall transmit certified copies to all governments whose names are set forth in Schedule A and to all governments whose membership is approved in accordance with Article II, Section 1 (b).

Schedule A. Subscriptions
Amounts expressed in millions of U.S. dollars

Australia	200	France	450	Paraguay	0.8
Belgium	225	Greece	25	Peru	17.5
Bolivia	7	Guatemala	2	Philippine	
Brazil	105	Haiti	2	Commonwealth	15
Canada	325	Honduras	1	Poland	125
Chile	35	Iceland	1	Union of South	
China	600	India	400	Africa	100
Colombia	35	Iran	24	Union of	
Costa Rica	2	Iraq	6	Soviet Socialist	
Cuba	35	Liberia	0.5	Republics	1,200
Czechoslovakia	125	Luxembourg	10	United Kingdom	1,300
Denmark[a]	—	Mexico	65	United States	3,175
Dominican Republic	2	Netherlands	275	Uruguay	10.5
Ecuador	3.2	New Zealand	50	Venezuela	10.5
Egypt	40	Nicaragua	0.8	Yugoslavia	40
El Salvador	1	Norway	50		
Ethiopia	3	Panama	0.2	Total	9,100

a. The quota of Denmark shall be determined by the Bank after Denmark accepts membership in accordance with these Articles of Agreement.

Schedule B. Election of Executive Directors

1. The election of the elective executive directors shall be by ballot of the Governors eligible to vote under Article V, Section 4 (b).

2. In balloting for the elective executive directors, each governor eligible to vote shall cast for one person all of the votes to which the member appointing him is entitled under Section 3 of Article V. The seven persons receiving the greatest number of votes shall be executive directors, except that no person who receives less than fourteen percent of the total of the votes which can be cast (eligible votes) shall be considered elected.

3. When seven persons are not elected on the first ballot, a second ballot shall be held in which the person who received the lowest number of votes shall be ineligible for election and in which there shall vote only (a) those governors who voted in the first ballot for a person not elected and (b) those governors whose votes for a person elected are deemed under 4 below to have raised the votes cast for that person above fifteen percent of the eligible votes.

4. In determining whether the votes cast by a governor are to be deemed to have raised the total of any person above fifteen percent of the eligible votes, the fifteen percent shall be deemed to include, first, the votes of the governor casting the largest number of votes for such person, then the votes of the governor casting the next largest number, and so on until fifteen percent is reached.

5. Any governor, part of whose votes must be counted in order to raise the total of any person above fourteen percent shall be considered as casting all of his votes for such person even if the total votes for such person thereby exceed fifteen percent.

6. If, after the second ballot, seven persons have not been elected, further ballots shall be held on the same principles until seven persons have been elected, provided that after six persons are elected, the seventh may be elected by a simple majority of the remaining votes and shall be deemed to have been elected by all such votes.

A-2. Excerpts from Articles of Agreement of the International Finance Corporation[1]

The Governments on whose behalf this Agreement is signed agree as follows:

INTRODUCTORY ARTICLE

The International Finance Corporation (hereinafter called the Corporation) is established and shall operate in accordance with the following provisions:

ARTICLE I. Purpose

The purpose of the Corporation is to further economic development by encouraging the growth of productive private enterprise in member countries, particularly in the less developed areas, thus supplementing the activities of the International Bank for Reconstruction and Development (hereinafter called the Bank). In carrying out this purpose, the Corporation shall:

(i) in association with private investors, assist in financing the establishment, improvement and expansion of productive private enterprises which would contribute to the development of its member countries by making investments, without guarantee of repayment by the member government concerned, in cases where sufficient private capital is not available on reasonable terms;

(ii) seek to bring together investment opportunities, domestic and foreign private capital, and experienced management; and

(iii) seek to stimulate, and to help create conditions conducive to, the flow of private capital, domestic and foreign, into productive investment in member countries.

1. Effective July 20, 1956, as amended by resolutions effective Sept. 21, 1961, and Sept. 1, 1965. The omitted provisions in most, but not all cases, are the same in substance as the corresponding provisions in the Bank's Articles of Agreement.

The Corporation shall be guided in all its decisions by the provisions of this Article.

ARTICLE II. Membership and Capital

SECTION 1. *Membership*

(a) The original members of the Corporation shall be those members of the Bank listed in Schedule A hereto which shall, on or before the date specified in Article IX, Section 2(c), accept membership in the Corporation.

(b) Membership shall be open to other members of the Bank at such times and in accordance with such terms as may be prescribed by the Corporation.

SECTION 2. *Capital Stock*

(a) The authorized capital stock of the Corporation shall be $100,000,000, in terms of United States dollars.[2]

(b) The authorized capital stock shall be divided into 100,000 shares having a par value of one thousand United States dollars each. Any such shares not initially subscribed by original members shall be available for subsequent subscription in accordance with Section 3(d) of this Article.

(c) The amount of capital stock at any time authorized may be increased by the Board of Governors as follows:

(i) by a majority of the votes cast, in case such increase is necessary for the purpose of issuing shares of capital stock on initial subscription by members other than original members, provided that the aggregate of any increases authorized pursuant to this subparagraph shall not exceed 10,000 shares;

(ii) in any other case, by a three-fourths majority of the total voting power.

(d) In case of an increase authorized pursuant to paragraph (c) (ii) above, each member shall have a reasonable opportunity to subscribe, under such conditions as the Corporation shall decide, to a proportion of the increase of stock equivalent to the proportion which its stock theretofore subscribed bears to the total capital stock of the Corporation, but no member shall be obligated to subscribe to any part of the increased capital.

(e) Issuance of shares of stock, other than those subscribed either on initial subscription or pursuant to paragraph (d) above, shall require a three-fourths majority of the total voting power.

(f) Shares of stock of the Corporation shall be available for subscription only by, and shall be issued only to, members.

SECTION 3. *Subscriptions*

(a) Each original member shall subscribe to the number of shares of stock set forth opposite its name in Schedule A. The number of shares of stock to be subscribed by other members shall be determined by the Corporation.

(b) Shares of stock initially subscribed by original members shall be issued at par.

(c) The initial subscription of each original member shall be payable in full within 30 days after either the date on which the Corporation shall begin operations pursuant to Article IX, Section 3(b), or the date on which such original

---

2. On September 3, 1963, the authorized capital stock was increased to 110,000 shares of $1,000 each.

member becomes a member, whichever shall be later, or at such date thereafter as the Corporation shall determine. Payment shall be made in gold or United States dollars in response to a call by the Corporation which shall specify the place or places of payment.

(d) The price and other terms of subscription of shares of stock to be subscribed, otherwise than on initial subscription by original members, shall be determined by the Corporation.

SECTION 4.   *Limitation on Liability*

No member shall be liable, by reason of its membership, for obligations of the Corporation.

SECTION 5.   *Restriction on Transfers and Pledges of Shares*

Shares of stock shall not be pledged or encumbered in any manner whatever, and shall be transferable only to the Corporation.

ARTICLE III. Operations

SECTION 1.   *Financing Operations*

The Corporation may make investments of its funds in productive private enterprises in the territories of its members. The existence of a government or other public interest in such an enterprise shall not necessarily preclude the Corporation from making an investment therein.

SECTION 2.   *Forms of Financing*[3]

The Corporation may make investments of its funds in such form or forms as it may deem appropriate in the circumstances (as amended Sept. 21, 1961).

SECTION 3.   *Operational Principles*

The operations of the Corporation shall be conducted in accordance with the following principles:

(i)   the Corporation shall not undertake any financing for which in its opinion sufficient private capital could be obtained on reasonable terms;

(ii) the Corporation shall not finance an enterprise in the territories of any member if the member objects to such financing;

(iii) the Corporation shall impose no conditions that the proceeds of any financing by it shall be spent in the territories of any particular country;

(iv) the Corporation shall not assume responsibility for managing any enterprise in which it has invested and shall not exercise voting rights for such purpose or for any other purpose which, in its opinion, properly is within the scope of managerial control (as amended Sept. 21, 1961);[4]

3. Originally, "(a) The Corporation's financing shall not take the form of investments in capital stock. Subject to the foregoing, the Corporation may make investments of its funds in such form or forms as it may deem appropriate in the circumstances, including (but without limitation) investments according to the holder thereof the right to participate in earnings and the right to subscribe to, or to convert the investment into, capital stock.

(b) The Corporation shall not itself exercise any right to subscribe to, or to convert any investment into, capital stock."

4. Originally, "(iv) The Corporation shall not assume responsibility for managing any enterprise in which it has invested."

(v) the Corporation shall undertake its financing on terms and conditions which it considers appropriate, taking into account the requirements of the enterprise, the risks being undertaken by the Corporation and the terms and conditions normally obtained by private investors for similar financing;

(vi) the Corporation shall seek to revolve its funds by selling its investments to private investors whenever it can appropriately do so on satisfactory terms;

(vii) the Corporation shall seek to maintain a reasonable diversification in its investments.

SECTION 4. *Protection of Interests*

Nothing in this Agreement shall prevent the Corporation, in the event of actual or threatened default on any of its investments, actual or threatened insolvency of the enterprise in which such investment shall have been made, or other situations which, in the opinion of the Corporation, threaten to jeopardize such investment, from taking such action and exercising such rights as it may deem necessary for the protection of its interests.

SECTION 5. *Applicability of Certain Foreign Exchange Restrictions*

[omitted]

SECTION 6. *Miscellaneous Operations*

In addition to the operations specified elsewhere in this Agreement, the Corporation shall have the power to:

(i) borrow funds, and in that connection to furnish such collateral or other security therefor as it shall determine; provided, however, that before making a public sale of its obligations in the markets of a member, the Corporation shall have obtained the approval of that member and of the member in whose currency the obligations are to be denominated; if and so long as the Corporation shall be indebted on loans from or guaranteed by the Bank, the total amount outstanding of borrowings incurred or guarantees given by the Corporation shall not be increased if, at the time or as a result thereof, the aggregate amount of debt (including the guarantee of any debt) incurred by the Corporation from any source and then outstanding shall exceed an amount equal to four times its unimpaired subscribed capital and surplus;[5]

(ii) invest funds not needed in its financing operations in such obligations as it may determine and invest funds held by it for pension or similar purposes in any marketable securities, all without being subject to the restrictions imposed by other sections of this Article;

(iii) guarantee securities in which it has invested in order to facilitate their sale;

(iv) buy and sell securities it has issued or guaranteed or in which it has invested;

(v) exercise such other powers incidental to its business as shall be necessary or desirable in furtherance of its purposes.

---

5. Last clause added by amendment effective Sept. 1, 1965.

SECTION 7.   *Valuation of Currencies* [omitted]

SECTION 8.   *Warning To Be Placed on Securities* [omitted]

SECTION 9.   *Political Activity Prohibited* [omitted]

ARTICLE IV.   Organization and Management

SECTION 1.   *Structure of the Corporation*

The Corporation shall have a Board of Governors, a Board of Directors, a Chairman of the Board of Directors, a President and such other officers and staff to perform such duties as the Corporation may determine.

SECTION 2.   *Board of Governors*

(a) All the powers of the Corporation shall be vested in the Board of Governors.

(b) Each Governor and Alternate Governor of the Bank appointed by a member of the Bank which is also a member of the Corporation shall *ex officio* be a Governor or Alternate Governor, respectively, of the Corporation. No Alternate Governor may vote except in the absence of his principal. The Board of Governors shall select one of the Governors as Chairman of the Board of Governors. Any Governor or Alternate Governor shall cease to hold office if the member by which he was appointed shall cease to be a member of the Corporation.

(c) The Board of Governors may delegate to the Board of Directors authority to exercise any of its powers, except the power to:

   (i)   admit new members and determine the conditions of their admission;

   (ii)   increase or decrease the capital stock;

   (iii) suspend a member;

   (iv)   decide appeals from interpretations of this Agreement given by the Board of Directors;

   (v)   make arrangements to cooperate with other international organizations (other than informal arrangements of a temporary and administrative character);

   (vi)   decide to suspend permanently the operations of the Corporation and to distribute its assets;

   (vii) declare dividends;

   (viii) amend this Agreement.

(d) The Board of Governors shall hold an annual meeting and such other meetings as may be provided for by the Board of Governors or called by the Board of Directors.

(e) The annual meeting of the Board of Governors shall be held in conjunction with the annual meeting of the Board of Governors of the Bank.

(f) – (i) [omitted]

SECTION 3.   *Voting*

(a) Each member shall have two hundred fifty votes plus one additional vote for each share of stock held.

(b) Except as otherwise expressly provided, all matters before the Corporation shall be decided by a majority of the votes cast.

SECTION 4.   *Board of Directors*

(a) [omitted]

(b) The Board of Directors of the Corporation shall be composed *ex officio* of each Executive Director of the Bank who shall have been either (i) appointed by a member of the Bank which is also a member of the Corporation, or (ii) elected in an election in which the votes of at least one member of the Bank which is also a member of the Corporation shall have counted toward his election. The Alternate to each such Executive Director of the Bank shall *ex officio* be an Alternate Director of the Corporation. Any Director shall cease to hold office if the member by which he was appointed, or if all the members whose votes counted toward his election, shall cease to be members of the Corporation.

(c) − (g) [omitted]

SECTION 5. *Chairman, President and Staff*

(a) The President of the Bank shall be *ex officio* Chairman of the Board of Directors of the Corporation, but shall have no vote except a deciding vote in case of an equal division. He may participate in meetings of the Board of Governors but shall not vote at such meetings.

(b) The President of the Corporation shall be appointed by the Board of Directors on the recommendation of the Chairman. The President shall be chief of the operating staff of the Corporation. Under the direction of the Board of Directors and the general supervision of the Chairman, he shall conduct the ordinary business of the Corporation and under their general control shall be responsible for the organization, appointment and dismissal of the officers and staff. The President may participate in meetings of the Board of Directors but shall not vote at such meetings. The President shall cease to hold office by decision of the Board of Directors in which the Chairman concurs. . . .

(c) − (d) [omitted]

SECTION 6. *Relationship to the Bank*

(a) The Corporation shall be an entity separate and distinct from the Bank and the funds of the Corporation shall be kept separate and apart from those of the Bank.[6] The provisions of this Section shall not prevent the Corporation from making arrangements with the Bank regarding facilities, personnel and services and arrangements for reimbursement of administrative expenses paid in the first instance by either organization on behalf of the other.

(b) [omitted]

SECTION 7. *Relations With Other International Organizations* [omitted]

SECTION 8. *Location of Offices* [omitted]

SECTION 9. *Depositories* [omitted]

SECTION 10. *Channel of Communication* [omitted]

SECTION 11. *Publication of Reports and Provision of Information* [omitted]

SECTION 12. *Dividends* [omitted]

ARTICLE V. Withdrawal; Suspension of Membership; Suspension of Operations

SECTION 1. *Withdrawal by Members* [omitted]

6. The original text included the following: "The Corporation shall not lend to or borrow from the Bank."

SECTION 2.   *Suspension of Membership* [omitted]

SECTION 3.   *Suspension or Cessation of Membership in the Bank*
Any member which is suspended from membership in, or ceases to be a member
of, the Bank shall automatically be suspended from membership in, or cease to
be a member of, the Corporation, as the case may be.

SECTION 4.   *Rights and Duties of Governments Ceasing To Be Members*
[omitted]

SECTION 5.   *Suspension of Operations and Settlement of Obligations*
[omitted]

Schedule A. Subscriptions to Capital Stock
of the International Finance Corporation

Amounts expressed in U.S. dollars

Country	Number of shares	Amount	Country	Number of shares	Amount
Australia	2,215	2,215,000	Iran	372	372,000
Austria	554	554,000	Iraq	67	67,000
Belgium	2,492	2,492,000	Israel	50	50,000
Bolivia	78	78,000	Italy	1,994	1,994,000
Brazil	1,163	1,163,000	Japan	2,769	2,769,000
Burma	166	166,000	Jordan	33	33,000
Canada	3,600	3,600,000	Lebanon	50	50,000
Ceylon	166	166,000	Luxembourg	111	111,000
Chile	388	388,000	Mexico	720	720,000
China	6,646	6,646,000	Netherlands	3,046	3,046,000
Colombia	388	388,000	Nicaragua	9	9,000
Costa Rica	22	22,000	Norway	554	554,000
Cuba	388	388,000	Pakistan	1,108	1,108,000
Denmark	753	753,000	Panama	2	2,000
Dominican			Paraguay	16	16,000
Republic	22	22,000	Peru	194	194,000
Ecuador	35	35,000	Philippines	166	166,000
Egypt	590	590,000	Sweden	1,108	1,108,000
El Salvador	11	11,000	Syria	72	72,000
Ethiopia	33	33,000	Thailand	139	139,000
Finland	421	421,000	Turkey	476	476,000
France	5,815	5,815,000	Union of South		
Germany	3,655	3,655,000	Africa	1,108	1,108,000
Greece	277	277,000	United Kingdom	14,400	14,400,000
Guatemala	22	22,000	United States	35,168	35,168,000
Haiti	22	22,000	Uruguay	116	116,000
Honduras	11	11,000	Venezuela	116	116,000
Iceland	11	11,000	Yugoslavia	443	443,000
India	4,431	4,431,000			
Indonesia	1,218	1,218,000	Total	100,000	100,000,000

ARTICLE VI. Status, Immunities and Privileges
[omitted]

ARTICLE VII. Amendments
[omitted]

ARTICLE VIII. Interpretation and Arbitration
[omitted]

ARTICLE IX. Final Provisions

SECTION 1. *Entry into Force*

This Agreement shall enter into force when it has been signed on behalf of not less than 30 governments whose subscriptions comprise not less than 75 percent of the total subscriptions set forth in Schedule A [page 786] and when the instruments referred to in Section 2(a) of this Article have been deposited on their behalf, but in no event shall this Agreement enter into force before October 1, 1955.

SECTION 2. *Signature* [omitted]

SECTION 3. *Inauguration of the Corporation* [omitted]

A-3. Excerpts from Articles of Agreement of the International Development Association[1]

The Governments on whose behalf this Agreement is signed,
Considering:

That mutual cooperation for constructive economic purposes, healthy development of the world economy and balanced growth of international trade foster international relationships conducive to the maintenance of peace and world prosperity;

That an acceleration of economic development which will promote higher standards of living and economic and social progress in the less-developed countries is desirable not only in the interests of those countries but also in the interests of the international community as a whole;

That achievement of these objectives would be facilitated by an increase in the international flow of capital, public and private, to assist in the development of the resources of the less-developed countries, do hereby agree as follows:

INTRODUCTORY ARTICLE

The INTERNATIONAL DEVELOPMENT ASSOCIATION (hereinafter called "the Association") is established and shall operate in accordance with the following provisions:

1. Effective September 24, 1960. The omitted provisions in most, but not all, cases are the same in substance as the corresponding provisions in the Bank's Articles of Agreement.

ARTICLE I. Purposes

The purposes of the Association are to promote economic development, increase productivity and thus raise standards of living in the less-developed areas of the world included within the Association's membership, in particular by providing finance to meet their important developmental requirements on terms which are more flexible and bear less heavily on the balance of payments than those of conventional loans, thereby furthering the developmental objectives of the International Bank for Reconstruction and Development (hereinafter called "the Bank") and supplementing its activities.

The Association shall be guided in all its decisions by the provisions of this Article.

ARTICLE II. Membership; Initial Subscriptions

SECTION 1. *Membership*

(a) The original members of the Association shall be those members of the Bank listed in Schedule A hereto which, on or before the date specified in Article XI, Section 2 (c), accept membership in the Association.

(b) Membership shall be open to other members of the Bank at such times and in accordance with such terms as the Association may determine.

SECTION 2. *Initial Subscriptions*

(a) Upon accepting membership, each member shall subscribe funds in the amount assigned to it. Such subscriptions are herein referred to as initial subscriptions.

(b) The initial subscription assigned to each original member shall be in the amount set forth opposite its name in Schedule A, expressed in terms of United States dollars of the weight and fineness in effect on January 1, 1960.

(c) Ten percent of the initial subscription of each original member shall be payable in gold or freely convertible currency as follows: fifty percent within thirty days after the date on which the Association shall begin operations pursuant to Article XI, Section 4, or on the date on which the original member becomes a member, whichever shall be later; twelve and one-half percent one year after the beginning of operations of the Association; and twelve and one-half percent each year thereafter at annual intervals until the ten percent portion of the initial subscription shall have been paid in full.

(d) The remaining ninety percent of the initial subscription of each original member shall be payable in gold or freely convertible currency in the case of members listed in Part I of Schedule A, and in the currency of the subscribing member in the case of members listed in Part II of Schedule A. This ninety percent portion of initial subscriptions of original members shall be payable in five equal annual instalments as follows: the first such instalment within thirty days after the date on which the Association shall begin operations pursuant to Article XI, Section 4, or on the date on which the original member becomes a member, whichever shall be later; the second instalment one year after the beginning of operations of the Association, and succeeding instalments each year thereafter at annual intervals until the ninety percent portion of the initial subscription shall have been paid in full.

(e) The Association shall accept from any member, in place of any part of the member's currency paid in or payable by the member under the preceding subsection (d) or under Section 2 of Article IV and not needed by the Association in its operations, notes or similar obligations issued by the government of the member or the depository designated by such member, which shall be non-negotiable, non-interest-bearing and payable at their par value on demand to the account of the Association in the designated depository.

(f) − (h) [omitted]

SECTION 3.   *Limitation on Liability* [omitted]

ARTICLE III. Additions to Resources

SECTION 1.   *Additional Subscriptions*

(a) The Association shall at such time as it deems appropriate in the light of the schedule for completion of payments on initial subscriptions of original members, and at intervals of approximately five years thereafter, review the adequacy of its resources and, if it deems desirable, shall authorize a general increase in subscriptions. Notwithstanding the foregoing, general or individual increases in subscriptions may be authorized at any time; provided that an individual increase shall be considered only at the request of the member involved. Subscriptions pursuant to this Section are herein referred to as additional subscriptions.

(b) Subject to the provisions of paragraph (c) below, when additional subscriptions are authorized, the amounts authorized for subscription and the terms and conditions relating thereto shall be as determined by the Association.

(c) When any additional subscription is authorized, each member shall be given an opportunity to subscribe, under such conditions as shall be reasonably determined by the Association, an amount which will enable it to maintain its relative voting power, but no member shall be obligated to subscribe.

(d) All decisions under this Section shall be made by a two-thirds majority of the total voting power.

SECTION 2.   *Supplementary Resources Provided by a Member in the Currency of Another Member*

(a) The Association may enter into arrangements, on such terms and conditions consistent with the provisions of this Agreement as may be agreed upon, to receive from any member, in addition to the amounts payable by such member on account of its initial or any additional subscription, supplementary resources in the currency of another member, provided that the Association shall not enter into any such arrangement unless the Association is satisfied that the member whose currency is involved agrees to the use of such currency as supplementary resources and to the terms and conditions governing such use. The arrangements under which any such resources are received may include provisions regarding the disposition of earnings on the resources and regarding the disposition of the resources in the event that the member providing them ceases to be a member or the Association permanently suspends its operations.

(b) The Association shall deliver to the contributing member a Special Development Certificate setting forth the amount and currency of the resources so contributed and the terms and conditions of the arrangement relating to such resources. A Special Development Certificate shall not carry any voting rights and shall be transferable only to the Association.

(c) Nothing in this Section shall preclude the Association from accepting resources from a member in its own currency on such terms as may be agreed upon.

ARTICLE IV. Currencies

SECTION 1.   *Use of Currencies*

(a) Currency of any member listed in Part II of Schedule A, whether or not freely convertible, received by the Association pursuant to Article II, Section 2(d), in payment of the ninety percent portion payable thereunder in the currency of such member, and currency of such member derived therefrom as principal, interest or other charges, may be used by the Association for administrative expenses incurred by the Association in the territories of such member and, insofar as consistent with sound monetary policies, in payment for goods and services produced in the territories of such member and required for projects financed by the Association and located in such territories; and in addition when and to the extent justified by the economic and financial situation of the member concerned as determined by agreement between the member and the Association, such currency shall be freely convertible or otherwise usable for projects financed by the Association and located outside the territories of the member.

(b) The usability of currencies received by the Association in payment of subscriptions other than initial subscriptions of original members, and currencies derived therefrom as principal, interest or other charges, shall be governed by the terms and conditions on which such subscriptions are authorized.

(c) The usability of currencies received by the Association as supplementary resources other than subscriptions, and currencies derived therefrom as principal, interest or other charges, shall be governed by the terms of the arrangements pursuant to which such currencies are received.

(d) All other currencies received by the Association may be freely used and exchanged by the Association and shall not be subject to any restriction by the member whose currency is used or exchanged; provided that the foregoing shall not preclude the Association from entering into any arrangements with the member in whose territories any project financed by the Association is located restricting the use by the Association of such member's currency received as principal, interest or other charges in connection with such financing.

(e) The Association shall take appropriate steps to ensure that, over reasonable intervals of time, the portions of the subscriptions paid under Article II, Section 2(d) by members listed in Part I of Schedule A shall be used by the Association on an approximately *pro rata* basis, provided, however, that such portions of such subscriptions as are paid in gold or in a currency other than that of the subscribing member may be used more rapidly.

SECTION 2.   *Maintenance of Value of Currency Holdings*

(a) Whenever the par value of a member's currency is reduced or the foreign exchange value of a member's currency has, in the opinion of the Association, depreciated to a significant extent within that member's territories, the member shall pay to the Association within a reasonable time an additional amount of its own currency sufficient to maintain the value, as of the time of subscription, of the amount of the currency of such member paid in to the Association by the member under Article II, Section 2(d), and currency furnished under the provisions of the present paragraph, whether or not such currency is held in the form of notes accepted pursuant to Article II, Section 2(e), provided, however, that the foregoing shall apply only so long as and to the extent that such currency shall not have been initially disbursed or exchanged for the currency of another member.

(b) Whenever the par value of a member's currency is increased, or the foreign exchange value of a member's currency has, in the opinion of the Association, appreciated to a significant extent within that member's territories, the Association shall return to such member within a reasonable time an amount of that member's currency equal to the increase in the value of the amount of such currency to which the provisions of paragraph (a) of this Section are applicable.

(c) The provisions of the preceding paragraphs may be waived by the Association when a uniform proportionate change in the par value of the currencies of all its members is made by the International Monetary Fund.

(d) Amounts furnished under the provisions of paragraph (a) of this Section to maintain the value of any currency shall be convertible and usable to the same extent as such currency.

Article V. Operations

Section 1. *Use of Resources and Conditions of Financing*

(a) The Association shall provide financing to further development in the less-developed areas of the world included within the Association's membership.

(b) Financing provided by the Association shall be for purposes which in the opinion of the Association are of high developmental priority in the light of the needs of the area or areas concerned and, except in special circumstances, shall be for specific projects.

(c) The Association shall not provide financing if in its opinion such financing is available from private sources on terms which are reasonable for the recipient or could be provided by a loan of the type made by the Bank.

(d) The Association shall not provide financing except upon the recommendation of a competent committee, made after a careful study of the merits of the proposal. Each such committee shall be appointed by the Association and shall include a nominee of the Governor or Governors representing the member or members in whose territories the project under consideration is located and one or more members of the technical staff of the Association. The requirement that the committee include the nominee of a Governor or Governors shall not apply in the case of financing provided to a public international or regional organization.

(e) The Association shall not provide financing for any project if the member in whose territories the project is located objects to such financing, except that it shall not be necessary for the Association to assure itself that individual members do not object in the case of financing provided to a public international or regional organization.

(f) The Association shall impose no conditions that the proceeds of its financing shall be spent in the territories of any particular member or members. The foregoing shall not preclude the Association from complying with any restrictions on the use of funds imposed in accordance with the provisions of these Articles, including restrictions attached to supplementary resources pursuant to agreement between the Association and the contributor.

(g) The Association shall make arrangements to ensure that the proceeds of any financing are used only for the purposes for which the financing was provided, with due attention to considerations of economy, efficiency and competitive international trade and without regard to political or other noneconomic influences or considerations.

(h) Funds to be provided under any financing operation shall be made available to the recipient only to meet expenses in connection with the project as they are actually incurred.

SECTION 2.   *Form and Terms of Financing*

(a) Financing by the Association shall take the form of loans. The Association may, however, provide other financing, either

  (i)   out of funds subscribed pursuant to Article III, Section 1, and funds derived therefrom as principal, interest or other charges, if the authorization for such subscriptions expressly provides for such financing; or

 (ii)   in special circumstances, out of supplementary resources furnished to the Association, and funds derived therefrom as principal, interest or other charges, if the arrangements under which such resources are furnished expressly authorize such financing.

(b) Subject to the foregoing paragraph, the Association may provide financing in such forms and on such terms as it may deem appropriate, having regard to the economic position and prospects of the area or areas concerned and to the nature and requirements of the project.

(c) The Association may provide financing to a member, the government of a territory included within the Association's membership, a political subdivision of any of the foregoing, a public or private entity in the territories of a member or members, or to a public international or regional organization.

(d) In the case of a loan to an entity other than a member, the Association may, in its discretion, require a suitable governmental or other guarantee or guarantees.

(e) The Association, in special cases, may make foreign exchange available for local expenditures.

SECTION 3.   *Modifications of Terms of Financing*

The Association may, when and to the extent it deems appropriate in the light of all relevant circumstances, including the financial and economic situation and prospects of the member concerned, and on such conditions as it may determine, agree to a relaxation or other modification of the terms on which any of its financing shall have been provided.

SECTION 4.   *Cooperation with Other International Organizations and Members Providing Development Assistance* [omitted]

SECTION 5.   *Miscellaneous Operations*

In addition to the operations specified elsewhere in this Agreement, the Association may:

  (i)   borrow funds with the approval of the member in whose currency the loan is denominated;

(ii) guarantee securities in which it has invested in order to facilitate their sale;

(iii) buy and sell securities it has issued or guaranteed or in which it has invested;

(iv) in special cases, guarantee loans from other sources for purposes not inconsistent with the provisions of these Articles;

(v) provide technical assistance and advisory services at the request of a member; and

(vi) exercise such other powers incidental to its operations as shall be necessary or desirable in furtherance of its purposes.

SECTION 6. *Political Activity Prohibited* [omitted]

ARTICLE VI. Organization and Management

SECTION 1. *Structure of the Association*

The Association shall have a Board of Governors, Executive Directors, a President and such other officers and staff to perform such duties as the Association may determine.

SECTION 2. *Board of Governors* [omitted]

SECTION 3. *Voting*

(a) Each original member shall, in respect of its initial subscription, have 500 votes plus one additional vote for each $5,000 of its initial subscription. Subscriptions other than initial subscriptions of original members shall carry such voting rights as the Board of Governors shall determine pursuant to the provisions of Article II, Section 1 (b) or Article III, Section 1 (b) and (c), as the case may be. Additions to resources other than subscriptions under Article II, Section 1 (b) and additional subscriptions under Article III, Section 1, shall not carry voting rights.

(b) Except as otherwise specifically provided, all matters before the Association shall be decided by a majority of the votes cast.

SECTION 4. *Executive Directors* [omitted]

SECTION 5. *President and Staff*

(a) The President of the Bank shall be *ex officio* President of the Association. The President shall be Chairman of the Executive Directors of the Association but shall have no vote except a deciding vote in case of an equal division. He may participate in meetings of the Board of Governors but shall not vote at such meetings.

(b) The President shall be chief of the operating staff of the Association. Under the direction of the Executive Directors he shall conduct the ordinary business of the Association and under their general control shall be responsible for the organization, appointment and dismissal of the officers and staff. To the extent practicable, officers and staff of the Bank shall be appointed to serve concurrently as officers and staff of the Association. . . .

(c) − (d) [omitted]

SECTION 6. *Relationship to the Bank*

(a) The Association shall be an entity separate and distinct from the Bank and the funds of the Association shall be kept separate and apart from those of the Bank. The Association shall not borrow from or lend to the Bank, except that this shall not preclude the Association from investing funds not needed in its financing operations in obligations of the Bank.

(b) The Association may make arrangements with the Bank regarding facilities, personnel and services and arrangements for reimbursement of administrative expenses paid in the first instance by either organization on behalf of the other.

(c) Nothing in this Agreement shall make the Association liable for the acts or obligations of the Bank, or the Bank liable for the acts or obligations of the Association.

SECTION 7. *Relations with Other International Organizations*

The Association shall enter into formal arrangements with the United Nations and may enter into such arrangements with other public international organizations having specialized responsibilities in related fields.

SECTION 8. *Location of Offices*

The principal office of the Association shall be the principal office of the Bank. The Association may establish other offices in the territories of any member.

SECTION 9. *Depositories* [omitted]

SECTION 10. *Channel of Communication* [omitted]

SECTION 11. *Publication of Reports and Provision of Information* [omitted]

SECTION 12. *Disposition of Net Income* [omitted]

ARTICLE VII. Withdrawal; Suspension of Membership; Suspension of Operations

SECTION 1. *Withdrawal by Members* [omitted]

SECTION 2. *Suspension of Membership* [omitted]

SECTION 3. *Suspension or Cessation of Membership in the Bank*

Any member which is suspended from membership in, or ceases to be a member of, the Bank shall automatically be suspended from membership in, or cease to be a member of, the Association, as the case may be.

SECTION 4. *Rights and Duties of Governments Ceasing To Be Members*
[omitted]

SECTION 5. *Suspension of Operations and Settlement of Obligations*
[omitted]

ARTICLE VIII. Status, Immunities and Privileges
[omitted]

ARTICLE IX. Amendments
[omitted]

ARTICLE X. Interpretation and Arbitration
[omitted]

ARTICLE XI. Final Provisions

SECTION 1. *Entry into Force*

This Agreement shall enter into force when it has been signed on behalf of governments whose subscriptions comprise not less than sixty-five percent of the total subscriptions set forth in Schedule A and when the instruments referred to in Section 2 (a) of this Article have been deposited on their behalf, but in no event shall this Agreement enter into force before September 15, 1960.

SECTION 2.   *Signature* [omitted]

SECTION 3.   *Territorial Application* [omitted]

SECTION 4.   *Inauguration of the Association*

(a) As soon as this Agreement enters into force under Section 1 of this Article the President shall call a meeting of the Executive Directors.

(b) The Association shall begin operations on the date when such meeting is held.

(c) Pending the first meeting of the Board of Governors, the Executive Directors may exercise all the powers of the Board of Governors except those reserved to the Board of Governors under this Agreement.

SECTION 5.   *Registration* [omitted]

Schedule A. Initial Subscriptions
Expressed in millions of U.S. dollars[a]

Part I Countries					
Australia	20.18	France	52.96	Norway	6.72
Austria	5.04	Germany	52.96	Sweden	10.09
Belgium	22.70	Italy	18.16	Union of South Africa	10.09
Canada	37.83	Japan	33.59	United Kingdom	131.14
Denmark	8.74	Luxembourg	1.01	United States	320.29
Finland	3.83	Netherlands	27.74		
				Subtotal	763.07
Part II Countries					
Afghanistan	1.01	Haiti	0.76	Panama	0.02
Argentina	18.83	Honduras	0.30	Paraguay	0.30
Bolivia	1.06	Iceland	0.10	Peru	1.77
Brazil	18.83	India	40.35	Philippines	5.04
Burma	2.02	Indonesia	11.10	Saudi Arabia	3.70
Ceylon	3.03	Iran	4.54	Spain	10.09
Chile	3.53	Iraq	0.76	Sudan	1.01
China	30.26	Ireland	3.03	Thailand	3.03
Colombia	3.53	Israel	1.68	Tunisia	1.51
Costa Rica	0.20	Jordan	0.30	Turkey	5.80
Cuba	4.71	Korea	1.26	United Arab Republic	6.03
Dominican Republic	0.40	Lebanon	0.45	Uruguay	1.06
Ecuador	0.65	Libya	1.01	Venezuela	7.06
El Salvador	0.30	Malaya	2.52	Viet-Nam	1.51
Ethiopia	0.50	Mexico	8.74	Yugoslavia	4.04
Ghana	2.36	Morocco	3.53		
Greece	2.52	Nicaragua	0.30	Subtotal	236.93
Guatemala	0.40	Pakistan	10.09		
				Total	1,000.00

a. As of January 1, 1960.

Presidents, Vice Presidents, Numbers of Members and Executive Directors, and Volume of Operations

Table B-1. *Bank Group Presidents and Vice Presidents, June 1946–June 1971*

Official	Term of service
Presidents of the World Bank and International Development Association[a]	
Eugene Meyer	June 18, 1946–December 18, 1946
John J. McCloy	March 17, 1947–June 30, 1949
Eugene R. Black	July 1, 1949–December 31, 1962
George D. Woods	January 1, 1963–March 31, 1968
Robert S. McNamara	April 1, 1968–Present
Vice Presidents of the World Bank and International Development Association[a]	
Harold D. Smith	June 20, 1946–January 23, 1947
Robert L. Garner	March 17, 1947–July 24, 1956
W. A. B. Iliff	July 24, 1956–October 31, 1962
J. Burke Knapp	July 24, 1956–Present
Davidson Sommers	July 24, 1956–December 31, 1959
Geoffrey M. Wilson	September 15, 1962–July 31, 1966
Simon Aldewereld	March 1, 1965–Present
Mohamed Shoaib	September 15, 1966–Present
Sir Denis Rickett	April 15, 1968–Present
Presidents of the International Finance Corporation[b]	
Robert L. Garner	July 24, 1956–October 15, 1961
Eugene R. Black	October 16, 1961–December 31, 1962
George D. Woods	January 1, 1963–March 31, 1968
Robert S. McNamara	April 1, 1968–Present
Executive Vice Presidents of the International Finance Corporation	
Martin M. Rosen	June 1, 1961–September 30, 1969
William S. Gaud	October 1, 1969–Present
Vice Presidents of the International Finance Corporation	
John G. Beevor	July 24, 1956–January 1, 1965
James S. Raj	June 6, 1966–June 30, 1970
Ladislaus von Hoffmann	July 1, 1970–Present

Source: IBRD, Secretary's Department.

a. After the IDA came into being in September 1960, presidents and vice presidents of the Bank served also as presidents and vice presidents of IDA.

b. After the retirement of Robert L. Garner as president of IFC, the presidents of the World Bank served also as presidents of IFC.

Table B-2. *Growth of World Bank Group Membership, Number of Executive Directors, and Volume of Operations, 1946–71*

Fiscal year	Number of member countries[a] Bank	IDA	IFC	Number of executive directors	Bank loans	IDA credits	IFC commitments	Total
1946	38	...	...	12	...	...	...	...
1947	44	...	...	12	250.0	...	...	250.0
1948	46	...	...	14	263.0	...	...	263.0
1949	48	...	...	14	137.1	...	...	137.1
1950	47	...	...	14	166.3	...	...	166.3
1951	49	...	...	14	297.1	...	...	297.1
1952	51	...	...	14	298.6	...	...	298.6
1953	54	...	...	16	178.6	...	...	178.6
1954	56	...	...	16	323.7	...	...	323.7
1955	56	...	...	16	409.6	...	...	409.6
1956	58	...	31[c]	16	396.0	...	...	396.0
1957	60	...	49	17	387.9	...	2.0	389.9
1958	67	...	55	17	710.8	...	8.7	719.5
1959	68	...	57	18	703.1	...	10.6	713.7
1960	68	...	59	18	658.7	...	23.7	682.4
1961	68	51	59	18	609.9	101.0	6.2	716.3
1962	75	62	63	18	882.3	134.1	21.3	1,037.7
1963	85	76	73	18	448.7	260.1	18.0	726.8
1964	102	93	78	19	809.8	283.2	20.8	1,113.8
1965	102	94	78	20	1,023.3	309.1	25.6	1,358.0
1966	103	96	81	20	839.2	284.1	35.3	1,158.6
1967	106	97	83	20	876.8	353.5	49.0	1,279.3
1968	107	98	86	20	847.0	106.6	50.4	1,004.0
1969	110	102	91	20	1,399.2	385.0	92.9	1,887.1
1970	113	105	94	20	1,680.4	605.6	111.8	2,397.8
1971	116	107	96	21[d]	1,896.4	584.0	101.3	2,581.7
Total	...	...	...	...	16,493.5[e]	3,406.2[e]	577.8[e]	20,477.5[e]

Sources: World Bank, IDA, and IFC annual reports, IBRD Secretary's Department, and IBRD Information and Public Affairs Department.

a. Numbers of member countries and numbers of executive directors are, in each case, the numbers at the end of the fiscal year. The executive directors of the Bank serve *ex officio* as executive directors of the IDA, provided that they represent at least one country that is a member of IDA. They also serve *ex officio* as members of the Board of Directors of the IFC, provided they represent at least one country that is a member of the IFC.

In IFC, from its inception until November 1966, the total number on the Board of Directors was one less than the total for the Bank. The Bank and IDA have had the same executive directors since the IDA came into being.

b. Expressed in millions of U.S. dollar equivalents.

c. Membership as of July 24, 1956.

d. Japan became the fifth largest stockholder on January 28, 1971. It appointed an executive director as of February 1, 1971, thereby raising the number of appointed directors to six and the total number of directors to twenty-one. After the next regular election of executive directors, with India no longer eligible to appoint an executive director, the numbers reverted to five and to twenty, respectively, as of November 1, 1972.

e. Unadjusted for cancellations, refundings, and terminations, which amount (in millions of U.S. dollars) to $425.1 (for Bank loans), $65.8 (for IDA credits), and $33.7 (for IFC commitments). Due to rounding, details may not add to totals.

Membership, Voting Power, and Subscriptions to Capital Stock

Table C-1. *IBRD Membership and Voting Power, 1947, 1951, 1961, and 1971*

Member	June 30, 1947 Number of votes	June 30, 1947 Percent of total	June 30, 1951 Number of votes	June 30, 1951 Percent of total	June 30, 1961 Number of votes	June 30, 1961 Percent of total	June 30, 1971 Number of votes	June 30, 1971 Percent of total
Afghanistan	...	...	...	...	350	0.16	550	0.21
Algeria	...	...	...	...	...	...	1,050	0.39
Argentina	...	...	...	...	3,983	1.83	3,983	1.49
Australia	...	...	2,250	2.35	5,580	2.56	5,580	2.08
Austria	...	...	750	0.78	1,250	0.57	2,117	0.79
Belgium	2,500	2.74	2,500	2.62	4,750	2.18	5,795	2.17
Bolivia	320	0.35	320	0.34	460	0.21	460	0.17
Botswana	...	...	...	...	...	...	282	0.11
Brazil	1,300	1.42	1,300	1.36	3,983	1.83	3,983	1.49
Burma	...	...	...	...	650	0.30	757	0.28
Burundi	...	...	...	...	...	...	400	0.15
Cameroon	...	...	...	...	...	...	450	0.17
Canada	3,500	3.84	3,500	3.66	7,750	3.56	8,170	3.05
Central African Republic	...	...	...	...	...	...	350	0.13
Ceylon	...	...	400	0.42	850	0.39	1,077	0.40
Chad	...	...	...	...	...	...	350	0.13
Chile	600	0.66	600	0.63	1,183	0.54	1,183	0.44
China	6,250	6.85	6,250	6.54	7,750	3.56	7,750	2.90
Colombia	600	0.66	600	0.63	1,183	0.54	1,183	0.44
Congo, Democratic Republic of	...	...	...	...	...	...	1,210	0.45
Congo, People's Republic of	...	...	...	...	...	...	350	0.13
Costa Rica	270	0.30	270	0.28	290	0.13	357	0.13
Cubaª	600	0.66	600	0.63	...	...	...	...
Cyprus	...	...	...	...	...	...	463	0.17
Czechoslovakiaᵇ	1,500	1.64	1,500	1.57	...	...	...	...
Dahomey	...	...	...	...	...	...	350	0.13
Denmark	930	1.02	930	0.97	1,983	0.91	2,461	0.92
Dominican Republicᶜ	270	0.30	270	0.28	...	...	393	0.15
Ecuador	282	0.31	282	0.30	378	0.17	421	0.16
El Salvador	260	0.28	260	0.27	310	0.14	357	0.13
Equatorial Guinea	...	...	...	...	...	...	314	0.12
Ethiopia	280	0.31	280	0.29	350	0.16	364	0.14
Fiji	...	...	...	...	...	...	361	0.14
Finland	...	...	630	0.66	1,010	0.46	1,583	0.59
France	5,500	6.03	5,500	5.75	10,750	4.93	10,750	4.02

Table C-1. *Continued*

Member	June 30, 1947 Number of votes	June 30, 1947 Percent of total	June 30, 1951 Number of votes	June 30, 1951 Percent of total	June 30, 1961 Number of votes	June 30, 1961 Percent of total	June 30, 1971 Number of votes	June 30, 1971 Percent of total
Gabon	...	...	...	...	...	...	350	0.13
Gambia, The	...	...	...	...	...	...	303	0.11
Germany	...	...	...	...	10,750	4.93	13,903	5.19
Ghana	...	...	...	...	717	0.33	984	0.37
Greece	500	0.55	500	0.52	750	0.34	917	0.34
Guatemala	270	0.30	270	0.28	330	0.15	357	0.13
Guinea	...	...	...	...	...	...	450	0.17
Guyana	...	...	...	...	...	...	410	0.15
Haiti	...	...	...	...	400	0.19	400	0.15
Honduras	260	0.28	260	0.27	310	0.14	330	0.12
Iceland	260	0.28	260	0.27	400	0.19	400	0.15
India	4,250	4.66	4,250	4.44	8,250	3.79	9,250	3.46
Indonesia	...	...	...	...	2,450	1.13	2,450	0.92
Iran	490	0.54	586	0.61	1,150	0.53	1,536	0.57
Iraq	310	0.34	310	0.33	400	0.19	890	0.33
Ireland	...	...	...	...	850	0.39	1,103	0.41
Israel	...	...	...	...	583	0.27	1,209	0.45
Italy	2,050	2.25	2,050	2.14	3,850	1.77	6,910	2.58
Ivory Coast	...	...	...	...	...	...	450	0.17
Jamaica	...	...	...	...	...	...	650	0.24
Japan	...	...	...	...	6,910	3.17	10,480	3.92
Jordan	...	...	...	...	310	0.14	413	0.15
Kenya	...	...	...	...	...	...	583	0.22
Khmer Republic	...	...	...	...	...	...	453	0.17
Korea	...	...	...	...	500	0.23	783	0.29
Kuwait	...	...	...	...	...	...	917	0.34
Laos	...	...	...	...	...	...	350	0.13
Lebanon	295	0.32	295	0.31	295	0.14	340	0.13
Lesotho	...	...	...	...	...	...	282	0.11
Liberia	...	...	...	...	...	...	463	0.17
Libya	...	...	...	...	450	0.21	450	0.17
Luxembourg	350	0.38	350	0.37	450	0.21	450	0.17
Malagasy Republic	...	...	...	...	...	...	450	0.17
Malawi	...	...	...	...	...	...	400	0.15
Malaysia	...	...	...	...	750	0.34	1,583	0.59
Mali	...	...	...	...	...	...	423	0.16
Mauritania	...	...	...	...	...	...	350	0.13
Mauritius	...	...	...	...	...	...	438	0.16
Mexico	900	0.99	900	0.94	1,983	0.91	2,330	0.87
Morocco	...	...	...	...	950	0.44	1,210	0.45
Nepal	...	...	...	...	...	...	350	0.13
Netherlands	3,000	3.29	3,000	3.14	5,750	2.64	6,173	2.31
New Zealand	...	...	...	...	...	...	1,917	0.72
Nicaragua	258	0.28	258	0.27	310	0.14	330	0.12
Niger	...	...	...	...	...	...	350	0.13
Nigeria	...	...	...	...	917	0.42	1,317	0.49
Norway	750	0.82	750	0.78	1,583	0.73	1,850	0.69
Pakistan	...	...	1,250	1.31	2,250	1.03	2,250	0.84
Panama	252	0.28	252	0.26	254	0.12	426	0.16
Paraguay	258	0.28	264	0.28	310	0.14	310	0.12
Peru	425	0.47	425	0.44	600	0.28	885	0.33
Philippines	400	0.44	400	0.42	1,250	0.57	1,423	0.53
Poland[d]	1,500	1.63	...	...	...	...	...	...
Portugal	...	...	...	...	1,050	0.48	1,050	0.39
Rwanda	...	...	...	...	...	...	400	0.15
Saudi Arabia	...	...	...	...	983	0.45	1,393	0.52
Senegal	...	...	...	...	...	...	583	0.22
Sierra Leone	...	...	...	...	...	...	400	0.15

Table C-1. *Continued*

Member	June 30, 1947 Number of votes	June 30, 1947 Percent of total	June 30, 1951 Number of votes	June 30, 1951 Percent of total	June 30, 1961 Number of votes	June 30, 1961 Percent of total	June 30, 1971 Number of votes	June 30, 1971 Percent of total
Singapore	...	...	...	...	...	...	570	0.21
Somalia	...	...	...	...	...	...	400	0.15
South Africa	1,250	1.37	1,250	1.31	2,250	1.03	2,383	0.89
Spain	...	...	...	...	2,250	1.03	2,917	1.09
Sudan	...	...	...	...	450	0.21	850	0.32
Swaziland	...	...	...	...	...	...	314	0.12
Sweden	...	...	...	...	2,250	1.03	2,650	0.99
Syrian Arab Republic[e]	315	0.35	315	0.33	...	...	650	0.24
Tanzania	...	...	...	...	...	...	583	0.22
Thailand	...	...	375	0.39	850	0.39	1,263	0.47
Togo	...	...	...	...	...	...	400	0.15
Trinidad and Tobago	...	...	...	...	...	...	717	0.27
Tunisia	...	...	...	...	550	0.25	623	0.23
Turkey	680	0.74	680	0.71	1,400	0.64	1,400	0.52
Uganda	...	...	...	...	...	...	583	0.22
United Arab Republic[e]	650	0.71	783	0.82	1,516	0.70	1,671	0.62
United Kingdom	13,250	14.52	13,250	13.85	26,250	12.04	26,250	9.81
United States	32,000	35.07	32,000	33.46	63,750	29.25	63,750	23.82
Upper Volta	...	...	...	...	...	...	350	0.13
Uruguay	355	0.39	355	0.37	355	0.16	661	0.25
Venezuela	355	0.39	355	0.37	355	0.16	2,117	0.79
Viet-Nam	...	...	...	...	550	0.25	677	0.25
Yemen Arab Republic	...	...	...	...	...	...	335	0.13
Yemen, People's Democratic Republic of	...	...	...	...	...	...	485	0.18
Yugoslavia	650	0.71	650	0.68	1,317	0.60	1,317	0.49
Zambia	...	...	...	...	...	...	783	0.29
Total	91,245	100.00	95,635	100.00	217,931	100.00	267,710	100.00
Number of member countries	44		49		68		116	

Source: IBRD, Secretary's Department, August 1971.
a. Cuba withdrew from the IBRD November 14, 1960.
b. Czechoslovakia ceased to be a member of the IBRD December 31, 1954.
c. Dominican Republic withdrew from the IBRD December 1, 1960; rejoined September 18, 1961.
d. Poland withdrew from the IBRD March 14, 1950.
e. Egypt and Syria became the United Arab Republics as of July 18, 1958; United Arab Republics became Syrian Arab Republic and United Arab Republic as of November 2, 1961.

Table C-2. *Subscriptions to Capital Stock of IBRD, as of June 30, 1971*

Amounts expressed in thousands of U.S. dollars

| | | | | | Amounts paid in[a] | | |
| | | Subscriptions | | In U.S. dollars | In currency of member other than United States[b] | In non-negotiable, non-interest-bearing demand notes[b] | Amounts subject to call to meet obligations of Bank[c] |
Member	Shares	Percent of total	Amount[a]				
Afghanistan	300	0.13	30,000	300	1,200	1,500	27,000
Algeria	800	0.34	80,000	800	72	7,128	72,000
Argentina	3,733	1.56	373,300	16,772	1,000	19,558	335,970
Australia	5,330	2.23	533,000	5,330	47,970	...	479,700
Austria	1,867	0.78	186,700	1,867	16,803	...	168,030
Belgium	5,545	2.32	554,500	5,545	40,594	9,311	499,050
Bolivia	210	0.09	21,000	210	13	1,877	18,900
Botswana	32	0.01	3,200	32	16	272	2,880
Brazil	3,733	1.56	373,300	3,733	33,597	...	335,970
Burma	507	0.21	50,700	507	1,207	3,356	45,630
Burundi	150	0.06	15,000	150	21	1,329	13,500
Cameroon[d]	200	0.08	20,000	200	29	1,771	18,000
Canada	7,920	3.32	792,000	7,920	71,280	...	712,800
Central African Republic	100	0.04	10,000	100	38	862	9,000
Ceylon	827	0.35	82,700	827	908	6,535	74,430
Chad	100	0.04	10,000	100	24	876	9,000
Chile	933	0.39	93,300	933	8,397	...	83,970
China	7,500	3.14	750,000	7,500	9,043	58,457	675,000
Colombia	933	0.39	93,300	9,330	...	...	83,970
Congo, Democratic Republic of	960	0.40	96,000	960	694	7,946	86,400
Congo, People's Republic of[d]	100	0.04	10,000	100	27	775	9,000
Costa Rica	107	0.05	10,700	467	603	...	9,630
Cyprus	213	0.09	21,300	213	21	1,896	19,170
Dahomey	100	0.04	10,000	100	31	869	9,000
Denmark	2,211	0.93	221,100	2,211	15,597	4,302	198,990
Dominican Republic	143	0.06	14,300	143	573	714	12,870
Ecuador	171	0.07	17,100	1,710	...	...	15,390
El Salvador	107	0.05	10,700	287	783	...	9,630
Equatorial Guinea	64	0.03	6,400	64	576	...	5,760
Ethiopia	114	0.05	11,400	1,014	126	...	10,260
Fiji	111	0.05	11,100	111	999	...	9,990
Finland	1,333	0.56	133,300	1,333	11,997	...	119,970
France	10,500	4.40	1,050,000	10,500	94,500	...	945,000
Gabon	100	0.04	10,000	100	32	868	9,000
Gambia, The	53	0.02	5,300	53	6	471	4,770
Germany	13,653	5.72	1,365,300	13,653	117,119	5,758	1,228,770
Ghana	734	0.31	73,400	734	1,892	4,714	66,060
Greece	667	0.28	66,700	667	6,003	...	60,030
Guatemala	107	0.05	10,700	467	603	...	9,630
Guinea	200	0.08	20,000	200	1,800	...	18,000
Guyana	160	0.07	16,000	160	15	1,425	14,400
Haiti	150	0.06	15,000	150	41	1,309	13,500
Honduras	80	0.03	8,000	620	...	180	7,200
Iceland	150	0.06	15,000	1,500	...	...	13,500
India	9,000	3.77	900,000	9,000	26,617	54,383	810,000
Indonesia	2,200	0.92	220,000	2,200	698	19,102	198,000
Iran[e]	1,286	0.54	128,600	1,286	8,100	3,474	115,740
Iraq	640	0.27	64,000	640	1,350	4,410	57,600
Ireland	853	0.36	85,300	853	6,841	836	76,770
Israel	959	0.40	95,900	4,644	1,219	3,727	86,310
Italy	6,660	2.79	666,000	6,660	59,900	...	599,400
Ivory Coast	200	0.08	20,000	200	1,800	...	18,000
Jamaica[e]	400	0.17	40,000	2,620	25	1,355	36,000

Table C-2. *Continued*

Member	Subscriptions Shares	Subscriptions Percent of total	Subscriptions Amount[a]	Amounts paid in[a] In U.S. dollars	Amounts paid in[a] In currency of member other than United States[b]	Amounts paid in[a] In non-negotiable, non-interest-bearing demand notes[b]	Amounts subject to call to meet obligations of Bank[c]
Japan	10,230	4.29	1,023,000	10,230	92,070	...	920,700
Jordan	163	0.07	16,300	163	61	1,406	14,670
Kenya	333	0.14	33,300	333	1,751	1,246	29,970
Khmer Republic	203	0.09	20,300	203	18	1,809	18,270
Korea	533	0.22	53,300	533	1,130	3,667	47,970
Kuwait	667	0.28	66,700	667	6,003	...	60,030
Laos	100	0.04	10,000	100	900	...	9,000
Lebanon	90	0.04	9,000	900	...	...	8,100
Lesotho	32	0.01	3,200	32	7	281	2,880
Liberia	213	0.09	21,300	213	13	1,904	19,170
Libya	200	0.08	20,000	2,000	...	...	18,000
Luxembourg	200	0.08	20,000	200	1,800	...	18,000
Malagasy Republic	200	0.08	20,000	200	41	1,759	18,000
Malawi	150	0.06	15,000	150	43	1,307	13,500
Malaysia	1,333	0.56	133,300	1,333	11,997	...	119,970
Mali	173	0.07	17,300	173	1,557	...	15,570
Mauritania	100	0.04	10,000	100	26	874	9,000
Mauritius	188	0.08	18,800	188	18	1,674	16,920
Mexico	2,080	0.87	208,000	2,080	18,720	...	187,200
Morocco	960	0.40	96,000	960	99	8,541	86,400
Nepal	100	0.04	10,000	100	9	891	9,000
Netherlands	5,923	2.48	592,300	5,923	49,500	3,807	533,070
New Zealand	1,667	0.70	166,700	1,667	129	14,874	150,030
Nicaragua	80	0.03	8,000	620	180	...	7,200
Niger[d]	100	0.04	10,000	100	26	776	9,000
Nigeria	1,067	0.45	106,700	1,067	396	9,207	96,030
Norway	1,600	0.67	160,000	1,600	14,400	...	144,000
Pakistan	2,000	0.84	200,000	2,000	2,049	15,951	180,000
Panama	176	0.07	17,600	212	...	1,548	15,840
Paraguay	60	0.03	6,000	60	540	...	5,400
Peru	635	0.27	63,500	3,785	44	2,521	57,150
Philippines	1,173	0.49	117,300	3,873	1,172	6,685	105,570
Portugal	800	0.34	80,000	800	7,200	...	72,000
Rwanda	150	0.06	15,000	150	1,350	...	13,500
Saudi Arabia	1,143	0.48	114,300	1,143	22	10,265	102,870
Senegal	333	0.14	33,300	333	37	2,960	29,970
Sierra Leone	150	0.06	15,000	150	20	1,330	13,500
Singapore	320	0.13	32,000	320	2,880	...	28,800
Somalia	150	0.06	15,000	150	14	1,336	13,500
South Africa	2,133	0.89	213,300	2,133	19,197	...	191,970
Spain	2,667	1.12	266,700	2,667	24,003	...	240,030
Sudan	600	0.25	60,000	600	1,800	3,600	54,000
Swaziland	64	0.03	6,400	64	6	570	5,760
Sweden	2,400	1.01	240,000	2,400	21,600	...	216,000
Syrian Arab Republic	400	0.17	40,000	400	44	3,556	36,000
Tanzania	333	0.14	33,300	333	106	2,891	29,970
Thailand	1,013	0.43	101,300	8,891	178	1,061	91,170
Togo[d]	150	0.06	15,000	150	35	1,168	13,500
Trinidad and Tobago[e]	467	0.20	46,700	2,190	24	2,456	42,030
Tunisia	373	0.16	37,300	373	74	3,283	33,570
Turkey	1,150	0.48	115,000	1,150	277	10,073	103,500
Uganda	333	0.14	33,300	333	78	2,919	29,970
United Arab Republic	1,421	0.60	142,100	1,421	159	12,630	127,890
United Kingdom[d]	26,000	10.89	2,600,000	26,000	231,674	...	2,340,000
United States	63,500	26.60	6,350,000	635,000	...	...	5,715,000

Table C-2. *Continued*

Member	Shares	Subscriptions Percent of total	Amount[a]	Amounts paid in[a] In U.S. dollars	In currency of member other than United States[b]	In non-negotiable, non-interest-bearing demand notes[b]	Amounts subject to call to meet obligations of Bank[c]
Upper Volta	100	0.04	10,000	100	26	874	9,000
Uruguay	411	0.17	41,100	2,301	63	1,746	36,990
Venezuela	1,867	0.78	186,700	18,670	...	...	168,030
Viet-Nam	427	0.18	42,700	427	3,843	...	38,430
Yemen Arab Republic	85	0.04	8,500	85	8	757	7,650
Yemen, People's Democratic Republic of	235	0.10	23,500	235	22	2,093	21,150
Yugoslavia	1,067	0.45	106,700	10,473	197	...	96,030
Zambia	533	0.22	53,300	533	48	4,749	47,970
Total	238,710	100.00	23,871,000	889,516	1,112,524	382,391	21,483,900

Source: World Bank/International Development Association, *Annual Report, 1971*, pp. 84–85, 89.

a. In terms of U.S. dollars of the weight and fineness in effect on July 1, 1944.

b. The portion of the subscriptions to the capital stock of the Bank payable in the currencies of the respective members (such portion being hereinafter called "restricted currency") can be used for lending purposes only with the approval of the members concerned. Article II, Section 9 of the Articles of Agreement of the Bank provides for the maintenance as of the time of subscription of the value of restricted currency, requiring the member to make additional payments to the Bank in the event of a reduction in the par value of its currency or a significant *de facto* depreciation of its currency in its territories and requiring the Bank to reimburse the member in the event of an increase in the par value of its currency. These obligations of the members and the Bank become effective immediately upon the happening of those events with respect to holdings of restricted currency represented by currency balances and notes, whereas with respect to restricted currency out on loan these obligations become effective only as and when such currency is recovered by the Bank.

Some members have converted part or all of the Bank's holdings of their restricted currency into U.S. dollars to be used without restriction in the Bank's operations, subject to the right of the Bank or the member to reverse the transactions at any time, with immediate effect as to dollars then held by the Bank, and, as to dollars loaned upon repayment of the loans. Such dollars amounting to $79,306,298 are not subject to the provision of Article II, Section 9 and are included in these financial statements, where relevant, as "unrestricted."

c. Subject to call by the Bank only when required to meet the obligations of the Bank created by borrowing or by guaranteeing loans. As to $19,096,800,000 the restriction on calls is imposed by the Articles of Agreement as to $2,387,100,000 by resolutions of the Board of Governors.

d. Amounts aggregating the equivalent of $2,669,321, receivable as a result of revaluation of these currencies, are not included in the "Amounts paid in" columns.

e. The equivalent of $408,000 has been received from members on account of increases in subscriptions which are in process of completion: Jamaica $46,000, Iran $294,000, and Trinidad and Tobago $68,000.

Table C-3. *Subscriptions to Capital Stock of IFC and Voting Power of IFC Members, as of June 30, 1971*

Amounts expressed in thousands of U.S. dollar equivalents

	Subscriptions		Voting power	
Member	*Amount*	*Per-cent of total*	*Num-ber of votes*	*Per-cent of total*
Afghanistan	111	*0.10*	361	*0.27*
Argentina	1,662	*1.55*	1,912	*1.46*
Australia	2,215	*2.07*	2,465	*1.88*
Austria	554	*0.52*	804	*0.61*
Belgium	2,492	*2.33*	2,742	*2.09*
Bolivia	78	*0.07*	328	*0.25*
Brazil	1,163	*1.09*	1,413	*1.08*
Burma	166	*0.16*	416	*0.32*
Canada	3,600	*3.36*	3,850	*2.94*
Ceylon	166	*0.16*	416	*0.32*
Chile	388	*0.36*	638	*0.49*
China	4,154	*3.88*	4,404	*3.36*
Colombia	388	*0.36*	638	*0.49*
Congo, Democratic Republic of	332	*0.31*	582	*0.44*
Costa Rica	22	*0.02*	272	*0.21*
Cyprus	83	*0.08*	333	*0.25*
Denmark	753	*0.70*	1,003	*0.77*
Dominican Republic	22	*0.02*	272	*0.21*
Ecuador	35	*0.03*	285	*0.22*
El Salvador	11	*0.01*	261	*0.20*
Ethiopia	33	*0.03*	283	*0.22*
Finland	421	*0.39*	671	*0.51*
France	5,815	*5.43*	6,065	*4.62*
Gabon	55	*0.05*	305	*0.23*
Germany	3,655	*3.41*	3,905	*2.98*
Ghana	166	*0.16*	416	*0.32*
Greece	277	*0.26*	527	*0.40*
Guatemala	22	*0.02*	272	*0.21*
Guyana	89	*0.08*	339	*0.26*
Haiti	22	*0.02*	272	*0.21*
Honduras	11	*0.01*	261	*0.20*
Iceland	11	*0.01*	261	*0.20*
India	4,431	*4.14*	4,681	*3.57*
Indonesia	1,218	*1.14*	1,468	*1.12*
Iran	372	*0.35*	622	*0.47*
Iraq	67	*0.06*	317	*0.24*
Ireland	332	*0.31*	582	*0.44*
Israel	50	*0.05*	300	*0.23*
Italy	1,994	*1.86*	2,244	*1.71*

Table C-3. *Continued*

Member	Subscriptions		Voting power	
	Amount	Per-cent of total	Number of votes	Per-cent of total
Ivory Coast	111	0.10	361	0.27
Jamaica	148	0.14	398	0.30
Japan	2,769	2.58	3,019	2.30
Jordan	33	0.03	283	0.22
Kenya	184	0.17	434	0.33
Korea	139	0.13	389	0.30
Kuwait	369	0.34	619	0.47
Lebanon	50	0.05	300	0.23
Liberia	83	0.08	333	0.25
Libya	55	0.05	305	0.23
Luxembourg	111	0.10	361	0.27
Malagasy Republic	111	0.10	361	0.27
Malawi	83	0.08	333	0.25
Malaysia	277	0.26	527	0.40
Mauritania	55	0.05	305	0.23
Mauritius	95	0.09	345	0.26
Mexico	720	0.67	970	0.74
Morocco	388	0.36	638	0.49
Nepal	55	0.05	305	0.23
Netherlands	3,046	2.84	3,296	2.51
New Zealand	923	0.86	1,173	0.89
Nicaragua	9	0.01	259	0.20
Nigeria	369	0.34	619	0.47
Norway	554	0.52	804	0.61
Pakistan	1,108	1.03	1,358	1.04
Panama	2	a	252	0.19
Paraguay	16	0.02	266	0.20
Peru	194	0.18	444	0.34
Philippines	166	0.16	416	0.32
Portugal	443	0.41	693	0.53
Saudi Arabia	111	0.10	361	0.27
Senegal	184	0.17	434	0.33
Sierra Leone	83	0.08	333	0.25
Singapore	177	0.17	427	0.33
Somalia	83	0.08	333	0.25
South Africa	1,108	1.03	1,358	1.04
Spain	1,108	1.03	1,358	1.04
Sudan	111	0.10	361	0.27
Swaziland	35	0.03	285	0.22
Sweden	1,108	1.03	1,358	1.04
Syrian Arab Republic	72	0.07	322	0.25

Table C-3. *Continued*

	Subscriptions		Voting power	
Member	Amount	Per-cent of total	Num-ber of votes	Per-cent of total
Tanzania	184	0.17	434	0.33
Thailand	139	0.13	389	0.30
Togo	83	0.08	333	0.25
Trinidad and Tobago	148	0.14	398	0.30
Tunisia	133	0.12	383	0.29
Turkey	476	0.44	726	0.55
Uganda	184	0.17	434	0.33
United Arab Republic	590	0.55	840	0.64
United Kingdom	14,400	13.44	14,650	11.17
United States	35,168	32.82	35,418	27.01
Uruguay	155	0.15	405	0.31
Venezuela	116	0.11	366	0.28
Viet-Nam	166	0.16	416	0.32
Yemen Arab Republic	47	0.04	297	0.23
Yugoslavia	591	0.55	841	0.64
Zambia	295	0.28	545	0.42
Total	107,157	100.00	131,157	100.00

Source: International Finance Corporation, *Annual Report, 1971*, p. 41.
a. Less than 0.005 percent.

Table C-4. *Subscriptions to IDA, Voting Power of IDA Members, and IDA Supplementary Resources, as of June 30, 1971*

Amounts expressed in thousands of U.S. dollar equivalents

Member[a]	Subscriptions Amount[b]	Subscriptions Per-cent of total	Voting Power Number of votes	Voting Power Per-cent of total	Supple-mentary resources Amount[b]	Total amount of sub-scriptions and supple-mentary resources
Part I member countries						
Australia	20,180	1.99	4,536	1.77	43,800	63,980
Austria	5,040	0.50	1,508	0.59	13,200	18,240
Belgium	8,250	0.81	2,150	0.84	28,650	36,900
Canada	37,830	3.72	8,066	3.14	116,700	154,530
Denmark	8,740	0.86	2,248	0.87	35,700	44,440
Finland	3,830	0.38	1,266	0.49	6,378	10,208
France	52,960	5.21	11,092	4.32	159,072	212,032
Germany	52,960	5.21	11,092	4.32	189,600	242,560
Italy	18,160	1.79	4,132	1.61	78,360	96,520
Japan	33,590	3.30	7,218	2.81	107,730	141,320
Kuwait	3,360	0.33	1,172	0.46	8,760	12,120
Luxembourg	375	0.04	575	0.22	975	1,350
Netherlands	27,740	2.73	6,048	2.35	45,780	73,520
Norway	6,720	0.66	1,844	0.72	18,600	25,320
South Africa	10,090	0.99	2,518	0.98	6,990	17,080
Sweden	10,090	0.99	2,518	0.98	94,135	104,225
United Kingdom	131,140	12.90	26,728	10.41	252,120	383,260
United States	320,290	31.51	64,558	25.14	792,000	1,112,290
Total	751,345	73.92	159,269	62.02	1,998,550	2,749,895
Part II member countries						
Afghanistan	1,010	0.10	702	0.27	...	1,010
Algeria	4,030	0.40	1,306	0.51	...	4,030
Argentina	18,830	1.85	4,266	1.66	...	18,830
Bolivia	1,060	0.10	712	0.28	...	1,060
Botswana	160	0.02	532	0.21	...	160
Brazil	18,830	1.85	4,266	1.66	...	18,830
Burma	2,020	0.20	904	0.35	...	2,020
Burundi	760	0.07	652	0.26	...	760
Cameroon	1,010	0.10	702	0.27	...	1,010
Central African Republic	500	0.05	600	0.23	...	500
Ceylon	3,030	0.30	1,106	0.43	...	3,030
Chad	500	0.05	600	0.23	...	500
Chile	3,530	0.35	1,206	0.47	...	3,530
China	30,260	2.98	6,552	2.55	...	30,260
Colombia	3,530	0.35	1,206	0.47	...	3,530
Congo, Democratic Republic of	3,020[c]	0.30	1,104	0.43	...	3,020
Congo, People's Republic of	500[c]	0.05	600	0.23	...	500
Costa Rica	200[d]	0.02	540	0.21	...	200
Cyprus	760	0.07	652	0.26	...	760
Dahomey	500	0.05	600	0.23	...	500
Dominican Republic	400	0.04	580	0.23	...	400
Ecuador	650	0.06	630	0.25	...	650
El Salvador	300	0.03	560	0.22	...	300
Ethiopia	500	0.05	600	0.23	...	500
Gabon	500	0.05	600	0.23	...	500
Gambia, The	267	0.03	553	0.22	...	267
Ghana	2,360	0.23	972	0.38	...	2,360
Greece	2,520	0.25	1,004	0.39	...	2,520
Guatemala	400	0.04	580	0.23	...	400
Guinea	1,010	0.10	702	0.27	...	1,010

Table C-4. *Continued*

Member[a]	Subscriptions Amount[b]	Per-cent of total	Voting Power Number of votes	Per-cent of total	Supple-mentary resources Amount[b]	Total amount of sub-scriptions and supple-mentary resources
Guyana	810	0.08	662	0.26	...	810
Haiti	760	0.07	652	0.26	...	760
Honduras	300	0.03	560	0.22	...	300
Iceland	100	0.01	520	0.20	...	100
India	40,350	3.97	8,570	3.34	...	40,350
Indonesia	11,100	1.09	2,720	1.06	...	11,100
Iran	4,540	0.45	1,408	0.55	...	4,540
Iraq	760	0.07	652	0.26	...	760
Ireland	3,030	0.30	1,106	0.43	...	3,030
Israel	1,680	0.17	836	0.32	...	1,680
Ivory Coast	1,010	0.10	702	0.27	...	1,010
Jordan	300	0.03	560	0.22	...	300
Kenya	1,680	0.17	836	0.32	...	1,680
Khmer Republic	1,020	0.10	704	0.28	...	1,020
Korea	1,260	0.12	752	0.29	...	1,260
Laos	500	0.05	600	0.23	...	500
Lebanon	450	0.04	590	0.23	...	450
Lesotho	160	0.02	532	0.21	...	160
Liberia	760	0.07	652	0.26	...	760
Libya	1,010	0.10	702	0.27	...	1,010
Malagasy Republic	1,010	0.10	702	0.27	...	1,010
Malawi	760	0.07	652	0.26	...	760
Malaysia	2,520	0.25	1,004	0.39	...	2,520
Mali	870	0.09	674	0.26	...	870
Mauritania	500	0.05	600	0.23	...	500
Mauritius	860	0.08	672	0.26	...	860
Mexico	8,740	0.86	2,248	0.87	...	8,740
Morocco	3,530	0.35	1,206	0.47	...	3,530
Nepal	500	0.05	600	0.23	...	500
Nicaragua	300	0.03	560	0.22	...	300
Niger	500[c]	0.05	600	0.23	...	500
Nigeria	3,360	0.33	1,172	0.46	...	3,360
Pakistan	10,090	0.99	2,518	0.98	...	10,090
Panama	20	[e]	504	0.20	...	20
Paraguay	300	0.03	560	0.22	...	300
Peru	1,770	0.17	854	0.33	...	1,770
Philippines	5,040	0.50	1,508	0.59	...	5,040
Rwanda	760	0.07	652	0.26	...	760
Saudi Arabia	3,700	0.36	1,240	0.48	...	3,700
Senegal	1,680	0.17	836	0.32	...	1,680
Sierra Leone	760	0.07	652	0.26	...	760
Somalia	760	0.07	652	0.26	...	760
Spain	10,090	0.99	2,518	0.98	...	10,090
Sudan	1,010	0.10	702	0.27	...	1,010
Swaziland	320	0.03	564	0.22	...	320
Syrian Arab Republic	950	0.09	690	0.27	...	950
Tanzania	1,680	0.17	836	0.32	...	1,680
Thailand	3,030	0.30	1,106	0.43	...	3,030
Togo	760[c]	0.07	652	0.26	...	760
Tunisia	1,510	0.15	802	0.31	...	1,510
Turkey	5,800	0.57	1,660	0.65	...	5,800
Uganda	1,680	0.17	836	0.32	...	1,680
United Arab Republic	5,080	0.50	1,516	0.59	...	5,080
Upper Volta	500	0.05	600	0.23	...	500
Viet-Nam	1,510	0.15	802	0.31	...	1,510

Table C-4. *Continued*

Member[a]	Subscriptions		Voting Power		Supple-mentary resources	Total amount of sub-scriptions and supple-mentary resources
	Amount[b]	Per-cent of total	Number of votes	Per-cent of total	Amount[b]	
Yemen Arab Republic	430	0.04	586	0.23	...	430
Yemen, People's Democratic						
Republic of	1,180	0.12	736	0.29	...	1,180
Yugoslavia	4,040	0.40	1,308	0.51	...	4,040
Zambia	2,690	0.26	1,038	0.40	...	2,690
Total	265,117	26.08	97,523	37.98	...	265,117
Total, Part I and Part II members	1,016,462	100.00	256,792	100.00	1,998,550	3,015,012

Source: World Bank/International Development Association, *Annual Report, 1971*, pp. 100–02.

Note: $32,000 has been received from Equatorial Guinea on account of its subscription pending admission to membership.

a. Members whose subscriptions may be freely used or exchanged by the Association and who have participated in the replenishment of the Association's resources are included in Part I. All other members are included in Part II.

b. Subscriptions and supplementary resources are expressed in terms of U.S. dollars of the weight and fineness as of January 1, 1960.

Article IV, Section 2, of IDA's Articles of Agreement provides for the maintenance as of the time of subscription of the value of the Association's holdings of the currency (or substituted notes) representing 90 percent of each member's initial subscription, to the extent that such currency has not been initially disbursed or exchanged for the currency of another member. This Section requires the member to make additional payments to the Association in the event of a reduction in the par value of its currency or a significant *de facto* depreciation of its currency in its territories and requires the Association to reimburse the member in the event of an increase in the par value of its currency or a significant *de facto* appreciation of its currency in its territories.

Supplementary resources of the Association have, by agreement, the same respective rights and obligations as to maintenance of value as are set forth in Article IV, Section 2, of the Articles of the Association.

The equivalent of $2,546,098 is due from four members, and the equivalent of $413,801 is payable to one member in order to maintain the value of the Association's currency holdings as required under Article IV, Section 2.

c. Includes amounts aggregating the equivalent of $2,546,098 receivable as a result of revaluation of the currencies of these members.

d. Does not include $2,720 paid as the first installment of Costa Rica's additional subscription under the third replenishment.

e. Less than 0.005 percent.

Chronology

1944

July 1–22   Articles of Agreement of Bank drawn up at Bretton Woods, New Hampshire.

1945

Dec. 27   Articles of Agreement become effective upon signature, in Washington, by twenty-eight governments.

1946

March 1–18   Inaugural meeting of board of governors held at Savannah, Georgia. First board of executive directors elected.

June 18   Eugene Meyer becomes president of Bank.

June 19   Harold D. Smith appointed vice president.

June 20   Calls for capital announced (2 percent portion plus 3 percent in national currencies).

July 12   Chester A. McLain appointed general counsel.

Aug. 13   Morton M. Mendels appointed secretary.

Aug. 28   Leonard B. Rist appointed research director.

Sept. 20   D. Crena de Iongh appointed treasurer.

Sept. 27   First annual meeting of governors convenes in Washington.

Sept. 27   Five percent of capital subscription called.

Oct. 14   Announcement made of loan applications from Chile, Czechoslovakia, Denmark, France, Luxembourg, and Poland.

Oct. 30   Announcement made of $250 million loan application from Iran.

Oct. 31   Charles C. Pineo appointed loan director.

Dec. 4   Eugene Meyer resigns as president of Bank.

Dec. 18   Harold D. Smith submits resignation, to become effective later.

1947

Jan. 23   Death of Vice President Harold D. Smith.

Feb. 28   John J. McCloy named as president of Bank; takes office March 17.

Feb. 28   Robert L. Garner appointed vice president; takes office March 17.

March 14	Eugene R. Black becomes U.S. executive director.
April 3	Chauncey G. Parker appointed director of administration.
April 29	Announcement made of applications from Mexico and the Netherlands for loans of $208,875,000 and $535,000,000, respectively.
May 9	Bank lends $250 million to Crédit National of France.
June 10	Small fact-finding mission to Poland announced.
July 15	Bank offers $250 million in bonds on U.S. market; and E. F. Dunstan, director of marketing, announces oversubscription of bonds.
July 16	Mission to Brazil departs.
Aug. 5	Australia joins Bank.
Aug. 7	Bank lends $195 million to the Netherlands.
Aug. 22	Bank lends $40 million to Denmark.
Aug. 28	Announcement of $250 million loan application from Italy.
Aug. 28	Bank lends $12 million to Luxembourg.
Sept. 11	Second annual governors meeting convenes in Washington.
Oct. 24	Charles C. Pineo resigns as loan director.
Nov. 26	W. A. B. Iliff appointed loan director; assumes duties on Feb. 9, 1948.
Dec. 5	Mission to Chile announced.
Dec. 31	Mission to the Philippines announced.

1948

Jan. 7	Announcement made of $500 million loan application from Yugoslavia.
March 10	Mission to Peru and Bolivia announced.
March 25	Bank lends $13.5 million to Fomento and $2.5 million to Endesa of Chile (first development loans and first loans in Latin America).
March 29	Visit by President McCloy to South America announced.
May 21	Visit by Vice President Garner to Europe announced.
June 4	Visit by Eugene Black (then U.S. executive director) to Netherlands East Indies announced.
July 19	Disbursement of Dutch loan proceeds completed.
July 19–23	Advisory Council holds first annual meeting.
July 26	Grant Forbes appointed to act as the Bank's liaison with the ECA and OEEC in Paris.
Aug. 9	Bank lends $12 million to four Dutch shipping companies (first post-reconstruction loans in Europe).
Aug. 16	Walter Hill appointed assistant in Paris office.
Sept. 15	The Philippines applies for a loan.
Sept. 27	Third annual governors meeting convenes in London.
Nov. 10	Visit by President McCloy to Central America announced.

1949

Jan. 6	Bank lends $34.1 million to two Mexican government agencies for electric power development (the first sector loan).

Jan. 10   Missions to India, Turkey, Colombia, and Peru announced.

Jan. 12   Dollar Savings Bank buys $1 million Dutch Shipping Notes (the first portfolio sale).

Jan. 16   Bank's first training course for positions on the permanent staff announced.

Jan. 27   Bank lends $75 million to Brazilian Traction, Light and Power, Ltd.

Jan. 31   General R. A. Wheeler appointed engineering adviser.

Feb. 16   Visit by Robert L. Garner to North Africa and the Middle East announced.

March 28   Mission to Egypt announced.

May 18   John J. McCloy resigns as president of the Bank; Eugene R. Black to succeed him.

June 2   Announcement made of technical assistance activities, in cooperation with (but not as part of) the UN joint program.

June 30   Mission to Colombia (first comprehensive economic survey mission) announced.

Aug. 18   Bank lends $34 million to India for railway reconstruction and development (first Asian loan).

Aug. 31   Davidson Sommers succeeds Chester A. McLain as general counsel of Bank.

Oct. 17   Walter Hill appointed special representative in Paris office.

Oct. 17   Bank lends $2.7 million to Yugoslavia and $2.3 million to Finland for timber-producing equipment (the Bank's first—and only—short-term loans).

Dec. 5   J. Burke Knapp appointed assistant director of Economic Department.

1950

Jan. 1   Bank announces that negotiations have been discontinued between the Bank and the U. K. Colonial Development Corporation for a loan of approximately $5 million.

Jan. 25   Bank announces sale, through competitive bidding, of $100 million of its bonds to syndicate headed by Chicago banks.

March 6   Bank announces sale of Swiss franc bond issue to a group of leading Swiss banks.

March 6   Norman M. Tucker goes to El Salvador in connection with marketing of Salvadorean *colones* bonds.

March 14   Poland withdraws from Bank.

April 18   Bank lends $18.5 million to India for further development of Damodar River Valley.

April 24   Black announces release from French franc subscription to Bank's capital.

May 3   Announcement made that a group of fourteen banks, headed by the Nederlandsche Handel Maatschappij NV, has applied for the listing on the Amsterdam Stock Exchange of Netherlands Trustee certificates to be issued against the 25-year, 3 percent bonds of the Bank.

May 11   Bank reports that steel facilities it has helped to finance in Western

	Europe are nearing completion and that some operations have already started.
May 24	Bank announces that six additional countries have taken action toward making their currencies available to the Bank for its lending operations: The Netherlands, Italy, Mexico, Honduras, El Salvador and Paraguay.
May 24	Bank announces that the Central Bank of Mexico has authorized domestic and foreign banks operating in Mexico to use part of their foreign exchange reserve deposits with the Central Bank to acquire International Bank bonds.
June 5	Bank announces that Costa Rica has agreed in principle to the use of its paid-in currency for Bank lending operations.
June 5	Bank reports that its mission to Turkey will undertake a broad survey of Turkish economy.
June 15	Bank lends $12.8 million to the Kingdom of Iraq for the construction on the Tigris River of a flood control system (first loan to Middle East).
July 7	Bank lends Turkey $16.4 million in the form of two loans—for port development and grain storage facilities.
July 11	Pakistan joins Bank.
Aug. 13	*The Basis of a Development Program for Colombia*, a report of the mission to Colombia, made available to the public.
Aug. 22	Bank lends Australia $100 million (first program loan).
Aug. 30	Yugoslavia approves use of its entire 18 percent paid-in currency, subject to consultation with Bank in each case.
Sept. 7	Fifth annual governors meeting in Paris.
Sept. 13	Two loans made to Ethiopia, one of $5 million for rehabilitation and maintenance of road system and another of $2 million for new development bank (first loans in Africa; first development bank loan).
Sept. 14	Iceland and Norway approve use of their paid-in currency.
Oct. 13	Bank and FAO jointly sponsor agricultural survey mission to Uruguay (first sector study).
Oct. 19	Bank announces $9 million loan to Industrial Development Bank of Turkey.
Oct. 19	Norman M. Tucker resigns as marketing director of the Bank to become general manager of the Industrial Development Bank of Turkey.
Oct. 26	George L. Martin appointed director of marketing.
Nov. 21	Harold N. Graves, Jr., appointed director of Public Relations Department of the Bank.

1951

April 4	Bank announces appointment of W. A. B. Iliff as assistant to Eugene R. Black, president.
April 27	A. Broches named assistant general counsel.
May 17	London banking firm of Baring Bros. and Co., Ltd. announces preparation of public offering of £5,000,000 issue of 3½ percent, 20-year Bank bonds.

May 24	Canadian government permits Bank to use for loans $7.5 million in Canadian dollars from paid-in capital subscription.
May 26	Agricultural mission to Chile named—jointly sponsored by FAO and Bank.
June 5	Report of economic survey mission to Turkey published.
June 20	Joint Bank-ECLA conference on economic programming opens at Pan-American Union, Washington, D.C.
July 3	Syndicate of leading Swiss banks announces first public offering in Switzerland of Bank bonds.
July 3	Recommendations for economic development of Guatemala made public in a report of a mission to Guatemala.
July 25	Program for the development of agricultural resources in Uruguay made public in a report by a joint mission of FAO and the Bank.
Aug. 31	Sweden becomes a member of the Bank.
Sept. 13	Loans announced of $40 million to Belgian Congo and $30 million to the Kingdom of Belgium—both to aid in carrying out ten-year development plan of the Belgian Congo (first "impact" loan).
Sept. 27	Bank economic survey mission to Ceylon announced.
Sept. 30	First loans repaid (Finland, Yugoslavia).
Oct. 11	Loan of $10 million made to Cassa per il Mezzogiorno of Italy ("impact loan").
Oct. 26	Bank economic survey mission to Surinam announced.
Nov. 6	Richard H. Demuth appointed director of technical assistance and liaison.
Dec. 31	Torkild Rieber and Hector Prud'homme arrive in Teheran, Iran, in connection with study of oil situation.

1952

Jan. 25	Eugene R. Black leaves for visit to Pakistan, India, Ceylon, Thailand, and Australia.
Feb. 11	Report of comprehensive economic survey mission to Iraq published.
Feb. 25	Comprehensive economic survey mission to Jamaica announced.
March 21	Loan of $7 million made to KLM Royal Dutch Airlines to help finance program to replace part of its air fleet.
March 27	Loan of $27.2 million to Pakistan for railway improvement announced.
April 3	Iranian oil problem: a review of Bank's negotiations issued.
May 1	Indus River meetings of engineers from India and Pakistan begin.
May 1	Report on a proposal to establish an International Finance Corporation announced.
May 6	Surinam survey mission report announced.
May 22	Canada releases $41 million (in Canadian dollars), freely convertible, from capital subscription.
June 26	Pieter Lieftinck of Netherlands appointed special representative in Turkey.
June 26	Indus River meetings held. Further studies and meetings planned.

June 30	Luis Machado appointed to deal with special matters in Latin America.
July 16	William Howell appointed director of administration, succeeding Chauncey Parker.
Aug. 13	Japan becomes member of Bank and Fund.
Aug. 14	Germany becomes member of Bank and Fund.
Sept. 5	Seventh annual governors meeting begins in Mexico City.
Oct.	Bank staff reorganized: area departments and Technical Operations Department created.
Oct. 2	J. Burke Knapp named director of operations for the Western Hemisphere.
Oct. 20	Economic mission to Japan announced.
Dec. 19	Loan of $31.5 million to India for iron and steel production announced.

1953

Jan. 7	Henry W. Riley appointed treasurer, succeeding Crena de Iongh.
Jan. 9	Jamaica survey mission report announced.
Jan. 30	Francois-Didier Gregh, of France, appointed director of Department of Operations for Asia and the Middle East.
Feb. 12	Eugene Black's seven-week trip to Egypt, Lebanon, Jordan, Iraq, Syria, Ethiopia, and Turkey announced (beginning of High Dam discussions).
Feb. 26	Milton C. Cross named director of technical operations.
March 5	Mission to Germany announced.
May 11	*The Economic Development of Mexico*, joint Mexican-Bank economic study, published.
Sept. 8	Eugene Black appointed president for another five-year term (to July 1, 1959).
Sept. 18	General survey mission to Nigeria announced.
Oct. 20	Dorsey Stephens named Bank's regional representative in Middle East, with offices in Beirut, Lebanon.

1954

Jan. 13	Bank announces general survey mission to Malaya and Singapore.
Feb. 3	Mission to Syria named to make general survey of the economy.
April 15	Indonesia joins Bank.
Sept. 21	First sale of dollar bond issue entirely outside United States announced.
Dec. 10	India and Pakistan representatives resume discussions on use of Indus system of rivers.
Dec. 15	Belgium receives loan of $20 million, with $30 million public offering of Belgian government bonds (first joint financing with market).
Dec. 23	Industrial Credit and Investment Corporation of India, Ltd., receives loan of $10 million.

1955

Jan. 24   John Duncan Miller appointed special representative in Europe.

March 11   Bank announces establishment of an Economic Development Institute.

March 24   Agricultural mission to Colombia, headed by Sir Herbert Stewart, announced.

March 25   General survey mission to Jordan announced—to be headed by Dr. Pieter Lieftinck.

April 15   Bank transmits charter of proposed International Finance Corporation to member governments for approval.

April 18   Report of general survey mission transmitted to Syrian government.

April 19   Investment market and World Bank engage in combined operation to lend $40 million to Norway.

May 11   Joseph Rucinski appointed director of Department of Operations for Asia and the Middle East.

May 25   Simon Aldewereld appointed director of Department of Technical Operations.

June 1   Loan of $70 million to Italy announced, for projects to increase agricultural production, industrial output, and electric power service in southern Italy.

June 6   S. R. Cope appointed director of operations, Europe, Africa, and Australasia.

June 21   Interim agreement on irrigation use of the Indus system of rivers signed by India, Pakistan, and the Bank.

Sept. 12   Tenth annual meeting opens in Istanbul.

Oct. 15   Indus Waters discussion—terminal date extended.

Oct. 24   Bank engineers visit Cairo; discuss Aswan High Dam.

Nov. 3   Indus Waters agreement extended to March 31, 1956.

Dec. 5   International Finance Corporation—U.S. deposits instruments of acceptance.

1956

Jan. 9   Economic Development Institute inaugurated, with A. K. Cairncross as director.

Jan. 24   President Black's visit to Egypt to discuss Aswan High Dam project announced.

July 20   IFC charter comes into force.

July 24   Robert L. Garner becomes president of IFC.

July 24   W. A. B. Iliff, J. Burke Knapp, and Davidson Sommers named vice presidents of Bank.

Sept. 18   Swiss government loans Bank 200 million Swiss francs—about $47 million.

Sept. 20   Michael L. Hoffman named director of Economic Development Institute.

Sept. 25   Eleventh annual meeting of governors of Bank convenes in Washington; IFC holds first meeting.

1957

Jan. 23 Bank lends $75 million to Iran to provide short-term financing for seven-year development plan.

April 2 Far East Department of Operations formed, with Martin Rosen director and I. P. M. Cargill assistant director.

June 20 IFC makes first investment—$2 million in Siemens do Brasil to expand manufacturing.

July 28 Report of general survey mission to Jordan published.

Aug. 2 Bank and Italy sponsor study expected to lead to construction o large nuclear power station.

Sept. 11 IFC makes first investment in a nonmanufacturing enterprise: $600,000 in Bristol de México.

Oct. 14 William Diamond's *Development Banks* published (first EDI publication).

Nov. 6 Eugene Black visits Cairo, Egypt (High Dam project).

1958

March 28 Discussions held concerning compensation of Suez Canal Company shareholders.

May 29 Jan Tinbergen's *The Design of Development* published.

July 7 IFC makes first investment in Asia: $630,000 in Steel Corporation of Pakistan, Ltd.

July 14 Final Suez Canal compensation agreement signed in Geneva.

Aug. 25–27 First meeting of India aid consortium held.

Oct. 7 Annual meetings convene in New Delhi (board of governors asks that consideration be given to increase in Bank's capital; IDA discussed).

Nov. 4 *Debt Servicing Capacity and Postwar Growth in International Indebtedness*, by Dragoslav Avramović, published by the Johns Hopkins Press.

1959

Feb. 9 IFC makes first investment in India: $1.5 million in Republic Forge.

Feb. 19 Eugene Black goes to Cairo (for mediation of U.K.-U.A.R. financial issues).

March 17 Second India aid consortium meeting held.

May 4 Report issued on nuclear power in southern Italy.

July 1 For second successive fiscal year, Bank lending exceeds $700 million (fiscal year 1959 as well as fiscal 1958).

Sept. 16 Bank capital increased from $10 billion to $21 billion.

Sept. 28 Annual meetings of Bank/IFC convene in Washington; governors ask that IDA charter be drafted.

Oct. 9 Robert W. Cavanaugh named treasurer of Bank, succeeding late Henry W. Riley.

Oct. 12 Agricultural survey mission goes to Peru.

Oct. 22 *Electric Power Regulation in Latin America* published by the Johns Hopkins Press.

Dec. 10	$50 million loaned for oil pipeline to Société Petrolière de Gérance in Algeria and Sahara.
Dec. 22	$56.5 million loaned to Suez Canal Authority.

1960

Jan. 20	"Three Wise Men" (Abs, Franks, and Sproul) begin visit to India and Pakistan.
Feb. 1	Articles of Agreement of International Development Association (IDA) are ready for acceptance by prospective member governments.
April 4	Eugene Black is to mediate settlement of City of Tokyo Bonds of 1912.
June 17	$15.5 million loan granted to Sudan for irrigation (first loan to "new" Africa).
Sept. 19	Indus Waters Treaty signed in Karachi.
Sept. 24	International Development Association (IDA) comes into being.
Sept. 25	IFC announces that a proposal to amend its charter (to permit equity investment) will be discussed informally during annual meeting of governors.
Sept. 30	Bank acts as executing agency for UN Special Fund in study of transportation in Argentina.
Oct. 5	First meeting of Pakistan aid consortium is held.
Nov. 15	Cuba withdraws from membership in Bank and IFC.

1961

April 4	Leonard Rist appointed special representative for Africa.
April 11	I. P. M. Cargill and A. G. Kheradjou appointed director and assistant director, Far East.
May 12	IDA extends first development credit, to Honduras.
June 1	Martin M. Rosen becomes executive vice president of IFC.
June 14	$19.5 million Bank loan and $13 million IDA credit granted to Sudan for Roseires Dam.
June 15	Special course to be held at Economic Development Institute for senior agricultural economists of FAO announced.
June 23	IFC announces first sale of an investment in a completed project.
Sept. 5	Adoption of amendment to IFC Articles of Agreement announced.
Sept. 8	IFC makes first investment in development banks: $2 million each in two Colombian financieras.
Sept. 19	Annual Bank–Fund meetings convene in Vienna.
Oct. 15	Eugene Black becomes president of IFC; Robert L. Garner retires.
Nov. 1	Development Services Department established.
Dec. 5	Geoffrey M. Wilson appointed director of operations for South Asia and Middle East.

1962

Jan. 31	New Industrial Development Bank Unit established in IFC; A. G. El Emary named director.

Feb. 5	New African Department created: Pierre L. Moussa, director; John H. Williams, assistant director.
Feb. 26	IFC establishes advisory panel of investment bankers.
March 5	Staff report on multilateral investment insurance published.
May 28	EDI begins special course on development planning for French-speaking officials of less developed countries.
July 2	Argentine transportation study, "A Long-Range Transportation Plan for Argentina," is published in Buenos Aires by Ministry of Public Works and Services (first UNDP feasibility study to be completed; Bank was executing agency).
July 26	Fifteen persons accept appointments in new Development Advisory Service.
Aug. 15	Geoffrey M. Wilson named to succeed Sir William Iliff as vice president; Escott Reid succeeds Wilson as director of operations for South Asia and Middle East.
Sept. 17	IDA lends for schools in Tunisia (first World Bank Group financing of education).
Nov. 20	Study undertaken of telecommunications needs in Central America and Panama; UN Special Fund finances the study; World Bank is executing agency.

1963

Jan. 1	George D. Woods succeeds Eugene R. Black as president of Bank, IDA, and IFC.
Jan. 16	IFC operates jointly with World Bank for first time—investment in Banque Nationale pour le Développement Economique, Morocco.
Aug. 2	Bank announces that its first loan of $250 million made in 1947 to Crédit National of France has been sold in its entirety and is no longer held by Bank.
Oct. 23	EDI begins first Project Evaluation Course conducted in Spanish.
Nov. 1	Marketing Department is designated "New York Office" and Howard C. Johnson is named director.
Dec. 17	Bank announces plan to send general survey mission to Morocco in February 1964.

1964

Jan. 7	First joint operation of IFC with Inter-American Development Bank.
March 25	George D. Woods delivers address before UN Conference on Trade and Development in Geneva, Switzerland.
March 30	EDI begins first course concerned primarily with evaluating industrial projects.
April 2	Bernard Chadenet appointed associate director of technical operations.
April 6	Supplemental Agreement to the Indus Basin Development Fund Agreement of 1960 comes into force. Provides additional foreign exchange resources to be applied toward the cost of works to be constructed by Pakistan in the Indus Basin, aggregating $315 million.

May 7	Announcement made that EDI, in cooperation with Indian Institute of Management, Calcutta, will give new course in evaluation of economic development projects in Jaipur, India, from Oct. 19 to Dec. 11 for participants from eight Asian countries.
May 26	Orvis A. Schmidt appointed special adviser to president on matters concerning Latin America; Gerald Alter succeeds Schmidt as director of operations, Western Hemisphere.
June 2	Féderico Consolo appointed to newly created post of special representative for United Nations organizations.
July 7	Loan equivalent to $82 million made to Nigeria to assist in financing Niger Dam.
Aug. 25	Michael L. Lejeune appointed director of administration to succeed the late William F. Howell.
Sept. 7	Annual meetings convene in Tokyo.
Oct. 1	Irving S. Friedman appointed as the economic adviser to George D. Woods, president.
Oct. 14	Bank makes first loan in the field of education, to the College of Agriculture of the University of the Philippines.
Nov. 24	Bank allocates $300,000 to meet foreign exchange costs of feasibility studies (an early grant for such studies) for three road construction projects in Peru; government of Peru to bear local currency costs.
Dec. 14	Bank announces that West African office in Abidjan, Ivory Coast, is expected to open in early 1965.
Dec. 22	Abdel G. El Emary, then with IFC, appointed to succeed Pierre L. Moussa as director of Department of Operations for Africa on Jan. 1, 1965.
Dec. 22	Ladislaus von Hoffmann appointed IFC director of investments, Africa, Asia, and the Middle East.

1965

Jan. 20	Alexander Stevenson appointed director of South Asia Department.
Jan. 22	Mahmud Burney appointed World Bank representative in Addis Ababa.
Jan. 22	Johns Hopkins Press publishes *Economic Growth and External Debt* by Dragoslav Avramović.
Feb. 15	Bank transmits to the United Nations a staff study on the proposal presented by David Horowitz, governor of the Bank of Israel, to UNCTAD.
March 1	Simon Aldewereld appointed a vice president of IBRD and IDA.
May 13	André de Lattre, Inspector of Finance (France), appointed to serve as personal adviser to George Woods for temporary period during discussions with Indian authorities.
July 6	World Bank agrees to pay up to $830,000 to help finance assistance provided by the Development Advisory Service of Harvard University to the Planning Commission of Pakistan and the Provincial Planning Departments.
Aug. 11	Leonard Rist heads Bank mission to review Gezira Irrigation Scheme. Bank to bear foreign exchange costs; Sudanese government local currency costs.

Aug. 17	Government of Indonesia withdraws from membership in World Bank.
Dec. 9	World Bank transmits to UN Secretary-General staff study on supplementary financial measures to prevent disruption of development programs in developing countries resulting from shortfalls in their export earnings.
Dec. 14	J. Burke Knapp visits Rhodesia and Zambia for talks on Kariba Dam.
Dec. 15	Johns Hopkins Press publishes *Development Planning—Lessons of Experience* by Albert Waterston.
Dec. 17	World Bank's Articles of Agreement amended to allow Bank to make loans to the IFC of up to four times IFC's unimpaired subscribed capital and surplus.

1966

Jan. 6	Appointment announced of David L. Gordon as chief of Bank's permanent mission in Eastern Africa, Nairobi.
Jan. 12	Bank/IFC join government of Brazil in study to develop a comprehensive expansion program for Brazilian steel industry.
March 16	Representatives of nine countries and the World Bank meet to set up the Nam Ngum Development Fund to be used to finance hydroelectric power project on Mekong River, with Bank acting as administrator.
April 1	John Duncan Miller appointed Bank's special representative in Europe. Arthur Karasz named deputy special representative and manager of European Office.
April 19	World Bank sends economic mission to Central America to make a comprehensive study of the development plans of Costa Rica, El Salvador, Guatemala, Honduras, and Nicaragua.
May 4	Nam Ngum Development Fund Agreement signed by representatives of nine countries and the World Bank. Seven participating countries agree to provide grants totaling the equivalent of $22,815,000.
July 20	World Bank convenes meeting in Paris to discuss the economic situation in Brazil.
July 21	World Bank convenes meeting in Paris to consider the establishment of a consultative group for Peru.
Aug. 29	Torgeir Finsaas appointed Bank's resident representative in Pakistan.
Sept. 15	Mohamed Shoaib appointed vice president of the Bank and IDA.
Oct. 14	Convention on the Settlement of Investment Disputes enters into force.
Oct. 19	World Bank approves a $100 million credit for IFC.
Oct. 20	Publication announced of *World Bank Staff Occasional Papers* (Paper No. 1 "The Economic Choice Between Hydroelectric and Thermal Power Developments," Paper No. 2 "Quantification of Road User Savings").
Dec. 8	IFC makes first investment in tourism.

1967

| Jan. 9 | World Bank lends $30 million equivalent to Compagnie des Potasses |

	du Congo, Brazzaville (loan for a state enterprise in the industrial sector).
Jan. 24	World Bank staff study on suppliers' credits, requested by UNCTAD, transmitted to UN secretary-general.
Feb. 14	World Bank announces establishment of a Department of Evaluation and Control, with J. H. Williams as director.
April 13	Indonesia rejoins World Bank (and is readmitted to IFC on April 23).
May 9	Appointment announced of Bernard Chadenet as director of the Bank's Projects Department.
May 19	World Bank announces publication by the Johns Hopkins Press of *Experiences with Agricultural Development in Tropical Africa*, by John C. de Wilde.
June 6	James S. Raj appointed vice president of IFC.
June 15	World Bank announces establishment of Middle East and North Africa Department. Michael L. Lejeune named director, Munir Benjenk deputy director. Hugh Ripman named new director of administration.
Sept. 25	Annual meetings convene in Rio de Janeiro.
Oct. 27	George D. Woods addresses Swedish Bankers Association, Stockholm (proposes the Pearson Commission).
Nov. 29	Executive directors agree to offer presidency of World Bank to Robert S. McNamara.
Dec. 11	World Bank joins governments of Kenya, Tanzania, and Uganda, and UNDP in providing study of existing surface transport systems in East Africa. Bank to act as executing agency.

1968

Jan. 8	Study of selected development projects and their appraisal, prepared by John A. King, Jr., published by the Johns Hopkins Press.
Jan. 24	Appointment of Arthur Karasz as director of the European office of the World Bank Group announced.
Feb. 19	Appointment of Sir Denis Rickett as a vice president of the Bank/IDA announced.
March 6	World Bank announces the setting up of a fund to finance the cost of constructing the Tarbela Dam project on the Indus River in West Pakistan.
April 1	Robert S. McNamara becomes president of the Bank/IFC/IDA.
April 29	World Bank arranges placement with the Saudi Arabian Monetary Agency of a $15 million issue of twenty-six-year bonds.
May 2	Tarbela Development Fund Agreement signed, to provide nearly $500 million of external financing for the project on the Indus River in West Pakistan; World Bank will be administrator.
June 26	World Bank announces loan of $90 million, with estimated $22 million in addition to come from major supplier countries, to help finance Mexico's power expansion program (joint financing).
Aug. 14	First public marketing of World Bank Bonds in the Middle East announced—$42 million of Kuwaiti dinar bonds.

Aug. 19	Lester B. Pearson's acceptance of chairmanship of an international commission to examine world development announced.
Sept. 30	President Robert S. McNamara addresses the Bank's board of governors.
Oct. 30	World Bank makes $25 million loan to Turkey for Keban electric power transmission (joint financing).
Oct. 31	Robert S. McNamara agrees to lend his offices in seeking a solution of the pending dispute between the government of the Democratic Republic of the Congo and the Union Minière, a Belgian company.
Nov. 4	Publication by the Johns Hopkins Press of a three-volume World Bank Report, *The Water and Power Resources in West Pakistan*, announced.
Nov. 19	McNamara announces appointment of Eugene H. Rotberg as treasurer of the World Bank Group.
Nov. 27	World Bank and major supplier countries agree to joint financing of $21.4 million for power interconnection in Colombia.
Dec. 16	World Bank arranges private placement of DM 400 million ($100 million) with the Rheinische Girozentrale und Provinzialbank, Düsseldorf, in cooperation with other German banks (the Bank's first savings bank issue).

1969

Jan. 2	IDA/UNDP provide $3.9 million to Pakistan to help finance employment of consultants for East Pakistan Water and Power Development Authority.
Jan. 15	IDA credit of $12.5 million to India to provide foreign exchange for imported production materials and components announced.
June 18	IDA credits totaling $44 million for agricultural production and highway improvement in Indonesia announced.
July 1	World Bank/IDA announce total loans and credits of $1,784 million in fiscal year 1969, compared with $953.5 million in preceding fiscal year. In addition, IFC financing totaled $93 million, compared with $51 million in fiscal 1968.
July 23	Second replenishment of IDA resources comes into effect with formal notification of U.S. agreement to participate.
Oct. 1	William S. Gaud succeeds Martin Rosen as executive vice president of IFC.
Dec. 23	World Bank agrees to lend an additional $100 million to IFC.

1970

Feb. 4	IDA announces $35 million credit (almost entirely for local currency expenditures) to help complete Kadana project for irrigation of about 700,000 acres in west central India.
Feb. 12	Japan's first loan to World Bank (equivalent to U.S. $100 million) announced.
Feb. 25	World Bank announces loan of $125 million to help finance Mexico's power expansion program.
March 26	IDA announces $26 million credit to United Arab Republic to assist

in largest tile drainage operation ever undertaken; project will provide drainage for nearly a million acres of irrigated land in Nile River delta.

April 24   IDA credit of $75 million to India for industrial imports signed.

May 7   Hollis B. Chenery appointed economic adviser to the president of the World Bank.

May 20   World Bank loan of $80 million to Brazil for electric power announced.

June 3   IDA provides credit of $35 million to India for an agricultural credit program in State of Gujarat.

June 4   IDA, Asian Development Bank, U.S. Agency for International Development, and Overseas Economic Cooperation Fund of Japan jointly provide Indonesia the equivalent of $68 million to finance foreign exchange costs of a fertilizer plant.

June 22   Loan approved of $2 million to Jamaica to support the government's family planning program (Bank's first loan for family planning).

July 1   Ladislaus von Hoffmann succeeds James S. Raj as vice president of IFC.

July 6   World Bank announces that it will open an office in Tokyo.

July 22   IDA announces agreement on third replenishment at a level to permit credits of approximately $813 million a year for a three-year period (first payments scheduled for Nov. 8, 1971).

Sept. 9   World Bank announces approval of a $30 million reconstruction loan to Peru for road improvement in area affected by the recent earthquake.

Sept. 10   Bank Group announces that its commitments in year ended June 30, 1970, exceeded $2 billion for the first time.

Dec. 31   Authorized capital of the World Bank increased from $24 billion to $27 billion.

1971

Jan. 13   McNamara announces $25 million IDA assistance for cyclone-devastated East Pakistan.

March 25   New Capital Markets Department in IFC announced as focal point within Bank Group for encouraging growth of capital markets in developing countries.

June 25   Twenty-five years since Bank opened for business on June 25, 1946.

Loans, Credits, and Investments

Table E-1. *IBRD Loans, IDA Credits, and IFC Investments by Purpose and Area, Net as of June 30, 1971*

In millions of U.S. dollar equivalents

| Purpose | Total, Bank, IDA, and IFC | Bank loans by area | | | | | | IFC |
		Total[a]	Africa	Asia and Middle East	Oceania	Europe	Western Hemisphere	
Grand total[a]	**19,953.1**	**16,068.6**	**2,342.4**	**4,978.6**	**576.3**	**2,963.5**	**5,007.8**	**200.0**
Electric power	5,284.0	5,010.6	600.4	1,075.3	171.4	700.6	2,462.9	...
Transportation	5,876.9	4,958.3	977.2	1,842.2	89.3	727.7	1,322.0	...
Telecommunications	575.2	348.6	37.1	113.1	7.0	40.3	151.1	...
Agriculture, forestry, and fishing	2,370.8	1,497.4	203.9	565.7	...	199.5	528.3	...
Industry	3,017.4	2,413.2	334.4	1,185.8	...	625.7	267.3	...
General development and industrial imports	1,318.4	637.7	120.0	103.8	308.5	100.0	5.4	...
Education	424.4	212.7	40.3	48.8	...	39.3	84.3	...
Population	9.8	5.0	...	...	...	...	5.0	...
Water supply and sewerage	328.7	277.7	28.3	44.0	...	23.7	181.7	...
Tourism	30.0	10.0	...	...	...	10.0	...	...
Post-war reconstruction	496.8	496.8	...	...	...	496.8	...	...
Project preparation and technical assistance[b]	21.1	0.9	0.9	...	...	...	...	...
Financing loan (IFC)	200.0	200.0	...	...	...	...	...	200.0

Table E-1. *Continued*

In millions of U.S. dollar equivalents

	IDA credits be area						IFC investments by area					
Purpose	Total[a]	Africa	Asia and Middle East	Oceania	Europe	Western Hemisphere	Total[a]	Africa	Asia and Middle East	Oceania	Europe	Western Hemisphere
Grand total[a]	**3,340.4**	**666.0**	**2,374.9**	**11.0**	**111.8**	**176.7**	**544.1**	**83.9**	**171.1**	**1.0**	**70.8**	**217.3**
Electric power	273.4	22.3	187.9	...	25.7	37.5	...	...	...	...	...	...
Transportation	918.5	300.7	536.0	4.5	...	77.3	...	...	...	...	...	...
Telecommunications	226.6	0.8	225.8	...	...	...	...	...	...	...	...	...
Agriculture, forestry, and fishing	850.2	158.7	586.7	6.5	51.4	46.9	23.2	14.5	...	...	...	8.7
Industry	104.0	5.0	64.3	...	34.7	...	500.2	55.8	170.4	1.0	70.8	202.2
General development and industrial imports	680.0	...	680.0	...	...	...	0.7	...	0.7	...	...	...
Education	211.7	150.0	49.7	...	...	12.0	...	...	...	...	...	...
Population	4.8	4.8	...	...	...	...	...	...	...	...	...	...
Water supply and sewerage	51.0	18.1	29.9	...	...	3.0	...	...	...	...	...	...
Tourism	...	...	...	...	...	...	20.0	13.6	...	...	...	6.4
Post-war reconstruction	...	...	...	...	...	...	...	...	...	...	...	...
Project preparation and technical assistance	20.2	5.6	14.6	...	...	...	...	...	...	...	...	...
Financing loan (IFC)	...	...	...	...	...	...	...	...	...	...	...	...

Source: World Bank Group, *Profiles of Development* (September 1971), pp. 32–33.

Note: Multipurpose loans have been distributed according to each purpose. Bank/IDA totals for specific sectors therefore differ from totals in corresponding sector working papers cited in Chapter 20.

a. Details may not add to totals due to rounding.
b. Only a small proportion of Bank/IDA technical assistance is covered by project preparation loans and credits. See Chapter 10, above.

Table E-2. *IBRD Loans and IDA Credits by Country, Net as of June 30, 1971*[a]

Amounts in U.S. dollar equivalents

Country	Bank loans		IDA credits		Total	
	Num-ber	Amount	Num-ber	Amount	Num-ber	Amount
Afghanistan	...	...	4	15,277,313	4	15,277,313
Algeria	3	80,500,000	...	...	3	80,500,000
Argentina	9	509,102,049	...	...	9	509,102,049
Australia	7	417,730,000	...	...	7	417,730,000
Austria	9	104,860,083	...	...	9	104,860,083
Belgium	4	76,000,000	...	...	4	76,000,000
Bolivia	1	23,250,000	6	32,600,000	7	55,850,000
Botswana	1	32,000,000	3	9,100,000	4	41,100,000
Brazil	34	998,291,274	...	...	34	998,291,274
Burma	3	33,123,943	...	...	3	33,123,943
Burundi	1	4,800,000	3	3,280,000	4	8,080,000
Cameroon	5	37,100,000	5	30,000,000	10	67,100,000
Central African Republic	...	...	2	8,500,000	2	8,500,000
Ceylon	8	74,128,601	4	19,646,000	12	93,774,601
Chad	...	...	3	8,100,000	3	8,100,000
Chile	18	232,537,762	1	18,997,755	19	251,535,517
China	14	312,613,133	4	13,073,716	18	325,686,849
Colombia	48	871,877,840	1	19,500,000	49	891,377,840
Congo, Democratic Republic of	5	91,582,854	3	18,000,000	8	109,582,854
Congo, People's Republic of	1	30,000,000	3	5,630,000	4	35,630,000
Costa Rica	11	84,876,251	1	4,550,243	12	89,426,494
Cyprus	6	39,493,510	...	...	6	39,493,510
Dahomey	...	...	2	8,100,000	2	8,100,000
Denmark	3	85,000,000	...	...	3	85,000,000
Dominican Republic	1	25,000,000	2	9,000,000	3	34,000,000
Ecuador	10	71,300,000	4	24,600,000	14	95,900,000
El Salvador	9	57,918,024	2	13,599,331	11	71,517,355
Ethiopia	11	97,800,000	6	44,500,000	17	142,300,000
Fiji	1	11,800,000	...	...	1	11,800,000
Finland	16	276,526,846	...	...	16	276,526,846
France	1	250,000,000	...	...	1	250,000,000
Gabon	4	54,788,722	...	...	4	54,788,722
Gambia, The	...	...	1	2,100,000	1	2,100,000
Ghana	2	53,000,000	6	31,900,000	8	84,900,000
Greece	4	71,300,000	...	...	4	71,300,000
Guatemala	5	50,500,000	...	...	5	50,500,000
Guinea	3	73,500,000	...	...	3	73,500,000
Guyana	4	14,219,017	2	5,100,000	6	19,319,017
Haiti	1	2,600,000	1	349,855	2	2,949,855
Honduras	10	58,085,959	5	24,027,974	15	82,113,933
Iceland	8	30,014,000	...	...	8	30,014,000
India	39	1,051,248,279	34	1,507,040,696	73	2,558,288,975
Indonesia	...	...	16	227,400,000	16	227,400,000
Iran	19	612,146,457	...	...	19	612,146,457
Iraq	2	25,293,946	...	...	2	25,293,946
Ireland	3	44,500,000	...	...	3	44,500,000
Israel	7	154,412,479	...	...	7	154,412,479
Italy	8	398,028,000	...	...	8	398,028,000
Ivory Coast[b]	10	75,991,567	...	...	10	75,991,567
Jamaica	8	59,959,421	...	...	8	59,959,421
Japan	31	857,041,004	...	...	31	857,041,004
Jordan	...	...	5	16,015,502	5	16,015,502
Kenya[c]	12	228,824,026	11	61,300,000	23	290,124,026
Korea	6	194,500,000	6	64,938,129	12	259,438,129
Lebanon	1	27,000,000	...	...	1	27,000,000
Lesotho	...	...	1	4,100,000	1	4,100,000
Liberia	4	15,249,812	...	...	4	15,249,812
Luxembourg	1	11,761,983	...	...	1	11,761,983
Malagasy Republic	3	11,100,000	4	29,100,000	7	40,200,000
Malawi	...	...	7	40,000,000	7	40,000,000

Table E-2. *Continued*

Country	Bank loans Number	Bank loans Amount	IDA credits Number	IDA credits Amount	Total Number	Total Amount
Malaysia	16	288,678,513	...	...	16	288,678,513
Mali[b]	...	...	2	16,800,000	2	16,800,000
Malta	1	6,040,080	...	...	1	6,040,080
Mauritania	1	66,000,000	2	9,700,000	3	75,700,000
Mauritius	1	6,973,119	1	5,200,000	2	12,173,119
Mexico	25	1,053,446,438	...	...	25	1,053,446,438
Morocco	10	186,720,830	2	18,300,000	12	205,020,830
Nepal	...	...	2	4,200,000	2	4,200,000
Netherlands	10	236,451,985	...	...	10	236,451,985
New Zealand	5	112,058,680	...	...	5	112,058,680
Nicaragua	15	59,858,828	1	2,994,834	16	62,853,662
Niger	...	...	4	13,903,224	4	13,903,224
Nigeria	13	338,800,000	2	35,304,820	15	374,104,820
Norway	6	145,000,000	...	...	6	145,000,000
Pakistan	31	633,459,647	38	497,190,454	69	1,130,650,101
Panama	6	60,047,426	...	...	6	60,047,426
Papua and New Guinea	3	34,700,000	3	11,000,000	6	45,700,000
Paraguay	6	21,838,549	4	21,400,000	10	43,238,549
Peru	24	244,102,066	...	...	24	244,102,066
Philippines	15	238,952,923	...	...	15	238,952,923
Portugal	5	57,500,000	...	...	5	57,500,000
Rhodesia[d]	3	86,950,000	...	...	3	86,950,000
Rwanda	...	...	1	9,300,000	1	9,300,000
Senegal[b]	2	4,000,000	6	24,150,000	8	28,150,000
Sierra Leone	3	11,400,000	2	6,500,000	5	17,900,000
Singapore	10	114,243,457	...	...	10	114,243,457
Somalia	...	...	4	12,350,000	4	12,350,000
South Africa	11	241,800,000	...	...	11	241,800,000
Spain	8	326,861,832	...	...	8	326,861,832
Sudan	6	129,000,000	2	21,500,000	8	150,500,000
Swaziland	2	6,950,000	1	2,800,000	3	9,750,000
Syria	...	...	1	8,500,000	1	8,500,000
Tanzania[c]	3	42,200,000	10	60,700,000	13	102,900,000
Thailand	22	361,698,461	...	...	22	361,698,461
Togo	...	...	1	3,700,000	1	3,700,000
Trinidad and Tobago	6	49,390,424	...	...	6	49,390,424
Tunisia	11	102,168,689	6	44,762,598	17	146,931,287
Turkey	16	238,679,609	10	111,815,987	26	350,495,596
Uganda[c]	1	8,400,000	7	44,300,000	8	52,700,000
United Arab Republic	1	56,500,000	1	26,000,000	2	82,500,000
Upper Volta[b]	...	...	2	7,000,000	2	7,000,000
Uruguay	9	130,461,803	...	...	9	130,461,803
Venezuela	10	329,114,641	...	...	10	329,114,641
Yemen, People's Democratic Republic of	...	...	1	1,600,000	1	1,600,000
Yugoslavia	19	565,490,547	...	...	19	565,490,547
Zambia[d]	11	168,250,000	...	...	11	168,250,000
International Finance Corporation	1	200,000,000	...	...	1	200,000,000
Total	783	16,068,465,389	274	3,340,398,431	1,057	19,408,863,820

Source: World Bank/IDA, *Annual Report, 1971*, pp. 110–11.
a. Initial commitments net of cancellations, refundings, and terminations.
b. One loan for $7.5 million shown against Ivory Coast is shared with Mali, Senegal, and Upper Volta.
c. Six loans aggregating $162.8 million shown against Kenya are shared with Tanzania and Uganda.
d. Three loans totaling $106.7 million have been assigned in equal shares to Rhodesia and Zambia.

Table E-3. *IBRD Loans and IDA Credits: Amounts and Disbursements by Fiscal Years through June 30, 1971*

Amounts and disbursements in U.S. dollar equivalents

Fis-cal year	World Bank loans[a]			IDA credits[a]		
	Num-ber	Amount	Disburse-ments	Num-ber	Amount	Disburse-ments
1947	1	250,000,000	92,000,000			
1948	5	263,000,000	378,055,751			
1949	10	137,100,000	56,235,263			
1950	12	166,345,000	87,871,146			
1951	21	297,080,000	77,564,969			
1952	19	298,608,000	184,777,004			
1953	10	178,633,464	226,756,982			
1954	26	323,682,000	302,296,920			
1955	20	409,610,000	274,169,870			
1956	26	396,050,000	283,926,916			
1957	20	387,858,000	332,379,283			
1958	34	710,846,429	498,683,137			
1959	30	703,125,000	582,630,254			
1960	31	658,700,000	543,879,250			
1961	27	609,890,000	398,488,190	4	101,000,000	...
1962	29	882,300,000	485,366,490	18	134,100,000	12,168,476
1963	28	448,650,000	620,417,274	17	260,050,000	56,192,417
1964	37	809,850,000	558,884,723	18	283,200,000	124,130,697
1965	38	1,023,300,000	605,723,972	20	309,090,000	222,197,090
1966	37	839,200,000	668,421,586	12	284,100,000	266,898,667
1967	46	876,750,000	790,442,920	20	353,540,000	342,090,922
1968	44	846,950,000	771,946,891	18	106,550,000	318,820,723
1969	84	1,399,250,000	762,039,490	38	385,000,000	255,790,731
1970	70	1,680,350,000[b]	771,839,154	56	605,614,000	143,347,903
1971	78	1,896,400,000	954,903,534	53	584,000,000	235,054,431
Total	783	16,493,527,893	11,309,700,969	274	3,406,244,000	1,976,692,057

Source: IBRD, Department of Information and Public Affairs.

a. The loan and credit figures in these columns are gross figures, unadjusted for cancellations, refundings, and terminations. In the case of Bank loans, the total of $16,493,527,893 includes cancellations, refundings, and terminations, totaling $425,062,504. In the case of IDA credits, the total of $3,406,244,000 includes cancellations, refundings, and terminations, totaling $65,845,570.

b. A $100 million Bank loan made to IFC in 1966 was consolidated into a single loan of $200 million in December 1969. The first $100 million is still shown in 1967.

Table E-4. *IBRD Loans by Area and Purpose, 1961–65, 1966–70, and January–June, 1971*[a]

Amounts expressed in millions of U.S. dollars

Purpose	1961–65		1966–70		Total 1961–70		Jan.–June 1971		Total Jan. 1961–June 1971	
	Amount	Per-cent	Amount	Per-cent	Amount	Per-cent	Amount	Per-cent	Amount	Per-cent
ALL AREAS										
Grand total	3,957.6	100.0	5,334.3	100.0	9,291.9	100.0	1,421.7	100.0	10,713.6	100.0
Electric power	1,525.9	38.6	1,662.6	31.2	3,188.5	34.3	217.7	15.4	3,406.2	31.8
Transportation	1,512.4	38.2	1,385.9	26.0	2,898.3	31.2	516.5	36.3	3,414.8	31.9
Railroads	531.7	13.4	333.6	6.3	865.4	9.3	205.7	14.5	1,071.1	10.0
Shipping	...	...	...	...	...	...	...	...	...	...
Ports and waterways	116.7	2.9	123.9	2.3	240.7	2.6	74.2	5.2	314.9	2.9
Roads	849.0	21.4	877.8	16.5	1,726.8	18.6	229.1	16.1	1,955.9	18.3
Airlines and airports	...	...	...	...	...	...	...	...	...	...
Pipelines	15.0	0.4	50.4	0.9	65.4	0.7	7.5	0.5	72.9	0.7
Telecommunications	64.1	1.6	191.8	3.6	255.9	2.8	68.7	4.8	324.6	3.0
Agriculture, forestry, and fishing	251.1	6.4	698.1	13.1	949.2	10.2	190.8	13.4	1,140.0	10.6
Farm mechanization	0.9	b	14.0	0.3	14.9	0.2	...	...	14.9	0.1
Irrigation and flood control	136.6	3.5	303.5	5.7	440.1	4.7	52.0	3.7	492.1	4.6
Land clearance, farm improvement	3.2	0.1	43.9	0.8	47.1	0.5	...	...	47.1	0.4
Crop processing and storage	-0.6[c]	b	6.8	0.1	6.2	0.1	16.2	1.1	22.4	0.2
Livestock improvement	30.7	0.8	163.6	3.1	194.3	2.1	83.0	5.8	277.3	2.6
Forestry and fishing	7.8	0.2	27.5	0.5	35.3	0.4	...	...	35.3	0.3
Agricultural credit	72.5	1.8	111.2	2.1	183.7	2.0	-3.5[c]	-0.2[e]	180.2	1.7
Smallholders and plantations	...	...	27.7	0.5	27.7	0.3	20.4	1.4	48.1	0.4

Table E-4. Continued

Purpose	1961–65		1966–70		Total 1961–70		Jan.–June 1971		Total Jan. 1961–June 1971	
	Amount	Per-cent	Amount	Per-cent	Amount	Per-cent	Amount	Per-cent	Amount	Per-cent
Agricultural industries	...	...	...	...	...	...	10.0	0.7	10.0	0.1
Agricultural research	...	...	...	...	...	...	12.7	0.9	12.7	0.1
Industry	535.3	13.5	924.8	17.3	1,460.1	15.7	147.5	10.4	1,607.6	15.0
Iron and steel	29.0	0.7	5.9	0.1	34.9	0.4	...	...	34.9	0.3
Pulp and paper	25.0	0.6	2.6	b	27.6	0.3	...	...	27.6	0.3
Fertilizer and chemicals	25.0	0.6	62.0	1.2	87.0	0.9	...	...	87.0	0.8
Other industries	128.5	3.2	58.7	1.1	187.2	2.0	−0.1c	b	187.1	1.7
Mining and mining infrastructure	19.5	0.5	24.9	0.5	44.4	0.5	32.0	2.3	76.4	0.7
Development finance companies	308.3	7.8	770.6	14.4	1,078.9	11.6	115.6	8.1	1,194.5	11.2
General development and industrial imports	29.1	0.7	−0.3c	b	28.8	0.3	85.4	6.0	114.2	1.1
Social services	39.7	1.0	270.6	5.1	310.3	3.3	195.2	13.7	505.5	4.7
Education	8.8	0.2	168.5	3.2	177.3	1.9	35.4	2.5	212.7	2.0
Family planning	...	...	2.0	b	2.0	b	3.0	0.2	5.0	b
Water systems	30.9	0.8	100.1	1.9	131.0	1.4	146.8	10.3	279.8	2.6
Hotels and tourism	...	...	...	...	...	...	10.0	0.7	10.0	0.1
Reconstruction	...	...	...	...	...	...	...	...	...	...
Miscellaneous	...	...	200.9	3.7	200.9	2.2	...	...	200.9	1.9
Technical assistance and project preparation	...	...	0.9	b	0.9	b	...	...	0.9	b
Financing loan (IFC)	...	...	200.0	3.7	200.0	2.2	...	...	200.0	1.9

WESTERN HEMISPHERE

Grand total	1,300.5	100.0	1,989.3	100.0	3,289.8	100.0	618.3	100.0	3,908.1	100.0
Electric power	715.7	55.0	1,050.1	52.8	1,745.8	53.7	70.0	11.3	1,835.8	47.0
Transportation	373.9	28.8	412.9	20.8	786.8	23.9	202.0	32.7	988.8	25.3
Railroads	43.3	3.3	12.1	0.6	55.4	1.7	84.0	13.6	139.4	3.6
Shipping	...	...	...	...	...	...	...	...	...	...
Ports and waterways	5.9	0.5	13.8	0.7	19.7	0.6	50.7	8.2	70.4	1.8
Roads	324.7	25.0	363.8	18.3	688.5	20.9	67.3	10.9	755.8	19.3
Airlines and airports	...	...	...	...	...	...	...	...	...	...
Pipelines	...	...	23.2	1.2	23.2	0.7	...	...	23.2	0.6
Telecommunications	56.4	4.4	22.5	1.1	78.9	2.4	50.0	8.1	128.9	3.3
Agriculture, forestry, and fishing	113.7	8.7	254.8	12.8	368.5	11.2	91.1	14.7	459.6	11.8
Farm mechanization	0.9	0.1	...	...	0.9	...	...	...	0.9	b
Irrigation and flood control	41.1	3.2	51.9	2.6	93.0	2.8	...	...	93.0	2.4
Land clearance, farm improvement	...	...	5.0	0.3	5.0	0.2	...	...	5.0	0.1
Crop processing and storage	...	...	...	...	...	...	...	...	...	...
Livestock improvement	31.7	2.4	129.9	6.5	161.6	4.9	83.0	13.4	244.6	6.3
Forestry and fishing	...	...	5.2	0.2	5.2	0.2	...	...	5.2	0.1
Agricultural credit	40.0	3.0	62.8	3.1	102.8	3.1	...	...	102.8	2.6
Smallholders and plantations	...	...	...	...	...	...	8.1	1.3	8.1	0.2
Agricultural industries	...	...	...	...	...	...	...	...	...	...
Agricultural research	...	...	...	...	...	...	...	...	...	...
Industry	38.0	2.9	132.8	6.7	170.8	5.2	47.9	7.7	218.7	5.6
Iron and steel	30.0	2.3	...	...	30.0	0.9	...	...	30.0	0.8
Pulp and paper	...	...	...	...	...	...	...	...	...	...
Fertilizer and chemicals	...	...	...	...	...	...	...	...	...	...
Other industries	8.0	0.6	20.4	1.0	28.4	0.9	-0.1c	b	28.3	0.7
Mining and mining infrastructure	...	...	24.9	1.3	24.9	0.7	...	...	24.9	0.6
Development finance companies	...	...	87.5	4.4	87.5	2.7	48.0	7.8	135.5	3.5

Table E-4. Continued

Purpose	1961-65		1966-70		Total 1961-70		Jan.-June 1971		Total Jan. 1961-June 1971	
	Amount	Per-cent	Amount	Per-cent	Amount	Per-cent	Amount	Per-cent	Amount	Per-cent
General development and industrial imports	...	...	...	...	...	...	5.4	0.9	5.4	0.1
Social services	2.8	0.2	116.3	5.8	119.1	3.6	151.9	24.6	271.0	6.9
Education	2.8	0.2	59.6	3.0	62.4	1.9	21.9	3.5	84.3	2.2
Family planning	...	...	2.0	0.1	2.0	0.1	3.0	0.5	5.0	0.1
Water systems	...	...	54.7	2.7	54.7	1.6	127.0	20.5	181.7	4.6
Hotels and tourism	...	...	...	...	...	...	...	...	...	...
Reconstruction	...	...	...	...	...	...	...	...	...	...
Miscellaneous	...	...	...	...	...	...	...	...	...	...
Technical assistance and project preparation	...	...	...	...	...	...	...	...	...	...
Financing loan (IFC)	...	...	...	...	...	...	...	...	...	...
EUROPE, OCEANIA, AND IFC										
Grand total	852.0	100.0	817.9	100.0	1,670.0	100.0	370.6	100.0	2,040.6	100.0
Electric power	341.6	40.1	94.7	11.6	436.3	26.1	77.7	21.0	514.0	25.2
Transportation	355.6	41.7	218.8	26.7	574.4	34.4	164.9	44.5	739.3	36.2
Railroads	212.0	24.9	100.0	12.2	312.0	18.7	105.1	28.4	417.1	20.4
Shipping	47.1	5.5	11.1	1.4	58.2	3.5	...	...	58.2	2.9
Ports and waterways	96.5	11.3	107.7	13.2	204.2	12.2	59.8	16.1	264.0	12.9
Roads	...	...	...	...	...	...	...	...	...	...
Airlines and airports	...	...	...	...	...	...	...	...	...	...
Pipelines	...	...	...	...	...	...	...	...	...	...

Telecommunications	...	...	47.0	5.7	47.0	2.8	...	...	47.0	2.3
Agriculture, forestry, and fishing	...	...	37.0	4.5	37.0	2.2	74.7	20.1	111.7	5.5
Farm mechanization	...	...	...	...	...	...	...	...	...	...
Irrigation and flood control	...	...	12.0	1.5	12.0	0.7	52.0	14.0	64.0	3.1
Land clearance, farm improvement	...	...	...	...	...	...	...	...	...	...
Crop processing and storage	...	...	...	...	...	...	...	...	...	...
Livestock improvement	...	...	25.0	3.1	25.0	1.5	...	...	25.0	1.2
Forestry and fishing	...	...	...	...	...	...	...	...	...	...
Agricultural credit	...	...	...	...	...	...	...	...	...	...
Smallholders and plantations	...	...	...	...	...	...	...	...	...	...
Agricultural industries	...	...	...	...	...	...	10.0	2.7	10.0	0.5
Agricultural research	...	...	...	...	...	...	12.7	3.4	12.7	0.6
Industry	151.0	17.7	194.6	23.8	345.6	20.7	10.0	2.7	355.6	17.4
Iron and steel	...	...	4.2	0.5	4.2	0.3	...	...	4.2	0.2
Pulp and paper	...	...	2.6	0.3	...	...	...	...	...	...
Fertilizer and chemicals	25.0	2.9	...	...	27.6	1.7	...	...	27.6	1.4
Other industries	100.0	11.7	38.3	4.7	138.3	8.3	...	...	138.3	6.8
Mining and mining infrastructure	...	...	...	...	...	...	...	...	...	...
Development finance companies	26.0	3.1	149.5	18.3	175.5	10.5	10.0	2.7	185.5	9.1
General development and industrial imports	...	...	...	...	...	...	...	...	...	...
Social services	3.9	0.5	25.8	3.2	29.7	1.8	43.3	11.7	73.0	3.6
Education	...	...	25.8	3.2	25.8	1.5	13.5	3.6	39.3	1.9
Family planning	...	...	...	...	...	...	...	...	...	...
Water systems	3.9	0.5	...	...	3.9	0.3	19.8	5.3	23.7	1.2
Hotels and tourism	...	...	...	...	...	...	10.0	2.7	10.0	0.5
Reconstruction	...	...	...	...	...	...	...	...	...	...
Miscellaneous	...	...	200.0	24.5	200.0	12.0	...	...	200.0	9.8
Technical assistance and project preparation	...	...	...	...	...	...	...	...	...	...
Financing loan (IFC)	...	...	200.0	24.5	200.0	12.0	...	...	200.0	9.8

Table E-4. Continued

AFRICA

Purpose	1961–65 Amount	1961–65 Per-cent	1966–70 Amount	1966–70 Per-cent	Total 1961–70 Amount	Total 1961–70 Per-cent	Jan.–June 1971 Amount	Jan.–June 1971 Per-cent	Total Jan. 1961–June 1971 Amount	Total Jan. 1961–June 1971 Per-cent
Grand total	448.5	100.0	824.0	100.0	1,272.6	100.0	241.4	100.0	1,514.0	100.0
Electric power	227.6	50.7	171.8	20.8	399.4	31.4	23.0	9.5	422.4	27.9
Transportation	127.0	28.3	314.5	38.2	441.5	34.7	61.0	25.3	502.5	33.1
Railroads	74.8	16.7	108.8	13.2	183.7	14.4	1.6	0.7	185.3	12.2
Shipping	...	...	...	...	...	...	...	...	...	...
Ports and waterways	20.4	4.5	75.5	9.2	95.9	7.5	7.4	3.1	103.3	6.8
Roads	31.8	7.1	130.2	15.8	161.9	12.7	44.5	18.4	206.4	13.6
Airlines and airports	...	...	...	...	...	...	...	...	...	...
Pipelines	...	...	...	...	...	...	7.5	3.1	7.5	0.5
Telecommunications	7.7	1.7	27.9	3.5	35.6	2.8	...	...	35.6	2.4
Agriculture, forestry, and fishing	48.8	10.9	113.2	13.7	162.0	12.7	10.7	4.4	172.7	11.4
Farm mechanization	...	...	5.0	0.6	5.0	0.4	...	...	5.0	0.3
Irrigation and flood control	19.5	4.3	46.0	5.6	65.5	5.1	...	...	65.5	4.3
Land clearance, farm improvement	3.4	0.7	7.2	0.9	10.6	0.8	...	...	10.6	0.7
Crop processing and storage	-0.6[c]	-0.1[c]	4.8	0.6	4.2	0.3	1.9	0.8	6.1	0.4
Livestock improvement	-1.0[c]	-0.2[c]	5.3	0.6	4.3	0.3	...	...	4.3	0.3
Forestry and fishing	...	...	7.9	1.0	7.9	0.6	...	...	7.9	0.5
Agricultural credit	27.5	6.1	9.4	1.1	36.9	2.9	-3.5[c]	-1.4[c]	33.4	2.2
Smallholders and plantations	...	...	27.7	3.4	27.7	2.2	12.3	5.1	40.0	2.6
Agricultural industries	...	...	...	...	...	...	...	...	...	...
Agricultural research	...	...	...	...	...	...	...	...	...	...

Industry	37.5	8.4	127.1	15.4	164.6	12.9	66.7	27.7	231.3	15.3
Iron and steel	...	...	...	...	...	...	...	...	...	...
Pulp and paper	...	...	...	...	...	...	...	...	...	...
Fertilizer and chemicals	...	...	30.0	3.6	30.0	2.4	...	...	30.0	2.0
Other industries	20.5	4.6	...	...	20.5	1.6	...	...	20.5	1.4
Mining and mining infrastructure	...	...	...	...	...	...	32.0	13.3	32.0	2.1
Development finance companies	17.0	3.8	97.1	11.8	114.1	8.9	34.7	14.4	148.8	9.8
General development and industrial imports	...	...	...	...	...	...	80.0	33.1	80.0	5.3
Social services	...	...	...	...	...	...	...	...	...	...
Education	...	...	68.6	8.3	68.6	5.4	...	...	68.6	4.5
Family planning	...	...	40.3	4.9	40.3	3.2	...	...	40.3	2.7
Water systems	...	...	28.3	3.4	28.3	2.2	...	...	28.3	1.9
Hotels and tourism	...	...	...	...	...	...	...	...	...	...
Reconstruction	...	...	...	...	...	...	...	...	...	...
Miscellaneous	...	...	0.9	0.1	0.9	0.1	...	...	0.9	0.1
Technical assistance and project preparation	...	...	0.9	0.1	0.9	0.1	...	...	0.9	0.1
Financing loan (IFC)	...	...	...	...	...	...	...	...	...	...
ASIA AND MIDDLE EAST										
Grand total	1,356.3	100.0	1,703.1	100.0	3,059.5	100.0	191.4	100.0	3,250.9	100.0
Electric power	241.0	17.8	346.0	20.4	587.0	19.1	47.0	24.5	634.0	19.5
Transportation	655.9	48.4	439.7	25.8	1,095.6	35.8	88.6	46.3	1,184.2	36.4
Railroads	201.6	14.9	112.7	6.6	314.3	10.2	15.0	7.9	329.3	10.1
Shipping	...	...	...	...	...	...	...	...	...	...
Ports and waterways	43.3	3.2	23.6	1.4	66.9	2.2	16.1	8.4	83.0	2.6
Roads	396.0	29.2	276.1	16.2	672.2	22.0	57.5	30.0	729.7	22.4
Airlines and airports	...	...	...	...	...	...	...	...	...	...
Pipelines	15.0	1.1	27.2	1.6	42.2	1.4	...	...	42.2	1.3
Telecommunications	...	...	94.4	5.5	94.4	3.3	18.7	9.8	113.1	3.5

Table E-4. *Continued*

Purpose	1961–65		1966–70		Total 1961–70		Jan.–June 1971		Total Jan. 1961–June 1971	
	Amount	*Per-cent*	*Amount*	*Per-cent*	*Amount*	*Per-cent*	*Amount*	*Per-cent*	*Amount*	*Per-cent*
Agriculture, forestry, and fishing	88.6	6.5	293.1	17.2	381.7	12.4	14.3	7.5	396.0	12.2
Farm mechanization	...	...	9.0	0.5	9.0	0.3	...	...	9.0	0.3
Irrigation and flood control	76.0	5.6	193.6	11.4	269.6	8.8	...	...	269.6	8.3
Land clearance, farm improvement	-0.2	b	31.7	1.9	31.5	1.0	14.3	7.5	31.5	1.0
Crop processing and storage	...	...	2.0	0.1	2.0	0.1	...	...	16.3	0.5
Livestock improvement	...	...	3.4	0.2	3.4	0.1	...	...	3.4	0.1
Forestry and fishing	7.8	0.6	14.4	0.8	22.2	0.7	...	...	22.2	0.7
Agricultural credit	5.0	0.4	39.0	2.3	44.0	1.4	...	...	44.0	1.4
Smallholders and plantations	...	...	...	...	...	...	...	...	...	...
Agricultural industries	...	...	...	...	...	...	...	...	...	...
Agricultural research	...	...	...	...	...	...	...	...	...	...
Industry	308.8	22.8	470.3	27.6	779.1	25.4	22.9	12.0	802.0	24.7
Iron and steel	-1.0e	-0.1c	1.7	0.1	0.7	0.1	...	...	0.7	b
Pulp and paper	...	...	...	...	...	...	...	...	...	...
Fertilizer and chemicals	25.0	1.8	32.0	1.9	57.0	1.9	...	...	57.0	1.8
Other industries	...	...	...	...	...	...	...	...	...	...
Mining and mining infrastructure	19.5	1.4	...	...	19.5	0.6	...	...	19.5	0.6
Development finance companies	265.3	19.6	436.5	25.6	701.8	22.5	22.9	12.0	724.7	22.3
General development and industrial imports	29.1	2.1	-0.3e	b	28.8	0.9	...	...	28.8	0.9
Social services	33.0	2.4	59.9	3.5	92.9	3.0	...	...	92.9	2.9
Education	6.0	0.4	42.8	2.5	48.8	1.6	...	...	48.8	1.5
Family planning	...	...	...	...	...	...	...	...	...	...

840

Water systems	27.0	2.0	17.1	1.0	44.1	1.4	...	...	46.1	1.4
Hotels and tourism	...	...	...	...	...	...	...	...	...	...
Reconstruction	...	...	...	...	...	...	...	...	...	...
Miscellaneous	...	...	...	...	...	...	...	...	...	...
Technical assistance and project preparation	...	...	...	...	...	...	...	...	...	...c
Financing loan (IFC)	...	...	...	...	...	...	...	...	...	...

Source: IBRD, Economic Program Department.

Notes: Multipurpose loans are distributed according to each purpose and not assigned to the major purpose. Details may not add to totals due to rounding.

a. Net of cancellations and refundings.
b. Less than 0.05 percent.
c. Minus signs indicate that cancellations or refundings exceeded new credits during the period.

Table E-5. *IDA Credits by Area and Purpose, 1961–65, 1966–70, and January–June, 1971*[a]

Amounts in millions of U.S. dollar equivalents

Purpose	1961–65		1966–70		Total 1961–70		Jan.–June 1971		Total Jan. 1961–June 1971	
	Amount	Per-cent	Amount	Per-cent	Amount	Per-cent	Amount	Per-cent	Amount	Per-cent
ALL AREAS										
Total	1,192.6	100.0	1,693.6	100.0	2,886.4	100.0	454.3	100.0	3,340.4	100.0
Electric power	96.7	8.2	89.1	5.3	185.8	6.4	87.7	19.3	273.4	8.2
Transportation	464.1	38.9	403.6	23.8	867.7	30.1	50.9	11.2	918.5	27.5
Railways	178.5	15.0	174.9	10.3	353.4	12.2	−0.4[c]	−0.1[c]	353.0	10.6
Ports and waterways	27.4	2.3	8.7	0.5	36.1	1.3	8.5	1.9	44.6	1.3
Roads	258.2	21.6	220.0	13.0	478.2	16.6	42.8	9.4	520.9	15.6
Telecommunications	75.0	6.3	73.6	4.3	148.6	5.1	78.0	17.2	226.6	6.8
Agriculture, forestry, and fishing	215.8	18.1	460.7	27.2	676.5	23.4	173.8	38.2	850.3	25.5
Farm mechanization	...	...	...	...	...	...	1.4	0.3	1.4	[b]
Irrigation and flood control	179.4	15.0	162.1	9.6	341.5	11.8	5.9	1.3	374.4	10.4
Land clearance, farm improvement	2.8	0.2	24.1	1.4	26.9	0.9	7.3	1.6	34.2	1.0
Crop processing and storage	...	...	25.9	1.5	25.9	0.9	11.2	2.5	37.1	1.1
Livestock improvement	3.6	0.3	39.4	2.3	43.0	1.5	23.3	5.1	66.3	2.0
Forestry and fishing	...	...	4.8	0.3	4.8	0.2	...	...	4.8	0.1
Agricultural credit	30.0	2.5	128.8	7.6	158.8	5.5	84.4	18.6	243.2	7.3
Smallholders and plantations	...	...	75.6	4.5	75.6	2.6	25.3	5.6	100.9	3.0
Agricultural industries	...	...	...	...	...	...	15.0	3.3	15.0	0.4
Industry	31.4	2.6	72.6	4.3	104.0	3.6	...	...	104.0	3.1
Fertilizer and chemicals	...	...	30.0	1.8	30.0	1.0	...	...	30.0	0.9

	1		2		3		4		5	
Other industries	6.5	0.5	2.9	0.2	9.4	0.3	...	...	9.4	0.3
Development finance companies	24.9	2.1	39.7	2.3	64.6	2.2	...	...	64.6	1.9
General development and industrial imports	190.0	15.9	465.0	27.5	655.0	22.7	...	...	655.0	19.6
Social services	119.6	10.0	109.0	6.4	228.6	8.0	38.9	8.6	267.5	8.0
Education	57.1	4.8	123.5	7.3	180.6	6.3	31.1	6.8	211.7	6.3
Family planning	...	...	...	...	...	...	4.8	1.1	4.8	1.1
Water systems	62.5	5.2	−14.5°	−0.9°	48.0	1.7	3.0	0.7	51.0	1.5
Reconstruction	...	...	...	...	...	...	25.0	5.5	25.0	0.7
Technical assistance and project preparation	...	...	20.2	1.2	20.2	0.7	...	...	20.2	0.6
WESTERN HEMISPHERE										
Total	100.5	100.0	54.8	100.0	155.3	100.0	21.4	100.0	176.7	100.0
Electric power	15.0	14.9	16.9	30.8	31.9	20.5	5.6	26.2	37.5	21.2
Transportation	78.9	78.5	−1.5°	−2.7°	77.4	49.8	...	...	77.4	43.8
Railways	...	...	...	...	...	...	...	...	...	...
Ports and waterways	...	...	...	...	...	...	...	...	...	...
Roads	78.9	78.5	−1.5°	−2.7°	77.4	49.8	...	...	77.4	43.8
Telecommunications	...	...	...	...	...	...	...	...	...	...
Agriculture, forestry, and fishing	3.6	3.6	31.5	57.5	35.1	22.6	11.8	55.1	46.9	26.5
Farm mechanization	...	...	...	...	...	...	...	...	...	...
Irrigation and flood control	...	...	...	...	...	...	...	...	...	...
Land clearance, farm improvement	...	...	...	...	...	...	...	...	...	...
Crop processing and storage	...	...	...	...	...	...	...	...	...	...
Livestock improvement	3.6	3.6	31.5	57.5	35.1	22.6	11.8	55.1	46.9	26.5
Forestry and fishing	...	...	...	...	...	...	...	...	...	...
Agricultural credit	...	...	...	...	...	...	...	...	...	...
Smallholders and plantations	...	...	...	...	...	...	...	...	...	...
Agricultural industries	...	...	...	...	...	...	...	...	...	...

Table E-5. *Continued*

Purpose	1961-65		1966-70		Total 1961-70		Jan.-June 1971		Total Jan. 1961-June 1971	
	Amount	Per-cent	Amount	Per-cent	Amount	Per-cent	Amount	Per-cent	Amount	Per-cent
Industry										
Fertilizer and chemicals	...	...	...	...	...	...	...	...	...	...
Other industries	...	...	...	...	...	...	...	...	...	...
Development finance companies	...	...	...	...	...	...	...	...	...	...
General development and industrial imports	...	...	...	...	...	...	...	...	...	...
Social services	3.0	3.0	8.0	14.5	11.0	7.1	4.0	18.7	15.0	8.5
Education	...	...	8.0	14.5	8.0	5.2	4.0	18.7	12.0	6.8
Family planning	...	...	...	...	...	...	...	...	...	...
Water systems	3.0	3.0	...	...	3.0	1.9	...	...	3.0	1.7
Reconstruction	...	...	...	...	...	...	...	...	...	...
Technical assistance and project preparation	...	...	...	...	...	...	...	...	...	...
EUROPE AND OCEANIA										
Total	65.7	100.0	37.6	100.0	103.3	100.0	19.5	100.0	122.8	100.0
Electric power	25.7	39.2	...	...	25.7	24.8	...	...	25.7	20.9
Transportation	...	...	4.5	12.0	4.5	4.4	...	...	4.5	3.7
Railways	...	...	...	...	...	...	...	...	...	...
Ports and waterways	...	...	...	...	...	...	...	...	...	...
Roads	...	...	4.5	12.0	4.5	4.4	...	...	4.5	3.7
Telecommunications	...	...	...	...	...	...	...	...	...	...

844

Agriculture, forestry, and fishing	20.0	30.4	18.4	48.9	38.4	37.2	19.5	100.0	57.9	47.1
Farm mechanization	...	...	...	...	...	...	...	...	...	...
Irrigation and flood control	20.0	30.4	11.9	31.6	31.9	30.9	...	...	31.9	26.0
Land clearance, farm improvement	...	...	...	...	...	...	...	...	...	...
Crop processing and storage	...	...	...	...	...	...	...	...	...	...
Livestock improvement	...	...	...	...	...	...	4.5	23.1	4.5	3.7
Forestry and fishing	...	...	...	...	...	...	...	...	...	...
Agricultural credit	...	...	...	...	...	...	...	...	...	...
Smallholders, plantations	...	...	6.5	17.3	6.5	6.3	...	...	6.5	5.3
Agricultural industries	...	...	...	...	...	...	15.0	76.9	15.0	12.2
Industry	20.0	30.4	14.7	39.1	34.7	33.6	...	...	34.7	28.3
Fertilizer and chemicals	...	...	...	...	...	...	...	...	...	...
Other industries	...	...	...	...	...	...	...	...	...	...
Development finance companies	20.0	30.4	14.7	39.1	34.7	33.6	...	...	34.7	28.3
General development and industrial imports	...	...	...	...	...	...	...	...	...	...
Social services	...	...	...	...	...	...	...	...	...	...
Education	...	...	...	...	...	...	...	...	...	...
Family planning	...	...	...	...	...	...	...	...	...	...
Water systems	...	...	...	...	...	...	...	...	...	...
Reconstruction	...	...	...	...	...	...	...	...	...	...
Technical assistance and project preparation	...	...	...	...	...	...	...	...	...	...
AFRICA										
Total	127.7	100.0	460.8	100.0	588.5	100.0	77.6	100.0	666.0	100.0
Electric power	...	...	15.3	3.3	15.3	2.6	7.1	9.1	22.4	3.4
Transportation	71.3	55.8	215.4	46.7	286.7	48.7	14.0	18.0	300.7	45.2
Railways	...	...	26.6	5.8	26.6	4.5	...	...	26.6	4.0
Ports and waterways	...	...	11.7	2.5	11.7	2.0	8.5	11.0	20.2	3.0
Roads	71.3	55.8	177.1	38.4	248.4	42.2	5.5	7.0	253.9	38.1

Table E-5. *Continued*

Purpose	1961–65		1966–70		Total 1961–70		Jan.–June 1971		Total Jan. 1961–June 1971	
	Amount	Per-cent	Amount	Per-cent	Amount	Per-cent	Amount	Per-cent	Amount	Per-cent
Telecommunications	...	...	0.8	0.2	0.8	0.1	...	...	0.8	0.1
Agriculture, forestry, and fishing	15.8	12.4	125.4	27.2	141.2	24.0	17.6	22.7	158.8	23.8
Farm mechanization	...	...	...	...	...	...	...	...	...	...
Irrigation and flood control	13.0	10.2	31.0	6.7	44.0	7.5	...	...	44.0	6.6
Land clearance, farm improvement	2.8	2.2	24.1	5.2	26.9	4.6	7.3	9.4	34.2	5.1
Crop processing and storage	...	...	6.7	1.5	6.7	1.1	...	...	6.7	1.0
Livestock improvement	...	...	7.9	1.7	7.9	1.3	...	...	7.9	1.2
Forestry and fishing	...	...	1.3	0.3	1.3	0.2	...	...	1.3	0.2
Agricultural credit	...	...	18.3	4.0	18.3	3.1	...	...	18.3	2.7
Smallholders and plantations	...	...	36.1	7.8	36.1	6.1	10.3	13.3	46.4	7.0
Agricultural industries	...	...	...	...	...	...	...	...	...	...
Industry	...	...	5.0	1.1	5.0	0.8	...	...	5.0	0.7
Fertilizer and chemicals	...	...	...	...	...	...	...	...	...	...
Other industries	...	...	...	...	...	...	...	...	...	...
Development finance companies	...	...	5.0	1.1	5.0	0.8	...	...	5.0	0.7
General development and industrial imports	...	...	...	...	...	...	...	...	...	...
Social services	31.8	31.8	93.4	20.3	134.0	22.8	38.9	50.2	172.9	26.0
Education	40.6	31.8	78.3	17.0	118.9	20.2	31.1	40.1	150.0	22.5
Family planning	...	...	...	...	...	...	4.8	6.2	4.8	0.7
Water systems	...	...	15.1	3.3	15.1	2.6	3.0	3.9	18.1	2.7

ASIA AND MIDDLE EAST

	Amount	%	Amount	%	Amount	%	Amount	%	Amount	%
Reconstruction	...	...	...	...	...	...	...	...	...	...
Technical assistance and project preparation	...	...	...	5.6	...	1.2	...	...	5.6	0.8
Total	898.7	100.0	1,140.3	100.0	2,039.0	100.0	335.9	100.0	2,374.9	100.0
Electric power	56.0	6.2	56.9	5.0	112.9	5.5	75.0	22.3	187.9	7.9
Transportation	313.9	34.9	185.2	16.2	499.1	24.5	36.9	11.0	536.0	22.6
Railways	178.5	19.9	148.3	13.0	326.8	16.0	-0.4[e]	-0.1[e]	326.4	13.7
Ports and waterways	27.4	3.0	-3.0[e]	-0.3[e]	24.4	1.2	...	...	24.4	1.0
Roads	108.0	12.0	39.9	3.5	147.9	7.3	37.3	11.1	185.2	7.8
Telecommunications	75.0	8.3	72.8	6.4	147.8	7.2	78.0	23.2	225.8	9.5
Agriculture, forestry, and fishing	176.4	19.6	285.4	25.1	461.8	22.6	124.9	37.2	586.7	24.7
Farm mechanization	...	...	...	...	...	...	1.4	0.4	1.4	0.1
Irrigation and flood control	146.4	16.3	119.2	10.5	265.6	13.0	5.9	1.8	271.5	11.4
Land clearance, farm improvement	...	...	...	...	...	...	...	...	...	...
Crop processing and storage	...	...	19.2	1.7	19.2	0.9	11.2	3.3	30.4	1.3
Livestock improvement	...	...	...	...	...	...	7.0	2.1	7.0	0.3
Forestry and fishing	...	...	3.5	0.3	3.5	0.2	3.5	...	3.5	0.1
Agricultural credit	...	...	110.5	9.7	140.5	6.9	84.4	25.1	224.9	9.5
Smallholders and plantations	30.0	3.3	33.0	2.9	33.0	1.6	15.0	4.5	48.0	2.0
Agricultural industries	...	...	...	...	...	...	...	...	...	...
Industry	11.4	1.3	52.9	4.6	64.3	3.2	...	...	64.3	2.7
Fertilizer and chemicals	...	...	30.0	2.6	30.0	1.5	...	...	30.0	1.3
Other industries	6.5	0.7	2.9	0.2	9.4	0.5	...	...	9.4	0.4
Development finance companies	4.9	0.6	20.0	1.8	24.9	1.2	...	...	24.9	1.0
General development and industrial imports	190.0	21.2	465.0	40.8	655.0	32.1	...	...	655.0	27.6

Table E-5. Continued

Purpose	1961-65		1966-70		Total 1961-70		Jan.–June 1971		Total Jan. 1961– June 1971	
	Amount	Per- cent	Amount	Per- cent	Amount	Per- cent	Amount	Per- cent	Amount	Per- cent
Social services	76.0	8.4	7.7	0.7	83.7	4.1	-4.0c	-1.1c	79.7	3.4
Education	16.5	1.8	37.2	3.3	53.7	2.6	-4.0c	-1.1c	49.7	2.1
Family planning	...	...	...	...	...	...	...	...	...	...
Water systems	59.5	6.6	-29.5c	-2.6c	30.0	1.5	...	...	30.0	1.3
Reconstruction	...	...	...	...	...	...	25.0	7.4	25.0	1.0
Technical assistance and project preparation	...	...	14.6	1.3	14.6	0.8	...	...	14.6	0.6

Source: IBRD, Economic Program Department.
Notes: Multipurpose loans are distributed according to each purpose and not assigned to the major purpose. Details may not add to totals due to rounding.

a. Net of cancellations and refundings.
b. Less than 0.05 percent.
c. Minus signs indicate that cancellations or refundings exceeded new credits during the period.

848

Table E-6. *Summary Statement of IBRD Loans by Country, Including Disbursed and Undisbursed Portions, as of June 30, 1971*[a]

In thousands of U.S. dollar equivalents

Members liable as borrower or guarantor[b]	*Disbursed portion*	*Undisbursed portion*[c]	*Effective loans*	*Loans not yet effective*[d]
Algeria	10,915	...	10,915	...
Argentina	194,560	130,094	324,654	149,975
Australia	124,975	9,483	134,818	22,275
Austria	46,316	...	46,316	...
Belgium	20,607	...	20,607	...
Bolivia	...	...	...	23,250
Botswana	...	...	...	32,000
Brazil	289,175	377,669	666,844	160,050
Burma	12,844	...	12,844	...
Cameroon	5,403	31,697	37,100	...
Ceylon	26,334	33,011	59,345	...
Chile	118,661	41,007	159,668	...
China	94,571	132,035	226,606	68,900
Colombia	372,772	194,773	567,545	152,530
Congo, People's Republic of	28,580	...	28,580	...
Costa Rica	40,842	26,320	67,162	...
Cyprus	16,059	14,408	30,467	5,400
Denmark	28,659	...	28,659	...
Dominican Republic	19,742	5,258	25,000	...
Ecuador	32,873	6,280	39,153	8,000
El Salvador	24,434	5,771	30,205	...
Ethiopia	51,142	25,611	76,753	...
Fiji	...	...	...	11,800
Finland	120,721	33,542	154,263	...
France	6,942	...	6,942	...
Gabon	15,449	2,886	18,335	...
Ghana	42,749	5,046	47,795	...
Greece	17,528	27,937	45,465	24,500
Guatemala	15,665	12,508	28,173	4,000
Guinea	36,337	28,163	64,500	9,000
Guyana	1,105	6,695	7,800	5,400
Haiti	269	...	269	...
Honduras	32,130	9,500	41,630	6,000
Iceland	20,146	3,348	23,494	...
India	488,157	88,387	576,544	...
Iran	181,752	247,816	429,568	36,000
Iraq	13,060	5,038	18,098	...
Ireland	6,289	27,238	33,527	10,000
Israel	84,003	41,843	125,846	...
Italy	137,789	...	137,789	...
Ivory Coast	8,163	33,017	41,180	27,500

Table E-6. *Continued*

Members liable as borrower or guarantor[b]	Dis-bursed portion	Undis-bursed portion[c]	Effective loans	Loans not yet effective[d]
Jamaica	31,779	12,976	44,755	13,500
Japan	459,620	...	459,620	...
Kenya	4,551	29,799	34,350	22,900
Kenya, Tanzania, and Uganda[e]	54,483	83,717	138,200	...
Korea	18,268	90,741	109,009	84,300
Lebanon	17,600	...	17,600	...
Liberia	7,243	7,707	14,950	...
Malagasy Republic	3,600	7,500	11,100	...
Malaysia	151,500	87,614	239,114	34,275
Mexico	620,828	143,464	764,292	73,600
Morocco	59,564	75,615	135,179	35,000
New Zealand	80,486	15,746	96,232	...
Nicaragua	28,009	8,857	36,866	...
Nigeria	150,266	141,064	291,330	7,200
Norway	76,119	...	76,119	...
Pakistan	343,239	119,482	462,721	...
Panama	7,135	41,624	48,759	...
Paraguay	7,721	9,329	17,050	...
Peru	125,068	52,327	177,395	...
Philippines	127,322	71,507	198,829	8,000
Portugal	51,015	263	51,278	...
Senegal	2,120	1,430	3,550	...
Sierra Leone	6,296	4,269	10,565	...
Singapore	60,098	29,004	89,102	...
South Africa	2,106	...	2,106	...
Spain	153,720	54,404	208,124	102,700
Sudan	92,340	9,888	102,228	...
Tanzania	4,487	37,623	42,110	...
Thailand	159,952	81,746	241,698	...
Trinidad and Tobago	9,106	15,629	24,735	3,000
Tunisia	30,180	43,621	73,801	23,825
Turkey	67,225	69,543	136,768	54,500
United Arab Republic	19,050	...	19,050	...
United Kingdom	84,540	...	84,540	...
Uruguay	50,194	21,595	71,789	4,000
Venezuela	214,434	48,126	262,560	33,850
Yugoslavia	255,259	156,433	411,692	89,950
Zambia	26,921	72,719	99,640	...
Subtotal	6,451,162	3,252,103	9,703,265	1,347,180
International Finance Corporation	57,900	142,100	200,000	...
Subtotal	6,509,062	3,394,203	9,903,265	1,347,180
Add: Exchange adjustments	76,916	...	76,916	...
Total	6,585,978	3,394,203	9,980,181	1,347,180

Summary of Currencies Repayable on Effective Loans

Currency	Amount	Currency	Amount
Argentine pesos	960	Malaysian dollars	16,577
Australian dollars	84,291	Mexican pesos	28,382
Austrian schillings	26,783	Netherlands guilders	159,909
Belgian francs	79,660	Norwegian kroner	23,928
Burmese kyats	1,561	Portuguese escudos	8,391
Canadian dollars	219,732	Pounds sterling	235,449
Ceylon rupees	295	Singapore dollars	3,098
Danish kroner	23,927	South African rand	36,452
Deutsche mark	1,374,597	Spanish pesetas	34,653
Finnish markkaa	16,969	Sudanese pounds	3,097
French francs	123,173	Swedish kronor	53,486
Ghanaian new cedis	3,913	Swiss francs	209,178
Indian rupees	48,107	New Taiwan dollars	9,415
Iranian rials	13,917	United States dollars	2,897,931
Iraqui dinars	2,281	Disbursed portion of effec-	
Irish pounds	11,104	tive loans held by Bank	6,509,062
Israel pounds	2,627	Add: Exchange adjustments	76,916
Italian lire	117,123		6,585,978
Japanese yen	559,059	Add: Undisbursed portion	
Kuwaiti dinars	47,699	of effective loans held	
Libyan pounds	28,078	by Bank	3,394,203
Luxembourg francs	3,260	Effective loans held by Bank	9,980,181

Source: World Bank/IDA, *Annual Report, 1971*, pp. 86–87.

a. Excludes principal repayments amounting to approximately $2.4 billion and sales of loans also amounting to approximately $2.4 billion. (It would be necessary to add this $4.8 billion to the total in this table for effective loans [approximately $10 billion] and loans not yet effective [approximately $1.3 billion] to obtain the $16.1 billion mentioned elsewhere in these appendixes as the total amount of Bank loans through June 30, 1971, net of cancellations, refundings, and terminations.)

b. Loans are made (a) to the member or (b) to a political subdivision or a public or a private enterprise in the territories of the member with the member's guarantee. In some instances loans were made, with the guarantee of a member, in territories which at the time were included in that member's membership but which subsequently became independent and members of the Bank in their own right (except Malta which although independent is not a member of the Bank). In all these instances (except in the case of a loan to the Public Utilities Board of Singapore guaranteed by Malaysia) these territories had assumed liability as a borrower or guarantor. In order to avoid double counting, liabilities for these loans are shown in the above table only under the name of the original member (whose guarantee continues unaffected). These loans, together with an indication of the member under whose name they are listed in the above table, are as follows (in thousands of U.S. dollar equivalents):

Belgium	
Burundi and Rwanda	1,079
Congo, Democratic Republic of	19,368
France	
Algeria	3,007
Congo, People's Republic of, and Gabon	2,172
Mauritania	1,762
Malaysia	
Singapore (Public Utilities Board)	5,710
United Kingdom	
Kenya	2,438
Kenya, Tanzania, and Uganda	107
Malta	23

Mauritius	2,022
Nigeria	14,570
Southern Rhodesia and Zambia	32,084
Singapore	11,415
Swaziland	4,250
Trinidad and Tobago	3,576
Uganda	64
Zambia	4,477

The loans to Burundi and Rwanda; People's Republic of the Congo; Kenya, Tanzania, and Uganda; and Southern Rhodesia and Zambia were made for the joint benefit of the territories listed (Southern Rhodesia is included in the membership of the United Kingdom). A loan has also been made to the International Finance Corporation.

c. This does not include $8,810,655 of effective loans which the Bank has agreed to sell. Of the undisbursed balance, the Bank has entered into irrevocable commitments to disburse $28,609,072.

d. Agreements providing for these loans have been signed, but the loans do not become effective and disbursements thereunder do not start until the borrowers and guarantors, if any, take certain action and furnish certain documents to the Bank. This amount is net of $8,570,000 of loans not yet effective which the Bank has agreed to sell. The total of effective and noneffective loans sold or agreed to be sold is the equivalent of $2,373,291,375. In addition the Bank has approved and indicated its willingness subject to certain conditions, to execute two loans equivalent to $24,700,000. These loans have since been signed.

e. Loan shared by the three members.

Table E-7. *Summary Statement of IDA Development Credits by Country,*
Including Disbursed and Undisbursed Portions, June 30, 1971

In thousands of U.S. dollar equivalents

Member in whose territories development credits have been made[a]	Disbursed portion	Undisbursed portion[b]	Effective development credits	Development credits not yet effective[c]
Afghanistan	849	9,428	10,277	5,000
Australia: Papua and New Guinea	2,950	8,050	11,000	...
Bolivia	18,985	6,815	25,800	6,800
Botswana	5,662	3,438	9,100	...
Burundi	1,485	1,795	3,280	...
Cameroon	10,176	19,824	30,000	...
Central African Republic	1,615	6,885	8,500	...
Ceylon	2,289	17,357	19,646	...
Chad	626	5,274	5,900	2,200
Chile	18,998	...	18,998	...
China	13,074	...	13,074	...
Colombia	19,500	...	19,500	...
Congo, Democratic Republic of	2,358	8,642	11,000	7,000
Congo, People's Republic of	597	1,533	2,130	3,500
Costa Rica	4,550	...	4,550	...
Dahomey	1,657	6,443	8,100	...
Dominican Republic	...	4,000	4,000	5,000
Ecuador	6,893	7,707	14,600	10,000
El Salvador	7,999	...	7,999	5,600
Ethiopia	24,719	10,281	35,000	9,500
Gambia, The	43	2,057	2,100	...
Ghana	11,659	13,141	24,800	7,100
Guyana	487	2,413	2,900	2,200
Haiti	350	...	350	...
Honduras	15,697	8,331	24,028	...
India	1,100,434	271,607	1,372,041	135,000
Indonesia	20,556	150,344	170,900	56,500
Jordan	9,248	767	10,015	6,000
Kenya	33,346	27,954	61,300	...
Korea	37,407	20,531	57,938	7,000
Lesotho	4,100	...	4,100	...
Malagasy Republic	11,884	17,216	29,100	...
Malawi	20,765	11,985	32,750	7,250
Mali	7,088	9,712	16,800	...
Mauritania	7,827	1,873	9,700	...
Mauritius	...	5,200	5,200	...
Morocco	6,820	11,480	18,300	...
Nepal	146	4,054	4,200	...
Nicaragua	2,995	...	2,995	...

Table E-7. *Continued*

Member in whose territories development credits have been made[a]	Disbursed portion	Undis- bursed portion[b]	Effective develop- ment credits	Develop- ment credits not yet effective[c]
Niger	5,097	8,806	13,903	...
Nigeria	17,494	17,811	35,305	...
Pakistan	297,564	195,314	492,878	4,000
Paraguay	19,266	2,134	21,400	...
Rwanda	172	9,128	9,300	...
Senegal	9,498	7,602	17,100	7,050
Sierra Leone	27	6,473	6,500	...
Somalia	8,455	561	9,016	3,300
Sudan	12,493	9,007	21,500	...
Swaziland	2,800	...	2,800	...
Syrian Arab Republic	4,981	3,519	8,500	...
Tanzania	38,292	22,408	60,700	...
Togo	2,352	1,348	3,700	...
Tunisia	18,741	21,222	39,963	4,800
Turkey	85,453	6,863	92,316	19,500
Uganda	17,815	15,185	33,000	11,300
United Arab Republic	...	26,000	26,000	...
Upper Volta	11	6,989	7,000	...
Yemen, People's Democratic Republic of	...	...	...	1,600
Total[d]	1,976,345	1,036,507	3,012,852	327,200

Source: World Bank/IDA, *Annual Report, 1971*, p. 99.

a. All development credits have been made to member governments or to the government of a territory of a member.

b. Of the undisbursed balance the Association has entered into irrevocable commitments to disburse $386,063.

c. Agreements in the amount of $327,200,000 providing for these development credits have been signed, but the development credits do not become effective and disbursements thereunder do not start until the borrower takes certain action and furnishes certain documents to the Association.

d. Excludes principal repayments totaling $347,000. The figures in this table, in thousands of U.S. dollar equivalents, for effective credits plus development credits not yet effective ($3,012,852 and $327,200) therefore do not add up to the total of $3,340,398 shown as the total amount of IDA credits, net of cancellations, refundings, and terminations, as of June 30, 1971, in Table E-2.

Table E-8. *IFC Investments, and Standby and Underwriting Commitments, by Regions and Countries, as of June 30, 1971*

Amounts in U.S. dollar equivalents

Region and country	Number of investments and standby and underwriting commitments	Operational investments	Standby and under-writing commit-ments	Total commit-ments
Australia				
Australia	3	975,000	...	975,000
Africa				
Congo, Democratic Republic of	1	756,345	...	756,345
Ethiopia	4	10,364,498	3,715,527	14,080,025
Ivory Coast	1	204,081	...	204,081
Kenya	3	17,724,201	...	17,724,201
Liberia	1	...	250,000	250,000
Mauritania	1	20,006,515	...	20,006,515
Mauritius	1	600,000	...	600,000
Morocco	2	2,884,260	...	2,884,260
Nigeria	4	1,574,909	1,400,000	2,974,909
Senegal	1	3,459,766	...	3,459,766
Sudan	1	688,893	...	688,893
Tanzania	2	4,657,485	...	4,657,485
Tunisia	4	14,613,175	...	14,613,175
Uganda	1	3,508,436	...	3,508,436
Africa (Regional)	1	500,000	...	500,000
Subtotal	28	81,542,564	5,365,527	86,908,091
Asia and the Middle East				
Ceylon	1	3,250,000	...	3,250,000
China	3	9,843,750	...	9,843,750
India	13	42,303,040	...	42,303,040
Indonesia	4	22,118,120	...	22,118,120
Iran	3	8,674,880	...	8,674,880
Korea	4	8,081,327	...	8,081,327
Lebanon	2	2,130,000	...	2,130,000
Malaysia	5	7,568,545	490,000	8,058,545
Pakistan	11	28,008,659	...	28,008,659
Philippines	6	23,908,029	8,255,711	32,163,740
Thailand	4	22,766,064	...	22,766,064
Subtotal	56	178,652,414	8,745,711	187,398,125
Europe				
Finland	4	2,989,001	158,644	3,147,645
Greece	6	14,945,002	...	14,945,002
Italy	1	960,000	...	960,000

Table E-8. *Continued*

Region and country	Number of investments and standby and underwriting commitments	Operational investments	Standby and under- writing commit- ments	Total commit- ments
Spain	5	3,947,639	...	3,947,639
Turkey	10	28,770,331	...	28,770,331
Yugoslavia	3	19,042,857	...	19,042,857
Subtotal	29	70,654,830	158,644	70,813,474
Western Hemisphere				
Argentina	8	26,210,000	3,000,000	29,210,000
Brazil	15	61,806,007	...	61,806,007
Chile	10	21,191,346	...	21,191,346
Colombia	35	19,332,534	352,109	19,684,643
Costa Rica	2	278,751	310,801	589,552
Ecuador	2	2,214,680	...	2,214,680
El Salvador	2	1,073,600	...	1,073,600
Guatemala	1	200,000	...	200,000
Honduras	4	452,500	...	452,500
Jamaica	2	3,137,000	...	3,137,000
Mexico	16	20,013,642	22,539,338	42,552,930
Nicaragua	1	2,071,428	...	2,071,428
Panama	1	1,472,500	...	1,472,500
Peru	9	8,979,941	...	8,979,941
Venezuela	9	17,476,712	9,607,142	27,083,854
Latin America (Regional)	1	10,000,000	...	10,000,000
Subtotal	118	195,910,641	35,809,390	231,720,031
Total[a]	234	527,735,449	50,079,272	577,814,721

Source: IBRD/IFC, Controller's Department, July 28, 1971.
a. Totals are gross commitments. Net commitments amounted to $544,085,114.

Sources of IBRD Funds

Table F-1. *IBRD Funds Available for Lending, from Borrowings, Sales of Loans, and Other Sources, June 30 Each Year, 1947–71*

Expressed in millions of U.S. dollar equivalents

Year	Net borrowings	Sales of loans	Usable subscriptions	Repayments of principal	Income from operations	Gross
1947	...	...	727	...	−0.9	726
1948	254	...	735	...	4	993
1949	254	28	746	...	15	1,043
1950	261	28	750	...	28	1,067
1951	325	31	761	...	43	1,160
1952	500	56	829	11	62	1,458
1953	556	71	867	13	82	1,589
1954	777	103	901	16	105	1,902
1955	852	200	942	139	130	2,263
1956	850	272	1,072	162	159	2,515
1957	1,078[a]	329	1,210	187	195	2,999
1958	1,704[a]	420	1,355	219	236	3,934
1959	1,937[a]	569	1,498	261	282	4,547
1960	2,124[a]	811	1,626	338	342	5,241
1961	2,303[a]	1,013	1,651	438	408	5,813
1962	2,528[a]	1,332	1,656	543	476	6,535
1963	2,524[a]	1,605	1,690	655	558	7,032
1964	2,492	1,778	1,705	773	605[b]	7,353
1965	2,742[a]	1,885	1,763	909	667[b]	7,966
1966	2,806	1,967	1,808	1,075	732[b]	8,388
1967	3,309[a]	2,035	1,855	1,263	892[b]	9,354
1968	3,524[a]	2,143	1,906	1,500	910[b]	9,983
1969	4,222[a]	2,177	1,912	1,798	965[b]	11,074
1970	4,612[a]	2,350	1,919	2,126	1,079[b]	12,086
1971	5,441[a]	2,373	1,958	2,445	1,177[b]	13,394[c]

Source: IBRD, Controller's Department, Accounting Division, August 1971.

a. Includes delayed deliveries in U.S. dollars and/or undrawn notes in German marks.

b. After deduction of transfer to IDA, land and buildings, and unamortized bond issuance costs.

c. Of this amount, $11,310 million was disbursed.

Table F-2. IBRD Cumulative Borrowing, Classified by Currency, Fiscal Years 1948–71

Expressed in millions of U.S. dollar equivalents

Fiscal year[a]	Belgian francs	Canadian dollars	German marks	Italian lire	Japanese yen	Kuwaiti dinars	Libyan pounds	Netherlands guilders	Pounds sterling	Swedish kronor	Swiss francs	U.S. dollars	Total
1948	...	...	...	...	...	...	...	...	...	...	4.0	250.0	254.0
1949	...	...	...	...	...	...	...	...	...	...	...	...	...
1950	...	...	...	...	...	...	...	...	...	...	6.6	100.0	106.6
1951	...	...	...	...	...	...	...	...	14.0	...	...	50.0	64.0
1952	...	13.6	...	...	...	...	...	...	...	...	11.6	150.0	175.2
1953	...	...	...	...	...	...	...	...	...	...	11.6	60.0	71.6
1954	...	22.8	...	...	...	...	...	...	...	...	34.9	175.0	232.7
1955	...	13.6	...	...	...	...	...	10.5	14.0	...	...	50.0	88.1
1956	...	...	...	...	...	...	...	10.5	...	...	11.6	...	22.1
1957	...	...	...	...	...	...	...	...	...	...	46.6	275.0	321.6
1958	...	...	...	...	...	...	...	...	...	...	...	650.0	650.0
1959	10.0	...	95.2	...	...	...	...	...	...	...	23.3	303.0	431.5
1960	...	...	50.0	...	...	...	...	...	28.0	...	14.0	282.5	374.5
1961	...	4.0[b]	227.4[b]	...	...	...	...	14.7[b]	...	...	45.1	508.0	799.2
1962	...	-3.2[c]	...	24.0	...	...	...	...	...	...	46.5	200.0	267.3
1963	...	...	...	...	...	...	...	11.0	...	...	...	110.0	121.0
1964	...	...	...	...	...	...	...	...	...	...	...	100.0	100.0
1965	...	23.1	162.5	...	...	...	...	...	...	...	14.0	398.0	597.6
1966	...	18.5	34.8	...	...	...	...	...	...	...	...	234.7	288.0
1967	...	18.5	32.0	...	...	...	...	...	...	...	21.7	657.0	729.2
1968	...	13.9	75.9	...	...	...	...	11.0	-6.0[d]	14.5	29.1	590.4	728.8
1969	...	...	561.0	...	...	42.0	...	...	...	...	18.6	602.2	1,223.8

858

1970	...	...	275.8e	...	200.0	...	...	28.0	...	...	...	...	349.5	825.3
1971	...	...	294.6	...	219.4	...	33.1	...	...	...	27.6f	775.0	1,377.7
Total	10.0	124.8	1,809.2	24.0	419.4	42.0	28.0	90.8	50.0	14.5	366.8	6,870.3	9,849.8

Source: IBRD, Controller's Department, Accounting Division, August 1971.
a. Including delayed deliveries.
b. Revaluation of previous issues (Canadian dollars +$4.0; German marks +$7.2; Netherlands guilders +$0.9).
c. Revaluation of previous issues (Canadian dollars –$3.2).
d. Revaluation of previous issues (pounds sterling –$6.0).
e. Revaluation of previous issues (German marks +$90.3).
f. Revaluation of previous issues (Swiss francs +$10.1).

Disbursements by Country of Supply and by Category of Goods

Table G-1. IBRD Disbursements, by Country of Supply for Selected Fiscal-Year Periods, 1947–71

Amounts in millions of U.S. dollar equivalents

Country of supply	1947–55		1956–60		1961–65		1966–70		1971		1947–71	
	Amount	Per-cent	Amount	Per-cent	Amount	Per-cent	Amount	Per-cent	Amount	Per-cent	Amount	Per-cent
Belgium	57.2	3.4	48.2	2.2	36.5	1.4	34.2	0.9	15.2	1.6	191.3	1.7
Canada	86.5	5.1	45.3	2.0	25.9	1.0	41.1	1.1	11.1	1.2	209.9	1.9
France	41.7	2.5	59.9	2.7	155.7	5.8	146.9	3.9	42.9	4.5	447.1	4.0
Germany	62.9	3.7	258.2	11.5	226.8	8.5	361.4	9.6	103.3	10.8	1,012.6	9.0
Italy	13.8	0.8	75.3	3.4	150.9	5.7	241.8	6.4	66.6	7.0	548.4	4.8
Japan	0.7	0.1	69.6	3.1	99.5	3.7	306.1	8.1	111.3	11.7	587.2	5.2
Netherlands	9.3	0.6	17.6	0.8	36.0	1.3	21.0	0.6	7.8	0.8	91.7	0.8
Sweden	11.7	0.7	29.6	1.3	54.3	2.0	110.3	2.9	19.0	2.0	224.9	2.0
Switzerland	32.2	1.9	34.4	1.5	69.1	2.6	89.6	2.4	26.2	2.7	251.5	2.2
United Kingdom	171.6	10.2	287.5	12.8	273.7	10.3	392.8	10.4	74.9	7.8	1,200.5	10.6
United States	982.3	58.5	588.0	26.2	497.6	18.6	615.6	16.4	192.1	20.1	2,875.6	25.4
All other countries	80.4	4.8	57.8	2.6	89.4	3.4	199.0	5.3	73.4	7.7	500.0	4.4
Subtotal	1,550.3	92.3	1,571.4	70.1	1,715.4	64.3	2,559.8	68.0	743.8	77.9	8,140.7	72.0
Other disbursements[a]	129.4	7.7	670.1	29.9	953.5	35.7	1,204.9	32.0	211.1	22.1	3,169.0	28.0
Total	1,679.7	100.0	2,241.5	100.0	2,668.9	100.0	3,764.7	100.0	954.9	100.0	11,309.7	100.0

Source: IBRD, Controller's Department, June 1972.
a. Includes "undetermined" and "local" expenditures.

Table G-2. *IDA Disbursements, by Country of Supply for Selected Fiscal-Year Periods, 1961–71*

Amounts expressed in millions of U.S. dollar equivalents

Country of supply	1961–65		1966–70		1971		1961–71	
	Amount	*Percent*	*Amount*	*Percent*	*Amount*	*Percent*	*Amount*	*Percent*
Belgium	8.1	2.0	29.5	2.2	1.9	0.8	39.5	2.0
Canada	10.3	2.5	41.0	3.1	1.6	0.7	52.9	2.7
France	10.9	2.6	59.4	4.5	21.6	9.2	91.9	4.6
Germany	34.9	8.4	181.1	13.7	32.0	13.6	248.0	12.5
Italy	9.5	2.3	50.5	3.8	9.4	4.0	69.4	3.5
Japan	66.1	16.0	89.4	6.7	25.4	10.8	180.9	9.2
Netherlands	8.3	2.0	7.8	0.6	1.7	0.7	17.8	0.9
Sweden	8.0	1.9	28.5	2.2	1.6	0.7	38.1	1.9
Switzerland	5.5	1.3	21.4	1.6	1.9	0.8	28.8	1.5
United Kingdom	67.2	16.2	261.7	19.7	27.2	11.6	356.1	18.0
United States	57.8	13.9	215.5	16.2	42.1	17.9	315.4	16.0
All other countries	15.3	3.7	141.7	10.7	23.7	10.1	180.7	9.1
Subtotal	301.9	72.8	1,127.5	85.0	190.1	80.9	1,619.5	81.9
Other disbursements[a]	112.8	27.2	199.4	15.0	45.0	19.1	357.2	18.1
Total	414.7	100.0	1,326.9	100.0	235.1	100.0	1,976.7	100.0

Source: IBRD, Controller's Department, June 1972.
a. Includes "undetermined" and "local" expenditures.

Table G-3. *Total IBRD/IDA Disbursements, by Categories of Goods, Fiscal Years 1967–71*

Amounts in millions of U.S. dollar equivalents

Category of goods	IBRD Amount	IBRD Per-cent	IDA Amount	IDA Per-cent	IBRD/IDA Amount	IBRD/IDA Per-cent
Chemicals	7.9	0.2	75.0	5.8	82.9	1.6
Livestock	32.4	0.8	3.2	0.2	35.6	0.7
Construction materials	139.4	3.4	26.3	2.0	165.7	3.1
Construction equipment	121.8	3.0	32.9	2.5	154.7	2.9
Mechanical equipment	565.3	14.0	113.7	8.8	679.0	12.7
Textile machinery	186.2	4.6	7.6	0.6	193.8	3.6
Agricultural machinery	37.0	0.9	72.4	5.6	109.4	2.0
Electrical equipment	799.7	19.7	215.8	16.7	1,015.5	19.0
Automotive machinery and equipment	32.0	0.8	174.3	13.5	206.3	3.8
Vessels and floating equipment	46.7	1.2	4.2	0.3	50.9	1.0
Materials and equipment for railways	313.3	7.7	165.9	12.8	479.2	9.0
School equipment and supplies	13.4	0.3	11.1	0.9	24.5	0.5
Civil works	1,260.0	31.1	278.7	21.5	1,538.7	28.8
Consultants' services	189.1	4.7	69.4	5.4	258.5	4.8
Freight and insurance	34.9	0.9	14.8	1.1	49.7	0.9
Loan charges	129.5	3.2	...	...	129.5	2.4
Miscellaneous	142.7	3.5	29.8	2.3	172.5	3.2
Total[a]	4,051.2	100.0	1,295.1	100.0	5,346.3	100.0

Source: IBRD, Controller's Department, June 1972.

a. Details may not add to totals due to rounding.

APPENDIX H

Organization and Personnel

Chart H-1. *IBRD Organization Chart, October 1947*

President: John J. McCloy

Vice President: Robert L. Garner

Assistant to the Vice President: Richard H. Demuth

Loan Department: Charles C. Pineo, Director

Research Department: Leonard B. Rist, Director

Marketing Department: E. F. Dunstan, Director

Treasurer's Department: D. Crena de Iongh, Treasurer

Secretary's Department: Morton M. Mendels, Secretary

Legal Department: Chester A. McLain, General Counsel

Public Relations Department: Drew Dudley, Director

Administration Department: Chauncey G. Parker, Director

Table H-1. *IBRD Executive Directors and Alternates, October 1947*

Executive Director	Alternate	Casting votes of
Appointed		
Eugene R. Black	John S. Hooker	United States
Sir Gordon Munro	Maurice H. Parsons	United Kingdom
Yuen-Ting Shen	Y. L. Chang	China
Pierre Mendes-France	Guy de Carmoy	France
N. Sundaresan	B. K. Madan	India
Elected		
J. W. Beyen (Netherlands)	W. Koster (Netherlands)	Netherlands, Union of South Africa
Franz De Voghel (Belgium)	Thomas Basyn (Belgium)	Belgium, Norway, Luxembourg, Iceland
Victor Moller (Chile)	Fernando Illanes (Chile)	Brazil, Chile, Philippine Republic, Bolivia, Costa Rica, Guatemala, Paraguay, Panama
Leon Baranski (Poland)	Stefan Michalski (Poland)	Czechoslovakia, Poland, Yugoslavia
Luis Machado (Cuba)	Joaquin Meyer (Cuba)	Mexico, Cuba, Peru, Uruguay, Ecuador, Dominican Republic, El Salvador, Honduras, Nicaragua
Graham F. Towers (Canada)	J. R. Parkinson (Canada)	Canada
Kyriakos Varvaressos (Greece)	F. Noury-Esfandiary (Iran)	Egypt, Greece, Iran, Iraq, Ethiopia
Constantino Bresciani Turroni (Italy)	Francesco Giordani (Italy)	Colombia, Denmark, Italy, Turkey, Venezuela

Chart H-2. *IBRD Organization Chart, May 1953*

President: Eugene R. Black
Vice President: Robert L. Garner
Assistant to the President: William A. B. Iliff

Office of the General Counsel: Davidson Sommers, General Counsel

Staff Loan Committee

Economic Staff: Leonard B. Rist, Director

Technical Assistance and Liaison Staff: Richard H. Demuth, Director

Department of Operations, Asia and Middle East: Francois-Didier Gregh, Director

Department of Operations, Europe, Africa, and Australasia: A. S. G. Hoar, Director

Department of Operations, Western Hemisphere: J. Burke Knapp, Director

Department of Technical Operations: Milton C. Cross, Director

Marketing Department: George L. Martin, Director

Office of the Secretary: Morton M. Mendels, Secretary

Administration Department: William F. Howell, Director

Treasurer's Department: Henry W. Riley, Treasurer

Office of Public Relations: Harold N. Graves, Jr., Director

Table H-2. *IBRD Executive Directors and Alternates, May 1953*

Executive Director	Alternate	Casting votes of
Appointed		
Andrew N. Overby	John S. Hooker	United States
Sir Edmund Hall-Patch	L. Waight	United Kingdom
Yueh-Lien Chang	...	China
Roger Hoppenot	Maurice Perouse	France
B. K. Nehru	B. R. Shenoy	India
Elected		
Luis Machado (Cuba)	Julio E. Heurtematte (Panama)	Mexico, Cuba, Peru, Uruguay, Venezuela, Costa Rica, Dominican Republic, Guatemala, El Salvador, Honduras, Nicaragua, Panama
Johannes Zahn (Germany)	A. Tasic (Yugoslavia)	Germany, Yugoslavia
Mohamed Shoaib (Pakistan)	Ali Asghar Nasser (Iran)	Pakistan, Egypt, Iran, Syria, Iraq, Lebanon, Ethiopia, Jordan
Cabir Selek (Turkey)	Felice Pick (Italy)	Italy, Austria, Turkey, Greece
Takeo Yumoto (Japan)	Boonma Wongswan (Thailand)	Japan, Burma, Ceylon, Thailand
Erling Sveinbjørnsson (Denmark)	Reino Rossi (Finland)	Sweden, Denmark, Norway, Finland, Iceland
Alfonso Fernandez (Chile)	Jorge Schneider (Chile)	Brazil, Chile, Colombia, Philippines, Bolivia, Ecuador, Paraguay
L. G. Melville (Australia)	L. H. E. Bury (Australia)	Australia, Union of South Africa
Louis Rasminsky (Canada)	G. Neil Perry (Canada)	Canada
D. Crena de Iongh (Netherlands)	L. R. W. Soutendijk (Netherlands)	Netherlands
Thomas Basyn (Belgium)	Ernest de Selliers (Belgium)	Belgium, Luxembourg

Chart H-3. *IBRD Organization Chart, September 1957*

President: Eugene R. Black
Vice President: William A. B. Iliff
Vice President: J. Burke Knapp
Vice President and General Counsel: Davidson Sommers

Staff Loan Committee

Economic Staff: L. B. Rist, Director

Technical Assistance and Liaison Staff: R. H. Demuth, Director

Department of Operations, Europe, Africa, and Australasia: S. R. Cope, Director

Department of Operations, Far East: M. Rosen, Director

Department of Operations, South Asia and Middle East: J. Rucinski, Director

Department of Operations, Western Hemisphere: O. A. Schmidt, Director

Department of Technical Operations: S. Aldewereld, Director

Marketing Department: G. L. Martin, Director

Office of the Secretary: M. M. Mendels, Secretary

Legal Department: A. Broches, Director and Associate General Counsel

Administration Department: W. F. Howell, Director

Treasurer's Department: H. W. Riley, Treasurer

Office of Information: H. N. Graves, Jr., Director

Economic Development Institute[a]: M. L. Hoffman, Director

a. An international staff college under the supervision of the management of the Bank.

Table H-3. *IBRD Executive Directors and Alternates, September 1957*

Executive Director	Alternate	Casting votes of
Appointed		
. . .	John S. Hooker	United States
G. F. Thorold	David B. Pitblado	United Kingdom
Kan Lee	. . .	China
René Larre	Jean-Maxime Leveque	France
V. Narahari Rao	P. J. J. Pinto	India
Elected		
Thomas Basyn (Belgium)	Max Thurn (Austria)	Belgium, Austria, Turkey, Korea, Luxembourg
Soetikno Slamet (Indonesia)	Carlo Gragnani (Italy)	Italy, Indonesia, Greece, Afghanistan
Mohamed Shoaib (Pakistan)	Ali Akbar Khosropur (Iran)	Pakistan, Egypt, Iran, Syria, Iraq, Lebanon, Ethiopia, Jordan
P. Lieftinck (Netherlands)	J. Smole (Yugoslavia)	Netherlands, Yugoslavia, Israel
Takeshi Watanabe (Japan)	U Thet Tun (Burma)	Japan, Burma, Ceylon, Thailand
B. B. Callaghan (Australia)	B. E. Fleming (Australia)	Australia, Union of South Africa, Vietnam
Luis Machado (Cuba)	Jorge A. Montealegre (Nicaragua)	Mexico, Cuba, Peru, Venezuela, Costa Rica, Guatemala, El Salvador, Honduras, Nicaragua, Panama
Sven Viig (Norway)	Bjorn Tryggvason (Iceland)	Sweden, Denmark, Norway, Finland, Iceland
Jorge Mejia-Palacio (Colombia)		Brazil, Colombia, Philippines, Ecuador, Dominican Republic, Haiti
Otto Donner (Germany)	Karl-Heinz Drechsler (Germany)	Germany
Louis Rasminsky (Canada)	Alan B. Hockin (Canada)	Canada
Victor A. Pane (Paraguay)		Argentina, Chile, Uruguay, Bolivia, Paraguay

Chart H-4. *IBRD Organization Chart, February 1960*

President: Eugene R. Black Vice President: William A. B. Iliff Vice President: J. Burke Knapp

- Staff Loan Committee
- Economic Staff: L. B. Rist, Director
- Technical Assistance and Liaison Staff: R. H. Demuth, Director
- Department of Operations, Europe, Africa, and Australasia: S. R. Cope, Director
- Department of Operations, Far East: M. Rosen, Director
- Department of Operations, South Asia and Middle East: J. Rucinski, Director
- Department of Operations, Western Hemisphere: O. A. Schmidt, Director
- Department of Technical Operations: S. Aldewereld, Director
- Marketing Department: G. L. Martin, Director
- Office of the Secretary: M. M. Mendels, Secretary
- Legal Department: A. Broches, General Counsel
- Administration Department: W. F. Howell, Director
- Treasurer's Department: R. W. Cavanaugh, Treasurer
- Office of Information: H. N. Graves, Jr., Director

Economic Development Institutea: M. L. Hoffman, Director

a. An international staff college under the supervision of the management of the Bank.

Table H-4. *IBRD Executive Directors and Alternates, February 1960*

Executive Director	Alternate	Casting votes of
Appointed		
T. Graydon Upton	John S. Hooker	United States
The Earl of Cromer	Geoffrey M. Wilson	United Kingdom
Kan Lee	. . .	China
René Larre	Jean Cottier	France
B. K. Nehru	C. S. Krishna Moorthi	India
Elected		
Mohamed Shoaib (Pakistan)	Ali Akbar Khosropur (Iran)	Pakistan, United Arab Republic, Iran, Afghanistan, Saudi Arabia, Sudan, Iraq, Lebanon, Ethiopia, Jordan
Thomas Basyn (Belgium)	Ernst A. Rott (Austria)	Belgium, Austria, Turkey, Korea, Luxembourg
Louis Rasminsky (Canada)	C. L. Read (Canada)	Canada, Ireland
P. Lieftinck (Netherlands)	Nikola Miljanic (Yugoslavia)	Netherlands, Yugoslavia, Israel
Takeshi Watanabe (Japan)	Prayad Buranasiri (Thailand)	Japan, Burma, Ceylon, Thailand
Luis Machado (Cuba)	Jorge A. Montealegre (Nicaragua)	Mexico, Cuba, Peru, Venezuela, El Salvador, Honduras, Nicaragua, Costa Rica, Guatemala, Panama
J. M. Garland (Australia)	A. J. J. van Vuuren (Union of South Africa)	Australia, Union of South Africa, Viet-Nam
T. L. Hammarskiold (Sweden)	Tyge Dahlgaard (Denmark)	Sweden, Denmark, Norway, Finland, Iceland
Jose Aragones (Spain)	Carlo Gragnani (Italy)	Italy, Spain, Greece
Jorge Mejia-Palacio (Colombia)	Jose Camacho (Colombia)	Brazil, Colombia, Philippines, Haiti, Ecuador, Dominican Republic
Otto Donner (Germany)	H. Gorn (Germany)	Germany
Ismail bin Mohamed Ali (Malaya)	Omar Saadi Elmandjra (Morocco)	Indonesia, Morocco, Malaya, Ghana, Tunisia, Libya
Carlos S. Brignone (Argentina)	L. Vartalitis (Argentina)	Argentina, Chile, Uruguay, Bolivia, Paraguay

Chart H-5. *IBRD/IDA Organization Chart, April 1965*

President: George D. Woods

- Personal Assistant to the President: G. C. Wishart
- Special Advisers to the President: L. Rist, O. Schmidt
- Consultant: E. Reid
- Vice President and Chairman, Loan Committee: J. B. Knapp
  - Africa Department: A. G. El Emary, Director
  - Europe and Middle East Department: S. R. Cope, Director
  - Far East Department: I. P. M. Cargill, Director
  - South Asia Department: A. Stevenson, Director
  - Western Hemisphere Department: G. Alter, Director
- Vice President: G. M. Wilson
  - Treasurer's Department: R. W. Cavanaugh, Treasurer
  - Office of the Secretary: M. M. Mendels, Secretary
  - Office of Information: H. N. Graves, Jr., Director
  - New York Office: H. C. Johnson, Director
  - European Office: J. D. Miller, Director
  - Economic Development Institute: J. H. Adler, Director
- Projects Department: S. Aldewereld, Vice President and Director
- Legal Department: A. Broches, General Counsel
  - Administration Department: M. L. Lejeune, Director
- Development Services Department: R. H. Demuth, Director
- Economic Adviser to the President, Chairman, Economic Committee: I. S. Friedman
  - Economics Department: A. M. Kamarck, Director
  - Director of Special Economic Studies: D. Avramović

Table H-5. *IBRD/IFC/IDA Executive Directors and Alternates, April 1965*

Executive Director	Alternate	Casting votes of
Appointed		
John C. Bullitt	. . .	United States
J. M. Stevens	N. M. P. Reilly	United Kingdom
René Larre	Jean Malaplate	France
Otto Donner	Helga Steeg	Germany
K. S. S. Rajan	S. Guhan	India
Elected		
Joaquín Gutiérrez Cano (Spain)	Sergio Siglienti (Italy)	Italy, Spain, Portugal,[a,b] Greece
John M. Garland (Australia)	A. J. J. van Vuuren (South Africa)	Australia, South Africa, New Zealand,[b] Viet-Nam[a]
Gengo Suzuki (Japan)	Eiji Ozaki (Japan)	Japan, Ceylon, Thailand, Burma, Nepal[a]
A. F. W. Plumptre (Canada)	L. Denis Hudon (Canada)	Canada, Ireland, Jamaica[b]
Mumtaz Mirza (Pakistan)	Ali Akbar Khosropur (Iran)	Pakistan, United Arab Republic, Iran, Saudi Arabia, Kuwait, Syrian Arab Republic, Iraq, Jordan, Lebanon
Abderrahman Tazi (Morocco)	Chedly Ayari (Tunisia)	Indonesia,[a,b] Malaysia, Algeria,[a] Morocco, Ghana, Afghanistan, Tunisia, Libya, Laos[a]
Pieter Lieftinck (Netherlands)	Aleksandar Bogoev (Yugoslavia)	Netherlands, Yogoslavia,[a] Israel, Cyprus
André van Campenhout (Belgium)	Othmar Haushofer (Austria)	Belgium, Turkey, Austria, Korea, Luxembourg
Reignson C. Chen (China)	. . .	China[a]
Vilhjálmur Thór (Iceland)	Odd Høkedal (Norway)	Sweden, Denmark, Norway, Finland, Iceland
Jorge Mejía-Palacio (Colombia)	José Camacho (Colombia)	Brazil, Philippines, Colombia, Ecuador, Dominican Republic
John M. Garba (Nigeria)	S. Othello Coleman (Liberia)	Nigeria, Congo (Democratic Republic of),[a] Kenya, Tanzania, Uganda, Trinidad and Tobago,[a,b] Guinea,[a,b] Sudan, Mali,[a] Burundi,[a] Liberia, Sierra Leone, Ethiopia
Luis Machado (Cuba)	Rufino Gil (Costa Rica)	Mexico, Venezuela,[b] Peru, Haiti, Costa Rica, El Salvador, Panama, Guatemala, Honduras, Nicaragua
Manuel San Miguel (Argentina)	Juan Haus-Solís (Bolivia)	Argentina, Chile, Bolivia, Uruguay,[a,b] Paraguay
Mohamed Nassim Kochman (Mauritania)	Said Mohamed Ali (Somalia)	Senegal, Cameroon,[a] Ivory Coast, Malagasy Republic, Rwanda,[a] Somalia, Togo, Central African Republic,[a] Chad,[a] Congo (Brazzaville),[a] Dahomey,[a] Gabon,[a] Mauritania,[a] Niger,[a] Upper Volta[a]

a. Not a member of IFC.
b. Not a member of IDA.

Chart H-6. *IBRD/IDA Organization Chart, March 1971*

President: Robert S. McNamara

- General Counsel: A. Broches
  - Legal Department: L. Nurick, Associate General Counsel
  - Secretary's Department: M. M. Mendels, Secretary
- Vice President, Finance: S. Aldewereld
  - Treasurer's Department: E. H. Rotberg, Treasurer
  - Programming and Budgeting Department: J. H. Adler, Director
  - Controller's Department: K. G. Gabriel, Controller
  - Internal Audit Office: L. N. Rapley
- Economic Adviser to the President and Chairman, Economic Committee: H. B. Chenery
  - Economics Department: P. D. Henderson, Director
  - Economic Program Department: J. P. Hayes, Director (effective May 1, 1971)
  - Department of Computing Activities: M. Muller, Director
  - Development Research Center: L. M. Goreux, Director
- Vice President and Chairman, Loan Committee: J. B. Knapp
  - Eastern Africa Department: M. L. Lejeune, Director
  - Western Africa Department: R. Chaufournier, Director
  - East Asia and Pacific Department: R. J. Goodman, Director
  - Central America and Caribbean Department: E. Guttierrez, Director
  - South Asia Department: I. P. M. Cargill, Director
  - South America Department: G. Alter, Director
  - Europe, Middle East, and North Africa Department: M. P. Benjenk, Director
- Director, Projects: S. Aldewereld
  - Agriculture Projects Department: L. J. C. Evans, Director
  - Education Projects Department: D. S. Ballantine, Director
  - Industrial Projects Department: H. Fuchs, Director
  - Population Projects Department: K. Kanagaratnam, Director
  - Public Utilities Projects Department: M. Weiner, Director
  - Special Projects Department: R. Sadove, Director
  - Tourism Projects Department: A. Koch, Director
  - Transportation Projects Department: A. D. Knox, Director
- Director, Development Services Department: R. H. Demuth
  - Development Services: M. L. Hoffman, Associate Director
  - Economic Development Institute: K. S. Krishnaswamy, Director
- Vice President: Sir Denis Rickett
- Vice President: M. Shoaib
- Information and Public Affairs: W. Clark, Director
- Administration: H. B. Ripman, Director
- Development Finance Companies Department: W. Diamond, Director

Overseas Offices and Missions

Table H-6. *IBRD/IFC/IDA Executive Directors and Alternates, March 1971*

Executive Director	Alternate	Casting votes of
Appointed		
Robert E. Wieczorowski	. . .	United States
D. J. Mitchell	M. P. J. Lynch	United Kingdom
Fritz Stedtfeld	Wolfgang H. Artopoeus	Germany
Marc Viénot	Jean P. Carrière	France
Seitaro Hattori	Masanari Sumi	Japan
S. R. Sen	M. R. Shroff	India
Elected		
Giorgio Rota (Italy)	Juan Moro (Spain)	Italy, Portugal,[b] Spain
S. Osman Ali (Pakistan)	Abdol Ali Jahanshahi (Iran)	Iran, Iraq, Jordan, Kuwait, Lebanon, Pakistan, Saudi Arabia, Syrian Arab Republic, United Arab Republic, Yemen Arab Republic, People's Democratic Republic of Yemen[a]
Claude Isbister (Canada)	Maurice Horgan (Ireland)	Canada, Guyana, Ireland, Jamaica[b]
R. L. Knight (New Zealand)	M. A. Cranswick (Australia)	Australia, New Zealand,[b] South Africa
Donatien Bihute (Burundi)	Bulcha Demeksa (Ethiopia)	Botswana,[a] Burundi,[a] Equatorial Guinea,[a,b] Ethiopia, Gambia (The),[a] Guinea,[a] Kenya, Lesotho,[a] Liberia, Malawi, Nigeria, Sierra Leone, Sudan, Swaziland, Tanzania, Trinidad and Tobago,[a,b] Uganda, Zambia
Reignson C. Chen (China)	Byong Hyun Shin (Korea)	China, Korea, Viet-Nam
Pieter Lieftinck (Netherlands)	Vladimir Cerić (Yugoslavia)	Cyprus, Israel, Netherlands, Yugoslavia
André van Campenhout (Belgium)	Viktor C. Wolf (Austria)	Austria, Belgium, Luxembourg, Turkey
Abderrahman Tazi (Morocco)	Mohammed Younos Rafik (Afghanistan)	Afghanistan, Algeria,[a] Ghana, Greece, Indonesia, Khmer Republic,[a] Libya, Morocco, Tunisia
Erik Törnqvist (Finland)	Carl I. Öhman (Sweden)	Denmark, Finland, Iceland, Norway, Sweden
Mohamed Nassim Kochman (Mauritania)	Benoît Boukar (Chad)	Cameroon,[a] Central African Republic,[a] Chad,[a] Congo (Democratic Republic of), Congo (People's Republic of),[a] Dahomey,[a] Gabon, Ivory Coast, Malagasy Republic, Mali,[a] Mauritania, Mauritius, Niger,[a] Rwanda,[a] Senegal, Somalia, Togo, Upper Volta[a]

Table H-6. *Continued*

Executive Director	Alternate	Casting votes of
Adrián Lajous-Martínez (Mexico)	Carlos Alzamora (Peru)	Costa Rica, El Salvador, Guatemala, Haiti, Honduras, Mexico, Nicaragua, Panama, Peru, Venezuela[b]
Virgilio Barco (Colombia)	Placido L. Mapa, Jr. (Philippines)	Brazil, Colombia, Dominican Republic, Ecuador, Philippines
Luis B. Mey (Argentina)	Oscar Vega-López (Bolivia)	Argentina, Bolivia, Chile, Paraguay, Uruguay[b]
Mrs. Suparb Yossundara (Thailand)	R. V. Navaratnam (Malaysia)	Burma, Ceylon, Laos,[a] Malaysia, Nepal, Singapore,[b] Thailand

a. Not a member of IFC.
b. Not a member of IDA.

Chart H-7. *IFC Organization Chart, September 1971*

President: Robert S. McNamara

Executive Vice President: William S. Gaud

Vice President: Ladislaus von Hoffmann

Legal Department: R. B. J. Richards, General Counsel

Engineering Department; H. Geoffrey Hilton, Director

Office of the Economic Adviser: Moeen A. Qureshi, Economic Adviser

Office of Portfolio Supervision: Douglas J. A. Dupré, Chief

Department of Investments, Central America, Australasia, Mexico, and Europe:Neil J. Paterson, Director

Department of Investments, South America: Rafael Talavera, Director

Department of Investments, Africa and Middle East: Albert Adomakoh, Director

Department of Investments, Asia: Ronald K. Jones, Director

Capital Markets Department: David B. Gill, Director

Note: The following departments and offices are common to the IBRD and the IFC: Administrative Services Department, Personnel Department, Information and Public Affairs Department, Programming and Budgeting Department, Secretary's Department, Treasurer's Department, Controller's Department, Department of Computing Activities, Office of the Internal Auditor, European Office.

Table H-7. *Nationality Distribution of IBRD/IDA Professional Staff, Selected Years, 1950–71*[a]

Country	1950	1953	1956	1959	1962	1965	1968	1971
Abu Dhabi	...	...	...	...	...	...	...	1
Afghanistan	...	...	...	...	...	...	...	5
Algeria	...	...	...	...	...	...	...	1
Argentina	...	...	...	...	2	3	5	10
Australia	1	1	2	2	5	7	9	22
Austria	...	...	1	1	3	4	5	11
Belgium	1	...	3	3	8	12	14	25
Bolivia	...	...	...	...	...	...	...	3
Brazil	...	...	...	1	...	...	...	5
Burma	...	...	...	...	...	...	1	3
Cameroon	...	...	...	...	...	...	...	1
Canada	8	13	12	10	8	14	21	50
Ceylon	...	...	...	...	...	2	3	8
Chad	...	...	...	...	...	...	...	1
Chile	...	...	...	...	1	1	3	18
China	3	2	3	4	5	7	10	11
Colombia	1	1	2	1	...	1	...	7
Cuba	...	...	...	...	...	...	...	7
Dahomey	...	...	...	...	...	...	...	1
Denmark	...	...	2	4	3	...	4	4
Ecuador	...	...	...	...	1	1	...	1
Ethiopia	...	...	...	...	...	...	...	2
Finland	1	1	1	1	2	1	2	5
France	6	5	11	16	20	34	44	88
Germany	...	...	3	3	16	24	40	77
Ghana	...	...	...	...	...	...	2	3
Greece	4	3	3	2	2	3	1	8
Guatemala	2	2	1	1	1	1	...	1
Haiti	...	...	...	...	...	...	...	1
British Honduras	...	...	...	...	...	...	...	1
Honduras	...	...	...	...	...	...	...	2
Iceland	...	1	1	...	...	...	...	1
India	1	1	2	5	9	13	34	59
Indonesia	...	...	...	...	...	...	...	4
Iran	...	...	...	1	1	2	4	4
Iraq	...	...	...	...	...	...	1	1
Ireland	...	...	...	1	1	...	1	7
Israel	...	...	...	...	...	4	9	8
Italy	2	2	6	4	6	11	15	16
Jamaica	...	...	...	...	...	...	1	5
Japan	...	...	...	1	1	3	5	23
Korea	...	...	...	1	1	2	3	13
Lebanon	...	...	...	1	...	...	2	7
Luxembourg	...	...	1	1	1	1	1	1

Table H-7. *Continued*

Country	1950	1953	1956	1959	1962	1965	1968	1971
Malagasy	...	...	...	...	...	...	...	1
Malaysia	...	...	...	...	...	...	...	2
Mexico	...	...	...	1	1	1	2	3
Morocco	...	...	...	...	1	...	...	1
Nepal	...	...	...	...	...	...	...	1
Netherlands	9	11	13	15	18	26	35	54
New Zealand	2	1	2	2	4	4	6	16
Nicaragua	...	1	1	2	1	1	1	2
Nigeria	...	...	...	...	...	...	3	3
Norway	...	2	3	4	6	7	6	9
Pakistan	...	...	1	2	3	4	11	26
Peru	...	...	...	1	3	...	3	7
Philippines	...	...	...	...	...	4	4	10
Portugal	...	...	...	...	...	...	...	1
Senegal	...	...	...	...	...	...	...	1
Sierra Leone	...	...	...	...	...	...	...	1
Singapore	...	...	...	...	...	...	...	1
South Africa	...	...	...	...	...	...	1	5
S. Rhodesia	...	...	...	...	...	...	1	4
Spain	...	...	...	...	2	2	5	14
Sweden	...	1	1	1	5	2	5	18
Switzerland	1	1	1	3	5	9	14	19
Sudan	...	...	...	...	...	...	...	1
Syrian Arab Republic	...	...	...	...	...	...	...	2
Tanzania	...	...	...	...	...	...	...	1
Thailand	...	...	...	...	...	1	1	3
Trinidad and Tobago	...	...	...	...	...	...	...	3
Tunisia	...	...	...	...	...	...	...	2
Turkey	...	...	1	1	1	6	6	5
Uganda	...	...	...	...	...	...	...	1
United Arab Republic	...	...	...	1	2	3	5	16
United Kingdom	23	19	24	34	52	83	133	198
United States	115	95	131	119	143	177	220	370
Upper Volta	...	...	...	...	...	...	...	1
Uruguay	...	...	...	...	...	...	...	3
Vietnam	...	...	...	...	...	1	1	3
Yugoslavia	...	...	...	1	1	1	1	5
Stateless staff members	...	5	3	3	...	1	1	3
Total	180	168	235	254	345	484	705	1,348

Source: IBRD, Administration Department, Personnel Division.
a. As of June 30.

Table H-8. *Nationality Distribution of IFC Professional Staff,*
Selected Years, 1959–71

Country	1959	1962	1965	1968	1971
Argentina	...	1	1	1	1
Australia	1	2	3	2	3
Austria	...	...	1	1	...
Belgium	1	1	1	...	1
Bolivia	...	...	...	...	...
Brazil	...	...	...	...	...
Canada	1	1	1	...	4
Ceylon	...	...	1	1	2
Chile	...	...	...	...	4
China	...	1	1	1	1
Colombia	...	1	2	2	...
Cuba	1	1	1	1	1
Egypt	...	1	...	...	...
France	1	...	4	2	4
Germany	3	3	5	5	8
Ghana	...	...	...	1	1
Greece	...	...	...	...	2
India	...	2	4	7	6
Iran	...	...	1	1	1
Italy	...	...	...	2	1
Japan	...	...	...	1	2
Jordan	...	1	1	...	...
Korea	...	...	1	...	...
Lebanon	...	...	...	1	2
Luxembourg	...	...	1	1	...
Mauritius	...	...	...	...	1
Netherlands	...	...	1	1	5
New Zealand	...	...	...	1	...
Norway	...	1	2	3	2
Pakistan	...	...	...	1	1
Peru	...	...	...	...	...
Philippines	...	...	...	1	2
Portugal	...	...	1	...	...
South Africa	1	...	...	...	...
Spain	...	1	1	...	1
Sweden	...	...	...	1	2
Switzerland	1	1	1	...	...
United Arab Republic	...	...	3	6	4
United Kingdom	6	12	7	10	7
United States	12	14	28	28	24
Vietnam	...	...	1	...	1
Total	28	44	74	82	94

Source: IBRD, Administration Department, Personnel Division.

APPENDIX I

Selected Readings
and Reference Materials

THE FOLLOWING LIST of readings and reference materials does not purport to be either the full bibliography of materials we consulted or a balanced set of readings on development and development assistance. Our emphasis is first on publications of the World Bank Group designed to provide information about its activities. Most of these are available from the Bank on request and without charge, often in other languages as well as English. A second focus is on so-called "sale publications of the World Bank Group"—longer studies and reports prepared by members and former members of the Bank staff and available through the Johns Hopkins University Press. Third, we list certain other books and articles that shed light directly or indirectly on the work of the Bank and its affiliates.

Informational Publications of the World Bank Group

Annual Reports on the activities of the World Bank, International Development Association, and International Finance Corporation are issued each year in September and cover activities for the preceding fiscal year (July 1 through June 30). The Bank's first annual report was issued in 1946, its second covered fiscal year 1946–47. IFC's first annual report was for 1956–57. IDA's first annual report was for 1960–61. Since 1963–64, Bank and IDA annual reports have been combined.

Similarly, annual reports covering the activities of the International Centre for Settlement of Investment Disputes are issued in September for the preceding fiscal year (July 1 through June 30). The first ICSID annual report covered 1966–67, that is, the 1967 fiscal year.

Summary Proceedings of annual meetings are published as soon as possible after the joint annual meeting in September of the boards of governors of the Bank, IFC, and IDA. The Bank's first proceedings were issued in 1946; IFC's in 1957. IDA's first proceedings (1961) were combined with the Bank's for that year. Beginning with the 1965 issue, a combined *Summary Proceedings* was issued for all three agencies.

Loan Agreements and *Development Credit Agreements* are printed for each Bank loan or IDA credit. *Guarantee Agreements* are printed for loans made to

882

borrowers other than member governments. Copies of agreements are mailed regularly to many libraries and other organizations. As is explained in Chapter 17 of this book—on the Bank and other international organizations—loan and credit agreements between the Bank and countries that are members of the United Nations are also printed in the UN treaty series. IFC investment agreements are not public documents. *General Conditions Applicable to Loan and Guarantee Agreements* (of the IBRD) and *General Conditions Applicable to Development Credit Agreements* (of the IDA) are issued periodically as brochures. The most recent editions as of this writing are dated January 31, 1969.

Basic explanatory pamphlets and booklets issued by the Bank Group include *Policies and Operations: The World Bank, IDA and IFC; World Bank and IDA: Questions and Answers; IFC General Policies; Guidelines for Procurement Under World Bank Loans and IDA Credits; Uses of Consultants by the World Bank and its Borrowers;* and *Economic Development Institute: Program and General Information.*

Ten sector working papers were published as pamphlets in 1971 and 1972. They were originally intended for internal Bank/IDA use in preparing projects, fixing priorities, and formulating policies in various sectors of the economies of developing countries. Because of the interest expressed outside the Bank, they were revised, edited, and made generally available under the titles *Agriculture, Education, Electric Power, Industry, Population Planning, Telecommunications, Tourism, Transportation, Urbanization,* and *Water Supply and Sewerage.* The subtitle in each case is *Sector Working Paper.*

Major speeches by the President of the World Bank Group and other high officials are published as brochures. Press releases are issued on virtually all loan and credit operations; on bond issues and major borrowings; and on organizational changes, mission departures, and other "events" in the life of the Bank.

Since June 1964, a quarterly entitled *Finance and Development* has been published jointly by the International Monetary Fund and the World Bank Group.

Sale Publications Available from the Johns Hopkins University Press

"Sale" publications of the World Bank Group issued by the Johns Hopkins University Press include the occasional papers, EDI studies, general survey mission reports, and miscellaneous publications listed below.

Adler, Hans A. *Sector and Project Planning in Transportation.* (1967).

Avramović, Dragoslav. *Debt Servicing Capacity and Postwar Growth in International Indebtedness, 1946–55.* (1958). Out of print.

————, and Ravi Gulhati. *Debt Servicing Problems of Low-Income Countries.* (1960). Out of print.

————, and associates. *Economic Growth and External Debt.* (1965).

————. *Economic Growth of Colombia: Problems and Prospects.* (1972). Report of a mission headed by Avramović.

Balassa, Bela, and associates. *The Structure of Protection In Developing Countries.* (1971).

Baranson, Jack. *Automotive Industries in Developing Countries.* (1969).

Boskey, Shirley. *Problems and Practices of Development Banks.* (1959).

Cavers, David F., and James R. Nelson. *Electric Power Regulation in Latin America.* (1959). Out of print.

Churchill, Anthony, and others. *A Study of Road User Charges in Central America.* (1972).

Cilingiroglu, Ayhan. *Manufacture of Heavy Electrical Equipment in Developing Countries.* (1969).

de Vries, Barend A. *The Export Experience of Developing Countries.* (1967).

de Weille, Jan. *Quantification of Road User Savings.* (1966).

de Wilde, John, and others. *Experiences with Agricultural Development in Tropical Africa.* 2 vols. (1967).

Diamond, William. *Development Banks.* (1957).

——— (ed). *Development Finance Companies: Aspects of Policy and Operation.* (1968).

Gittinger, J. Price. *Economic Analysis of Agricultural Projects.* (1972).

King, Benjamin B. *Notes on the Mechanics of Growth and Debt.* (1968).

King, John A., Jr. *Economic Development Projects and Their Appraisal: Cases and Principles from the Experience of the World Bank.* (1967).

Lieftinck, Pieter, A. Robert Sadove, and Thomas C. Creyke. *Water and Power Resources of West Pakistan: A Study in Sector Planning.* 3 vols. (1968).

Pouliquen, Louis Y. *Risk Analysis in Project Appraisal.* (1970).

Reports of General Survey Missions. The twenty-five country economic reports prepared by survey missions of the World Bank between 1950 and 1965 are listed, with dates of publication, on page 302, above.

Reutlinger, Shlomo. *Techniques for Project Appraisal under Uncertainty.* (1970).

Thias, Hans Heinrich, and Martin Carnoy. *Cost-Benefit Analysis in Education: A Case Study on Kenya.* (1972).

Tinbergen, Jan. *The Design of Development.* (1958).

van der Tak, Herman G. *The Economic Choice Between Hydroelectric and Thermal Power Developments.* (1966).

———, and Anandarup Ray. *The Economic Benefit of Road Transport Projects.* (1971).

———, and Jan de Weille. *Reappraisal of a Road Project in Iran.* (1969).

Walters, Alan A. *The Economics of Road User Charges.* (1968).

Waterston, Albert. *Planning in Morocco.* (1962).

———. *Planning in Yugoslavia.* (1962).

———. *Planning in Pakistan.* (1963).

———. *Development Planning: Lessons of Experience.* (1965). Revised fourth edition. (1971).

Zaidan, George C. *The Costs and Benefits of Family Planning Programs.* (1971).

Others Books and Articles

Adler, Hans A. *Economic Appraisal of Transport Projects: A Manual with Case Studies.* Bloomington: Indiana University Press, 1971.

Adler, John H., and Paul W. Kuznets (eds.). *Capital Movements and Economic Development.* New York: St. Martin's Press, 1967; London: Macmillan, 1967.

Adler, John H. "The Economic Development Institute of the World Bank," *International Development Review,* Vol. 5 (March 1963).

Adler, Robert W., and Raymond F. Mikesell. *Public External Financing of Development Banks in Developing Countries.* Eugene: University of Oregon, Bureau of Business and Economic Research, 1966.

Aldewereld, S. *The Challenge of Development Aid.* Address to the Swedish International Development Authority, Stockholm. May 6, 1966.

Alexandrowicz, Charles Henry. *International Economic Organisations.* Published under the auspices of the London Institute of World Affairs. New York: Praeger, 1953.

Baldwin, David A. "The International Bank in Political Perspective." *World Politics,* Vol. 18 (October 1965).

Baldwin, George B. "A Layman's Guide to Little/Mirrlees," *Finance and Development,* Vol. 9 (March 1972).

Basch, Antonin. "International Bank for Reconstruction and Development, 1944–1949," *International Conciliation,* No. 455. New York: Carnegie Endowment for International Peace, November 1949.

———. *Financing Economic Development.* New York: Macmillan, 1964; London: Collier-Macmillan, 1964.

———. *A Pragmatic Approach to Economic Development.* New York: Vantage Press, 1970.

Baum, Warren C. "The Project Cycle," *Finance and Development,* Vol. 7 (June 1970).

Beyen, J. W. *Money in a Maelstrom.* New York: Macmillan, 1949.

Bitterman, Henry J. "Negotiation of Articles of Agreement of the International Bank for Reconstruction and Development," *The International Lawyer,* Vol. 5 (January 1971).

———. "The Negotiating History of the Bank." Processed; 1967.

Black, Eugene R. *The Diplomacy of Economic Development.* Cambridge: Harvard University Press, 1960.

———. "Development Revisited," *Virginia Quarterly Review,* Vol. 47 (Winter 1971).

———. "Challenge of Underdeveloped Lands," *Virginia Quarterly Review,* Vol. 32 (Winter 1956).

———. "The World Bank at Work," *Foreign Affairs,* Vol. 30 (April 1952).

———. "The Indus: A Moral for Nations," *New York Times,* December 11, 1960.

Blanco Vidal, Manuel. *Organizaciones Internacionales de Créditos.* Antofagasta, Chile: Editorial La Portada, 1962.

Bleicher, Samuel A. "UN v. IBRD: A Dilemma of Functionalism," *International Organization,* Vol. 24 (Winter 1970).

Blelloch, David. "One Developing World," Graduate School of Citizenship and Public Affairs, Syracuse University, September 1963.

Bonnet, Henri. *Les Institutions Financières Internationales.* Paris: Presses Universitaires de France, 1968.

Boskey, Shirley, and Piero Sella. "Settling International Disputes," *Finance and Development,* Vol. 2 (September 1965).

Broches, A. "Development of International Law by the International Bank for Reconstruction and Development," *Proceedings of the American Society of International Law* (April 1965).

―――. "International Legal Aspects of the Operations of the World Bank," *Recueil des Cours,* Académie de Droit International (Tome 98, Vol. 3, 1959). Leiden: A. W. Sijthoff, 1960.

―――, and Shirley Boskey. "Theory and Practice of Treaty Registration, with Particular Reference to Agreements of the International Bank." *Netherlands International Law Review* (Issue 2–3, 1957). Leiden: A. W. Sijthoff.

Cairncross, Alexander K. *The International Bank for Reconstruction and Development.* Essays in International Finance, No. 33. Princeton: International Finance Section, Princeton University, 1959.

Carlin, A. "Project versus Program Aid: From the Donor's Viewpoint," *Economic Journal,* Vol. 77 (March 1967).

Creyke, Thomas C. *Financing Water Resource Development.* Melbourne: Committee for Economic Development of Australia, 1969.

Demuth, Richard H. "The International Agricultural Research Consultative Group," *International Development Review,* Vol. 13, No. 3, 1971.

Development Assistance: Efforts and Policies of the Members of the Development Assistance Committee. Review by the chairman of the DAC, published annually since 1962. Paris: OECD.

The Development of Brazil. Report of the Joint Brazil–United States Economic Development Commission. Washington: Government Printing Office, December 21, 1954.

Elwell-Sutton, L. P. *Persian Oil, a Study in Power Politics.* London: Lawrence and Wishart, Ltd., 1955.

Fatemi, Nasrollah Asifpour. *Oil Diplomacy.* New York: Whittier Books, Inc., 1954.

Ford, Alan W. *The Anglo-Iranian Oil Dispute, 1951–1952.* Los Angeles: University of California Press, 1954.

Frank, Charles, Jr. *Debt and Terms of Aid.* Washington: Overseas Development Council, 1970.

Fromm, Gary (ed.). *Transport Investment and Economic Development.* Brookings Institution, 1965.

Gardner, Richard N. *Sterling-Dollar Diplomacy.* London: Oxford University Press, 1956. New, expanded edition published in New York, Toronto, Sydney, and London by McGraw-Hill, 1969.

―――, and Max F. Millikan (eds.). *The Global Partnership: International Agencies and Economic Development.* New York, Washington, and London: Praeger, 1968.

Gilbert, Richard V. "The Works Programme in East Pakistan," *International Labour Review,* Vol. 89 (March 1964).

Goldenweiser, E. A., and Alice Bourneuf. "Bretton Woods Agreements," *Federal Reserve Bulletin,* Vol. 30 (September 1944).

Gordon, David L. "The World Bank's Mission in Eastern Africa," *Finance and Development,* Vol. 5 (March 1968).

Gulhati, N. D. *Indus Waters Treaty: A Successful Exercise in International Mediation.* New Delhi: Allied Publishers, 1972.

Gulhati, Ravi. "The Question of India's External Debt," *India Quarterly* (New Delhi), Vol. 28 (January–March 1972).

Hadwen, John G., and Johan Kaufman. *How United Nations Decisions Are Made.* Leiden: A. W. Sijthoff, 1960.

Haq, Mahbub ul, "Employment in the 1970s: A New Perspective, *International Development Review,* Vol. 13, No. 4, 1971.

Harrod, Roy F. *The Life of John Maynard Keynes.* London and New York: Harcourt, Brace, 1951.

Hayter, Teresa. *Aid as Imperialism.* Baltimore: Penguin Books, 1971.

Hirschman, Albert O. *Development Projects Observed.* Washington: Brookings Institution, 1967.

———, and Richard M. Bird. *Foreign Aid: A Critique and a Proposal.* Essays in International Finance, No. 69. Princeton: International Finance Section, Princeton University, 1968.

Hoffman, Michael. "The Co-ordination of Aid," in *Effective Aid.* London: Overseas Development Institute, Ltd., 1967.

IBRD. *Bankers' Mission to India and Pakistan, February–March 1960.* Washington: 1960.

———. "Economic Mission to India, 1964–1965." Washington: September 3, 1965.

———. "The Horowitz Proposal, A Staff Report." Processed; February 1965.

———. *Inaugural Meeting of the Board of Governors of the International Bank for Reconstruction and Development, Savannah, Georgia, March 8–18, 1946, Selected Documents.* Washington: May 1946.

———. "Indus Waters Agreement between the Government of India and the Government of Pakistan for *Ad Hoc* Transitional Arrangements for —" Three agreements, the first "for 1955," June 21, 1955; the second, "for Rabi 1955–56," Oct. 31, 1955; the third, "for the period from April 1, 1956 to March 21, 1957," Sept. 24, 1956.

———. "Indus Basin Development Fund Agreement." Processed; September 19, 1960.

———. *Report of the Executive Directors on the Articles of Agreement of the International Development Association.* Washington: January 26, 1960.

———. "Report on the Proposal for an International Finance Corporation." Processed; April 29, 1952.

———. "Review of the International Bank's Negotiations Concerning the Iranian Oil Problem." Washington: IBRD Press release, No. 285, April 3, 1952.

IMF: *The International Monetary Fund, 1945–1965: Twenty Years of International Monetary Cooperation.* J. Keith Horsefield, ed. Washington: International Monetary Fund, 1969.

Vol. 1: *Chronicle.* By J. Keith Horsefield.

Vol. 2: *Analysis.* By Margaret G. de Vries and J. Keith Horsefield, with Joseph Gold, Mary H. Gumbart, Gertrud Lovasy, and Emil G. Spitzer.

Vol. 3: *Documents.* Edited by J. Keith Horsefield.

Jackson, Sir Robert. "A Study of the Capacity of the United Nations Development System" (the Jackson Report). UN Document DP/5. 2 vols. Processed; Geneva: United Nations, 1969.

Jacobsson, Per. *International Monetary Problems, 1957–1963*. Washington: International Monetary Fund, 1964.

Kamarck, Andrew M. "The Appraisal of Country Economic Performance," *Economic Development and Cultural Change*, Vol. 18 (January 1970).

Knorr, Klaus. "The Bretton Woods Institutions in Transition," *International Organization*, Vol. 2 (February 1948).

Lewis, John P., and Ishan Kapur (eds.). *The World Bank, Multilateral Aid, and the 1970s*. New York: D. C. Heath and Company, forthcoming.

Lilienthal, David E. "Another 'Korea' in the Making?," *Collier's* (August 4, 1959).

———. "The Road to Change," *International Development Review*, Vol. 6 (December 1964).

Little, Ian, Tibor Scitovsky, and Maurice Scott. *Industry and Trade in Some Developing Countries: A Comparative Study*. Published for the Development Centre of the OECD by the Oxford University Press, London, 1971.

———, and James A. Mirrlees. *Social Cost-Benefit Analysis*. Paris: OECD Development Centre, 1969.

Little, Tom. *High Dam at Aswan*. New York: John Day, 1965.

Louchheim, W. C., Jr. "The Marketing of World Bank Bonds," *Commercial and Financial Chronicle*, Vol. 163, Part I (March 28, 1946).

Love, David. "Controlling the Chao Phya," *Finance and Development*, Vol. 4 (December 1967).

Love, Kennett. *Suez, the Twice-Fought War*. New York and Toronto: McGraw-Hill, 1969.

Luard, Evan (ed.). *The Evolution of International Organizations*. New York: Praeger, 1966.

McCloy, John J. "The Lesson of the World Bank," *Foreign Affairs*, Vol. 27 (July 1949).

McNamara, Robert S. "Interview," *The Banker* (London), Vol. 119 (March 1969).

Maddison, Angus. *Foreign Skills and Technical Assistance in Economic Development*. Paris: Development Centre of the Organisation for Economic Co-operation and Development, 1965.

Matecki, B. E. *Establishment of the International Finance Corporation and United States Policy*. New York: Praeger, 1957.

Michel, Aloys Arthur. *The Indus Rivers*. New Haven: Yale University Press, 1967.

Mikesell, Raymond F. *Public International Lending for Development*. New York: Random House, 1966.

Ministère d'État Chargé de la Réforme Administrative. *La Politique de Coopération avec les Pays en Voie de Développement*. Paris, 1963.

Moore, Frederick T. "The World Bank and Its Economic Missions," *Review of Economics and Statistics*, Vol. 42 (February 1960).

Morris, James. *The Road to Huddersfield: A Journey to Five Continents*. New York: Pantheon Books, 1963.

Nehru, B. K. "The Way We Looked for Money Abroad," in Vadilal Dagli (ed.), *Two Decades of Indo-U.S. Relations.* Bombay: Vora and Company, 1969.

Oliver, Robert W. "The Origins of the International Bank for Reconstruction and Development." Ph.D. dissertation, Princeton University, 1959.

————. *Early Plans for a World Bank.* Studies in International Finance, No. 29. Princeton: International Finance Section, Princeton University, 1971.

Ozaki, Eiji. *The World Bank.* Tokyo: Research Association of Japan on International Problems, 1969.

Partners in Development. Report of the Commission on International Development, Lester B. Pearson, chairman. New York and London: Praeger, 1969.

Patel, I. G. *Foreign Aid.* New Delhi: Allied Publishers Private, Ltd., 1968.

Please, Stanley. "Saving Through Taxation—Reality or Mirage?," *Finance and Development,* Vol. 4 (March 1967).

Proceedings and Documents of United Nations Monetary and Financial Conference, Bretton Woods, New Hampshire, July 1–22, 1944. Washington: U.S. Department of State, 1948.

Pryor, Donald J. "Livestock: The Recognition of a Stepchild," *Finance and Development,* Vol. 7 (September 1970).

Reid, Escott. *The Future of the World Bank: An Essay.* Washington: World Bank/IDA, 1965.

————. *Strengthening the World Bank.* Chicago: Adlai Stevenson Institute of International Affairs, forthcoming.

Reisman, William M. "The Role of the Economic Agencies in the Enforcement of International Judgments and Awards: A Functional Approach," *International Organization,* Vol. 19 (Autumn 1965).

Rubin, Seymour J. *The Conscience of the Rich Nations: The Development Assistance Committee and the Common Aid Effort.* New York: Harper and Row, 1966.

Salter, Sir Arthur. *Foreign Investment.* Essays in International Finance, No. 12. Princeton: International Finance Section, Princeton University, 1957.

Sewell, James Patrick. *Functionalism and World Politics: A Study Based on United Nations Programs for Financing Economic Development.* Princeton: Princeton University Press, 1966.

Shonfield, Andrew. *The Attack on World Poverty.* New York: Random House, 1960.

Singh, Manmohan. *Regional Development Banks.* New York: Carnegie Endowment for International Peace, International Conciliation Pamphlet No. 576, January 1970.

Taylor, K. W. "The Pre-Investment Function in the International Development System," *International Development Review,* Vol. 12, No. 2, 1970.

Tendler, Judith. *Electric Power in Brazil.* Cambridge: Harvard University Press, 1968.

————. "Foreign Aid: A Study in Atypical Bureaucracy." Unpublished manuscript, December 1970.

Trevelyan, Humphrey. *The Middle East in Revolution.* Boston: Gambit, Inc., 1970.

Trewhitt, Henry L. *McNamara: His Ordeal in the Pentagon.* New York and London: Harper and Row, 1971.

United Nations, Department of Economic Affairs. *Measures for the Economic Development of Under-Developed Countries.* Report of a Group of Experts Appointed by the Secretary-General of the United Nations (Alberto Baltra Cortez, D. R. Gadgil, George Hakim, W. Arthur Lewis, and Theodore W. Schultz). Doc. E/1986, ST/ECA/10, May 3, 1951.

United Nations, Department of Economic Affairs. *Report on a Special United Nations Fund for Economic Development,* by a Committee Appointed by the Secretary-General. Doc. E/2381, November 18, 1953.

United Nations Secretariat, Department of Economic Affairs. *Methods of Financing Economic Development in Under-Developed Countries.* Doc. II.B.4, 1949.

U.S. Congress. House. Committee on Banking and Currency. *Bretton Woods Agreements Act.* Hearings. 79 Cong. 1 sess. Washington: Government Printing Office, 1945.

U.S. Congress. Senate. Committee on Banking and Currency. *Bretton Woods Agreements Act.* Hearings. 79 Cong. 1 sess. Washington: Government Printing Office, 1945.

U.S. Congress. Senate. Committee on Banking and Currency. *Study of Export-Import Bank and World Bank.* Hearings. 83 Cong. 2 sess. Washington: Government Printing Office, 1954.

U.S. International Development Advisory Board. *Partners in Progress: A Report to the President by the International Development Advisory Board.* Washington, 1951.

Vinson, Fred M. "After the Savannah Conference," *Foreign Affairs,* Vol. 24 (July 1946).

Weaver, James H. *The International Development Association: A New Approach to Foreign Aid.* New York: Praeger, 1965.

White, John. *Pledged to Development: A Study of International Consortia and the Strategy of Aid.* London: Overseas Development Institute, Ltd., 1967.

———. *Regional Development Banks.* London: Overseas Development Institute, Ltd., 1970; and New York: Praeger Publishers, 1972.

Williams, J. H. "International Bank for Reconstruction and Development." Paper delivered to Fourth Maxwell Institute on the United Nations, Bretton Woods, New Hampshire, August 27–September 1, 1967. (Processed version dated February 28, 1968.)

Wilson, George W., Barbara R. Bergmann, Leon V. Hirsch, and Martin A. Klein. *The Impact of Highway Investment on Development.* Washington: Brookings Institution, 1966.

Woods, George D. "The Development Decade in Balance," *Foreign Affairs,* Vol. 44 (January 1966).

———. *Address to the United Nations Conference on Trade and Development.* March 25, 1964.

———. *Development—the Need for New Directions.* Address to the Swedish Bankers Association. Stockholm, October 27, 1967.

Index

891

lem, 221; five-year lending programs, 452n; IBRD loan policy under, 134–35, 138, 205, 216, 226n, 279–81, 375, 473–77, 480, 738; as IBRD president, 66, 83–86, 88, 91, 93, 100–01, 146, 696–98; and IDA, 411, 415–16; IDA credits to India, 286, 288; and IDB, 581; and IFC, 352, 357, 745; and IMF, 552; relations with UN and its agencies, 567n, 594, 754; reorganization of IBRD, 740n; sale of IBRD bonds, 136–37; selection of, 89n

Maddison, Angus, 332n

Madigan, Michael J., 159, 164

Maintenance imports. *See* Import credits; Program loans

Makins, Roger, 600

Malawi, 584, 713–14

Malaya, 302, 304

Malaysia, 330n, 403, 482, 524, 713n, 716, 727

Management of IBRD, 6, 69n, 87, 92, 94, 96, 737–42. *See also* Board of Governors; Executive directors; President

Management of IBRD projects, 251–56, 291, 319–20, 363, 365, 420, 441–42; covenants re, 436, 652; political and cultural constraints on, 423–24, 445–46; skill-transfer difficulties, 312

Manpower: analysis, 468; human resource development, 469–70, 473, 481; shortage of trained, 423

Manufacturing projects: Bank Group loans for, 80, 202–03, 336, 371, 375, 378, 499, 745; IFC investment in, 352, 355, 359. *See also* Industrial projects

Marcos, Ferdinand E., 433

Marjolin, Robert, 84n

Marshall Plan, 2, 52–53, 109, 170–71, 174, 494, 497, 504, 568n, 705

Martin, Edwin M., 207n, 577n, 686n

Martin, George, 95–96

Martin, William McChesney, Jr., 496

Marxian theory, 486

Mason, Edward S., 666n

Matecki, B. E., 349n

Mathew, P. M., 363n

Mauritania, 199, 534

Mauritius, 304

Mediation attempts, by IBRD, 8, 97–98, 339, 595–643, 697

Médici, Emilio Garrastazú, 663n

Mejia-Palacio, Jorge, 94n

Membership (IBRD), 3–4, 17, 19, 63–65, 469–70, 695; withdrawal provisions, 32

Membership (IDA), 81, 391, 394–95

Mendels, Morton M., 43, 51, 92, 96n, 545n

Mendes-France, Pierre, 22, 47

Menzies, Robert, 272

Merchant, Livingston, 89n

Mexico, 19n, 22–23, 292, 302n, 486n, 535–36, 648, 731n; Bank Group loans to, 158–60, 166, 194, 198–99, 202, 237–38, 359, 470, 580, 707; irrigation projects, 712; livestock project, 318; loan application, 53, 159n; maize and wheat research in, 574; power consumption, 687n; power projects, 233, 246, 276, 462, 498–99, 531–32, 536, 702, 715–16; steel project, 582n; transport-sector study, 710

Meyer, Eugene, 41–44, 46–48, 61, 87, 95–96, 128, 696, 698

Michel, Aloys Arthur, 624n

Middle East, 64–65, 141, 176–79

Millikan, Max F., 571n

Minhas, Bagicha S., 328

Mining projects: Bank Group loans for, 80, 203, 336, 371, 375, 378, 499, 700n, 745; IFC investment in, 352, 355

Mirrlees, James, 244n

Missions (IBRD), 72–74, 185–86, 256, 297–307, 315, 320–24, 427, 474, 741–43, 745–46; Africa, 323, 404; Australia, 273; Bolivia, 176; Brazil, 661; collaboration with IMF, 546–47, 551, 553; Colombia, 162, 297, 299–303, 464, 546, 650, 656, 741n; Ethiopia, 165, 741; India, 196; Iran, 172; Norway, 274; Pakistan, 668–69; Peru, 176, 305, 452–53; Poland, 170; Thailand, 690–91

Missions (IMF), 545–47, 553

Moe, Finn, 57

Mohammed, Ghulam, 611

Monnet Plan, 265

Monroney, A. S. Mike, 386–87, 393, 395

Moody's Investors Service, 117, 132

Moore, Frederick T., 303n

Morgan Stanley and Co., 132, 135–36

Morgenthau, Henry, 11, 14, 17–18, 41

Morocco, 205, 302, 331, 525, 721

Morozov, Alexander P., 57

Morris, James, 71n, 98n

Morse, Wayne, 638n

Mossadegh, Mohammed, 598–99, 601–10

Mueenuddin, G., 617, 621–22

Murphy, Robert D., 640

Mutual funds, 370n

to, 258, 357, 364, 375, 743–45; IBRD
opposition to financing of government-
owned industries, 150–51, 371–72, 374;
need for investment planning in, 459
Public utilities, 151–52, 190, 366, 700n;
charges (rates), 166, 238–39, 554,
556–57, 652; IFC investment in, 352,
355; loans for, 201–02, 308; studies
of, 309. *See also* Communication facility loans; Electric power projects;
Transport projects; Water supply projects
Public works projects, 721, 725, 731

Quadros, Janio, 663

Rahman, Fazlur, 507
Railways, 151–52, 201, 700n; appraisal
procedures, 249; in Brazil, 660, 662;
rate covenants, 238–39
Railways, Bank Group loans for, 134,
177–78, 296, 706–09, 734: Brazil, 197,
556, 657–58, 663–64; Chile, 155–56;
Colombia, 650n, 652; Guinea, 297;
India, 163, 168, 195, 201–02, 231, 283,
433, 437, 677, 680; Nigeria, 253–54;
Pakistan, 668; Spain, 230, 433; Thai-
land, 168–69, 253, 684n, 687–89
Raj, James, 365
Rao, V. K. R. V., 382–83
Rasminsky, Louis, 94n
Rate covenants, in loan agreements, 76–
77, 160–61, 237–39, 255, 420, 436–38,
652–53
Rates, foreign exchange, 541, 554–55,
557. *See also* Interest rates
Rates of return: economic and financial,
247–54; internal, 241–42; for power
projects, 716
Ratification of IBRD Articles of Agree-
ment, 33–35
Rating, of IBRD bonds, 132
Razmara, Ali, 597
Reconstruction, 2, 13, 21–23, 28. *See also*
Marshall Plan; Relief and rehabilita-
tion
Reconstruction loans (IBRD), 25, 52–53,
72, 177n; to Western Europe, 109, 150,
153–54, 229, 264–68, 289, 494, 705
Reddaway, W. Brian, 328
Refugee problem, 517, 519
Regional development banks, 7–8, 358,
417, 534, 561, 578–86, 593, 749, 752–
53. *See also* African Development
Bank; Asian Development Bank; Euro-

pean Investment Bank; Inter-American
Development Bank
Regional offices (IBRD), provision for,
32
Reid, Escott, 418, 735n, 736–37
Relief and rehabilitation, 2–3, 16–17, 154,
274. *See also* Reconstruction
Repayments, effect on net lending of Bank
Group, 217–21
Research: agricultural, 204, 317, 574,
585, 715; by AsDB, 585; by IBRD,
473, 477, 551 (*see also* Country eco-
nomic reports); need for economic,
324–25; by OECD Development Cen-
tre, 577. *See also* Preinvestment
studies; Sector studies
Reserve funds (IBRD), 119–24, 148–49
Resident representatives (IBRD), 72–73,
83, 320–21, 323, 333, 741–43. *See also*
Consultants; Missions
Rhodesia, 175, 177, 201, 262, 591
Rickett, Denis, 92, 411
Rieber, Torkild, 602–04, 606–07, 609
Ripman, Hugh B., 158n
Rist, Leonard B., 43, 70, 269, 271n, 330
Roads. *See* Highway projects
Robichek, E. Walter, 540n
Rockefeller Foundation, 325–26, 331, 574
Rockefeller, Nelson, 346–49, 384–85
Romania, 724
Roosevelt, Franklin D., 17, 33, 102
Rosen, Martin M., 43, 112n, 352–53, 356–
58
Rosenstein-Rodan, Paul N., 181, 257n,
269, 324, 468
Rubin, Seymour J., 520n, 576n

Sadove, A. Robert, 230n, 240, 241n, 248n,
627n, 717n
Salaries (IBRD), 38–39, 45, 72, 79
Salter, James Arthur, 126
Sanctions, legal, 434–35
Sanitation projects, 82, 151, 385, 393.
See also Health projects; Sewerage
projects
Saudi Arabia, 141
Savannah meeting (*1946*) of IBRD Gov-
ernors, 36–40
Savings and loan associations, and the
IFC, 370n
Savings rate, in developing countries, 239,
443–46, 450, 464–66
Scandinavia, 7, 506, 511
Schmidt, Orvis A., 165n, 166n, 175, 183n
Schultz, Theodore W., 384n, 462n
Schweitzer, Pierre-Paul, 550